D0138939

Shelley: The Golden Years

Shelley The Golden Years

Kenneth Neill Cameron

Harvard University Press Cambridge, Massachusetts 1974

Library of Congress Catalog Card Number 73–80566
SBN 674–03160–1
Printed in the United States of America

The world's great age begins anew,
  The golden years return,
The earth doth like a snake renew
  Her winter weeds outworn:
Heaven smiles, and faiths and empires gleam,
Like wrecks of a dissolving dream.

. . . . .

O cease! must hate and death return?
  Cease! must men kill and die?
Cease! drain not to its dregs the urn
  Of bitter prophecy.
The world is weary of the past,
O might it die or rest at last!

—Shelley, *Hellas*

Preface

In *The Young Shelley: Genesis of a Radical,* published in 1950, I examined Shelley's transition from a "votary of romance" to a political and antireligious radical, from the schoolboy novels *Zastrozzi* and *St. Irvyne; or, The Rosicrucian,* to *Queen Mab* and *A Refutation of Deism.* In *Shelley and His Circle,* vols. I-II (1961), and *The Esdaile Notebook: A Volume of Early Poems* (1964) I dealt further with this period, and in *Shelley and His Circle,* vols. III-IV (1970), I discussed the later period up to the suicide of Harriet Shelley.

The present book is a continuation of these studies. Biographically, it sketches Shelley's life from the breakdown of his marriage with Harriet Westbrook in 1814 to his death in Italy in 1822; critically, it concentrates on the major later works in both prose and poetry. In *The Young Shelley* I examined the life and works together within a chronological framework because Shelley's intellectual evolution in those years was closely related to the events of his life. In later years, however, such evolution was less marked; once Shelley's ideas were formed, they underwent little basic change. It is preferable, therefore, to examine the later works by category: biographical poems, political poems, philosophical poems, drama, literary criticism, etc. I begin with the biographical section, indicating, as I go along, what works were being written when and under what circumstances. In discussing the works, I consider the prose, where Shelley's ideas are easier to grasp, before the poetry.

The biographical section concentrates on the events in Shelley's life that have become the subject of particular controversy; the breakup of his marriage with Harriet, his elopement with Mary Godwin, his relations with Claire Clairmont, Mary Shelley, and Thomas Jefferson Hogg, the suicides of Fanny Imlay and Harriet Shelley, the trial for the custody of Shelley's children by Harriet, the relations between Shelley, Mary, Byron, and Claire Clairmont at Geneva, the "Neapolitan child" mystery, and the sinking of Shelley's boat. In Chapter 7, dealing with the autobiographical poems, some of these matters are explored further, in particular the relationship of Shelley and Mary.

This biographical examination is necessary, because Shelley has remained a controversial figure. Few writers have provoked such hostility or inspired such affection. Hostile critics have distorted the facts with so much malice that even Shelley's defenders have not always realized the degree of the distortion and have tended to write defensively. As a result, the prevailing views of Shelley as a person have been largely false, and these views have inevitably affected the approach to his poetry.

In recent decades the scope of the attack has widened—from Irving Babbit to T. S. Eliot, from the New Critics to F. R. Leavis. This development is understandable, for the reactionary, the conservative, or the "common sense" pragmatist is not going to be sympathetic toward the iconoclast, the revolutionary, or the romantic. Because of the severity of the attacks on Shelley, the impression has arisen in some quarters that he has declined in popularity. But in fact he has never been so widely read. Over the past twenty years, an average of about eight books and thirty-five articles dealing with him have appeared each year, and his works have been translated into Norwegian, Dutch, Japanese, Danish, Russian, Chinese, Italian, Polish, Serbo-Croatian, Greek, Spanish, Yugoslavian, Rumanian, Bulgarian, Czech, Lettish, and other languages, including those of India. Shelley, in short, has become a world poet.

Work on this book was assisted by grants from Indiana University, The Philosophical Society of Philadelphia, the Graduate School of Arts and Sciences at New York University, and a Guggenheim Fellowship. The typescript was read and annotated by John Lavelle of Monmouth College and Gloria Deak of the New York Public Library, both of whom caught many errors and made valuable critical suggestions.

I received permission to quote material under copyright from a number of sources: the Clarenden Press, Oxford, for *The Letters of Percy Bysshe Shelley* (1964), edited by Frederick L. Jones; the University of Oklahoma Press, for *The Letters of Mary W. Shelley* (1946) and *Mary Shelley's Journals* (1947), both edited by Frederick L. Jones; The Carl and Lily Pforzheimer Foundation and Harvard University Press, for *Shelley and His Circle*, vols. I-IV (1961, 1970), edited by Kenneth Neill Cameron; and The Carl and Lily Pforzheimer Foundation and Knopf, for *The Esdaile Notebook* (1940), also edited by Kenneth Neill Cameron. This last acknowledgment brings up a debt of a special kind. In 1952 I was asked by the late Carl H. Pforzheimer to edit the Shelley and His Circle manuscripts in his library, which contains a Shelley collection second only to that in the Bodleian; and after his death in 1957, his son, Carl H. Pforzheimer, Jr., asked me to continue the work. For a number of years I was allowed access to the original manuscripts of Shelley and his associates, and even though the present work, being essentially critical, relies primarily on printed texts, working with those manuscripts provided additional insights that are lasting and valuable. In quoting from Shelley's works, I have generally used *The Complete Works of Percy Bysshe Shelley* (1927–1930), edited by Roger Ingpen and Walter E. Peck, published by Scribner's in 10 volumes.

New York University
April 1973

Contents

Part One Biography

1
The Last Years in England

> A heavy weight of hours has chained and bowed
> One too like thee: tameless and swift and proud.

So Shelley, in 1819, contemplating his own past and the west wind of the Italian Mediterranean. The years in which he was "tameless and swift and proud" were those preceding the breakdown of his marriage to Harriet Westbrook. Of those years, 1811 was the watershed, for it was then that Shelley was expelled from Oxford with his friend, Thomas Jefferson Hogg, for writing *The Necessity of Atheism,* was finally rejected by his boyhood sweetheart and cousin, Harriet Grove, a young woman of his own class, and eloped with Harriet Westbrook, daughter of a wealthy London tavern owner. These events, alienating him from both his family and his class, gave birth to others. Within a few months of his marriage he was campaigning in Ireland for Irish freedom and Catholic emancipation, speaking on the same platform as Daniel O'Connell, and issuing *An Address to the Irish People.* Returning from Ireland, he engaged in the defense of an imprisoned radical, Daniel Isaac Eaton, on whose behalf he wrote *A Letter to Lord Ellenborough,* and was put under surveillance by the government (with its army of spies). In the summer of 1813 he published *Queen Mab,* later known as the Chartists' Bible. In the fall came the first signs of a faltering in the marriage. The following summer he eloped with Mary Wollstonecraft Godwin, daughter of William Godwin and Mary Wollstonecraft, and a new chain of events was begun, one that ended—more than two years later—with the suicide of Harriet and Shelley's loss by legal action of their children, Ianthe and Charles.

Harriet and Mary

In popular accounts these events were telescoped into a picture of the radical poet abandoning his wife and driving her to suicide. When Edward Dowden began his monumental two-volume biography of Shelley (1886), its most important objective, it was felt by Shelley's son and daughter-in-law, Sir Percy Florence and Lady Shelley, was to clear Shelley of these charges. Harriet's champions, including Mark Twain, rallied to her defense; and the battle assumed a gossip column aspect which has continued into the present century.[1] As is not unusual in such conflicts, it is difficult to find a simple documentary account of the events. Furthermore, until recently important material has not been available.

Shelley, as we now know from the *Esdaile* poems, was deeply in love with his cousin, Harriet Grove. When the affair was broken off by his and Harriet's parents because of his antireligious views, he was plunged—age nineteen—into a suicidal depression:

> God! Nature! Chance! remit this misery—
> It burns! why need he live to weep who does
> not fear to die?

When he wrote this poem in the early summer of 1811, he had already met Harriet Westbrook but had not fallen in love with her. Within a few weeks the situation had changed rapidly.

Among other popular fallacies about Shelley is one that his interests in women were solely intellectual (despite the fact that he fathered six children). That his pursuit of Harriet Westbrook was both sexual and romantic is now clear both from these early poems and from his "Keswick" letters to Hogg.

For instance, in telling Hogg to stay away from Harriet, he wrote, "*presence* without the fullest satiation will kindle the passions to an inextinguishable flame." And to Harriet he was writing:

> That hour which tears thee from me
> Leaves nothing but death and despair.[2]

These lines were probably written in July 1811. In August, Harriet and Shelley eloped to Edinburgh; in the fall they were joined at York by Harriet's older sister, Eliza—thirty years old to Harriet's sixteen—who thereafter became a fixture in the household. Although the early poems show that tensions between Shelley and Eliza set in almost immediately, the first evidence of actual strain within the marriage comes in a letter by Shelley from Edinburgh in the fall of 1813 to Hogg in London: "I am happy to hear that you have returned to London, as I shall shortly have the pleasure of seeing you again.—I shall return to London alone. My evenings will often be spent at the Newtons, where I presume you are no infrequent visitor."[3]

When a young married man tells his best friend that he is returning to town without his wife, leaving her, in fact, several hundred miles away for an apparently indefinite period, the indications are that all is not well. By the following March, the marriage began to show definite signs of disintegration. Shelley was then living at the village of Bracknell, thirty miles from London, at the house of Mrs. Jean Baptiste Chastel de Boinville, the sister-in-law of his vegetarian friend John Frank Newton. Mrs. Boinville had married a French *émigré* whose property had been confiscated during the revolution but who had returned to France under Napoleon and died on the retreat from Moscow. She was a person of charm and culture—"the most admirable specimen of a human being I had ever seen," Shelley commented six years later—and a revolutionary: "Round her slight figure," wrote her grandson, "she wore the badge of republicanism—a wide red band—and I have often heard her call herself *une enfant de la Revolution.*" Around her and her lovely daughter Cornelia—married to Thomas Turner, a lawyer and protégé of William Godwin—she had built a circle of fellow radicals.[4] Shelley had never before encountered such a group and was enchanted by its atmosphere of revolutionary culture, as well as by Mrs. Boinville and her daughter.

It was from Mrs. Boinville's house on March 16, 1814, that Shelley wrote the following revealing letter (again to Hogg):

I have been staying with Mrs. B[ ] for the last month; I have escaped, in the society of all that philosophy and friendship combine, from the dismaying solitude of myself. They have revived in my heart the expiring flame of life. I have felt myself translated to a paradise, which has nothing of mortality but its transitoriness; my heart sickens at the view of that necessity, which will quickly divide me from the delightful tranquillity of this happy home—for it has become my home. The trees, the bridge, the minutest objects, have already a place in my affections . . .

Eliza is still with us—not here!—but will be with me when the infinite malice of destiny forces me to depart. I am now but little inclined to contest this point. I certainly hate her with all my heart and soul. It is a sight which awakens an inexpressible sensation of disgust and horror, to see her caress my poor little Ianthe, in whom I may hereafter find the consolation of sympathy. I sometimes feel faint with the fatigue of checking the overflowings of my unbounded abhorrence for this miserable wretch. But she is no more than a blind and loathsome worm [snake], that cannot see to sting.

I have begun to learn Italian again . . . Cornelia [Turner] assists me in this language. Did I not once tell you that I thought her cold and reserved? She is the reverse of this, as she is the reverse of everything bad. She inherits all the divinity of her mother.

What have you written? I have been unable even to write a common letter. I have forced myself to read Beccaria and Dumont's *Bentham.* I have sometimes forgotten that I am not an inmate of this delightful home—that a time will come which will cast me again into the boundless ocean of abhorred society.

I have written nothing but one stanza, which has no meaning, and that I have only written in thought:

Thy dewy looks sink in my breast;
  Thy gentle words stir poison there;
Thou hast disturbed the only rest
  That was the portion of despair!
Subdued to Duty's hard control,
  I could have borne my wayward lot:
The chains that bind this ruined soul
  Had cankered then—but crushed it not.

This is the vision of a delirious and distempered dream, which passes away at the cold clear light of morning. Its surpassing excellence and exquisite perfections have no more reality than the colour of an autumnal sunset.[5]

From this letter it appears that Shelley had not been living at home for a month (Harriet and Eliza were away) but had a room at Mrs. Boinville's. He had not only been feeling solitary and loveless in his marriage, but had developed an obsessive hatred for Eliza. Harriet—by implication—had nothing to offer and was, in fact, part of the "abhorred society." For sympathy and love Shelley was turning to Cornelia Turner. The poem in the letter, which clearly refers to Cornelia, is obviously the poem of a deeply disturbed young man. He had fallen, the poem implies, into "despair," which he had learned to live with because of the marriage tie ("Duty"), but this acceptance had been shattered by the "poison" of desire implanted by the "dewy looks" and "gentle words" of Cornelia.

A few months later, Harriet Shelley went to see Mrs. Godwin: "She related that last November he had fallen in love with Mrs. Turner, Madame de Boinville's daughter, and paid her such marked attentions Mr. Turner, the husband, had carried off his wife to Devonshire."[6] This may be exaggerated—and November is certainly wrong because Shelley was then in Edinburgh—but Turner's later enmity toward Shelley indicates that it contains some truth, and if so, Harriet's implied picture—accepted by the biographers—of a villainous Shelley pursuing a reluctant Cornelia can hardly be true. Lawyer Turner—to judge by his letters—was scarcely inspiring, and Cornelia may have been as attracted to Shelley as he was to her.[7] At any rate, within a few weeks Shelley was out of Mrs. Boinville's, back at his own house, and living alone again. The poem *Stanzas—April, 1814* reflects his feelings at returning to his "sad and silent" home: "Duty and dereliction guide thee back to solitude." In that solitude he would remember "the music of two voices and the light of one sweet smile." The voices are clearly Mrs. Boinville's and Cornelia's, the smile Cornelia's.

Further light is thrown on the situation by a letter of Shelley's to Hogg seven months later, on October 4, 1814:

> In the beginning of spring, I spent two months at Mrs. Boinville's without my wife. If I except the succeeding period these two months were probably the happiest of my life: the calmest the serenest the most free from care. The contemplation of female excellence is the favorite food of my imagination. Here was ample scope for admiration: novelty added a peculiar charm to the intrinsic merit of the objects: I had been unaccustomed to the mildness the intelligence the delicacy of a cultivated female. The presence of Mrs. Boinville & her daughter afforded a strange contrast to my former friendless & deplorable condition. I suddenly perceived that the entire devotion with which I had resigned all prospects of utility or happiness to the single purpose of cultivating Harriet was a gross & despicable superstition. Perhaps every degree of affectionate intimacy with a female, however slight, partakes of the nature of love. Love makes men quicksighted, & is only called blind by the multitude because he perceives the existence of relations invisible to grosser optics. I saw the full extent of the calamity which my rash & heartless union with Harriet: an union over whose entrance might justly be inscribed.

Lasciate ogni speranza, voi ch'entrate!

had produced. I felt as if a dead & living body had been linked together in loathsome & horrible communion. It was no longer possible to practise self deception: I believed that one revolting duty yet remained, to continue to deceive my wife.[8]

Before Shelley left to live with Mrs. Boinville, his home life had been "deplorable." He hints that he had even ceased his humanitarian writings—"I had resigned all prospects of utiity"—in order to devote himself to Harriet, but Harriet had proved incapable of development. His feeling for Harriet was not love but "friendship"; she was—the implication runs—too immature to feel true passion. He had held the marriage together only from a sense of "duty," the word used also in both the poems of the spring of 1814. He had not, he tells Hogg—and the poem to Cornelia supports this—realized the extent of his unhappiness until he left Harriet to live at Mrs. Boinville's. He implies that he had been in love with Cornelia. Certainly her qualities made him perceive the impossibility of achieving happiness in his own marriage. He felt—like Milton, whose words he echoes—that "a dead & living body had been linked together in loathsome & horrible communion." But he did not yet feel ready to break up the marriage; he still had to "deceive" Harriet by pretending affection for her.

In spite of these strains and tensions, Shelley remarried Harriet on March 24, 1814, only one week after the March 16 letter to Hogg. Why? The answer is given on the marriage certificate:

Percy Bysshe Shelley and Harriet Shelley (formerly Harriet Westbrook, Spinster, a Minor), both of this Parish, were remarried in this Church by Licence (the parties having been already married to each other according to the Rites and Ceremonies of the Church of Scotland), in order to obviate all doubts that have arisen, or shall or may arise, touching or concerning the validity of the aforesaid Marriage (by and with the consent of John Westbrook, the natural and lawful father of the said Minor), this Twenty-fourth day of March, in the Year 1814.[9]

The remarriage was instigated by legal motives—to ensure the legitimacy and hence the inheritance rights of Shelley's child and any future children of the marriage. That the instigation came from the Westbrooks seems certain, in view of Shelley's feelings as revealed in his letters to Hogg, but the fact that Shelley acquiesced shows that he was not at this time prepared to leave Harriet. Furthermore, he and Harriet were having sexual relations in March or April, for their son, Charles Bysshe, was born on November 30, and Harriet referred to him as "an eight months' child."[10] Charles was perhaps conceived in London when Shelley was there for the second marriage ceremony. By April 14 Harriet and Shelley were again separated.

Neither the remarriage nor the sexual relationship contradict the evidence that Shelley was deeply discontented with his marriage. In Shelley's day, marriages—whether good, bad, or indifferent—were supposed to last for a lifetime. Even under the most miserable circumstances people did not seriously consider a separation. Nor does the fact that Shelley had sexual relations with Harriet mean that he was in love with her.

In April there is one other piece of evidence to show that things were still not going smoothly, a letter of the eighteenth from Mrs. Boinville to Hogg: "Shelley is again a widower; his beauteous half went to town on Thursday [April 14] with Miss Westbrook, who is gone to live, I believe, in Southampton"[11] From this it appears that Eliza had remained in the household after the remarriage. This time Harriet had gone to London ("town"), later in the spring she was at Bath. And if Eliza had in fact gone to Southampton, she was not away long, for in May Shelley was again urging Harriet to get rid of her.

In May, Shelley encountered Mary Godwin.[12] A poem, *To Harriet* ("Thy look of love"), written shortly afterward and apparently sent in a letter to Harriet, reveals him in a turmoil of conflicting emotions as his loyalty to Harriet was being overwhelmed by his growing passion for Mary. Torn by guilt and frightened by the prospects of the moral struggle opening up before him, he urges Harriet to take him back, implying that they could perhaps be happy still if she would only get rid of Eliza:

> O trust for once no erring guide!
> Bid the remorseless feeling flee;
> 'Tis malice, 'tis revenge, 'tis pride,
> 'Tis any thing but thee;
> O, deign a nobler pride to prove,
> And pity if thou canst not love.[13]

A few weeks later this moral conflict had broken out of control. "Between his old feelings for Harriet, *from whom he was not then separated,*" wrote T. L. Peacock, who was with him much of the time, "and his new passion for Mary, he showed in his looks, in his gestures, in his speech, the state of a mind 'suffering, like a little kingdom, the nature of an insurrection.' His eyes were bloodshot, his hair and dress disordered." The poem in May reveals the beginning of this conflict. "He might well have said, after first seeing Mary Wollstonecraft Godwin," Peacock continued, 'Ut vidi! ut perii!' "[14]

The inhabitants of the rather motley Godwin menage were seven in number: William Godwin (previously married to Mary Wollstonecraft); Mary Jane Godwin, his second wife (married 1801); Fanny Imlay (born May 14, 1794), the daughter of Mary Wollstonecraft and Gilbert Imlay (with whom Mary had lived prior to her marriage with Godwin); Mary Godwin (born August 30, 1797), daughter of Mary Wollstonecraft and William Godwin; Clara Mary Jane ("Claire") Clairmont (born April 27, 1798), daughter of Mary Jane Godwin and a Swiss lover known as Clairmont; Charles Clairmont, son of Mary Jane Godwin and Clairmont; and William Godwin Junior, son of Mary Jane Godwin and William Godwin.[15] Shelley had started corresponding with Godwin in January 1812 and met him in the fall of that year. In the spring and summer of 1814 he was attempting to help Godwin financially. In March, Mary Godwin returned from a vacation in Scotland; Shelley and she met in May, fell in love, and in July eloped to the Continent. The most interesting contemporary account of these events is in a letter by Godwin on August 27 to a friend, John Taylor of Norwich. Godwin related the story to explain why—as a result of this misfortune—he was unable to pay him a debt:

You are already acquainted with the name of Shelley, the gentleman who more than twelve months ago undertook by his assistance to rescue me from my pecuniary difficulties. Not to keep you longer in suspense, he, a married man, has run away with my daughter. I cannot conceive of an event of more accumulated horror.

Mary, my only daughter, was absent in Scotland for her health during Shelley's former visits in London. She returned to me finally on the 30th of March last. Shelley came to London on the 18th of June; & as we expected every day the conclusion of the loan that has been raised it was necessary he should continue on the spot. He was under apprehension of arrests (for debt); & from this consideration I invited him to make my house his principal home, his known haunts being all at the west end of town. He lodged at an inn in Fleet Street, & took his meals with me. I had the utmost confidence in him; I knew him susceptible of the noblest sentiments; he was a married man, who had lived happily with a wife for three years. Accordingly the first week of his visit passed in perfect innocence; he was every day impatient to be spared to go into Wales, to secure a retreat he had fixed on, where he might reside with his wife & child, shut out from the rest of the world. When he found that for the moment impracticable, he desired to be absent one night only, that he might visit them at Bracknell, 30 miles from London, where he had left them. On Sunday, June 26, he accompanied Mary, & her sister, Jane Clairmont, to the tomb of Mary's mother, one mile distant from London; and there, it seems, the impious idea first occurred to him of seducing her, play[ing] the traitor to me, & deserting his wife. On Wednesday, the 6th of July, the transaction of the loan was completed; & on the evening of that very day he had the madness to disclose his plans to me, & to ask my consent. I expostulated with him with all the energy of which I was master, & with so much effect that for the moment he promised to give up his licentious love, & return to virtue. I applied all my diligence to waken up a sense of honour & natural affection in the mind of Mary, & I seemed to have succeeded. Mary & her sister Jane escaped from my house; and the next morning when I rose, I found a letter on my dressing table, informing me what they had done. I had been of opinion from the first that Mary could only be withheld from ruin by her mind; & in that, by a series of the most consumate dissimulation, she made me believe I had succeeded. I formed the plan of sending her from home, knowing the violence of Shelley's temper & far from certain what scenes he might be capable of acting: but I was well aware that in sending her from home I should be doing good, if she concurred with me, & concealed her retreat from her betrayer, but that she were capable of opposite conduct, I should be rather throwing her into his power.

You will imagine our distress. If anything could have added to it, it was this circumstance of Jane's having gone with her sister. Fanny has been for a month or two on a visit to a friend in Wales, & her aunts had come over from Ireland to meet her there; so that Mrs. Godwin & I were left in a moment without a female in the house. We enquired at the neighbouring livery-stables, & found that they had set off post for Dover in their way to France. Jane we were, & still are, most anxious to recover immediately; & therefore, after much deliberation, it was agreed that Mrs. G. should set off after them by the evening's mail. She overtook them at Calais. I had made it a condition in suffering her to depart, that she should avoid seeing Shelley, who had conceived a particular aversion to her as a dangerous foe to his views, & might be capable of any act of desperation. Mrs. Godwin wrote to Jane the very moment she reached Calais, July 29, who came to her at a separate inn, spent the night with her, & promised to return with her to England the next morning. But when morning arrived, she said she must see the fugitives for a few minutes, & in that interview all her resolutions were subverted. Not the most earnest intreaties of a mother could turn her from her purpose; & on Sunday, July 31, Mrs. Godwin returned once more, alone.[16]

To this must be added Mrs. Godwin's view that "all our troubles began in May," not in June; and Godwin's diary shows that Shelley was a frequent visitor in May.[17] As *To Harriet* ("Thy look of love") was written in May, Mrs. Godwin was doubtless right, although Shelley's involvement, both with Godwin and with Mary, was much deeper in June. From this information may be drawn the following salient facts: Mary returned to London on March 30; Shelley and she met in May; Shelley had many meals at the Godwins' from June 18 on; Shelley was thinking of going to Wales with Harriet and Ianthe, who were then at Bracknell, but whether this was in May or June is not clear; on June 26 he and Mary declared their love for each other; on July 28 they eloped, taking Claire Clairmont with them; Mrs. Godwin caught up with them at Calais on July 29, tried to persuade Claire to leave them but without success, and returned home on July 31.

Shelley's own account of some of these events, given in his letter to Hogg of October 4, 1814, differs somewhat from Godwin's:

In the month of June I came to London to accomplish some business with Godwin that had been long depending. The circumstances of the case required an almost constant residence at his house. Here I met his daughter Mary. The originality & loveliness of Mary's character was apparent to me from her very motions & tones of voice. The irresi[s]tible wildness & sublimity of her feelings shewed itself in her gestures and her looks—Her smile, how persuasive it was, & how pathetic! She is gentle, to be convinced & tender; yet not incapable of ardent indignation & hatred. I do not think that there is an excellence at which human nature can arrive, that she does not indisputably possess, or of which her character does not afford manifest intimations.

I speak thus of Mary—now & so intimately are our natures now united, that I feel whilst I describe her excellencies as if I were an egoist expatiating upon his own perfections—*Then,* how deeply did I not feel my inferiority, how willingly confess myself far surpassed in originality, in genuine elevation & magnificence of the intellectual nature until she consented to share her capabilities with me.

I speedily conceived an ardent passion to pos[s]ess this inestimable treasure. In my own mind this feeling assumed a variety of shapes, I disguised from myself the true nature of affection. I endeavored also to conceal it from Mary: but without success. I was vacillating & infirm of purpose: I shuddered to transgress a real duty, & could not in this instance perceive the boundaries by which virtue was separated from madness, *where* self devotion becomes the very prodigality of idiotism. Her understanding was made clear by a spirit that sees into the truth of things, & affections preserved pure & sacred from the corrupting contamination of vulgar superstitions. No expressions can convey the remotest conception of the *manner* in which she dispelled my delusions. The sublime & rapturous moment when she confessed herself mine, who had so long been her's in secret cannot be painted to mortal imaginations—Let it suffice to you, who are my friend to know & to rejoice that she is mine: that at length I possess the inalienable treasure, that I sought & that I have found.

To Godwin's factual picture this letter supplies psychological substance. Although Shelley, at Mrs. Boinville's, had begun to realize the hopelessness of his marriage, he went back to Harriet (and Eliza) and tried to hold the marriage together. In March he remarried Harriet, and in May or June was planning to take her and their child on a trip to Wales. When, however, he met Mary in May, his intentions of continuing his marriage on a basis of "friendship" and affection began to dissolve ("so long hers in secret"). Mary was not only a lovely, intelligent girl with similar views to his own, but she was the daughter of two people whom he almost worshiped, Mary Wollstonecraft and William Godwin. She reciprocated his passion. Yet on the surface all apparently looked calm to Godwin (and to Peacock—"It always appeared to me that you were very fond of Harriet").[18] Shelley seemed outwardly on good terms with his wife, but underneath he was disturbed and unhappy, as he had been for months; encountering Mary at first churned up and then concentrated his emotions.

To this picture can be added a few details from other sources. On June 8 Hogg witnessed a meeting between Shelley and Mary at Godwin's house which shows that they were by then either in love or close to it: "A thrilling voice called 'Shelley!' A thrilling voice answered 'Mary!' And he darted out of the room, like an arrow from the bow of the far-shooting king. A very young female, fair and fair-haired, pale indeed, and with a piercing look, wearing a frock of tartan, an unusual dress in London at that time, had called him out of the room."[19] In the last days of June, Shelley wrote a poem, *To Mary Wollstonecraft Godwin*:

thy lips did meet
Mine tremblingly; thy dark eyes threw
Their soft persuasion on my brain,
Charming away its dream of pain.

In July, Shelley inscribed a copy of *Queen Mab* to Mary, and Mary added a note to the inscription: "This book is sacred to me and as no other creature shall ever look into it I may write in it what I please—yet what shall I write —that I love the author beyond all powers of expression and that I am parted from him dearest and only love—by that love we have promised to each other although I may not be yours I can never be another's. But I am thine exclusively thine."[20]

On July 6 or 7, Harriet, who seems to have been at Bath again, wrote in alarm to their mutual friend, Thomas Hookham, the publisher: "You will greatly oblige me by giving the enclosed to Mr. Shelley. I would not trouble you but it is now four days since I have heard from him which to me is an age. Will you write by return of post and tell me what has become of him as I always fancy something dreadful has happened if I do not hear from him. If you tell me that he is well I shall not come to London; but if I do not hear from you or him I shall certainly come as I cannot endure this dreadful state of suspence. You are his friend and can feel for me."[21] Newman I. White commented on this letter: "No estranged couple corresponds so frequently that a hiatus of four days causes serious alarm."[22] But Shelley certainly by this time felt himself "estranged" from Harriet, and Harriet's absences from home do not indicate a normal situation. Shelley's hatred of Eliza was unconcealed, and neither his continuous pleas to Harriet to get rid of her (as in his poem in May) nor his complaints about the house being made "desolate" by Harriet's frequent absences can have been confined to his poetry. In fact, the indication is that there were frequent and bitter scenes, probably mostly, but not entirely, between Shelley and Eliza. Of these months Shelley declared three years later at the trial for the custody of his children: "at the commencement of my union with the present Mrs. Shelley, I was legally married to a woman of whom delicacy forbids me to say more than that we were disunited by incurable dissensions."[23] The implication is that the "dissensions" were between husband and wife. Harriet and the Westbrooks, however, in an age when divorce was virtually impossible, apparently felt that such "dissensions" constituted no actual threat to the marriage as a legal entity.

On July 12 or 13, Shelley called Harriet to Bracknell from Bath and told her of his love for Mary. Following the interview, he wrote to her: "Our connection was not one of passion & impulse. Friendship was its basis, & on this basis it has enlarged & strengthened. It is no reproach to me that you have never filled my heart with an all-sufficing passion—perhaps, you are even yourself a stranger to these impulses, which one day may be awakened by some nobler & worthier than me, and may you find a lover as passionate and faithful, as I shall ever be a friend affectionate & sincere!"[24] The next day—according to Mrs. Godwin—Harriet, weeping and badly frightened, visited the Godwins:

Shortly after, Harriet Shelley came up from Bracknell suddenly, and saw me and my husband alone. She was very much agitated, and wept, poor dear young lady, a great deal, because Mr. Shelley had told her yesterday at Bracknell that he was desperately in love with Mary Godwin. She implored us to forbid him our house and prevent his seeing Mary. We sympathized with her, and she went away contented, feeling as she said, quite sure that, not seeing Mary, he would forget her. We then spoke to Mary on the subject, and she behaved as well as possible—approved our renouncing his acquaintance, and wrote a few lines to Harriet to pray her not to be unhappy, as she would not see Mr. S. again.[25]

A day or so later, Mary—according to Claire Clairmont—went with Claire to see Harriet and told her she would "not think of Shelley's love for her." This reduced Shelley to desperation. Sometime after the middle of July he burst into the Godwin household with a pistol and a bottle of laudanum and proposed a suicide pact to Mary. He next tried to kill himself with laudanum and was nursed back to life by Mrs. Boinville. Mary relented and on July 28 they eloped in a post chaise with four horses (to "outstrip pursuit"), headed for Dover, and traveled thence by boat to Calais, taking Claire Clairmont with them.[26]

These events, which led to the end of the marriage of Shelley and Harriet, were not a unique melodrama but followed a pattern common in the breakdown of marriage: the husband, feeling unloved but still having some affection for his wife, turns toward other women, finds one with whom he falls in love, then suffers a moral crisis as he faces the alternatives of either continuing the old relationship on an unsatisfactory level or plunging boldly into a new one, with all the social opprobrium it would engender and the hurt it would inflict on his wife. Nor is the depth of the psychological disturbance suffered by Shelley unique. It can be paralleled every day in the newspapers—even to the attempted suicide.

These events must also be examined in relation to their underlying social and psychological motives. As Shelley was nineteen and Harriet sixteen when they married, the marriage relation was an immature one, in which, for the groom, the bride's character and mind were obscured by his sexual desire, and the bride was unready for the responsibilities of marriage or motherhood. Shelley, who had previously been in love with a young woman of his own social class, turned toward Harriet Westbrook in a turmoil of anger, despair, and hurt pride; he had known her for only a short time when they were married; and they were married after an elopement, without his family's participation. Furthermore, Shelley came from a landowning, county family, recently granted a baronetage, while Harriet's father, John Westbrook, although quite wealthy and living in a respectable neighborhood, was still a tavern owner. Hence, a family conflict was inherent in the marriage from the beginning, the Shelleys being convinced that the Westbrooks had arranged the marriage in order to acquire the family name and fortune, the Westbrooks determined that their Harriet should in time come into her own as mistress of Field Place. Shelley, although of aristocratic background, was a young man of radical principles with little interest in family or fortune. Nevertheless, although he had renounced his background in ideas and action, it was still there, and having been brought up with the ways and speech of the English landed gentleman, he must at times have found Harriet and

Eliza—especially Eliza—intolerably "Cockney." With these instabilities and conflicts built into the marriage from the beginning, its only hope for survival was for either Shelley or the Westbrooks to give in. If Shelley had agreed to return to home and orthodoxy, all would doubtless have been forgiven in time. Or the Westbrooks could have decided to accept their son-in-law as he was and to let Harriet lead a rambling, subversive existence for a while in the hope that matters might improve. But given the nature of the situation, no yielding was possible either way.

Shelley had already been expelled from Oxford and broken with his family for the sake of his principles. He was prepared to sacrifice his marriage also if it became necessary. He had written in the Notes to *Queen Mab*: "How long then ought the sexual connexion to last? What law ought to specify the extent of the grievances which should limit its duration? A husband and wife ought to continue so long united as they love each other: any law which should bind them to cohabitation for one moment after the decay of their affection would be a most intolerable tyranny, and the most unworthy of toleration."[27] In 1811, only a few months after the elopement, he had informed Harriet in the presence of Robert Southey that he would remain with her only so long as he continued to love her.[28] These things he meant quite literally. Thus, what doubtless seemed merely to be youthful aberrations to the Westbrooks, who were conservative and orthodox,[29] were in fact the principles on which he based his life.

It was clearly to attain the Westbrook family aims that Eliza entered the household. Eliza, about ten years older than Shelley, was in effect the Westbrook family manager for the marriage. That the family thought the marriage needed a manager is understandable, and Eliza, in spite of the "bad notices" she usually gets from Shelley's biographers, seems to have been a well-intentioned woman devoted to her younger sister. The move, nevertheless, was a serious blunder. The Westbrooks would have done better to leave the two young people to themselves. Eliza, doubtless only trying to help, fell into the classic pattern of the mother-in-law in the home, and the marriage turned into a long, relentless struggle between her and Shelley, with Harriet in the middle. The depth and continuousness of this struggle is revealed in Shelley's rather juvenile poems written in the early days of the marriage, for instance, in the conclusion of *To Harriet* ("Thy kiss to my soul"):

Harriet! adieu to all vice and care,
  Thy love is my Heaven, thy arms are my world;
While thy kiss and thy look to my soul remain dear
  I should smile tho' Earth from its base be hurled.
For a heart as pure and a mind as free
  As ever gave lover, to thee I give,
And all that I ask in return from thee
  Is to love like me and with me to live.

This heart that beats for thy love and bliss,
  Harriet! beats for its country too;
And it never would thrill with thy look or kiss
  If it dared to that country's cause be untrue.
Honor, and wealth and life it spurns,
  But thy love is a prize it is sure to gain,
And the heart that with love and virtue burns
  Will never repine at evil or pain.[30]

It appears from this poem that Harriet had been remonstrating with Shelley about his radical political activities, most probably those in Devon in the fall of 1812, which resulted in a government spy being put on his trail. It is clear from the early poems and Harriet's own remarks that the instigator of this quarrel was Eliza, as part of her attempt to bring Shelley into line. Harriet had listened to Eliza and then taken the matter up with Shelley. Shelley replies that his "country's cause"—by which he means democratic reforms and antiwar activities—must come first, that he can not condone "evil or pain," such as were at the time provoking food riots in nearby Cornwall. That Shelley realized the source of Harriet's protest is apparent in the phrase "with me to live." The emphasis is on "me"—to live with me, your husband, and get rid of your sister. By the spring of 1814 Eliza's interference had spread to all aspects of Shelley's domestic life. She had become "this miserable wretch."

What of the third member of the household, caught in this conflict of "mighty opposites"? What kind of a person was Harriet Shelley? In view of the rather malicious pictures of her drawn by Hogg and Dowden, it is only fair to give Peacock's tribute to her, which has the ring of truth as well as of impassioned vindication:

> Few are now living who remember Harriet Shelley. I remember her well, and will describe her to the best of my recollection. She had a good figure, light, active, and graceful. Her features were regular and well proportioned. Her hair was light brown, and dressed with taste and simplicity. In her dress she was truly *simplex munditiis*. Her complexion was beautifully transparent; the tint of the blush rose shining through the lily. The tone of her voice was pleasant; her speech the essence of frankness and cordiality; her spirits always cheerful; her laugh spontaneous, hearty, and joyous. She was well educated. She read agreeably and intelligently. She wrote only letters, but she wrote them well. Her manners were good; and her whole aspect and demeanour such manifest emanations of pure and truthful nature, that to be once in her company was to know her thoroughly. She was fond of her husband, and accommodated herself in every way to his tastes. If they mixed in society, she adorned it; if they lived in retirement, she was satisfied; if they travelled, she enjoyed the change of scene.[31]

Peacock's picture may be supplemented with a typical letter by Harriet, that of August 25, 1814, to her Irish friend Catherine Nugent:

I am afraid you will think I am not sincere, when I tell you what pleasure the sight of your handwriting caused me. I think as you do with the greatest horror on the present state of things—giving the slave trade to France for seven years. Can anything be more horrible? Peace has been dearly purchased at this price. I am dreadfully afraid America will never hold out against the numbers sent to invade her. How senseless all these rejoicings are! Deluded beings, they little know the many injuries that are to ensue. I expect France will soon have another revolution. The present king is not at all fitted to govern such a nation. Mr. Shelley is in France. You will be surprised to find I am not with him; but times are altered, my dear friend, and tho' I will not tell you what has passed, still do not think that you cloud my mind with your sorrows. Every age has its cares. God knows, I have mine. Dear Ianthe is quite well. She is fourteen months old, and has six teeth. What I should have done without this dear babe and my sister I know not. This world is a scene of heavy trials to us all. I little expected ever to go thro' what I have. But time heals the deepest wounds, and for the sake of that sweet infant, I hope to live many years. Write to me often. My dear friend, you know what pleasure your letters give me. I wish you lived in England that I might be near you. Tell me how you are in health. Do not despond, tho' I see nothing to hope for when all that was virtuous becomes vicious and depraved. So it is—nothing is certain in this world. I suppose there is another where those that have suffered keenly here will be happy. Tell me what you think of this. My sister is with me. I wish you knew her as well as I do. She is worthy of your love. Adieu, dear friend, may you still be happy is the first wish of your ever faithful friend.[32]

The impression given by Peacock is that if Eliza had not been present, Shelley and Harriet could have had a reasonably happy marriage. Harriet was beautiful, natural, and unaffected, "pure and truthful," "fond of her husband" and ready to "accommodate herself" to him, "well-educated," and not unintelligent. Her letter to Catherine Nugent shows that she was kind and thoughtful, with liberal and humanitarian views. Disturbed by an element of despondency in Catherine Nugent's letter, she answers that she wishes that she could be with her to help her. Her liberal views no doubt originally came from Shelley, but when she wrote this letter, Shelley was no longer with her. Catherine Nugent, a veteran of the 1798 Irish uprising, had evidently made some political comments, to which Harriet is responding. Both hatred of the slave trade and her fear that America would lose the war seem to reflect her own thinking; moreover, the latter sentiment was, in England at the time, subversive. Her feeling that the French situation was unstable proved to be true the next year when Napoleon escaped from Elba. Harriet was certainly still following world events with interest.

In the light of Peacock's picture and this letter, one can see why Shelley was attracted to Harriet and why, even after Eliza had entered the household, he wrote of her with warm affection and sometimes, as in the *Sonnet. to Harriet on Her Birthday*, with playful innuendo:

> O thou, whose radiant eyes and beamy smile—
> Yet even a sweeter somewhat indexing.

There is, however, another characteristic of Harriet, apparent alike in Peacock's account, the letter to Catherine Nugent, and Shelley's poems. Peacock reports that she "accommodated herself" and was "satisfied" no matter what Shelley did; he does not say that she loved Shelley but that she was "fond of" him—all of which suggests a certain passivity; and this is supplemented by a curious childlike quality in the letter to Catherine Nugent. Events seem to be just going on around Harriet, without her really participating in them: her husband has left her, and the only explanation she offers is that "all that was virtuous" has somehow become "vicious and depraved." Shelley's poems contain affection, though never passion, and also a note of failure to move Harriet to a deeper level of communion, either intellectual or emotional (*To Harriet*— "It is not blasphemy"):

> when life's aestival sun
> To deeper manhood shall have ripened me,
> . . . when some years have added judgement's store
> To all thy woman sweetness, all the fire
> Which throbs in thine enthusiast heart, not then
> Shall holy friendship (for what other name
> May love like ours assume?) . . .

Although Shelley here recognizes his own immaturity as well as Harriet's, the emphasis is on hers, and the key word is "friendship." So, too, in another early poem, *The Retrospect, Cwm Elan, 1812*:[33]

> Thou fair in form and pure in mind,
> Whose ardent friendship rivets fast
> The flowery band our fates that bind . . .

The most serious consequence of this passive aspect of Harriet's personality for the marriage was her dependence on Eliza. In the letter to Catherine Nugent, written a month after her husband had left her, there is no word of criticism of Eliza, no feeling that Eliza might have wrecked the marriage, but, on the contrary, evidence of continuing dependence. "Trust" in the "erring guide" was as strong as ever, and remained so until the end of Harriet's life.

It has been assumed that because Mary Godwin was only sixteen at the time, her role must have been negligible. But clearly this was not so. In his letter to Hogg in the fall of 1814, Shelley reveals that despite his theoretical belief that marriage should not outlast love, he was "vacillating and infirm" and felt that he had a "real duty" toward Harriet. He hesitated even to tell Mary that he was in love with her. Here Mary stepped in: she "confessed herself mine." When Shelley still hesitated, her "clear spirit," which had been "preserved pure and sacred" by the ministrations of William Godwin "from the contamination of vulgar superstitions," successfully "dispelled" Shelley's "delusions" in regard to his own marriage.

Doubtless there was more give and take than this picture indicates. Shelley, in his "ardent passion to pos[s]ess this inestimable treasure," and Mary, in her reciprocation of his passion, must step by step have jointly come to the brink where they faced the prospect of Shelley's leaving Harriet and his child. If Shelley quailed at this prospect, Mary did not. In the final oscillations of a passion whose direction must already have been fixed ("so long hers in secret"), it was she who made the final move. If Mary had not been in love with Shelley, determined to live her life with him and bold enough to act out her convictions, there could have been no elopement.

That Shelley should have fallen passionately in love with Mary Godwin was inevitable, as even Peacock realized, despite his admiration of Harriet. Not only was she beautiful and the daughter of Mary Wollstonecraft and William Godwin, but even at sixteen the creative talent that two years later produced *Frankenstein* must have been apparent. But it was also inevitable, that Mary should fall in love with Shelley. One must not be deceived by the caricature of the young Shelley as dreamy and ineffectual. On the contrary, as his actions and writings show, he had vigor and daring, sensitivity and warmth. His appeal to Mary must have been irresistible, and her determination to possess him, come what may, must have matched his to possess her. In addition, Mary's beliefs were similar to his. Had not her mother penned the *Vindication of the Rights of Woman*, and her father written in *Political Justice* that the "institution of marriage is a system of fraud . . . an affair of property and the worst of all properties"?[34] Armed with such beliefs, the two young people justified their actions. "It will be sufficient to say that, in all he did, he at the time of doing it believed himself justified to his own conscience," wrote Mary of these events in her Note on *Alastor* (1815), and doubtless she was speaking of herself also. "I am innocent of ill, either done or intended," Shelley declared to Southey six years later.[35]

Shelley apparently rationalized matters as follows. He did not love Harriet, and though she was "fond" of him, her primary dependence was on Eliza. He would not, then, be really abandoning Harriet and Ianthe, for they would simply go on living as they had, away from him and with Eliza. Furthermore, Harriet would come to no real harm, because her father was wealthy. Yet Shelley's letters and actions reveal an underlying guilt, for the simple fact was that, principles or no principles, when it came to a crisis, he put himself first and Harriet second. True, she had been foolish in keeping Eliza in the household and had proved incapable of being the kind of wife he needed; but she was still in love with him, even if not passionately. She had borne him one child and was pregnant with another. She did not want to end the marriage. The picture of the hurt and frightened girl given by Mrs. Godwin is borne out by Harriet's letter to Hookham before the elopement and that to Catherine Nugent after it. Shelley's interview with her in mid-July must have been shattering. He did have a duty toward her, and it was not just that of a legal tie. Nor was it a question of an abstract moral duty. The marriage had not deteriorated to a point where the husband hated the wife from whom he wished to be free. On the contrary, as the May poem shows, Shelley still felt a considerable attachment to Harriet. Her sweetness of character, her beauty, her very helplessness must have held great appeal to him. The thought of leaving her must at times have been almost intolerable, and the fact that he suppressed it did not mean that he had killed it.

Shelley, then, in June and July 1814 was in the not uncommon situation of a man with an unsatisfactory marriage who was passionately in love with another woman. Few alternatives were open to him. Divorce was then granted in England only after a hearing in the House of Lords, and only two or three were granted each year. In 1827 his sister Mary went through such a divorce proceeding, and those who wish to see the almost insuperable difficulty of obtaining a divorce and the nightmare of publicity that accompanied it—with evidence by detectives and chambermaids—should read her story.[36] Today, of course, hundreds of cases similar to Shelley's and Harriet's, involving young people marrying in haste, are daily handled in the divorce courts.

Divorce being, in fact, impossible, for even if the Shelleys had been willing to try their influence with the Lords, the Westbrooks certainly would not have consented, Shelley could either give up Mary and return to Harriet (and Eliza), or run away with Mary or continue his marriage with Mary as his mistress. The last was both the usual and the acceptable solution at the time, as Leigh Hunt indicated.[37] It was, in fact, what Shelley's grandfather had done. Sir Bysshe had a mistress in London who bore him several children.[38]

Alarms and Excursions

As soon as Mrs. Godwin had left the three fugitives at Calais, they went first to Paris, where Shelley raised £60 from a French banker or moneylender,[39] and then set out on what was in effect a honeymoon trip. It took them through France, Switzerland, Germany, and Holland, and was later described by Mary and Shelley in a little book published in 1817 called *History of a Six Weeks' Tour.*[40] On a map the trip is seen to form a large irregular arc beginning at Calais and ending at Rotterdam. They first journeyed southeast through Paris, Troyes, and Besançon to Switzerland, crossing the border at Pontarlier; thence to Lucerne and Brunnen, on the shores of Lake Lucerne. At Brunnen their money began to fail and they went by boat up the Reuss River to the Rhine, then up the Rhine through Strassburg to Cologne. At Cologne they went overland to Rotterdam, whence they sailed for England. The trip began on July 28, 1814, from London and ended back in London on September 13. From Mary's and Claire's journals and from the *History of a Six Weeks' Tour* it appears to have been a happy, carefree trip with many interesting minor adventures, including a pack donkey so feeble that it had to be carried.[41] But Shelley was shocked by the war devastation of France:

"I cannot describe to you the frightful desolation of this scene. Village after village entirely ruined and burned; the white ruins towering in innumerable forms of destruction among the beautiful trees. The inhabitants were famished; families once perfectly independant now beg their bread in this wretched country. No provisions, no accom[m]odation; filth, misery & famine everywhere." [42]

Two aspects of this trip have aroused discussion: first, Claire's being along, and second, the fact that Shelley wrote a letter to Harriet on August 13 urging her to come to Geneva—"where you will at least find one firm and constant friend, to whom your interests will be always dear"—and to bring with her some legal papers Shelley had arranged to have drawn up providing for her maintenance. "Do not," he counseled her, "part with any of your money."[43]

By taking Claire on the trip, Shelley laid himself open to the charge that he was having sexual relations with her as well as with Mary. But, although he was certainly having sexual relations with Mary, who gave birth to a seven-month baby in February 1815, there is no indication in the girlish and outspoken journals of Mary and Claire of a *ménage à trois*.[44] It seems understood that Shelley and Mary are lovers and Claire is a kind of sister to both. Any other arrangement would probably not have occurred to two sixteen-year-old girls who, up to this time, had led sheltered lives.

Why, then, did Claire go along? Dowden, who had access not only to documents but to oral tradition, commented: "It was stated by Jane [Claire] that she left the house in Skinner Street on the morning of July 28, believing that no more was intended than an early walk, and that on meeting Shelley at the corner of Hatton Garden, she was pressed by him and Mary to enter the post-chaise and accompany them to France, because she was skilled in the language of that country, with which they were unfamiliar."[45] Although this statement has been ridiculed, it is probably true. Claire was of Swiss background and knew French well. It was frightening enough for Mary to be eloping, let alone eloping to a foreign country recently ravaged by British and allied armies. Taking Claire along at the last minute as an interpreter fits the mood of youthful impetuosity that animates the scene.

Moreover, the decision to continue on the trip was made by Claire. After the party arrived in Calais, Claire spent the night with her mother. The next day, according to Shelley's entry in Mary's diary, she told them that she was "unable to withstand the pathos of Mrs. Godwin's appeal. She appealed to the Municipality of Paris—to past slavery and to future freedom. I counselled her to take at least half an hour for consideration. She returned to Mrs. Godwin and informed her that she resolved to continue with us."[46] Shelley seems not to have cared greatly whether Claire came or not.

Shelley's suggestion that Harriet come to Geneva has been interpreted as an invitation to her to join the elopement trip. But to judge from the letter, he appears to have thought of settling for a while at or near Geneva, and he is merely urging Harriet to settle there also so that he can help her financially and personally—an impractical enough suggestion, to be sure, but one dictated neither by lust nor delusion but by feelings of guilt and a desire to get her away from her sister. That he did not intend Harriet to live in the same household with himself and Mary is clear from another paragraph of the letter in which he speaks of a "retreat I will procure for you among the mountains." The confusion has perhaps arisen in part because of a letter by Harriet in which she stated that Shelley, in the first tumult of telling her of his love for Mary, had the "folly" to believe that she could continue to live with him "as his sister" and Mary "as his wife."[47] This was obviously impractical, but people throw out such thoughts in emotional trauma. By the time of the elopement trip, Shelley's guilt feelings had assumed less desperate form.

Back in London, the travelers found a cold reception.[48] They were snubbed by most of their old friends, including Godwin (forgetful of the free love doctrines of *Political Justice*), Mrs. Boinville (from whom Shelley had borrowed £40), the Newtons, and Mary's Scottish friends the Baxters. Hogg inquired wryly after Shelley's "two wives." Even Shelley's mother no longer wanted to see him. He had little money, being cut off from the £200 a year that Harriet had received from her father and having to subsist on the £200 a year provided by his own father, a portion of which he turned over to Harriet. In addition, he was burdened by debts dating back to former days and was being pursued by bailiffs trying to collect for a carriage he had bought for Harriet. It became necessary to shift lodgings continually and to see Mary clandestinely, usually only for an hour or two. "Dearest Shelley," wrote Mary in a typical letter, "you are solitary and uncomfortable why cannot I be with you to cheer you and to press you to my heart oh my love you have no friends why then should you be torn from the only one who has affection for you—But I shall see you tonight and this is the hope that I shall live on through the day."[49]

At the same time Shelley was trying to make a permanent financial arrangement for Harriet. Although he had no ready funds, he was still heir to the family estate and was hoping that legal measures could be devised whereby part of this inheritance could be obtained in advance. Copies of some of Shelley's letters to Harriet were preserved because they were introduced by the Westbrooks into the trial two years later over the custody of their children.[50] In the second letter in the series, Shelley informs Harriet that there is no hope of a reconciliation: "My attachment to Mary neither could nor ought to have been overcome. Our spirits & [ ] are united. We met with passion, she has resigned all for me."[51] (The blank left by the legal transcriber presumably read "bodies"; as he seemed to have no difficulty with Shelley's hand elsewhere, the omission must have been deliberate.)

Shortly thereafter the atmosphere changed. Shelley writes to Harriet:

You say that you have employed an attorney, but that you intend to take no legal measures. This is itself a legal measure—wherefore not let Hookham or any common friend, be the arbiter of our differences if any difference exists. He can explain to you my resources, my powers my intentions. I repeat that I consider this application as an act of determined hostility.

I desire to renew no intercourse of whatsoever nature with you, whilst you act under the principles, which you recently avowed these you were formerly the for[e]most to stigmatize & abhor. A common love for all that the world detests, was once the bond of union between us. This you have been the first to break: & you have lost a friend whom you will with difficulty replace. Your contumelious language toward Mary is equally impotent & mean. You appeal to the vilest superstitions of the most ignorant & slavish of mankind. I consider it an insult that you address such Cant to me.[52]

In reading these letters, we have to keep in mind that they were written by a young man for whom law and social conventions were merely forms to be tested against principles. The fact that Harriet was legally his wife was of no consequence. There were only two things that mattered: whether she could be turned into a person who would work for human betterment, and whether he loved her. When both questions were answered in the negative, she ceased to be his wife in what he considered the real sense of the word. And another woman whom he did love, and who shared his humanitarian ideals, became in fact his wife, regardless of what the law or society dictated. Harriet, unresponsive to these ethical abstractions, reacted by hiring a lawyer to get money out of Shelley, by calling Mary names, and by spreading a story that Godwin, apostle of free love, had "favored" Shelley's "passion" for Mary.[53] One puzzling aspect of the correspondence is Harriet's apparent lack of funds for her father was a wealthy man.

A few months later Shelley's financial difficulties were resolved by the death of his grandfather, Sir Bysshe Shelley, on January 6, 1815. His will and the negotiations that followed were long and complex, but they ended with Shelley's receiving an annuity of £1,000, of which he signed over £200 to Harriet.[54] Shelley, brought up as heir to a great estate, was knowledgeable about financial and legal affairs, and his letters of 1816 explaining these and other matters to Godwin are direct and businesslike. For example:

I possessed in January, 1815, a reversion expectant on the death of the survivor of my grandfather and father, approaching so nearly to the nature of an absolute reversion, that by a few ceremonies I could, on these contingencies falling, possess myself of the fee-simple and alienate the whole. My grandfather had exerted the utmost power with which the law invested him to prevent this ultimate alienation, but his power terminated in my person, and was exercised only to the restraint of my father. The estate of which I now speak is that which is the subject of the settlement of 1792.

My grandfather's will was dictated by the same spirit which had produced the settlement. He desired to perpetuate a large mass of property. He therefore left the moiety of about £240,000 to be disposed of in the following manner. My father was to enjoy the interest of it during his life. After my father's death I was to enjoy the interest alone in like manner conditionally on my having previously deprived myself of the absolute power which I now possess over the settled estates of 1792, and so accept of the reversion of a life annuity of £12,000 or £14,000 per an. in exchange for a reversion of landed property of 6, 7, or 8000 per an. All was reversion. I was entitled, in no view of the case, to any immediate advantage.[55]

During those stormy months from the spring of 1814 to the summer of 1815, Shelley had little time for writing. While on the Continent he worked on his fragmentary novel, *The Assassins,* and after returning to London, he was connected with a radical magazine called *The Theological Enquirer,* which published the first part of *A Refutation of Deism* and ran a series of articles on *Queen Mab* with copious quotations from the poem.[56]

During these months a set of relationships among Shelley, Claire, Mary, and Hogg developed that, with the publication of previous unknown letters by Mary and Shelley in 1944,[57] has resulted in still another controversy. When Mary's pregnancy became hampering, Claire took Mary's place on Shelley's trips to lawyers and moneylenders; and Mary tried to get rid of her. "Shelley and I go upstairs and talk of Clara's going," she wrote in her journal. "The prospect appears to me more dismal than ever; not the least hope. This is, indeed hard to bear."[58] During March, April, and the first part of May, the journal shows that Shelley and Claire were together a good deal, with Mary's comments becoming increasingly caustic. In July, when Shelley was away looking for a house near London and Mary was at Clifton in Devon, she wrote to him: "Pray is Clary with you? for I have enquired several times & no letters—but seriously it would not in the least surprise me if you have written to her from London & let her know that you are there without me that she should have taken some such freak—. . . Tomorrow is the 28th of July—dearest ought we not to have been together on that day— . . . dearest best Shelley pray come to me—pray pray do not stay away from me—this is delightful weather and you better we might have a delightful excursion to Tintern Abbey."[59]

Although Mary places the emphasis on Claire's difficult personality and impetuousness, there is an undercurrent of fear that she may be pursuing Shelley and he ready to encourage her. Whether they actually had an affair is a matter of controversy.[60] When Claire was involved with Byron the following year and Byron twitted her about Shelley, she seems to have denied that they had had an affair and to have given him Shelley's letters to her as evidence (letters now apparently lost): "If I had not been hurried out of town yesterday, I should certainly have sent you Shelley's letters. Pray compare them and acquit me, I entreat you from the list of those you suspect. Nothing could give me greater happiness than to be believed by you for what I am; one who loves you disinterestedly for your beauty and talents alone."[61]

At the time of the "Neapolitan child" crisis, Shelley implied in a letter to Mary that Claire had never been his mistress: "Elise says that Clare was my mistress—that is all very well & so far there is nothing new: all the world has heard so much & people may believe or not believe as they think good."[62] At the same time Mary, in a letter defending her husband to a third party, called such an insinuation "so wickedly false, so beyond all imagination fiendish."[63] The evidence of Shelley's autobiographical poetry, however, especially *Epipsychidion*, indicates that an affair took place, if not at this time, perhaps somewhat later. But whether it did or not Mary clearly had grounds for anxiety. She was pregnant, Claire was in the household, and Shelley was restless.

This, then, is one side of the picture. The other side involves Mary and Hogg. Hogg had begun to visit the household in November 1814. By January 1815 he was sending Mary presents and suggesting that they become lovers. Mary wrote him two sets of letters, the first in January (when she was pregnant), which promises future bliss, the second in April (after the birth of her child), written at the village of Salt Hill where she was vacationing with Shelley, which are in a gay, flirtatious mood. The following, written on January 7, is typical of the first set:

Dearest Hogg

I send you what you asked me for [a lock of hair].—I sincerely believe that we shall all be so happy. My affection for you although it is not now exactly as you would wish will I think dayly become more so—then what can you have to add to your happiness—I ask but for time—time which for other causes beside this—phisical causes—that must be given—Shelley will be subject to these also—& this dear Hogg will give time to for that love to spring up which you deserve and will one day have

All this—you know is sweet hope but we need not be prudent now—for I will try to make you happy & you say it is in my power

Most affectionately yours
Mary[64]

A letter of April 25 is typical of the Salt Hill letters:

My dear Jefferson

I am no doubt a very naughty dormouse [here follows a tiny drawing of a dormouse] but indeed you must forgive me—Shelley is now returned—he went to Longdills—did his business & returned he heard from Harriets attorney that she meant (if he did not make a handsome settlement on her) to prosecute him for atheism.—

How are you amusing yourself with the Pecksie away very doleful no doubt but my poor Jefferson Id shall soon be up again & you may remember that even if we had staid you would not have seen much of me as you must have been with me—

Do you mean to come to us—I suppose not Prince Prudent well as you please but remember I should be *very* happy to see you. If you had not been a lawyer you might have come with us—

Rain has come after a mild beautiful day but Shelley & I are going to walk as it is only showery How delightful it is to read Poetry among green shades Tintern Abbey thrilled me with delight—

But Shelley calls me to come, for

The sun is set
and night is coming.

I will write perhaps by a night coach or at least early tomorrow—

I shall return soon & remain till then an affectionate but

Runaway Dormouse[65]

Enclosed with two letters by Mary on April 26 was one by Shelley:

I shall be very happy to see you again, & to give you your share of our common treasure of which you have been cheated for several days. The Maie knows how highly you prize this exquisite possession, & takes occasion to quiz you in saying that it is necessary for me to absent from London, from your sensibility to its value. Do not fear. A few months [these words crossed out]. We will not again be deprived of this participated pleasure—

I did all the requisite acts at Longdill's yesterday at one o'Clock & returned immediately to the Pecksie. I could not persuade her to come to London.[66]

These letters have been interpreted in various ways. Some argue that they mean that Mary was having an affair with Hogg with Shelley's approval,[67] others that although there was no actual affair the situation was "slightly insane" or "beyond belief."[68] That Mary and Hogg were not lovers in January is indicated in Mary's first letter, quoted above, where "phisical causes" were said to prevent such relations. By this, Mary meant that she was pregnant and that Shelley was therefore not having relations with her either. In early nineteenth century England, intercourse seems to have been medically discouraged throughout pregnancy. She and Hogg, therefore, need not "be prudent now," for everyone would realize that they could not be lovers.

The baby was born prematurely on February 22 and died on March 6. Mary, as shown by her journal, was in no state for romance in the following weeks. And for the period of the April letters, there is evidence involving another pregnancy. Mary's next child, William, was born on January 24, 1816. He was healthy and red-cheeked and appears to have been a full-term baby; at least there is no mention of his being premature, as with the first baby.[69] He must therefore have been conceived in the spring of 1815. If Mary had been having relations with both Hogg and Shelley during this period, one would find indications of uncertainty with regard to his paternity. There is, however, no such uncertainty either in the letters and journals of Shelley and Mary or in the comments of those close to them. References to William are no different from those to Shelley's other children by Mary, Clara and Percy Florence; William is always taken as their child. In fact, there is more actual evidence regarding the paternity of William than usual, because he died while still a child, and his final illness and death evoked expressions of fear and grief that are simultaneously testimony of parenthood.

William died on June 7, 1819, in Rome. On June 5 Mary wrote to Maria Gisborne: "William is in the greatest danger—We do not quite despair yet we have not the least possible reason to hope."[70] Shelley, Mary informed Marianne Hunt, "watched 60 miserable—deathlyke hours without closing his eyes" over the deathbed.[71] The next day Shelley wrote to Peacock: "Yesterday after an illness of only a few days my little William died. There was no hope from the moment of the attack. You will be kind enough to tell all my friends, so that I need not write to them—It is a great exertion to me to write this, & it seems to me as if, hunted by calamity as I have been, that I should neve[r] recover any cheerfulness again—"[72] On July 2, Hogg, presumably informed of the death by Peacock, wrote to Shelley: "I have hitherto been unwilling to mention my main reason for writing to you now—I mean your unfortunate loss of that sweet little boy. You have been a most unlucky father in all respects."[73]

Shelley's grief poured out in two poems, the first beginning:

> My lost William, thou in whom
> Some bright spirit lived, and did
> That decaying role consume
> Which its lustre faintly hid,—
> Here its ashes find a tomb,—
> But beneath this pyramid
> Thou art not—if a thing divine
> Like thee can die—thy funeral shrine
> Is thy Mother's grief and mine.[74]

All these utterances—by Shelley, by Mary, and by Hogg—are sincere and spontaneous. Placed beside other similar references at other times, they establish beyond reasonable doubt that William was Shelley's child.

There are other indications that the "affair" between Mary and Hogg did not go beyond a flirtation. It is clear that Mary was in love with Shelley. When they were separated in November 1814, for example, a typical passage in one of her letters reads: "so goodnight—May you sleep as well as though it were in my arms—but I know you wont—dearest love Goodnight." Moreover, Mary's later feelings about Hogg do not imply a previous love affair, for they have in them neither the sentiment that would linger over from a tender affair, nor the hatred that might result from a broken one. She merely finds Hogg unpleasant and selfish. That she had this attitude from a period not too long after her letters of the spring of 1815 is implied by a comment on Hogg to Leigh Hunt and his wife in March 1817: "I do not like him and I think he is more disagre[e]able than ever. I would not have him come every week to disturb our peace by his ill humour and noise for all the w[orld]."[75]

If the letters of Mary to Hogg are read as though they were written by a mature, sophisticated woman, they could certainly imply an actual love affair. But if they are read as the product of a girl of seventeen, in love with Shelley, they have a different sound. Why, however, did Mary write the letters? Why did she get involved with Hogg at all? Various motives appear in the letters themselves and in Mary's journal. One is her jealousy of Claire and her exasperation with Shelley for his reluctance to eject her from the household. Her first letter to Hogg complains, "they have both left me and I am here all alone."[76] When Claire was finally leaving, Mary's jealousy is clear from her journal comments: "Shelley goes out with his friend [Claire] . . . Shelley and the lady [Claire] walk out. After tea, talk; write Greek characters. Shelley and his friend have a last conversation."[77] Furthermore, Mary was undoubtedly at first somewhat attracted to Hogg, whom she had known only a few weeks. Hogg was gallant, witty, and full of masculine assurance. When her baby died, she wrote asking him to come to see her: "You are so calm a creature & Shelley is afraid of a fever from the milk."[78] Hogg's "calm" was clearly a relief from Shelley's excitability. It took time for Mary to recognize Hogg's limitations—his lack of sensitivity, his self-centered caution, his opportunism. That by April some of this was becoming apparent is shown in her teasing of "Prince Prudent." Nor was Mary averse, at least in theory, to a free love adventure, for she had, after all, been brought up by the high priest of such doctrines. Finally, to Godwinian theory was added Shelleyan persuasion. Shelley was always—as her letters to Hogg made clear—to be first in her heart; and if Shelley believed that a *ménage à trois* arrangement would be desirable, she was willing to consider it.

However, it is most unlikely that Mary had any serious intention of embarking upon an affair with Hogg. She promised it for the future; "phisical causes" safely precluded it in the present. When those causes had been removed, she went away on a vacation in April, not with Hogg but with Shelley. Hogg, left behind in London, had to be content with teasing letters. In May she apparently put her foot down and insisted that Claire be turned out. In June, she and Shelley are off in Devon, and Hogg is still at his Inns of Courts in London.

Such seem to have been Mary's views and motives. What were Shelley's? They are illuminated by two previous episodes involving Shelley, Hogg, and a woman. When at Oxford, Shelley created for Hogg's benefit a romantic picture of his favorite sister, Elizabeth, and Hogg became so excited that he made the long coach trip to Field Place simply on the chance of catching a glimpse of her. Shelley's delight in this situation was obvious. He wrote sensuously suggestive letters to excite Hogg further. But when Hogg became too ardent, he tired of the game and began to discourage him.[79] Shelley's language in the letters indicates that he was getting sensual pleasure from the fantasy of the union of his sister with Hogg, but they show also that when there seemed to be any chance of the fantasy becoming reality, his interest slackened.

A few months later Shelley eloped with Harriet Westbrook, and Hogg joined them on their honeymoon. Shelley left them alone at York while he went in search of funds in Sussex and London; Hogg attempted to seduce Harriet. When Shelley returned, he whisked Harriet off to the Lake District. Hogg wrote, expostulating: if Shelley believed in free love, as he claimed, why should he have taken Harriet away? Shelley replied that free love was, after all, love, and love on both sides. Hogg might love Harriet, but Harriet did not love Hogg, and the choice was hers. Once again Shelley was placing Hogg in the path of temptation, then blocking his gratification.

In Shelley's letter of April 26, 1815, such phrases as "our common treasure" and "deprived of this participated pleasure" certainly could be taken to mean that Mary was having sexual relations with both Shelley and Hogg. Yet the weight of the evidence indicates that Mary and Hogg were not lovers. If so, Shelley must simply mean that both he and Hogg received pleasure from Mary's company. Shelley, however, was certainly aware of the sexual implications of the phrases. Why, then, did he write them? The fact that the letter was addressed by Mary and was enclosed inside two letters by her to Hogg indicates that Mary almost certainly read the letter. If she did, Shelley must have derived excitement from showing it to her as well as from writing it in the first place. A state of excitement is perhaps indicated also by the occasionally awkward wording in the letter, and by the handwriting, which is rather ragged. These phrases seem to have been designed to whet Hogg's appetite; and Shelley enjoyed writing them. Both psychological patterns are apparent in the earlier letters to Hogg on Elizabeth Shelley.

In spite of his April 26 letter, Shelley probably had no more intention of allowing a serious affair to develop than did Mary. He knew as well as Mary of the "phisical" barrier. And he always had in reserve, when this barrier was removed, the final club that he had used in the case of Harriet: Mary must be willing. He probably sensed that Mary, despite her flirtatious letters, was not willing. How much of this motivation was conscious and how much unconscious or semiconscious is difficult to say. If the accusation had been made that Shelley was simply tormenting Hogg, he would doubtless have denied it and stoutly reaffirmed his free love principles. But these principles gave him an out: both parties must be in love.

What, finally, were Hogg's motives? Hogg seems to have been particularly interested in having love affairs with women associated with Shelley. Not only did he pursue Elizabeth, Harriet, and Mary, but after Shelley's death he married Jane Williams, to whom Shelley had written love poems and with whom he wanted to have an affair.[80]

Hogg's intention toward Elizabeth became apparent in a theory he developed of "perfectibility" in love, a theory that Shelley regarded with suspicion, as it seemed to imply a primarily physical scale of ascension.[81] Hogg's letters to Shelley on Harriet (now lost) appear to have been rather wild and impassioned (with threats of suicide). That he wanted an affair with Mary seems clear from both Mary's and Shelley's letters. But for Hogg, love and sex did not necessarily go together, and it was on this question that Shelley broke with him, as he indicates in a review of Hogg's novel, *Memoirs of Alexy Haimatoff*:

> But we cannot regard his commendation to his pupil to indulge in promiscuous concubinage without horror and detestation. The author appears to deem the loveless intercourse of brutal appetite, a venial offence against delicacy and virtue! he asserts that a transient connection with a cultivated female, may contribute to form the heart without essentially vitiating the sensibilities. It is our duty to protest against so pernicious and disgusting an opinion. No man can rise pure from the poisonous embraces of a prostitute, or sinless from the desolated hopes of a confiding heart . . . [the] mind must be pure from the fashionable superstitions of gallantry, must be exempt from the sordid feelings which with blind idolatry worship the image and blaspheme the deity, reverence the type, and degrade the reality of which it is an emblem.[82]

In essence, this is the same criticism that Shelley implied in regard to Hogg's "perfectibility in love" scheme. Hogg, though sensitive, is primarily sensual; he analyzes love but does not understand it in its true fullness or beauty; he would degrade a woman by possessing her without love, and would not scruple to use the insincerities of "gallantry," as he had with Harriet.[83] In short, he is not much better—in these regards—than the:

> Things whose trade is, over ladies
> To lean, and flirt, and stare, and simper.[84]

It seems unlikely, then, that if it had come to a showdown, Shelley would have been willing for Hogg and Mary to have an affair.

In July 1815, Shelley found a house near London, a quiet cottage just outside Windsor Forest, near the Bishopsgate road into the forest. In August, he and Mary moved in. Here he began to write again producing *Alastor,* his first major poem since *Queen Mab* (written more than two years previously). At Bishopsgate, he began to see a good deal of the third of his biographical "sons of light," Thomas Love Peacock, whom he had first met in London in the fall of 1812 and who had gone with him and Harriet to Edinburgh the following year. In 1815, Peacock had not hit upon his true literary medium, the satiric novel of manners, but his *Palmyra* and other poems had attracted Shelley, and the two men became good friends.

In the years 1858, 1860, and 1862 Peacock published in *Fraser's Magazine* a series of articles on Shelley, which were later issued in his book *Memoirs of Shelley.* These memoirs, like Hogg's biography, cannot be used uncritically but have to be sifted and evaluated. Although Peacock was a liberal—Jefferson and Cobbett were among his heroes—and favored parliamentary reform, he was not a social revolutionary nor egalitarian. And even his political liberalism was muted by a pose of satiric aloofness which, although it gave a brilliant intellectual sparkle to his novels, caused people to consider him "cold."[85] Shelley's expansive hopes for humanity's future seemed extravagant to him, and although a poet himself, he was out of tune with the new poetry of the age. In short, the framework within which he viewed Shelley was a narrow one, and within it, his penchant for the comic distorted the picture. In his novels, most notably in the character of Scythrop in *Nightmare Abbey,* Shelley is depicted as a well-meaning but impractical idealist. In the *Memoirs,* Peacock, like Hogg, provided a series of personal anecdotes and individual eccentricities, some of which he called "semi-delusions." An account of any great poet that confines itself largely to anecdotes and eccentricities will by its very omissions inevitably give a demeaning impression. Within his limits, however, Peacock was accurate and often acute. For instance, he was correct in dismissing a ridiculous story that Shelley had told him of a mysterious visit from Williams of Tremadoc (who, Shelley said, later sent him a diamond necklace in a letter).[86] But such a story was not a "semi-delusion"—Shelley knew perfectly well that the story was not true—but was an imaginative invention in which the teller, having created an incident partly tongue-in-cheek, built up others to substantiate it rather than admitting its falsity, and took ironic delight in stringing his listener along.

In addition to anecdotes and other narrative material, Peacock examined the breakdown of Shelley's marriage to Harriet. Although openly a champion of Harriet—reacting specifically to Hogg's unfavorable picture of her—he tried to give an objective account. Yet either he was slanting his material, or he was curiously unobservant. For instance, he was with Shelley, Harriet, and Eliza in Edinburgh in 1813 when Shelley wrote the letter to Hogg in late November that suggests alienation and dissension, and he must have known something of the situation a few months later at Bracknell—of Harriet's absences, Shelley's hatred of Eliza and interest in Cornelia Turner—for he knew Mrs. Boinville and Mrs. Newton, yet he stated in the *Memoirs* that there "was no estrangement, no shadow of a separation, till Shelley became acquainted" with Mary Godwin.[87] This statement, which has been accepted by some biographers at face value, places, in effect, the sole responsibility for the breakdown of the marriage on Shelley.

Geneva and Byron

In the spring of 1816, Claire Clairmont—then seventeen—wrote a series of love letters to Byron. The first, signed "E. Trefusis," informed Byron that she was a "woman whose reputation has yet remained unstained," and who was now placing her happiness in his hands.[88] The other letters follow a similar pattern. The upshot was that Byron obliged her, and she became pregnant. When Byron, soon after their apparently brief series of meetings, left for Geneva, Claire wanted to follow him, and Shelley and Mary were only too happy to go with her.[89] About May 15, 1816, Shelley, Mary, and Claire arrived in Geneva, and with the arrival ten days later of Byron (who had taken a circuitous route) the first period in the friendship of the two poets began.

We have grown so used to thinking of Shelley and Byron as two of the great poets of the age that it is necessary to recall that in the spring of 1816, while Byron was already famous, Shelley was virtually unknown. Byron was the great "milord," Shelley an obscure radical with perhaps a certain clandestine fame as the author of *Queen Mab* (which Byron had admired). When Byron's physician, John Polidori, met Shelley, he jotted down in his diary: "Dined P[ercy] S[helley], the author of Queen Mab, came; bashful, shy, consumptive; twenty-six; separated from his wife; keeps the two daughters of Godwin, who practice his theories; one L[ord] B[yron]'s."[90] To Polidori, then, Shelley was merely a consumptive-looking young man with extreme ideas on sex and a bent for radical literature.

When English society heard of this visit of Shelley, Mary, and Claire to Byron, a story spread (perhaps begun by Southey) of a "league of incest" at Geneva.[91] Although slander of this kind directed at Shelley or Byron was political in motive, there was certainly food for gossip. Mary and Shelley were unmarried, Shelley's deserted wife and two children were in England, and Byron and Claire were continuing their affair: "I would have come to you tonight [wrote Claire to Byron] if I thought I could be of any use to you. If you want me I am sure Shelley would come and fetch me. I am afraid to come dearest for fear of meeting anyone. Can you present the copying? . . . Shelley says he won't look at my note, so don't be offended." Moreover, Claire had written to Byron on the way to Geneva virtually offering him Mary: "You will, I suppose, wish to see Mary, who talks and looks at you with admiration. You will, I daresay, fall in love with her; she is very handsome and very amiable, and you will no doubt be blessed in your attachment. Nothing can afford me such pleasure as to see you happy in any of your attachments. If it should be so, I will redouble my attentions to please her. I will do everything she tells me whether it be good or bad, for I would not stand low in the affection of the person so beyond blest as to be beloved of you.[92]

In Claire's letters to Byron she was apparently telling him what she thought he wanted to hear. She had discussed Shelley's free love views with him, and he seems to have assumed, or pretended to assume, that the Shelley circle lived in accordance with them. He was obviously amused by Claire's stories, and Claire was willing to tell him anything that kept up his interest in her. In this instance it is most unlikely that Mary knew anything of Claire's vicarious generosity. In fact, it appears from Claire's early letters to Byron that she felt Mary would disapprove even of Claire's own affair. At any rate, to give Byron's testimony—and Byron was not reticent about his conquests—nothing came of Claire's offer of Mary:

> I have been in some danger on the lake (near Meillerie), but nothing to speak of; and, as to all these "mistresses," [he was writing to his half-sister, Augusta Leigh] Lord help me—I have had but one. Now don't scold; but what could I do?—a fool-

ish girl, in spite of all I could say or do, would come after me, or rather went before —for I found her here—and I have had all the plague possible to persuade her to go back again; but at last she went. Now, dearest, I do most truly tell thee, that I could not help this, that I did all I could to prevent it, and have at last put an end to it. I was not in love, nor have any love left for any; but I could not exactly play the Stoic with a woman, who had scrambled eight hundred miles to unphilosophize me.[93]

As a balance to Claire one might also take a letter from Byron's friend, John Cam Hobhouse to Lady Melbourne a few months later:

It is true that a neighbouring farm-house did, until lately give shelter to an establishment of a singular description, between whom and my friend malicious report assigned some small intimacy, but as I never saw either of the inmates of this same mansion except a good natured being, the son of one Sir Timothy Shelley, I really have no evidence to bring upon this scandalous topic. Whatever has passed, everything has been conducted with the utmost decency, and you may safely contradict, if worth while, every story told of the irregularities said to have been imported from Piccadilly amongst the Maids of the Lake.[94]

The indication is that Geneva witnessed no more than the de facto marriage of Shelley and Mary and the continuation of the affair between Byron and Claire. Nevertheless, Byron obviously thought that Shelley had been a previous lover of Claire's, and he apparently continued to believe it after her denial, for he felt—how seriously it is hard to say—that Shelley could be the father of her daughter Allegra.[95]

In view of the unfavorable impression often given of Claire in Shelley and Byron biographies, especially in connection with this affair with Byron, one might consider the rather different picture that Shelley's cousin Thomas Medwin gave of her a few years later in Florence: "She was a brunette, with very dark hair, and eyes that flashed with the fire of intelligence, and might have been taken for an Italian. Her history was a profound secret. As she possessed considerable talents—spoke French and Italian, particularly the latter, with all its *nuances* and niceties—she was much courted by the Russian *coterie,* a numerous and fashionable one in that city. Though not strictly handsome, she was animated and attractive, and possessed an *esprit de société* rare among our countrywomen."[96] Here, certainly, is a woman who could have attracted Shelley. She obviously had a sparkle that Mary did not.

A record of other aspects of these days at Geneva appears in the letters of Shelley and Mary. On July 12, Shelley tells of a trip around the lake with Byron in which they visited the castle of Chillon, a trip that Byron later recorded in Book III of *Childe Harold's Pilgrimage,*[97] and which inspired *The Prisoner of Chillon*:

There are seven pillars of Gothic mould,
In Chillon's dungeons deep and old.

Shelley also commented on the dungeons: "Close to this long and lofty dungeon was a narrow cell, and beyond it one larger and far more lofty and dark, supported upon two unornamented arches. Across one of these arches was a beam, now black and rotten, on which prisoners were hung in secret. I never saw a monument more terrible of that cold and inhuman tyranny, which it had been the delight of man to exercise over man."[98] Following this trip with Byron, Shelley went on an expedition with Mary and Claire to the valley of Chamonix, during which Mary began *Frankenstein*[99] and Shelley wrote *Mont Blanc*. This expedition also led to attacks on Shelley. In the visitor's book at several inns Shelley described himself, in Greek: "lover of mankind, democrat and atheist."[100] One of these inscriptions Byron later saw and erased; another was seen by Southey, who copied it down and took it back to England, where it became the basis for attacks on Shelley in *The Quarterly Review* and the *London Chronicle*, the latter concluding: "Mr. Shelley is understood to be the person who, after gazing on Mont Blanc, registered himself in the Album as *Percy Bysshe Shelley*, Atheist; which gross and cheap bravado he, with the natural tact of the new school, took for a display of philosophic courage; and his obscure muse has been since constantly spreading all her foulness on those doctrines which a decent infidel would treat with respect, and in which the wise and honourable have in all ages found the perfection of wisdom and virtue."[101]

About a month after the conclusion of this trip—July 21–27—Shelley, Mary, and Claire set out for England. The month of August had yielded nothing of special interest at Geneva except the arrival for a brief visit of Matthew Gregory Lewis, author of *The Monk*, which Shelley had admired as a schoolboy. Shelley must have been interested also in Hobhouse (later Lord Broughton) for he was then one of the more advanced parliamentary reformers and an associate of Shelley's first political hero, Sir Francis Burdett. On his way back to England, Shelley visited Versailles:

> We saw the Library of Louis XVI. The librarian had held some place in the ancient court near Marie-Antoinette. He returned with the Bourbons, and was waiting for some better situation. He showed us a book which he had preserved during the Revolution. It was a book of paintings, representing a tournament at the Court of Louis XIV; and it seemed that the present desolation of France, the fury of the injured people, and all the horrors to which they abandoned themselves stung by their long sufferings, flowed naturally enough from expenditures so immense, as must have been demanded by the magnificence of this tournament. The vacant rooms of this palace imaged well the hollow show of monarchy.[102]

Two Suicides

On September 8, 1816, Shelley, Mary, and Claire arrived back in England. They soon settled in Bath, pending the renting of a house near London.

Shelley doubtless had literary plans, but they were not to be put into effect, for the next few months were the most tragic and troubled in his life. First came the suicide of Fanny Imlay, then that of Harriet Shelley, and finally the court battle with the Westbrooks for the custody of the children.

The death of Fanny was reported in a Swansea paper on October 12, 1816:

> A melancholy discovery was made in Swansea yesterday. A most respectable looking female arrived at the Mackworth Arms Inn on Wednesday night by the Cambrian Coach from Bristol; she took tea and retired to rest, telling the chambermaid she was exceedingly fatigued, and would take care of the candle herself. Much agitation was created in the house by her non-appearance yesterday morning, and in forcing her chamber door, she was found a corpse, with the remains of a bottle of laudanum on the table, and a note, of which the following is a copy:—"I have long determined that the best thing I could do was to put an end to the existence of a being whose birth was unfortunate, and whose life has only been a series of pain to those persons who have hurt their health in endeavouring to promote her welfare. Perhaps to hear of my death will give you pain, but you will soon have the blessing of forgetting that such a creature ever existed as ——"
>
> The name appears to have been torn off and burnt, but her stockings are marked with the letter "G.," and on her stays the letters "M. W." are visible. She was dressed in a blue-striped skirt with a white body, and a brown pelisse, with a fur trimming of a lighter colour, lined with white silk, and a hat of the same. She had a small French gold watch, and appears about 23 years of age, with long brown hair, dark complexion, and had a reticule containing a red silk pocket handkerchief, a brown berry necklace, and a small leather clasped purse, containing a 3s. and 5s. 6d. piece. She told a fellow-passenger that she came to Bath by the mail from London on Tuesday morning, from whence she proceeded to Bristol, and from thence to Swansea by the Cambrian coach, intending to go to Ireland. We hope the description we have given of this unhappy catastrophe, will lead to the discovery of the wretched object, who has thus prematurely closed her existence.[103]

Fanny had left London on October 7, arrived in Bath on October 8 by the London mail coach, took a local coach to Bristol (14 miles away by the coach-road), then went from Bristol to Swansea in Wales (about 86 miles). She cannot have gone to see Shelley and Mary when she stopped at Bath between coaches or Mary would have recorded it in her journal. As it is, the entry for October 8 reads: "Letter from Fanny [written at Bristol]. Drawing lesson. Walk out with Shelley to the South Parade, read Clarendon, and draw. In the evening work, and Shelley reads 'Don Quixote'; afterwards read 'Memoirs of the Princess of Barieth' aloud."[104] Shelley and Mary must have thought it strange that Fanny would pass through Bath without seeing them, but Fanny was known to be moody, and her letter from Bristol does not seem to have contained anything alarming. The indication is that Fanny had determined to commit suicide before she left London, perhaps many weeks before: her suicide note stated that she had "long determined" on such a course; she had only 8s 6d left; and Godwin later wrote that he had expected it to happen. Thus determined on ending her life, Fanny presumably did not wish to see anyone she knew.

Godwin, in London, also received a letter from Fanny, and he set out at once for Bristol. There he learned of the tragedy and wrote to Mary on October 13:

> I did indeed expect it.
>
> I cannot but thank you for your strong expressions of sympathy. I do not see, however, that that sympathy can be of any service to me; but it is best. My advice and earnest prayer is that you would avoid anything that leads to publicity. Go not to Swansea; disturb not the silent dead; do nothing to destroy the obscurity she so much desired that now rests upon the event. It was, as I said, her last wish; it was the motive that led her from London to Bristol and from Bristol to Swansea . . .
>
> The following is one expression in her letter to us, written from Bristol on Tuesday: "I depart immediately to the spot from which I hope never to remove."[105]

From this letter it appears that Fanny went to Swansea so that she could die in a place where her identity could not be ascertained (but to which she could be traced by those close to her). Godwin did not claim the body, and as his letter indicates, he did not wish Shelley or Mary to claim it either. Fanny was presumably buried in a pauper's grave; the coroner's inquest verdict was simply "found dead."[106] Godwin put out the story that she had died from natural causes while on the way to visit her aunts in Ireland.[107]

Why did Fanny kill herself? Four years later Maria Gisborne visited Godwin while on a trip from Italy and recorded a conversation with him in her journal: "Mr. G[odwin] told me that the three girls were all equally in love with —— and that the eldest put an end to her existence owing to the preference given to her younger sister."[108] The blank obviously stands for Shelley. This statement could be—and has been—read as meaning that Shelley and Fanny had a love affair and that Fanny killed herself because Shelley refused to give up Mary. However, we have to remember that Shelley and Mary eloped in July 1814 and Fanny did not commit suicide until October 1816. In a letter to his friend William Thomas Baxter, six months after Fanny's suicide, Godwin wrote: "From the fatal day of Mary's elopement Fanny's mind had been unsettled, her duty kept her with us: but I am afraid her affections were with them."[109] Fanny had doubtless been attracted by Shelley and probably Shelley by Fanny,[110] for Fanny, to judge by her letters, was both intelligent and radical.[111] But Godwin's implication to Baxter is that Shelley's elopement with Mary was a blow to her, not so much because of her interest in Shelley but because of her desire to escape from the Godwin household—as Claire had.

Godwin, then, apparently did not really believe that Shelley and Fanny had been having a love affair which resulted in her death. Certainly there is no suggestion of such a belief in his letters or journals, nor is there any evidence to support it.[112] Indeed, it seems doubtful that Fanny even continued to nurse a secret love for Shelley. Mary apparently did not think so, for she wrote to Shelley immediately on hearing of the death of Harriet (an event that left them free to marry): "Poor dear Fanny if she had lived until this moment she would have been saved for my house would then have been a proper asylum for her."[113] After her problems with Clàire, Mary would hardly have thought of inviting Fanny into her home if she had believed she was in love with Shelley.

Other reasons have been advanced for the suicide, such as that an aunt in Ireland refused to offer her a home.[114] But the only solid indications are those in the suicide note itself. The overall tenor of that note suggests a deep depression—which apparently was also the state underlying the letter Fanny sent to Godwin—a depression passing beyond conscious control. Perhaps there was even an element of delusion in her reference to injuring the health of others. Two specific reasons for suicide are given, namely, her "unfortunate" birth and the "pain" she had inflicted on those who had tried to help her.

A clue to the '"pain" reference comes from a letter that Fanny wrote to Mary only six days before her suicide. After speaking of her differences with her stepmother—"whatever she chooses to say in a passion to me alone" —she continues:

> It is very painful to me to have to mention Papa's affairs, particularly as you appear to wish to avoid them; but you must be aware that he has been made very uneasy by Shelley's letter. I should have been obliged to Shelley if he had seen me when he came to town to sign; though, to own the truth and not offend either of you, I cannot help thinking that he had arranged everything with Longdill before I parted from him in Piccadilly the other day, and for these reasons he chose not to be frank with me. I think, in the present state of Papa's spirits, it is of the utmost consequence to keep his mind as easy as possible, and to endeavour to prevent any sudden shock.[115]

The situation in the Godwin household explains these references. Fanny was the daughter of Godwin's first wife; the second Mrs. Godwin was apt to fly into rages with her. Godwin, overwhelmed by debts, was in a constant and desperate search for funds. Lately Fanny had been trying to raise money for him herself, but had failed. She began to feel that she had injured his "health" by her failure. Fanny's home life, then, was miserable and discordant. That it was bad enough to drive her to suicide is implied in Mary's comment to Shelley.

Even more oppressive, perhaps, was the fact that Fanny was the illegitimate child of Gilbert Imlay and Mary Wollstonecraft. As an advocate of women's rights, Mary had, both during her lifetime and after, been the subject of scurrilous attacks; for example:

> Whilom this dame the Rights of Women writ,
> That is the title to her book she places,

Exhorting bashful womankind to quit
All foolish modesty, and coy grimaces;
And name their backsides as it were their faces;
Such license loose-tongued liberty adores,
Which adds to female speech exceeding graces;
Lucky the maid that on her volume pores,
A scripture, archly fram'd, for propagating w——s.[116]

The "shame" of Fanny's birth had long been known to the town (and to Fanny).[117] Wherever she went, she must have felt the gnawing of gossip.

Hardly had Shelley begun to recover from the shock of Fanny's suicide than he was struck by that of Harriet. Harriet "had left her father's house" for some reason in October 1814; but had returned by November 30 to give birth to Charles. In January 1815 she was apparently getting ready to leave again: "When I shall quit this house I know not . . . I am so restrained here that life is scarcely worth having." Sometime in this year she was at the village of Stanmore, ten miles out of London by the Edgeware Road—whether alone, for how long, or why is not known. Shelley's last recorded visit to her was in April 1815, when he went to try to persuade her to allow their infant son, Charles, to be shown at a trial connected with Shelley family property.[118] The trial did not actually take place until a year later, in March of 1816. Harriet had refused to allow Charles to appear and was served with a court order appointing a guardian-ad-litem to represent him. Shelley was present at the trial, but because the infant was represented by the guardian there was no need for Harriet to be there.[119] The next record of her is a letter she wrote to John Frank Newton, Shelley's vegetarian friend, in June 1816, after hearing that Mrs. Newton had been ill. The letter is addressed from her father's house and concludes: "if there is any kind of Fruit I can send you do tell me; at present there is but little variety owing to our cold spring. If it will fatigue you too much to write an answer let my favorite Augustus give me a line just to say how you all are, or Mary. Pray don't take any trouble yourself; my sister unites with me in kindest regards and best wishes to you all."[120]

Sometime during the summer she visited Mrs. Boinville at Bracknell. After her return to London she wrote to Mrs. Boinville threatening suicide. The letter was delayed in the post, and by the time Mrs. Boinville arrived in London, "she found that she was too late."[121]

Shelley, then at Bath with Mary, received the news in a letter from Thomas Hookham, written on December 13:

It is nearly a month since I had the pleasure of receiving a letter from you, and you have no doubt felt surprised that I did not reply to it sooner. It was my intention to do so, but on enquiry I found the utmost difficulty in obtaining the information you desire relative to Mrs. Shelley and your children.

While I was yet endeavouring to discover Mrs. Shelley's address, information was brought to me that she was dead—that she had destroyed herself. You will believe that I did not credit the report. I called at the house of a friend of Mr. Westbrook! My doubt led to conviction. I was informed she was taken from the Serpentine river on Tuesday last apparently in an advanced state of pregnancy. Little or no information was laid before the jury which sat on the body. She was called Harriet Smith, and the verdict was—*found drowned.*

Your children are well, and are both, I believe, in London.

This shocking communication must stand single and alone in the letter which I now address you: I have no inclination to fill it with subjects comparatively trifling: you will judge of my feelings and excuse the brevity of this communication.[122]

On December 11 *The Sun* had carried a brief and anonymous notice: "Yesterday [December 10th] a respectable female far advanced in pregnancy was taken out of the Serpentine River and brought home to her residence in Queen Street, Brompton, having been missed for nearly six weeks. She had a valuable ring on her finger. A want of honour in her own conduct is supposed to have led to this fatal catastrophe, her husband being abroad."[123]

Harriet's body was taken from the Serpentine to the receiving station of the Royal Humane Society (which had charge of drownings) at the Fox and Bull tavern, the back yard of which opened into Hyde Park. On the next day, December 11, a coroner's inquest was held at the tavern. Though the body was "called" that of "Harriet Smith," it was recognized as that of Harriet Shelley by the daughter of the proprietor of the Fox and Bull.[124]

Four witnesses testified: John Leavsley, an old soldier who had found the body, which he stated "must have lain in the water some days"; William Alder, a plumber by trade, who seems to have known Harriet and her family quite well; Mrs. Jane Thomas, widow and owner of the lodgings where Harriet had stayed; and Mary Jones, a servant in the lodgings.

The last three witnesses testified as follows:

William Alder: "I knew the deceased she resided at No. 7 Elizabeth Street Hans Place she was a married Woman but did not live with her husband—she had been missing as I was informed from her House upwards of a Month, and at the request of her Parents when she had been absent about a week I dragged the Serpentine River and all the ponds near thereto without effect the deceased having for sometime labored under lowness of Spirits which I had observed for several months before and I conceived that something lay heavy on her Mind. On hearing yesterday that a Body was found I went and recognized it to be the deceased—she was about 21 years of age and was married about 5 years."

Jane Thomas: "The deceased occupied the second floor in my House she took them accompanied by a Mr. Alder, she stated that she was a married lady & that her Husband was abroad she took them from month to month—she had been with me about 9 weeks on the 9th of November last, she paid her month's Rent on the Thursday preceding—she appeared in the family way and was during the time she lived in my house in a very desponding and gloomy way—on the 9th of

November last she left my house as I was informed by my servant Mary Jones. I did not see the deceased that day."

Mary Jones: "On Saturday the ninth of November last the deceased breakfasted and dined in her Apartments, she told me previously that she wished to dine early & she dined about 4 o'clock—she said very little, she chiefly spent her time in Bed. I saw nothing but what was proper in her Conduct with the exception of a continual lowness of Spirits—she left her Apartment after Dinner which did not occupy her more than 10 minutes—I observed she was gone out on my going into her room about 5 o'clock that day. I never saw or heard from her afterwards."[125]

From these documents the following facts emerge: Harriet had ceased to live at home at least by early September 1816; she was pregnant; she had been in "continual" low spirits for some time; she lived in lodgings from early September until November 9; she left her lodgings between four and five on the afternoon of November 9; after she had been absent from "her House" for a week, the Westbrooks asked a friend, William Alder, to have the river dragged; and on December 10 her body was found, after having been in the water "some days."[126] There is, however, one major problem inherent in the testimony of three of the witnesses. The impression is given by William Alder, Mrs. Thomas, and Mary Jones that Harriet drowned herself after leaving her lodgings on November 9, although they do not make a definite statement to that effect. But this was impossible. A body will normally surface within a week, or two weeks at the outside, unless it is held down by artificial means. If it is so held down or is even floating in the water for four weeks, it becomes so bloated and decayed as to be unrecognizable.[127] But there is no evidence of artificial means holding Harriet's body down, and a body could not float in the Serpentine in Hyde Park for several weeks without being seen. It would, in fact, normally be found within a few hours. That Harriet's body was not unrecognizable is clear from other evidence at the inquest. Alder stated that he "recognized" it. Leavsley seems even at first to have thought that there might be some life in it, but looking more closely he saw that it was "quite dead" and had been in the water for "some days." This is not at all the impression one would get from a corpse a month old. To the inquest record should be added the following from an affidavit by Eliza Westbrook several months later at the trial for custody of Shelley's children: "until a short time previously to her death she [Harriet] lived with or under the protection of the said John Westbrooke her Father. And that in the month of December last she died."[128] On a Saturday evening, apparently just before her suicide, Harriet wrote a farewell letter to her sister Eliza, Shelley, and her parents:

To you my dear Sister I leave all my things as they more properly belong to you than any one & you will preserve them for Ianthe. God bless you both. My dearest & much belod Sister

When you read this letr. I shall be [no] more an inhabitant of this miserable world. do not regret the loss of one who could never be anything but a source of vexation & misery to you all belonging to me. Too wretched to exert myself lowered in the opinion of everyone why should I drag on a miserable existence embittered by past recollections & not one ray of hope to rest on for the future. The remembrance of all your kindness which I have so unworthily repaid has often made my heart ache. I know that you will forgive me because it is not in your nature to be unkind or severe to any dear amiable woman that I had never left you oh! that I had always taken your advice. I might have lived long & happy but weak & unsteady have rushed on my own destruction I have not written to Bysshe. oh no what would it avail my wishes or my prayers would not be attended to by him & yet I should he see this perhaps he might grant my last request to let Ianthe remain with you always dear lovely child, with you she will enjoy much happiness with him none My dear Bysshe let me conjure you by the remembrance of our days of happiness to grant my last wish—do not take your innocent child from Eliza who has been more than I have, who has watched over her with such unceasing care.—Do not refuse my last request—I never could refuse you & if you had never left me I might have lived but as it is, I freely forgive you & may you enjoy that happiness which you have deprived me of. There is your beautiful boy. oh! be careful of him & his love may prove one day a rich reward. As you form his infant mind so you will reap the fruits hereafter Now comes the sad task of saying farewell—oh I must be quick. God bless & watch over you all. . You dear Bysshe. & you dear Eliza. May all happiness attend ye both is the last wish of her who loved ye more than all others. My children I dare not trust myself there. They are too young to regret me & ye will be kind to them for their own sakes more than for mine My parents do not regret me. I was unworthy your love & care. Be happy all of you. so shall my spirit find rest & forgiveness. God bless you all is the last prayer of the unfortunate Harriet S——[129]

The exact details of how this lovely and lovable woman, so vividly sketched by Hogg and Peacock, had come to be in lodgings, alone and pregnant, may never be known, but an examination of various contemporary versions of the story in relation to the other evidence suggests its main outline. Different versions of her story were supplied by Shelley, Thornton Hunt (from his father, Leigh Hunt, who was with Shelley in London at the time), William Godwin (from an unnamed informant not of the Shelley circle), Claire Clairmont (from Eliza Westbrook), and Trelawny (from Claire Clairmont, Hookham, and others):

Immediately after receiving Hookham's letter at Bath, Shelley went to London. The next day he wrote to Mary:

It is thro' you that I can entertain without despair the recollection of the horrors of unutterable villainy that led to this dark dreadful death . . . It seems that this poor woman—the most innocent of her abhorred & unnatural family—was driven from her father's house, & descended the steps of prostitution until she lived with a groom of the name of Smith, who deserting her, she killed herself —There can be no question that the beastly viper her sister, unable to gain profit from her connexion with me—has secured to herself the fortune of the old man—who is now dying—by the murder of this poor creature. Everything tends to prove, however, that beyond the mere shock of so hideous a catastrophe having fallen on a human being once so nearly connected with me, there would, in any case have been little to regret. Hookham, Longdill—every one, does *me* full justice; —bears testimony to the up[rightness &] liberality of my conduct to her:— T[here] is but one voice in condemnation of the dete[s]table Westbrooks. If they should dare to bring [it] before Chancery—a scene of such fearful horror would be unfolded as would cover them with scorn & shame.[130]

Thornton Hunt's account is essentially the same as Shelleys: Harriet was "driven from the paternal roof" so that Eliza might get their father's money, then "deserted" by "a man in a very humble grade of life; and it was in consequence of this desertion that she killed herself."[131] Whether Leigh Hunt got this version from Shelley or was present when Shelley heard it from someone else (for he was with Shelley "all day") is not known.

Godwin's story is somewhat different. In the spring following Harriet's suicide he wrote to his friend William Baxter: "The late Mrs. Shelley has turned out to have been a woman of great levity. I know, from unquestionable authority, wholly unconnected with Shelley (though I cannot with propriety be quoted for this) that she had proved herself unfaithful to her husband before their separation . . . Afterwards, she was guilty of repeated acts of levity, and had latterly lived in open connection with a colonel Maxwell. Peace be to her shade!"[132]

Claire Clairmont's account appeared in a letter to Trelawny in 1875:

She did not form after S's leaving her, a connexion with some low man, as Mr. Rossetti in his desire of making S a model of moral perfection hints and more than hints. Her lover was a Captain in the Indian or Wellington Army I forget which and he was ordered abroad. His letter did not reach her—with her sister's concurrence, she retired for her accouchement to live with a decent couple in a Mews ["at the rear of" *crossed out*] near Chapel St—her sister without telling either Harriett's or her own name, placed her there, saying she was her lady's maid, was married and that her husband was abroad as a Courier. The parents were told that H—— was gone on a visit of some weeks to a friend in the country—it was of consequence in Miss W's opinion to conceal the affair from Shelley. One morning Miss W—— visited H—— and the later was very low at receiving no letters from her lover—and expressed a fear that he did not really love her and meant to abandon her—for she remarked I don't think I am made to inspire love, and you know my husband abandoned me—the Eg of that day, a dark November Eg—with rain—at eight o'clock she went into the park and threw herself into the Serpentine—Her body was not found till next Morning—was taken to St. George's workhouse, an inquest held—and verdict returned—An unknown woman found drowned. Miss W—— made no stir, nor any of the family appeared to claim her—and Harriet was buried at the expence of the parish in the small burial ground called St. George's which may now have disappeared, but which in former years was in the Baywater road, opposite Hyde Park. To me it appears that Mr. Rossetti has written his memoir to suit Lady Shelley's predilections—and she is a warm partisan of Shelley and Mary, and like all warm partisans does not care much about Truth. Miss Westbrook related all the above particulars to my Mother.[133]

Trelawny's account appeared in 1878 in his *Records of Shelley, Byron and the Author.* After Shelley's elopement, Trelawny writes, "Harriet sought a refuge with her father." Then:

The father at last was confined to his room by sickness, and the sister refused her entrance there. Friendless, and utterly ignorant of the world and its ways, deserted by her husband and family, Harriet was the most forlorn and miserable of her sex—poor and outcast. It is too painful to trace her faltering steps. She made one effort to hold on to life. A man professed to be interested and to sympathize in her fate. He was a captain in the army, and was suddenly ordered to join his regiment abroad. He promised to correspond with her. Her poverty compelled her to seek a refuge in a cheaper lodging; her former landlady refused to forward her letters to her new address. In this deplorable state, fancying that no human being could take the least interest in her, and believing in Shelley's doctrine—that when our last hopes are extinguished, and life is a torment, our only refuge is death—blighted, benighted, and crushed, with hurried steps she hastened into the Park, and threw herself off the bridge into the Serpentine.[134]

Although Trelawny mainly follows Claire's account in her letter to him, he adds to it Eliza's harshness, the two lodgings, the bridge, and other details. Trelawny had not known Shelley in England but, as he explained, derived information from those who had: "the few friends who knew both Shelley and his wife—Hookham, who kept the great library in Bond Street; Jefferson Hogg, Peacock, and one of the Godwins."[135] The "one of the Godwins" was presumably Claire. The other details must have come from Hookham and perhaps Hogg. Peacock was too staunch a champion of Harriet to have been an informant along these lines.

Together, these five accounts form two basic patterns: one a sordid tale of prostitution, the other a tragic story of a broken love affair. According to Shelley, Harriet was "driven" from the Westbrook house—apparently at Eliza's instigation—then "descended the steps of prostitution until she lived with a groom of the name of Smith, who deserting her, she killed herself." To this, Hunt and Trelawny add that she was living in "poverty." Where Shelley heard this story is not known—possibly from Hookham, possibly from his attorney, Longdill; perhaps he even visited Harriet's lodgings or the Fox and Bull tavern. Wherever he heard it, however, it does not fit the facts established at the inquest and in other records. Harriet had no need to descend "the steps of prostitution," for she was getting £200 a year from her father and £200 more from Shelley. That she had money is shown by the fact that she rented a "floor" from her landlady, Jane Thomas, in which she had an "apartment." She was referred to in *The Sun* as "a respectable female" who wore a "valuable" ring, and the Hans Place area

—to judge by the listings in *Boyle's Court Guide* (1813)—was a respectable middle-class neighborhood.[136] None of this fits a picture of prostitution and degradation. Furthermore, if there was an, descent down "the steps of prostitution," it must have been both rapid and brief. In June, Harriet was living at home and sending kind regards from her sister to John Frank Newton. By early September she was in her apartment at Mrs. Thomas', where her "Conduct" was described as "proper" until she left on November 9. Nor does there seem to be any foundation for the story that she had been badly treated by Eliza. At least Harriet did not appear to think so, to judge from the expressions of gratitude and affection in her suicide letter.

Whether Shelley continued to believe the prostitution story is not known, but he certainly did continue to believe that something appalling had happened. "If you were my friend," he wrote four years later to Robert Southey, who was charging him with responsibility for Harriet's death, "I could tell you a history that would make you open your eyes; but I shall certainly never make the public my familiar confidant."[137]

Though the prostitution story may be safely rejected, the question remains of whether Harriet had a love affair while still living with Shelley. Godwin had heard this story, and Shelley expressed doubts to Mary about the paternity of his son Charles. But that this latter was a wild accusation, made in the heat of the emotional turmoil of his pursuit of Mary, is indicated by the other evidence. In his will, both in the drafts written before and after Harriet's death, he left equal sums to Ianthe and "my son" Charles.[138] In the custody suit he demanded custody of both children. In a letter to Eliza on December 18, 1816, he wrote: "My friend Mr. Leigh Hunt, will take charge of *my children* & prepare them for their residence with me.[139] At the time of Charles's birth it was assumed by Shelley and Mary that Charles was his child,[140] and he was later brought up by Sir Timothy Shelley as a grandson (until his death at the age of twelve). Harriet referred to him as "very like his unfortunate father" in a letter to Catherine Nugent shortly after the birth,[141] and in her suicide letter wrote to Shelley: "There is your beautiful boy. Oh! be careful of him, & his love may prove one day a rich reward."

Clearly Harriet and Shelley, both believed that Charles was Shelley's son, so that if Harriet had an affair "before their separation," as Godwin stated, it cannot have been a long one. She could hardly have had a prolonged affair while living with Shelley without Shelley's knowing of it. But she could have had a brief affair in the early part of 1814 when she was away from Shelley with Eliza for two months or more. This is indicated also in Shelley's comment to Mary on January 11, 1817, that Godwin told him that Harriet had been unfaithful to him "*four months*" before he ran away with Mary in July 1814. Godwin's testimony on this cannot be discarded. Although Godwin could become evasive when pressed by money difficulties, his general conduct was honest and straightforward—he had once been an idealistic minister—and if he said that he had "unquestionable authority" for his information, he certainly believed it to be true, as apparently Shelley did also. Who was this "authority"? It was most likely Eliza Westbrook, who told Mrs. Godwin the story of the suicide and may have told her much else beside at the same time. If Harriet did have an affair, however, it was neither long nor psychologically deep, as indicated both by her anguish—reported by Mrs. Godwin—at the thought that she was about to lose Shelley, and by a letter to Catherine Nugent in January 1815 when, looking back on the events of the spring and summer, she wrote: "Oh no, with all the affections warm, a heart devoted to him, and then to be so cruelly blighted."[142]

There remains, finally, the story that Harriet had a lover in the spring of 1816. Obviously she must have had sexual relations with someone then in order to be "far advanced in pregnancy" at the time of her death, and the indication is that he was a lover rather than a casual acquaintance, and that he was an army officer. On the latter point, it should be noted that Hans Place was in a military neighborhood. Nearby were the two great Knightsbridge barracks, one for foot regiments and one for cavalry (both—as shown on Horwood's map—dominating the area). From an early age Harriet must have been acquainted with this neighborhood, just across the park from her house, for she told Elizabeth Hitchener: "When quite a child I admired these Red Coats. This grew up with me, & I thought the military the best as well as most fascinating men in the world."[143]

The specific story heard by Godwin, that the officer in question was a "Colonel Maxwell" has been ridiculed without investigation by critics hostile to Godwin. There are, however, indications of some truth to it. Claire Clairmont, on going through her mother's letters to Lady Mount Cashell on Shelley's elopement with Mary, added a note to one of them, which was transcribed by Dowden as follows: "He [Shelley] succeeded in persuading her [i.e., persuading Mary Godwin to elope with him] by declaring that Harriet did not really care for him; that she was in love with a Major Ryan; and the child she would have was certainly not his. This Mary told me herself, adding that this justified his having another attachment. I spoke to my mother and to the Boinvilles on this point in after years. Neither had ever seen or heard of any such person as Ryan."[144]

This Major Ryan, according to Newman I. White, who searched the British Army Lists, was probably Major Matthew Ryan of the Thirtieth Foot Regiment.[145] White, however, had not heard of Godwin's Colonel Maxwell, as that part of Godwin's letter to Baxter had not been published when he wrote his biography of Shelley.[146] If he had, he would have noticed that the Thirtieth Foot Regiment also contained a lieutenant colonel named Christopher Maxwell. This can hardly be a coincidence, for the odds against a Major Ryan and a Colonel Maxwell both belonging to the same regiment of the British army (then having about 140 regiments) are of a very high order. Godwin, moreover, as Claire indicated, had never heard of Ryan, so the stories must have come from different sources. That Claire was telling the truth is shown by references in Harriet's letters (which Claire never saw) and in Mary's journal (which Claire may or may not have seen), which show that Shelley and Harriet did, in fact, have a friend named Ryan. They had met him in Dublin; he dined with them in London in 1813; and after Shelley left Harriet, he apparently attempted to get money from Shelley on Harriet's behalf.[147]

It seems virtually certain, then, that Harriet's lover in early 1816 was an army officer, and it is probable that Godwin's informant was correct in stating that his name was Maxwell. If Harriet lived "in open connection" with him, quite a few people must have known of it. Whether or not he was Lieutenant Colonel Christopher Maxwell of the Thirtieth Foot is of course not known. The son of Sir David Maxwell of Cardoness, Christopher Maxwell, was thirty-six in 1816.[148] According to the regimental records, the regiment was in India in March 1816, but there is no indication whether Maxwell was with them or not. Claire stated only that he "was ordered abroad" and that he may have belonged to the "Indian" army. Trelawny, however, implies that the regiment was already "abroad" and that he was ordered to "join" it. Whoever Harriet's lover was, the indication is that the love affair was a serious one. He did not leave her voluntarily but went away because of an army order, and he wrote to her.

Among the various accounts of Harriet's last days, Eliza Westbrook's, told to Mrs. Godwin and recounted by Claire, seems to be closest to the truth. This may seem surprising because of the unfavorable pictures given of Eliza in biographies of Shelley. But the fact that Shelley hated Eliza does not mean that she was either unreliable or less than devoted to Harriet, who in her last weeks of life must have been most difficult to handle. She was surely heartbroken by Harriet's death, and there is no reason to suppose that she would not in this state have given an essentially true picture to Mrs. Godwin. The Godwins had been as distressed as she when Shelley left Harriet and eloped with Mary. They had apparently tried to comfort Harriet when she went to London from Bracknell, and they forced Mary to say that she would see Shelley no more. Eliza may well at that time—prior to the marriage of Shelley and Mary—have felt kindly toward the Godwins.

There are, however, certain inconsistencies or apparent inconsistencies between Eliza's story as given by Claire and the other evidence. According to Claire, Eliza stated that she took Harriet to lodge with "a decent couple in a mews near Chapel Street," the street on which the Westbrooks lived. But according to the inquest, she was in lodgings in Hans Place, across Hyde Park from Chapel Street, with Mrs. Thomas, a widow, and had been taken there by William Alder. The solution to this problem may lie in entries in the register of burials in the parish of Paddington discovered by Roger Ingpen, which show that on December 11, 1816, a burial ceremony was performed for Benjamin Smith, age fifty-four, of Mount Street, and on December 13 for "Harriet Smith," age twenty-one of Mount Street. That "Harriet Smith" was, as Ingpen contends, Harriet Shelley seems certain. "She was accustomed at times to spell her name with the double *t*, she was twenty-one at the date of her death, and Mount Street was close to her father's residence and in the neighborhood of *the Mount* coffee-house, where he had made his fortune."[149] To this should be added the evidence that the "Harriet Smith" of the December 11 inquest was Harriet Shelley.

Who, however, was the "Benjamin Smith" who was buried two days before Harriet and had probably died on December 9 or 10? Was he somehow connected with the fact that Harriet Shelley was "called" Harriet Smith? Was he Shelley's "groom by the name of Smith?" Did his death have some connection with Harriet Shelley's? Granted that Smith is a common name, there are too many "Smiths" here for it to be purely a coincidence. Ingpen did not find Benjamin Smith of Mount Street in Johnstone's *Commercial Directory* for 1816, "corrected to August 31, 1817," but he did find a Benjamin Smith, "Shopkeeper," of 61 Mount Street in directories for 1817 to 1824. Ingpen suggests that Smith's business was "continued after his death, his name being retained." The most interesting thing, however, is the address, 61 Mount Street. According to Horwood's detailed map of London, number 61 was located either in or just behind "Reeves Mews."[150] This location suggests that Benjamin Smith and his wife might be Eliza's "decent couple in a Mews near Chapel Street," for that is exactly where they were—"in the rear" of Chapel Street almost exactly behind the Westbrook's house, one street over. Furthermore, Eliza stated that she took Harriet there for the "accouchement," expected within "some weeks," which raises the possibility that she took Harriet there after Harriet had left Mrs. Thomas' on November 9. That this is indeed what happened is indicated by other evidence. Trelawny heard that Harriet had been in two sets of lodgings, the first with a "landlady" who "refused" to forward her mail. There is also the discrepancy between the implication that Harriet had drowned herself on November 9 and the fact that the body had been in the water only a short time. Finally, in her affidavit Eliza placed the date of the death in December. The probability is then, that after Harriet left Mrs. Thomas' on November 9 following her four o'clock dinner she went to Eliza and was taken—then or later—to the Smiths on Mount Street. Shelley, getting a garbled version of these events on first coming to London after Harriet's suicide, talked about her being "driven from her father's home" and living with "a groom of the name of Smith."

There are other differences between Eliza's story and the rest of the evidence. Eliza stated that Harriet was buried in St. George's cemetery on "the Bayswater road." If so, why was the burial registered in the parish of Paddington? The answer must be either that Harriet was buried in Paddington and Eliza was mistaken, or, more likely, the Paddington record was made deliberately to cover up Harriet's trail.[151] If so, Eliza's story that the Westbrooks did not "appear to claim her" cannot be quite true, for only the Westbrooks would have had the motive or the influence to have a record falsified. That they did, in fact, intervene is shown in the spelling of Harriet's name with two "t's" in the Paddington register. Perhaps Eliza actually said only that the Westbrooks did not claim Harriet's body at the inquest, which they obviously did not, as she was known at the inquest as Harriet Smith. But they may have claimed it privately later. It must be remembered that Eliza's story comes from Claire, who had heard it many years before from her mother and was telescoping it for Trelawny's benefit in a letter. One other error must be Claire's or Mrs. Godwin's, namely, the statement that Harriet died on a "November" evening. Godwin also believed that Harriet had died in November. Yet Eliza's affidavit giving December as the month of death is certainly preferable evidence on this point. In telling the story, Eliza may not even have mentioned the month.

Eliza stated, according to Claire, that Harriet's body was found the "next morning" and taken to "St. George's workhouse." According to *The Sun*, the body was taken to Queen's Street, Brompton, which may be the same as the Hans Place address.[152] Possibly the body was taken from there to the St. George's workhouse so that the Westbrooks could make arrangement's for burial in an institution in their own parish where they perhaps had influence with the directors.

The assertion that Harriet's body was found the next morning seems to be contradicted by the evidence at the inquest. Leavsley said it seemed to have been in the water "for some days," and this conclusion is supported by Harriet's suicide letter, which was dated "Sat. eve." Eliza stated that Harriet died in December, and the only Saturday in December 1816 prior to December 10 was December 7. If, as seems likely, Harriet committed suicide shortly after writing that letter, the most probable day of her death was Saturday, December 7.

One final point of difference between Eliza's story and the inquest occurs in the testimony of William Alder that he dragged the Serpentine at the request of Harriet's parents after she had been missing from her "House" about a week. The indication is that he meant a week following November 9. But if Harriet did not die until December and Alder was telling the truth, the dragging must have taken place while she was still alive. If so, again one can only guess at the explanation, but it may lie in Eliza's statement to Mrs. Godwin that she had not informed her parents of the true situation. Eliza also said that she had taken Harriet to lodgings, whereas Harriet implied that she had left Eliza. Perhaps both were true. Harriet may have left home to go with her lover, later returned home, and then been taken to lodgings. Eliza would have tended to eliminate from her narrative any conflict between herself and Harriet.

What, finally, of Eliza's statement, as reported by Claire, that she did not tell the couple in the mews Harriet's or her name and claimed that Harriet was "her lady's maid." It seems impossible that a couple living so close to the Westbrooks could be thus deceived. Claire, however, seems to have accepted the story, so perhaps Eliza gave some explanation for it that Claire did not include in her shortened version to Trelawny.[153]

Two more related and much discussed questions remain to be considered, namely, the degree of Shelley's responsibility for Harriet's suicide and his attitude toward it. In considering the matter of Shelley's responsibility, one should make a distinction between the situation in which Harriet found herself in the fall of 1816 and the fact that she took suicide as a way out of it. Shelley was no doubt in good part responsible for the situation. Harriet herself felt this: "if you had never left me I might have lived . . ." But Shelley cannot be held responsible for the fact that Harriet chose suicide as the solution. Harriet's situation was far from desperate. She had a wealthy father and two children. She could have given birth to her child and placed it for adoption—which was perhaps Eliza's plan—and then continued to live as a mother with Ianthe and Charles. Many women have been in much more difficult situations and have not killed themselves. Harriet chose suicide because she was already predisposed to it.

In an early letter to Elizabeth Hitchener, Shelley stated that even before their marriage, "suicide was with her a favorite them[e and] her total uselessness was urged as its defence."[154] "She spoke of self-murder serenely before strangers," Hogg commented in regard to his first period of acquaintance with Harriet in 1811. When he met her again in 1813, he observed, "she had not renounced her eternal purpose of suicide; and she still discoursed of some scheme of self-destruction, as coolly as another lady would arrange a visit to an exhibition or a theatre."[155] In January 1815, nearly two years before her suicide, she wrote to her friend Catherine Nugent: "For myself happines is fled. I live for others. At nineteen I could descend a willing victim to the tomb. How I wish those dear children had never been born. They stay my fleeting spirit, when it would be in another state. How many there are who shudder at death. I have been so near it that I feel no terrors."[156]

All threats of suicide, psychiatrists maintain, have to be taken seriously. Hogg's description and Harriet's 1815 letter reveal the psychological patterns that developed under stress into the psychotic state of depression, divorce of thought and emotion from reality, self-abasement, and guilt disclosed in the suicide letter. That Harriet was, indeed, in a psychotic state at the time of her death is shown by the circumstances of the suicide, for she not only killed herself but also took the life of her unborn child and left her two children motherless. The indications are that she would have been driven to such a state by any major crisis, whether or not she had had any association with Shelley.

Shelley's letter to Mary on December 16, 1816, was written under the first impact of a shattering personal tragedy. Like others caught in such a situation he felt the need for immediate communication with someone close to him and for self-justification. But his attitude was not heartless.[157] Leigh Hunt, who was with him throughout the day, wrote that the suicide "tore his being to pieces," and "he never forgot it."[158] "The feeling for Harriet's death," wrote Peacock, who saw him frequently in the succeeding months, "grew into a deep and abiding sorrow."[159] His anguish came out in two poems on Harriet's death and five years later in the passage on Harriet and his children in *Epipsychidion*: "The wandering hopes of one abandoned mother."[160] Shelley, however, was obviously not going to express his anguish on Harriet's suicide in a letter to Mary. Only in the phrase "this dark, dreadful death" is there a hint of its intensity.

Shelley's deep sense of guilt for having left Harriet in the first place was now compounded by the horror of the suicide. It was, however, psychologically impossible for Shelley fully to accept this guilt, for to do so would have destroyed his sustaining image of himself as a man who lived according to the highest principles of social justice and self-sacrifice. Instead, he threw his guilt out upon those he hated—his wife's "abhorred and unnatural family" in general, and Eliza in particular.

The conflict between Shelley and Eliza indeed, provides the key to much of Shelley's reaction. His hatred for Eliza—that "blind and loathsome worm"[161] —was so obsessive that when he faced the naked fact of the suicide he pushed the blame away from himself and onto her. In a letter to Byron a month later he wrote: "My late wife is dead. The circumstances which attended this event are of a nature of such awful and appalling horror, that I dare hardly avert to them in thought. The sister of whom you have heard me speak may be truly said (though not in law, yet in fact) to have murdered her for the sake of her father's money."[162]

Mingled with the anguish and guilt in the letter to Mary is a general psychological trait that can be early observed in Shelley, as in his boyhood rages. In 1811, when he was in a disturbed state, he had made wild charges of sexual relations between his mother and his young friend Edward Fergus Graham.[163] These charges grew more and more fantastic in a mounting erotic spiral until they got out of conscious control. It was apparently this same tendency—although the specific situation was different which whipped him to a point of frenzy in his charges against Harriet and Eliza. As Shelley matured, this tendency receded, and he bore the deaths of his children Clara and William in Italy with a quiet if bitter suffering. The death of Harriet had had a sobering effect on him.[164]

About two weeks after the suicide of Harriet, Shelley legalized his union with Mary ("so good a match," wrote William Godwin, hopefully viewing the end of his days of penury).[165] A few weeks later, on February 18, 1817, Shelley rewrote his will. On September 24, 1816, he had drawn up a will with the following main provisions: £6,000 to Harriet; £5,000 each for his children by Harriet; £6,000 to Claire Clairmont for herself and another £6,000 for someone to be named by her (that is, her coming child by Byron—born in January 1817); £2,000 to Hogg; £2,000 to Byron; to Peacock £500 in cash and £2,000 to be invested as an annuity; and the residue of the estate (the bulk of it) to Mary. These provisions he now left unchanged except for deleting the bequest to the deceased Harriet, raising that to his children by her to £6,000 each, and providing a similar sum for William, his child by Mary.[166]

The Fight for the Children

One of Shelley's main objects in going to London on hearing of the death of Harriet was to obtain possession of his children. In his letter to Mary of December 16, 1816, he wrote: "The children I have not yet got. I have seen Longdill who recommends proceeding with the utmost caution and resoluteness."[167] In her suicide letter, Harriet had urged him to take Charles only and leave Ianthe to Eliza. But this compromise Shelley was unwilling to make. In a letter to Eliza two days later, on December 18, he informed her that he wanted both children.[168] He also sent Mrs. Boinville to her and called at the Westbrook house himself. It soon became clear that Eliza had determined to hold on to both children. Thus, the old struggle between Shelley and Eliza began in a new form.

On January 10, 1817, the children (such was the legal fiction) filed a bill in the Chancery Court urging that the court appoint guardians for them, as their father was immoral and atheistic:

> To the right Honorable the Lord High Chancellor of Great Britain. The Humble Petition of the said Plaintiffs—SHEWETH . . . that the sd. Percy Bysshe Shelley about 3 years ago deserted his sd. wife and unlawfully cohabited with the sd. Mary Godwin . . . That the sd. Defendant Percy Bysshe Shelley vows himself to be an Atheist and that he hath since his sd. Marriage written, published a certain Work called "Queen Mab" with notes and other Works that he hath therein blasphemously derided the Truth of the Christian revelation and denied the existence of a God as the Creator of the Universe.[169]

These charges, Shelley wrote to Mary the next day, he must—according to Chancery law—"*deny* or *admit* upon oath, and then it seems that it rests in the *mere* discretion of the Chancellor to decide whether those are fit grounds for refusing me my chidren."[170] Sir Timothy Shelley's solicitor, William Whitton, urged Shelley not to oppose the Westbrooks, for as he wrote to Sir Timothy, "I know not what a Court of Justice may be induced to [do to] the author of so much unjustifiable matter as is stated throughout the pages of his books."[171] Whitton feared that Shelley—like Daniel Isaac Eaton, Richard Carlile, William Hone, and Leigh Hunt—might be tried for blasphemy or sedition as well as having his children taken from him.

But Shelley decided to fight the case and on January 18 filed his answer to the bill of complaint. He denied that he had deserted Harriet: "This Defendant saith that the said Complainants are the only issue of the said marriage, and that after the birth of the said Complainant Eliza Ianthe Shelley, this Defendant and his said late wife agreed, in consequence of certain differences between them, to live separate and apart from each other, but this Defendant denies that he deserted his said wife, otherwise than by separating from her as aforesaid."[172] As for the children, he had wanted them with him but had deferred to Harriet's wish that she be allowed to bring them up while they were of "tender age," and he had always intended "to provide for their education himself, as soon as they should be of proper age, or in case of the death of his wife, and never having in any manner abandoned or deserted them, or had any intention of so doing."[173]

That the Westbrooks were determined to spare no effort to prevent Shelley from getting his children became obvious when they retained Sir Samuel Romilly as their attorney, for Romilly was one of the most prominent lawyers in England, a member of Parliament, and a former solicitor general. (He was retained by Byron, but in the separation case of 1816 had advised Lady Byron.)[174] He was a leading Whig who, unlike many Whigs in those years, still retained some liberal principles, as shown by his advocacy of Catholic emancipation, his support of Sir Francis Burdett's reform motion in 1817, and his argument in Parliament against the restoration of the Bourbons in 1816. In retaining him, the Westbrooks presumably intended not only to stress their own wealth and importance but also to show that even prominent liberals would not condone Shelley's conduct.

Shelley, for his part, retained three attorneys—Basil Montagu, John Bell, and Sir Charles Wetherell—all competent men but not of the stature of Romilly. Montagu, a liberal friend of Godwin's, was presumably chosen because of his sympathy for Shelley's beliefs, and Bell and Wetherell because they were conservative and highly regarded by the lord chancellor. The lord chancellor was Lord Eldon, who occupied, with Sidmouth and Castlereagh, the apex of the Tory pyramid of the Establishment. He it was who was to decide whether the "atheist" and "republican"[175] should be allowed to bring up his own children. The radical press—as shown by the following passage from Leigh Hunt's *Examiner* for January 26—realized that the trial had implications beyond its apparent bounds:

> A cause is now privately pending before the Chancellor, which involves considerations of the greatest importance to all the most tolerant and best affections of humanity, public and private. It is of a novel description, and not only threatens to exhibit a most impolitic distinction between the prince and the subject, but trenches already upon questions which the progress of liberality and self-knowledge has been tacitly supposed to have swept aside, and the return of which would be bringing new and frightful obstacles in the way of the general harmony.[176]

The case was heard on January 24, but except for a newspaper account in the *Globe*,[177] little is known of the actual proceedings. There is extant, however, a copy of some "Observations" on the learned infants' bill of complaint by Wetherell, which indicates the line of the defense. Wetherell makes six main points, all of them legally telling but none of them really defending Shelley:

(1) "Little can be said in defence of 'Queen Mab.' It was, however, written and printed by Mr. Shelley when he was only nineteen and . . . it was merely distributed to some few of his personal friends."

(2) In spite of Shelley's attacks on marriage, he had married twice before he was twenty-five.
(3) There is no precedent for taking children from their father because of his religious views.
(4) Shelley is no longer living with Mary Godwin in an unmarried state.
(5) It would be unwise to deprive the children of the economic and other benefits which Shelley as the heir to a great estate could bestow upon them.
(6) "Part of the prayer of the petition is that Mr. and Miss Westbrooke should be appointed guardians. That part of the prayer, it is presumed, cannot, in the present state of the affair, be granted, but it is thought right to say that Mr. Westbrooke formerly kept a coffee-house, and is certainly in no respect qualified to be the guardian of Mr. Shelley's children. To Miss Westbrooke there are more decided objections: she is illiterate and vulgar, and what is perhaps a still greater objection, it was by her advice and with her active concurrence, and it may be said by her *management*, that Mr. Shelley, when of the age of nineteen, ran away with Miss Harriet Westbrooke, then of the age of seventeen, and married her in Scotland."[178]

Basil Montagu seems to have spoken along similar lines. The "liberal" Romilly emphasized Shelley's irreligious views as expressed in *Queen Mab*. At the end of the day's proceedings the lord chancellor declared that he would postpone judgment until he had held private hearings in his chambers and had studied the evidence more at leisure.

The weakness of the case from Shelley's point of view was that his attorneys felt their hands were tied. Even Montagu could not (or would not) come out and really support Shelley. It was tacitly taken for granted that Shelley's views on marriage, religion, and politics were indefensible. The strategy, therefore, was to play down these views and emphasize other considerations. Shelley himself apparently resented this lack of aggression and, though he realized that a full-fledged defense of his views might be injudicious, believed that a more positive attitude might bring better results. Shortly after the trial he sat down to pen a declaration to submit to Eldon during the period of deliberation:

I understand the opinions which I hold on religious matters to be abandoned as a ground of depriving me of the guardianship of my children; the allegations from which this unfitness is argued to proceed are reduced to a simple statement of my holding doctrines inimical to the institution of marriage as established in this country, and my having contravened in practice, as well as speculation, that institution. If I have attacked religion, it is agreed that I am punishable, but not by the loss of my children; if I have imagined a system of social life inconsistent with the constitution of England, I am punishable, but not by the loss of my children.

I understand that I am to be declared incapable of the most sacred of human duties and the most inestimable of human rights, because I have reasoned against the institution of marriage in its present state; because I have in my own person violated that institution, and because I have justified that violation by my reasoning . . . I consider the institution of marriage, as it exists precisely in the laws and opinions of this country, a mischievous and tyrannical institution, and shall express publicly the reasonings on which that persuasion is founded. If I am judged to be an improper guardian for my children on this account, no men of a liberal and inquiring spirit will remain in the community, who, if they are not more free from human feelings or more fortunate in their development and growth than most men can sincerely state their own to be, must not for some protest against the opinions of the multitude, equivalent to my tenets, live in the daily terror lest a court of justice should be converted into an instrument of private vengeance, and its edicts be directed, under some remote allegement of public good, against the most deep and sacred interests of his heart . . . It was matter of the deepest grief to me, to instance my particular case, that, at the commencement of my union with the present Mrs. Shelley, I was legally married to a woman of whom delicacy forbids me to say more than that we were disunited by incurable dissensions.[179]

Shelley thus refuses to back down from his principles on marriage or religion and simply denies that holding such principles is a sufficient reason for depriving him of his children. The statement that he and Harriet were "disunited by incurable dissensions," however, is at best a half-truth. That there were such "dissensions" and that they were bitter and had gone on for some time is clear, but the indication is that Eliza rather than Harriet was responsible. Moreover, the phrase gives the impression that Harriet had agreed to a separation, a suggestion made explicit in the statement in Shelley's answer to the bill of complaint that he and Harriet "agreed . . . to live separate and apart from each other."[180] But Harriet certainly did not so "agree." She was confronted by a fait accompli in Shelley's leaving her for Mary Godwin and had to make the best of it.

On March 27 the lord chancellor gave his judgment:

This is a case in which, as the matter appears to me, the father's principles cannot be misunderstood; in which his conduct, which I cannot but consider as highly immoral, has been established in proof, and established as the effect of those principles; conduct, nevertheless, which he represents to himself and others not as conduct to be considered as immoral, but to be recommended and observed in practice, and as worthy of approbation.

I cannot, therefore, think that I should be justified in delivering over these children for their education exclusively to what is called the care to which Mr. Shelley wishes it to be entrusted.[181]

Shelley, therefore, was deprived of his children. That Eldon was moved by political motives—the chastisement of a young radical—no one who is acquainted with the political temper of England in those times can doubt. If the verdict had been given on moral grounds alone, one has only to ask why, in view of the moral code of London society under the Regency, similar trials were not everyday occurrences? In fact, the Shelley trial actually set a precedent, and it is still cited in legal circles as a classic case of its kind. Shelley's statement to Byron in a letter of January 17, 1817, aimed at arousing Byron, is essentially true: "So I am here, dragged before the tribunals of tyranny and superstition, to answer with my children, my property, my liberty, and my fame, for having exposed their frauds, and scorned the insolence of their power."[182]

Following Eldon's judgment, there ensued a long period of disputation in which Shelley proposed one set of guardians, the Westbrooks another. Finally on July 25, 1818, Lord Eldon approved of a Dr. Thomas Hume and his wife, who agreed to a plan for rearing the children that Shelley's solicitor, P.W. Longdill, had drawn up.[183] The following extract indicates the general nature of this plan:

> On the Subject of Religion, which though here mentioned so late Mr. Longdill thinks the very first in point of consideration and importance, he [Longdill] would bring up the Children in the Faith and Tenets of the Church of England; he would deem it an imperative Duty to inculcate in them solemn, serious, and orthodox Notions of Religion, but at the same time he would be cautious not prematurely to lead their unripe minds to that momentous Subject. To a morning and evening prayer and Thanksgiving, and to Grace before and after Meals, he would regularly accustom them, and take occasion as circumstances might arise to inculcate in them a general religious feeling, without bringing to their Notice controversial Points that might excite doubts which they would be unable to solve, and entangle them in difficulties from which they would be unable to extricate themselves. What is clearly revealed Mr. Longdill would endeavour to teach them fervently to embrace, and what the limited powers of human Intellect would not permit them to understand, he would endeavour to make them feel it their Duty silently to revere. A regular attendance at Divine Service on Sundays Mr. Longdill would, when the Children arrived at a proper age, consider an indispensible Duty.[184]

Such were the lengths to which Shelley had to go in order to even secure the right of appointing a guardian for his children.

The Marlow Period

During this troubled time from the suicide of Fanny Imlay to the trial for the children, October 1816–February 1817, Shelley produced only one piece of writing, a political tract entitled *A Proposal for Putting Reform to the Vote*. In March he and Mary moved to the little town of Marlow, thirty miles from London, and there he produced *The Revolt of Islam*, his longest poem and *An Address to the People on the Death of the Princess Charlotte*, a pamphlet protesting the execution of three working-class radicals.

Life at Marlow was quiet. Peacock was a neighbor, and the Shelleys were visited by the Hunts and the Godwins. Among those in the village he became friendly with a Mr. Brooks, who admired Robert Owen, and a local businessman named Madocks from whom he rented a house.[185] "Marlow," Mary Shelley later wrote, "was inhabited . . . by a very poor population. The women are lace makers and lose their health by sedentary labour, for which they are very ill paid."[186] Shelley assisted them in every way that he could. "He . . . visited the sick in their beds," Hunt noted, " . . . and kept a regular list of the industrious poor, whom he assisted with small sums to make up their accounts."[187] "Every spot," wrote Mrs. Madocks in recollection, "is sacred that he visited; he was a gentleman that seldom took money about with him, and we received numerous little billets, written sometimes on the leaf of a book, to pay the bearer the sum specified, sometimes as much as half a crown; and one day he came home without shoes, saying that he had no paper, so he gave the poor man his shoes."[188] And the following bill for blankets and sheets for the poor is as "well deserving of admiration," Dowden suggests, as any stanza in *The Revolt of Islam:*

P. B. Shelley, Esq.	December 29, 1817		
	L.	S.	D.
20 blankets, at 7s per blanket	7	0	0
2 pieces sheeting, at 1s. 2d.	9	8	0
Packing, porterage	0	12	9
12 (?) at 2d.	0	2	0
	17	2	9
cash by cheque	15	9	6
Balance due	1	13	3[189]

Shelley's day-to-day existence at Marlow was described by Leigh Hunt in *The Examiner* in October 1819, when Shelley was under attack by *The Quarterly Review*:

> This was the round of his daily life: He was up early; breakfasted sparingly; wrote this *Revolt of Islam* all the morning; went out in his boat or into the woods with some Greek author or the Bible in his hands; came home to a dinner of vegetables (for he took neither meat nor wine); visited (if necessary) "*the sick and the fatherless,*" whom others gave Bibles to and no help; wrote or studied again, or read to his wife and friends the whole evening; took a crust of bread or a glass of whey for his supper; and went early to bed. This is literally the whole of the life he led, or that we believe he now leads in Italy.[190]

The variety of his reading may be judged by his reading list for the year 1817, which includes Coleridge's *Lay Sermon,* Defoe's *Journal of the Plague Year* (perhaps for the plague scenes in *The Revolt of Islam*), Paine's *Rights of Man, The Faerie Queen* (the *Revolt* is in the Spenserian stanza), the plays of Ben Jonson, Godwin's *Political Justice, Antony and Cleopatra, The Decline and Fall of the Roman Empire,* and Ovid's *Metamorphoses.*[191]

In spite of the apparent tranquillity of life at Marlow, forces were astir that were to drive Shelley and Mary not merely out of Marlow but out of England: a desire to take Claire's child by Byron—temporarily named Alba and later Allegra—to her father in Italy, financial difficulties, the general air of persecution (felt also by Byron and other radicals), and poor health. Regarding the first of these Mary was especially insistent. It was troublesome and embarrassing to have an unmarried woman and her child in the house, especially as rumors were spreading that the child was Shelley's. She contended that the expense of sending Allegra to Italy would be nearly as great as taking her there themselves and urged Shelley to action: "You do not seem enough to feel the absolute necessity there is that she should join her father with every possible speed."[192] As to Shelley's financial condition, a letter of Whitton's of October 22, 1817, stated that Shelley had recently been arrested for debt at the instigation of his uncle, Captain Pilfold, and that his debts totaled about £1,500.[193]

Shelley had rented a large house at Marlow (whose furnishings he neglected to pay for) and kept three servants.[194] He had also given more than £5,000 to Godwin and others, including £1,400 to Hunt at one stroke alone. In Italy, life would be less expensive, and he would be free from Godwin's importunities. The atmosphere of persecution is reflected in a letter to Godwin written just before Shelley left for Geneva in 1816: "Continually detained in a situation where what I esteem a prejudice does not permit me to live on equal terms with my fellow beings I resolved to commit myself by a decided step."[195] In 1816, however, Shelley had wavered in his determination and returned to England. After two more years of the same "prejudice," his mind was made up.

The final reason for leaving England, Shelley's health has not received much attention. I secured an opinion on it from the chief of medical services at a large metropolitan hospital, after supplying him with the following pieces of evidence:

Mary Shelley wrote in her Note to *Alastor:* "In the Spring of 1815 an eminent physician pronounced that he was dying rapidly of a consumption; abscesses were formed on his lungs, and he suffered acute spasms. Suddenly a complete change took place . . . every symptom of pulmonary disease vanished. His nerves, which nature had formed sensitive to an unexampled degree, were rendered still more susceptible by the state of his health."[196]

Thornton Hunt recalled in the article "Shelley, by One Who Knew Him": "I can remember one day at Hampstead; it was soon after breakfast, and Shelley sat reading, when he suddenly threw up his books and hands, and fell back, his chair sliding sharply from under him, and he poured forth shrieks, loud and continuous, stamping his feet madly on the ground. My father rushed to him, and, while the women looked out for the usual remedies of cold water and hand-rubbing, applied a strong pressure to his side, kneading it with his hands; and the patient seemed gradually to be relieved by that process . . . Again, accident has made me aware of facts which give me to understand, that, in all its paths, Shelley did not go scathless,—but that, in the tampering with venal pleasures, his health was seriously, and not transiently, injured. The effect was far greater on his mind than on his body;

and the intellectual being greater than the physical power, the healthy reaction was greater. But that reaction was also, especially in early youth, principally marked by horror and antagonism."[197]

Leigh Hunt wrote in *Lord Byron and Some of His Contemporaries*: "Mr. Shelley, when he died, was in his thirtieth year. His figure was tall and slight, and his constitution consumptive. He was subject to violent spasmodic pains, which would sometimes force him to lie on the ground till they were over; but he had always a kind word to give those about him, when his pangs allowed him to speak . . . though his habits of temperance and exercise gave him a remarkable degree of strength, it is not supposed that he could have lived many years."[198]

Shelley wrote to Godwin on December 7, 1817: "My health has been materially worse. My feelings at intervals are of a deadly & torpid kind, or awakened to a state of such unnatural & keen excitement that only to instance the organ of sight, I find the very blades of grass & the boughs of distant trees present themselves to me with microscopical distinctness. Towards evening I sink into a state of lethargy & inanimation, & often remain for hours on the sofa between sleep & waking a prey to the most painful irritability of thought. Such with little intermission is my condition . . . I have experienced a decisive pulmonary attack, & although at present it has past away without any considerable vestige of its existence, yet this symptom sufficiently shows the true nature of my disease to be consumptive. It is to my advantage that this malady is in it's nature slow, & if one is sufficiently alive to its advances is susceptible of cure from a warm climate."[199]

Medwin reported in his *Life of Shelley*: "After my departure from Pisa, he was magnetised [hypnotized] by a lady . . . during which operation, he made the same reply to an inquiry as to his disease, and its cure, as he had done to me,—'What would cure me would kill me,'—meaning lithotomy."[200]

Shelley wrote to Claire Clairmont on October 29, 1820: "I have suffered within this last week a violent access of my disease, with a return of those spasms that I used to have. I am consoled by the persuasion that the seat of the disease is in the kidneys, and consequently not mortal. As to the pain, I care little for it; but the nervous irritability which it leaves is a great and serious evil to me, and which, if not incessantly combated by myself and soothed by others, would leave me nothing but torment in life. —I am now much better . . . I expect the water of Pisa to relieve me, if indeed the disease be what is conjectured."[201]

Shelley again wrote to Claire Clairmont in January 1821: "I have not been able to see until the last day or two . . . My eyes are still weak. I have suffered also considerably from my disease; and am already in imagination preparing to be cut for the stone, in spite of Vacca's consolatory assurance."[202]

Finally, Shelley had six children. Born to Harriet were: Ianthe Elizabeth, born June 23, 1813, died June 1876; and Charles Bysshe, born November 30, 1814, died of tuberculosis in 1826.[203]

Born to Mary were: a daughter, born prematurely (seven month) February 22, 1815, died in London, March 5, 1815; William, born January 24, 1816, died June 7, 1819, of a "severe gastric attack" (Mary remarked during the winter of 1817–1818 that he suffered from the cold and was of a "delicate complexion"[204]); Clara Everina, born September 3, 1817, died September 25, 1818 in Venice of dysentery; and Percy Florence, born November 12, 1819, died 1889. Mary suffered a miscarriage in June 1822 (about four months).

On the basis of this evidence, the physician I consulted made the following points: "From the evidence of Thornton Hunt and Leigh Hunt on Shelley's spasms, from Medwin's reference to lithotomy (an operation for kidney stone), and from Shelley's letter to Claire in January 1821, it is evident that Shelley suffered from attacks of kidney stone (nephrolithiasis). The stone, which is formed in the kidney, lodges in the narrower portion of the ureter and causes terrific pain, one of the worst known. Now kidney stones are not the usual thing in a young person. Perhaps he had a tuberculous kidney in which stones are easily formed since there is tissue disintegration.

"The evidence on pulmonary tuberculosis is less certain, but it seems likely that he once had the disease and that it cleared up.

"As to venereal disease there is no evidence beyond the statement of Thornton Hunt in the material you sent me. If Shelley had had untreated syphilis his wives would have had one miscarriage after another, three or four times, and then the fourth or fifth child would have lived. The deaths of some of his children in their first year of life or late infancy is explicable on the basis of gastrointestinal infections (dysentery, etc) so common a cause of infant mortality in his day and even as late as 1900. He might have had gonorrhea at college, which cleared up without leaving any particular symptoms, and this may be the base for Thornton Hunt's story.

"Superimposed on these physical symptoms there was doubtless some element of neurotic self-absorption with his health as *vide* his letter to Godwin, but while this may have aggravated some of his symptoms it certainly did not cause those of them that originated from his kidney stones. In conclusion, I would say from the evidence that Shelley was a young man who had an attack of pulmonary tuberculosis from which he recovered and suffered attacks of kidney stones all his adult life, possibly on the basis of a t.b. kidney. There is no evidence from the material that he had syphilis or gonorrhea."

Once it is realized that Shelley periodically suffered from the agonies of a descending kidney stone, the allusions to his ill health—especially a pain in the side—in his letters and the journals become intelligible. As described in the letter of October 28, 1820, this pain left him, as it does all such patients, in a condition of nervous tension, partly from shock and partly from fear of a recurrence, and in these periods it was not unnatural that he should become obsessed with his health. The implication deriving from Peacock, Hogg, and others that all his symptoms were hypochondriacal is unjustified. Shelley may have had pulmonary tuberculosis in the spring of 1815 and a recurrence in the fall of 1817; his sister, Elizabeth, as well as his son Charles, subsequently died of tuberculosis.[205] But Shelley showed no signs of it later, and his activities during these earlier periods indicate that if he had the disease, his resistance to it must have been strong. Evidence that he had syphilis is lacking; in fact, the evidence points in the opposite direction. Thornton Hunt's statement, however, is difficult to understand, for he was an admirer of Shelley's and unlikely to make such a statement unless he believed it had some foundation.[206] It seems likely that Shelley (like Keats) picked up gonorrhea in Oxford. Hunt, knowing this and of Shelley's kidney disease, perhaps thought that the two were connected, and hence that Shelley's health "was seriously, and not transiently, injured" by his Oxford experience.

That ill health provided an incentive for quitting the damp of England for the warmth of Italy (as with Keats also) there can be no doubt, even if Shelley exaggerated somewhat in the December 7, 1817, letter to Godwin, who viewed the departure of his financial benefactor with terror. After a period of indecision, Shelley, Mary, and Claire finally left Marlow early in February 1818, spent a month or so in London, and then on March 12, accompanied by three children and a Swiss nurse, Elise, and a maid, Amelia (Milly) Shields, left Dover for the Continent, their journey financed by the purchase of £2,000 in *post obit* bonds for a promised £4,500. Shelley, therefore, had adequate reasons—physical, financial, and social—for leaving England and was not, as Peacock alleged, and subsequent biographers have repeated, overcome by a "spirit of restlessness."[207]

With Shelley's sojourn in Italy (1818–1822), a new chapter in his life opened. It was there that he wrote the poems which slowly brought about the realization that he was one of England's greatest poets. But he was not so regarded when he left England. In 1813, 1814, and 1815 Shelley was known only in a very limited circle, and known primarily not as a poet but as a radical and atheist. In the spring of 1816 his first attempt to break into orthodox literary circles with the publication of the *Alastor* volume failed. Only two reviews are known, and both were unfavorable.[208] It was not until the end of 1816 that the first recognition of Shelley as a poet took place. This was in an article in *The Examiner* entitled "Young Poets," in which he was noted (along with Keats) as a promising poet and a "very striking and original thinker."[209] Five weeks later, on January 19, 1817, *The Examiner* printed *Hymn to Intellectual Beauty* with a favorable comment.[210] Then in the February 1, February 22, and March 1, 1818, numbers appeared the first important review of one of Shelley's works, *The Revolt of Islam*:

> This is an extraordinary production. The ignorant will not understand it; the idle will not take the pains to get acquainted with it . . . but, we will venture to say, that the intelligent and the good . . . will find themselves amply repaid by

breaking through the outer shell of this production . . . The beauties of the poem consist in depth of sentiment, in grandeur of imagery, and a versification remarkably sweet, various, and noble, like the placid playings of a great organ. If the author's genius reminds us of any other poets, it is of two opposite ones, Lucretius and Dante . . . [yet] the work cannot possibly become popular . . . the author must forget his metaphysics and sea-sides a little more in his future works, and give full effect to that nice knowledge of men and things which he otherwise really possesses to an extraordinary degree. We have no doubt he is destined to be one of the leading spirits of his age, and indeed has already fallen into his place as such.[211]

In addition to this review, a sonnet to "The Author of 'The Revolt of Islam' " by Horace Smith appeared in the February 8, 1818, *Examiner*, and the March 2 issue contained comments on Shelley's pseudonymous political pamphlet *A Proposal for Putting Reform to the Vote*.[212]

From this period there are also various accounts of Shelley as a person. For instance, Crabb Robinson wrote of an evening at Godwin's house: "Mr. Shelley was there. I had never seen him before. His youth and a resemblance to Southey, particularly in his voice, raised a pleasing impression which was not altogether destroyed by his conversation, which is vehement and arrogant and intolerant. He was very abusive towards Southey, whom he spoke of as having sold himself to the Court, and this he maintained with the usual party slang. His pension and his laureateship, his early zeal and his recent virulence, are the proofs of gross corruption.[213]

Shelley thus impressed Robinson as a rather violent young man, who attacked his political enemies with virulence in left Whig "party slang."

Horace Smith, liberal coauthor of the comic *Rejected Addresses*, received a different impression when first meeting Shelley at Leigh Hunt's late in 1816:

In a short time Shelley was announced, and I beheld a fair, freckled, blue-eyed, light-haired, delicate-looking person, whose countenance was serious and thoughtful; whose earnest voice, though never loud, was somewhat unmusical. Manifest as it was that his pre-occupied mind had no thought to spare for the modish adjustment of his fashionably-made clothes, it was impossible to doubt, even for a moment, that you were gazing upon a *gentleman*; a first impression which subsequent observation never failed to confirm, even in the most exalted acceptation of the term, as indicating one that is gentle, generous, accomplished, brave. "Never did a more finished gentleman than Shelley step across a drawing-room," was the remark of Lord Byron.[214]

Keats's artist friend Joseph Severn was less favorably impressed at his first meeting with Shelley at Hunt's in 1817:

Shelley, in our first interview, went out of his way to attack me on my Christian creed. He repeated to Leigh Hunt the plan of a poem he was about to write, being a comparison of the Blessed Saviour with a mountebank, whose tricks he identified with the miracles. I was shocked and disturbed, and breaking in upon his offensive detail, I exclaimed, "That the fact of the greatest men having been Christians during the Christian period placed the religion far above such low ridicule." Shelley immediately denied this fact, and we at once began enumerating on our fingers the great men who were Christians, and the few who were not. When we got to Shakespeare he attempted to deny the great poet's belief, and quoted the sailor in "Measure for Measure." My counter quotations were from the utterances of Portia, Hamlet, Isabella, and numerous others; so that Leigh Hunt and Keats declared I had the best of the argument—whereupon Shelley declared that he would study the subject and write an essay upon it.[215]

Benjamin Robert Haydon—Tory, artist, and religious fanatic—had a similar experience in 1817 at a dinner at Horace Smith's attended by Leigh Hunt and Keats:

It was now, too, I was first invited to meet Shelley, and readily accepted the invitation. I went a little after the time, and seated myself in the place kept for me at the table, right opposite Shelley himself, as I was told after, for I did not then know what hectic, spare, weakly yet intellectual-looking creature it was, carving a bit of broccoli or cabbage on his plate, as if it had been the substantial wing of a chicken. [Hunt] and his wife and sister, Keats, Horace Smith, and myself made up the party.

In a few minutes Shelley opened the conversation by saying in the most feminine and gentle voice, "As to that detestable religion, the Christian—" I looked astounded, but casting a glance round the table easily saw by [Hunt?]'s expression of ecstasy and the women's simper, I was to be set at that evening *vi et armis.* No reply, however, was made to this sally during dinner, but when the dessert came and the servant was gone to it we went like fiends. [Hunt] and [Smith] were deists. I felt exactly like a stag at bay and resolved to gore without mercy. Shelley said the Mosaic and Christian dispensations were inconsistent. I swore they were not, and that the Ten Commandments had been the foundation of all the codes of law in the earth. Shelley denied it. [Hunt] backed him. I affirmed they were,—neither of us using an atom of logic.[216]

Long after *Queen Mab,* Shelley, then, was still anticlerical in his conversation and took a certain Voltairean delight in battling the orthodox. He apparently liked to open the fray with an iconoclastic shocker in a "gentle" voice, waiting for his opponent to take the bait.

In September 1817 William Thomas Baxter, an old friend of Godwin's, visited the Shelleys at Marlow. His daughter Isabel had been compelled by her husband to break off her friendship with Mary. On October 3 Baxter wrote to his daughter:

As to Shelley, I confess to you I was very much deceived in the preconceived estimate I had formed of him, and very agreeably disappointed in the man I found him to be. I had somehow or other imagined him to be an ignorant, silly, half-witted enthusiast, with intellect scarcely sufficient to keep him out of a madhouse, and morals that fitted him only for a brothel. How much, then, was I surprised and delighted to find him a being of rare genius and talent, of truly republican frugality and plainness of manners, and of a soundness of principle and delicacy of moral tact that might put to shame (if shame they had) many of his detractors; and, with all this, so amiable that you have only to be half an hour in his company to convince you that there is not an atom of malevolence in his whole composition! Is there any wonder that I should become attached to such a man, holding out the hand of kindness and friendship towards me? Certainly not.[217]

The most important biographer of Shelley for this period was Leigh Hunt. Hunt first penned a sketch of Shelley in his answer to the *Quarterly* attack on him in 1819. Then in *The Literary Examiner* for August 23, 1823, he told the following anecdote, repeated in his *Autobiography*:

Shelley, in coming to our house that night, had found a woman lying near the top of the hill, in fits. It was a fierce winter nignt, with snow upon the ground; and winter loses nothing of its fierceness at Hampstead. My friend, always the promptest as well as most pitying on these occasions, knocked at the first houses he could reach, in order to have the woman taken in. The invariable answer was, that they could not do it . . . At last my friend sees a carriage driving up to a house at a little distance. The knock is given; the warm door opens; servants and lights pour forth. Now, thought he, is the time. He puts on his best address, which any body might recognize for that of the highest gentleman as well as an interesting individual, and plants himself in the way of an elderly person, who is stepping out the carriage with his family. He tells his story. They only press on the faster. "Will you go and see her?" "No, Sir; there's no necessity for that sort of thing, depend on it; imposters swarm every where; the thing cannot be done: Sir, your conduct is extraordinary." "Sir," cried Mr. Shelley at last, assuming a very different appearance, and forcing the flourishing householder to stop out of astonishment, "I am sorry to say that *your* conduct is *not* extraordinary: and if my own seems to amaze you I will tell you something that may amaze you a little more, and I hope will frighten you. It is such men as you who madden the spirits and patience of the poor and wretched: and if ever a convulsion comes in this country, (which is is very probable,) recollect what I tell you;—you will have your house, that you refuse to put the miserable woman into, burnt over your head." "God bless me, Sir! Dear me, Sir!" exclaimed the frightened wretch, and fluttered into his mansion. The woman was then brought to our house, which was at some distance, and down a bleak path; and Shelley and her son were obliged to hold her, till the doctor could arrive.[218]

In the *Atlantic Monthly* for February 1863, Leigh Hunt's son, Thornton, came out with the article "Shelley, by One Who Knew Him." Hogg's picture of Shelley, he asserted, was "like a figure seen through fantastically distorting panes of glass," for Hogg was cynical to the point of irresponsibility. Peacock, a "dry wit . . . was not the man exactly to discern the form of Shelley's mind, or to portray it with accuracy and distinctiveness." His father suffered from an overrefinement and a delicacy of temperament that were "scarcely suited to comprehend the strong instincts, indomitable will, and complete unity of ideas which distinguished Shelley." All three of these biographers were charged with failing to bring out Shelley's essential decisiveness and determination:

The real man was reconcilable with all these descriptions. His traits suggested everything that has been said of him; but his aspect, conformation, and personal qualities contained more than any one has ascribed to him, and more indeed than all put together. A few plain matters-of-fact will make this intelligible. Shelley was a tall man,—nearly, if not quite, five feet ten in height. He was peculiarly slender, and, as I have said already, his chest had palpably enlarged after the usual growing period. He retained the same kind of straitness in the perpendicular outline of each side of him; his shoulders were the reverse of broad, but yet they were not sloping, and a certain squareness in them was naturally incompatible with anything feminine in his appearance. To his last days he still suffered his chest to collapse; but it was less a stoop than a peculiar mode of holding the head and shoulders,—the face thrown a little forward, and the shoulders slightly elevated; though the whole attitude below the shoulders, when standing, was unusually upright, and had the appearance of litheness and activity. I have mentioned that bodily vigour which he could display; and from his action when I last saw him, as well as from Mary's account, it is evident that he had not abandoned his exercises, but the reverse. He had an oval face and delicate features, not unlike those given to him in the well-known miniature. His forehead was high. His fine, dark brown hair, when not cut close, disposed itself in playful and very beautiful curls over his brows and round the back of his neck. He had brown eyes, with a colour in his cheek "like a girl's"; but as he grew older his complexion bronzed. So far the reality agrees with the current descriptions; nevertheless they omit material facts. The outline of the features and face possessed a firmness and *hardness* entirely inconsistent with a feminine character. The outline was sharp and firm; the markings distinct, and indicating an energetic physique . . . The beard also, although the reverse of strong, was clearly marked especially about the chin. Thus, although the general aspect was peculiarly slight, youthful, and delicate, yet, when you looked to "the points" of the animal, you saw well enough the indications of a masculine vigor, in many respects far above the average. And what I say of the physical aspect of course bears upon the countenance. That changed with every feeling. It usually looked earnest,—when joyful, was singularly bright and animated, like that of a gay young girl,—when saddened, had an aspect of sorrow peculiarly touching, and sometimes it fell into a listless weariness still more mournful; but for the most part there was a look of active movement, promptitude, vigor, and decision, which bespoke a manly, and even a commanding character . . . The impulsiveness which is ascribed to him is a wrong expression, for it is usually interpreted to mean the action of sudden motives waywardly, capriciously, or at least intermittently working; whereas the character which Shelley so constantly displayed was an overbearing strength of conviction and feeling, a species of audacious but chivalrous readiness to act as promptly as possible, and, above all, a zealous disposition to say out all that was in his mind. It is better expressed by the word which some satirist put into the mouth of Coleridge, speaking of himself, and, instead of impulsiveness, it should have been called an "utterancy," coupled with decision and promptitude of action.[219]

If we could cross the years and see Shelley as he was during his final months in England, our first impression would be that of a young English gentleman,—educated, gracious, cosmopolitan, speaking in the cultured tones of the upper classes, dressed in "fashionably made clothes." He was tall, with a rather boyish figure and scholarly stoop, and possessed a light, easy humor; a friendliness in the eyes, voice, and gestures; and a sense of energy and power of character integrated by suffering and conviction. If the conversation turned to serious matters—as in a "discussion until 3 in the morning with Hazlitt concerning Monarchy and Republicanism"[220]—one would be immediately struck by his animation, the intensity of his intellectual interest, and his desire to penetrate to the bottom of everything, the voice sweeping rapidly along on the stream of tumbling thoughts. If challenged by an opponent, he would stab back with quick flashes of logic, skillfully holding to the main point, not allowing the issue to be confounded by secondary questions, and scornfully disposing of the claims of orthodoxy. Nothing was sacred; truth was all. If establishing the truth meant goring sacred cows, he gored them. The existing religion was vicious and ossified, the existing marriage system repressive; the existing social order a madhouse of inequality, fraud, bigotry, despotism, crime, prejudice, war, and prostitution. He had little respect for tradition. The thinkers of the past had to be judged anew at the bar of a higher logic, for a new kind of society was visible in embryo, one of equality, peace, justice and freedom.[221] For the first time in history such a society was possible, and to achieve it required bold, fresh thinking. It was this vision that gave Shelley the confidence to challenge all that had been written and believed. The good in the old had to be retained, but the new was the essence. The will and intelligence of humanity must be freed for the task of establishing an egalitarian world.

Shelley supported these views by a varied array of evidence: facts from the morning *Chronicle* on the condition of the Lancashire weavers, an analysis of the sinking fund for the national debt, the opinions of Spinoza on superstition and of Hume on miracles, the political principles of Plato's *Republic*, the foreign policy of Castlereagh, Rousseau's views on education, the virtues and weaknesses of Cobbett's latest *Political Register*, Holbach's analysis of the origin of religion, the fallacies of Malthus, Sir William Drummond's views on Kant, the legal aspects of the jury system, the evolutionary theories of Erasmus Darwin, the chemical discoveries of Sir Humphrey Davy, the Greek view of sexual morality, the significance of the restoration of the Bourbons, the historical perspectives of Condorcet, Bentham's views on parliamentary reform, the current history of Ireland, the unjust game laws, and the laws on marriage and divorce. His voice would sweep on, getting somewhat thinner as it grew more intense, the jabs of logic and fact becoming more telling and—to his opponents—more exasperating. An opponent, sensing this intensity, might feel that it was directed against him; but was not. The young man was in deadly earnest about his beliefs, about society, and about mankind. As he grew more heated, he reckoned little with personal feelings and sometimes mangled with a curt derisiveness ideas that perhaps had become important to those listening. If one was an intellectual cynic like Hogg or Peacock, one would observe him with amusement taking for granted that his ideas were fantastic but assuming that in time he would grow more reasonable. If one was a sentimental liberal, like Hunt or Horace Smith, one would sigh over the beauties of the vision and the naive charm of the poet who conjured it like a magician from the depths. If one was an intelligent and rebellious boy, like Thornton Hunt, drawn close to the adult rebel, one would perceive in him direction, power, courage, and determination.

2

Shelley in Italy

Shelley's life in Italy falls into two periods, one between April 1818 and the end of January 1820, in which he and Mary wandered from city to city—Milan, Leghorn, Venice, Naples, Rome, Florence—and one from the end of January 1820 until his death in July 1822, in which he and Mary were settled in or near Pisa with a group of friends around them. During the first period there were no future biographers present, and we have to depend mainly on letters and diaries. For the second period, we have also the observations of Thomas Medwin, who stayed with Shelley at Pisa, and Edward John Trelawny, who was with him much of the time from January to July 1822.

Milan, Leghorn, Bagni di Lucca, Venice, Este, Rome, Naples: April 1818–February 1819

The Italy that Shelley entered in the spring of 1818 was not the unified Italy of today but consisted of several small separate states, each with its own government, including the kingdom of Sardinia, the duchy of Tuscany, the states of the Church, and the kingdom of the Two Sicilies. In pre-Napoleonic Italy they had all been feudal despotisms. Then the general bourgeois Napoleonic regimes produced reforms and developed the political consciousness of the business and professional classes. But with the defeat of France and the rise of the Quadruple Alliance, the despotisms were re-established. They were, however, re-established over peoples who had meanwhile had a taste of liberty and were no longer willing to submit passively. The seeds of the movement that later resulted in the unification of Italy under Garibaldi and Mazzini were already stirring during Shelley's years there.

In the northwest of Italy lay the state through which Shelley entered the country, the kingdom of Sardinia, with Turin and Genoa as its principal cities. Sardinia was ruled by a native feudal cabal indirectly under the thumb of Metternich's Austria. A revolt in 1821 was crushed violently. Below Sardinia came two minor duchies, Parma and Modena, both client states of Austria, and then the grand duchy of Tuscany, with Florence, Pisa, Lucca, and Leghorn (Livorno) as its principal towns. Of the four larger states, Tuscany was the only one that retained anything of the comparative liberalization of the Napoleonic times, and it was largely for this reason that Shelley eventually settled there. As he wrote to Peacock from Pisa in March 1820:

"I have no news from Italy. We live here under a nominal tyranny, administered according to the philosophic laws of Leopold, & the mild opinions which are the fashion here. Tuscany is unlike all the other Italian states, in this respect."[1]

The grand duke of Tuscany left most matters in the hands of his Secretary of State, Vittorio Fossombroni, who according to W. J. Stillman had "an easy going tolerance of liberal opinions . . . During all of these years Tuscany was the Italian Arcadia, where, as nowhere else in the peninsula, a certain freedom of thought and discussion existed undisturbed."[2] Political exiles from the other Italian states took refuge in Tuscany.

To the south of Tuscany and stretching along its eastern and northeastern borders lay the states of the Church, with their center in Rome. These states were ruled by papal dictate, but in their northern towns (Ravenna, for instance, where Byron lived for a time) the spirit of revolt was high, and three attacks were made on the liberals by the government between 1817 and 1823. Below the states of the Church and including all southern Italy lay the kingdom of the Two Sicilies, dominated by the kingdom of Naples. The two northern provinces, Lombardy (with Milan as its center) and Venetia (with Venice as its center), were politically part not of Italy but of Austria.

Shelley, accompanied by a not inconsiderable retinue—Mary, Claire, Elise (the Swiss nurse), Milly (the English maid), his two children, Clara (six months) and William (three years), and Claire's child by Byron, Allegra (one year)—crossed from France to the kingdom of Sardinia on March 26, 1818, where his books were immediately seized and sent to a censor, "a priest who admits nothing of Rousseau, Voltaire, &c., into the dominions of the King of Sardinia."[3] By April 4 the party had arrived in Milan, and then spent the next month near the lake of Como waiting for Byron and Claire to come to an agreement on Allegra. Claire had been told by Byron that he would let her live near Allegra in Venice (where Byron was then staying), posing as the child's aunt, but he now demanded sole custody.[4] As a result, Allegra was sent to Venice attended by Elise, "in whom," Shelley informed Byron, "Mrs. S[helley] entirely confides."[5] Shelley and the rest of the party moved south to Tuscany, where they stayed about four months, first at Leghorn, then at the watering resort of the baths of Lucca, some fifteen miles north of the town. At Leghorn they met the Gisbornes, John and Maria (to whom Godwin had once proposed), and Maria's son by a previous marriage, Henry Reveley, an engineer.

In the meantime, Claire, who was still living with the Shelleys, became insistent on going to Venice to see her child. In August, Shelley and she set out for Venice, while Mary remained behind at the baths with her children. At Florence they stopped to get a passport to enter the domains of the emperor of Austria, for Venice along with Turin had been taken from Italy at the Congress of Vienna. Byron received Shelley warmly, took him on a tour of the town, and placed his villa at Este, in the southern section of the beautiful Euganean Hills, at his disposal. He agreed to allow Allegra to go there for a time. Mary was sent for and hastened across Italy with her children. About three weeks after her arrival her younger child, Clara, died from dysentery. These events form the background for Shelley's narrative poem *Julian and Maddalo*.

From Este, the Shelleys and Claire left for a brief stay in Rome, passing through Ferrara and Bologna on their way south. At Ferrara, they stopped to see the cell where the poet Tasso had been imprisoned two hundred years before:

> Tasso's situation was widely different from that of any persecuted being of the present day, for from the depth of dungeons public opinion might now at length be awakened to an echo that would startle the oppressor. But then there was no hope. There is something irresistibly pathetic to me in the sight of Tasso's own hand writing moulding expressions of adulation & entreaty to a deaf & stupid tyrant in an age when the most heroic virtue would have exposed its possessor to hopeless persecution, and—such is the alliance between virtue & genius—which unoffending genius could not escape.[6]

Following a week of sightseeing at Rome, the party moved south to Naples, where they settled for three months (November 27, 1818–February 28, 1819). There, as usual, they lived quiet, rather solitary lives (*Stanzas, Written in Dejection, near Naples*), broken by expeditions to Vesuvius, Pompeii, and Baiai.[7]

It was at Naples that the mysterious affair of the "Neapolitan child" took place. In view of the controversy aroused by this affair, with theories and counter-theories created almost yearly, the main facts should be outlined so that a reader may draw his own conclusions. A day or so before January 24, 1819, the Shelleys discharged their Italian servant, Paolo Foggi, and at the same time their Swiss nurse, Elise, left them. "Elise," Shelley wrote to Peacock on January 24, "has just married our Italian servant & has quitted us; the man was a great rascal & cheated enormously; this match was very much against our advice."[8]

On February 27, 1819, Shelley appeared before a Neapolitan magistrate bringing with him a baby girl. He declared that the child had been born to him and "Mary Godwin" in Naples on December 27, 1818, and requested a birth certificate. He was accompanied by Francesco Florimente, described as a cheesemonger, and Antonio Di Lorenzo, a hairdresser, who lived near the Shelleys. On the same day the child was baptized as Elena Adelaide Shelley and a certificate of baptism was issued.[9]

On June 10, 1820, Antonio Liguari, cheesemonger, and Pasquale Fiorenzano, potteryman, appeared before a registrar of vital statistics in Naples to declare that Elena Adelaide Shelley, daughter of Percy Bysshe Shelley and Mary Godwin, had died in Naples, on June 9, aged fifteen months and twelve days, the parents then having residence at Leghorn.[10]

On March 8, 1820, Shelley, then at Pisa, wrote to the Gisbornes at Leghorn: "I enclose an outside calculation of the expenses at Naples calculated in ducats—I think it is as well to put into the hands of Del Rosso [an attorney] or whoever engages to do the business 150 ducats.—or more, as you see occasion.—but on this you will favour me so fa{r as} t{o} allow your judgment to regulate mine." On March 19, 1820, he wrote again to the Gisbornes: "If it [is] necessary to *write* again on th{e subject o}f Del Rosso, address not Medwin, nor Shelley, but simply 'Mr. Jones.' "[11]

On June 18, 1820, Mary Shelley wrote from Leghorn to Mrs. Gisborne, then on a visit to England:

The truth is, my dear friend, a variety of circumstances have occurred not of the most pleasant nature, since you left us and [we] have been obliged to reform our plans—We could not go to the baths of Lucca and finding it necessary to consult an attorney we thought of Del Rosso & came here—Are you pleased or vexed? Our old friend Paolo was partly the cause of this—by entering into an infamous conspiracy against us—there were other circumstances that I shall not explain till we meet—That same Paolo is a most superlative rascal—I hope we have done with him but I know not—since as yet we are obliged to guess as to his accomplices.[12]

On June 30, 1820, Shelley wrote to Mr. and Mrs. Gisborne: "My poor Neapolitan, I hear, has a severe fever of dentition. I suppose she will die, and leave another memory to those which already torture me. I am waiting the next post with anxiety, but without much hope . . . We have had a most infernal business with Paolo, whom, however, we have succeeded in crushing." On July 2 he wrote again to the Gisbornes: "I have later news of my Neapolitan. I have taken every possible precaution for her, and hope that they will succeed. She is to come as soon as she recovers." And later in July he wrote to them from Leghorn: "My Neapolitan charge is dead. It seems as if the destruction that is consuming me were as an atmosphere which wrapt & infected everything connected with me. The rascal Paolo has been taking advantage of my situation at Naples in December 1818 to attempt to extort money by threat[en]ing to charge me with the most horrible crimes. He is connected with some English here, who hate me with a fervour that almost does credit to their phlegmatic brains, & listen & vent the most prodigious falsehoods."[13]

On September 10, 1820, Byron wrote his friend R. B. Hoppner, the British consul at Venice, who had been kind to Shelley during his visit to Byron there in 1818: "You seem lately to have got some notion against him." In reply, Hoppner wrote out for Byron the story he had heard and which had made him change his mind about Shelley:

You are surprised, and with reason, at the change of my opinion respecting Shiloe [Shelley]: it certainly is not that which I once entertained of him: but if I disclose to you my fearful secret, I trust, for his unfortunate wife's sake, if not out of regard to Mrs. Hoppner and me, that you will not let the Shelleys know that we are acquainted with it. This request you will find so reasonable that I am sure you will comply with it, and I therefore proceed to divulge to you, what indeed on Allegra's account it is necessary that you should know, as it will fortify you in the good resolution you have already taken never to trust her again to her mother's care.

You must know then that at the time the Shelleys were here Clara [Claire Clairemont] was with child by Shelley: you may remember to have heard that she was constantly unwell, and under the care of a Physician, and I am uncharitable enough to believe that the quantity of medicine she then took was not for the mere purpose of restoring her health. I perceive too why she preferred remaining alone at Este, notwithstanding her fear of ghosts and robbers, to being here with the Shelleys. Be this as it may, they proceeded from here to Naples, where one night Shelley was called up to see Clara who was very ill. His wife, naturally, thought it very strange that he should be sent for; but although she was not aware of the nature of the connexion between them, she had had sufficient proof of Shelley's indifference, and of Clara's hatred for her: besides as Shelley desired her to remain quiet she did not dare to interfere. A Mid-wife was sent for, and the worthy pair, who had made no preparation for the reception of the unfortunate being she was bringing into the world, bribed the woman to carry it to the Pieta, where the child was taken half an hour after its birth, being obliged likewise to purchase the physician's silence with a considerable sum. During all the time of her confinement Mrs. Shelley, who expressed great anxiety on her account, was not allowed to approach her, and these beasts, instead of requiting her uneasiness on Clara's account by at least a few expressions of kindness, have since increased in their hatred to her, behaving to her in the most brutal manner, and Clara doing everything she can to engage her husband to abandon her. Poor Mrs. Shelley, whatever suspicions she may entertain of the nature of their connexion, knows nothing of their adventure at Naples, and as the knowledge of it could only add to her misery, 'tis as well that she should not. This account we had from Elise, who passed here this summer with an English lady who spoke very highly of her.

To this Byron replied on October 8: "The Shiloh story is true no doubt, though Elise is but a sort of *Queen's evidence* . . . Of the facts, however, there can be little doubt; it is just like them."[14]

Nearly a year later, on August 6, 1821, Shelley visited Byron at Ravenna, and Byron told him the story that Elise had told the Hoppners. On August 7 Shelley outlined the story to Mary:

Lord Byron has also told me a circumstance that shocks me exceedingly, because it exhibits a degree of desperate & wicked malice for which I am at a loss to account . . . Elise says that Claire was my mistress—that is all very well & so far there is nothing new: all the world has heard so much & people may believe or not believe as they think good.—She then proceeds to say that Claire was with child by me—that I gave her the most violent medicines to procure abortion—that ["I did not" *canceled*] this not succeeding she was brought to bed & that I immediately tore the child from her & sent it to the foundling hospital—I quote Mr. Hoppner's words—and this is stated to have happened in the winter after we left Este. In addition she says that both I & Claire treated *you* in the most shameful manner that I neglected & beat you, & that Claire never let a day pass without offering you insults of the most violent kind in which she was abetted by me . . . *You* should write to the Hoppners a letter refuting the charge, in case you believe & know & can prove that it is false; stating the grounds & the proofs of your belief.—I need not dictate what you should say, nor I hope inspire you with warmth to rebut a charge which you only can effectually rebut.—If you will send the letter to me here, I will forward it to the Hoppners.—Lord Byron is not up, I do not know Hoppners address—& I am anxious not to lose the post.

The next day he wrote that the story "shall be suppressed: even if I am to be reduced to the disagreeable necessity of prosecuting Elise before the Tuscan tribunals."[15]

On August 10, Mary wrote to Mrs. Hoppner:

Before I speak of these falsehoods permit [me] to say a few words concerning this miserable girl. You well know that she formed an attachment with Paolo when we proceeded to Rome, and at Naples their marriage was talked of. We all tried to dissuade her; we knew Paolo to be a rascal, and we thought so well of her that we believed him to be unworthy of her. An accident led me to the knowledge that without marrying they had formed a connexion; she was ill, we sent for a doctor who said there was danger of a miscarriage. I would not turn the girl on the world without in some degree binding her to this man. We had them married at Sir W. A'Court's—she left us; turned Catholic at Rome, married him, and then went to Florence. After the disastrous death of my child we came to Tuscany. We have seen little of them; but we have had knowledge that Paolo has formed a scheme of extorting money from Shelley by false accusations—he has written him threatening letters, saying that he w[oul]d be the ruin of him, &c. We placed these in the hands of a celebrated lawyer here who has done what he can do to silence him. Elise has never interfered in this, and indeed the other day I received a letter from her, entreating with great professions of love that I would send her money. I took no notice of this; but although I knew her to be in evil hands, I would not believe that she was wicked enough to join in his plans without proof.

And now I come to her accusations—and I must indeed summon all my courage while I transcribe them; for tears will force their way, and how can it be other wise? You knew Shelley, you saw his face, and could you believe them? Believe them only on the testimony of a girl whom you despised? I had hopes that such a thing was impossible, and that although strangers might believe the calumnies that this man propagated, none who had ever seen my husband could for a moment credit them.

She [Elise] says Clare was Shelley's mistress, that—upon my word, I solemnly assure you that I cannot write the words, I send you a part of Shelley's letter that you may see what I am now about to refute—but I had rather die that [*sic*] copy anything so vilely, so wickedly false, so beyond all imagination fiendish.

I am perfectly convinced in my own mind that Shelley never had an improper connexion with Clare—at the time specified in Elise's letter, the winter after we quitted Este, I suppose while she was with us, and that was at Naples, we lived in lodgings where I had momentary entrance into every room, and such a thing could not have passed unknown to me. The malice of the girl is beyond all thought —I now remember that Clare did keep her bed for two days—but I attended on her—I saw the physician—her illness was one that she had been accustomed to for years—and the same remedies were employed as I had before ministered to her in England.

Clare had no child—the rest must be false—but that you should believe it—that my beloved Shelley should stand thus slandered in your minds—he the gentlest and most humane of creatures, is more painful to me, oh far more painful than any words can express.

It is all a lie—Clare is timid; she always showed respect even for me—poor dear girl! She has some faults—you know them as well as I—but her heart is good, and if ever we quarreled, which was seldom, it was I, and not she, that was harsh, and our instantaneous reconciliations were sincere and affectionate.

Need I say that the union between my husband and myself has ever been undisturbed. Love caused our first imprudence, love which improved by esteem, a perfect trust one in the other, a confidence and affection which, visited as we have been by severe calamities (have we not lost two children?) has encreased daily, and knows no bounds.[16]

This letter Mary sent to Shelley, as he had requested, for forwarding to the Hoppners, and with it she enclosed a note to Shelley:

Shocked beyond all measure as I was I instantly wrote the enclosed—if the task be not too dreadful pray copy it for me I cannot—

Send that part of your letter which contains the accusation—I tried but I could not write it—I think I could as soon have died—I send also Elise's last letter—enclose it or not as you think best . . . Pray get my letter to Mrs. H[oppner] copied for a thousand reasons.

Adieu dearest take care of yourself all yet is well—the shock for me is over and I now despise the slander—but it must not pass uncontra[di]cted—I sincerely thank Lord Byron for his kind unbelief . . . Do not think me imprudent in mentioning Clares illness at Naples—It is well to meet facts—they are as cunning as wicked—I have read over my letter it is written in haste—but it were as well that the first burst of feeling sh[oul]d be expressed.[17]

On April 12, 1822, Elise wrote in French to Mary: "Having met Mademoiselle [Claire Clairmont] in a home here in Florence I was very sorry when she accused me of having said horrid things about her to Mrs. Hoppner—she also told me that you & Monsieur [Shelley] were both angry with me because of them: I assure you, my dear Mrs. Shelley, that you can believe my word of honor that I have never said anything to Mrs. Hoppner, neither against you, nor against Mlle, nor against Monsieur & from whatever party from which it comes it is a lie against me." On the same day Elise wrote to Mrs. Hoppner, denying that she had ever "seen anything in Mlle's conduct which could give rise to the least [ ] evil."[18]

Finally, Medwin reports that Shelley said he was in fear of arrest in Naples and Trelawny informed Rossetti that Shelley had attempted suicide in Naples.[19]

This tangle of facts, charges, countercharges, rumors, and innuendoes might be summarized as follows. A child was born in Naples on December 27, 1818, which Shelley declared to be his and "Mary Godwin's." However Mary Shelley had no child at the time.[20] The child died on June 10, 1820. Shortly before January 24, 1819, Elise, who perhaps was pregnant, and Foggi were married and left Naples for Florence.[21]

By March 1820, Shelley was being blackmailed by Foggi and was handling negotiations through the Gisbornes and Frederico Del Rosso, an attorney at Leghorn. By June 1820, Shelley had informed the Gisbornes that he had a child as a "charge" in Naples, and in two letters seems to associate this with Paolo's blackmailing attempts. He also stated that he intended to bring the child into his household. In the summer of 1820 Elise told the Hoppners that Shelley had had a child by Claire in Naples, but that Mary was unaware of it. This charge both Shelley and Mary heatedly denied, but they failed to mention the child in Naples. In April 1822, Elise denied to the Shelleys that she told any such story to the Hoppners and asserted to Mrs. Hoppner that she had never seen anything incorrect in Claire's conduct.

To explain these facts, several theories have been advanced. Shelley once told Medwin and Byron a long and curious story about a high-born lady who had been in love with him since 1816, had followed him to Naples, and had died there. It has been conjectured that the lady might have been the mother of the child.[22] Others, rejecting this story, have argued that the child was of unknown parentage and adopted by Shelley in order to solace Mary for the loss of their daughter Clara.[23] Still others have variously conjectured Shelley as the father and Claire as the mother, Elise as the mother and Foggi as the father, and Elise as the mother and Shelley as the father.[24]

The view that Claire gave birth to a child at Naples has nothing to support it except Elise's story, which she later denied. All other evidence is against it. An "X" mark in Claire's journal indicates that she was menstruating and her activities do not suggest pregnancy.[25] She was riding horseback in late July, when she would hypothetically have been four months pregnant, and a few days before the birth of the child she went with the Shelleys on a trip up Mount Vesuvius.[26] Furthermore, if Claire had been pregnant, she would hardly have gone to Naples, a city with an English colony of three hundred, to live in a street inhabited by English visitors.[27]

It is not possible for the child's parents to have been Elise and Foggi, for Foggi did not join the household until May or June at Leghorn, and at that time Elise was not with the Shelleys; she was with Allegra at Venice and then at Este. Paolo did not arrive at Este until September 5, when he drove Mary there from the baths of Lucca.[28] Paolo, then, cannot have been the father of a child born to Elise in December.

Could Elise have been the mother and someone other than Foggi the father? The only evidence that Elise was pregnant is the statement by Mary that a doctor examining her shortly before she married Paolo said that she was in "danger" of a miscarriage.[29] If this was true, she cannot have been the mother of Elena Adelaide, for the child was born on December 27, 1818, and Elise was married just before January 24, 1819. Even if the doctor's visit is placed as far back as December 1, when Mary and Elise arrived in Naples, the problem would not have been one of a miscarriage but of a premature birth, which Mary would hardly refer to as a "danger." If Elise was pregnant at all in December, the probability is that she was only a few months pregnant. Mary's implication is that she was pregnant when she married Foggi in January, and that she was pregnant by Foggi. It is most unlikely, then, that Elise was the mother of Shelley's "Neapolitan charge."[30]

What, then, of the mysterious lady? Although the story sounds more like romance than reality, there was perhaps some truth to it. Medwin begins his account: "A singular circumstance occurred to Shelley, which, after his death, I talked over with Lord Byron at Pisa—for he was equally acquainted with the story, as told to us mutually and which he more than once made a subject of conversation with me during my visit to Pisa. The night before his departure from London, in 1814 [1816], he received a visit from a married lady, young, handsome, and of noble connections, and whose disappearance from the world of fashion, in which she moved, may furnish to those curious in such inquiries a clue to her identity."[31] Shelley, then, told Medwin the name of the lady. Byron apparently accepted at least part of the story: "There was a Mrs. —— once fell in love with Shelley for his verses."[32] Finally, Claire Clairmont told Rossetti that she had once seen the lady in Naples.[33] Apparently there actually was a young English married lady who told Shelley in the spring of 1816 that she had fallen in love with him, and Shelley met her again in Naples. Even so, it is unlikely that she was the mother of Elena Adelaide. Shelley told Medwin that he had met her on the trip from Rome to Naples, which would place the meeting at the beginning of December 1818, and since the baby was born on December 27, a woman would not normally have been traveling from Rome to Naples by coach if she was eight months pregnant. She may, however, have been somehow connected with the child. Perhaps it was the child of someone she knew, and perhaps she did "charge" Shelley with its care.[34] Shelley's letter of March 8, 1820, to the Gisbornes suggests that he was paying for the child's upkeep. In the light of the known facts, therefore, one cannot make even a reasonable guess as to the identity of either the father or the mother of the child, though some obviously false speculations can be cleared away.

There is a more substantial clue to the basis for Paolo's blackmailing scheme. Once Shelley had signed a birth certificate declaring himself the father of the child, he laid himself open to blackmail. It could easily be shown that Mary was not the mother. It might not have been so easy to show that Shelley was not the father. Presumably Foggi knew of the birth certificate and perhaps had a copy of it. Elise had perhaps told him of the rumors in Marlow that Shelley was the father of Allegra. He knew also of Claire's illness because he was in the household. He must soon have become aware of the hostility toward Shelley in the English colonies in Italy as a free love advocate, radical, and atheist—a hostility so bitter that a minister in Pisa preached a sermon against him.[35]

Rome, Leghorn, Florence: February 1819–January 1820

On February 28, 1819, the Shelleys and Claire left Naples for Rome. There they led a less solitary life and made their first attempt to move into Italian intellectual society through the famed *conversazioni* of Marianna Dionigi, artist and author. In Rome, Shelley met two compatriots in whom he had a special interest: Sir William Drummond, whose work on metaphysics, *Academical Questions*, he had long admired; and Amelia Curran, daughter of the Irish nationalist John Philpot Curran, an old friend of William Godwin's on whom Shelley had called while in Dublin in 1812. As Amelia Curran was an amateur painter and Shelley had no painting of himself, he sat for his portrait by her. She produced an idealized picture, which in later years was further etherealized by the Victorian artist George Clint. Such portraits, according to Thornton Hunt, resemble Shelley "about as much as a lady in a book of fashions resembles real women."[36] Fortunately a partial corrective to the Curran portrait appears in the long-lost water-color miniature of Shelley by his friend Edward Ellerker Williams.[37]

Shelley responded to the art and archaeology of Rome with delighted excitement, as shown by his *Notes on Sculptures in Rome and Florence*, but he was bitterly aware of the contrast between the arts of Rome and the social scene, with its everpresent poverty and brutality:

> In the square of St. Peter there are about 300 fettered criminals at work, hoeing out the weeds that grow between the stones of the pavement. Their legs are heavily ironed, & some are chained two by two. They sit in long rows, hoeing out the weeds, dressed in party-coloured clothes. Near them sit or saunter, groupes of soldiers armed with loaded muskets. The iron discord of those innumerable chains clanks up into the sonorous air, and produces, contrasted with the musical dashing of the fountains, & the deep azure beauty of the sky & magnif-[ic]ence of the architecture around a conflict of sensations allied to madness. It is the emblem of Italy: moral degradation contrasted with the glory of nature & the arts.[38]

In Rome the first three acts of *Prometheus Unbound*, begun at Este seven months before, were finished and the somber drama of the Cenci begun, based on a manuscript story of the Cenci family that Mary had copied out the previous year at Leghorn. These months in Rome (March–June 1819) were in fact among the most productive in Shelley's career. But all writing and social life ended with the sudden death of William Shelley at the age of three. Shelley, Mary told Marianne Hunt, "watched 60 miserable—deathlyke hours without closing his eyes" over his dying son.[39] The child was buried in the Protestant cemetery, where a little more than three years later his father's ashes were buried also. The two graves may still be seen today, with that of Keats nearby.

The death of William, coming so soon after Clara's, was almost insupportable. Three days later, on June 10, the Shelleys, now childless, left Rome for Leghorn, where their friends the Gisbornes lived and where the (Tuscan) air was less heavy with oppression. At Leghorn the Shelleys found, about a mile out of town, "an airy little country house," known as the Villa Valsovano, where Shelley sought refuge from grief in work.[40] Here he finished *The Cenci,* and here too, infuriated by the news of the wanton riding-down of the people known as the "Manchester massacre," he rapidly composed *The Masque of Anarchy,* with its revolutionary refrain "Rise like Lions after slumber," which he sent to Hunt for immediate publication. The routine of life at the villa Shelley described in a letter to Peacock: "My employments are these, I awaken usually at 7, read half an hour, then get up, breakfast. After breakfast *ascend my tower,* and read or write until two. Then we dine—After dinner I read Dante with Mary, gossip a little, eat grapes & figs, sometimes walk, though seldom; and at ½ past 5 pay a visit to Mrs. Gisborne who reads Spanish with me until near seven. We then come for Mary & stroll about till suppertime."[41]

After four months the Shelleys moved again, still within the borders of Tuscany, to Florence. Mary was pregnant, and at Florence was then living a Scottish physican, Dr. J. Bell, who had attended little William at Rome and in whom the Shelleys had confidence. There is an interesting glimpse of Shelley's life at Florence in the journal of Sophia Stacey, the ward of an uncle and aunt of Shelley's, who visited him there. Her journal account was summarized by Helen Rossetti Angeli:

"He keeps his carriage, not horses, being more humane to keep fellow-creatures," Miss Stacey writes in her diary; and adds: "They see no company and live quite to themselves." She refers to many talks with him, and to his discourses on politics and religion; "his observation of the Established Church and Radicalism," and on "Love, Liberty, Death" . . . That Miss Stacey had the discernment to find Shelley a "very interesting man" is clear enough; later she refers to him as a "mysterious, yet interesting character." Like Trelawny, she was impressed by his devotion to books, which he always carried about with him. "As usual he held in his hand a book," she notes elsewhere; and again: "He is always reading, and at night has a little table with pen and ink, she [Mary] the same."

On the 14th November Shelley showed Miss Stacey his baby, saying "it could do no mischief now," but might some day or other be the "conqueror of provinces" . . . Miss Stacey was gifted with a very sweet and well-trained voice . . . Shelley took a keen delight in her singing, and she often sang to him, or he would come in and listen to her practising. After hearing her sing on the evening of the 17th November, he handed her the exquisite verses, "I arise from dreams of thee," having promised to write her some poetry the day before . . . Shelley was in very poor health during the latter part of Miss Stacey's sojourn in Florence. "He was suffering much from the pain in his side," she wrote on the 17th December, and on the 24th: "Mr. Shelley was talking to me when he was seized with spasma: he is in a very delicate state of health . . . Shelley was an admirable Italian scholar, and was kind enough to read daily with me in that language. I shall never forget his personal appearance. His face was singularly engaging, with strongly marked intellectuality. His eyes were however the most striking portion of his face, blue and large, and of a tenderness of expression unsurpassed. In his manner there was an almost childish simplicity combined with much refinement.

"Shelley was also passionately fond of music, but no executant himself A song of mine *'Non temer, o madre amata'* was the especial favourite, also de Thierry's ballad 'Why declare how much I love thee.' "[42]

Sophia Stacey had heard much of the famed black sheep of the family from her guardian and Shelley's aunt, Mrs. Robert Parker, and doubtless approached him with a fluttering heart.[43] She found him both "interesting" and "mysterious," with a tendency to talk freely about "the Established Church and Radicalism" and a flair for flattering lyrics. He led a retired, studious life, while suffering from a pain in his side that at times produced spasms. In his comment on babies growing into men who become "conquerors" she perhaps missed the irony. Later, as she looked back, she remembered that his manners were pleasantly unaffected and that he had extraordinary blue eyes and an intellectual expression. Such was Shelley to a young English belle meeting him in Florence in the winter of 1819.

At no period of his life did Shelley produce such a variety of works as at Florence: the political tract *A Philosophical View of Reform*; his passionate defense of the republican and anticlerical radical Richard Carlile in an open letter to *The Examiner;* a *jeu d'esprit* satire on Wordsworth as renegade radical, *Peter Bell the Third,* the light love lyrics to Sophia Stacey, including *The Indian Serenade;* the fourth act of *Prometheus Unbound;* a translation of *The Cyclops* of Euripides; and some translations from Spinoza's *Tractatus theologico politicus.* It was probably here, too, that he planned to put together a little book of poems for the English workers for which he wrote, among others, *Song to the Men of England* and *Sonnet: England in 1819.*[44]

On November 12, 1819, Mary gave birth to a child, named after the father and place of birth, Percy Florence Shelley. On January 26, 1820, the Shelleys left for Pisa.

Pisa, Leghorn, the Baths of Pisa: January 1820–August 1821

With this transfer to Pisa at the beginning of the year 1820 the second period of Shelley's life in Italy began. From then on he lived mainly in Tuscany and mostly in or near Pisa, where he gradually began to build up a circle of friends. During this first stay in Pisa, from January to June, the Shelleys became friendly with a "Mrs. Mason" whom they had met briefly several months before on their way from Leghorn to Florence. "Mrs. Mason" was Lady Mount Cashell, who thirteen years previously had left her husband and run off with George William Tighe ("Mr. Mason"), an absentee Irish landlord with literary interests. She and Tighe had two daughters. Years before, when she was a child, Lady Mount Cashell had been a pupil of Mary Wollstonecraft's in Ireland, and appears in her letters as her favorite "dear Margaret."[45] The name "Mason," in fact, came from Mary's *Original Stories,* in which the governess (Mary herself) was "Mrs. Mason" and Margaret one of her charges.[46] Lady Mount Cashell was a woman of advanced political views. William Godwin, meeting her in 1800, characterized her as a "democrat and a republican in all their sternness."[47] Like so many of the "Shelley circle" in Italy, she was an author. One of her books, on child rearing, became a standard household work in England and America.[48]

One other friend acquired by the Shelleys during this visit to Pisa was Andrea Vacca Berlinghieri, a well-known Italian physician, whom Mary delightedly described as "a great republican and no Xtian."[49] Shelley became his patient and was diagnosed by him as having kidney trouble complicated by a nervous temperament.[50] In 1825, when T. J. Hogg was passing through Pisa, Vacca told him that "no man was ever so much loved by his friends as S[helley]."[51] In this early stay at Pisa, however, the Shelleys, still in a state of shock from William's death lived rather solitary lives: "I ought to tell you that we do not enter into society. The few people we see are those who suit us—& I believe nobody but us. I find saloons & compliments too great bores; though I am of an extremely social disposition."[52]

Yet neither Shelley nor Mary lost interest in the affairs of the world. It was during this stay in Pisa that Shelley made one of his best-known political comments, in a letter to Leigh Hunt:

> The system of society as it exists at present must be overthrown from the foundations with all its superstructure of maxims & of forms before we shall find anything but disappointments in our intercourse with any but a few select spirits. This remedy does not seem to be one of the easiest. But the generous few are not the less held to tend with all their efforts towards it. If faith is a virtue in any case it is so in politics rather than religion; as having a power of producing that a belief in which is at once a prophesy, & a cause.[53]

Mary penned a diatribe against the Establishment and Castlereagh, Byron's "intellectual enunuch," that doubtless reflected the conversations in the Shelley household:

> Not that I much wish to be in England if I could but import a cargo of friends & books from that island here. I am too much depressed by its enslaved state, my inutility; the little chance there is for freedom; & the great chance there is for tyranny to wish to be witness of its degradation step by step & to feel all the sensations of indignation & horror which I know I sh[oul]d experience

were I to hear daily the talk of the subjects or rather the slaves of King Cant whose dominion I fear is of wider extent in England than anywhere else . . . but that nook of ci devant free land, so sweetly surrounded by the sea is no longer England but Castlereagh land or New Land Castlereagh—heaven defend me from being a Castlereaghish woman . . . The form of their oath sh[oul]d be—The King shall have my wealth—Castlereagh my obedience—his parliament my love—the Courier my trust—the Quarter[l]y my belief—Murray my custom—down with the Whigs & Radicals—So God help me.[54]

In March, Shelley heard of the January revolution in Spain, which almost overnight and almost bloodlessly had overthrown the medieval tyranny of Ferdinand. He hailed this event in *Ode to Liberty* as marking perhaps the first break in the dikes of the Quadruple Alliance. The next month, the revolution continuing, he considered going to Spain.[55] This ode and the very different *The Sensitive Plant* (perhaps inspired by Lady Mount Cashell and her garden) were apparently the only works he produced during his stay at Pisa.

For the summer the Shelleys went to the seaside town of Leghorn, where they lived in the house of their other British friends the Gisbornes, who were on a visit to England. There Shelley wrote *To a Skylark* and the playful *Letter to Maria Gisborne.* In August they returned to the vicinity of Pisa, settling at the baths of Pisa, a resort about five miles from the town. Shelley had for some time been following with rising hopes the second revolution of the year, in the kingdom of Naples, where the people overthrew their despotic ruler and were then attacked by the Austrian army. These events inspired his *Ode to Naples.* He also produced two poems of sharply contrasting types, the Puckish *Witch of Atlas* and the bluntly satirical *Swellfoot the Tyrant,* directed against the Castlereagh administration. In late October a cousin of Shelley's arrived, Thomas Medwin, who had been with him as a boy at school (Sion House). Medwin would probably never have written his *Life of Percy Bysshe Shelley,* published in 1847, if he had not made this visit to Shelley. Since last seeing Shelley in England, Medwin had been in India as a lieutenant in the Dragoon Guards and had retired in 1819 on half pay.

Medwin's faults as a biographer have been greatly exaggerated.[56] Certainly he is often muddled, especially on details, and he tones down Shelley's views to make him more acceptable to the Victorian reading public, but he had a deep affection for Shelley, and unlike Hogg, for whom cleverness was all, he tried to present an honest picture. He gives an unforgettable description of Shelley on their reunion:

It was nearly seven years since we had parted, but I should immediately have recognized him in a crowd. His figure was emaciated, and somewhat bent, owing to nearsightedness, and his being forced to lean over his books, with his eyes almost touching them; his hair, still profuse, and curling naturally, was partially interspersed with grey; but his appearance was youthful, and his countenance, whether grave or animated, strikingly intellectual. There was also a freshness and purity in his complexion that he never lost.

Medwin found Shelley discouraged by his failure to secure readers. At times he was "affected with a prostration of spirits that bent him to the earth." At others he was infectiously gay, as when reading Wordsworth's *Peter Bell* or some of the lesser works of the Leigh Hunt school: " 'But the adoption of such a barbarous jargon in translation from the Greek!' and here he turned to a travesty of Homer, whilst tears of laughter ran out of his large, prominent eyes." Treading through his variation of mood from enervated depression to humorous high spirits was Shelley's native kindness and compassion: "During a long and severe attack of illness, aggravated by the fatigues of my journey from Geneva, Shelley tended me like a brother. He applied my leeches, administered my medicines, and during six weeks that I was confined to my room, was assiduous and unintermitting in his affectionate care of me,—care I shall never forget."[57]

A week after Medwin's arrival, the Shelleys moved from the baths to Pisa, and from October 29, 1820, with the exception of a visit to Byron at Ravenna in August 1821, they resided continuously either at Pisa or the baths until the spring of 1822. At Pisa they acquired for the first time since their arrival in Italy a circle of friends. Three of these were Italian, Professor Francesco Pacchiani, Tommaso Sgricci, and Teresa Emilia Viviani; one was Greek, Prince Alexander Mavrocordato; two were English, Captain Edward Ellerker Williams and Jane Williams. Later the circle was joined by Byron (November 1821) and Edward John Trelawny (January 1822). Previous friendships with the "Masons" and Dr. Berlinghieri continued.

Pacchiani, who held a professorial chair at the University of Pisa, was famed both as a conversationalist (compared by Shelley to Coleridge) and an eccentric.[58] Sgricci was a professional "improviser": he would take a classical subject, such as the death of Hector or Iphigenia, and improvise a long dramatic poem on it before a theater audience. Shelley rated his talents high but deprecated his disdain for the common people (during the Neapolitan revolution):

I hate the cowardly envy which prompts such base stories as Sgricci's about the Neapolitans: a set of slaves who dare not to imitate the high example of clasping even the shadow of Freedom, alledge the ignorance {&} excesses of a populace, which oppression has made savages in sentiment & understanding. That the populace of the city of Naples are brutal, who denies to be taught? They cannot improvise tragedies as Sgricci can, but is it certain that under no excitement they would be incapable of more enthusiasm for their country? Besides it is not of them we speak, but of the people of the Kingdom of Naples, the cultivators of the soil; whom a sudden & great impulse might awaken into citizens & men, as the French & Spaniards have been awakened, & may render instruments of a system of future social life before which the existing anarchies of Europe will be dissolved & absorbed.[59]

The third of the Shelleys' Italian friends, the young and lovely Emilia Viviani, who inspired *Epipsychidion*, had been a pupil of Professor Pacchiani's and was kept in a convent by a jealous stepmother, where Shelley, and sometimes Mary and Claire, used to visit her.

Of Shelley's new friends in Italy, Prince Mavrocordato—then in exile in Pisa—was the most worthy of record. After the outbreak of the Greek war for independence he returned to Greece and became president of the new Greek republic. We first hear of him in the Shelley circle in a letter by Mary Shelley to Leigh Hunt:

> We have made acquaintance with a Greek, a Prince Mauro Codarti—a very pleasant man profound in his own language and who although he has applied to English little more than a month begins to relish its beauties & to understand the genius of its expressions in a wonderful manner—He was *done up* by some alliance I believe with Ali Pacha and has taken refuge in Italy from the Constantinopolitan bowstring. He has related to us some very infamous conduct of the English powers in Greece of which I sh[oul] exceedingly like to get the documents & to place them in Grey Bennett's or Sir F[rancis] B[urdett]'s hands—they might serve to give another knock to this wretched system of things.[60]

Captain Edward Ellerker Williams (1783–1822) had, like Medwin, served with the British armed forces in India, from which he had retired in 1816 on half pay. In India he had met a young, attractive married woman, Jane Johnson (*nee* Cleveland), who went first to England and then to the Continent with him under the name of Jane Williams. Why she broke with her husband, a ship's captain whom she had married at sixteen, is not known. After Williams' death in Italy she returned to England. There she lived with and, on the death of her husband, married Shelley's old friend, Thomas Jefferson Hogg.[61]

The Williamses had heard of Shelley from Medwin while they were staying at Geneva. They arrived in Pisa in January 1821 and soon became close friends with the Shelleys. Williams seems to have been open, honest, and good-natured, with some talent for writing (two plays, a journal and several poems), and was an amateur draftsman and painter.

Thus settled at Pisa, and with a circle of friends about him, Shelley produced—between February and June 1821—three of his greatest works: *Epipsychidion*, *Adonais*, and *A Defence of Poetry*. During much of this time he was also following with eager interest the course of the Greek revolution, which Prince Mavrocordato went to join in June.

Ravenna, Pisa: August 1821–May 1822

Since the summer of 1819 Byron had been residing at Ravenna in the house of his mistress, the Countess Teresa Guiccioli. The countess, her father, and her brother, the Count Pietro Gamba, were ardent Italian nationalists, and Byron joined in their plans for liberalizing the states of the Church—where Ravenna was situated—and freeing Italy from Austrian domination. He became a member of the Carbonari revolutionary organization, established contact with other leaders in Italy, and built a veritable arsenal in the Guiccioli mansion. With the outbreak of the Neapolitan revolution in the summer of 1820, these preparations were given added impetus. Byron drew up a plan for a revolutionary uprising, using the Guiccioli house as headquarters, and sent an impassioned address to the Neapolitan revolutionaries, offering to join their army. "The powers mean to war with the people," he wrote in his journal, "Let it be so—they will be beaten in the end. The king-times are fast finishing. There will be blood shed like water, and tears like mist; but the people will conquer in the end. I shall not live to see it, but I foresee it."[62] In February 1821 the Austrian army began to march against the Neapolitans. In order to reach Naples, they had to pass through the states of the Church. Byron and his fellow revolutionaries laid plans to hinder their advance by cutting off their artillery, which came last in line. Owing to a series of miscalculations, however, the plan failed. The decisive defeat of the Neapolitan army and the penetration of spies into the Carbonari enabled the papal authorities to thwart the uprising. To Byron, as an English lord, nothing could be done, but the Countess Guiccioli's father and brother were exiled and the countess found it expedient to follow them to Florence. Byron considered leaving Italy for Switzerland with the countess and taking Allegra with them. Faced with these multiple problems, he sent for Shelley.[63]

Shelley arrived at Ravenna on August 6, and he and Byron sat up talking until five in the morning about poetry (including the "killing" of Keats by the *Quarterly*), the Paolo-Elise slander, and politics. "The interest which he took in the politics of Italy," Shelley wrote to Mary, & "the actions he performed in consequence of it, are subjects not fit to be *written* [for fear of reprisals], but are such as will delight & surprise you."[64] A letter to Peacock gives an interesting glimpse of his life with Byron and incidentally reveals the humor that was characteristic of Shelley's conversation but which seldom appears in his writings:

Lord Byron is in excellent cue both of health and spirits. He has got rid of all those melancholy and degrading habits which he indulged at Venice. He lives with one woman, a lady of rank here, to whom he is attached, and who is attached to him, and is in every respect an altered man. He has written three more cantos of "Don Juan." I have yet only heard the fifth, and I think that every word of it is pregnant with immortality. I have not seen his late plays, except "Marieno Faliero," which is very well, but not so transcendently fine as the "Don Juan." Lord Byron gets up at *two*. I get up, quite contrary to my usual custom, but one must sleep or die, like Southey's sea-snake in "Kehama," at 12. After breakfast we sit talking till six. From six till eight we gallop through the pine forests which divide Ravenna from the sea; we then come home and dine, and sit up gossiping till six in the morning. I don't suppose this will kill me in a week or fortnight, but I shall not try it longer. Lord B.'s establishment consists, besides servants, of ten horses, eight enormous dogs, three monkeys, five cats, an eagle, a crow, and a falcon; and all these, except the horses, walk about the house, which every now and then resounds with their unarbitrated quarrels, as if they were the masters of it . . . After I have sealed my letter, I find that my enumeration of the animals in this Circean Palace was defective, and that in a material point. I have just met on the grand staircase five peacocks, two guinea hens, and an Egyptian crane. I wonder who all these animals were before they were changed into these shapes.[65]

In spite of their friendship, Shelley felt a strain in his relationship with Byron, for Byron, as he once remarked in a letter to Leigh Hunt, had never really uprooted the "canker of aristocracy." A member of the House of Lords and a celebrated writer, Byron somehow always made Shelley aware that he was from a "county" family and had few readers: "Lord Byron & I are excellent friends, & were I reduced to poverty, or were I a writer who had no claims to a higher station than I possess—or did I possess a higher than I deserve, we should appear in all things as such, & I would freely ask him any favour. Such is not now the case—The demon of mistrust & of pride lurks between two persons in our situation poisoning the freedom of their intercourse."

One unfortunate by-product of Shelley's friendship with Byron was a reinforcement of his own feeling of failure: "He has read to me one of the unpublished cantos of Don Juan, which is astonishingly fine.—It sets him not above but far above all the poets of the day: every word has the stamp of immortality.—I despair of rivaling Lord Byron, as well I may: and there is not other with whom it is worth contending." Sometimes this feeling was distorted into masochistic self-abasement:

the worm beneath the sod
May lift itself in homage of the God.[66]

Although Shelley was virtually without conceit, he was certainly too acute a critic not to have recognized his superiority on some counts to Byron. It was not only Byron's poetical powers that oppressed him but Byron's popularity. Byron was recognized both in England and on the Continent as a major poet, as well as a nonconformist and a liberal. Shelley, writing poetry with a message similar to Byron's, although more radical and more profound, was receiving little but vituperation. His attacks on the English Establishment, political and religious, seemed utterly in vain: "I write nothing, and probably shall write no more. It offends me to see my name classed among those who have no name. If I cannot be something better, I had rather be nothing, and the accursed cause to the downfall of which I dedicated what powers I may have had—flourishes like a cedar and covers England with its boughs."

After a visit of about ten days, Shelley persuaded Byron to come to Pisa, where the Countess Guiccioli could join him, since it was in Tuscany, and he would find a group of English and Italian admirers. Shelley himself had determined to settle there. "Our roots," he wrote to Mary, "were never struck so deeply as at Pisa & the transplanted tree flourishes not."[67]

While at Ravenna, Shelley and Byron talked over a plan for establishing a liberal periodical to serve as an effective counterblast to the Tory *Quarterly Review*. Both poets had independently thought of such a project. More than two years before, Shelley had written to Peacock: "I have just seen the *Quarterly* for September (not from my own box). I suppose there is no chance now of your organizing a review! This is a great pity. The *Quarterly* is undoubtedly conducted with talent great talent & affords a dreadful preponderance against the cause of improvement. If a band of staunch reformers, resolute yet skilful infidels were united in so close & constant a league as that in which interest & fanaticism have bound the members of that literary coalition!" Eight months previously Byron had suggested that Tom Moore and he "set up jointly a [weekly] *newspaper*" which would "give the age some new lights upon policy, poesy, biography, criticism, morality, theology, and all other *ism, ality*, and *ology* whatsoever." He had reminded Moore of the project only a day or two before Shelley's arrival. A few days after his return from Ravenna, Shelley wrote to Leigh Hunt:

> He [Lord Byron] proposes that you should come and go shares with him and me, in a periodical work, to be conducted here; in which each of the contracting parties should publish all their original compositions, and share the profits. He proposed it to Moore, but for some reason it was never brought to bear. There can be no doubt that the *profits* of any scheme in which you and Lord Byron engage, must, from various yet co-operating reasons, be very great. As to myself, I am, for the present, only a sort of link between you and him, until you can know each other and effectuate the arrangement; since (to entrust you with a secret which, for your sake, I withhold from Lord Byron), nothing would induce me to share in the profits, and still less in the borrowed splendour, of such a partnership.[68]

There has been speculation as to which of the two really initiated the periodical (named *The Liberal*).[69] Byron doubtless mentioned the newspaper project to Shelley, as he had just written to Moore about it and had perhaps complained about Moore's lack of enthusiasm. Shelley probably responded with a suggestion for a review, as he had to Peacock, with Hunt as editor, instead of a newspaper with Moore as editor. Certainly Hunt must have been Shelley's suggestion, for Byron had mixed feelings about him. Although he admired Hunt's courage and was in general agreement with *The Examiner's* policy, especially on foreign affairs, he felt that Hunt was rather "Cockney" in his radicalism and something of "an honest charlatan."[70] Shelley, however, admired Hunt almost unreservedly. If such was the course of events, it means that Shelley changed Byron's Whig newspaper scheme into one for a radical review. But the final decision must have been Byron's for only he had the wealth and influence to launch such a project.

After his return from Ravenna to the baths of Pisa, Shelley composed his last completed long poem, *Hellas,* an impassioned tribute to the Greek revolution. In October he went to Pisa. On November 1, Byron arrived with an extensive retinue of people and animals and moved into a mansion opposite the Shelley-Williams house. Under his dynamic influence the Pisa circle became more active. A group consisting of Byron, Shelley, Williams, a Captain Hay, John Taaffe, an Irish eccentric, Medwin (for a brief period), and Trelawny (from January 1822) joined in the daily activities of riding, shooting, dining, and talking, and Mary found a new companion in the Countess Guiccioli.[71] Interesting reflections of this period in Shelley's life appear in Williams' journal, Medwin's *The Conversations of Lord Byron,* and Trelawny's *Recollections of the Last Days of Shelley and Byron.* Of these, Williams' journal was written at the time, Medwin's book was published two years later from notes taken at the time, and Trelawny's book was written thirty-six years later.[72]

The following excerpts give the flavor of Williams' journal (1821–1822):

Friday, October 26 . . . As a Poet S[helley] is certainly the most imaginative of the day, and if he addressed himself more to human affections he would be the greatest. His greatest fault is ignorance of his own worth. He asked me yesterday what name he should give to the drama he is now engaged with. I proposed "Hellas" which he will adopt. I mention this circumstance as I was proud at being asked the question, and more so that the name pleased him.

Friday, November 9. Fine, but a sharpness in the air I have not felt before. Continue writing and finish . . . In the evening S reads aloud "The Vision of Judgment" a satirical poem of Lord B[yron]'s, a sublime composition which displays the greatness of his genius above any other of his works; but I am in doubt if it can be published or rather I fear no publisher can be found for it in these times.

Thursday, November 29. Cloudy. Rise early, and S accompanies us to Leghorn . . . While S was waiting for the carriage, standing at a shop-door in the Via Grande a well-dressed but vulgar Italian approaching asked if he might be allowed to address a few words to him. "Certainly" said S——"Then, Sir," said he "as you seem to be a stranger in this Country, and would probably be happy to find any one who could judiciously point out its many classical and natural beauties, if you will give me ten thousand crowns a year, I will undertake to be your companion and guide; every wish of your heart shall be anticipated, and every sense gratified in its turn; nay, you shall enjoy those pleasures now unknown to you."

"For how much" said S—— seriously.—"Ten thousand crowns, Sir,—for which you will be disburthen'd from all care—a carriage at your command will be ever in readiness—a sumptuous table will be provided for you and you will be introduced to the first families, and enter into every fashionable gaiety—in short—" The carriage now arrived, and S—— stepping into it said—

"I thank you for your polite and *generous* offer, but my means are proportion-

ate to my wishes which are both extremely moderate—and—" —"Sir," said the man, "I know to the contrary"—He was about to continue when we drove off.
Returned to dinner with S—— at 6 o'clock. Rain on the way home.

Sunday, December 2 . . . Walk with Jane in the evening and meet Lord B's party —with whom we shoot. Lord B. hit, at the distance of 14 yards, the bulls eye four times, and a half-crown piece three. The last shot struck the piece of money so exactly in the centre that it was afterwards found with the ball enclosed within it— the sides being drawn to the centre like a three-cornered cocked hat.

Monday, December 3. S hit the half-crown.

Saturday, January 5. . . . Played at billiards with S almost the whole day—Mary & M[edwin] dine with us—

Tuesday, January 8 . . . Mary read to us the first two acts of Lord B's "Werner" . . . As to S's "Charles the First"—on which he sat down about 5 days since, if he continues it in the spirit [of] some of the lines which he read to me last night, it will doubtless take place before any other that has appear[ed] since Shakespeare, and will be found a valuable addition to the historical Pla[y.]

It is exceedingly to be regretted that S [does] not meet with greater encouragement. [A] mind such as his, powerful as it is, requires gentle *leading*.—[73]

Shelley had brought pistols with him from England[74] and was a good shot. The January 8 entry reflects a conflict situation: Mary, anxious for Shelley to achieve recognition, urged him to write in a more popular style, sometimes, Williams felt, crudely pushing rather than subtly "leading" him.

Medwin's *Conversations of Lord Byron* were the result of his visits to Byron during his second stay with Shelley at Pisa (November 15, 1821–March 9, 1822). He begins with an interesting account of his first visit, accompanied by Shelley:

20th November.—"This is the Lung' Arno. He has hired the Lanfranchi palace for a year:—it is one of those marble piles that seem built for eternity, whilst the family whose name it bears no longer exists" said Shelley, as we entered a hall that seemed built for giants. "I remember the lines in the 'Inferno,' " said I: "a Lanfranchi was one of the persecutors of Ugolino."—"The same," answered Shelley; "you will see a picture of Ugolino and his sons in his room. Fletcher, his valet, is as superstitious as his master, and says the house is haunted, so that he cannot sleep for rumbling noises overhead, which he compares to the rolling of bowls. No wonder; old Lanfranchi's ghost is unquiet, and walks at night."

The palace was of such size, that Lord Byron only occupied the first floor; and at the top of the staircase leading to it was the English bulldog, whose chain was long enough to guard the door, and prevent the entrance of strangers; he, however, knew Shelley, growled, and let us pass. In the anti-room we found several servants in livery, and Fletcher . . . who had been in his service since the time he left Harrow. "Like many old servants, he is a privileged person," whispered Shelley. "Don Juan had not a better Leporello, for imitating his master. He says that he is a Larel struck by a *Metre*, and when in Greece remarked upon one of the bas-reliefs of the Parthenon, 'La! what mantel-pieces these would make, my Lord!' "

When we were announced, we found his Lordship writing. His reception was frank and kind; he took me cordially by the hand, and said: "You are a relation and schoolfellow of Shelley's—we do not meet as strangers—you must allow me to continue my letter on account of the post. Here's something for you to read, Shelley, (giving him part of his MS. of 'Heaven and Earth;') tell me what you think of it."

A few days later they had a discussion with Byron on Christianity:

Calling on him the next day, we found him, as was sometimes the case, silent, dull, and sombre. At length he said:

"Here is a little book somebody has sent me about Christianity, that has made me very uncomfortable: the reasoning seems to me very strong, the proofs are very staggering. I don't think you can answer it, Shelley; at least I am sure I can't, and what is more, I don't wish it . . . You believe in Plato's three principles; —why not in the Trinity? One is not more mystical than the other. I don't know why I am considered an enemy to religion, and an unbeliever. I disowned the other day that I was of Shelley's school in metaphysics, though I admired his poetry; not but what he has changed his mode of thinking very much since he wrote the Notes to 'Queen Mab,' which I was accused of having a hand in."

Medwin recorded Byron's views on Shelley and Keats:

"A man who means to be a poet should do, and should have done all his life, nothing else but make verses. There's Shelley has more poetry in him than any man living; and if he were not so mystical, and would not write Utopias and set himself up as a Reformer, his right to rank as a poet, and very highly too, could not fail of being acknowledged. I said what I thought of him the other day; and all who are not blinded by bigotry must think the same. The works he wrote at seventeen are much more extraordinary than Chatterton's at the same age" . . .

"I know no two men," said he, "who have been so infamously treated, as Shelley and Keats . . . Milman [was] the author of that article on 'The Revolt of Islam' . . . In consequence of the shameless personality of that and another number of 'The Quarterly,' every one abuses Shelley,—his name is coupled with every thing that is opprobrious: but he is one of the most moral as well as amiable men I know. I have now been intimate with him for years, and every year has added to my regard for him" . . . "I know no lines more cutting than those in 'Adonais,' or more feeling than the whole elegy."

. . . "As Keats is now gone, we may speak of him. I am always battling with the Snake [Shelley] about Keats, and wonder what he finds to make a god of, in that idol of the Cockneys: besides, I always ask Shelley why he does not follow his style, and make himself one of the school, if he think it so divine. He will, like me, return some day to admire Pope, and think 'The Rape of the Lock' and its sylphs worthy fifty 'Endymions,' with their faun and satyr machinery."[75]

As with the entries in Williams' journal, each of these passages gives a certain insight into Shelley. The first passage has something of the flavor of his daily conversation. His comment on the Lanfranchi Palace existing beyond the line whose fame it was meant to perpetuate shows the same ironical attitude toward the efforts of a ruling class to preserve its fame in monuments as *Ozymandias*. The remark about old Lanfranchi's ghost walking at night exemplifies the playful humor of Shelley's day-to-day conversation. The discussion of Christianity and Plato shows that although Byron respected Shelley for both his learning and his intellect, he was sardonic about some of Shelley's ideas. He admits that Shelley might be able to refute a book supporting Christianity, as he himself could not, but he jibes at Shelley for attacking Christianity while at the same time being attracted by Platonism. Some of this was obviously good-humored joshing, but behind some of it lurks an attitude of aristocratic condescension. It was doubtless this attitude that the poet Samuel Rogers, who visited Byron at Pisa, spoke of when he told Moore that Byron "treats his companion Shelley very cavalierly," and which, in time, wore Shelley's patience thin: "Certain it is, that Lord Byron has made me bitterly feel the inferiority which the world has presumed to place between us."[76] This attitude is visible also in Byron's reference to Shelley as "the Snake"—explained by Byron in a letter to Tom Moore: "Goethe's Mephistofilus calls the serpent who tempted Eve 'my aunt, the renowned snake;' and I always insist that Shelley is nothing but one of her nephews, walking about on the tip of his tail."[77] Another source of annoyance to Shelley must have been Byron's failure really to grasp his poetry (especially such "Utopias" as *Prometheus Unbound*). This negative aspect of the relationship of the two poets, however, should not be exaggerated. No doubt Byron was often exasperating and Shelley angry, but the two nevertheless had strong links of mutual regard and affection.[78]

The importance of Byron's comments on Shelley is that they are those of a man of rare intelligence and insight who saw Shelley almost every day for several periods in his life, and if allowance is made for Byron's penchant for ridicule and his love of gossip, a great deal can be learned from him. He and Shelley were together at a number of times and places: at Geneva from May 25 to August 28, 1816; at Venice from August 23 to the end of October 1818; at Ravenna from August 6 to about August 22, 1821; and at Pisa from November 1, 1821 to the end of April 1822. In 1820 during the Neapolitan child scandal, Byron commented on Shelley in a letter to Hoppner: "Surely he has talent and honour but is crazy against religion and morality." Although Byron bows in his second clause to Hoppner's prejudices, the remark, in view of the current picture of Shelley, was really a rebuke to Hoppner and a defense of Shelley. Few people in 1820 had the courage to assert that Shelley had either talent or honor. In a journal for October 15, 1821, Byron noted that in general he did not like literary men with the exception of "men of the world, such as Scott, and Moore, etc., or visionaries out of it, such as Shelley etc." To this may be added the following from Trelawny, quoting Byron: "Today I had another letter warning me against the Snake [Shelley]. He, alone, in this age of humbug, dares stem the current, as he did to-day the flooded Arno in his skiff, although I could not observe he made any progress. The attempt is better than being swept along as all the rest are, with the filthy garbage scoured from its banks."[79]

On February 18, 1822, Thomas Moore wrote to warn Byron against his association with Shelley:

> Boldness and even licence, in politics, does good,—actual present good; but in religion, it profits neither here nor hereafter; and, for myself, such a horror have I of both extremes on this subject, that I know not which I hate most, the bold, damning bigot, or the bold, annihilating infidel . . . You will easily guess that, in all this, I am thinking not so much of you, as of a friend, and, at present, companion of yours, whose influence over your mind . . . I own I dread and deprecate most earnestly.

To this Byron, who had just spent six months as Shelley's neighbor at Pisa, replied sharply:

> As to poor Shelley, who is another bugbear to you and the world, he is, to my knowledge, the *least* selfish and the mildest of men—a man who has made more sacrifice of his fortune and feelings for others than any I have heard of. With his speculative opinions I have nothing in common, nor desire to have. The truth is, my dear Moore, you live near the *stove* of society, where you are unavoidably influenced by its heat and its vapours . . .
>
> If you speak of your *own* opinions, they ever had, and will have, the greatest weight with *me*. But if you merely *echo* the *monde*, (and it is difficult not to do so, being in its favour and its ferment,) I can only regret that you should ever repeat any thing to which I cannot pay attention.[80]

On August 3, after the drowning of Shelley and the consequent distress of Mary, Byron wrote to Murray: "I never saw such a scene, nor wish to see another. You were all brutally mistaken about Shelley, who was, without exception, the best and least selfish man I ever knew. I never knew one who was not a beast in comparison." And on August 8, he wrote to Moore: "There is another man gone, about whom the world was ill-naturedly, and ignorantly and brutally mistaken. It will, perhaps do him justice now, when he will be no better for it." "You should have known Shelley," he commented several months later to the Countess of Blessington, "to feel how much I must regret him. He was the most gentle, most amiable, and *least* worldly-minded person I ever met; full of delicacy, disinterested beyond all other men, and possessing a degree of genius, joined to a simplicity, as rare as it is admirable. He had formed to himself a *beau ideal* of all that is fine, high minded, and noble, and he acted up to the ideal even to the very letter. He had a most brilliant imagination, but a total want of worldly wisdom."[81]

Edward John Trelawny, born in the same year as Shelley—1792—had a long and adventurous life. He had entered the navy in 1805, voyaged to South America, India, and Borneo, saw naval action, left the navy in 1812, went to Italy and then to Greece with Byron, returned to England in 1828, traveled in the United States from 1833 to 1835, where he swam the rapids above Niagara Falls and freed a slave, returned once more to England, settled uneasily into Victorian life, died in 1881 and was buried, at his own request, beside Shelley in Rome. In 1831 he published an autobiography dealing with his early life, called *Adventures of a Younger Son*, which, as naval and other records show, is mostly fictional, although some of its incidents are based on fact.[82] "Trelawny's inability to apprehend the truth in its fixity," his biographer comments, "was due to a looseness of adjustment in his mental lenses."[83] This "looseness of adjustment" also afflicted his view of Shelley, as shown in one of his best-known anecdotes:

> I was bathing one day in a deep pool in the Arno, and astonished the Poet by performing a series of aquatic gymnastics, which I had learnt from the natives of the South Seas. On my coming out, whilst dressing, Shelley said mournfully "Why can't I swim, it seems so very easy?" I answered: "Because you think you can't. If you determine, you will; take a header off this bank, and when you rise turn on your back, you will float like a duck; but you must reverse the arch in your spine, for it's now bent the wrong way."
>
> He doffed his jacket and trousers, kicked off his shoes and socks, and plunged in; and there he lay stretched out on the bottom like a conger eel, not making the least effort or struggle to save himself. He would have been drowned if I had not instantly fished him out.[84]

This story has been repeated endlessly since its publication in 1858, yet it is manifestly untrue in at least one respect: the human body will not lie stretched out at the bottom of a "deep" pool but will float to the surface. That Trelawny made up the story out of whole cloth, however, is unlikely. There probably was a pool, and Shelley probably did go into it and was helped out by Trelawny. But the "poet" had to be shown as impetuous and nonhuman— a visionary elf requiring the guidance of a practical man of the world. Although there is none of Hogg's sardonic intent in Trelawny, and he shared Shelley's liberal and anticlerical views, the picture he gives is a variation of the same stereotype.[85]

If, however, we sift Trelawny carefully, we can learn a good deal from him about Shelley. And sometimes we do not even have to sift. For instance, he relates that Shelley was as "strong-limbed and vigorous" as "a young Indian . . . there were few men who would walk on broken ground at the pace he kept up."[86] This contradicts the popular caricature of the effete intellectual and bears out Thornton Hunt's picture of Shelley's masculine vigor. Or he gives the following description of Shelley's conversation, from a letter to him by Williams: "Shelley is certainly a man of most astonishing genius, in appearance extraordinarily young, of manners mild and amiable, but withal full of life and fun. His wonderful command of language, and the ease with which he speaks on what are generally considered abstruse subjects, are striking; in short, his ordinary conversation is akin to poetry, for he sees things in the most singular and pleasing lights; if he wrote as he talked, he would be popular enough." He supplies an interesting anecdote of a visit to an American ship at Leghorn, which reveals Shelley's admiration for American democracy and its leaders, in contrast to his opinion of Napoleon or Nelson. Trelawny and Shelley followed the captain down to a cabin:

I seduced Shelley into drinking a wine-glass of weak grog, the first and last he ever drank. The Yankee would not let us go until we had drunk, under the star-spangled banner, to the memory of Washington, and the prosperity of the American commonwealth.

"As a warrior and statesman," said Shelley, "he was righteous in all he did, unlike all who lived before or since; he never used his power but for the benefit of his fellow-creatures."[87]

However, Trelawny's most famous anecdotes—his first meeting with Shelley, the adventure with Jane Williams in the boat, Shelley in his woodland "study," the visit to the Greek ship—while doubtless having some basis in fact, all betray Trelawny's weakness for dressing up a good story. And his accounts of the shipwreck and Shelley's cremation are filled with invention, as the variations in the existing manuscripts show.

In company with Byron, Trelawny, Williams, and others, the months at Pisa were pleasant ones for Shelley. Three disturbing incidents took place, however: a local preacher, Dr. Nott, preached a sermon against Shelley's atheism (and was attacked in witty doggerel by Byron); a rumor spread that a man was to be burned alive in the states of the Church for a sacrilegious act, whereupon Byron and Shelley made plans for rescuing him by force (the man escaped and fled to Tuscany); and the Byron-Shelley party got mixed up in an affray with an Italian dragoon, which led to considerable litigation.

Medwin tells of the second of these episodes:

Being one day at Moloni's the bookseller's at Pisa, a report was in circulation that a subject belonging to the Lucchese States had been taken up for sacrilege, and sentenced to be burnt alive . . . I quitted him with disgust, and immediately hastened to Lord Byron's.

"Is it possible?" said he, after he had heard my story. "Can we believe that we live in the nineteenth century?" . . . Shelley entered at this moment horror struck: he had just heard that the criminal was to suffer the next day. He proposed that we should mount and arm ourselves as well as we could, set off immediately for Lucca, and endeavour to rescue the prisoner when brought out for execution, making at full speed for the Tuscan frontiers, where he would be safe. Mad and hopeless as the scheme was, Lord Byron consented, carried away by his feelings, to join in it, if other means should fail. We agreed to meet again in the evening, and in the mean time to get a petition signed by all the English residents at Pisa, to be presented to the Grand Duke.[88]

The third episode arose when Byron, Shelley, Trelawny, Captain Hay, Count Gamba, and Taaffe were returning with their horses to Pisa after a bout of pistol shooting and a sergeant on horseback brushed against Taaffe. The party demanded apologies, and Gamba apparently struck the soldier with his whip. A scuffle ensued, in which Captain Hay was slashed by the man across the face, and Shelley was hit by the hilt of his saber, knocked off his horse, and lay stunned and vomiting on the ground. Byron, seeing the scuffle begin, rode to his house where a servant gave him a sword-stick. The sergeant, leaving the scene of the fight, encountered Byron returning to it. They exchanged words. The sergeant rode on. As he passed Byron's house, Byron's coachman rushed out and stabbed him with a lance, seriously wounding him. The Tuscan authorities began a lengthy investigation, which ended with the clearing of Byron's servants of the crime, apparently after the distribution of lavish bribes. Byron decided to move to Leghorn. A short time after the incident the Shelleys left to spend the summer on the Gulf of Spezia.[89]

During this period at Pisa with Byron, Shelley worked on his historical drama *Charles the First*, projected a play on the Timon of Athens theme, "adapted to modern times," and began his last poem, *The Triumph of Life*.[90]

San Terenzo: May–July 1822

About forty-five miles to the north of Pisa, along the western coast of Italy, lies the Gulf of Spezia, with Spezia, its principal town, in the center of the shoreline and the village of Lerici at its southeastern tip. A little to the north of Lerici lay, in Shelley's time, the tiny fishing village of San Terenzo, and it was to a house on the outskirts of this village that the Shelleys and the Williamses moved in the spring of 1822.[91] The months ahead promised much pleasure, as Shelley had just had a sailboat built (temporarily named the *Don Juan*, at Trelawny's suggestion, as a tribute to Byron's satire).[92] The daily routine of their life by the sea is reflected in Williams' journal:

Thursday, May 2. Cloudy, with intervals of rain. Went out with Shelley in the boat—fish on the rocks—bad sport. Went in the evening after some wild ducks—saw nothing but sublime scenery, to which the grandeur of a storm greatly contributed.

Saturday, May 4. Fine. Went fishing with Shelley. No sport. Loitered away the whole day. In the evening tried the rocks again, and had no less than thirty baits taken off by the small fish. Returned late—a heavy swell getting up.

Sunday, May 5. Fine. Kept awake the whole night by a heavy swell which made a noise on the beach like the discharge of heavy artillery. Tried, with Shelley, to launch the small, flat-bottomed boat through the surf. We succeeded in pushing it through, but shipped a sea on attempting to land. Walk to Lerici along the beach, by a winding path on the mountain's side. Delightful evening—the scenery most sublime.[93]

This idyllic existence was broken by two saddening events. On May 2, Shelley told Claire the news he had withheld from her for some days—that Allegra had died in the convent where Byron had placed her. And on June 16, Mary had a miscarriage.[94]

During this period, there occurred three more of those psychological episodes which—along with one earlier at Tremadoc in Wales—have been much debated.[95] The first is recorded in Williams' journal for May 6:

> After tea, walking with S[helley] on the terrace, and observing the effect of moonshine on the waters, he complained of being unusually nervous, and stopping short he grasped me violently by the arm and stared steadfastly on the white surf that broke upon the beach under our feet. Observing him sensibly affected I demanded of him if he was in pain—but he only answered, saying "There it is again! —there!"—He recovered after some time, and declared that he saw, as plainly as then he saw me a naked child rise from the sea, clap its hands as if in joy and smiling at him. This was a trance that it required some reasoning and philosophy entirely to awaken him from, so forcibly had the vision operated on his mind. Our conversation which had been at first rather melancholy lead to this, and my confirming his sensations by confessing that I had felt the same, gave a greater activity to his ever wandering and lively imagination.

The second and third episodes were related by Mary in a letter to Maria Gisborne after Shelley's death:

> As I said Shelley was at first in perfect health but having over fatigued himself one day, & then the fright my illness gave him caused a return of nervous sensations & visions as bad as in his worst times. I think it was the saturday after my illness [22nd] while yet unable to walk I was confined to my bed—in the middle of the night I was awoke by hearing him scream & come rushing into my room; I was sure that he was asleep & tried to waken him by calling on him, but he continued to scream which inspired me with such a panic that I jumped out of bed & ran across the hall to Mrs. W[illiam]'s room where I fell through weakness, though I was so frightened that I got up again immediately—she let me in & Williams went to S who had been wakened by my getting out of bed—he said that he had not been asleep & that it was a vision that he saw that had frightened him—But as he declared that he had not screamed it was certainly a dream & no waking vision—What had frightened him was this—He dreamt that lying as he did in bed Edward & Jane came in to him, they were in the most horrible condition, their bodies lacerated—their bones starting through their skin, the faces pale yet stained with blood, they could hardly walk, but Edward was the weakest & Jane was supporting him—Edward said—Get up, Shelley, the sea is flooding the house & it is all coming down." S got up, he thought, & went to the his window that looked on the terrace & the sea & thought he saw the sea rushing in. Suddenly his vision changed & he saw the figure of himself strangling me, that had made him rush into my room, yet fearful of frightening me he dared not appro[a]ch the bed, when my jumping out awoke him, or as he phrased it caused his vision to vanish. All this was frightful enough, & talking it over the next morning he told me that he had had many visions lately—he had seen the figure of himself which

met him as he walked on the terrace & said to him—"How long do you mean to be content"—no very terrific words & certainly not prophetic of what has occurred.[96]

Beside these episodes should be placed one other, told by Byron's physician, John William Polidori, concerning the famed ghost-story evening at Geneva in 1816 that resulted in *Frankenstein*:

> Among other particulars mentioned, was the outline of a ghost story by Lord Byron. It appears that one evening Lord B., Mr. P.B. Shelly, two ladies and the gentleman before alluded to, after having perused a German work, entitled Phantasmagoriana, began relating ghost stories; when his lordship having recited the beginning of Christabel, then unpublished, the whole took so strong a hold of Mr. Shelly's mind, that he suddenly started up and ran out of the room. The physician [Polidori himself] and Lord Byron followed, and discovered him leaning against a mantle-piece, with cold drops of perspiration trickling down his face. After having given him something to refresh him, upon enquiring into the cause of his alarm, they found that his wild imagination having pictured to him the bosom of one of the ladies with eyes (which was reported of a lady in the neighbourhood where he lived) he was obliged to leave the room in order to destroy the impression.[97]

On this episode Byron later commented—contrasting it with Shelley's conduct when he faced drowning in a storm on Lake Geneva: "And yet the same Shelley, who was as cool as it was possible to be in such circumstances, (of which I am no judge myself, as the chance of swimming naturally gives self possession when near shore,) certainly had the fit of phantasy which Polidori describes, though *not exactly* as he describes it."[98]

That Shelley was not hallucinating in the Geneva episode is shown by his rapid recovery and by his generally normal conduct. He did not see, as a psychotic does, something that was not there. Byron's reaction was that he was a generally normal person who had experienced a "fit of phantasy," that is, that he had worked up his imagination to a point of terror in a midnight session of mutual escalation of fears. The extraordinary thing about the episode is the intensity of Shelley's reaction. He was obviously deeply agitated and seems to have been unable to control his actions. The three later episodes must be seen in relation to the situation at Lerici. Shelley and Mary had originally rented the house for themselves; Jane and Edward Williams were taken in because they could not find another place. Consequently, the house was crowded, with the Shelleys and Williamses living on one floor—Shelley in one bedroom, Mary and their son in another, the Williamses in a third. Mary had a miscarriage, then Allegra died, which brought the wildly grief-stricken Claire in as an additional guest for a time. Shelley and Mary were not sleeping together, for Mary was either pregnant or recovering from her miscarriage, and Shelley, as his poems show, was turning toward Jane Williams. It is difficult to conceive of a situation more designed to create psychological stress. That Shelley was, in fact, disturbed and depressed is shown by a letter he wrote to John Gisborne on June 18, four days before the nightmare episode:

I write little now. It is impossible to compose except under the strong excitement of an assurance of finding sympathy in what you write. Imagine Demosthenes reciting a Philippic to the waves of the Atlantic! Lord Byron is in this respect fortunate. He touched a chord to which a million hearts responded, and the coarse music which he produced to please them disciplined him to the perfection to which he now approaches. I do not go on with "Charles the First." I feel too little certainty of the future, and too little satisfaction with regard to the past, to undertake any subject seriously and deeply. I stand, as it were, upon a precipice, which I have ascended with great, and cannot descend without *greater*, peril, and I am content if the heaven above me is calm for the passing moment.

On the same day he wrote to ask if Trelawny could secure prussic acid for him: "I need not tell you I have no intention of suicide at present,—but I confess it would be a comfort to me to hold in my possession that golden key to the chamber of perpetual rest—["Let this rest" *and two or three words more are smeared out.*] The *prussic acid* is used in medicine in infinitely minute doses, but that preparation is weak, & has not the concentration necessary to medicine all ills infallibly.—A single drop, even less, is a dose & it acts by paralysis."[99] This, if not a direct threat of suicide, was certainly close to it; and Shelley, as his final sentence shows, was thinking about it more obsessively than he admits. A depression of this nature obviously could not have arisen suddenly, nor from the Lerici situation alone, but must have had roots going back for several months at least.

One of the most important of these roots was Shelley's growing sense of his failure and isolation as a writer, which meant he was losing his purpose in life. Added to this was his growing feeling of alienation from Mary, shown in the poems to Emilia Viviani and then to Jane Williams. What the situation at Lerici apparently did was to intensify and bring to the surface an already developing disturbance.

Nor was Shelley the only one affected by that situation. Mary, in her letter to Maria Gisborne, after describing Shelley's "vision" of encountering his own figure, continues:

But Shelley had often seen these figures when ill; but the strangest thing is that Mrs. W[illiams] saw him. Now Jane though a woman of sensibility, has not much imagination & is not in the slightest degree nervous—neither in dreams or otherwise. She was standing one day, the day before I was taken ill, at a window that looked on the Terrace with Trelawny—it was day—she saw as she thought Shelley pass by the window, as he often was then, without a coat or jacket—he passed again—now as he passed both times the same way—and as from the side towards which he went each time there was no way to get back except past the window again (except over a wall twenty feet from the ground) she was struck at seeing him pass twice thus & looked out & seeing him no more she cried—"Good God can Shelley have leapt from the wall? Where can he be gone?" Shelley, said Trelawny—"no Shelley has past—What do you mean?" Trelawny says that she trembled exceedingly when she heard this & it proved indeed that Shelley had never been on the terrace & was far off at the time she saw him.[100]

The first of Shelley's Lerici "visions" was that of the child in the waves. Williams' reaction was similar to that of Byron five years previously, namely, that Shelley was an essentially normal person whose imagination had run away with him. The stimulus this time was not a ghost-story atmosphere but a melancholy conversation, presumably on death, perhaps on the death of Allegra. Shelley must have been brooding over Allegra's death, and the formation of waves and surf in the moonlight may have seemed like the body of a child.

That Shelley was not sleepwalking in the second of the Lerici episodes is shown, as Mary notes, by the fact that he was screaming. Presumably he had had a nightmare and rushed into Mary's room in a frightened state, from which Williams finally aroused him. Beside Mary's account of this episode we might put Williams' journal entry: "*Sunday, June 23.* Calm—Painting and fitting rigging. During the night S[helley] sees *spirits* and alarms the whole house."[101] Williams apparently did not regard the episode as seriously as did Mary and ironically hints that Shelley was conscious of his actions. Whether or not this was true, the content of the nightmare, as given by Mary, reveals Shelley's state of mind at the time. Laceration, strangulation, death, the whelming of a sea—these are typically expressive of fear and hostility. It is interesting, too, that Mary was the one being strangled, and that Jane appeared as stronger than Edward (who was "the weakest").

In the "doppelgänger" episode, in which Shelley "met" his own figure on the terrace, he must again have been experiencing one of his heightened-imagination fantasies. In the first act of *Prometheus Unbound* he had written that Zoroaster "Met his own image walking in the garden."[102] And Mary reports his saying that he had "often seen these figures when ill," presumably when he had a fever. Shelley obviously felt attracted by the doppelgänger fantasy, perhaps morbidly so, for the dopplegänger was supposed to be a premonition of death.

The psychological mechanisms inherent in these episodes seem similar to those involved in two other psychological phenomena observed in Shelley. Peacock called some of Shelley's fantasies "semi-delusions," which Shelley half-believed even as he made them up. The "vision" of Shelley meeting himself was perhaps of similar nature and motivation. In telling Mary of "visions" that he knew were unreal but had imagined vividly, Shelley is taking a kind of perverse delight in mystifying and frightening her, much as he used to do as a child with his sisters and later with Harriet.[103]

The second component in these episodes is Shelley's lack of control at a certain point of mounting emotion, as when under the stress of Harriet's suicide he hurled charges recklessly in an emotional orgy, charges that he must have known were untrue but which he had a compulsion to believe. If this kind of emotional escalation was triggered by a deep fear and swept up into the poetic imagination, it could conceivably produce such imaginative-emotional extravaganza as the Geneva episode and the aftermath of the nightmare. The "vision" of the child in the waves is of similar nature to that of the Geneva episode. Both were fantasies which seized Shelley's mind so firmly that they frightened and confused him.

Why, one might ask—and the question obviously puzzled Byron—could a man as intelligent as Shelley be so swayed at times by fantasies? The answer is in part that such matters are determined primarily not by intelligence but by early psychological patterns. They are, however, often subject to a degree to conscious control, which Williams apparently felt Shelley was not trying to exert. Usually, one would assume from the infrequency of such episodes in Shelley's life that he exercised such controls. But when he lost control, he seemed to feel that the fantasies could really have been "visions." Although this kind of credulity seems at odds with intelligence, there is evidence in Shelley's prose works, *One Life* and *Speculations on Metaphysics*, that he took a somewhat Humean view of the difficulty of distinguishing internal from external sensations. He could thus feel that he had some philosophical backing for his "visions," which might have made him feel freer to yield to his imaginative impulses and also, perhaps, made him really wonder about their nature and origin.

It has been argued, on the basis of these and other episodes, that Shelley was psychotic or neurotic. That he was not psychotic is self-evident. Psychotics do not lead normal daily lives and produce an uninterrupted series of great works of literature. The word "neurotic" has unfortunately come to be applied loosely to anyone who may need psychological guidance, and few, if any, could not at some periods in their lives benefit from such guidance—as Shelley certainly could have at Lerici. But if the word is taken in the basic sense of a seriously disturbed person who, though still in contact with reality, has little sense of his own identity, is ineffective, weak, and drifting—sometimes manifesting his state in alcoholism—then Shelley was not a neurotic. He had a sharp, clear sense of identity, was purposeful and aggressive, was capable of both giving and inspiring love, and was, in general, a strong person on whom others relied. It is against this central core of personality that one must view these psychological episodes.

The Last Days

About the middle of June, Leigh Hunt, his wife Marianne, and their six children, including the precocious Thornton, arrived in Genoa. On June 21 Hunt wrote to Shelley that they were sailing from Genoa for Leghorn and would look for Shelley's house at San Terenzo as they passed.[104] On July 1 Shelley set out in the *Don Juan* with Williams, Captain Daniel Roberts, and an eighteen-year-old English boy, Charles Vivian, who looked after the boat, on "a run of 45 to 50 miles" to Leghorn to greet Hunt and assist in launching *The Liberal*.[105] On July 2 Shelley met the Hunts at Leghorn and proceeded with them to Pisa, where they were to live with Byron. He stayed in Pisa until July 7.

The meeting of Shelley and Hunt was recorded by Thornton:

> Some years elapsed between the night when I saw Shelley pack up his pistols —which he allowed me to examine—for his departure for the South, and the moment when, after our own arrival in Italy, my attention was again called to his presence by the shrill sound of his voice, as he rushed into my father's arms, which he did with an impetuousness and a fervour scarcely to be imagined by any who did not know the intensity of his feelings and the deep nature of his affection for that friend. I remember his crying out that he was "so *inexpressibly* delighted! —You cannot think how inexpressibly happy it makes me!"[106]

When Shelley and the Hunts first arrived at Pisa, events seemed to bode ill for the projected *Liberal*, because Byron, the Gambas, and the Countess Guiccioli were again in trouble. Byron had aroused the suspicions of the authorities by christening his yacht the *Bolivar* after the South American revolutionary hero and requesting permission to move passengers in it up and down the coast (permission that was immediately denied). Then on June 28 a fight broke out between Byron's and the Gambas' servants, which was only controlled with the aid of the police. The Tuscan authorities promptly exiled the Gambas and the countess. When Shelley and the Hunt ménage arrived on July 3, the household was in confusion, with the Gambas preparing for exile, Byron at first thinking of leaving for America, then for Switzerland, and Trelawny talking of hauling the *Bolivar* overland to the Lake of Geneva.

Furthermore, Byron was being pressured to abandon *The Liberal*. Even before the periodical had appeared, he was attacked for associating himself with such notorious radicals as Shelley and Hunt. *Blackwoods* predicted that the alliance would soon break up: "Shelley will henceforth rave only to the moon. Hunt will sonneteer himself, and 'urge tear on tear,' in memory of Hampstead butter and Chelsea buns; and Byron, sick of his companions, and ashamed of his career, will at length ask his daemon, how it is that he has cast himself out of all the advantages that life lavished on him?" "Is an English nobleman," the editors queried, "to have no correspondent but his bookseller? No friends but a vulgar group, already shaken out of English society?"[107] The Whig outcry was as loud as the Tory. Thomas Moore wrote to Byron in protest:

> I heard some days ago that Leigh Hunt was on his way to you with all his family; and the idea seems to be, that you and Shelley and he are to *conspire* together in the Examiner. I cannot believe this,—and deprecate such a plan with

all my might. *Alone* you may do anything; but partnerships in fame, like those in trade, make the strongest party answerable for the deficiencies or delinquencies of the rest, and I tremble even for *you* with such a bankrupt *Co.*—* * * *. They are both clever fellows, and Shelley I look upon as a man of real genius; but I must again say, that you could not give your enemies (the * * *'s, "et hoc genus omne") a greater triumph than by forming such an unequal and unholy alliance.[108]

Moore, in fact, seems to have appointed himself chief abortionist for the threatened journal. "Mr. Moore," wrote Hazlitt, "darted backwards and forwards from Cold-Bath-Fields' Prison to the Examiner-Office, from Mr. Longman's to Mr. Murray's shop, in a state of ridiculous trepidation, to see what was to be done to prevent this degradation of the aristocracy of letters, this indecent encroachment of plebeian pretensions, this undue extension of patronage and compromise of privilege."[109]

Mary Shelley implied later that Byron was weakening under this pressure. "Shelley," she informed Maria Gisborne, "had past most of the time a[t] Pisa—arranging the affairs of the Hunts—& skrewing L[ord] B[yron]'s mind to the sticking place about the journal."[110] Whatever waverings Byron may have had at this time, however, were obviously not serious, for on the day after Shelley's departure Hunt wrote to his sister in England:

Though not ill, the change of climate has affected me at first with a lethargic tendency, which you will easily imagine I shall get over for our new work, especially since Lord B. enters into it with great ardour. He has given directions to Murray to put a variety of MS. into the hands of my brother John for it, and Shelley has some excellent MS. ready also . . . Lord B. made me a present the other day of a satire on Southey, called the *Vision of Judgment*, which my brother has accordingly to get from the hands of Murray, and print for our mutual benefit."[111]

The Liberal, as it turned out, was the last project of Shelley's life; and it was typical of that life that it should end with a challenge to the Establishment: "God defend us from the morality of slaves and turncoats, and from the legitimacy of half a dozen lawless old gentlemen, to whom, it seems, human nature is an estate in fee." True, *The Liberal* was not a political but a literary magazine. However, as the editors pointed out, there was a connection: "The object of our work is not political, except inasmuch as all writing now-a-days must involve something to that effect, the connexion between politics and all other subjects of interest to mankind having been discovered, never again to be done away."[112]

The effectiveness of the magazine was shown by the Tory reaction: "If this contagion must exist among us, let it exist unspoken of, if possible unnamed; like some talisman of fiendish construction and pestilential tendency, whose influence must remain suspended in our silence, only to break and become capable of harm from our communion with it."[113] Nor did the opposition stop with words. In December, John Hunt was indicted by a

Middlesex grand jury for the publication of Byron's *Vision of Judgment* in the first number: "John Hunt . . . bookseller, being a person of wicked and malicious disposition . . . did print and publish, and cause to be printed and published, in a certain printed book, to wit in a certain printed book called "*The Liberal*," a certain false, scandalous, malicious, and defamatory libel, of and concerning his said late Majesty, and also of and concerning his reign, death, and burial." Hunt was found guilty, but this time—in contrast to his previous imprisonments—was let off with a fine.[114]

After Shelley's death, Byron began to waver: "I am afraid the Journal *is* a *bad* business, and won't do; but in it I am sacrificing *myself* for others."[115] He might have continued if the paper had been a financial success, but it was not.[116] In its brief life, however, *The Liberal* made a considerable impact. It had not only Byron, Shelley, and Hunt among its contributors but Hazlitt and Mary Shelley as well. In addition to *The Vision of Judgment* it included Byron's *Heaven and Earth* and *The Blues*. Hazlitt contributed several essays, including *My First Acquaintance with Poets*.

On July 7, Shelley left Pisa for Leghorn. On the eighth, he, Williams, and Charles Vivian set sail from Leghorn to proceed north along the coast to Lerici. About fifteen or twenty miles beyond Leghorn they ran into a storm and were drowned.[117] Their bodies were washed ashore some ten days later.

There has been considerable controversy over the sinking of the *Don Juan*. Was the boat swamped by the waves or run down by another boat, either accidentally or deliberately? Shelley's earlier biographers favored the "swamped" theory; more recent ones, the "run-down" theory.[118] And the controversy has broadened out into speculation on whether Shelley's death was accidental or suicidal.

The *Don Juan*, according to Mary Shelley and Trelawny, was twenty-four by eight feet. A sketch plan (by Williams or Roberts) shows the center section, not counting the stern or bow, to have been fifteen feet long. The boat had no deck and was hollow, like a large rowboat. The sketch shows bookshelves around the sides and a folding table in the middle.[119] When completed, the boat rode dangerously high in the water, and "it took two tons of iron ballast to bring her down to her bearings, and then she was very crank in a breeze." In June, Captain Roberts, who in building the boat had followed, with some hesitation, a design by Williams, came to San Terenzo and fitted "2 topmasts to her," besides adding a false stern and a false bow to give the impression of greater length. Williams recorded the changes: "Finished the billet head and painted both that and the stern—a great improvement that gives two actual feet in length with the appearance of as many more. Fitted the topmasts ataunt, with these up she looks like a vessel of 50 tons . . . With all her ballast in she floats 3 inches lighter than before. This difference is caused I imagine by her planks having dried while on shore." A drawing of the ship by Williams shows exceptionally high masts for so short a ship, with topsails and three jib sails, two of them attached to the bowsprit.[120]

The *Don Juan's* departure from Leghorn—with Shelley, Williams, and Charles Vivian aboard—was witnessed by Trelawny:

On Monday, 8 July 1822, I went with Shelley to his bankers, and then to a store. It was past one p.m. when we went to board our respective boats—Shelley and Williams to return to their home in the Gulf of Spezzia; I in the *Bolivar* to accompany them into the offing. When we were under weigh, the guard-boat boarded us to overhaul our papers. I had not got my port clearance, the captain of the port having refused to give it to the mate as I had often gone out without. The officer of the Health Office consequently threatened me with forty days' quarantine. It was hopeless to think of detaining my friends. Williams had been for days fretting and fuming to be off; they had no time to spare, it was past two o'clock, and there was very little wind.

Suddenly and reluctantly I re-anchored, furled my sails, and with a ship's glass watched the progress of my friend's boat. My Genoese mate observed: "They should have sailed this morning at three or four a.m., instead of three p.m. They are standing too much in shore; the current will set them there."

I said: "They will soon have the land breeze."

"May be," continued the mate, "she will soon have too much breeze; that gaff topsail is foolish in a boat with no deck and no sailor on board." Then pointing to the S.W.: "Look at those black lines and the dirty rags hanging on them out of the sky—they are a warning; look at the smoke on the water; the devil is brewing mischief."

There was a sea-fog, in which Shelley's boat was soon after enveloped, and we saw nothing more of her.

After the storm broke: "Fishing craft and coasting vessels under bare poles rushed by us in shoals, running foul of the ships in the harbour."[121]

"About three—"wrote Mary to Maria Gisborne on August 15, 1822, "Roberts, who was still on the mole—saw wind coming from the Gulph —or rather what the Italians call a temporale—anxious to know how the boat w[oul]d weather the storm, he got leave to go up the tower & with the glass discovered them about ten miles out at sea."[122]

The *Don Juan* was reported to have been seen by sailors on another vessel after Roberts lost sight of her. By August 12 an account had appeared in the London *Morning Chronicle*, which John Gisborne, then in England, paraphrased:

At about 5 in the afternoon in the midst of this tempest, a fisherman saw their boat, and in a moment looked again and saw it no more. He had observed a boy, who was with them, aloft, attempting to furl the sail. This it appears was off Via Reggio, and their boat must have foundered. The bodies were washed ashore a few days afterwards. Our poor friend had been reading the last Volume of the works of Keats. It was found in his pocket, doubled back, and thrust open into his pocket. The writer of the account observes that something fatal was to be expected from the over daring of S[helley] and his friend Williams.[123]

Mary continued in her August 15 letter to Maria Gisborne:

A Fishing boat saw them go down—It was abou[t] 4 in the afternoon—they saw the boy at mast head, when baffling winds struck the sails they had looked away a moment & looking again the boat was gone—This is thei[r] story but there is little down [doubt] that these men might have saved them, at least Edward who could swim. They c[oul]d not they said get near her—but 3 quarters of an hour after passed over the spot where they had seen her—they protested no wreck of her was visible, but Roberts going on board their boat found several spars belonging to her—perhaps they let them perish to obtain these.

In 1826 John Taaffe gave the following account to Clarissa Trant at Pisa:

The crew of a vessel going into Leghorn had seen them soon after they put to sea, and foreseeing that they could not long contend with such tremendous waves, bore down upon them and offered to take them on board. A shrill voice, which is supposed to have been Shelley's, was distinctly heard to say "NO." The Captain, amazed at their infatuation, continued to watch them with his telescope. The waves were running mountains high—a tremendous surf dashed over the boat which to his astonishment was still crowded with sail. "If you will not come on board for God's sake reef your sails or you are lost," cried a sailor thro' the speaking trumpet. One of the gentlemen (Williams, it is believed), was seen to make an effort to lower the sails—his companion seized him by the arm as if in anger.

The next wave which rose between the Boat and the vessel subsided—not a splash was seen amidst the white foam of the breakers. Every trace of the boat and of its wretched crew had disappeared.[124]

The three bodies were washed ashore between July 17 and 18—Williams' near the mouth of the Serchio River, about fifteen miles north of Leghorn; Shelley's at Viareggio, about seven miles further north; Vivian's opposite Massa, about seven miles still further north.[125]

On September 12, the governor of Viareggio wrote to the secretary of state of Lucca:

I hasten to apprize your Excellency that the two fishing smacks belonging to Sig. Stefano Baroni of Viareggio have, while fishing, discovered, at the bottom of the sea, at the distance of about 15 miles from shore, a small vessel, schooner rigged, and one of the masters of the same, having warned the Captain of the Sanitary Guard of this harbour of the fact, the same Captain put a Sanitary Guard on board to escort the smacks into Viareggio in company with the schooner which had been found, where they arrived towards noon this morning, and have been placed with the crew, in quarantine and watched with the most scrupulous care according to sanitary rules.

We, however, having certain evidence that this may be the same vessel which was wrecked in the past month of July, on the occasion on which Mr. Shelley, an English gentleman, and Captain Williams of H.B.M.'s Service left Leghorn for the gulf of Spezia, on board of the same, accompanied by one sailor only, who unfortunately perished with them.[126]

Years later, one of the sailors who had been on one of these fishing boats was found and questioned:

The next morning at 10 a.m. (August 31st) we examined, in the Office of the Captain of the Port, Antonio Canova, son of Giovanni, born at Viareggio in 1803. He was a fine type of an old sailor, quite strong and well, with a full beard and flowing hair and a frank, ready manner of speaking. "At the age of 19 years he was a fisherman, and belonged to the crew of Baroni's *paranzelle,* commanded by Giampieri, who recovered the schooner in the roads at Viareggio, precisely five miles out, in the direction of the Tower of Migliarino. The schooner caught in their net. They towed her westward, beached her, bailed her, and found on board a trunk with clothes and cheques and other papers, besides a hundred francs in silver; sixteen sand-bags for ballast, some iron spades, and several hampers full of bottled beer. Canova and another sailor, accompanied by two Leghornese, afterwards towed the schooner into the port of Leghorn."[127]

Of the two distances from shore—five or fifteen miles—at which the ship was said to have been found, that of the official document of the time seems preferable to that of the fisherman's memory. Trelawny in an early narrative gave the distance as about "13 miles."[128] According to the map, a point about fifteen miles out from Viareggio would be on a straight line between Leghorn and Lerici. Shelley and Williams seem to have been going on a direct course over the open sea.

At Leghorn the boat was inspected by Captain Roberts, who wrote to Mary Shelley on September 14: "We have got fast hold of the Don Juan at last and she is safe at anchor at Via reggio. She has been got up entire but much damaged from being so long under Water, everything is complete in her and clearly proves that she was not upset, but I think must have filled by a heavy sea."[129]

Two days later, Roberts sold the boat at auction, himself buying the "shell."[130] On September 18 he wrote to Trelawny: "The Two masts carried away just above board—bowsprit off close to the bows—Two gaffs good—boomb good, pump good, false stern carried away—the rudder lost. The Gunwale stove in in many places—the boat half full of a blue mud among which we picked out Cloths of all Sorts (mostly rotten), books and Spyglass (broken)."[131] When Trelawny published this letter in his *Recollections* in 1858, a postscript appeared with it as though by Roberts, but it is not in the manuscript of Roberts' letter (now in the British Museum): "On a close examination of Shelley's boat, we find many of the timbers on the starboard quarter broken, which makes me think for certain that she must have been run down by some of the feluccas in the squall."[132] Trelawny had himself come to this conclusion shortly after the ship was found—perhaps after communicating with Roberts—for it appears in a narrative that he dated "Sep.br 1822." But that he wavered in this opinion is shown by a note he added at the end: "Shelley's boat might have foundered & the damage of her hull done in getting her up—and not by having been run down."[133]

The running-down theory Trelawny passed on to Mary, who wrote to Jane Williams on October 15 after talking to Trelawny: "The Don Juan was found her topsails down and her other sails fast. Trelawny tells me that in his, Roberts' & every other sailor's opinion that she was *run down*; of course by that fishing boat." Six months later, after actually talking to Roberts, she gave more details: "On bringing her up from 15 fathom all was in her—books, telescope, ballast, lying on each side of the boat without any appearance of shifting or confusion—the topsails furled—topmasts lowered—the false stern (Jane can explain) broken to pieces and a great hole knocked in the stern timbers. When she was brought to Leghorn, every one went to see her—and the same exclamation was uttered by all—She was run down by that wretched fishing boat which owned that it had seen them."[134] In editing Shelley's poems in 1839, however, Mary in a *Note on the Poems of 1822* did not refer to the running-down story but commented simply: "Ours was to be an open boat, on a model taken from one of the royal dock-yards. I have since heard that there was a defect in this model, and that it was never sea-worthy."

The story was next taken up by Leigh Hunt, in 1828, in *Lord Byron and Some of His Contemporaries*: "Among the various conjectures respecting this lamentable event, a suspicion was not wanting, that the boat had been run down by a larger one, with a view to plunder it. Mr. Shelley was known to have taken money on board. Crimes of that nature had occurred often enough to warrant such a suspicion; and they could be too soon washed out of the consciences of the ignorant perpetrators by confession. But it was lost in the more probable conclusions arising from the weather."[135] Hunt did not repeat the conjecture is his *Autobiography* of 1850, but in the 1860 edition, published after his death, his son Thornton added a note:

> A story was current in Leghorn which conjecturally helped to explain the shipwreck of Shelley's boat. It went out to sea in rough weather, and *yet* was followed by a native boat. When Shelley's yacht was raised, a large hole was found stove in the stern. Shelley had on board a sum of money in dollars; and the supposition is, that the men in the other boat had tried to board Shelley's piratically, but had desisted because the collision caused the English boat to sink; and they abandoned it because the men saved would have become their accusers. The only facts in support of this conjectural story are the alleged following of the native boat, and the damage to the stern of Shelley's boat, otherwise not very accountable.[136]

In November 1875, Trelawny's daughter, Letitia Call, wrote to her father that she had heard that an old sailor who had died "a little while ago" at Spezia had confessed to his priest "that he was one of the crew that ran down the boat containing Shelley and Williams." The following month, Sir Vincent Eyre, a retired officer and diplomat then living in Rome, wrote to the *Times* indicating that he was the source for this story. He had heard it in May 1875 from an unnamed hostess, "who owned a villa" on the Bay of Spezia and who, in turn, had heard it from "an Italian noble residing in the vicinity," who had heard it from the priest. The sailor, according to Sir Vincent, had died not "a little while ago" but twelve years previously. Sir Vincent continued: "I will now give the story itself in the very words of my friend:—A boatman dying near Sarzana, confessed, about twelve years ago, that he was one of five who, seeing the English boat in great danger, ran her down, thinking milord Inglese was on board, and they should find gold."

Trelawny also wrote to the *Times* supporting the story of the deliberate running down: "After a course of dredging she was found in ten fathoms water, about two miles off the coast of Via Reggio. The cause of her loss was then evident. Her starboard quarter was stove in, evidently by a blow from the sharp bows of a felucca; and, as I have said, being undecked and having three tons and a half of iron ballast, she would have sunk in two minutes. Had she been decked it would have been otherwise."[137]

Three years later Richard Garnett cast doubt on the confession story:

> A similar explanation of Shelley's fate is suggested in Leigh Hunt's *Byron and his Contemporaries*, and the story of the confession itself is referred to in Dr. Lee's work on the health-resorts of the Mediterranean, edition of 1872. Since the appearance (December, 1875) of the correspondence in the *Times* reprinted by Mr. Trelawny, the matter has been further investigated by two English ladies, honourably known in literature, who, during an Italian tour, turned aside to Lerici at the request of the writer of these pages. It seems established that such a declaration was made, but under circumstances which precluded all possibility of examining or verifying it; nor is it quite certain whether it related to Shelley's catastrophe or to some other.[138]

In trying to reach some conclusions from this mass of evidence, one should note at the outset that the running-down hypothesis is not necessary to explain the sinking. The storm was dangerous enough to set all ships within range of Leghorn scurrying back to harbor, many of them much larger vessels than the *Don Juan*. The *Don Juan* was clearly a nautical monstrosity—a hollow shell containing a writing table and book shelves, weighed down by two tons of pig iron yet still riding high, with a false stern and false prow, special topmasts, and sail enough for a schooner. Such a boat, as both Roberts and Trelawny realized, would sink rapidly if swamped by a heavy sea, and in a high wind her towering mass of sail, unless quickly furled, would tilt her over into the waves. Roberts' concern is clear from Mary Shelley's description. Byron commented in a letter to John Murray on August 3, 1822: "I presume you have heard that Mr. Shelley and Capt. Williams were lost on the 7th. Ulto. in their passage from Leghorn to Spezia in their own open boat."[139] By "open boat" Byron meant a boat without a deck, and the implication is that the sinking of such a boat required no special explanation. If Byron had thought that the boat had been run down, he would have mentioned it.

At about the same time, Edward Dawkins, British chargé d'affaires at Florence, wrote to an official of the Tuscan government: "Two English gentlemen, Captain Williams and Mr. Shelley embarked on the 12th of last month at Leghorn to rejoin their families at Spezia. Surprised by the storm which took place on the following day, their vessel, the property of Mr. Shelley, sank with all on board, consisting of the above-mentioned gentlemen, and a young English sailor."[140] Dawkins had obviously heard that the ship was sunk by the storm. So, too, had Medwin, who witnessed the storm from a larger vessel in the Gulf of Genoa and commented on its severity:

The squall at length came, the precise time of which I forget, but it was in the afternoon; and neither in the bay of Biscay or Bengal, nor between the Tropics, nor on the Line, did I ever witness a severer one; and being accompanied by a heavy rain, it was the more felt . . . The only chance of their safety would have been to tack or wear, and drive before the wind, and return to Leghorn. But this idea probably never entered into Shelley's or Williams's mind, and from my knowledge of both their characters, they would, I am sure, have incurred any risk rather than have given up the voyage. Perhaps they were insensible to the danger till it was too late.[141]

Trelawny himself, in an early version of his narrative, believed the storm and the nature of the *Don Juan* sufficient explanation:

The headlands projecting boldly and far into the sea, forming a deep and exceedingly dangerous Gulph, with a heavy swell & strong current generally running right into it. A vessel embayed in this Gulph overtaken by one of the squalls is common upon the coast, if it continued for any length of time, is almost certain to be wrecked, the loss of small craft is incalculable, and the shallowness of the water and the breaking of the surf, preventing their approaching the beach, or boats going out to assist them, the loss of lives is equally great. It was in the centre of this bay, about four or five miles at sea, in 15 or 16 fathom water, with a light breeze under a crowd of sail, that the Don Juan was suddenly taken slap aback by a sudden and very violent squall, and it is supposed that in attempting to bear up under such a press of canvas, all the sheets fast, being unprepared, and with only three persons on board, she filled to leeward, and having two tons of iron ballast, and not decked, went down on the instant, not giving them a moment to prepare themselves by even taking off their boots, or seizing an oar.[142]

The running-down theory is based on four points: the departure of the fishing boat from Leghorn at about the same time as the *Don Juan*, the damage to the *Don Juan*, the rumor at Leghorn, and the confession. These items seem more impressive in toto than when examined separately. On the first point, Thornton Hunt had heard that a large fishing boat left Leghorn just after the *Don Juan* in spite of the fact that the weather was "rough." But the weather cannot have been rough, for Trelawny noted that "there was very little wind," and there were many boats out. The storm did not break for at least two hours after the sailing, and it cannot have been anticipated at the time of the sailing.[143] This fact, taken by itself, means no more than that another ship happened to leave Leghorn at the same time as the *Don Juan*.

On the second point, the damage to the boat, when Roberts first saw the *Don Juan* after she had been towed into the harbor at Leghorn (September

12–14), he apparently did not notice any particular damage. He told Mary on September 14 that he thought the boat "must have been filled by a heavy sea." On September 18 he told Trelawny that the false stern had been "carried away" and that the gunwale (the board running around the top edge of the side) was "stove in in many places," which sounds like a number of small breaks. When Roberts talked to Mary about eight months later, this had grown to "the false stern . . . broken to pieces" and "a great hole knocked in the stern timbers." By 1875 the hole had, in Trelawny's description, become enormous: "Her starboard quarter was stove in." What was at first an injury to the upper board of the side became "a great hole" in the stern. By this Roberts—Trelawny did not see the boat—must mean a hole in the actual stern knocked in by the prow of a large ship, a hole large enough to flood and sink the *Don Juan*.[144] But if there had been a hole of this size, why did he not notice it at once? This obviously bothered Trelawny and perhaps caused him to add his crude postscript. Clearly, one does not notice that a ship has a "great hole in the stern" only on "a close examination." Neither the governor of Viareggio nor the fisherman who towed the boat into Leghorn mentioned any damage—although they gave other less important details—or hinted at a collision. The probability is that there was no damage to the ship so extensive as to warrant a view that she had been rammed by another vessel. The damage—as Trelawny earlier suggested—probably came from the salvage operations.[145] A ship twenty-four by eight feet with pig iron ballast and "half full of blue mud" in 60-80 feet of water must have been difficult to salvage.[146]

Roberts clearly had a special motive for advancing a running-down theory. Although the original design had been by Williams, Roberts had actually built the boat and added the topsails. If she was unseaworthy, the blame was his, and the deaths of three men rested on his head. His first letter to Mary shows his desire to absolve himself from guilt: the boat was not "upset"—a result of bad design—but was overwhelmed by a "heavy sea." As for Trelawny, not only did exaggeration and invention come naturally to him, but in regard to the *Don Juan* he was specially motivated, for it was he who had recommended Roberts. He was clearly eager to clutch at any straw that would remove the blame and guilt from himself and Roberts. Mary at first believed the Roberts-Trelawny running-down story, but later, on being told that the ship's construction and design were faulty, apparently changed her mind.

When the running-down rumor started at Leghorn, who started it, or how widespread it was are not known. The story came from the Hunts, who were not at Leghorn but at Pisa and then at Genoa. As they had little if any contact with the Italian community, it may be that Roberts himself was the source.

The confession of the dying "boatman" makes no sense. If fishermen wished to secure gold, they would not ram an undecked ship, for—as Sir Arthur Quiller-Couch once pointed out—it would obviously fill and sink instantly.[147] Furthermore, the confession came third-hand twelve years later, and it is not clear that it referred to the *Don Juan*.

There is, then, no firm evidence for a collision, and there are strong indications against it. Moreover, fishermen, whether Italian or English, are not usually thieves or pirates. The ramming and robbery story has in it more than a touch of English chauvinistic anti-Italian and anti-Catholic prejudice. The "crimes" could be easily "washed out of the consciences of the ignorant perpetrators by confession." If they had been "sturdy" Devon fishermen the story would never have been born. An accidental collision is also unlikely, because the wreck took place on the uncrowded, open sea, fifteen miles out.

If, then, the ship was sunk by the action of the waves and wind, the three stories of the fishermen who claimed to have seen the ship have to be taken seriously. There are obvious divergences among the three accounts, but they all agree on two points: all or most of the sails were still up, and the ship sank almost instantly.[148] These points are confirmed by other evidence. As Peacock long ago suggested, the fact that the masts and bowsprit were broken off when the ship was found indicates that the sails had been up when the wind struck; and Captain Roberts observed with his telescope that the mainsails were up as the storm moved in, but that the topsails were being furled.[149] An undecked ship, loaded with ballast, would sink rapidly, as Roberts and Trelawny recognized. The probability is that the ship tilted to leeward, filled, and sank, and that a fishing boat captain and crew did indeed see her just before she went down and so witnessed the last moments of Shelley, Williams, and Vivian.[150]

On the other hand, some of the details of the story as given by Taaffe cannot be accepted without question. For instance, it is not clear how close the two ships came or how well the fishing ship crew was able to see the Don Juan in what Roberts called the "haze" of the storm. Taaffe stated that the ships were sufficiently close to talk or shout back and forth; yet the captain used a telescope. The captain is said to have offered to take the crew of the *Don Juan* aboard in "tremendous" waves. Possibly he did, but he is also said to have told Trelawny that there was no "possibility of assisting her."[151] It is also obvious that no one on the Italian fishing ship could know which of the figures was Shelley and which Williams, or which voice was which. Nor could others who knew Shelley and Williams have told after hearing their story, for both men were of about the same age and of slender build; and voices in the roar of a storm are apt to sound shrill. That Shelley would restrain Williams if he wished to furl the sails seems unlikely, for as Trelawny's descriptions of their earlier sailings and other evidence indicate, Williams was in charge of the ship.[152] All one can say is that the captain and crew of the fishing vessel yelled across the waters to furl the sails, that something was yelled back, and that the crew observed some movement in the figures aboard which they (or Taaffe) thought might have been a gesture of restraint.[153]

It is sometimes suggested that—regardless of the manner of sinking—the wreck was the result of Shelley's irresponsible "daring." One finds, especially in popular accounts, the contention that he should not have put to sea when a storm was brewing. But when the *Don Juan* sailed, the weather was "fine" and "the wind right fair."[154] The storm did not come up until at least two hours later. When it did begin to threaten, Williams and Shelley—and Williams as well as Shelley was involved—were caught in a very difficult situation. To return to Leghorn would have taken two hours or more. If they were fifteen or even only five miles from the nearest shore, they had no chance of reaching a haven, for the storm swept down suddenly. Their only hope was to furl the sails and try to ride it out. What they did was to furl the topsails, which would be the most likely to upset the ship, and to see if that would prove sufficient. If they had had time, they would probably have furled the mainsails and jib sails also; but they had no time. That there was some "daring" involved in not at once furling all the sails is possible but unlikely. Neither Shelley nor Williams was an experienced sailor, and as Medwin suggests, probably they did not realize the full extent of their danger until it was too late.

What, finally, of the "suicide" theory? This theory is based mostly on the fact that Shelley had been depressed in the months before his death. But in his last days he was energetically pursuing *The Liberal* project with Hunt and Byron at Pisa, and his letters show that he had every intention of returning to Lerici. He wrote to Mary Shelley:

> How are you my best Mary? Write especially how is your health & how your spirits are, & whether you are not more reconciled to staying at Lerici at least during the summer.
>
> You have no idea how I am hurried & occupied—I have not a moments leisure—but will write by next post—Ever dearest Mary.[155]

A letter to Jane Williams informed her that Williams might return before Shelley: "You will probably see Williams before I can disentangle myself from the affairs with which I am now surrounded—I return to Leghorn tonight & shall urge him to sail with the first fair wind without expecting me."[156] Williams, however, did not leave ahead of Shelley. Two days later, on July 6, he wrote to his wife from Leghorn:

> I have just left the quay, my dearest girl, and the wind blows right across to Spezia, which adds to the vexation I feel at being unable to leave this place—For my own part I should have been with you, in all probability on Wednesday evening, but have been kept day after day waiting for Shelleys definitive arrangements with Lord B[yron] relative to poor Hunt . . . Would I could take the present gale by the wings and reach you tonight, hard as it blows I would venture across for *such* a reward—! However, tomorrow something decisive shall take place, and if S is still detained I shall depart in a Felucca and leave the boat to be brought round in company with Trelawny in the Bolivar, who talks of visiting Spezia again in a few days.

I am tired to death of waiting. This is our longest separation, and seems a year to me.[157]

Shelley, involved in *The Liberal* arrangements at Pisa with Byron and Hunt, was in no hurry to return, but Williams, at Leghorn, with nothing to do, was bored and lonely. His comment also shows that Shelley and Vivian would not have attempted to sail the ship without him, which reinforces Trelawny's observation that he was the de facto captain. More than suicide, however, is implied in the suicide hypothesis. The implication is that Shelley, in effect, murdered two other people.[158] Such an action clearly runs counter to Shelley's character, for few men have been more selflessly dedicated to their fellow beings than he. For Shelley to kill Williams and Vivian would imply a deep psychiatric disturbance; but Shelley in the days before his death, was acting with energy and purpose, and his letters are normal. In short, there is no evidence to support the suicide-murder theory, and all indications are against it.

The two main factors involved were the nature of the *Don Juan* and the inexperience of Shelley and Williams. The *Don Juan* would almost certainly have sunk in the first real storm. It was simply by chance that the storm struck when the ship was so far from port or shore. The inexperience of Shelley and Williams was shown in the fact that they allowed such a boat to be built in the first place and then commissioned Roberts to add the false stern and bow and the top masts. Here, however, a psychological element was perhaps involved. On June 13 the *Don Juan* had raced with Byron's larger ship, the *Bolivar*, and was beaten; on June 16 Roberts began the refitting.[159] Perhaps the additions were made in order to rival the *Bolivar* in speed and appearance. Whatever the motive, the responsibility was Captain Roberts', for Roberts was a shipbuilder. So far as sailing was concerned, Shelley had little experience. Country-bred, he had never taken to the sea and had previously only handled boats on English rivers or a small skiff on the Arno. Williams, an army officer, had some experience but, as Trelawny observed, was "over-anxious and wanted practice." He refused to take an experienced sailor aboard when Trelawny suggested it, "thinking I undervalued his efficiency as a seaman."[160]

While Shelley and Williams were at Leghorn and Pisa, Mary Shelley and Jane Williams were home at San Terenzo. Their feelings and experiences Mary communicated to Maria Gisborne a month later:

On Monday 8th Jane had a letter from Edward, dated saturday, he said that he waited at Leghorn for S[helley] who was at Pisa. That S's return was certain, "but" he continued, "if he should not come by monday I will come in a felucca, & you may expect me tuesday evening at furthest." This was Monday, the fatal monday, but with us it was stormy all day & we did not at all suppose that they could put to sea. At twelve at night we had a thunderstorm; Tuesday [9th] it rained all day & was calm—the sky wept on their graves—on Wednesday [10th] —the wind was fair from Leghorn & in the evening several felucca's arrived thence

—one brought word that they had sailed Monday, but we did not believe them—thursday [11th] was another day of fair wind & when twelve at night came & we did not see the tall sails of the little boat double the promontory before us we began to fear not the truth, but some illness—some disagre[e]able news for their detention. Jane got so uneasy that she determined to proceed the next day to Leghorn in a boat to see what was the matter—friday [12th] came & with it a heavy sea & bad wind—Jane however resolved to be rowed to Leghorn (since no boat could sail) and busied herself in preparations—I wished her to wait for letters, since friday was letter day—she would not—but the sea detained her, the swell rose so that no boat would venture out—At 12 at noon our letters came—there was one from Hunt to Shelley, it said—"pray write to tell us how you got home, for they say that you had bad weather after you sailed monday & we are anxious"—the paper fell from me—I trembled all over—Jane read it—"Then it is all over!" she said.[161]

Mary and Jane went by coach to Leghorn, but no one there had any news. On the way back they stopped at Viareggio:

When at 2 miles from Via Reggio we rode down to that town to know if they knew any thing—here our calamity first began to break on us—a little boat & a water cask had been found five miles off—they had manufactured a *piccolissima lancia* of thin planks stitched by a shoemaker just to let them run on shore without wetting themselves as our boat drew 4 feet [of] water.—the description of that found tallied with this—but then this boat was very cumbersome & in bad weather they might have been easily led to throw it overboard—the cask frightened me most—but the same reason might in some sort be given for that. I must tell you that Jane & I were not now alone—Trelawny accompanied us back to our home. We journied on & reached the Magra about 1/2 past ten P.M. I cannot describe to you what I felt in the first moment when, fording this river, I felt the water splash about our wheels—I was suffocated—I gasped for breath—I thought I should have gone into convulsions, & I struggled violently that Jane might not perceive it—looking down the river I saw the two great lights burning at the *foce*—A voice from within me seemed to cry aloud that is his grave. After passing the river I gradually recovered. Arriving at Lerici we [were] obliged to cross our little bay in a boat—San Arenzo [Terenzo] was illuminated for a festa—What a scene—the roaring sea—the scirocco wind—the lights of the town towards which we rowed—& our own desolate hearts—that coloured all with a shroud—We landed; nothing had been heard of them. This was saturday July 13. & thus we waited until Thursday July 25 [*error for* 18] thrown about by hope & fear. We sent messengers along the coast towards Genoa & to Via Reggio—nothing had been found more than the *lancetta*; reports were brought us—we hoped—& yet to tell you all the agony we endured during those 12 days would be to make you conceive a universe of pain—each moment intolerable & giving place to one still worse. The people of the country too added to one's discomfort—they are like wild savages—on festas' the men & women & children in different bands—the sexes always separate—pass the whole night in dancing on the sands close to our door running into the sea then back again & screaming all the time one perpetual air—the most detestable in the world—then the scirocco perpetually blew & the sea for ever moaned their dirge. On thursday 25th [*should be* 18th] Trelawny left us to go to Leghorn to see what was doing or what could be done. On friday [19th] I was very ill but as evening came on I said to Jane—"If any thing had been found on the coast Trelawny would have returned to let us know. He has not returned so I hope." About 7 oclock P.M. he did return—all was over—all was quiet now, they had been found washed on shore—Well all this was to be endured.[162]

According to the strict quarantine laws of the time, the bodies had either to be buried near the beach or burned. Vivian's body was buried near the beach; those of Shelley and Williams were burned, with Trelawny in charge of operations. He had an iron grill constructed—"four feet & a half long by twenty inches broad with a rim of three or four inches" and supported on "four iron legs"—on which the body of Williams was burned on August 15, that of Shelley on August 16.[163] Trelawny proposed (to Bryon) that he write an account of the ceremony for *The Liberal*, and two manuscripts found among his papers perhaps represent drafts for this article.[164] As the earlier of these accounts was written close to the events and before Trelawny's imagination could dress up the narrative, it is probably the most accurate :

Having collected together his remains I set fire to the pile and we went through the same ceremonies as the previous day. The Poem of Lamia and Issabella which had been found open in Shelley's Jacket Pockett—and buried with him, I was anxious to have—but we could find nothing of it remaining but the leather binding. Lord B. wished much to have the skull if possible—which I endeavoured to preserve—but before any part of the flesh was consumed on it, on attempting to move it—it broke to pieces—it was unusually thin and strikingly small.

Although we made a tremendous fire—it burnt exceedingly slow; and it was three hours before the body separated—it then fell open across the breast—and the heart, which was now seen, was likewise small. The body was much longer consuming than the other—it was nearly four o'clock before the body was wholly consumed, that part nearest the heart being the last that became ashes—and the heart itself seemed proof against fire, for it was still perfect and the intensity of heat everything now even the sand on which the furnace stood the furnace itself being red hot and fierce fire still kept up the largest bones reduced to white cinders and nothing perfect distinguishable—but the heart which although bedded in fire —would not burn—and after awaiting an hour continually adding fuel it becoming late we gave over by mutual conviction of its being unavailing—all exclaiming it will not burn—there was a bright flame round it occasioned by the moisture still flowing from it—and on removing the furnace nearer to the Sea to immerse the iron I took the heart in my hand to examine it—after sprinkling it with water; yet it was still so hot as to burn my hand badly and a quantity of this oily fluid still flowed from it—we now collected the dust and ashes and placed them in the box made for the occasion, and shipped it on board Lord Byron's schooner. There had been—during the whole ceremony—a solitary sea bird crossing and recrossing the fire—which was the only intruder our guards had not kept away—yet it was with much difficulty being so near a Town they kept off the people! We then returned slowly in the carriage drawn by buffaloes to the Inn L.B. proceeding to Pisa—and weighed anchor for Leghorn.[165]

Following this ceremony, Shelley's ashes were removed to the Protestant cemetery in Rome (where Keats had been buried the previous year) and were buried there on January 21, 1823. A solitary pastor, the Reverend Richard Burgess, was found courageous enough to brave church hostility toward the dead atheist and read the burial service.[166]

After the death of Shelley and Williams, the circle of friends and relatives connected with them broke up. Mary, after another year in Italy, left for England, where she devoted herself to writing novels, editing Shelley's works and raising her son, Percy Florence Shelley. Claire left for Vienna and thereafter led a frustrated existence as tutor and governess in various places—Vienna, Moscow, London, Dresden, and Florence—finally dying in 1879 at the age of eighty-one. Byron left Italy to take part in the Greek revolution and died in Greece in 1824. Trelawny, accompanying Byron to Greece, stayed there till 1827, resumed his adventurous career on a lesser scale in America, and then settled down in England, dying at the age of eighty-nine in 1881. Jane Williams returned to England, married Thomas Jefferson Hogg, and survived both Claire and Trelawny, dying at the age of eighty-six in 1884. Medwin married a baroness in 1825, deserted her, and led a rambling and unsettled life as a free-lance writer, finally returning to Shelley's and his native village of Horsham to die in 1869, loving Shelley, Trelawny reports, to the last days of his life.[167] After editing *The Liberal* for a time, Leigh Hunt returned with his family to England in 1825, where he again took up work as a publicist for the cause of moderate reform, receiving a pension for his pains from the Whigs after the passing of the Reform Act in 1832. Percy Florence Shelley grew up to be a quiet English Tory with an interest in yachting and the drama. His aged countenance peers out with grizzled amiability from a photograph taken about 1880.[168] He died without issue. Shelley's other son, Charles, child of Shelley and Harriet, survived his father by only four years, dying apparently of tuberculosis at the age of twelve in 1826. Charles's sister Ianthe, however, lived on; in 1837 she married Edward Jeffries Esdaile, of a well-known banking family. Descendants of this marriage are alive today.

Part Two Prose

3

Political Philosophy

Letter in Defence of Richard Carlile. A Proposal for Putting Reform to the Vote. An Address to the People on the Death of the Princess Charlotte. A Philosophical View of Reform

Shelley's prose works provide important keys to his poetry. But they are significant in their own right also—in social thought, ethics, philosophy, and literary criticism. Shelley had an evolutionary vision of history, which was rare in his age. In examining the politics and social issues of this age, which encompassed the industrial revolution, the Napoleonic Wars, and insurgent democracy, he threw light on problems that were then first emerging and are still unresolved. With *A Defence of Poetry* he became one of the earliest critics to analyze the relationships of literature and society. His views on ethics also socially oriented, embody many original insights. His philosophical views anticipate such later scientific agnostics as Thomas Henry Huxley and in some respects go beyond them. It was, in fact, Shelley the thinker rather than Shelley the poet who influenced such late nineteenth and early twentieth-century radicals as Mahatma Gandhi, George Bernard Shaw, Thomas Hardy, H. G. Wells, and Bertrand Russell.

Some may wonder how one who was not a "specialist" in these various subjects could make significant contributions to them. Here, our modern emphasis on specialization misleads us. The "specialist" in a field is not always the best-equipped to form generalizations. In fact, he is often trained to refrain from them. An intelligent and informed observer, drawing on the discoveries of specialists, can make important generalizations in such fields as social thought or aesthetics. When the observer is young, creative, and thrown into the maelstrom of a revolutionary age, he is all the more likely to do so. Although some of the general frameworks within which Shelley makes his observations are today outmoded, his particular views on society and humanity offer new and sometimes striking insights. His views on love as a social force, for instance, have special significance in an age when new societies are emerging in all quarters of the globe. And many of the questions he raises in regard to religion, politics, ethics, and literary history are precisely those that are still unanswered, despite contemporary pretenses of omniscience or indifference. Shelley's social and political writings should be considered first because they often provide foundations for the others. His ethics flow from his egalitarian concepts; his metaphysics are subordinate to his ethics; and his view of literary history is derived largely from his social views.

Shelley, it is often forgotten, grew up in a political atmosphere. His father was a Whig member of Parliament, and it was intended that Shelley should succeed him. Both his father and grandfather were political dependents of the duke of Norfolk, a radical Whig who supported the American Revolution, opposed the war with France, and championed Irish independence. The radical Whigs were at times—especially when out of office—quite fiery, and Shelley imbibed some of their fire. Even when an Eton schoolboy—as *Henry and Louisa* shows—he was opposed to war and colonial oppression. But by his last year at Eton he had begun to move beyond the Whigs, first into republicanism and then into Godwinian egalitarianism. The republicans of the Thomas Paine and Mary Wollstonecraft school showed him the futility of the monarchical-aristocratic system and the virtues of democracy. The French revolutionary thinkers, Condorcet and Volney, inspired him with a glowing faith in the ever-ascending future of mankind. William Godwin pointed out that the basic evils of society stemmed rather from economic than political injustice and tried to give philosophical body to the utopian visions of Condorcet and Volney.

Moreover, Paine, Godwin, and the others were read by Shelley not as intellectual exercises but as political guidebooks, for the issues of the age of the American and French revolutions continued into his own century: war, revolution, dictatorship, colonialism, and parliamentary reform. Without these continuities, the theoretical writings of Paine and Godwin would have lost their present impact, and neither *Hellas* nor *Prometheus Unbound* would have been written.

In Shelley's day there were four vital streams of radical thought: egalitarianism, Owenite socialism, republicanism, and parliamentary reform. Of these, the most immediately pertinent was reform. Although economic egalitarianism in the form of equality of private property had been a main doctrine of *Political Justice* (1793), this aspect of Godwin's teachings was little regarded in the new century. In his day-to-day politics Godwin was a Whig, as were many of the young radicals who had imbibed his doctrines in the nineties. But although by 1815 *Political Justice* had ceased to be a major radical influence, an egalitarian stream continued and entered the political realm from Thomas Spence. Son of a Scottish shoemaker and twice imprisoned on political charges, Spence was the intellectual heir of the levelers and diggers of the British (Cromwellian) Revolution. He was not primarily interested, as was Godwin, in an intellectual radicalism but in the property rights of the poor farmers and city workers. Although his proposals for self-contained land communities were theoretically no more radical than Godwin's, he addressed himself to the farmers and city workers, who might take egalitarian action, whereas Godwin addressed himself to the city middle class, who would not. Furthermore, Spence wrote with a truly revolutionary verve (anticipating Bronterre O'Brien and the Chartists), as in his Preface to *The Constitution of a Perfect Commonwealth* (1798):

> The reader on finding that according to this constitution, the landed property is all engrossed by the parishes, will naturally conclude that it tolerates no landed

interest; none of that lofty generation called quality; no lords nor gentlemen; in a word, that there will be no amphibious class or intermediate body, between the government and the people; and such a conclusion will certainly be right. For I did not mean such a nest of wasps to have a place in my Commonwealth, to devour the honey, which the working bees had toiled for, and ill-treat them into the bargain. No; in truth the world has long enough experienced the blessings of this combination of wolves, and common sense teaches us, that a nation may exist without beasts of prey.[1]

Articles 3 and 6 of the Declaration of Rights for the "Perfect Commonwealth" give the essence of Spence's view: "All men are equal by nature, and before the law; and have a continual property in, and right to earth's natural productions," and "Thus, after deducting the land tax for support of the state, and all local contingent expenses, the residue of the rents ought to be equally divided among all the living inhabitants, of every age and sex, having right by residence."

Spence died in 1814, but the Spencean movement continued, led by a chemist, Dr. James Watson, and an ex-army officer and farmer, Arthur Thistlewood. In December 1816, when the postwar economic depression had created great pockets of unemployment, Watson and Thistlewood organized a radical meeting in Spa Fields, London. A "riot" took place, apparently instigated by a government labor spy named John Castle, after which the Spenceans were put on trial for high treason. The reformers and other opposition elements, however, became alarmed at the possible consequences for themselves of such trials, and a London jury refused to convict.

Although the Spenceans are usually pictured as a small set of fanatics, contemporary accounts show that they had a considerable following among the London workers. They may also have served to swing a segment of the reform movement further to the left and probably had greater potential power than has usually been recognized. Certainly, the government considered them dangerous, for in 1820 another government spy initiated a plot to assassinate the Cabinet—the "Cato Street conspiracy"—and involved Thistlewood. As a result, Thistlewood and four other Spenceans, including a Jamaican Negro radical, were beheaded.[2] After this, the movement dwindled.

Shelley's attitude on the Spenceans was ambivalent. His charge in *A Philosophical View of Reform* that "secret associations" were leading to "partial and premature" results is clearly directed against them; and he disapproved of the Cato Street conspiracy;[3] but the Spencean revolutionary pictures in both the *View* and *Swellfoot the Tyrant* are written with considerable gusto.[4] Shelley's dislike of the landed aristocracy was such that he found a certain joy in the concept of their being overrun by an aroused populace. The pictures, however, were intended not as ideals but as a warning to the ruling class to adopt more liberal policies or face mass revolution. If such a revolution were to break out, Shelley indicates that he would support it, but he also makes clear that he wishes to avoid it if possible.

English socialist thought, although having roots in Godwin and others, really begins with Robert Owen. Owen agreed with two of Godwin's major contentions: the real roots of social evil were economic, and human nature was molded by the social system. But he disagreed with Godwin's belief that the solution lay in the equalization of private property. The real error Godwin made, he implied, was to regard the economic system as a set of static property units, not seeing that the industrial revolution had made it an integrated machine. True, economic inequality lay at the foundation of the trouble, but this no longer manifested itself primarily in individual property holdings, but in a lack of balance between industrial production and consumption: "the want of beneficial employment for the working classes, and the consequent public distress, were owing to the rapid increase of the new productive power, for the advantageous application of which, society had neglected to make the proper arrangements." And further: "The deficiency of employment for the working classes cannot proceed from a want of wealth or capital, or of the means of greatly adding to what now exists, but from some defect in the mode of distributing this extraordinary addition of new capital throughout society."[5] The solution to this situation lay not in equalizing private property but in having the state take over the total economic system and run it rationally, balancing production and consumption. Society, he argued, either had to learn to harness the immense new productive forces of the industrial revolution or dissolve in chaos. He was not clear as to what form a "socialist" state should take or just how it was to be achieved. At first he hoped, as had Godwin, for "conversions" among the wealthy, but later he turned to trade unionism and cooperatives. After Owen, socialist thinking in England was taken up first by the Chartists and then by Karl Marx and Friedrich Engels.

Owen knew Godwin and sometimes visited him. But if Owen and Shelley had met, there or elsewhere, surely one of them would have said so.[6] Of their admiration for each other there is no doubt. Shelley sent Owen a copy of his first reform pamphlet.[7] Leigh Hunt in a letter refers to Owen as Shelley's "new counsellor." Owen in his later, spiritualist days claimed that the ghost of "my friend" Shelley—presumably his "spirit" friend—appeared to him in a seance.[8] Medwin reports that Owen later sold *Queen Mab* in his socialist meeting places in London and spoke of Shelley with great admiration.[9] But Owen did not tell Medwin that he had met Shelley, as he almost certainly would have if he had done so.

Owen's influence on Shelley is manifested in *A Philosophical View of Reform* when he treats the twin themes of the unprecedented industrial expansion of the economy and its inability to satisfy consumption. The thinking in the passage is typical of Owen and would have been so recognized at the time. For instance, the London *Times* for July 30, 1817, reported as uniquely Owen's the argument that the then prevailing economic crisis resulted from "a misapplication of the existing powers of production to the wants and demands for those productions." According to him, it continued:

"Much of the natural power, consisting of the physical and intellectual faculties of human beings is now, not only altogether unproductive, but a heavy burden to the country, under a system too, which is rapidly demoralizing it; while a large part of our artificial or mechanical agency is employed to produce that which is of little value to society." Owen also argued against "the artificial law of supply and demand, arising from the principles of individual gain in opposition to the general well-being of society." Finally he claimed, apparently following the Spenceans, that the masses lived in such poverty that they would "further demoralize and finally subvert the whole social system." Shelley writes: "The benefit of this increase in the powers of man became, in consequence of the inartificial [crude] forms into which society came to be distributed, an instrument of his additional evil . . . Modern society is thus a[n] engine assumed to be for useful purposes, whose force is by a system of subtle mechanism augmented to the highest pitch, but which, instead of grinding corn or raising water acts against itself and is perpetually wearing away or breaking to pieces the wheels of which it is composed."[10]

Some of Shelley's comments in *A Philosophical View of Reform* on the exploitation of children may also have received inspiration from Owen, who brought the horrors of this practice to light in 1815 in his *Observations on the Effect of the Manufacturing System.* It was Owen who persuaded Robert Peel to bring in a bill for the abolition of child labor.[11] But while Owen and Shelley agreed on such matters, there are no indications in Shelley of Owen's distinctively socialist utopia. In his own concept of a new order Shelley did not advance markedly beyond the Godwinian picture of the equality of property with an anarchistic minimum of government. He nowhere reflects Owen's vision of a cooperative commonwealth based on expanding productivity in an industrial economy of balanced production and consumption. Owen himself however, did not expound this particular theory in a published work until 1821.

The Carlile Case

The main proponents of the anticlericalism and republicanism of Thomas Paine in early nineteenth-century England were Daniel Isaac Eaton and Richard Carlile. Both of them, when under government prosecution, were defended by Shelley, Eaton in a *Letter to Lord Ellenborough* in 1812, Carlile in an open letter sent to *The Examiner* in 1819.

Carlile, a tinner by trade, became one of the outstanding exponents of radical thought at the time in England. Through Paine and others he was converted to deism and republicanism, and being a man of extraordinary courage, he did not hesitate to express his opinions fully. Associated at first with the "radical" reformer Thomas Jonathan Wooler and his journal *The*

Black Dwarf, he in 1819 founded a journal of his own, *The Republican.*[12] Although he sometimes worked along with the reformers, he believed that their proposed remedy of merely *reforming* Parliament was inadequate: "These political writers who urge the necessity of preserving and adhering to that part of the English legislature which at present consists of Kings and Lords, and who wish to extend the suffrage of representation to every man, evasively argue an absurdity which they previously know to be impracticable."[13] Carlile, however, did not agree with the Spenceans in their communistic visions or with Owen in his socialist ones. His ultimate proposal was, in essence, that which Paine had expounded in the 1790s, namely, to establish a democratic republic on the American model.

In the spring of 1819, Carlile was charged under the blasphemy laws for the publication of Paine's *Age of Reason* and Elihu Palmer's *Principles of Nature,* and in the Fall he was sentenced to three years' imprisonment and £1,500 fine (which actually ended in six years imprisonment because he was unable to pay the fine). As he continued to run *The Republican* from jail with the aid of his wife, the Tories started a subscription, with the duke of Wellington's name at the head of the list, for the prosecution of his assistants. They succeeded in raising £6,000 and in putting his wife in prison for two years. In spite of the fact that altogether he spent nine years in prison, Carlile did not falter; in 1830, for instance, he organized the largest free speech meeting that England had witnessed.

In all probability, Shelley had never met Carlile, but there may have been some connection between them, for Carlile published an edition of *Queen Mab,* printed Shelley's *Declaration of Rights* in *The Republican,* and published articles and poems in praise of him.[14] As soon as Shelley heard of Carlile's trial (but before he knew of the sentence), he sat down to the essay headed simply *For the Examiner.* Hunt, however, did not publish it (just as, in the same year, he did not publish *The Masque of Anarchy*) even though he reported the Carlile case and supported Carlile.[15] Shelley's defense was apparently too radical and anticlerical in tone for *The Examiner.*

Shelley begins his letter, written in November 1819, by tying in the Carlile case with his *Masque of Anarchy* theme, namely, the cavalry attack on a reform meeting, known as the Manchester Massacre. He cites both as examples of the execrable rule of the Tory government:

> In the name of all we hope for in human nature what are the people of England about? Or rather how long will they, & those whose hereditary duty it is to lead them, endure the enormous outrages of which they are one day made the victim & the next the instrument? Post succeeds post, fresh horrors are forever detailed. First we hear that a troop of the enraged master-manufacturers are let loose with sharpened swords upon a multitude of their starving dependents & in spite of the remonstrances of the regular troops that they ride over them & massacre without distinction of sex or age, & cut off women's breasts and dash the heads of infants against the stones. Then comes information that a man has been found guilty of some inexplicable crime, which his prosecutors call blasphemy; one of the

features of which, they inform us, is the denying that the massacring of children, & the ravishing of women, was done by the immediate command of the Author & preserver of all things. And thus at the same time we see on one hand men professing to act by the public authority who put in practice the trampling down & murdering an unarmed multitude without distinction of sex or age, & on the other a tribunal which punishes men for asserting that deeds of the same character, transacted in a distant age & country were not done by the command of God. If not for this, for what was Mr. Carlisle prosecuted? For impugning the Divinity of Jesus Christ? I impugn it. For denying that the whole mass of antient Hebrew literature is of divine authority? I deny it. I hope this is no blasphemy, & that I am not to be dragged home [from Italy] by the enmity of our political adversaries to be made a sacrifice to the superstitious fury of the ruling sect. But I am prepared both to do my duty & to abide by whatever consequences may be attached to its fulfilment.

In the main body of the letter Shelley argues that if Carlile is to get a fair trial, he should be tried by a jury of deists (his "peers"), and that he is being persecuted not so much for his religious as for his political views: "And the prosecutors care little for religion, or care for it only as it is the mask & the garment by which they are invested with the symbols of worldly power. In prosecuting Carlisle they have used the superstition of the jury as their instrument for crushing a political enemy, or rather they strike in his person at all their political enemies." He suggests a campaign for the repeal of the blasphemy laws and a subscription for Carlile's defense. He sees Carlile's case not as a simple matter of free speech but as a symptom of the general political forces of the age:

These, my dear Hunt, are awful times. The tremendous question is now agitating, whether a military & judicial despotism is to be established by our present rulers, or some form of government less unfavourable to the real & permanent interests of all men is to arise from the conflict of passions now gathering to overturn them: *We* cannot hesitate which party to embrace; and whatever revolutions are to occur, though oppression should change names & names cease to be oppressions, our party will be that of liberty & of the oppre[ss]ed. Whatever you may imagine to be our differences in political theory, I trust that I shall be ab[le] to prove that they are less than you imagine, by [ag]reeing, as from my soul I do, with your principles [of] political practice.[16]

Shelley was always well to the left of Hunt—who was neither republican nor egalitarian—but agreed with him on the "political practice" of striving for the reform of Parliament. What was to Hunt the ultimate objective, however, was to Shelley only a stepping stone along the way.

The 1817 Pamphlets

Whereas on the continent of Europe the revolutionary struggle for "liberty" was waged against absolutist dictatorial states and hence had to be settled by arms, in England it took the shape of a movement for the reform of Parliament. The House of Lords was controlled by the aristocracy by the simple method of having nobody but themselves (and their churchmen) sit in it; the House of Commons they controlled by purchasing seats and narrowing the franchise. John Wilson Croker, Tory publicist and politician, computed as late as 1827 that 276 Commons seats were under direct aristocratic control and, of these, 51 were owned by 8 peers. While tiny hamlets elected two members, the new industrial centers of Manchester, Birmingham, Leeds, and Sheffield had none.[17] The most expedient remedy for the city commercial and professional men lay in extending the franchise just enough to enable them to elect their own representatives to Parliament, and this was the object of that branch of the reform movement which had its birth in John Wilkes's stormy campaigns of the late eighteenth century and which culminated in the Reform Act of 1832. Wilkes, Horne Tooke, and others demanded the abolition of the rotten boroughs and the extension of the vote on a property basis. In the 1790s this battle was taken up by the Foxite Whigs, who in two notable debates of 1793 and 1797 urged, with much eloquent generalization on "freedom" and "tyranny", that the upper middle class be given the franchise.

These, however, were not the only classes who wanted the vote. The industrial revolution that had produced the industrial capitalists also produced an industrial working class. Agricultural production, although not having advanced at the same rate as industrial production, had nevertheless advanced in both efficiency and output. A large new group of independent farmers had come into being. And finally, the city middle class of small tradesmen and professionals had grown considerably. Representing these various classes, often in rather mixed forms, were the "radical" reformers. The radicals, first led by the indomitable Major John Cartwright, scorned the Whig demand for "limited suffrage" (the vote for certain property owners only) and called for "universal suffrage" (the vote for every adult male).

In Shelley's childhood and early youth, the leading figure in the reform movement was Sir Francis Burdett, to whom Shelley sent many letters, all now apparently lost. Burdett, a "moderate" reformer standing for limited suffrage, was ably assisted within the House of Commons by Lord Cochrane and, outside the House, by Francis Place, a behind-the-scenes organizer, and a veritable phalanx of moderate journals: *The Examiner, the Morning Chronicle, The Statesman,* and the *Independent Whig.*[18]

The most influential leader of the radical reformers, pressing for universal suffrage, was William Cobbett. His *Political Register,* issued in an untaxable form at 2d in 1816, had a weekly circulation of 40,000 to 50,000 (the *Times* had only 8,000).[19] Cobbett proposed the vote for all adult males, a secret ballot, annual election of Parliament, and the abolition of both government corruption and the national debt, to which he attributed most of the social miseries of the age.[20] The most active and for a time the most popular figure of the movement was Henry ("Orator") Hunt, the hero of the Manchester

Massacre (no relation to Leigh Hunt).[21] Cobbett supported Hunt and his energetic organizing tours with all the vigor of his powerful pen.

Another group of radical reformers were those still clustered around the venerated "Father" of the movement, Major Cartwright.[22] Cartwright never had the mass following of Cobbett and Hunt, but he was everywhere highly regarded. Associated with him for a time was a radical journalist, Thomas Jonathan Wooler, whose periodical *The Black Dwarf* had a weekly circulation of 12,000 and appealed largely to a working class audience. Castlereagh declared with alarm in 1819 that in some northern collieries one could find a copy of *The Black Dwarf* in the cap of "almost every pitman you meet."[23] In 1817 the radical reformers received an unexpected addition to their ranks in Jeremy Bentham with his *Plan of Parliamentary Reform,* which they hastened to bring out in a popularized version.[24]

"The cause of reform" declared Henry Hunt in his autobiography, "languished until the year 1816, although Major Cartwright, Sir Francis Burdett, Mr. Cobbett, myself and many others, had made frequent efforts to call the people's attention to the only measure calculated to check the progress—the fatal progress of corruption, and its consequent effects, unjust and unnecessary war, profligate expenditure, the funding or *swindling* system, and the rapid annual increase of a ruinous and irredeemable debt."[25] The great social upheavals of the postwar depression—economic crisis, a renewal of Luddite rioting, a hundred thousand jobless men streaming back from the battlefields—turned reform into a popular movement. In the days of the Foxite reformers, Cobbett notes, a large meeting consisted of 500, but in the stormy days following the end of the war in 1815, of 30,000 or more.[26] One of the most immediate effects of this growth was a widening of the division between the moderates and the radicals. Bitter quarrels broke out between Cobbett and Burdett, and between the *Political Register* and *The Examiner;* the moderates refused to grace the same platform as the radicals or to drink toasts to their leaders; the two groups ran rival candidates in elections. To the moderates, the radicals were irresponsible extremists; to the radicals, the moderates were weak-kneed opportunists; and to the republicans or the Spenceans, both were mere tinkerers.

Such was the situation in the midst of which Shelley issued his first reform pamphlet, *A Proposal for Putting Reform to the Vote,* by "the Hermit of Marlow." The pamphlet was written at Marlow, probably in February 1817, was published in March, received two brief puffs in *The Examiner,* gave rise to a caustic attack on the "Hermit" by Robert Southey in the *Quarterly Review,* received a third comment in *The Examiner* in 1819, and was heard of no more.[27] That Shelley regarded it seriously is shown by his offer to give up one-tenth of his income to assist in his scheme for "putting reform to the vote" by a national canvass, and by the imposing a list to whom he ordered the pamphlet to be sent, including Sir Francis Burdett, Lord Grey, Henry Brougham (later Lord Brougham), Lord Holland, Cobbett, Alderman Robert Waithman, John Philpot Curran, Douglas Kinnaird, Lord Cochrane,

Francis Place, Major Cartwright, Robert Owen, George Ensor, William Madocks, and two Hampden clubs.[28] The thing that stands out about this list is that it was primarily a moderate one, including the more liberal Whig leaders, but only Cartwright and Cobbett of the radical reformers. The pamphlet was also sent to the moderate reform press—*The Examiner, The Statesman,* the *Morning Chronicle,* the *Independent Whig*—whereas the radical reform press is represented only by Cobbett. Other radical organs—*The Black Dwarf,* William Sherwin's *Republican,* and Hone's *Reformists' Register*—are omitted.[29] Nor was a copy sent to the man who at the time was the outstanding popular leader of the radical reformers, Henry Hunt.

The moderate position is advocated in the pamphlet, although with some qualifications:

> With respect to Universal Suffrage, I confess I consider its adoption, in the present unprepared state of public knowledge and feeling, a measure fraught with peril. I think that none but those who register their names as paying a certain small sum in *direct taxes* ought, at present, to send Members to Parliament. The consequences of the immediate extension of the elective franchise to every male adult, would be to place power in the hands of men who have been rendered brutal and torpid and ferocious by ages of slavery. It is to suppose that the qualities belonging to a demagogue are such as are sufficient to endow a legislator. I allow Major Cartwright's arguments to be unanswerable; abstractedly it is the right of every human being to have a share in the government. But Mr. Paine's arguments are also unanswerable; a pure republic may be shewn, by inferences the most obvious and irresistible, to be that system of social order the fittest to produce the happiness and promote the genuine eminence of man. Yet, nothing can less consist with reason, or afford smaller hopes of any beneficial issue, than the plan which should abolish the regal and the aristocratical branches of our constitution, before the public mind, through many gradations of improvement, shall have arrived at the maturity which can disregard these symbols of its childhood.[30]

This rather snobbish attack on the radical reformers as "demagogues" and their followers as "brutal and torpid" is typical of *The Examiner* attitude.[31] Because the *Proposal* was written at a time when Shelley, then new to the reform movement, was in frequent association with Leigh Hunt, it doubtless directly reflects Hunt's influence.

The distinction, however, between Shelley and Hunt must again be emphasized. Hunt looked for little beyond an extension of the franchise to the middle class and was indeed quite satisfied with the Reform Bill of 1832 (and his own consequent pension). Shelley not only favored in theory the universal suffrage demands of the radicals but wished to push beyond them into a republican and then an equalitarian state. He attacked Cartwright and the radicals, he made clear, not because he disagreed with their aims but because he felt that those aims could more safely be accomplished in two stages than in one; an attempt to gain complete franchise at once might precipitate revolution and put those in power who were untrained to rule. This was a common argument of the moderates, and one which Jeremy Bentham ridiculed later that very same year (1817): "No, no:—it is not *anarchy* that ye are afraid of: what ye are afraid of is *good government*."[32]

On one of their demands, however, Shelley sided with the radicals: "Annual Parliaments have my entire assent. I will not state those general reasonings in their favour, which Mr. Cobbett and other writers have already made familiar to the public mind." The moderates as a rule demanded only triennial parliaments. Cartwright had long demanded annual parliaments, and Cobbett in his *Political Register* for October 19, 1816 (the issue to which Shelley is here referring), made an extended attack on the moderate view and supported Cartwright.[33]

In spite of his leaning toward the moderate reformers, Shelley urged that the radical-moderate split be healed and both views be subjected to a national democratic process: "A certain degree of coalition among the sincere Friends of Reform, in whatever shape, is indispensable to the success of this proposal. The friends of Universal or of Limited Suffrage, of Annual or Triennial Parliaments, ought to settle these subjects on which they disagree, when it is known whether the nation desires that measure on which they are all agreed. It is trivial to discuss what species of Reform shall have place, when it yet remains a question whether there will be any Reform or no."[34] This theme of unity for immediate aims was a part of Shelley's political thinking throughout his life.

Shelley's second political pamphlet of 1817, *An Address to the People on the Death of the Princess Charlotte*, was not strictly a reform pamphlet, but it did deal with an issue taken up by the reformers in that year, namely, the execution of three workingmen, Jeremiah Brandreth, Isaac Ludlam, and William Turner, the leaders of the so-called "Derbyshire Insurrection."[35] The Tory administration, becoming alarmed at the spread of unrest in the postwar depression, routinely employed *agents provocateurs* to turn anti-government demonstrations into riots. They would then seize the "ringleaders" and execute them in order to demoralize their followers. Of these *agents provocateurs*, the most notorious was the man known as "Oliver" (attacked by Charles Lamb in *The Three Graves*).[36] In the summer of 1817 "Oliver," representing himself as a delegate from the London "Physical Force Party," succeeded in penetrating radical working-class organizations in Derbyshire. One of these, led by Brandreth, may or may not already have been planning to lead an armed working-class march into Nottingham. It is difficult to get the true story because Brandreth and his followers did not take the stand at their trial and the evidence presented was mainly that of government spies. Certainly "Oliver" played a major part in the plot and either engineered the whole scheme or inflamed the workers by tales of supporting insurrections in London and elsewhere. At any rate, Brandreth's "army" failed to materialize, and his band grew smaller as it approached Nottingham, where it was routed by the militia. Brandreth and the other leaders were put on trial, and three of them were sentenced to be executed. On November 7, the day following the death of the Princess Charlotte, heir to the throne, sentence was carried out. The three men were hanged and then beheaded, their heads held aloft to the crowd.

The reformers, who had done little during the trial, were roused to action by the executions. *The Examiner* in a lead article condemned the government, pointing out the incongruity of national mourning for the princess on a day of wanton bloodshed. *The Black Dwarf* was even more bitter: "That the death of the Princess Charlotte should have been immediately followed by such a scene of blood as that exhibited upon the scaffold at Derby, is as shocking to the understanding, as it is abhorrent to the feelings. Was the vulture of law so eager for the banquet of mangled carcases, that it could not fast through the solemnity of these funeral preparations?" Henry Hunt, who alone of the reform leaders had attended the trial at Derby in an unavailing effort to save the three men, now used all his powers of oratory and organization to arouse feeling against the government.[37] Cobbett devoted a large part of three numbers of his *Political Register* to the executions and started a fund for Mrs. Brandreth. But the most powerful and eloquent statement that the whole horrible episode inspired was Shelley's pamphlet.[38]

While retaining an attitude of respectful regret toward the death of the princess (in contrast to Byron's rather maudlin rhetoric),[39] Shelley points out that thousands of poor women die in childbirth every week and have no days of national mourning decreed for them. He follows the reform journals' pattern of contrasting the death of the princess with the execution of the men at Derby,[40] but he subordinates political agitation to humanitarian protest and strikes out at capital punishment as such:

> The execution of Brandreth, Ludlam, and Turner, is an event of quite a different character from the death of the Princess Charlotte. These men were shut up in a horrible dungeon, for many months, with the fear of a hideous death and of everlasting hell thrust before their eyes; and at last were brought to the scaffold and hung . . . What these sufferers felt shall not be said. But what must have been the long and various agony of their kindred may be inferred from Edward Turner, who, when he saw his brother dragged along upon the hurdle, shrieked horribly and fell in a fit, and was carried away like a corpse by two men. How fearful must have been their agony, sitting in solitude on that day when the tempestuous voice of horror from the crowd, told them that the head so dear to them was severed from the body! Yes—they listened to the maddening shriek which burst from the multitude: they heard the rush of ten thousand terror-stricken feet, the groans and the hootings which told them that the mangled and distorted head was then lifted into the air. The sufferers were dead. What is death? Who dares to say that which will come after the grave? Brandreth was calm, and evidently believed that the consequences of our errors were limited by that tremendous barrier. Ludlam and Turner were full of fears, lest God should plunge them in everlasting fire. Mr. Pickering, the clergyman, was evidently anxious that Brandreth should not by a false confidence lose the single opportunity of reconciling himself with the Ruler of the future world. None knew what death was, or could know. Yet, these men

were presumptuously thrust into that unfathomable gulf, by other men, who knew as little and who reckoned not the present or the future sufferings of their victims.[41]

Shelley excoriates the government labor spy system, noting, as also did *The Examiner* and *The Black Dwarf*, that Turner cried out with the hangman's rope around his neck, "This is all Oliver and the government," when the chaplain stepped up and put his hand over his mouth. He concludes on a republican note: "Let us follow the corpse of British Liberty slowly and reverentially to its tomb: and if some glorious Phantom should appear, and make its throne of broken swords and sceptres and royal crowns trampled in the dust, let us say that the Spirit of Liberty has arisen from its grave and left all that was gross and mortal there, and kneel down and worship it as our Queen."[42]

A Philosophical View of Reform

A few months after writing the *Address*, Shelley left for Italy, but his interest in the political situation in England, as his letters show, remained as keen as ever. In July 1818 he wrote to Peacock in condemnation of the "apostate" Wordsworth's electioneering activities on behalf of the Tories in Westmoreland—activities that also disturbed Keats, who had called at the Wordsworths' during a walking tour of the Lakes.[43] On the same day he wrote with delight to Godwin on hearing that the liberals Sir Francis Burdett and Sir Samuel Romilly had been elected for Westminster, and concluded: "I wish that I had health or spirits that would enable me to enter into public affairs, or that I could find words to express all that I feel I know."[44] When Romilly committed suicide in the fall, Henry Hunt nominated Cobbett for the vacant seat as a radical reformer, and the Burdett-Place faction countered with John Cam Hobhouse (Byron's "Hobby-O") as a moderate. Shelley, although he had previously declared that he had "a very slight opinion" of Hobhouse, now supported him, feeling that Hunt and Cobbett had uselessly split the reform vote, for Cobbett had no chance: "I am yet ignorant of the event of Hobhouse's election. I saw the last numbers were [George] Lamb 4200 & Hobhouse 3900 14th day. There is little hope. That michievous Cobbet [sic] has divided & weakened the interests of the popular party so that the factions who prey upon our country have been able to coalesce to its exclusion."[45] In June 1819 he was more favorably disposed toward Cobbett: "Cobbet still more & more delights me, with all my horror of the sanguinary commonplaces of his creed. His design to overthrow Bank notes by forgery is very comic."[46] In the fall he began his most ambitious attempt to express his political philosophy, in *A Philosophical View of Reform*.

Shelley, as he later informed Leigh Hunt, intended this work to occupy a place in the reform movement similar to Bentham's recent *Plan of Parlia-*

mentary Reform, which, as a result of Bentham's surprising endorsement of radical reform, was creating a sensation: "Do you know any bookseller who wd publish for me an octavo volume entitled 'A philosophical View of Reform'? It is boldly but temperately written & I think readable. It is intended for a kind of standard book for the philosophical reformers politically considered, like Jeremy Bentham's something [somewhat], but different & perhaps more systematic."[47]

While other reform pamphlets of the period are taken up almost entirely by details of program, Shelley places the movement in its historical perspective and sketches its economic background. He divides the work into three chapters. In the first he outlines the struggle for political liberty from the medieval Italian city-states through the British (Cromwellian), American, and French revolutions, implying that the English reform movement should be seen as part of this general historical development. In the second chapter, he argues that much of the social disorganization of contemporary Britain results from the financial burden imposed by the national debt and currency inflation. In the third chapter he considers methods for the achievement of reform. Unfortunately his failure to get a publisher discouraged him from continuing, and the work is unfinished.

In the first chapter, history is viewed not as a static series of past political events but as a continuing social stream driven by the forces of "freedom" and "tyranny." In his own age, "freedom" had received an impetus of such unprecedented power from the American and French revolutions that the counterrevolutionary repression of Metternich, Castlereagh, and the Quadruple Alliance could not long contain it. New democratic states would arise and, in time, blend into a world republic—a concept that also underlies *Prometheus Unbound* and *Hellas.*

The first liberterian state—hailed in *Hellas*—was Athens. But in regard to Athens, Shelley had some reservations: "Before [reading Godwin's *Political Justice*] I was a republican—Athens appeared to me the model of a government, but afterwards Athens bore in my mind the same relation to perfection that Great Britain did to Athe[ns]."[48] The stricture clearly applies not only to Athens but, in one or another degree, to all states and political systems past and present: political liberty without economic and social equality is imperfect and limited. Thus, when Shelley speaks of the rise of liberty in this or that century or state, he is aware that it is not liberty for the many but for the few (in Athens mostly the male slave owners; in Florence the great aristocrats, bankers, and merchants). Liberty for humanity can come only in the future egalitarian order. The concept of equality—"Eldest of things, divine Equality"—[49] was always, it should be understood, uppermost in Shelley's thinking even though he did not always wish to make it explicit for fear of alienating his less "enlightened" readers.

A Philosophical View of Reform begins, however, not with Athens but with the dissolution of the Roman Empire, for in this work Shelley was discussing modern history, and although he believed that the culture of

Athens had greatly influenced Europe and America, their historical traditions began with the collapse of the Roman Empire:

> From the dissolution of the Roman Empire, that vast and successful scheme for the enslaving [of] the most civilized portion of mankind, to the epoch of the present year, have succeeded a series of schemes, on a smaller scale, operating to the same effect. Names borrowed from the life and opinions of Jesus Christ were employed as symbols of domination and imposture; and a system of liberty and equality (for such was the system preached by that great Reformer) was perverted to support oppression.—Not his doctrines, for they are too simple and direct to be susceptible of such perversion—but the mere names. Such was the origin of the Catholic Church, which together with the several dynasties then beginning to consolidate themselves in Europe, means, being interpreted, a plan according to which the cunning and selfish few have employed the fears and hopes of the ignorant many to the establishment of their own power and the destruction of the real interests of all.

Such is the opening paragraph of *A Philosophical View of Reform.* Its hatred of tyranny, political or religious, its underlying humanitarianism, its clarity and compact power continue throughout. So, too, does its sense of history as an evolutionary process:

> The Republics and municipal Governments of Italy opposed for some time a systematic and effectual resistance to the all-surrounding tyranny . . . When this resistance was overpowered (as what resistance to fraud and [tyranny] has not been overpowered?) another was even then maturing. The progress of philosophy and civilization which ended in that imperfect emancipation of mankind from the yoke of priests and kings called the Reformation, had already commenced.

Shelley's sympathies lie not with Luther and his princely backers but with the peasants (whom Luther had first courted but, when they revolted, called "mad dogs" and demanded their bloody suppression):

> Exasperated by their long sufferings, inflamed by the spark of that superstition from the flames of which they were emerging, the poor rose against their natural enemies, the rich, and repaid with bloody interest the tyranny of ages. One of the signs of the times was that the oppressed peasantry rose like the negro slaves of West Indian Plantations, and murdered their tyrants when they were unaware. For so dear is power that the tyrants themselves neither then, nor now, nor ever, left or leave a path to freedom but through their own blood.

Among the products of the Reformation were the republics of Holland and Switzerland. These, however, were soon outshone by the first great national revolution in the modern world, that of Cromwell:

> Shakespeare and Lord Bacon and the great writers of the age of Elizabeth and James the 1st were at once the effects of the new spirit in men's minds, and the

causes of its more complete development. By rapid gradation the nation was conducted to the mighty example which, "in teaching nations how to live," England afforded to the world—of bringing to public justice one of those chiefs of a conspiracy of privileged murderers and robbers whose impunity has been the consecration of crime.

Following the Revolution came the Restoration, a "compromise" between the "unextinguishable spirit of Liberty and the ever watchful spirit of fraud and tyranny," for at least the power of Parliament remained. This compromise was reflected intellectually in the "exact and intelligible but superficial school" of Locke and his followers. Later, these views spread to France and America:

> The system of government of the United States of America was the first practical illustration of the new philosophy. Sufficiently remote, it will be confessed, from the accuracy of ideal excellence is that representative system which will soon cover the extent of that vast Continent. But it is scarcely less remote from the insolent and contaminating tyrannies under which, with some limitation of these terms as regards England, Europe groaned at the period of the successful rebellion of America.
>
> America holds forth the victorious example of an immensely populous, and as far as the external arts of life are concerned, a highly civilized community administered according to republican forms. It has no king, that is it has no officer to whom wealth and from whom corruption flows. It has no hereditary oligarchy, that is it acknowledges no order of men privileged to cheat and insult the rest of the members of the state, and who inherit a right of legislating and judging which the principles of human nature compel them to exercise to their own profit and to the detriment of those not included within their own peculiar class. It has no established Church . . . no false representation, whose consequences are captivity, confiscation, infamy and ruin, but a true representation.

The American Revolution represented the first great advance of mankind into republican democracy. Whereas most radicals regarded it as an ultimate goal, however, to Shelley its "representative system" was still "remote" from "the accuracy of ideal excellence," because it lacked economic and social equality. Without these, political liberty is stunted.

Following fast on the heels of the American came the French Revolution, both foreshadowed by the Enlightenment: "The just and successful Revolt of America corresponded with a state of public opinion in Europe of which it was the first result. The French Revolution was the second." But in France things were even less "ideal" than in America. The political accomplishments of the early days of the National Assembly and Legislative Assembly had been largely thwarted as the revolution turned into the violence from which emerged the successive despotisms of Napoleon and the new monarchy: "The usurpation of Bonaparte and then the Restoration of the Bourbons were the shapes in which this reaction clothed itself, and the heart of every lover of liberty was struck as with palsy by the succession of these events."[50]

But new movements for liberty are stirring in Germany and Spain (then on the brink of revolution against Ferdinand). In South America, in India and Persia, in Syria and Arabia (the Wahabee movement), in Egypt and the West Indies (the revolts in Santa Domingo and Haiti, the latter under the guidance successively of Toussaint L'Ouverture and Henri Christophe), a revolutionary spirit is abroad:

> Lastly, in the West Indian islands, first from the disinterested yet necessarily cautious measures of the English Nation, and then from the infection of the spirit of Liberty in France, the deepest stain upon civilized man is fading away. Two nations of free negroes are already established; one, in pernicious mockery of the usurpation over France, an empire, the other a republic;—both animating yet terrific spectacles to those who inherit around them the degradation of slavery and the peril of dominion.

England—"the particular object for the sake of which these general considerations have been stated"—is "at a crisis in its destiny," and this crisis is reflected, as were similar movements in the past, in a new intellectual temper: "we live among such philosophers and poets as surpass beyond comparison any who have appeared in our nation since its last struggle for liberty."

Shelley's view of history is not cyclical, although there are cyclical elements in it, for true cyclical theory posits inevitable stages of rise and decline with no underlying pattern of progress. Although Shelley depicts conflicting successions of liberty and despotism, the underlying pattern is an expanding spiral rising from ancient Athens to the French Revolution. Shelley implies that this spiral will continue, but he does not state that its path will be direct or smooth. In *Hellas,* he even brings up the possibility of future serious setbacks. In spite of these doubts and cyclical elements, however, Shelley's theory looks forward not to Spengler but to Marx. He stands, in fact, about halfway between Godwin and Marx, and as such his theory has a special historiographical interest. A glance forward to Marx might help to set Shelley's view in its proper nineteenth-century perspective.

The key problem facing an evolutionary theory, whether in biology or history, is what causes the evolution. Marx's answer is rooted in his famous propositions: "The mode of production of the material means of existence conditions the whole process of social, political, and intellectual life. It is not the consciousness of men that determines their existence, but, on the contrary, it is their social existence that determines their consciousness." Historical evolution arises not from applied human intelligence but from the struggle for existence. This struggle assumes the form of conflicts between classes and within classes—economic competition, war, revolution, and so on. Although this struggle is not consciously directed toward the advancement of society, it nevertheless results in that advancement because it brings about the expansion of the economy ("the mode of production"), and as the economy "conditions" the processes of society, the processes of society—social, political, and intellectual—change when the economy changes.

At a certain point economic expansion comes into conflict with existing "property relationships," and a revolution ensues which frees the economy for another advance:

> At a certain stage of their development the material productive forces of society come into contradiction with the existing productive relationships, or, what is but a legal expression for these, with the property relationships within which they had moved before. From forms of development of the productive forces these relationships are transformed into their fetters. Then an epoch of social revolution opens. With the change in the economic foundation the whole vast superstructure is more or less rapidly transformed.[51]

Although arguing abstractly, Marx is actually describing the European bourgeois revolutions of 1789, 1830, and 1848 against the feudal state (with his mind's eye on future working-class revolutions against capitalism). Starting in about the 1780's, the industrial section of the "mode of production"—not the whole of it—began a significant expansion, which encountered a barrier in feudal "property relationships." Nobody had planned this expansion. It arose out of business competition, and although each businessman was conscious of his own immediate goals, the total pattern formed without being planned. So, too, there was no general realization that what was blocking further expansion was the feudal landowning system as such. It was realized only that the great aristocrats held political power and used this power to hamper business development. This, of course, was not new; it had gone on for centuries. What was new was the great growth of the business class, both in social power and numbers, a growth sufficient to enable the class to challenge successfully the aristocracy's political monopoly. In this challenge they were supported in an uneasy but necessary alliance by the middle class and the industrial working class. The result was that in three successive revolutionary movements (1789, 1830, and 1848) the business class achieved political power. Again there was no overall plan for the shape of the new society. Its shape resulted from the resolution of the crosscurrents of various immediate objectives in political and other struggles. These crosscurrents and their resolution brought about changes in people's ways of thinking, in their art, religion, and literature (such as the so-called "romantic" movement) which the people were aware of even though they did not fully understand what was producing them.

This kind of process in social change Marx believed to be a general one. As a result of it, society had moved from "primitive communism" to slavery (in Greece and Rome) to feudalism, to capitalism. Marx, although describing this as a universal process, was actually thinking in European rather than world terms. There was no predominantly slave society in Asia, for example, where continuous feudalism followed the early farming society in Sumer, the Indus valley, and elsewhere. Nor were the major developments—as from an early farming society to feudalism—the result of revolutions. Most of them were gradual processes of many centuries in duration. After capitalist civilization, Marx argued, society will advance to communism, to a lower stage first, then a higher one—the lower one to consist of national states run by the industrial working class with limited economic resources, the higher one, a classless world community with abundance for all.

Some of the fragments that went into this theory can be seen, directly or indirectly, not only in Godwin but in Condorcet, Volney, Holbach, Paine, Mary Wollstonecraft, and Blake. Both Blake and Condorcet, for instance, developed the concept of historical progress taking place in response to forces beyond conscious human control. Condorcet maintained that there were laws governing social as well as natural development; if one could but understand them, one could predict the outlines of the future. Society had advanced through nine stages and was about to move into the tenth—the egalitarian. Blake developed a mythology of spiritual forces that controlled nature and society. "Orc," for instance, was the spirit of energy in nature and of revolution in society. In *America,* it was the power of Orc and not the human characters that created and directed the American Revolution: the individual could not act until the proper social and psychological atmosphere had been created. Blake, too, was sure that the general direction of society was upward. Even if conservative elements ("Urizen") should begin to contaminate the American scene, about which was writting in 1793, revolution was triumphing in France and would spread to Europe, Asia, and Africa in time to culminate in the worldwide "New Jerusalem."

Although Blake and Condorcet, as well as Paine, believed that society had advanced and was still advancing, they did not really delve into causes. It was to this problem that Godwin addressed himself. He, too, argued that natural and social laws must be similar to each other, possibly in some way connected. Of one thing he felt certain: one general law governed both, namely, that of necessity. The universe must be "connected and cemented in all its parts, nothing in the boundless progress of things being capable of happening otherwise than it has actually happened." The events of history show a like interdependence and inevitability. Moreover, the pattern of these events has, from the time of the ancients, been one of "improvement." In the past few centuries these "improvements"—in society, science, art—have been "incessant." If they are not halted by some "concussion of nature or barbarism," they will eventually result in an egalitarian state. In seeking the reason for this upward spiral, Godwin searched not, as did Marx, in the nature of society but in the nature of mind: "The inherent tendency of intellect is to improvement."[52] Mind was to Godwin something apart and unique, even though it was subject to the laws of necessity, and if mind had an "inherent tendency" to improve, one need not seek further to find what caused that tendency. It was simply the nature of mind. And it is mind, the assumption runs, that controls society, which is exactly the reverse of Marx's proposition.

According to Godwin's concept, if the improvements of society resulted from this tendency to improvement in the mind, then one could affect the rate of social improvement by becoming an "indefatigable votary of justice and truth" and trying to convert others, including political leaders, aristocrats, and businessmen. One must, however, shun political "associations" and above all revolutionary movements: "Amid the barbarous rage of war, and the clamorous rage of civil contention, who shall tell whether the event will be prosperous or adverse?"[53] Godwin, unlike Paine, was not a revolutionary but a radical scholar. His prime interests were centered in the English middle class.

Shelley had early read Condorcet, Godwin, and Paine. There is no evidence that he had read Blake, and it is most unlikely that he had, for not only was Blake virtually unknown, but his method of producing his works by engraving limited his market to a handful of readers. Of *America,* for instance, only seventeen copies are known. The fact that both Shelley and Blake viewed society as progressive shows only that the idea was in the air; and the fact that both shadowed forth this concept in symbolic poetry—as, indeed, did Keats in *Hyperion*—probably means no more than that poets living in the same age tend to use similar techniques. Futhermore, the symbolic worlds of the two were very different. Blake developed his own mythology and mixed religious and social messages; Shelley utilized existing mythologies and shunned religious connotations. He would, in fact, have been shocked by Blake's crude "everlasting gospel" ideas, though he would have responded warmly to his social revolutionary message.

Shelley, like Godwin, tried to find the "why" of social progress. If he did not pursue this general question with the formal assiduity of Godwin, his conclusions are nonetheless significant. Perhaps the closest he came to a general statement is in the following passage in *A Philosophical View of Reform.* After discussing the political philosophy of the eighteenth and early nineteenth centuries—listing Rousseau, Godwin, and Bentham among others —he continued:

> Contemporary with this condition of the intellect all the powers of man seemed, though in most cases under forms highly inauspicious to develop themselves with uncommon energy. The mechanical sciences attained to a degree of perfection which, though obscurely foreseen by Lord Bacon, it had been accounted madness to have prophesied in a preceding age. Commerce was pursued with a perpetually increasing vigour, and the same area of the Earth was perpetually compelled to furnish more and more subsistence. The means and sources of knowledge were thus increased together with knowledge itself, and the instruments of knowledge. The benefit of this increase of the powers of man became, in consequence of the inartificial forms into which society came to be distributed, an instrument of his additional evil. The capabilities of happiness were increased, and applied to the augmentation of misery. Modern society is thus a[n] engine assumed to be for useful purposes, whose force is by a system of subtle mechanism augmented to the highest pitch, but which, instead of grinding corn or raising water acts against itself and is perpetually wearing away or breaking to pieces the

wheels of which it is composed. The result of the labours of the political philosophers has been the establishment of the principle of Utility as the substance, and liberty and equality as the forms according to which the concerns of human life ought to be administered . . . The system of government in the United States of America was the first practical illustration of the new philosophy.[54]

Shelley, then, viewed historical progress as resulting from a combination of intellectual, social, and technological factors. For instance, in the eighteenth century the rise of scientific knowledge, the mechanical inventions of science and technology, the expansion of commerce, the increase in farm productivity, and the spread of knowledge all went hand in hand ("increased together"). This increase, however, came into conflict with the "inartifical [crude] forms" of modern society. What these "forms" are is indicated by his comments on the views of the "political philosophers" Godwin and Bentham. By the "principle of Utility" he means the Benthamite principle of "the greatest good for the greatest number," a state that can be realized, however, only through the political and economic "forms" of "liberty and equality." By equality, Shelley means not primarily political but economic equality, which is the Godwinian position. What the great increase in knowledge, commerce, farming, and technology came into conflict with were therefore the "forms" whereby modern society would not permit the equitable distribution of its products—an argument having roots in Owen. The new bounties of agriculture went to the landed aristocracy, and those of commerce and technology to the merchants, manufacturers, and bankers. Hence, society was faced by the situation that followed the Napoleonic wars, of accumulated riches and a hungry populace, with political rights and knowledge alike reserved for the "few." This situation, Shelley argues, will produce a "change" in England, which will in time fall in with the revolutionary advances of the age.

Shelley thus envisaged historical progress as resulting from the interactions of social and intellectual forces. On the question of which of the two is primary, he does not commit himself but is content with simply stating the fact of interconnection. For instance, in discussing the increase in technology, commerce, and agriculture, he does not state that the "condition of the intellect" caused the increase but simply that it was "contemporary" with it. Similarly, in discussing the English Revolution, he does not assert that the preceding intellectual development brought it about but only that Shakespeare and Bacon were both "the effect of the new spirit" (the Reformation) and "the causes of its more complete development." Then he begins a new sentence without any direct causal link: "By rapid graduation the nation was conducted to the temporary abolition of aristocracy and episcopacy." He does not state what the sources of the "new spirit" were, but his previous descriptions suggest both social and intellectual factors (such as the German peasant's revolt and the Dutch struggle for independence). He does, it is true, state that this spirit, once created, could cause further intellectual development, but he does not state that it caused the revolution. And in other places, for instance, the Preface to *Hellas,* he implies the primacy of social factors. The only certainty, however, is that society is progressive, and that this progress results from the interweaving of intellectual and social factors.

On two basic and related questions, Shelley was in general agreement with Godwin. He believed that history moved in accordance with the laws of necessity, and he felt that although human beings could not control this movement, they could in his own age direct it to a limited degree. For instance, in a rejected fragment of *Julian and Maddalo* (1818) he wrote:

> tho all the past cd not have been
> Other than as it was—yet things foreseen
> Reason and Love may force beneath their yoke
> Warned by a fate foregone.[55]

In the past, Shelley is arguing, people were the victims of blind historical forces. The cycles of despotism and liberty ran their inevitable course. But now some control is possible, for humanity is beginning to understand history, and understanding brings power. True, necessity is a blind force, bringing indifferently evil or good, but if "Reason and Love" and not evil are the dominant elements that this force has to work with, it will produce a higher form of society. One must, therefore, work to spread "Reason and Love." How is one to do this? As *A Philosophical View of Reform* indicates, by participating in political movements—revolutions on the Continent, reform in England—and not simply, as Godwin suggested, by educating an elite. Thus, although Shelley still based himself on the general Godwinian concepts of progress and necessity, he broke with their mechanical abstractions and their practical ineffectuality. Godwin's small enlightened bands of intellectuals could accomplish little, whereas revolutionary or reform movements could accomplish much.

In all the respects in which Shelley moved beyond Godwin he advanced toward Marx: in his concept of the interaction of social and intellectual factors, his theory that economic and technological advances are checked by the "forms" of society, his revolutionary sense of social conflict and the interests of the different classes involved, his hatred for "the oppressors," and his championing of the people. The concepts of necessity and the ultimate egalitarian society, which he shared with Godwin, were also fragmented foreshadowings of Marx. Shelley, in fact, comes closer to Marx than do any of the other writers or thinkers of his age. This affinity is true of style as well as content: the revolutionary fervor of, say, the Preface to *Hellas* —"This is the age of the war of the oppressed against the oppressors" —has the ring of *The Communist Manifesto.* Yet there is a great gulf between Marx's total concept and Shelley's, as even the above brief excerpt from *The Critique of Political Economy* shows. Shelley did not, as did Marx, have a rounded sociological theory, but rather a series of brilliant insights into parts of historical patterns. He did not see the future path as one of industrial expansion or predict that new forms of society would be based on it, but remained within the older confines of egalitarian anarchism. He had a sharp sense of class differences and class conflicts, but he did not perceive their full historical significance. Shelley however, was writing in 1819, Marx in 1859, and Shelley did not live to see either the 1848 revolutions or the rise of Chartism.

The first chapter of *A Philosophical View of Reform* outlines the past development that has led to the present. In the second chapter Shelley comes to the present and examines the specific socio-economic situation in England which has rendered the reform of Parliament urgent. Here, especially for his economic analysis, he is indebted to William Cobbett's unorthodox treatise *Paper Against Gold*, which sold more than 100,000 copies.[56]

In *Paper Against Gold*, Cobbett dealt with two outstanding financial problems, "paper money" and the national debt, which in 1815 stood at the then colossal total of £902,000,000. The national debt had begun with the founding of the Bank of England in 1694 as a device to raise credit for the wars of William III, and it owed its enormous growth to government expenditure during the war against the American colonies and the "anti-Jacobin war" against the French Republic. The necessity for paying the interest on this debt, which in 1815 amounted to £30,458,000, had imposed a tremendous tax burden, which was moved down the social scale when the repeal of the income tax in 1816 was compensated for by new taxes on commodities. It was calculated that a laborer earning 10 shillings a week paid half of his earnings in these taxes. Thus, Cobbett argued, a large group of financial parasites—"the omnium-eaters; all the innumerable swarm of locusts, who, without stirring ten miles from the capital, devour three-fourths of the produce of the whole land"—were living on the backs of the people.[57]

In addition to this burden, the government introduced inflationary measures after the Bank of England went off the gold standard in 1797. By 1809, inflation had reached a point sufficiently alarming for David Ricardo to call attention to it in the columns of the *Morning Chronicle*.[58] As a result, a "Bullion Committee" was appointed, which recommended a return to the gold standard. Numerous pamphleteers, parliamentary debaters, and editorial writers supported the recommendation, but not until 1821 was it carried into effect.

Of these two issues—paper money and "the debt"—the former was respectable, the latter was not. The very gentlemen who feared that their business would suffer if too great a depreciation of the currency took place —and hence were opposed to "paper money"—were alarmed lest their holdings in the debt should be lost. Cobbett, however, was troubled by no such scruples. He not only attacked the debt but argued that it was responsible for "paper money": the depreciation of the currency had resulted from the Bank of England's inability to pay the interest on the debt in gold. The only way to solve the paper money problem was to solve the debt problem—a conclusion the orthodox economists denied.

On most of these points Shelley follows Cobbett, but with differences.[59] Although the national debt might have begun in the days of William III, it received its great increases in the reactionary wars against America and France: "The national debt was chiefly contracted in two liberticide wars, undertaken by the privileged classes of the country—the first for the ineffectual purpose of tyrannizing over one portion of their subjects, the second, in order to extinguish the resolute spirit of obtaining their rights, in another."[60] The debt created a group of parasitical fundholders, who constituted a "second aristocracy." Partly under the influence of Hume's *Essay on Public Credit* as well as of Cobbett's "omnium-eaters," Shelley develops the concept of a "second aristocracy":[61]

> Instead of one aristocracy, the condition [to] which, in the present state of affairs, the friends of justice and liberty are willing to subscribe as to an inevitable evil, they have supplied us with two aristocracies. The one, consisting [of] great land proprietors, and merchants who receive and interchange the produce of this country with the produce of other countries . . . The other is an aristocracy of attornies and excisemen and directors and government pensioners, usurers, stock jobbers, country bankers, with their dependents and descendants. These are a set of pelting wretches in whose employment there is nothing to exercise, even to their distortion, the more majestic faculties of the soul.[62]

The national debt, he points out, is not really a *national* debt at all, but a debt that one section of the upper classes owes to another section:

> The fact is that the national debt is not a debt contracted by the whole nation towards a portion of it, but a debt contracted by the whole mass of the privileged classes towards one particular portion of those classes . . . The payment of the principal of what is called the national debt, which it is pretended is so difficult a problem, is only difficult to those who do not see who is the creditor, and who the debtor, and who the wretched sufferers from whom they both wring the taxes which under the form of interest is given by the [latter] and accepted by the [former].[63]

It is in arguments such as this that Shelley's value as an independent radical observer is most apparent. It was precisely the obvious fact that the national debt was a class debt that the government and orthodox economists wished to obscure; in obscuring it, they distorted the framework within which their technical arguments were offered.

The concept of the two aristocracies next leads Shelley to a distinction between two kinds of property, that which is acquired by labor, either manual or intellectual, and that which comes from financial manipulation:

> When I speak of persons of property I mean not every man who possesses any property; I mean the rich. Every man whose scope in society has a plebeian and intelligible utility, whose personal exertions are more valuable to him than his capital; every tradesman who is not a monopolist, all surgeons and physicians

> and those mechanics and editors and literary men and artists, and farmers, all those persons whose profits spring from honourably and honestly exerting their own skill and wisdom or strength in greater abundance than from the employment of money to take advantage of the necessity of the starvation of their fellow-citizens for their profit, are those who pay, as well as those more obviously understood by the labouring classes, the interest of the national debt.[64]

He supports, here and elsewhere, as he had in the Notes to *Queen Mab,* a pre-Marxist and somewhat Ricardian labor theory of value: "The labour which this money represents . . . would, if properly employed, have covered our land with monuments of architecture exceeding the sumptuousness and the beauty of Egypt and Athens . . . But the labour which is expressed by these sums has been diverted from these purposes of human happiness to the promotion of slavery, or the attempt at dominion."[65]

He switches rather suddenly from the national debt to paper money, silently accepting Cobbett's explanation that it was the debt which had forced the government off the gold standard. He denies the claim of government apologists that inflation is a sign of national prosperity, declaring (again with Cobbett) that inflation cheats those who own gold, silver, or goods, all of which exchange for less than their value in an inflated paper currency. (Shelley's "county" bias against city speculators is obvious.) He argues that inflation places added burdens on the working class because of the lower purchasing power of paper money wages and the rise in prices caused by the abandoning of the gold standard: "Since the institution of this double aristocracy, however, they have often worked not ten but twenty hours a day. Not that all the poor have rigidly worked twenty hours, but that the worth of the labour of twenty hours now, in food and clothing, is equivalent to the worth of ten hours then." And again: "One of the vaunted effects of this system is to increase the national industry. That is, to increase the labours of the poor and those luxuries of the rich which they supply. To make a manufacturer work 16 hours where he only worked 8. To turn children into lifeless and bloodless machines at an age when otherwise they would be at play before the cottage doors of their parents."[66]

Shelley agreed with Cobbett that the solution to this situation had to lie with the national debt, and that a return to the gold standard of itself would accomplish little, but he disagreed with Cobbett in the nature of the solution to be offered. Cobbett, in the end, advocated nothing more drastic than a reduction of the interest rate or, in more angry moods, the abolition of interest. Shelley argued that this did not go to the root of the problem because it left the principal of the debt untouched. Carrying out his view that the debt was an exploitive mechanism created by "the privileged classes," he advocated that the members of these classes pool the debt between them, that is, simply abolish the debt: "It would be a mere transfer among persons of property. Such a gentleman must lose a third of his estate, such a citizen a fourth of his money in the funds; the persons who borrowed would have paid, and the juggling and complicated system of paper finance be at an end."[67] Ricardo had proposed a similar extreme solution about six months previously, although so far as is known, Shelley in Italy was unaware of it.[68]

Shelley places so much emphasis on the national debt, devoting almost a whole chapter to it, because he believed that the debt was at the root of the grossest forms of exploitation and injustice:

—That the majority [of the people of England] are destitute and miserable, ill-clothed, ill-fed, ill-educated.
—That they know this, and that they are impatient to procure a reform of the cause of their abject and wretched state.
—That the cause of this peculiar misery is the unequal distribution which, under the form of the national debt, has been surreptitiously made of the products of their labour and the products of the labour of their ancestors; for all property is the produce of labour.
—That the cause of that cause is a defect in the government.[69]

Shelley's point of view in his arguments against the national debt and paper money is essentially humanitarian. No doubt both the debt and paper money were important stimulants to business at a time when the industrial revolution was first getting into high gear. They forshadowed future capitalist economic policies. Their abolition was, in fact, impossible. They could have been abolished only by the abolition of the economy on which they were based, and that economy was on the upswing. It was to dominate the whole century, although neither Shelley nor Cobbett nor anyone else at that time realized this. Shelley, in any case, was not interested in business profits but in the human suffering that the system caused. He was thinking of the lifeless children in the textile factories and not the prosperity of the textile manufacturers.

Having thus completed his examination of the existing situation and argued that the only immediate palliative lay in parliamentary reform, Shelley next discusses reform, presenting his own reform platform:

We would abolish the national debt.
We would disband the standing army.
We would, with every possible regard to the existing interests of the holders, abolish sinecures.
We would, with every possible regard to the existing interests of the holders, abolish tithes, and make all religions, all forms of opinion respecting the origin and government of the Universe, equal in the eye of the law.
We would make justice cheap, certain and speedy, and extend the institution of juries to every possible occasion of jurisprudence.[70]

With this program it is interesting to compare Cobbett's reform plan given in the *Political Register* for October 12, 1816. Cobbett lists ten points: abolition of the "profligacy, bribery, and perjury of elections"; the merit system for all government services; abolition of all pensions and sinecures not granted for public services; reduction of salaries of those "in public employ"; extension of the merit system to the army and navy; abolition of the system of government spies for domestic purposes; reform of the bar; a free press, with "the hireling crew of editors and authors" removed; reform of the civil lists and crown lands; and cessation of interest payments on the national debt to those undeserving of them. Shelley's plan, while more detailed than, say, Sir Francis Burdett's or anything put forward in *The Examiner*, is less detailed than Cobbett's, who was in daily contact with the problems of the reform movement.

Shelley's second point, abolition of the standing army, was unusual in the reform movement, for although Burdett and *The Examiner* insistently pointed out the evils of the military system, they—like Cobbett and Bentham—advocated only its reform. Shelley's special hatred of the army was perhaps owing to its use as a domestic force, notably against the Luddites.[71]

The third point, the abolition of sinecures, was a commonplace of reform agitation, stemming back at least to the Whig "corruption" debates of the late eighteenth century. Cobbett and Henry Hunt took particular delight in publicizing lists of sinecure holders, but Burdett and Cochrane (the "moderates") discussed them also.[72]

The abolition of tithes was not a prominent part of reform agitation and apparently was first brought in by Cobbett, who directed his *Political Register* largely toward farming communities, where tithes were a special burden.[73] Shelley, as the heir to a great country estate, had particular interest in this question.

The making of all religions equal in "the eye of the law" is a renewal of Shelley's old plea for Catholic emancipation, a cause supported by the Foxite Whigs and the Duke of Norfolk.[74] Among the reformers it was pursued with some vigor by Burdett—whose trip to Ireland in 1817 turned into a triumphal procession—but it was not taken up by Cobbett until 1824.[75]

The sanctioning of "all forms of opinion respecting the origin and government of the Universe" was not a demand of the reform movement at all. It perhaps harkens back to Paine's arguments for the toleration of freethinking, a cause that was most conspicuously championed in Shelley's day by Richard Carlile and his *Republican*.

Shelley's final point, on juries, may go back to his reading of *Political Justice*, where its eloquent treatment had perhaps inspired his little essay *A System of Government by Juries*. His plan for making "justice cheap, certain and speedy" is along the same lines as Cobbett's advocacy of the reform of the bar.

All these objectives, however, were subordinate to the basic one, namely, the extension of the franchise. Shelley in 1817 had supported the moderates on this question, urging the vote only for propertied taxpayers. Now, in 1819, he feared that the time had passed when such gradual reform was a practical possibility, and he was prepared to risk the consequences of too swift a transition to full suffrage:

> Two years ago it might still have been possible to have commenced a system of gradual reform. The people were then insulted, tempted and betrayed, and *the petitions of a million* of men rejected with disdain. Now they are more miserable, more hopeless, more impatient of their misery . . . It is possible that the period of conciliation is past, and that after having played with the confidence and cheated the expectations of the people, their passions will be too little under discipline to allow them to wait the slow, gradual and certain operation of such a Reform as we can imagine the constituted authorities to concede.

If this was really the case, there was no other course open but to support the radical reformers: "If the Houses of Parliament obstinately and perpetually refuse to concede any reform to the people, my vote is for universal suffrage and equal representation" (the abolition of the rotten borough system through the granting of franchise rights on a density of population basis —a point stressed by Cobbett and other radical reformers).[76]

In considering radical reform, Shelley does not agree with Cartwright, Cobbett, and Bentham in their advocacy of the secret ballot, but repeats Godwin's arguments in *Political Justice* that it tends to build a secretive character. "The elector and the elected," Shelley maintained, "ought to meet one another face to face . . . There ought to be the common sympathy of the excitements of a popular assembly among the electors themselves."[77] Shelley's opinion that democracy must be grass-roots and give-and-take if it was to be real democracy was apparently behind his argument. He evidently did not realize the degree to which discrimination would be practiced in open voting.

It is not always sufficiently stressed that in the conflicts between radicals and moderates on the extent of the franchise, only male suffrage was being discussed. Even Cobbett declared that to propose votes for women would render the cause of reform "ridiculous." Only Bentham, a newcomer in the reform ranks, advocated women's suffrage. Although Shelley's sympathies were with Bentham, he felt that women's suffrage might be impractical as a plank in the immediate platform: "Mr. Bentham and other writers have urged the admission of females to the right of suffrage; this attempt seems somewhat immature.—Should my opinion be the result of despondency, the writer of these pages would be the last to withhold his vote from any system, which might tend to an equal and full development of the capacities of all living beings."[78] Shelley's "despondency" arose not from his attitude toward women—for he was a strong feminist—but from his realization of the extent of antifeminist prejudice in the society of his day. To advocate so extreme a measure as the vote for women in a reform platform in 1819 might jeopardize the whole platform. It was, in fact, not until 1928 that women in Great Britain were granted suffrage on the same basis as men.

A major problem confronting the reform movement, as Shelley seemed to realize more clearly than most reform leaders, was the multifaceted opposition of the Establishment: "My vote is—but, it is asked, how shall this be accomplished, in defiance of and in opposition to the constituted authorities of the Nation, they who possess whether with or without its consent the command of a standing army and of a legion of spies and police officers, and hold all the strings of that complicated mechanism with which the hopes and fears of men are moved like puppets." Shelley's statement here, brief though it is, represents a most advanced concept for the time regarding the oppressive aspects of the state—its use of force, of espionage, and by implication, of the press, Parliament, and pulpit. As a persecuted ex-member of the ruling class, he had no illusions about either its ruthlessness or its competence. Furthermore, he had none of the unspoken deference toward it that clouded the attitudes of some reformers.

On the key problem of how actually to achieve reform, Shelley urges first and foremost, as he had in 1817, that the reformers unite their ranks and forget their internal quarrels: "The true patriot ... will endeavor to rally round one standard the divided friends of liberty, and make them forget the subordinate objects with regard to which they differ by appealing to that respecting which they are all agreed." However much Shelley suspected the motives behind Tory flag-waving, he is not willing to surrender nationalistic or patriotic appeal into their hands. The "true patriot" is he who really has the interests of the nation at heart, and the interests of the nation are those of the majority of its inhabitants. Shelley wished to convert the reform movement into a national crusade against the two aristocracies. Such a movement must be legal and open in character and shun "secret organizations"—apparently a reference to the "Spenceans." It was to be built by a nationwide campaign embracing everything from what is known today as mass "civil disobedience" to defiance of the courts and petitioning:

All questions relating to the jurisdiction of magistrates and courts of law respecting which any doubt could be raised ought to be agitated with indefatigable pertinacity. Some two or three of the popular leaders have shown the best spirit in this respect; they only want system and co-operation. The tax-gatherer ought to be compelled in every practicable instance to distrain, whilst the right to impose taxes, as was the case in the beginning of the resistance to the tyranny of Charles the 1st is formally contested by an overwhelming multitude of defendants before the courts of common law. Confound the subtlety of lawyers with the subtlety of the law. All of the nation would thus be excited to develop itself, and to declare whether it acquiesced in the existing forms of government . . . Simultaneously with this active and vigilant system of opposition, means ought to be taken of solemnly conveying the sense of large bodies and various denominations of the people in a manner the most explicit to the existing depositaries of power. Petitions, couched in the actual language of the petitioners, and emanating from distinct assemblies, ought to load the tables of the House of Commons.[79]

The general method that Shelley here advocates is an extension to the national scene and national movement of techniques employed by the radical reformers on specific issues, namely, the organization of social protests centered on the House of Commons, a method that Cobbett employed with conspicuous success in the Queen Caroline affair and which was later used by the Chartists. The "two or three popular leaders" whom Shelley had in mind as battling against legal injustice were William Hone, Thomas Jonathan Wooler (both of whom had been tried for seditious libel in 1817), and Henry Hunt. Shelley had made a contribution to Hone's defense fund and on Hunt's conduct following the Manchester Massacre he commented: "H. Hunt has behaved, I think, with great spirit and coolness in the whole affair."[80] The suggestion of having a monster petition campaign "to load the tables of the House of Commons" was also "radical" in origin, being identified especially with Major Cartwright, who carried out such campaigns indefatigably. Byron had presented one of his petitions to the House of Lords in 1813.

This movement Shelley hoped would be nonviolent. Whether it was would depend not so much on the people as on the nature of the opposition to them, particularly that of the armed forces: "From the moment that a man is a soldier, he becomes a slave. He is taught obedience; his will is no longer, which is the most sacred prerogative of man, guided by his own judgement. He is taught to despise human life and human suffering."[81] Shelley, in anticipation of Gandhi, urged the people to use massive, passive resistance, arguing that if they fought or ran, the soldiers would, in natural response to their training, attack them, as at Manchester: "But the soldier is a man and an Englishman. This unexpected reception would probably throw him back upon a recollection of the true nature of the measures of which he was made the instrument, and the enemy might be converted into the ally." Shelley was opposed to revolution not only on humanitarian grounds but also because of the political risks of failure:

A Republic, however just in its principle and glorious in its object, would through violence and sudden change which must attend it, incur a great risk of being as rapid in its decline as in its growth. It is better that they should be instructed in the whole truth; that they should see the clear grounds of their rights, the objects to which they ought to tend; and be impressed with the just persuasion that patience and reason and endurance [are the means of] a calm yet irresistible progress. A civil war, which might be engendered by the passions attending on this mode of reform, would confirm in the mass of the nation those military habits which have been already introduced by our tyrants, and with which liberty is incompatible.[82]

His reasoning on this point (which underlies the message of *Prometheus Unbound*) derives from his view of the French Revolution:

If there had never been war, there could never have been tyranny in the world; tyrants take advantage of the mechanical organization of armies to establish and defend their encroachments. It is thus that the mighty advantages of the French

Revolution have been almost compensated by a succession of tyrants (for demagogues, oligarchies, usurpers and legitimate kings are merely varieties of the same class) from Robespierre to Louis 18. War, waged from whatever motive, extinguishes the sentiment of reason and justice in the mind.[83]

With political change, revolutionary armies can become the tool of tyranny and be used to defend despotic regimes. This danger was inherent in all revolutions.

"Shelley," wrote Mary Shelley, "loved the people . . . He believed that a clash between the two classes of society was inevitable, and he eagerly ranged himself on the people's side."[84] He did so, moreover, without illusions about the nature of either the "clash" or the "people": "The savage brutality of the populace is proportioned to the arbitrary character of their government . . . They eat less bread, wear worse clothes, are more ignorant, immoral, miserable, and desperate. This then is the condition of the lowest and largest class, from whose labour the whole materials of life are wrought, of which the others are only the receivers or the consumers."[85]

This vast mass of men and women, huddled in their gray slums, rendered desperate and brutal by the new industrial exploitation, roused in Shelley both sympathy and fear; and although the sympathy was deeper, the fear—especially fear of militaristic response if the people turned to violent action—was never far behind. Hence, his hesitancies on revolution and his stress on the (superficial) similarity of the use of force in the efforts of Robespierre to set up a middle class republic and in those of Napoleon to establish a military dictatorship.

Yet Shelley had no hope that either of the two upper classes—commercial or aristocratic—could bring about a higher order of society: "All monopolies are bad. I do not however when condemning commercial aggrandizement think it in the least necessary to panegyrize hereditary accumulation—Both are flagrant encroachments on liberty, neither can be used as an antidote for the poison of the other."[86] Thus, hating both the ruling aristocracy and the new capitalists who aspired to supersede them, fearing the people and yet passionately sympathetic with their aims, Shelley had only one path to follow: he placed his faith in the alliance of the people with middle or upper class reformers, liberals, and advanced intellectuals. Unless these men and women took the lead and moved the people into constructive action and away from "the paths of blood," violence would break out, and violence might lead, as it had in France, to renewing and even strengthening the existing oligarchy: "the change should commence among the higher orders or anarchy will only be the last flash before despotism."[87] Later in his pamphlet he named Godwin, Hazlitt, Bentham, and Leigh Hunt as representative of the intellectuals he had in mind, but he would doubtless also have included Sir Francis Burdett, Henry Brougham, Lord Grey, Francis Place, Cobbett, Owen, and others to whom he had sent his *Proposal for Putting Reform to the Vote*. Shelley probably had not given up hope that in a showdown some of the more advanced Whigs would join with the people. Who would join and who would not he doubtless expected to be brought out in the course of his national civil disobedience and petition campaign. It was this desire for a union of the radicals and liberals (the "higher orders") with the people that was at the root of Shelley's emphasis on unity in the reform movement.

But Shelley had to face the prospect that this campaign would either never get underway or prove inadequate. Either the people or their rulers might at some point precipitate a revolution. What was to be done then? Much as he hated violence, Shelley did not hesitate in his reply: "The last resort of resistance is undoubtedly insurrection.—The right of insurrection is derived from the employment of armed force to counteract the will of the nation. Let the government disband the standing army, and the purpose of resistance would be sufficiently fulfilled by the incessant agitation of the points of dispute before the courts of common law, and by an unwarlike display of the irresistible number and union of the people."[88]

A revolution would mean "the abolition of monarchy and aristocracy," of "a House of Lords and a bench of Bishops." It would thus result in the establishment of a democratic republic on the American model. It might even pass beyond these bounds into "the levelling of inordinate wealth, and an agrarian distribution, including the Parks and Chases of the rich, of the uncultivated districts of the country," as advocated by Thomas Spence.[89]

Some of this revolutionary projection was designed, it is true, merely to warn the ruling class that unless they gave reform, revolution was the alternative, but Shelley was nevertheless serious in his profession of support for a revolution if it broke out: "insurrection" was a "right." Though he feared the people, he feared their rulers more, as he showed also in *The Masque of Anarchy*. His embittering experiences with poverty and social ostracism had given him a deeper feeling of kinship with the people—the "many"—and a deeper hatred of the upper classes than is found in Hunt, Hazlitt, or Byron. The austerity of a Grey or a Burdett toward the people had no counterpart in Shelley.[90] Hence, while most intellectual or upper class reformers established an uneasy relationship with the new industrialists or liberal aristocrats, Shelley urged a popular alliance. That the people, if left to themselves, could set up a lasting liberal republic he doubted; but he doubted also that the intellectuals or professionals alone could establish it or, for that matter, could achieve parliamentary reform. On the one hand, the industrial working class was only beginning to abandon such primitive forms of struggle as machine wrecking and to move toward trade unionism and politics. The farmers, in spite of their political interests—on which Cobbett largely relied—were unable to achieve coordination in plan or action. There was, therefore, in these years from 1815 to about 1820 little possibility of advanced political change coming from the people alone; and without them, the intellectuals had no mass leverage.

On the other hand, there is no doubt that Shelley exaggerated the dangers inherent in revolution, especially his fears about "anarchy" resulting from the extension of the franchise on a nonproperty basis, and that Bentham was right in ridiculing such fears as Tory bogey men. The full extension of the franchise would have alleviated, not aggravated the situation. If Shelley had had day-to-day experience in the reform movement, he would have realized this; deeply humanitarian as he was, he would have lost his fear of the people by working beside them, as did Cobbett or Henry Hunt. Had he remained in England, he might well have done so. As *The Masque of Anarchy* indicates, he could hardly have resisted joining in the anti-Manchester Massacre demonstrations of 1819, and he would certainly have been active in the cause of Greek independence. Not that Shelley would have become a professional reformer, for he was already set in his career as a poet. But he would have become, even more than he did, the poet of the people and perhaps, in time an Owenite socialist.

If Shelley falls below Cobbett and other radical reformers in some regards, he towers above them in others. The reformers pursued their objectives, such as extension of the franchise or abolition of the rotten boroughs, with houndlike persistence. But these were for them the be-all and the end-all. Even Cobbett wished to retain the House of Lords and the monarchy, his ultimate ideal being really a return to the past—the (fictional) merrie England of guilds and yeomen. Leigh Hunt would have been content with the existing order if the middle class had the vote and the army stopped flogging soldiers. The reformers, that is, even the intellectual ones, had no such ultimate goal as did Shelley:

> Equality in possessions must be the last result of the utmost refinements of civilization; it is one of the conditions of that system of society, towards which with whatever hope of ultimate success, it is our duty to tend. We may and ought to advert to it as to the elementary principle, as to the goal, unattainable, perhaps, by us, but which, as it were, we revive in our posterity to pursue. We derive tranquility and courage and grandeur of soul from contemplating an object which is, because we will it, and may be, because we hope and desire it, and must be if succeeding generations of the enlightened sincerely and earnestly seek it.
>
> But our present business is with the difficult and unbending realities of actual life, and when we have drawn inspiration from the great object of our hopes it becomes us with patience and resolution to apply ourselves to accommodating our theories to immediate practice.

Strong though the passage is, Shelley is in it actually making a less positive statement than his full convictions required. As he had written in his *Essay on Christianity*: "Jesus Christ did what every other reformer who had produced any considerable effect upon the world has done. He accommodated his doctrines to the prepossessions of those whom he addressed . . . All reformers have been compelled to practice this misrepresentation of their own true feelings and opinions."[91] Although one had to accommodate one's "theories" to "immediate practice," one was not to deny the theories; it was simply not always practical to develop their full implications.

Shelley was well aware that egalitarianism was a dangerous topic, one likely to alienate some of the liberal readers to whom he was addressing his tract. That he believed an egalitarian society would eventually be realized is clear from *Queen Mab* (1813) and *Prometheus Unbound* (1819), but he prefers here to treat it rather as an ideal to inspire than a goal decreed by necessity. His phrasing is deliberately neutral: "with whatever hope"; "Unattainable, perhaps, by us." He does not state either that there is no "hope" or great "hope." It "must," however, come about "if succeeding generations" fight for it. Shelley had little doubt that they would. It is this egalitarian society that he had in mind when he wrote to Leigh Hunt: "The system of society as it exists at present must be overthrown from the foundations with all its superstructure of maxims & of forms before we shall find anything but disappointment in our intercourse with any but a few select spirits."[92] The "foundations" of society, as Shelley was well aware, included economic inequality with its consequent poverty and injustice. Only when these and other barriers were removed could true cultural enlightenment spread to humanity as a whole.

The reformers, and even Byron, as *Julian and Maddalo* shows, were, Shelley believed, encircled by the shell of the past. They accepted a society based on inequality and wished to do little more than patch it up. In doing so, they accepted the fact that humanity's potential was never to be realized, that there would always be the "few" and the "many," that war, poverty, and oppression would forever be part of the human condition.

At the same time, Shelley did not get lost in his vision of the future. That future could only be realized by work in the present; one must turn to the "unbending realities of actual life." The essence of his position on this matter he put in a letter to Hunt in November 1819:

> I fear that in England things will be carried violently by the rulers, and that they will not have learned to yield in time to the spirit of the age. The great thing to do is to hold the balance between popular impatience and tyrannical obstinacy; to inculcate with fervour both the right of resistance and the duty of forbearance. You know my principles incite me to take all the good I can get in politics, for ever aspiring to something more. I am one of those whom nothing will fully satisfy, but who am ready to be partially satisfied by all that is practicable.[93]

If "all that is practicable" meant "moderate reform," Shelley would fight for that but aim at "radical reform"; if "radical reform" became "practicable" at some point, he would fight for that but aim at a democratic republic. At each step he would have the next step in mind and be sustained throughout by his vision of the ultimate Godwinian egalitarian order.

This combination of the ultimate with the immediate permeates Shelley's social thinking. In Ireland in 1812 he had advocated building a large general organization around the issues of Catholic emancipation and the repeal of the Union Act, with a smaller group of "philanthropists" giving it guidance and focusing its ultimate sights on an egalitarian republic. In *Queen Mab* he had depicted the egalitarian society and stated that it was to be achieved by "the gradual paths of an aspiring change."[94] A similar dual emphasis on the present and the future appears in his public letter on the Eaton case.

In 1817 his friendship with Hunt had brought him into contact with the reform movement. *A Proposal for Putting Reform to the Vote* was a "moderate" reform pamphlet of *The Examiner* type. Though it did not bring out his ultimate republican and egalitarian goals, he had not given them up, as *The Revolt of Islam,* written a few months later, adequately demonstrated. He simply did not wish in this tract to alienate reform readers. In examining any particular work by Shelley, one must take into account its purpose and the audience for which it was written.

A Philosophical View of Reform is wider in scope and appeal than the *Proposal for Putting Reform to the Vote.* The *Proposal* was on a specific topic; the *Philosophical View* is a general statement of reform policies. Nevertheless, it is a reform tract, not primarily an examination of history or economic theory, and if these matters were to be discussed—and Shelley obviously thought it important to discuss them in order to set the reform movement and its ideas in perspective—they had to be discussed as background. Shelley unfortunately never wrote a work in which he concentrated primarily on his general social theories. He did, however, succeed in working them into the fabric of his tract, and in so doing, he gave it a scope beyond that of any other reform tract, even Bentham's. He placed the present in the perspectives of history, and history in the perspectives of the future. He neither bogged down in the details of the movement nor, as did Godwin, become so immersed in general concepts as to forget specifics. It is this combination of the general and the particular, of vision and practicality, that makes *A Philosophical View of Reform* the most advanced work of political theory of the age.

This may seem a strange claim to make for Shelley, who was primarily a poet, not a political philosopher. But he was also a man of genius, writing, like Dante, in the sharp air of persecution and exile. Certainly among the political writers of the period there is no one who even approached him either for his sharp insights into the present or his vision of the future. His view that reform would come in stages, with the granting first of limited suffrage, was proved correct by subsequent events: limited suffrage was granted by the Reform Bills of 1832 and 1867, and under popular pressure the franchise was gradually extended by a series of acts, until with the passage of women's suffrage in 1928 the long battle for English parliamentary reform that had begun in the middle of the eighteenth century with Wilkes was finally brought to an end. Shelley's conviction that new social turmoil would bring about social change never before seen is being borne out in the present century. And although the Godwinian concept of private property egalitarianism has long gone by the boards, other aspects of Shelley's ultimate society are being realized or are within reach in various parts of the globe.

4

Philosophy, Religion, and Ethics

Speculations on Metaphysics. On Life. Essay on Christianity. On the Devil and Devils. Speculations on Morals. On Love. A Discourse on the Manners of the Antient Greeks. The Assassins. The Coliseum. Una Favola

Shelley was—like Lucretius or Goethe—primarily a poet of ideas, ranging widely into social thought, philosophy, science, and ethics. His greatest poetry combines ideas from all four. Unfortunately he wrote no later prose works embodying his views on science, which underlie much of *Prometheus Unbound,* and on philosophy and ethics he wrote only short or fragmentary pieces. He also wrote essays on religious topics and made some attempts at fiction.[1]

The British Empiricists

The general ideas of philosophy as Shelley knew them fall mainly into four groups: materialist, idealist, dualist, and skeptic. Materialists, such as Lucretius or Holbach, argue that the universe is a material entity, consisting of matter in various forms—solid, liquid, gaseous—and having qualities such as motion and energy inherent within it. It was not "created" but has existed from all time. The human mind is only another manifestation of matter. It follows that there is no God, either as creator or as a force within the universe. The idealist view falls into two main streams, the Platonic and the Berkeleian, although both, in fact, had early origins in Asia. According to the Platonists, there is both matter and God, but the world of matter is an imperfect shadow of the mind of God, the One, which has as its attributes the Good, the True, and the Beautiful. Berkeley simplified this concept by asserting that the world *is* the mind of God, that what looks like matter is, in fact, a spiritual substance. The dualists, such as Locke, argue that both mind and matter exist and are different entities, each subject to its own laws of action. The external world is simply a world of shapes and solidity; the mind supplies it with colors, sounds, and so on. The skeptics, such as Hume, argue that all one can know are sensations. There may be an external world, there may be a God, there may be mind, or there may be none of them.

The earliest influences on Shelley's philosophy came from Locke, Hume, Godwin, and Holbach. At Oxford he had accepted the proposition from Locke that the mind is a blank tablet at birth and all ideas come from the senses. He also accepted Locke's dualistic concept of an external world of matter clothed by the mind with color and sound. From the first of these propositions he derived the argument, put forward in *The Necessity of Atheism*, that the idea of God cannot be a divine implantation but must come from the senses. Hence the existence of God is a matter for reasoned argument, not merely acceptance as an article of "faith" (with the corollary that a lack of acceptance implies "sin").

The Necessity of Atheism also presents two propositions from Hume: it is more likely that those reporting miracles lied than that the miracles took place; and if God created the world, who created God (and so on in an infinite regress of creating and created Gods)? In the *Queen Mab* Note on necessity Hume's arguments on causality are used against the existence of a deity: if we know only sequence and not cause, then we do not know that there was a First Cause. Shelley did not at this time, however, accept Hume's skeptical epistemological views, as he told his friend Hogg: "I have examined Hume's reasonings with respect to the non-existence of external things, & I confess, they appear to me to follow from the doctrines of Locke. What am I to think of a philosophy which conducts to such a conclusion?"[2] From Godwin, first read in 1809 at Eton, came the idea of necessity: both mind and matter operate by inexorable laws, inherent in their nature, to produce an inevitable chain of events in the universe and in society. But Shelley disagreed with Godwin's idealistic concepts that mind was a unique entity, quite different from matter, was always active, even in sleep, and was the source of motion.[3] On the contrary, he agreed with Holbach that mind was similar to certain manifestations of matter, such as electricity, and that motion was inherent in the nature of matter. Holbach also strengthened his concept of necessity.

At Keswick in 1812 Robert Southey introduced Shelley to Berkeley's subjective idealism—the universe *is* the mind of God; there is no mind-matter dilemma, for all is mind—and Shelley rejected it: "I have read Berkeley, and the perusal of his arguments tended more than anything to convince me that immaterialism & other words of general usage deriving all their force from mere *predictates* in *non* were invented by the pride of philosophers to conceal their ignorance even from themselves."[4]

Later, however, according to Mary Shelley, he became a "disciple of the Immaterial Philosophy of Berkeley. This theory gave unity and grandeur to his ideas, while it opened a wide field for his imagination."[5] Shelley had perhaps discussed these matters with Mary, but it seems more likely that she was basing her views on an interpretation of his essay *On Life*. She may have been echoing the phrasing of that essay, and by the time of its composition (1819–1820), Shelley seems to have been discussing his works very little with her. Few critics have gone so far as to consider Shelley a Berkeleian, but some have argued that he was an immaterialist. More have contended that he became a Platonist, others a Neoplatonist. In recent years the "Platonist" tide has begun to turn, and the emphasis has been placed on the British empiricists, especially Hume.

Shelley's later views on mind, matter, and perception—his epistemology

—were expressed primarily in two works, the short essay *On Life* and the first fragment of *Speculations on Metaphysics*.[6] *On Life* also contains his repudiation of "materialism." In 1814, following the publication of *Queen Mab*, Shelley had advanced a materialist position in *A Refutation of Deism*:

> The greatest, equally with the smallest motions of the Universe, are subjected to the rigid necessity of inevitable laws. These laws are the unknown causes of the known effects perceivable in the Universe. Their effects are the boundaries of our knowledge, their names the expressions of our ignorance.
>
> To assert that God is intelligent, is to assert that he has ideas; and Locke has proved that ideas result from sensation. Sensation can exist only in an organized body, an organized body is necessarily limited both in extent and operation. The God of the rational Theosophist is a vast and wise animal.
>
> Mind cannot create, it can only perceive. Mind is the recipient of impressions made on the organs of sense, and without the action of external objects we should not only be deprived of all knowledge of the existence of mind, but totally incapable of the knowledge of any thing. It is evident therefore that mind deserves to be considered as the effect, rather than the cause of motion.[7]

Shelley here presumes four entities: a material universe, a biological body, sensation, and mind. The material universe is controlled by natural laws that can be investigated by science but whose fundamental nature is unknown. Sensation arises from the interaction of biological body and universal matter and provides the material for thought. Mind is not basically creative but works with what is provided for it by the senses. It can, of course, create new combinations from this sense data—as in poetry or art—but it does not create the sense data. In the mind-matter relationship, matter is primary. Mind is perhaps a form of material motion. Without matter, mind would not be aware of its own existence. If there is any divine mind or God, it too must have a similar nature and be dependent on sensation, body, and the material universe; hence, by implication, there is no divine mind.

The repudiation passage in *On Life* (1819–1820), runs as follows:

> I confess that I am one of those who am unable to refuse my assent to the conclusions of those philosophers who assert that nothing exists but as it is perceived.
>
> It is a decision against which all our persuasions struggle, and we must be long convicted before we can be convinced that the solid universe of external things is "such stuff as dreams are made of." The shocking absurdities of the popular philosophy of mind and matter, its fatal consequences in morals, and their violent dogmatism concerning the source of all things, had early conducted me to materialism. This materialism is a seducing system to young and superficial minds. It allows its disciples to talk, and dispenses them from thinking. But I was discontented with such a view of things as it afforded; man is a being of high aspirations, "looking both before and after," whose "thoughts wander through eternity," disclaiming alliance with transience and decay; incapable of imagining to himself annihilation; existing but in the future and the past; being, not what he is, but

> what he has been and shall be. Whatever may be his true and final destination, there is a spirit within him at enmity with nothingness and dissolution. This is the character of all life and being. Each is at once the centre and the circumference; the point to which all things are referred, and the line in which all things are contained. Such contemplations as these, materialism and the popular philosophy of mind and matter alike forbid; they are only consistent with the intellectual system.[8]

Although the statement that "the solid universe of things is 'such stuff as dreams are made of' " gives the impression that Shelley is advocating immaterialism, a comparison with other passages shows that he is really advancing a skeptical position. He is not denying the existence of an external universe, but is arguing only that whatever is known is known only through the senses, and the senses disclose nothing more than sensation. Knowledge is knowledge of thought substance only. Some sensations or thoughts are stronger than others. Although the stronger ones are presumed to have an origin in "external objects," all we actually know is that they are stronger:

> Thoughts, or ideas, or notions, call them what you will, differ from each other, not in kind, but in force. It has commonly been supposed that those distinct thoughts which affect a number of persons, at regular intervals, during the passage of a multitude of other thoughts, which are called *real*, or *external objects*, are totally different in kind from those which affect only a few persons, and which recur at irregular intervals, and are usually more obscure and indistinct, such as hallucinations, dreams, and the ideas of madness . . . A specific difference between every thought of the mind, is, indeed, a necessary consequence of that law by which it perceives diversity and number; but a generic or essential difference is wholly arbitrary.[9]

Those who have argued that Shelley became an immaterialist have usually argued also that he abandoned his beliefs in an ordered universe, in science, and in rational logic, substituting for them God, intuition, and mysticism. But that this cannot be so is apparent even in *On Life:*

> The relations of things remain unchanged, by whatever system. By the word things is to be understood any object of thought, that is, any thought upon which any other thought is employed, with an apprehension of distinction. The relations of these remain unchanged; and such is the material of our knowledge.
>
> What is the cause of life? that is, how was it produced, or what agencies distinct from life have acted or act upon life? All recorded generations of mankind have wearily busied themselves in inventing answers to this question; and the result has been,—Religion. Yet, that the basis of all things cannot be, as the popular philosophy alleges, mind, is sufficiently evident. Mind, as far as we have any experience of its properties, and beyond that experience how vain is argument! cannot create, it can only perceive. It is said also to be the cause. But cause is only a word expressing a certain state of the human mind with regard to the manner

in which two thoughts are apprehended to be related to each other. If any one desires to know how unsatisfactorily the popular philosophy employes itself upon this great question, they need only impartially reflect upon the manner in which thoughts develop themselves in their minds. It is infinitely improbable that the cause of mind, that is, of existence, is similar to mind.[10]

Shelley here seems almost to be harking back to *A Refutation of Deism*, with his attack on Christian theology ("the popular philosophy" of such theologians as Paley), his argument on the noncreativity of mind and his implication that this rules out a creative God (the divine cosmic mind). Shelley also includes his former *Necessity of Atheism* argument from Hume that causation may be simply unmotivated succession; hence, there is no First Cause (or God). Regardless of one's epistemological view, the "relations of things" remain "unchanged," a position also implied in Hume and other skeptics. Only in their specific philosophical arguments do they assert their epistemological skepticism. Usually they write and act as though they were, like the rest of us, inhabiting a universe of "things." So also in Shelley's poetry. Unless he is directly expressing his epistemological view, he writes in terms of things and thoughts. Presumably in his poems written before his repudiation of "this materialism" he actually meant things, and afterward meant only the more powerful sensations, but there is usually no way of telling. A star is a star in both cases, or a bird a bird.

Not only do the "relations of things" remain the same, but the laws of nature also remain: "By considering all knowledge as bounded by perception, whose operations may be indefinitely combined, we arrive at a conception of Nature inexpressibly more magnificent, simple and true, than accord [s with] the ordinary systems of complicated and partial consideration. Nor does a contemplation of the Universe, in this comprehensive and synthetical view, exclude the subtlest analysis of its modifications and parts."[11] If the universe is still to be analyzed in all its "modifications and parts," such analysis—as Shelley's interest in science and use of it in his poetry indicate—must be carried on by scientific investigation.

Shelley's empirical and scientific attitude holds true also for the analysis of mind itself: "Mind, so far as we have any experience of its properties, and beyond that experience how vain is argument!" Mind is not only noncreative in essence and neither a unique nor an ultimate substance, but it has to be examined and its properties determined by analysis and "experience."

The epistemological picture is further developed in another passage in *On Life*:

What follows from the admission [that "nothing exists but as it is perceived"]? It establishes no new truth, it gives us no additional insight into our hidden nature, neither its action nor itself. Philosophy, impatient as it may be to build, has much work yet remaining, as pioneer for the overgrowth of ages. It makes one step towards this object; it destroys error, and the roots of error. It leaves, what is too often the duty of the reformer in political and ethical questions to leave, a vacancy. It reduces the mind to that freedom in which it would have acted, but for the misuse of words and signs, the instruments of its own creation.[12]

Skepticism does not, of itself, contribute to knowledge, but it does clear away "error" and its "roots." Shelley is apparently referring primarily to theological concepts. If skepticism shows that all we know are our own sensations, then we cannot know whether God exists (which was one of Hume's points in his attack on Berkeley). Philosophy, if it is to move ahead, must begin with a "vacancy"—"we grow dizzy to look down the dark abyss of how little we know"—but it is better to begin with a vacancy that one can build from than to be lost in theological fantasies. Light can be thrown into the "abyss" only by philosophical investigation and the "subtlest analysis" of science. Eventually, Shelley indicates, in a future higher social order, the fundamental nature of the universe and of mankind will be known: "That there is a true solution of the riddle, and that in our present state the solution is unattainable by us are propositions which may be regarded as equally certain."[13]

Shelley implies that he was convinced of the falsity of "materialism" by the argument that "nothing exists but as it is perceived," a proposition that was basic to Berkeley and Hume alike. Berkeley used it to support his contention that "there is not any other substance than *Spirit*, or that which perceives."[14] Hume used it to support his skeptical view that all cognition can be reduced to "a bundle of perceptions." Shelley differed from Berkeley in that he did not believe in the Berkeleian all-inclusive "Spirit", and from Hume in that he posited the existence of mind. The materialist view was both "complicated" and "partial"—complicated because, assuming both mind and matter, it had to account for their interaction; partial because it placed an exclusive emphasis on matter. Once, however, we realize that our knowledge is limited by our perceptions, everything becomes much simpler. The so-called world of matter and the world of mind blend into one. This latter thought Shelley derived from neither Berkeley nor Hume but from a contemporary philosopher, Sir William Drummond: "Perhaps the most clear and vigorous statement of the intellectual system is to be found in Sir William Drummond's Academical Questions. After such an exposition, it would be idle to translate into other words what could only lose its energy and fitness by the change."[15]

Sir William Drummond became known mainly for his anticlerical argument in *Oedipus Judaicus* (1811) that the biblical stories were myths.[16] Shelley had early read this work and by the time of writing *A Refutation of Deism* had also read Drummond's philosophical study *Academical Questions,* and was impressed by Drummond's argument for the nonexistence of God, which Shelley summarized: "If Power be an attribute of existing substance, substance could not have derived its origin from power."[17]

This is simply an extension of the argument that if motion is inherent in matter, a "prime mover" is not needed, but Drummond placed it in a skeptical framework[18] and added to it, rather incongruously, the contention of Parmenides that all existence was a unity (the one "ens"): "There is One that is all, which is the principle of all, by which extension and mind exist, and in which all things are contained contractedly and unitedly, in one unity . . . the nominal difference between physical forces, and mental faculties, concealed from the inattentive observer their common origin and their real similitude."[19] It was perhaps this concept that inspired Shelley's comment: "It is difficult to find terms adequate to express so subtle a conception as that to which the Intellectual Philosophy had conducted us."[20] In Drummond, Shelley found a philosopher who was anticlerical and yet avoided the sterility of an absolute skepticism, imaginatively viewing all reality as essentially one.

By "materialism" Shelley must mean mainly the doctrines of Holbach, for Halbach was the only materialist who had deeply unfluenced him, and in regard to Holbach he appears to be thinking mainly of his scoffing at all hope of immortality and his mechanistic picture of man: "The moral man is nothing more than this physical being considered under a certain point of view."[21] On the contrary, man is "a being of high aspirations . . . disclaiming alliance with transience and decay." Shelley felt that the concept of man as a primarily "physical being" responding to self-serving instincts (as Hobbes had earlier argued and Malthus implied) was a degrading one. Such a "being" could never build a new world based on humanitarian principles. Whatever Shelley's reasoning, he is certainly cavalier in his sweeping dismissal of materialism, implying that its arguments are over simplified and its "disciples" superficial. A more modest appraisal might have been in order, especially as his new philosophy was not without pitfalls:

> The view of life presented by the most refined deductions of the intellectual philosophy, is that of unity. Nothing exists but as it is perceived. The difference is merely nominal between those two classes of thought, which are vulgarly distinguished by the names of ideas and of external objects. Pursuing the same thread of reasoning, the existence of distinct individual minds, similar to that which is employed in now questioning its own nature, is likewise found to be a delusion. The words *I, you, they,* are not signs of any actual difference subsisting between the assemblage of thoughts thus indicated, but are merely marks employed to denote the different modifications of the one mind.
>
> Let it not be supposed that this doctrine conducts to the monstrous presumption that I, the person who now write and think, am that one mind. I am but a portion of it.[22]

Shelley, then, was uneasily aware of the solipsism inherent in his new epistemology: if "I" know nothing except "my" sensations, how do I know that the world is not just my dream? This awkward question—the bugbear of idealism and skepticism alike—he chose not to pursue but contented himself with labeling it a "monstrous presumption."

As corollaries of this solipsist theme came other problems. If "the" mind is not "my" mind but a universal mind, then there are really no individual minds. But in *Speculations on Metaphysics* as in his works in general Shelley assumes the existence of individual minds: "We are intuitively conscious of our own existence, and of that connection in the train of our successive ideas, which we term our identity. We are conscious also of the existence of other minds; but not intuitively." It was perhaps partly in response to this problem—which gave Berkeley and Hume trouble also—that Shelley suggested the rather desperate expedient of a graduated "scale" by which one could measure the "intensity, duration, connexion" and so on of one's sensations.[23] But he failed to provide a reference base for such a scale.

Such, then, were the main epistemological changes in Shelley's philosophy. The indications are that these changes took place in 1816–1817. In a passage in *The Queen of the Universe*, probably written in the fall of 1815, Shelley presumes the existence of a "universal mind" or "Spirit," the individual human mind, and the "vast world" of matter.[24] In the summer of 1816, a similar dualistic assumption apparently underlies *Mont Blanc*. In fragment IV of *Speculations on Metaphysics* and in the essay *On the Punishment of Death*, both written circa 1816–1817, the change is apparent. In the essay, Shelley refers to the "accurate philosophy" of the "modern Academy" (of Drummond), which shows "the prodigious depth and extent of our ignorance respecting the causes and nature of sensation."[25] The fragment contains the following observation: "It imports little to inquire whether thought be distinct from the objects of thought. The use of the words *external* and *internal*, as applied to the establishment of this distinction, has been the symbol and the source of much dispute. This is merely an affair of words and as the dispute deserves, to say, that when speaking of the objects of thought, we indeed only describe one of the forms of thought —or that, speaking of thought, we only apprehend one of the operations of the universal system of beings."[26] The position in this fragment is the same as that in *On Life* (1819–1820).

Just as it was formerly assumed that Shelley was a Platonist, now there seems to be a tendency to assume that he was a thoroughgoing skeptic, both in philosophy and in social thought. But an all-embracing philosophical skepticism should not be confused with a selective reserving of judgment where evidence is lacking or with a specifically epistemological skepticism. Shelley's own efforts to solve "the riddle" had been in vain. There might perhaps be an ultimate creative force behind phenomena, but then again there might be nothing beyond what can be perceived, and the whole answer might lie in scientific analysis. Whatever the answer, Shelley believed, as the true skeptic does not, that mankind would in time discover it. But for the present, evidence on which to base a conclusion was lacking, and rather than propose one, he withheld judgment. However, he was always hopefully seeking for answers, and often he felt he had found them. When he did, he expressed them vigorously and positively. He was not skeptical about the existence of God; he was sure there was none. He was certain that mind was not creative but perceptive, its deductions and fantasies alike ultimately dependent on "sensation." In *A Defence of Poetry* he included Hume among the "mere reasoners" and not among the great creative intellects. Shelley, that is, resorted to noncomittal and agnostic responses on certain questions because intellectual honesty demanded that he do so, but he felt that skepticism as a system of philosophy, while essential for the abolition of theological "error," was negative rather than creative. It made for the beginning of wisdom, but the beginning only.

This was true also of Shelley's concept of political thought. As he stated, it is often the "duty" of the philosopher as well as of the "reformer in political questions to leave a vacancy."[27] He did this himself from time to time in *A Philosophical View of Reform;* for instance, when he did not know whether intellectual or social forces were primary in causing social change, he argued only that change arose from their interaction. Yet his political and social views were essentially positive. Although he withheld judgment on some social questions, he had a clear position on others. Human nature was conditioned by social forces. The source of political oppression lay in the ruling classes, with their "standing army," their "legion of spies," and their control of the press and pulpit. He was confident that this "tyranny" would be eliminated by "reform" or "revolution." He was convinced that humanity was advancing to an egalitarian society. He dedicated his life and writing to the battle against social evils. Indeed, it is difficult to think of works that are more the antithesis of social skepticism—with its cynical concept of the uselessness of human endeavor—than *A Philosophical View of Reform* or *Prometheus Unbound.*

Platonism

Unfortunately, in view of later controversies, Shelley left no such explicit comments on Platonism as he did on British empiricism. The closest he comes is in a few sentences in the Preface to his translation of Plato's *Symposium*:

> His [Plato's] views into the nature of mind and existence are often obscure, only because they are profound; and though his theories respecting the government of the world, and the elementary laws of moral action, are not always correct, yet there is scarcely any of his treatises which do not, however stained by puerile sophisms, contain the most remarkable intuitions into all that can be the subject of the human mind. His excellence consists especially in intuition, and it is this faculty which raises him far above Aristotle, whose genius, though vivid and various, is obscure in comparison with that of Plato.[28]

That Shelley admired what he believed to be Plato's political philosophy is evident from the well-known comment in the Preface to *Prometheus Unbound*: "Let this opportunity be conceded to me of acknowledging that

I have, what a Scotch philosopher characteristically terms, 'a passion for reforming the world:' what passion incited him to write and publish his book, he omits to explain. For my part, I had rather be damned with Plato and Lord Bacon, than go to Heaven with Paley and Malthus." The reference is to *The Republic,* which Shelley believed to embody the "principle of equality" (a general belief until twentieth-century scholars demonstrated that Plato's "equality" was limited to a small ruling class in a slave state).[29]

To understand Shelley's attitudes toward Platonic metaphysics, one must take into account a distinction he made between "philosophical" and "metaphorical" expressions of ideas. In his *Essay on Christianity,* after stating that Jesus attributed "the faculty of will" to God, Shelley continues: "How far such a doctrine in its ordinary sense may be philosophically true, or how far Jesus Christ intentionally availed himself of a metaphor easily understood, is foreign to the subject to consider." In *Speculations on Morals* he complained of "the abuse of a metaphorical expression to a literal purpose." Shelley felt that it was legitimate to express metaphorically ideas that might be dubious philosophically if they would assist human progress. As he put it in a note to *Hellas* (1821):

> The received hypothesis of a Being resembling men in the moral attributes of his nature, having called us out of non-existence, and after inflicting on us the misery of the commission of error, should superadd that of the punishment and the privations consequent upon it, still would remain inexplicable and incredible. That there is a true solution of the riddle, and that in our present state the solution is unattainable by us, are propositions which may be regarded as equally certain; meanwhile, as it is the province of the poet to attach himself to those ideas which exalt and ennoble humanity, let him be permitted to have conjectured the condition of the futurity towards which we are all impelled by an inextinguishable thirst for immortality. Until better arguments can be produced than sophisms which disgrace the cause, this desire itself must remain the strongest and the only presumption that eternity is the inheritance of every thinking being.[30]

Shelley here makes a distinction between himself as poet and as philosopher.[31] As a poet, he felt free to use ideas of which he was not philosophically convinced if they would "exalt and ennoble humanity." This dichotomy was one he had long made. As early as June 1811 he wrote that, although a "personification" of God as a "Deity of virtue" might be "beautiful in Poetry," it is "inadmissible in reasoning." And in the *Essay on Christianity*, after expounding Jesus' doctrine of immortality, he comments: "How delightful a picture even if it be not true! How magnificent & illustrious is the conception which this bold theory suggests to the contemplation, even if it be no more than the imagination of some sublimest and most holy poet, who impressed with the loveliness and majesty of his own nature, is impatient and discontented, with the narrow limits which this imperfect life and the dark grave have assigned for ever as his melancholy portion."[32]

The belief of Shelley's that it is permissible to express ideas in poetry which are "inadmissible to reasoning" adds a complicating factor to the interpretation of his poetry, though it is a less formidable one than at first appears. The ideas on which Shelley allows himself these liberties are few in number, and they usually concern immortality. Hence, the philosophical-metaphorical distinction is of particular importance in determining Shelley's relation to Platonic metaphysics.

That Shelley had no reasoned belief in the doctrine of immortality is clear from the Note to *Hellas*, written only nine months before his death. His most extended comments on the subject appear in his essay *On a Future State* (1820–1821). As James A. Notopulos has noted, this essay echoes Plato's *Phaedo*. It also questions some of the *Phaedo's* well-known arguments for immortality: that the soul is indivisible, that it existed before birth, and that it can exist in some general mindlike form after death. On the indivisibility of the soul, Shelley writes: "They have clung to the idea that sensibility and thought, which they have distinguished from the objects of it, under the several names of spirit and matter, is, in its own nature, less susceptible of division and decay, and that, when the body is resolved into its elements, the principle which animated it will remain perpetual and unchanged." This argument, Shelley continues, can be supported only by claiming the "interposition of a supernatural power," a concept that he rejects. On the existence of the soul before birth, he asks: "Have we existed before birth? It is difficult to conceive the possibility of this." And on the soul's existence after death, he states: "It is said that it is possible that we should continue to exist in some mode totally inconceivable to us at present. This is a most unreasonable presumption. It casts on the adherents of annihilation the burthen of proving the negative of a question, the affirmative of which is not supported by a single argument, and which, by its very nature lies beyond the experience of the human understanding." Because death is beyond human experience, there can be no valid, reasoned argument for immortality. Furthermore, the available evidence militates against it:

> How can a corpse see or feel? its eyes are eaten out, and its heart is black and without motion. What intercourse can two heaps of putrid clay and crumbling bones hold together? When you can discover where the fresh colours of the faded flower abide, or the music of the broken lyre, seek life among the dead. Such are the anxious and fearful contemplations of the common observer, though the popular religion often prevents him from confessing them even to himself.
>
> The natural philosopher, in addition to the sensations common to all men inspired by the event of death, believes that he sees with more certainty that it is attended with the annihilation of sentiment and thought. He observes the mental powers increase and fade with those of the body, and even accommodate themselves to the most transitory changes of our physical nature. Sleep suspends many of the faculties of the vital and intellectual principle; drunkenness and disease will either temporarily or permanently derange them. Madness or idiocy may

utterly extinguish the most excellent and delicate of those powers. In old age the mind gradually withers; and as it grew and was strengthened with the body, so does it together with the body sink into decrepitude. Assuredly these are convincing evidences that so soon as the organs of the body are subjected to the laws of inanimate matter, sensation, and perception, and apprehension, are at an end.[33]

In view of the specific anti-Platonic arguments in the essay as a whole, this passage must be intended as a repudiation of Plato's arguments in the *Phaedo.* In fact, if Shelley's comments on Plato's "puerile sophisms" in the Preface to his translation of *The Symposium* are compared with his remark in the note to *Hellas* "on sophisms which disgrace the cause [of belief in immortality]," it is apparent that among Plato's "puerile sophisms" he included his arguments for immortality.

A few days before his death, Shelley wrote to his friend Horace Smith: "Let us see the truth, whatever that may be. The destiny of man can scarcely be so degraded that he was born only to die—and if such should be the case, delusions, especially the gross and preposterous ones of existing religion, can scarcely be supposed to exalt it."[34] The "delusions" that are not of "existing religion" must refer to Plato's, for the Platonic and the Christian (heaven and hell) arguments on this matter are the only two that he discusses, and, indeed, the only two that were then generally known to English intellectuals.

So far as rational argument is concerned, there is no doubt, Shelley implies, that the "natural philosopher" is right: the mind depends on its relationship with the body and dies with it. But Shelley is not convinced that this argument reflects the whole truth. There are two other factors that may have a bearing on the subject: man has "an inextinguishable thirst for immortality," and the utter degradation of death seems to conflict with the nature of humanity. Though man's obsession with immortality might signify nothing, it is nevertheless a fact and must have had some origin. The second concept, hinted in the letter to Horace Smith, is spelled out in *On Life*: "man is a being of high aspirations . . . disclaiming alliance with transcience and decay."[35] Surely such a being could not end as a rotting corpse. Yet it certainly seemed so, and if such was the truth, one must face it. Shelley's hopes for immortality were not only personal, but were also part of his hopes for humanity. Death was degradation for all; the vision of the untold millions of the dead of the past and the thought that the present and the future held nothing better appalled him. An egalitarian utopia in which man was "born only to die" was still a society in half-shadows.

Not only did Shelley repudiate the Platonic arguments on immortality, but he also refused to accept Plato's related concept of mind as a unique entity existing before birth and acquiring knowledge from divine sources. Shelley remained an empiricist: mind is at birth a blank tablet, essentially noncreative, and knowledge comes only from experience. The third main Platonic argument, that this world is the imperfect shadow of a divine pattern (depicted most notably in the allegory of the cave in *The Republic*), Shelley nowhere accepts and his general philosophical agnosticism would, in fact, have prevented his accepting it.

Shelley viewed Plato as a precursor of modern skepticism. In *A Defence of Poetry* he referred to Plato's "intellectual system." In *On Life* he spoke of the views of Drummond and others as "the intellectual philosophy" and, in *On the Punishment of Death*, as "the modern academy."[36] Since Plato's was the original academy, the implication is that Shelley believed the modern "intellectual philosophy" to have roots in the ancient. By "intellectual philosophy," Shelley meant essentially a skeptical epistemology.[37] The word "intellectual" was commonly used to designate mind as such, as in "intellectual beauty," not quality of intelligence; hence, "intellectual philosophy" is the philosophy that sees all in terms of idea or sensation. That anyone should regard Plato as a skeptic may seem curious, but his method of questioning by dialogue and Socrates' ironical pose of ignorance had given rise to such a belief—from Cicero to Montaigne. But Shelley also felt that Plato's skepticism was limited, for when he treats Plato at any length, he places the emphasis on his "sophisms" on immortality or his poetical visionings.[38]

It is difficult to determine to what degree Shelley felt that Plato had anticipated "the modern academy," but the indication is that he thought him a remote precursor, who lacked the foundations provided by science and anticipated intuitively in flashes rather than systematically. He regarded Plato as a precursor also of other views: "Plato is eminently the greatest among the Greek philosophers, and from him, or, rather, perhaps through him, from his master Socrates, have proceeded those emanations of moral and metaphysical knowledge in which a long series and an incalculable variety of popular superstitions have sheltered their absurdities from the slow contempt of mankind."[39] The reference is once more to Plato's views on immortality. Plato was the greatest "among the Greek philosophers," however, not among all philosophers, for modern philosophy, Shelley implies, had gone beyond Plato. But great though Plato was, he—or Socrates—propagated ideas that gave shelter to "popular superstitions." It was doubtless because he felt that the Platonic doctrine of immortality had provided cover for Christian beliefs in hell and punishment that Shelley was so bitter about Plato's "puerile sophisms."

Although Shelley rejected Plato's philosophic assumptions, his general admiration for him is everywhere apparent. The ambivalence is explained in *A Defence of Poetry*: "The distinction between philosophers and poets has been anticipated. Plato was essentially a poet—the truth and splendour of his imagery, and the melody of his language, is the most intense that it is possible to conceive."[40] Plato, then, was not "essentially" a philosopher, a thinker like Aristotle or Locke, who could construct a logical philosophical system, but "a poet," who caught glimpses of reality in "remarkable intuitions." Because Shelley considered poets—"the unacknowledged legislators of the world"—to be greater stimulators of human progress than philosophers, this places Plato in the forefront of the leading intellectual spirits of the past. Plato, he believed, for all his "sophisms," looked to an egalitarian society and had fleeting visions of truth, particularly in regard to the nature of love (Shelley translated Plato's *Symposium*), which were often more evocative of good than the systems of the "mere reasoners."

Essay on Christianity

Along with the view that Shelley in his later years became a Platonist is sometimes found the view that he became a Christian. Here, too, it is helpful to break the question up into its constituent parts and to make a distinction between Shelley's views on ethics and theology, and on Jesus and the church. Shelley's most comprehensive expression of his later opinions on Christianity and Jesus of Nazareth are found in his *Essay on Christianity* (1817), an essay that also provides further insights into his philosophical views. His object in writing the essay is most succinctly expressed in his fragmentary *Moral Teachings of Jesus Christ*, apparently written two years later: "Doctrines of Reform were never carried to so great a length as by Jesus Christ. The republic of Plato and the Political Justice of Godwin are probable and practical systems in the comparison." If these doctrines were acted upon, he continues, "no political or religious institution could subsist a moment"; they would demonstrate "the falsehood of Christianity" (the doctrines of the established church) and reveal that the Christian religion "is the strongest ally and bulwark of that system of successful force and fraud . . . from which it has derived its origin and permanence," a system against which Jesus himself "declared the most uncompromising war."[41] One of Shelley's motives in writing the *Essay on Christianity*, then, was to use the humanitarian and communistic views of Jesus as a bludgeon against the church.

The *Essay on Christianity*, after an introductory fragment, falls into three parts, headed in the manuscript: "God," "To belong to some other part/ Introduction," and "Equality of Mankind."[42] In "God" Shelley presents Jesus' concept of God, indicating that it contradicts the currently accepted anthropomorphic picture; in the second part he emphasizes Jesus' reformist views and shows that they constitute an attack on Old Testament doctrines; and in the third he brings out Jesus' egalitarian philosophy, comparing it with the similar doctrines of Plato, Diogenes, and Rousseau.

In the introductory fragment, Shelley's object is to show that the social gospel of Jesus sprang from the conditions of his age, which appear curiously parallel to Shelley's own:

The birth of Christ occurred at a period which may be considered as a crisis the most stupendous and memorable in the progress of the human race. The splendour of the Roman name, the vital spirit of the Roman power [the Republic] had vanished. A race of despicable usurpers had assumed the dominion of the world power and was no longer distributed but as the price of the basest artifices of slavery. Sentiments of liberty and heroism no longer lived but in the lamentations of those who had felt, but had survived their influence. Even from these they were speedily effaced. Accumulations of wealth and power were inordinately great . . . The intercourse of man with man was that of Tyrant with slave, the one stipulating as the price of his submission, the other as the prerogation of his superiority, some personal advantage.[43]

Shelley adds in a footnote: "The dominion which Rome had usurped over the civilized world was essentially iniquitous. It was procured by a series of aggressions, and preserved by sanguinary despotism." Jesus formulated his political and moral views, then, in protest against inequality, despotism, and imperialism—as did Shelley. In fact, the final sentence in the footnote is doubtless aimed as much at the British as at the Roman Empire.

In the first section Shelley takes the salient doctrines of Jesus—mainly from the Sermon on the Mount—and shows that the accepted interpretation of them is wrong. He begins with, "Blessed are the pure in heart, for they shall see God." Does this, he sarcastically enquires, mean that after death the faithful shall "stand in awe before the golden throne on which he sits, and gaze upon the venerable countenance of the paternal Monarch?" Such ideas are "the pernicious representations of imposters" (the clergy). Jesus meant that if a man lived a good life, his clear conscience would enable him to feel in tune with the spirit of beauty in nature and humanity. Shelley's exposition of this concept is important for understanding both his philosophy and his poetry:

God, it has been asserted, was contemplated by Jesus Christ as every poet and every philosopher must have contemplated that mysterious principle. He considered that venerable word to express the overruling Spirit of the collective energy of the moral and material world . . . He affirms that a being of pure and gentle habits will not fail in every thought, in every object of every thought, to be aware of benignant visitings from the invisible energies by which he is surrounded. Whosoever is free from the contamination of luxury and licence may go forth to the fields and to the woods, inhaling joyous renovation from the breath of Spring, or catching from the odours and the sounds of Autumn some diviner mood of sweetest sadness, which improves the solitary heart. Whosoever is no deceiver or destroyer of his fellow-man, no liar, no flatterer, no murderer, may walk among his species, deriving from the communion with all which they contain of beautiful or of majestic, some intercourse with the Universal God. Whoever has maintained with his own heart the strictest correspondence of confidence, who dares to examine and to estimate every imagination which suggests itself to his mind, who is that which he designs to become, and only aspires to that which the divinity of his own nature shall consider and approve—he, has already seen God. We live and move and think, but we are not the creators of our own origin and existence, we are not the arbiters of every motion of our own complicated nature; we are not the masters of our own imaginations and moods of mental being. There is a Power by which we are surrounded, like the atmosphere in which some motionless lyre is suspended, which visits with its breath our silent chords, at will. Our most imperial and stupendous qualities—those on which the majesty and the power of humanity is erected—are, relatively to the inferior portion of its mechanism, indeed active and imperial; but they are passive slaves of some higher and more omnipresent Power. This Power is God. And those who have seen God, have, in the period of their purer and more perfect nature, been harmonized by their own will to so exquisite [a] consentaneity of powers as to give forth divinest melody when the breath of universal being sweeps over their frame.[44]

Some critics have felt that in this passage Shelley is expressing a belief in a personal God, but this he denies, both for Jesus and implicitly also for himself: "The doctrine of what some fanatics have termed a peculiar Providence, that is of some power beyond and superior to that which ordinarily guides the operations of the Universe, interfering to punish the vicious and reward the virtuous—is explicitly denied by Jesus Christ." Others have felt that the passage expresses an idealist or mystical viewpoint. But a careful reading shows that Shelley makes no positive statements to support this argument and that his phrasing, though poetic, is carefully neutral.

Shelley is arguing that Jesus himself was no "Christian" and would have repudiated the doctrines being propounded in his name. In this respect the essay continues the ironical manner of *A Refutation of Deism.* But it is more subtle in both intent and tone. Shelley is not attempting, as in the earlier tract, to disprove the existence of God or convert deists to atheism, but to demonstrate that the doctrines of Jesus were philosophical and ethical rather than religious. These doctrines, as Shelley expounds them, are obviously close to his own; and he no doubt wished to emphasize this fact in order to link Jesus with the social radicalism of his own day.

This aim presented problems in exposition, however. Shelley did not believe in God; but in expressing the doctrines of Jesus, he could hardly avoid using the word. Yet if he used it in the orthodox sense, he would be distorting the views of Jesus and playing into the hands of the church; if he expressed his own views fully, he would lose the audience of liberal Christians and deists to whom he was appealing. He gets around the difficulty by defining God ambiguously as "the overruling Spirit of the collective energy of the moral and material world." If Shelley had been expounding his own ideas directly, he would doubtless have chosen some other word than "overruling," with its anthropomorphic overtones, but that he was using "Spirit" in its natural and not its supernatural sense is indicated by his equating it with "principle" and "Power" and by his studious avoidance of claiming that it is either creative or transcendent. The term designates the essence of the "collective energy" of both nature and humanity. Like the Wordsworthian "spirit" of *Tintern Abbey,* it exists both in nature ("the fields and woods") and the mind. It cannot, however, be felt by everyone. The military "destroyer of his fellow men," the petty "flatterer," and the priestly "deceiver" are all cut off by their own evil from seeing the "beautiful or the majestic" in humanity. When one does see these things, he has "some intercourse" with the "universal God," that is, with the essence of the "collective energy." Only one who lives up to the self-sacrificing humanitarian potential within all—"the divinity of his own nature"—can see them (and realize what they portend for the future of society).

Although Shelley did not believe that the essence of the "Power" (or "Spirit," "Principle," "invisible energy," "breath of universal being," for they are all clearly the same) could be defined in the existing state of knowledge, he did believe that something of its nature could be determined:

If Power be an attribute of existing substance, substance could not have derived its origin from power. One thing cannot be at the same time the cause and the effect of another.—The word power expresses the capability of any thing to be or act. The human mind never hesitates to annex the idea of power to any object of its experience. To deny that power is the attribute of being, is to deny that being can be. If power be an attribute of substance, the hypothesis of a God is a superfluous and unwarrantable assumption.[45]

"Power" is not separate from "substance" or "being" but one of its "attributes," something inherent in the universe, not transcendent or supernatural. Matter has within it a power of motion. Living matter has a power for growth and reproduction:

There is, in the generative principle of each animal and plant, a power which converts the substances by which it is surrounded into a substance homogeneous with itself. That is the relations between certain elementary particles of matter undergo a change and submit to new combinations. For when we use the words *principle, power, cause, &c.*, we mean to express no real being, but only to class under those terms a certain series of co-existing phenomena; but let it be supposed that this principle is a certain substance which escapes the observation of the chemist and anatomist. It certainly *may be;* though it is sufficiently unphilosophical to allege the possibility of an opinion as a proof of its truth.[46]

Although Shelley makes a distinction between the realm of the "chemist" and the "anatomist," the biological sciences were but little developed in his day. He apparently believed that the line between dead and living matter was a thin one. The "elementary particles of matter" operate in both. Science in the early nineteenth century could not differentiate atoms from molecules or cells. Changes in the form of matter and growth in biological life were alike the result of new "combinations" of the "elementary particles." What the "principle" or "power" was that activated these new combinations Shelley did not pretend to know. He admitted the possibility that it might be a "general substance" that the lowly science of his own day had failed to detect, but he seemed skeptical about this.

Although the essential character of the power or principle inherent in nature cannot yet be known, some of its attributes can be perceived. From the fact of motion one can deduce that it is somehow akin to life—a "spirit" of "activity and life." From the fact of universal generation one can deduce that biological life is infused with love, a concept perhaps ultimately derived from Plato. And because the same "particles" exist in both life and matter, both partake to some degree of the qualities of the other. The "spirit" or essence of nature is one of life and love. It is also necessitarian:

> Spirit of Nature! all-sufficing Power,
> Necessity! thou mother of the world![47]

Power is manifested in motion; but motion is not random. The planets move in set orbits. Necessity must therefore be of the essence of the power of matter. So, too, in biological life: the form that the seed will take as a plant or an animal is predetermined; it can take no other. And in social and psychological life: "We live and move and think, but we are not the creators of our own origin and existence, we are not the arbiters of every motion of our own complicated nature; we are not the masters of our own imaginations and moods of mental being." The power inherent in nature is not only necessitarian, it is also beautiful, bountiful, and egalitarian: "that merciful and benignant power who scatters equally upon the beautiful earth all the elements of security and happiness."[48]

Shelley, then, uses "power" in different ways, all of which are related to a basic concept. "Power" as such is simply a capacity for existence, motion, or growth. As it is inherent in matter, one need not assume a creative God. There is also a "power" within biological life. And there is a "benignant power" that affects human thought and actions and is associated with the "collective energy of the moral and material universe." The source of this energy is unknown.

Although Shelley nowhere actually states that the attributes of the power or principle of existence are the same in physical matter, biological life, society, and mind, he implies that they are, or at least are similar. He certainly seems to believe that the qualities of the natural world penetrate into the moral world, presumably because man is biologically part of nature. People are "naturally" egalitarian, benignant, loving, and sensitive to beauty, but society has, to one or another degree, corrupted them and turned them to selfishness and hatred. Only those who have resisted these social influences and have led lives dedicated to humanity are in tune with nature. But "there will come a time when the human mind shall be visited exclusively by the influences of the benignant power,"[49] namely, when the present social system is replaced by an egalitarian one in tune with nature, as depicted in Acts III and IV of *Prometheus Unbound*.

Behind Shelley's philosophical views lie moral and social ones, for much though he loved philosophy and science, his overriding interest was humanity; and his philosophical thinking is sometimes guided by this interest. The degree of priority that he assigned to the moral sphere is revealed in a sentence in *Speculations on Metaphysics.* Following his usual epistemological argument on "thoughts" and "external objects," he continues: "No essential distinction between any one of these ideas, or any class of them, is founded on a correct observation of the nature of things, but merely on a consideration of what thoughts are most invariably subservient to the security and happiness of life."[50] It does not matter so much what ideas as such are; the really important thing is whether or not they contribute to human happiness and economic security.

In the second section of *Essay on Christianity,* headed "To belong to some other Part/Introduction," Shelley tries to establish that the doctrines of Jesus cannot always be taken at face value because Jesus himself modified his views at times with regard to "the opinions of his auditors," and because his disciples were not trustworthy recorders of them. As the disciples sometimes "impute sentiments to Jesus Christ which flatly contradict each other," such sentiments must be examined in the light of what is known of Jesus' character and philosophy. Examples of erroneous recordings are the miracles and the view that Jesus was "vindictive." With respect to Jesus' modifications of his doctrine to his hearers, Shelley comments: "Jesus Christ did what every other reformer who had produced any considerable effect upon the world has done. He accommodated his doctrines to the prepossessions of those whom he addressed . . . All reformers have been compelled to practice this misrepresentation of their own true feelings and opinions."[51]

That Shelley himself used such accommodations on occasion is clear both in this essay and elsewhere.[52] Though the point is often forgotten, it must be borne in mind. Just as Shelley did not always wish to present all the implications of his political views, so too with his philosophical and antireligious ones. Sometimes he will shade his phrasing ambiguously, without, however, compromising his root meaning.

In the final section, "Equality of Mankind," Shelley elaborates his concept of Jesus as a social radical, who, along with Plato and Diogenes, believed in "the equality of mankind": "They saw that the great majority of the human species were reduced to the situation of squalid ignorance, and moral imbecility, for the purpose of purveying the luxury of a few, and contributing to the satisfaction of their thirst for power." Jesus believed that eventually mankind would attain an egalitarian republic: "The only perfect and genuine republic is that which comprehends every living being . . . In proportion as mankind becomes wise, yes, in exact proportion to that wisdom should be the extinction of the unequal system under which they now subsist . . . The whole frame of human things is infected by the insidious poison."[53]

These egalitarian views of Jesus, Shelley points out, are similar to Rousseau's; indeed, Rousseau's are superior to those of Jesus in being "more connected and systematic." Following the death of Jesus, his disciples attempted to put these views into practice; but the "system of equality which they established, necessarily fell to the ground, because it is a system which must result from, rather than precede the moral improvement of human kind."[54] Shelley does not mean by this that an egalitarian state would come about through individual moral indoctrination. If he had believed this, he would not have written his political tracts. It was, in fact, precisely on this question that he parted company with Godwin, arguing in effect that widespread moral improvement could come only through political actions and the new social forms they would bring into being—a reformed Parliament, a republic, and so on. Individualistic preaching, whether by the disciples of Jesus or of Godwin, would have little effect. A true advance must entail the "moral improvement" not of a few but of "human kind."

In one other fragment apparently connected with the *Essay on Christianity,* titled *On Miracles,* Shelley reaffirms his old Humean disbelief in miracles, which arise from "imposture, fabrication and a heated imagination," and he claims that since miracles are supposed to prove doctrine and doctrine is supposed to imply miracles, the theologians are arguing in a circle.[55]

On the Devil and Devils

Perhaps the best way to set the stage for *On the Devil and Devils* is to note a conversation that Trelawny records as having taken place "within a month of Shelley's death":

> SHELLEY: Religion itself means intolerance. The various sects tolerate nothing but their own dogmas. The priests call themselves shepherds. The passive they drive into their folds. When they have folded you, then they are satisfied, they know you fear them; but, if you stand aloof, *they* fear *you.* Those who resist they consider as wolves, and, where they have the power, stone them to death. I said, "You are one of the wolves." SHELLEY: I am not in sheep's clothing.

That Trelawny's account is reliable is indicated by a comment in a letter of about the same time to Shelley's Irish friend John Taaffe: "Remember that I am predestined to everlasting damnation, merely because I doubt whether I or anyone else will ever be damned, and therefore if I arrive in Hell before you do in Heaven I will endeavour to inform you how far I desire to be punished everlastingly."[56] It is this Voltairean anticlerical irony—reminiscent of *A Refutation of Deism*—that animates *On the Devil and Devils.*

Shelley was apparently stimulated to write the essay by an article by a young English critic, Julius Charles Hare, who commented both on Shelley and on the fact that loss of faith in the Devil leads to loss of faith in God.[57] The reference to himself doubtless led Shelley to read the article carefully, and the loss of faith idea tickled his fancy: "I was immeasurably amused by the quotation from Schlegel about the way in which the popular faith is destroyed—first the Devil, then the Holy Ghost, then God the Father."[58]

Shelley begins by pointing out that the Greeks and other peoples got along quite well without the Devil. Neither Democritus nor Aristotle believed in the existence of a "living and thinking agent," either good or bad, as "the author or superintendent" of the universe. Socrates and Plato, however, "struck with the beauty and novelty of the theistical hypothesis . . . supposed the existence of a God" and based their moral theory on it—a procedure of which Shelley disapproved. The Greek idealists accounted for evil by supposing that God "in making the world, made not the best that he, or even inferior intelligence could conceive; but that he moulded the reluctant and stubborn materials ready to his hand, into the nearest arrangement possible to the perfect archetype existing in his contemplation."

Although the Christian theologians rejected this theory "on the grounds that the eternity of matter is incompatible with the omnipotence of God," they were nevertheless faced with a world in which "good and evil are inextricably entangled," and with the necessity of reconciling this fact with the concept of a God of "omnipotence, and benevolence, and equity." In order to "extricate themselves from this difficulty," they "invented or adopted the Devil." In the old jibing style of the antireligious Notes to *Queen Mab*, Shelley then gives one of his satirical accounts of the Christian "mythology"—a form of clerical tail-twisting made popular by Paine and others:

> They then proceed to relate, gravely, that one fine Morning, a chief of these spirits took it into his head to rebel against God, having gained over to his cause a third part of the eternal angels, who attended upon the Creator and Preserver of Heaven and Earth. After a series of desperate conflicts between those who remained faithful to the ancient dynasty, and the insurgents, the latter were beaten, and driven into a place called Hell, which was rather their empire than their prison, and where God reserved them to be first the tempters, and then the jailors and tormentors of a new race of beings, whom he created under the same conditions of imperfection and with the same foresight of an unfortunate result. The motive of this insurrection is not assigned by any of the early mythological writers. Milton supposes that on a particular day God chose to adopt as his son and *heir*, (the reversion of an estate with an immortal incumbent, would be worth little) a being unlike the other Spirits, who seems to have been and approved to be a detached portion of himself, and afterwards figured upon the earth in the well-known character of Jesus Christ.[59]

Shelley argues the moral superiority of Milton's Satan to God, and asserts that only through *Paradise Lost* will future generations know the Christian religion, which in time will be added as "one more superstition to those which have already arisen and decayed upon the earth."[60]

The rest of the essay is taken up with a satirical account of the nature and function of the Devil and devils. The Devil, according to Biblical accounts, "is at once the Informer, the Attorney General, and the jailor of the Celestial tribunal," a concept that Shelley develops in a passage dictated by his own hatred of the British government's system of sending *agents provocateurs* among the English workers: "The dirty work is done by the Devil, in the same manner as some starving wretch will hire himself out to a King or Minister to work with a stipulation that he shall have some portion of the public spoil, as an instrument to betray a certain number of other starving wretches into circumstances of capital punishment, when they may think it convenient to edify the rest, by hanging up a few of those whose murmurs are too loud."[61]

Such, then, is the function of the Devil, but what is his nature—"is the Devil, like God, omnipresent? If so he interpenetrates God, and they both exist together"—and where does he live? Are there Devils on the other planets (a notion perhaps borrowed from Paine)? If so, is not our Devil perhaps an inferior Devil, much less important than, say, the Devil of a large planet like Jupiter? It has been suggested that perhaps the Devil lives on the Sun and that the Sun is Hell. This is at least an improvement over the idea that the Devil's abode is in the center of the earth, for "the Devils and the damned would be exceedingly crowded in process of ages" if they were all bottled up in the earth. The Devil has been represented as a serpent, but among the Greeks the serpent was considered a symbol of good and among the Egyptians "an hieroglyphic of eternity."[62] With these comments, the fragment ends.

Speculations on Morals

In a letter to Leigh Hunt's *The Examiner* in December 1817 Shelley complained that "all that is temporary in the fame of Godwin has suffered from his daring to announce the true foundation of morals." What Shelley had in mind is indicated in *Political Justice*: "Morality is that system of conduct which is determined by a consideration of the greatest general good." This and similar ideas formed the basis for Shelley's early comments on ethics in his letters and in the Notes to *Queen Mab*. One observation from the Notes, in fact, is based directly on Godwin: "But utility is morality; that which is incapable of producing happiness is useless." Godwin had described "utility" as the doctrine that morality should "contribute to the general good." Although Shelley believed that Godwin had provided the "foundation" for morality, and was doubtless also aware of similar views in Bentham, Priestley, and Beccaria, he went beyond it to create an ethical philosophy of his own.[63]

Shelley's early thinking on ethics is tied up with his hatred of religious intolerance: "The state of society in which we exist is a mixture of feudal savageness and imperfect civilisation. The narrow and unenlightened morality of the Christian religion is an aggravation of these evils." In his *Letter to Lord Ellenborough* he rejected the concept that moral values rest either on religion or law:

Morality, or the duty of a man and a citizen, is founded on the relations which arise from the association of human beings, and which vary with the circumstances produced by the different states of this association.—This duty in similar situations must be precisely the same in all ages and nations. The opinion contrary to this has arisen from a supposition that the will of God is the source or criterion of morality: It is plain that the utmost exertion of Omnipotence could not cause that to be virtuous which actually is vicious. An all-powerful Demon might indubitably annex punishments to virtue and rewards to vice, but could not by these means effect the slightest change in their abstract and immutable natures.[64]

Shelley's ethical views, as even these few excerpts indicate, are an extension of his social philosophy. The laws of ethics are based neither on religious principles nor on abstract logic but arise from human association in society. As such, they transcend national and temporal standards; their purpose is to increase human happiness. Although in his later writings Shelley went deeper into these matters, these early concepts remained as his intellectual base.

The work that Mary Shelley called *Speculations on Morals* in her edition of Shelley's prose in 1840 consists of two sets of fragments, the first of which is in manuscripts watermarked 1814 and 1815 and was most probably written in 1817 in England, the second of which is in an Italian notebook and was most probably written in 1821.[65] Shelley apparently began—perhaps at Marlow—to put down his thoughts on the subject and then started a more systematic effort after he had settled in Italy. For those unacquainted with the classics of moral philosophy, some of these fragments might seem unduly formalized, but Shelley is simply following the practice of the genre, accepting—as did Godwin and others—such established Aristotelian categories as virtue, benevolence, and justice. But he accepts them only to shatter their traditional social framework.

In the fragment placed first by Shelley's editors, *Plan of a Treatise of Morals,* and clearly of an introductory nature, Shelley advances once again the "greatest good of the greatest number" argument: "The object of the forms according to which human society is administered, is the happiness of the individuals composing the communities which they regard, and these forms are perfect or imperfect in proportion to the degree in which they promote this end . . . It is not enough, if such a coincidence can be conceived as possible, that one person or class or persons should enjoy the highest happiness, whilst another is suffering a disproportionate degree of misery."

Presenting his own concepts of the traditional categories, Shelley calls the propensity within each individual to spread good among his fellow beings, "benevolence"; and the science of directing it through egalitarian channels he calls "justice." In regard to benevolence, he argues that the psychological roots for morality lie in the imagination:

If a child observes without emotion its nurse or its mother suffering acute pain, it is attributable rather to ignorance than insensibility. So soon as the accents and gestures significant of pain are referred to the feelings which they express, they awaken in the mind of the beholder a desire that they should cease. Pain is thus apprehended to be evil for its own sake, without any other necessary reference to the mind by which its existence is perceived than such as is indispensable to its perception. The tendencies of our original sensations, indeed, all have for their object the preservation of our individual being. But these are passive and unconscious. In proportion as the mind acquires an active power, the empire of these tendencies becomes limited. (Every one has experience of the fact, that to sympathise with the sufferings of another, is to enjoy a transitory oblivion of his own.) Thus an infant, a savage, and a solitary beast, is selfish, because its mind is incapable of receiving an accurate intimation of the nature of pain as existing in beings resembling itself. The inhabitant of a highly civilised community will more acutely sympathize with the sufferings and enjoyments of others, than the inhabitant of a society of a less degree of civilization . . .

The imagination thus acquires by exercise a habit as it were of perceiving and abhorring evil, however remote from the immediate sphere of sensations with which that individual mind is conversant . . . The only distinction between the selfish man, and the virtuous man, is that the imaginaton of the former is confined within a narrow limit, whilst that of the latter embraces a comprehensive circumference. In this sense, wisdom and virtue may be said to be inseparable, and criteria of each other. Selfishness is the offspring of ignorance and mistake; it is the portion of unreflecting infancy, and savage solitude, or of those whom toil or evil occupations have blunted and rendered torpid; disinterested benevolence is the product of a cultivated imagination.[66]

In these arguments Shelley aligns himself with those who, like Hume, Hartley, Bentham, Adam Smith, Godwin, or Hazlitt, wished to establish a rational and nonreligious basis for ethics.[67] There is no "moral sense" within the individual at birth, no fragment of divine mind "trailing clouds of glory," no "sinful" human nature resulting from a "fall." All begins not with a garden or abstract "Man" but with the embryonic psychological mechanism of the individual acting instinctively for his own self-preservation. In response to "unconscious" instincts he avoids pain and seeks pleasure. At first these actions are directed toward the self only; then with increasing mental development and experience they are applied to others. If they are applied for the pleasure of others, the resulting conduct is "good"; if they are applied for the pain of others, it is "evil." They are applied more frequently for the pleasure of others as one's imagination develops and one visualizes one's own reactions in others. There is, then, no Platonic "Pattern" of "the good," no Aristotelian abstractions of "good" and "evil." Conduct is the result of human instincts responding to social forces.

Following the discussion of benevolence, Shelley presents his concept of "justice": "It is through this principle that men are impelled to distribute any means of pleasure which benevolence may suggest the communication of to others, in equal portions among an equal number of applicants. If ten men are shipwrecked on a desert island, they distribute whatever subsistence may remain to them, into equal portions among themselves. If six of them conspire to deprive the remaining four of their share, their conduct is termed unjust."[68] Justice is thus essentially a matter of egalitarianism. Shelley, in fact, believed with Godwin that real justice can not exist until the egalitarian society arises. In the present essentially unjust order each individual can only protest the most outrageous perversions of justice—such as war, the persecution of Richard Carlile, or the execution of Brandreth, Ludlam, and Turner—and make his personal conduct an example for others.

The next fragment, headed "Chapter II," begins: "It is foreign to the general scope of this little Treatise to encumber a simple argument by controverting any of the trite objections of habit or fanaticism. But there are two; the first, the basis of all political mistake, and the second, the prolific cause and effect of religious error, which it seems useful to refute." Because Shelley's manuscript has both a gap and an unplaced insert following this initial paragraph for Chapter II, it is difficult to follow his argument, but apparently the concept he has in mind as underlying both "political" and "religious" errors is that conduct should not be determined by reward or punishment, either on earth (political) or in Heaven or Hell (religious):

> A person who should labour for the happiness of mankind lest he should be tormented eternally in Hell, would, with reference to that motive, possess as little claim to the epithet of virtuous, as he who should torture, imprison, and burn them alive, a more usual and natural consequence of such principles, for the sake of the enjoyments of Heaven . . .
>
> A king, or an assembly of men, may publish a proclamation affixing any penalty to any particular action . . .
>
> Some usurper of supernatural energy might subdue the whole globe to his power; he might possess new and unheard of resources for induing his punishments with the most terrible attributes of pain. The torments of his victims might be intense in their degree, and protracted to an infinite duration. Still the "will of the lawgiver" would afford no surer criterion as to what actions were right or wrong. It would only increase the possible virtue of those, who, refusing to become the instruments of his [end of fragment]

Conduct, then, is intrinsically either right or wrong. Its nature is determined neither by theological obfuscations nor legal codes but by universal, ultimately egalitarian standards of benevolence and justice. In these propositions lies the theoretical basis for Shelley's advocacy of civil disobedience. All human laws have to be evaluated by these intrinsic moral standards. The intellectual, if he is to be worthy of the name, must be prepared to flout the laws of his country and defy its punishments in the interests of humanity. Furthermore, in so doing, he must have utterly selfless motives. If he is undaunted by the threat of punishment, he must be unmoved also by the enticement of reward.

A final separate fragment, on a detached sheet beginning *in media res* and bearing an English 1815 watermark, moves off into deeper waters with a discussion of "the difference between social and individual man." If we "visit, in imagination, the proceedings of some metropolis," we perceive "social man" going about his business: "The trader holds a train of conduct from which he never deviates. The ministers of religion employ an accustomed language, and maintain a decent and equable regard . . . The actions which are classed under the general appellations of marriage, education, friendship &c., are perpetually going on, and [to] a superficial glance, are similar one to the other." Only, however, to the "superficial glance."

But, if we would see the truth of things, they must be stripped of this fallacious appearance of uniformity. In truth, no one action has, when considered in its whole extent, an essential resemblance with any other. Each individual, who composing the vast multitude which we have been contemplating, has a peculiar frame of mind, which, whilst the features of the great mass of his actions remain uniform, impresses the minuter lineaments with its peculiar hues. Thus, whilst his life, as a whole, is like the lives of other men, in detail, it is most unlike; and the more sub-divided the actions become; that is, the more they enter into that class which have a vital influence on the happiness of others and his own, so much the more are they distinct from those of other men.

—"those little, nameless unremembered acts
Of kindness and of love,"

as well as those deadly outrages which are inflicted by a look, a word—or less—the very refraining from some faint and most evanescent expression of countenance; these flow from a profounder source than the series of our habitual conduct, which, it has been already said, derives its origin from without.[69]

Each individual, then, leads two lives: the mechanical and structured life or work and social actions, and the life of truly individual relationships. In the former, one adopts certain set attitudes: the minister puts on his ministerial countenance; the trader adopts the attitudes of business dealings; even marriage and friendship have their masks.

The actual relationships between individuals as individuals are more complex and subtle. In this sphere ideas and attitudes can be conveyed by the slightest gestures or changes of expression, even by silence. It is thought that this aspect of life is of secondary importance, but on the contrary, even though its forms are largely unrecognized and unrecorded, it is in them that one must look for the essence of morality:

Internally is all conducted otherwise; the efficiency, the essence, the vitality [of actions] derives its colour from what is no wise contributed to from any external source. Like the plant, which whilst it derives the accident of its size and shape from the soil in which it springs, and is cankered, or distorted, or inflated, [yet] retains those qualities which essentially divide it from all others; so that hemlock continues to be poison, and the violet does not cease to emit its odour in whatever soil it may grow.

We consider our own nature too superficially. We look on all that in ourselves with which we can discover a resemblance in others; and consider those resemblances as the materials of moral knowledge. It is in the differences that it actually consists.

It might seem at first that in the opening sentences of this passage Shelley is simply distinguishing between the biologically inherited nature of each mind and the social influences acting on it. But he is not really saying this, and indeed, such a concept only became prevalent later in the century in the works of Spencer, Huxley, and others. Shelley is contending that there is a part of the mind which is not in its *essence* subject to the social influences of the existing order. It is this core of the mind that produces truly "individual" relationships. Some of these relationships are good ("those little, nameless unremembered acts/Of kindness and of love."); some are bad ("those deadly outrages which are inflicted in a look"). Why they constitute the true "materials of moral knowledge" is suggested in the first (incomplete) sentence of the fragment: " . . . happiness or misery of this state, that which produces that peculiar modification of those actions which makes them intrinsically good or evil, is—the internal influence derived from the constitution of the mind frcm which they flow." What Shelley had been discussing before this (on a missing sheet) we can only guess, but apparently his argument is that what makes these actions "intrinsically"—not legally or relatively—moral or immoral is their roots in the "internal" influences of the mind. They are, once again, actions which are not prescribed by convention or influenced by reward or punishment.

Incomplete though it is, the sentence also implies that Shelley did not make an absolute distinction between "social" and "individual" actions. And this is borne out by his statement that the "distinction" between social and individual man is not "definite"—not, that is, a matter of exact boundary.[70] That "social" forces could influence and sometimes corrupt, "individual" actions he states in the existing fragment; in the previous and now missing portion he apparently indicated that "individual" forces could modify social thoughts and actions. He cannot mean, then, in the phrase "in no wise contributed to from any external source" that individual ideas are not in any way influenced by social ones, but only that their "essence" is not so influenced. The answer to the question as to why some "individual" actions are evil is presumably that they are "modified" by evil social influences.

The final paragraph on "differences" rather than "resemblances" forming the basis for "moral knowledge" is apparently intended to be a restatement of the previous argument. The "resemblances" are those of "social man," such as the mechanical actions of business life. Nothing of basic ethical knowledge is to be found in these actions because they are formed by outside influences, largely by rewards and punishments. They are considered important only by those who do not look beyond them. If one does look beyond them, one penetrates to the layer of "individual" man. Both aspects of life have their types of ideas. Those of "social" man are those of "habit" and "prejudice," looking to the past; those of "individual" man are, or rather can be, enlightened and looking toward an egalitarian brotherhood.

Shelley's views on these questions result in a concept of mind having two aspects: one peripheral, which is easily affected by corrupting social influences; the other central, which is less susceptible to such influences. This theory is developed further in *On Love* and *A Defence of Poetry*. It is not difficult to see how he came to think in this direction: he recognized that he, Hunt, and others stuck to humanitarian principles in a socially corrupt society; in asking how this was possible, he decided that the answer must lie in the nature of the mind itself, that there must be a core of the mind which was remote from social inflluences. Shelley, no more than Locke, took the Lockean position to its logical conclusion, namely, that all ideology must be shaped in its general outlines by environmental factors, some of them retrograde, others progressive. Consequently he ended up with a curious dualism involving a virtually inviolate area of the mind for which he could really present no explanation.

Marriage, Sex, and Love

Although the basic principles of Shelley's ethics are laid down in the *Speculations on Morals* fragments, there are important extensions of them in *On Marriage* (1817–1818) and *A Discourse on the Manners of the Antient Greeks Relative to the Subject of Love* (1818). In the second paragraph of *On Marriage* Shelley further develops the theme that ethics must have a "universal" standard:

> To consider whether any particular action of any human being is really right or wrong we must estimate that action by a standard strictly universal. We must consider the degree of substantial advantage which the greatest number of the worthiest beings are intended to derive from that action. I say thus much to distinguish what is really right and wrong from that which from equivocal application of the idea of criminality, has falsely been called right and wrong.[71]

Laws are of two kinds, those that have "a tendency to produce in every case the greatest good," and those that are "partial and unjust." In the first case, "what is lawful" corresponds with "what is right," but in the second case there is no such correspondence and "the greatest evils" flow from it. This distinction and this appeal to a "universal" standard were not, for Shelley, simply theoretical questions. Whenever he concluded that a law or custom had not a sound moral or social basis, he defied it.

In the first paragraph of the *On Marriage* fragment Shelley treats the origin of marriage and the status of women. In primitive times there was no marriage, the man used his superior strength to subdue the woman, and she became his "property." It was from this primitive property relationship that the institution of marriage arose. The notion has roots in Godwin and partly anticipates the socialist view developed by Friedrich Engels and others later in the century. Shelley puts it thus: "Women therefore, in rude ages and in rude countries have been considered as the property of men, because they are the materials of usefulness or pleasure. They were valuable to them in the same manner as their flocks and herds were valuable, and it was as important to their interests that they should retain undisturbed possession."[72]

In *A Discourse on the Manners of the Antient Greeks Relative to the Subject of Love*—probably written about two years later—Shelley attacks the degradation of women in Greece: "Among the antient Greeks the male sex, one half of the human race, received the highest cultivation and refinement; whilst the other, so far as intellect is concerned, were educated as slaves, and were raised but few degrees in all that related to moral or intellectual excellence above the condition of savages." As a result of this degradation, women were unable to develop their capacities; and here Shelley considers mind and personality development primarily a matter of social conditioning: "The women, thus degraded, became such as it was expected they would become. They possessed, except with extraordinary exceptions, the habits and qualities of slaves." As for the present age, the "practices and customs of modern Europe" are "incomparably less pernicious," but still "remote from what an enlightened mind cannot fail to desire as the future destiny of human beings." Shelley, here as elsewhere, aligns himself with Mary Wollstonecraft and others on the subject of the emancipation and education of women.

In discussing the asserted lack of "sentimental love" among the Greeks—a lack he denies—Shelley makes some interesting comments on the relation of sex to love:

> Man is in his wildest state a social being: a certain degree of civilization and refinement ever produces the want of sympathies still more intimate and complete; and the gratification of the senses is no longer all that is sought in sexual connexion. It soon becomes a very small part of that profound and complicated sentiment, which we call Love, which is rather the universal thirst for a communion not merely of the senses, but of our whole nature, intellectual, imaginative and sensitive; and which, when individualised, becomes an imperious necessity, only to be satisfied by the complete or partial, actual or supposed, fulfilment of its claims. This want grows more powerful in proportion to the development which our nature receives from civilization; for man never ceases to be a social being. The sexual impulse, which is only one, and often a small part of those claims, serves, from its obvious and external nature, as a kind of type or expression of the rest, a common basis, an acknowledged and visible link. Still it is a claim which even derives a strength not its own from the accessory circumstances which surround it, and one which our nature thirsts to satisfy.

In another passage Shelley refers to the sexual act as "the act which ought always to be the link and type of the highest emotions of our nature."[73]

In considering these statements, we have to remember that in Shelley's day a taboo of almost primitive intensity surrounded sex. It was not so much that the Society for the Suppression of Vice stood ever ready to prosecute, but that sex was tacitly considered, even by enlightened intellectuals, a subject not for open discussion. A writer could, of course, depict romantic love, and sexual intercourse was, as ever, a fit topic for male humorous commentary, but the two were regarded as separate phenomena.

It appears from the ambivalence of his language that Shelley is aware of this taboo and is to some degree quailing before it. By the "gratification of the senses" he clearly means the expression of "the sexual impulse," that is, sexual intercourse, but he hesitates to say so directly. This "gratification" is a "small part" of the total love relationship between a man and a women, yet "when individualized," as in a love affair or marriage, it "becomes an imperious necessity," which is increased by the psychological development of the individual in a civilized society. Furthermore, such gratification is a "type or expression" of the whole relationship and forms a "basis" for it; it is an impulse which "our nature thirsts to satisfy." Clearly Shelley regarded sexual intercourse as essential for the fulfillment of a love relationship, and it also seems likely that he considered its part in that relationship to be greater than the word "small" would indicate, as is borne out by passages of sexual imagery in his poetry. But he also felt that a true love relationship could not be formed on a purely sexual attraction or be expressed solely by physical contacts. Love is a "communion," of the senses, of the mind ("intellectual"), of the imagination, "of our whole nature." Regardless of how much emphasis is placed on Shelley's views of the importance of sexual intercourse in this communion, the fact remains that he has thrown out the accepted dichotomy between romantic and physical love by declaring that both are, or should be, part of one relationship. It would be another three-quarters of a century before similar views became current in English thought with Edward Carpenter and Havelock Ellis, and a full century before they received literary expression in the works of D. H. Lawrence.

By sexual love Shelley meant a relationship between a man and a woman. He did not consider a homosexual relationship as a love relationship. Between members of the same sex there could be friendship—"a profound and sentimental attachment to one of the same sex, wholly divested of the smallest alloy of sensual intermixture"—but not love.[74] Homosexual practices he condemned. He criticized Byron in Venice for associating "with wretches who seem almost to have lost the gait & phisiognomy of man, & who do not scruple to avow practices which are not only not named but I believe seldom even conceived in England."[75] The roots of homosexuality were, he thought, sociological rather than biological or psychological, and grew out of the social degradation of women: "Among the Greeks these feelings, being thus deprived of their natural object, sought a compensation and a substitute."[76] If in a given society, such as that of Plato's Athens, women are not allowed to develop intellectually, men will turn to other men, but such a relationship is inferior and degrading.

Further light on Shelley's views of sexual morality is shed by his review of his friend T. J. Hogg's novel *Memoirs of Prince Alexy Haimatoff*, in which he condemns Hogg's advocacy of sexual promiscuity. The "sexual impulse" might be "an imperious necessity" in a love relationship, but this did not make its indiscriminate fulfillment moral. Indeed, if divorced from the "profound and complicated sentiment" of love, it is self-centered and hence immoral. Nor should love have any truck with "chivalry" or with "the fashionable superstitions of gallantry." Shelley was thus neither a sensualist nor an ascetic. He considered both prostitution and sensuality degrading, but he had no use for the "monkish and evangelical superstition" of "chastity." Love is a deep relationship, physical, asthetic, and intellectual, between a man and a woman, which should be neither denied nor perverted by homosexuality, lust, commercialism, or lies.[77]

In the above passages Shelley is using "love" in a sexual sense. Usually, however, he used it in a broader sense, anticipating the views of such modern psychologists as Erich Fromm.[78] In *On Love*, brief though it is, he gives the core of this concept:

> *Thou* demandest what is love? It is that powerful attraction towards all that we conceive, or fear, or hope beyond ourselves, when we find within our own thoughts the chasm of an insufficient void, and seek to awaken in all things that are, a community with what we experience within ourselves. If we reason, we would be understood; if we imagine, we would that the airy children of our brain were born anew within another's . . . This is Love. This is the bond and the sanction which connects not only man with man, but with every thing which exists. We are born into the world, and there is something within us which, from the instant that we live, more and more thirsts after its likeness. It is probably in correspondence with this law that the infant drains milk from the bosom of its mother; this propensity develops itself with the development of our nature. . . . in solitude, or in that deserted state when we are surrounded by human beings and yet they sympathise not with us, we love the flowers, the grass, and the waters, and the sky.

There are, Shelley is arguing, certain qualities in every human being at birth which develop as he grows—fear, hope, reason, and feeling. Yet the essence of love lies not in these but in some special force that turns the mind and emotions outward for communication with others. This need for communication is part of a general "law" of nature. In infancy it manifests itself in the physical relationship of mother and child. Later it takes the form of seeking for qualities in others that one finds within the self. Love is an expansive force, a going outward of the individual—to other individuals, to humanity, to nature—breaking through the barrier of the self in a passionate communication of sentiments and ideas.

One seeks, however, for correspondences not only with the total self but particularly with the inner "individual" part of the self:

We dimly see within our intellectual nature a miniature as it were of our entire self, yet deprived of all that we condemn or despise, the ideal prototype of every thing excellent or lovely that we are capable of conceiving as belonging to the nature of man. Not only the portrait of our external being, but an assemblage of the minutest particles of which our nature is composed [*here Shelley adds a footnote*: "These words are ineffectual and metaphorical. Most words are so—No help!"]; a mirror whose surface reflects only the forms of purity and brightness; a soul within our soul that describes a circle around its proper paradise, which pain, and sorrow, and evil dare not overleap. To this we eagerly refer all sensations, thirsting that they should resemble or correspond with it . . . this is the invisible and unattainable point to which Love tends.[79]

The root idea from which Shelley's later ethics derived was succinctly expressed in a letter in 1811: "What does man exist for? Surely not for his own happiness, but as a more perfect instrument of that of others."[80] He then expanded this idea in the light of his social philosophy. Ethics and politics cannot be divided. It is of little value to talk about "the good" in a society of war, hunger, and oppression. The real basis for justice must be economic and political equality. The claims of humanity for this justice transcend all laws and governments. The roots of morality are neither religious nor legal but lie deep in the human mind.

Fiction and Allegory

Shelley intended *The Assassins* (1814) to be a full-length "romance," but he finished only the first four chapters, of which the first two discuss the characteristics and philosophy of the Assassins.[81] Historically a Moslem sect who fought the Christian Crusaders, the Assassins held unorthodox views similar to those of the Gnostics. They fled from Jerusalem to "the solitudes of Lebanon, and there settled in a beautiful and secluded valley. In this valley—the description of which contains echoes of the "happy valley" in Samuel Johnson's novel *Rasselas*—the Assassins set up an egalitarian society: "Every impulse conspired to one end, and tended to a single object. Each devoted his powers to the happiness of the other. Their republic was the scene of the perpetual contentions of benevolence; not the heartless and assumed kindness of commercial man, but the genuine virtue that has a legible superscription in every feature of the countenance, and every motion of the frame."[82]

Once the "insidious poison" of inequality and despotism, which in society infects "the whole frame of human things," is removed, human nature changes. Acting in accordance with the nature of their society, the Assassins strive ardently for social justice. Their credo is Shelley's own:

Can the power derived from the weakness of the oppressed, or the ignorance of the deceived, confer the right in security to tyrannise and defraud?

The subject of regular governments, and the disciple of established superstition, dares not to ask this question. For the sake of the eventual benefit, he endures what he esteems a transitory evil, and the moral degradation of man disquiets not his patience. But the religion of an Assassin imposes other virtues than endurance, when his fellow-men groan under tyranny, or have become so bestial and abject that they cannot feel their chains. An Assassin believes that man is eminently man, and only then enjoys the prerogatives of his privileged condition, when his affections and his judgment pay tribute to the God of Nature. The perverse, and vile, and vicious—what were they? Shapes of some unholy vision, moulded by the spirit of Evil, which the sword of the merciful destroyer should sweep from this beautiful world. Dreamy nothings; phantasms of misery and mischief, that hold their death-like state on glittering thrones, and in the loathsome dens of poverty.[83]

In this exposition of the Assassins' creed, Shelley is clearly thinking of his own age, the age of Castlereagh, Napoleon, and Czar Alexander (*The Assassins* was written between Leipzig and Waterloo) and prophesying the destruction of its despotic states. "The prominent feature of Shelley's theory of the destiny of the human species," wrote Mary Shelley (correctly) "was, that evil is not inherent in the system of the creation, but an accident that might be expelled."[84] Political despotisms based on the ignorance or weakness of the people cannot last, and when they go, the evils they have engendered go with them. Furthermore, political oppression ("on glittering thrones") and economic exploitation ("the loathsome dens of poverty") are but "dreamy nothings" and "phantasms." The thought is paralleled in *The Revolt of Islam,* where Shelley states that the strength of tyrants is based on "Opinion," that is, on false views which deceive the people:

Alas, what strength? Opinion is more frail
   Than yon dim cloud now fading on the moon
Even while we gaze, though it awhile avail
   To hide the orb of truth—and every throne
   Of Earth or Heaven, though shadow, rests thereon,
One shape of many names:—for this ye plough
   The barren waves of ocean, hence each one
Is slave or tyrant, all betray and bow,
Command, or kill, or fear, or wreak, or suffer woe.[85]

The power of the despots and exploiters rests ultimately on the frail foundations of falsehood. As these falsehoods are perceived by the people when they begin to "feel their chains," the tyrants will be overthrown—as outlined in *A Philosophical View of Reform.*

With Chapter III of *The Assassins* the story begins. A young Assassin called Albedir is horror-struck to find, while wandering in the woods, the body of a man impaled on the branch of a cedar tree. A vulture hovers above, a snake approaches from below. The man is still alive and, as Albedir approaches, cries out: "The great tyrant is baffled, even in success. Joy! joy! to his tortured foe! Triumph to the worm whom he tramples under his feet . . . I was thy slave—I am thy equal, and thy foe.—Thousands tremble before thy throne, who, at my voice, shall dare to pluck the golden crown from thine unholy head!"[86]

The man in the tree, according to Mary Shelley, was Shelley's "old favourite," the immortal Wandering Jew.[87] He has been impaled on the branch by God—"the Eternal Avenger"—and is bidding defiance to his ancient foe. Albedir removes the Wandering Jew from the branch and takes him to his home. The next morning the Wandering Jew accompanies Albedir and his wife, Khaled, to see their little boy and girl. The children are playing with a small boat in a creek; on a rock, asleep, lies a pet snake. The children call to the snake, who creeps into the boat. The children then set the boat loose and run along the shore singing. The snake raises its head to their singing; but when the wind threatens to take the boat out beyond the little creek, it leaps into the water and swims back to the children. The girl takes it to her bosom; the boy sings to it and it comes to him. The children then see their parents and run toward them. With this the fragment ends.

That this scene has symbolic significance is shown by the first canto of *The Revolt of Islam* (*Laon and Cythna,*) where there are a man, a woman, a boat, and a snake that symbolizes freedom and love. Perhaps *The Assassins* would have followed a story pattern similar to *The Revolt of Islam,* with the little boy and girl later turning out to be Laon and Cythna figures who, inspired by the Wandering Jew, would war against evil.

On November 25, 1818, according to Mary Shelley's journal, Shelley began "the Tale of the Coliseum."[88] Whether he worked on it later is not known, but if so, it cannot have been often, for the tale is short and fragmentary. It opens with an old blind man and a little girl entering the ruins of the Coliseum in Rome at noon on the feast of the Passover. They are joined by a young man who, Medwin tells us, was to have been an idealized portrait of Shelley.[89] Mary with whom Shelley perhaps talked over the story, supplies the following information: "The stranger was a Greek—nurtured from infancy exclusively in the literature of his progenitors—and brought up as a child of Pericles might have been; and to heighten the resemblance, Shelley conceived the idea of a woman, whom he named Diotima, who was his instructress and guide."[90]

Una Favola (A Fable) is an allegorical fragment written in 1821, probably for Emilia Viviani, as was *Epipsychidion.*[91] The story concerns a young man who encounters, at the age of fifteen, "a certain one calling himself Love," who is accompanied by "a great troop of female forms." For a year the youth follows Love and the enticing forms through deserts and caverns, while the forms, who refuse to unveil themselves, act as intermediary between the youth and Love. Finally one of them does unveil herself, one "tall of person and beautiful, cheerful and easy in her manners, and richly adorned," whose name is Life. Life, the youth soon finds, is "more false than any Siren," for she gets Love to abandon him and then leaves him herself to go to the cavern of "a certain sister of hers" called Death.

When Love leaves the youth, the rest of the female forms unveil themselves and are seen to be of "horrible aspect and loathsome figure." They mock and threaten the youth. In fleeing from them, he comes to the cavern of Death. He asks Death to protect him from these figures, "the wicked companions of Life," and she takes him to "a chamber of her cavern" where they cannot follow him. The youth then falls in love with Death, but Death leaves him, saying that if he did not love her, she might love him, but as he loves her, she must hate him and fly from him.

The youth spends many years hunting for Death until "sorrows . . . had blanched his locks and withered the flower of his beauty." One day in the forest he discovers a "lady" of whom he had been earlier "enamored" weeping sympathetically beside him: "And lifting up his eyes he saw her, and it seemed to him never to have beheld so glorious a vision." The two fall in love and walk off together through the forest. Suddenly the figure of Death appears before them: "Whilst, O youth, thou didst love me, I hated thee, and now that thou hatest me, I love thee." Death has a special place set aside in Paradise for the youth and the lady. The lady, jealous of this past love of the youth's (Death), calls for Life, who appears "with a gay visage, crowned with a rainbow." Death, seeing Life, goes away in tears, crying out as she goes that they will one day find that she and not Life is their true friend, for she dwells with "Love and Eternity, with whom the souls whose love is everlasting must hold communion." She urges Life not to injure the lovers. The story ends with an incomplete sentence: "The youth, mindful of how great evil she had wrought him in that wood, mistrusted Life; but the lady, although she doubted, yet being jealous of Death . . ."

This fable perhaps reflects the moods and retrospections of the Emilia Viviani episode: the search for love that led to disillusionment by "life" (beginning at the age of fifteen with Harriet Grove); the discovery of the "glorious . . . vision" (Emilia); an obsession (as in *Alastor*) with death following these early disappointments; the proposal of the hopeless lover to the lady that death is perhaps the only path before them, a proposal that is rejected by the lady (Emilia's marriage), who seeks life, not knowing that its values will prove to be the opposite of those of a true, selfless love.[92]

In considering Shelley's philosophy as expressed in his later prose, one must keep in mind a certain imbalance caused by the fact that it includes no work on science. Since Shelley's poetry continued to be imbued with science, the gap in the prose does not indicate a cessation of interest. Carl Grabo in *A Newton among Poets* and Desmond King-Hele, himself a scientist, in *Shelley: The Man and the Poet* have shown that Shelley's insights into science were so deeply integrated into his thinking that they form an essential part of the fabric of *Queen Mab, Prometheus Unbound, Hellas,* and other poems. Shelley, as King-Hele notes, had "a belief in the possibilities of science which would have seemed out of proportion until modern times."[93] But although Shelley recognized the possibilities of science, the science of his own age was severely limited in scope and depth. Great though the advance had been, it was mainly in physics and astronomy. Chemistry was just beginning with Priestley, Davy, and Lavoisier, as was geology; biology and psychology had hardly even begun.

Shelley's philosophy was thus the product of an age in which science had made certain advances but was just short of others that would supply vital links, such as the discovery of the cell or the theory of evolution. Shelley and his contemporaries had no explanation for the origin of man or the diversity of biological life and no conception of the connections between biological, neurological, and psychological phenomena. Astronomy and physics had advanced to a point where natural explanations for the universe and its workings were emerging, as in Kant's nebular hypothesis, and one could assume that further explanations would solve other problems. But Pasteur was still unborn, and although something like the conditioned reflex was inherent in Hartley's "associationism," there was really no psychological science.

Eighteenth and early nineteenth century thinkers, confronting both these advances and apparent dead-ends, moved in various directions in search of a general theory. Diderot and Holbach argued that mind must be a form of matter. Godwin maintained that mind and matter were antithetical entities and, although the laws of necessity operated in both, they functioned in basically different ways. Shelley felt that neither the materialism of his day nor dualism provided satisfactory answers and, following the lead of Drummond, tried to formulate a subjectivist skepticism which posited the unity of all phenomena. In doing so, however, he retained his belief in science, arguing that reality, whatever it was, was governed by natural laws. As society advanced, humanity might uncover the fundamental nature of the universe, of life, and of man. In the meantime, there was little point in speculating philosophically in areas not illumined by knowledge. Here he was, as philosopher, "content"[94] to let matters rest; as poet, he believed that he should fill in the gaps "metaphorically" by "idealisms" that might encourage and ennoble mankind.

Shelley's opposition to Christian theology and its church never ceased. He felt as bitterly about the doctrine of Heaven and Hell or the concept of a vengeful God in his later years as he had in *A Refutation of Deism,* although he did not always express his feelings as directly as he had earlier. Some modification of language seemed advisable, he began to believe, if he wished to convince others. Thus, when he writes in *On Life* about being moved to materialism by the "shocking absurdities of the popular philosophy of mind and matter, its fatal consequences in morals, and their violent dogmatism concerning the source of all things," he means the Christian theology of his own day, with its anthropomorphism, its concept that morality depends on fear of punishment after death, its naive concept of the creation, and its substitution of miracles, revelation, and dogma for thought. He rejected also such semitheological "arguments" as Plato's on immortality.

Shelley's age was not an age of philosophers. Although knowledge was making possible an advance beyond abstract empiricism, it had not gone far enough to open the way for a new synthesis. In the previous generation Kant (1724–1804) had attempted to shore up the ruins left by Hume and in the process had created new if nebulous structures. But Shelley had little regard for Kant.[95] The only major philosopher of Shelley's age, Hegel (1770–1831), pursued a different track, ignoring scientific advances and returning to the Platonic divine pattern, though he regarded it not as a static but as an evolving "dialectical" entity. Shelley, as poet, might have taken considerable interest in this concept, but Hegel's name does not appear in his reading list. Hegel, in fact, was virtually unknown in England; and England itself was to produce no philosophers until later in the century, when Huxley and others began to explore the philosophical implications of Darwinism.

Shelley's moral philosophy reflects the social and ideological changes of his age. The American and French revolutions had rocked political thought to its foundations and, in so doing, had given wider scope to ethics. Previously, from Aristotle to Kant, ethics had been essentially concerned with the individual. It now began to focus on nations and society. The old concept—implied rather than stated—that the happiness of only a narrow segment of society really counted was being broadened under the blows of a spreading democracy until it found its ultimate expression in the Godwinian and Benthamite "greatest happiness of the greatest number." And the morality of nations and governments, hitherto considered outside the scope of ethics, was being forced within it by a quarter-century of bloody and devastating war.

It was with this current of thought that Shelley stood. Governments and laws could be immoral, and when they were, they must be defied. He had early accepted Godwin's view that morality should form the basis of politics and so should be considered primarily a social rather than personal matter. But he went beyond Godwin, and beyond Bentham also. "Until the mind can love, and admire, and trust, and hope, and endure," he wrote in the Preface to *Prometheus Unbound*, "reasoned principles of moral conduct are seeds cast upon the highway of life which the unconscious passenger tramples into dust, although they would bear the harvest of his happiness."[96] Ethical theories and systems, though useful, miss the essential point, namely, that the achievement of a higher morality is not a matter of maxims but of human feelings, and these are part of a larger social complex. Love, Shelley had declared two years previously in the Preface to *The Revolt of Islam*, should be "the sole law which should govern the moral world."[97] But he realized that this would not be possible until there was "a great and important change in the spirit which animates the social institutions." Thus,

Shelley's moral and sociopolitical views form a synthesis: since morality is not primarily an individual but a social matter, the moral level depends on the social level; political change can bring about a society in which moral forces have greater play; this, in turn, will effect further social change; the hatreds aroused by tyranny and oppression will in time be abolished, and love, born of egalitarian living (as exemplified by the Assasins), will become the dominant force in society.

5
Shelley As Critic

A Defence of Poetry

A Defence of Poetry, written at Pisa in 1821 and often considered Platonic or even mystical, is primarily empirical and radical—arguing that literature arises from a confluence of social, psychological, and cultural forces that in different historical situations produce different kinds of literature. The misinterpretations arose in part from the determination of some critics to see Platonism in everything that Shelley wrote, but the essay itself presents difficulties in interpretation. Its metaphorical style sometimes gives an impression of transcendental intent, which is not supported by a critical examination. It was unfinished; only Part One of a projected three-part work remains; and the last, unwritten part, on the literature of Shelley's age, would doubtless have made his basic concepts more explicit. Finally, as Shelley wished the work to be accepted in circles that had shunned him, he sometimes softened—although without basically changing—his more radical views on the relations between art and society.[1]

In the early nineteenth century the social orientation of literary theory had its beginnings in Hazlitt's "Spirit of the Age" approach, in August Wilhelm Schlegel, and in Madame de Stael's pioneer work *De la littérature: Considérée dans ses rapports avec les institution sociales* (1800).[2] It was to be expected that in a period of such unprecedented upheavals as the American and French revolutions, the industrial revolution and the Napoleonic Wars, critics would begin to emphasize the social connections of literature, for they were highlighted in a way that they had not been in quieter epochs. As in the 1930s in the United States, writers reflected the social issues of the age and reflected them from differing points of view. Blake was aware that he was expressing the viewpoint of the lower strata of society and that his outlook was fundamentally revolutionary. The novel *Caleb Williams* was as much a vehicle for Godwin's views as was *Political Justice.* It was perfectly clear to critics on both sides that Wordsworth's *Thanksgiving Ode* was not so much an emanation of the spirit of poetry as of jingoism, and that Byron's *Don Juan* was just the opposite. Wordsworth himself was well aware that his experiences in the French Revolution had permeated his early poetry. To minds brought up on the formalism of Aristotle or Johnson, the discovery of such social determinants came with disturbing impact, as the *Biographia Literaria* with its snobbish attack on Wordsworth testifies. It became clear that the ways in which a writer reflected life depended not only on his talent but on his political views and social position.

The Nature of Poetry

Not only was *A Defence of Poetry* unfinished, but it was written specifically as an answer to Thomas Love Peacock's *The Four Ages of Poetry*, and so places a disproportionate emphasis on points raised by Peacock. Peacock's *The Four Ages of Poetry* (1820) is on the surface an amusing spoof on poetry, but as Shelley perceived, it has a caustic undercurrent directed against the new poetry of Coleridge, Wordsworth, Hunt, Moore, Byron, and Shelley himself. The reason for this lay, in part, as Shelley hints, in Peacock's thwarted ambitions as a poet. The fact that he had outlined in detail and written two books of a projected twelve-book epic, *Ahrimanes* (which influenced Shelley's *The Revolt of Islam*), shows how lofty these ambitions had been. Furthermore, there was a personal as well as an ideological element in the dispute. When Peacock wrote of "the degenerate fry of modern rhymsters," he could hardly have intended to exclude Shelley; and when Peacock read in Shelley's defense of the "low-thoughted envy which would under-value contemporary merit," he might well have felt that the barb was aimed at him.

The essence of Peacock's argument is that poetry has twice passed through four ages—iron, gold, silver, and brass—once in the ancient world and once in the modern, and that it is now, in its second brass age, a childish, outmoded art. A man with intelligence would do better to turn to science or politics. Peacock begins with the four ages of the ancient world. Poetry in its origins, the iron age, was despicable, arising from the untutored superstition of savages hymning the deeds of brutal chieftains. The poets were regarded as prophets only because of the ignorance of the people, whom they misled: "delivering their oracles *ex cathedra,* and being indeed often themselves (as Orpheus and Amphion) regarded as portions and emanations of divinity; building cities with a song, and leading brutes with a symphony; which are only metaphors for the faculty of leading multitudes by the nose." In the next age, "the age of Homer, the golden age of poetry," poetry is supreme only because it stands alone and "has no rivals in history, nor in philosophy, nor in science." From this point on, poetry must of necessity decline. In the next period, the silver age, stretching from Aristophanes to Virgil, this decline is apparent, as poetry degenerates into mere polished repetition of past glories, and other arts develop. With the brass age, the age of Nonnus (a Christian Greek epic poet of the fifth century), this degeneration is complete. Thus ended the four ages of poetry in the ancient world.

In the modern world, the iron age was the time of the troubadours and romance writers with their absurd "semi-deification of women" and hero-worship of knights and chivalry. The golden age was the age of Ariosto in Italy and Shakespeare in England. The silver age was the Augustan period, "beginning with Dryden, coming to perfection with Pope, and ending with Goldsmith, Collins and Gray." The "brass" age was the romantic period. It is this last that Peacock has really been working toward, and once he gets to it, he lets loose with full force, inveighing against "the herd of desperate imitators, who have brought the age of brass prematurely to its dotage," namely, Wordsworth, Coleridge, Southey, Byron, Campbell, and Moore. Poetry has become a cultural anachronism, the poet "a simi-barbarian in a civilized community." As poetry possesses no utility value, "intellectual power and intellectual acquisition have turned themselves into other and better channels"—mathematics, astronomy, chemistry, ethics, history, politics, political economy—and "have abandoned the cultivation and the fate of modern poetry to the degenerate fry of modern rhymsters."[3]

Shelley received the copy of *Ollier's Literary Miscellany* in which Peacock's essay appeared in January 1821 and began a first tentative reply in the form of a letter to the editor. In his first draft, Shelley lists what he considers to be Peacock's main arguments: there are "four ages of poetry . . . in which this art or faculty has progressively deterioriated"; the early poets were "savages" who wrote only to flatter "semibarbarians"; poetry has "deteriorated," as civil society and the "arts of life" have progressed; and every intelligent person should desert poetry for "political economy."[4] Although he ultimately produced not a "reply" but an independent work, these points still determined much of his structure.

In the first section of the essay, Shelley apparently set out originally to counter the argument on the barbarous and contemptible origins of poetry, which led him into a discussion of the nature of poetry. In examining any general question, Shelley usually analyzes by logical reduction, first establishing his main categories and then determining how the secondary ones are related to them. In considering the nature of poetry, he argues that whatever poetry is, it cannot in its essence be different from the other arts. All are an expression of the human creative spirit, and must therefore have common roots. The problem of the critic is to perceive what they have in common and in what they differ. The former will reveal the essential nature of all art; the latter, the nature of each particular art.

All artistic expression, he argues, is "connate [cognate] with the origin of man." It is cognate in two senses, psychological and sociological. This relationship can be perceived in the child and can be assumed in the origins of society:

> A child at play by itself will express its delight by its voice and motions; and every inflexion of tone and every gesture will bear exact relation to a corresponding antitype in the pleasurable impressions . . . The savage (for the savage is to ages what the child is to years) expresses the emotions produced in him by surrounding objects in a similar manner; and language and gesture, together with plastic or pictorial imitation, become the image of the combined effect of those objects and his apprehension of them.

Poetry, then, did not arise out of a desire to flatter savage chieftains but is the expression of an elemental force within human nature, one that turns the personality outward in imitative and rhythmic response to its environment. At first, this response was to "objects," natural or man-made. But later it broadened out:

> Man in society, with all his passions and pleasures, next becomes the object of the passions and pleasures of man; an additional class of emotions produces an augmented treasure of expressions; and language, gesture, and the imitative arts, become at once the representation and the medium, the pencil and the picture, the chisel and the statue, the chord and the harmony. The social sympathies, or those laws from which, as from its elements, society results, begin to develop themselves from the moment that two human beings coexist; the future is contained within the present as the plant within the seed; and equality, diversity, unity, contrast, mutual dependence, become the principles alone capable of affording the motives according to which the will of a social being is determined to action, inasmuch as he is social; and constitute pleasure in sensation, virtue in sentiment, beauty in art, truth in reasoning, and love in the intercourse of kind. Hence men, even in the infancy of society, observe a certain order in their words and actions, distinct from that of the objects and the impressions represented by them, all expression being subject to the laws of that from which it proceeds. But let us dismiss those more general considerations which might involve an inquiry into the principles of society itself, and restrict our view to the manner in which the imagination is expressed upon its forms.[5]

It is apparent from this passage that although Shelley believes with Locke that the mind at birth is a blank tablet so far as ideas are concerned, he also believes that it has certain capacities which have developed as the result of psychological and social forces reacting upon each other. He is noncommittal on which of these forces is primary, stating only that the "social sympathies" develop from the interactions of human beings in society. These interactions result in certain basic socio-psychological "principles," namely, "equality, diversity, unity, contrast, mutual dependence." These "principles" form the basic structure of the "social being." They provide a base for—"constitute"—the qualities that form the essence of cultural and psychological life: "pleasure in sensation, virtue in sentiment, beauty in art, truth in reasoning, and love in the intercourse of kind." Shelley does not imply an item-by-item correlation—that "equality" produces "pleasure," "diversity" produces "virtue," and so on—but suggests that all of the first in their mingled complex result in all of the second. Pleasure, virtue, beauty, truth, and love are not innate qualities. They would not develop in any human being in isolation from his fellows, for they result from the human psychological mechanism with its natural capacities—among which is one for the "social sympathies"—acting in response to social intercourse. It is because of these socio-psychological reactions that art arose. They were, in fact, operative in the very first societies, those of the "savage," and were responsible for turning him to "language and gesture" in dance and song, and to "plastic" and "pictorial imitation." They constitute the "laws" from which art "proceeds."

Shelley is not in this argument idealizing "savage" society. As he explains in the conclusion of *Essay on Christianity*: "Later and more correct observations have instructed us that uncivilized man is the most pernicious and miserable of human beings," even more the victim of "violence and injustice" than is civilized man.[6] Shelley means only to argue that certain artistic responses are inherent in humanity in its origins.

These responses "next" develop to a higher state. When "next" was supposed to be, Shelley does not indicate, but he must have had in mind either what Condorcet and others called the "pastoral" stage or the early civilizations that produced Homer and the Biblical prophets. Although artistic qualities developed further in this "next" stage of society, Shelley recognized that they could not develop fully until mankind entered an egalitarian society, as depicted in *Prometheus Unbound*. From the beginnings of society to his own day they had to one degree or another been distorted. There exists, as it were, a constant battle between the qualities that naturally arise out of the intercourse of people as people and those instilled in them by a corrupt social order.

Although in regard to "art" Shelley mentions only "beauty," this is not because he felt that the other qualities listed are not also associated with art, but because he considered that beauty constitutes the essence of art—as "truth" constitutes the essence of "reasoning." Pleasure, virtue, and love are obviously all as much a part of art as they are of human intercourse. And all of them arise from the basic "principles" of socio-psychological interaction. In searching for the roots of art, as in searching for the roots of ethics, Shelley attempts to find a natural and social explanation that is in accord with the science of his day. His approach is based on the cumulative views of such thinkers as Locke, Hume, Hartley, and Godwin.

Shelley wished to establish at the outset that poetry is not different in essence from the other arts (nor they from each other), and that all the arts grow from socio-psychological processes. In seeking the particular qualities of mind which, interacting with these processes, result in artistic creativity, Shelley, like Blake, Wordsworth, Coleridge, Hazlitt, and Keats, singles out the imagination. It cannot, he argues, be reason, or at least not reason alone, because reason is primarily analytic, concerned with "the enumeration of quantities already known," whereas imagination is primarily synthetic. Reason and imagination, however, are not antithetical; they work in harmony: "According to one mode of regarding those two classes of mental action, which are called reason and imagination, the former may be considered as mind contemplating the relations borne by one thought to another, however produced; and the latter, as mind acting upon those thoughts so as to colour them with its own light, and composing from them, as from the elements, other thoughts, each containing within itself the principle of its own integrity."

The law by which the imagination operates is that of "association."[7] True, it creates new concepts but it does so by combining materials presented to it by the senses and analyzed by reason. Shelley's general dependence on Locke is still evident, but he has now turned to Hartley as well. If Hartley's psychological associationism can explain how the elements of poetry are combined, however, it does not explain the nature ("power") of the imagination as such, anymore than the law of gravity explains the nature of gravity. Whatever imagination is, however, it is not intuitive nor unique but operates according to known psychological processes.

In thus defining imagination, Shelley has left implicit a thought that underlies much of his argument. It is clear that he considers poetry in general to be a force for good. In *Speculations on Morals,* when discussing the development of the child and the savage, he argues that so long as they are unable to comprehend pain in others, they cannot have sympathy with others. This comprehension can come only as the imagination develops: "Selfishness is thus the offspring of ignorance and mistake . . . disinterested benevolence is the product of a cultivated imagination, and has an intimate connexion with all the arts which add ornament, or dignity, or power, or stability to the social state of man."[8]

Imagination, then, is both creative and expansive. It sends the mind outward and encourages generous and humanitarian feelings. Such is also the general function of "the arts," including poetry. Here Shelley is on familiar ground. The imagination lies at the root of love, and love is a many-sided force—love between man and woman, between the individual and humanity, between humanity and nature. As poetry is akin to imagination, it is also akin to love.

Although all human beings have these qualities, there is something special about the creative artist:

> In the youth of the world, men dance and sing and imitate natural objects, observing in these actions, as in all others, a certain rhythm or order. And, although all men observe a similar, they observe not the same order, in the motions of the dance, in the melody of the song, in the combinations of language, in the series of their imitations of natural objects. For there is a certain order or rhythm belonging to each of these classes of mimetic representation, from which the hearer and the spectator receive an intenser and purer pleasure than from any other: the sense of an approximation to this order has been called taste by modern writers.[9]

In the arts there are some performers and artists who have "a certain order of rhythm" different from that of the rest; from this "order" the audience receives "an intenser and purer pleasure" than from any other. The performers and artists who create this particular "order" have a special "Faculty of approximation to the beautiful": "Those in whom it exists in excess are poets, in the most universal sense of the word; and the pleasure resulting from the manner in which they express the influence of society or nature upon their own minds, communicates itself to others, and gathers a sort of reduplication from that community. Their language is vitally metaphorical;

that is, it marks the before unapprehended relations of things and perpetuates their apprehension."

Poets and artists in all fields differ not in kind but in degree from their fellows, for as all people have something of this "order or rhythm" in them they can respond to it in others. Hence, there can be a close link between the artist and his audience. Turning specifically to the poet as writer, Shelley argues that he has more insight into reality than most people, which is conveyed in a language that by its imaginative insights ("metaphorical") and beauty of rhythm starts a resonance in the mind, giving new insights into life and new meaning to language. The poet, however, is not, as the creative artist in general is not, of a different species, but is a person with an unusual imagination and sense of beauty (an idea stemming from Wordsworth's 1800 Preface to *Lyrical Ballads*).[10] He does not create something from nothing or have mystic vision but remolds what he takes in from society and nature.

Shelley believed that truth could be discovered either by reason or by imaginative insight or, best of all, by both acting together. Conveying truth to others can be done by rational analysis alone, but it can be done in greater depth if the mind is put in a responsive state through imaginative, emotional, and rhythmic language, or by music or graphic representation. Shelley is not abandoning logic, reason, or science but is arguing only that poetry has its own pathways to truth. He himself used both methods, analysis and synthesis, usually blended together, but the former is dominant in his prose, the latter in his poetry. The concept implies a repudiation of the neoclassical distrust of emotion and imagination as deterrents to "reason"; Shelley argues that, in fact, they can assist reason.

Shelley's use of the word "poet" in its "universal sense" has a fuller scope than at first appears: "But Poets, or those who imagine and express this indestructible order, are not only the authors of language and music, of the dance and architecture, and statuary, and painting; they are the institutors of laws, and the founders of civil society, and the inventors of the arts of life, and the teachers, who draw into a certain propinquity with the beautiful and the true, that partial apprehension of the agencies of the invisible world which is called religion." Such are "the Poets" in the "universal sense" of the word. But even in its "restricted sense" Shelley's concept is broad. He regards certain writers as poets regardless of whether they write in prose or verse, arguing that the real division is not between prose and verse but between "measured" or "unmeasured language." Even if a truly creative writer writes in prose, his language still has the "harmony" that is the "essence" of poetry: "The distinction between poets and prose writers is a vulgar error . . . Plato was essentially a poet . . . Lord Bacon was a poet. His language has a sweet and majestic rhythm which satisfies the sense, not less than the almost superhuman wisdom of his philosophy satisfies the intellect.[11]

For some of the ideas in these passages Shelley may be indebted to Sidney, Johnson, Wordsworth, and Hazlitt, but he develops them in his own way.[12]

For instance, he is not simply arguing, as Wordsworth is, that the language of prose and poetry should be the same and that artificial diction should be avoided, but that the essence of poetry transcends form. Similarly, although he is indebted to Wordsworth for the concept of the poet as a "man"—albeit a man of special gifts—"talking to men," he goes beyond Wordsworth. The "Poet" is the type of the highest human intellect, the imaginative, creative mind, a representative of those "imperial spirits" of the "past" who have made human progress possible.[13] The concept follows from his definition of the imagination and was, indeed, inherent in his comments on it in *Speculations on Morals*: "Imagination or mind employed in prophetically imaging forth its objects, is that faculty of human nature on which every gradation of its progress, nay, every, the minutest, change, depends.[14]

By means of his creative intellect, the poet is able to project the "laws" underlying present historical conditions into the future, and to see, at least in general outline, the next forms of society: "For he not only beholds intensely the present as it is, and discovers those laws according to which present things ought to be ordered, but he beholds the future in the present, and his thoughts are the germs of the flower and the fruit of latest time." Shelley warns the reader not to take his words in a mystical sense: "Not that I assert poets to be prophets in the gross sense of the word, or that they can foretell the form as surely as they foreknow the spirit of events: such is the pretence of superstition, which would make poetry an attribute of prophecy, rather then prophecy an attribute of poetry." There is no such thing as supernateral prophecy (a concept perhaps developed from Spinoza). The poet is able to foresee only in so far as he can understand the nature of the present.[15] Shelley then elaborates his thought:

> A poet participates in the eternal, the infinite, and the one; as far as relates to his conceptions, time and place and number are not. The grammatical forms which express the moods of time, and the differences of persons, and the distinction of place, are convertible with respect to the highest poetry without injuring it as poetry; and the choruses of Aeschylus, and the book of Job, and Dante's Paradise, would afford, more than any other writings, examples of this fact, if the limits of this essay did not forbid citation. The creations of sculpture, painting, and music, are illustrations still more decisive.

Although the phrase "participates in the eternal, the infinite and the one" has a Platonic ring, the rest of the statement shows that Shelley intended the phrase in an Aristotelian rather than a Platonic sense; the concepts of the human condition in Aeschylus, the *Book of Job*, or Dante are essentially the same. The creative artist expresses the thoughts and emotions of different people and different periods, but all have basic similarities, and the general forms in which they are expressed are the same ("one") in all times and places. In depicting these forms, the artist "participates" in this realm of universal values: "A poem is the image of life expressed in its eternal truth There is this difference between a story and a poem, that a story is a catalogue of detached facts, which have no other bond of connexion than time, place, circumstance, cause and effect; the other is the creation of actions according to the unchangeable forms of human nature, as existing in the mind of the creator, which is itself the image of all other minds."[16]

Although Shelley was doubtless well acquainted with Aristotle's works, more direct sources for his thinking here are Sidney's *Apologie for Poesie* and Imac's discourse on poetry in Johnson's *Rasselas.* Sidney, following Aristotle, argued: "*Poesie* dealeth with . . . the universall consideration, and Historie with . . . the particular." Johnson wrote: "He [the poet] must divest himself of the prejudices of his age or country; he must consider right and wrong in their abstracted and invariable state; he must disregard present laws and opinions, and rise to general and transcendental truths, which will always be the same."[17]

As Aristotle made clear, a major point of dispute between himself and Plato lay in the matter of "forms"—Plato deriving them from a divine "pattern," Aristotle abstracting them from reality. On this question Shelley—though in general no Aristotelian—is on the Aristotelian side. Some of his metaphorical expressions are, it is true, more reminiscent of Plato than of Aristotle or Johnson, but the metaphors can be taken in various ways, and the nonmetaphorical passages make the meaning clear. The "creator" is not God, as it is sometimes taken to be, but the poet, whose mind is similar to all other minds. One concept, associated with Plato and other philosophers, that he seems to have found attractive was that of the eternal nature of mind: "But mind seems to govern the world without visible or substantial means. Its birth is unknown; its actions and influence unperceived; and its being seems eternal."[18] By this he does not mean that each individual mind is immortal but only that mind as such (like matter as such) "seems" eternal. And, unlike Plato or Berkeley, he is not thinking of a transcendent, divine mind but of mind as actually manifested in man and society. As in his philosophical writings, he withholds judgment on the basic nature or origin of mind.

By the phrase "unchangeable forms of human nature," Shelley does not mean that human nature cannot be changed. He shows many times in his works how people's characters can be changed by poverty, war, or oppression, and that in a future egalitarian society "man" will undergo a psychological transformation. He means that there are certain general "forms" which do not change, such as love or fear. The forms remain, but the specific content changes in each society.

Poetry and Society

Shelley concludes the first section of his essay with the orienting sentence: "Having determined what is poetry, and who are poets, let us proceed to estimate its effect upon society." The second, historical section is the main part of the work. Peacock's argument that poetry passes through four ages into inevitable deterioration was, as Shelley perceived, his weakest point. There was simply no sense to it. Why would poetry mechanically parade through these set stages, not once but twice? Peacock certainly expressed much of this tongue-in-cheek, as Shelley was aware, but Shelley chose to answer him seriously, in part because it gave him an opportunity to depict, in a brief historical sketch, his views on the relationship of literature to society. In this sketch he develops two points he had previously made in *A Philosophical View of Reform,* namely, that literature responds to social forces and the function of the poet is to assist humanity.

The underlying tenet of this second section is that in every age the sum total of potential talent is the same, the degree of its development depending on historical factors. Shelley made the concept explicit in the Preface to *Prometheus Unbound*:

> The mass of capabilities remains at every period materially the same; the circumstances which awaken it to action perpetually change. If England were divided into forty republics, each equal in population and extent to Athens, there is no reason to suppose but that, under institutions not more perfect than those of Athens, each would produce philosophers and poets equal to those who (if we except Shakespeare) have never been surpassed. We owe the great writers of the golden age of our literature to that fervid awakening of the public mind which shook to dust the oldest and most oppressive form of the Christian religion. We owe Milton to the progress and development of the same spirit: the sacred Milton was, let it ever be remembered, a republican, and a bold inquirer into morals and religion.[19]

The general argument here is similar to that in *A Philosophical View of Reform* on the interrelationship of social and cultural phenomena, as specifically exemplified by the cultural revival of the Renaissance arising from the bitter struggle against the feudal state and church. But in this passage Shelley applies the argument particularly to literature and places the emphasis more decisively on the priority of social factors. The implication is that the "institutions" create the intellectual "spirit," which then molds the literature. This doctrine provides a basis for a general theory of literary history. Shelley is, in effect, repudiating the common, though often only implict view that the ups-and-downs of literary periods depend on unexplained variations in the supply of talent: if the Restoration period lacks great literature and the Elizabethan is rich in it, this is because the latter had a golden rain of "genius" and the former a drought. Shelley points to the elementary fact that roughly the same number of potentially great writers must have been alive in both periods. The Elizabethan and Cromwellian (prerevolutionary and revolutionary) periods awakened such writers to an intensive use of their powers, whereas the (conservative and aristocratic) Restoration did not. In the first period one finds wide-ranging speculation on man, nature, and society; in the second, a narrow anti-humanitarian cynicism. The first period is marked by free-flowing and soaring verse; the second, by clever conformity. The literature of any age, then, both in content and form, is determined by its sociocultural roots. If Athens was great not because it had a large number of "naturally" talented individuals but because it had social forms ("institutions") that developed artistic potential, then any industrial town of England—such as Manchester—could produce a drama equal to the Athenian if it had the same "institutions" as Athens.

Shelley begins his sketch of literary history with Homer. Of the mercantile society that gave rise to Homer little was then known (Schliemann's discovery of Troy was sixty years in the future). Far apart though their ages and ideas were, Shelley felt a kinship with Homer:

> Homer embodied the ideal perfection of his age in human character; nor can we doubt that those who read his verses were awakened to an ambition of becoming like to Achilles, Hector, and Ulysses: the truth and beauty of friendship, patriotism, and persevering devotion to an object, were unveiled to their depths in these immortal creations: the sentiments of the auditors must have been refined and enlarged by a sympathy with such great and lovely impersonations, until from admiring they imitated, and from imitation they identified themselves with the objects of their admiration.[20]

The comment reveals how Shelley reconciled his dislike of "didactic poetry" with his belief that literature had a social purpose. Although the function of the poet is not to package moral precepts, it is legitimate for him to depict ideals in character or situation that indirectly might bring about moral improvement. Shelley, too, "embodied the ideal perfections of his age," sometimes, as did Homer, "in human character" (Laon and Cynthia) but more often (as in *Prometheus Unbounds*) in ideas and symbols. For Homer in his age, Shelley implies, the only path open was one of personal idealization; the great ideas that would move mankind to an egalitarian state had not yet been born, but in Shelley's own age, these ideas were abroad and could be used not just for individual moral improvement but for "reforming the world." Poetry often works not directly but indirectly: "Ethical science arranges the elements which poetry has created, and propounds schemes and proposes examples of civil and domestic life: nor is it for want of admirable doctrines that men hate, and despise, and censure, and deceive, and subjugate one another. But Poetry acts in another and diviner manner. It awakens and enlarges the mind itself by rendering it the receptacle of a thousand unapprehended combinations of thought." The concept is put more explicitly in the Preface to *Prometheus Unbound:* "until the mind can love and admire, and trust, and hope, and endure, reasoned principles of moral conduct are seeds cast upon the highway of life." The implication is that one of the functions of literature, like that of ethics, is to better the human condition. Ethics cannot function in a world of minds closed by prejudice and selfishness, and literature can help to remove these barriers. One way of doing so is by assisting that development of the imagination which leads to selflessness and love: "A man, to be greatly good, must imagine intensely and comprehensively; he must put himself in the place of another and of many others; the pains and pleasures of his species must become his own. The great instrument of moral good is the imagination."[21]

Because of this function of the imagination, even poets who are not themselves progressive in their political beliefs can, to some degree, help the cause of "liberty." As Shelley succinctly wrote of contemporary poets in *A Philosophical View of Reform*, referring no doubt to Wordsworth, Coleridge, and Southey: "And whatever systems they may [have] professed by support, they actually have advanced the interests of liberty." Shelley is not, of course, arguing that only by such indirect methods can poets assist social advancement. He believed that poets should actively support humanitarian causes, such as the Carlile case, and work for political reform. He wrote *A Philosophical View of Reform* with this purpose in mind.

> The poets, philosophers and artists ought to remonstrate, and the memorials entitled their petitions might shew the diversit[y of] convictions they entertain of the inevitable connection between national prosperity and freedom, and the cultivation of the imagination and the cultivation of scientific truth, and the profound development of moral and metaphysical enquiry. Suppose these memorials to be severally written by Godwin, Hazlitt, Bentham and Hunt, they would be worthy of the age and the cause; these, radiant and irresistible like the meridian sun would strike all but the eagles who dared to gaze upon its beams, with blindness and confusion. These appeals of solemn and emphatic argument from those who have already a predestined existence among posterity, would appal the enemies of mankind by their echoes from every corner of the world in which the majestic literature of England is cultivated; it would be like a voice from beyond the dead of those who will live in the memories of men, when they must be forgotten; it would be Eternity warning Time.[22]

Shelley believed that the poet should assist political movements by speaking and writing for them: "I wish that I had health or spirits that would enable me to enter into public affairs, or that I could find words to express all that I feel & know."[23] In fact, he did this in his Irish and reform pamphlets. The poet should write poems on specific events in order to arouse popular opposition to reaction. This was Shelley's object in such poems as *The Masque of Anarchy, Swellfoot the Tyrant, Ode to Naples,* and *Hellas.* The poet should write about his age in general and point out both present evils and future directions: hence, *Queen Mab, The Revolt of Islam,* and *Prometheus Unbound.* Though the significance of these works might not be recognized in his own age, they would at least be "ashes and sparks" for future ages: "it is reserved for future generations to contemplate and measure the mighty cause and effect in all the strength and splendour of their [the poet and his audience's] union."[24] Finally, Shelley believed that even the poetry of conservative poets had some progressive tendencies, though this did not prevent him from condemning such poets: "What a beastly and pitiful wretch that Wordsworth! That such a man should be such a poet! I can compare him with no one but Simonides, that flatterer of the Sicilian tyrants, and at the same time the most natural and tender of lyric poets."[25] Wordsworth's "tender" lyrics might develop one's humanitarian senses (the *Prelude* was still unpublished and unknown), but this did not excuse Wordsworth's political support of the aristocracy.

Shelley's essay next moves into a brief sketch of the history of the drama, which he selects as especially appropriate because "the connexion of poetry and social good is more observable in the drama than in whatever other form." Here Shelley has more background material than he had for Homer. The drama of democratic Athens rose to great heights, uplifting and stimulating its audience, developing alike the imagination and the moral sense. "But," Shelley continues, "in periods of the decay of social life, the drama sympathizes with that decay. Tragedy becomes a cold imitation of the form of the great masterpieces of antiquity." One of these "periods of decay" was the English Restoration: "At such periods the calculating principle pervades all the forms of dramatic exhibition, and poetry ceases to to be expressed upon them. Comedy loses its ideal universality: wit succeeds to humour; we laugh from self-complacency and triumph, instead of pleasure; malignity, sarcasm, and contempt, succeed to sympathetic merriment; we hardly laugh, but we smile."[26] Shelley's objection to the Restoration drama was not the usual one, against which Lamb humorously argued, namely, that it depicted personal immorality. He opposed it as the drama of an aristocratic caste cynically indifferent to the people. A similar reaction underlies Peacock's anecdote of Shelley's reaction to a passage in Beaumont and Fletcher that made fun of a poor woman and a maid servant:

> He [Shelley] said, "There is comedy in its perfection. Society grinds down poor wretches into the dust of abject poverty, till they are scarcely recognizable as human beings; and then, instead of being treated as what they really are, subjects of the deepest pity, they are brought forward as grotesque monstrosities to be laughed at." I said, "You must admit the fineness of the expression." "It is true," he answered; "but the finer it is the worse it is, with such a perversion of sentiment."[27]

Behind jokes on the lower class characters Shelley sensed the odor of exploitation and the complacency of the exploiter.

Following his brief comments on the drama, Shelley takes up where he had left off with Homer and continues to sketch the history of poetry, beginning with the "bucolic writers" of the second and third centuries B.C.,—Theocritus, Bion, and Moschus. These writers, living neither in democratic Athens nor in an absolute dictatorship but "under the lettered tyrants of Sicily and Egypt," neither descend to the depths nor rise to the heights. In completely degenerate periods, Shelley argues, people lose even "the sensibility to pleasure, passion, and natural scenery . . . For the end of social corruption is to destroy all sensibility to pleasure; and, therefore, it is corruption. It begins at the imagination and the intellect as at the core, and distributes itself thence as a paralysing venom, through the affections into the very appetites, till all become a torpid mass in which sense hardly survives."[28]

Applying these arguments to the "bucolic writers," Shelley concludes that they could not achieve "equal sensibility to the influences of the senses and the affections" but were primarily sensuous. They were unable to rise above the senses into the higher realms of the imagination, for "social corruption . . . begins at the imagination." They had not become deadened to all finer sensations; beauty still had a hold on them; but it was a beauty with roots in the pleasures of self, not the higher beauty of humanitarian love. "Their poetry is intensely melodious; like the odour of the tuberose, it overcomes and sickens the spirit with excess of sweetness." Despotic regimes infect "the whole frame of human things" with their "insidious poison."[29]

Moving chronologically upward, Shelley turns to the Roman poets. Only Lucretius, the radical, intellectual poet of the Republic, does he consider a "creator" in the "highest sense." Virgil, although creative "in a very high sense," he objects to for his "chosen delicacy of expression," and perhaps for his subservience to Augustus and Mycenas. He praises Livy, but Horace, Catullus, and Ovid he regards as imitators of the Greeks, a judgment that seems curiously blind to the earthy originality of the *Ars Amatoria* and to the passion of Catullus. On the whole Shelley objected to the Roman poets because they did not attempt the renovation of their age: "poetry in Rome, seemed to follow, rather than accompany, the perfection of political and domestic society."[30]

After the collapse of Rome, "the world would have fallen into utter anarchy and darkness" if it had not been for the poets of "the Christian and chivalric systems of manners and religion, who created forms of opinion and action never before conceived." Here Shelley is answering Peacock's attack on the troubadours and his slighting of Dante and Petrarch, but he is also interested in developing favorite themes of his own.[31] The rebirth of literature in the Middle Ages both resulted from and was affected by several factors: "the abolition of personal and domestic slavery," the partial emancipation of women, the spread of the equalitarian aspects of Christian doctrine, and (following Madame de Stael) "the incorporation of the Celtic nations with the exhausted populations of the south." The rebirth of culture in medieval Italy was also, Shelley asserted in *A Philosophical View of Reform*, owing to the rise of the Italian mercantile city-states, especially Florence: "Florence long balanced, divided, and weakened the strength of the Empire and the Popedom. To this cause, if to any thing, was due the undisputed superiority of Italy in literature and the arts over all its contemporary nations, that union of energy and of beauty which distinguish[es] from all other poets the writings of Dante."[32]

Responding to Peacock's antifeminism, Shelley regarded the "emancipation of women from a great part of the degrading restraints of antiquity" as one of the great advances of the modern over the ancient world. He had previously commented in *Discourse on the Manners of the Antient Greeks Relative to the Subject of Love*:

> The fact is, that the modern Europeans have in this circumstance [the greater freedom of women], and in the abolition of slavery, made an improvement the most decisive in the regulation of human society; and all the virtue and the wisdom of the Periclean age arose under other institutions, in spite of the diminution which personal slavery and the inferiority of women, recognised by law and opinion, must have produced in the delicacy, the strength, the comprehensiveness, and the accuracy of their conceptions, in moral, political, and metaphysical science, and perhaps in every other art and science.

As a result of this advance over the ancients, there arose a new and highly inspired genre, the literature of love:

> The abolition of personal slavery is the basis of the highest political hope that it can enter into the mind of man to conceive. The freedom of women produced the poetry of sexual love. Love became a religion, the idols of whose worship were ever present . . . the Provencal Trouveurs, or inventors, preceded Petrarch, whose verses are as spells, which unseal the inmost enchanted fountains of delight which is in the grief of love. It is impossible to feel them without becoming a portion of that beauty which we contemplate: it were superfluous to explain how the gentleness and elevation of mind connected with these sacred emotions can render men more amiable, and generous and wise, and lift them out of the dull vapours of the little world of self.

One advantage of modern over ancient literature, then, lay in the integration of women into social and cultural life. In the male-dominated society of ancient Greece, women were "educated as slaves," and as a consequence, homosexuality was rife. In medieval Italy women came into intellectual society, as depicted in the *Decameron* or Castiglione's *Courtier*. Otherwise mankind would not have had Dante's *Vita nuovo*—"an inexhaustible fountain of purity of sentiment and language"—or the works of the other poets who "celebrated the dominion of love."[33]

From "the astonishing poetry of Moses, Job, David, Solomon, and Isaiah" and from Plato's doctrines of social equality and love came the gospel of Jesus Christ. For a time this gospel was obscured by "night's black agents" (the church), but by the eleventh century it became known again and in the thirteenth was incorporated by Dante in the *Divine Comedy*. His *Paradiso* is "a perpetual hymn of everlasting love," and Dante himself is "the Lucifer of that starry flock which in the thirteenth century shone forth from republican Italy, as from a heaven, into the darkness of the benighted world." Along with Milton he shared the honor of conferring "upon modern mythology a systematic form." For Boccaccio, Shelley also had considerable admiration, though he says little about him in *A Defence of Poetry.*[34] Following the great trio of "poets" of republican Italy—Dante, Petrarch, and Boccaccio,—Italian literature declined:

I consider the three first as the productions of the vigour of the infancy of a new nation, as rivulets from the same spring as that which fed the greatness of the republics of Florence and Pisa, and which checked the influence of the German Emperors, and from which through obscure channels Raphael and Michel Angelo drew the light and the harmony of their inspiration. When the second-rate Poets of Italy wrote, the corrupting blight of tyranny was already hanging on every bud of genius. Energy and simplicity, and unity of idea were no more. In vain do we seek in the finest passages of Ariosto and Tasso any expression which at all approaches, in this respect, to those of Petrarch and Dante.[35]

Before this decline took place, Chaucer had received inspiration from Italy: "The father of our own literature, Chaucer, wrought from the simple and powerful language of a nursling of this Republic [Florence] the basis of our own literature. And thus we owe, among other causes, the exact condition belonging to [our own] intellectual existence to the generous disdain of submission which burned in the bosoms of men who filled a distant generation and inhabited another land."[36]

The Contemporary Scene

Shelley begins the final section of his *Defence* with a consideration of political science and economics (exalted by Peacock). It is true, he argues, that great improvements are needed in these fields, but many of those who have tried have only made matters worse:

Whilst the mechanist abridges, and the political economist combines, labour, let them beware that their speculations, for want of correspondence with those first principles which belong to the imagination, do not tend, as they have in modern England, to exasperate at once the extremes of luxury and want. They have exemplified the saying, "To him that hath, more shall be given; and from him that hath not, the little that he hath shall be taken away." The rich have become richer, and the poor have become poorer; and the vessel of the state is driven between the Scylla and Charybdis of anarchy and despotism. Such are the effects which must ever flow from an unmitigated exercise of the calculating faculty.

By "those first principles which belong to the imagination" Shelley means the selfless humanitarianism that would enable inventors and economists to look beyond narrow interests and plan for the good of all. Lacking it, they have created the material and ideological basis for an increasing inequality, which has confronted humanity with a choice between military despotism and mass revolution. Social science and technology, in fact, have trapped humanity in an economic system that it cannot control:

> The cultivation of those sciences which have enlarged the limits of the empire of man over the external world, has, for want of the poetical faculty, proportionally circumscribed those of the internal world; and man, having enslaved the elements, remains himself a slave. To what but a cultivation of the mechanical arts in a degree disproportioned to the presence of the creative faculty, which is the basis of all knowledge, is to be attributed the abuse of all invention for abridging and combining labour, to the exasperation of the inequality of mankind? From what other cause has it arisen that these inventions which should have lightened, have added a weight to the curse imposed on Adam? Thus Poetry, and the principle of Self, of which Money is the visible incarnation, are the God and Mammon of the world.[37]

Shelley is obviously thinking not of agricultural but of industrial activity, specifically of the growth of factories and of the slum-dwelling proletariat that was rising as a consequence. Both in this concept and in that of the inability of mankind to control the economic monster it had created he was probably indebted to Robert Owen, who was the most prominent advocate of such ideas.

In *A Philosophical View of Reform*, a political tract, Shelley proposed a political solution; here he considers the psychological and cultural implications. Like Blake, he associates capitalist greed with mechanistic reasoning: "accumulation of facts and calculating processes." (No doubt he had his arch-enemy, Malthus, partly in mind.) He associates the spirit of poetry with imagination and love. The function of the poet is to spread the spirit of love in order to counteract greed, self-interest, and cold, mechanical thinking. The advances made by mere "reasoners," such as Locke, Hume, Gibbon, and Voltaire, could not have been made at all if it had not been for the opening of new horizons by the truly imaginative thinkers, "the Poets and poetical philosophers," among whom Shelley includes Bacon and Rousseau: "The human mind could never, except by the intervention of these excitements, have been awakened to the invention of the grosser sciences, and that application of analytical reasoning to the aberrations of society, which it is now attempted to exalt over the direct expression of the inventive and creative faculty itself."[38] Shelley is here certainly less than just to the "reasoners," and his concept of the role of cultural influences in social progress is exaggerated, but that he was thinking of social change as coming only from those influences is disproved by—among other things—his revolutionary Preface to *Hellas*, written in the same year as the *Defence*.

For his answer to Peacock's next argument, on the superiority of science to poetry, he was indebted to Wordsworth: "Poetry is the breath and finer spirit of all knowledge; it is the impassioned expression which is in countenance of all Science." Shelley considers poetry to be "at once the centre and circumference of knowledge; it is that which comprehends all science, and that to which all science must be referred."[39] Without creative thinking, science becomes a sterile compilation of facts to be used by the "mechanist."

The poet is sensitive to the finest shades of emotional and aesthetic experience, experience which expands the being beyond the confines of self:

> We are aware of evanescent visitations of thought and feeling, sometimes associated with place or person, sometimes regarding our own mind alone, and always arising unforeseen and departing unbidden, but elevating and delightful beyond all expression: so that even in the desire and the regret they leave, there cannot but be pleasure, participating as it does in the nature of its object. It is as it were the interpenetration of a diviner nature through our own; but its footsteps are like those of a wind over a sea, which the coming calm erases, and whose traces remain only, as on the wrinkled sand which paves it. These and corresponding conditions of being are experienced principally by those of the most delicate sensibility and the most enlarged imagination; and the state of mind produced by them is at war with every base desire. The enthusiasm of virtue, love, patriotism, and friendship, is essentially linked with these emotions; and whilst they last, self appears as what it is, an atom to a Universe.[40]

The passage has been interpreted in various ways. Are the "evanescent visitations" natural or supernatural? Is the "interpenetration of a diviner nature through our own" a religious or psychological experience? Once more, as in the *Essay on Christianity*, when the metaphorical phrasing is examined, it actually turns out to be noncommittal, but with the emphasis on the natural and rational. Shelley does not claim that there is an "interpenetration of a diviner nature," only that "it is as it were." What he means is indicated later in the passage: the "enthusiasm of virtue, love, patriotism, and friendship, is essentially linked with these emotions."[41] He is using "divine" in a moral sense, the sense of responding to and sharing humanitarian feelings. These feelings sometimes come as "evanescent visitations"; but that they are not mystic in origin is indicated in the fact that they are aroused by some "place or person," or by some set of associations within the mind itself. The statement that such experiences come mainly to those of "delicate sensitivity" and "enlarged imagination" implies that they are the result of the person's innate characteristics. Sensitive, imaginative people are more likely to respond to their fellow beings sympathetically and lose their self-interest in humanitarian feelings.

Shelley turns next to the creative process itself: "Poetry is not like reasoning, a power to be exerted according to the determination of the will. A man cannot say, 'I will compose poetry.' The greatest poet even cannot say it; for the mind in creation is as a fading coal, which some invisible influence, like an inconstant wind, awakens to transitory brightness." And again: "Poetry, as has been said, in this respect differs from logic, that it is not subject to the controul of the active powers of the mind, and that its birth and recurrence has no necessary connexion with conciousness or will."[42]

The "invisible influence, like an inconstant wind" is clearly the same as the "evanescent visitations." Whether this "evanescent" character is primarily the result of external or internal factors, Shelley does not indicate. He knows only that it is from such "visitations" that poetry is created and that one cannot control it by the "active powers" of the mind. It cannot be forced into existence by "labor and study." It is not subject to simple logic, but operates in accordance with complex laws of mental being beneath the surface of consciousness.

Shelley's plans for the projected second part of the essay included the application of principles laid down in Part I to "the present state of the cultivation of Poetry" and a "defence of the attempt to idealize the modern forms of manners and opinions, and compel them into a subordination to the imaginative and creative faculty." On the latter subject he says no more, though he had obviously intended to expound his "beautiful idealisms" technique in *Prometheus Unbound* and other works, whereby he projected present trends into the future. The probable direction that his study of "the present state of the cultivation of Poetry" would have taken is amply indicated in his concluding sentences, which were originally written for *A Philosophical View of Reform.* The essence of Shelley's view in the *Defence*—repudiating the "brass age" sardonics of Peacock—was that the present was a kind of new Elizabethan period, which was leading to a new English revolution:

For the literature of England, an energetic development of which has ever preceded or accompanied a great and free development of the national will, has arisen as it were from a new birth. In spite of the low-thoughted envy which would under-value contemporary merit, our own will be a memorable age in intellectual achievements, and we live among such philosophers and poets as surpass beyond comparison any who have appeared since the last national struggle for civil and religious liberty. The most unfailing herald, companion, and follower of the awakening of a great people to work a beneficial change in opinion or institution, is Poetry. At such periods there is an accumulation of the power of communicating and receiving intense and impassioned conceptions respecting man and nature. The persons in whom this power resides, may often as far as regards many portions of their nature, have little apparent correspondence with that spirit of good of which they are the ministers. But even whilst they deny and abjure, they are yet compelled to serve, the Power which is seated upon the throne of their own soul. It is impossible to read the compositions of the most celebrated writers of the present day without being startled with the electric life which burns within their words. They measure the circumference and sound the depths of human nature with a comprehensive and all-penetrating spirit, and they are themselves perhaps the most sincerely astonished at its manifestations; for it is less their spirit than the spirit of the age. Poets are the hierophants of an unapprehended inspiration; the mirrors of the gigantic shadows which futurity casts upon the present; the words which express what they understand not; the trumpets which sing to battle, and feel not what they inspire; the influence which is moved not, but moves. Poets are the unacknowledged legislators of the world.[43]

There has been a good deal of controversy over this passage, but there is really no problem in perceiving Shelley's meaning if one has followed his previous argument. The germ of the concept that poets are the "legislators of the world" came from the passage in Johnson's comment in *Rasselas* to the effect that the poet is "the interpreter of nature, and the legislator of mankind." By the second phrase Johnson meant that the poet should, as it were, draw up a kind of code of moral conduct for mankind. Shelley, however, broadens the concept. By "Poets" he means all truly creative thinkers, including Plato and Rousseau. In the first version of the passage, in *A Philosophical View of Reform,* he wrote "poets and philosophers." Once the new ideas of the poets get abroad, social and moral changes follow. But though the poets provide the creative spark, the reasoners often get the credit (as in Peacock's essay): "poets have been challenged to resign the civic crown to reasoners and mechanists on another plea." Thus, for instance, the coming British (Puritan) revolution was both sensed and assisted by the Elizabethan poets—among whom Shelley included Bacon—but their role has not been acknowledged by the historians. Shelley clearly considered himself, Byron, Leigh Hunt, Hazlitt, and others as the poets who in his age were paving the way for a new order. Shelley, then, does not mean that poets draw up moral codes or make laws, but that they create the intellectual atmosphere which brings about new political and legal structures. It is in this sense that they are "legislators," and usually "unacknowledged" ones. As Shelley put it in another passage: poets are "not only the authors of language and of music, of the dance and architecture, and statuary, and painting; they are the institutors of laws, and the founders of civil society, and the inventors of the arts of life."[44]

In the Preface to *Prometheus Unbound,* Shelley comments that the "great writers of our own age are . . . the companions and forerunners of some unimagined change in our social conditions." Hence, poets are "the mirrors of the gigantic shadows which futurity casts upon the present." In describing their vision as an "*unapprehended* inspiration" of "what they understand not," Shelley means that poetry is not the product of deliberate reason but of unconscious processes. The poet does not—as a poet—analyze society, as does the political scientist, but imaginatively senses changes in the offing. Even poets who have a reactionary political outlook sense progress and by the very nature of their language stimulate people to the love of liberty and justice.

In his more extended treatment of this concept—for instance, in *A Philosophical View of Reform*—Shelley makes clear that writers do have conscious understanding of their age and can directly assist it by their writings and actions, but in this summary he places the emphasis on the poet's unconscious sensitivity.

Had Shelley completed this essay, he would have evaluated his contemporaries within the general concept of an age leading to political and social renovation. What some of these evaluations would have been can be gathered from his other works. For instance, he would have treated Wordsworth as one of the great poets of the age, even though he condemned his desertion of the cause of liberty. As he wrote in his review of Godwin's *Mandeville*:

> Godwin has been to the present age in moral philosophy what Wordsworth is in poetry. The personal interest of the latter would probably have suffered from his pursuit of the true principles of taste in poetry, as much as all that is temporary in the fame of Godwin has suffered from his daring to announce the true foundation of morals, if servility, and dependence, and superstition, had not been too easily reconcilable with Wordsworth's species of dissent from the opinions of the great and the prevailing.

The comment, as in Shelley's sonnet to Wordsworth, contains both praise and condemnation, with the emphasis perhaps on the praise. By calling Wordsworth the equivalent in poetry of Godwin in moral philosophy, Shelley in effect ranked him as the most significant germinal poet of the age, for he believed that Godwin had provided "the true foundation of morals." Shelley apparently regarded Wordsworth as the founder of the new school of poetry of which he himself, Byron, Hunt, and Keats were part, for it was Wordsworth who had established "the true principles of taste in poetry." By this Shelley meant not only Wordsworth's style—his renunciation of the artificial manner of eighteenth century verse—but his content:

> In honoured poverty thy voice did weave
> Songs consecrate to truth and liberty.

To judge from Shelley's own works, the poems of Wordsworth that most attracted him were either those on humanitarian themes, such as *The Female Vagrant*, which influenced such early poems as *A Tale of Society as it is* and *Zeinab and Kathema*, or those of a Rousseauistic and Godwinian cast, such as *Tintern Abbey*, which is echoed in the invocation to *Alastor*. He no doubt rejoiced as well in such political poems as the sonnets to Milton and Toussaint L'Ouverture.[45]

So far as style is concerned, the influence of Coleridge on Shelley was more pervasive than that of Wordsworth. After *Alastor*, in fact, direct verbal Wordsworthian influence virtually disappears, but influences from Coleridge persist and can be found at least as late as *Prometheus Unbound* (1819). Nevertheless, Shelley regarded Wordsworth as the more important of the two poets. Coleridge as poet is not compared to Godwin as moral philosopher. Whereas Shelley emphasizes Wordsworth's past greatness rather than his later retreat, Coleridge is depicted as the renegade, who in his backsliding befuddled a great mind and killed a great promise:

He was a mighty poet—and
A subtle-souled psychologist;
All things he seemed to understand
Of old or new—of sea or land—
But his own mind—which was a mist.

This was a man who might have turned
Hell into Heaven—and so in gladness
A Heaven unto himself have earned;
But he in shadows undiscerned
Trusted,—and damned himself to madness.[46]

The third of the "Lakers," Robert Southey, Shelley had read during his "votary of romance" schoolboy days, and in the fall of 1812 he visited Southey at Keswick. He soon came to detest Southey's political and religious views but retained a liking for his early poems of social protest (which influenced some *Esdaile* poems and *Queen Mab*). Sending Southey a copy of *Alastor* in March 1816, he wrote that he viewed him with "admiration as a poet" and "respect as a man" and suggested that their wide difference "in moral and political opinions" might not prevent Southey from viewing his work charitably.[47] From 1817 on, however, he had nothing favorable to say about Southey, and he seems to have considered him a minor figure.

In the next generation of poets, he regarded Byron as outstanding. He discerned that *Don Juan* was Byron's masterpiece—a judgment showing the range of his taste, for nothing could be further removed in style and content from his own work: "It sets him not above but far above all the poets of the day: every word has the stamp of immortality."[48] Shelley was also able, as few modern critics have been, to perceive the greatness of Byron's best political verse: "the 'Prophecy of Danté' . . . is indeed sublime." He praised the *Cain, Sardanapalus, Foscari* volume warmly—"In my opinion it contains finer poetry than has appeared in England since the publication of Paradise Regained"—no doubt having the antireligious rebel Cain especially in mind: "Cain is apocalyptic—it is a revelation not before communicated to man."[49]

On Keats his judgment was uneven. For instance, on the volume containing *Hyperion*, the odes *To a Nightingale* and *On a Grecian Urn, Lamia, Isabella,* and *The Eve of St. Agnes*, he commented: "Keats's new volume has arrived to us, & the fragment called Hyperion promises for him that he is destined to become one of the first writers of the age.—His other things are imperfect enough, & what is worse written in the bad sort of style which is becoming fashionable among those who fancy they are imitating Hunt & Wordsworth." After this first reaction, Shelley acquired a higher appreciation for some of the "other things," as indicated by Medwin: "*The Pot of Basil,* and *The Eve of St. Agnes,* he read and re-read with ever new delight, and looked upon *Hyperion* as almost faultless, grieving that it was but a fragment, and that Keats had not been encouraged to complete a work worthy of Milton." But it seems strange that Shelley did not mention the odes. Perhaps he felt that they were too self-centered and sensuous, in the "bucolic" tradition. *Hyperion,* on the other hand, with its epic magnificence and suggestions of incipient revolution, coming at times close to his own treatment of the Titan theme in *Prometheus Unbound,* he would immediately appreciate to the full—as did Byron, who called it "as sublime as Aeschylus."[50]

If Shelley had continued the *Defence* to the survey of his own age, he would have selected Wordsworth and Byron as the most significant figures, with Coleridge perhaps not far behind them. Keats would, as in *Adonais,* have been depicted as a young genius of "unfulfilled renown." Moore would doubtless have been praised, as he is in the Preface to *Peter Bell,* for his witty political satires. To these would have been added—some of them as true poets—such prose writers as Godwin, Hazlitt, Bentham, and Hunt. As to Peacock, Shelley had mixed feelings about his verse but found his novels amusing.[51] All writers in poetry or prose would have been viewed as part of a general movement having roots in the "spirit of the age."

> The only remark worth notice in this piece is the assertion that I imitate Wordsworth. It may as well be said that Lord Byron imitates Wordsworth, or that Wordsworth imitates Lord Byron, both being great poets, and deriving from the new springs of thought and feeling, which the great events of our age have exposed to view, a similar tone of sentiment, imagery, and expression. A certain similarity all the best writers of any particular age inevitably are marked with, from the spirit of that age acting on all.[52]

Although *A Defence of Poetry* was Shelley's main work of literary criticism, other works need to be taken into account. In addition to the *Defence,* Shelley wrote three reviews: on Hogg's novel *Memoirs of Prince Alexy Haimatoff,* on Godwin's *Mandeville,* and on Peacock's *Rhododaphne.* He began one other work, *On the Revival of Literature,* which he apparently intended to turn into a fairly full exposition of his views. The prefaces to many of his poems and *A Philosophical View of Reform* contain important critical comments, as do his letters.

In the *Haimatoff* review, Shelley's condemnation of the book's sexual morality of "promiscuous concubinage" and its false ideal of chivalry is matched by his comment on an incident in which Haimatoff cynically switches from Whiggism to Toryism in order to gain the hand of a nobleman's daughter: "An instance of more deplorable perversity of the human understanding we do not recollect ever to have witnessed. It almost persuades us to believe that scepticism or indifference concerning certain sacred truths may occasionally produce a subtlety of sophism, by which the conscience of the criminal may be bribed to overlook his crime." Both sets of comments show once more that although Shelley abhorred didacticism, he nevertheless felt that literature had for one of its objectives as an art form the creation of a humanitarian ethic.

The reviews of *Mandeville* and *Rhododaphne* are of no particular consequence, although that on *Rhododaphne* gives further revelations of Shelley's love for Greek life and literature.[53]

In *On the Revival of Literature*, Shelley treats a theme he also handles in the *Defence*: the rebirth of literature in medieval Italy with Dante and Petrarch. Previous to this revival, literature had been held back by religious superstition: "The monks in their cloisters were engaged in trifling and ridiculous disputes . . . Morality,—the great means and end of man,—was contained, as they affirmed, in the extent of a few hundred pages of a certain book [the Bible]." Once this intellectual tyranny was ended, the revival began, and the influence of "Grecian literature,—the finest the world has ever produced,—was at length restored."[54]

Much of Shelley's approach to literature is tied up with his concept of his own function as a writer. In what might be called his *Queen Mab* period he felt that his main purpose in writing was to diffuse moral and political truths that would assist the progress of humanity: "Many with equally confined talents to my own are by publications scattering the seeds of prejudice and selfishess. Might not an exhibition of truth with equal elegance and depth suffice to counteract the deleterious tendency of their principles?" As an example of literary reaction, he cited Southey, "the servile champion of every abuse and absurdity."

Seven years later, he wrote to Peacock:

> I consider Poetry very subordinate to moral & political science, & if I were well, certainly I should aspire to the latter; for I can conceive a great work, embodying the discoveries of all ages, & harmonizing the contending creeds by which mankind have been ruled. Far from me is such an attempt & I shall be content by exercising my fancy to amuse myself & perhaps some others, & cast what weight I can into the right scale of that balance, which the Giant [of Arthegall] holds.

To this comment Peacock added the following footnote:

> The allusion is to the *Fairy Queen,* book v, canto 3. The Giant has scales, in which he professes to weigh right and wrong, and rectify the physical and moral evils which result from inequality of condition. Shelley once pointed out this passage to me, observing: "Artegall argues with the Giant; the Giant has the best of the argument; Artegall's iron man knocks him over into the sea and drowns him. This is the usual way in which power deals with opinion." I said: "That was not the lesson which Spenser intended to convey." "Perhaps not," he said; "it is the lesson which he conveys to me. I am of the Giant's faction."[55]

Although it is true that Spenser did not have this "lesson" in mind, Shelley's interpretation is legitimate enough. By the "Giant's faction" Spenser meant the revolutionary, communistic Anabaptists, led by Dr. Thomas Muenzer, who were prominent in the German Peasant Wars of the early sixteenth century. They were something of a bogyman to the English Establishment, and Spenser was expressing the expected condemnation, advocating short shrift for all such rebels. Shelley understands that the giant is expressing egalitarian views and aligns himself with him.

In the same year (1819) Shelley wrote in his Dedication of *The Cenci* to Leigh Hunt:

Those writings which I have hitherto published, have been little else than visions which impersonate my own apprehensions of the beautiful and the just. I can also perceive in them the literary defects incidental to youth and impatience; they are dreams of what ought to be, or may be. The drama which I now present to you is a sad reality. I lay aside the presumptuous attitude of an instructor, and am content to paint, with such colours as my heart furnishes, that which has been.[56]

In such works as *Queen Mab, Alastor, The Revolt of Islam* or *Rosalind and Helen,* Shelley considered his role as that of "instructor." He was trying to instruct by presenting ennobling pictures of the "just" and the "beautiful." But this intention was true only in a very general sense and served to hide his real purpose, which he did not wish to emphasize publicly. *The Revolt of Islam* gives a grim, realistic picture of the contemporary scene of war and tyranny. *Queen Mab* depicts exploitation, poverty, and oppression as well as the future egalitarian society. *Rosalind and Helen* portrays political persecution, *Alastor,* psychological deterioration. Nor is he quite candid about his intent in regard to *The Cenci.* True, he is dealing with the past, but he intends its picture of injustice and despotism to reflect the present.

In August 1821 Shelley told Peacock that he considered his writings to be directed against social reaction: "the accursed cause to the downfall of which I dedicated what powers I may have had—flourishes like a cedar and covers England with its boughs." During the same period he commented in the Notes to *Hellas*: "it is the province of the poet to attach himself to those ideas which exalt and ennoble humanity." In the Prefaces he took a similar position. The preface to *Alastor* argues that isolation from humanity results in the destruction of the creative artist. *The Revolt of Islam* was written with "the view of kindling within the bosoms of my readers, a virtuous enthusiasm for those doctrines of liberty and justice, that faith and hope in something good, which neither violence, nor misrepresentation, nor prejudice, can ever totally extinguish among mankind." *Prometheus Unbound* was similarly oriented:

Let this opportunity be conceded to me of acknowledging that I have, what a Scotch philosopher characteristically terms, "a passion for reforming the world" . . . But it is a mistake to suppose that I dedicate my poetical compositions solely to the direct enforcement of reform . . . My purpose has hitherto been simply to familiarize the highly refined imagination of the more select classes of poetical readers with beautiful idealisms of moral excellence.[57]

Here Shelley implies that although the "direct enforcement of reform" was one of his motives in writing poetry, in *Prometheus Unbound* he was attempting to bring about change mainly by stimulating the intellectuals ("select classes of poetical readers") to a higher ideal of social justice and morality. Although his purpose was in fact more "direct" than he admits, in the Preface he apparently did not want to frighten off potential readers. Finally, the prefaces to *Adonais* and *Hellas,* both written in 1821, were intended, respectively, to expose the unscrupulousness of Tory critics and to arouse British support for the Greek revolution.

In a letter to John Gisborne of October 22, 1821 Shelley made a frequently misunderstood remark: "The Epipsychidion is a mystery—As to real flesh & blood, you know I do not deal in those articles,—you might as well go to a ginshop for a leg of mutton, as expect anything human or earthly from me." By the word "mystery," on which he is making a pun, Shelley means the Eucharist, as "real flesh and blood" shows. *Epipsychidion,* in other words, deals with spiritual or psychological not material matters. As Shelley put it in a later letter to Gisborne: "It [*Epipsychidion*] is an idealized history of my life and feelings."[58] In the "ginshop" analogy he implies that his other works are imaginative rather than factual. Although this is true in a general sense, it is not wholly true, and the comment about his not depicting "anything human or earthly" is not true at all. But in the letter he is accepting—mockingly and sardonically—the kind of criticism which Mary Shelley and others had made of his work, namely, that it was too visionary and ideal to be popular. He answered the same charge, in a playful mood, in the dedicatory verses to *The Witch of Atlas.*

In addition to his literary criticism, Shelley did a series of Notes on sculptures in Rome and Florence, and his letters contain a good many comments on art. The range of his appreciation is wide. He responded equally to the quiet classical beauty of Greek art and the wild horror of Leonardo's Medusa. But sometimes his social or anticlerical views are dominant: "His [Michelangelo's] famous painting in the Sistine Chapel seems to me deficient in beauty and majesty, both in the conception and the execution; it might have combined all the forms of terror and delight—and it is a dull and wicked emblem of a dull and wicked thing. Jesus Christ is like an angry pot-boy and God like an old alehouse-keeper looking out of the window."[59]

Often Shelley's art criticism is impressionistic as he attempts to recreate the spirit of the original in words, for instance, on a sculpture of the maenads:

> The tremendous spirit of superstition aided by drunkenness and producing something beyond insanity, seems to have caught them in its whirlwinds, and to bear them over the earth as the rapid volutions of a tempest bear the ever changing trunk of a water-spout, as the torrent of a mountain river whirls the leaves in its full eddies. Their hair loose and floating seems caught in the tem-

pest of their own tumultous motion, their heads are thrown back leaning with a strange inanity upon their necks, and looking up to Heaven, while they totter and stumble even in the energy of their tempestuous dance.

The theme of this sculpture suggests a difference between Greek and Roman art:

> This was indeed a monstrous superstition only capable of existing in Greece because there alone capable of combining ideal beauty and poetical and abstract enthusiasm with the wild errors from which it sprung. In Rome it had a more familiar, wicked and dry appearance—it was not suited to the severe and exact apprehensions of the Romans, and their strict morals once violated by it, sustained a deep injury little analogous to its effects upon the Greeks who turned all things, superstition, prejudice, murder, madness—to Beauty.[60]

The Greeks, with their higher civilization based on "liberty," could make beauty even out of madness and superstition, but the more rigidly minded Romans could not.

Shelley loved literature and art in all their forms. He could enter alike into the spirit of the Greek drama, the religious vision of Dante, the sophisticated satire of *Don Juan,* Shakespeare and Milton, Raphael and Spenser, Moore's Fudge Family and Keats' *Hyperion.* He reveled in "the flowery and starry Autos" of Calderon and could laugh at Wordsworth's *Peter Bell* till the tears ran down his cheeks.[61] But he could not tolerate literature or art that compromised with reaction, whether it was Spenser's aristocratic prejudice, MacHeath's callousness in *The Beggars' Opera,* upper-class decadence in Sheridan's comedies, a slur on the common people in Beaumont and Fletcher, or the "superstitions" of Michelangelo. Much though he admired *Rasselas,* he condemned Johnson's religious conservatism.[62] His "theory of poetry" was not, as Newman White has stated, linked to his "View of history" by a "semi-mystical faith" but was a logical extension of it.[63] History is a struggle between liberty and tyranny, affecting all aspects of social life; literature, as part of society, is conditioned by it and reflects it, even though writers themselves may not be fully aware of it. Shelley was primarily interested not in detailed analyses of form but, like Wordsworth, in determining the roots of his subject. He was concerned with the origins of poetry, with its relationship to society and to the human mind and personality, with the nature of the creative process. Some of his answers to these problems were unsurpassed in his age for depth of understanding, indeed, were well in advance of many present day schools of critical thought. He did not fall into the fallacy of considering style or structure in isolation from content, or content in isolation from cultural and social currents; and although he placed the emphasis on the social relations of literature, he never forgot that literature is after all literature, not sociology. He was not a professional critic like Hazlitt, constantly lecturing and writing on critical matters. But if he lacked Hazlitt's scope he more than made up for it by a deeper understanding of socio-literary processes and a finer sensitivity to poetry. His comments on his contemporaries, for instance, brief and scattered though they were, are truer than any others at the time, unmarred by the envy or malice which blurred Hazlitt's judgment on Byron or Coleridge's on Wordsworth.

Part Three Poetry

6
New Directions

Alastor. Prince Athanase. Hymn to Intellectual Beauty. Mont Blanc

Alastor, wrote Mary Shelley in a Note on the poem, "is written in a very different tone from *Queen Mab.* In the latter, Shelley poured out all the cherished speculations of his youth—all the irrepressible emotions of sympathy, censure, and hope, to which the present suffering, and what he considers the proper destiny, of his fellow-creatures, gave birth. *Alastor,* on the contrary, contains an individual interest only." It is true that *Queen Mab* is primarily social, *Alastor,* essentially psychological. The style of *Queen Mab* is direct and sharp, even at times harsh; that of *Alastor* is connotative, rich, and sinuous. But these differences do not mark an absolute break with the past. *Alastor* was not a new form for Shelley. He had written personal poetry before, as in *The Retrospect, Cmw Elan, 1812.* And the subjectivism of *Alastor* did not mean that he was abandoning revolutionary poetry—as *The Revolt of Islam* was soon to show. But *Alastor* does, as Mary implies, mark a stage in his development. It reveals new psychological insight and narrative power. It was the first mature, long poem in which Shelley employed the aesthetic style that in varied forms was to dominate his poetry from then on and which characterized his revolutionary poems (*Hellas*) as much as his personal ones (*Epipsychidion*). Although Shelley never really abandoned the matter of *Queen Mab,* he did abandon its manner.

Mary Shelley states in her Note that *Alastor* was begun following a boating expedition up the Thames in 1815 made by her, Shelley, Peacock, and Charles Clairmont. They had left Bishopsgate shortly after August 26 and returned on September 9 or 10. The Preface to the poem is dated December 14, 1815. By January 6, 1816, Shelley had printer's sheets in hand. *Alastor,* then, was probably completed by December 14. It was published in February in a volume entitled *Alastor; or, The Spirit of Solitude: and Other Poems.*[1]

Alastor deals with the solitary wanderings of a young poet. He journeys through many strange lands and cities—Memphis, Thebes, Ethiopia, Babylon—and even stranger scenes—red volcanoes towering over ice-topped mountains, secret gem-filled caverns. During these travels he is alone and oblivious to the human society around him. Then one day while sleeping in "the vale of Cashmire," he has a dream of a passionate Asian girl with "glowing limbs" offering herself to him. As he reaches out for her, shuddering and gasping, she vanishes in the enfolding darkness. He awakes, feeling wan and empty. The dream marks a turning point in the poem. The poet's journeyings become more bizarre and are marked by a "pursuit of death" restlessness: he goes up an ascending whirlpool in a cracked mountain; near an isolated well in a forest he feels the presence of a strange Spirit beside him. Finally he follows an ever-expanding river to the edge of the mountain, where he sees its waters dissipated in the "void." There he dies, alone in a silent nook.

Some of the questions raised by the poem are immediately apparent.[2] What is the significance of the dream? Why do the poet's journeyings become more frenzied afterward? What is the poet seeking? Who is the Spirit in the forest? Do the river, the mountain, the well, and so on have symbolic meaning? Why does the poet die? Within what framework are these questions to be answered? Is the poem a romance or an allegory? To assist his readers in these matters, Shelley provided a Preface.

The main theme of the Preface is the destructive effect of shutting out love, with love including, as in the essay *On Love*, both personal love and love for humanity. Shelley indicates the results of such a shutting out for the hero, who is described as a poet, and then treats the subject in general terms. There are two groups that shut themselves off from love. The first group consists of "selfish, blind, and torpid" people, intent only —like the "second aristocracy" of the business world—on pursuing their own special interests. The second consists of sensitive intellectuals who, although possessing potentialities for love, shut themselves away from their fellow beings in "self-centered seclusion." The results of their loveless states differ for each group. The first dies a slow spiritual death, shut off from humanitarian or creative impulse:

> They who, deluded by no generous error, instigated by no sacred thirst of doubtful knowledge, duped by no illustrious superstition, loving nothing on this earth, and cherishing no hopes beyond, yet keep aloof from sympathies with their kind, rejoicing neither in human joy nor mourning with human grief; these, and such as they, have their apportioned curse. They languish, because none feel with them their common nature. They are morally dead.

In contrast, the self-centered intellectuals are stricken with "sudden darkness and extinction" as the sterility of their mode of life bursts upon them: "Among those who attempt to exist without human sympathy, the pure and tender-hearted perish through the intensity and passion of their search after its communities, when the vacancy of their spirit suddenly makes itself felt."[3]

The *Alastor* poet, as depicted in the Preface, represents the second group. He is an imaginative idealist in love with nature—the "magnificence and beauty of the external world sinks profoundly into the frame of his conceptions"—and with books—he "drinks deep of the fountains of knowledge"—but shut off from his fellow beings. He lives in "self-centered seclusion." For some years he is satisfied with beautiful idealizations of art and nature, but after a time "these objects cease to suffice . . . His mind is at length suddenly awakened and thirsts for intercourse with an intelligence similar to itself. He images to himself the Being whom he loves." This would seem to be a harmless procedure, but the results are devastating: "The Poet's self-centered seclusion was avenged by the furies of an irresistible passion pursuing him to speedy ruin."

The poem is "allegorical" of a state or "situation" of "the human mind." The situation is that of a man imagining "to himself the Being whom he loves," and then seeking its "prototype." He does this because he has lived in "self-centered seclusion." Beyond this the Preface does not go. It does not explain what kind of "prototype" the poet is seeking, where he sought it, why he did not find it, nor why he should die.

The poem itself pivots around the poet's dream. One narrative sequence leads up to it, another away from it. There is also an introduction of forty-nine lines and a conclusion of forty-nine lines.

The introduction consists of an invocation to the "Mother of this unfathomable world," which seems almost deliberately reminiscent of Wordsworth.[4] But the "great Mother" is clearly necessity (hailed in *Queen Mab* as the "Mother of the world"), and the tenor of the invocation is antireligious.

In lines 50–149 the poet is pictured as in the opening of the Preface: "a youth of uncorrupted feelings and adventurous genius led forth by an imagination inflamed and purified through familiarity with all that is excellent and majestic, to the contemplation of the universe." The youth having left, as had Shelley in 1811, "His cold fireside and alienated home" (76), lives "in solitude" (60), and rejoices in the beauties of nature:

Nature's most secret steps
He like her shadow has pursued. (81–82)

He loves animals, in contrast to his lack of communion with human beings, and is a vegetarian:

the doves and squirrels would partake
From his innocuous hand his bloodless food. (100–101)

He voyages through strange lands studying the ruins and history of past empires:

Athens, and Tyre, and Balbec, and the waste
Where stood Jerusalem, the fallen towers
Of Babylon, the eternal pyramids,
Memphis and Thebes. (109–112)[5]

While thus improving his mind, he spurns human companionship and the love of women. He is oblivious to an "Arab maiden" who tends to his needs and is in love with him:

then, when red morn
Made paler the pale moon, to her cold home,
Wildered, and wan, and panting, she returned. (137–139)

Up to this point the poet has been a self-centered, ivory-tower intellectual eagerly searching for knowledge but remote from human interests. Then suddenly, to quote the Preface, his mind "thirsts for intercourse with an intelligence similar to itself," and he "images" this "Being." In the poem the "imaging" is depicted thus:

He dreamed a veiled maid
Sate near him, talking in low solemn tones.
Her voice was like the voice of his own soul
Heard in the calm of thought.

. . . . .

Knowledge and truth and virtue were her theme,
And lofty hopes of divine liberty,
Thoughts the most dear to him, and poesy,
Himself a poet. (151–154, 158–161)

At first the poet in his dream does not even look at the girl, so remote is he from communication, and simply listens to her as she sits beside him talking and then singing. But when she rises, overwhelmed by the power of her love, he faces her and sees her naked beauty:

Sudden she rose,
As if her heart impatiently endured
Its bursting burthen: at the sound he turned,
And saw by the warm light of their own life
Her glowing limbs beneath the sinuous veil
Of woven wind, her outspread arms now bare,
Her dark locks floating in the breath of night,
Her beamy bending eyes, her parted lips
Outstretched, and pale, and quivering eagerly.
His strong heart sunk and sickened with excess
Of love. He reared his shuddering limbs, and quelled
His gasping breath, and spread his arms to meet
Her panting bosom: . . . she drew back a while,
Then, yielding to the irresistible joy,
With frantic gesture and short breathless cry
Folded his frame in her dissolving arms.
Now blackness veiled his dizzy eyes, and night
Involved and swallowed up the vision. (172–189)

The poet awakes, bewildered and shaken. He seeks desperately for the vision, but it has fled, and he gazes blankly on "the cold white light of morning" (194).

It is clear from the Preface that the dream reflects the poet's imaginary ideal of love, an ideal arising from his neglect of human love. True, he has loved the beauties of nature and art, but this is not sufficient. The heart must also have human love:

> The spirit of sweet human love has sent
> A vision to the sleep of him who spurned
> Her choicest gifts. (203–205)

The ignoring of the "Arab maiden" thus represented a "spurning" of love; and it is because of this "spurning" that the poet has the dream, metaphorically represented as coming from the "spirit of sweet human love" but psychologically evoked by the neglect of the "Arab maiden."

The poet's dream is not purely sensuous. The dream-girl sings of "truth" and "liberty," ideals the poet has admired but done nothing about. She is, indeed, the perfect mate, her inner being corresponding to that of the poet: "Her voice was like the voice of his own soul" (153). But the correspondence is deceptive, for the poet has simply projected something of himself—"embodies his own imaginations"—and not actually found an affinity in another person. However, there is a strong sexual element both in the vision of the girl and in the wild desires, burning like "poison," which almost immediately begin to attack the poet, driving him madly over the earth. The dream clearly has the elements of a sexual dream, mounting sharply to orgasm. That Shelley consciously intended these sexual elements is indicated by the fact that he had depicted fellatio in an early poem, *Fragment Supposed To Be an Epithalamium of Francis Ravaillac and Charlotte Corday*, and he later used sex-act symbolism in such works as *Prometheus Unbound*, *Epipsychidion*, and *The Triumph of Life*.[6]

Following the fading of the vision, the poet's wild quest for "a prototype of his conception" begins.[7] That by "prototype" Shelley does not mean a living woman who would have the characteristics of the dream-girl is shown by the fact that the poet does not hunt for her among people. He has, in fact, been unfitted by his solitary, introspective existence for relationships with women:

> but youthful maidens, taught
> By nature, would interpret half the woe
> That wasted him, would call him with false names
> Brother, and friend, would press his pallid hand
> At parting, and watch, dim through tears, the path
> Of his departure from their father's door. (266–271)

The "youthful maidens" have some understanding of his state. They perceive that he needs love. But they mistakenly feel that he is still part of humanity and call him "Brother, and friend," not realizing that since he has become essentially nonhuman, these names are "false." His rejection of love has shriveled his spirit into something alien and monstrous. He can no longer communicate with his fellow beings, men or women. Nature, although an original molding force of humanity, is not itself a sufficient object for human love. Either physical solitude or psychological isolation can in time destroy one's capacity for love itself: "So soon as this want or power is dead, man becomes the living sepulchre of himself, and what yet survives is the mere husk of what once he was."[8] Such is the state that the *Alastor* poet is approaching at this point in the narrative.

On these matters the poem and the Preface not unexpectedly differ somewhat, for one is creative, the other expository. In the poem the poet dreams of a beautiful and intellectual girl akin to "his own soul"; in the Preface he has a "vision in which he embodies his own imaginations" of beauty and wisdom. In the poem he seeks for the dream-girl; in the Preface he "seeks for a prototype of his conception." Yet despite these differences, the basic concepts are the same.[9] Seeking beauty and love, the poet turns first to nature and then to his own imagination, but, though he may not be aware of it, all he can actually seek is a narcissistic projection of himself, for the denial of love has turned his life energies destructively inward.

Lost, lost, for ever lost,
In the wide pathless desert of dim sleep,
That beautiful shape! Does the dark gate of death
Conduct to thy mysterious paradise,
O Sleep? (209–213)

There was considerable speculation in Shelley's day on the nature of sleep, and here Shelley metaphorically represents the state of sleep as a realm of its own. It is in this realm, the poet-hero feels, that the dream-girl must exist, because it was in sleep that he saw her. The realm of sleep, however, is envisaged as akin not to life but to death. In *Queen Mab* (I, 2) Shelley had spoken of "Death and his brother Sleep."

This concept of the affinity of death and sleep provides the rationale for the poet's search, which dominates the rest of the poem. But it soon becomes clear that the poet has, in fact, lost conscious control and is caught up in an elemental drive to self-destruction:

By the bright shadow of that lovely dream,
Beneath the cold glare of the desolate night,
Through tangled swamps and deep precipitous dells,
Startling with careless step the moon-light snake,
He fled. Red morning dawned upon his flight,
Shedding the mockery of its vital hues
Upon his cheek of death. (233–239)

Some critics regard *Alastor* as a dreamy, gentle romance, but in fact there is little dreamy or gentle about it. The perverse "passion" that "shook him from his rest" is searing and brutal. To Shelley, the deprivation of love was a soul-shaking experience. The poet is no longer wandering with elevated curiosity among the ruins of Babylon or Thebes. The present has gripped him and thrown him out into the world, alone, frustrated and directionless, headed only for death. Arriving at the shore of a sea (the Caspian),[10] he perceives a small boat near the bank:

> A restless impulse urged him to embark
> And meet lone Death on the drear ocean's waste;
> For well he knew that mighty Shadow loves
> The slimy caverns of the populous deep. (304–307)

He embarks and, although now seeking death, is still seeking it not for its own sake but as the pathway to the realm where he will find the dream-girl. He looks at the swirling waves:

> As if their genii were the ministers
> Appointed to conduct him to the light
> Of those beloved eyes. (330–332)

With the embarkation, the tempo of the poem becomes more rapid, its events fantastic, and its style symbolic. The symbolism begins with the description of the boat:

> its sides
> Gaped wide with many a rift, and its frail joints
> Swayed with the undulations of the tide. (301–303)

The boat is without a sail. The poet removes his cloak and spreads it "aloft on the bare mast." Immediately, sitting there in "his lonely seat," he feels:

> the boat speed o'er the tranquil sea
> Like a torn cloud before the hurricane. (314–315)

The boat is driven by the "boiling torrent" (358) to a "shattered mountain" (360) in the Caucasus and swept into a cavern in the mountain. It follows the "windings" (370) of the stream in this cavern until it comes to an open gorge through which the side of the shattered mountain and the sky above it are visible. Here the current becomes calm and the boat moves "slowly" (374). Some distance down the gorge is a great waterfall pouring its waters into the stream. This current, coming in from the opposite direction to that from the sea, is apparently the force which has slowed the current from the sea. The two currents then meet in the gorge and create a great whirlpool that spirals upward: "Stair above stair the eddying waters rose,/ Circling immeasurably fast" (380–381). The boat is caught in the whirlpool and swept upward to an "opening" (391) in the side of the gorge through which the waters spill over into a placid stream before the whirlpool reverses itself and roars back down like water in a drain. The boat hesitates on the edge but is caught by a "wandering stream of wind,/Breathed from the west" (397–398) and moves over into the stream before the "reverting stress" (395) of the whirlpool can seize it. (Why the whirlpool goes back down is not made clear; perhaps at some point the current from the waterfall proves stronger than that from the sea and the whole mass of water moves out through the cavern.)

The stream on which the boat now moves, fed by the spilled-over waters from the whirlpool, ends shortly in a "cove . . . closed by meeting banks" (405–406), where the poet gets out and begins to walk through the forest. Night falls—"More dark/And dark the shades accumulate" (430–431)—and he comes to a "darkest glen" containing a well, from whose "secret springs" (478) a new stream flows. At the well the poet senses the presence of a "Spirit" and of two "starry eyes, which, hung in the gloom of thought," seem to "beckon him" (492). He follows the stream, which at first is small and its surroundings pleasant as it goes through the forest. But soon it flows with "larger volume" and sweeps in "descending curves" with "wintry speed" (540–543) through a canyon, until it comes to a point at which the "abrupt mountain" ends (the same "shattered mountain" the poet had entered with his boat) and the stream—now a "broad river"—plunges over a "grey precipice," falling into an "immeasurable void,/Scattering its waters to the passing wind" (569–570). Beside the top of the waterfall the poet finds a small "silent nook" (572). There, looking out on the void, he dies.

That this story has meaning beyond the narrative, Shelley stresses at the outset, when the hurricanelike wind arises to strike the cloak-sail and drive the boat out into the sea. Inasmuch as in both the Preface and the first part of the narrative Shelley makes clear that he is not writing a mere romance, the wind must have symbolic meaning. So too must such features as the cavern and the well in the forest on the mountain. Sometimes Shelley makes his symbolic meaning explicit. For instance, in his comments on the stream that flows from the well:

> The rivulet
> Wanton and wild, through many a green ravine
> Beneath the forest flowed. Sometimes it fell
> Among the moss, with hollow harmony
> Dark and profound. Now on the polished stones
> It danced; like childhood laughing as it went:
> Then, through the plain in tranquil wanderings crept,
> Reflecting every herb and drooping bud
> That overhung its quietness.—"O stream!
> Whose source is inaccessibly profound,
> Whither do thy mysterious waters tend?
> Thou imagest my life. Thy darksome stillness,

Thy dazzling waves, thy loud and hollow gulphs,
Thy searchless fountain, and invisible course
Have each their type in me: And the wide sky,
And measureless ocean may declare as soon
What oozy cavern or what wandering cloud
Contains thy waters, as the universe
Tell where these living thoughts reside, when stretched
Upon thy flowers my bloodless limbs shall waste
I' the passing wind!" (494–514)

The stream, then, symbolizes the course of life. At first it runs "like childhood laughing"; toward the end it flows downward with "wintry speed" and falls into the "immeasurable void." If the stream is life, the well from which it flows must be the source of life, and the void into which it falls must be eternity: "The space [of time]/When Time shall be no more."[11] The source of life itself is an unknown element: the "dark fountain" rises from "secret springs" (477, 478); it is "searchless"; its "source" is "inaccessibly profound" (503, 507). The poet-hero is surveying life from its unknown source to its eternal end.

Shelley also gives a clue to the meaning of the cavern and the mountain:

A cavern there
Yawned, and amid its slant and winding depths
Ingulfed the rushing sea. The boat fled on
With unrelaxing speed.—"Vision and Love!"
The Poet cried aloud, "I have beheld
The path of thy departure. Sleep and death
Shall not divide us long!" (363–369)

Since the cavern is the entrance to the realm of sleep and death, the symbol of the mountain must embrace this realm. However, as the poet also finds on the mountain the source of life, its course, and its end, it appears that in the mountain Shelley means to symbolize not just sleep and death but the universal "power" of which sleep and death are manifestations, the necessitarian "Mother of this unfathomable world."

The sea over which the poet journeys is presumably the sea of life, and the wind and currents—to judge from their role in the action—are necessitarian symbols.[12] The fact that the poet uses his own cloak as a sail perhaps signifies that it is because of his own actions—something of himself—that the forces of necessity are driving him to his doom. The poet's rejection of love starts a chain reaction over which he has no control.

Because Shelley is apparently providing symbolic parallelism for his major objects and events, the boat in which the poet journeys presumably also has symbolic meaning. As it is described as having "many a rift" and "frail sides," a plausible suggestion has been made that it represents the human body.[13] What, then, of the vast waterfall in the chasm in the mountain, the whirlpool and the little stream made of the spilled-over water where the poet precariously balances? These appear to be symbols of death. If so, the total symbolism revolves around transmigration. The poet beholds the end of life in the whirlpool—the conflicting currents of life and death?—and its new beginning in the well, and then at the end, again with a waterfall image, death once more. Shelley is apparently anticipating a (metaphorical) concept put forward later in *The Triumph of Life* and *Hellas* (201–203):

> But they are still immortal
> Who, through birth's orient portal,
> And death's dark chasm hurrying to and fro . . .

Vivid though these symbols be, they are nevertheless essentially tools in a basically psychological poem—"allegorical of one of the most interesting situations of the human mind." The boat, the journey, and the stream project various aspects of this situation, namely that of a man deprived of love.

The poem, in fact, proceeds on two levels, the narrative and the psychological. On the narrative level, it is a story of the fantastic adventures of a young intellectual in a setting which, though geographically located (the Caspian Sea, the Caucasus), is unreal. On the psychological level, no action is really taking place. The poet is not journeying across Asia Minor or being transported to a mountain top by a whirlpool. All these are poetic forms designed to illustrate the development of the psychological "situation."

On one point, however, Shelley runs into a conflict, namely, the death of the poet. This presents him with a difficulty in the Preface also: "He seeks in vain for a prototype of his conception. Blasted by his disappointment, he descends to an untimely grave." This really makes no sense. An intellectual might suffer psychological deterioration in such a situation, but he would not physically die. In the poem, the poet's death is not really motivated, despite his identification of sleep with death. Only on the psychological level of meaning does the "death" make sense—as Shelley put it in the final sentence of *On Love*: "So soon as this want or power of love is dead, man becomes the living sepulchre of himself, and what yet survives is the mere husk of what once he was." The poet, in killing the "power" of love within himself, destroys his human essence. Shelley might, then, simply have shown the poet ending as a broken recluse; but such an ending would have reduced the dramatic impact he needed to drive home his psychological and ethical concepts. And if the poet died in the poem, he had to die in the Preface as well.

The death of the poet, however illogical, was needed also to emphasize the philosophical message of the poem. At the well in the forest, the poet feels a mysterious presence:

A Spirit seemed
To stand beside him—clothed in no bright robes
Of shadowy silver or enshrining light,
Borrow'd from aught the visible world affords
Of grace, or majesty, or mystery;—
But, undulating woods, and silent well,
And leaping rivulet, and evening gloom
Now deepening the dark shades, for speech assuming,
Held commune with him, as if he and it
Were all that was,—only . . . when his regard
Was raised by intense pensiveness, . . . two eyes,
Two starry eyes, hung in the gloom of thought,
And seemed with their serene and azure smiles
To beckon him.

Obedient to the light
That shone within his soul, he went, pursuing
The windings of the dell. (479–494)

This Spirit must be intended to represent the "Power" mentioned in the Preface—"which strikes the luminaries of the world with sudden darkness and extinction, by awakening them to too exquisite a perception of its influences"—and described in the *Essay on Christianity* as the "collective energy of the moral and material world."[14] When people refuse to live in accordance with this power by failing to dedicate themselves selflessly to humanity, they perish spiritually—the intellectuals swiftly, the others slowly. The poet in the poem has denied the power, for he has lived for himself alone. Now, when he finally perceives the power he does not see its moral (human) qualities but only its natural ones, and not even all its natural qualities but only those of decline—"evening gloom" and "dark shades"—not those of "grace, or majesty, or mystery." The poet, having bypassed humanity, as it were, stands alone facing an alien universe. He also faces his own delusions, for the two eyes do not belong to the Spirit but are those of the dream-girl. Because she was a product of his own mind, they are "hung in the gloom of thought." The unhealthy "light/That shone within his soul," the creatures of his own involuted imagination, "beckon him" to death.

Shelley's view of death is one of pessimistic skepticism. The river of life pours over the precipice, "Scattering its waters to the passing wind" (570). Not only the body but the mind—"these living thoughts" (512)—are dissipated at death. As the poet lies dying in his solitary nook, the atmosphere is one of loneliness and despair.

That Shelley intends a skeptical questioning of immortality to be the central philosophical theme of the poem is shown by the fact that he deliberately stresses it in various places (especially 502–514) and concludes with a long passage (672 to the end) in which he rejects concepts of immortality as delusions. One cannot indulge even the "passionate tumult of a clinging hope." There is nothing to do but face the grim fact that one who lived has gone forever, leaving his survivors only "pale despair and cold tranquility." The passage puts into poetry what Shelley expressed in *On a Future State* in prose.

Shelley was not, however, driven to these thoughts only by his own recent illness, as Mary Shelley implies, but also by his horror at the Napoleonic Wars and despotic reaction:

O, storm of death!
Whose sightless speed divides this sullen night:
And thou, colossal Skeleton, that, still
Guiding its irresistible career
In thy devastating omnipotence,
Art king of this frail world, from the red field
Of slaughter, from the reeking hospital,
The patriot's sacred couch, the snowy bed
Of innocence, the scaffold and the throne,
A mighty voice invokes thee. Ruin calls
His brother Death. (609–619)

Two of the most influential early commentators on *Alastor,* Thomas Love Peacock and Mary Shelley, although helpful in some respects, have misled later critics in others. Peacock commented in his *Memoirs of Percy Bysshe Shelley*: "At this time Shelley wrote his *Alastor.* He was at a loss for a title, and I proposed that which he adopted: *Alastor: or, the Spirit of Solitude.* The Greek word [Alastor] is an evil genius . . . The poem treated the spirit of solitude as a spirit of evil. I mention the true meaning of the word because many have supposed Alastor to be the name of the hero of the poem."[15] The poet's difficulties arise, however, not because he lives in solitude but because he lives in a state of "self-centered seclusion." His solitude is psychological, not physical. Nor is there anything in the Preface about an avenging "spirit" in the sense that Peacock intended it. Although the poet is pursued by "the furies of an irresistible passion," these furies are his own creations arising from his "self-centered seclusion." True, the poet lives in physical solitude in the second part of the narrative, but the "situation" of his "mind," as the Preface indicates, had already been created by his spurning of human companionship, especially that of women. Physical solitude has very little to do with it. Why, then, did Shelley accept Peacock's suggestion for the title? Perhaps he felt that it was appropriate because he was in a way dealing with an avenging spirit, even though a self-created one, and because its psychological character would be apparent. Moreover, he had once had a similar experience to that of the *Alastor* poet.

In the summer of 1811, following his expulsion from Oxford, his rejection by Harriet Grove, and his alienation from his father, Shelley went for a vacation to "Cwm Elan," the isolated estate in Wales of Thomas Grove, Harriet's older brother. There he wrote, crudely but feelingly, of the "Dark Spirit" that presided over "this awful solitude." The following year, describing this experience in *The Retrospect,* he revealed that it had been of a suicidal intensity:

Then would I stretch my languid frame
Beneath the wild-woods' gloomiest shade
And try to quench the ceaseless flame
That on my withered vitals preyed;
Would close mine eyes and dream I were
On some remote and friendless plain,
And long to leave existence there
If with it I might leave the pain
That with a finger cold and lean
Wrote madness on my withering mien.

Before his rescue from this melancholy state by Harriet Westbrook, he had felt driven toward death:

O Thou,
Whose dear love gleamed upon the gloomy path
Which this lone spirit travelled, drear and cold,
Yet swiftly leading to those awful limits
Which mark the bounds of Time and of the space
When Time shall be no more.[16]

In the early summer of 1811, then, Shelley had experienced social and physical solitude and suffered from them so intensely that they must have seemed like a manifestation of an avenging spirit. True, the social solitude did not come—as it did to the *Alastor* poet—from his rejection of others, but by others, particularly Harriet Grove, but his psychological state must have been similar to that of the *Alastor* poet's. As in *Alastor,* the social and not the physical solitude was primary. If Harriet Grove had continued their relationship, the woods and waterfalls of Cwm Elan would not have seemed forbidding.

Mary Shelley contended not only that *Alastor,* in contrast to *Queen Mab,* contained "an individual interest only," but also that the reason for this lay in the fact that "the ardour" of Shelley's "political hopes" had been checked. She referred also to the events of Shelley's life during the preceding two years:

This is neither the time nor place to speak of the misfortunes that chequered his life. It will be sufficient to say, that, in all he did, he at the time of doing it believed himself justified to his own conscience; while the various ills of poverty and loss of friends brought home to him the sad realities of life. Physical suffering had also considerable influence in causing him to turn his eyes inward;

inclining him rather to brood over the thoughts and emotions of his own soul, than to glance abroad, and to make, as in "Queen Mab," the whole universe the object and subject of his song. In the spring of 1815, an eminent physician pronounced that he was dying rapidly of a consumption; abscesses were formed on his lungs, and he suffered acute spasms.[17]

Mary's emphasis is on the past: the "misfortunes" of the breakup of his marriage in the spring of 1814, the days of poverty and ostracism in the fall of 1814 and early months of 1815, and the previous ill-health and gloomy medical verdict, to which might be added the death of their first baby in early 1815. The implication is that just as Shelley's health had cleared up in the fall of 1815, so too had his psychological state, and he was happy in the bucolic cottage at Bishopsgate with Mary by his side. And certainly the immediate past, with its present reminders in his separation from his children and the coldness of Godwin and others, must still have been with him as he wrote. So too must the more recent shock of the doctor's diagnosis.[18] But the atmosphere of *Alastor* is so heavy with loneliness and despair that it must also reflect Shelley's situation at the time of writing. It is impossible to conceive of a happy man writing such a poem. Furthermore, there are indications that Shelley was, in fact, far from happy in the fall and winter of 1815–1816.

The basic theme of *Alastor*—the effects of a lack of love—is mingled with a suicidal despair. Both themes are reflected in a comment by Shelley in a letter to T. J. Hogg, written from Bishopsgate just before the composition of the poem: "Yet who is there that will not pursue phantoms, spend his choicest hours in hunting after dreams, & wake only to perceive his error & regret that death is so near?" Shelley had long been in the habit of discussing with Hogg, either directly or in hints, the intimate problems of his domestic life. He had done so in regard to Harriet. He is doing so here in regard to Mary, for as he was alone with Mary at Bishopsgate at the time, the reference in "dreams" and "error" must be to Mary.[19] He had pursued a phantom of love and found only disillusionment. As for "death," either Shelley was still depressed by the doctor's verdict of a few months before, or he was speaking of the shortness of human life in general. The facts behind these hints to Hogg were spelled out later in *Epipsychidion* (277–300), where it becomes apparent that in the months preceeding *Alastor* Shelley had begun to realize that Mary was unable to give him the love he had hoped for and he was to lie unsatisfied in "a chaste cold bed." His loneliness was doubtless aggravated by the fact that Claire was no longer in the household, having been driven out by Mary some months before. The girl who fades from the poet's arms in his dream in *Alastor* has a vivacity and coquettish quality that remind one of Claire rather than Mary.

Yet the autobiographical element should not be exaggerated. The hero of *Alastor* reflects Shelley only in a fragmentary way. Shelley did not turn his back on love and humanity. On the contrary, he dedicated his life to humanity and was unceasing in his search for love. He was not drifting but was generally purposeful and, when events demanded it, decisive. Nevertheless, he had periods of despair, loneliness, and self-pity. At Bishopsgate, the events of the past turbulent years blended with his discovery of Mary's lack of passion. At Bishopsgate also he was cut off from the mainstream of English political and literary life. He had not yet met Leigh Hunt nor plunged into the parliamentary reform movement. Whereas two years later at Marlow, when he wrote *The Revolt of Islam* and was beginning to gain recognition in radical and liberal circles, this isolation had been broken, in late 1815 it must have been oppressive.

That there was some autobiographical context in *Alastor* must have been apparent to a few readers at the time. The hero is described as a poet who has left an "alienated home" and is a vegetarian. Furthermore, that the poem reflected something of the situation of Shelley and Mary must have been apparent to Claire Clairmont, Hogg, Peacock, Godwin, and others. Perhaps another reason for Shelley's adopting Peacock's misleading title was to obscure this autobiographical element.

Alastor is an intensely personal poem. Just how personal is especially apparent today because Shelley's life is known in more detail, through letters and journals, than he anticipated. Nevertheless, Shelley was able to objectify his emotions to produce a work of art, indeed, a unique work of art. He created a narrative style whose techniques anticipate both impressionism and surrealism. The poem's symbolism makes an almost Daliesque use of the bizarre; it reflects inner states by external objects, scenes, and actions; it builds a mood of tormented, hopeless seeking in a wildly beautiful but indifferent universe, and ends on a shattering philosophical note. There had been nothing like it in English literature before, and several generations of readers have responded intensely to its strange and disturbing beauty, its haunting sense of loneliness, although often without realizing its hidden depths.

Prince Athanase

Prince Athanase (1817) is in some respects similar to *Alastor*. It was intended to be a long narrative poem, but Shelley wrote only one "Part" and some fragments. Mary Shelley commented on it:

> The idea Shelley had formed of Prince Athanase was a good deal modelled on *Alastor*. In the first sketch of the poem, he named it *Pandemos and Urania*. Athanase seeks through the world the One whom he may love. He meets, in the ship in which he is embarked, a lady who appears to him to embody his ideal of love and beauty. But she proves to be Pandemos, or the earthly and unworthy Venus; who, after disappointing his cherished dreams and hopes, deserts him. Athanase, crushed by sorrow, pines and dies. "On his deathbed, the lady who can really

reply to his soul comes and kisses his lips" (*The Deathbed of Athanase*). The poet describes her. This slender note is all we have to aid our imagination in shaping out the form of the poem, such as its author imagined.[20]

Not much of this intended plot appears in the published fragments. Part I comprises a character sketch of the prince. Fragment 3 describes Athanase's father as a Greek chieftain who died fighting the Turks and tells of the coming of the old philosopher Zonoras to Athanase's home when Athanase was a child.[21] Fragments 1 and 3 give pictures of Zonoras and Athanase as tutor and pupil. Apparently considerable time elapsed between these two fragments and the next, for Fragment 4 notes that one spring Athanase "Passed the white Alps." Presumably, the sea voyage and the first meeting with the lady described in Mary's note took place somewhere between Fragment 3, set in Greece, and Fragment 4. Fragment 5 is a hymn to love, anticipating *Ode to the West Wind.* A final fragment of six lines describes a beautiful woman with brown hair and eyes who, according to Mary, is "the lady who can really reply to his soul" and who comes to his deathbed.

The description of the prince in Part I is similar in some respects to that of the poet in *Alastor.* Like the poet, he is an idealistic young man who travels restlessly, has "a gentle yet aspiring mind," and is "with varied learning fed." He has a marked "lustre" in his eye, his hair is prematurely gray, and he is driven "from land to land" by "inner griefs." The root of these "griefs" is explained by Zonoras in Fragment 3:

> "Thou lovest, and thy secret heart is laden
> With feelings which should not be unrequited." (73–74)

There is, however, an important difference between Prince Athanase and the *Alastor* poet. Prince Athanase is a humanitarian and a radical:

> Yet even in youth did he not e'er abuse
> The strength of wealth or thought, to consecrate
>
> Those false opinions which the harsh rich use
> To blind the world they famish for their pride;
> Nor did he hold from any man his dues,
>
> But, like a steward in honest dealings tried,
> With those who toiled and wept, the poor and wise,
> His riches and his cares he did divide. (35–42)

In spite of this interest in society, Prince Athanase is, like the *Alastor* poet, without love in his personal life. He feels rejected and hated:

> a snake which fold by fold
> Pressed out the life of life, a clinging fiend

Which clenched him if he stirred with deadlier hold;—
And so his grief remained—let it remain—untold.
(121–124)

That Prince Athanase is in large part a psychological self-portrait is clear from the parallels between him and Shelley. The reference to unrequited love can hardly point to anyone but Mary.[22]

The Alastor Volume

Alastor was not published alone but as part of a volume, entitled *Alastor, or, The Spirit of Solitude; and Other Poems.* Besides *Alastor,* the volume contains eleven poems, two of them translations. Some are personal; others are political or antireligious. Some of the personal poems reveal characteristics similar to *Alastor.* For instance, three of them—*Mutability,* the poem entitled *On Death* by Mary, and *A Summer-Evening Church-Yard, Lechlade, Gloucestershire*—deal with death. Two others—*Stanzas: April, 1814* and an untitled poem beginning "Oh! there are spirits in the air"—stem from the breakup of Shelley's marriage to Harriet.[23]

On Death is a revision of an early poem that appears in *The Esdaile Notebook.* A comparison of the two versions provides insight into Shelley's development in the intervening years. In *The Esdaile Notebook,* stanza three reads:

All we behold, we feel that we know;
  All we perceive, we know that we feel;
And the coming of death is a fearful blow
  To a brain unencompassed by nervestrings of steel—
When all that we know, we feel and we see
Shall fleet by like an unreal mystery.

In the *Alastor* volume this stanza is revised:

This world is the nurse of all we know,
  This world is the mother of all we feel,
And the coming of death is a fearful blow,
  To a brain unencompassed with nerves of steel;
When all that we know, or feel, or see,
Shall pass like an unreal mystery.[24]

The rather flabby first two lines are changed entirely, except for the rhyme words. The awkward and overlong "nervestrings" becomes "nerves." The loose and dragging "we feel and we see" is tightened to "or feel, or see." And the last two lines are given a firm beat, the trite "fleet by" being changed to the simple but strong "pass."

The poems with political or antireligious implications are *To Wordsworth, Feelings of a Republican on the Fall of Bonaparte, Superstition,* and *The Daemon of the World.* The first deals with Wordsworth's desertion of the cause of liberty:

> In honoured poverty thy voice did weave
> Songs consecrate to truth and liberty,—
> Deserting these, thou leavest me to grieve,
> Thus having been, that thou shouldst cease to be. (11–14)

The poem on Napoleon reveals the difference between Shelley's views and those of Byron, Hunt, and Hazlitt. Shelley could not, as they could, champion Napoleon as the destroyer of feudal regimes, because he felt that his suppression of the French Revolution and his military invasions overshadowed his other actions.[25]

Superstition and *The Daemon of the World* are extracts from *Queen Mab,* with minor revisions. Shelley's comment on *The Daemon of the World* reveals his continuing regard not only for *Queen Mab's* subject matter but also for its style: "The Fragment, entitled 'THE DAEMON OF THE WORLD,' is a detached part of a poem which the author does not intend for publication. The metre in which it is composed is that of Samson Agonistes and the Italian pastoral drama, and may be considered as the natural measure into which poetical conceptions, expressed in harmonious language, necessarily fall."[26] This poem, which depicts the coming egalitarian society, together with the poems on Wordsworth and Napoleon, show clearly that the *Alastor* volume does not signify a retreat by Shelley from his previous views but only that he had acquired a wider poetic range in both subject matter and style.

Hymn to Intellectual Beauty

Alastor was published in February 1816. In May, Shelley, Mary, and Claire left for Geneva and their meeting with Byron, a visit that produced not only the "atheist-in-guestbook" and the "league-of-incest" scandals but Shelley's *Hymn to Intellectual Beauty* and *Mont Blanc,* Mary Shelley's *Frankenstein* and Byron's *Childe Harold,* Canto III. The *Hymn,* Mary Shelley notes, was "conceived during his voyage round Lake Geneva with Lord Byron" in late June; *Mont Blanc* was written just after a trip to the mountain in July.[27]

Hymn to Intellectual Beauty presents a number of unresolved problems, and the commentaries have not always been helpful, such as Newman I. White's influential claim that intellectual beauty "supplanted Necessity in Shelley's mind."[28] If this was so, then intellectual beauty would have become central to Shelley's social philosophy from 1816 on, but that it did not is shown by the fact that in *The Revolt of Islam* and other works written later than the *Hymn*, the ruling force in society and the universe is necessity. Furthermore, nowhere in any of his other poems does Shelley mention intellectual beauty. In actual fact, he does not use the term in the text of the *Hymn*, only in the title. In his prose it appears only once, in the translation of Plato's *Symposium*.

In Shelley's day, "intellectual" often did not refer to degree of intelligence but simply to mind as such. Thus, he writes in *Queen Mab*:

> The Spirit's intellectual eye
> Its kindred beings recognized. (II. 98–99)

By "intellectual eye" Shelley simply means the eye of a creature endowed with mind. In his translation of the *Symposium*, he writes: "The lover would then conduct his pupil to science, so that he might look upon the loveliness of wisdom . . . would turn towards the wide ocean of intellectual beauty, and from the sight of the lovely and majestic forms which it contains, would abundantly bring forth his conceptions in philosophy." Shelley here uses "intellectual beauty" to designate the beauty of things of the mind in contrast to those of nature. His concept, however, differed from Plato's, for whereas Plato felt that this beauty was a reflection of God (the One) and was essentially philosophical, Shelley had no belief in the Platonic God and placed the emphasis not on "philosophy" but on artistic creation: "Poetry turns all things to loveliness; it exalts the beauty of that which is most beautiful, and it adds beauty to that which is most deformed." Poetry, then, is akin to "intellectual beauty." Although Shelley never defined the creative source of poetry, he argued that it entailed forces beyond those of the individual poet's mind. In the mind it was tantalizingly fleeting:

> We are aware of evanescent visitations of thought and feeling sometimes associated with place or person, sometimes regarding our own mind alone, and always arising unforeseen and departing unbidden, but elevating and delightful beyond all expression: so that even in the desire and the regret they leave, there cannot but be pleasure, participating as it does in the nature of its object. It is as it were the interpenetration of a diviner nature through our own; but its footsteps are like those of a wind over a sea, which the coming calm erases, and whose traces remain only, as on the wrinkled sand which paves it.

The source for these "evanescent visitations" is a "Power": "There is a Power by which we are surrounded, like the atmosphere in which some motionless lyre is suspended, which visits with its breath our silent chords, at will." Shelley never defined this power—and indeed did not believe that its nature was known—but contented himself with equating it with "the collective energy of the moral and material world." He put the concept into poetry in some rejected stanzas, perhaps intended for *The Revolt of Islam*:

There is a Power whose passive instrument
Our nature is—a Spirit that with motion,

Invisible and swift, its breath hath sent
Amongst us, like the wind on the wide Ocean.

. . . . .

The lamps of mind which make this night of earth
So beautiful, were kindled thus of yore—.[29]

The power (or spirit) and its "breath," then, appears "among us" like the "wind" on the ocean and kindles "lamps of mind" in the "night of earth."

The *Hymn* opens:[30]

I

The awful shadow of some unseen Power
   Floats though unseen among us,—visiting
   This various world with as inconstant wing
As summer winds that creep from flower to flower;
Like moonbeams that behind some piny mountain shower,
   It visits with inconstant glance
   Each human heart and countenance.

. . . . .

II

Spirit of BEAUTY that dost consecrate
   With thine own hues all thou dost shine upon
   Of human thought or form, where art thou gone?

. . . . .

III

Love, Hope, and Self-esteem, like clouds, depart
   And come, for some uncertain moments lent.
   Man were immortal, and omnipotent,
Didst thou, unknown and awful as thou art,
Keep with thy glorious train firm state within his heart.

The general line of thought is clearly similar to that in the prose works and the rejected stanzas. The "shadow" of the "Power" that "visits" the "human heart" is the same as the "breath" of the "Power" that "visits" our "silent chords" and the "footsteps" of the "diviner nature" that interpenetrates "our own." Again, the "visitations" are "evanescent."

This parallel, however, raises a problem. The "Power" represents "the collective energy of the moral and material world,"[31] and the "diviner nature" is apparently much the same thing. But this "collective energy" is clearly a more general phenomenon than is "intellectual beauty," which is specifically the beauty of the mind and its creations. The "collective energy" is, in fact, a synonym for the universal "power" inherent in society and nature.

In the *Hymn* the poet describes his sudden inspiration one spring day "While yet a boy" by a force that one would assume from the title was intellectual beauty and which convinced him to dedicate his life to humanity and to the eradication of superstition:

> Sudden, thy shadow fell on me
> I shrieked, and clasped my hands in ecstacy.
>
> I vowed that I would dedicate my powers
> To thee and thine.
>
> . . . . .
>
> never joy illumed my brow
> Unlinked with hope that thou wouldst free
> This world from its dark slavery.

In the Dedication to *The Revolt of Islam*, III–IV, Shelley describes what is clearly the same experience, without, however, mentioning intellectual beauty:

> I do remember well the hour which burst
> My spirit's sleep: a fresh May-dawn it was,
> When I walked forth upon the glittering grass,
> And wept, I knew not why; until there rose
> From the near schoolroom, voices, that, alas!
> Were but one echo from a world of woes—
> The harsh and grating strife of tyrants and of foes.
>
> And then I clasped my hands and looked around—
> —But none was near to mock my streaming eyes,
> Which poured their warm drops on the sunny ground—
> So without shame, I spake:—'I will be wise,
> And just, and free, and mild, if in me lies
> Such power, for I grow weary to behold
> The selfish and the strong still tyrannise
> Without reproach or check.' I then controlled
> My tears, my heart grew calm, and I was meek and bold.

Both poems describe the determination engendered in the poet on a spring day in his boyhood, probably in 1810, to dedicate his life to humanity—a determination apparently resulting from his reading Godwin's *Political Justice*: "It is now [Shelley wrote to Godwin in January 1812] a period of more than two years since first I saw your inestimable book on 'Political Justice'; it opened to my mind fresh & more extensive views, it materially influenced my character, and I rose from its perusal a wiser and a better man.—I was no longer the votary of Romance; till then I had existed in an ideal world; now I found that in this universe of ours was enough to excite the interest of the heart, enough to employ the discussions of Reason. I beheld in short that I had duties to perform." Shelley referred to this early experience also in *Julian and Maddalo* (379–382):

I am prepared—in truth with no proud joy—
To do or suffer aught, as when a boy
I did devote to justice, and to love
My nature, worthless now![32]

It is revealing to look at *Hymn to Intellectual Beauty* as though it were a poem without a title. In the opening stanza there are two entities, an "unseen Power" and its "shadow." The title gives the impression that the power is intellectual beauty, but actually there is no mention of beauty in the stanza, intellectual or otherwise. There is, however, some distinction indicated between the power and its shadow. It is the shadow, not the power, that "visits" the "human heart" with an "inconstant glance." The distinction, however, is not absolute, for the shadow is after all the shadow of the power; but the shadow is depicted as a force within the human mind. (The natural images—"winds," "clouds"—are simply analogies. The power is not manifested in them but in the "human heart and countenance.")

In the second stanza comes the first reference to beauty. That the "Spirit of Beauty" here is synonymous with the power, not its shadow, is indicated by Shelley's equating of power and spirit in the rejected stanzas perhaps intended for *The Revolt of Islam.* Again, there is no sharp or absolute division between the spirit (or power) and the shadow, but the emphasis is again on the mind. The spirit affects "human thought" and "form," corresponding to "human heart and countenance" in the first stanza. The spirit is shown as not directly affecting the world—the "vale of tears"—but rather affecting the human reactions to it.[33] When the effects of the spirit pass, the world seems to be "vacant and desolate." This spirit itself is not confined to the human mind but is a vaster force that affects the mind—as the wind makes music on the "motionless lyre."

The phrase "Spirit of Beauty" (not capitalized in the manuscript) can be taken in two ways. Either the spirit is the essence of beauty and nothing else, or it is simply a beautiful spirit which can also have other attributes. It was not stated in the first stanza that the power was the essence of beauty; in fact, the impression given by "awful" and "unseen" is of a force more comprehensive than beauty alone.

In the third stanza the poet states that the search for answers to the riddle of life has produced religious superstition: "The names of God and Ghosts and Heaven,/Remain the records of their vain endeavour." Or, as he put it in *On Life:* "All recorded generations of mankind have wearily busied themselves in inventing answers to this question; and the result has been,—Religion."[34] It is only the "light" emanating from the power that "Gives grace and truth to life's unquiet dream." The indication is again that the power is more than beauty alone, for it is apparently the force which some have called God. A similar concept is found in the invocation to *Alastor*:

> Mother of this unfathomable world!
> Favour my solemn song, for I have loved
> Thee ever, and thee only; I have watched
> Thy Shadow, and the darkness of thy steps
> And my heart ever gazes on the depth
> Of thy deep mysteries. (18–23)

The spirit addressed is clearly the same as the "Spirit of Nature" and "Necessity! thou mother of the world!" in *Queen Mab* (VI, 197–198) and in *The Daemon of the World* (175, 291), published with *Alastor*. The "shaddow" is similar to the shadow in the *Hymn*. In both poems Shelley tells how as a boy he sought in false beliefs and "poisonous names" (God, Christ) for the nature of the spirit or power.

The fourth stanza begins:

> Love, Hope, and Self-esteem, like clouds, depart
> And come, for some uncertain moments lent.
> Man were immortal and omnipotent,
> Didst thou, unknown and awful as thou art,
> Keep with thy glorious train firm state within his heart.

Here again is the distinction between the universal and the subjective, between "thou" (the power) and the "train within his heart" of "Love, Hope, and Self esteem." Beauty is not mentioned.

The fifth stanza describes the conversion—when "thy shadow fell on me." The sixth stanza is the dedication of the poet to "thee and thine." It concludes:

> They know that never joy illumed my brow
> Unlinked with hope that thou wouldst free
> This world from its dark slavery,
> That thou—O awful LOVELINESS
> Would give whate'er these words cannot express.

The "awful LOVELINESS" is again the same as the "Power" and the "Spirit." As with the "Spirit of Beauty," the phrase can be taken in two ways, as a spirit that is the essence of loveliness, or as a spirit one of whose attributes is "loveliness." That the second is intended is indicated by the fact that Shelley expects the power to "free the world from its dark slavery"—by which, he means, in part at least, organized religion, as the third stanza implies. It makes little sense to expect beauty, intellectual or otherwise, to be the instrument for social or religious change. Shelley nowhere expresses such a concept, and his general social philosophy would exclude it. He does, however, in *Queen Mab* and *The Revolt of Islam*—one written before, one after the *Hymn*—expect that the universal power associated with necessity will bring about such change.

The final stanza concludes:

Thus let thy power, which like the truth
Of nature on my passive youth
Descended, to my onward life supply
Its calm, to one who worships thee,
And every form containing thee.
Whom, SPIRIT fair, thy spells did bind
To fear himself, and love all human kind.

The phrase "Spirit fair" indicates that by "Spirit of Beauty" Shelley did indeed mean simply "beautiful spirit" (and so too with "awful LOVELINESS"). It is the "power" emanating from this spirit—or redundantly but still logically, the power of the power—which has taught him to love humanity.

In view of all the evidence, internal and external, there can be no question but that the "Power" in *Hymn to Intellectual Beauty* is not intellectual beauty. Why then did Shelley give the poem this title? Presumably because he wanted a title that would disguise the poem's antireligious character: whatever power may exist is of an unknown nature; the search for it has produced the superstitions of the established religions; and the "dark slavery" of the church should be overthrown. Furthermore, although the power is not "intellectual beauty," there is an element of "intellectual beauty" in the poem. The power is itself beautiful, and its "shadow" produces elements in the mind—"grace and truth," "Love, Hope and Self-esteem"—which could be associated with "intellectual beauty" as Shelley uses the phrase in his translation from Plato. In the stanzas apparently rejected for *The Revolt of Islam*, the power kindles the "lamps of mind which make this night of earth [vale of tears] so beautiful." It was doubtless this element in the poem that gave Shelley the idea for the title and made him feel that it had a certain justification.

Shelley sometimes liked to be mysterious and enigmatic—as in the title to *Alastor. Prometheus Unbound, Epipsychidion,* and other poems are full of what can only be considered deliberate puzzles. He gave an innocuous title to radical works, such as *Queen Mab, Laon and Cythna* or *Rosalind and Helen,* thinking that his "enlightened" readers would grasp his meaning and that his deviousness might prevent the less enlightened from being alienated at the outset.

Hymn to Intellectual Beauty, is an agnostic or skeptical poem; the word "*Hymn*" is doubtless sardonic. Although the power is "unknown," Shelley feels free to speculate metaphorically on its relation to humanity. He himself had had an experience that he did not quite comprehend, but which confirmed him in the humanitarian and anticlerical direction in which he had already begun to move. The experience in the poem is neither mystical nor Platonic.[35] Shelley had no faith in a "supernatural agency," and although there is a parallel in form between the power's effect on the mind and Platonic communion with the One, the specific concepts are very different. The power is not depicted as a divine pattern of which nature is a reflection, but is an "unknown" force that leaves fleeting impressions on the human mind.

Nevertheless, it is true that the language of the poem conveys a sense of hope and feeling beyond skepticism, as do some prose passages in the *Essay on Christianity* and *A Defence of Poetry*. The reason is doubtless the same in all three works, namely that Shelley believed such ideas "exalted" mankind. Furthermore, in impassioned creative writing, the emotions tend to take over and to force the writer's language beyond what he may rationally believe. Shelley did not know whether there was any basic force behind the universe beyond what was revealed by reason and science, but he passionately hoped that there was, and that it was allied to permanence and beauty—that life was not, as it seemed, a fleeting dream ended by death:

> Depart not as thy shadow came:
> Depart not, lest the grave should be,
> Like life and fear, a dark reality.

Mont Blanc

The trip that resulted in *Mont Blanc, Lines Written in the Vale of Chamouni,* was described by Shelley in a letter to Peacock on July 22, 1816. The letter gives the setting—the mountain above and the ravine below—and something of the feeling that inspired the poem:

> We ascended winding between mountains whose immensity staggers the imagination . . . From Servox, three leagues remain to Chamounix. Mont Blanc was before us. The Alps with their innumerable glacie[r]s on high, all around; closing in the complicated windings of the single vale:—forests inexpressibly beautiful—but majestic in their beauty—interwoven beech & pine & oak overshadowed our road or receded, whilst lawns of such verdure as I have never seen before, occupied these opening[s], & extending gradually becoming darker into their recesses.—Mont Blanc was before us but was covered with cloud, & its base furrowed with dreadful gaps was seen alone. Pinnacles of snow, intolerably bright, part of the chain connected with Mont Blanc shone thro the clouds at intervals on high. I never knew I never imagined what mountains were before. The immensity of these aerial summits excited, when they suddenly burst upon the sight, a sentiment of extatic wonder, not unallied to madness—And remember this was all one scene. It all pressed home to our regard & to our imagination.—Though it embraced a great number of miles the snowy pyramids which shot into the bright blue sky seemed to overhang our path—the ravine, clothed with gigantic pines and black with its depth below.—so deep that the very roaring of the untameable Arve which rolled through it could not be heard above—was close to our very footsteps. All was as much our own as if we had

been the creators of such impressions in the minds of others, as now occupied our own.—Nature was the poet whose harmony held our spirits more breathless than that of the divinest.

When the poem was published in *History of a Six Weeks' Tour* (1817), Shelley commented in the Preface: "It was composed under the immediate impression of the deep and powerful feelings excited by the objects which it attempts to describe; and as an undisciplined overflowing of the soul, rests its claim to approbation on an attempt to imitate the untameable wildness and inaccessible solemnity from which these feelings sprang." Since the poem is concerned essentially with philosophy and not nature, the emphasis on its descriptive aspects is apparently an attempt to divert attention from its antireligious nature. The phrase "undisciplined overflowing" is intended to prepare readers for syntactical and philosophical complexities. *Mont Blanc* is, in fact, the most difficult of Shelley's shorter poems and has received more diverse interpretations than any other.[36]

The philosophical note is struck immediately in the first section:

> The everlasting universe of things
> Flows through the mind, and rolls its rapid waves
> Now dark—now glittering—now reflecting gloom—
> Now lending splendour, where from secret springs
> The source of human thought its tribute brings
> Of waters,—with a sound but half its own,
> Such as a feeble brook will oft assume
> In the wild woods, among the mountains lone,
> Where waterfalls around it leap for ever,
> Where woods and winds contend, and a vast river
> Over its rocks ceaselessly bursts and raves. (1–11)

The second section begins, "Thus thou, Ravine of Arve," and then describes the poet's reaction to the ravine. The overall structure of the two sections shows that they are parallel. The first is a statement of a general philosophical proposition, on the relation of mind to the universe, and has no specific reference either to the poet or to Mont Blanc; the second, as the word "Thus" indicates at the outset, particularizes the proposition in relation to the poet and the scene before him. The two sections have to be read and examined together.

In the first section, some critics consider the "human mind" to be the basic entity; others, the "universe of things." According to the first group, Shelley is maintaining that the universe is a passive "flow" and the significant element in the mind-matter relationship is added by the mind. The universe is like a "feeble brook" which increases its sound by echoing and blending with the sound of a "vast river" and other natural objects. According to the second group, the human mind is the "feeble brook" and the surrounding scene which it echoes is the universe. The exponents of the first view argue their case in part on syntactical grounds, namely, that the dash after "waters" in line 7 indicates that the "its" of "but half its own" in the same line refers back to the original substantive—the "universe of things." The syntactical argument, however, proves nothing one way or the other, for the dash could equally serve the purpose of providing introductory emphasis, a common use of the dash in Shelley's poetry. In this case "its" would refer to "tribute" rather than "source": as external phenomena pass into the mind, the mind adds to them. The general tenor of the passage indicates that such is indeed Shelley's meaning. In the opening two lines the emphasis is on the vast "everlasting universe," in an implied contrast to the human mind. After this beginning it would be incongruous to reverse the roles by treating the universe as a "feeble brook" and the mind as the surrounding world with its "vast river."

The nature of the "tribute" that the mind adds to the "flow" of the external universe is indicated in the difficult and much debated second section:

> Thus thou, Ravine of Arve—dark, deep Ravine—
> Thou many-coloured, many-voiced vale,
> Over whose pines, and crags, and caverns sail
> Fast cloud-shadows and sunbeams: awful scene,
> Where Power in likeness of the Arve comes down
> From the ice gulphs that gird his secret throne,
> Bursting through these dark mountains like the flame
> Of lightning thro' the tempest;—thou dost lie,
> Thy giant brood of pines around thee clinging,
> Children of elder time, in whose devotion
> The chainless winds still come and ever came
> To drink their odours, and their mighty swinging
> To hear—an old and solemn harmony;
> Thine earthly rainbows stretched across the sweep
> Of the ethereal waterfall, whose veil
> Robes some unsculptured image; the strange sleep
> Which when the voices of the desart fail
> Wraps all in its own deep eternity;—
> Thy caverns echoing to the Arve's commotion,
> A loud, lone sound no other sound can tame;
> Thou art pervaded with that ceaseless motion,
> Thou art the path of that unresting sound—
> Dizzy Ravine! and when I gaze on thee
> I seem as in a trance sublime and strange
> To muse on my own separate phantasy,
> My own, my human mind, which passively
> Now renders and receives fast influencings,
> Holding an unremitting interchange
> With the clear universe of things around;
> One legion of wild thoughts, whose wandering wings

Now float above thy darkness, and now rest
Where that or thou art no unbidden guest,
In the still cave of the witch Poesy,
Seeking among the shadows that pass by
Ghosts of all things that are, some shade of thee,
Some phantom, some faint image; till the breast
From which they fled recalls them, thou art there! (12–48)

This complex section, like the first, involves the question of Shelley's general philosophical framework in the poem. Had he, at the time of writing *Mont Blanc*, arrived at a position of epistemological skepticism? By "things" (42) did he mean only more intense sensations of unknown origin or was he still a dualist? It is difficult to say, for as Shelley himself declared in *On Life*: "The relation of *things*, remains unchanged, by whatever system."[37] One would in either case refer to "things" in the same way. Nevertheless, there is no specific statement of epistemological skepticism in the poem—as there is in *Ahasueras'* speeches in *Hellas* (1821)—and no denial of the existence of the individual mind—as in *On Life*. The general impression is of the existence of both mind and an external universe, as in Shelley's letter to Peacock. Yet the "interchange" is clearly not one of orthodox Lockean dualism. Shelley does not present the "universe of things" as pure extension and solidity, and the "tribute" of the mind as that of the "secondary qualities" of color, sound, and so on, but implies a more fluid interaction. Like Wordsworth in Shelley's much admired *Tintern Abbey* ("both what they half create,/And what perceive"), Shelley does not say where mind begins and the universe leaves off. The only thing he specifically indicates as the "tribute" of the mind to the complex is "thought." The mind, that is, arranges and thinks about the raw material submitted by the senses, then takes off imaginatively from it. Though this may seem to be a creative function of the mind, it is not creative in the philosophical sense; the mind does not create the "flow" but simply arranges its parts. As in the letter to Peacock, "Nature" is the creative force.

These general concepts seem also to lie behind the difficult and much discussed lines 34–48. The thought in the opening lines of this passage (34–40) is a repetition of the first section, where the external "universe . . . Flows through the mind" and the mind brings its own "tribute" to the flow. In the second section, a specific manifestation of the external universe, the "ravine" (34), is being contemplated by a specific manifestation of mind, the "human mind" of the poet (37). As there was in section one a general "interchange" between mind and "things," so is there now a particular interchange. The poet's mind "passively" receives impressions (passively because mind is not a creative force) and "renders" them—which is the same thing as the "tribute" of section one, namely, the mind's contribution to the process. The character of this rendering is spelled out in the succeeding lines. The mind, taking in the "flow" of the universe—specifically the ravine—

from the senses, develops from it "one legion of wild thoughts." There is just "one" legion because the poet is not sure where the external begins and the internal leaves off in so complex a process; he is not clear, that is, exactly what is contributed by nature and what by the mind. The poet is as though in a "trance" (35), which seems similar to "the state called reverie" in *On Life*, in which people feel "as if their nature were dissolved into the surrounding universe."[38]

As a result, then, of the interaction between the poet's mind and the ravine, the mind gives birth to a "legion of wild thoughts." These thoughts sometimes directly reflect and contemplate the ravine; sometimes they visit "the still cave of the witch Poesy." Some have taken this cave to be simply the poet's own creative imagination. But Shelley indicates—by "that" and "thou" (43)—that the cave is inhabited by other entities as well as the poet's particular thoughts. The meaning of "that" and "thou" is indicated by their antecedents. The antecedent of "thou" is the same as that of "thy" in the preceding line, namely, the ravine. "That" has been variously taken to refer to "darkness," to the "legion of wild thoughts," and to the "human mind" of the poet. Most probably it refers to the mind. Both the image of the ravine and the mind are sometimes "guests" in the "still cave of the witch Poesy"—witch as in "Witch of Atlas," in the sense of a creative spirit. It must be the "image" of the ravine and not the ravine itself which is in the cave, for all things in it are images, phantoms, or "ghosts." The poet's mind and the image of the ravine are not "unbidden," which implies that they are "bidden" there and that it is natural for them to be there. It is natural for the mind of the poet to be there presumably because his mind is associated with "Poesy." It is natural for the image of the ravine to be there because the "ghosts of all things that are " are there.

Those who believe that the cave is simply the mind of the poet interpret "that" of line 43 to refer not to "mind" (37) but to the "legion of wild thoughts" (41), which is grammatically possible, though strained, because it requires that both "that" and "seeking" refer back to the "thoughts." But if Shelley had meant "legion" or "darkness" to be the antecedent, he would normally have used "it." The unusual use of "that" indicates—as elsewhere in Shelley's poetry—an unusual, nonimmediate antecedent. Furthermore, if the cave is understood as the poet's mind, then the "breast" of line 47 would have to refer to his mind also, but this is contrary to Shelley's view of mind as noncreative, for the "breast" is clearly a creative agent.

If, the cave of "Poesy" is not simply that of the mind of the poet himself, it must refer to the creative imagination in general, the totality of creative imagination of which the individual poet's is, as it were, only part. This individual imagination is stirred by a larger power; or as Shelley wrote in *A Defence of Poetry*: "The mind in creation is as a fading coal, which some invisible influence, like an inconstant wind, awakens to transitory brightness." Poetry, Shelley added, "makes us the inhabitants of a world to which the familiar world is as a chaos."[39] This "world" built by poetry—that is, by the total creative imagination of all the poets of all the ages,—is the "cave of the witch Poesy." Within this cave are the "Ghosts of all things that are," including the image of the ravine. These images have come from the creative power—the wind that makes the coals of the mind glow, the power which creates intellectual beauty. In the poem, this power is the "breast" from which the images "fled" into the "cave" or, to vary the metaphor, entered the stream of the imagination. The power, not the cave, is the essential creative force. The cave is "still." If the power should die, the poetic imagination would die. But so long as the power exists and creates, the image of the ravine will exist in the imagination. The thoughts of the poet fly outward to the material ravine and inward to the poetic imagination, seeking some image of the ravine that reflects its spiritual essence—in other words, searching in the realm of intellectual beauty for some "shadow" of the "unseen Power." The same concepts underlie both *Mont Blanc* and *Hymn to Intellectual Beauty*, which is not surprising since the two poems were written within a few weeks of each other.

In the first two sections, Shelley does not mention Mont Blanc itself but only the river and the valley below. In section three, his gaze moves upward:

> Some say that gleams of a remoter world
> Visit the soul in sleep,—that death is slumber,
> And that its shapes the busy thoughts outnumber
> Of those who wake and live.—I look on high;
> Has some unknown omnipotence unfurled
> The veil of life and death? or do I lie
> In dream, and does the mightier world of sleep
> Spread far around and inaccessibly
> Its circles? For the very spirit fails,
> Driven like a homeless cloud from steep to steep
> That vanishes among the viewless gales!
> Far, far above, piercing the infinite sky,
> Mont Blanc appears,—still, snowy, and serene—
> Its subject mountains their unearthly forms
> Pile around it, ice and rock. (49–63)

As the poet looks "on high," his mind—to borrow a metaphor from Yeats—is "driven wild" by the immensity of the scene. This experience is so intense that he speculates on one of two things as having happened: either the power permeating and sustaining the universe ("unknown omnipotence") has disclosed the essence that lies beyond mind and matter, or the poet's mind has somehow been gathered into the boundless realm of death preceding birth and is now looking out from it at the world. The phenomenon, that is, can come from either external or internal causes, from a change in either the "universe of things" or the "mind."

The first four lines of the section are introductory. Their function —as in *Alastor*—is to link the world of sleep with that of death or, more exactly, with the state that precedes life. The concept originally came from Indian philosophy, where it involves both transmigration and death as sleep, and then it passed on to Plato. In his concluding speech in the *Apology* Socrates likens sleep to death, and in the *Phaedo* he pursues the concept of preexistence. Shelley could have taken some of these ideas either from Indian sources (Sir William Jones, perhaps, or other orientalists of the time) or from Plato, or from Wordsworth or other contemporaries. The poet's trance is not simply a personal dream but a participation of the mind in this death-sleep world.

Certain of the concepts in the poem Shelley is advancing philosophically, to take his own distinction, and others metaphorically. That Shelley intends the mind-matter-perception views of the first two sections as serious philosophical concepts is clear from his unequivocal and systematic statement of them in the first section. That he is simply speculating metaphorically on the ideas in the opening of section three is indicated by his qualification "Some say." That he himself had no reasoned belief in a life after death or before birth is clear from his prose works.

Stanza three ends on an antireligious note:

> The wildness has a mysterious tongue
> Which teaches awful doubt, or faith so mild,
> So solemn, so serene, that man may be
> In such faith with nature reconciled;
> Thou hast a voice, great Mountain, to repeal
> Large codes of fraud and woe; not understood
> By all, but which the wise, and great, and good
> Interpret, or make felt, or deeply feel. (76–83)

When the poem was originally published in 1817 at the end of *History of a Six Weeks' Tour,* line 79 read: "But for such faith with nature reconciled." The reading given here is that of a draft manuscript by Shelley, transcribed by Richard Garnett and noted in the standard editions of Shelley's poems. The 1817 text has been defended by various scholars, perhaps most skillfully by C. D. Locock: "The wilderness teaches doubt in the current beliefs; or, at the most, a faith in them so mild, so undemonstrative, that if man can only rid himself of these remaining traces of faith he may be made one with Nature."[40] This is ingenious certainly, but hardly persuasive when one considers the total context. Shelley clearly favors the kind of "mild faith" that can come from a contemplation of nature, in implied contrast to the superstitious "faith" of religion. He has faith that the "Spirit of Nature" or the power, working outside and through mankind, will help to restore the balance between nature and society and, in the process, will destroy social and other evils. The concept is similar to that in the conclusion of the *Hymn to Intellectual Beauty.* After having declared himself in favor of this kind of faith—"So solemn, so serene"—Shelley would hardly have reversed himself in the next line and denounced it as an evil that man should get rid of. The "faith," furthermore, is specifically a faith in the "voice" of the mountain of the following lines, the "voice" of the power; it is the good "faith" that will destroy the evil "faith" of the church.

The antireligious, skeptical theme is present also in the next two sections. For instance:

> Power dwells apart in its tranquillity
> Remote, serene, and inaccessible:
> And *this*, the naked countenance of earth,
> On which I gaze, even these primaeval mountains
> Teach the adverting mind. (96–100)

It is almost as though Shelley were responding to Coleridge's *Hymn Before Sunrise, in the Vale of Chamouni*, with its provocative footnote, "Who *would* be, who *could* be an atheist in this valley of wonders?"—and its fundamentalist raptures:

> God! let the torrents, like a shout of nations,
> Answer! and let the ice-plains echo, God!
> God! sing ye meadow-streams with gladsome voice!

Perhaps it was Coleridge's note that spurred Shelley defiantly to write "atheist" in the inn guestbook.

The "adverting mind" (100) is apparently an echo from Godwin's chapter "Of the Mechanism of the Human Mind" in *Political Justice*: "Consciousness is a sort of supplementary reflection, by which the mind not only has the thought, but adverts to its own situation, and observes that it has it. Consciousness therefore, however nice the distinction, seems to be a second thought." Godwin's passage perhaps also influenced the speculations in the conclusion of section two on the distinction between the impressions coming into the mind and the mind's concepts arising from them.[41]

In the final stanza Shelley returns to the epistemological question with which he began:

> Mont Blanc yet gleams on high:—the power is there,
> The still and solemn power of many sights,
> And many sounds, and much of life and death.
> In the calm darkness of the moonless nights,
> In the lone glare of day, the snows descend
> Upon that Mountain; none beholds them there,
> Nor when the flakes burn in the sinking sun
> Or the star-beams dart through them:—Winds contend
> Silently there, and heap the snow with breath

Rapid and strong, but silently! Its home
The voiceless lightning in these solitudes
Keeps innocently, and like vapour broods
Over the snow. The secret Strength of things
Which governs thought, and to the infinite dome
Of heaven is as a law, inhabits thee!
And what were thou, and earth, and stars, and sea,
If to the human mind's imaginings
Silence and solitude were vacancy? (127–144)

The "secret Strength of things" (139) is, once more the "Power" of the previous sections and of the first line of this one, a power that is allied with necessity and pervades both mind and matter, man and nature, a concept similar to that in *Tintern Abbey*:

a sense sublime
Of something far more deeply interfused,
Whose dwelling is the light of setting suns,
And the round ocean and the living air,
And the blue sky, and in the mind of man.

In the first section, Shelley depicted the intermingling of mind and nature in perception. In the second, he gave an example of it and speculated about the character of natural phenomena when no mind is present to observe them. So, too, in this stanza. The winds still heap the snow, but there is no sound; the lightning is "voiceless." In the final three lines he seems to put the same philosophical question in a different way: if there is no unifying power pervading both mind and nature, if there is nothing in unbeheld nature but "vacancy," how would the universe seem to human conception? The question is left open, but the implication is that there could be no communication between man and nature.

7
Shelley and Mary

Rosalind and Helen. Julian and Maddalo. Lines Written among the Euganean Hills. Letter to Maria Gisborne. The Witch of Atlas. Epipsychidion. The Sensitive Plant. Fragments of an Unfinished Drama. Lyrics. Translations

The first life of John Donne was written not because he was a poet but because he was a churchman. In the ages of feudal social dominance, the only individuals who were considered important were members of the ruling class—monarchs, aristocrats, churchmen—and in writings about them the stress was placed not so much on their personal characteristics as on their administrative actions, political or ecclesiastical. Professional writers like Shakespeare, Spenser, or Jonson did not rate biographies. As the commercial and professional classes in the cities grew and developed their own writers—Defoe and Fielding in England; Voltaire and Rousseau in France—a reaction to this snobbish downgrading of the writer set in. With it came an increasingly aggressive assertion of the importance of the individual, particularly the middle-class individual. What Rousseau implied in his *Confessions* was that he, Jean-Jacques, was as worthy of consideration as any aristocrat, because like all people, he had an individual mind, character, and life. Values should be based on personal characteristics not social status; to reveal oneself was to reveal general psychological or moral truth. Once the assertions were proclaimed, they could not be downed. By the turn of the century the movement to autobiographical searching was in full swing. Even a comparatively nonintrospective person such as Wordsworth wrote his major poem about his own life and personality. Childe Harold (first called Childe Biron) is unabashedly Byron. The *Don Juan* narrator is also Byron, or rather, another aspect of Byron, the debonaire, liberal cosmopolite in contrast to the suffering, romantic Childe. *Manfred* is a psychological confessional of Byron's love affair with his half-sister, Augusta Leigh. Keats' *Endymion* is a spiritual autobiography, and *The Fall of Hyperion* begins with deep, painful self-questioning.

The autobiographical elements in Shelley's poetry add a new dimension to the biographical material found in journals, letters, and early biographies. In range, variety, and depth of probing his autobiographical poetry is unmatched in the age. It includes *Alastor*, many of the lyrics and passages in *Adonais* and other poems, as well as the works to be treated here. True, none of these poems is exclusively autobiographical. *Epipsychidion* has philosophical overtones; *Lines Written among the Euganean Hills* centers on Italian history and its revolutionary potential; *The Witch of Atlas* is biographical only in background. But taken together, they form an autobiographical sequence, some with more, some with less depth of revelation. And all of them reveal aspects of the relations of Shelley and Mary.

Rosalind and Helen

Rosalind and Helen was mostly written at Marlow in 1817 and finished in Italy the next year.[1] It is the story of two contrasting marriages or, more exactly, one marriage and one free-love union. Rosalind falls in love with a youth who turns out to be her brother (an incest theme similar to that in *The Revolt of Islam*). He collapses and dies on their wedding day after learning of the relationship. Rosalind then marries a businessman of a hard and grasping nature. After his death she discovers that in his will he has declared her unfit to care for their three children, and she is legally deprived of them.

Helen, a girlhood friend of Rosalind's, enters into a free-love union with a young revolutionary named Lionel, whereupon Rosalind breaks off their friendship. Lionel works hard in a revolutionary movement, which is finally crushed. He wanders away in semimadness for three years, returns home, and is imprisoned. Upon his release, he and Helen journey to his beautiful estate by the sea in Wales, and there, like the hero of *Alastor*, he romantically expires. Helen and their one child leave for Italy. There they meet Rosalind, and the two women are reconciled. One of Rosalind's children, a daughter, is somehow restored to her and later marries Helen's son.

The value of *Rosalind and Helen* as a poem has little to do with this implausible story. That Shelley took only a minor interest in the narrative itself is shown by such inconsistencies as having Rosalind's daughter at one point her youngest child and at another her eldest.[2] The story, in fact, is simply a peg used by Shelley to support a passionate exposition of his social beliefs. It was written under the stress of the embittering ostracism to which he and Mary had been subjected since their elopement.

One incident had affected him especially. William Godwin had a Scottish friend named William Thomas Baxter, to whose home in Dundee he used to send Mary on vacations. There she and Baxter's daughter Isabella became good friends. Isabella married a lexicographer and brewer named David Booth, who was over fifty years of age and had previously been married to her older sister. Booth demanded that his bride break off relations with Mary, who had espoused, without benefit of clergy, an atheist and radical.[3] On September 1, 1817, Baxter began a visit to Mary and Shelley at Marlow, during which he confided to Mary that his daughter was being ill-treated by her husband: "I was much pained last night to hear from Mr. B[axter] that Mr. Booth is ill tempered and *jealous* towards Isabell—& Mr. B[axter] thinks that she half repents her marriage—so she is to [be] another victim of that ceremony."[4] Baxter, unlike Booth, was much impressed by Shelley, but he failed to convince Booth that the friendship should be renewed. When the Shelleys left for Italy the following March, although the Booths were in London, Booth refused to allow his wife to visit Mary.[5]

Apparently Shelley wrote *Rosalind and Helen* for Mary—who referred to it with pleased possessiveness as "my pretty eclogue"—in order to give a comforting picture of the happiness of their own union in contrast to the harsh but respectable one of Isabella and Booth.[6] But the poem broke beyond these bounds, and its "prettiness" vanished in an eruption of social protest. Rosalind's embittered description of poverty as breeding "foul self-contempt" (479) is a reflection of the hand-to-mouth existence of Shelley and Mary in 1814 as they dodged bailiffs, shuttling from lodging to lodging, and made frantic and humiliating deals with moneylenders.

The taking of Rosalind's children by a "sallow lawyer cruel and cold" (491) on the grounds that she was adulterous and believed "In secret that the Christean creed is false," and then the trial of Lionel for blasphemy (855-901) reflect Shelley's feelings on being deprived of his own children.[7] He presumably split the episodes in two so that the autobiographical background would not be too obvious. The picture of Rosalind's husband as "Pale with the quenchless thirst of gold" (424) is not so much a portrait of Booth himself as a composite picture of those "moneyed men" at whose hands Shelley and Mary had suffered.

The most powerfully executed part of the poem is the self-portrait in Lionel. Whereas the poet in *Alastor* is a distorted picture of Shelley, lacking his social philosophy, Lionel is Shelley not only with that philosophy intact but engaging in the kind of revolutionary activity that Shelley hoped to be granted the health and opportunity for, and which he felt he had carried out to some degree in his trip to Ireland and by the publication of *Queen Mab*, the *Letter to Lord Ellenborough*, and *A Proposal for Putting Reform to the Vote.* Like Shelley himself, Lionel refuses to be depressed by the collapse of the French Revolution, and he receives a call to social action like those described in *Hymn to Intellectual Beauty* and the Dedication to *The Revolt of Islam:*

> Yet through those dungeon walls there came
> Thy thrilling light, O Liberty!
> And as the meteor's midnight flame
> Startles the dreamer, sun-like truth
> Flashed on his visionary youth. (614–618)

People are unable to understand why one so wealthy should take up social causes:

> That poor and hungry men should break
> The laws which wreak them toil and scorn,
> We understand; but Lionel
> We know is rich and nobly born. (667–672)

Shelley had doubtless heard such sentiments expressed about himself. Lionel, like Shelley, indulges in humorous antireligious stories (such as those that had affronted Benjamin Haydon):

> For he made verses wild and queer
> On the strange creeds priests hold so dear.
>
> . . . . . .
>
> So this grew a proverb: "Don't get old
> Til Lionel's 'banquet in Hell' you hear,
> And then you will laugh yourself young again." (680–681, 686–688)[8]

His words on entering prison epitomize Shelley's own political credo, repeated in *To William Shelley:*

> 'Fear not the tyrants shall rule for ever,
> Or the priests of the bloody faith;
> They stand on the brink of that mighty river,
> Whose waves they have tainted with death:
> It is fed from the depths of a thousand dells,
> Around them it foams, and rages, and swells,
> And their swords and their sceptres I floating see,
> Like wrecks in the surge of eternity.' (894–901)

Julian and Maddalo

Shortly after Shelley's arrival in Italy, Claire Clairmont sent her child Allegra to Byron, the father, at Venice. Some months later, when Claire and the Shelleys were settled at the baths of Lucca, she decided to go to Venice to ask Byron to let her have the child for a time. Thus was started the chain of events that resulted in *Julian and Maddalo.*

Shelley, realizing that Claire could have no influence with Byron, decided to go with her. They set off for Venice on August 17, 1818. On August 20 Shelley wrote to Mary from Florence on the way to Venice describing a typically "Clairish" scheme that he had agreed to: Claire was to remain in Padua, about twenty miles south of Venice, because she felt that Byron would be more likely to part with the child if Claire was not in Venice. This plan was later modified: Claire would go to Venice, but Shelley was to tell Byron that both she and Mary were at Padua, presumably on the grounds that Byron was more likely to part with Allegra if he believed Mary was present.[9]

Claire and Shelley arrived in Venice on August 22. The next afternoon Shelley visited Byron, whom he had not seen since their days together in Switzerland two years previously. Byron was "delighted" to see him, quite willing to part with Allegra for a time and offered Shelley the use of his villa at Este, twenty miles beyond Padua. Shelley and he then went out for a horseback ride along the sands of the Lido which is commemorated in *Julian and Maddalo* and which Shelley described in a letter to Mary:

> When we disembarked, we found his horses waiting for us, & we rode along the sands of the sea talking. Our conversation consisted in histories of his wounded feelings, & questions as to my affairs, & great professions of friendship & regard for me. He said that if he had been in England at the time of the Chancery affair, he would have moved Heaven & Earth to have prevented such a decision. We talked of literary matters, his fourth Canto which he says is very good, & indeed repeated some stanzas of great energy to me; & Foliage which he quizzes immoderately.[10]

Shelley, having agreed to Claire's brainstorm told Byron that Claire and Mary were together at Padua and sent an urgent appeal to Mary to leave the baths "instantly" and speed to Este. Mary bundled her things together and started off with her two little children, Clara and William, on the long, tedious journey across Italy. When she arrived at Este, almost two weeks later, on September 5, baby Clara had dysentery and, as she wrote to Maria Gisborne, was "reduced so thin in this short time that you would hardly know her again."[11]

On September 16 Shelley and Claire went from Este to Padua, and on September 22 they went there again, the second time to visit a physician because Shelley was suffering from a digestive upset and Claire was indefinably unwell. Mary had apparently expected them to come back to Este that night, but for some unknown reason Shelley set off for Venice and sent Claire back to Este by coach. He wrote to Mary to inform her of his change of plans and then referred to Clara's illness: "My poor little Clara how is she today? Indeed I am somewhat uneasy about her, and though I feel secure there is no danger, it would be very comfortable to have some reasonable person's opinion about her. The Medico at Padua is certainly a man in great practise, but I confess he does not satisfy me."

On September 24, Mary, Claire, and baby Clara set out for Padua, and Shelley returned from Venice to meet them. Then Shelley and Mary went on to Venice with the baby to look for a physician, and Claire returned to Este. What ensued is best told in a letter from Shelley to Claire on the next day:

> We arrived at Venice yesterday [24 September] about five o'clock. Our little girl had shewn symptoms of increased weakness and even convulsive motions of the mouth and eyes, which made me anxious to see the physician. As she past from Fusina to the Inn, she became worse. I left her on landing and took a gondola for Dr. Alietti. He was not at home.—When I returned, I found Mary in the hall of the Inn in the most dreadful distress.
>
> Worse symptoms had appeared. Another Physician had arrived. He told me there was no hope. In about an hour—how shall I tell you—she died—silently, without pain. And she is now buried.

The Hoppners instantly came and took us to their house—a kindness I should have hesitated to accept, but that this unexpected stroke reduced Mary to a kind of despair.

That this misfortune affected Shelley as deeply is apparent from a letter of October 8 to Peacock: "But I have not been without events to disturb & distract me, amongst which is the death of my little girl. She died of a disorder peculia[r] to the climate. We have all had bad spirits enough, & I in addition bad health.—I *intend* to be better soon—there is no malady bodily or mental which does not either kill or is killed."[12]

Julian and Maddalo falls into two sharply different parts. The first depicts the happy meeting in Venice of Byron (Maddalo) and Shelley (Julian, presumably from Julian the Apostate, of whose anti-Christian and radical views Shelley had read in his old favorite, Gibbon).[13] The second part presents a tormented portrait of a "madman" whom Julian and Maddalo visit. The poem was probably begun at Este in the fall of 1818 and completed in Rome early in 1819.[14]

The first part consists of a penetrating picture of the two revolutionary poets: Byron, dynamic and cynically brilliant; Shelley, intense, subtle and humanitarian. Maddalo (Byron) agrees with Julian's (Shelley's) attacks on the ruling class but evinces little faith in his vision of future emancipation. Julian speaks first:

"—it is our will
That thus enchains us to permitted ill—
We might be otherwise—we might be all
We dream of happy, high, majestical.
Where is the love, beauty, and truth we seek
But in our mind? and if we were not weak
Should we be less in deed than in desire?"
"Ay, if we were not weak—and we aspire
How vainly to be strong!" said Maddalo:
"You talk Utopia." (170–179)

Maddalo delights in Julian's anticlerical witticisms:

"You talk as in years past," said Maddalo.
"Tis strange men change not. You were ever still
Among Christ's flock a perilous infidel,
A wolf for the meek lambs—if you can't swim
Beware of Providence." (113–118)

This part of the poem provides an interesting study in contrasts. Byron, the poet of national liberation, opposed feudal oppression and, in the end, gave his life in the struggle against it. Of his collaboration with the Carbonari in Italy, he declared to Medwin: "I felt for Romagna as if she had been my own country and would have risked my life and fortune for her."

But he saw little immediate hope for England beyond a revival of Whiggism along the lines of the old Fox-Sheridan tradition, and wavered between his hatred of the Castlereagh clique and his fear of the reformers, especially the Cobbett "blackguard" variety. And deeply though he hated European dictatorial governments, he did not think of replacing them with anything more drastic than a British-type parliamentary system. In line with these views he urged Shelley to cease writing "Utopias" and stop setting up "as a reformer." He had little use for organized religion but was notoriously superstitious. His main trouble, Shelley thought, was his failure to rid himself of the "canker of aristocracy."[15] Yet he could write in his journal:

> But onward!—it is now the time to act, and what signifies *self,* if a single spark of that which would be worthy of the past can be bequeathed unquenchedly to the future? It is not one man, nor a million, but the *spirit* of liberty which must be spread. The waves which dash upon the shore are, one by one, broken, but yet the *ocean* conquers, nevertheless.
>
> The king-times are fast finishing. There will be blood shed like water, and tears like mist; but the peoples will conquer in the end.[16]

And he expressed similar views in *The Prophecy of Dante* and other poems.

The second part of the poem turns from this fascinating interplay between two creative minds—"the swift thought,/Winging itself with laughter" (28–29)—to the agonized portrait of the "madman." Count Maddalo takes Julian in his gondola to visit a madhouse on an island near Venice. Maddalo describes the madman as "one like you . . . /With whom I argued in this sort" (195–197). His "wild talk," Maddalo claims, will reveal "how vain" are the "aspiring theories" (200–201) of Julian for humanity. Presumably this will be done by demonstrating that the path of the idealist ends in madness. Actually, however, there is little link between the two sections of the poem. "What," asks Julian, "made him mad?" Apparently, Maddalo replies, his desertion by a lady:

> "A lady came with him from France, and when
> She left him and returned, he wandered then
> About yon lonely isles of desert sand
> Till he grew wild." (246–249)

The two poets then go to the madman's room and listen to his ravings.

The madman begins by complaining that he is wearing a "mask of falsehood even to those/Who are most dear" (308–309). He cannot tell the truth, because this would result in even more coldness than he now endures:

> But that I cannot bear more altered faces
> Than needs must be, more changed and cold embraces. (312–313)

He implies that if he has done wrong, it has brought him no pleasure, and even his penitence has resulted only in pain:

If I have erred, there was no joy in error,
But pain and insult and unrest and terror;
I have not as some do, bought penitence
With pleasure, and a dark yet sweet offence,
For then,—if love and tenderness and truth
Had overlived hope's momentary youth,
My creed should have redeemed me from repenting. (326–332)

If his "spirit's mate . . . compassionate and wise" could see this "sad writing," she would "weep tears bitter as blood to know" her "lost friend's incommunicable woe" (337–343). He cannot tell others of his "secret load" (346). Having been led into this "misery" by "love," he now knows that only through truth can one find peace. He will not give up his radical beliefs:

Believe that I am ever still the same
In creed as in resolve, and what may tame
My heart, must leave the understanding free,
Or all would sink in this keen agony—
Nor dream that I will join the vulgar cry;
Or with my silence sanction tyranny. (358–363)

The madman implies that he can no longer keep his secret locked in torment within him: "I must remove/A veil from my pent mind. 'Tis torn aside!" (382–383) The rest of the poem is presumably a declaration of the secret. No sooner does he cry out, " 'Tis torn aside," than he is confronted with a vision of a woman, "pallid as Death's dedicated bride" (384), sitting beside him. This woman has deserted him for the "ghastly paramour" of death and "made the tomb" her "bridal bed" (388–390). The madman, "wide awake tho' dead" and in his "winding sheet" (390–391) will watch her and the paramour on their ghastly bridal bed. The vision of the woman then vanishes and does not return, much though he pleads.

Next follow a series of asterisks, presumably intended to indicate the disconnected nature of the madman's thoughts. Then his speech continues:

Nay, was it I who wooed thee to this breast,
Which, like a serpent, thou envenomest
As in repayment of the warmth it lent?
Didst thou not seek me for thine own content?
Did not thy love awaken mine? I thought
That thou wert she who said, "You kiss me not
Ever, I fear you cease to love me now"—
In truth I loved even to my overthrow
Her, who would fain forget these words: but they
Cling to her mind, and cannot pass away. (398–407)

That this is addressed to the "pallid" woman of the vision seems clear for the "thee" of the first sentence apparently is meant to refer back to the "thou art gone,/Thy work is finished," of the final lines of the preceding paragraph. The madman claims that she who has now turned against him, envenoming his bosom, once loved him deeply, indeed had taken the initiative in arousing his love for her, and was troubled when she feared he did not reciprocate it. He, too, had loved the woman, "even to my overthrow." The purpose of the passage is apparently to contrast the woman's former aggressive love for him with her present poisonous hatred.

The madman has tried to win back the woman's love, humbling himself and writhing in the dust like a worm. But she turned on him hysterically and with sexual sadism:

> That you had never seen me—never heard
> My voice, and more than all had ne'er endured
> The deep pollution of my loathed embrace—
> That your eyes ne'er had lied love in my face—
> That, like some maniac monk, I had torn out
> The nerves of manhood by their bleeding root
> With mine own quivering fingers, so that ne'er
> Our hearts had for a moment mingled there
> To disunite in horror—these were not
> With thee, like some suppressed and hideous thought
> Which flits athwart our musings, but can find
> No rest within a pure and gentle mind . . .
> Thou sealedst them with many a bare broad word,
> And ceredst my memory o'er them,—for I heard
> And can forget not . . . they were ministered
> One after one, those curses. Mix them up
> Like self-destroying poisons in one cup. (420–436)

To treat anyone like this would be cruel, but to treat one like the madman in such a way is torment, for the madman is sensitive to all human suffering:

> *Me*—who am as a nerve o'er which do creep
> The else unfelt oppressions of this earth. (449–450)

The woman told him that she had ceased to love him and that it was a horrible experience to have him—especially as he was so physically unattractive—make love to her:

> Thou wilt tell,
> With the grimace of hate, how horrible
> It was to meet my love when thine grew less;
> Thus wilt admire how I could e'er address
> Such features to love's work . . . this taunt, tho' true,
> (For indeed Nature nor in form nor hue
> Bestowed on me her choicest workmanship)
> Shall not be thy defence. (460–467)

This abuse by the woman makes the madman worry about their child:

> Those who inflict must suffer, for they see
> The work of their own hearts, and this must be
> Our chastisement or recompense—O child!
> I would that thine were like to be more mild
> For both our wretched sakes. (482–486)

Yet he does not end his misery by suicide out of feeling for the woman; it would give her an even more "bitter cause to grieve."

With this the speech of the madman ends, and Julian and Maddalo leave. Maddalo comments:

> "Most wretched men
> Are cradled into poetry by wrong,
> They learn in suffering what they teach in song." (544–546)

Many years later Julian returns to Venice. Maddalo's daughter tells him that the madman's lady came back to him but left again. Julian asks for details, and after much coaxing, she tells him "how/All happened—but the cold world shall not know."

That the speech of the madman reflects a situation in which Shelley was involved, Shelley himself implies, for Maddalo introduced the madman as "one like you." Shelley informed Hunt that the madman was "in some degree a painting from nature but, with respect to time and place, ideal." Hunt, reading the sketch of the madman, could hardly be expected by Shelley to come to any other conclusion than that the "painting" was "in some degree" one of Shelley himself ("from nature"). In December 1819 Shelley wrote to Charles Ollier: "Have you seen my poem, *Julian and Maddalo*? Suppose you print that in the manner of Hunt's *Hero and Leander;* for I mean to write three other poems, the scenes of which will be laid at Rome, Florence, and Naples, but the subjects of which will be all drawn from dreadful or beautiful realities, as that of this was."[17] Clearly the madman section was a reflection of a "dreadful," not a "beautiful" reality, and the kind of reality—personal, detailed, and psychological—that could only have come from the author's life. In view of the accepted reticences of the day on such matters, these are quite broad hints to Hunt and Ollier of autobiographical content.

The mood of the madman is similar to the mood displayed by Shelley in poems of a distinctly personal nature. Thus, in *Lines Written among the Euganean Hills*, composed at Este in September, 1818, he complains that he has been bitterly abused (as was the madman), imagines himself as dead and the one who abused him as relenting. In the personal, first-person *Invocation to Misery* (1818), the vision of misery is similar to that of "Death's dedicated bride" in *Julian and Maddalo:*

Come, be happy!—sit near me,
Shadow-vested Misery:
Coy, unwilling, silent bride.
. . . . .
Hasten to the bridal bed—
Underneath the grave 'tis spread:
In darkness may our love be hid.
Oblivion be our coverlid—
We may rest, and none forbid. (1–3, 41–45)

The sketch of the madman is similar in some ways to those of Lionel, Prince Athanase, Laon, and the *Alastor* poet. The madman, Maddalo tells Julian, "was ever talking in such sort as you do" but "far more sadly" (236–237). Like Shelley and the poet of *Alastor,* he is thin (279) and has "lustrous" eyes and wind-blown hair (276–277). Like Shelley, he has been "weighed in friendship" by only a "few" (344–345). As a "boy," he was devoted "to justice and to love" (380–382). Like Lionel and Laon, he fears he may die at the hands of his political enemies on "the red scaffold as our country bends" (375). Like the hero of *Alastor* and Lionel he has a romantic nostalgia for death. His political philosophy is similar to Shelley's, though now, like Lionel and the poet in *Ode to the West Wind,* he is somewhat "subdued." Moreover, Shelley instructed his publishers to publish *Julian and Maddalo* in the same volume as *Prince Athanase,* a clearly autobiographical poem giving a portrait of Shelley in search of love and suffering from a secret "grief."[18]

Finally, the picture of the maniac is not consistent with his situation in the poem. The maniac speaks of a "child" as though he and the woman had a child and the child was present, but it is not indicated in the poem that they had a child, and neither child nor woman is present in the asylum. The maniac's ravings, to which Julian and Maddalo are listening, are referred to as "writings": "If this sad writing thou shouldst ever see" (340); "And from my pen the words flow as I write" (476). All these characteristics fit Shelley himself: he was surrounded by those whose good opinion he wished to retain; he and Mary had a child (William), who was in the household; and he did at this time, as Mary reported, hide "writings" from her.[19] Thus there can be little doubt that the madman is Shelley and that this section of *Julian and Maddalo* reflects an actual situation in his life. And if the madman is Shelley the woman must be Mary for there was no other woman who stood in the kind of relationship depicted in the poem to Shelley.[20] Newman White, accepting this identification, argued that the bitter abuse of the madman (Shelley) by the scornful lady (Mary) arose from Mary's feeling that Shelley was responsible for the death of their baby, Clara: "Mary must have seen clearly and bitterly that Clara's death was directly traceable to Claire Clairmont's restless and reckless insistence upon visiting Allegra, to Shelley's yielding to Claire, and to his initial deception of Byron that had caused Shelley to insist upon the hot and hurried journey from Bagni di Lucca to Este, with its tragic results for their child."[21] The "mask of falsehood" that so disturbed the madman (Shelley) was his keeping secret his feelings of neglect from the woman (Mary) and from his friends. The kindly "spirit's mate" and the "Death's dedicated bride" were, White argued, not two persons but one, namely, Mary as her real self and in her temporary state of hysterical alienation from Shelley.

That White was essentially correct in this hypotheses is borne out by further examination of the text and other documents. Although the "mask of falsehood" might at first seem to refer to some wrong the madman had hidden from the lady, the structure of the poem indicates that it refers to his concealing the hurt the lady had inflicted upon him. From line 300 to 382 he speaks of a "secret grief" that weighs him down. In lines 382–383 he declares that he must release the secret. He goes on, however, to describe not any wrong done to the lady but the lady's abuse of him. It is thus the hiding of the hurt caused by this abuse that is the secret grief. This is borne out also by the reaction of Julian and Maddalo on leaving the madman:

> And we agree his was some dreadful ill
> Wrought on him boldly, yet unspeakable,
> By a dear friend; some deadly change in love
> Of one vowed deeply which he dreamed not of;
> For whose sake he, it seemed, had fixed a blot
> Of falsehood on his mind which flourished not
> But in the light of all-beholding truth. (525–531)

The "truth" must be the abuse previously depicted, the "falsehood" must be the hiding of that truth. He hid it because the woman, despite her vows (wedding vows?), had turned against him. It was this that drove him mad. Mary was perhaps referring specifically to the madman's remark that, if the spirit's mate could "see this sad writing," she would pity him, when she commented in her Note to the poems of this year: "and then he escaped to solitude, and in verses, which he hid from fear of wounding me, poured forth morbid but too natural bursts of discontent and sadness. One looks back with unspeakable regret and gnawing remorse to such periods; fancying that, had one been more alive to the nature of his feelings, and more attentive to soothe them, such would not have existed."[22]

That not only the "spirit's mate" but also the scornful lady is Mary is indicated by the fact that there was no other woman from whom abuse and neglect would have brought about so traumatic a disturbance as that described by the madman. Mary seemed to accept this identification also. In her poem *The Choice*, again written after Shelley's death, she bitterly regretted her "cold neglect, averted eyes/That blindly crushed thy soul's fond sacrifice."[23]

The vision of the scornful lady as "Death's dedicated bride" is explained by Julian's words to Maddalo:

> there are some by nature proud,
> Who patient in all else demand but this—
> To love and be beloved with gentleness;
> And being scorned, what wonder if they die
> Some living death? (206–210)

Mary by her bitterness and abuse had turned their love into something akin to death. The picture resembles that given in *Alastor, Rosalind and Helen* and *Invocation to Misery.*

Another characteristic of the woman, as depicted by the madman, is sadistic hysteria, including castration phantasies: "tear out/The nerves of manhood by their bleeding root." Mary's hysteria was no doubt set off by her grieving for the death of her child. Hysteria, however, is not necessarily a part of grief. And when it is, it is not necessarily hostile. Indeed, grief as such can bring a husband and wife closer together. But in the picture drawn by Shelley, the wife is striking out at her mate in a fury of sexual aggression. Why? The answer must lie in Mary's feelings about Shelley and Claire.

Shelley and Claire left the baths of Lucca on August 17 accompanied by Paolo Foggi, their Italian servant. Paolo left them at Florence on August 20 and returned to Mary at the baths of Lucca. Shelley and Claire then traveled alone to Venice, arriving on August 22 at midnight. Thus, they spent the nights of August 20 and 21 unchaperoned and passed the previous nights, Mary might well have felt, under a not too inflexible surveillance. On August 23 Shelley wrote to Mary that he, Claire, and Elise the nursemaid, who was then with Byron, were going to Byron's villa at Este and would await her there. Here, Shelley and Claire, with only Elise as potential chaperone, lived from August 24 until September 5, when Mary arrived. Then on September 16 and again on September 22, just two days before little Clara's death, Shelley and Claire were alone together in Padua.[24]

Trelawny, in his conversations with Rossetti, stated that Mary was "excessively jealous of Shelley, both sexually and as regards the influence of other women over his mind." This jealousy must have been directed with special force against Claire, for Shelley and Claire had either had an affair or come close to having one in 1815, following which Claire was ejected from the household amid "a turmoil of passion and hatred." In 1817 the "Constantia" poems reveal a passionate interest in Claire and contain derogatory comments on Mary. In later years, when Claire was about to visit her, Mary is said to have cried out to her daughter-in-law: "Don't go, dear! don't leave me alone with her! she has been the bane of my life ever since I was three years old." Certainly jealousy is emphasized in the scenes of Mary's autobiographical novel *Mathilda* that apparently reflect the situation at Este: "I called him [Lovel-Shelley] my friend but I viewed all he did with jealous eyes . . . 'but [said Lovel] if my friendship can make you look on life with less disgust beware how you injure it with suspicion—love is a delicate sprite & easily hurt by rough jealousy.' "[25]

Mary was perhaps impelled to hasten across the country with her children more from jealousy of Shelley and Claire, mingled with chagrin that others (Elise and Paolo, Byron, the Gisbornes, and the Hoppners) knew of their being together, than from fear that Byron might discover that she had been at the baths of Lucca instead of at Padua.[26] In fact, Shelley informed Byron on September 13 that Mary had arrived the previous Sunday, apparently without any feelings that Byron might think it strange she should take from August 24 to September 6 to make what should have been only a few hours' trip if she had been at Padua. Shelley must at some point have informed Byron that Mary had actually been at the baths of Lucca.[26]

Shelley's letters of the period, although not giving, as indeed, they could not, detailed corroboration for this reconstruction, do not contradict it and could in fact fit it. On August 24, writing from Este to urge Mary to join him and Claire, Shelley is friendly but apprehensive: "I have been obliged to decide on all these things without you.—I have done for the best & my own beloved Mary you must come & scold me if I have done wrong & kiss me if I have done right—for I am sure I do not know which—& it is only the event that can shew."[27]

His letter from Padua on September 22, two weeks after Mary's arrival, also indicates a friendly relationship. Thus, if Mary made protests, they cannot have resulted in any serious strain. But with the death of Clara the situation changed. On September 25 Shelley tells Claire that the death of the child had "reduced Mary to a kind of despair." On October 8 he comments to Peacock: "We have all had bad spirits enough," which sounds more like quarreling than despair.

The situation and state of the madman are consistent with this hypothesis. He begins by complaining of the "mask of falsehood," the "secret load" within his breast that is crushing him. At first it appears that he has committed a crime, but it later emerges that what is troubling him is the abuse and coldness of the lady. In being unable to speak of her treatment and pretending that it had not occurred, he is living a lie. If such was Shelley's own situation, there can be no doubt that he would write about it, for, like Byron and Hazlitt, he had a strong urge for self-dramatization and confession, sometimes of an extraordinarily frank character. Moreover, the reactions of the madman are what one might expect of Shelley. If he was faced by an elemental emotional tirade released by Mary's hysteria, he would at first be shocked and bewildered, and later, as he brooded alone, filled with resentment and self-justification.

In the poem, Shelley apparently throws it up at Mary that it was she who had taken the initiative in their affair (at the tomb of Mary Wollstonecraft), had "sought" him out for her own "content." For her he had sacrificed everything—"loved even to my overthrow." Despite this, she had rejected him and turned viciously against him, telling him she wished that she had never had sexual relations with him and screaming at him to castrate himself. Yet *he* had not changed, for he still loved her; his love, in fact, had kept him from revealing to her how deeply he was hurt. For her sake he was living a lie—he whose mind flourished only "in the light of all-beholding truth." This love on his part—in contrast to her hatred—had led him "astray to misery." He would not, as would she or other "perverted beings," find refuge in scorn or hate: "I give thee tears for scorn and love for hate." For her sake, too, he would refrain from suicide:

> And that thy lot may be less desolate
> Than his on whom thou tramplest, I refrain
> From that sweet sleep which medicines all pain. (497–499)

Furthermore, he had done nothing to deserve such abuse. He had blundered unthinking—"wandering heedlessly" (324)—into a situation that had brought him nothing but "pain and insult and unrest and terror" (that is participating in Claire's schemes in an effort to help her had brought about the death of his child and the frenzied alienation of his wife). Mary had driven him to admit he was in the wrong. If he had lived up to his "creed" (presumably on love relations), he would never have retreated and, consequently, would never have undergone such humiliation. Indeed, if she had still loved him and still believed in this creed, as once she did, she would not have demanded "penitence." This is self-dramatization and self-pity with a vengeance; but in view of Shelley's masochistic—"I fall upon the thorns of life"—and self-idealizing impulses, it rings remarkably true. Apparently this was a husband-and-wife quarrel of unusual vehemence—the wife, almost mad with grief and jealousy, hurling hysterical recriminations; the husband retiring to brood resentfully.

At one point, apparently, Mary lashed out at Shelley's physical appearance:

> Thou wilt tell
> With the grimace of hate, how horrible
> It was to meet my love when thine grew less;
> Thou wilt admire how I could e'er address
> Such features to love's work . . . this taunt, tho' true,
> (For indeed nature nor in form nor hue
> Bestowed on me her choicest workmanship)
> Shall not be thy defence. (460–467)

If this picture does not fit that of Shelley in the Curran and Clint portraits, it must be remembered that those portraits are idealized. The Williams watercolor shows him as prematurely grey, and Thornton Hunt, while speaking of his lithe vigor and delicate features, also stated that he was thin and hollow-chested. It is possible that Shelley himself emphasized these negative features. He seldom refers to his physical appearance, but once when he did, he spoke deprecatingly of his "little turn up nose."[28] The physical picture obtained from Shelley's self-portraits, such as that in *Alastor*, does not indicate any pride in appearance; in fact, rather the contrary.

Lines Written among the Euganean Hills

As Shelley dated the *Lines Written among the Euganean Hills* "October, 1818," the poem must have been written shortly after his and Mary's return to Este on September 29, following the death of Clara on September 24. It was published in the *Rosalind and Helen* volume in 1819, and in the "Advertisement" to that volume, dated "Naples, *Dec. 20*, 1818," Shelley comments on it:

> If any one is inclined to condemn the insertion of the introductory lines, which image forth the sudden relief of a state of deep despondency by the radiant visions disclosed by the sudden burst of an Italian sunrise in autumn, on the highest peak of those delightful mountains, I can only offer as my excuse, that they were not erased at the request of a dear friend, with whom added years of intercourse only add to my apprehension of its value, and who would have had more right than any one to complain, that she has not been able to extinguish in me the very power of delineating sadness.[29]

On the face of it, this apology is needless, for a poet does not have to apologize for writing despondent lines. The implication is that the apology is connected with the "dear friend," who has always been taken to be Mary, and indeed, could hardly be anyone else. Shelley indicates here that he showed these lines of "deep despondency" to Mary and asked her if she wished him to publish them. The lines, then, must concern Mary. Apparently they do so and in a most personal sense:

> Senseless is the breast, and cold,
> Which relenting love would fold;
> Bloodless are the veins and chill
> Which the pulse of pain did fill;
> Every little living nerve
> That from bitter words did swerve
> Round the tortured lips and brow,
> Are like sapless leaflets now
> Frozen upon December's bough. (36–44)

This sounds once more like the quarrel revealed in *Julian and Maddalo*: Mary's attack left Shelley "chill" and "bloodless," and even her "relenting" has not revived him. He has, as it were, suffered a spiritual death. Indeed, in the "introductory lines," which consist of two sections (1-44, 45-65), the theme of death, actual and spiritual, is clear, no doubt reflecting both Shelley's grief at the death of his daughter and his shock at Mary's abuse. Life, to the poet, seems a "deep wide sea of misery" over which "the mariner" travels (1-2).

The autobiographical nature of the whole passage becomes clear in the second section, which although cryptic and esoteric, is obviously personal:

On the beach of a northern sea
Which tempests shake eternally,
As once the wretch there lay to sleep,
Lies a solitary heap,
One white skull and seven dry bones,
On the margin of the stones,
Where a few gray rushes stand,
Boundaries of the sea and land:
Nor is heard one voice of wail
But the sea-mews, as they sail
O'er the billows of the gale;
Or the whirlwind up and down
Howling, like a slaughtered town,
When a king in glory rides
Through the pomp of fratricides:
Those unburied bones around
There is many a mournful sound;
There is no lament for him,
Like a sunless vapour, dim,
Who once clothed with life and thought
What now moves nor murmurs not. (45–65)

A reading of this section along with the first reveals that "the wretch" and "the mariner" are the same and both stand for Shelley himself. A clue to the "beach" image comes from Mary Shelley's poem, *The Choice*, written after Shelley's death and expressing her regret for her ill-treatment of him. In one passage she speaks of the death and burial of their daughter Clara:

First my dear girl, whose face resembled *his*,
Slept on bleak Lido, near Venetian seas.

Clara, then, was buried on the shore of the Adriatic. The probability is that this is the "beach of a northern sea." But that the skull and bones cannot be those of Clara is shown by the fact that they are referred to as "unburied" and appear to be those of a man ("him"). The context implies that they are the skull and bones of "the wretch," namely, those of Shelley himself. This is also indicated by the fact that they are said to be "unlamented," which again sounds like the self-pity theme of *Julian and Maddalo*. But what is meant by the "wretch" lying down "to sleep" on the beach? And why "seven dry bones"? The Advertisement suggests that Mary knew the meaning of these expressions and that they had a private significance to her and Shelley. What this could be one can only guess. Perhaps Shelley means that he was numb with grief or was seeking forgetfulness. Perhaps Mary broke down on the beach when Clara was buried and made some of the accusations that Shelley records in *Julian and Maddalo*. As a result, he died emotionally (the bones—the body) and spiritually (the skull) and had remained in this state: "what now moves nor murmurs not." The lines would thus parallel those in the first section: "Bloodless are the veins and chill." Is there any special significance to the "seven" bones? Possibly they stand simply for the body, but Shelley usually has a specific meaning in such phrases. The poem was written in October 1818. In August 1811, Shelley had eloped with Harriet Westbrook; in October 1811, her sister Eliza had joined the household. If Shelley were speaking generally, he could be referring to the first event; if specifically, to the latter. He could, on looking back, have regarded either event as leading to the withdrawal of love from his life:

> Hard hearts, and cold, like weights of icy stone,
> Which crushed and withered mine.[30]

This coldness, as *Epipsychidion* states, Mary had continued. Shelley, then, may be saying that he laid seven, loveless ("dry") years of his life beside his daughter's grave on the bleak Adriatic beach.

The historical and political section of the poem was perhaps intended as an answer to Byron's rather despondent *Ode to Venice*, which Mary Shelley copied out for him at Este. After the two introductory sections, the poem switches to the poet, as narrator, in the Euganean hills at sunrise. The sun lights up the towers of Venice, bringing to his mind a contrast between its past glories and its present subordination to Austria. As Shelley put it in a letter to Peacock written at the same time (October 8): "But Venice which was once a tyrant, is now the next worse thing, a slave. For in fact it ceased to be free, or worth our regret as a nation from the moment that the oligarchy usurped the rights of the people. Yet I do not imagine that it ever was quite so degraded as it has been since the French, and especially the Austrian yoke."

But Venice and the other Italian states might yet arise and overthrow the Metternich oppression:

> But if Freedom should awake
> In her omnipotence, and shake
> From the Celtic Anarch's hold
> All the keys of dungeons cold,
> Where a hundred cities lie
> Chained like thee, ingloriously. (150–155)[31]

Turning to another oppressed Italian city in the vicinity, Padua, Shelley speculates that in it too, from the tiny spark of freedom yet alive in Italy, a forest fire of revolution might arise. Two years later, with the outbreak of revolution in Naples, he saw some confirmation of his hopes for Italian national revolt, a revolt that finally triumphed in the days of Mazzini and Garibaldi. In the conclusion of the poem Shelley returns to his image of a "green isle" in the sea of life, using it now in a historical sense. As in Act

IV of *Prometheus Unbound,* he looks forward to the "flowering isles" of the future world order. The "rage" of the now "polluting multitude" will be quiescent, nature and humanity will blend in a "mild brotherhood," and "the earth grow young again."

Letter to Maria Gisborne

Maria Gisborne, daughter of an English merchant, was born in 1770 and spent part of her childhood in Constantinople, where she knew Jeremy Bentham. Marrying an English architect, Willey Reveley, she returned to England. During the stormy 1790s the couple, who were on the liberal side in politics, became friendly with William Godwin. So close was the friendship that when Mary Wollstonecraft Godwin died in 1797, Maria Reveley took the baby, Mary Godwin (later Mary Shelley), into her own home and cared for her for a time. When Reveley died suddenly two years later, Godwin asked the widow to marry him, but she refused. The following year she married John Gisborne, a merchant, and they left for Italy accompanied by her son, Henry Reveley.[32]

When the Shelleys left England eighteen years later, they took with them a letter of introduction to the Gisbornes, whom they visited at Leghorn in May 1818. Mrs. Gisborne they found charming and intelligent, Mr. Gisborne rather dull. Shelley's comment on him to Peacock, who always appreciated a joke, exemplifies the good-natured humor that was apparently typical of his daily conversation:

> His nose is something quite Slawkenburgian—it weighs on the imagination to look at it,—it is that sort of nose which transforms all the *g*s its wearer utters into *k*s. It is a nose once seen never to be forgotten and which requires the utmost stretch of Christian charity to forgive. I, you know, have a little turn up nose; Hogg has a large hook one but add them both together, square them, cube them, you would have but a faint idea of the nose to which I refer.[33]

Maria Gisborne's son, Henry Reveley, had in the intervening years become an engineer (he later achieved distinction in his profession in England, South Africa, and Australia) and was currently engaged in constructing an engine for a steamboat to ply between Leghorn, Genoa, and Marseilles, a pioneering project in the days of sailing ships. Shelley, with his interest in science —especially scientific undertakings like the Tremadoc embankment which would aid the advancement of mankind—took up the project enthusiastically and raised money for it. He heralds (with anticlerical touch) the casting of a cylinder:

> Your volcanic description of the birth of the cylinder is very characteristic both of you & of it. One might imagine God when he made the earth, & saw the gran-

ite mountains & flinty promountories flow into their craggy forms, & the splendour of their fusion filling millions of miles of the void space, like the tail of a comet, so looking, & so delighting in his work. God sees his machines spinning round the sun & delights in its success, & has taken out patents to supply all the suns in space with the same manufacture.—Your boat will be to the Ocean of Water what the earth is to the Ocean of Æther—a prosperous & swift voyager.[34]

The following year, after Shelley had put up money for the project, Henry decided to abandon it, whereupon Shelley angrily wrote to Claire, with overtones from Swift: "I absolutely refused to take any further part in the concern, except to receive whatever money they choose to give me as proceeding from the sale of the materials . . . The Gisbornes are people totally without faith.—I think they are altogether the most filthy and odious animals with which I ever came in contact." The comment has been used to support the picture of Shelley as irresponsibly swinging from extreme to extreme, but actually it shows only that he was very angry, which he had good reason to be in view of the amount of money he stood to lose. He expressed this anger not for publication, but in a private letter to a close friend. A few months later the quarrel was patched up, and according to Reveley, the engine and hull were sold and the money returned to Shelley.[35]

Following their visit to the Gisbornes in 1818, the Shelleys lived in various places. In the summer of 1819 they returned for a time to Leghorn, where they lived outside the town in the Villa Valsovano. During this period Maria Gisborne turned Shelley's attention to another language and literature—Spanish—in addition to those he already knew, which included Greek, Latin, German, Italian, and French. He became an admirer of the plays of Calderon and began to translate them. The next year the Gisbornes went on a trip to England, and the Shelleys took over their house in Leghorn from June 15 to August 4. It was during this period and in this house that Shelley wrote his *Letter to Maria Gisborne*, dated "July 1, 1820."

Shelley, as he tells Maria in the poem, is writing in Reveley's workshop (where the steam engine was coming to birth). After an introductory comment on a favorite theme, that if he could not achieve fame in his own age he could at least look for it in posterity, he breaks into the first part of the poem proper, a semihumorous description of objects in the workshop and of thoughts they inspire. He looks first at the "dread engines" on the wall, and his recent absorption with the Prometheus myth raises the thought that Jove never had such engines for the torture of Prometheus. The image of engines of torture touches off a stream of ironical associations from his early antireligious reading: "that man of God, St. Dominic," never had such fine instruments of torture, nor did the Spanish Inquistion ("that philanthropic council") when it thought to bring its "thumbscrews" and "wheels" to Elizabethan England:

to pay some interest for the debt
They owed to Jesus Christ for their salvation,

By giving a faint foretaste of damnation
To Shakespeare, Sidney, Spenser and the rest
Who made our land an island of the blest. (28–32)

Spain calls to mind the Spanish revolution of a few months earlier:

lamp-like Spain, who now relumes her fire
On Freedom's hearth. (33–34)

A bowl of quicksilver on the workshop table leads him into a fantasy on underground gnomes, reminiscent of Spenser's fiends in the Cave of Mammon, who toast the "demons of the earthquake" in quicksilver. In the bowl he has playfully "made to float/A rude idealism of a paper boat" (60, 75–76).[36] After listing humorously the other odds and ends scattered around the workshop, something calls to mind the attacks on him by the *Quarterly* and other reviews. He warns that one should not heed the

shriek of the world's carrion jays,
Their censure, or their wonder, or their praise. (130–131)

The second section of the poem (132–192), beginning with a light invocation to hope and memory, speaks of the good times that he and Maria Gisborne have had together. He remembers the days when they studied Spanish—the language of the revolution against the "tyrant" Ferdinand:

The language of a land which now is free,
And winged with thoughts of truth and majesty,
Flits round the tyrant's sceptre like a cloud,
And bursts the peopled prisons, and cries aloud,
"My name is Legion!" (175–180)

The third section (192–253) switches to a series of thumbnail sketches of people whom the Gisbornes will meet in London: Godwin, "greater none than he/Though fallen"; Coleridge, "A hooded eagle among blinking owls"; Leigh Hunt with his "eternal puns"; Hogg, hiding his "virtues" behind a barricade of sarcasm; Peacock with his "fine wit"; and the delightful Horace Smith (197–198, 208, 219, 227).

The fourth section presents contrasting descriptions of London and Italy. That of London combines cameo-like realism with humanitarian irony:

But what see you beside? A shabby stand
Of Hackney-coaches—a brick house or wall
Fencing some lonely court, white with the scrawl
Of our unhappy politics;—or worse—
A wretched woman reeling by, whose curse
Mixed with the watchman's, partner of her trade,
You must accept in place of serenade. (265–271)

The poem concludes with a light and fanciful picture of the good times they will all have when Maria returns to Italy:

> we'll have tea and toast;
> Custards for supper, and an endless host
> Of syllabubs and jellies and mince-pies,
> And other such lady-like luxuries,—
> Feasting on which we will philosophize!

The sprightly informality of such passages makes it difficult to realize that they are written in the heroic couplet with its traditional balanced counterpoise of line and phrase.

The Witch of Atlas

On August 5, 1820, the Shelleys moved from the Gisborne house at Leghorn to the summer resort of the baths of Pisa. On August 12 they took a trip with Claire Clairmont to the nearby town of Lucca, and while Claire and Mary explored the town, Shelley went off on his own:

> During some of the hottest days of August [writes Mary with wifely disapproval], Shelley made a solitary journey on foot to the summit of Monte San Pellegrino—a mountain of some height, on the top of which there is a chapel, the object, during certain days of the year, of many pilgrimages. The excursion delighted him while it lasted; though he exerted himself too much, and the effect was considerable lassitude and weakness on his return. During the expedition he conceived the idea, and wrote, in the three days immediately succeeding to his return, the *Witch of Atlas*.[37]

The poem, she felt, consisted of Shelley's "airiest flights of fancy," a judgment that was perhaps influenced by Shelley's playful Dedication:

> How, my dear Mary,—are you critic-bitten,
> (For vipers kill, though dead,) by some review,
> That you condemn these verses I have written,
> Because they tell no story, false or true!
> What, though no mice are caught by a young kitten,
> May it not leap and play as grown cats do,
> Till its claws come? Prithee, for this one time,
> Content thee with a visionary rhyme. (1–8)

That Shelley is being ironical here he indicates in the final stanza of the Dedication, which suggests the presence of a below-surface meaning: "if you unveil my Witch" (46). The surface mood is one of light fantasy—reminiscent of the early stanzas of Wordsworth's Peter Bell—and when

Shelley does not wish to go below this level, he does not. On this level, the Witch is simply the Witch, an imaginary, prankish goddess, a female counterpart of the youthful god Hermes in the so-called Homeric *Hymn to Mercury* that Shelley had been translating.[38] But beneath the surface she is another manifestation of "the benignant power":

> with the living form
> Of this embodied Power, the cave grew warm. (79–80)

Her mother, "one of the Atlantides" (57), is perhaps a symbol for nature (she is successively a "vapour," a "cloud," a "meteor," and a "star"); her father is the sun. The Witch is akin to "Universal Pan" (113), that is, to biological life. Like the power in the *Hymn to Intellectual Beauty* with its "shadow," she has a "veil" (151) and is seen only in passing glimpses. She is immortal and unchanging, in contrast to the things of this world. She visits "destined minds" (176) in youth, then vanishes. Her realm is not the earth but a "remoter world" (*Mont Blanc*), wherein, from a "well of crimson fire" (279) or in a frozen lake, she gazes at the flickering surface of life. Like the power in the *Hymn* and in the Dedication to *The Revolt of Islam*, those to whom she appears become devoted to something beyond themselves:

> And lived thenceforward as if some controul,
> Mightier than life, were in them. (596–597)

The Witch has a magic boat, originally "wrought for Venus," which is drawn by a winged hermaphrodite. The boat is clearly a manifestation of love, and the hermaphrodite, it has been plausibly suggested, is imagination,[39] for the relationship of the hermaphrodite and the Witch is similar to that of the creative imagination and the power in *A Defence of Poetry* and other works. Like the "fading coal" of the mind that comes to life under the wind of the power, the hermaphrodite comes to life when the Witch commands it. Normally it lies passive, "with folded wings and unawakened eyes," but when she calls, it unfurls "its heaven-coloured pinions" and sweeps gloriously upward, pulling the boat.

The Witch's "choice sport" is to visit human habitations in ancient Egypt, a land on the same continent as her Mount Atlas dwelling:

> her light feet
> Passed through the peopled haunts of humankind,
> Scattering sweet visions from her presence sweet. (522–524)

She gazes on the evils of religious and social oppression:

> Distortions foul of supernatural awe,
> And pale imaginings of visioned wrong;

And all the code of Custom's lawless law
Written upon the brows of old and young. (491–494)

She believes that these, like all evil (as in *The Assassins*), are transient phenomena:

"This," said the wizard maiden, "is the strife
Which stirs the liquid surface of man's life." (495–496)

Like the power in the Dedication to *The Revolt of Islam* and elsewhere, she acts against social injustice, "all harsh and crooked purposes" (619), but does so in her own prankish way. She makes the priests deny the divinity of the bull Apis, has the king dress an ape up in his crown to be worshiped by courtiers (apparently suggested by Spenser's *Mother Hubbard's Tale*),[40] and makes the "lying scribe . . . his own lies betray without a bribe"—in obvious reference to such Tory reviewers as Robert Southey. Her puckish acts against war and dictatorship are satiric reflections on Shelley's own age:

The soldiers dreamed that they were blacksmiths, and
   Walked out of quarters in somnambulism;
Round the red anvils you might see them stand
   Like Cyclopses in Vulcan's sooty abysm,
Beating their swords to ploughshares;—in a band
   The gaolers sent those of the liberal schism
Free through the streets of Memphis, much, I wis,
To the annoyance of king Amasis. (641–648)

The underlying mood of *The Witch of Atlas* is one of skeptical exasperation. Shelley had complained in *A Defence of Poetry*, *Hymn to Intellectual Beauty*, and elsewhere that the visitations of the "benignant power" to the human mind were brief and flickering. Yet this was the power that could "free the world from its dark slavery" if only it moved mankind sufficiently. Whether this power was an inner psychological force or some mysterious agency connected with nature Shelley did not know, but the implicit appeal of the *Hymn* that the power remain and exert its full force is turned in the *Witch* into a wryly sardonic picture of its inconstancy.

Epipsychidion

Emilia Viviani, who inspired *Epipsychidion*, was a member of the Tuscan aristocracy. Her father, Count Niccolo Viviani, the governor of Pisa, had placed her in a convent against her will and apparently at the instigation of her mother. The Shelleys first heard of her situation in November 1820 through Professor Franchesco Pacchiani of the University of Pisa, who had formerly been her tutor. Soon they and Claire began to visit her. On December 29 Mary wrote to Leigh Hunt: "It is grievous to see this beautiful girl wearing out the best years of her life in an odious convent where both mind and body are sick from want of the appropriate exercise of each—I think she has great talent if not genius."[41]

Shortly after the first visit by Mary on December 1, Shelley went to see the fair "prisoner."[42] His cousin, Thomas Medwin, who accompanied him, recorded the occasion:

The next day, accompanied by the priest, we came in sight of the gloomy, dark convent, whose ruinous and dilapidated condition told too plainly of confiscation and poverty. It was situated in an unfrequented street in the suburbs, not far from the walls. After passing through a gloomy portal, that led to a quadrangle, the area of which was crowded with crosses, memorials of old monastic times, we were soon in the presence of Emilia . . . Emilia was indeed lovely and interesting. Her profuse black hair, tied in the most simple knot, after the manner of a Greek Muse in the Florence gallery, displayed to its full height her brow, fair as that of the marble of which I speak. She was also of about the same height as the antique. Her features possessed a rare faultlessness, and almost Grecian contour, the nose and forehead making a straight line,—a style of face so rare, that I remember Bartolini's telling Byron that he had scarcely an instance of such in the numerous casts of busts which his studio contained. Her eyes had the sleepy voluptuousness, if not the color of Beatrice Cenci's. They had indeed no definite colour, changing with the changing feeling, to dark or light, as the soul animated them. Her cheek was pale, too, as marble, owing to her confinement and want of air, or perhaps "to thought." There was a lark in the *parloir*, that had lately been caught. "Poor prisoner," said she, looking at it compassionately, "you will die of grief! How I pity thee! What must thou suffer, when thou hearest in the clouds, the songs of thy parent birds, or some flocks of thy kind on the wing, in search of other skies—of new fields—of new delights! But like me, thou wilt be forced to remain here always—to wear out thy miserable existence here. Why can I not release thee?"

Medwin also quoted a little essay, "Il Vero Amore" (The True Love), written by Emilia in her convent. A heightened piece in the Italian neo-Platonic style, it gives a picture of an intellectual and romantic girl (who had apparently read Bembo's apostrophe to love in Castiglione's *The Courtier*): "Love! soul of the world! Love, the source of all that is good, of all that is lovely. What would the universe be failing thy sacred flame? A horrible desert." The lover is one who is "sublimed" and raised above other men by love's mystic power; "all energetic, all pure, all divine," he "inspires none but actions that are magnanimous . . . The soul of him who loves disdains restraint—nothing can restrain it. It lances itself out of the created and creates in the infinite a world for itself." Such is true love, a harmony of the human spirit with the divine, urging man to virtue. But such, unfortunately, is not what men always mean by love. The name of love has been "profaned" —presumably by associating it with sex, though Emilia is too delicate to say so. This unnamed profanation she rejects: "Every other sentiment dissimilar from this, than this less pure, deserves not the sacred name of love."[43] Clearly Emilia Viviani was a young woman of talent, histrionic as well as literary, whose situation and temperament would almost seem to have been expressly created by some Shelleyan cosmic dynast. Shelley's feelings for Emilia have been depicted as "Platonic" and lightly romantic, but that he was passionately aroused by her is clear both in *Epipsychidion* itself and in other poems on her:

> Oh my beloved why have you
> Sent sweet basil & mignionette?—
> Why when I kiss their leaves find I them wet
> With thine adored tears dearer than heavens dew?[44]

When Emilia married, Shelley was deeply disturbed, and his feelings flowed over into the tale *Ginevra* and the lyrics "Music, when soft voices die" and "O World! O Life! O Time!"

Mary's reaction to Emilia, following her initial sympathy, was simply that she was a threat to their marriage. Six months after Emilia's wedding, her bitterness spilled over in a letter to Maria Gisborne:

> Emilia married Biondi–we hear that she leads him & his mother (to use a vulgarism) *a devil of a life*—The conclusion of our friendship *a la Italiana* puts me in mind of a nursery rhyme which runs thus—
>
> As I was going down Cranbourne lane,
> Cranbourne lane was dirty,
> And there I met a pretty maid,
> Who dropt to me a curtsey;
> I gave her cakes, I gave her wine,
> I gave her sugar candy,
> But oh! the little naughty girl!
> She asked me for some brandy.
>
> Now turn Cranbourne lane into Pisan acquaintances, which I am sure are dirty enough, & brandy into that wherewithall to buy brandy (& that no small sum *pero*) & you have the whole story of Shelley's Italian platonics.[45]

Epipsychidion falls into three parts. The first (1–245) begins with a sustained apostrophe to Emilia and the spirit of love, and ends with a passage on free love. The second part (246–387) is mostly disguised autobiography. The third (388–591) depicts an imaginary elopement with Emilia to a romantic isle. The basically autobiographical nature of the poem was acknowledged by Shelley in a letter to John Gisborne: "If you are anxious, however, to hear what I am and have been, it will tell you something thereof. It is an idealized history of my life and feelings. I think one is always in love with something or other; the error, and I confess it is not easy for spirits cased in flesh and blood to avoid it, consists in seeking in a mortal image the likeness of what is perhaps eternal."[46]

The title of the poem, it has been suggested, means "little soul song," on analogy with an epithalamion or marriage song.[47] As there is no such Greek word as *epipsyche*, Shelley apparently constructed it from *epi* meaning on and *psyche* meaning inner self. He perhaps intended the title, and indeed, the poem itself as a rejoinder to epithalamion poems—of which Spenser's *Epithalamium* is the best known in English—with the implication that the only unions worthy of celebration are those of men and women whose inner "selves" seek for love without concern for legal ties: "the meeting with an understanding capable of clearly estimating our own; an imagination which should enter into and seize upon the subtle and delicate peculiarities which we have delighted to cherish and unfold in secret."[48] Shelley believed that he had found such a person in Emilia.

The antimarriage theme is taken up in a central passage in the poem:

> I never was attached to that great sect,
> Whose doctrine is, that each one should select
> Out of the crowd a mistress or a friend,
> And all the rest, though fair and wise, commend
> To cold oblivion, though it is in the code
> Of modern morals, and the beaten road
> Which those poor slaves with weary footsteps tread,
> Who travel to their home among the dead
> By the broad highway of the world, and so
> With one chained friend, Perhaps a jealous foe,
> The dreariest and the longest journey go. (149–159)

The "dreariest and the longest journey" (the latter phrase taken as a title by E. M. Forster) is clearly marriage, and the sentiment an echo of the antimatrimonial Note to *Queen Mab*:

> How long then ought the sexual connection to last? what law ought to specify the extent of the grievances which should limit its duration? A husband and wife ought to continue so long united as they love each other: any law which should bind them to cohabitation for one moment after the decay of their affection would be a most intolerable tryanny, and the most unworthy of toleration . . . Love is free: to promise for ever to love the same woman is not less absurd than to promise to believe the same creed: such a vow, in both cases, excludes us from all inquiry.[49]

By the time of writing *Epipsychidion*, Shelley had linked his free love views to philosophical and social concepts:

> True Love[50] in this differs from gold and clay,
> That to divide is not to take away.
> Love is like understanding, that grows bright,
> Gazing on many truths; 'tis like thy light,

Imagination! which from earth and sky,
And from the depths of human fantasy,
As from a thousand prisms and mirrors, fills
The Universe with glorious beams, and kills
Error, the worm, with many a sun-like arrow
Of its reverberated lightning. Narrow
The heart that loves, the brain that contemplates,
The life that wears, the spirit that creates
One object, and one form, and builds thereby
A sepulchre for its eternity.

Mind from its object differs most in this:
Evil from good; misery from happiness;
The baser from the nobler; the impure
And frail, from what is clear and must endure.
If you divide suffering and dross, you may
Diminish till it is consumed away;
If you divide pleasure and love and thought,
Each part exceeds the whole; and we know not
How much, while any yet remains unshared,
Of pleasure may be gained, of sorrow spared:
This truth is that deep well, whence sages draw
The unenvied light of hope; the eternal law
By which those live, to whom this world of life
Is as a garden ravaged, and whose strife
Tills for the promise of a later birth
The wilderness of this Elysian earth. (160–189)

The elements of love, imagination, mind, good, and happiness in this passage are those that Shelley identified with the "benignant power" which stimulates the mind to overthrow the "dark slavery" of this world. These entities are inherently prolific—in contrast to such non-natural, social evils as "misery" and "suffering"—and it is in this realization that the social revolutionary ("sages" like Godwin, Hunt, or Shelley himself) is able to fight on, knowing that a future egalitarian society will come about in time (the "promise of a later birth" depicted in *Queen Mab* and *Prometheus Unbound*). Of this general process, sexual love is part and, hence, has the same characteristics: "to divide is not to take away."

Shelley, however, is not advocating promiscuity. He believed that sexual relations without love were self-centered and degrading, as he indicated in his review of Hogg's novel, *Alexy Haimitoff*. On the contrary, sexual relations should form part of a pattern of emotional and intellectual "communion."[51] When a man and a woman feel this communion, they should become lovers. In the existing society, however, their relationship has to take place within marriage or they face persecution. Hence, love suffers distortion and repression. But in the future egalitarian state love will be open, free, and beautiful among men and women who have been transformed in a transformed world. To the "soul within our soul," the code of "modern morals" is an embittering restriction on its natural tendency to embrace love to the fullest, not sexual love only but love in all its aspects: "To live as though to love and live were one." Later in the century, with the revolt against Victorianism similar views again appeared, and Shelley was hailed as a pioneer spirit by H. G. Wells, Bertrand Russell, and others, but in his own day he had little support.

In the second section of the poem, Shelley describes a strange encounter:

> There,—One, whose voice was venomed melody
> Sate by a well, under blue nightshade bowers;
> The breath of her false mouth was like faint flowers,
> Her touch was as electric poison,—flame
> Out of her looks into my vitals came,
> And from her living cheeks and bosom flew
> A killing air, which pierced like honey-dew
> Into the core of my green heart, and lay
> Upon its leaves; until, as hair grown gray
> O'er a young brow, they hid its unblown prime
> With ruins of unseasonable time. (256–266)

The obvious meaning of this passage is that Shelley, early in life, encountered a prostitute and contracted a venereal disease. This interpretation was supported by Thornton Hunt: "Again, accident has made me aware of facts which give me to understand, that in passing through the usual curriculum of a college life in all its paths, Shelley did not go scatheless,—but that, in the tampering with venal pleasures, his health was seriously, and not transiently, injured."[52] Furthermore, the passage in *Epipsychidion* does not seem to apply to any known woman in Shelley's life and is separate from the main autobiographical section where such women are treated. If Shelley did have an experience with a prostitute, the probability is that it happened at Oxford, for a "well" is a common symbol for learning, and the passage occurs at the approximate point in the symbolic narrative where his Oxford days would be.

Following this passage comes the central autobiographical section (267–387), representing the "idealized history of my life and feelings." The section opens:

> In many mortal forms I rashly sought
> The shadow of that idol of my thought.
> And some were fair—but beauty dies away:
> Others were wise—but honeyed words betray:
> And One was true—oh! why not true to me?
> Then, as a hunted deer that could not flee,
> I turned upon my thoughts, and stood at bay,
> Wounded and weak and panting; the cold day
> Trembled, for pity of my strife and pain,

When, like a noon-day dawn, there shone again
Deliverance. One stood on my path who seemed
As like the glorious shape which I had dreamed,
As in the Moon, whose changes ever run
Into themselves, to the eternal Sun. (267–280).

The identification of the Moon is indicated in a letter from Mary to Byron in October 1822, following Shelley's death: "Where also is he, who gone has made this quite, quite another earth from that which it was? There might have been something sunny about me then, now I am truly *cold moonshine.*" She recorded in her journal on October 5, 1822: "Well, I shall commence my task, commemorate the virtues of the only creature worth loving or living for, and then, maybe, I may join him. Moonshine may be united to her planet, and wander no more, a sad reflection on all she loved on earth."[53] Later in *Epipsychidion,* having identified the Sun as Emilia Viviani (344), Shelley represents himself as being ruled by the "twin spheres" of the Sun and Moon in terms that make the identification of Mary with the Moon inescapable. Thus, the events implied in the early lines of the passage took place before Shelley fell in love with Mary; those in the lines following the passage occurred afterward.

The "fair," the "wise," and the one "not true to me" represents some of the women who influenced Shelley's life before he met Mary: his sister Elizabeth, Harriet Grove, Harriet Westbrook, Elizabeth Hitchener, Mrs. Boinville and her daughter Cornelia Turner. Of these, Elizabeth Hitchener and Mrs. Boinville would approximate "the wise," the others, the "fair." The "honeyed words" betraying could reflect both Mrs. Boinville's turning against Shelley after the elopement with Mary and Elizabeth Hitchener's malicious threats to inform the government of his radical activities. The One who was "true" but "not true to me" is clearly either Harriet Grove or Harriet Shelley. If she is Harriet Grove, the "hunted deer" crisis must encompass the period from the winter of 1810–1811, when the relationship with Harriet Grove broke off and Shelley was in a suicidal turmoil, to the spring of 1814, when his marriage with Harriet Shelley was disintegrating. If she is Harriet Shelley, the reference is to the latter period only. That the reference is to Harriet Grove is indicated by an earlier, incomplete draft of some lines in the autobiographical section of the Dedication to *The Revolt of Islam* addressed to Mary Shelley in 1817:

One whom I found was dear but false to me;
The other's heart was like a heart of stone
Which crushed and withered mine

Whose touch made all my hopes and be
Withered until revived by thee.[54]

As "thee" is Mary, the one with the "heart of stone" must be Harriet Shelley; and as the "one" before Harriet Shelley was Harriet Grove, the one who was "dear but false to me" must be Harriet Grove, who had rejected Shelley and married someone else. That the "One" in *Epipsychidion* is also Harriet Grove is indicated by the fact that Shelley's bitterness about his marriage to Harriet Shelley and its break-up was such that he would not have referred to Harriet in a poem as having ever been "true." Nor, conversely, would he have referred to her as having been "not true" for this would have been to make what amounted to a public charge of marital infidelity. Finally, Harriet is referred to a few lines later under a special symbol, and as Shelley in the poem meticulously reserves one symbol for each of the leading women characters in the poem, he would not be likely to refer to her also in another way.[55]

Up to this point, Shelley has been describing, in disguised form, certain aspects of his life prior to his meeting Mary. The succeeding lines (277-307) describe his early life with Mary:

> One stood on my path who seemed
> As like the glorious shape which I had dreamed,
> As is the Moon, whose changes ever run
> Into themselves, to the eternal Sun;
> The cold chaste Moon, the Queen of Heaven's bright isles,
> Who makes all beautiful on which she smiles.
> That wandering shrine of soft yet icy flame
> Which ever is transformed, yet still the same,
> And warms not but illumines. Young and fair
> As the descended Spirit of that sphere,
> She hid me, as the Moon may hide the night
> From its own darkness, until all was bright
> Between the Heaven and Earth of my calm mind,
> And, as a cloud charioted by the wind,
> She led me to a cave in that wild place,
> And sate beside me, with her downward face
> Illumining my slumbers, like the Moon
> Waxing and waning o'er Endymion.
> And I was laid asleep, spirit and limb,
> And all my being became bright or dim
> As the Moon's image in a summer sea,
> According as she smiled or frowned on me;
> And there I lay, within a chaste cold bed:
> Alas, I then was nor alive nor dead:—
> For at her silver voice came Death and Life,
> Unmindful each of their accustomed strife,
> Masked like twin babes, a sister and a brother,
> The wandering hopes of one abandoned mother,
> And through the cavern without wings they flew,
> And cried "Away! he is not of our crew."
> I wept, and, though it be a dream, I weep.

During his agitation in the summer of 1814, when his marriage with Harriet was crumbling, Shelley met Mary, who was "young and fair," with a quality of character and mind that made "all beautiful on which she smiled." Of a tender ("soft") and loving nature, she nursed him back to psychological health. At first she appeared to be a true soul-mate, but then he found that, although she was affectionate ("soft"), she was sexually unresponsive; he lay in "a chaste cold bed." Nor was she ever really deeply stirred by anything, emotional or intellectual, but viewed all with a Godwinian calm: "ever is transformed, yet still the same." Nevertheless there was between them companionship and some sharing of intellectual interests ("warms not but illumines"). He was not in the "heart of stone" situation he had endured in his life with Harriet and Eliza, but still he felt that he was receiving just enough affection to keep some life in body and mind ("nor alive nor dead"), existing, as it were, in a pale shadow-world between life and death. The picture of loneliness and love-starvation is similar to that in *Alastor,* written in the fall of 1815. Nor is it really contradicted by the affectionate *Dedication* to Mary of *The Revolt of Islam* in the fall of 1817. The coming of Mary is hailed gratefully in the *Dedication*:

> Thou Friend, whose presence on my wintry heart
> Fell, like bright Spring upon some herbless plain;
> How beautiful and calm and free thou wert
> In thy young wisdom. (55–58)

Here the emphasis on affection and companionship—"no more companionless" (64)—is stronger, and the poet speaks fondly of their two children, who "fill our home with smiles, and thus are we/Most fortunate beneath life's beaming morn" (78-79). Yet there is no hint of a truly passionate relationship, and the selection of qualities for praise seems almost to exclude it:

> Yet in the paleness of thy thoughtful cheek,
> And in the light thine ample forehead wears,
> And in thy sweetest smiles, and in thy tears,
> And in thy gentle speech, a prophecy
> Is whispered, to subdue my fondest fears:
> And through thine eyes, even in thy soul I see
> A lamp of vestal fire burning internally. (93–99)

In the *Dedication,* of course, Shelley was paying an open tribute to Mary, whereas the "cold chaste Moon" passage in *Epipsychidion* was to be understood only by their immediate circle. Shelley could hardly criticize Mary in the *Dedication.* Furthermore, *Epipsychidion* was written four years later, after the bitter quarrel depicted in *Julian and Maddalo* and other domestic crises. Looking back on these earlier years in 1821, Shelley might well place the emphasis differently. The essential picture, however, is the same, namely, that of a "thoughtful," "gentle," and "vestal" character.

Immediately following the "cold, chaste Moon" revelation in *Epipsychidion* comes an enigmatic passage:

What storms then shook the ocean of my sleep,
Blotting that Moon, whose pale and waning lips
Then shrank as in the sickness of eclipse;—
And how my soul was as a lampless sea,
And who was then its Tempest; and when She,
The Planet of that hour, was quenched, what frost
Crept o'er those waters, till from coast to coast
The moving billows of my being fell
Into a death of ice, immovable;—
And then—what earthquakes made it gape and split,
The white Moon smiling all the while on it,
These words conceal:—If not, each word would be
The key of staunchless tears. Weep not for me! (308–320)

In the preceding passage, Shelley described his loneliness and desperation as his first marriage crumbled, his meeting with Mary, and their life together. Next comes a series of events that obviously shook him deeply and must represent a major crises in his life. The biographical evidence points clearly to the suicide of Harriet and the subsequent seizure of his children.

The first, rather obvious point of correspondence between these events and the passage is the suicide itself and Shelley's reaction to it. The "quenching" of the Planet corresponds to the drowning of Harriet. Shelley was so shaken by her suicide that after the first shock had passed, with its frenzied rationalizations of his own guilt as shown in his December 16, 1816, letter to Mary, he fell into an agony of grief and despair. Leigh Hunt, who was with him at the time, wrote: "It was a heavy blow to him and he never forgot it. For a time it tore his being to pieces." Peacock, who saw him shortly afterward, commented: "Harriet's untimely fate occasioned him deep agony of mind, which he felt the more because for a long time he kept the feeling to himself." Trelawny stated that even in 1822, "the impression of extreme pain which the end of Harriet had caused the poet was still vividly present and operative."[56] Shelley, then, went through a psychological crisis following the suicide of Harriet, corresponding to the "death of ice" state that in the poem followed the "quenching" of the planet.

While the poet was still in this state, a second blow, or rather series of blows, struck him: "And then—what earthquakes made it gape and split." This could also refer to Shelley's grief for Harriet, but the structure (a separate line beginning "And then") seems to imply a second crisis. If so, it must be the moves of the Westbrooks to deprive him of his children, which followed immediately upon the suicide. That Shelley's disturbance during this period was strong enough to warrant a parallel to a spiritual earthquake is apparent from his letters to Mary on January 11, 1817, and to Byron on January 17. There is also the testimony of Leigh Hunt: "His children, a girl and a boy, were taken from him. They were transferred to the care of a clergyman of the Church of England. The circumstance deeply affected Shelley: so much so, that he never afterwards dared to trust himself with mentioning their names in my hearing, though I had stood at his side throughout the business; probably for that reason."[57] Further evidence comes from *Rosalind and Helen,* in the "agony" of Rosalind when she is similarly deprived of her children, and from *To the Lord Chancellor* and *To William Shelley:*

> They have taken thy brother and sister dear,
> They have made them unfit for thee;
> They have withered the smile and dried the tear
> Which should have been sacred to me.

That Shelley was tormented by thoughts of Harriet and his children is indicated also by the vision of the "abandoned mother" and her children, which immediately precedes the Planet-Tempest passage. The parallels between the "abandoned mother" and Harriet, and between the "wandering" children, "a sister and a brother," and Ianthe and Charles are clear. Mary's soothing rationalizations, Shelley seems to be saying, roused conscience-stabbing images of his abandoned wife and children, which drove him even further into a state of semi-being between life and death. He was then hurled into the "storms" of the suicide and litigation.

A third problem of identification is that of the Tempest:

> And how my soul was as a lampless sea,
> And who was then its Tempest; and when She,
> The Planet of that hour, was quenched, what frost
> Crept o'er those waters. (311–314)

The syntax allows us to take the Planet and the Tempest as either the same entity or separate ones. If they are the same, the Tempest must also be Harriet. Harriet, however, was hardly tempestuous, and a contiguous reference to one character under two such different symbols is not paralleled elsewhere in the poem. Each symbol seems precise, designating a specific character. The tempest, then, most probably represents a separate person; and the person whom Shelley regarded in this period as a veritable tempest, responsible for turning his soul into a "lampless sea," was Eliza Westbrook. Shelley not only hated Eliza with an almost pathological hatred but blamed her for the suicide of Harriet and the litigation over his children. As he bluntly declared to Byron at the time: "The sister . . . may be truly said . . . to have murdered her"; and to Mary: "There can be no question that the beastly viper her sister, unable to gain profit from her connexion with me—has secured to herself the fortune of the old man—who is now dying—by the murder of this poor creature." Shelley wrote bitterly to Byron of Eliza's attempts to deprive him of his children:

> The sister has now instituted a Chancery process against me, the intended effect of which is to deprive me of my unfortunate children, now more than ever dear

to me; of my inheritance, and to throw me into prison, and expose me in the pillory, on the ground of my being a REVOLUTIONIST, and an *Atheist*. It seems whilst she lived in my house she possessed herself of such papers as go to establish these allegations. The opinion of Counsel is, that she will certainly succeed to a considerable extent, but that I may probably escape entire ruin, in the worldly sense of it.[58]

Eliza, then, fits the role of the Tempest.

The final problem of the passage involves the "storms" of the initial lines and the role of the Moon during these storms:

> What storms then shook the ocean of my sleep,
> Blotting that Moon, whose pale and waning lips
> Then shrank as in the sickness of eclipse!—
>
> . . . . .
>
> And then—what earthquakes made it gape and split,
> The white Moon smiling all the while on it. (308–310, 317–318)

The "storms" are not intended to be separate experiences from the "sea of ice" or the "earthquakes," but represent a general introductory metaphor for the poet's disturbances throughout the period, doubtless including the suicide of Fanny Godwin in October 1816. They reflect Shelley's life in the harrowing months of the two suicides and his struggle for custody of his children—a situation he put succinctly in the opening sentence of a letter to Byron on January 17, 1817: "I write to you, my dear Lord Byron, after a series of the most unexpected and overwhelming sorrows, and from the midst of a situation of peril and persecution."

The lines on the Moon clearly fit what must have been Mary's role during this period from the late fall of 1816 to the spring of 1817 and Shelley's reaction to her: Shelley's mind was in such a turmoil that she was, as it were, "blotted" from his consciousness, and she in her anxiety for him "shrank" in body and spirit; but she persisted in her loving care, and as his mind became normal again, he found that she had been "smiling" on him "all the while." That Mary was eager to help him, urging him to bring his children by Harriet back to her, and yet was extremely worried and disturbed herself, is indicated by her letter to him of December 17, 1816, written in the early stages of the crisis: "You tell me to write a long letter and I would but that my ideas wander and my hand trembles come back to reassure me my Shelley & bring with you your darling Ianthe & Charles."[59]

Neither in his early loves nor in the Moon did the poet find a woman capable of deep, passionate love. On encountering Emilia, however, he believed that he had at last found such a woman. In "Emily" (344) he sensed a warm and passionate affection different from the moon-glow of Mary:

> Soft as an Incarnation of the Sun
> When light is changed to love. (335–336)

Poised between these two influences—though clearly leaning toward the Sun—he hopes to achieve happiness and inspiration:

> Twin Spheres of light who rule this passive Earth,
> This world of love, this *me*; and into birth
> Awaken all its fruits and flowers, and dart
> Magnetic might into its central heart. (345–348)

Beside these two celestial bodies there looms a third, a Comet:

> Thou too, O Comet beautiful and fierce,
> Who drew the heart of this frail Universe
> Towards thine own; till, wreckt in that convulsion,
> Alternating attraction and repulsion,
> Thine went astray and that was rent in twain;
> Oh, float into our azure heaven again! (368–373)

As at the time of his writing *Epipsychidi*on, Claire was the only other woman who stood in any relation to Shelley intimate enough to be listed with Mary and Emilia, the Comet must be Claire.[60] This is further indicated by the final line, "Oh, float into our azure heaven again," for Claire was not then a part of the Shelley household but was living in Florence, and Shelley is apparently urging her return.

Claire, unlike the "cold, chaste Moon," is "beautiful and fierce." She has not, it is implied, the deep love-warmth of the sun, but she is tempestuous and exciting. There is also the implication that she had once loved Shelley ("drew the heart of this frail universe/Towards thine own") and they had an ardent but unstable relationship ("convulsion,/Alternating attraction and revulsion"). As a result, Claire's heart went "astray" and Shelley's was "rent in twain." The reference here must be to Claire's love affair with Byron which, as was abundantly clear by 1821, had ended disastrously, with Byron's refusal to let her bring up their child and Claire's obsessive hatred for Byron. The implication is that Shelley and Claire were deeply involved with each other before her affair with Byron in the early spring of 1816 and that it was somehow as a result of this involvement that she virtually threw herself at Byron.

The final section of the poem proper (388–591) describes an imaginary elopement with Emilia to a Mediterranean island. The intent and nature of the section have been misunderstood, for instance, the climactic lines on the lovers:

> Our breath shall intermix, our bosoms bound,
> And our veins beat together; and our lips
> With other eloquence than words, eclipse
> The soul that burns between them, and the wells
> Which boil under our being's inmost cells,

The fountains of our deepest life, shall be
Confused in passion's golden purity,
As mountain-springs under the morning Sun. (565–572)

It almost passes comprehension that some commentators have considered this passage as purely spiritual, for the sexual imagery is obvious and intentional. Once Shelley's feelings for Emilia are recognized, the final section is seen to be not an exercise in escapism but a passionate expression of need and longing. It is, in fact, the very essence of romantic love poetry.

The Sensitive Plant; Fragments of an Unfinished Drama; Marenghi; A Vision of the Sea; Ginevra

The Sensitive Plant consists of three parts and a conclusion. The first part describes a beautiful garden, in the midst of which grows the Sensitive Plant (*mimosa pudica*, whose leaves fold up when touched):

For the Sensitive Plant has no bright flower;
Radiance and odour are not its dower;
It loves, even like Love, its deep heart is full,
It desires what it has not, the beautiful! (74–77)

Part Two tells of the lady who looks after the garden:

There was a Power in this sweet place,
An Eve in this Eden; a ruling Grace
Which to the flowers, did they waken or dream,
Was as God is to the starry scheme. (1–4)

The lady tended the garden from early spring until late summer, and then died. Part Three describes the subsequent deterioration of the garden from neglect and its destruction by winter. The Sensitive Plant and other lovely flowers die, but the weeds and poisonous plants live; when spring returns, only the latter revive:

When Winter had gone and Spring came back,
The Sensitive Plant was a leafless wreck;
But the mandrakes, and toadstools, and docks, and darnels,
Rose like the dead from their ruined charnels. (110–113)

The Sensitive Plant, like other poems by Shelley, has a number of interlocking levels. On the surface it is simply the story of a beautiful garden and the lady who tends it. Shelley may have remembered a garden he once saw with Hogg at Oxford, or he may, as Medwin stated, have had in mind his friend Lady Mount Cashell ("Mrs. Mason") and her garden at Pisa.

That he, Mary, and others in the Pisa circle had talked over the poem on this level, regarding the lady simply as a loving and beautiful woman, is apparent from his comments to Leigh Hunt on Jane Williams: "a most delightful person whom we all agree is the exact antitype of the lady I described in the sensitive plant though this must have been *pure anticipated cognition* as it was written a year before I knew her."[61]

On a second level the poem restates the concept in the Preface to *Alastor* that the more sensitive persons perish spiritually, while those who poison the world with greed, apathy, and selfishness survive. On this level the garden is society, the lady, like the Witch, is a manifestation of the "benignant power" under whose warmth those "of pure and gentle habits" flourish, and the Sensitive Plant represents "the Poets," ever aspiring to communion with "the Beautiful."[62] Both levels were supposed to be understood by the reading public.

The third level is psychological: Shelley is the Sensitive Plant, the lady is perhaps, as Newman White suggested, Mary, and her death represents Mary's withdrawal of love.[63] But unlike the systematic autobiographical content of *Epipsychidion*, these correspondences reflect only a mood or state of mind, which is woven haphazardly throughout the narrative. And it was not supposed to be apparent to the general reader.

The conclusion of *The Sensitive Plant* is a kind of metaphysical addendum:

It is a modest creed, and yet
Pleasant if one considers it,
To own that death itself must be
Like all the rest, a mockery.

That garden sweet, that lady fair,
And all sweet shapes and odours there,
In truth have never pass'd away:
'Tis we, 'tis ours, are changed! not they.

For love, and beauty, and delight,
There is no death nor change: their might
Exceeds our organs, which endure
No light, being themselves obscure. (126–137)

The benignant power and its manifestations in the mind ("love, and beauty, and delight") are eternal; if the death of human beings ("we" and "ours") gives a sense of unreality ("mockery") to life, then, death, too, may be unreal. The sense organs (the brain) endure "no light" because they are basically noncreative (dark, "obscure"), passively accepting the love and beauty and delight provided by the power, just as the Hermaphrodite came to life when stimulated by the Witch of Atlas, or the poet when inspired by the wind of creation. The individual sense organs perish, but the total world of the imagination and its creations, including the lady and the garden, continue to live on—as Shelley wrote in *Mont Blanc*—in "the still cave of the witch poesy" which is given life by the power ("the breast/From which they fled"). All this, Shelley indicates, is a "metaphorical" concept, put forward tentatively, even wistfully—"a pleasant creed"—not a statement of philosopher belief. Death was more likely the "dark reality" of *Hymn to Intellectual Beauty* than "a mockery."

On April 10, 1822, Williams wrote in his journal: "Trelawny dined here and passed the evening. We talked of a play of his singular life, and a plot to give it the air of Romance & ca." Shelley may have begun such a play, and the piece titled in his works *Fragments of an Unfinished Drama* may be a draft for it. It is a light romantic piece, intended only, as Mary noted, "for the amusement of the individuals who composed our intimate society" at Pisa, namely, the Williamses, Trelawny, Byron, and their Italian friends. She outlines its apparently involved plot as follows. An Enchantress on an enchanted island in the Indian archipelago saves the life of a Pirate. The Pirate makes love to the Enchantress, but after a time "returns to his Lady." But setting out to sea once again, he is again ensnared on the isle by the Enchantress. Fortunately, a Good Spirit whose function it is to thwart the schemes of the Enchantress conveys the Pirate's Lady to the island and provides her with a companion in an Indian Youth, "who loves the Lady, but whose passion she returns only with a sisterly affection."[64] Mary's account ends there, but presumably the Enchantress would have ultimately been defeated and the Pirate and the Lady have escaped together.

The parts of the drama that were actually written consist of two fragmentary scenes. In the first scene, of only 28 lines, the Enchantress laments a lost lover, presumably the Pirate. She makes a spell that will return him to her and is answered by a mysterious Spirit, whose customary abode, he informs her, is the center of the earth.

In the next scene (216 lines) the lady and the Indian Youth are on the "mysterious island" discussing her previous lover, again presumably the Pirate. The Lady explains that she knew him when he was only a "simple innocent boy" (85), and he left her in the "dawn" of life. In spite of calumnies directed against him, she wishes to join him:

> Some said he was a man of blood and peril,
> And steeped in bitter infamy to the lips.
> More need was there I should be innocent,
> More need that I should be most true and kind,
> And much more need that there should be found one
> To share remorse and scorn and solitude,
> And all the ills that wait on those who do
> The tasks of ruin in the world of life.
> He fled, and I have followed him. (112–120)

The Indian Youth asks the Lady how she came to leave India and travel to the island. In reply, she tells of a mysterious dream in which she saw in the midst of the light of a glowing meteor, "a spirit like a child," who placed something "like melon seeds" in a vase, whereupon:

> A soft hand issued from the veil of fire,
> Holding a cup like a magnolia flower,
> And poured upon the earth within the vase
> The element with which it overflowed,
> Brighter than morning light, and purer than
> The water of the springs of Himalah. (144–150)

The next day the Lady found a little plant sprouting in the vase. She nurtured it, and it grew to a large and rare beauty, trailing outside her window through a garden and lawn until its end lay floating on a fountain. Here the fragment breaks off.

The description of the seeding and growth of the plant is so detailed that Shelley must have considered it of special importance. On the basis of a similar apparition in *The Revolt of Islam* (I, xxxix-xliii), it would seem to represent, once more, some aspect of the "benignant power." At any rate, it somehow got the Lady from India to the island, which she calls "this/ Realm of abandonment" (99).

From the entry in Williams' journal, one would presume the previous lover to be sketched after Trelawny, but as Sylva Norman pointed out, he resembles Shelley more than Trelawny, and the Lady, "who plays on the double flute and delights in flowers," is very like Jane Williams.[65] The explanation is perhaps that Shelley intended the lover ostensibly to be Trelawny (the scene is Trelawny's old stamping ground of *Adventures of a Younger Son*, the Indian archipelago), and it was so understood in the Pisan circle, but he also contrived to bring in certain elements of self-portraiture. Certainly the relationship of the Lady and the Indian seems rather like that of Shelley and Jane Williams. Jane had lived in India and gone from there to a "Realm of abandonment," namely, Italy, the "Paradise of Exiles."

The text of the poem raises questions about the reliability of Mary Shelley's outline. The Indian Youth had a previous love (32–35), a condition Mary assigned to the Pirate, and he refers to the Lady's encounters with her previous beloved (identified as the Pirate by Mary) in such a strange way (88–92) that he himself seems to be the previous beloved, through either a magic spell or reincarnation. The Lady gives no indication of having known her beloved twice (as Mary stated) but seems to have left him when he was merely a "boy." Nor does he appear to have been a pirate; rather, he is a reviled youthful idealist, like "Lionel." Finally, Mary did not mention the mysterious plant, although it was obviously going to play an important role in the play. Possibly Shelley changed his plot outline after talking to Mary, perhaps he misled her with regard to some aspects of it, or perhaps she saw more in it than she wished to disclose.

Marenghi, a narrative poem written in Italy in 1818, is also fragmentary. Shelley took the story from an incident recorded in Sismondi's *Histoire des republiques italiennes du Moyen Age.* During a war between Pisa and Florence, Pisa was being blockaded by the Florentines, a Pisan galley attempted to run the blockade but was destroyed by Marenghi, a man who had been exiled from Florence and had since lived in the Pisan marshes. Marenghi plunged into the river with a flaming torch in hand and, daring the might of the Pisans, set the galley on fire. He was later reinstated to Florentine citizenship with honor.

Shelley's poem displays that partiality for the Florentine republic which is also evident in *A Philosophical View of Reform*:

> A nation amid slaveries, disenchanted
> Of many impious faiths. (26–27)

Marenghi, while living in the marshes, could have survived only by keeping the torch of liberty alive in his heart:

> There must have burned within Marenghi's breast
> That fire, more warm and bright than life and hope.

One day, rather like Zeinab in the early *Zeinab and Kathema:*

> he saw beneath the sunset's planet
> A black ship walk over the crimson ocean.

Presumably this ship is the Pisan galley, but the fragment ends with this stanza.

Two minor narrative poems written in Pisa are *A Vision of the Sea* and *Ginevra,* the first probably written in April 1820, the second in 1821.[66] *A Vision of the Sea,* a fragment, is something of a puzzle. A ship that has been becalmed for eight weeks and whose crew is mysteriously dead is adrift in a storm. Two tigers, who were in the hold, get loose in the storm. At the helm sits a beautiful woman clutching a child to her bosom. When the storm subsides, one tiger jumps overboard and battles a sea serpent. What is apparently a ship's boat appears; the men in it shoot the other tiger, which is still on the deck; and presumably the lady and her child are rescued. The poem ends:

> Like a sister and brother
> The child and the ocean still smile on each other,
> Whilst——

Possibly Shelley began to write a long narrative poem, perhaps inspired by something he was reading at the time, then abandoned it but thought the opening lines worth saving. Certainly, as it stands, the poem makes little sense. It does not appear to have either symbolic or autobiographical meaning. The verse, however, in skillful anapaests, is often strong, and the descriptions, as of the ship in storm, are sometimes powerful. In one passage

Shelley expresses compactly and poignantly his doubts on immortality. The lady is addressing her child during the storm:

> Alas! what is life, what is death, what are we,
> That when the ship sinks we no longer may be?
> What! to see thee no more, and to feel thee no more?
> To be after life what we have been before?
> Not to touch those sweet hands? Not to look on those eyes. (82–86)[67]

The plot of *Ginevra,* which Shelley took from an Italian paper, is of a standard romantic type. Ginevra, in love with Antonio, is forced by her father to marry Gherardi. On her wedding day Antonio appears and they hold an impassioned conversation, in which she tells him that she will die before she is married. In the final scene the wedding guests find Ginevra dead. According to the Italian story, Ginevra was not really dead but in a coma; she came to in the tomb, escaped, was rejected by her husband and parents as a ghost, and ended up with Antonio. It has been suggested that Shelley was attracted to this wild tale by its application to Emilia Viviani and himself, Emilia having been forced by her father to marry and so desert her devoted Shelley. Since the poem was written in the period of Shelley's obsession with Emilia and fits in with other poems concerning her marriage, the suggestion is plausible.[68] It should not, however, be pushed too far. Antonio is certainly not a Shelley self-portrait.

Lyrical Poems

The most famous of Shelley's lyrics, *Ode to the West Wind,* has been generally considered as a personal poem, the "winter" referring to personal sorrows, the "spring" to their alleviation. But although Shelley does have this concept in mind, it is secondary to the sociohistorical meaning. What this is may be seen by comparing the ode with some stanzas in *The Revolt of Islam,* written two years earlier. In the *Revolt,* the revolution in the "Golden City" (the "beau ideal" of the French Revolution) has been put down, the revolutionary armies have been routed, and its leaders, Laon and Cythna, are in flight. Cythna speaks to Laon:

> The blasts of autumn drive the winged seeds
> Over the earth,—next come the snows, and rain,
> And frosts, and storms, which dreary winter leads
> Out of his Scythian cave, a savage train;
> Behold! Spring sweeps over the world again,
> Shedding soft dews from her aetherial wings.
> . . . . .
> The seeds are sleeping in the soil: meanwhile
> The tyrant peoples dungeons with his prey,

Pale victims on the guarded scaffold smile
Because they cannot speak; and, day by day,
The moon of wasting Science wanes away
Among her stars, and in that darkness vast
The sons of earth to their foul idols pray,
And gray Priests triumph, and like blight or blast
A shade of selfish care o'er human looks is cast.

"This is the winter of the world;—and here
We die, even as the winds of Autumn fade,
Expiring in the frore and foggy air.—
Behold! Spring comes, though we must pass, who made
The promise of its birth,—even as the shade
Which from our death, as from a mountain, flings
The future, a broad sunrise; thus arrayed
As with the plumes of overshadowing wings,
From its dark gulf of chains, Earth like an eagle springs." (3649–54, 3676–93)

"Autumn" and the "winter of the world" clearly refer to the decades following the defeat of the French Revolution. The "winged seeds" driven by autumn "blasts" are the social forces and ideas that will bring about a revival of liberty; and this new age will be the "spring" of mankind.

In the ode also, there are two winds, the west wind of autumn ("thou breath of Autumn's being") and the west wind of spring ("thine azure sister of the spring"). The autumn wind scatters the "winged seeds"; the west wind of spring brings them to life. That Shelley has in mind here also the spring of mankind, the new social order, is clear from the final stanza: "The trumpet of a prophecy!" The same kind of symbolism appears also in *Prometheus Unbound* (I, 790–800), written in the same year as the ode.

In the ode, however, the framework is personal, as is usual in a lyrical poem. The poet is Shelley himself as he thinks of both his own suffering and that of the world around him. The despairing cry, "I fall upon the thorns of life! I bleed!" has been attacked as excessive, but it does not appear so in light of the experiences of the previous months: the deaths of Shelley's daughter Clara at Este, with Mary's subsequent depression, and of his son William after those "60 miserable—deathlike hours" of watching over his deathbed.[69]

In the conclusion the personal and political elements are blended, as the poet hopes that his own writings may assist in the coming of the new order, which, like Cythna, he will never witness himself:

Drive my dead thoughts over the universe
Like withered leaves to quicken a new birth!

Shelley's volatile imagination with its fluid combining of diverse images has been a bugbear for the literal-minded, as witness F. R. Leavis' comment on the lines:

Thou on whose stream, 'mid the steep sky's commotion,
Loose clouds like earth's decaying leaves are shed,
Shook from the tangled boughs of Heaven and Ocean.

Leavis stated that the "boughs" stand for "nothing that Shelley could have pointed to in the scene before him." Richard Harter Fogle replied aptly: "It is quite true—in fact self-evident—that there are no 'boughs' in the sky, no boughs in the sea. But the clouds derive from these 'tangled boughs'—tangled because Heaven and Ocean intermingle, boughs because the clouds derive from the sky and sea in just such an organic process as causes the leaves to grow on the tree."[70]

The message of *To a Skylark* is similar to that of the *Ode to the West Wind*.[71] To Shelley, gazing at both the despotic world about him and his own inner discontents, the song of the soaring skylark becomes a symbol of liberty and happiness, a force from nature that might, like the message of those "unacknowledged legislators," the poets, inspire others to produce a better world:

Like a poet hidden
In the light of thought,
Singing hymns unbidden,
Till the world is wrought
To sympathy with hopes and fears it heeded not. (34–36)

Such was Shelley's own deepest wish:

Teach me half the gladness
That thy brain must know,
Such harmonious madness
From my lips would flow
The world should listen then—as I am listening now. (101–105)

The theme of the third of Shelley's best-known lyrics, *The Cloud*, is that of the permanence behind flux and change:

I am the daughter of earth and water,
And the nursling of the sky;
I pass through the pores of the ocean and shores;
I change, but I cannot die.
For after the rain when with never a stain,
The pavilion of heaven is bare,
And the winds and sunbeams with their convex gleams,
Build up the blue dome of air,
I silently laugh at my own cenotaph,
And out of the caverns of rain,
Like a child from the womb, like a ghost from the tomb,
I arise and unbuild it again. (73–84)

Desmond King-Hele, who is both a Shelleyan and a physicist, commented:

The "sweat" of the ocean is the chief raw material for the cloud, and the pores of the shores are the rivers and rivulets which return the cloud's remains to the sea. (*Pores* is a word used by Adam Walker which may have stuck in Shelley's memory.) During its life-cycle the cloud material may assume any of the three states of matter: as vapour, a liquid droplet or an ice particle. *I change* thus covers changes of state as well as of shape, size and colour. The second notable image is the *sunbeams with their convex gleams.* The earth's atmosphere bends a ray of sunlight into a curve concave downwards, or convex to an observer in a cloud looking down. Few poets, probably, have been aware of this, and fewer still would think of putting it in a poem.[72]

A fourth often anthologised lyric, *Stanzas, Written in Dejection Near Naples,* is a product of Shelley's period of depression in Naples in the winter of 1818–1819. In the opening stanzas he describes the beauty of Naples and its surroundings.[73] The concluding stanzas contrast in simple, poignant words this beauty with the weariness in his heart:

> Yet now despair itself is mild,
>   Even as the winds and waters are;
> I could lie down like a tired child,
>   And weep away the life of care. (28–31)

Part of the reason for the despair is loneliness and isolation: "How sweet! did any heart now share in my emotion." The reference must be to Mary's alienation from him in the days following the death of Clara.

Beyond these poems, Shelley's lyrics fall mainly into four groups, inspired by four women: Claire Clairmont, Sophia Stacey, Emilia Viviani, and Jane Williams. The poems to Claire were written at Marlow, where she, Shelley, and Mary occupied the same house (1817–1818). The best known of them is *To Constantia, Singing,* which, Claire said, Shelley hid from Mary. It reveals a rather desperate turning toward Claire—"I have no life, Constantia, now, but thee"—and a passionate intensity of feeling:

> Even while I write, my burning cheeks are wet—
> Alas, that the torn heart can bleed but not forget.[74]

Shelley seems to be deeply shaken. The second lyric, *To Constantia,* is fragmentary:

> I
> The rose that drinks the fountain dew
>   In the pleasant air of noon,
> Grows pale and blue with altered hue—
>   In the gaze of the nightly moon;
> For the planet of frost, so cold and bright,
> Makes it wan with her borrowed light.

II

Such is my heart—roses are fair,
  And that at best a withered blossom;
But thy false care did idly wear
  Its withered leaves in a faithless bosom!
And fed with love, like air and dew,
Its growth—

These two poems are illuminated by a fragment, appearing on the same manuscript page as stanza four of *To Constantia, Singing*:

To thirst and find no fill—to [wail] and wander
With short unsteady steps—to pause and ponder—
To feel the blood run through the veins and tingle
Where busy thought and blind sensation mingle;
To nurse the image of unfelt caresses
Till dim imagination just possesses
The half-created shadow, then all the night
Sick[75]

Together, the three poems reflect the same general situation as *Epipsychidion*. "I have no life, Constantia, now but thee" indicates the lack of a passionate relationship with Mary. "To thirst and find no fill" gives the impression of an *Alastor*-like loneliness and frustration. The "planet of frost" or the "nightly moon" is clearly parallel to the "cold chaste moon" in *Epipsychidion*, where the reference is unmistakably to Mary. The implication is that after Shelley's heart became "a withered blossom," he sought an affair with Claire, who accepted his love, but in an idle, "faithless" fashion. The reference of "faithless" can hardly be to anything but Claire's affair with Byron in 1816.[76] Again the situation is similar to that reflected in *Epipsychidion*, where the Comet alternated "attraction and repulsion." Viewed in this context, the "Constantia" poems must mean that in late 1817 or early 1818 Shelley was trying to persuade Claire to become his mistress. Again, however, as in *Epipsychidion*, there is no sense of a warm, reciprocal love but rather of an unstable, tormented relationship. Apparently Claire did not want an affair with Shelley at this time, perhaps because she had not yet given up hope of Byron or was afraid that Mary would again eject her from the household. One curious aspect of some of the poems is that they show almost as much obsession with the coldness of Mary as with the desirability of Claire. The situation seems to be that of a husband, feeling neglected and lonely, turning to an exciting woman in the same household, with whom he may have had a previous affair.

The lyrics presented to Sophia Stacey, Shelley's pretty cousin who lived in the same boarding house in Florence with the Shelleys for a few weeks in 1819, are very different from the "Constantia" poems. Both Sophia's journal and Shelley's and Mary's comments indicate a mild flirtation, with

Shelley, the black sheep of the family, talented but dangerous, gallantly courting his wide-eyed country cousin. He writes verses complimenting her on her singing (*To Sophia*) and lyrics for her to sing, which though not ostensibly intended to have any direct reference to her, could be so taken (*The Indian Serenade, Love's Philosophy,* and *Good-Night*). Shelley also presented her with poems written on other subjects and other occasions: *On a Faded Violet* (probably written to Mary at Este) and *Time Long Past.* The poems to Sophia are light troubadour-and-lady pieces, saved from the usual artificiality of such verse by Shelley's lyrical magic.[77]

The *Indian Serenade* has received adverse attention from the New Critics and others on the grounds that it is sentimental and overemotional, qualities that are presumed to be alien to a truly masculine lover:

> Let thy love in kisses rain
> On my lips and eyelids pale.

But these are matters of relative taste and judgment. The view that the male is to be stolidly dominant has received hard knocks in recent years, and Shelley was among the first to imply a basic similarity of masculine and feminine roles in a love relationship and suggest that men should uninhibitedly display tenderness, dependence, and sensitivity. The poem combines passion with grace and charm in a manner reminiscent of the Indian drama of Shakuntala.

Shelley's reaction to Emilia Viviani went through the two stages of romantic excitement on first meeting her and despondency after her marriage the next fall. The second stage, which may have provided the initial impetus for *Ginevra,* probably also inspired a series of lyrics, apparently written late in 1821, including *To ——"Music when soft voices die"* and *To——"When passion's trance is overcast."*[78]

One other "To——" poem of this year, *To——"One word is too often profaned,"* has been traditionally regarded as having been inspired not by Emilia but by Jane Williams. It has not the nostalgic tone of the later Emilia poems but reflects an awakening romantic interest. Whereas the later poems to Jane express sexual passion rather directly, in this early stage, when Shelley was just getting to know Jane and her husband, he is tentatively probing. He cannot, he protests, think of offering love, although he is happy to accept her "pity"; perhaps she might accept in return an airy and spiritual passion. The lyric's power comes from its blending of a growing love for Jane with the longing for a better world: "The desire of the moth for the star."

One of Shelley's most delightful short poems was written not to Jane but to Edward Williams, namely, *The Boat on the Serchio.* It is in the easy, informal style that he handled with such verve in *Letter to Maria Gisborne.* It reveals a warm companionship between the two men, who had both gone to Eton:

Ay, heave the ballast overboard,
And stow the eatables in the aft locker.
"Would not this keg be best a little lowered?"
"No, now all's right." "Those bottles of warm tea—
(Give me some straw)—must be stowed tenderly;
Such as we used, in summer after six,
To cram in greatcoat pockets, and to mix
Hard eggs and radishes and rolls at Eton,
And, couched on stolen hay in those green harbours
Farmers called gaps, and we schoolboys called arbours,
Would feast till eight." (73–83)

Another poem, although titled *To Edward Williams*, is really addressed jointly to Edward and Jane. It depicts, again with extraordinary frankness, Shelley's discontent with Mary:

Of hatred I am proud,—with scorn content;
Indifference, that once hurt me, now is grown
Itself indifferent.

. . . . .

When I return to my cold home, you ask
Why I am not as I have ever been.
You spoil me for the task
Of acting a forced part in life's dull scene. (9–11, 25–28)

The reference in "hatred," "scorn," and "indifference," are clearly directed at Mary. They are, in fact, a repetition of the charges in *Julian and Maddalo*.

Following "*One word is too often profaned*," the developing relationship of Shelley and Jane is revealed in a series of lyrics: *The Magnetic Lady to Her Patient; To Jane: The Invitation; To Jane: The Recollection; The Pine Forest of the Cascine Near Pisa; With a Guitar, To Jane; To Jane: The keen stars were twinkling; Lines Written in the Bay of Lerici;* and *Lines: "We meet not as we parted."*

The Magnetic Lady to Her Patient—that is, Jane to Shelley, who was being mesmerized by her to reduce his kidney stone pains—reveals that Jane responded sympathetically to Shelley's tales of a lack of affection—"My pity on thy heart, poor friend"—but refused to become his mistress:

Forget lost health, and the divine
Feelings which died in youth's brief morn;
And forget me, for I can never
Be thine. (24–27)

To Jane: The Invitation, To Jane: The Recollection, and *The Pine Forest of the Cascine Near Pisa* describe a walk by Shelley and Jane through a pine forest near the sea. The poems show that Shelley was becoming increasingly attracted by Jane. *The Recollection* contains some puzzling lines:

And still I felt the centre of
  The magic circle there
Was one fair form that filled with love
  The lifeless atmosphere.

. . . . .

Like one beloved the scene had lent
  To the dark water's breast,
Its every leaf and lineament
  With more than truth exprest;
Until an envious wind crept by,
  Like an unwelcome thought,
Which from the mind's too faithful eye
Blots one dear image out.
Though thou art ever fair and kind,
  The forests ever green,
Less oft is peace in Shelley's mind,
  Than calm in waters, seen. (49–52, 77–88)

The identity of the "envious wind," and of the "dear image" that blots it out, is found in Mary Shelley's journal entry for February 2, 1822: "Go through the Pine Forest to the sea with Shelley and Jane."[79] Mary, that is, was along on the walk, as the poems fail to mention. The "envious wind," then, must be Mary, the "dear image," Jane. Likewise, Jane is the "fair form," Mary the "lifeless atmosphere." The poem was sent to Jane with a note: "To Jane—not to be opened unless you are alone or with Williams."

The best-known of the poems is *With a Guitar, To Jane.* The love between Jane and Williams is recognized, at least on the surface, and Shelley appears in the role of a worshiping poet-sprite (Ariel speaking to Miranda, with Ferdinand present). The poem is light and pleasant, without the gossipy overtones of *The Invitation* and *The Recollection.* So, too, is *To Jane: The keen stars were twinkling*", a tribute to Jane's guitar playing. As Newman White commented, the verse itself seems to reproduce the tinkling of a guitar.[80]

Lines Written in the Bay of Lerici must have been composed between early May 1822, when the Shelleys and Williamses first settled in the Bay of Lerici region, and July 1, when Shelley and Williams left for Leghorn, never to return. A reference in the poem to a full moon points to June 21–24.[81] Both it and *We meet not as we parted* deal with Shelley and a woman to whom he declares his love. Jane was the only woman with Shelley at the Bay of Lerici who would fit the situation, and the feelings expressed are a natural development from those in previous poems to her.

In *Lines Written in the Bay of Lerici*, the poet is sitting alone in the moonlight by the shore after the woman has left:

She left me, and I staid alone
Thinking over every tone,
Which though now silent to the ear

The enchanted heart could hear
Like notes which die when born, but still
Haunt the echoes of the hill:
And feeling ever—o too much
The soft vibrations of her touch
As if her gentle hand even now
Lightly trembled on my brow
And thus although she absent were
Memory gave me all of her
That even fancy dares to claim.

. . . . .

I dare not speak
My thoughts; but thus disturbed & weak
I sate and watched the vessels glide
Along the Ocean bright & wide.

The second poem, *We meet not as we parted,* was apparently written a day or so later:

We meet not as then we parted—
We feel more than all may see
My bosom is heavy hearted
And thine full of doubt for me
A moment has bound the free

That moment is gone for ever
Like lightning it flashed and died
Like a snowflake upon the river
A sunbeam upon the tide—
Which the dark shadows hide—

That moment from time was singled
As the price of a life of pain.—
In the cup of its joy was mingled
Delusion too sweet though vain
Too sweet to be mine again

Sweet lips, could my soul not have hidden
That its life was consumed by you
Ye would not have then forbidden
The death which a heart so true
Sought in your burning dew—
That methinks were too little cost
For a moment so found, so lost!

In the first poem, the poet is pictured weak and shaken after the woman's departure; yet the beauty of her voice and the touch of her hand are still with him and in remembrance stimulate his imagination to envisage complete possession of her. In the second poem he centers on the "moment" of confrontation, feeling that it has changed the lives of both himself and the woman. They are no longer "free" but bound by love. In the fourth stanza, "not" in the first line was doubtless intended to be canceled, and the last two lines may belong to an unfinished fifth stanza. Shelley's meaning in stanza four seems to be: "If I had been able to conceal the fact that I was seriously in love, you would not have forbidden me to kiss you" (with a double meaning perhaps suggested by "death" and "burning dew"). The final lines appear to refer to a canceled line: "The peace that I now have lost." The intensity of the "moment" is revealed in two fragmentary lines:

That moment was   mingled
With delusion & madness too sweet.

The situation reflected in the two poems seems to be that the poet made a passionate declaration of love and tried to embrace and kiss the woman, who, although aroused ("burning"), refused him, while at the same time indicating that all was not hopeless. The poet was left in a turmoil of emotions. That this situation had been building up for some time is revealed in *The Magnetic Lady to Her Patient*, with its implication of similar proposals, though presumably of a less vehement nature, and in *To Jane: The Recollection*, with its contrast between the "dear image" and the "envious wind." When *The Magnetic Lady* was written is not known, but *The Recollection* can be dated in early February 1822 on the basis of Mary Shelley's and Williams' journal entries. Shelley and Jane had carried on a kind of troubadour play for several months, with Shelley cast as the hopeless lover-poet, but by June, Shelley's feeling for Jane had become deeply passionate.

Translations

Shelley had remarkable facility in languages. He translated works from Greek, Latin, French, Italian, Spanish, and German. Although he enjoyed translating, he usually turned to it only when not engaged in creative work. He apparently regarded it as form of relaxation and never embarked on an extensive project, but contented himself with translating some of his own favorites. In poetry, he translated the *Cyclops* of Euripides, a number of the so-called *Homeric Hymns*, three scenes from Calderon's *Magico prodigioso*, and two scenes from Goethe's *Faust*, and in prose he translated Plato's *Ion* and *Symposium* and Spinoza's *Tractatus theologico-politicus*, now mostly lost.[82]

The translation of the *Cyclops* is reprinted in the Everyman edition of Euripides, whose editor considered it the "most poetical translation of *Euripides* into any tongue," and Edward Dowden considered that the *Homeric*

Hymns were "admirably executed."[83] The best of them is the long *Hymn to Hermes,* whose puckish and hurly-burly spirit Shelley catches admirably. The translation of the *Magico prodigioso* was praised by Salvador de Madariaga:

> Shelley's translation is indeed a striking proof of his insight into Calderon's art and style. Expression is not always crystal-like in Calderon. He sometimes strains his thought to suit his images and twists his sentences in order to cage them within the narrow walls of his versification. But Shelley's ingenuity in disentangling the sense overcomes all obstacles. At times the younger poet improves the melody of the original, though, perhaps, at the expense of the image.[84]

As for the *Faust* fragments, Bayard Taylor commented on the Walpurgis-Night scene: "His version of the Walpurgis-Night, although not very faithful, and containing frequent lines of his own interpolation, nevertheless admirably reproduces the hurrying movement and the weird atmosphere of the original. This is the more remarkable since he disregards, for the most part, the German metres."[85] Shelley's shorter verse translations include some fragments from Bion and Moschus that a classical editor has referred to as "beautifully done," two short passages from Virgil, several excerpts from Dante (including the first canzone of the *Convivio* and the lovely description of Matilda from the *Purgatorio*), and the early *Marseillaise.*[86]

Of the Greek prose translations, that of the *Symposium* has been widely accepted. According to Benjamin Farrington, it catches more of Plato's essentially poetic beauty than the more literally correct versions: "Nor is it only in the more exalted passages . . . that the superiority of Shelley [to Jowett] manifests itself . . . Shelley's Alcibiades carries about him, with something of a Byronic air and with an incommunicable verve and charm and freshness, the atmosphere of an accomplished man of the world, a spoilt darling of the gods." Shelley's feat is all the more remarkable in view of the fact that in his day Plato was neglected, not even being among the required authors at Oxford or Cambridge. The existing translations were, according to James A. Notopoulos, "harsh and un-English."[87]

Shelley and Mary

Some of the poems discussed in this chapter have raised biographical questions on the relationship of Shelley and Mary. In the early months of their marriage, as shown by *Epipsychidion,* Shelley was enthralled by Mary, who seemed like a "glorious shape." Later, however, he found that although she was loving and affectionate, she was apparently incapable of any deep emotional response—"cold" and "chaste." Letters and other poems bear out the picture. The letters of October, November, and December 1814 depict the first glow of enthusiasm, in which the hours they are forced to spend apart are agony to them, and they live only that they may be together again. But in the ensuing months, the Hogg-Mary "affair" indicates that something was wrong. *Alastor,* written in the autumn, suggests a state of almost suicidal depression. By late 1817 or early 1818 the "Constantia" poems show Shelley turning to Claire and complaining of "the planet of frost." The Dedication to *Laon and Cythna* in the fall of 1817 indicates that, despite his frustration and loneliness, he and Mary had built up a bond of mutual affection but reveals no true passion. In the crisis following Harriet's suicide in December 1816 Mary had given him all the aid and comfort in her power, and Shelley wrote in thankful affection: "Do you, dearest & best, seek happiness—where it ought to reside in your own pure & perfect bosom: in the thoughts of how dear & how good you are to me—how wise & how extensively beneficial you are perhaps now destined to become."[88]

During this period the marriage had apparently adjusted itself, not on the level of passionate warmth that Shelley had hoped for, but on a basis of companionship and common intellectual interests.

Julian and Maddalo in the fall of 1818, however, reveals hidden hostilities, which Clara's death brought explosively to the surface:

> That you had never seen me—never heard
> My voice, and more than all had ne'er endured
> The deep pollution of my loathed embrace. (420–422)

That at least the acute phase of this 1818 crisis had ended within a few months can be gathered from Shelley's tribute to his "friend" Mary in the Advertisement to the *Rosalind and Helen* volume, dated December 20, 1818.

Two years later, Shelley became passionately attracted to Emilia Viviani and then deeply upset by her plans for marriage. Mary, although clearly angry and frightened, nevertheless made an unequivocal statement to Mrs. Hoppner a few months later: "Need I say that the union between my husband and myself has ever been undisturbed. Love caused our first imprudence, love which improved by esteem, a perfect trust one in the other, a confidence and affection which, visited as we have been by severe calamities (have we not lost two children?) has encreased daily, and knows no bounds."[89] That this statement was not really true, *Epipsychidion* alone suffices to show, but perhaps Mary believed that it was.

The pattern, then, up to the period of the final crisis involving Jane Williams, seems to have been that Shelley and Mary had an affectionate but not a passionate relationship, which Mary apparently found mainly satisfying but Shelley did not. Inwardly lonely and frustrated, he turned to other women, first to Claire, then to Emilia, hoping for a warmth and passion that Mary seemed incapable of providing.

The biographical background for the final crisis—the crowded house at San Lorenzo, Mary's pregnancy and miscarriage, Shelley's "visions" and nightmares—is supplemented by the poems to Edward and Jane Williams. To these, other evidence may be added, both for Shelley's discontent with

Mary and for his turning to Jane. On June 18, 1822, Shelley wrote to John Gisborne: "I only feel the want of those who can feel, and understand me. Whether from proximity and the continuity of domestic intercourse, Mary does not. The necessity of concealing from her thoughts that would pain her, necessitates this, perhaps. It is the curse of Tantalus, that a person possessing such excellent powers and so pure a mind as hers, should not excite the sympathy indispensable to their application to domestic life." In his final days at Leghorn and Pisa, Shelley made similar complaints to Williams and Leigh Hunt after receiving a letter from Mary that disturbed him.[90] These remarks, together with the poems, make clear that in the last months of his life Shelley was complaining openly about his wife's deficiencies.

Shelley and Williams left San Terenzo for Leghorn on July 1. Williams remained at Leghorn; Shelley went on to Pisa. On July 4 Shelley wrote to Jane Williams from Pisa. He told her that he would urge Williams to sail home immediately: "I have thus the pleasure of contributing to your happiness when deprived of every other." He concluded: "How soon those hours past, & how slowly they return to pass so soon again, & perhaps for ever, in which we have lived together so intimately so happily!—Adieu, my dearest friend—I only write these lines for the pleasure of tracing what will meet your eyes.—Mary will tell you all the news. S.——" Jane replied on July 6, complaining that Williams had not written to her: "my own Neddino does not deign to lighten my darkness by a single word: surely I shall see him tonight!" She added a postscript: "Why do you talk of never enjoying moments like the past, are you going to join your friend Plato or do you expect I shall do so soon? Buona notte."[91]

This exchange, taken in conjunction with Jane's letters to Williams and Shelley's poems to Jane, indicates that there was no actual love affair but that Shelley was seriously turning toward Jane and that Jane was not quite closing the door on him. Shelley's lament that their happy hours of intimacy might return no more must include reference to the scene depicted in *Lines Written in the Bay of Lerici*. If so, Jane's letter was telling him, in effect, not to lose hope; there was no need for him to die and certainly she did not intend to. She provocatively reminded him that Williams might come to her "tonight!" and ended with "Buona Notte." Moreover, there was no need either for Shelley to write to Jane or for Jane to reply, as Shelley was expected back at San Terenzo within a few days.

Further insights into these recurrent marital crises come from the observations of those acquainted with Shelley and Mary. Although Trelawny was hostile to Mary and virtually worshiped the memory of Shelley, he was an intelligent man of the world, and his observations must contain an element of truth. In 1870 Trelawny wrote to Claire Clairemont: "She [Mary] was conventional in everything and tormented him by jealousy and would have made him like Tom Moore if she could—she had not the capacity to comprehend him or his poetry."[92] Again: "As the poet used to exclaim when Mary teased [tormented] him, 'I bear what I can and suffer what I must'—

how she worried him with her jealousy and wailing . . . she would have been better matched with a conventional man of the world—that went to church and parties."[93] According to Rossetti, Trelawny commented to him in a similar vein: "He [Trelawny] did not greatly like Mrs. Shelley, thinking her too eager to stand well with society, and, as regards Shelley, too fractious and plaguey—also she had none of the habits of a housewife, and dinner etc. had very much to take care of themselves." "He insists that Shelley would have separated from Mary, but for the unhappy result to Harriet: says M[ary] was excessively jealous of S[helley], both sexually and as regards the influence of other women over his mind. But he seems to think (as far as I can make out) that the sexual jealousy was baseless." As a result of these deficiencies in Mary, Shelley lived a life of "utter desolation and isolation . . . forlorn and dejected with no one to sympathize or soothe him."[94]

The accounts of Jane Williams and Hogg—though they too were prejudiced against Mary—cannot be discounted. Jane wrote to Leigh Hunt two years after Shelley's death:

> I had always heard you spoken of by Mary as her most intimate friend; as one who had known her long, and had lived for some time under her roof—Now it is utterly impossible to do this, and not know whether a person's temper be bad or good: you I imagined as well as myself had seen that the intercourse between Shelley & Mary was not as happy as it should have been; and I remember your telling me that our Shelley mentioned several circumstances on that subject that distressed you during the short week you were together and that you witnessed the pain he suffered on receiving a letter from Mary at that period.[95]

Hogg wrote to Jane on Mary's return to England:

> Her conversation will be painful, just as her letters are, because, to those, who saw behind the scenes, the subject of it is a mere fable; our loss is real, your's, dearest girl, I acknowledge, in spite of my hopes, irreparable, mine bad enough, but her's, however painful, is in fact imaginary for to suppose that matters co[ul]d have continued as they were, wo[ul]d have been the vanity of vanities, & any other termination wo[ul]d have been for her, except as to money-matters, infinitely worse.[96]

Finally there are Leigh Hunt's views, given in a letter to his sister-in-law, Elizabeth Kent:

> A cloud hung over her connexion with her husband, which as I latterly thought, only wanted a certain kind of address to explain to both of them and do away. This it was my intention to do, had he lived. It has been my fate to do it afterwards: & oh poor thing, how bitterly she repents not having considered it all before! and how sorry was I, when I found that during all my cold & almost ["contemptuous" *canceled*] cruel treatment of her, on her first residing here, she had been recording her remorse in private! . . . Mrs. S. one day and in evident allusion to what Mrs. W.

perhaps might allow herself to say of her, said that though others had seen the worst part of her tempers toward S., they had not seen the amends, & requests for pardon, which she always made to him in private.[97]

Some obvious corrections need to be made in these views. Trelawny was certainly wrong in contending that Mary had little understanding of Shelley and his works. On the contrary, her notes to his poems reveal a considerable grasp of both; her comments, in fact, are unsurpassed among early nineteenth-century critics, Hunt not excepted. The political opinions in her letters are similar to Shelley's. That she wanted Shelley to sacrifice his ideals is doubtful; rather, she seems to have wanted him to express them in a more easily understood form, as in *The Cenci.* Mary must have seen that his failure to reach an audience of any size comparable, say, to Byron's was seriously undermining his spirit. Hogg's comment to Jane Williams was certainly malicious, for Mary was deeply shaken by her husband's death.[98]

Yet after all such adjustments, considerable truth remains in these reports. Given the mores of the time, Shelley's statement about Mary to Gisborne, in which he charges that she could not "excite the sympathy indispensible to . . . domestic life," is an extreme one; he is, in effect saying that Mary was unfit to be a wife. Trelawny's observations on her "jealousy and wailing" are borne out by Shelley's poems and by the comments of Jane Williams. He had apparently witnessed some of Mary's temper tantrums. His description of Shelley's loneliness, which is vivid and heart-felt, again accords with the evidence of the poems, dating back at least to 1817 in England and growing stronger in the Italian years. His comments on Mary's domestic slovenliness are borne out by other evidence. Hogg's comments, although influenced by what he had heard of the Pisa and Lerici days from Jane Williams, must also have been based partly on his own observations of the marriage in England. He appears convinced that it would have broken down. Jane's comments to Hunt are clearly modified, for she was writing to one sympathetic to both Shelley and Mary. But again the emphasis is on Mary's temper. Hunt, of course, had not witnessed the marriage in Italy. A naturally kindly man, he clearly did not feel, from what he knew of it in England, that it was beyond salvage. Yet Hunt, too, placed the blame mainly on Mary.

Mary herself recognized the strain in the marriage. In her pathetic poem, *The Choice*, composed only a few weeks after Shelley's death she wrote:

First let me call on thee! Lost as thou art,
Thy name aye fills my sense, thy love my heart.
Oh, gentle Spirit! thou hast often sung,
How fallen on evil days thy heart was wrung;
Now fierce remorse and unreplying death
Waken a chord within my heart, whose breath,
Thrilling and keen, in accents audible
A tale of unrequited love doth tell.

It was not anger,—while thy earthly dress
Encompassed still thy soul's rare loveliness,
All anger was atoned by many a kind
Caress or tear, that spoke the softened mind.—
It speaks of cold neglect, averted eyes,
That blindly crushed thy soul's fond sacrifice:—
My heart was all thine own,—but yet a shell
Closed in its core, which seemed impenetrable,
Till sharp-toothed misery tore the husk in twain,
Which gaping lies, nor may unite again.
Forgive me! let thy love descend in dew
Of soft repentance and regret most true.[99]

The ill temper and the subsequent scenes of forgiveness reflected in the lines "All anger was atoned by many a kind/Caress or tear" parallel Mary's statement to Hunt on "amends" made in "private."[100] She apparently did not feel that her ill temper and abuse of her husband were matters of major consequence. Evidently they did seem so to Shelley, to Trelawny and the Williamses. Mary's belief that a private reconciliation could undo the damage of public abuse, with the hurt, humiliation, and anger that such scenes must have engendered in Shelley, seems at the very least naive. And if there were public quarrels, there must have been private ones also. That these could sometimes be bitter and violent, leaving lasting scars, is indicated in *Julian and Maddalo.*

However, *The Crisis* reveals Mary as disturbed by the charge of coldness, and so, too, does her journal.[101] The comment on "cold neglect, averted eyes" must refer to the "cold chaste moon" passage in *Epipsychidion* as well as to various shorter poems and perhaps to *Julian and Maddalo.*[102] Mary appeared to accept, at least in part, the portrait of her in these poems, while adding the explanation in *The Choice* that although she loved her husband deeply, she was unable to properly express this love. The evidence from Shelley, Mary, and their friends, in short, shows that the marriage was undergoing serious strain in the last months of Shelley's life, and Shelley's poetry indicates that for some years it had been inadequate.

Among the basic problems that contributed to this situation, one factor stands out: Mary was only sixteen when she eloped with Shelley, and thereafter she was almost continuously pregnant. A middle-class girl of sixteen, as Kinsey's and other studies have shown, is unlikely immediately to respond with deep sexual passion. And in Shelley's day, sexual intercourse during pregnancy seems to have been generally forbidden. But there also seems to have been a lack of depth in Mary's emotional responses in general. She herself felt that there was a deficiency in her character that made it difficult for her to express love fully. If so, the root of the problem probably lay in the fact that she was brought up without a mother. The chief formative factor in her early personality development, as reflected in her fragmentary novel *Mathilda*, was her father, William Godwin. Although

Godwin was not the emotional robot that hostile critics have depicted, he was hardly warm or outgoing. As she had little rapport with her stepmother, Mary's parental image was restricted to her father, and she was very much William Godwin's daughter, having been brought up to place almost entire emphasis on intellectual values. She was herself a writer. As such, her attitude toward her husband and his work can hardly have been other than ambivalent. Much though she admired him, she must also, on some level of consciousness, have regarded him as a rival.

Shelley himself, in spite of his basic kindness and gentleness, cannot have been easy to live with. His dedication to his work and his determination to pursue it in his own way were such that Mary must have been conscious of always coming second. Much though she may, as a Godwinian intellectual, have understood the necessity for this, she must, as a wife, have resented it. Furthermore, Shelley's conduct, especially in the last months of his life, was sometimes reprehensible. He must have known that he was tormenting Mary by his attention to Claire, Emilia, and Jane, some of it embodied in poetry that she read. His comments to Jane on Mary's coldness and envy, his portrait of her hysterical raging in *Julian and Maddalo* and of her frigidity in *Epipsychidion*, his gossip about her to the Williamses and Gisbornes, may have been the result of frustration, but they can hardly be condoned, and their net effect must have been to undermine Mary's morale.

Shelley may have hurt Mary in another way also, though he would doubtless have denied it. Harriet he once laughingly called a "little Cockney," but behind the laughter was an implication of superiority.[103] Mary, too, was a Cockney, a middle-class Londoner, whereas Shelley came out of the county aristocracy and had attended Eton and Oxford. Mary must always, in caste-conscious nineteenth-century England, have been aware of this. Her manners and accent were undoubtedly in some ways different from his. Although Shelley, as a principled egalitarian and liberal, would never have reminded her of this distinction, he may unconsciously have implied it. It is hard, for instance, to imagine him gossiping about a young woman of his own class, such as Harriet Grove, to the Williamses as he did about Mary.

One other factor is Shelley's tendency to become ungovernable when frustrated, of which there is ample evidence and which Shelley himself recognized. He could also become aggressive and destructive. He was prone to indulge in emotional orgies, as he had against his father or Eliza Westbrook, and in the quarrels with Mary he can hardly have been so passive as he implies, for instance, in *Julian and Maddalo*. Finally, there is the obvious parallel between Shelley's charges of coldness leveled at both Mary and at Harriet (the "cold heart"). On the one hand, this may mean merely that Shelley married two very young women who could not respond sexually. On the other hand, it may indicate an underlying phobia of the deprivation of love that exaggerated reservations and inhibited expressions of affection both by his partners and himself. Shelley seems to have been brought up without deep maternal or paternal affection. His mother married late and, as an intelligent and perhaps talented woman, may have lacked any deep love or respect for her farm-oriented husband. That she never corresponded with her son in all the tragedies which later befell him, such as the deaths of his children, does not indicate a warm, maternal interest. Although Shelley as a child manifested affection for his father, this must have early been mixed with the condescension that appeared in him later, perhaps derived in part from his mother's attitude. In his childhood Shelley seems to have turned toward his sisters rather than his parents. He had no close friends. That his boyhood on the family estate was lonely is suggested by his early Cwm Elan poems, whose desolation of spirit must have had deep roots.[104]

Whatever the reasons for Shelley's failing to find love, they were not his search for an unrealizable ideal in woman, one that neither Mary nor anyone else could have lived up to. His poetry and letters show that this was not true. What Shelley wanted was a woman who was both intellectual and passionate. He was simply unfortunate in not having encountered her.

It is apparent, then, that both Shelley and Mary had psychological and social-background characteristics that made a really deep, warm marriage relationship between them difficult. Mary, although clearly in love with Shelley, was sexually cold, domestically slovenly, and nagging. Shelley was constantly threatening to break the bonds of the marriage. Yet despite these problems, the two had by 1817 at least arrived at a modus vivendi based on mutual respect and "friendship."

A new factor appeared in the final crisis, namely that Shelley was rather obviously provoking it. He does not seem to have previously gossiped openly about Mary to their friends. Hunt, coming to Italy from England after four years' absence, was clearly taken by surprise at the deterioration of the relationship. But if Shelley was provoking a crisis, he must have decided to end the marriage, and the indication is that he would have left Mary. When a couple, especially a nineteenth-century English couple, reaches the point of public quarrels and of spreading destructive gossip, and their close friends feel a break is near, it probably is.

Had Shelley lived, it seems unlikely that the break would have come over Jane Williams, or that Shelley and she would have run away together. Although Shelley was apparently ready to go off with Jane, Jane seems to have been too devoted to her "Nedino" and their children to abandon them for Shelley. She felt pity for him, admired him, and was willing to engage in flirtation, but she was not in love with him. She may have felt, in fact, that she was getting into a situation that she could not handle, and to judge from Shelley's last letter to her, she had perhaps suggested that she and Williams move away. Nevertheless, the situation during the last few months of Shelley's life indicates that before long Shelley would have found someone else.

8

The International Scene

The Revolt of Islam

In *The Revolt of Islam* Shelley abandoned the individualism of *Alastor* and returned to the iconoclastic, social sweep of *Queen Mab*. But instead of treating all three of *Queen Mab's* components (the past, present and future), he concentrated on the present, in order to give a comprehensive picture of his own age. The poem, comprising twelve books and replete with battles and adventures, was clearly intended to have an epic aspect. And Shelley, as he told Godwin, felt that it epitomized his message to mankind; indeed, he thought of it as a kind of intellectual last will and testament: "The Poem was produced by a series of thoughts which filled my mind with an unbounded and sustained enthusiasm. I felt the precariousness of my life, and I engaged in this task resolved to leave some record of myself. Much of what the volume contains was written with the same feeling, as real, though not so prophetic, as the communication of a dying man."[1]

Of all Shelley's major poems, *The Revolt of Islam* is the most neglected. True, it is often poorly written, perhaps partly because Shelley's sense of "precariousness" urged him to haste, and partly because in his mood of "sustained enthusiasm" his ideas tumbled out one after the other and he paid little attention to the niceties of style. Furthermore, the poem is overlong and sometimes lacks unity of structure and mood, incongruously mixing realism and fantasy. Yet it is a poem of great power, giving in impressionistic form, a panoramic picture of the age. It penetrates—as a more brilliant work such as *Don Juan* does not—deeply into the forces behind international events, depicting the savage brutality of the European ruling class, the revolutionary potential of the people, and the massiveness of the conflict between the two. The very directness that sometimes aborts the evocative qualities of the verse gives it a realistic impact and ensures that ideas are plainly expressed, which in more sophisticated poems, such as *Prometheus Unbound*, are veiled in symbolism. The poem is, in fact, an invaluable storehouse of Shelley's ideas, and a touchstone for the interpretation of other poems.

Shelley apparently began composition shortly after moving to the village of Marlow in Buckinghamshire in March 1817, and as shown by Mary's journal, he finished it on September 23 of the same year.[2] After having been declined by one publisher, the work was accepted by the newly founded firm of Charles and James Ollier, friends of Leigh Hunt and publishers of Hunt and Lamb, as well as of Keats's first volume. Shelley was particularly eager to have the poem published. When it was being held up by the printer, he wrote impatiently to Charles Ollier: "That McMillan is an obstinate old dog . . . Let him print the errata, and say at the top if he likes, that it was all the Author's fault, and that he is as immaculate as the Lamb of God."[3] When the poem was first published, it was entitled not *The Revolt of Islam* but *Laon and Cythna; or, The Revolution of the Golden City: A Vision of the Nineteenth Century.* It has been estimated that perhaps as many as 1,000 copies of *Laon and Cythna* were printed, some being sent out by Shelley at the time, but many of them not getting into circulation until later in the century. Sometime between December 3 and 11, Ollier decided not to publish the poem because as Peacock wrote, Shelley "had carried the expression of his opinions, moral, political and theological beyond the bounds of discretion," and Ollier "in those days of persecution of the press," feared for the consequences. On December 11, Shelley wrote to Ollier urging him to stand fast:

I don't believe that, if the book was quietly and regularly published, the Government would touch anything of a character so refined, and so remote from the conceptions of the vulgar. They would hesitate before they invaded a member of the higher circles of the republic of letters. But, if they see us tremble, they will make no distinctions; they will feel their strength. You might bring the arm of the law down on us both by flinching now. Directly these scoundrels see that people are afraid of them, they seize upon them and hold them up to mankind as criminals already convicted by their own fears. You lay yourself prostrate and they trample on you. How glad they would be to seize on any connexion of Hunt's by this most powerful of all their arms—the terrors and self-condemnation of their victim. Read all the *ex officio* cases, and see what reward booksellers and printers have received for their submission.[4]

Following the receipt of this letter, Ollier wrote indicating that he would publish the poem if alterations were made. On December 14 he went to see Shelley at Marlow, and by the next day the alterations were finished.[5] A comparison of the two texts shows that these were not extensive, although some were important. Ollier objected to the fact that the lovers in the poem were brother and sister, and he felt that the attacks on religion were too forthright. The result was, as Shelley wrote to Thomas Moore on December 16: "The present edition of 'Laon and Cythna' is to be suppressed, & it will be republished in about a fortnight under the title of 'The Revolt of Islam,' with some alterations which consist in little else than the substitution of the words *friend* or *lover* for that of *brother* & *sister*"—and, Shelley might have added, the substitution of Heaven or Power for God.[6] Afterward all went smoothly; Shelley busied himself calling in the copies of *Laon and Cythna* that had been sent out (unfortunately he did not get *The Quarterly Review's* copy, which was later used against him) and pushing the advertizing for *The Revolt of Islam.*

Preface and Sources

Shelley's Preface informs his readers that the poem depicts, in a kind of impressionistic panorama, the major events of recent history:

> the awakening of an immense nation from their slavery and degradation to a true sense of moral dignity and freedom; the bloodless dethronement of their oppressors, and the unveiling of the religious frauds by which they had been deluded into submission; the tranquillity of successful patriotism, and the universal toleration and benevolence of true philanthropy; the treachery and barbarity of hired soldiers; vice not the object of punishment and hatred, but kindness and pity; the faithlessness of tyrants; the confederacy of the Rulers of the World, and the restoration of the expelled Dynasty by foreign arms; the massacre and extermination of the Patriots, and the victory of established power; the consequences of legitimate despotism,—civil war, famine, plague, superstition, and an utter extinction of the domestic affections; the judicial murder of the advocates of Liberty; the temporary triumph of oppression, the secure earnest of its final and inevitable fall; the transient nature of ignorance and error, and the eternity of genius and virtue. Such is the series of delineations of which the Poem consists.[7]

To any educated reader of the year 1817, most of the references here to recent history would be clear enough even though the passage is representational rather than literal. The "awakening of an immense nation" suggests the beginning of the French Revolution; the "bloodless dethronement," "the tranquillity of successful patriotism," and the "benevolence of true philanthropy" represent the period of the flourishing of the National Assembly and the Legislative Assembly, which destroyed the worst abuses of the ancient regime and produced the Declaration of the Rights of Man. The "unveiling of religious frauds" refers to the breaking of the power of the church in France and the elevation of the goddess of Reason, "the treachery and barbarity of hired soldiers" to the brutal Swiss and German guards of Louis XVI, the "faithlessness of tyrants" to the intrigues of Louis and the aristocracy with the foreign powers who were conspiring to overthrow the revolutionary government. The "confederacy of the Rulers of the World" suggests both the early coalition of the European powers against the French republic and the later one at the Congress of Vienna, solidified by the Holy Alliance and Quadruple Alliance. The "restoration of the expelled dynasts by foreign arms" reflects the restoration of the Bourbons by the allied powers in 1814; the "massacre and extermination of the Patriots" refers to the 1792 "September massacres" conducted by the Jacobins and probably also to the "White Terror" massacres of the Republicans by the Royalists after their return in 1815–1816; the "civil war, famine and plague" is a composite picture of the Napoleonic Wars and their aftermath, which Shelley had himself witnessed in France in 1814 and 1816; the "judicial murder of the advocates of liberty" perhaps refers to the execution of Danton, Herbert, and their followers by Robespierre, whom Shelley regarded as a dictator; and the "temporary triumph of oppression" relates to the unstable restoration of the Bourbons.[8]

Further light is shed on the poem by a letter that Shelley wrote to a publisher on October 13: "It is in fact a tale illustrative of such a Revolution as might be supposed to take place in an European nation, acted upon by the opinions of what has been called (erroneously as I think) the modern philosophy, & contending with antient notions & the supposed advantage derived from them to those who support them. It is a Revolution of this kind, that is, the beau ideal as it were, of the French Revolution, but produced by the influence of individual genius & out of general knowledge."[9] That Shelley believed such a revolution, or revolutions, would in fact take place is indicated by his original subtitle, "A Vision of the Nineteenth Century," and although *The Revolt of Islam* reflects recent history, Shelley is not interested in it primarily as a historian but as a political prophet. He is projecting past and present patterns imaginatively into the future to illustrate what he believes will be the course of events, hoping, in so doing, to influence present actions.

Shelley had long believed that the greatest blow suffered by the liberal cause in Great Britain had been the retreat following the Pitt repression. In the early 1790s the Whigs and reformers had been moving to the left, with the Whigs championing the cause of the French republic and fighting the Tories on the franchise issue. Some of the Foxite Whigs, under Grey, had formed an alliance for parliamentary reform with Major Cartwright and the working class radicals called the "Friends of the People." Wordsworth, Coleridge, and Southey, swinging beyond the Whigs, had followed Paine into revolutionary republicanism, and for a time Wordsworth even hovered close to atheism and Godwinian egalitarianism. A new and glorious future seemed to be dawning for mankind; the "budding rose" seemed about to burst into the "rose full blown." But as the war gathered momentum, panic and hysteria gave the Tories their chance. Those who opposed the government were stigmatized as traitors. The Whigs sulked but capitulated. Wordsworth began his retreat to nature and the British revenue service, Coleridge took to opium and *The Courier*, and Southey became the literary hatchet-man of *The Quarterly Review*.

Shelley, surveying the scene in 1817, saw that the rout had been halted and believed that a revival had begun: the parliamentary battles of Burdett and the Independent Whigs; a new radical poet in Byron, philosopher in Bentham, and critic in Hazlitt; the popular "reform" agitation; the rise of the Hunts and *The Examiner*; and the renewed struggle in Ireland under O'Connell. This new movement must be encouraged. *The Revolt of Islam* was written to encourage it:

The panic which, like an epidemic transport, seized upon all classes of men during the excesses consequent upon the French Revolution, is gradually giving place to sanity. It has ceased to be believed, that whole generations of mankind ought to consign themselves to a hopeless inheritance of ignorance and misery, because a nation of men who had been dupes and slaves for centuries, were incapable of conducting themselves with the wisdom and tranquillity of freedom so soon as some of their fetters were partially loosened . . . Our works of fiction and poetry have been overshadowed by the same infectious gloom. But mankind appear to me to be emerging from their trance. I am aware, methinks, of a slow, gradual, silent change. In that belief I have composed the following Poem.[10]

Shelley's "belief" was, ironically enough, the same as one that the young Coleridge had urged upon Wordsworth some eighteen years before, when he had observed with alarm the beginnings of the reaction that was even then engulfing both Wordsworth and himself: "My dear friend: I do entreat you to go on with 'The Recluse'; and I wish you would write a poem in blank verse, addressed to those, who, in consequence of the complete failure of the French Revolution, have thrown up all hope of the amelioration of mankind, and are sinking into an almost epicurean selfishness, disguising the same under the soft titles of domestic attachment and contempt for visionary *philosophes*. It would do great good."[11]

In writing his poem, Shelley derived inspiration from one of the most popular radical works of the day, Constantin François Volney's *Ruins of Empire*. Volney's distinguished career of service to the French Revolution would have endeared him to Shelley. He had been elected to the States General in 1789 and later to the Constituent Assembly. In 1793 he was imprisoned by the Jacobins but was released after the overthrow of Robespierre and appointed professor of history in the Sorbonne. He visited the United States in 1795 and wrote an interesting account of his travels.

In *Les ruines, ou méditations sur les révolutions des empires*, first published in 1791, Volney traced, in idealized form, the history of the French Revolution, in order to arouse his liberal colleagues from their "plague on both your houses" lethargy. His hero, the "traveler," having fallen into despair, is accosted by a "Genius," who decides that the traveler can be saved by a vision revealing the true meaning of the revolution:

Here, sunk in sorrow, my heart suppressed my speech. The Genius answered not; but I heard him whisper to himself: Let us revive the hope of this man; for if he who loves his fellow creatures be suffered to despair, what will become of nations? The past is perhaps too discouraging; let us then disclose to the eye of virtue the astonishing age that is ready to begin; that on viewing the object she desires, she may be animated with new ardour, and redouble her efforts to attain it.[12].

The genius goes on to depict, as in Shelley's Preface, an immense nation awakening and bloodlessly dethroning its oppressors, with the dethroned oppressors then forming a confederacy but being defeated by the people. The vision has the desired effect, for the traveler, representing the European intelligentsia, is roused from his gloom.[13]

Once Shelley had decided on a project of this nature, he felt, perhaps with the apparent failure of *Queen Mab* in mind, that it should be presented not as a historical vision but a narrative, combining, as in his earliest long poem, *Henry and Louisa*, antiwar and antireligious views with a story of two young lovers. To turn once more to his letter to the publisher:

> The whole poem, with the exception of the first canto & part of the last is a mere human story without the smallest intermixture of supernatural interference. The first Canto is indeed, in some measure a distinct poem, tho' very necessary to the wholeness of the work. I say this because if it were all written in the manner of the first canto, I could not expect that it would be interesting to any great number of people. I have attempted in the progress of my work to speak to the common elementary emotions of the human heart, so that though it is the story of violence and revolution, it is relieved by milder pictures of friendship and love and natural affections.[14]

With this popularizing purpose in mind, Shelley selected as his framework a love story of two young Greek revolutionaries, Laon and Cythna, who vow to end the despotic rule of "Islam" (foreshadowing *Hellas*). The two are early separated: Cythna is captured by sailors of the Turkish emperor and taken to his seraglio; Laon is left to die in chains in a remote tower, but is rescued by a hermit. When Cythna is found to be pregnant, she is imprisoned in a cave by the emperor. Shortly after her baby has been born it is taken away from her. An earthquake opens the cave; Cythna escapes, returns to the Golden City, and leads a revolution. Laon there joins her. They help to overthrow the dictatorship and establish a republic. The emperor, however, helped by his fellow monarchs, returns to make war on the people. Famine and pestilence follow. Laon and Cythna escape from the city, but later return and are executed. After death, their spirits and that of Cythna's child voyage to a strange island in a lake fed by four (obviously symbolic) waterfalls.

For this narrative story, too, Shelley had a model, Peacock's abandoned epic *Ahrimanes*.[15] *Ahrimanes*, as Peacock planned it, was to depict the adventures of two lovers, Darassah and Kelasris, struggling against the Zoroastrian power of evil, Ahrimanes. The poem, like *The Revolt of Islam*, was to consist of twelve cantos in the Spenserian stanza; of the projected twelve cantos, Peacock finished only two but fortunately left prose outlines that indicate his general plan.[16] The lovers, living on an island "in the Araxes," vow to fight the evil reign of Ahrimanes. They arrive at an unnamed Asian city, whose Sultan "sees Kelasris, forcibly takes her from her lover, and confines her in his seraglio." But when an enemy army enters the city, the lovers escape in the confusion. They retreat into the desert and "live peacefully in an oasis." Then a "band of robbers" seizes them and sells them separately into slavery. Darassah somehow escapes and by chance finds Kelasris. They travel to another city, this time on the Persian Gulf, which "is afflicted by pestilence and famine." Next the lovers are shipwrecked on an island, which is devastated by a "volcanic eruption." A good "Oromazic spirit" appears and "directs them to embark on a small boat which will bear them to the dwelling of Oromazes." Their voyage is said to symbolize "the course of virtue through the storms of life."

Although *Ahrimanes* differs in intent and spirit from the revolutionary *Revolt of Islam,* certain parts of the two stories are so similar that there is obviously a connection between them: the pair of lovers opposing evil, the confinement in the seraglio, the attack on the city, the seizure of the lovers, the earthquake, the pestilence and famine, and the final magical voyage. One cannot necessarily conclude, however, that the borrowing was all Shelley's, for Shelley himself had long been fascinated by the concept of star-crossed lovers harassed by social forces, as shown by *Zeinab and Kathema* as well as by *Henry and Louisa.* The concept of *Ahrimanes* might have arisen in conversations between Peacock and Shelley. This possibility is heightened by the fact that some parts of *Ahrimanes* express typically Shelleyan views, apparently including echoes from *Queen Mab.*[17]

Canto I

This canto is, as Shelley informed the publisher to whom he first sent the work, "in some measure a distinct poem." It also appears to be a symbolic treatment of the central theme. The poet, in despair at the overthrow of the French Revolution, "when the last hope of trampled France had failed," climbs a cliff overlooking the sea. There he witnesses an aerial fight between an eagle and a serpent, in which the serpent is defeated:

when lifeless, stark, and rent,
Hung high that mighty Serpent, and at last
Fell to the sea, while o'er the continent,
With clang of wings and scream the Eagle past,
Heavily borne away on the exhausted blast. (248–252)

The poet hastens down the cliff. There by the shore a beautiful woman sits near a small boat. The serpent swims haltingly to her, and she sings to it in a strange language, which the poet cannot understand:

She spake in language whose strange melody
Might not belong to earth. I heard, alone,
What made its music more melodious be,
The pity and the love of every tone. (289–292)[18]

The woman turns and speaks to the poet:

"To grieve is wise, but the despair
Was weak and vain which led thee here from sleep." (311–312)

She then carries the serpent into the boat and is joined by the poet.

As they sail, the woman explains the meaning of the fight between the eagle and the serpent. In early society there was a struggle between good and evil forces, symbolized by "the Morning Star" (Venus, love) and a "blood red Comet" (war, oppression).[19] The evil spirit, becoming "One Power of many shapes . . . One Shape of many names," triumphed and changed the good power into "a dire Snake": good is made to appear evil in an evil society. But the snake fought back, and their struggle, became the modern one between feudal reaction and social progress:

> "Such is this conflict—when mankind doth strive
> With its oppressors in a strife of blood,
> Or when free thoughts, like lightnings, are alive,
> And in each bosom of the multitude
> Justice and truth with custom's hydra brood
> Wage silent war;—when priests and kings dissemble
> In smiles or frowns their fierce disquietude,
> When round pure hearts, a host of hopes assemble,
> The Snake and Eagle meet—the world's foundations tremble!" (415–423)

Their latest struggle, which the poet has just witnessed, was presumably the French Revolution, which ended in the triumph of a militaristic dictatorship. In the next encounter the victory will be the serpent's, the woman asserts, in a recapitulation of the belief expressed in the Preface in a coming "change" and a rejection, in effect, of the Peacockian cyclical concept of the Ahrimanes-Oromazes conflict.[20]

As for the sources of the eagle and serpent symbolism, the eagle was perhaps suggested by the Roman eagle, a warlike symbol. The concept of the serpent as an agent of good doubtless was based in part on Shelley's reading about the Gnostics, some of whose sects perversely depicted the snake of the Garden of Eden as a symbol for wisdom. But Shelley might also have been influenced by Volney: " 'The Persians,' says Chardin, 'call the constellation of the serpent Ophicus, serpent of Eve: and this serpent Ophiucus or Ophioneus plays a similar part in the theology of the Phoenicians,' for Pherecydes, their disciple and the master of Pythagoras, said 'that *Ophioneus Serpentinus had been chief of the rebels against Jupiter.*' "[21] To Shelley, "the chief of the rebels against Jupiter" would be, as in *Prometheus Unbound*, a good, not an evil figure.

One other serpent symbol also could have been influenced by Volney. According to Volney, a school of "physical theologians" in the ancient world used as a symbol of the universe "a great round serpent (representing the heavens where they placed the moving principle, and for that reason of an azure colour, studded with spots of gold, the stars) devouring his tail, that is folding and unfolding himself eternally, like the revolutions of the spheres." This is apparently the basis for the image that Shelley used in Canto IV to depict Laon's awakening in the home of the old hermit:

did my spirit wake
From sleep, as many-coloured as the snake
That girds eternity? (1444–1446)[22]

Shelley also speaks of the "wreathed Serpent" (215), and refers to the combatants as "an Eagle and a Serpent wreathed in fight" (193). Apparently he had in mind that linking of liberty with eternal forces and reaction with temporary ones that he stressed in the Preface and in *A Philosophical View of Reform:* "It would be Eternity warning Time."[23]

The woman next tells the poet of her youth, which is rather like Shelley's own. At first she was absorbed by the beauties of nature and art. Then came the French Revolution:

"When first the living blood thro' all these veins
Kindled a thought in sense, great France sprang forth
And seized, as if to break, the ponderous chains
Which bind in woe the nations of the earth." (469–472)

At night she had a vision of the "benignant power" in the form of:

"A winged youth [whose] radiant brow did wear
The Morning Star [Venus, Love]." (500–501)

Now she is no longer content with nature and art. But unlike the hero of *Alastor,* she does not turn self-destructively inward, but outward, toward people, love, and society. She abandons "the path of the sea shore" and, inspired by the presence of the spirit, goes out among mankind:

"How, to that vast and peopled city led,
Which was a field of holy warfare then,
I walked among the dying and the dead,
And shared in fearless deeds with evil men." (514–517)

Although when she "braved death for liberty and truth," she found that her hopes were not realized, she was not, like "others," left "cold and dead," for the spirit revitalized her hopes for mankind. The analogy with Mary Wollstonecraft and the French Revolution—also suggested in the Dedication—is unmistakable, even though Shelley draws on his own reactions to fill out the picture. Mary, unlike Wordsworth or Coleridge—who were doubtless included among the "others"—did not abandon her revolutionary views.

The boat arrives at a calm sea in whose midst, surrounded by beautiful islands, is a mighty temple. Inside, beneath the temple dome:

there sate on many a sapphire throne,
The Great, who had departed from mankind,
A mighty Senate; some, whose white hair shone
Like mountain snow, mild, beautiful, and blind.
Some, female forms, whose gestures beamed with mind. (604–608)

The symbolism of the temple here is similar to the temple of nature in *Queen Mab* (I, 275–277; II, 31–35, 41–42), repeated with minor changes in *The Daemon of the World* in 1816:

> Spirit of Nature! thou!
> Imperishable as this scene,
> Here is thy fitting temple
> . . . . .
> As Heaven, low resting on the wave, it spread
> Its floors of flashing light,
> Its vast and azure dome,
> Its fertile golden islands
> Floating on a silver sea
> . . . . .
> The Fairy and the Spirit
> Entered the Hall of Spells.

In *The Daemon of the World* the temple is described as "The temple of the mightiest daemon" (208), namely, necessity. The concept in *The Revolt of Islam* is along the same general lines, although with specific differences. There is no senate of the great in the "hall of Spells" in *Queen Mab*. The senate in *The Revolt of Islam* represents the minds of the great creative thinkers of the past, "the Poets," with the "blind" obviously referring to Homer and Milton, and the "female forms" including Mary Wollstonecraft. Later in the poem Shelley repeats the concept more succinctly:

> The good and mighty of departed ages
> Are in their graves, the innocent and free,
> Heroes, and Poets, and prevailing Sages,
> Who leave the vesture of their majesty
> To adorn and clothe this naked world;—and we
> Are like to them—such perish, but they leave
> All hope, or love, or truth, or liberty,
> Whose forms their mighty spirits could conceive,
> To be a rule and law to ages that survive. (3712–3720)

In the final canto Shelley refers to this temple as the Temple of the Spirit, in which the great minds of the past are imagined as a continuing chain influencing future generations. As the woman, the poet, and the serpent enter the hall of the temple, one throne is vacant. Unlike the other thrones, this one is special:

> Reared on a pyamid like sculptured flame,
> Distinct with circling steps. (614–615)

The woman shrieks the name of the spirit to whom the throne belongs and then vanishes. Two "glittering lights" like small "serpent eyes" appear and form into a "clear and mighty planet," which hangs over a cloud enwrapping the vacant throne. As the cloud is "cloven," a beautiful "form" appears on the throne:

He sat
Majestic, yet most mild—calm, yet compassionate. (638–639)

His "blue" eyes looking into those of the poet, he tells him that "two mighty Spirits" will "return" to tell him a "tale of human power." A beautiful young man then stands forth, with an even more beautiful woman beside him, and the young man tells the poet the story of the revolt of Islam to inspire him (as did Volney's "genius") to humanitarian hope and action:

They pour fresh light from Hope's immortal urn;
A tale of human power—despair not—list and learn! (647–648)

The man and woman are obviously Laon and Cythna, and the spirit on the throne is the serpent returned to his proper form as the "benignant power."[24] The planet is again, no doubt, Venus, the planet of love. The supreme spirit on the throne presides over the council of great humanitarians; or in other words, he animates their works and deeds.

Canto II

Laon was born in Greece, in "Argolis beside the echoing sea." Greece, as part of the Turkish Empire, was ruled by a despotism that warped people's lives and characters:

The land in which I lived, by a fell bane
Was withered up. Tyrants dwelt side by side,
And stabled in our homes,—until the chain
Stifled the captive's cry, and to abide
That blasting curse men had no shame. (694–698)

Laon determines, as had Shelley himself, to dedicate his life to the eradication of such evils. Although it is often assumed that *Queen Mab* is the apex of Shelley's social radicalism, *The Revolt of Islam* in some ways surpasses it. In the four years since writing *Queen Mab* Shelley had suffered further persecution and ostracism, had witnessed at first hand the misery of the French people in 1814 and 1816 resulting from the Napoleonic Wars, had seen the social effects of the economic crisis in England following those wars, had joined the movement for parliamentary reform, and had watched with growing anger and frustration the ever-increasing social conflicts between Toryism and Luddism, between a brutalized military and desperate hunger-marchers ("blanketeers"). Consequently, his radicalism had become less abstract. He began to see practical political solutions to social problems.

Laon's announcement of his dedication has a positive, revolutionary ring (the metaphor is volcanic):

"It must be so—I will arise and waken
The multitude, and like a sulphurous hill,
Which on a sudden from its snows has shaken
The swoon of ages, it shall burst, and fill
The world with cleansing fire; it must, it will—
It may not be restrained!" (784–789)

A young girl named Cythna (Laon's sister in the original version), who was brought up in the same home with him and became his companion, also determines to wage war against a corrupt social order, taking, like Mary Wollstonecraft, as her special function the emancipation of women:

Can man be free if woman be a slave?
. . . . .
Can they whose mates are beasts, condemned to bear
Scorn, heavier far than toil or anguish, dare
To trample their oppressors? (1045, 1048–1050)

In Cythna we have the first intellectual, radical heroine in English literature, anticipating the "new woman" heroines of Shaw and others later in the century.

Canto III

The revolutionary hopes of Laon and Cythna are shattered by a raid in which the sailors of the Turkish emperor carry Cythna off to captivity and leave Laon imprisoned, naked and in chains, in a cage on a high tower. There, in delirium, Laon has strange sexual and cannibalistic dreams:

Methought that grate was lifted, and the seven
Who brought me thither four stiff corpses bare,
And from the frieze to the four winds of Heaven
Hung them on high by the entangled hair:
Swarthy were three—the fourth was very fair:
As they retired, the golden moon upsprung,
And eagerly, out in the giddy air,
Leaning that I might eat, I stretched and clung
Over the shapeless depth in which those corpses hung.

A woman's shape, now lank and cold and blue,
The dwelling of the many-coloured worm,

Hung there; the white and hollow cheek I drew
To my dry lips—what radiance did inform
Those horny eyes? whose was that withered form?
Alas, alas! it seemed that Cythna's ghost
Laughed in those looks, and that the flesh was warm
Within my teeth!—A whirlwind keen as frost
Then in its sinking gulfs my sickening spirit tossed.

Then seemed it that a tameless hurricane
Arose, and bore me in its dark career
Beyond the sun, beyond the stars that wane
On the verge of formless space—it languished there,
And dying, left a silence lone and drear,
More horrible than famine:—in the deep
The shape of an old man did then appear,
Stately and beautiful; that dreadful sleep
His heavenly smiles dispersed, and I could wake and weep. (1325–1350)

The "old man" turns out to be a hermit who rescues Laon, and who, according to Mary Shelley, represents Dr. James Lind, Shelley's mentor of his Eton days, who is said to have nursed him through a delirious fever.[25] Whether or not Shelley had similar delusions during his fever is not recorded, but the dream is interesting psychologically and aesthetically. It is, in fact, a revelation of the unconscious, unmatched in previous literature for psychiatric frankness, embodying both sadistic and masochistic fantasies—the cannibalism, the chains on the naked body. Aesthetically the stanzas are among the best in the poem, indicating that Shelley was excited by their subject matter. They anticipate surrealism in their blending of horrifying detail with a wavering unreality and existentialism in their projection of self-annihilation in the cosmos.

Canto IV

Before Laon recovers in the hermit's home, seven years have passed. The hermit tells him that the country is on the verge of revolution. In the capital, the Golden City (Constantinople), the corruption of the ruling class is mingled with a haunting fear:

"The tyrants of the Golden City tremble
At voices which are heard about the streets,
The ministers of fraud can scarce dissemble
The lies of their own heart; but when one meets
Another at the shrine, he inly weets,
Tho' he says nothing, that the truth is known;
Murderers are pale upon the judgement seats,

And gold grows vile even to the wealthy crone,
And laughter fills the Fane, and curses shake the Throne." (1531–1539)

The stanza reveals both Shelley's haste in writing ("he inly weets") and the flexibility of his "beau ideal" method. Clearly he is not thinking primarily of Constantinople nor, despite his general French-Revolution framework, of Paris, but of the London of his own day, the London of Tory "ministers" and corrupt judges and lawyers, of Castlereagh and Eldon and the prince regent.[26]

The hermit informs Laon that the people, led by a woman, have already risen, but "the tyrant's guards"—doubtless suggested by the Swiss guards of Louis XVI—are still fighting, "fearless and fierce and hard as beasts of blood" (1639–1640). The hermit is afraid that unless they can be subdued by peaceful means, a violent struggle will break out, and anarchy result. "Anarchy," Shelley informed Peacock in 1819, might be "the last flash before despotism." The hermit fears also that revolution may lead to military dictatorship. But perhaps Laon can check this trend and lead the people to the peaceful establishment of a new order:

"If blood be shed, 'tis but a change and choice
Of bonds,—from slavery to cowardice
A wretched fall!—Uplift thy charmed voice,
Pour on those evil men the love that lies
Hovering within those spirit-soothing eyes—
Arise, my friend, farewell!" (1657–1662)

This belief Shelley had maintained for some time—as in the early Irish pamphlet *Proposals for an Association*: "Had there been more of those men [enlightened intellectuals] France would not now be a beacon to warn us of the hazard and horror of Revolutions, but a pattern of society, rapidly advancing to a state of perfection, and holding out an example for the gradual and peaceful regeneration of the world."[27] The thought appears again in *Swellfoot the Tyrant* and *Prometheus Unbound*.

Canto V

As Laon approaches the city, he meets a young man he had known intimately in his youth and who he felt had been "false" to him (825). He now learns that he had been "deluded" (1761) and his friend had been "innocent" (presumably a reference to the story that Hogg had attempted to seduce Harriet at York in 1811). Laon also finds that the tyrant's guards have treacherously slaughtered ten thousand people. The danger now is that the people might take matters into their own hands. Even though the "tyrants, as usual, were the aggressors," nevertheless "the oppressed, having been rendered brutal, ignorant, servile and bloody by long slavery," might arise and take "a dreadful revenge on their oppressors."[28] Once more, it is implied, the despotism-anarchy-despotism cycle will result.

Laon therefore proceeds to fulfill the pacifist but revolutionary function assigned to him by the hermit. When his arm is thrust through with a spear by one of the tyrant's guards, he does not retaliate but remonstrates that vengeance leads only to more vengeance:

"Oh wherefore should ill ever flow from ill,
And pain still keener pain for ever breed?" (1810–1811)

His speech so impresses the soldiers on both sides that they fraternize with each other and then sweep after him into the city in "a mighty brotherhood":

Lifting the thunder of their acclamation,
Towards the City then the multitude,
And I among them, went in joy—a nation
Made free by love. (1836–1840)

They find the fallen tyrant alone in his palace except for a little girl, who is dancing gracefully before him. The people want to kill him. They ask whether only Othman shall "unavenged despoil" while they:

by the stress of grinding toil
Wrest from the unwilling earth his luxuries. (2003–2004)

Laon, however, intervenes and saves the tyrant's life.

The masses, with Laon, then swarm into the vast plain before the city, where the people have "Decreed to hold a sacred Festival, A rite to attest the equality of all Who live" (2047–2049). The people have built a huge pyramid, on whose summit sits a female lawgiver (Cythna) whom "men have chosen . . . to be the Priestess of this holiest rite" (2145–2146). Several lines recall *The Prelude,* XI, 108 ff—"Bliss was it in that dawn to be alive"—published in Wordsworth's 1815 *Poems:*

To hear, to see, to live, was on that morn
Lethean joy! so that all those assembled
Cast off their memories of the past outworn. (2089–2091)

The scene is a poetical representation of revolutionary fetes, and celebrates accomplishments like those of the early days of the French Revolution, namely, the reforms of the Legislative Assembly, which found condensed expression in the Declaration of the Rights of Man. However, Shelley also had in mind a similar scene in Volney: "And the people immediately raised a great standard, inscribed with these three words, in three different colours. They displayed it over the pyramid of the legislators; and for the first time the flag of universal justice floated on the face of the earth. And the people raised before the pyramid a new altar, a sword, and a book with this inscription: To equal law, which judges and protects."[29]

On the pyramid are three images, standing for equality, love, and wisdom. Of these, the first, Cythna declares, beginning a speech to the people, is equality:

> "Eldest of things, divine Equality!
> Wisdom and Love are but the slaves of thee." (2212–2213)

Equality, Volney's lawgiver declares, "is the primordial basis, the physical origin of all justice and of all right." Volney complained that "in the Declaration of Rights there is an inversion of ideas in the first article, liberty being placed before equality, from which it in reality springs."[30]

The revolution, Cythna continues, has triumphed. The power of religion has been broken, and legal marriage has been abolished:

> "man and woman,
> Their common bondage burst, may freely borrow
> From lawless love a solace for their sorrow!" (2229–2231)

Cythna ends her speech with a stirring invocation to the other nations of the world to follow America and France in throwing off the chains of feudalism and colonialism:

> "Victory, Victory to the prostrate nations!
> Bear witness Night, and ye, mute Constellations,
> Who gaze on us from your crystalline cars!
> Thoughts have gone forth whose powers can sleep no more!" (2257–2260)

Canto VI

The new state has hardly been set up when the armies of the emperor and his fellow kings attack. Among those killed are the hermit and the friend of Laon's youth, and one wonders if Laon would not have done better to have let the people execute the emperor:

> Then, rallying cries of treason and of danger
> Resounded: and—"they come! to arms! to arms!
> The Tyrant is amongst us, and the stranger
> Comes to enslave us in his name! to arms!" (2353–2356)

The inspiration for this action was clearly the attack of Prussia and Austria, aided by the French aristocrats under the leadership of the king's brother, the count of Artois, against the newly established French republic. The

French aristocrats—declared traitors by the Legislative Assembly—were later put in power by the allied armies and instigated the reprisals of the White Terror against the republicans.

The people fight gallantly—"myriads flocked in love and brotherhood to die" (2424)—but the cause is lost:

and ever
Our myriads, whom the swift bolt overthrew,
Or the red sword, failed like a mountain river
Which rushes forth in foam to sink in sands forever. (2457–2460)

The episode illustrates an apparent weakness in the logic of the poem. If the action really represents, as Shelley wrote to the publisher, a "*beau ideal* as it were of the French Revolution, but produced by the influence of individual genius out of general knowledge," then presumably the revolution should not have failed. If the masses are really guided out of the path of revenge by love-inspired intellectuals, anarchy could not come about, and the despots could not take advantage of it to assume power.

Laon and Cythna do so guide the masses; nevertheless, the despots come back with their armies, wreck the new state, and hound its champions to destruction. Shelley perhaps intended to suggest that although the revolution itself was a "beau ideal," it was overthrown by foreign intervention; but if so, he does not make this clear. In any case the despots attack, regardless of whether the people love them or hate them:

into the plain
Disgorged at length the dead and the alive
In one dread mass, were parted, and the stain
Of blood, from mortal steel fell o'er the fields like rain. (2385–2388)

In the midst of the battle, Cythna appears on a large black horse and rescues Laon, in a piece of melodramatic heroics that again illustrates the conflict between Shelley's social and romantic purposes. In a fantastic, Southey-type narrative such an event would not be discordant, but in a realistic scene of civil war it is. The two lovers (originally brother and sister) find a green and remote "recess" on a promontory, where they make love:

What are kisses whose fire clasps
The failing heart in languishment, or limb
Twined within limb? or the quick dying gasps
Of the life meeting, when the faint eyes swim
Thro' tears of a wide mist boundless and dim,
In one caress? What is the strong controul
Which leads the heart that dizzy steep to climb,
Where far over the world those vapours roll,
Which blend two restless frames in one reposing soul? (2650–2658)

Again, physical love and romantic love are viewed as one. Men and women seek both the gratification of the senses in "sexual connexion" and a "universal thirst for a communion . . . of our whole nature, intellectual, imaginative and sensitive."[31]

Returning to the devastated countryside to look for food, Laon finds a village, which is reminiscent of those Shelley had seen in war-devastated France. There, in one of the few scenes in which the Spenserian manner as well as verse form is manifest, Laon encounters a mad woman who believes herself to be the spirit of pestilence. Leaving her, he returns to Cythna.

Canto VII

With this canto Cythna begins a flash-back story of her adventures since the day when she was abducted by the sailors of the emperor. The sailors, she tells Laon, took her to the royal seraglio, where she was raped by the tyrant.[32] In a state of semimadness she was imprisoned in a cave located in a cliff above the sea, which could be entered only by an underwater route. There she gave birth to a baby girl. Since the girl is later described as the "tyrant's child" (4592) and by Cythna as "mine own child" (4645) she must be the product of the rape. But the child feels herself to be intellectually akin to Laon, whose words, she states later in the poem, "Kindled a clinging dream within my brain" (4662), and she joins Laon and Cythna after death in the final canto.

Cythna, after a brief time with her baby—"I watched the dawns of her first smiles" (3001)—finds herself alone, with the baby gone:

> "I was no longer mad, and yet methought
> My breasts were swoln and changed." (3037–3038)

The child had been stolen from her and taken to the emperor. All this seems to her to have taken place in a kind of delirium. The account is clearly based in part on the death of Mary Shelley's first child shortly after birth in the spring of 1815, including the detail of the swollen breasts.[33] After several years, Cythna was miraculously freed from her cave by an earthquake, which broke open the cavern, and she was picked up by a passing ship.

Canto VIII

With this canto the tempo changes as the action moves from the personal to the social in a description of the rise of the revolution and its tragic aftermath of civil war. As the canto opens, Cythna is still telling her story to

Laon and quoting a speech she made to the sailors of the ship that rescued her, a speech which contains one of Shelley's most compact expressions of his radical and anticlerical views. Cythna attacks the use of religion as a social narcotic—a use freely admitted by such pillars of the Establishment as Malthus or Southey. If there is a "cause" behind life and the universe, she asserts, its nature is unknown. Certainly it has neither mind nor sense. Attempts to envisage it as "God" are merely attributions of human characteristics to the universal force. Although this self-projection is harmless in itself, reactionary rulers have used it to terrify and subdue:

"What is that God? Ye mock yourselves, and give
A human heart to what ye cannot know:
As if the cause of life could think and live!"

. . . . .

"What is that God? Some moon-struck sophist stood
Watching the shade from his own soul upthrown
Fill Heaven and darken Earth, and in such mood
The Form he saw and worshipped was his own,
His likeness in the world's vast mirror shown;
And 'twere an innocent dream, but that a faith
Nursed by fear's dew of poison, grows thereon,
And that men say, that Power has chosen Death
On all who scorn his will, to wreak immortal wrath."
(3235–3237, 3244–3252)

In the same year (1817), Shelley expressed similar views in a talk with Horace Smith: "Any attempt at an impersonation of the Deity, or any conception of Him as otherwise than as the pervading spirit of the whole illimitable universe, he [Shelley] held to be presumptuous; for the finite cannot grasp the infinite . . . All the present evils of mankind he attributed to the erroneous views of religion in which had originated the countless wars, the national hatreds, the innumerable public and private miseries that make history a revolting record of suffering and crime."[34]

In the coming egalitarian society, Cythna continues, love will rule—"To live as if to love and live were one" (3304)—but in the existing society, family life and love are warped:

"But children near their parents tremble now,
Because they must obey—one rules another,
For it is said God rules both high and low,
And man is made the captive of his brother,
And Hate is throned on high with Fear his mother,
Above the Highest—and those fountain-cells,
Whence love yet flowed when faith had choked all other,
Are darkened—Woman, as the bond-slave, dwells
Of man, a slave; and life is poisoned in its wells." (3307–3315)

Economic exploitation and social degradation form the lot of the mass of humanity:

> "Man seeks for gold in mines, that he may weave
> A lasting chain for his own slavery;—
> In fear and restless care that he may live
> He toils for others, who must ever be
> The joyless thralls of like captivity;
> He murders, for his chiefs delight in ruin;
> He builds the altar, that its idol's fee
> May be his very blood; he is pursuing,
> O, blind and willing wretch! his own obscure undoing." (3316–3324)

The function of the social reformer, Cythna explains, is to awaken the people to a sense of their own revolutionary power:

> "This need not be; ye might arise, and will
> That gold should lose its power, and thrones their glory;
> That love, which none may bind, be free to fill
> The world, like light; and evil faith, grown hoary
> With crime, be quenched and die.—Yon promontory
> Even now eclipses the descending moon!—
> Dungeons and palaces are transitory—
> High temples fade like vapour—Man alone
> Remains, whose will has power when all beside is gone." (3334–3342)

The "will" of "Man" can change the world, but its instrumentality ("ye might arise, and will") must be social revolution.

Cythna's words stir the sailors and they release a group of young women whom they were taking—as Cythna herself had formerly been taken—to imprisonment in the seraglio of the Turkish emperor.

Canto IX

As the ship sails on to the port, the revolutionary spirit of the sailors spreads contagiously to other vessels, and their journey, as Cythna describes it, becomes a triumphal pageant of awakening humanity:

> "The many ships spotting the dark blue deep
> With snowy sails, fled fast as our's came nigh,
> In fear and wonder; and on every steep
> Thousands did gaze, they heard the startling cry,
> Like earth's own voice lifted unconquerably
> To all her children, the unbounded mirth,
> The glorious joy of thy name—Liberty!
> They heard!—As o'er the mountains of the earth
> From peak to peak leap on the beams of morning's birth." (3486–3495)

Their arrival in port touches off a spark that flames into a great mass movement. "Millions" gather around the city "in the high name of truth and liberty" (3570). The tyrant, to counteract the growing revolutionary fervor, sends Malthusian and other demagogues among the people to disrupt their movement:

"And grave and hoary men were bribed to tell
From seats where law is made the slave of wrong,
How glorious Athens in her splendour fell,
Because her sons were free,—and that among
Mankind, the many to the few belong,
By God, and Nature, and Necessity.
They said, that age was truth, and that the young
Marred with wild hopes the peace of slavery,
With which old times and men had quelled the vain and free." (3586–3594)

This attempt fails, the "sneers of calumny" (3629) are in vain, and the revolution continues. As Laon himself has witnessed developments from this point on (having been convalescing in the hermit's home while the earlier events were taking place), Cythna does not describe the further progress of the movement, but goes on to state what Shelley perhaps considered the central message of his poem—that, in spite of the triumph of the tyrants, a new and successful revolution will arise. As is clear from the Preface, Shelley was here thinking of the Europe of his own day, a Europe dominated by Metternich and the Quadruple Alliance. His remarks are addressed to those intellectuals who, like Wordsworth, had given up "in despair." In *Ode to the West Wind*, Shelley saw his words as seeds for a new spring for humanity; so too, Cythna:

"This is the winter of the world;—and here
We die, even as the winds of Autumn fade,
Expiring in the frore and foggy air.—
Behold! Spring comes, though we must pass, who made
The promise of its birth." (3685–3689)

The ultimate and perhaps direct source for the concept both here and in the ode may be Tom Paine: "What pace the political summer may keep with the natural, no human foresight can determine. It is, however, not difficult to perceive that the spring is begun."[35] That the concept was tied up in Shelley's mind with the necessitarian forces of social evolution becomes apparent a few stanzas later:

"And tho' some envious shade may interlope
Between the effect and it, one comes behind,
Who aye the future to the past will bind—
Necessity, whose sightless strength forever
Evil with evil, good with good, must wind
In bands of union, which no power may sever:
They must bring forth their kind, and be divided never!" (3705–3711)

The "spring" of the new social order will come about because of the workings of necessity, the force that controls both the universe and society. However, why, if necessity is "sightless" and can work only with whatever good or evil already exists in society should it produce the new egalitarian order of "spring" rather than further despotism? Cythna gives the answer in the next stanza:

> "The good and mighty of departed ages
> Are in their graves, the innocent and free,
> Heroes, and Poets, and prevailing Sages,
> Who leave the vesture of their majesty
> To adorn and clothe this naked world;—and we
> Are like to them—such perish, but they leave
> All hope, or love, or truth, or liberty,
> Whose forms their mighty spirits could conceive,
> To be a rule and law to ages that survive." (3712–3720)

The answer in short, is, that "good" is increasing more rapidly than "evil" as a result of the deeds and writings of the great progressive thinkers, which have a cumulative effect. As Shelley makes clear in the Preface to *Prometheus Unbound* and in *A Philosophical View of Reform*, he believed that his own age was uniquely endowed with such thinkers. The concept is similar to that expressed in the *Julian and Maddalo* fragment, to the effect that good deeds and works can tilt toward progressivism the social forces with which the "sightless" forces of necessity must work. Hence, society moves in a progressive spiral. People cannot control the process as such, but they can control what goes into it and hence, indirectly, what comes out. In other words, necessity is like a flowing river, which human power cannot do away with but can divert, one way or the other. In Shelley's own age, the American and French revolutions showed that necessity could be diverted into the channels of social progress.

After their death, Cythna continues, their deeds, like those of all radical intellectuals, will be distorted by the powers that be:

> "And Calumny meanwhile shall feed on us,
> As worms devour the dead." (3739–3740)

Nevertheless, their words and deeds will live on in the hearts of the people and be added to the ever-increasing stream of human enlightenment:

> "Our many thoughts and deeds, our life and love,
> Our happiness, and all that we have been,
> Immortally must live, and burn, and move,
> When we shall be no more." (3730–3733)

Although their works will endure, the enlightened intellectuals themselves face annihilation. The thought of herself and Laon as dead strikes Cythna with horror in the midst of her vision of the future:

"The while we two, beloved, must depart,
And Sense and Reason, those enchanters fair,
Whose wand of power is hope, would bid the heart
That gazed beyond the wormy grave despair:
These eyes, these lips, this blood, seems darkly there
To fade in hideous ruin; no calm sleep
Peopling with golden dreams the stagnant air,
Seems our obscure and rotting eyes to steep
In joy;—but senseless death—a ruin dark and deep!

"These are blind fancies—Reason cannot know
What sense can neither feel, nor thought conceive;
There is delusion in the world—and woe,
And fear, and pain—we know not whence we live,
Or why, or how, or what mute Power may give
Their being to each plant, and star, and beast,
Or even these thoughts.—Come near me! I do weave
A chain I cannot break—I am possessed
With thoughts too swift and strong for one lone human breast." (3748–3765)

The concept of the decay of the body in the grave and the fear that this means also the death of the mind is the same as that in *On a Future State.* "Senseless death" (death without sense perception) echoes Cythna's earlier comment, "the grave—I fear 'tis passionless" (1094). The horror of this vision is compounded by man's ignorance of the powers controlling life. Even of the source of thought nothing is known. All the powers are "mute."

Canto X

Cythna's story completed, the poem returns to the mainstream of the narrative. While Laon and Cythna are in hiding, the war continues:

For, from the utmost realms of earth, came pouring
The banded slaves whom every despot sent
At that thron'd traitor's summons.

. . . . .

the continent
Trembled, as with a zone of ruin bound,
Beneath their feet, the sea shook with their Navies' sound. (3820–3822, 3826–3828)

To convey his hatred of the professional soldier, Shelley uses an image that may have come from his own boyhood experiences on the family's sheep farms around Field Place:

From every nation of the earth they came,
The multitude of moving heartless things,
Whom slaves call men: obediently they came,
Like sheep whom from the fold the shepherd brings
To the stall, red with blood. (3829–3833)

Shelley, here and throughout this canto, is apparently painting an impressionistic picture of the Napoleonic Wars. As the *Esdaile* poems show, he had followed the course of these wars since childhood, and their horrors had helped to shake him out of his "votary of romance" fantasies. His disgust was compounded when in 1814 and 1816, he saw for himself the war's devastation. The poem does not, of course, rigidly follow historical events. The emphasis is on a general scene of mounting reactionary military might, as in the successive coalitions against France. The implied climax doubtless reflects the English declaration of war against the new French republic. For the tyrant there is no definite historical prototype; he is a composite of such European rulers as Napoleon and Metternich.

As more and more armies appear—"Myriads had come—millions were on their way" (3856)—the slaughter increases:

They rushed into the plain.—Loud was the roar
Of their career: the horsemen shook the earth;
The wheeled artillery's speed the pavement tore;
The infantry, file after file, did pour
Their clouds on the utmost hills. Five days they slew
Among the wasted fields; the sixth saw gore
Stream thro' the city; on the seventh, the dew
Of slaughter became stiff, and there was peace anew. (3884–3891)

The peace is, if anything, more ghastly than the war itself:

Peace in the desert fields and villages,
Between the glutted beasts and mangled dead!
Peace in the silent streets! (3892–3894)

Then comes famine to pile the corpses high:

Sometimes the living by the dead were hid.
Near the great fountain in the public square,
Where corpses made a crumbling pyramid
Under the sun, was heard one stifled prayer
For life, in the hot silence of the air. (3991–3995)

After famine comes disease, which unlike famine is no respecter of class:

Famine had spared the palace of the king:—
He rioted in festival the while,

He and his guards and priests; but Plague did fling
One shadow upon all. (4000–4003)

The scenes are vivid and realistic, told with power and passion, inspired, as Shelley indicated in the Preface, by the sights he had himself witnessed: "I have seen the theatre of the more visible ravages of tyranny and war, cities and villages reduced to scattered groups of black and roofless houses, and the naked inhabitants sitting famished upon their desolated thresholds."[36]

The rulers themselves, formerly so arrogant and ruthless, are now terror-stricken at the horrors they have let loose, and grovel in superstitious panic:

"O God Almighty! Thou alone hast power!
Who can resist thy will? who can restrain
Thy wrath, when on the guilty thou dost shower
The shafts of thy revenge, a blistering rain?
Greatest and best, be merciful again!
Have we not stabbed thine enemies, and made
The Earth an altar, and the Heavens a fane,
Where thou wert worshipped with their blood, and laid
Those hearts in dust which would thy searchless works have weighed?"
(4036–4044)

The reference, as in the Preface to *Hellas*, is to the Holy Alliance, whose founders—the kings of Russia, Austria, and Prussia—had piously declared God to be the ultimate repository of political power: "The rulers of Austria, Prussia, and Russia thus confess that the Christian world of which they and their people form a part has in reality no other sovereign than Him to Whom alone power rightfully belongs."[37] Shelley's rulers sadistically vow to crush the enemies of God:

"Give sanction, from thine hell of fiends and flames,
That we will kill with fire and torments slow,
The last of those who mocked thy holy name,
And scorned the sacred laws thy prophets did proclaim." (4050–4053)

The rulers in *The Revolt* begin to quarrel among themselves (as in Volney's *Ruins*) over which God is the true one, but their squabbling is dramatically cut short before it can lead to bloodshed:

each raging votary 'gan to throw
Aloft his armed hands, and each did howl
'Our God alone is God' and slaughter now
Would have gone forth, when, from beneath a cowl,
A voice came forth, which pierced like ice through every soul.

He was a Christian Priest from whom it came,
A zealous man, who led the legioned west

With words which faith and pride had steeped in flame,
To quell the rebel Atheists.

. . . . .

He loathed all faith beside his own, and pined
To wreak his fear of Heaven in vengeance on mankind.
(4067–4075, 4079–4080)

The reference is apparently, in part at least, to Lord Castlereagh, who represented the "legioned West" (Great Britain) at the Congress of Vienna. Castlereagh, although supporting the counterrevolutionary objectives of the Holy Alliance, scoffed at its aura of nebulous piety: "a piece of sublime mysticism and nonsense."[38] Like the "Christian Priest," he played a dominant part at the congress. Unlike Metternich and others, he had not actually intervened with armed force to put down revolutions:

He dared not kill the infidels with fire
Or steel, in Europe. (4090–4091)

Nevertheless, he supported his absolutist and Catholic partners in such acts:

So he made truce with those who did despise
His cradled Idol, and the sacrifice
Of God to God's own wrath,—that Islam's creed
Might crush for him those deadlier enemies. (4093–4096)

"Islam's creed" is in this context, Catholicism (Russian and Roman), and the "deadlier enemies" are those champions of democracy who had rejoiced "to hear/That Faith and tyranny were trampled down" (4085—4086). Castlereagh feared democracy more than he did the menace of the absolutist systems of Russia, Austria, and Prussia; or as Shelley wrote in the Preface to *Hellas*, the European sovereigns "look to each other for aid against the common enemy, and suspend their mutual jealousies in the presence of a mightier fear." The advice of the "Christian Priest" is to capture Laon and Cythna and burn them alive. But just as the emperor is a composite figure, so too is the priest. If in his political aspect he resembles Castlereagh, in his priestly one he resembles Malthus, whom Shelley attacked in *A Philosophical View of Reform* as "a priest of course," whose "doctrines are those of a eunuch and a tyrant."[39] The "Christian Priest" is a Castlereagh-type political leader infected by the antihumanitarian Malthusian doctrine, which in its original form condoned wars, famine, and pestilence as means for reducing the population.

As a result of the priest's fanatic urgings, an orgy of reprisals begins; and Shelley's primary source of inspiration moves from the Napoleonic Wars to earlier wars of religious persecution:

And Priests rushed through their ranks, some counterfeiting
The rage they did inspire, some mad indeed

With their own lies; they said their god was waiting
To see his enemies writhe, and burn, and bleed. (4189–4192)

Canto XI

The scene shifts back to Laon and Cythna on their remote promontory. Laon has been making expeditions into the countryside and is aware of what has been going on. One day Cythna falls into a melancholy, *Alastor*-like mood:

Which only clothes the heart in solitude,
A thought of voiceless death. (4229–4230)

Leon steals away, determined to sacrifice his own life in order to save hers. Once more the historical and personal narrative elements come into conflict when, disguised as a monk, Laon gains admittance to the council of the kings:

"Ye Princes of the Earth, ye sit aghast
Amid the ruin which yourselves have made,
Yes, desolation heard your trumpet's blast,
And sprang from sleep!—dark Terror has obeyed
Your bidding." (4351–4355)

Blood, conflict, and hatred, he charges, make a long, difficult struggle inevitable; the rulers themselves have been caught up in the web of lies, prejudices, and superstitions that they wove for the subjugation of the people. Laon exhorts them to abandon their evil power:

"Fear not the future, weep not for the past.
O, could I win your ears to dare be now
Glorious, and great, and calm! that ye would cast
Into the dust those symbols of your woe
Purple, and gold, and steel!" (4378–4382)

The passage perhaps has reference to Robert Owen, for it was in 1817, during the months when Shelley was writing *The Revolt of Islam*, that Owen was promulgating, with wide publicity (including whole pages of *The London Times*), the notion that the ruling classes of England and Europe could be converted to socialistic progress. Although Shelley placed great emphasis upon the power of ideas, he had little faith in such a conversion. It was, in fact, in 1817 that he wrote a tract advocating broad political action. His reservations are evident, indeed, in this scene, for even though Laon does succeed in swaying some of the younger members of the "Senate," before they can act, they are coldly assassinated by the others:

> The men of faith and law then without ruth
> Drew forth their secret steel, and stabbed each ardent youth. (4394–4395)

Laon, still in his monkish guise, tells the rulers that he will deliver Laon into their hands if they will allow Cythna to go free. His hope is that she may be able to go to America. To Shelley, as to other English liberals and radicals in the dark days of the Quadruple Alliance, America seemed to be the hope of the world, a steady beacon from the west shining across the wreck of the French Revolution and the subsequent dark decades of war. Laon advises, with clear reference to the current scene, that the England which gave birth to America, but, now is "oppressed" by a corrupt oligarchy must turn to her offspring for help:

> "There is a People mighty in its youth,
> A land beyond the Oceans of the West,
> Where, tho' with rudest rites, Freedom and Truth
> Are worshipped; from a glorious Mother's breast,
> Who, since high Athens fell, among the rest
> Sate like the Queen of Nations, but in woe,
> By inbred monsters outraged and oppressed,
> Turns to her chainless child for succour now,
> It draws the milk of Power in Wisdom's fullest flow." (4414–4422)

The kings swear that Cythna shall be pardoned if the supposed stranger deliver Laon to them. Laon then naively reveals his identity.

Canto XII

As the canto opens, Laon is being led in a priestly procession to the pyre. The tyrant watches, his and Cythna's child by his side. The child pleads for Laon's life "without avail" (4500). When the torch is about to be applied Cythna makes a melodramatic entrance on a black charger, sarcastically announcing: "God has sent his other victim here" (4548). The king is prepared to stand by his oath and grant her freedom, but the "Christian priest," crying out that the extinction of "an Atheist" is always justified before God, condemns her to the flames along with Laon. The priest, here veering more toward the Malthusian component of his character, typifies the sadistic religious fanatic:

> "Were it not impious," said the King, "to break
> Our holy oath?"—"Impious to keep it, say!"
> Shrieked the exulting Priest—"Slaves, to the stake
> Bind her, and on my head the burthen lay
> Of her just torments:—at the Judgment Day
> Will I stand up before God's golden throne
> And cry, O Lord, to thee did I betray
> An Atheist; but for me she would have known
> Another moment's joy!—the glory be thine own." (4549–4557)

Laon feels the flames sweeping round him and Cythna:

> the mighty veil
> Which doth divide the living and the dead
> Was almost rent, the world grew dim and pale. (4581–4583)

At the same moment he sees the child fall to the ground, a victim of the plague.

Laon and Cythna awake to find themselves in a realm beyond life, with a crystal pool before them and a wide sky above. A boat with the spirit of the child approaches. She tells them that their deaths were not in vain. True, the people had stood in dismay for a time after the execution, but one of them, inspired by the heroism of Laon and Cythna, arose to condemn the tyrants:

> "These perish as the good and great of yore
> Have perished, and their murderers will repent."
>
> . . . . .
>
> "And to long ages shall this hour be known;
> And slowly shall its memory, ever burning,
> Fill this dark night of things with an eternal morning."
> (4693–4694, 4708–4710)

But as the time for revolution had not yet come, the speaker stabs himself in order to arouse others by his death:

> "For me the world is grown too void and cold,
> Since Hope pursues immortal Destiny
> With steps thus slow—therefore shall ye behold
> How Atheists and Republicans can die." (4711–4714)[40]

Here, as earlier, historical change is regarded as being in the hands of necessity ("immortal Destiny"), but since necessity moves at its own pace, the hour of change has not yet come. Therefore, one can only add to the storehouse of good, in this instance by unselfish and inspiring sacrifice, so that when the hour does come, the change will be for the better.

The child's brain then "grew dark in death," but as she died, she heard "a murmur from the crowd to tell/Of deep and mighty change which suddenly befell" (4718–4719). She awoke to find herself "a winged Thought / Before the immortal Senate" (4720–4721)—the senate of great minds depicted in the first canto—and confronted by the throned spirit (the "benignant power"):

> Of that star-shining spirit, whence is wrought
> The strength of its dominion, good and great,
> The better Genius of this world's estate. (4722–4724)

Laon and Cythna get into the boat with the child and journey down a rushing river, which enters the calm lake depicted in Canto I, containing the "Temple of the Spirit."

The final scenes though decorative, are also symbolic. For instance, the second to last stanza reads:

> The torrent of that wide and raging river
> Is passed, and our aerial speed suspended.
> We look behind; a golden mist did quiver
> Where its wild surges with the lake were blended:
> Our bark hung there, as on a line suspended
> Between two heavens, that windless waveless lake,
> Which four great cataracts from four vales, attended
> By mists, aye feed, from rocks and clouds they break,
> And of that azure sea a silent refuge make. (4801–4809)

The lake, as in Canto I, is a symbol for the essence of nature, similar to the spirit of nature in *Queen Mab* and *The Daemon of the World*. The "four great cataracts" are perhaps also explained in *Queen Mab* (II, 91–92). In the realm of the spirit of nature, "matter, space and time . . . cease to act." The fairy tells Ianthe that her power is limited to the area of things as they are (VIII, 48–50):

> To me is given
> The wonders of the human world to keep,
> Space, matter, time, and mind.

On the basis of this analogy, the four cataracts would be space, matter, time, and mind. None of these entities, Shelley indicates, is part of the essential, unifying force inherent in the universe. Everything we know is known in terms of space, matter, time, and mind, and all four are basically noncreative. Whether there is some creative entity behind them is not known, but if there is, it is perhaps sustained by them, although different from them (as the calm lake is supplied by and yet left undisturbed by the four cataracts). All four entities, however, while they are changing in form, are eternal in essence. Mind, although not a creative substance, is immortal, just as matter is: its parts change, but the whole continues. One of its characteristics is that its thoughts can influence mankind long after the individual mind that gave birth to those thoughts has perished. Hence, the "Senate" of great minds is "immortal." Laon and Cythna have symbolically journeyed through the unknown (misted) essence of the universe to join them.

The Reception of *The Revolt of Islam*

With publication of *The Revolt of Islam*, Shelley first began to gain recognition as a poet. In spite of its weaknesses, the poem was too massive and challenging to be ignored by the major journals, as the *Alastor* volume had been. Whereas some later critics have had doubts about the poem's radical connotations, contemporary reviewers did not. Its revolutionary and anti-clerical nature was immediately perceived, and with alarm. The Tory *Quarterly Review* gave it a full, if hostile, treatment:

> Mr. Shelley would abrogate our laws—this would put an end to felonies and misdemeanours at a blow; he would abolish the rights of property, of course there could thenceforward be no violations of them, no heart-burnings between the poor and the rich, no disputed wills, no litigated inheritances, no food in short for sophistical judges, or hireling lawyers; he would overthrow the constitution, and then we should have no expensive court, no pensions or sinecures, no silken lords or corrupt commoners, no slavish and enslaving army or navy; he would pull down our churches, level our Establishment, and burn our bibles—then we should pay no tithes, be enslaved by no superstitions, abused by no priestly artifices: marriage he cannot endure, and there would at once be a stop put to lamented increase of adulterous connections amongst us, whilst by repealing the canon of heaven against incest, he would add to the purity, and heighten the ardour of those feelings with which brother and sister now regard each other; finally, as the basis of the whole scheme, he would have us renounce our belief in our religion, extinguish, if we can, the light of conscience within us, which embitters our joys here, and drown in oblivion the hopes and fears that hang over our hereafter.

Blackwoods took a more subtle line. Shelley was clearly a radical, but he was also a poet and a gentleman. Perhaps the one could be weaned away from the other by praising the poetry and condemning the radicalism.[41]

In contrast, the *Examiner* rejoiced. It perceived, through the poem's many imperfections, a creative talent rising to support the liberal cause:

> This is an extraordinary production. The ignorant will not understand it; the idle will not take the pains to get acquainted with it; even the intelligent will be startled at first with its air of mysticism and wildness; the livelier man of the world will shake his head at it good naturedly; the sulkier one will cry out against it; the bigot will be shocked, terrified, and enraged; and fall to proving all that is said against himself . . . but we will venture to say, that the intelligent and the good, who are yet healthy-minded, and who have not been so far blinded by fear and self-love as to confound superstition with desert, anger and hatred with firmness, or despondency with knowledge, will find themselves amply repaid by breaking through the outer shell of this production, even if it be with the single reflection, that so much ardour for the happy virtues, and so much power to recommend them, have united in the same person. To will them with hope indeed is to create them; and to extend that will is the object of the writer before us . . . We have no doubt he is destined to be one of the leading spirits of his age.[42]

After the publication of *The Revolt of Islam*, Shelley might be attacked, but he could never again be ignored.

9
Political Poems

The Masque of Anarchy. Peter Bell the Third. Swellfoot the Tyrant

In 1820, shortly after writing *A Philosophical View of Reform,* Shelley thought of compiling a book of political poems. "I wish to ask you," he wrote to Leigh Hunt, "if you know of any bookseller who would like to publish a little volume of *popular songs* wholly political, & destined to awaken direct the imagination of the reformers." He discussed the project with Mary, who commented on it in her Note to the poems of 1819: "Shelley loved the people, and respected them as often more virtuous, as always more suffering, and therefore more deserving of sympathy, than the great. He believed that a clash between the two classes of society was inevitable, and he eagerly ranged himself on the people's side."[1]

Unfortunately, Shelley never completed his plans for the book, probably because of the difficulty of finding a publisher. He did, however, compose seven of the poems: three directed to the English working class—*The Masque of Anarchy; Song, to the Men of England;* and *An Ode to the Assertors of Liberty;* two attacking the ruling clique—*Lines Written During the Castlereagh Administration* and *To Sidmouth and Castlereagh;* one on the general political situation in England—*Sonnet: England in 1819;* and *A New National Anthem,* hailing liberty in the place of monarchy. Perhaps he intended also to include in the book the political poems he had written in previous years, some of which had appeared in the *Alastor* volume: *To Wordsworth, Feelings of a Republican on the fall of Bonaparte, To the Lord Chancellor,* and *To William Shelley.*

Of the shorter 1819 poems, *Sonnet: England in 1819* pivots around the contrast between the people—"starved and stabbed in the untilled field"—and the ruling class, with its old mad king, George III, the decadent prince regent, and corrupt officials:

Rulers, who neither see, nor feel, nor know,
But leech-like to their fainting country cling,
Till they drop, blind in blood, without a blow.

The same bitterness permeates *Lines Written during the Castlereagh Administration* and *To Sidmouth and Castlereagh* in the second of which the home secretary and foreign minister are compared to "a shark and dog-fish" lurking under a slave ship waiting for human food.

An Ode to the Assertors of Liberty, written in October, 1819, was inspired by the "Manchester Massacre."[2] Shelley, indignant at the "massacre," urges the workers to take justice into their own hands, but hopes that though they are driven by hunger and exploitation ("Famine and Toil"), the result will be a democratic republic ("Freedom"). He urges them to abjure the violence bred of "injury."

The theme of *Song to the Men of England* is similar, and though it lacks the revolutionary sweep of the *Ode*, it has a steadier pace and more solid movement. Its Spencean egalitarianism foreshadows later socialist views.

Men of England, wherefore plough
For the lords who lay ye low?
Wherefore weave with toil and care
The rich robes your tyrants wear?

. . . . .

Sow seed,—but let no tyrant reap;
Find wealth,—let no impostor heap;
Weave robes,—let not the idle wear;
Forge arms,—in your defence to bear.

The conclusion is at first puzzling:

With plough and spade, and hoe and loom,
Trace your grave, and build your tomb,
And weave your winding-sheet, till fair
England be your sepulchre.

Shelley, after urging the workers to arise and take back the wealth they have created, defending themselves by armed force, here seemingly tells them to retreat. The mood, however, is sardonic, the motive that of shaming the workers into action, implying that unless they act, they will become lethargic.

The theme of the last of these poems, *A New National Anthem,* is that liberty is the only true ruler, an idea that Shelley had earlier used at the conclusion of his Princess Charlotte pamphlet. His antipathy to patriotic songs goes back at least to the days of his Irish pamphlet, *Proposals for an Association,* where he assailed "God Save the King" and "Rule Brittannia" as "political cant . . . abstracts of the caterpillar [i.e., rapacious, imperialistic] creed of courtiers."[3]

If Shelley had been able to publish the volume, the central poem would doubtless have been *The Masque of Anarchy.* He brought out the political burlesque drama, *Oedipus Tyrannus;* or, *Swellfoot the Tyrant,* in 1820 as a separate volume, and he intended to do the same with the political-literary satire, *Peter Bell the Third.*

The Masque of Anarchy

The Masque of Anarchy was inspired by a cavalry attack upon a parliamentary reform meeting at St. Peter's Field, Manchester, on August 16, 1819, which became known as the "Manchester Massacre" or "Peterloo." "Many thanks for your attention in sending the papers which contain the terrible and important news of Manchester," Shelley wrote from Italy on September 9, 1819. "These are, as it were, the distant thunders of the terrible storm which is approaching. The tyrants here, as in the French Revolution, have first shed blood. May their execrable lessons not be learnt with equal docility!"[4]

By the year 1819 the massive new movement for parliamentary reform created by the depression following the war had spread beyond London into the new industrial north. Powerful reform groups in Manchester, Birmingham, and Leeds were led by local reformers, such as the Lancashire weaver and poet Samuel Bamford. The object of these men was to turn the working people from rioting to political action. In January and February, large reform meetings were held in Manchester, Oldham, Royton, and Stockport; during June, in Leeds, Glasgow, and other towns. At Leeds, a reform petition was circulated for the signature of every adult in the town.[5] On July 12 the greatest meeting of all, attended by fifty thousand men and women, was held in Birmingham. Jubilant at this success, the reformers planned similar meetings for Leeds and Manchester. The government, however, now thoroughly alarmed, forbade both meetings. The Leeds group capitulated, but the Manchester reformers refused.

To the workers of Manchester and the surrounding towns, it was a gala occasion. Dressed in their Sunday best, they marched in procession, with banners flying and bands playing, into St. Peter's Fields, eighty thousand strong. They were to be addressed by the great "Orator" from London, Henry Hunt, who had come, not to incite them to riot, but to point out that, while such tiny "rotten boroughs" as Old Sarum had two seats in Parliament, Manchester, a town of one hundred thousand, had only one. A vivid, eyewitness account of the events was given by Samuel Bamford himself. He first described his own contingent (from Middleton and Rochdale) in the grand procession:

> First were selected twelve of the most comely and decent-looking youths, who were placed in two rows of six each, with each a branch of laurel held presented in his hand, as a token of amity and peace; then followed the men of several districts in fives . . .
>
> Our whole column, with the Rochdale people, would probably consist of six thousand men. At our head were a hundred or two women, mostly young wives, and mine own was amongst them. A hundred or two of our handsomest girls, sweethearts to the lads who were with us, danced to the music, or sung snatches of popular songs; a score or two of children were sent back, though some went forward; whilst on each side of our line walked some thousands of stragglers. And thus, accompanied by our friends and our dearest and most tender connections, we went slowly towards Manchester.

Orator Hunt, arrived in a carriage accompanied by Richard Carlile, the much-jailed editor of *The Republican,* and began to address the meeting.

Bamford suggested to a friend that they leave for a while and walk back to town. There they were surprised to find "a party of cavalry in blue and white uniform come trotting sword in hand, round the corner of a garden-wall." Although they presumed that the cavalry were just there in case of disturbance they decided to go back to the meeting to find out. Then, suddenly, the attack began:

On the cavalry drawing up they were received with a shout of good-will, as I understood it. They shouted again, waving their sabres over their heads; and then, slackening rein, and striking spur into their steeds, they dashed forward and began cutting the people.

"Stand fast," I said, "they are riding upon us; stand fast." And there was a general cry in our quarter of "Stand fast." The cavalry were in confusion. They evidently could not, with all the weight of man and horse, penetrate that compact mass of human beings; and their sabres were plied to hue a way through naked held-up hands and defenceless heads; and then chopped limbs and wound-gaping skulls were seen; and groans and cries were mingled with the din of that horrid confusion. "Ah! Ah!" "For shame! for shame!" was shouted. Then, "Break! break! they are killing them in front, and they cannot get away;" and there was a general cry of "break! break!" For a moment the crowd held back as in a pause; then there was a rush, heavy and resistless as a headlong sea, and a sound like low thunder, with screams, prayers, and imprecations from the crowd-moiled and sabre-doomed who could not escape. . .

On the breaking of the crowd the yeomanry wheeled, and dashing whenever there was an opening, they followed, pressing and wounding. Many females appeared as the crowd opened; and striplings or mere youths also were found. Their cries were piteous and heart-rending, and would, one might have supposed, have disarmed any human resentment: but here their appeals were in vain. Women, white-vested maids, and tender youth, were indiscriminately sabred or trampled; and we have reason for believing that few were the instances in which that forbearance was vouchsafed which they so earnestly implored.

In ten minutes from the commencement of the havoc the field was an open and almost deserted space. The sun looked down through a sultry and motionless air. The curtains and blinds of the windows within view were all closed. A gentleman or two might occasionally be seen looking out from one of the new houses before mentioned, near the door of which a group of persons (special constables) were collected, and apparently in conversation; others were assisting the wounded or carrying off the dead. The hustings remained, with a few broken and hewed flagstaves erect, and a torn and gashed banner or two drooping; whilst over the whole field were strewed caps, bonnets, hats, shawls, and shoes, and other parts of male and female dress, trampled, torn, and bloody. The yeomanry had dismounted—some were easing their horses' girths, others adjusting their accoutrements, and some were wiping their sabres. Several mounds of human beings still remained where they had fallen, crushed down and smothered. Some of these still groaning, others with staring eyes, were gasping for breath, and others would never breathe more. All was silent save those low sounds, and the occasional snorting and pawing of steeds.[6]

The response to this terroristic attack was not what the authorities had anticipated. Far from being intimidated, the reformers rallied around Henry

Hunt and his colleagues, holding meetings of protest from one end of England to the other, the "radicals" and "moderates" forgetting their differences in a common indignation. The wrath of Thomas Jonathan Wooler and William Cobbett in *The Black Dwarf* and the *Political Register* respectively was matched by *The Examiner* and Sir Francis Burdett. *The Examiner*, in its issues for August 22 and 29, fulminated against the government in editorials, gave detailed accounts of the "massacre," and printed an open letter from Burdett (which cost him several months in prison) as well as letters from William Hone and Henry Hunt. The August 22 editorial made a scathing comparison between the Tories' attitudes to war and to domestic oppression:

With what feelings can these Men in the Brazen Masks of power dare to speak lamentingly of the wounds or even the death received by a constable or a soldier or any other person concerned against an assemblage of Englishmen irritated by every species of wrong and insult, public and private? With what feelings can they dare to speak of such things in such a tone, after they have so long been inciting the whole world under false pretences to shed their blood in the impudent cause of Divine Right? After they have been hallooing, and shouting, and clapping their "deluded countrymen" on the back, and *paying* them to make charge after charge upon their fellow-creatures with bloody swords and bayonets, not for poverty's sake and right, but that hereditary masters and their hirelings might wallow to all eternity at their pleasure in superfluities and wrong? . . . So it is an innocent, admirable, and desirable thing for thousands of human beings to slaughter and be slaughtered for the greater security of a corrupt Government but if the corruptions of that Government provoke a half-starved populace to the destruction of a single constable or a soldier, we are allowed to return to our abstract lamentations on the shedding of blood! In the former case, "Carnage is God's daughter;"—so says a pathetic court poet.[7]

Shelley, in Italy, must have read both this and the next issue of *The Examiner* avidly for *The Masque of Anarchy* contains a poetic transmutation of material found in them.[8] His purpose in writing the poem was not so much to expose the oppressive nature of the rulers of England as to propagate, according to Mary Shelley, "the great truth that the many, if accordant and resolute, could control the few."[9] This purpose animates the whole work.

The first specific problem is Shelley's meaning in the title, his final choice for the spelling of the second word of which was "masque" and not "mask."[10] As he indicates in stanza seven, he uses the word in the sense not of a courtly play but of a masquerade or revel, in which the participants are disguised by masks.

I met Murder on the way—
He had a mask like Castlereagh. (5–6)

The idea doubtless came from *The Examiner's* excoriation of the Tories as "Men in the Brazen Masks of Power." Shelley, that is, although using the word ironically in its sense of a revel, also wanted to imply the secondary sense of masks as a disguise. The participants in the revels are the spirits of oppression and destruction that have plagued mankind since the beginning of history—murder, fraud, hypocracy, and anarchy—seen in their present guises as Castlereagh, Eldon, Sidmouth, and others:

> And many more Destructions played
> In this ghastly masquerade,
> All disguised, even to the eyes,
> Like Bishops, lawyers, peers, or spies. (26–29)

Castlereagh is singled out as Murder because he was the main architect of a foreign policy of war and oppression, from the bloody suppression of the Irish rebellion in 1798 to the Napoleonic Wars (as Byron also noted in the Dedication to *Don Juan*). The "seven bloodhounds" who follow Castlereagh probably represent the seven nations that in 1815 agreed with Britain to put off the abolition of the universal slave trade: Austria, France, Russia, Prussia, Spain, Portugal, and Sweden.[11] The "human hearts" which Castlereagh throws to them to keep them (economically) "fat" are those of the slaves. Eldon, the lord chancellor who had deprived Shelley of his children and was known for his tearful rendering of harsh verdicts, is personified as a weeping fraud. Sidmouth, the home secretary, who had built churches for the poor and then implemented a policy of police repression such as that at Manchester, is "Clothed with the Bible" and represents Hypocrisy.

Shelley's use of "anarchy" is unusual. The word meant the breakdown of law and government and was generally applied to the rule of the masses following a revolution. Its opposite was "despotism," which referred to the dictatorial rule of the military and aristocracy. Inasmuch as in Shelley's poem it is the ruling classes who are in control and are the followers of Anarchy, one might expect the poem to be called *The Mask of Despotism*. Shelley's meaning, however, is that the ruling classes, by blind oppression such as that at Manchester, the introduction of paper money, and the wild escalation of the national debt, are themselves bringing about the anarchic breakdown of law and government. In the grisly procession, Anarchy, "on a white horse, splashed with blood . . . Like Death in the Apocalypse" (31–33), is raised by his groveling followers, the "Destructions," to the position of "GOD, AND KING, AND [ironically] LAW" (37).[12]

> And Anarchy, the Skeleton,
> Bowed and grinned to every one,
> As well as if his education
> Had cost ten millions to the nation.
>
> For he knew the Palaces
> Of our Kings were rightly his;
> His the sceptre, crown, and globe,
> And the gold-inwoven robe. (74–81)

Anarchy seizes control of the "Bank" (economic dislocation through the national debt and paper money) and the "Tower" (the threat of prison for reform leaders), then marches off to meet "his pensioned parliament."

The triumph of Anarchy is about to be completed when "a maniac [i.e., desperate] maid" named Hope throws herself into the path of the ghastly cavalcade. As she is about to be trampled, a mist arises beside her and forms into an airy "Shape," which scatters Anarchy and his followers in a mighty wind of death and destruction:

And Anarchy, the ghastly birth,
Lay dead earth upon the earth;
The Horse of Death, tameless as wind
Fled, and with his hoofs did grind
To dust, the murderers thronged behind. (130–134)

Upon the people, who had so far looked on hopelessly, there descended a new strength, "a sense awakening yet tender." The shape is apparently once more the "benignant power" of *Essay on Christianity*. As in *The Revolt of Islam*, one of its components is love:

On its helm, seen far away,
A planet, like the Morning's, lay. (114–115)

And "arrayed in mail" (110), it stimulates people to libertarian thought (as did the Witch of Atlas):

As flowers beneath May's footsteps waken,
As stars from Night's loose hair are shaken,
As waves arise when loud winds call,
Thoughts sprung where'er that step did fall. (122–125)

A voice is then heard addressing the people (and does so to the end of the poem). It is as if "their own indignant Earth/Which gave the sons of England birth" (139–140) were speaking. A similar representation appeared in *The Revolt of Islam*, where at the beginning of the revolution, before moving into action, the people:

heard the startling cry
Like Earth's own voice lifted unconquerably
To all her children. (IX, iii)

As in the *Masque*, Shelley did not say that the voice *is* the Earth's, only that it is "like" the Earth's. The voice, then, is presumably that of the "power" as inherent in nature.

The third and final section of the poem, containing the speech itself, falls into the two parts of an impassioned analysis of freedom (stanzas 37 to 64), and a call for a national meeting. The first part expresses the same deep sympathy for the working class as does the *Song to the Men of England.*[13] Shelley gives a vivid picture of the slum-huddled proletariat of the early nineteenth century. The indictments are hammered out one by one, in simple but searing verse. The workers are virtually slaves, turned into tools of production, living in a prisonlike hell of poverty and misery:

> " 'Tis to work and have such pay
> As just keeps life from day to day
> In your limbs, as in a cell
> For the tyrants' use to dwell.
>
> So that ye for them are made
> Loom, and plough, and sword, and spade,
> With or without your own will bent
> To their defence and nourishment." (160–167)

The workers are exploited even more than previously by the special burdens of inflation imposed by the "forgery" of "paper coin" (180). If they try to rebel, they are beaten down by armed force, as at Manchester:

> "And at length when ye complain
> With a murmur weak and vain
> 'Tis to see the Tyrant's crew
> Ride over your wives and you—
> Blood is on the grass like dew." (188–192)

Freedom to the worker is not primarily political but economic, not so much the freedom to speak as to eat:

> "Thou art clothes, and fire, and food
> For the trampled multitude." (225–226)

The workers should call meetings of protest—represented here for poetical effect as one vast gathering—to force the hand of the government. If at such a meeting the cavalry charges the people, they are not to resist, for as Shelley put it in *A Philosophical View of Reform* (where he recapitulated the argument of these stanzas), "the soldier is a man and an Englishman," and "this unexpected reception would probably throw him back upon a recollection of the true nature of the measures of which he was made the instrument, and the enemy might be converted into the ally."[14]

The pacifist element in this section of the poem has been exaggerated and sometimes misunderstood. That there is such an element is true:

> "Stand ye calm and resolute,
> Like a forest close and mute,
> With folded arms and looks which are
> Weapons of unvanquished war." (323–326)

It is not, however, the pacifism of the individual conscience, but a pacifism of massive nonviolent resistance, the tactic of Gandhi more than a century before Gandhi (who read and admired the poem).[15] Shelley hoped that such mass actions might break the morale of the troops and bring about fraternization between them and the people:

> "And the bold, true warriors
> Who have hugged Danger in wars
> Will turn to those who would be free,
> Ashamed of such base company." (360–363)

But the closing note of the passage is, in effect, revolutionary without any suggestion of passivity:

> "And these words shall then become
> Like oppression's thundered doom
> Ringing through each heart and brain,
> Heard again—again—again—
>
> "Rise like Lions after slumber
> In unvanquishable number—
> Shake your chains to earth like dew,
> Which in sleep had fallen on you—
> Ye are many—they are few." (368–376)[16]

This is the dominant note, too, of Shelley's other poem on Peterloo, the stirring *Ode to the Assertors of Liberty*:

> Arise, arise, arise!
> There is blood on the earth that denies ye bread;
> Be your wounds like eyes
> To weep for the dead, the dead, the dead.

In the final passage of *The Masque of Anarchy*, as in the conclusion of *A Philosophical View of Reform*, Shelley is torn between his love for the people, his hatred of the ruling class, and his fear that insurrectionary violence, should it fail, would lead to a military dictatorship. He (rather naively) urges the people not to fight the military, but he advocates a massive action that would clearly have had revolutionary consequences.

Peter Bell the Third

There is still a considerable range of opinion on the merits of Wordsworth's *Peter Bell*. Few would argue that it is a great poem, but the older concept that it is virtually doggerel is fading as its psychological insights, sly humor, and narrative skill become more widely appreciated. In its own day, however, it stood virtually no chance for a fair reception. To the large and generally conservative section of the reading public that still adhered to what were basically feudal cultural values—as Wordsworth himself indicated in his 1800 Preface to *Lyrical Ballads*—the fact that it dealt sympathetically with the ordinary life of common people was enough to condemn it, and the liberals and radicals rejected it because they regarded Wordsworth as a political renegade. When *Peter Bell* was announced for publication in the spring of 1819 and was rumored to deal with the religious regeneration of a hardened sinner through a chance meeting with a noble donkey, the wits of all factions prepared for a field day. As early as April 15, Keats wrote to his brother and sister-in-law that his friend, John Hamilton Reynolds (who had been linked with Keats and Shelley in Hunt's "young poets" *Examiner* article in December 1816), "hearing that said Peter Bell was coming out, took it into his head to write a skit upon it called Peter Bell."[17] This skit actually came out about a week before Wordsworth's own poem.[18] In *The Examiner* for April 25, an anonymous review of Reynolds' poem appeared, which is now known to have been written by Keats, and in the next issue (May 2) there was a review of Wordsworth's own *Peter Bell* by Leigh Hunt.[19] Shelley received these reviews at Leghorn, probably in early July, but he apparently did not begin *Peter Bell the Third* until October, when he and Mary had moved from Leghorn to Florence.[20] The indication is that the actual impetus for writing it came from Wordsworth's poem itself.[21]

Keats in his review quoted part of Reynolds' witty burlesque of Wordsworth, of which the following sample is typical:

> 'Tis Peter Bell—'tis Peter Bell,
> Who never stirreth in the day;
> His hand is wither'd—he is old!
> On Sundays he is us'd to pray,
> In winter he is very cold.
>
> I've seen him in the month of August,
> At the wheat-field, hour by hour,
> Picking ear—by ear—by ear,—
> Through wind,—and rain,—and sun,—and shower,
> From year,—to year,—to year.
>
> You never saw a wiser man,
> He knows his Numeration Table;
> He counts the sheep of Harry Gill
> Every night that he is able,
> When the sheep are on the hill.[22]

Shelley, like Reynolds, begins with prefatory material, a Dedication to "Thomas Brown, Esq., the Younger, H. F." As "Thomas Brown" was the name under which Thomas Moore had written his satire *The Fudge Family* the "H.F.," it has been suggested, stands for "Historian of the Fudges" in sarcastic reference to Wordsworth's dedication of *Peter Bell* to "Robert Southey, Esq. P.L." (Poet Laureate).[23] Shelley's Dedication, with its political overtones, indicates an important difference between his poem and Reynolds'. Whereas Reynolds is largely occupied in parodying Wordsworth's style, Shelley is interested in the psychological effect on Wordsworth of abandoning radical and humanitarian views. How strongly Shelley felt on this matter is shown in Mary Shelley's comments:

> He conceived the idealism of a poet—a man of lofty and creative genius—quitting the glorious calling of discovering and announcing the beautiful and good, to support and propagate ignorant prejudices and pernicious errors; imparting to the unenlightened, not that ardour for truth and spirit of toleration which Shelley looked on as the sources of the moral improvement and happiness of mankind; but false and injurious opinions, that evil was good, and that ignorance and force were the best allies of purity and virtue. His idea was that a man gifted even as transcendently as the author of *Peter Bell,* with the highest qualities of genius, must, if he fostered such errors, be infected with dulness.[24]

Shelley himself regarded the poem, in part at least, as a political attack—a "party squib"—on a Tory poet.[25]Although he was aiming at Wordsworth more directly than Mary suggests, he did not mean to attack such earlier poems as *Tintern Abbey,* which was a favorite of his. He had perhaps first become aware of the later Wordsworth's dullness, as had Byron, from reading *The Excursion* in 1814, and it may be that he mainly had this poem in mind in his charge of dullness.

Shelley in his Dedication explains that, having learned of two Peter Bells from *The Examiner*, he has been inspired to add a third: "You know Mr. Examiner Hunt; well—it was he who presented me to two of the Mr. Bells. My intimacy with the younger Mr. Bell naturally sprung from this introduction to his brothers. And in presenting him to you, I have the satisfaction of being able to assure you that he is considerably the dullest of the three." The three Peter Bells, he continues—referring not to the character Peter Bell but to Wordsworth—form a kind of trinity, for all three have in common the basic qualities of treachery, dullness, and royalist reaction:

> There is this particular advantage in an acquaintance with any one of the Peter Bells, that if you know one Peter Bell, you know three Peter Bells; they are not one, but three; not three, but one . . . Peter is a polyhedric Peter, or a Peter with many sides. He changes colours like a chameleon, and his coat like a snake. He is a Proteus of a Peter. He was at first sublime, pathetic, impressive, profound; then dull; then prosy and dull; and now dull—O, so very dull! it is an ultra-legitimate dulness.[26]

In Part One, Peter Bell (Wordsworth himself) is represented as dying and his soul is spirited away to Hell—"a city much like London" (147). Part Two is a sketch of the devil, who in one of his metamorphoses is clearly

Southey—"a bard bartering rhymes/For sack" (83–84).[27] In Part Three, the description of Hell (London) is pithy, direct, and bitter:

> There is a Chancery Court; a King;
>   A manufacturing mob [factory owners]; a set
> Of thieves who by themselves are sent
> Similar thieves to represent;
>   An army; and a public debt. (162–166)

Chastity exists in Hell only by courtesy of the lightning rod of prostitution, and women are ruined by the false values of "gallantry":

> There are mincing women, mewing,
>   (Like cats, who *amant misere,*)
> Of their own virtue, and pursuing
> Their gentler sisters to that ruin,
>   Without which—what were chastity?
>
> Things whose trade is, over ladies
>   To lean, and flirt, and stare, and simper,
> Till all that is divine in woman
> Grows cruel, courteous, smooth, inhuman,
>   Crucified 'twixt a smile and whimper. (182–186, 192–196)

To the first of these stanzas Shelley adds a note: "What would this husk and excuse for a virtue be without its kernal prostitution, or the kernal prostitution without this husk of a virtue? I wonder the women of the town do not form an association, like the Society for the Suppression of Vice, for the support of what may be called the 'King, Church, and Constitution' of their order. But this subject is almost too horrible for a joke."[28] He plays bitterly on the damnation theme, pointing out that the only damnation is on this earth, and arises not, as the church contends, from evil in human nature but from flaws in the social system:

> The rich are damned, beyond all cure,
>   To taunt, and starve, and trample on
> The weak and wretched; and the poor
> Damn their broken hearts to endure
>   Stripe on stripe, with groan on groan. (232–236)

In Part Four Shelley turns more directly to Wordsworth, charging that his prudery gives an air of unnatural restraint even to his nature poetry:

> But from the first 'twas Peter's drift
> To be a kind of moral eunuch,
> He touched the hem of Nature's shift,
> Felt faint—and never dared uplift
> The closest, all-concealing tunic. (313–317)

Part Five treats the beginning of Wordsworth's decline as a poet, a theme developed in Parts Six and Seven. The point is not original with Shelley. Godwin, Hazlitt, Hunt, and Byron had argued that Wordsworth (along with Coleridge and Southey), in going over to the Tories, had declined as a poet. The later Wordsworth lives on as an empty echo of his own past:

And these obscure remembrances
  Stirred such harmony in Peter,
That, whensoever he should please,
He could speak of rocks and trees
  In poetic metre. (418–422)

Having changed his coat, Peter is greeted with enthusiasm by the Tory reviewers, faithful as ever to their master's bidding:

Yet the Reviews, who heaped abuse
  On Peter while he wrote for freedom,
So soon as in his song they spy
The folly which soothes tyranny,
  Praise him, for those who feed 'em. (619–623)

Wordsworth's sanctimonious apology for the slaughter of the Napoleonic Wars in his *Ode, 1815* receives a well-deserved drubbing. Peter is now adopted completely by the upper classes, whereupon a strange disease of dullness suddenly attacks him:

Peter was dull—he was at first
  Dull—oh, so dull—so very dull!
Whether he talked, wrote, or rehearsed—
Still with this dulness was he cursed—
  Dull—beyond all conception—dull. (703–707)

Peter Bell is a jeu d' esprit and, as such, is uneven, as Shelley himself was doubtless aware, but this is a characteristic of the genre.[29] He had an ear for the rollicking effortlessness of the form and combined it in the best stanzas with a neat crispness of phrase. He was able also to achieve a considerable variety of effects, from intellectual satire to slapstick farce. His deep contempt for establishment values and their protagonists is never far from the surface.

Swellfoot the Tyrant

The last, and longest, of Shelley's political poems was *Oedipus Tyrannus; or, Swellfoot the Tyrant,* a dramatic burlesque on George IV and the Liverpool administration. The occasion for the work, was the Queen Caroline scandal. George IV, when prince of Wales, had in 1795 married a German princess, Caroline of Brunswick, activated mainly, according to William Cobbett, by his desire to have a wealthy wife to pay off gambling debts. Catered to by innumerable mistresses (one of whom he had secretly married in 1785), he schemed to get rid of Caroline, who finally in the year 1814 agreed to live abroad. No sooner had she set up house on the Continent than George put spies on her trail to obtain or to falsify evidence of riotous living. In 1818 a committee, known as the Milan Commission, was formed to gather this evidence systematically. The commission hired a group of discharged servants of the queen and collected their testimony in one of the customary containers of legal evidence at the time, a green bag. The members of the commission were Sir John Leach, chairman, who according to Brougham had risen in society "by the art of making himself useful to the powerful and the wealthy," a Colonel Browne, and two lawyers, Cooke and Powell. The farsightedness of George's policy appeared when in 1820 the old King died and Caroline decided to return to claim her rightful place as queen.[30]

From that moment on, confusion reigned. The queen was determined to ascend the throne; the king was equally determined that she should not. The government, with Lord Liverpool as prime minister, supported the king; the people supported the queen—for as an eminent historian drily remarked, the "subjects of the land were in some doubt as to the Queen's character, but in none at all about the king's." The queen's progress from the seacoast to London turned into a triumphal procession. According to *The Examiner*, she was cheered at every step of her way by tumultous crowds, the women crying out, "God bless her . . . she must be innocent!" and the men unharnessing the horses from her carriage and pulling it through the flag-decked streets.[31]

On June 6, Castlereagh laid the green bag before the House of Commons, and Liverpool did the same in the House of Lords. On June 7, Castlereagh stated the administration's position in a speech reported by *The Examiner* of June 11, where it was read and made use of by Shelley. Castlereagh expressed surprise, according to *The Examiner*, that the ministers "should be suspected of a design or wish to deprive an accused person of all those safeguards, which in this country, where the laws were more purely administered than in *any other nation upon earth*, the Legislature had provided!" He therefore proposed the establishment of a secret committee to investigate the evidence against the queen, "on the grounds of decorum and justice, . . . not in order to fetter or bias the judgement of the House, but to do the duty of a Grand Jury." The queen's method of appealing "to the lowest orders of the people," Castlereagh felt, was to be deprecated. He hoped that she would stop being advised by people who wished to "make this question the means of agitating the public tranquility at present imperfectly restored [i.e., after the Peterloo agitation]." *The Examiner* was bitter in its denunciation of the tactics of the king and warm in its newfound loyalty to the queen: "An animal . . . sets itself down, month after month, at Milan to watch the doors and windows, to intercept discarded servants and others who knew what deposition might be worth, and thus to gather poison for one of those venemous Green Bags, which have so long infected and nauseated the people, and are now to infect the QUEEN." In the June 25 issue, *The Examiner* carried an account of Sir Francis Burdett's defense of the Queen: "He believed the Green Bag was as false as it was filthy." But the queen was not afraid: "With a royal spirit she exclaimed, 'Proceed! spatter me with filth at your own discretion. I proudly retort your charges upon yourself . . . I defy you.' "[32]

Not only Burdett and *The Examiner* but the reformers in general flocked to the defense of the queen, her greatest champion being the leader of the radical reformers, William Cobbett, whose *Political Register* carried on an even more extreme agitation than *The Examiner*, and whose *History of the Regency and Reign of King George the Fourth* contains the most lively and comprehensive account of the case. Political satirists and cartoonists had a field day. Hundreds of pamphlets and broadsides were issued, the best of them by the master craftsman of the genre, William Hone. In many of these appeared the same dramatic personae—a rat, a leech—and the same paraphernalia—the green bag and swine—as in *Swellfoot the Tyrant*. Whether Shelley, in Italy, saw any of them before composing his play is not known.[33] Similar productions on the affairs of the royal couple had been common for several years, inspiring, for example, Keat's *The Cap and Bells*.[34] To one of these earlier works, published in *The Examiner* on August 30, 1818, Shelley seems to have been directly indebted, namely a skit entitled *A New Catechism*. In it the radical image of the people as wretched swine (taken from Burke's "swinish multitude," and applied in Thomas Spence's *Pig's Meat*) was further developed:

Q. What is your name?—A. Hog or Swine.

Did God make you a hog?—No! God made me man in his own image; the Right *Honourable* Sublime and Beautiful made me a Swine.

How did he make you a swine?—By muttering uncouth words and dark spells: he is a dealer in the black art.

Who feeds you?—Our drivers, the only *real men* in the County.

How many hogs are you in all?—Seven or eight millions.

How many drivers?—Two or three hundred thousand.

With what do they feed you?—Generally with husks, swill, draft, malt-grains; now and then with a few potatoes; and when they have too much butter-milk for themselves, they spare us some.

What are your occupations?—To be yoked to the plough; to do all hard work; for which purpose we still, as you see, retain enough of our original form, speech, and reason, to carry our drivers on our shoulders, or draw them in carriages.[35]

Shelley perceived, as did Cobbett and other reformers, that the question had long ceased to be primarily a personal one between the king and the queen. But unlike Cobbett, he was no partisan of the queen and hoped only that her situation might help to bring down the Tory administration and advance the cause of parliamentary reform: "My only hope is that the mistake into which the ministers have fallen will precipitate them into ruin."[36] It was in this hope that he penned *Swellfoot the Tyrant* and sent it to Horace Smith for publication.[37] The authorities, however, knew just as well as did Shelley the kind of impact his work might have, and after only seven copies had been sold, all the remaining issue was burned at the demand of the Society for the Suppression of Vice. The story is told by Horace Smith:

> Scarcely had it appeared in the bookseller's window, when a burly alderman called upon me on the part of "The Society for the Suppression of Vice," to demand the name of the author, in order that he might be prosecuted for a seditious and disloyal libel. On my denying its liability to this accusation, and refusing to disclose the writer's name, I was angrily apprised, that unless I consented to give up the whole impression to the Society, an action would instantly be commenced against the publisher, who stood by the side of the alderman in deep tribulation of spirit. To save an innocent man from fine and imprisonment, and the chance of ultimate ruin, I submitted to this insolent dictation of the Society, and made holocaust of "Swellfoot the Tyrant" at the Inquisition Office, in Bridge Street, Blackfriars.[38]

The opening of the play exposes—in a tone of savage burlesque—the horrors of slum exploitation. Swellfoot (George IV) has come to worship in the Temple of Famine—"A Magnificent Temple, built of thigh-bones and death's-heads." He is interrupted by a chorus of swine, whose presence he has failed to note:

> Alas! the Pigs are an unhappy nation!
> Now if your Majesty would have our bristles
> To bind your mortar with, or fill our colons
> With rich blood, or make brawn out of our gristles,
> In policy—ask else your royal Solons—
> You ought to give us hog-wash and clean straw,
> And sties well thatched; besides it is the law!
>
> *Swellfoot.* This is sedition, and rank blasphemy!
> Ho! there, my guards! (I, 63–71)

At Swellfoot's command, a guard summons Solomon, the court porkman, Moses, the sow-gelder, and Zephaniah, the hog-butcher (representing Malthus and his followers, who advocated the sterilization of the poor). As the pigs dash out, pursued by these three, in come Mammon, "the Arch Priest" (Liverpool, the prime minister), and Purganax, "Chief of the Council of Wizards" (Castlereagh, the foreign secretary). Purganax has a sense of impending doom:

> There's something rotten in us—for the level
> Of the State slopes, its very bases topple,
> The boldest turn their backs upon themselves! (I, 102–104)

Mammon answers with cavalier cynicism:

> Why what's the matter, my dear fellow, now?
> Do the troops mutiny?—decimate some regiments;
> Does money fail?—come to my mint—coin paper. (I, 105–107)

Purganax answers that the situation is complicated by the fact that Mammon once uttered an "oracle" to the effect that when their queen returned, Boeotia would have to choose between "reform or civil war"; and oracles were popularly supposed to be fulfiled. Purganax contends that the queen must be kept away. To accomplish this, he has hired a leech, a gadfly, and a rat (the Milan commission of Leach, Cooke, and Browne), whom he now summons. The leech sings:

> I will suck
> Blood or muck!
> The disease of the state is a plethory,
> Who so fit to reduce it as I? (264–267)

Their songs are interrupted by the entrance of Swellfoot, who announces in panic that the queen has returned. He calls for General Laoctonos (the Duke of Wellington, who with Castlereagh represented the king in negotiations with the queen's advisors). The general comes in, accompanied by Dakry (Lord Eldon, the lord chancellor, who was to preside at the trial). As in *The Masque of Anarchy*, Shelley plays up Eldon's hypocritical weeping:

> And how I loved the Queen!—and then I wept
> With the pathos of my own eloquence. (336–337)

Now that the queen has actually arrived, Mammon proposes a new scheme. He exhibits a green bag filled with poison collected by the leech, the gadfly, and the rat, and sealed up by "Fraud, Who is the Devil's Lord High Chancellor" (again Eldon). He suggests that they persuade the pigs of the "Public Sty" (the House of Commons) that the bag will really reveal innocence and that for this purpose it should be poured over the queen. Purganax (Castlereagh) is given the task of thus persuading the pigs.[39]

The second act opens with Purganax's speech, which was clearly suggested by Castlereagh's address to the House on June 6 (reported in *The Examiner* on June 11). Like Castlereagh, Purganax compliments the "Boars" (members of the House) on the glories of their country (whose laws, said Castlereagh, were more purely administered than in "any other nation on earth"). Purganax argues that all is going well owing to the excellent policies of the government: the decline in foreign trade is small; the national debt is increasing gloriously and hence enriching the upper classes; the lower classes, though somewhat impoverished, are only temporarily so; and as for those who oppose the government, they have been beaten into subjection. The speech is a skillful takeoff on political sanctimoniousness, accurately catching the manners and rhythms of parliamentary oratory (Shelley's father was a member of Parliament and Shelley had visited the House of Commons with him).

Act II opens:

SCENE I.—*The Public Sty. The* BOARS *in full Assembly.*
Enter PURGANAX.

Purganax. Grant me your patience, Gentlemen and Boars,
Ye, by whose patience under public burthens
The glorious constitution of these sties
Subsists, and shall subsist. The lean-pig rates
Grow with the growing populace of swine,
The taxes, that true source of piggishness
(How can I find a more appropriate term
To include religion, morals, peace, and plenty,
And all that fit Boeotia as a nation
To teach the other nations how to live?)
Increase with piggishness itself; and still
Does the revenue, that great spring of all
The patronage, and pensions, and by-payments,
Which free-born Pigs regard with jealous eyes,
Diminish, till at length, by glorious steps,
All the land's produce will be merged in taxes,
And the revenue will amount to—nothing!
The failure of a foreign market for
Sausages, bristles, and blood-puddings,
And such home manufactures, is but partial;
And, that the population of the pigs,
Instead of hog-wash, has been fed on straw
And water, is a fact which is—you know—
That is—it is a state necessity—
Temporary, of course. Those impious Pigs,
Who, by frequent squeaks, have dared impugn
The settled Swellfoot system, or to make
Irreverent mockery of the genuflexions
Inculcated by the arch-priest, have been whipt
Into a loyal and an orthodox whine.

Purganax goes on to say that he wants only to be fair to the queen and hence is presenting them with a green bag containing a magic fluid which, if poured over anyone, will reveal guilt or innocence. (Castlereagh had presented the green bag to the House of Commons.) When an "honorable Boar" shouts that green is an evil color, the color of jealousy and of scorpions, Purganax suavely replies:

Honourable swine,
In piggish souls can prepossessions reign?
Allow me to remind you, grass is green—
All flesh is grass;—no bacon but is flesh—
Ye are but bacon.

In the midst of the discussion a large number of pigs break in, followed by the queen, Iona Taurina—Joan Bull.[40] The queen alone, of course, and not the public, appeared in the House of Commons; Shelley simply means that the popular power, as expressed in mass demonstrations that sometimes numbered as many as 30,000, was felt in Parliament.[41] To the relief of Purganax, the queen agrees to the test of the green bag.

In the final scene, the action takes on a grimmer tone. In the earlier scenes Shelley was interested mainly in exposing the duplicity and unscrupulousness of the Tories. Now his theme (as in *A Philosophical View of Reform*) is that England faces the alternative of despotism or revolution. The opening chorus of priests of Famine paints a bitter, psychologically acute picture of the autocratic ruling class, with its self-centered, cynical smugness, and its hard brutality. The scene opens:

> SCENE II.—*The interior of the Temple of* FAMINE. *The statue of the Goddess, a skeleton clothed in parti-coloured rags, seated upon a heap of skulls and loaves intermingled. A number of exceedingly fat Priests in black garments arrayed on each side, with marrow-bones and cleavers in their hands.* SOLOMON *the Court Porkman. A flourish of trumpets.*
> *Enter* MAMMON *as arch-priest,* SWELLFOOT, DAKRY, PURGANAX, LAOCTONOS, *followed by* IONA TAURINA *guarded. On the other side enter the* SWINE.
>
> *Chorus of* PRIESTS, *accompanied by the* COURT PORKMAN *on Marrow-bones and cleavers.*
> Goddess bare, and gaunt, and pale,
> Empress of the world, all hail!
> What though Cretans old called thee
> City-crested Cybele?
> We call thee FAMINE!
> Goddess of fasts and feasts, starving and cramming!
> Through thee, for emperors, kings, and priests and lords,
> Who rule by viziers, sceptres, bank-notes, words,
> The earth pours forth its plenteous fruits,
> Corn, wool, linen, flesh, and roots—
> Those who consume these fruits through thee grow fat,
> Those who produce these fruits through thee grow lean,
> Whatever change takes place, oh, stick to that!
> And let things be as they have ever been.

In contrast comes the chorus of swine (the common people). They, too, thank Famine, not, however, like the priests (the rulers), for ensuring the continuance of rule, but for representing the force that will drive them to the revolutionary seizure of power:

Hail to thee, hail to thee, Famine!
  Thy throne is on blood, and thy robe is of rags;
Thou devil which livest on damning;
  Saint of new churches, and cant, and GREEN BAGS,
Till in pity and terror thou risest,
Confounding the schemes of the wisest.
When thou liftest thy skeleton form,
  When the loaves and the skulls roll about,
We will greet thee—the voice of a storm
  Would be lost in our terrible shout!

This matches the peasant vision of Thomas Spence in his *Constitution of a Perfect Commonwealth*—the vision that Shelley reiterated, warningly, in *A Philosphical View of Reform:* "the immediate abolition, for instance, of monarchy and aristocracy, and the levelling of inordinate wealth, and an agrarian distribution, including the parks and chases of the rich, or the uncultivated districts of the country."[42] But despite all his sympathy with the ultimate establishment of an egalitarian state, Shelley did not wish a mass revolution to take place, although—so intense was his hatred of the Tory aristocracy—he was prepared to support it if it did. He still hoped that the road to the third alternative, reform, was not yet closed, and this hope he expresses in the appearance of *"a graceful figure in a semi-transparent veil,"* called Liberty, who comes up to expostulate with the hideous goddess, Famine:

            by thy dread self, O Famine!
I charge thee! when thou wake the multitude,
Thou lead them not upon the paths of blood.
The earth did never mean her foizon
For those who crown life's cup with poison
Of fanatic rage and meaningless revenge—
  But for those radiant spirits, who are still
The standard-bearers in the van of Change.
  Be they th' appointed stewards, to fill
The lap of Pain, and Toil, and Age!—
Remit, O Queen! thy accustom'd rage!
Be what thou art not! In voice faint and low
FREEDOM calls *Famine,* her eternal foe,
To brief alliance, hollow truce.—Rise now! (II, ii, 90–103)

For this Liberty-Famine scene Shelley was indebted to the conclusion of the young Coleridge's *Letter of Liberty to Her Dear Friend Famine* in the *Conciones ad populum* volume (1795), and perhaps assumed that his more literate readers would perceive the reference. Coleridge's argument was that unless the rulers of England changed to more liberal policies, they would be overwhelmed by the forces of revolution generated by economic distress (famine). Liberty concluded her letter:

Thus baffled and friendless, I was about to depart, and stood a fearful lingerer on the Isle, which I had so dearly loved—when tidings were brought me of *your* approach. I found myself impelled by a power superior to me to build my last hopes on you.—Liberty, the MOTHER OF PLENTY, calls Famine to her aid. O FAMINE, most eloquent Goddess! plead thou my cause. I meantime will pray fervently that Heaven may unseal the ears of its vicegerents, to that they may listen to your first pleadings, *while yet your voice is faint and distant,* and your counsels peaceable.[43]

Following the grimly powerful scene in the Temple of Famine, the action reverts to burlesque as the queen seizes the green bag and splatters her enemies with it, whereupon they turn into "filthy and ugly animals" and rush out. The figure of John Bull arises as the pigs, metamorphosed into bulls, pursue Swellfoot and his accomplices out of the temple. The final scene represents the hope of the reformers that Queen Caroline would be able to turn the lying testimony of the "mangy" Milan Commission witnesses against the Tories, and that the people of England would regain their self-respect in the old John Bull tradition and overturn the administration.

Swellfoot the Tyrant is, like *The Masque of Anarchy,* fundamentally revolutionary. Shelley may have feared mass insurrection, but he nevertheless wanted to see the world of the Castlereaghs and Wellingtons, with its war, poverty, oppression, and exploitation, utterly eliminated. He had no interest in tinkering with the top of the structure. The people would take over—hopefully guided by enlightened intellectuals and reform leaders—and in time would build a new world, the world of Promethean egalitarianism. This expectation enabled Shelley to observe the present with greater understanding and to see the extent of its destruction of the human potential. The masses, kept ignorant and made desperate by a corrupt society, had the capacity within them for humanitarian love and creativity in all fields. This knowledge made the actuality almost unbearable to Shelley. As he said of prostitution, the subject was too horrible for jest. And in *Swellfoot the Tyrant,* while there is savage indignation, hatred, and compassion, there is little laughter. It pictures the age as a hell of human misery and brutality, divided between a cynical ruling class and an exploited mass. If knowledge of the distortion of the potential in the past and present gives depth to the scene, the certainty of future emancipation gives it perspective—a perspective not found in Byron, Hazlitt, or Hunt, all of whom believed, of course, that eventually the "king-times" would vanish, but believed also that inequality would remain and human nature would ever be what it had been. To think otherwise was to "talk Utopia." It was this outlook that enabled Byron to laugh over what made Shelley only suffer, and to ridicule upper class follies which to Shelley seemed irrelevant. *Swellfoot* exposes a depth of social reality not revealed in the brilliant panorama of *Don Juan* nor, indeed, elsewhere in the literature of the age.

10

The Lightning of the Nations

Ode to Liberty. Ode to Naples. Hellas

It is not difficult to see why Shelley characterized the period from the defeat of the French Revolution to the Congress of Vienna as an "age of despair."[1] Seldom had an international outlook seemed blacker. With the defeat of Napoleon, reaction reigned from one end of Europe to the other. In Russia, czarist autocracy continued unchallenged (the Decembrist revolt did not come until 1825); in France, the Bourbons were restored with the blessings of the British government; King Ferdinand had returned to Spain, and with him returned the Inquisition; Germany was split into petty duchies, each ruled by a medieval autocrat; the numerous kingdoms of disjointed Italy had become, directly or indirectly, "client" states of Metternich's Austria; and in England the Tory administration of Liverpool and Castlereagh was solidly entrenched. Yet such diverse British liberal and radical thinkers as Byron, Blake, Leigh Hunt, William Cobbett, Richard Carlile, and Thomas Jonathan Wooler felt that this suppression of progress was temporary and that in spite of the brave words of the chieftains of the Quadruple Alliance, the peoples of Europe would rise again. None of them held to this view more confidently than Shelley. As there were in the first years after the Congress of Vienna few specific events to which he could point to justify this perspective he expressed it as a future "beau ideal" in *The Revolt of Islam* in 1817 and in *Prometheus Unbound* in 1819.

It was in 1820 that the first cracks appeared in Metternich's *festung Europa*. In January, revolution broke out in Spain; in February, the Bourbon duc de Berri, nephew to the king, was assassinated in Paris; in July, a revolutionary war against Austria began in the kingdom of Naples; then came an uprising in Piedmont; and in August, revolution broke out in Portugal. In England the Cato Street Conspiracy had shaken the Liverpool cabinet, and hard on its heels came the Queen Caroline affair. In the spring of 1821 Continental events rose to a climax when Greece, then part of the Turkish Empire, began a national revolutionary war which was successful after eight years of bitter struggle. Shelley was quick to perceive in these events a confirmation of his historical extrapolation, and he responded with three poems on the three most important of them: the *Ode to Liberty* on the Spanish revolution; the *Ode to Naples* on the Neapolitan revolution; and *Hellas* on the Greek war for independence. One of Shelley's main sources for all three poems was *The Examiner*, and for the modern reader it is also the most valuable background source, because it not only related the events as they actually happened but held views similar to Shelley's.

Ode to Liberty

After the re-establishment of the Spanish monarchy at the point of British muskets in 1814, the liberties that the people had secured during the Napoleonic regime were withdrawn. The press was muzzled, liberals were jailed or exiled, the Jesuits (who had been banished in the eighteenth century) were brought back, and King Ferdinand issued a proclamation abolishing the constitution. Shelley, however, was convinced that beneath the surface, revolutionary forces were stirring—as he demonstrated in *A Philosophical View of Reform*:

In Spain and in the dependencies of Spain good and evil in the forms of Despair and Tyranny are struggling foot to foot. That great people have been delivered bound hand and foot to be trampled upon and insulted by a traitorous and sanguinary tyrant . . . the persons who have thus delivered them were that hypocritical knot of conspiring tyrants, who proceeded upon the credit they gained by putting down the only tyrant among them who was not a hypocrite, to undertake the administration of those *arrondissements* of consecrated injustice and violence which they deliver to those who the nearest resemble them under the name of the "kingdoms of the earth" . . . Those men of understanding, integrity, and courage who rescued their country from one tyrant are exiled from it by his successor and his enemy and their legitimate king. Tyrants, however they may squabble among themselves, have common friends and foes. The taxes are levied at the point of the sword. Armed insurgents occupy all the defensible mountains of the country. The dungeons are peopled thickly, and persons of every sex and age have the fibres of their frame torn by subtle torments . . . These events, in the present condition of the understanding and sentiment of mankind, are the rapidly passing shadows, which forerun successful insurrection, the ominous comets of our republican poet perplexing great monarchs with fear of change. Spain, having passed through an ordeal severe in proportion to the wrongs and errors which it is kindled to erase must of necessity be renovated. [The country which] producd Calderon and Cervantes, what else did it but breathe, thro the tumult of the despotism and superstition which invested them, the prophecy of a glorious consummation.[2]

In January 1820, Shelley's prediction became reality. Revolt broke out among soldiers who were to be shipped to South America to subdue the insurgent Spanish colonists. Led by General Raphael Reigo and supported by the antifeudal middle class, the movement spread. In March, Ferdinand agreed to recall the Cortes and to re-establish the constitution. On July 9 the Cortes was convened. It was a great and practically bloodless triumph.

The Examiner gave its readers excited, detailed reports. On March 26 the lead article, "Spanish Insurrection Triumphant," began: "We have most heartily to congratulate our readers, and every body of sense and feeling throughout the world, upon the final, irrepressible rise of Spanish Liberty." With one eye clearly cocked at the English Tories, it announced the results of the revolution: all men who could read and write had the franchise, parliaments were to be elected every two years, no governmental officers could hold seats in parliament, and representation was to be proportional to the division of the population—all demands of the English reformers.[3]

Shelley's enthusiasm was such that he thought of emigrating to Spain: "Much stress is laid upon a still more southern climate for my health, which has suffered dreadfully this winter, and if I could believe that Spain would be effectual, I might possibly be tempted to make a voyage thither, on account of the glorious events of which it is at this moment the theatre. You know my passion for a republic, or anything which approaches it."[4] Late in June he included a tribute to the revolution, in *Letter to Maria Gisborne* (Mrs. Gisborne had taught him Spanish):

> Or how I, wisest lady! then indued
> The language of a land which now is free,
> And winged with thoughts of truth and majesty,
> Flits round the tyrant's sceptre like a cloud,
> And bursts the peopled prisons, and cries aloud,
> "My name is Legion!" (175–180)

It was probably early in July that he composed the *Ode to Liberty*.[5] He saw in the Spanish revolution the first important break in the counterrevolutionary dam of the Quadruple Alliance, perhaps signifying that the movement begun by the American and French Revolutions was about to resume with renewed force. This feeling for the possible implications of the Spanish Revolution rather than the revolution itself forms the substance of the *Ode to Liberty*. This note is struck immediately. The first stanza hails the Spanish Revolution as a "contagious" force, a fire destined to spread throughout Europe:

> A glorious people vibrated again
> The lightning of the Nations: Liberty,
> From heart to heart, from tower to tower, o'er Spain,
> Scattering contagious fire into the sky,
> Gleamed. (1–5)

The poet is then seized by a power, a "voice out of the Deep" (15), like the "wind" of inspiration in *A Defence of Poetry*, and he records its words.

After this introductory emphasis on Spain, the ode begins to trace the history of humanity's long struggle for liberty. In the earliest societies (the stage of "savagery" noted in *A Defence of Poetry*) humanity existed in a brutal state: "beasts warr'd on beasts . . . And men on men; each heart was as a hell of storms" (29–30). As in his prose works, Shelley exhibits no faith in a primitive "golden age." He moves next to Egypt and other early empires with their "human living multitude" of slaves exploited by "Anarchs and priests, who feed on gold and blood" (33, 36, 43). Then came the early dawnings of liberty in Homeric Greece:

like unfolded flowers beneath the sea,
Like the man's thought dark in the infant's brain. (54–55)

These early stirrings led to the culture of Athens, a culture that arose not from a chance conglomeration of genius but—in accordance with Shelley's theory of historical and cultural development—from the liberterian nature of Athenian democracy:

For thou [liberty] wert, and thine all-creative skill
Peopled, with forms that mock [represent] the eternal dead
In marble immortality, that hill
Which was thine earliest throne and latest oracle. (72–75)

Athens continues to live on as an indestructible inspiration to humanity:

Within the surface of Time's fleeting river
Its wrinkled image lies, as then it lay
Immovably unquiet, and for ever
It trembles, but it cannot pass away! (76–79)[6]

These lines are not, as some have thought, Platonic. Shelley is simply saying, in metaphorical language, that the culture of Athens has continued in the minds of men, in the "time" sequences of history, not in a mystic One. He is repeating and developing the thought of the previous stanza. The culture of Athens, having been created by a democratic society, embodies the antireligious, antidictatorial philosophy of such a society, and that philosophy has inspired mankind through the ages:

The voices of thy bards and sages thunder
With an earth-awakening blast
Through the caverns of the past;
Religion veils her eyes; Oppression shrinks aghast. (80–83)

In prose, Shelley might have modified the sentiment. He believed that Plato's arguments in favor of immortality had assisted the spread of Christian theological delusions, and he was aware that Athens, though a democracy, was also a slave state. But he felt that on the whole Athens had been a progressive influence, the source of egalitarian and anticlerical concepts, and of a new beauty in art and literature.

The ode next provides a poetical counterpart of the first chapter of *A Philosophical View of Reform,* with a sketch of the historical struggle between liberty and despotism from the days of the Roman Empire on. As in the opening of *A Philosophical View,* Shelley condemns the Rome of the empire, "profaned" by "gold" and ruled by "the senate of the tyrants" (100, 102), and laments the Dark Ages dominated by the medieval church, "the Galilean serpent" (119), which reduced civilization to an "indistinguishable heap." This tyranny was first challenged by King Alfred (an idea perhaps drawn from Leigh Hunt, who was something of a champion of Alfred) and then by the Italian city-states, which "frowned" above the "tempestuous sea / Of kings, and priests, and slaves, in tower-crowned majesty" (127–128). As Shelley wrote in *A Philosophical View*, the "republics and municipal Governments of Italy opposed for some time a systematic and effectual resistance to the all-surrounding tyranny." Outside the city walls raged the "multitudinous anarchy" (129) of feudalism and its church.[7]

After Florence and the other Italian city-states had fallen, the next advance came with the Reformation:

> Luther caught thy wakening glance:
> Like lightning, from his leaden lance
> Reflected, it dissolved the visions of the trance
> In which, as in a tomb, the nations lay. (141–144)

It might seem surprising, in view of Shelley's anticlerical views, that he would speak thus of Luther, but Shelley made distinctions between different religions and their social effects at different times. He believed that the Reformation, though "imperfect," had assisted the cause of liberty by cracking the feudal monolith of the Catholic Church—the "most oppressive form of the Christian religion"; yet he was not really an admirer of Luther. Luther's thought was marked by "rudeness and acrimony" rather than by "boldness" or originality.[8] His lance was "leaden."

From the Continent the Reformation spread to England, where it was taken up by "England's prophets" (145), including the "spirit-sighted" (148) Milton. Afterward came the "night" (150) of the Restoration in England and general reaction on the Continent. But even then the powers of liberty, though repressed, were gathering to strike again:

> The eager hours and unreluctant years
>   As on a dawn-illumined mountain stood,
> Trampling to silence their loud hopes and fears,
>   Darkening each other with their multitude,
> And cried aloud, Liberty! (151–155)

The metaphor is that of the "hours" of future freedom struggling to be born. Shelley conveys a sense of the immensity of the coming movement: "Darkening each other with their multitude." Finally, release comes when "desolation" calls upon "the destroyer" (158) to save the world, and the new era of revolution begins. The "destroyer" in this context can only mean necessity, the power that destroys the old order. The thought is that revolution is made inevitable by the "desolation" of war, dictatorship, and exploitation. British oppression of the American colonies gave birth to revolutionary war, French feudal dictatorship to revolution. The American Revolution first shattered the darkness of the long night that succeeded the destruction of the English Commonwealth:

as if day had cloven the skies
At dreaming midnight o'er the western wave,
Men started, staggering with a glad surprise,
Under the lightnings of thine unfamiliar eyes. (162–165)

France, driven to violent revolution by the feudal monarchy and the church—"Destruction's sceptered slaves, and Folly's mitred brood" (173)—had suffered reverses in the regimes of Napoleon and the restored Bourbons. Shelley's feelings on Napoleon were somewhat mixed. He was a tyrant—"the military project of government of the great tyrant"—and a ruthless militarist:

Napoleon's fierce spirit rolled
In terror, and blood, and gold,
A torrent of ruin to death from his birth.[9]

But Shelley also felt that Napoleon was superior to the rulers of the Quadruple Alliance—"one, like them, but mightier far than they" (174)—and gave some measure of liberty to the previously feudal nations of Europe: "The Anarch of thine [Liberty's] own bewildered powers" (174–175).

Turning to the contemporary scene, Shelley notes that the Spanish Revolution has already borne fruit in the revolutions in Naples and Sicily ("From Pithecusa to Pelorus"—185), but England "yet sleeps" (181) and fails to fulfill her heritage of libertarian struggle:

Her chains are threads of gold, she need but smile
And they dissolve; but Spain's were links of steel,
Till bit to dust, by virtue's keenest file. (189–191)

Hope lies in America—"in the dim West" (194)—by which Shelley may refer not only to the United States but also to Latin America, whose new "republics" he hailed in *A Philosophical View of Reform.* By "threads of gold" for England but "chains of steel" for Spain, he means that as Spain was a feudal dictatorship, liberty could be achieved only through revolution, but as England was at least a partial democracy, fuller freedom could be achieved by reform.

Shelley next invokes revolt in the peoples of "King-deluded" (201) Germany and Italy—"island of eternity" (206—home of works of eternal value). He then turns to a general attack on the forces of reaction in the contemporary world:

O that the free would stamp the impious name
Of KING into the dust! or write it there,
So that this blot upon the page of fame
Were as a serpent's path, which the light air
Erases, and the flat sands close behind! (211–215)

When Shelley sent the poem to Peacock to give to his publishers, he felt that it might be necessary to substitute asterisks for some of these "expressions," and Peacock duly substituted four asterisks for KING. When the reviewer in the Tory *Quarterly Review* quoted the lines, however, he put in six asterisks instead of four, in order to imply, as Hunt pointed out in *The Examiner*, that the omitted word was "Christ" and not "King."[10]

If man could see through the deceptions of religion and its "Priests," (228) he would stand before his real "Lord" (240), the "unknown" (233) power that runs through both nature and society. Shelley next strikes a note of hope for the future, in spite of the restrictions of the present:

He who taught man to vanquish whatsoever
  Can be between the cradle and the grave
Crowned him the King of Life. O vain endeavour!
  If on his own high will a willing slave,
He has enthroned the oppression and the oppressor.
    What if earth can clothe and feed
    Amplest millions at their need,
And power in thought be as the tree within the seed? (241–248)

The "He" at the beginning of this stanza either refers back to the "Lord" of the proceeding stanza—i.e., Man's own powers have shown him how to control the social and natural world through science and art—or, more likely, it is used in an indefinite sense, meaning "whoever." (If the first reading is correct, there should be commas after "He" and "grave.") If only the truth, now a "seed" in the human mind, could come to fruition, the end of the old order would be in sight. But in the modern world, although man has the potential to "feed" and "clothe" the millions of the earth and to achieve an egalitarian society, he does not do so, for he has created a social order which dams up this potential. This situation, as Shelley indicated in *A Philosophical View of Reform*, will be changed by social movements and the ideas connected with them. In the poem Shelley is more succinct, as well as more aesthetically oriented, than in the tract, and as in *Julian and Maddalo*—"it is our will/That thus enchains us to permitted ill" (170–171)—he emphasizes the intellectual side.

Shelley urges "Liberty" to lead "Wisdom" to abolish economic inequality: "life's ill-apportioned lot" (263). In this task humanity will be aided by the traditions of struggle in the past and by a social philosophy that anticipates the coming egalitarian order:

                                        the Fame
Of what has been, the Hope of what will be. (264–265)

The final stanza returns to the "Power" of the first. This power (as in the *Hymn*) is like an external force, which has entered the poet's mind to enlist him in its service. Having done so, it departs, leaving him exhausted but realizing that, although he may die, the necessitarian power will continue.

Shelley's verse has sometimes been criticized as being "thin" or "shrill." Such criticisms, usually aimed at an isolated passage or a single lyric, often turn out to be based more on ideological differences than on aesthetics. To the conservative, ideas that he dislikes can easily seem "thin." But it would be impossible to sustain such a charge against *Ode to Liberty* even if argued solely on the basis of style, for the ode clearly has power and dignity. It rolls with a magnificent, organlike crescendo through the central movement of the rise of liberty in the past to the final upsurge of its projection into the future. One can see why the humanitarian John Stuart Mill, when he read it aloud to his friends, was moved to tears.

Ode to Naples

On July 2, 1820, only a week before the climax of the Spanish revolution in the convening of the Cortes, a revolt broke out in the kingdom of the Two Sicilies—the state of Naples plus the island of Sicily. This revolution was, in one sense, more significant than that in Spain, for the kingdom of the Two Sicilies was a puppet state of a major power, Austria. Its king, Ferdinand IV, had made a secret agreement with Metternich to effect no changes not approved by him for the administration of his "Italian provinces." The revolt, led by General Guglielmo Pepe and supported mainly by the upper classes, spread rapidly. On July 7 Ferdinand, following the example of his uncle, Ferdinand of Spain, proclaimed a constitution. On October 1, a national parliament was opened, and by January 30 it had drawn up the new constitution. But these initial successes were deceptive. Even as the constitution was being formulated, events were developing that were to break the new national power.

The people of Sicily refused to accept the new constitution and demanded the restoration of the more liberal constitution of 1812, which they had obtained under British influence. The Neapolitan government sent an army into Sicily to bring the Sicilians into line; and the strange spectacle arose of the kingdom of Naples fighting for its freedom against Austria and at the same time attempting to subordinate Sicily. Then in October Metternich summoned a meeting of monarchs at Troppeau to decide on action against the Italian rebels; in January, the meeting shifted to Laibach to be nearer the actual scene of events, and on February 5 the Austrian armies invaded Italy. On March 7, General Pepe was defeated at Rieti. On May 9, Ferdinand returned to his throne, the Jesuits were recalled to take over the educational system, and the works of Voltaire and Rousseau were publicly burned. The revolution had been crushed.

The spirit of enthusiasm that swept the liberal world at the outbreak in Naples was reflected in *The Examiner*. This new revolution, coming so hard upon that in Spain, might, it was hoped, be the signal for a general European revolt against the powers of the Quadruple Alliance. On July 23, *The Examiner* rejoiced that "the Revolution in Spain has been succeeded by a Revolution in Naples. We thought Prussia would go next"; and it reported the duc de Richelieu's statement that "all Italy is preparing for an explosion." On July 30 it ran a lead article, "Neapolitan Revolution": "But what a poor figure the Kings of Spain and Naples make! . . . The King of Prussia will infallibly have to go through the same course of dishes. We expect to hear of it every day. So will the King of Sardinia; so will the Emperor of Austria, or his successor . . . The fire is kindled; it warms the nations; they are interested in seeing it spread; and who shall say where it will stop?" Following this the article quoted twenty-eight lines from Shelley's *Lines Written among the Euganean Hills*, to the effect that the spark of revolution would grow into a European holocaust—though without mentioning Shelley's name, as Hunt apparently feared that he might alienate some of his more conventional readers by identifying the radical, "atheist" author. In succeeding issues, the editors noted the alarming preparations of the monarchs at Troppeau and Laibach for the invasion: "the Allied Ruffians are conscious that their repulse would be the signal for an universal struggle on the continent, which would only end in the total destruction of the 'monarchical principle.' " When the invasion began, they watched, heartsick with anxiety: "We feel the approach of the Austrians as if they were against our own homes." But not until the very end did they lose hope that the Neapolitans would hold out.[11]

Shelley, living in Tuscany, just to the north of these stirring events, followed them with "breathless interest," as Medwin reported. Deep though his sympathy for Naples was, however, when he heard of the July outbreak in Sicily, he supported the people of Sicily against the Neapolitans: "There are bad news from Palermo—the soldiers resisted the people, and a terrible slaughter amounting it is said to 4000 men, ensued. The event [conclusion] however was as it should be—Sicily like Naples is free."[12] On September 1, he notes with approval the decision of the revolutionary party to execute the royal family if Austria declared war: "That kings should be every where hostages for liberty were admirable!"[13] On February 15, 1821, he watches the approach of the two armies with mingled fear and hope:

> We are now in the crisis and point of expectation in Italy. The Neapolitan and Austrian armies are rapidly approaching each other, and every day the news of a battle may be expected. The former have advanced into the Ecclesiastical States, and taken hostages from Rome, to assure themselves of the neutrality of that power, and appear determined to try their strength in open battle. I need not tell you how little chance there is that the new and undisciplined levies of Naples should stand against a superior force of veteran troops. But the birth of liberty in nations abounds in examples of a reversal of the ordinary laws of calculation: the defeat of the Austrians would be the signal of insurrection throughout all Italy.[14]

The *Ode to Naples*, written before the victory of the Austrian forces, concentrates on the actual events rather than, like the *Ode to Liberty*, emphasizing the European historical perspective of which those events were part.[15] The revolution in Spain was over quickly, and the danger of intervention negligible, for it did not directly threaten the central fortress of European absolutism. But in the case of Naples, the threat was direct, and the implications of victory or defeat were considerable. A victory would almost certainly have meant uprisings in other subject states; defeat might kill the prospects of further resistance for years. Shelley, realizing both the potentialities and the dangers more keenly than did Hunt, concentrated on the immediately urgent issues. He followed events avidly: "Day after day, he read the bulletins of the Austrian army, and sought eagerly to gather tokens of its defeat."[16] Shelley's sympathy for the people of Naples and his hatred for their Austrian oppressors, his fluctuating hopes and fears as he watched the march of events so close at hand, hoping always for victory but dreading in his heart the specter of defeat—all these form the substance of the *Ode to Naples.*

The poem, in the form of a classic Greek ode, begins with a scene from Shelley's visits to Pompeii and Baiae during his residence at Naples in 1818–1819. "This," he writes in a note to the first stanza, "has given a tinge of picturesque and descriptive imagery to the introductory Epodes, which depicture the scenes and some of the majestic feelings permanently connected with the scene of this animating event." The opening lines capture the eerie feeling of the visitor to Pompeii:

> I stood within the city disinterred;
> And heard the autumnal leaves like light footfalls
> Of spirits passing through the streets. (1–3)

They also convey the curious sensation of looking at seascape brilliance through an architectural framework, the ruined temples at Baiae:

> through white columns glowed
> The isle-sustaining Ocean-flood,
> A plane of light between two heavens of azure. (9–11)

Through the beauty comes a sense of the presence of the "benignant power:"

> Because the crystal silence of the air
> Weighed on their life; even as the Power divine,
> Which then lulled all things, brooded upon mine. (20–22)

As in *A Defence of Poetry* and elsewhere, "divine" means simply universal and life-giving. Shelley had no more belief in a supernatural "divine" power than in the "spirits" of the first stanza. Nor did he believe in "prophesy," even though he states that he felt as if he were expressing "Prophesyings which grew articulate" (50). But he did believe that poets, although not "prophets in the gross sense of the word," were able to perceive general future historical directions from present trends, and that the psychological stimulations of the power, whatever they were, heightened the creative faculty. The revolution is then hailed:

> Thou youngest giant birth,
> Which from the groaning earth
> Leap'st, clothed in armour of impenetrable scale! (66–68)

The "leagued Oppressors" from the lands of northern darkness (the Austrians and their allies in the Quadruple Alliance) are warned that, should they advance, their soldiers might mutiny and join the Neapolitans:

> What though Cimmerian Anarchs dare blaspheme
> Freedom and thee [Naples]? thy shield is as a mirror
> To make their blind slaves see, and with fierce gleam
> To turn his hungry sword upon the wearer;
> A new Actaeon's error
> Shall theirs have been—devoured by their own hounds! (77–82)

The combined examples of Spain and Naples might serve to set all Italy aflame:

> Didst thou not start to hear Spain's thrilling pæan
> From land to land re-echoed solemnly,
> Till silence became music? From the Ææan
> To the cold Alps, eternal Italy
> Starts to hear thine! (102–106)

Genoa, Milan, Florence, and Rome may yet follow the path of Naples. Shelley's hopes, though premature, were not unfounded, for a revolt broke out in Piedmont in March, an uprising took place in Genoa, and the Papal States were the scene of considerable discontent. If Naples had held out, perhaps it could have become a "signal of insurrection," if not "throughout all Italy," at least in a good part of it.[17]

Shelley next turns to the opposite side of the picture, the gathering forces of the Austrians, of whom Byron was writing at the time: "The Austrian barbarians will march . . . the hounds of hell! Let it still be a hope to see their bones piled up."[18] Shelley pictures a ruthless feudal reaction, desolating alike cities and the beauty of the earth:

> The Anarchs of the North lead forth their legions
> Like Chaos o'er creation, uncreating;
> An hundred tribes nourished on strange religions
> And lawless slaveries,—down the ærial regions
> Of the white Alps, desolating,
> Famished wolves that bide no waiting,

Blotting the glowing footsteps of old glory,
Trampling our columned cities into dust,
    Their dull and savage lust
On Beauty's corse to sickness satiating—
They come! The fields they tread look blue and hoary
With fire—from their red feet the streams run gory! (139–148)

In the final stanza, Shelley complexly blends the natural and philosophical themes touched on in the opening lines with the social:

    Great Spirit, deepest Love!
    Which rulest and dost move
All things which live and are, within the Italian shore
    Who spreadest Heaven around it,
    Whose woods, rocks, waves, surround it;
Who sittest in thy star, o'er Ocean's western floor;
  Spirit of beauty! at whose soft command
  The sunbeams and the showers distil its foison
    From the Earth's bosom chill;
Oh, bid those beams be each a blinding brand
  Of lightning! bid those showers be dews of poison!
    Bid the Earth's plenty kill!
    Bid thy bright Heaven above
    Whilst light and darkness bound it,
    Be their tomb who planned
    To make it ours and thine!
Or, with thine harmonizing ardours fill
And raise thy sons, as o'er the prone horizon
Thy lamp feeds every twilight wave with fire—
Be man's high hope and unextinct desire
The instrument to work thy will divine! (149–169)

These difficult lines are illuminated somewhat by a letter from Shelley to Claire Clairmont on the Neapolitan events:

As to the Austrians I doubt not they are strong men, well disciplined, obeying the master motion like the wheels of a perfect engine: they may even have, as men, more individual excellence & perfection (not that I believe it) than the Neapolitans,—but all these things if the spirit of Regeneration is abroad are chaff before the storm, the very elements & events will fight against them, indignation & shameful repulse will burn after them to the vallies of the Alps—Lombardy will renew the league against [the] Imperial power, which once was so successful, & as the last and greatest consummation, Germany itself will wrest from its oppressors, a power confided to them under [sti]pulations which after having assumed they refused to carry into effect.[19]

Shelley realized, that the material forces of the Austrians were superior to those of the Neapolitans, that they had the usual well-disciplined and brutal army of a despotic state, but he believed that even such an army could not defeat a truly revolutionary people. If the Neapolitans were awakened by "a sudden and great impulse," they would win because the processes of necessity would then be working with progressive social forces. Indeed, a general European revolution might result, and the people might become "instruments of a system of future social life before which the existing anarchies of Europe will be dissolved and absorbed."

That Shelley also had in mind some combination of natural and social forces is implied in both the letter and the poem. In the poem, the "Great Spirit" addressed is once more the power of the earlier stanzas and the *Ode to Liberty*, whose attributes include necessity, love (biological creativity), and beauty, and which permeated nature, society, and the human mind. The theme is similar to that in *Hymn to Intellectual Beauty*, as is the mode of address to the "Spirit of beauty," and similar also to that in *Mont Blanc*:

> Thou hast a voice, great Mountain, to repeal
> Large codes of fraud and woe. (80–81)

It is this inspirational aspect of the power that Shelley has in mind in the final lines. In the earlier ones (and in the letter) he is also expressing a hope the nature might by flood or lightning aid the Neapolitans. That he did not have any rational belief in such actions is clear from his philosophical views, but his hatred of the Austrian invaders and his hopes for the revolution were so intense that he apparently felt this to be a justified rhetorical expression. Although the *Ode to Naples* lacks the scope and massiveness of the *Ode to Liberty*, it has a swifter movement and perhaps, because of its focus on one subject, a more concentrated brilliance. In it Shelley achieves the difficult technical feat of combining highly structured form with fluid and lyrical lightness.

Hellas

Scarcely had the defeat of the Neapolitan armies been announced than Shelley received news of the outbreak of the Greek war against the Turkish Empire, and soon he was eagerly following its development in the papers. In October 1821 he was working on *Hellas*, and it was completed in November, along with its Preface and Notes.

The Greek revolutionary war, like the American or the Mexican (which Shelley had earlier celebrated), was a war for national independence. Although it had economic roots in the opposition of Greek merchants to Turkish taxation and trade restrictions, it soon turned into a national war supported by a fairly large section of the population—"a people's war, a war revolt of peasants and Klephts [guerrillas] against an intolerable subjection, and it succeeded only because of this irresistible popular impulse."[20]

Its international implications were, as both sides quickly realized, far greater than the Spanish or the Neapolitan revolutions. In fact, it kept alight the torch of revolt for eight years in Metternich's Europe, almost to the verge of the "year of revolutions," 1830. These elementary facts require emphasis in view of a tendency to view the war as a meaningless struggle between corrupt Greeks and brutal Turks.

Liberals and revolutionaries everywhere rallied to the Greek cause, writing poems and manifestoes, holding meetings and organizing committees, collecting funds and arms. Out of their activities came the movement known as philhellenism, which attracted Chateaubriand, Victor Hugo, and Alfred de Vigny in France, Daniel Webster and James Monroe in America, with Byron first in Italy and then in Greece, as its most dramatic and influential champion.[21] *Hellas* was its greatest work of art.

Enthusiasm everywhere ran high. "This is an age of revolutions," rejoiced *The Examiner.* "The Greeks have risen in arms! What an inspiring sound!" The editors opened a subscription to purchase arms for the Greek rebels. From the British government, they noted with scorn, nothing could be expected. It had "squandered" the people's money on "useless colonies, on ridiculous feastings of neighbour despots, on the dirty runaway Noblesse of France, and on hosts of sinecurists at home." Only from the people themselves could help be enlisted for the Greeks: "send to the oppressed a speedy supply of arms . . . and for yourselves—you will earn what no potentate on earth can grant—the immortal title of DELIVERERS OF GREECE"[22] *The Examiner* followed the events of the war in detail. So, too, did Shelley.

The Greek nationalists had for years planned a revolt against Turkey. which was scheduled to break out in 1825. But in 1821 they decided to strike immediately, when Ali, pasha of Janina, one of the most powerful of the Turkish rulers in Albania, and a rather colorful tyrant earlier celebrated in *Childe Harolds's Pilgrimage*, rebelled and attempted to set up a separate state. As soon as it became apparent that some of the best Turkish regiments would be tied up at Janina, Price Alexander Ypsilanti, a Greek general in the Russian army, on March 6, 1821, led his forces across the Pruth River in Rumania, expecting to advance from the north into Greece. He seems to have undertaken this venture only upon assurance that the czar would declare war against Turkey, the Russians' traditional foe. The czar, however, was persuaded by Metternich's argument that support of any revolutionary movement was dangerous, and Ypsilanti was left on his own. On June 19 his forces were routed by the Turks at the town of Dragashan, northwest of Bucharest. Ypsilanti fled across the frontier to Austria, where he was promptly imprisoned. The only notable event of an otherwise disastrous campaign was the gallant fight put up at Dragashan by a corps of patriotic Greek youths known as the "Sacred Legion," who were left to bear the brunt of the battle and "fell bravely fighting round their standard."[23]

Ypsilanti's expedition, however, was only the prologue. Even as he was advancing toward Greece from the north, revolution broke out in the

Morea (all of Greece south of the Gulf of Corinth); and it was this southern outbreak that expanded into the war which finally liberated Greece. On April 2, a Greek nationalist leader, Archbishop Germanos, "raised the standard of the cross and occupied Kalavryta." Four days later he placed the cross in the town square of Patras and besieged the Turkish fortress. Other towns fell one after the other, including Coron, Modon, Navarino, Monemvasia, and Tripolitza, whose names, Shelley discovered, made for sonorous, if overly Miltonic, effect. The revolt spread with such fury that by April the Morea was freed from Turkish rule, and the revolution swept north to Athens. The Turks were besieged in the Acropolis. In April, too, naval power was added to military when the islands of Psara, Hydra, and Spezzia (off the southeast coast) joined the struggle. Two Greek fleets put to sea in search of the Turkish navy, one sailing eastward into the Aegean, and one westward into the Ionian Sea. Early in June the fleet in the Aegean encountered two Turkish battleships and some smaller craft. One of the battleships became separated from the rest of the fleet and was pursued into the Bay of Eroseos on the northwest coast of the island of Mitylene, where the Greeks destroyed it with the aid of fireships. In effect, as *The Examiner* noted, the Turkish navy had been put out of commission. The fleet in the Ionian Sea engaged in no such spectacular naval action but did sail into the Gulf of Corinth under the guns of the Turkish fortresses.[24]

The Turks, in revenge for these actions, massacred the Greek population in Asiatic Turkey and on April 22 hanged the Greek patriarch of Constantinople. The Turkish Empire, however, was in a far from stable condition in other places besides Greece. The pasha of the Palestinian port of Acre rebelled; the Syrians took up arms against the officers of the sultan; in Arabia the holy cities of Mecca and Medina were threatened by a Mohammedan army; Persian resistance to the sultan forced him to declare war against Persia; and rebellion broke out in Wallachia (Rumania). In the midst of these events came the angry withdrawal of the Russian ambassador, which alarmed the Turkish government, for it could hardly have survived if war against Russia had been added to its other problems. By October 1821, when Shelley was writing *Hellas*, except for the initial disaster of Dragashan, the Greek armed forces had been extraordinarily successful. All of southern Greece had been freed by a series of spectacular victories, and the Greek navy seemed to control the seas. But over this bright prospect a cloud was growing, for Metternich and Castlereagh had agreed on a policy of nonintervention. The Greek revolt should be allowed, they stated in the elegent language of international diplomacy, to "burn itself out beyond the pale of civilization."[25] A proposal for a joint pro-Christian demonstration of the European powers at Constantinople was vetoed by the British ambassador, Lord Strangford. The revolutionaries were to be left in isolation to face what seemed to the experts to be certain defeat at the hands of Turkey. Such, then, was the situation as seen by Shelley in the fall of 1821. In the end, public pressure for intervention forced the British and French fleets to move against the Turkish navy at Navarino in 1827, and Russia declared war on Turkey. In February 1830, Greece was declared an independent nation.

It so happened that one of the exiled Greek nationalist leaders, Prince Alexander Mavrocordato, a cousin of Ypsilanti's, was living in Pisa during the Shelleys' residence there from 1820 to 1821. Mavrocordato, formerly secretary for foreign affairs for Wallachia, had sought refuge from the Turks in Italy. Along with other Greek exiles, he settled in Pisa, Tuscany being the only Italian state with a moderately liberal government. In June 1821 he left for Greece, and in January 1822 he was elected the first president of the new republic, later becoming recognized as "the most celebrated statesman of the Greek Revolution."[26]

The first record of a report on the Greek war reaching the Shelley household is a note in Mary Shelley's journal for March 16, 1821, on "the taking of the citadel of Candia [Crete] by the Greeks." On April 1, Mavrocordato called at the Shelley house, "gay as a caged eagle just free" with "news of Greece." The following day he returned with the revolutionary proclamation of Ypsilanti: "The hour has struck, valiant Greeks . . . the hour has come to destroy their [the Persians'] successors, more barbarous and still more detestable. Let us do this or perish. To arms, then, my friends, your country calls you."[27] The enthusiasm engendered in the Shelley household by news of the invasion of Ypsilanti appears in Mary Shelley's letters: "Greece has declared its Liberty—has declared the war of the cross against the Crescent. Alexander Ipsilanti—a Greek General in the Russian service and an Aide de camp of the Emperor Alexander has advanced as far as Buchareste with 10,000 Greeks collected from the Russian service, has issued an eloquent & Beautiful Cry of War to his countrymen & is hastening to join the Sulliotes, Servians, Epirotes & the people of the Morea who have all revolted —My Master, the Prince Mavrocordato, is hastening to join the army."[28]

Shelley shared in these enthusiasms: "the news . . . filled him with exultation." But it may be that not until he visited Byron at Ravenna in August was he aroused to the point of considering a poem on the revolution. In three letters to Byron before his visit he did not mention the Greek situation, although in the second of them he noted the failure of the Neapolitan Revolt.[29] The first comment in one of his letters occurs four days after his arrival at Ravenna: "We have good rumours of the Greeks here, & [of] a Russian war." Obviously he and Byron were discussing the war together. And on September 14, after returning from Ravenna, he wrote to Horace Smith: "All public attention is now centred on the wonderful revolution in Greece. I dare not, after the events of last winter, hope that slaves can become freemen so cheaply; yet I know one Greek of the highest qualities, both of courage and conduct, the Prince Mavrocordato, and if the rest be like him, all will go well."[30] On October 21, Williams recorded in his diary that Shelley had given him an inspiring account of the "Sacred Legion" at Dragashan, which he had received from some Greek survivors of the battle, and Byron stated that Shelley intended to go with him to Greece.[31]

The first mention of *Hellas* itself is in a letter from Shelley to John Gisborne on October 22: "I am just finishing a dramatic poem called *Hellas* upon the contest now waging in Greece."[32] The Dedication to Mavrocordato —"as an imperfect token of the admiration, sympathy, and friendship of the author"—is dated "Pisa, November 1, 1821." On November 11 Shelley sent a manuscript copy to Ollier: "What little interest this poem may ever excite, depends upon it's *immediate* publication; I entreat you therefore to have the goodness to send the Ms. instantly to a Printer, & the moment you get a proof, despatch it to me by the Post."[33] When by January 11 he had received no proofs, he wrote again: "I had exceedingly desired the immediate publication of 'Hellas' from public no less than private reasons." The next day he wrote to Gisborne, then in London, authorizing him to take the poem from Ollier and give it to some other publisher if it had not by then been printed.[34] Shelley was even more anxious to secure speedy publication of this poem than he had been for the *Ode to Liberty* and the *Ode to Naples*, for not only did he realize that the implications of the Greek struggle were greater than those in Spain or Naples, but he also felt that haste was essential if he was to add his voice effectively to the already considerable chorus of opposition to Castlereagh's nonintervention policy.

Shelley's awareness of the implications of the Greek war is clear from his Preface, which contains what is perhaps the most concentrated revolutionary statement of the age. The struggle in Greece is viewed both in itself and "as a portion of the cause of civilisation and social improvement" —a "portion," that is, of the growing revolutionary movement which he had outlined in the first chapter of *A Philosophical View of Reform*. The Greeks have within them, he argues, the power to defeat the Turks, for "they have gained more than one naval victory," and "their defeat in Wallachia [under Ypsilanti] was signalised by circumstances of heroism more glorious even than victory," that is, by the last stand of the "Sacred Legion." He attacks those who believe that the modern Greeks were degenerate, claiming that, on the contrary, their growing opposition to the Turks within recent years has transformed them, for "habits which subsist only in relation to a peculiar state of social institution may be expected to cease as soon as that relation is dissolved."[35] Shelley, who often seems noncommital on the question of the primacy of social or psychological factors in a historical complex, here clearly places the emphasis on social conditioning.

The courageous struggle resulting from this regeneration of national character is being jeopardized, Shelley continues, by the foreign policy of the great powers: "The English permit their own oppressors to act according to their natural sympathy with the Turkish tyrant . . . Russia desires to possess, not to liberate Greece; and is contented to see the Turks, its natural enemies, and the Greeks, its intended slaves, enfeeble each other, until one or both fall into its net." The rulers of Europe hesitate to intervene because they realize that the Greek struggle grows out of "the same spirit before which they tremble throughout the rest of Europe"—the spirit of revolution.[36]

Despite this sabotage of the cause of liberty by the great powers, Shelley concludes, the outlook is not black. The monarchs are riding against the tide, and the tide is rising:

Should the English people ever become free, they will reflect upon the part which those who presume to represent their will have played in the great drama of the revival of liberty, with feelings which it would become them to anticipate. This is the age of the war of the oppressed against the oppressors, and every one of those ringleaders of the privileged gangs of murderers and swindlers, called Sovereigns, look to each other for aid against the common enemy, and suspend their mutual jealousies in the presence of a mightier fear. Of this holy alliance all the despots of the earth are virtual members. But a new race has risen throughout Europe, nursed in the abhorrence of the opinions which are its chains, and she will continue to produce fresh generations to accomplish that destiny which tyrants foresee and dread.

The Spanish Peninsula is already free. France is tranquil in the enjoyment of a partial exemption from the abuses which its unnatural and feeble government are vainly attempting to revive. The seed of blood and misery has been sown in Italy, and a more vigorous race is arising to go forth to the harvest. The world waits only the news of a revolution of Germany, to see the tyrants who have pinnacled themselves on its supineness precipitated into the ruin from which they shall never arise.[37]

When *Hellas* was first published in 1822, it did not contain the fragmentary Prologue now appended to it.[38] Shelley's object in writing the Prologue was apparently to develop some of the general ideas underlying the drama and to place the Greek struggle in historical perspective, but for some reason —perhaps a fear that its composition might delay publication—it was discarded.

The setting for the Prologue (reminiscent of Goethe's *Faust*) is eternity; the actors are Christ, Satan, and Mahomet, who have come before the" senate of the Gods" to plead for or against Greece. Christ, speaking first, urges that God send forth "Fate, Thy irrevocable child" (100–101) to assist the Greeks, and hopes that in spite of the machinations of the Quadruple Alliance and the Holy Alliance—"hollow leagues" (105)—Greece will rise victorious. Satan declares that fate is his instrument too, and by means of it he will destroy progress itself:

War shall hover
Above, and Fraud shall gape below, and Change
Shall flit before thee on her dragon wings,
Convulsing and consuming. (147–150)

(The powerful picture of change results from Shelley's characteristic uniting of the abstract and the concrete in his images, sometimes in a kind of surrealistic setting.) Satan's main weapon will be "Anarchy," here used in its primary sense of the social chaos and violence which, Shelley believed, had led to the defeat of the French Revolution after its first promising days:

> The first is Anarchy; when Power and Pleasure,
> Glory and science and security,
> On Freedom hang like fruit on the green tree,
> Then pour it forth, and men shall gather ashes. (156–159)

Anarchy will be followed by tyranny (Napoleon followed Robespierre). Christ answers that Satan has based his observations on the past alone, not realizing that new forces are abroad:

> Obdurate spirit!
> Thou seest but the Past in the To-come.
> Pride is thy error and thy punishment. (160–162)

Satan, like the Bourbons, learns nothing and forgets nothing. Mahomet next speaks, also apparently calling on fate to assist the Turkish cause, but the Prologue ends before either his message or his function becomes clear.

It might seem strange that Shelley, with his anticlerical views, made Christ the spokesman for progress, but Shelley, as the *Essay on Christianity* shows, drew a distinction between Christ and the Christian Church. Christ he regarded as an egalitarian moralist, indeed, as something of a revolutionary. Furthermore, in *Hellas* he wished to stir up Christian support for the Greeks against the Turks.

Hellas is frequently treated as though it were a poetic drama without structure, significant only for its lyrical choruses. But it has a dramatic structure, formed by Shelley's central purpose, namely, to rally English public opinion behind the Greeks. The drama goes through two movements, the first depicting the initial triumphs of the Greeks and the internal disintegration of the Turkish Empire, the second the treachery of the great powers in leaving Greece to its fate. In the first movement Shelley depicts the heroism of the Greeks, and in the second, he implies that victory may be thwarted by the cynical policy of the British government, which had allied itself with Russian and other despotic states. The first movement falls into a number of sections: an opening chorus, striking the initial theme of the victorious advance of liberty; a conversation between the Sultan Mahmud and his adviser Hassan, designed in part to motivate the later appearance of the soothsayer Ahasuerus; the "Worlds on worlds" chorus, prophesying the destruction of Mohammedan power; the central section, consisting of a series of announcements of victories of the Greeks and Mahmud's dismayed reactions to them; a third chorus, hailing the libertarian and cultural traditions of Greece; and finally, the calling up of the Phantom of Mahomet the Second by Ahasuerus to prophesy further ruin, which throws Mahmud into despair. The second movement consists of announcements of the betrayals by the great powers and defiantly answering semichoruses spiraling into the final chorus: "The world's great age begins anew."

A secondary influence on the structure of the drama was Aeschylus' *The Persians*, which depicted an earlier Greek struggle against an Asiatic power, one that ended in triumph at Salamis.[39] The excessive gloom of Mahmud, for example, derives in part from the consistently gloomy moods of Atossa, Xerxes' mother, of the chorus, and at the end, of Xerxes himself. The announcements in *Hellas* of the routing of the Turks on land and sea have a parallel in Aeschylus' Persian Messenger's account of the Greek victory at Salamis and the consequent Persian defeats on land. And finally, the calling up of the spirit of Mahomet the Second is parallelled in the calling up of the spirit of Darius, who gave a similarly gloomy message.

Shelley's drama opens at Constantinople. Mahmud is sleeping on a terrace in the seraglio while the chorus of captive Greek women sing a hymn to liberty:

Semichorus I

Life may change, but it may fly not;
Hope may vanish, but can die not;
Truth be veil'd, but still it burneth;
Love repulsed,—but it returneth!

Semichorus II

Yet were life a charnel where
Hope lay coffin'd with Despair;
Yet were truth a sacred lie,
Love were lust—

Semichorus I

If Liberty
Lent not life its soul of light,
Hope its iris of delight,
Truth its prophet's robe to wear,
Love its power to give and bear. (34–45)

The historical concept behind the deceptively tenuous lines is similar to that in *A Philosophical View of Reform* and *A Defence of Poetry*: even the most dictatorial states cannot wholly stamp out the beauty of life, the hope for a better society, the search for truth, or the comradeship of love (and, as Shelley added in the *Defence*, the creativity of art). Yet in such states these qualities, though not dead, may be reduced to a faint glow and sometimes perverted—truth into religious superstition, love into lust. Only to the degree that liberty is fought for or achieved can the human potential for beauty, love, and happiness be realized. The struggle for liberty also enables one to foresee future developments (the poets' sensing historical change).

Following these stanzas, the chorus depicts the historical rise of liberty, repeating the theme of the *Ode to Liberty* and introduced here with a similar purpose, namely, to proclaim that the struggle in Greece, like that in Spain, is part of a rising revolutionary tide in Europe and America:

From far Atlantis its young beams
Chased the shadows and the dreams.
France, with all her sanguine steams,

Hid, but quench'd it not; again
Through clouds its shafts of glory rain
From utmost Germany to Spain. (70–75)

Mahmud, his sleep penetrated by the women's song, wakes troubled and gloomy. His adviser, Hassan, enters and suggests that he consult a Jewish soothsayer, Ahasueras. But Mahmud cannot shake his sense of foreboding:

Kings are like stars—they rise and set, they have
The worship of the world, but no repose. (195–196)

As he leaves, the captive Greek women sing in chorus:

Worlds on worlds are rolling ever
  From creation to decay,
Like the bubbles on a river
  Sparkling, bursting, borne away. (197–200)

As Desmond King-Hele pointed out, Shelley had an extraordinary capacity for selecting from the sparse scientific knowledge of his day those basic truths that later science would verify and develop. Here, in one compact image, is conveyed something of the fluid essence of the universe as modern astrophysics has revealed it, a picture very different from the static, mechanical one common in the encyclopedias of Shelley's day.

The next passage of the chorus is more difficult. Shelley contrasts the transience of material bodies to the continuity of mind:

  But they are still immortal
  Who, through birth's orient portal
And death's dark chasm hurrying to and fro,
  Clothe their unceasing flight
  In the brief dust and light
Gather'd around their chariots as they go;
  New shapes they still may weave,
  New Gods, new laws receive,
Bright or dim are they, as the robes they last
    On Death's bare ribs had cast. (201–210)

The general reference in the passage is to transmigration ("to and fro"). Shelley had discussed transmigration in his early letters to Elizabeth Hitchener:

One of the properties of animal soul is consciousness of identity—if this is destroyed, in consequenc[e] the *soul* whose essence this is, must perish; but as I conceive, & as is certainly capable of demonstration that nothing can be annihilated, but that everything appertaining to nature, consisting of constituent parts infinitely divisible, is in a continu[al] change, then do I suppose, & I think I have a right to draw this inference, that neither will soul perish; that in a future existence it will lose all consciousness of having formerly lived elsewhere, will begin life anew, possibly under a shape of which we have now no idea.[40]

The concept in the letter is that of the individual mind at death going back into a general mind substance, from which it may again emerge, retaining its individuality but without any recollection of its past existence. The concept in *Hellas* is similar. Matter is everlasting, although its individual parts—"the worlds"—perish. Mind too may be everlasting, and even the minds of individuals may retain something of their individuality after death. Although Shelley presumably meant the minds of all individuals rather than only some, he is here speaking only of those that have made a special contribution to society, utilizing whatever "light" they had as their bodies ("chariots") made their brief passage through life. Some of these persons were the great creative intellects, "the Poets," who were able to make "new shapes" in philosophy, art, and social thought. Others, the political and religious leaders, were able only to "receive." Shelley's meaning becomes clearer in the next two stanzas, in which he notes that there has been a progression in both religions and social institutions. In the final two lines of the above stanza, "robes" refers to the contribution made by these minds to the world, and "Death's bare-ribs" refers to the world of mortality itself. The leaders of mankind can in each incarnation take up from the point at which they had previously arrived ("last")—the implication being that they go progressively higher as mankind advances.

Nevertheless, Shelley had no firm belief in transmigration, and he adds a Note to indicate this to his readers: "The concluding verses indicate a progressive state of more or less exalted existence, according to the degree of perfection which every distinct intelligence may have attained. Let it not be supposed that I mean to dogmatise upon a subject, concerning which all men are equally ignorant, or that I think the Gordian knot of the origin of evil can be disentangled by that or any similar assertions." "Meanwhile," he continued, " . . . it is the function of the poet to attach himself to those ideas which exalt and ennoble humanity," especially those expressing man's "inextinguishable thirst for immortality," even though these ideas may prove to be untrue.[41] Perhaps, too, in a corner of his mind lurked the hope that there might be some truth in them, but as he indicates, he did not put the doctrine forward as a serious philosophical view. Moreover, he hesitates to make a clear affirmation that he is depicting transmigration in the poem. A "progressive state of more or less exalted existence" is a vague phrase, though it can hardly refer to anything else. Perhaps Shelley feared the ridicule of reviewers on the point.

In the next stanza of the chorus, Christ is hailed as one of the "Immortals" described in the previous stanza: "A Promethean conqueror" (212). This again is consistent with Shelley's view of Christ as an egalitarian radical. And once more the Christian Church with its doctrines of "hell, Sin and

Slavery" is attacked as having betrayed its founder's ideals: "Nor prey'd until their Lord had taken flight" (220). But the attack is modified, for a reason Shelley gives in a Note: "The popular notions of Christianity are represented in this chorus as true in their relation to the worship they superseded, and that which in all probability they will supersede, without considering their merits in a relation more universal."[42] Christian theology, that is, poor though it may be when measured by a philosophical yardstick, is yet superior to those of Greece and Rome that preceded it, and to the Mohammedan which it will displace:

The moon of Mahomet
Arose, and it shall set:
While blazon'd as on heaven's immortal noon
The cross leads generations on. (221–224)

Shelley's main objection to the Mohammedan Church was doubtless its subjugation of women. The chorus women in *Hellas* are slaves in a seraglio, and Shelley had earlier expressed his abhorrence of the harem system in *The Revolt of Islam.* He was here, furthermore, writing his play in the hope of rallying Christian sentiment against a Mohammedan power. Nevertheless, the sentiment that the "cross leads generations on" is a strange one coming from Shelley, for he must have been aware that the record of the Christian Church for persecution and religious wars at least equaled that of the Mohammedan. He does, however, suggest that the "leading on" will not last long. It will vanish with the coming of the egalitarian order—"the golden years" of the final line of the chorus—and a "more universal" outlook will take its place.

With the re-entrance of Mahmud and Hassan, the central scene of the drama begins—the history of the war and its international implications. Mahmud, oppressed by gloom, vividly pictures an empire torn by internal strife (not only Ali, pasha of Janina, but also, others, had risen against the Turkish authority), threatened by external conflict, and moving to inevitable destruction:

Ruin above, and anarchy below;
Terror without, and treachery within;
The Chalice of destruction full, and all
Thirsting to drink; and who among us dares
To dash it from his lips? and where is Hope? (268–272)

Hassan tries to cheer Mahmud by describing the mobilization of the forces of his empire and the inactivity of England, Russia, and Austria. Indeed, in the case of Metternich's Austria, fresh from exterminating the revolution in Naples, it is more than inactivity; it is true sympathy:

But recreant Austria loves thee as the Grave
Loves Pestilence, and her slow dogs of war

Flesh'd with the chase, come up from Italy,
And howl upon their limits. (312–315)

But Mahmud refuses to be comforted. Though he admits there are fine words of support from the great powers, he asks where the deeds are that alone can ensure success. His foreboding has, if anything, grown deeper. (The gloomy atmosphere here is particularly reminiscent of *The Persians*.) Mahmud now sees not only his own doom but also that of his fellow despots. He is a fragment of an outmoded social system crumbling before a democratic tide:

Far other bark than ours were needed now
To stem the torrent of descending time:
The spirit that lifts the slave before his lord
Stalks through the capitals of armed kings,
And spreads his ensign in the wilderness;
Exults in chains; and when the rebel falls,
Cries like the blood of Abel from the dust;
And the inheritors of the earth, like beasts
When earthquake is unleased, with idiot fear
Cower in their kingly dens—as I do now.
What were Defeat when Victory must appal?
Or Danger, when Security looks pale? (349–360)

Hassan again attempts to reverse his master's mood by giving a long account of the defeat of Ypsilanti at Dragashan. He makes the mistake, however, of describing the heroic defense of the Sacred Legion and repeating (rather out of character) the dying speech of one of its members, a speech passionate with revolutionary hatred, defiance, and hope:

Famine, and Pestilence,
And Panic, shall wage war upon our side!
Nature from all her boundaries is moved
Against ye: Time has found ye light as foam. (439–442)[43]

Hassan next reports the defeat of the Turkish fleet in the Aegean, in which one of their two battleships has been destroyed by Greek fireships.[44] Shelley, perhaps influenced by the description of Salamis in *The Persians*, makes the engagement out to be rather more extensive than in reality it was.

As Hassan finishes, a messenger arrives to announce the withdrawal of the Russian ambassador from Constantinople, an event which spread panic in Turkish governing circles, because they realized that Russia was being held back from a declaration of war against Turkey only by the influence of Metternich.[45] A second messenger enters with news of the sudden and spectacular success of the revolution in the Morea:

Nauplia, Tripolizza, Mothon, Athens,
Navarin, Artas, Monembasia,
Corinth and Thebes are carried by assault,
And every Islamite who made his dogs
Fat with the flesh of Galilean slaves
Passed at the edge of the sword: the lust of blood
Which made our warriors drunk, is quench'd in death. (546–552)

Furthermore, the continuing resistance of Ali at Janina "Holds our besieging army like a spell." (568) Shelley, although always hoping for peaceful solutions, was clearly no absolute pacifist, for he obviously takes considerable joy in these Greek victories. A third messenger then arrives to announce the spread of revolt within the empire, involving Damascus, Medina, Persia, Crete and Cyprus. A fourth messenger announces that the Greek squadron that had sailed into the Ionian Sea had been sighted off the northwest coast of the Peloponnesus, where it was moving toward the Bay of Corinth.

In these speeches of Hassan and the messengers, Shelley is surveying the four main events of the early months of the war: the Ypsilanti campaign in the north, the uprising in the Morea, the successes of the Greek navy, and the revolt in the Turkish Empire. The spirit that animates the scene—inversely conveyed through the alarm and gloom of the speakers—reflects the joyous exultation with which liberal Europe watched the insurgent advance of the Greeks. "The Standard of the Cross floats on the Parthenon," *The Examiner* exclaimed on July 22; the Turks had been "driven from the ramparts by the Greeks." "A great naval victory obtained by the Greeks over the combined Turkish and Egyptian fleets," was reported on October 7. Two weeks later: "With the exception of two fortresses, the Greeks have liberated the whole of the Morea . . . they continue masters of the sea." In December came reports of revolt within the Turkish Empire: "a situation of greater peril than it ever experienced before." It would require "a political miracle to rescue it from such a coincidence of foreign and domestic assaults."[46] Such was the kind of "newspaper erudition" on which Shelley, as he explained in his Preface, based the events of his drama, and which he was able to transmute into poetry.

Following this series of gloomy recitations, Mahmud leaves to meet the soothsayer, Ahasuerus. When he has gone, the chorus of captive Greek women sings again, first in answering semichoruses, then in a full chorus, lamenting their own condition and that of all Greeks, but asserting the continuity and greatness of the Greek spirit:

Temples and towers,
Citadels and marts, and they
Who live and die there, have been ours,
And may be thine, and must decay;
But Greece and her foundations are
Built below the tide of war,

Based on the crystalline sea
Of thought and its eternity;
Her citizens, imperial spirits,
  Rule the present from the past,
On all this world of men inherits
  Their seal is set. (692–703)

As in the "Worlds on worlds" chorus, Shelley contrasts the general continuity of mind with the passing of material objects. Specifically the concept is that of the chain of great minds (here particularly the ancient Greeks) handing on their evolving wisdom and immortal creations to aid present development. This inspiring and progressive body of thought will join with historical necessity to secure Greek victory:

The world's eyeless charioteer,
  Destiny is Hurrying by!
What faith is crushed, what empire bleeds
Beneath her earthquake-footed steeds? (711–714)

But if this victory is to be permanent and not, it is implied, to end in internal military despotism, the Greeks must reject vengeance:

Revenge and wrong bring forth their kind,
  The foul cubs like their parents are. (729–730)

The object of this chorus, coming immediately after the successive reports of Greek victories, is to foreshadow the drama's final message of hope.

As the chorus ceases, Mahmud enters with Ahasuerus, who turns out to be Shelley's old favorite, the Wandering Jew, in philosophic garb.[47] Mahmud asks if the soothsayer can conjure up "the unborn hour" of the future fate of his empire. Ahasuerus replies:

Sultan! talk no more
Of thee and me, the future and the past;
But look on that which cannot change—the One
The unborn and the undying. Earth and ocean,
Space, and the isles of life or light that gem
The sapphire floods of interstellar air,
This firmament pavilioned upon chaos,
With all its cressets of immortal fire,
Whose outwall, bastioned impregnably
Against the escape of boldest thoughts, repels them
As Calpe the Atlantic clouds—this Whole
Of suns, and worlds, and men, and beasts, and flowers,
With all the silent or tempestuous workings
By which they have been, are, or cease to be,
Is but a vision;—all that it inherits
Are motes of a sick eye, bubbles and dreams;

Thought is its cradle and its grave, nor less
The future and the past are idle shadows
Of thought's eternal flight—they have no being;
Nought is but that which feels itself to be. (766–785)

To this passage Shelley added a Note: "I have preferred to represent the Jew as disclaiming all pretension, or even belief, in supernatural agency, and as tempting Mahmud to that state of mind in which ideas may be supposed to assume the force of sensation through the confusion of thought with the objects of thought, and excess of passion animating the creations of the imagination."

According to the empiricists, "sensations" had greater force than "thoughts" or "ideas." Locke argued that the difference arose from the fact that "sensations" originated in external objects, while "thoughts" or "ideas" came from within the mind. Thus, if a person saw a house, he had a more vivid picture (sensation) than if he closed his eyes and envisaged it (idea). Hume, in accordance with his general skepticism, argued that all we know is that some sensations are stronger than others. Shelley maintains in the above Note that sometimes the visions of the imagination are so vivid that the distinction between sensation and thought is obscured. In the poem, he has Ahasueras restate the argument of the essay *On Life*, that "nothing exists but as it is perceived," but with particular reference to "the state called reverie," in which people are "conscious of no distinction" between "the surrounding universe" and "their being." In the poem, as in the essay, there is no hint of a Berkeleian divine cosmic mind, and the "One" is not the Platonic One, of which reality is a reflection, but the One of Parmenides as found in Drummond, namely, the unchanging common element running through all the variations of perceived reality. Unlike the *On Life* presentation, however, Shelley puts these concepts forward not as philosophical doctrine but (almost apologetically) as ideas that might arise in a certain "state of mind."

Mahmud, feeling such an almost hypnotic "state of mind" coming upon him, is frightened, and his fear perhaps reflects something of Shelley's own feelings on the implications of the "intellectual system" (which in the essay he described as "startling to the apprehension"):

They cast on all things, surest, brightest, best,
Doubt, insecurity, astonishment. (790–791)[48]

Ahasuerus replies:

Mistake me not! All is contained in each.
Dodona's forest to an acorn's cup
Is that which has been or will be, to that
Which is—the absent to the present. (792–795)

The present, then, grows necessarily out of the past and the future out of the present as a tree grows from a seed. One set of events inevitably creates another. If one could, like "the Poets," grasp something of present patterns, future ones could be predicted:

> The coming age is shadowed on the past
> As on a glass. (805–806)

At the same time, Ahasuerus seems to be going beyond this statement of the inevitability of future developments to a concept that everything exists, as it were, simultaneously within the thought substance, which is the only reality of which we are aware. This idea is not discussed in Shelley's prose expositions of his philosophical views. Presumably it could be part of the state of "reverie" and a legitimate concept to be expressed by a soothsayer. Certainly Shelley had no belief, as he emphasizes in his Note, in a "supernatural agency."

Ahasuerus then calls up (or so it appears to Mahmud) the spirit of Mahomet, the conqueror of Constantinople in 1453.[49] The spirit prophesies doom:

> Islam must fall, but we will reign together
> Over its ruins in the world of death. (887–888)

Ahasuerus' purpose now becomes clear. The state of reverie will produce visions that will undermine Mahmud's morale by convincing him of the inevitable end of his empire. In this, Ahasuerus succeeds. As the phantom vanishes, Mahmud is left in despair, clinging to his "gloomy crag of time" and looking hopelessly into the future. With his exit after this realization, the final movement of the drama opens. "Voices without" announcing the successive treacheries of the great powers are answered by defiant semichoruses of the Greek women, the whole winding up in the final chorus of hope for a rejuvenated Greece in an egalitarian world.

The Greeks were, as Shelley wrote, enjoying a series of startling victories. But as yet the full might of the Turkish Empire had not be exerted against them. The danger was that they would be crushed unless the great powers could be persuaded to change their policy of nonintervention. Of this danger, as the Preface shows, Shelley, in common with other liberals, was constantly aware. *The Examiner* hammered away at British policy in issue after issue. "Anything short of Greek independence and the expulsion of the Turks from Europe," it argued, "can only be the clumsy botching of a rotten system . . . it is peculiarly the interest of France and England to take immediate measures in the furtherance of these noble objects." Greek victory was essential, explained *The Examiner*, with a twin solicitude for commerce and Christianity not previously emphasized in its pages. Such victory would vindicate "our professions as Christians . . . overthrow a debasing and bloody despotism . . . provide a solid and permanent check" to absolutist Russia, and "open a new, extensive and glorious field for the enterprise and industry of our merchants and manufacturers." Yet the British government could not see these manifest advantages while remaining part of the reactionary Holy Alliance, whose "simple object is to suppress, by its *combined* power, every attempt at liberal change."[50] And so the great fear hung over all that British foreign policy, unless changed, would leave the Greeks to perish. It is on this policy that Shelley focuses the final movement of his drama, where he attempts to reveal the danger, display the heroic spirit of the Greeks, and shame the British people into joining forces with them.

The movement begins with a "Voice without," announcing the new advance of the Turks. The answer of the semichorus reflects the horror of a small nation watching the inevitable gathering of immense destructive power:

> Victorious Wrong, with vulture scream,
> Salutes the risen sun, pursues the flying day!
> I saw her, ghastly as a tyrant's dream,
> Perch on the trembling pyramid of night,
> Beneath which earth and all her realms pavilioned lay
> In visions of the dawning undelight.
> Who shall impede her flight?
> Who rob her of her prey? (940–947)

Shelley's interest in science, as A. N. Whitehead noted, formed "part of the main structure of his mind, permeating his poetry through and through." Whitehead specifically pointed out that "pyramid of night" here embodies the astronomical picture of the earth throwing a long, conelike shadow into sunlit space.[51] Shelley was one of the few poets of the past with a real sense of the earth as a planet. It was this feeling that produced the image of war's destruction as hovering not locally in the sky but monstrously out in space over the darkened side of the earth, as though about to swoop down and devastate mankind—an image even more appropriate to our century than to Shelley's.

To the desperate plea of the chorus for salvation there is only the news of further disaster. Russia has decided not to intervene against the Turks. Another voice announces that Austria, Russia, Britain, and France have agreed on a joint policy of nonintervention. The chorus, aroused from its initial mood of bewilderment by these fast-falling reports of international treachery, asserts again the immortality of the Greek ideal. Hope for mankind still remains in democratic America ("young Atlantis"), no matter what happens in Europe, and in time a new world state will arise in which the traditions of Greek culture are revived. In two powerfully revolutionary stanzas the chorus defies the gathering forces of reaction:

> Let the tyrants rule the desert they have made;
> Let the free possess the Paradise they claim;
> Be the fortune of our fierce oppressors weighed
> With our ruin, our resistance, and our name!
>
> Our dead shall be the seed of their decay,
> Our survivors be the shadow of their pride,
> Our adversity a dream to pass away—
> Their dishonour a remembrance to abide! (1008–1015)

The announcement then comes of the decision to keep the British navy from intervening against the Turks:

The bought Briton sends
The keys of ocean to the Islamite. (1016–1017)

In answer, the semichorus again takes up the theme of hope now residing in America, which Shelley emphasizes in order to shame the British into action:

Darkness has dawn'd in the East
  On the noon of time:
The death-birds descend to their feast,
  From the hungry clime.
Let Freedom and Peace flee far
  To a sunnier strand,
And follow Love's folding star!
  To the Evening land! (1023–1030)[52]

The poem concludes with the great chorus hailing mankind in the new world order to come:

The world's great age begins anew,
  The golden years return,
The earth doth like a snake renew
  Her winter weeds outworn:
Heaven smiles, and faiths and empires gleam,
Like wrecks of a dissolving dream.

. . . . .

Another Athens shall arise,
  And to remoter time
Bequeath, like sunset to the skies,
  The splendour of its prime;
And leave, if nought so bright may live,
All earth can take or heaven can give.

Saturn and Love their long repose
  Shall burst, more bright and good
Than all who fell, than One who rose,
  Than many unsubdued:
Not gold, not blood, their altar dowers,
But votive tears and symbol flowers.

O cease! must hate and death return?
  Cease! must men kill and die?
Cease! drain not to its dregs the urn
  Of bitter prophecy.
The world is weary of the past,
O might it die or rest at last!

The final vision of *Hellas* revolves, like *The Revolt of Islam* or *Ode to the West Wind,* around the passing of the "winter of the world" and the coming of the "spring" of a new society. It anticipates, the Note comments, "a period of regeneration and happiness." In the new world society, equality ("They represented equality as the reign of Saturn" wrote Shelley elsewhere) and human brotherhood (Love) will rule, for they constitute a finer basis for morality and philosophy than either Christianity ("One who rose"), the religion of Greece ("all who fell"), or other religions, especially the Asiatic ("many unsubdued").[53] By "altar dowers" Shelley does not mean that any kind of formal religion will continue in the new order. He is speaking metaphorically. People will abandon the old religions of persecution ("blood") and exploitation ("gold") and will be thankful to live in a society of love and equality. The possibility that sometime in the future the new order might be torn apart and persecution ("hate") and war ("death") return, the chorus refuses to contemplate, for the world has suffered enough already. It would be better for the world to die if the horrors of war, exploitation, and injustice that have plagued it so far are to "return" and mankind is not to live hereafter undisturbed in the peaceful era of the egalitarian society.

11

Shelley As Dramatist

The Cenci. Charles the First

Shelley scholars have often underestimated both Shelley's dramatic gifts and the extent of his interest in playwriting. It was a professional drama critic, St. John Ervine, who began to redress the balance. Ervine contended that Shelley had dramatic abilities which in another age might have made him a leading playwright. *The Cenci,* long tagged as a "closet drama," is, he argued, actually a "stage play," and *Charles the First,* if it had been completed might, he believed, have surpassed *The Cenci.*[1] Shelley also wrote *Fragment of an Unfinished Drama,*[2] and a few lines of a play on the life of Tasso, which give tantalizing promise of a play rich with intrigue (anticipating Browning's dramatic monologues):

> The Duke was leaning,
> His finger on his brow, his lips unclosed.
> The Princess sate within the window-seat,
> And so her face was hid; but on her knee
> Her hands were clasped, veined, and pale as snow,
> And quivering—young Tasso, too, was there.[3]

In addition, Shelley planned plays on Job, Timon of Athens (to deal with "present social and political evils"), and Troilus and Cressida.[4] The total comes to one completed play, three fragmentary plays, and three plans for plays. Of these, *Job* was perhaps intended to be a lyrical drama of the *Hellas* or *Prometheus Unbound* type, but the rest probably fall within Shelley's comment to Trelawny on *Charles the First*: "I am now writing a play for the stage. It is affectation to say we write a play for any other purpose."[5]

Shelley, although brought up to "country" living, and more often out of London than in it, went more frequently to the theater than is usually recognized. While still a schoolboy, he ran off with his cousin Thomas Medwin to the provincial theater at Richmond to see Dora Jordan, a leading comic actress, in her famous role in *The Country Girl,* Garrick's toned-down version of William Wycherley's *The Country Wife.*[6] On October 13, 1814, he saw Edmund Kean in Hamlet at Drury Lane. According to Mary Shelley, he was "displeased with what he saw of Kean."[7] His next recorded visit to a theater came in 1817, when on January 29 he saw Eliza O'Neill in George Coleman's *The Jealous Wife,* and on February 11 he, Mary, and Leigh Hunt saw *The Merchant of Venice.* Three years later, Hunt remembered Mary giggling at the antics of "Master Launcelot." On February 16, 1818, Shelley went with Peacock to Covent Garden to see Henry Hart Milman's *Fazio*, featuring Eliza O'Neill.[8] With Peacock, too, he saw *A School for Scandal* but disliked its association of "virtue with bottles and glasses, and villainy with books."[9] On February 21, 1818, at Drury Lane he saw the stage version of Byron's *The Bride of Abydos*. Apparently he was impressed by this production, for on March 2 he returned to Covent Garden to see a new comedy, *The Castle of Glyndower*, which survived only one performance. Since the journals of Mary and Claire show that Shelley attended the opera on January 29, February 7, 10, 14, 21, 24, 28, and March 10, 1818, it would appear that during his last weeks in England he was cramming in all the "theater" possible. He is not known to have seen any more plays in London, but his interest had been whetted. Passing through Lyons on his way to Italy, he went "to the Comedie," Mary noted, "which is very amusing"; and he and Mary attended the opera in Turin, Milan, Naples, and Pisa. In addition, he was an extensive reader of plays, both ancient and modern.[10]

The Cenci

Shelley began *The Cenci* in May 1819 in Rome and finished it in September.[11] He had stage production in mind from the start: "What I want you to do," he wrote to Peacock in England, "is, to procure for me its presentation at Covent Garden. The principal character Beatrice is precisely fitted for Miss O'Neill, & it might even seem to have been written for her—(God forbid that I shd. see her play it—it wd. tear my nerves to pieces) and in all respects it is fitted only for Covent Garden. The chief male character I confess I should be very unwilling that any one but Kean shd. play—that is impossible, & I must be contented with an inferior actor."[12]

Eliza O'Neill, though now forgotten, was regarded as one of the most accomplished actresses of the day. That Shelley did not overevaluate her is apparent from the praise of Hazlitt and Macready (who had acted with her).[13] Shelley was much impressed by her performance in Milman's *Fazio*. "I remember his absorbed attention to Miss O'Neill's performance of Bianca in *Fazio* "wrote Peacock," and it is evident to me that she was always in his thoughts when he drew the character of Beatrice in *The Cenci*." As Eliza O'Neill first became famous on the Dublin stage before going to England in 1814, Shelley may have seen her or at least heard of her during his visits to Dublin in 1811–1812 and in 1813. His selection of her and of Kean for the leads were regarded by St. John Ervine as "clear proof of Shelley's skill in casting a play . . . He had disliked Kean's Hamlet so deeply that he had left the theatre, but he must have remembered enough of the performance to realize how excellent Kean would be in the part of Count Cenci: a furious part for a furious actor."[14]

But all Shelley's plans came to wreck on the rocks of censorship and reaction. The Tory Establishment, only partially able to dominate book and periodical publishing, maintained firm control over the theater. The lord chamberlain could legally keep any play off the boards, and the resulting stultifying theatrical atmosphere prevented playwrights and managers alike from experimentation. *The Cenci*, as a play by an "atheist" and dealing with incest, obviously stood no chance. Peacock, however, duly submitted it to Covent Garden, whose manager, Henry Harris, turned it down; and it was turned down also at Drury Lane.[15] That it would have become a center of controversy if it had been produced, and perhaps even been driven off the boards, is clear from the reviews that appeared on its publication, as in *The Literary Gazette*: "Of all the abominations which intellectual perversion, and poetical atheism, have produced in our times, this tragedy appears to us to be the most abominable. We have much doubted whether we ought to notice it; but, as watchmen place a light over the common sewer which has been opened in a way dangerous to passengers, so have we concluded it to be our duty to set up a beacon to this noisome and noxious publication." Such attacks, as Stuart Curran has pointed out, were not so much directed at the play itself as at Shelley, the atheist and nonconformist.[16]

A play starting its career without staging in its author's lifetime is at a disadvantage ever after. The author is not able to make alterations in the light of actual performance, and if the delay between writing and production is long, the play becomes dated. Nevertheless, as has become recognised in recent years, *The Cenci* has had a quite respectable stage history. For instance, it ran at the Korsch Theater in Moscow in the 1919–1920 season for twenty-six performances, with a total audience of 26,880.[17] In 1922, when the centenary of Shelley's death was being observed, it was produced at the Municipal Theater, Prague, with the Capek brothers in charge, and at the New Theatre, London, with Sybil Thorndyke playing the role of Beatrice, a production that was well received by the leading English theatrical critics. In 1926 the play was revived in London, again with Sybil Thorndyke as Beatrice, and in 1959 it ran at the Old Vic in London from April to June and received good reviews in the theatrical journals.

Although Shelley read many plays in several languages, of the English dramas being acted at the time he appears to have read only four: *Orra* by Joanna Baillie, *Bertram* by Charles Robert Maturin, *Osorio (Remorse)* by Coleridge, and *Fazio* by Milman.[18] This fact, as well as his lack of stage experience, left a certain mark upon the play. Some of the speeches are overlong, the action flags at times, notably in the second act, and the use of dramatic devices is sometimes too obvious.

An even deeper mark was left on the play by the generally enfeebled condition of the theater at the time, the boards being almost wholly occupied with pantomimes, spectacles, extravaganzas, farces, and melodramas (one of the most popular including the rescue of the heroine from a tank of water by a dog). The little legitimate drama being acted, whether comedy or tragedy, consisted almost wholly of revivals, especially Shakespeare and Sheridan.

The only original tragedies of any consequence were *Remorse, Fazio,* and *Bertram,* all three of which are essentially melodramas. In *Remorse,* a wronged lover returns disguised as a Moor, is not recognized by his beloved, sees his villainous brother stabbed by a wild Morrosco woman, and finally wins the heroine. In *Fazio,* the most actable play of the period, the hero deserts the virtuous Bianca for the vampirish Aldebella, is betrayed by the vengeful Bianca for a murder he did not commit and is executed, whereupon Bianca goes mad and dies of a broken heart. *Bertram* concerns a Byronic pirate—Byron recommended the play to Drury Lane—who seduces Imogene, wife of Lord Aldobrand, and stabs her husband to death; Imogene, as usual, goes mad. The conclusion illustrates the level of the drama at the time:

Imo. Have I deserved this of thee?
(*She dies slowly, with her eyes fixed on Bertram, who continues to gaze on her, unconscious of her having expired.*)
Prior. 'Tis past (*to the Monks*). Brethren, remove the corpse.
(*The Knights and Monks advance. Bertram waves them off, still supporting the body.*)
Ber. (*Starting up*) She is not dead;
She must not, shall not die, till she forgives me!
(*Kneeling to the corpse. Turning to the Monks.*)
Speak, speak to me!
Yes, she will speak with me anon.
(*A long pause; he drops on the corpse.*)
She speaks no more. Why do you gaze on me?
I loved her; yea, I love, in death I love her;
I killed her, but I loved her.
What arm shall loose the grasp of love and death?
(*The Knights and Monks surround, and attempt to tear Bertram from the body; he snatches a sword from one of the Knights, who retreats in terror, as it is pointed at him; Bertram, resuming all his former sternness, bursts into a disdainful laugh.*)
Thee! against thee! Oh, thou art safe, thou worm!
Bertram hath but one fatal foe on earth,
And he is here!
(*Stabs himself*)
Prior. (*Rushing forward*) He dies, he dies!
Ber. (*Struggling with the agonies of death*) I know
Thee, holy Prior; I know thee, brethren!
Lift up your holy hands in charity.
(With a burst of wild exultation)
I died no felon's death;
A warrior's weapon freed a warrior's soul.
(*Dies*)[19]

The only original movement in the contemporary theater occurred not in England but in Germany, in the plays of Friedrich Schiller, whose *The Rob-*

bers Shelley early admired, but he makes only one reference to him (to the *Maid of Orleans*) and his drama does not appear to have been influenced by him. In England the only serious attempt at innovation came from Byron, who wrote two types of drama—heroic romantic plays centering around a Byronic figure (*Marino Faliero, Sardanapalus*), and philosophical or psychological drama (*Manfred, Cain*)—neither of which became part of the living stage. Shelley particularly admired the second type, especially *Cain* with its powerful anticlericalism, and some of *Manfred*, with its brilliant alternation of chorus and dialogue, wove its way into *Prometheus Unbound*, but he rejected both types when it came to writing his own play for the stage. Perhaps he felt that the Byronic romantic manner was not suited to a penetrating depiction of life and character, and he must also have been aware of Byron's limitations as a stage dramatist (his centering a play around a self-projection character, his tendency to wordiness, and his paucity of dramatic action).

Shelley, then, unlike Shakespeare or Racine, Shaw or O'Neill had no contemporary theater to turn to for either models or inspiration. In his poetry he could—like Keats—rise on the crest of the new movement begun by Wordsworth and Coleridge and continued by Byron, creating his own style within a general pattern. But in the theater there was no such movement and Shelley, like Coleridge or Wordsworth, was virtually forced to return to past models, especially Shakespeare.[20] This imposed certain limitations on *The Cenci*, for it signified that he was not writing as part of a dramatic movement expressing the style and spirit of his age but imposing the forms of a former period on an age to which they were no longer wholly appropriate. *The Cenci*, with its archaisms and soliloquies, strikes the reader as old-fashioned in a way that Shelley's nondramatic poetry does not. On the stage, however, these defects are lost in the dramatic movement of the play or are glossed over by audiences conditioned to the Shakespearean manner. Furthermore, in spite of its "thous" and "tweres," the dialogue is more natural than the Elizabethan, as is apparent in the first line (surely one of the best opening lines of any play): "That matter of the murder is hushed up." Certainly the stage history of *The Cenci* shows beyond question that, when it is properly produced, it has powerful theatrical impact. It is, in fact the only major tragedy in English between Thomas Otway's *Venice Preserved* in 1682 and O'Casey's *Juno and the Paycock* or Shaw's *Saint Joan* in 1924. Unlike other nineteenth century poets who wrote plays, Shelley had a true dramatic sense. He was able to visualize stage and audience reaction as he composed; and he wrote the play, as he himself said, not primarily to be read but to be acted.

Fortunately the basic source that Shelley used for *The Cenci*, has survived, copied out by his wife, and a comparative study provides unusual insights into Shelley's creative process.[21] The actual Cenci family history, as later unearthed by the Italian historian A. Bertolotti, is a sordid tale of decadence, crime, and, retribution.[22] Count Francesco Cenci, born in 1549, was twice imprisoned, once for sodomy, and once tried for seduction. His son Christofer was murdered in a fight over another man's wife; his son Rocco, who along with a notorious ruffian named Mario Querro stole clothes from his father, was also murdered. His daughter Beatrice, born in 1577, appears to have had an affair with the keeper of the family castle, Olimpio, and to have had an illegitimate child by him, which she placed, without her father's knowledge, in the charge of a country woman. In fact, it seems not unlikely that the discovery of this child was what led to Cenci's ill treatment of his daughter. At any rate, he did mistreat her, and she, along with her brothers Giacomo and Bernardo, the villainous Querro, and her stepmother, Lucrezia, formed a plot to murder him. She and Lucrezia drugged the old man with opium at supper; Lucrezia then lay asleep by his side in bed while Olimpio and a fellow villain named Marzio beat him to death with a hammer. The murder was discovered, the murderers admitted their guilt under torture, and all except Bernardo, who was presented by his lawyer as an imbecile, were executed in 1599.

Out of this grim history there grew in the succeeding century the Cenci legend. "Relazioni" sprang up in which Count Cenci was represented as a monster of wickedness and Beatrice as a martyr. Some of these versions even provided her with a romantic lover in her accomplice Guerra (Querro), a relationship that probably never existed, for Beatrice had testified against him when he was accused of stealing clothes from her father. As the story grew, it acquired political significance as a heroic struggle against feudal and papal tyranny. As such, it entered Italian and other literature, often quite independently of Shelley. Several novels and plays have been written on it, and in the present century the Cenci story has been distributed in the Italian quarters of American cities as a document in the history of Italian liberty.[23]

The source that Shelley used for his play was one of the seventeenth or eighteenth century "relazioni," which treated the story in sensational style as a struggle against inhuman oppression. According to this version, Count Cenci was a monster of wickedness: "Sodomy was the least, and atheism the greatest of the vices of Francesco." He hated his sons Rocco, Giacomo, and Cristofero, and kept them short of money, refusing to "dress or maintain them" until he was forced to do so by the pope. When Rocco and Cristofero were murdered, the "inhuman father showed every sign of joy on hearing this news, saying that nothing would exceed his pleasure if all his children died, and that when the grave should receive the last he would, as a demonstration of joy, make a bonfire of all that he possessed."

His treatment of his daughter Beatrice was even more disgraceful: "Francesco . . . often endeavoured, by force and threats, to debauch his daughter Beatrice, who was now grown up, and exceedingly beautiful." Presumably he raped her, because at this point Mary Shelley in her copy (the only extant text) supplied a series of asterisks with the note: "The details here are horrible, and unfit for publication."

As a result of this treatment, Beatrice, her stepmother Lucretia, her brother Giacomo, and a young prelate, "Monsignore Guerra," who was "somewhat in love with Beatrice," planned the murder of the count. Giacomo hired two murderers, Olympio and Marzio, who were to lie in wait for Cenci's carriage on the road to his country castle of La Petrella and there slay him, but they arrived too late and Cenci escaped. It then became necessary to commit the murder inside the castle, and here Beatrice took the lead:

About midnight his daughter herself led the two assassins into the apartment of her father, and left them there that they might execute the deed they had undertaken, and retired to a chamber close by, where Lucretia remained also, expecting the return of the murderers, and the relation of their success. Soon after the assassins entered, and told the ladies that pity had held them back, and that they could not overcome their repugnance to kill in cold blood a poor sleeping old man. These words filled Beatrice with anger, and after having bitterly reviled them as cowards and traitors, she exclaimed, "Since you have not courage enough to murder a sleeping man, I will kill my father myself; but your lives shall not be long secure." The assassins, hearing this short but terrible threat, feared that if they did not commit the deed, the tempest would burst over their own heads, took courage, and re-entered the chamber where Francesco slept, and with a hammer drove a nail into his head, making it pass by his eye, and another they drove into his neck. After a few struggles the unhappy Francesco breathed his last. The murderers departed, after having received the remainder of the promised reward; besides which, Beatrice gave Marzio a mantle trimmed with gold. After this the two ladies, after drawing out the two nails, enveloped the body in a fine sheet, and carried it to an open gallery that overhung a garden, and had underneath an elder-tree; from thence they threw it down, so that it might be believed that Francesco, attending a call of nature, was traversing this gallery, when, being only supported by feeble beams, it had given way, and thus had lost his life.

This story was believed for some time, but suspicions were later aroused and the body was exhumed. Guerra, hearing of the investigation, hired other murderers to kill, in their turn, Olympio and Marzio, to prevent their turning state's evidence. Olympio was killed, but Marzio fell into the hands of the authorities and confessed. Beatrice, Lucretia, Giacomo, and a younger brother, Bernardo, whose body and mind "seemed formed in the same model as that of his sister," were thereupon arrested (Guerra having escaped): "They were here examined, and all constantly denied the crime, and particularly Beatrice, who also denied having given to Marzio the mantle trimmed with gold, of which mention was before made; and Marzio, overcome and moved by the presence of mind and courage of Beatrice, retracted all that he had deposed at Naples, and, rather than again confess, obstinately died under his torments."

Giacomo, Bernardo, and Lucretia were tortured and confessed. "But the Signora Beatrice, being young, lively, and strong, neither with good nor ill treatment, with menaces, nor fear of torture, would allow a single word to pass her lips which might inculpate her; and even, by her lively eloquence, confused the judges who examined her." The rest of the family, however, urged her to confess:

They began altogether to exhort her to confess; saying, that since the crime had been committed, they must suffer the punishment. Beatrice, after some resistance, said, "So you all wish to die, and to disgrace and ruin our house?—This is not right; but since it so pleases you, so let it be:"—and turning to the jailors, she told them to unbind her, and that all the examinations might be brought to her, saying, "That which I ought to confess, that will I confess; that to which I ought to assent, to that will I assent; and that which I ought to deny, that will I deny" and in this manner she was convicted without having confessed.

Various influential people urged the pope to be lenient, but he remained adamant. When Beatrice first heard that the sentence of death by beheading was to be carried out, she "broke into a piercing lamentation, and into passionate gesture, exclaiming, 'How is it possible, O my God! that I must so suddenly die?' " But later she "courageously supported herself, and gave every one certain proofs of a humble resignation." She sent for plain, nunlike dresses for herself and Lucretia: "When these dresses came, Beatrice rose, and turning to Lucretia—'Mother', said she, 'the hour of our departure is drawing near, let us dress therefore in these clothes, and let us mutually aid one another in this last office.' Lucretia readily complied with this invitation, and they dressed, each helping the other showing the same indifference and pleasure as if they were dressing for a feast."[24] At the last minute Bernardo was pardoned on condition that he witness the execution of his relatives. Lucretia died first, then Beatrice, and finally Giacomo.

Shelley introduces his play based on this account with a Preface and Dedication. The Dedication is addressed rather defiantly to Leigh Hunt: "In that patient and irreconcilable enmity with domestic and political tyranny and imposture, which the tenor of your life has illustrated, and which, had I health and talents, should illustrate mine, let us, comforting each other in our task, live and die."[25]

In the Preface, Shelley reviews the Cenci legend and states some critical principles. The language of a verse play should, he feels, be less lavish than that of a poem. Imagery should be subordinated to content and not used for purely aesthetic ends: "In a dramatic composition the imagery and the passion should interpenetrate one another, the former being reserved simply for the full development and illustration of the latter." He agrees with the dictum of Wordsworth's Preface to *Lyrical Ballads*, that "in order to move men to true sympathy we must use the familiar language of men." And his style throughout the play, despite its Elizabethan echoes, is direct and terse. Shelley also makes a distinction between didactic poetry, which aims at teaching moral lessons (a form he abhorred), and poetry that endeavors indirectly and by example to show "the human heart, through its sympathies and antipathies, the knowledge of itself." He states that he has tried to avoid depicting the characters in accordance with his own "conceptions of right or wrong" and to interpret them objectively. Thus, while he feels that Beatrice's urge for revenge is morally condemnable, he nevertheless intends to show her as she was. "Beatrice Cenci," he concludes, in a comment apparently reflecting his concept of himself, "appears to have been one of those rare persons in whom energy and gentleness dwell together without destroying one another."[26]

The Cenci has usually been examined as a literary work. Its dependence on the Elizabethans has been analyzed, as has its structure and imagery, and some attention has been given to its psychological attitudes, particularly as shown in the character of Beatrice. It has not, however, been examined sufficiently for what it essentially is, namely, a play intended for the stage. Such examination has been made easier in recent years by reviews of various performances, particularly one presented at a little theater in Bellingham, Washington, the producers of which kept a detailed record of both the production and audience reaction.[27]

In the opening scene Cardinal Camillo (a character not in Shelley's source) is attempting to move Count Cenci from his evil ways. Shelley's object is to establish the wickedness of Cenci, which he does not by volume of talk—so often the pitfall of the new dramatic writer—but by a conflict of wills between two contrasting characters: the cardinal, disturbed and pleading; Cenci, cynically disdainful. The picture of an evil, unscrupulous, miserly old man is sharply and briefly drawn. His final words to a servant sent a rustle of suspenseful anticipation through the Bellingham audience:

> Bid Beatrice attend me in her chamber
> This evening:—no, at midnight and alone. (I. i. 145–146)

To the objection of some critics that Cenci is "too monstrous to be credible," one can only reply that credible or not, he existed. The deeds with which Shelley charges him are historical facts.[28] Furthermore, they are consistent with the character as drawn by Shelley and with the corrupt society depicted in the play.

The next scene further reveals character, that of Beatrice and of the wily, unscrupulous prelate Orsino. Orsino and Beatrice had been youthful lovers, and he had broken off with her to satisfy his ambitions in the church. He is now a wealthy churchman, whom she is trying to persuade to plead with the pope to help her and her family. Orsino, for his part, hopes to make her his mistress and has no intention of approaching the pope. The picture of a self-seeking, corrupt society is further implied. The dialogue is at times crisp and bitter:

> *Orsino.* You said you loved me then.
> *Beatrice.* You are a priest,
> Speak not to me of love.

But the scene ends with an overly long and villainous soliloquy by Orsino. The picture of Beatrice is one of a spirited, intelligent, practical but not very scrupulous girl, caught in an intolerable situation and ready to use any weapons she can to break out of it.

The action then moves into a colorful and dramatic banquet scene, which the critics usually consider one of the most impressive in the play. As a factual basis for this scene, Shelley had no more than the bare statement in his source that Cenci "showed signs of joy" on hearing of the death of his sons. The scene opens with the guests and the family entering to take their places at the table. Cenci appears in high spirits, which everyone presumes to mean that he has a happy announcement to make—everyone except Beatrice:

> I fear that wicked laughter round his eye,
> Which wrinkles up the skin even to the hair. (I.iii.37–38)

When he rises to speak, the guests look up in anticipation, only to be shocked by the announcement that the occasion for the banquet is the death of his sons. Several guests attempt to seize him but are forced back in confusion by his threats. Beatrice rises, and attention switches from the count to her as she berates him. For a time, Cenci pretends to ignore her, talking on to Camillo, but he finally turns and orders her to her chamber. She continues to defy him. The frightened guests leave. When she and Cenci are alone on the stage—the protagonists at last face to face—he wheels on her with a chilling threat: "I know a charm shall make thee meek and tame." The curtain drops—"to thunders of applause."[29]

The second act opens with a vivid portrayal of a family cowed by paternal tyranny. Shelley's intent in the scene is to make Cenci's coming attack on his daughter plausible by showing the depths of his infamy and to win the sympathy of the audience for the family. Bernardo, the youngest son, is attempting to comfort Lucretia, who has been struck by Cenci. Beatrice enters, distracted and fearful. Her father has renewed and made more explicit his threats to her. Seeing her thus disturbs the others, for, as the audience now begins to see, Beatrice is the force that holds them together. "Your firm mind," Lucretia tells her, "has been our only refuge and defence" (II.i.48–49). In the midst of their talk, Cenci dramatically enters. Seizing Beatrice by the wrist, he curses her and Bernardo from the stage. Left alone with his terrified wife, he sadistically baits her with false accusations, obviously feeling a perverted pleasure in her bewildered denials. The next day, he tells her, they will all leave for the castle of Petrella.

The second scene of the act introduces another member of the family, Beatrice's brother Giacomo, who is seen talking to Orsino. Giacomo is weak and vacillating, subject to unstable extremes, from blustering braggadocio to slobbering remorse. In the hands of Orsino he is a puppet. The scene closes with an overlong soliloquy by Orsino, one of Shelley's heritages from the Elizabethans.

Although Shelley allows the tension generated by the two previous scenes to falter somewhat in this Orsino-Giacomo encounter, by this time it is apparent to the audience that Shelley has a clear sense of character: the self-centered and coldly manipulative Orsino, the sympathetic and troubled Cardinal Camillo, the simple and dependent Lucretia, the vacillating Giacomo, and the youthful Bernardo. None of these characters as such was in his source; from the merest hints—the general wickedness of Cenci and the strong-mindedness of Beatrice—he built up a sadistic, egocentric tyrant and an intellectual, sensitive rebel. Nor are the characters statically conceived. Shelley is not implying that they need inevitably have been such but, in accordance with his view that "their institutions made them what they were," is showing the distortion of a personality under social pressures. The state tyranny that bred the personal tyranny of Cenci transmits itself to his family. Lucretia, it appears, was naturally of a simple, affectionate nature, which had been distorted by the sadistic despotism of a husband whom she once loved. Her tragedy is summed up in her words to Beatrice:

> Nay, Beatrice; have courage, my sweet girl,
> If any one despairs it should be I
> Who loved him once, and now must live with him
> Till God in pity call for him or me. (II.i.80–83)

Giacomo would have lived placidly with his family if Cenci had not turned them against him and generated in him a turmoil of alternating hate and fear. Bernardo is a tragic picture of a boy broken by the contempt of his father: "Thy milky, meek face makes me sick with hate!" (II.i.122). Beatrice is a character of natural warmth, nobility, and honesty, who under the impact of tyranny neither falters, as does Giacomo, nor gropes blindly, as does Lucretia, but resists firmly and finally, under unbearable pressure, turns to savage revenge.

The transition from resistance to revenge takes place in the first scene of the third act. As Beatrice staggers on stage talking wildly, the audience realizes with horror that Cenci has raped her. She is depicted as having gone temporarily insane. Her speeches, really soliloquies, are uncoordinated and hallucinative. If to the modern audience sometimes they seem psychologically unrealistic, one must remember that in Shelley's day little was known of psychiatry, and that Elizabethan-type mad scenes were almost standard fare in tragedies, as in *Orra*, *Bertram*, and *Fazio*. Eliza O'Neill specialized in them. Furthermore, Shelley, aware of the taboo that hung over his theme, must perforce handle it indirectly. Nevertheless, Beatrice's description of the deep, inner revulsion she feels is often penetrating:

> The beautiful blue heaven is flecked with blood!
> The sunshine on the floor is black! The air
> Is changed to vapours such as the dead breathe
> In charnel pits! Pah! I am choked! There creeps
> A clinging, black, contaminating mist
> About me—'tis substantial, heavy, thick;
> I cannot pluck it from me, for it glues

My fingers and my limbs to one another,
And eats into my sinews, and dissolves
My flesh to a pollution, poisoning
The subtle, pure, and inmost spirit of life! (III.i.13–23)

As the scene progresses, her shattered thoughts and emotions begin to swirl into a pattern of murder. Hatred has eaten deep into her, and revenge becomes an obsession. When Orsino wonders what has happened, she replies coldly:

What it can be, or not,
Forbear to think. It is, and it has been;
Advise me how it shall not be again. (III.i.146–148)

With Orsino, Giacomo, and Lucretia, she plots quite calmly to kill her father. A hanging rock on the way to Petrella is to be pushed onto him as he passes along the road. Almost the whole of the stirring and often psychologically acute dialogue in this scene arises from a single statement in the source: "In one of these conversations Beatrice let fall some words which plainly indicated that she and her mother-in-law contemplated the murder of their tyrant, and Monsignore Guerra not only showed approbation of their design, but also promised to co-operate with them in their undertaking."[30]

One question that has puzzled Shelley's critics is Cenci's motive in raping his daughter. Newman White argued that, as it is apparently not lust, "a dramatic motive comprehensible enough," it must lie in a "deep, unexplained hatred and love of evil for its own sake." And Stuart Curran wrote: "Cenci, old and failing, whose life consists solely in power, seeks restoration at the fountainhead of his daughter's spiritual annihilation, her concession to his absolute authority." Shelley "distills the act from its physical to its metaphysical nature."[31] There is certainly an element of truth in both these views. Cenci, as he himself states, is out to break Beatrice's spirit. He does not plan to do this by rape alone. Rather, he intends to turn his daughter into his mistress, to make her learn to like incestuous pleasures, and hence to wholly degrade her. But for this, Cenci clearly has a sexual motivation:

My blood is running up and down my veins!
A fearful pleasure makes it prick and tingle:
I feel a giddy sickness of strange awe:
My heart is beating with an expectation
Of horrid joy. (IV.i.163–167)

Yet he feels reluctance to perpetrate this final evil:

For, strange to say, I feel my spirits fail
With thinking what I have decreed to do. (I.iii.171–172)

He also feels that he is in the power of forces that he cannot consciously control:

> I do not feel as if I were a man,
> But like a fiend appointed to chastise
> The offences of some unremembered world. (IV.i.160–162)

These forces drive him not only to the destruction of Beatrice but to his own destruction also:

> The act I think shall soon extinguish all
> For me: I bear a darker deadlier gloom
> Than the earth's shade, or interlunar air,
> Or constellations quenched in murkiest cloud,
> In which I walk secure and unbeheld
> Towards my purpose.—Would that it were done! (II.i.188–193)

Cenci, Shelley implies, has become so immersed in evil that his pleasures come mostly from inflicting it, and he has now reached a stage of perversity in which unconscious forces are driving him—like the poet of *Alastor*—to his doom. He feels that he has become a kind of demoniacal agent whose mission is not only to break Beatrice's spirit but also to corrupt her soul for all eternity:

> Her spirit shall approach the throne of God
> Plague-spotted with my curses. I will make
> Body and soul a monstrous lump of ruin. (IV.i.93–95)

Clearly, in Count Cenci Shelley has created no simple "Renaissance villain" but a complex, developing character, prey to human fears and vacillations and swept along, in spite of his apparent triumph, like a cork on a necessitarian stream of deepening evil.

Finally, Beatrice and her father are not only individual characters but types of the tyrant and his defier. One of the main motives of all Shelley's tyrants—Jupiter in *Prometheus Unbound*, the emperor in *The Revolt of Islam*, the priests in *Rosalind and Helen*—is to break the spirits of those who oppose them. Beatrice, however, is not only a rebel but a woman, and a woman can be broken by sexual as well as by social oppression:

> From this day and hour
> Never again, I think, with fearless eye,
> And brow superior, and unaltered cheek,
> And that lip made for tenderness or scorn,
> Shalt thou strike dumb the meanest of mankind;
> Me least of all. Now get thee to thy chamber! (II.i.115–120)

The tyrant can brook no opposition, especially from those whose inherent goodness increases both his own sense of guilt and his sadism. Cenci, having failed to break his daughter by other torments, thinks by rape to begin to breed in her that "self-contempt, bitterer to drink than blood,"[32] which will render her impotent to oppose him.

The next scene opens with Giacomo alone in a poverty-stricken room, brooding over the supposed death of his father. A solitary lamp is on the table in front of him, and he enters into an Othello-like comparison between it and his father's life. Suddenly Orsino enters, startling him (and the audience) with the news that Cenci has escaped their murder trap. For this turn of events Shelley is indebted to his source, of which he makes skillful use to build up suspense as the audience realizes that Cenci has still to be dealt with. Orsino unfolds a new plan to Giacomo, who has characteristically, swung from remorse to unstable vengefulness. Orsino knows two villains, Marzio and Olimpio, both of whom bear a grudge against Cenci. On this note of a new conspiracy, the third act closes.

In the opening scene of Act IV, Cenci makes his last appearance and as usual—except perhaps in the conclusion of the banquet scene—dominates the stage. The scene ripens with dramatic conflict as he sends messages to Beatrice, via Lucretia and a servant, to come to him, and as her defiant replies are brought back. The curse that Cenci vents on Beatrice when her final refusal reaches him is a dramatic highlight. At the end of the scene Cenci, worn out by the vehemence of his own lusts and hatreds, goes to bed.

For the outline of the two following scenes, involving the murder of Cenci, Shelley relied on his source. In both the source and the play, Marzio and Olimpio return once, saying that they are overwhelmed by pity, and are upbraided by Beatrice, who threatens to lead them into the room to do the deed herself. In the source, she did actually lead them into the bedroom the first time, but Shelley omitted this, perhaps fearing that it would lose audience sympathy. When the deed is finally done, she gives a bright cloak (a "mantle trimmed with gold" in the source) to Marzio. As the murderers prepare to leave, the sharp sound of a horn announcing the arrival of visitors startles both actors and audience. Beatrice, however, refuses to panic: "Some tedious guest is coming" (IV.iii.58). Now that the murder is over, she feels a quiet calm and confidence:

> The spirit which doth reign within these limbs
> Seems strangely undisturbed. I could even sleep
> Fearless and calm: all ill is surely past. (IV.iii.63–65)

The "ill," however, is only beginning.

It was thought by earlier critics that with the murder of Cenci the action of the play faltered. Most modern critics disagree. The reason for the old view lay in the belief that the flamboyant count was the main character and that the conflict between him and Beatrice was central and personal. But Shelley clearly intended Beatrice to be the main character, and the central conflict is not primarily personal but is directed against social oppression in some form or other. As Giacomo put it:

> And now no more, as once, parent and child,
> But man to man; the oppressor to the oppressed. (III.i.283–284)

With Cenci's death this conflict, far from disappearing, is intensified, as Beatrice comes up against oppression in the new and more terrifying form of the papal state.

The first stage in this new conflict comes with the entrance of the papal legate bearing, ironically but not too convincingly, a warrant for the arrest and execution of Cenci. Lucretia, to the horror of the audience (whose sympathies are wholly with the family), goes to pieces when she is questioned. Beatrice enters to give her strength and the legate leaves, but a moment later the cry of "Murder" rings out and he reenters. The forebodings of the audience are confirmed when the wretched Marzio is dragged in by guards. The legate announces that the family is under arrest. Lucretia is in panic, but Beatrice boldly asserts her innocence, and her bitter speech when her mother faints reveals the typically Shelleyan social concept behind the play:

> My Lord,
> She knows not yet the uses of the world.
> She fears that power is as a beast which grasps
> And loosens not: a snake whose look transmutes
> All things to guilt which is its nutriment.
> She cannot know how well the supine slaves
> Of blind authority read the truth of things
> When written on a brow of guilelessness:
> She sees not yet triumphant Innocence
> Stand at the judgement-seat of mortal man,
> A judge and an accuser of the wrong
> Which drags it there. (IV.iv.176–187)

The final act opens with the last of the Giacomo-Orsino scenes. Giacomo, terrified by the news of the murder of his father, turns on Orsino in blustering defiance. Orsino cunningly soothes him and then coolly sends him into a trap, while he himself—as in the source—escapes in disguise.

The concluding scenes of trial and condemnation are among the most powerful in the play. Shelley, avoiding the long lapse between the murder and its discovery in his source, and the delays as Marzio is finally captured and the defendants are led from prison to prison, focuses immediately on the drama of Beatrice's final conflict with tyranny. Marzio, fresh from the torture, is dragged in and confesses, a confession that provokes the cryptic comment from one of the judges, "This sounds as bad as truth" (V.ii.19). When Beatrice is brought in, she boldly denies everything, as she had previously to the legate. She upbraids Marzio with such vehemence that he retracts his confession and, as in the source, dies in silence under further tortures.

Some have argued that by having Beatrice deny her guilt, Shelley detracts from her character. Shelley, however, is following the source: "They were here examined, and all constantly denied the crime, and particularly Beatrice, who also denied having given to Marzio the mantle trimmed with gold."[33] Moreover, Beatrice's character, as Shelley depicts it, leads logically to such a denial, for Beatrice does not really believe herself guilty of murder but of a simple act of justice, a "high and holy deed" (IV.ii.35). She, like her father in his own perverted way, has a sense of a divine mission:

Our act
Will but dislodge a spirit of deep hell
Out of a human form. (IV.ii.6–8)

As Shelley points out in his Preface, the characters are Catholic believers, and each—ironically—interprets the will of God in his own way. Furthermore, just as Count Cenci is no stock villain, so Beatrice is no unspotted heroine. After all, she has her father murdered, and Shelley indicates that she, too, has been corrupted by the very society against which she is fighting. She is perfectly prepared to lie and to throw others, such as Marzio, to the dogs in order to save herself and her family. Her motives apparently come through clearly in stage presentation and the audience views them sympathetically: "This court scene has profoundly stirred the audience, who sympathize with Beatrice in her bold and resourceful defense. They share her conviction of her own innocence, and they realize that she is defending herself and her family in the only way possible before a court that weighs justice in very crude scales."[34]

The moral conviction of Beatrice, is not shared by the rest of the family. Giacomo is subject to remorseful vacillations, and Lucretia collapses when confronted by the papal legate. In the next scene, Beatrice is awakened by Bernardo to be told that Giacomo and Lucretia have confessed under torture. When the judge enters her cell and threatens her, she turns on him in scornful anger:

Torture your dog, that he may tell when last
He lapped the blood his master shed. (V.iii.63–64)

She paints a vivid and concise picture of the world of medieval tyranny:

And with considering all the wretched life
Which I have lived, and its now wretched end,
And the small justice shown by Heaven and Earth
To me or mine; and what a tyrant thou art,
And what slaves these; and what a world we make,
The oppressor and the oppressed. (V.iii.70–75)

But she realizes that all is now hopeless and, as in the source, is "convicted without having confessed":

Say what ye will. I shall deny no more.
If ye desire it thus, thus let it be,
And so an end of all. Now do your will;
No other pains shall force another word. (V.iii.86–89)

The final scene opens with Cardinal Camillo speaking with Bernardo in a hall in the prison. The cardinal has been to see the pope, as did "many cardinals and princes," according to Shelley's source, but the pope is adamant:

He looked as calm and keen as is the engine
Which tortures and which kills, exempt itself
From aught that it inflicts. (V.iv.2–4)

Beatrice, Lucretia, and Giacomo enter, to learn the hopelessness of their situation. From the merest hint in his source—"Beatrice on hearing it broke into a piercing lamentation, and into passionate gesture, exclaiming, 'How is it possible, O my God! that I must so suddenly die!' "[35]—Shelley creates one of his most moving speeches, in which Beatrice's faith begins to crumble:

My God! Can it be possible I have
To die so suddenly? So young to go
Under the obscure, cold, rotting, wormy ground!
To be nailed down into a narrow place;
To see no more sweet sunshine; hear no more
Blithe voice of living thing; muse not again
Upon familiar thoughts, sad, yet thus lost—
How fearful! to be nothing! Or to be . . .
What? Oh, where am I? Let me not go mad!
Sweet Heaven, forgive weak thoughts! If there should be
No God, no Heaven, no Earth in the void world;
The wide, gray, lampless, deep, unpeopled world! (V.iv.48–59)

As she recovers from this nihilistic vision, reminiscent of Cythna, she turns again to scornful excoriation of a society in which:

hard, cold men,
Smiling and slow, walk through a world of tears
To death as to life's sleep. (V.iv.112–114)

Such speeches show clearly what Shelley meant in his comments on the difference between the language of dramatic and nondramatic poetry. The words of Beatrice are stark and ironic, in contrast to the intricate lyrical fire of, say, *Epipsychidion.*

At the end Beatrice is resigned, and the play closes in tones of simple, natural pathos:

Give yourself no unnecessary pain
My dear Lord Cardinal. Here, Mother, tie

My girdle for me and bind up this hair
In any simple knot; ay, that does well.
And yours I see is coming down. How often
Have we done this for one another; now
We shall not do it any more. My Lord,
We are quite ready. Well, 'tis very well. (V.iv.158–165)

Although the 1922 London performance lasted three hours, with only one short break, a critic wrote of the production: "the audience listened with rapt attention from start to finish, and, exhausted as it must have been by the effort required to grasp Shelley's magnificent imagery, it would not leave until everybody had been called again and again." And W. J. Turner wrote in *The Spectator*:

Well, now that we have seen *The Cenci* on the stage what are we to think of it? I can say at once that I did not find it a moment too long. When one considers the extraordinary difficulty of the theme and the entire absence of any relief from its pitch of sustained gloom and suffering it must be reckoned a marvel of dramatic construction. It holds our attention from the first moment to the last. It might be thought that after the murder of Count Cenci the interest would flag, but, on the contrary, it deepens. In fact, the last act of the play is the most moving of all. It is what it should be, the culmination of the tragedy, the moment when its meaning flowers with a complete and extraordinary beauty.[36]

Charles the First

Shelley had high hopes for *The Cenci,* and its refusal by the theaters must have been a heavy blow to him. Nevertheless, under prodding by Mary, he soon started to plan a second play, and when he realized that, despite the reviewer's attacks, *The Cenci* was having some success with the reading public, he was encouraged to go ahead with his plans.[37] For his second play Shelley turned to what he considered the most significant period in English history, the revolutionary overthrow of the monarchy of Charles I and the rise of the republic under Cromwell.

The idea that developed into *Charles the First* arose from a suggestion by William Godwin in June 1818 that Shelley or Mary write a book on the Cromwellian revolutionary leaders, depicting them as "great and admirable personages." Shelley suggested a dramatic treatment, and Mary considered doing a play on the subject.[38] Two years later, in July 1820, Shelley informed Medwin that he himself intended to write a play "without prejudice or passion, entitled 'Charles the First.' "[39] Apparently he began work on it about January 3, 1822.[40] On January 11, he wrote with enthusiasm to his publishers that it "promises to be good" and "will be ready by the Spring."[41] By January 26, however, he had become discouraged, claiming that he could not "seize the conception of the subject as a whole" and could "seldom now touch the *Canvas.*"[42] Shortly afterward he laid it aside and turned to *The Triumph of Life.* Only one act of the play was attempted, and two of the scenes for that act are incomplete, but enough remains to show that it could have become a major English historical drama.

During the brief period that Shelley actually spent on the play, he appears to have worked hard at it. Medwin reported that his manuscript gave evidence of much reworking, and he did a good deal of serious historical reading. To follow his use of the sources provides, once again, an interesting revelation of the creative process, showing what he accepted and rejected, and how he changed the stuff of history into that of literature. His main sources were Bulstrode Whitelocke's *Memorials of the English Affairs from the Beginning of the Reign of Charles the First to the Happy Restoration of King Charles the Second* and David Hume's *History of England.* He also used Catherine Macaulay's *History of England from the Accession of James I to the Elevation of the House of Hanover*, and possibly the earl of Clarendon's *The History of the Rebellion and Civil Wars in England.* Materials from the first three works are mingled, often inextricably, in the play. But Shelley used each for a special purpose. From Whitelocke he took detailed material not present in the others; and Whitelocke is the only one of the four to have noticeably influenced his wording. Hume he liked for his concise marshaling of the facts and his ironic objectivity. Catherine Macaulay was a late eighteenth-century radical, whose eight-volume history treats the subject in much more detail than the others. Her staunch pro-Commonwealth attitudes—not to mention Mary Wollstonecraft's praise of her as "the woman of the greatest abilities, undoubtedly, that this country has ever produced"—certainly must have endeared her to Shelley.[43]

Shelley's attitude toward Charles I and the Commonwealth men is evident in *A Philosophical View of Reform*: "From England then first began to pass away the stain of conquest . . . By rapid gradation the nation was conducted to the temporary abolition of aristocracy and episcopacy, and to the mighty example which, 'in teaching nations how to live,' England afforded to the world—of bringing to public justice one of those chiefs of a conspiracy of privileged murderers and robbers whose impunity has been the consecration of crime." And again: "The Long Parliament, questionless, was the organ of the will of all classes of people in England since it effected the complete revolution in a tyranny consecrated by time."[44]

Its author holding such views, it was inevitable that *Charles the First* would take on a strong political slant. Indeed, it is clear from passage after passage in the play that, if performed before a contemporary audience, it would have been understood as advocating parliamentary reform or republicanism. Shelley, nevertheless, intended to give what he believed was a true portrait of the king and to present royalist views fairly. The guidelines that he laid down for a dramatist in the Preface to *The Cenci* would certainly have held for *Charles the First*: "to represent the characters as they probably were" and "avoid the error of making them actuated by my own conceptions of right and wrong." He was not writing a propaganda play. Yet his declaration to his publishers that the play "is not coloured by the party spirit of the author" is not entirely true.[45] Shelley's political views obviously slanted both his selection of material and his characterizations.

Shelley, along with Hunt and others, believed that the period to be covered by the first two acts, 1633–1641, was similar to his own age, involving a struggle against aristocratic domination that might possibly end in revolution. The king, William Laud, archbishop of Canterbury, and Thomas Wentworth, earl of Strafford, formed a triumvirate of aristocratic reaction. They introduced the burdensome penalties and taxes that led to the trial of John Hampden for refusing payment. Hoping to break the power of Parliament, they were already attempting to exert dictatorial rule through the Star Chamber. In ecclesiastical affairs they intended to undermine the power of the Dissenters and to subordinate them to the Church of England. It was here that they met with the most stubborn opposition and consequently used the most terroristic methods of subjection. Alexander Leighton, a preacher and physician, was sentenced to be whipped, branded, and to have his ears cut off and his nose slit for an attack on the Anglican hierarchy. William Prynne, a Puritan lawyer, was fined £5,000 and sentenced to have his ears removed and to be imprisoned for an alleged slight on the queen in his *Histriomastix: A Scourge of Stage Players*.[46] When he continued his defiance, he was again tried—and branded "S.L." (seditious libeler) on both cheeks—this time with two other offenders, John Bastwick, a physician, and Henry Burton, a preacher.

It was the first trial of Prynne that inspired the event which Shelley used for his opening scene. The lawyers of the Inns of Court, fearing that Prynne's *Histriomastix* might bring them under suspicion of disloyalty, put on a processional masque in honor of the king on his return from Scotland in 1633. James Shirley, as the leading court playwright, was requested to write the text, and Bulstrode Whitelocke, then master of the revels, was placed in charge of the musical arrangements. The whole spectacle was reputed to have cost £20,000.

The most elaborate account of the masque was given by Whitelocke, and it was this account that inspired Shelley's opening scene:

> The first that marched [Whitelocke wrote] were twenty footmen, in scarlet liveries with silver-lace, each one having his sword by his side, a baton in one hand, and a torch lighted in the other hand; these were the marshal's men who cleared the streets, made way, and were all about the marshal, waiting his commands . . . [Then came] one hundred gentlemen of the inns of court . . . gallantly mounted on the best horses, and dressed in very rich clothes . . . After the horsemen came the antimaskers; and as the horsemen had their music, about a dozen of the best trumpeters proper for them, and in their livery, sounding before them so the first antimask, being of cripples and beggars on horseback, had their music of keys and tongs, and the like, snapping and yet playing in a consort before them. These beggars were also mounted, but on the poorest leanest

jades that could be gotten out of the dirt-carts or elsewhere; and the variety and change from such noble music and gallant horses as went before them unto their proper music and pitiful horses, made both of them the more pleasing.

Later came the parade of the chariots, a colorful scene that obviously caught Shelley's eye:

Then came the first chariot of the grand maskers, which was not so large as those which went before, but most curiously framed, carved, and painted with exquisite art, and purposely for this service and occasion. The form of it was after that of the Roman triumphal chariots, as near as could be gathered by some old prints and pictures extant of them . . . The colours of the first chariot were silver and crimson, given by the lot to Gray's Inn, as I remember; the chariot was all over painted richly with these colours, even the wheels of it, most artificially laid on, and the carved work of it was as curious for that art, and it made a stately show. It was drawn with four horses abreast, and they were covered to their heels all over with cloth of tissue, of the colours of crimson and silver, huge plumes of red and white feathers on their heads and buttocks; the coachman's cap and feather, his long coat, and his very whip and cushion, of the same stuff and colour. The torches and flaming huge flambeaus borne by the sides of each chariot made it seem lightsome as at noonday, but more glittering, and gave a full and clear light to all the streets and windows as they passed by. The march was slow, in regard of their great number, but more interrupted by the multitude of the spectators in the streets, besides the windows, and they all seemed loath to part with so glorious a spectacle.[47]

In Shelley's picturesque opening scene, headed "The Masque of the Inns of Court," he tried to capture the magnificence of this masque, following Whitelocke closely, even to the contrast with the antimasque, but giving it an ironic, anti-establishment twist:

The Youth. How glorious! See those thronging chariots
Rolling, like painted clouds before the wind,
Behind their solemn steeds: how some are shaped
Like curved sea-shells dyed by the azure depths
Of Indian seas; some like the new-born moon;
And some like cars in which the Romans climbed
(Canopied by Victory's eagle-wings outspread)—
The Capitolian—See how gloriously
The mettled horses in the torchlight stir
Their gallant riders.

. . . . .

Second Citizen. Lo, giving substance to my words, behold
At once the sign and the thing signified—
A troop of cripples, beggars, and lean outcasts,
Horsed upon stumbling jades, carted with dung,
Dragged for a day from cellars and low cabins
And rotten hiding-holes, to point the moral

Of this presentment, and bring up the rear
Of painted pomp with misery! (I.i.135–149.167–174)

Shelley used this spectacle as a background to the sullen and mounting opposition of the London citizens. When Strafford, Laud, and the queen pass by, the spectators murmur. Stafford is an "apostate," Laud is "drunken with blood and gold," and the "papist" queen walks "as if her nice feet scorned our English earth" (I.i.54,61,67–68). To add fuel to these fires, the Puritan Leighton comes in among the spectators, his face branded and disfigured: "I *was* Leighton: what I *am* thou seest" (I.i.88–89).[48]

As the chariots, lit by flambeaus, the gentlemen in rich clothes, the magnificent marshal, and his assistants, all parade by, the bitterness of the populace bursts out in the speech of the second citizen, in words that are virtually a poetic rendering of the views of the Spenceans and other social radicals of Shelley's day:

Here is the pomp that strips the houseless orphan,
Here is the pride that breaks the desolate heart.
These are the lilies glorious as Solomon,
Who toil not, neither do they spin,—unless
It be the webs they catch poor rogues withal.
Here is the surfeit which to them who earn
The niggard wages of the earth, scarce leaves
The tithe that will support them till they crawl
Back to her cold hard bosom. (I.i.155–162)

Scene II shifts to a large chamber in the royal palace some time after the performance of the masque. A group of lawyers from the Inns of Court have come to thank the king for his attendance at the masque and to receive his thanks in turn. In Whitelocke, these gentlemen were identified as "Sir John Finch, Mr. Gerling, Mr. Hyde [Clarendon], and myself," and the interview is reported as most amiable. Shelley mentions none of these but introduces Oliver St. John, a well-known Puritan supporter, as the spokesman for the group.[49] His object in doing so was both to show growing opposition to the monarchy and to familiarize his audience with St. John, who would doubtless have come into the second act as he was Hampden's counsel at his trial.

The king thanks the gentlemen graciously, but the queen takes advantage of the occasion to lecture St. John on the behavior of Prynne and to hint that an absolutist monarchy on the French model is what England needs. St. John answers scornfully:

Madam, the love of Englishmen can make
The lightest favour of their lawful king
Outweigh a despot's.—We humbly take our leaves,
Enriched by smiles which France can never buy. (II.29–32)[50]

Still smarting under this rebuff, the king, Laud, Strafford, and Lord Cottington, the chancellor of the exchequer, settle down to a discussion of policy, which soon turns into a general squabble on how to raise money, whether or not to call Parliament, and how to handle the rebellious Scots. Shelley gives a vivid picture of a tyrannical cabal intent on maintaining its own despotic rule no matter what the cost to the country. The new rise of democratic power is seen by them only as a challenge to their ancient prerogative of unchecked taxation. The Parliament that represents this power they hate and fear, intending to counteract it through the Star Chamber or, if necessary, by armed force.

The king somewhat blusteringly strikes the opening note for the discussion:

> The uttermost
> Farthing exact from those who claim exemption
> From knighthood: that which once was a reward
> Shall thus be made a punishment, that subjects
> May know how majesty can wear at will
> The rugged mood. (II.75–80)

The queen approves—with aristocratic contempt for the people:

> My dearest lord,
> I see the new-born courage in your eye
> Armed to strike dead the Spirit of the Time
> Which spurs to rage the many-headed beast. (II.113–116)

Strafford's cynical, cunning speech is reminiscent of Purganax (Castlereagh) before Parliament in *Swellfoot the Tyrant*, and would have been taken by a contemporary audience as aimed at the policy of the government:

> Fee with coin
> The loudest murmurers; feed with jealousies
> Opposing factions,—be thyself of none;
> And borrow gold of many, for those who lend
> Will serve thee till thou payest them; and thus
> Keep the fierce spirit of the hour at bay. (II.160–165)

The most blindly reactionary of all is Laud, the very type of the religious tyrant for whom Shelley had long had a special hatred, as witness the "Iberian priest" in *The Revolt of Islam*, and he depicts his sadistic, self-righteous fanaticism with a sure hand. Laud is obsessed with the notion of persecuting the dissenting Scots for their stubborn opposition to his rule:

> Let ample powers and new instructions be
> Sent to the High Commissioners in Scotland.
> To death, imprisonment, and confiscation,
> Add torture, add the ruin of the kindred

Of the offender, add the brand of infamy,
Add mutilation: and if this suffice not,
Unleash the sword and fire, that in their thirst
They may lick up that scum of schismatics. (II.225–232)

But if war is to be declared on Scotland, money will be needed, and money can be raised in large sums only by calling Parliament. Laud's hatred of the Scots is such that he is willing to attempt even this, but the queen opposes it. Strafford suggests a policy bordering on treason:

The engine of parliaments
Might be deferred until I can bring over
The Irish regiments: they will serve to assure
The issue of the war against the Scots.
And, this game won—which if lost, all is lost—
Gather these chosen leaders of the rebels
And call them, if you will, a parliament. (II.344–350)

For this, and for other touches in the scene, Shelley was indebted to a report, included by both Whitelocke and Catherine Macaulay, of an actual conference produced at Strafford's trial:

King Charles. How can we undertake offensive war, if we have no more money?
Lord Strafford. Borrow of the city one hundred thousand pounds. Go on vigorously to levy ship-money. Your majesty having tried the affection of your people, is absolved and loosed from all rules of government, and to do what power will admit. Your majesty having tried all ways, and being refused, shall be acquitted before God and man; and you have an army in Ireland that you may employ to reduce this kingdom to obedience; for I am confident the Scots cannot hold out five months.
Archbishop Laud. You have tried all ways, and have always been refused; it is now lawful to take it by force.[51]

Shortly after the Strafford speech, Laud, Cottington, and Strafford leave, and the king and queen are left alone with Archy, the king's fool. Archy had appeared earlier in the scene, when he was sentenced to stand ten minutes in the rain for making fun of Laud.[52] Now, on his return, it becomes apparent what Shelley intends his role to be. It is not only, as Charles said of him, to "weave about himself a world of mirth, out of the wreck of ours" (II.107–108). Archy is, ironically, the only one who senses the coming deluge. Through his meandering, insinuating patter is heard the somber note of disaster: "Thus Baby Charles, and the Twelfth-night Queen of Hearts, and the overgrown schoolboy Cottington, and that little urchin Laud—who would reduce a verdict of 'guilty. death,' by famine, if it were impregnable by composition—all impannelled against poor Archy for presenting them bitter physic the last day of the holidays." Archy has a poet's faculty for sensing the changes in the weather of history and, in a broken way, has something of a poet's language.

Archy's chatter finally becomes oppressive, and Henrietta sends him off on an errand. After he leaves, she adds to her advocacy of French absolutism and of despotic rule in England a subtle insinuation toward Catholicism:

And, as we pass
The gallery, we'll decide where that Correggio
Shall hang—the Virgin Mother
With her child, born the King of heaven and earth,
Whose reign is men's salvation. (II.463–467)

Shelley's picture of Henrietta, as well as that of Charles and his ministers, seems to reflect something of Catherine Macaulay, who depicts Charles as ruling England "four years despotically" by usurping "the power of raising money without consent of the people" and by imposing, through the Star-Chamber, "rigorous and arbitrary penalties on offenses not legally punishable."[53] Shelley has him say:

My Lord of Coventry,
Lay my command upon the Courts below
That bail be not accepted for the prisoners
Under the warrant of the Star Chamber. (II.80–83)

Shelley's picture, however, is perhaps somewhat tempered by Hume's (and possibly Clarendon's) concept of Charles as vacillating, and led astray by the extremes of his advisers:

Oh, be our feet still tardy to shed blood,
Guilty though it may be! (II.351–352)[54]

As for the queen, Shelley would find the fact of her influence over the uxorious Charles in all his sources.

For the third scene Shelley depicts the trials of Prynne, Bastwick, and Bishop Williams, who was accused of having written libelous statements about Laud. The scene is the Star Chamber. Laud, Juxon, and Strafford are on the bench, Prynne and Bastwick before them as prisoners. In Bastwick, Shelley intends to portray the typical Puritan revolutionary, scornful of his oppressors, confident of the future, and in his own way, as fanatical as Laud. Between the two is Juxon, a "moderate" royalist. The conflict in the courtroom reflects the conflict of the age:

Bastwick. I bid ye grudge me not
The only earthly favour ye can yield,
Or I think worth acceptance at your hands,—
Scorn, mutilation, and imprisonment.

. . . . .

Laud. Officer, take the prisoner from the bar,
And be his tongue slit for his insolence.

Bast. While this land holds a pen—
Laud. Be his hands—
Juxon. Stop!
Forbear, my lord! The tongue, which now can speak
No terror, would interpret, being dumb,
Heaven's thunder to our harm; . .
And hands, which now write only their own shame,
With bleeding stumps might sign our blood away.
Laud. Much more such "mercy" among men would be,
Did all the ministers of Heaven's revenge
Flinch thus from earthly retribution. I
Could suffer what I would inflict. (III.23–26, 32–44)[55]

Bastwick is led off, and Bishop Williams brought in. He, too, begins a defiant speech, just as the act breaks off. Shelley, perhaps, had some doubts on how to proceed with Williams because he later capitulated.

The plan for the fragmentary fourth scene, the projected flight of Hampden, Pym, and Cromwell to America, could have been found by Shelley in both Macaulay and Hume. Macaulay wrote:

The enormous, yet increasing height of monarchical tyranny which raged at this time in England, together with the small prospect of redress which the times promised, occasioned numbers of the natives to sell their estates, and to ship themselves off for America, there to enjoy a liberty lost to the inhabitants of Great Britain. But these avowed destroyers of all the rights of humanity, the bosom-friends and ministers of Charles, unwilling that their fellow-citizens should anywhere possess the blessings of Freedom, prevailed with their master to issue out a proclamation, debarring the adventurous access to those uncultivated shores. Eight ships laying in the Thames, and ready to sail, were stayed by an order of the council. Earmarked in these were Sir Arthur Hazelrig, John Hampden, and Oliver Cromwell, three men of spirit, who resolved for ever to abandon a country where the laws had lost their power to protect, and fly to the other extremity of the globe, there to endure a painful solitude in wild deserts, rather than submit to a government that degraded their species beneath the condition of beasts.[56]

Shelley barely began the scene. Cromwell does not speak, but Hampton voices (somewhat anachronistically) one of Shelley's finest tributes to America:

Oh, light us to the isles of the evening land!
Like floating Edens cradled in the glimmer
Of sunset, through the distant mist of years
Touched by departing hope, they gleam! lone regions,
Where Power's poor dupes and victims yet have never
Propitiated the savage fear of kings
With purest blood of noblest hearts. (IV.22–28)[57]

With this scene, the manuscript breaks off,[58] but Shelley's plan for his second act can be gathered from one of his notebooks:

> Act 2^d Scene 1
>
> Chiefs of the Popular Party, Hampden's trial and its effects—Reasons of Hampden and his colleag[u]es for resistance-young Sir H. Vane's reasons: The first rational and logical, the Second impetuous and enthusiastic.
>
> Reasonings on Hampden's trial p. 222.
>
> The King zealous for the Church inheriting this disposition from his father.
>
> This act to open between the two Scotch Wars.
>
> Easter Day 1635
>
> The reading of the Liturgy
>
> Lord Traquai
>
> The Covenant
>
> The determined resistance against Charles and the Liturgy—
>
> Worse than the worse is indecision
>
> Mary di Medici the Queen came to England in 1638. It was observed that the sword and pestilence followed her wherever she went and that her restless spirit embroiled everything she approached
>
> The King annulled at York
>
> Many unlawful grants, & in wh
>
> [This concluded Shelley's plan, but at the top of one of the pages is penciled:]
>
> Act 2
>
> After the 1st Scottish War
>
> [and at the bottom:]
>
> The End—Strafford's death[59]

In the first act, Shelley had been treating the events of 1633–1637: the masque of the Inns of Court; the debates between Charles and his ministers following his return from Scotland; the trials of Prynne, Bastwick, and Bishop Williams; the projected emigration of Pym, Hampden, and Cromwell. In the second act he intended to treat the events of 1637–1641. The first scene was to deal with Hampden's trial, either portraying it directly or showing its effects on a gathering of Puritan leaders. A second scene apparently was to represent Charles's attempts to impose the liturgy on the Scots. "Lord Traquai" is an abbreviation for "Lord Traquaire." The Earl of Traquaire went to London to represent the Scottish cause to Charles, and Shelley's noting of the name may indicate that London and not Scotland was to provide the setting for this scene, and that he intended to represent Scottish opposition to Charles by showing its repercussions in the English court. The scene would thus be a continuation of Scene II in Act I, where

Charles and his ministers discuss war against Scotland. The final, climactic scene of the act was to be the execution of Strafford, an historical episode that, with its last meeting between Laud and Strafford, was highly dramatic. The main purpose of the act as a whole was to reveal the mounting opposition to Charles and his ministers, including the stormy and defiant trial of Hampden and the subsequent increase of popular opposition, the commotions in Scotland foreshadowing the outbreak of war, and finally the execution of Strafford.

The notation on "Mary di Medici" apparently does not imply a separate scene. She had visited England in 1638 at the time of the Scottish trouble, and Shelley probably intended to introduce her during one of the other scenes, perhaps the third. The notation on Charles at York indicates a suggestion for Act III, as Charles did not retire to York until after the execution of Strafford, and Shelley indicates that Act II was to end with Strafford's execution.

It is also possible to discover from these notes something of the source material that Shelley intended to use for the act. The comments on Mary di Medici, for instance, are taken almost word for word from Whitelocke: "In October, Mary de Medicies, the queen-mother of France, came into England. The people were generally discontented at her coming and her followers, which some observed to be the sword or pestilence; and that her restless spirit embroiled all where she came."[60]

That Shelley would have completed the play, had he lived, seems likely, even though he faced considerable difficulties. The story of Charles I, with its innumerable characters and crosscurrents is complex and diffuse, in contrast to the neatly unified story of the Cenci family. It was doubtless this structural difficulty that Shelley had in mind when he wrote that he could not seize "the conception of the subject as a whole."[61] But this kind of difficulty is one that playwrights have constantly to cope with and usually solve. Plays are often laid aside, sometimes for a considerable period, before being resumed, for the fitting of material into the confines of the traditional dramatic structure is a special kind of problem that may require time and ingenuity. That Shelley was seriously involved in the play is shown not only by what he wrote but also by the amount of historical reading he did in preparation for it. The unfinished play gives the impression of a great work of art struggling to be born, like Michelangelo's captives emerging from the rock. If it had been completed on the same level on which it was begun, it might have been a play of greater power and significance than *The Cenci.* In it Shelley began to break with his Elizabethan models and was creating a new dramatic language and structure.

12
The Poet and the Critic

Adonais

"Poetry," Shelley informed Medwin, who had submitted some poetry to him, "although its source is native and involuntary, requires in its development severe attention."[1] It is probably not fortuitous that the next sentence begins, "I am happy to hear that 'Adonais' pleased you," for *Adonais*, combining subtle thought and soaring emotion in disciplined Spenserian stanzas, perfectly illustrates his meaning. The combination, however, also presents difficulties. *Adonais* is one of the most complex of Shelley's poems. Often presented as asserting Platonism and immortality, it in fact asserts neither. And it has psychological depths and hidden motifs that have generally gone unperceived.

Part of the problem lies in the fact that *Adonais* is written on three levels. On the surface it is an elegy on the death of a beautiful youth called Adonais, mourned by Urania—echoing the tale of Adonis, slain by a wild boar and mourned by Venus. On the next level it is, as the Preface notes, an elegy for John Keats and an attack on the critic whose slanderous review of his poems in *The Quarterly Review* was said to have caused or hastened his death. This, the central level, mingles social and philosophical content. The deepest level is partly conscious and partly unconscious, blending Shelley's own persecution, which he attributed in part to the same critic, and his projected death with Keats's death and persecution.

Shelley and Keats

So far as the reading public was concerned, Keats had begun his career as one of Leigh Hunt's "young poets." On December 1, 1816, he had been so linked with Shelley in an article in *The Examiner*. Shortly afterward he dedicated his first book of poems to Hunt, in which he included a sonnet hailing Hunt's release from prison and attacking the prince regent. He was a regular reader and supporter of the radical *Examiner* and the liberal *Champion*, for both of which he wrote reviews. He rejoiced in Hazlitt's annihilating attack on Southey for the *Letter to Mr. Smith*, in which Southey had attempted to justify his own backsliding.[2] He supported William Hone and Thomas Jonathan Wooler in their free speech trials.[3] He was a skeptic in religion.[4] And he was as strongly antiwar as any radical, sharing Shelley's view that Napoleon was more of a reactionary than a progressive influence. "I would," he once declared, "jump down Aetna for any great Public Good."[5]

This outlook is reflected in the *Hyperion* vision of society as advancing to higher and higher stages of beauty and in the humanitarian dedication of *The Fall of Hyperion*:

> "Are there not thousands in the world," said I,
> Encourag'd by the sooth voice of the shade,
> "Who love their fellows even to the death,
> Who feel the giant agony of the world,
> And more, like slaves to poor humanity,
> Labour for mortal good?" (154–159)

Yet except for the sonnets to Hunt and Kosciusko, Keats wrote little directly political poetry (although the sharp antiregency satire of the *Cap and Bells* shows that he had talents in this field which his early death left only partly developed). Although a humanitarian, he was not, like Shelley, a revolutionary in his social philosophy, and he sometimes showed little understanding of the political reform movement: "There are many Madmen in the Country, I have no doubt, who would like to be beheaded on tower Hill merely for the sake of eclat, there are many Men like Hunt who from a principle of taste would like to see things go on better, there are many like Sir F. Burdett who like to sit at the head of political dinners—but there are none prepared to suffer in obscurity for their Country—the motives of our worst Men are interest and of our best Vanity—We have no Milton, no Algernon Sidney."[6] Keats, a middle class Londoner, had a healthy distrust for the aristocratic radical Sir Francis Burdett, much admired by Shelley and Hunt, but his general attitude is clearly impractical. It would have done no good for anyone to "suffer in obscurity." Shelley and Hunt were willing to support reform advocates not only because they believed in reform but also because they regarded it as a steppingstone to further advances, and they viewed the reform movement not as a break with past struggles for liberty but as their continuation. They could hardly have regarded Keats as more than a promising neophyte in political matters, whereas Keats, while agreeing with much of their outlook, considered that, for poets, they were overobsessed with politics.

Shelley first met Keats at Leigh Hunt's home in December 1816, and thereafter until his departure for Italy in March 1818 the two met from time to time at the homes of mutual friends. On one occasion they wrote sonnets ("to the Nile") in competition, and Shelley told Medwin that he and Keats "mutually agreed, in the same given time, (six months each) to write a long poem, and that the *Endymion*, and *Revolt of Islam* were the fruits of this rivalry." "I had not known the young poet long," wrote Hunt in his *Autobiography*, "when Shelley and he became acquainted under my roof. Keats did not take to Shelley as kindly as Shelley did to him . . . Keats, being a little too sensitive on the score of his origin, felt inclined to see in every man of birth a sort of natural enemy. Their styles in writing also were very different; and Keats ... was so far inferior in universality to his great acquaintance, that he could not accompany him in his daedal rounds with nature, and his Archimedean endeavours to move the globe with his own hands." "I went to Hunt's and Haydon's who live now as neighbours," Keats wrote to his friend, Benjamin Bailey, "Shelley was there—I know nothing about any thing in this part of the world ... You see Bailey how independent my writing has been—Hunt's disuasion was of no avail—I refused to visit Shelley, that I might have my own unfettered scope—and after all I shall have the Reputation of Hunt's elevé." And again (to his brothers): "The fact is he [Hunt] & Shelley are hurt & perhaps justly, at my not having showed them the affair [*Endymion*] officiously & from several hints I have had they appear much disposed to dissect & anatomize, any trip or slip I may have made.—But whose afraid Ay! Tom! demme if I am." And on another occasion Keats wrote to his brothers: "Shelley's poem [*The Revolt of Islam*] is out & there are words about its being objected to, as much as Queen Mab was. Poor Shelley I think he has his Quota of good qualities, in sooth la!!"[7]

Keats's attitude toward Shelley was clearly ambivalent, his regard for his "good qualities" modified by some underlying antagonism. Feeling the impact of, yet at the same time distrusting, Shelley's revolutionary philosophy (his "Archimedean endeavors to move the globe"), he resisted its encroachment on his own "commonsense" liberalism and fought for his "own unfettered scope." He felt out of his depth in the knowledgeable Shelley-Hunt circle: "I know nothing of anything in this part of the world." He retreated from their criticism of his work and rebuffed Shelley's attempts at a closer friendship.

Nevertheless, Shelley did have an influence on Keats. It must be remembered that Shelley and Keats were Leigh Hunt's promising "young poets," and there were no others of consequence at the time. The fact that Shelley was older and had published more must mean that Keats regarded him as his main rival, and must, therefore, have reacted to him strongly, both positively and negatively. The positive influence is clear in *Endymion*, which embodies some of Shelley's views on sexual love and was influenced by *Alastor*. But that Keats was determined not to become in any way an echo of Shelley is clear from his letters. And this very determination influenced his development. The fact that Keats's liberal and antireligious ideas penetrated so little of his major poetry suggests that he was deliberately avoiding their expression. Perhaps, indeed, Keats's philosophy of "negative capability"—a skeptical objectivity—arose in part from his reaction to Shelley's positive views on politics and religion and their expression in *Queen Mab*, *The Revolt of Islam*, and the *Alastor* volume poems. Keats's fear of Shelley's influence—at a time when his own original genius was still being formed—doubtless also lay behind his rebuffing of Shelley's attempts at a closer relationship. This situation Shelley aggravated by an overly critical attitude toward Keats's early poetry, even at one time advising Keats not to publish his "first-blights."[8]

Such is the written record on the relationship of Shelley and Keats in England. It seems impossible to doubt, however, that there was a deeper feeling between the two poets than appears from this record. One so sensitive to others as Shelley must have felt the essential nobility of Keats's character, and one with Keats's insight must have been aware of Shelley's genius and humanity. That a stronger feeling did exist is evident in the celebrated exchange of letters between the two poets in 1820, when Shelley, on hearing of Keats's illness, wrote to invite him to spend the winter with him in Italy. This was a warm and generous gesture, for Shelley was neither over burdened with money nor room, and he would not have made the offer unless he had had strong affection and admiration for Keats. Keats, for his part, was deeply moved: "I am very much gratified that you, in a foreign country, and with a mind almost over occupied, should write to me in the strain of the Letter beside me." The critical comments in these letters should not be taken as personal reflections. Shelley, it is true, states that the "treasures" of *Endymion* were "poured forth with indistinct profusion," and Keats hints that Shelley might spend more time on style and less on social philosophy: "curb your magnanimity and be more of an artist, and 'load every rift' of your subject with ore." But these were objective criticisms honestly given by both poets. Shelley, thinking his views about *Endymion* to be correct, felt that he had to express them, for poetry was above personal relations; and so, too, with Keats. Neither would have been apt to take offense at such judgments. It seems likely, in fact, that if the two men had lived longer, they might have become close friends. Shelley certainly seems to have hoped so: "Where is Keats now? I am anxiously expecting him in Italy when I shall take care to bestow every possible attention on him. I consider his a most valuable life, & I am deeply interested in his safety. I intend to be the physician both of his body & his soul, to keep the one warm & to teach [the] other Greek & Spanish. I am aware indeed in part, [tha]t I am nourishing a rival who will far surpass [me] and this is an additional motive & will be an added pleasure."[9]

A few months after Shelley left England, the first of the attacks on Keats took place in *Blackwoods* for August 1818. These attacks were not so much literary as political. Keats's avant-garde poetry was beyond the narrow traditionalist scope of the Tory critics, and whatever merits they may have seen in it they buried, partly consciously, partly unconsciously, in a desire to conform to the general policy of their journals of hitting out at *The Examiner* group. Following the attack in *Blackwoods* came one in *The Quarterly Review*, in which, as in the *Blackwoods* article, the political bias of the reviewer was frankly displayed:

He is unhappily a disciple of the new school of what has been somewhere called 'Cockney Poetry,' which may be defined to consist of the most incongruous ideas in the most uncouth language. Of this school Mr. Leigh Hunt . . . aspires to be the hierophant . . . This author is a copyist of Mr. Hunt, but he is more unintelligible, almost as rugged, twice as diffuse, and ten times more tiresome and absurd, than his prototype, who though he impudently presumed to seat himself in the chair of criticism, and to measure his own poetry by his own standard, yet generally had a meaning. But Mr. Keats had advanced no dogmas which he was bound to support by examples. His nonsense, therefore, is quite gratuitous; he writes it for its own sake, and, being bitten by Mr. Leigh Hunt's insane criticism, more than rivals the insanity of his poetry.[10]

Shelley's first reaction to these reviews appeared in November 1820 in an indignant letter to the *Quarterly* editor, William Gifford, which embodied several of the motifs that went the following year into *Adonais* and its Preface. Shelley begins with a statement not about Keats but about himself, referring to the slanderous attack on him in the April 1819 *Quarterly*. Such attacks do not trouble him: "I feel in respect to the writer in question, that 'I am there sitting, where he durst not soar—' " The effect was different, however, on Keats: "Poor Keats was thrown into a dreadful state of mind by this review, which I am persuaded was not written with any intention of producing the effect, to which it has at least greatly contributed, of embittering his existence, & inducing a disease from which there are now but faint hopes of his recovery." Although Shelley does not completely defend Keats's poetry, he maintains that *Endymion*—which was the center of the attack—has some good passages and that "the great proportion" of *Hyperion* "is surely in the very highest style of poetry."[11]

That Keats's tuberculosis could have been either caused or seriously aggravated by adverse reviews is medically impossible.[12] He doubtless caught the disease from his brother, Tom, and once begun, it would—before the days of rest-cures or antibiotics—simply pursue its course. Keats himself, however, apparently felt that the reviews had an adverse effect on his condition. On hearing of his death, his friend Benjamin Bailey wrote to John Taylor, Keats's publisher: "Reynolds told me, when I was last in London, that poor Keats attributed his approaching end to the poisonous pen of Lockhart [in *Blackwoods*]."[13] Such rumors had appeared in print before Shelley's letter to the *Quarterly*. For instance, in Leigh Hunt's *The Indicator* for August 9, 1820, there appears the comment that Keats, already "sickened and shaken," had to "contend with . . . critical malignity."[14] Shelley had previously heard from John Gisborne of Keats's ill health, and Gisborne may also have relayed the rumor that this illness had been caused by the reviews, for the Gisbornes on their trip to England had met Keats at Hunt's house in June and July 1820, and they must have talked about him with Hunt.[15] Shelley apparently also had a letter from Hunt on the subject.[16] But no matter what Shelley may have heard, there was no solid indication that the reviews had seriously damaged Keats's health. Shelley seemed determined to accept any rumors that came his way, whereupon he became their most influential publicist, not only directly in *Adonais* but also indirectly through Byron, for Byron would almost certainly not have written the "snuffed out by an article" stanza in *Don Juan* if it had not been for Shelley.[17]

Other letters by Shelley also express regard for Keats, respect for his poetry, indignation against the Tory reviewers and a the linking of himself and Keats as fellow victims. In August 1819 he asked his publisher, Charles Ollier, to be sure always to send copies of his works to Keats. In July 1820, on hearing that Keats was ill with tuberculosis, he sent him the invitation to winter in Italy. In October 1820 he wrote to Mrs. Hunt that Keats's *Hyperion* "promises for him that he is destined to become one of the first writers of the age." In November he told Peacock that *Hyperion* is "an astonishing piece of writing, and gives me a conception of Keats which I confess I had not before." With his reading of *Hyperion*, in fact, Shelley began to realize for the first time that Keats was not simply a young poet of promise but a "great genius."[18] On February 18, 1821, hearing that Keats was ill in Naples (he was actually dying in Rome at the time), Shelley once more thought of inviting him to Pisa. By April 11—probably in fact *on* April 11—he had heard of Keats's death, and on April 16 he wrote to Byron: "Young Keats, whose 'Hyperion' showed so great a promise, died lately at Rome from the consequences of breaking a blood-vessel, in paroxysms of despair at the contemptuous attack on his book in the *Quarterly Review*."[19] Shelley apparently began *Adonais* shortly after April 11, writing it first in about forty stanzas, which he sent to the press on June 16, and then composing another series of stanzas, to make a total of fifty-five, between that date and shortly before the poem's issuance from the press on July 12.[20]

The Preface to *Adonais* displays the same sentiments and motifs as do these various letters. Shelley begins by asserting his admiration for Keats's talents, again selecting *Hyperion* for special praise and remarking that Keats should be "classed among the writers of the highest genius who have adorned our age."[21] He hints at his own persecution by *The Quarterly Review*—"One of their associates is, to my knowledge, a most base and unprincipled calumniator"—and launches into a bitter attack on such reviewers in general and on the one responsible for the review of *Endymion* in particular.

In some discarded first drafts of this Preface the attack on the reviewer is less restrained. He is called a "hell-hate animal slave," who has "prostituted his soul for twenty pounds per sheet," an accusation similar to the one made against the reviewer of *The Revolt of Islam* in Shelley's November 1820 letter to the *Quarterly*: "the 30 guineas a sheet or whatever it is you pay him." In these drafts Shelley's own persecution is stressed: "Persecution contumely and calumny have been heaped upon me in profuse measure . . . domestic conspiracy and legal oppression have violated in my person the most sacred rights of nature and humanity."[22]

It is clear, then, that one of Shelley's purposes in writing *Adonais* was to attack the Tory reviewers, especially the *Quarterly* reviewer, and that his sense of identity with Keats lent fire to his purpose. Both motifs ultimately blended with Shelley's obsessive hatred of Robert Southey, the poet laureate and leading man of letters associated with *The Quarterly Review*.

Shelley and Southey

Southey and Shelley had met during Shelley's stay at Keswick in 1811–1812, and Southey, his own radical past long forgotten, had tried unsuccessfully to convert the young iconoclast to conservatism. Four years later he spread the rumors of a "league of incest" between Byron, Claire, Shelley, and Mary at Geneva, and brought back from the Continent the story of Shelley's signing "atheist" in the guest book at Montanver. In the January 1817 *Quarterly* he reviewed, along with two other works, Shelley's first reform pamphlet, the *Proposal for Putting Reform to the Vote* by the "Hermit of Marlow." In the midst of this review occur several passages that Shelley would certainly have taken as a personal attack.[23] That Southey intended them as such is indicated by the fact that they are the same charges as he made against Shelley in his correspondence.[24] In the review Southey hinted that "a youth of ardent mind" whom it is "difficult" to "advise" had committed "the act of moral suicide," that his writings dealt in "scandal, sedition, obscenity, or blasphemy," and that his radicalism was based on "vanity, presumption and half knowledge." He hinted that his only hope for salvation was to turn to religion. He condemned "literary adventurers" who turn to "political warfare" without a true "compass": "*From the first their bias is on the wrong side: vanity, presumption, and half-knowledge, make them believe that they are wiser than their elders, and capable of reforming the world;* add to these *errors by which youth is so easily beset, false philosphy to which they lead, and irreligion in which that philosophy ends, and you have a revolutionist complete.*"[25]

It was little wonder that Crabb Robinson, running into Shelley a few months later at Godwin's, found him "very abusive toward Southey, whom he spoke of as having sold himself to the Court, and this he maintained with the usual party slang. His pension and his laureateship, his early zeal and his recent virulence, are the proofs of gross corruption." The following year Shelley began to manifest an *idée fixé* that every attack on him in *The Quarterly Review* was by Southey. When a few slurring remarks on Shelley appeared in a review of Hunt's *Foliage* in the May 1818 *Quarterly*, Shelley wrote to Hunt asserting that Southey was the author and commenting on the "dreadful hatred" that he displayed.[26] Such an imputation of authorship—as Southey himself later pointed out—was decidedly strained in view of the fact that the author of the article mentioned having been at Eton with Shelley, which Southey was not. Hunt wrote back assuring Shelley that he was mistaken; Southey was not the author.[27] But the next year Shelley jumped to the conclusion that Southey was the author of the scurrilous review of *The Revolt of Islam* in the April 1819 *Quarterly*.[28] Once again he wrote an indignant letter to Hunt, and he also began a letter to *The Quarterly*, which apparently was intended as an attack on Southey. A year later he wrote to Southey himself, asking whether he were the author and taking the opportunity to deliver some sharp blows at the Tory laureate:

> That an unprincipled hireling, in default of what to answer in a published composition, should, without provocation, insult the domestic calamities of a writer of the adverse party—to which perhaps their victim dares scarcely advert in thought—that he should make those calamities the theme of the foulest and the falsest slander—that all this should be done by a calumniator without a name—with the cowardice, no less than the malignity, of an assassin—is too common a piece of charity among Christians (Christ would have taught them better), too common a violation of what is due from man to man among the pretended friends of social order, to have drawn one remark from me, but that I would have you observe the arts practised by that party for which you have abandoned the cause to which your early writings were devoted.[29]

In reply, Southey denied that he had written the review but took advantage of the occasion to lecture Shelley on his morals and opinions:

> I reply to you sir, because I cannot think of you without the deepest compassion. Eight years ago you were somewhat displeased when I declined disputing with you upon points which are beyond the reach of the human intellect—telling you that the great difference between us was, that you were then nineteen and I was eight-and-thirty. Would that the difference were no greater now! You wrote to me when you sent me your 'Alastor,' that as you tolerated my opinions, you supposed I should tolerate yours. Few persons are less intolerant than myself, by disposition as well as by principle, but I cannot admit that any such reciprocity is justly to be claimed. Opinions are to be judged by their effects—and what has been the fruit of yours? Do they enable you to look backward with complacency or forward with hope? Have you found in them a rule of life conducive either to your own happiness, or to that of those who were most nearly and dearly connected with you? Or rather, have they not brought immediate misery upon others, and guilt, which is all but irremediable, on yourself?

Shelley answered with some heat:

> I confess your recommendation to adopt the system of ideas you call Christianity has little weight with me, whether you mean the popular superstition in all its articles, or some more refined theory with respect to those events and opinions which put an end to the graceful religion of the Greeks . . . You select a single passage out of a life otherwise not only spotless but spent in an impassioned pursuit of virtue, which looks like a blot, merely because I regulated my domestic arrangements without deferring to the notions of the vulgar . . . I need not to be instructed that the opinion of the ruling party to which you have attached yourself always exacts, contumeliously receives, and never reciprocates, toleration.

Moreover, Southey's protestations had apparently not eliminated Shelley's suspicions that Southey was connected with the *Quarterly* attacks on him: "I recollect expressing what contempt I felt, in the hope that you might meet the wretched hireling who has so closely imitated your style as to deceive all but those who knew you into a belief that he was you."[30] Southey replied with further aspersions on Shelley's private life:

It is a matter of public notoriety that your wife destroyed herself. Knowing in what manner she bore your desertion, I never attributed this to her sensibility on that score. I have heard it otherwise explained: I have heard that she followed your example as faithfully as your lessons, and that the catastrophe was produced by shame. Be this as it may, ask your own heart, whether you have not been the whole, sole, and direct cause of her destruction. You corrupted her opinions; you robbed her of her moral and religious principles; you debauched her mind. But for you and your lessons she might have gone through the world innocently and happily . . . your offence is moral as well as political, practical as well as speculative . . . You would have found me as strongly opposed in my youth to Atheism and immorality of any kind as I am now, and to that abominable philosophy which teaches self-indulgence instead of self-control.

The Christianity which I recommended to your consideration is to be found in the Scriptures and in the Book of Common Prayer. I would fain have had you to believe that there is judgment after death, and to learn, and understand, and feel all sins may be forgiven through the merits and mediation of Jesus Christ.[31]

In the same year (1820) as this exchange of letters, and probably in the same weeks, Shelley penned a fifty-four line verse diatribe on Southey:

who that has seen
What Southey is and was, would not exclaim,
"Lash on!" and be the keen verse dipped in flame.[32]

Shelley's obsession in regard to Southey and the *Quarterly* was next transferred to the *Quarterly* attack on Keats, for which Shelley seemed determined to believe that Southey was also responsible. In the discarded first draft of the Preface to *Adonais* he assails the attackers of Keats:

At what gnat did they strain here after having swallowed all those camels? Mr. Southey and Mr. Gifford well knew what true poetry is; they could not have been mistaken with respect to the indications afforded by portions of this poem of such astonishing descriptive power which they will have observed in the *Hyperion*. Surely such men as these hold their repute cheap in permitting to their subordinate associates so great a license, not of praise which can do little mischief, but of censure which may destroy—and has destroyed one of the noblest specimens of the workmanship of God.

Shelley thus held Southey and Gifford responsible for the attack on Keats on the grounds that, even though neither of them may actually have penned it, they were the directing figures behind the *Quarterly* literary policy. That Shelley held Southey more to blame than Gifford is indicated by the phrase "Mr. Southey especially" as well as by the fact that Shelley nowhere exhibits a hatred of Gifford sufficient to produce a diatribe of this nature. Furthermore, Shelley ignores the more virulent and notorious attack on Keats in *Blackwoods*. Always it is the *Quarterly*, and always Southey.[33]

The above excerpt from Shelley's discarded first draft of the Preface should be read against the passage that corresponds to it in the published version:

> It may well be said, that these wretched men know not what they do. They scatter their insults and their slanders without heed as to whether the poisoned shaft lights on a heart made callous by many blows or one like Keat's, composed of more penetrable stuff. One of their associates is, to my knowledge, a most base and unprincipled calumniator. . . . What gnat did they strain at here, after having swallowed all those camels? Against what woman taken in adultery dares the foremost of these literary prostitutes to cast his opprobrious stone? Miserable man! you, one of the meanest, have wantonly defaced one of the noblest specimens of the workmanship of God. Nor shall it be your excuse, that, murderer as you are, you have spoken daggers, but used none.

A comparison between the earlier and later drafts shows that by "these wretched men" Shelley means Gifford and Southey and that by the "foremost of these literary prostitutes," the "unprincipled calumniator," and "the miserable man" he means Southey. This is indicated also in a passage from Shelley's letter to Southey of August 17, 1820:

> You accuse me, on what evidence I cannot guess, of *guilt* . . . a bold word, sir, this, and one which would have required me to write to you in another tone, had you addressed it to anyone except myself. Instead, therefore, of refraining from "judging that you not be judged," you not only judge but condemn, and that to a punishment which its victims must be either among the meanest or the loftiest not to regard as bitterer than death. But you are such a pure one as Jesus Christ found not in all Judea to throw the first stone against the woman taken in adultery![34]

Shelley must have let it be known—probably by hints to Byron, Hunt, and others—that this attack in the Preface was directed against Southey, for Southey himself had heard that it was. In a letter three years later to the Tory newspaper *The Courier,* he wrote: "In the preface to his Monody on Keats, Shelley, as I have been informed, asserts that I was the author of the criticism in the *Quarterly Review* upon that young man's poems, and that his death was occasioned by it. There was a degree of meanness in this (especially considering the temper and tenour of our correspondence) which I was not then prepared to expect from Shelley, for that he *believed* me to be the author of that paper, I certainly do not believe."[35]

Classical Sources

Moved to poetry by these diverse feelings, Shelley had to find a poetic form that would encompass grief and rage without descending either to sentimentality or to direct diatribe. Like Milton before him when faced by a similar problem, he turned to the classical elegy, taking as his models Bion's *Lament for Adonis* and Moschus' *Lament for Bion*, both of which he translated in part. From the first he probably derived the idea of using, although indirectly, the Venus and Adonis story, and from the second the lament-for-a-poet motif.

Bion began his elegy on Adonis with a lamentation: "I cry woe for Adonis and say the beauteous Adonis is dead; and the Loves cry me woe again and say the beauteous Adonis is dead." Venus is urged to awake and lament the death of Adonis. She hastens to his side, finds him dying from the tusk of the boar, and wails, "Awake Adonis, awake for a little while, and give me one latest kiss."[36] She complains that she is "a God and may not go with thee," and asks why he was so mad as to pit himself against a wild beast. The "Loves" are pictured as grieving over the body: "There he lies, the delicate Adonis, in purple wrappings, and the weeping Loves lift their voices in lamentation; they have shorn their locks for Adonis' sake. This flung upon him arrows, that a bow, this a feather, that a quiver. One hath done off Adonis' shoe, others fetch water in a golden basin, another washes the thighs of him, and again another stands behind him and fans him with his wings." Bion concluded: "Give over thy wailing for today, Cytherea, and beat not now thy breast any more; thou needs wilt wail again and weep again, come another year."

Moschus' elegy takes the simple form of listing the mourners, both animate and inanimate, for the dead Bion: "Lament you now, good orchards; gentle groves, make ye your moan; be your breathing clusters, ye flowers, dishevelled for grief"; "Echo, too, she mourns among the rocks that she is silent and can imitate your lips no more. For sorrow that you are lost the trees have cast their fruit on the ground and the flowers are withered away." The nightingales and the swallows alike lament. The world of nature lives on, but man is mortal; Bion is said to have died from eating poison; Moschus wishes that he could join him in the other world and that, as a fellow poet, he had his gifts.

According to the myth, after the death of Adonis, Zeus, affected by the grief of Aphrodite (Venus), agrees that Adonis shall spend half of each year on earth and half in Hades. In this respect Adonis is one with Syrian, Hebrew, and other nature gods, the myth representing the regeneration of the earth in spring. His name was alternatively given as "Adonai," and the yearly mourning ceremonies for him were called the "adonias." It was presumably from "Adonai" and "adonias" that Shelley formed the name "Adonais." In doing so, however, he did not intend to heap on his creation all the attributes of all the deities associated with the myth.[37]

Just as Adonis is transformed into Adonais, Aphrodite is transformed into Urania. In Greek literature, two aspects of Aphrodite were emphasized, spiritual love and sexual love—Aphrodite Urania ("heavenly") and Aphrodite Pandemos ("all the people's"). The name Urania, however, was also applied to the muse of astronomy, perhaps deriving from Aphrodite Urania.

This muse was addressed as a source of poetic inspiration by Dante, Spenser, Milton, and Wordsworth.[38] In *Adonais* Shelley combines both the goddess and the muse, though the primary emphasis is on the muse, as shown by the fact that he makes Urania the "mother," not the lover, of Adonais. Urania—"my mistress Urania," as Shelley half jestingly calls her in a letter to Peacock—is one more of Shelley's symbols for the creative spirit of poetry or poetic inspiration—the wind that sets the coals of the mind aglow.[39]

Adonais

Adonais pivots on the three themes of mourning for the dead poet, an attack on the critic, and death. In the first eight stanzas, which are a general exhortation to mourning, a contemporary reader opening the volume would have been struck most by the implied comparison between Keats and Milton. Milton is hailed as the great republican poet who died in unyielding strife against aristocratic reaction:

> Most musical of mourners, weep again!
> Lament anew, Urania!—He died,
> Who was the Sire of an immortal strain,
> Blind, old, and lonely, when his country's pride,
> The priest, the slave, and the liberticide,
> Trampled and mocked with many a loathed rite
> Of lust and blood; he went, unterrified,
> Into the gulf of death; but his clear Sprite
> Yet reigns o'er earth; the third among the sons of light. (28–36)

Urania now must mourn her "youngest dearest one." As the other two sons of light were most likely Homer and Dante, Keats is placed in, or at least near, some rather distinguished company. This placement would have seemed ridiculous, indeed an insult and a challenge, to conservative critics; and even to most liberal ones it would have seemed greatly exaggerated. Shelley, in fact, felt that he owed an explanation to Byron: "Although I feel the truth of what I have alleged about his 'Hyperion,' and I doubt, if you saw that particular poem, whether you would not agree with me; yet I need not be told that I have been carried too far by the enthusiasm of the moment; by my piety, and my indignation, in panegyric. But if I have erred, I console myself by reflecting that it is in defence of the weak—not in conjunction with the powerful."[40] In thus early presenting Keats as an important poet, Shelley was building up to his attack on the Establishment critic, implying the enormity of his crime. And this accusation is implicit throughout the poem. Today we tend to miss it because we think of Keats's reputation as it now is, not as it was in 1821.

The next nine stanzas are developed from Bion and Moschus: the mourning Loves, which Shelley expands into the concept of the poet's own creative thoughts lamenting his passing; and the mournings of nature, especially the picture of lorn Echo and the blighted buds of spring.

With the introduction of the death theme the verse begins to rise to a new level. The opening note is one of skeptical questioning:

> Nought we know, dies. Shall that alone which knows
> Be as a sword consumed before the sheath
> By sightless lightning?—the intense atom glows
> A moment, then is quenched in a most cold repose. (176–179)

Nothing of what we perceive through the senses ("know") dies; that is, the world of nature is eternal. Its parts may change or disappear, but the whole remains. Yet if matter as such is eternal, is mind perishable? Does the human mind (the "sword") perish as the result of blind, necessitarian ("sightless") forces, in fact, even before the body (the "sheath") has decayed?[41] Certainly it appears so. The mind seems to vanish like a particle of matter, coming to glowing birth but disappearing in an instant.

The note of skeptical but tormented questioning deepens in the next stanza:

> Alas! that all we loved of him should be,
> But for our grief, as if it had not been,
> And grief itself be mortal! Woe is me!
> Whence are we, and why are we? of what scene
> The actors or spectators? Great and mean
> Meet massed in death, who lends what life must borrow.
> As long as skies are blue, and fields are green,
> Evening must usher night, night urge the morrow,
> Month follow month with woe, and year wake year to sorrow. (181–189)

So long, that is, as natural forces control the world, there will be death and "sorrow." Shelley may mean that death will always be a part of life, but he apparently felt—as he hinted in the conclusion of the third act of *Prometheus Unbound*—that in time there might come to pass an ultimate Utopia in which even death might be conquered by science.

Next comes Shelley's depiction of the traditional flight of Venus to the wounded Adonis, which he transforms into the flight of Urania to the dead Adonais, that is, the flight of the creative spirit of poetry to the bier of Keats. This creative spirit, allied to love and beauty, is rejected by society. Like the Witch of Atlas, she finds as she passes through the world that men are intent on war and material things, that their hearts are cold and their tongues bitter:

> Out of her secret Paradise she sped,
> Through camps and cities rough with stone, and steel,

And human hearts, which to her aery tread
Yielding not, wounded the invisible
Palms of her tender feet where'er they fell:
And barbed tongues, and thoughts more sharp than they,
Rent the soft Form they never could repel,
Whose sacred blood, like the young tears of May,
Paved with eternal flowers that undeserving way. (208–216)

People in the present society have little use for poetry or beauty. But though they attack them, they are unable to destroy them. Even in the worst of tyrannies, as Shelley argued in *A Defence of Poetry,* some core of beauty and love remains in the human heart.

When Urania arrives to find Adonais dead, her lament passes into rage against those who killed him. Up to this point there had been only two passing references to the critics. In stanza two the poet was pictured as slain by "the shaft that flies in darkness" (anonymous criticism); and in stanza seventeen the "curse of Cain" is called down on the head of his slayer. Now Shelley, in the voice of Urania, directly assails the critics:

"O gentle child, beautiful as thou wert,
Why didst thou leave the trodden paths of men
Too soon, and with weak hands though mighty heart
Dare the unpastured dragon in his den?"

. . . . .

"The herded wolves, bold only to pursue,
The obscene ravens, clamorous o'er the dead;
The vultures to the conqueror's banner true
Who feed where Desolation first has fed,
And whose wings rain contagion;—how they fled,
When, like Apollo, from his golden bow
The Pythian of the age one arrow sped
And smiled!—The spoilers tempt no second blow,
They fawn on the proud feet that spurn them lying low."
(235–238, 244–253)

Despite the veiled nature of the language, the allusions are specific. "Too soon" is a reference to Keats's early *Poems* and *Endymion,* the lines embodying, rather ungenerously, Shelley's earlier urging that Keats not publish too soon.[42] The "unpastured dragon" is either a direct allusion to the *Quarterly* reviewer—later specifically attacked—or to the Tory reviewers collectively, most likely the former. The reference in the "Pythian" (Apollo, who slew the python) is to Byron, who in *English Bards and Scotch Reviewers* attacked those who had denounced his early volume, *Hours of Idleness.* After this blow, the sycophantic reviewers had acclaimed his *Childe Harold's Pilgrimage* and other works.

In contrast to the critics, the poets mourn their lost brother. Four poets only are selected: Byron, Moore, Shelley himself, and Leigh Hunt. From some manuscript fragments it appears that Horace and James Smith were also originally included.[43] Wordsworth, Coleridge, Southey, and Scott are conspicuously omitted. The reason for the omissions would have been apparent to a contemporary reader: Shelley was deliberately choosing radical and liberal poets, even in the case of Moore forcing the point, for Moore, though the author of liberal political satires, had shown no particular interest in Keats. The mere choice was thus a challenge to the conservative reviewers: they may have killed one of the group, but the rest continue. The reviewers, moreover, got the point: "For what," wrote the *Literary Gazette* in reviewing *Adonais*, "is the praise of the cockneys [the Hunt radicals] but disgrace, or what honorable inscription can be placed over the dead by the hands of notorious libellers [Hunt], exiled adulterers [Byron], and avowed atheists [Shelley]?"[44]

Shelley's portrait of himself in this section has been attacked as sentimental, self-pitying, and over-long, all of which it doubtless is; it is also in places artificially decorative. But at the same time it has power and truth:

> he, as I guess,
> Had gazed on Nature's naked loveliness
> Actaeon-like, and now he fled astray
> With feeble steps o'er the world's wilderness,
> And his own thoughts, along that rugged way,
> Pursued, like raging hounds, their father and their prey. (274–279)

Acteon, seeing Diana bathing naked, was turned by the goddess into a stag and torn to pieces by his own hounds. Shelley had early divined what humanity could become if the beautiful spirit in nature should prevail in society—and the contrast between the potential and the actual endlessly tormented him. The length of the portrait is justified, at least in part, by the fact that Shelley's own situation—of neglect and persecution—was similar to Keats: "Who in another's fate now wept his own" (300).

The bitterness of Shelley's feelings on this subject are revealed in an agitated passage from an early rough draft of the Preface to *Adonais*:

> As a man, I shrink from notice and regard; the cea[seless] ebb and flow of the world vexes me; my habits are simple I know. I desire to be left in peace. I have been the victim of a monstrous and unheard of tyranny. I am the victim of a despotic power which has violated in my home the rights of nature and has . . .
>
> The bigot will say it was the recompense of my errors, the man of the world will call it the result of my imprudence but never was calumny heaped in so profuse a measure upon any head as upon mine.[45]

This passage shows more directly than the verse how keenly Shelley resented the campaign of vilification against him (the "bigot" seems aimed at Southey) and how badly he was hurt by the seizure of his children by the courts. In his personal life he is lonely, alienated from his wife ("companionless"—272), and heartsick ("on a cheek/The life can burn in blood, even while the heart may break"—287–288). As a writer, he is isolated, sinking beneath unbearable persecution and the failure of readers to understand his message (he wrote as though "in the accents of an unknown land"—301).[46]

The mourning of the poets leads, as did that of Urania, into the anti-critic theme, this time narrowing down to an attack on one critic:

> Our Adonais has drunk poison—oh!
> What deaf and viperous murderer could crown
> Life's early cup with such a draught of woe?
> The nameless worm would now itself disown.[47]
>
> . . . . .
>
> Live thou, whose infamy is not thy fame!
> Live! fear no heavier chastisement from me,
> Thou noteless blot on a remembered name!
> But be thyself, and know thyself to be!
> And ever at thy season be thou free
> To spill the venom when thy fangs o'erflow:
> Remorse and Self-contempt shall cling to thee;
> Hot Shame shall burn upon thy secret brow,
> And like a beaten hound tremble thou shalt—as now. (316–319, 325–333)

When Byron was Shelley's neighbor in Pisa a few months after the composition of *Adonais*, Byron commented to Shelley's cousin, Thomas Medwin:

> I might well say he [Southey] had impudence enough, if he could confess such infamy [spreading the story about "atheist" in the guestbook] . . . Shame on the man who could wound an already bleeding heart,—he barbarous enough to revive the memory of a fatal event [the suicide of Harriet] that Shelley was perfectly innocent of,—and found scandal on falsehood! Shelley taxed him with writing that (*Quarterly*) article some years ago; and he had the audacity to admit that he had treasured up some opinions of Shelley's ten years before; when he was on a visit at Keswick, and had made a note of them at the time. But his bag of venom was not full; it is the nature of the reptile. Why does a viper have a poison-tooth, or the scorpion claws?

Shelley, then, had discussed with Byron his persecution by Southey, and it seems likely that he had told him that Southey—with his reptilelike "venom"—was the critic under attack in *Adonais*. And he had perhaps told others also.[48] Furthermore, as Southey himself was aware that he was under attack in the Preface as the murderous assailant of Keats he would also have recognized that he was the critic singled out in the poem.

This attack on the critic combines with the death theme as Shelley explores the contrast, previously hinted at, between the enduring fame of the poet and the passing infamy of the critic:

Nor let us weep that our delight is fled
Far from these carrion kites that scream below;
He wakes or sleeps with the enduring dead;
Thou canst not soar where he is sitting now—
Dust to the dust! but the pure spirit shall flow
Back to the burning fountain whence it came,
A portion of the Eternal, which must glow
Through time and change, unquenchably the same,
Whilst thy cold embers choke the sordid hearth of shame. (334–342)

That the sentiment here rises once more out of Shelley's blending of his own persecution with that of Keats is indicated by his comment in the letter to the *Quarterly* on the critic who had attacked the *Revolt of Islam* and who he believed to be Southey: "But I feel, in respect to the writer in question, that 'I am there sitting where he durst not soar.'" The philosophical attitude underlying the stanza is skeptical: "wakes or sleeps." Yet Keats, in contrast to the critic, does enjoy a certain kind of immortality. He has joined the "immortal Senate" of great minds described in *The Revolt of Islam*, the "imperial spirits" of *Hellas* who "Rule the present from the past" and whose power is "Based on the crystalline sea/Of thought and its eternity" (696–699). In doing so, he has become, as it were, part of the "unseen power" that makes the mind glow with inspiration and moves one to humanitarian endeavor. As the *Essay on Christianity* made clear, only the good and unselfish feel this power. Keats has become part of it because his mind was "pure." The critic will not because he is corrupt and time-serving.

This theme of literary immortality is continued as Shelley depicts Keats being welcomed into their ranks by the great poets of the past who also died young: Chatterton, Sidney, and Lucan. Obviously Shelley does not mean that these three poets exist as spirits. He is speaking metaphorically of their works: poets and other creative thinkers, the "splendors of the firmament of time," live in "lofty thought," and their "transmitted effluence cannot die" (388, 392, 407). Artistic creativity is part of the enduring human force; it is not, like evil, transient or part of "time." As in *Hellas*, Shelley envisions a chain whereby the humanitarian creative spirits of the past "Rule the present." The next stanza carries the thought a step further:

Peace, peace! he is not dead, he doth not sleep—
He hath awakened from the dream of life—
'Tis we, who lost in stormy visions, keep
With phantoms an unprofitable strife,
And in mad trance, strike with our spirit's knife
Invulnerable nothings.—*We* decay
Like corpses in a charnel; fear and grief
Convulse us and consume us day by day,
And cold hopes swarm like worms within our living clay. (343–359)

A few months after finishing *Adonais*, Shelley wrote in a Note to *Hellas*: "Until better arguments can be produced than sophisms [the arguments of Plato and the theologians] which disgrace the cause, this desire itself [for immortality] must remain the strongest and the only presumption that eternity is the inheritance of every thinking being."[49] What Shelley is expressing in such lines as "He lives, he wakes—'tis Death is dead not he" is not a serious philosophical argument but an expression of this deeply felt "desire." The mood is one of tormented hope, not reasoned affirmation —a revulsion from the intolerable sufferings of life ("cold hopes swarm like worms"). Shelley does not say in what sense Keats has "awakened." A succeeding stanza states only:

> He is made one with Nature; there is heard
> His voice in all her music, from the moan
> Of thunder, to the song of night's sweet bird. (370–372)

Again this is a variation of the theme of literary immortality. Poets and others responding to the beauties of nature will now feel them in part in the way Keats depicted them, as in the *Ode to a Nightingale*.[50] Shelley asserts again that Keats has, as it were, become part of the "benignant power" within nature, "which has withdrawn his being to its own" (376). And he continued the thought in the next stanza:

> He is a portion of the loveliness
> Which once he made more lovely: he doth bear
> His part, while the one Spirit's plastic stress
> Sweeps through the dull dense world, compelling there
> All new successions to the forms they wear;
> Torturing th' unwilling dross that checks its flight
> To its own likeness, as each mass may bear;
> And bursting in its beauty and its might
> From trees and beasts and men into the Heaven's light. (379–387)[51]

If there is any poem of Shelley's to which those who argue he was a Platonist can point for confirmation, it is *Adonais*, and in places the language in fact does resemble that of Platonism, as here in "the one Spirit's plastic stress." But again the "one" concept is rather that of Parmenides than of Plato, a unifying force within matter rather than a transcendent spiritual godhead of which the world is an imperfect reflection. As Shelley early put it in *Queen Mab*:

> Throughout these infinite orbs of mingling light
> Of which yon earth is one, is wide diffused
> A Spirit of activity and light,
> That knows no term, cessation or decay. (VI.146–149)

This power exists also within society and the human mind, it is a power of love and beauty as well as activity and light, and Keats's works have become a part of it as "intellectual beauty" is part of the general "Spirit of Beauty."

The young, dead poets who greet Keats were chosen with particular appropriateness: Sidney, who fought against the conservative critics of his day in his *Defence of Poetry;* Chatterton, who like Keats died young and in neglect; and Lucan, who was executed at the age of twenty-six for joining a conspiracy against the tyrant Nero. They hail Keats as worthy to join their high company: "Thou art become as one of us" (410). Shelley once more is underlining the enormity of the critic's crime by emphasizing the genius of the man he had killed.

This thought leads him into a third attack on the critic:

Who mourns for Adonais? Oh, come forth,
Fond wretch! and know thyself and him aright.
Clasp with thy panting soul the pendulous Earth;
As from a centre, dart thy spirit's light
Beyond all worlds, until its spacious might
Satiate the void circumference: then shrink
Even to a point within our day and night;
And keep thy heart light lest it make thee sink
When hope has kindled hope, and lured thee to the brink. (415–423)

The critical commentaries on these stanzas have often been misleading, some assuming that they refer to a mourner or mourners for Keats; but that the critic is again the person under attack is shown not only by the stanzas themselves but by their relationship to the previous attacks. First, the whole despicable crowd of reactionary reviewers—"the herded wolves," "the many reptiles"—was assailed, then one critic was singled out for specific abuse as the "murderer," the "nameless worm" who was ashamed to admit his authorship of the review. In this third attack the assault is taken a step further. The critic is now urged to realize his own contemptible character and to pay homage to the genius he has slain. He is urged, in the stanza just quoted, to recognize his insignificance in relation to the universe, and then is bidden to "go to Rome," where Keats was buried:

Or go to Rome, which is the sepulchre,
Oh, not of him, but of our joy: 'tis nought
That ages, empires, and religions there
Lie buried in the ravage they have wrought;
For such as he can lend, they borrow not
Glory from those who made the world their prey;
And he is gathered to the kings of thought
Who waged contention with their time's decay,
And of the past are all that cannot pass away. (424–432)

Again the emphasis is on the contrast between the critic and the poet. The critic is a time-server, one who "borrows" whatever "Glory" he has from his masters in power: "those who made the world their prey." Adonais, however, is now secure in his literary immortality, joined with those "kings of thought" who courageously struggled through the ages against reaction and corruption ("their time's decay"), as, it is again implied, the critic has not.

The critic, after recognizing his own insignificance, in relation to both the universe and the poet, is exhorted to expiate his crime at the grave of Keats in the Protestant Cemetery at Rome, as well as at another recent grave there:

> Here pause: these graves are all too young as yet
> To have outgrown the sorrow which consigned
> Its charge to each; and if the seal is set,
> Here, on one fountain of a mourning mind,
> Break it not thou! too surely shalt thou find
> Thine own well full, if thou returnest home,
> Of tears and gall. From the world's bitter wind
> Seek shelter in the shadow of the tomb.
> What Adonais is, why fear we to become? (451–459)

The implications in all these stanzas can only be fully understood in the light of Shelley's correspondence with Southey. The exhortation to the critic not to break the seal of grief for one buried in the same cemetery as Keats refers to Shelley's son, William, who was also buried in the Protestant Cemetery. Among the drafts for the Preface to *Adonais* appears the following passage: "My beloved child is buried there. I envy death the body far less than the oppressor the mind of those whom they have torn from me."[52] In the poem Shelley asks the critic not to renew his sorrow for his dead son because Southey had expressed the hope that personal suffering might bring Shelley to a belief in Christianity:

> You rejected Christianity before you knew—before you could possibly have known—upon what evidence it rests. How utterly unlike in this, and in every other respect to the superstitions and fables of men's devices, with which you in your presumptuousness have classed it. Look to that evidence while you are yet existing in Time, and you may yet live to bless God for any visitation of sickness and suffering which, by bringing you to a sense of your miserable condition, may enable you to hope for forgiveness, and teach you where to look for it. God in his infinite mercy bring you to this better mind!"[53]

This smug piety Shelley answered as follows: "I ought not to omit that I have had sickness enough . . . All this is of no account in the favor of what you, or anyone else, calls Christianity; surely it would be better to wish me health and healthful sensations. *I* hope the chickens will not come home to roost!" The reference, as Edward Dowden pointed out, is to the motto of Southey's *The Curse of Kehama*: "Curses are like young chickens, they always come home to roost."[54]

The implications of the poem are similar to those of the correspondence. Southey, with his primitive Christian beliefs, knows little of "Time" or the universe. It is he, not Shelley, who needs to realize the nature of the earth and of earth-time relative to the infinite and eternal universe, which would make both him and his beliefs look small indeed. He should also think of the many religions that have perished in the past, as Christianity itself will perish. The death of William is referred to in connection with Southey's hope that whatever "suffering" God might decide to visit on Shelley would be for his own good—to bring him to religious belief and, hence, to Christian salvation. In effect, Shelley is saying that Southey should have the decency to realize that he had already undergone great personal suffering, which had not served to change his antireligious views. The assertion that in the future the critic will suffer from remorse for killing Keats—"tears and gall" "if thou returnest home"—is similar to the warning of the chickens ("curses") coming "home" to roost.

Shelley cannot, of course, have intended his general readers to understand these specific references. But he doubtless did intend them to recognize the "wretch" as the critic; and he perhaps expected more readers than in fact did so to pick up the hint from the Preface that Southey was under attack. Certainly if it had not been for Shelley's quarrel with Southey, the stanzas would not have been written.

The attack on the critic blends with the death theme in the famous stanza:

> The One remains, the many change and pass;
> Heaven's light forever shines, Earth's shadows fly;
> Life, like a dome of many-coloured glass,
> Stains the white radiance of Eternity,
> Until Death tramples it to fragments.—Die,
> If thou wouldst be with that which thou dost seek!
> Follow where all is fled!—Rome's azure sky,
> Flowers, ruins, statues, music, words, are weak
> The glory they transfuse with fitting truth to speak. (460–468)[55]

Despite the usual interpretation of this stanza, Shelley could not have been referring to the Platonic "One" or to a supernatural "Heaven" or "eternity," because he had no belief in any of them. He did, however, use the word "heaven" as a synonym for the spirit of nature, and "Eternity" to designate lasting values. Nature, as people perceive it, is infinitely varied, but behind the variety probably lies one unifying force, of unknown character —"one Spirit's plastic stress" (381). Shelley's general concept is, moreover, as in *Essay on Christianity*, more ethical than metaphysical. The "benignant power" awakens eternal truths in the truly moral, humanitarian few, but these are distorted by the social evils afflicting the mass of humanity. The dome is the "painted veil" of "Life." It remains, with its distorting influences, throughout each life, and when death does "trample" it to "fragments," the result may simply be nothingness. No one knows. Neither nature nor man nor history has given an answer. We see only that in a world of natural beauty and art, all things perish. The essential philosophical note is again one of tormented skepticism.

In the midst of these speculations comes the exhortation: "Die / If thou wouldst be with that which thou dost seek." Once again, the person being addressed can only be the critic. The attack continues from the preceding stanza, its motive and theme still rooted in Shelley's correspondence with Southey. In effect, Shelley is saying to Southey: "If you are so fanatically religious as you claim and seek salvation and Paradise, why do you not simply commit suicide? Come to Rome and die here near the graves of my son and of Keats in the Protestant Cemetery."

The last three stanzas of *Adonais* are essentially personal. The deep unhappiness that has lain below the surface throughout the poem wells up in a dark longing for death:

Why linger, why turn back, why shrink, my Heart?
Thy hopes are gone before: from all things here
They have departed; thou shouldst now depart!
A light is passed from the revolving year
And man, and woman; and what still is dear
Attracts to crush, repels to make thee wither.

Life seems to have become a dim shadow, friendship and love lack the meaning they once had, and his marriage is embittered.

It seems to Shelley as though the power of the universe were concentrating its rays, like the sun through a magnifying glass, to transmute him into a part of it, as it had Keats:

That light whose smile kindles the Universe,
That Beauty in which all things work and move,
That Benediction which the eclipsing Curse
Of birth can quench not, that sustaining Love
Which through the web of being blindly wove
By man and beast and earth and air and sea,
Burns bright or dim, as each are mirrors of
The fire for which all thirst; now beams on me,
Consuming the last clouds of cold mortality. (478–486)

The power, being blind ("blindly wove"), is necessitarian. It is also the "Spirit of activity and life" inherent in the material universe. As in *Hymn to Intellectual Beauty,* it gives beauty to nature. It manifests itself as biological creativity and human love. In a world where death ("the eclipsing curse of birth") exists, it gives value to life.

In the final stanza, through the dark, inevitable swirling toward death comes a note of pride and defiance:

The breath whose might I have invoked in song
Descends on me; my spirit's bark is driven,
Far from the shore, far from the trembling throng
Whose sails were never to the tempest given. (487–490)

Poetic creation, as in *A Defence of Poetry,* is itself a manifestation of the power, the necessitarian power, which the poet now feels to be destroying him. Yet he can still assert that, should he die, he will do so knowing that he dared to live, defying authority no matter how powerful, fighting evil no matter what the consequences—unlike those who conformed and obeyed (the "trembling throng").

> I am borne darkly, fearfully, afar;
> Whilst, burning through the inmost veil of Heaven,
> The soul of Adonais, like a star,
> Beacons from the abode where the Eternal are. (492–495)[56]

The "abode" of the "Eternals" is, once more, the "Senate" of "the Poets," the immortality of intellectual being. Like Keats, Shelley will become part of the collective chain of creative intellect that has moved mankind upward through the centuries.

13

Masks and Shadows

The Triumph of Life

Following *Adonais*, Shelley completed only one longer poem, *Hellas*. After *Hellas*, he began work in January 1822 on *Charles the First*, but finding its intricacies of construction baffling, he temporarily dropped it and began the poem of which only a fragment remains, called *The Triumph of Life*.[1] Mary wrote that he was working on it in his boat at Lerici in May and June 1822 and that he was "employed" on it "at the last."[2]

The Narrative

To unravel the symbolism of *The Triumph of Life* is by no means an easy task, and the best way to approach it is perhaps by outline. Formerly the poem was less studied than Shelley's other longer poems; but in recent years it has received considerable critical attention.[3] The poem opens magnificently, with Dantean speed and directness. The poet—"I"—has been kept awake all night by "thoughts which must remain untold" (21). As the sun rises, he goes up into the Apennines, which are behind Lerici, where Shelley was then living:

> Swift as a spirit hastening to his task
> Of glory & of good, the Sun sprang forth
> Rejoicing in his splendour, & the mask
>
> Of darkness fell from the awakened Earth.
> The smokeless altars of the mountain snows
> Flamed above crimson clouds, & at the birth
>
> Of light, the Ocean's orison arose. (1–7)

The atmosphere then changes to one similar to a medieval dream poem. A "strange trance"—which was "not slumber"—"grew" over the poet's "fancy" (29, 30), and he began to feel that he had known this somewhere before:

> That I had felt the freshness of that dawn,
> Bathed in the same cold dew my brow & hair
> And sat as thus upon that slope of lawn. (34–36)

Then, as in a "waking dream," a "vision" unfolded before him (40, 42). He seemed to be sitting "beside a public way," on which—as in the vision of Piers the Plowman or of Mirza—was "a great stream Of people hurrying to & fro" (43, 44–45):

> All hastening onward, yet none seemed to know
> Whither he went, or whence he came, or why
> He made one of the multitude. (47–49)

A few were philosophically obsessed by morbid thoughts, but most were mechanically engaged in their daily tasks:

> But more with motions which each other crost
> Pursued or shunned the shadows the clouds threw
> Or birds within the noonday ether lost,
>
> Upon that path where flowers never grew;
> And weary with vain toil & faint for thirst
> Heard not the fountains whose melodious dew
>
> Out of their mossy cells forever burst
> Nor felt the breeze which from the forest told
> Of grassy paths, & wood lawns interspersed
>
> With overarching elms & caverns cold,
> And violet banks where sweet dreams brood, but they
> Pursued their serious folly as of old. (62–73)

Soon the poet perceived a change:

> And as I gazed methought that in the way
> The throng grew wilder, as the woods of June
> When the South wind shakes the extinguished day. (74–76)

These new agitated motions of the crowd are produced by a bright, "icy cold" light so intense that it dims the sun. The light comes from a rushing chariot, which is driven by a strange, shadowlike charioteer with four faces, on each of which the eyes are bandaged. He stands "upon the chariot's beam." In the chariot sits a vague "Shape," which reminds the poet of:

> one whom years deform
>
> Beneath a dusky hood & double cape
> Crouching within the shadow of a tomb. (88–90)

Over its head is a "cloud" like a "crape" (substituted for the more concrete "like a widows veil of crape").[4] The chariot is drawn by "wonder-winged . . . Shapes . . . lost" in "thick lightnings" (95–97).

Behind the chariot is chained a "captive multitude" (119), which seems to contain most of the recognized leaders of mankind. A few, including "they of Athens and Jerusalem" (134), have not been made captive. Around the chariot and the captives surge vast masses of people. These masses fall into two groups: young people, who are dancing and making love in wild abandonment in front of the chariot until, falling, they are mowed down by it; and old people behind the chariot, still trying feebly to perform the sensual dance but being left "Farther behind & deeper in the shade" (169).

The poet, depressed by this spectacle, cries out:

And what is this?
Whose shape is that within the car? (177–178)

A voice beside him answers, "Life!" (180). Turning in astonishment—for he had seen no one near him—he perceives that a gnarled object, which he had taken to be "an old root" (182), was in reality a man withered almost beyond recognition as human, one of the "deluded crew" of old people who had toiled behind the chariot. The man identifies himself as Rousseau. He reads the thoughts of the poet, which are that Rousseau would have done well to have "forborne" (189) joining the dance. Rousseau agrees, stating that he will tell how he and his "companions" (192) were caught up in the dance, in hopes that the story will dissuade the poet from joining it also.

In answer to a question as to who are the persons chained to the car, Rousseau indicates that they are the past religious, military, political, and intellectual leaders of mankind:

The Wise,

The great, the unforgotten: they who wore
Mitres & helms & crowns, or wreathes of light,
Signs of thought's empire over thought. (208–211)

He lists some of them by name: Napoleon, Voltaire, Frederick the Great, Kant (substituted for Pitt), Catherine of Russia, and Leopold II, Tuscan conqueror of Hungary. They were made captive because:

their lore

Taught them not this—to know themselves; their might
Could not repress the mutiny within. (211–213)

Rousseau himself, however, he explains, was:

overcome
By my own heart alone, which neither age

Nor tears nor infamy nor now the tomb
Could temper to its object. (240–243)

That he was so overcome, he earlier implied, was not so much his fault as society's:

> And if the spark with which Heaven lit my spirit
> Earth had with purer nutriment supplied
>
> Corruption would not now thus much inherit
> Of what was once Rousseau. (201–204)

He points out other captives, this time not those of recent history but the "mighty phantoms of an elder day": Plato, Aristotle, Alexander the Great, the Roman emperors from Caesar to Constantine, and the popes "Gregory and John" (253, 288).[5]

The poet asks Rousseau where he is from, where he is going, and how and why he started on his present path. Rousseau replies that he has some grasp of his origins; what his path has been and how he came to take it even the poet might be able to guess; but as to "why" or "Whither the conqueror hurries me" (303–304), he has no answer. If, however, the poet should cease to be a "spectator" (305) and should join the pageant of life, perhaps he could in time answer some of these questions for Rousseau. For the present, all Rousseau can do is to describe the facts of his experience.

With this story the second part of the poem begins. Rousseau states that, of his origins, he only knows that one spring morning he "found" himself "asleep" in a "high and deep" cavern under a mountain (311–313). Out of a "well" in the cavern flowed a "gentle rivulet," which passed through the cavern and into a "grove" just outside the entrance (314, 317, 346). It filled this grove:

> With sound which all who hear must needs forget
>
> All pleasure & all pain, all hate & love,
> Which they had known before that hour of rest. (318–320)

Rousseau walked out of the cavern into the grove, a "scene of woods and water" (336), which broadened out into a forested valley. Everything seemed lit up by:

> a gentle trace
> Of light diviner than the common Sun
> Sheds on the common Earth. (337–339)

But soon, as he looked back, "Though it was now broad day" (337):

> the bright omnipresence
> Of morning through the orient cavern flowed,
> And the Sun's image radiantly intense

> Burned on the waters of the well that glowed
> Like gold, and threaded all the forest maze
> With winding paths of emerald fire. (343–348)

From this, one would gather that the cavern went right through the mountain, like a large tunnel, and the mountain stretched north and south.[6] Rousseau had walked out of one entrance, the one to the west, into the grove. As he looked back, he saw the morning sun fill the cavern from its eastern exit ("orient"); between the east and west exits was the "well," from which the "rivulet" flowed westward into the grove; the light of the sun, striking this well, lit up both it and the rivulet. As the sun did not shine through the tunnel-like cavern until later in the morning—"broad day"—the tunnel must have sloped upward toward the east and downward toward the west, as is also indicated by the direction of the rivulet.

As Rousseau looked back into the sun-filled cavern, he saw on "the vibrating Floor of the fountain" (350–351)—the "fountain" and the "well" being the same—a female "shape all light" (352). This shape was so bright that it stood:

> Amid the sun, as he amid the blaze
> Of his own glory. (349–350)

In her right hand she carried "a crystal glass Mantling with bright Nepenthe." (357–358) With her left hand she flung "dew on the earth" (353)—presumably from the "crystal glass." Standing in the grove, he saw that the shape was moving toward him through the cavern along the surface of the rivulet. As she moved, the intensity of her light steadily diminished:

> the fierce splendour
> Fell from her as she moved under the mass
>
> Of the deep cavern. (359–361)

The effect of this approaching vision on Rousseau was to "blot" out his thoughts as dawn blots out the stars. Before she faded, he asked her the questions the poet had asked of him:

> "If, as it doth seem,
> Thou comest from the realm without a name,
>
> Into this valley of perpetual dream,
> Shew whence I came, and where I am, and why—
> Pass not away upon the passing stream." (395–399)

In answer, she held out the glass of Nepenthe to him with the injunction: "Arise and quench thy thirst" (400). As he did so, his "brain became as sand" (405) and "a new Vision never seen before" (411) burst upon it. As the vision materialized, the shape faded; yet as he "moved along the wilderness" (426), he realized that she was still silently and invisibly beside him.

The vision came in two sequences. The first was that of the "cold bright car" and its chained captives crossing the forested valley before him, with "solemn speed and savage music" (435), moving:

as if from some dread war
Triumphantly returning, the loud million
Fiercely extolled the fortune of her star. (436–438)

As the car swept down the nearer valley slope, there was a kind of magnificence to it, but as it started to climb the "Opposing slope of that mysterious dell" (470), a strange metamorphosis took place, representing the second sequence of the "new Vision." From the "great crowd" (527) "shadows" arose, until "the grove / Grew dense" (480–481) with them. These shadows were then apparently formed into "phantoms" by "the car's creative ray" (533), and the phantoms took various forms and performed a variety of tasks. For instance, some "like restless apes" (493) inhabited "kingly mantles" (496); others "like small gnats & flies . . .thronged about the brow / Of lawyer, statesman, priest & theorist" (508–510).

The poem ends:

thus, on the way
Mask after mask fell from the countenance
And form of all, and long before the day

Was old, the joy which waked like Heaven's glance
The sleepers in the oblivious valley, died,
And some grew weary of the ghastly dance

And fell, as I have fallen by the way side,
Those soonest from whose forms most shadows past
And least of strength & beauty did abide.—

"Then, what is Life?" I said . . . the cripple cast
His eye upon the car which now had rolled
Onward, as if that look must be the last,

And answered . . . "Happy those for whom the fold
Of" (535–548)

The Chariot and the Captives

The existing fragment of the poem thus falls into two sections: first, the poet's vision of the chariot and Rousseau's comments on it; second, Rousseau's account of his origins and of his two visions. The problems involved in the poem are apparent. What is the strange, dusky "Shape" in the chariot? Who is the charioteer? Why are his eyes bandaged? Why does he have four pair of eyes? What is the cold light emitted by the chariot? Why are some of the leaders of mankind captives, but not others? Who are the others? What is the symbolism of the cavern, the mountain, the well, the rivulet, and the other entities connected with Rousseau's origin? Who is the "shape all light" that appears to him? Why does she "blot" out his thoughts? Why does a drink from her glass bring on the "new vision"? Is she good or evil? What is the meaning of the strange metamorphosis of phantoms at the end? Why is it caused by the light from the chariot? How would the poem have continued?

To begin with the chariot and its occupants, the identity of the "Shape" is explicitly stated. When the poet asks, "Whose shape is that within the car?" (178), Rousseau answers, "Life."[7] Shelley describes the scene further:

such seemed the jubilee
As when to greet some conqueror's advance
Imperial Rome poured forth her living sea. (111–113)

He is basing his picture on a Roman triumph, in which the conqueror sat in the chariot, with captive leaders chained behind.

The shape, then, is life—the "conqueror." In English, "life" is used to designate either biological or social life and Shelley sometimes refers to both in the same passage, as, for instance, in speaking of the effect of the "shadows" that emanate from the multitude.

after brief space
From every form the beauty slowly waned,

From every firmest limb & fairest face
The strength & freshness fell like dust, & left
The action & the shape without the grace

Of life. (518–523)

By "life" here he means the physical and psychological energy that animates the human body and gives it "beauty" and "grace." But this energy is drained mainly by the stresses of social life. And it is apparent from the poem's social emphasis that it is concerned primarily with life in the social sense. This is the emphasis also in a letter that Shelley wrote to his friend Horace Smith during the period in which he was composing the poem, a letter that helps to elucidate some of its mysteries:

It seems to me that things have now arrived at such a crisis as requires every man plainly to utter his sentiments on the inefficacy of the existing religious, no less than political systems, for restraining and guiding mankind. Let us see the truth, whatever that may be. The destiny of man can scarcely be so degraded that he was born only to die—and if such should be the case, delusions, especially the gross and preposterous ones of the existing religion, can scarcely be supposed to exalt it. If every man said what he thought, it could not subsist a day. But all, more or less, subdue themselves to the element that surrounds them, and contribute to the evils they lament by the hypocrisy that springs from them—

England appears to be in a desperate condition, Ireland still worse; and no class of those who subsist on the public labour will be persuaded that *their* claims on it must be diminished. But the government must content itself with less in taxes, the landholder must submit to receive less rent, and the fundholder a diminished interest, or they will all get nothing. I once thought to study these affairs, and write or act in them—I am glad that my good genius said *refrain*—I see little public virtue, and I foresee that the contest will be one of blood and gold, two elements which however much to my taste in my pockets and my veins, I have an objection to out of them.[8]

This letter, taken in conjunction with the range of historical epochs covered by the poem—from fifth century Athens to the Napoleonic Wars of Shelley's own age—indicates that Shelley was thinking of life primarily in its social and political aspects, in the past and the present. Some critics have taken the word in the poem in an absolute sense, to include life in the future, as though Shelley was saying, "This is the way life is, has been, and always will be." But as *A Philosophical View of Reform* and other works show, he believed that society was going into a new period of revolutionary change in which it would advance first to a republican and then to an egalitarian state. Nor is there any indication that Shelley, as is sometimes suggested, changed his mind in the last months of his life. *Hellas*, completed in the fall of 1821, is one of the most revolutionary of his poems, climaxing with a vision of the future world state, and *Charles the First*, begun after *Hellas* and temporarily laid aside to begin *The Triumph of Life*, is animated by revolutionary fervor.

Nor in the letter to Horace Smith is there any indication that Shelley is renouncing his basic social philosophy. He is simply saying that he will no longer write pamphlets on the reform of Parliament and allied subjects, nor, if he returns to England, will he "act" in them. He feels that the reform program he favored stands little chance of success. Because the landholding ruling class refuses to make concessions, the people are being forced to achieve their objectives by violence, so that the anarchy-despotism cycle may begin anew. He is not, however, saying that he will no longer write poetry or prose expressing his radical social philosophy. This is apparent in his urging that "every man" should say "what he thought," and in the phrase, "I am glad that my good genius said refrain," for although Shelley had refrained from entering the political arena directly, he had certainly not refrained from writing radical poetry or prose. Even as he was writing the letter, he had plans afoot for the launching of *The Liberal*, along with Hunt and Byron, as an anti-Establishment journal, and it was in pursuit of these plans that he met his death.

One can assume, then, that the over-all social philosophy of Shelley's works from *Queen Mab* to *Charles the First* also underlies *The Triumph of Life*. The view he had earlier expressed to Leigh Hunt still held good and, in fact, is particularly pertinent to this poem: "The system of society as it exists at present must be overthrown from the foundations with all its superstructure of maxims & of forms before we shall find anything but dissappointment in our intercourse with any but a few select spirits." Life in the existing social order is "infected" by an "insidious" poison, which erects barriers of mistrust between friends, turns love into lust, plants the seeds of "self-contempt," and corrupts by lies, hypocrisy, and greed. Thus it has always been, in ancient Athens (based on slavery), under the tyranny of ancient Rome and the Holy Roman Empire, in the Florence that expelled Dante, in the Rome of the Cenci, and in the England of the Regency. The future will witness "the extinction of the unequal system under which they [mankind] now subsist," the "poison" will dissipate, and all humanity, rather than only "a few select spirits" will be able to communicate each with each in a world without hatred, war, lust, or superstition.[9]

The charioteer of the chariot of life is described as follows:

Upon the chariot's beam
A Janus-visaged Shadow did assume

The guidance of that wonder-winged team;
The shapes which drew it in thick lightnings
Were lost:—I heard alone on the air's soft stream

The music of their ever-moving wings.
All the four faces of that charioteer
Had their eyes banded . . . little profit brings

Speed in the van and blindness in the rear,
Nor then avail the beams that quench the Sun,—
Or that his banded eyes could pierce the sphere

Of all that is, has been or will be done,
So ill was the car guided—but it passed
With solemn speed majestically on. (93–106)

Although Shelley does not give so specific an indication of the character of the charioteer as he does of the shape, the evidence shows that the charioteer stands for necessity. His chariot, with its "Shapes" lost in "thick lightnings," is similar to the chariot of the daemon in *The Daemon of the World*, and the daemon is necessity. The daemon's car is pulled by vague shapes that symbolize forms of energy:

Four shapeless shadows bright and beautiful
Draw that strange car of glory, reins of light
Check their unearthly speed. (65–67)[10]

The "banded eyes" of the charioteer are paralleled in *Hellas*:

The world's eyeless charioteer,
  Destiny, is hurrying by!
What faith is crushed, what empire bleeds
Beneath her earthquake-footed steeds? (711–714)

In *The Revolt of Islam* the concept is made explicit:

One comes behind,
  Who aye the future to the past will bind—
Necessity, whose sightless strength for ever
  Evil with evil, good with good must wind
In bands of union, which no power may sever. (3706–3710)

The charioteer, then, is necessity, which Shelley regarded as a universal force, permeating both nature and society. In nature it controlled everything from the motions of planets to biological growth; in society, everything from historical development to individual psychological reactions. In *The Triumph of Life*, or at least in the fragment that was completed, Shelley is thinking of it primarily in its sociohistorical functions. In his own age, as he indicated to Horace Smith, necessity was about to produce a revolutionary conflict of "blood and gold." People, caught up in this struggle acted in set patterns. This was true also in past epochs. Life was dominated by necessity. In *The Triumph of Life* it is necessity that drives life, not life that controls necessity. His bandaged eyes signify that necessity is a blind, insensate force without consciousness or purpose, a "sightless" power, an "eyeless charioteer." In *The Triumph of Life* the *Hellas* picture is elaborated by giving the charioteer four pairs of "banded" eyes. Shelley indicates his meaning here in "all that is, has been or will be done"[11] The eyes in the back of the head represent the blind workings of necessity in the past, those on each side of the head represent them in the present, and those in front represent them driving into the future. But the charioteer could have understanding—that is, society could be guided consciously rather than blindly—if the "beams that quench the sun" could only "avail"; if his eyes were unbandaged, in other words, he could see by the light of life, and he would wind "good with good" and not "evil with evil." As it is, the chariot moves rapidly but without conscious direction, impelled by the blind forces of necessity in a frenzied, unthinking drive: "speed in the van and blindness in the rear."

The same concepts apply to the "million" people around the chariot. When the poet first sees this great multitude, before the appearance of the chariot, they are "hurrying to & fro" along the "public way" of his "waking dream" (42, 43, 45). Some of them are "flying from the thing they feared & some/Seeking the object of another's fear" (54–55). As Donald H. Reiman indicated, this refers not so much to personal as to political relations, those who are in fear being the "oppressed," and those who are maliciously playing on their fears being the "oppressors."[12] Some are absorbed in thoughts of their own death: "mournfully within the gloom / Of their own shadow walked, and called it death" (58–59). The implication seems to be that what makes them gloomy is their own self-preoccupation, not death as such. But more are engaged in useless, self-defeating activities:

more with motions which each other crost
Pursued or shunned the shadows the clouds threw
Or birds within the noonday ether lost. (62–64)

The picture is generally similar to that in the Preface to *Alastor*: "Among those who attempt to exist without human sympathy, the pure and tender-hearted perish through the intensity and passion of their search after its communities, when the vacancy of their spirit suddenly makes itself felt. All else, selfish, blind, and torpid, are those unforeseeing multitudes who constitute, together with their own, the lasting misery and loneliness of the world. Those who love not their fellow-beings, live unfruitful lives, and prepare for their old age a miserable grave."[13] There is actually no need for this situation of lonely intellectuals and "unforeseeing multitudes," for although the "public way" is, it is true, a "path where flowers never grew," just beyond it is a "forest" with "fountains," "grassy paths," "caverns," and "violet banks where sweet dreams brood" (43, 65, 67, 69, 70, 71, 72). The multitude, however, obsessed with their "serious folly" (73), do not hear the fountains nor feel the breeze from the forest. They live in a loveless world and do not respond to the "benignant power" around and within them. If they did, they could change the social order "from its foundations." The same general contrast is implied in the opening lines of the poem, between the "smokeless altars" of nature and the bloodstained, sacrificial altars of society.

Regardless of what may be its potential, however, life must be faced as it is, and in *The Triumph of Life*, as in *The Revolt of Islam*, the confrontation is harsh. In the first section of the poem Shelley depicts the degrading influence of loveless sensuality:

And in their dance round her who dims the Sun

Maidens & youths fling their wild arms in air
As their feet twinkle; they recede, and now
Bending within each other's atmosphere

Kindle invisibly; and as they glow
Like moths by light attracted & repelled,
Oft to their bright destruction come & go.

Till like two clouds into one vale impelled
That shake the mountains when their lightnings mingle
And die in rain,—the fiery band which held

Their natures, snaps . . . ere the shock cease to tingle
One falls and then another in the path
Senseless, nor is the desolation single,

Yet ere I can say *where* the chariot hath
Past over them. (148–162)

The imagery is clearly sexual. By the maidens and youths "Bending within each other's atmosphere," Shelley means essentially the sexual act. "The sexual impulse," he wrote elsewhere, "serves, from its obvious and external nature, as a kind of type or expression of the rest."[14] In love this act may sometimes be "a small part" of the total psychological complex, but in sensuality it is almost everything, for which reason it is ultimately unsatisfying: "the fiery band . . . snaps," and the young people fall "senseless" before the chariot of life, not one by one but in pairs, as a result of their sensual but loveless unions. In the phrase "nor is the desolation single," Shelley implies that the man and woman involved in a purely sensual relationship mutually destroy each other. Their lives are really ended when the life force, thus misused, begins to fade. Having no other pattern to their existence, they try vainly and mechanically to hold on to this one: "Limp in the dance" (167). In time they can no longer even limp and are left "Farther behind and deeper in the shade" (169).

Shelley neither here nor elsewhere in the poem is advocating the "Monkish superstition" of "chastity" which he scorned in the Notes to *Queen Mab*.[15] He was no ascetic moralist. On the contrary, he felt that people should live life to the full. His joy in love, physical and emotional, is evident in his works and in his life, but it must be a joy in self-giving, not in self-indulgence. Love is fertile to the spirit; sensuality is destructive.

These passages on the young and old raise several problems. The old people—who are really the young ones grown old, for Shelley's chariot moves in time as well as in space—have clearly been conquered by life. They are captives, even though they are not chained to the chariot. In a Roman triumph only the leaders of the conquered peoples were chained. As a selfish and sensual existence leads to a lonely and purposeless old age, their captivity consists in essentially this condition of loneliness and lack of purpose, a "vacancy" of the "spirit."[16] It thus appears that young people are not actually conquered by life, although the germs of that conquest are planted in them. For a time they dance in front of the chariot, sustained by their own sensuous vitality. The conquest—biological and social—comes with age.

The people around the chariot represent the masses of mankind; the chained captives, their leaders. Moreover, the masses around the chariot are millionfold, even the captives themselves form a "multitude." Like the throngs in Dante's hell, the crowds stretch out to infinity. They fade off into the distance in all directions as the chariot with its grim, black 'Shape" and unseeing charioteer ploughs them under. Shelley's technique, however, in contrast to Dante's direct realism, is preimpressionist, like a picture by Turner in which the attention is directed toward a vivid center with the edges hazing off—except that the picture is in motion.

Almost all the past leaders of mankind are represented as captives chained to the chariot of life. To understand what Shelley means by this captivity, it is necessary to consider those who are not captive:

> All but the sacred few who could not tame
> Their spirits to the Conqueror, but as soon
> As they had touched the world with living flame
>
> Fled back like eagles to their native noon,
> Or those who put aside the diadem
> Of earthly thrones or gems, till the last one
>
> Were there;—for they of Athens & Jerusalem
> Were neither mid the mighty captives seen
> Nor mid the ribald crowd that followed them
>
> Or fled before. (128–137)

There are thus two groups who are not captives, those who died young, and those who rejected power or wealth. Among the first were doubtless "the inheritors of unfulfilled renown" of *Adonais* (397)—Chatterton, Sidney, and Lucan. Among the second were Socrates and Jesus, as the Prologue to *Hellas* confirms:

> and I add
> Three vials of the tears which demons weep
> When virtuous spirits through the gate of Death
> Pass triumphing over the thorns of life,
> Sceptres and crowns, mitres and swords and snares,
> Trampling in scorn, like Him and Socrates. (150–155)

The word "like," however, shows that Jesus and Socrates were not the only ones. Although the existing fragment of the *Triumph* mentions only one other great figure who is not among the captives, Francis Bacon, no doubt in a later section Shelley would have discussed the "sacred few" in more detail. They were doubtless, in the main, the same as "the poets" of *A Defence of Poetry*.[17]

If a rejection of power and wealth prevents one from becoming a captive of life, then an acceptance of them must lead to captivity. The implication is that a person is more likely to accept them as he grows older and as the pressures of society increase. The reason for such an acceptance of power or riches Shelley gives, though in rather cryptic form, in the first passage describing the captives of the modern world:

The Wise,

The great, the unforgotten: they who wore
  Mitres & helms & crowns, or wreathes of light,
Signs of thought's empire over thought; their lore

  Taught them not this—to know themselves; their might
Could not repress the mutiny within,
  And for the morn of truth they feigned, deep night

Caught them ere evening. (208–215)

The key phrase is clearly "the mutiny within."[18] Socrates, Jesus, and others were able to suppress this "mutiny," and by so doing, they escaped captivity. But if one does not suppress it, he becomes a captive.

If Shelley had finished the poem, he would doubtless have developed this thought further, as he did in his *Sonnet to the Republic of Benevento* (1821):

Nor happiness, nor majesty, nor fame,
Nor peace, nor strength, nor skill in arms or arts,
Shepherd its herds whom tyranny makes tame;
Verse echoes not one beating of their hearts,
History is but the shadow of their shame,
Art veils her glass, or from the pageant starts
As to oblivion their blind millions fleet,
Staining that Heaven with obscene imagery
Of their own likeness. What are numbers knit
By force or custom? Man who man would be
Must rule the empire of himself; in it
Must be supreme, establishing his throne
On vanquished will, quelling the anarchy
Of hopes and fears, being himself alone.[19]

The general thought in the sonnet is similar to that in other passages of *The Triumph of Life* and elsewhere. The "herd," made "tame" by "tyranny," has never known happiness, and its members pass into the "oblivion" of the grave like the "unforeseeing multitudes" of the Preface to *Alastor*, without fulfilling their human potential. Their minds are formed by reactionary and stultifying social agencies: "force or custom." They are representatives of social man, not individual man. He who would be a true leader of humanity must resist these forces with their "anarchy of hopes and fears," which is clearly the same as "the mutiny within," and must conquer the urge to use or control others ("will").[27] He must be "himself alone"; that is he must be guided by the "benignant power." People have innate noble characteristics that they can develop, or they can substitute for them evil ones supplied by society. If a person does the former, his inner life is one of moral and intellectual harmony; if the latter, it is one of anarchic, unruly, contending forces.

Shelley explains his concept more specifically in *Essay on Christianity*, in an unfinished passage:

Plato wrote the scheme of a republic in which law should watch over the equal distribution of the external instruments of unequal power: honours, property and Diogenes devised a nobler and more worthy system of opposition to the system of slave and tyrant. He said, It is in the power of each individual to level the inequality which is the topic of the complaint of mankind. Let him be aware of his own worth and the station which he really occupies in the scale of moral beings. Diamonds and gold, palaces and sceptres derive their value from the opinion of mankind. The only sumptuary law which can be imposed on the use and fabrication of these instruments of mischief and deceit, these symbols of successful injustice, is the law of opinion. Every man posesses [sic] the power in this respect, to legislate for himself. Let him be well aware of his own worth, and moral dignity. Let him yield in to any wiser or worthier than he so long as he accords no veneration to the splendour of his apparel, the luxury of his food, the multitude of his flatterers and slaves. It is because, o mankind, ye value and seek the empty pageantry of wealth and social power that ye are enslaved to its possessions.[21]

The fundamental evil of society, past and present has been inequality—in "property," "honours," and other regards. An "insidious poison," inequality affects society from top to bottom and is expressed in injustices of various kinds. Its open manifestations are in "diamonds and gold, palaces and sceptres." These inequalities and the injustices they breed exist by virtue of governmental power and the clichés or prejudices that support them—the "numbers knit by force or custom" of the sonnet. These false values form within each individual a discordant psychological state at war with his natural tendencies toward equality and love, in short, a "mutiny within." If one is not misled by these values but is "aware of his own worth, and moral dignity" and uses the "power" within him to try to "level the inequality which is the topic of the complaint of mankind," then he can be said to know himself, is "himself alone." He is able to "quell" the harmful, cacophonous forces of hate, lust, and ambition. But after quelling them, he does not retire from life. Shelley is not advocating an ascetic ideal or urging a life of pure contemplation. The man who conquers the evil forces that drive him to act in an antihumanitarian manner substitutes for them positive, not negative, qualities. He participates in life to the full but in a selfless way, preaching, like Jesus or Socrates, an egalitarian gospel.

If it seems surprising that almost all the past leaders of mankind in every field are pictured as captives of life, the reason is that Shelley has adopted an absolute humanitarian standard by which to judge them. Either a person puts himself first or he puts humanity first; to the degree that he favors his own interests at the expense of others, he is corrupted. The emancipation of mankind from its "dark slavery" will come about only if its leaders are utterly selfless. It is they who hold the fate of mankind in their hands. If they falter, the horrible, antihuman society of poverty, brutalization, war, and tyranny that has existed from the beginning of civilization will continue. Misery will remain the lot of the great majority of the inhabitants of the planet. Hence, those who are leaders bear a heavy responsibility, and any element of corruption must be condemned.

Even when judged by the high moral standard that Shelley is adopting, the presence of some leaders among the captives is at first puzzling, for instance, Plato, for whom Shelley had in some ways so high a regard. Plato, however, is treated as an exception:

> All that is mortal of great Plato there
> Expiates the joy & woe his master knew not;
> That star that ruled his doom was far too fair—
>
> And Life, where long that flower of Heaven grew not
> Conquered the heart by love which gold or pain
> Or age or sloth or slavery could subdue not. (254–259)

Shelley's language here is clearly of the riddling kind he sometimes delighted in, but his specific reference is apparent from the following epigram by Plato, which he translated:

> Thou wert the morning star among the living,
> Ere thy fair light had fled;
> Now, having died, thou art as Hesperus, giving
> New splendour to the dead.[22]

The "star that ruled" Plato's "doom," then, was the person to whom this little love poem was written. As the poem was written to a boy ("Aster"—the star) with whom Plato had a love affair, the implication is that Plato yielded to what seemed to Shelley the corrupting influences of society not from selfishness or ambition but in a search for love.

Shelley's comment on Plato is notable in another respect. He states that the figure behind the chariot was "All that is mortal of great Plato." This implies that only Plato's body and senses, perhaps even the outer socially-conditioned ring of his mind, were conquered by life. The creative core of his mind, which had produced his great works, was not conquered, as shown by the fact that Shelley regarded him as an egalitarian.

Rousseau's status in the drama is somewhat ambiguous. He is not chained to the chariot, as he should be by virtue of being a leader of mankind, but is standing on the hillside by the poet. He is said to be one of that "deluded crew" (184), which seems to refer only to the dancers before and behind the chariot. The chained captives have not at this point been mentioned. Furthermore, Rousseau later states that he "among the multitude was swept" (460), a reference that clearly excludes "the captives" (457). At the end of the poem he implies that he was one of the dancers and voluntarily dropped out:

> And some grew weary of the ghastly dance
>
> And fell, as I have fallen by the way side. (540–541)

He could hardly have dropped out if he had been chained.

Rousseau, then, for some reason that perhaps would have been explained later, was not among the "mighty captives." He was nevertheless, as were all those in the "multitude" before and behind the chariot, in fact a captive of life. He explains his subjugation as follows:

> Frederick, and Kant, Catherine, and Leopold,
> Each hoary anarch and demagogue and sage
> Whose name the fresh world thinks already old
>
> For in the battle Life and they did wage
> She remained conqueror—I was overcome
> By my own heart alone, which neither age
>
> Nor tears nor infamy nor now the tomb
> Could temper to its object. (236–243)

The concept is clearly similar to that for Plato. Unlike Frederick and the others, Rousseau did not yield to self or ambition. On the contrary, he was conquered "By my own heart alone." The reference is apparently to Rousseau's later book *The Reveries of a Solitary*. There, as in *The Triumph of Life*, Rousseau as an old man is looking back on his life with some bewilderment: "I am upon this earth as on a strange planet . . . I was made for living and I am dying before I have lived." Having finished with the struggle of life, he finds the world in a state of flux. He was led astray by his love for his fellow men: "But from these first acts of goodness, poured out with effusions of heart, were born chains of successive engagements that I had not foreseen, and of which I could no longer shake off the yoke."[23] In the pursuit of love and humanitarian ideals he had suffered from persecution, malice, and slander, and in his old age he is left lonely and bewildered. Part of the reason for his defeat, as Shelley saw it, must also have been his relations with women. As a youth, Shelley had been shocked by the sensualism of *The Confessions*, and perhaps by Rousseau's placing his five children by Therese le Vasseau in a foundling hospital.[24]

Like Plato, Rousseau, then, was led into captivity by a search for love. Like Plato, too, he was only partly conquered by life:

> I feared, loved, hated, suffered, did & died,
> And if the spark with which Heaven lit my spirit
> Earth had with purer nutriment supplied
>
> Corruption would not now thus much inherit
> Of what was once Rousseau—nor this disguise
> Stained that within which still disdains to wear it.—
>
> If I have been extinguished, yet there rise
> A thousand beacons from the spark I bore. (200–207)

Rousseau's natural "spirit," though essentially good, could not completely withstand the pressures of an evil society ("earth"). Even so, the creative core of his mind—"that within"—remained dedicated to humanitarian ideals, and his works have inspired mankind.

In another passage Rousseau states that his "words" have become "seeds of misery" (280) to him, leading to his persecution—"Even as the deeds of others" (281) have done. This parallel the poet denies:

> "Not as theirs,"
> I said—and pointed to a company
>
> In which I recognized amid the heirs
> Of Caesar's crime from him to Constantine,
> The Anarchs old whose force & murderous snares
>
> Had founded many a sceptre bearing line
> And spread the plague of blood & gold abroad,
> And Gregory and John and men divine. (281–288)

Although Rousseau's life and works may have brought him "misery," they were not at all the same kind of thing as the "crimes" of the Roman emperors or of church leaders against mankind. Rousseau's contribution to humanity has been essentially good; theirs, essentially evil. The implication is that the conquest of those political and religious leaders by life is more complete than that of Rousseau or Plato. This concept of degrees of corruption was implied also in Shelley's letter to Horace Smith: "But all, more or less, subdue themselves to the element which surrounds them." Plato and Rousseau were among those who subdued themselves "less." This must have been true to some degree, for other captives as well. Shelley must certainly have regarded Voltaire as less "subdued" than Frederick, Aristotle as less "subdued" than Alexander; but his image of the chained captives does not allow him to show degrees of captivity. As all are chained, except Rousseau, he can indicate such degrees only by specific comments, such as those for Plato, but he can hardly do this for each one.

The Visions of Rousseau

Among the problems posed by the second part of the poem, the first concerns the "cavern" in which Rousseau awoke and from which he emerged to look back on the "shape all light" above the well. Shelley gives several clues to the meaning, the first in the lines:

> Whether my life had been before that sleep
> The Heaven which I imagine, or a Hell
>
> Like this harsh world in which I wake to weep,
> I know not. (332–335)

The "Heaven" that Rousseau imagines does not, as some have suggested, refer to a divine preexistence, but to the future society which Rousseau envisaged, either directly or by implication, in his works, a society of equality and love. The general concept, echoing the final chorus of *Hellas,* is of an imagined previous age of "golden years," in which Rousseau's spirit might have lived, a concept that also suggests reincarnation. The sound of the rivulet in the cavern is described as "Lethean" (463). According to Greek mythologists, the river of oblivion, Lethe, was a river in Hades whose waters were drunk both by the souls of the dead arriving and by the souls of those about to be born as they left to begin a new incarnation.

Further light is shed on the meaning of the cavern by another chorus in *Hellas*:

> But they are still immortal
> Who, through birth's orient portal
> And death's dark chasm hurrying to and fro,
> Clothe their unceasing flight
> In the brief dust and light
> Gather'd around their chariots as they go. (201–206)

The concept in *Hellas* is that the minds of the great creative leaders of mankind, the "poets," are reborn in different bodies in different ages. The image is similar in general, though not in detail, to that of Rousseau's "orient cavern." Apparently Shelley's idea is that the immortal spirit known as Rousseau enters the cavern from the east when the body it last inhabited dies, stays for a period, and emerges from the western entrance into life. Rousseau himself has no memory of a past existence—"So sweet & deep is the oblivious spell" (331)—although he has some feeling that he has lived before. That Shelley did not accept reincarnation as a philosophical doctrine he indicated in the Notes to *Hellas,* but he also indicated there that it was legitimate to make metaphorical use of it in poetry as a beautiful, uplifting notion, in contrast to the degradation of death: "born only to die." He does not state that the mind of Rousseau had previously existed; he simply hints it as a fancy in a realm in which all is ignorance: "I know not."

Rousseau's emergence from the cavern, then, simply represents his birth. He emerges into a forest, with the rivulet from the cavern running beside him. The forest at first is pleasant and inspiring:

> I arose & for a space
> The scene of woods & waters seemed to keep,
>
> Though it was now broad day, a gentle trace
> Of light diviner than the common Sun
> Sheds on the common Earth, but all the place
>
> Was filled with many sounds woven into one
> Oblivious melody, confusing sense
> Amid the gliding waves & shadows dun. (335–342)

Shelley's symbolism here is not hard to penetrate. A forest has, at least since Dante, been a standard symbol for life or the world, and Shelley so used it in *Epipsychidion* ("the wintry forest of our life").[25] The forest occupies a valley, which is another standard symbol for the world, as in the Biblical "vale of tears" of *Hymn to Intellectual Beauty.* Rousseau is thus moving out into the forest and valley of the world, where he is to see the vision of the chariot of life. But first he is in the pleasant woods with its singing rivulet and unnatural light. This is the same period depicted in *Alastor* (67-75) for the young poet-hero and in *Epipsychidion* (192-194) for Shelley, in all of which the beauties of nature and the imagination shut the mind off from social realities—blend all into "one Oblivious melody."

Looking back eastward into the cavern, Rousseau sees the sun strike the waters of the bubbling well from which the rivulet flows, turning it to brilliant gold and the rivulet to "emerald fire" as it flows into the forest. If the symbolism of the forest and valley is obvious, that of the spring, the stream, the cavern, and the mountain is not. The fact that the mountain fronts the forest, however, and that the cavern opens into it provides a clue. Moreover, in *Alastor,* too, there was a mountain, with a cavern at one end, which was said to be the entrance to the realm of sleep and death, then a rising whirlpool in the middle of the mountain, and on top a wellspring from which a stream flowed. The stream grew into a river and fell off into a great gulf. That the stream and river in *Alastor* represent life Shelley made explicit in the narrative, and as the cavern is the entrance to the realm of death and sleep, then the mountain must stand for that realm. But, as the well and stream show, it is also the site of the beginning of life. It must, then, be a symbol for the "power" that is inherent both in the motions of matter and the life cycle. Like Rousseau, the *Alastor* poet apparently undergoes reincarnation, finding, in his new life, the well and its stream, which he follows.

The symbolic structure in *The Triumph of Life,* however, although similar, is not quite the same as that in *Alastor.* In the *Triumph of Life,* the cavern goes straight through the mountain, there is no whirlpool, no river, no waterfall, and no gulf. Toward one end of the cavern are the well and the rivulet that leads into the forest of life. But in spite of these differences, the mountain in *The Triumph of Life* seems by its role in the poem to stand for the same general concept of the power as it does in *Alastor*. It also seems intended to suggest eternity: the great mountain looming over the valley of the world and time, the mountain from which life emerges—the "cradles of eternity."[26] As for the cavern, the spring and the stream within it may indicate that Shelley intended it to symbolize the biologically creative aspect of power, consciously or unconsciously a womb symbol. The emphasis with regard to the well is on light:

> the Sun's image radiantly intense
>
> Burned on the waters of the well that glowed
> Like gold, and threaded all the forest maze
> With winding paths of emerald fire. (346–348)

The most obvious explanation is probably the correct one, namely, that the spring is the source of life in its natural essence of love and beauty, and that the stream represents the flow of this essence into social life (the forest). The light comes not from internal forces within the spring but externally from the sun; in other words, it is natural and not mystical. The source of the spring, in both *Alastor* and *The Triumph of Life*, is unknown.

The "shape all light" is clearly similar to the "Being" of *Epipsychidion*. Rousseau observes the "shape" in his confused youth just as Shelley observes the "Being" in "the clear golden prime of my youth's dawn" (191). Rousseau, looking back from the woods just beyond the cavern, sees above the well and then over the stream:

> A shape all light, which with one hand did fling
> Dew on the Earth, as if she were the dawn,
> Whose musical rain forever seemed to sing
>
> A silver melody on the mossy lawn. (352–355)

The shape has a supernaturally light step and is accompanied by a strange music that brings forgetfulness:

> the fierce splendour
> Fell from her as she moved under the mass
>
> Of the deep cavern, and with palms so tender
> Their tread broke not the mirror of its billow.
>
> . . . . .
>
> And still her feet, no less than the sweet tune
> To which they moved, seemed as they moved, to blot
> The thoughts of him who gazed on them. (359–362, 382–384)

Though the shape disappears, its continuing presence is felt:

> And the fair Shape waned in the coming light
> As veil by veil the silent splendour drops
> From Lucifer, amid the chrysolite
>
> Of sunrise ere it strike the mountain tops,
> And as the presence of that fairest planet,
> Although unseen, is felt by one who hopes
>
> That his day's path may end as he began it.
>
> . . . . .
>
> So knew I in that light's severe excess
> The presence of that Shape. (412–418, 424–425)

In these and other respects the Shape is parallel to the "Being" in *Epipsychidion*:

> An antelope,
> In the suspended impulse of its lightness,
> Were less ethereally light: the brightness
> Of her divinest presence trembles through her limbs.
>
> . . . . .
>
> And from her lips, as from a hyacinth full
> Of honey dew, a liquid murmur drops,
> Filling the sense with passion; sweet as stops
> Of planetary music heard in trance.
>
> . . . . .
>
> But She, whom prayers or tears then could not tame,
> Past, like a God throned on a winged planet.
>
> . . . . .
>
> And as a man with mighty loss dismayed,
> I would have followed, though the grave between
> Yawned like a gulf whose spectres are unseen:
> When a voice said:—"O Thou of hearts the weakest,
> The phantom is beside thee whom thou seekest."
> (75–79, 83–86, 225–226, 229–233)

The "Being" of *Epipsychidion* was a manifestation of the "benignant power" that "surrounds us" and "visits with its breath our silent chords at will." This power is of the essence of nature, and those who lead self-sacrificing, humanitarian lives can come into contact with it in "the fields and woods" and take something of it into themselves. And this is what Rousseau does in *The Triumph of Life*.[27] The "shape all light," when first seen above the well, stands "Amid the sun, as he amid the blaze / Of his own glory" (349–350). In other words, she is a manifestation of nature, and she comes "from the realm without a name" (396), that is, from the unknown essence of the universe.

Some critics have denied the identification of the shape with any good quality because she is followed by the hideous vision of life and because her effect on Rousseau's mind is described in what appears to be a destructive sense.[28] She "blotted" out his "thoughts" until:

All that was, seemed as if it had been not,
As if the gazer's mind was strewn beneath
Her feet like embers, and she, thought by thought,

Trampled its sparks into the dust of death,
As Day upon the threshold of the east
Threads out the lamps of night, until the breath

Of darkness reillumines even the least
Of heaven's living eyes—like Day she came,
Making the night a dream. (285–290)

But the idea here is not primarily one of destruction but of rebirth, and rebirth to a finer existence—the change from stars to the sun, from night to day. The poet in *Epipsychidion* undergoes a similar experience:

Soft as an Incarnation of the Sun
When light is changed to love, this glorious One
Floated into the cavern where I lay,
And called my Spirit, and the dreaming clay
Was lifted by the thing that dreamed below
As smoke by fire, and in her beauty's glow
I stood, and felt the dawn of my long night
Was penetrating me with living light. (335–342)

Shelley's meaning in both poems is that the natural power, if received, tramples out the old life of selfishness; and once the old is destroyed, the new can arise: "that powerful attraction towards all that we conceive, or fear, or hope beyond ourselves."[29]

Such also is Shelley's meaning in the "nepenthe" that the shape gives Rousseau to drink, which makes him forget his egocentric self.[30] Why, however, if Rousseau is thus regenerated, does he see as his second vision the hideous chariot of life? This question may be answered with another: what else was there for him to see? The world is in fact the scene of hatred, war, poverty, dictatorship, injustice, and corruption—which Shelley had depicted in poems from *Zeinab and Kathema* to *Hellas*. Rousseau, having encountered the "benignant power," plunges into this world in order to change it:

me sweetest flowers delayed not long,
Me not the shadow nor the solitude,

Me not that falling stream's Lethean song,
  Me, not the phantom of that early form
Which moved upon its motion,—first among

  The thickest billows of the living storm
I plunged, and bared my bosom to the clime
  Of that cold light, whose airs too soon deform. (461–468)

To understand Shelley's meaning more fully, one must remember the esteem in which he held Rousseau and the extent to which he identified with him. Rousseau, like Shelley, was a political radical, an exponent of the doctrine of universal love, and a man who felt himself misunderstood by his age. In *A Defence of Poetry* Shelley had gone out of his way to add a footnote asserting Rousseau's claim to be considered a poet, and listed him with the great poets who "have celebrated the dominion of love, planting as it were trophies in the human mind of that sublimest victory over sensuality and force."[31] Rousseau's *Nouvelle Heloise* he considered a work "of sublimest genius and more than human sensibility," and Rousseau himself was "the greatest man the world has produced since Milton." In the *History of a Six Weeks, Tour* he wrote: "It is nearly a fortnight since I have returned from Verai. This journey has been on every account delightful, but most especially because then I first knew the divine beauty of Rousseau's imagination." When on a visit to the lake of Geneva Byron gathered some acacia in memory of Gibbon, Shelley commented: "I refrained from doing so, fearing to outrage the greater and more sacred name of Rousseau, the contemplation of whose imperishable creations had left no vacancy in my mind for mortal things." His greatest tribute to Rousseau comes in the *Essay on Christianity*, where he compares him with Jesus, somewhat to Rousseau's advantage:

It is impossible to read those passionate words in which Jesus Christ upbraids the pusillanimity and sensuality of mankind, without being strongly reminded of the more connected and systematic enthusiasm of Rousseau . . . Rousseau certainly did not mean to persuade the immense population of his country to abandon all the arts of life, destroy their habitations and their temples, and become the inhabitants of the woods. He addressed the most enlightened of his compatriots, and endeavoured to persuade them to set the example of a pure and simple life, by placing in the strongest point of view his conceptions of the calamitous and diseased aspect which, overgrown as it is with the vices of sensuality and selfishness, is exhibited by civilized society.[32]

In *The Triumph of Life* Shelley depicts Rousseau as "plunging" into the turmoil of pre-Revolutionary France in order to expose the "diseased aspect" of the existing society and to establish an ideal based on the "dominion of love." The situation parallels that in the Dedication to *The Revolt of Islam*, in which Shelley depicts himself as not blinded by the promise of a regenerated humanity but seeing the world as it is and growing determined to change it:

> for I grow weary to behold
> The selfish and the strong still tyrannise
> Without reproach or check.
>
> . . . . .
>
> Wrought linked armour for my soul, before
> It might walk forth to war against mankind. (33–35, 41–42)

Rousseau, having felt the power—the "collective energy of the moral and material world"—abadoned his early fancies and obsessions with death, the allurements of abstract philosophy, the "phantom" of the ideal, and "plunged" into life. In so doing, he was hurt and to some degree corrupted ("whose airs too soon deform").

Rousseau's view of the chariot of life and its accompanying phenomena differs in some respects from the poet's. Although the poet feels that the chariot has a certain "rushing splendor" and he manifests curiosity in it, his main reactions are those of revulsion and fear. The emphasis is on the death-like figure within the chariot and its blindly driving charioteer. He feels no attraction toward the sensual dance of the young dancers in front of the chariot and is disgusted by the sight of the old people stumbling behind. But when Rousseau as a young man first sees the chariot, it holds a definite attraction for him:

> But the new Vision and its cold bright car,
> With solemn speed and stunning music, crost
>
> The forest, and as if from some dread war
> Triumphantly returning, the loud million
> Fiercely extolled the fortune of her star.—
>
> A moving arch of victory the vermilion
> And green & azure plumes of Iris had
> Built high over her wind-winged pavilion,
>
> And underneath aetherial glory clad
> The wilderness, and far before her flew
> The tempest of the splendour which forbade
>
> Shadow to fall from leaf or stone. (434–445)

The poet had made no mention of the "stunning music"; and here, instead of the destroyed dancers, a jubilant throng crowds around the chariot. Rousseau does not comment on the charioteer; nor does he seem to be repelled by the gloomy figure of life. In fact, he does not specifically mention it. He does, however, convey an underlying sense of evil. The "arch of victory" is only a rainbow ("Iris"). The bright light permits no shadows, having substituted for the gentle, natural light of the sun a harsh and garish glow from which there is no escape. But there is at least a superficial air of exultation:

> And more did follow, with exulting hymn,
>
> The chariot & the captives fettered there,
> But all like bubbles on an eddying flood
> Fell into the same track at last & were
>
> Borne onward.—I among the multitude
> Was swept. (456–461)

Both groups—the captives and the masses—after excitedly greeting the chariot, fall into line and march behind it, blended together in "the same track."

These differences in emphasis between the two visions presumably mean that the poet's vision is of life in Shelley's day, in the aftermath of the defeat of the French Revolution, whereas Rousseau's vision is of life in the years before the Revolution—Rousseau died in 1778—and may also reflect the early days of the Revolution, when Rousseau's spirit if not his body was still alive. In those heady days life had a wild attraction, and the line between rulers and masses was blurred. It may also have been for this reason that Rousseau was not among the chained captives.[33]

As the crowd streaming behind the chariot begins to move up the "opposing" (470) slope of the valley, the metamorphosis begins:

> the grove
> Grew dense with shadows to its inmost covers,
> The earth was grey with phantoms, & the air
> Was peopled with dim forms. (480–483)

So thick are these shadows and forms that the air behind the marching multitude is "stained" with them. At first it seems as though the phantoms and the shadows are the same, but later in the passage Shelley indicates that the shadows come from the people and are shaped into the phantoms by the light from the chariot:

> each one
> Of that great crowd sent forth incessantly
> These shadows, numerous as the dead leaves blown
>
> In Autumn evening from a poplar tree—
> Each, like himself & like each other were,
> At first, but soon distorted, seemed to be
>
> Obscure clouds moulded by the casual air;
> And of this stuff the car's creative ray
> Wrought all the busy phantoms that were there
>
> As the sun shapes the clouds. (526–535)

The phantoms take a variety of forms:

Some made a cradle of the ermined capes

Of kingly mantles, some upon the tiar
Of pontiffs sate like vultures, others played
Within the crown which girt with empire

A baby's or an idiot's brow, & made
Their nests in it; the old anatomies
Sat hatching their bare brood under the shade

Of demon wings, and laughed from their dead eyes
To reassume the delegated power
Arrayed in which these worms did monarchize

Who made this earth their charnel.—Others more
Humble, like falcons sate upon the fist
Of common men, and round their heads did soar,

Or like small gnats & flies, as thick as mist
On evening marshes, thronged about the brow
Of lawyer, statesman, priest & theorist,

And others like discoloured flakes of snow
On fairest bosoms & the sunniest hair
Fell, and were melted by the youthful glow

Which they extinguished. (495–514)

The phantoms, then, are the phantoms of power, exploitation and corruption. As Shelley wrote in *The Assassins*: "The perverse, and vile and vicious—what are they? Shapes of some unholy vision, moulded by the spirit of Evil, which the sword of the merciful destroyer should sweep from this beautiful world. Dreamy nothings; phantasms of misery and mischief, that hold their death-like state on glittering thrones, and in the loathsome dens of poverty."[34] The reactionaries of the world are "phantasms" or "phantoms" because their power rests essentially upon ideas. Shelley expressed the same general thought in *Essay on Christianity* and *The Revolt of Islam:*

Opinion is more frail
Than yon dim cloud now fading on the moon
Even while we gaze, though it awhile avail
To hide the orb of truth—and every throne,
Of Earth or Heaven, though shadow, rests thereon,
One shape of many names:—for this ye plough
The barren waves of ocean, hence each one
Is slave or tyrant; all betray and bow,
Command, or kill, or fear, or wreak, or suffer woe. (3271–3279)

The specific concept in *The Triumph of Life* seems to be that in the existing social order the false "shadows" of superstition, hypocrisy, prejudice, hatred, and so on, which plague the common people, form into the constructs of power and corruption, the "phantoms." If the people could only penetrate to the truth, the "phantoms," mighty though they seem, would vanish. As Shelley put it in his letter to Horace Smith: "The destiny of man can scarcely be so degraded that he was born only to die—and if such should be the case, delusions, especially the gross and preposterous ones of the existing religion, can scarcely be supposed to exalt it—if every man said what he thought, it could not subsist a day." Shelley, of course, did not expect the old ideas to be overthrown easily or by the directly countering of ideas to ideas. *A Philosophical View of Reform* envisaged a long, difficult struggle to destroy the social order with which the ideas were enmeshed. But the new ideas would provide essential "sparks."

By the raw "stuff" from which false ideas are formed by the cold light of life, Shelley must mean the substance of mind itself. In the existing order, the forms this substance takes are largely those of subservience and superstition: people's concepts of monarchy and of the church ("pontiffs"); delusions about law and government and their hypocritically "humble" practitioners. Although the young idealist fights off these ideas, in so doing he is often himself destroyed. All are, in fact, to one degree or another corrupted:

> From every firmest limb & fairest face
> The strength & freshness fell like dust. (520–521)

Apparently *The Triumph of Life* passage reflects the disenchantment that Rousseau expressed in his *Confessions* and elsewhere—the warm-hearted young man entering the French social scene who at first was praised and befriended but soon began to feel persecuted and betrayed. It also clearly embodies comments by Shelley on life in the existing order. Some of the forms of that life resulted from the overthrow of the French Revolution and the restoration of the Bourbons as well as other reactionary regimes: the "old anatomies" and their "base brood" who, by means of the Congress of Vienna, reassumed "the delegated power" in which to "monarchize." The "crown which girt with empire/A baby's or an idiot's brow" is presumably a reference to the insane George III, and Napoleon's declaration of his infant son as king of Rome in 1811. Lower down on the pyramid of power are the hypocritically "humble" corruptors, lawyers and priests and so on.

How the poem would have continued, whether it would have run to several thousand lines in three or more parts, of which Shelley almost completed only the first part, or whether it is half-complete or almost complete, are matters of dispute. The only indications come from within the poem itself and from the fact that Shelley was making use in it of Petrarch's *Triumphs*.[35] On that usage, A. C. Bradley remarked:

> [The *Triumphs*] form a series of six poems in *terza rima,* describing in turn the triumph of Love over man, especially in his youth; the triumph of Chastity over Love; that of Death over all mortality; that of Fame over Death; that of Time over Fame; and that of Divinity over Time. Shelley owes little to the last five of the *Trionfi,* but a good deal to the first, as a few words will show. Here Petrarch, lying in early morning on the grass in a solitary place, and wearied with sad thoughts of the past, falls asleep. In his sleep he sees a great light, and within this light four white coursers drawing a car, in which sits Love, like a conqueror in a Roman triumph. Around the car he sees innumerable mortals, dead and alive; and one of them, a friend who recognizes him, points out and describes to him the most famous of the victims.[36]

If Shelley was in fact following the structure of Petrarch's first *Triumph* so closely as this in the initial 548 lines of his poem, he perhaps intended to follow at least Petrarch's general framework for the rest of it also. If such was his plan, perhaps *The Triumph of Life* was meant not to be a title for the whole work but a subtitle for the first part only.

That this was Shelley's intention may be indicated by the concluding fragmentary lines. The chariot of life has vanished, with no hint of its return, and the poet seems to be turning to another theme: "Happy those for Whom the fold of . . ." As Reiman noted, Shelley used "folding-star"—the star that guides the shepherd—as a symbol for love, as in *Hellas*:

> And follow Love's folding star
> To the Evening land.[37]

Since the "Evening land" was America, that passage depicted the new hope for humanity growing out of the American republican democracy. If in the later, unfinished poem Shelley did intend a "triumph" of love or at least a dialogue on it between the poet and Rousseau, he would perhaps have discussed various literary and historical figures, especially those not noted in *The Triumph of Life,* such as Aeschylus, Sophocles, Dante, Tasso, Bacon, Chatterton, and Mary Wollstonecraft. He might also have shown how "love" and similar qualities—the "benignant power"—sustained and inspired those figures. In *The Triumph of Life* all the great figures discussed are dead, but in another "triumph" or section Shelley would almost certainly have depicted living ones also, for instance, those discussed by him in other poems: Wordsworth, Coleridge, Godwin, Malthus, Hunt, Byron, and Keats. He had stated in the conclusion of the Preface to *Prometheus Unbound* (1819) that he intended at some time to produce a "systematical history of what appears to me to be the genuine elements of human society."[38] Perhaps he felt that in the "triumph" form he had found a poetical medium for presenting such an idea.

The autobiographical element would probably have continued in the rest of the poem, for Rousseau says to the poet narrator:

> But follow thou, & from spectator turn
> Actor or victim in this wretchedness,
> And what thou wouldst be taught I then may learn
> From thee. (305–308)

That the poet narrator—"I"—is Shelley in his early youth is suggested in various passages. The implication of Rousseau's words could thus be that the young poet will plunge into life, as Rousseau had, and will then tell him what conclusions he has reached. If so, it seems unlikely that the poet would have taken the path that Rousseau took, for the chariot of life did not have the attraction for him that it did for Rousseau. When the poet saw it, there was no "stunning music" associated with it, and even had it reappeared later in the poem, it is virtually certain that Shelley would not have depicted himself among the captives, for he believed that he was one who had resisted the blandishments of society and remained true to the ideals of equality, love, and beauty. He was, however, aware of the dangers of love as a "snare," and his remarks on Plato and Rousseau in this regard doubtless have some application to himself. He may have felt that he had risked such captivity by following his heart into a "cold" marriage or by engaging in humanitarian action, as had Rousseau, but his letter to Horace Smith implies that he had not in fact been trapped by those activities into either self-seeking or blindly partisan involvement.

14
The Contemporary World and Its Promise

Prometheus Unbound, Acts I and II

In *Queen Mab* and then in *The Revolt of Islam,* Shelley had tried to express the essence of his social philosophy in a major work. Although he still held to the main tenets of each and, indeed, considered a new edition of *The Revolt of Islam* as late as 1821, he was troubled by what he felt were stylistic crudities in the first and by faults, apparently mainly structural, in the second.[1] On his arrival in Italy, with his poetical powers rapidly maturing and his mind stimulated by the turmoil of postwar Europe, he made a third attempt—*Prometheus Unbound.*[2] This time he felt that he had succeeded. As he wrote to the Olliers on October 15, 1819: "The 'Prometheus,' a poem in my best style, whatever that may amount to, will arrive with it, but in MS., which you can print and publish in the season. It is the most perfect of my productions." And he wrote them again on March 6 in the following year: " 'Prometheus Unbound,' I must tell you, is my favourite poem; I charge you, therefore, specially to pet him and feed him with fine ink and good paper."[3] He was also aware, however, that this "favourite," aimed, unlike *The Masque of Anarchy,* at an intellectual and not a mass audience, was a difficult poem, for in it he used a complex symbolic technique (rather like that of Blake in his longer poems, in which the characters represent clusters of meaning).[4] The problem in interpretating *Prometheus Unbound* (or *The Four Zoas*) is to find the meaning of the symbols. Unlike Blake, however, Shelley did not make up his own mythology but turned to his wide knowledge of the classics, especially Aeschylus, for a base for his symbolism.

Hesiod and Aeschylus

The importance of fire to the human race, today taken for granted, was a living tradition as late as the age of Lucretius. Fire not only gave people a means to heat food and conquer cold but provided the power to fashion metal tools and weapons. Consequently, myths on its origin are everywhere part of folk history. One of the oldest and most sophisticated is the legend, common to both Indian and Greek mythology, of a god who brought fire from heaven (lightning) as a gift to mankind—Matarisvan among the Indians, Prometheus among the Greeks.[5]

In Greek literature, the basic written source of the myth is Hesiod's *Theog-*

ony, a work that Shelley read and which throws light on many aspects of his poem.[6] According to Hesiod, first there was Chaos; then, apparently out of Chaos, came Earth, who gave birth to "starry Heaven, equal to herself, to cover her on every side." Earth, the mother, and Heaven, the father, produced the Titans, among whom were Oceanus, Tethys, Iapetus, Rhea, and Kronos (Saturn). Earth and Heaven also produced three gigantic creatures with fifty heads and a hundred arms, but these their father hated so much that he hid them in "a secret place of Earth" as soon as they were born. This so enraged Earth that she plotted with her son Kronos to castrate his father Heaven. After he did so, Kronos ruled as king of the Titans.[7] The rule of Kronos, as described in Hesiod's other major poem, *Works and Days,* was a golden age. Men "lived like gods without sorrow of heart," the "fruitful earth unforced bare them fruit abundantly," and "when they died it was as though they were overcome with sleep."[8]

Kronos, having seized power from his father and fearing lest any of his own sons should follow his example, swallowed them as fast as his wife, Rhea, produced them. In the case of their son Zeus, however, Rhea deceived Kronos by wrapping a large stone in swaddling clothes for him to swallow, while the child was hidden in a cave by his grandmother, Earth. When Zeus grew up, what Kronos had feared happened, for Zeus led a revolt against him and the other Titans and established the reign of the gods.

Although the Titans were overthrown, some of their children were allowed to live as before, including the four daughters of Oceanus and Tethys: Asia, Ianeira ("Lady of the Ionians"), Ianthe, and Clymene. Clymene bore several sons to the Titan Iapetus, among them a stupid son, Epimetheus (the "after-thinker"), and a brilliant son, Prometheus (the "forethinker"). When Zeus withheld the knowledge of fire from mankind, Prometheus stole some from heaven. Zeus, seeing "amongst men the farseen ray of fire," was enraged and sent all manner of evil upon the human race (the Pandora legend), while the "ready witted Prometheus he bound with inextricable bonds, cruel chains, and drove a shaft through his middle, and set on him a long-winged eagle, which used to eat his immortal liver." (According to other sources, Prometheus was first fettered to a rock in Scythia, which was hurled by Zeus's thunderbolt into Tartary. After a time he was brought again into the upper world and fettered in the Caucasus. It was there that the eagle preyed on him.)[9] Many years later, Hercules, with Zeus's permission, killed the eagle and released Prometheus.

Hesiod's account does not include one vital part of the myth that later developed, growing out of the successive seizures of power by Kronos and Zeus. According to Hyginus and other mythologists, after Zeus had succeeded to the throne, he was beset by the same fear that had troubled Kronos, namely, that a son would be born to him greater than he, who would overthrow him as he had overthrown Kronos. Prometheus and his grandmother Earth knew of a prophecy that the son of the sea goddess Thetis, whom Zeus was then wooing, would be greater than his father.[10] This secret either Prometheus or Earth finally told to Zeus, who hastily turned Thetis over to Peleus, to whom she bore Achilles. Thus, the prophecy was fulfilled, for Achilles was certainly greater than Peleus, and Zeus's throne was saved.

Three centuries after Hesiod, Aeschylus wrote two plays based on these myths, *Prometheus Bound* and *Prometheus Unbound*, and possibly a third, *Prometheus the Torchbearer*. Of these, only *Prometheus Bound* is extant; the second exists only in fragments.[11] From *Prometheus Bound* Shelley not only received the initial inspiration for his own work but took some of his basic structure from it. Some commentators have missed Shelley's meanings by not seeing that he is in places echoing or developing ideas from Aeschylus.

The Prometheus of Aeschylus is a very different figure from that of Hesiod. In Hesiod he is merely one character among the multitude of the *Theogony*; in *Prometheus Bound* he is the central figure. In Hesiod, he is rather condescendingly depicted as a sly and cunning fellow, fond of playing tricks on the father of the gods and foolishly defying him in order to bring fire to mankind. In Aeschylus, he is a titanic symbol of rebellion, bringing to mankind not fire alone but science, art, and wisdom—a tradition that Plato in his *Protagoras* also followed.

Aeschylus' play opens with Prometheus, guarded by two daemons of Zeus, Might and Force, about to be fettered by Hephaistos to a rock on the shore of Ocean in Scythia. Hephaistos, addressing Prometheus as a "child of Themis" (Earth), laments that he must chain him, for he does the work of Zeus unwillingly. But although he does not agree with Zeus, he also feels that Prometheus' defiance is foolish: "Lo, the reward of all thy love for man." The daemons drive Hephaistos on to complete his unwilling task. Only after they have departed and Prometheus is left alone against the desolate rock, a mighty and scornful figure, does he speak. The powers of "Necessity" will, Prometheus is certain, ultimately overthrow Zeus:

> One thing being certain, that no victory
> Is his who wars 'gainst That which Needs must be.

Prometheus hears a great rushing of wings, and the chorus of the Daughters of Oceanus sweeps up in winged chariots. The chorus hails him as unconquerable:

> Oh, thou art valiant! None shall teach
> By torment that proud heart to quail.

Prometheus informs the chorus that Zeus owes his throne to him, for it was he who showed him how to defeat the Titans. In this he had been aided by Earth (designated as his mother by Aeschylus). After a visit by Oceanus, who informs Prometheus that he intends to intercede with Zeus for him, Prometheus lists the good things that he has bestowed on mankind. He gave them "new mastery of thought," taught them how to build houses and to know the coming of seasons by the stars. He gave them the arts of writing and arithmetic, showed them how to domesticate animals and build ships, taught them divination and the science of medicine:

> Ye have heard
> A tale that can be summed in one brief word:
> All that of art man has, Prometheus gave.

He once more prophesies the overthrow of Zeus by the powers of necessity; necessity is stronger than Zeus: "The doom that is ordained he cannot break."

Then follows a long discussion with another victim of Zeus's persecution, Io, princess of Argos. It has little direct bearing on the main theme except for the prophecy that a descendant of hers (Hercules) will one day free Prometheus. Prometheus outlines her gloomy future, divination being one of his arts, and then, in answer to the imprecations of the chorus, hints at the secret of Zeus's downfall, which he alone knows:

> I swear that yet, for all his stubborn pride,
> Zeus shall bow low his head. There is a bride
> He woos and wins; and winning, shall be hurled
> From that high throne and sceptre of the world
> To darkness.
>
> . . . . .
>
> So dire a thing of death
> 'Gainst him and his even now he gendereth . . .

Hermes now enters and presumptuously demands that Prometheus reveal the secret to Zeus. Prometheus retorts scornfully:

> let his jagged flame be hurled,
> With white-winged snow and earthquake, let the world
> Be racked till chaos come. I warn thee well,
> Naught of all these shall move my lips to tell
> What hour, what hand, shall cast him to the abyss.[12]

The play ends with Prometheus and his rock being hurled, amid divine lightnings and whirlwinds, into the abyss. The daughters of Oceanus remain faithful and are swept down with him.

Aeschylus' play, as even so brief an outline indicates, is a sophisticated and radical work. Zeus is not just Zeus, king of the gods, but a symbol for political and religious tyranny, ruling by the "daemons" of Might and Force. Prometheus is the rebellious intellectual, standing for reason, science, and art against blind authority. He is defiant, courageous, and scornful. Although there are hints of a future compromise, he rejoices vengefully at the thought of Zeus's ultimate, inevitable humiliation. The concept of fate or necessity hangs over the play. Necessity is greater than the gods, greater than tyranny, greater than man. Aeschylus clearly had thunderbolts of his own to hurl at the Athenian Establishment.

In the sequel, *Prometheus Unbound*, as indicated in a fragment quoted by Cicero, Prometheus is back on the rock, still defiant:

> Offspring of Titans, linked in blood to ours,
> Children of Heaven, see bound to rugged cliffs . . .
> Pierced through, I make this Furies' fort my home.[13]

The goddess Earth is with him. It was she who told him of the prophecy concerning the child of Thetis, and perhaps in the end Prometheus himself did not divulge this to Zeus but permitted Earth to do so. Shelley's opening scene appears to have been influenced by this fragment.[14]

Characters and Action

Shelley's play opens with Prometheus already bound to his "Precipice," which, however, is neither in Scythia nor the Caucasus but in the "Indian Caucasus." Shelley's shift of scene is deliberate, for the Indian Caucasus or Hindu Kush Mountains were, in his day, thought to be connected with the origins of mankind.[15] The locale of the play is, in fact, not Greek but Indian.

Instead of a chorus of Oceanides (daughters of Oceanus), Prometheus has with him only two, Ione (Hesiod's Ianeira) and Panthea. A third Oceanid, Asia, sister to Ione and Panthea, has been separated from him by Jupiter and lives in a valley of the Indian Caucasus (apparently the Vale of Cashmere).[16] According to Hesiod, Asia was a sister of Clymene, mother of Prometheus, but according to Herodotus, who was apparently following another mythological tradition, she was the wife of Prometheus. This last relationship is the one that Shelley, for dramatic purposes, chose to accept.

In his opening speech, Prometheus reveals himself as the same defiant, intellectual rebel as in Aeschylus, but while he still defies Jupiter, he now wishes to "recall" the curse he formerly uttered against him. His mother, Earth (Shelley here follows Aeschylus in making Prometheus the son of Earth) tells him to summon a phantom from the underworld and to have it repeat the curse. Prometheus calls up the phantasm of Jupiter, and, after hearing the curse, revokes it. Hardly has he done so than a swirling of wings is heard, and "an endless crowd" (330) of winged Furies, led by Mercury, come sweeping through the mountain chasm to the precipice. Their mission is to torture Prometheus, but Mercury holds them back while urging Prometheus to disclose the secret of the overthrow of Jupiter. Mercury's attitude toward Prometheus seems to combine that of Aeschylus' Hermes, with his insolent mockery, and Hephaistos, who pitied Prometheus and regretted his mission but saw no other choice than to obey Jupiter. For the torturing Furies, who spectacularly take the place of the classical eagle, Shelley turns to another of Aeschylus' plays, *The Eumenides,* where they are described as wingless (but flying) Harpies or Gorgons. Like Shelley's Furies, they inflict havoc and torment. They pursue men like hounds tracking a wounded fawn, rejoice in the smell of blood, and sing hymns of hate and madness. They are associated with the old tribal order, with Zeus and the rule of brute force. Shelley's Furies torment Prometheus with two visions of the futility of humanitarian endeavor: the perversion of the gospel of Jesus by a corrupt church, and the collapse of the French Revolution. One Fury remains behind to drive home this message of despair, but on hearing Prometheus express pity for those who have lost feeling for the sufferings of humanity, it too vanishes, apparently baffled.

There next appears, as an antidote to the Furies, a chorus of Spirits, summoned by Earth, who sing of a revival of love that was followed by "Ruin." They predict that Prometheus will conquer this "Ruin" and that a new order of "Wisdom, Justice, Love, and Peace" will be born. When they have departed, Panthea—who, with Ione, has been sitting near Prometheus throughout the scene—leaves to go to her sister Asia. With this, the first act ends.

The second act depicts Asia in her "lovely Vale" waiting for the arrival of Panthea. It is dawn, and spring is in the air. Panthea enters, to tell Asia she has had two dreams. In one she saw Prometheus transfigured by love; the second she cannot remember. A "shape" from the second dream, with golden morning dew gleaming through its gray robes, appears and calls Asia to "follow" it. "Echoes" take up the cry:

> In the world unknown
> Sleeps a voice unspoken;
> By thy step alone
> Can its rest be broken;
>   Child of Ocean! (II.i. 190–194)

The sisters follow "To the deep, to the deep,/Down down!" (II.iii.54–55) and come to the cave of Demogorgon, a "mighty darkness/Filling the seat of power" (II.iv.2–3). Demogorgon comes not from classical but from medieval mythology, where he figures as the ruler of the underworld and master of the Fates.[17] Asia challenges Demogorgon to explain how, if there is a God, evil exists, to which he answers that "the deep truth is imageless" and that only "eternal Love" is beyond the control of "Fate, Time, Occasion, Chance and Change" (II. iv. 116, 119, 120). Two chariots appear. Demogorgon ascends in the first, Asia and Panthea in the second. As they arise, Asia is transfigured by love and hailed as "Life of Life" by a "voice in the air" (II.v.48).

The third act opens in "Heaven," with Jupiter on his throne and Thetis and other gods and goddesses near him. He informs them that he and Thetis have produced a "fatal child, the terror of the earth" (III. i. 19), evidently derived from the "dire thing of death" prophesied by Prometheus in Aeschylus' play. The child exists in spirit only, but Jupiter expects him to take over the body of Demogorgon—in fact, to be become Demogorgan. He now awaits this phenomenon. Instead of the child, however, Demogorgon himself appears. Jupiter, in amazement and growing fear, asks who he is. Demogorgon replies cryptically, "Eternity. Demand no direr name" (III. i. 52). And he adds, "I am thy child, as thou wert Saturn's child;/Mightier than thee" (III. i. 54-55). The traitional prophecy is thus somehow fulfilled. Jupiter's "child," greater than his father, is Demogorgon. Demogorgon informs Jupiter that his reign is now over, that he and Demogorgon will "dwell together/Henceforth in darkness" (III. i. 55–56). Jupiter resists but is helpless before the might of Demogorgon: "The elements obey me not (III. i. 80). He is driven from his throne and sinks "down, ever, forever down" (81), while:

> like a cloud, mine enemy above
> Darkens my fall with victory. (III.i.82–83)

In the second scene of the act, the god Ocean (the Oceanus of Aeschylus), and Apollo, the sun god, discuss the fall of Jupiter. In the third scene, Prometheus is released from the rock by Hercules, who is accompanied by Asia, Panthea, Ione, and Earth. Ione is commanded by Prometheus to give a "curved shell" (III. iii. 65) to the Spirit of the Hour in whose chariot Asia and Panthea had traveled. The Spirit is to blow the "mighty music" (III. iii. 81) of the shell to mankind. Prometheus, Asia, Panthea, and Ione retreat to a cave in which they will view the future world and its creations:

> the progeny immortal
> Of Painting, Sculpture, and rapt Poesy,
> And arts, tho' unimagined, yet to be. (III.iii.54–56)

In the final scene of the act, the Spirit of the Hour returns to report on the new order arising in response to the music from the shell:

> The loathsome mask has fallen, the man remains,—
> Sceptreless, free, uncircumscribed, but man—
> Equal, unclassed, tribeless and nationless. (III.iv.193–195)

The fourth act is a sustained lyrical tribute to this new society. A chorus of Hours and a chorus of Spirits "from the mind/Of human kind" (IV.93–94) reveal that man has control not only of the Earth but of the other planets as well. Models of the Earth and the Moon, themselves transformed, rejoice in the overthrow of the old order and celebrate the beauties of the new. Demogorgon arises to give the final message of the play. If, he announces cryptically, the serpent that would bind eternity should ever get free, order can be restored by human endeavor:

To defy Power, which seems omnipotent;
To love, and bear; to hope till Hope creates
From its own wreck the thing it contemplates. (IV. 572–574)

The Preface

That behind the characters and action there lies a symbolic intent Shelley indicates in his Preface. For this, he had precedent in Aeschylus. Yet he is not following Aeschylus mechanically:

Had I framed my story on this model [that of Aeschylus] I should have done no more than have attempted to restore the lost drama of Aeschylus; an ambition, which, if my preference to this mode of treating the subject had incited me to cherish, the recollection of the high comparison such an attempt would challenge might well abate. But, in truth, I was averse from a catastrophe so feeble as that of reconciling the Champion with the Oppressor of mankind. The moral interest of the fable, which is so powerfully sustained by the sufferings and endurance of Prometheus, would be annihilated if we could conceive of him as unsaying his high language and quailing before his successful and perfidious adversary . . . But Prometheus is, as it were, the type of the highest perfection of moral and intellectual nature, impelled by the purest and truest motives to the best and noblest ends.[18]

Shelley thus takes Aeschylus' Prometheus to be a symbolic character—the "Champion . . . of mankind"—as is his Zeus the "Oppressor of mankind."[19] Shelley implies that they have the same general meaning in his own play. In his final sentence, however, he seems to envisage the symbolism of Prometheus in more complex terms than did Aeschylus. He objects to having Prometheus surrender to Zeus, as Aeschylus is said to have done in his lost *Prometheus Unbound*, and states that he is reversing this action. Although he does not discuss the meaning of the other main characters, it can be assumed that if Prometheus and Jupiter are symbolic, so are they.

Shelley then outlines his general purpose:

Let this opportunity be conceded to me of acknowledging that I have, what a Scotch philosopher characteristically terms, "a passion for reforming the world": what passion incited him to write and publish his book, he omits to explain. For my part, I had rather be damned with Plato and Lord Bacon, then go to Heaven with Paley and Malthus. But it is a mistake to suppose that I dedicate my poetical compositions solely to the direct enforcement of reform, or that I consider them in any degree as containing a reasoned system on the theory of human life. Didactic poetry is my abhorrence; nothing can be equally well expressed in prose that is not tedious and supererogatory in verse. My purpose has hitherto been simply to familiarize the highly refined imagination of the more select classes of poetical readers with beautiful idealisms of moral excellence; aware that until the mind can love, and admire, and trust, and hope, and endure, reasoned principles of moral conduct are seeds cast upon the highway of life which the unconscious passenger tramples into dust, although they would bear the harvest of his happiness. Should I live to accomplish what I purpose, that is, produce a systematical history of what appear to me to be the genuine elements of human society, let not the advocates of injustice and superstition flatter themselves that I should take Aeschylus rather than Plato as my model.[20]

This passage is more complex than it at first seems. For instance, Shelley is not saying that in *Prometheus Unbound* he is unconcerned with social change. On the contrary, he implies that, like other works of his, it is intended to assist in "reforming the world." He states only that it is not aimed at "the direct enforcement of reform," that is, in the specific sense of parliamentary reform. He did have such a purpose in mind in *The Masque of Anarchy,* written during the period of composition of *Prometheus Unbound,* and the word "solely" indicates that he had it in mind as a secondary purpose in other works. *Prometheus Unbound* is, he implies, one of these other works. Although it is not aimed "solely" at the "direct" enforcement of parliamentary reform, it may help that cause indirectly. This, however, is not its main purpose. That purpose is one of "reforming the world;" and here he uses "reform" in a general sense of changing society "from its foundations."[21] Rather than spelling out this goal in the Preface, he implies it through references to Plato and Bacon, for Plato he regarded as an advocate of an egalitarian society and Bacon in his *New Atlantis* projected a rational society run by science. In one draft Shelley also added the names of Rousseau, whom he believed looked forward to a society permeated by love, and Milton, whom he called a "republican" in the Preface.[22]

Shelley has so far in his poetry, he implies, attempted to reform the world by creating "beautiful idealisms of moral excellence," which would help his liberal-minded readers to learn to "love, and admire, and trust, and hope, and endure." This statement is only partially true and, in its overall effect, rather misleading. Certainly in *The Masque of Anarchy* Shelley was not primarily concerned with presenting "beautiful idealisms of moral excellence," nor was he the following year in *Swellfoot the Tyrant,* nor had he been in *Queen Mab.* What is uppermost in his mind, apparently, is the hostile reception of *The Revolt of Islam* in the previous year (1818) by the reviewers. Through *The Revolt of Islam,* a kind of modern epic, he had hoped to have an impact on his age. It was his first work to be widely reviewed, and when *The Quarterly* and other major journals descended on it with savage hostility, tagging its author as an atheist, a dangerous radical, and a Godwinian dogmatist, Shelley became seriously concerned. Unless he could break that image, he could not reach the audience he most desired—the audience that Byron, with a less extreme message, had reached—namely, the middle class and aristocratic liberals. What he is implying here is that in Laon and Cythna, the hero and heroine of *The Revolt of Islam,* he was creating ideal models of "moral excellence." His object in presenting these models was to encourage others to imitate them, and learn to "love, and admire, and trust, and hope, and endure." This latter statement has been taken in an abstract moral sense by some critics, and certainly Shelley's wording leaves such an interpretation open, as he no doubt intended, because he was trying to present himself in as innocuous a light as possible, in hopes of blunting the hostility of the reviewers and lulling the prejudices of less radical readers. He had followed the same policy in his prefatory comments on *Mont Blanc* in the *Alastor* volume, as well as in his choice of such innocuous titles as *Queen Mab* or *Hymn to Intellectual Beauty*. Shelley, however, is not primarily venturing the hope that his readers would become better men and women in their personal relations but that they might become radicals, like Laon and Cythna. By "love," he means love for humanity; by "hope," hope for radical change; and by "endure," to endure persecution for one's principles. In short, he is hoping by his poetry to influence uncommitted intellectuals, particularly those with potential creativity ("highly refined imaginations"), to ally themselves with Byron, Hunt, Hazlitt, Bentham, and other dedicated liberals. Much of this would have been clear to the sophisticated reader of his time.

Even in Shelley's day, however, some readers might well have been puzzled by the distinction he makes between "reasoned principles of moral conduct" and love, admiration, trust, hope, and endurance which are also moral concepts. How is one to acquire these qualities if not by "reason"? Shelley's answer is related to his old difference with Godwin on the way in which a better society might be achieved. Godwin argued that a little band of disciples, dedicated to an enlightened system of ethics, could in time convert sufficient people and thereby change society. But Shelley was convinced that society could only be changed fundamentally by political means, reformist or revolutionary. He felt also that people themselves must change if a disaster such as the failure of the French Revolution was to be avoided in the future, but that kind of change would come about in the course of the political and social movement, as Laon and Cythna preached in the revolution in the Golden City. During this movement, people would learn to "love, and admire, and trust, and hope, and endure," and poets could assist them toward that end by presenting "beautiful idealisms" embodying these qualities. But without the movement, there would be nothing. One could not bring about social change by a static preaching of ethical abstractions. It would, in fact, take successive "generations" of radicals to make such a change, as he stated in the Preface to *Hellas*, and Shelley's hope was that his writings might play some part in this long struggle. Nor did he feel that his only contribution was to present "beautiful idealisms." His writings were diverse, aimed at different publics, and often grimly realistic, as in the pictures of war in *The Revolt of Islam* or of the brutal upper classes in *Swellfoot the Tyrant*. But he was convinced that the delineation of the qualities most needed by the leaders of the new movement was of particular importance, and that he was especially well equipped to provide it.

These various objectives were clearly part of a general social philosophy, and much of Shelley's writing was aimed at changing both social conditions and people's minds. What, then, of his statements in the Preface that he did not consider his poetry as "in any degree containing a reasoned system on the theory of human life" and that he abhorred "didactic" poetry? Both statements contain an essential truth, but both, again, are misleading, especially when taken in conjunction with the unqualified comments on "beautiful idealisms." Shelley did reserve judgment on certain basic questions, but he also had firm beliefs—on necessitarian forces in historical development, on the inevitability of an egalitarian society. Apparently he felt that his areas of agnostic doubt were sufficiently large to prevent his views from forming a "system." And again, he was eager to deny that he was a doctrinaire disciple of Godwin and the French materialists.

By "didactic poetry" Shelley meant the kind of verse that flows from a set system of ideas, particularly moral ones, as in Samuel Johnson's *The Vanity of Human Wishes.* It was this that he abhorred. Although he was eager to convey ideas, he was also writing poetry, and he realized that if ideas are to be conveyed in verse, they have to be handled creatively, not wrapped in moral-lesson packages.

The Furies and Mercury

No doubt Shelley thought that the hints of meaning given in the Preface and scattered throughout the play would enable his readers to interpret the symbolism. Unfortunately, this has not been the case. No work by Shelley has been more "guessed at" than *Prometheus Unbound.* And the field for guessing is endless. There seem, in fact, to be very few suggestions that have not been made, many of them patently ridiculous.[23]

In the first act a number of questions virtually ask themselves. At what time is the action supposed to be taking place? If Prometheus, as the Preface reveals and the act confirms, is not simply the Greek Titan, what is he? What exactly does Shelley mean by "the Champion . . . of mankind"? Who are the Furies? Why do they show Prometheus the visions of the rise and fall of the French Revolution and the suffering of Christ? Who are the spirits that are summoned after the Furies depart? What do their songs signify? What is the meaning of the revocation of the curse?

The answer to the first question, the time of the action, is suggested almost immediately. In line 12 Prometheus says that he has been on the rock for "Three thousand years," which indicates that the action takes place in modern times. That this was indeed Shelley's intention is confirmed by the vision of the French Revolution and its aftermath shown to Prometheus by the Furies. The revolution collapses, whereupon the "world" is conquered by "slaves and tyrants" (577), that is, by Jacobins, Napoleon and the Bourbons in France, and the Holy Alliance in Europe. "It it thus," Shelley wrote in *A Philosophical View of Reform*, "that the mighty advantages of the French Revolution have been almost compensated by a succession of tyrants . . . from Robespierre to Louis 18."[24] The world on which Prometheus gazes, then, is Shelley's own age, from about 1789 to 1819.

Some of the most important indications of Shelley's general concept come in the vision of the rise and fall of the French Revolution, which the Furies show to Prometheus in order to break his spirit (their words "Grant a little respite now" are ironical):

Semichorus I. Drops of bloody agony flow
From his white and quivering brow.
Grant a little respite now:
See a disenchanted nation
Springs like day from desolation;
To Truth its state is dedicate,
And Freedom leads it forth, her mate;
A legioned band of linked brothers,
Whom Love calls children—
Semichorus II. 'Tis another's:
See how kindred murder kin:
'Tis the vintage-time for Death and Sin:
Blood, like new wine, bubbles within:
Till Despair smothers
The struggling world, which slaves and tyrants win. (564–577)

When the Furies have left and Panthea asks Prometheus the nature of the torments he underwent at their hands, he reports the picture he saw:

Names are there, Nature's sacred watchwords—they
Were borne aloft in bright emblazonry;
The nations thronged around, and cried aloud,
As with one voice, Truth, Liberty, and Love!
Suddenly fierce confusion fell from Heaven
Among them: there was strife, deceit, and fear:
Tyrants rushed in, and did divide the spoil.
This was the shadow of the truth I saw. (648–655)[25]

In the great days of the National Assembly, the fall of the Bastille, and the proclamation of the Rights of Man, people were like "a legioned band of linked brothers," dedicated to "Truth, Liberty and Love"; in the Terror and the militarist conquest, "kindred" murdered "kin"; with the successive assumption of power by Robespierre, Napoleon, and the Bourbons, "Tyrants rushed in and did divide the spoil," and "Despair" smothered the hearts of men.

As early as 1812, Shelley in his juvenile novel *Hubert Cauvin*, now lost, had discussed "the causes of the failure of the French Revolution to benefit humankind."[26] In the Irish pamphlets, he argued that the French Revolution collapsed because it had too few dedicated, humanitarian leaders, which implied that as a new age of revolution was at hand in Europe, new leaders must arise to guard against another failure. *A Philosophical View of Reform* returned to this theme, intimating that the revolution collapsed because French intellectuals were unable to guide it into constructive channels, and implying that as Europe, Asia, and Latin America now stood on the threshold of revolution, the lesson of France was of universal importance. The most explicit and illuminating account of the concept was that in the Preface to *The Revolt of Islam*:

The panic which, like an epidemic transport, seized upon all classes of men during the excesses consequent upon the French Revolution, is gradually giving place to sanity. It has ceased to be believed, that whole generations of mankind ought to consign themselves to a hopeless inheritance of ignorance and misery, because a nation of men who had been dupes and slaves for centuries were incapable of conducting themselves with the wisdom and tranquillity of freemen so soon as some of their fetters were partially loosened. That their conduct could not have been marked by any other characters than ferocity and thoughtlessness, is the historical fact from which liberty derives all its recommendations, and falsehood the worst features of its deformity. There is a reflux in the tide of human things which bears the shipwrecked hopes of men into a secure haven, after the storms are past. Methinks, those who now live have survived an age of despair.

The French Revolution may be considered as one of those manifestations of a general state of feeling among civilized mankind produced by a defect of correspondence between the knowledge existing in society and the improvement or gradual abolition of political institutions. The year 1788 may be assumed as the epoch of one of the most important crises produced by this feeling. The sympathies connected with that event extended to every bosom. The most generous and amiable natures were those which participated the most extensively in these sympathies. But such a degree of unmingled good was expected, as it was impossible to realize . . . The revulsion occasioned by the atrocities of the demagogues, and the re-establishment of successive tyrannies in France was terrible, and felt in the remotest corner of the civilized world. Could they listen to the plea of reason who had groaned under the calamities of a social state, according to the provisions of which, one man riots in luxury whilst another famishes for want of bread? Can he who the day before was a trampled slave, suddenly become liberal-minded, forbearing, and independent? This is the consequence of the habits of a state of society to be produced by resolute perseverance and indefatigable hope, and long-suffering and long-believing courage, and the systematic efforts of generations of men of intellect and virtue. Such is the lesson which experience teaches now. But on the first reverses of hope in the progress of French liberty, the sanguine eagerness for good overleapt the solution of these questions, and for a time extinguished itself in the unexpectedness of their result. Thus many of the most ardent and tender-hearted of the worshippers of public good have been morally ruined by what a partial glimpse of the events they deplored, appeared to shew as the melancholy desolation of all their cherished hopes. Hence gloom and misanthrophy have become the characteristics of the age in which we live, the solace of a disappointment that unconsciously finds relief only in the wilful exaggeration of its own despair. This influence has tainted the literature of the age with the hopelessness of the minds from which it flows. Metaphysics, and enquiries into moral and political science, have become little else than vain attempts to revive exploded superstitions, or sophisms like those of Mr. Malthus, calculated to lull the oppressors of mankind into a security of everlasting triumph. Our works of fiction and poetry have been overshadowed by the same infectious gloom. But mankind appear to me to be emerging from their trance. I am aware, methinks, of a slow, gradual, silent change. In that belief I have composed the following Poem.[27]

The passage emphasizes the reaction of intellectuals and other liberal-minded individuals: "the most generous and amiable natures . . . the most ardent and tender-hearted of the worshippers of public good," those who had created "the literature of the age," its philosophy, its ethics, and its "political science." Among them Shelley certainly included Wordsworth, Coleridge, and Southey, who saw in the collapse of the Revolution "the melancholy desolation of all their cherished hopes." As a result, they were "morally ruined"; that is, they had ceased to dedicate themselves to humanitarian effort and supported an exploitive, corrupt system. But the damage was still more extensive. A spirit of "gloom and misanthropy" had spread out to infect the whole of the literature and thought of the age. The defection of the liberals paved the way for the domination of intellectual life by reactionaries like Malthus, who gleefully preached the hopelessness of all humanitarian effort, or of theologians, like Paley, who tried to substitute long-discredited religious "superstitions" for philosophy and ethics. The total effect was disastrous. It was believed that "whole generations of mankind" were doomed to continue in the old way of life, their only lot being "a hopeless inheritance of ignorance and misery." However, this was no longer everywhere accepted. A new generation of intellectuals and liberals was arising, and a "slow, gradual silent change" was taking place. Or as Shelley puts it in the Preface to *Prometheus Unbound*, "The cloud of mind is discharging its collected lightning." In a passage in *A Philosophical View of Reform* he named some of the bearers of this lightning: Godwin, Hazlitt, Bentham, and Hunt.[28] To these one could certainly add Byron, Shelley himself, perhaps such liberal reformers and radicals as Sir Francis Burdett and Robert Owen, and such enlightened philosophers as Sir William Drummond.

It appears, then, that in the Furies scene Shelley regards Prometheus as a composite of the radical intellectuals of his own day, temporary assailed by the vision of the failure of the French Revolution. The Furies are attempting to enfold him in that "gloom and misanthropy" which will make him despair of the future of humanity, turn him from his traditional role as "Champion," and ruin him "morally," as the previous intellectual generation had been ruined.

The Greek Erinyes or Eumenides (Furies to the Romans) were the goddesses of vengeance. Usually three in number (Tisiphone, Alecto, and Megaera), they were the daughters, according to some mythologists, of Earth, or according to others, of Night. They dwelt in Tartarus. Aeschylus in *The Eumenides* depicted them as snake-haired. Sometimes they had wings. They punished violations of filial duty and crimes such as murder or perjury. For Aeschylus or Euripides they became dramatic representations of conscience or the spirit of vengeance.

In the extant fragment of Aeschylus' *Prometheus Unbound* Prometheus spoke of his rock as "this Furies' fort."[29] Possibly it was this remark that first gave Shelley the idea for using the Furies in the play, to take the place of the eagle. But Shelley was not indebted to classical sources alone. He was also acquainted with later mythologists who added touches of their own. For instance, in a book that he mentioned in the Notes to *Queen Mab*, Abbé Banier's *The Mythology and Fables of the Ancients Explained from History*, he could have read: "The Furies were employed not only in punishing the Guilty, but also in chastising Men by Diseases, by War, and the other Strokes of the Celestial Wrath . . . Tisiphone was employed for contagious Distempers, while Alecto's Functions particularly related to the Disorders of War . . . Henceforth [after Aeschylus] they came to be represented no otherwise but with a grim Aspect and a frightful Mien, with Attire black and bloody, having instead of Hair, Serpents wreathed about their Heads, a burning Torch in one Hand, and a Whip of Scorpions in the other, and for their Attendants, Terror, Rage, Paleness and Death. Thus seated around Pluto's Throne, whose Prime Ministers they were, they waited his Orders with an Impatience that marked out all the Fury they were possessed of."[30] And Lemprière's *Classical Dictionary*, the most popular of Shelley's time, commented on the Furies: "They inflicted their vengeance upon earth by wars, pestilence, and dissensions, and by the secret strings of conscience." Shelley's use of them in his play certainly indicates that he was aware of the modern concept of them as agents of war and other social evils, as well as of the classical one of them as conscience spirits persecuting individuals.

The Furies come in two groups. The first group announces itself as follows:

> We are the ministers of pain and fear,
> And disappointment and mistrust and hate
> And clinging crime; and as lean dogs pursue
> Through wood and lake some struck and sobbing fawn,
> We track all things that weep and bleed and live
> When the great King betrays them to our will. (452–457)

Prometheus is acquainted with this group of Furies, for they have evidently assailed him before during his long martyrdom on the precipice:

> O many fearful natures in one name,
> I know ye; and these lakes and echoes know
> The darkness and the clangour of your wings. (458–460)

These Furies thus represent the general evils of civilized society from its inception—a society of hate, pain, and fear. They hound to death those who have humanitarian feelings. They are the agents of the despotic state ("the great King").

When Prometheus sees approaching the second group of Furies, who are even more "hideous" and numerous than the first, he indicates that he has not seen them before:

> But why more hideous than your loathed selves
> Gather ye up in legions from the deep? (461–462)

The first group hails the approaching Furies:

> From the ends of the earth, from the ends of the earth,
> Where the night has its grave and the morning its birth,
> Come, come, come!
> O ye who shake hills with the scream of your mirth,
> When cities sink howling in ruin, and ye
> Who with wingless footsteps trample the sea,
> And close upon Shipwreck and Famine's track,
> Sit chattering with joy on the foodless wreck;
> Come, come, come!
> Leave the bed, low, cold, and red,
> Strewed beneath a nation dead;
> Leave the hatred, as in ashes
> Fire is left for future burning:
> It will burst in bloodier flashes
> When ye stir it, soon returning;
> Leave the self-contempt implanted
> In young spirits sense-enchanted,
> Misery's yet unkindled fuel:
> Leave Hell's secrets half unchanted
> To the maniac dreamer; cruel
> More than ye can be with hate
> Is he with fear.
> Come, come, come!
> We are steaming up from Hell's wide gate
> And we burthen the blast of the atmosphere,
> But vainly we toil till ye come here. (495–520)

As the second group "steam" up from Hell, their songs proclaim their nature and their mission:

> *First Fury.* Your call was as a wingèd car,
> Driven on whirlwinds fast and far;
> It rapt us from red gulfs of war;
> *Second Fury.* From wide cities, famine-wasted;
> *Third Fury.* Groans half heard, and blood untasted;

Fourth Fury. Kingly conclaves stern and cold,
Where blood with gold is bought and sold;
Fifth Fury. From the furnace, white and hot,
In which—
A Fury. Speak not: whisper not:
I know all that ye would tell,
But to speak might break the spell
Which must bend the Invincible,
The Stern of thought;
He yet defies the deepest power of Hell.
Fury. Tear the veil!
Another Fury. It is torn! (525–539)

In the "red gulfs of war" Shelley may be referring to the general wars of the past few centuries, but he must primarily have the Napoleonic Wars in mind, as in the "wide cities, famine wasted," which doubtless included Moscow, whose burning he referred to in *Queen Mab*.[31] And the "kingly conclaves" certainly include the Congress of Vienna. It is a society of civil war, whose "hatred" will result in further violence, of cities "in ruin," of psychological distortion ("self-contempt") and religions that drive people to insanity ("maniac dreamer").[32] The reference of the "furnace white and hot" is apparently to the burning alive of antireligious rebels.[33] All these horrors, which were supposed to break the spirit of the modern Prometheus, have failed to do so. New weapons are needed. The "veil" must be torn.

After "veil," Shelley added a stage direction in his manuscript: "The Furies having ming'd [sic] in a strange dance divide, & in the background is seen a plain covered with burning cities."[34] This direction helps to explain the next chorus of the Furies:

One came forth of gentle worth,
Smiling on the sanguine earth;
His words outlived him, like swift poison
Withering up truth, peace, and pity.
Look! where round the wide horizon
Many a million-peopled city
Vomits smoke in the bright air. (546–555)

The smoking cities must be the same as the burning cities of the stage direction, which are apparently in flames as the result of war. That the "One" of "gentle worth" is Jesus is made clear in the dialogue following the chorus, when Ione asks Panthea what she saw during the attack of the Furies. Panthea answers "A youth/With patient looks nailed to a crucifix" (584–585). Prometheus then repeats the vision he himself had:

Remit the anguish of that lighted stare;
Close those wan lips; let that thorn-wounded brow
Stream not with blood; it mingles with thy tears! (597–599)

The cities here seem to be burning as the result of religious wars, the theme being Shelley's familiar contrast between the humanitarian gospel of Jesus and religious persecution, such as that, noted in *Queen Mab*, of the Albegenses.[35] But he may also have in mind the general horrors of war in a presumably Christian society, the "bright air" again suggesting Moscow.

After the vision of the French Revolution all the Furies vanish except one, who is left to drive home the lesson of the two visions:

> Behold an emblem: those who do endure
> Deep wrongs for man, and scorn, and chains, but heap
> Thousandfold torment on themselves and him. (594–596)

Prometheus is obviously disturbed both by the visions and the words of the Fury. After again conjuring up in his mind the picture of Jesus on the cross—"Remit the anguish of that lighted stare" (597)—he adds: "Thy name I will not speak,/It hath become a curse" (603–604).

The Fury hastens to press home what it believes to be an advantage. There is, it tells Prometheus, even worse evil than everything he has so far seen:

> In each human heart terror survives
> The ravin it has gorged: the loftiest fear
> All that they would disdain to think were true:
> Hypocrisy and custom make their minds
> The fanes of many a worship now outworn.
> They dare not devise good for man's estate,
> And yet they know not that they do not dare.
> The good want power but to weep barren tears;
> The powerful goodness want: worse need for them;
> The wise want love; and those who love want wisdom;
> And all best things are thus confused to ill. (618–628)

What the Furies mean by tearing the "veil" now begins to appear. They have shown Prometheus physical and social evils, but the sight has not broken his will. The new torture must be more subtle. It must penetrate beyond a vision of society as such into the realm of the mental or psychological ("Speak not; whisper not"). The Furies try to show that not only are social evils horrible but they cannot be eradicated, and humanitarian effort only makes them worse: "all best things are thus confused to ill." This they demonstrate, first by showing that all the suffering of Jesus resulted only in intolerance and persecution, then that the ideals of the French radicals, such as Rousseau, ended in war and dictatorship. The hopelessness of the situation is shown by an examination of modern society: the "good" lack ("want") power, those who have power are evil, and people are held back from taking action by the stultifying bonds of "custom." This uselessness of all effort for good is the truth that lies behind the "veil" of things as they are.

Whereas Prometheus represents the radical intellectuals, the Furies are primarily subjective or mental phenomena. Prometheus refers to them as "Phantasms" from "the all-miscreative brain of Jove" (447–448). They tell him that they will become "dread thought within thy brain" and "foul desire round thine astonished heart" (488–489). Prometheus also calls them a "torturing and conflicting throng within" (493) his mind. They are clearly, therefore, mental or emotional states of some kind. The Furies themselves earlier indicated of what kind:

> We are the ministers of pain and fear,
> And disappointment, and mistrust, and hate.

The new group of Furies was hailed by the old as leaving "hatred," "self-contempt," and superstitious "fear" behind them when they came to torment Prometheus. When Prometheus first saw them, he cried out: "Oh! many fearful natures in one name,/I know ye" (458–459). This calls to mind the passage on opinion in *The Revolt of Islam*:

> Opinion is more frail
> Than yon dim cloud now fading on the moon
> Even while we gaze, tho' it awhile avail
> To hide the orb of truth—and every throne
> Of Earth or Heaven, tho' shadow rests thereon,
> One shape of many names. . .
>
> Its names are each a sign which maketh holy
> All power—aye, the ghost, the dream, the shade,
> Of power—lust, falsehood, hate, and pride, and folly;
> The pattern whence all fraud and wrong is made,
> A law to which mankind has been betrayed. (3271–3276, 3280–3284)

In *The Revolt of Islam* the emphasis was on the "One shape" ("Opinion") rather than its "many names"; in *Prometheus Unbound* the emphasis is on the "many names," the "many fearful natures in one name" (that name presumably being Jupiter); but the basic concept is the same in both works. Thus, the Furies are, in general, personifications of lust, falsehood, hate, pride, pain, fear, and so on. They are not defined, however, simply in a personal psychological sense, for Shelley had a special theory about such thoughts, emotions, and moral states. They do not come from the inner "natural" part of the mind but are imposed on the mind by an oppressive society, creating a "mutiny within." They are, in fact, the ideas and emotional states that hold that society together, as do the phantoms and shadows of *The Triumph of Life*. They are the "exploded superstitions" and "sophisms like those of Mr. Malthus" which bring about "infectious gloom." They give only a "partial glimpse" of "events," a "shadow of the truth" (655), as Prometheus declared, which is designed to make intellectuals feel "the melancholy desolation of all their cherished hopes." They are the hatreds and fears instilled in the mind by opinion and retained by custom. They arise from the pyramidal social complex at whose top sits the ruling class—"the all-miscreative brain of Jove." The Furies, in brief, symbolize the ideas, emotions, and moral states whereby the ruling class maintains the existing order. As such, they try to undermine the will of radical intellectuals and bring to their minds visions of the hopelessness of resistance (the vain suffering of Jesus, the collapse of the French Revolution). They are the tormenting Furies by which Shelley and his liberal contemporaries were constantly being bombarded—in the press, the pulpit, letters, and conversation. Having subverted the previous generations of intellectual rebels, they now hoped to succeed with the new. They came in two waves, those representing the general ideas common to any inegalitarian order, and those resulting from the special conditions of the particular age.

The scene as a whole represents the intellectual rebels, as it were, carrying on a dialogue with themselves, one part of their mind conversing with another part of their mind, the "natural" inner circle, the center of unselfish love, struggling against the demoralizing swarm of ideas and emotions in the outer or socially conditioned circle. However, the Furies are also, as in *The Eumenides*, characters in a play. When Shelley does not wish to go below the dramatic, representational level he does not do so. When the Furies, for example, taunt Prometheus—"Dost imagine/We will but laugh into thy lidless [unclosed] eyes?" (478–479)—they are primarily Furies, and Prometheus is the Titan on the stage precipice. But when they sing of the collapse of the French Revolution, they are primarily symbols for the sophisms and superstitions that enable such visions of despair to enter the mind. Shelley's approach, as in *Adonais*, embraces several levels of meaning.

According to some versions of the Greek myth, Mercury was assigned by Zeus, his father (his mother being Maia, daughter of Atlas), to bind Prometheus to the rock. In Aeschylus, this function is carried out by Hephaestus, and Mercury is simply Zeus's messenger to Prometheus.[36] In Shelley's drama, Mercury has a more important role. As the Furies strain to attack Prometheus, Mercury holds them back and addresses the Titan:

Awful Sufferer
To thee unwilling, most unwillingly
I come, by the great Father's will driven down,
To execute a doom of new revenge.
Alas! I pity thee, and hate myself
That I can do more: aye from thy sight
Returning, for a season, Heaven seems Hell,
So thy worn form pursues me night and day,
Smiling reproach. Wise art thou, firm and good,
But vainly wouldst stand forth alone in strife
Against the Omnipotent. (352–362)

Using a typically Shelleyan metaphor that combines the abstract with the concrete, Mercury urges Prometheus to tell the secret of the overthrow of Jupiter, for in the end all rebels, even the most confirmed must yield:

> Let the will kneel within thy haughty heart;
> For benefits and meek submission tame
> The fiercest and the mightiest. (378–380)

Prometheus replies scornfully:

> Let others flatter Crime where it sits throned
> In brief Omnipotence. (401–402)

Mercury next tries to break Prometheus' spirit by contrasting the perhaps endless years of torment that are yet to come and the easy life ahead, "Lapped in voluptuous joy" (426), if he will only yield. Prometheus answers brusquely that the prospect of such a luxurious future would never make him "quit/This bleak ravine, these unrepentant pains" (426–427). To Mercury's reply—"Alas! I wonder at, yet pity thee" (428)—Prometheus scornfully answers, "Pity the self-despising slaves of Heaven" (429)—those who, like Mercury himself, carry out the will of the despotic state not because they agree with it but because they prefer the soft life of the "Gods" to the "bleak ravine" of the rebel. Mercury admires Prometheus but fears Jupiter more. This fear and his certitude of the hopelessness of rebellion have broken any spirit he ever had. He threatens Prometheus by implying that unless he yields, he will have to deal with the Furies. In Mercury, Shelley probably had in mind those he attacked in the Preface to *The Revolt of Islam* and elsewhere for dispensing the "sophisms" and "superstitions" of the age, such as Malthus, Paley, and Southey. It was their task to lead the Furies of moral and mental corruption to the liberal intelligentsia.

The Poet As Prophet

As Prometheus has been on his precipice for three thousand years and was before assailed by some of the Furies, those reflecting the general evils of civilized society, he cannot represent only the intellectual rebels of Shelley's day. Although he is a modern Prometheus, he is still Prometheus, the "type" of the "highest perfection of moral and intellectual nature." What is this "type"?

Shelley, as he explained in *A Defence of Poetry*, had a special theory of the historical role of "the Poets," those "unacknowledged legislators of the world." Every new age of social and cultural advance was both foreshadowed and assisted by them: "Shakespeare and Lord Bacon and the great writers of the age of Elizabeth and James the Ist were at once the effects of the new spirit in men's minds, and the cause of its more complete development." And in Shelley's own age: "It is impossible to read the productions of our most celebrated writers, whatever may be their system relating to thought or expression, without being startled by the electric life which there is in their words."

The argument is recapitulated in the Preface to *Prometheus Unbound*:

> We owe the great writers of the golden age of our literature to that fervid awakening of the public mind which shook to dust the oldest and most oppressive form of the Christian religion. We owe Milton to the progress and development of the same spirit: the sacred Milton was, let it ever be remembered, a republican, and a bold inquirer into morals and religion. The great writers of our own age are, we have reason to suppose, the companions and forerunners of some unimagined change in our social condition or the opinions which cement it. The cloud of mind is discharging its collected lightning and the equilibrium between institutions and opinions is now restoring, or is about to be restored.

In *A Defence of Poetry* the argument was developed in more general terms, with the poets being hailed as "the mirrors of the gigantic shadows which futurity casts upon the present."[37] It was Prometheus, Asia informed Demogorgon (II. iv.72–94), who gave humanity "speech," which "created thought," as well as poetry, music, art, and science. This concept of Prometheus, which derived from Aeschylus, clearly fits with Shelley's view of "the Poets"—all creative thinkers. It is apparent, then, that although Shelley intended Prometheus to stand primarily for the intellectual rebels of his own age, he also represented all those creative intellectuals, from Homer to Hazlitt, who had advanced culture and the cause of humanity.

This symbolism of Prometheus as the poet provides a clue to the Spirits scene, which immediately follows the Furies scene. The "Poets," Shelley noted in *A Defence of Poetry*, not only help to bring about social advance but are able to sense such advance before it begins: "For he not only beholds intensely the present as it is, and discovers those laws according to which present things ought to be ordered, but he beholds the future in the present, and his thoughts are the germs of the flower and the fruit of latest time." This aspect of the poet as prophet ("though not in the gross sense of the word") also had particular relevance to Prometheus, because, according to Aeschylus, "divination" was one of his "arts."[38]

Whereas the Furies scene showed "the Poets" of Shelley's age being afflicted by visions of its horrors and by thoughts of despair, the Spirits scene shows them perceiving the elements of hope in the age and projecting them into the future. The significance of the Spirits is indicated by the speech of Earth which heralds them:

> To cheer thy state
> I bid ascend those subtle and fair spirits

Whose homes are the dim caves of human thought,
And who inhabit, as birds wing the wind,
Its world-surrounding ether; they behold
Beyond that twilight realm, as in a glass,
The future—may they speak comfort to thee! (657–663)

By "future," Shelley does not mean the future in general but the decades about to begin. The Spirits can tell the future from signs that they observe in the spirit of the age. Just how poets are able to do this, Shelley did not presume to understand. He felt that inspiration is a strange phenomenon, whose origins are obscure. It comes and goes like wind moving the water or stirring the coals of a fire, but whether it comes from within the mind or outside it, or from a combination of the two, he did not say, although his emphasis was on its being primarily a psychological (unconscious mind) phenomenon, which can or cannot be initiated by external impression. So that if Shelley here represents it as coming from the Spirits, he does not necessarily mean that it is an external force. As he was writing a dramatic poem, the Spirits like the Furies are dramatic characters. That they are also, and primarily, mental phenomena is shown by the Earth's statement that their "homes are the dim caves of human thought," and in their initial chorus they state that the "atmosphere" they "breathe" is that of "human thought." Like the Furies, to whom they are a deliberate contrast, they both present or report ideas and events on the dramatic level, and on the symbolic level are themselves mental phenomena. They represent inspiration and insight coming to the poets.

The first Spirit conveys in swift, staccato lines the excitement of revolutionary change:

On a battle-trumpet's blast
I fled hither, fast, fast, fast,
'Mid the darkness upward cast.
From the dust of creeds outworn,
From the tyrant's banner torn,
Gathering 'round me, onward borne.
There was mingled many a cry—
Freedom! Hope! Death! Victory!
Till they faded thro' the sky;
And one sound, above, around,
One sound beneath, around, above,
Was moving; 'twas the soul of love;
'Twas the hope, the prophecy,
Which begins and ends in thee. (694–707)

This song of the first Spirit clearly reflects a time in which tyrants were being overthrown and "outworn" religious creeds cast aside, a time of the coming of love to humanity, when the slogans of "Freedom! Hope! Death! Victory!" rang out. Yet there was no such upheaval in 1819 when Shelley was writing the play; in fact, just the contrary, for the counterrevolution of Metternich and Castlereagh was in the ascendency. The reference must be to the early days of the French Revolution.

The same general theme of love is embodied in the song of the second Spirit, who has just witnessed a storm in which two rival naval forces were destroyed. He saw a sailor "who gave an enemy/His plank, then plunged aside to die" (721–722). The specific form of love depicted here is similar to that drawn in *Ode to Naples*, namely, fraternization among the armed forces. The third Spirit reports that it sat beside the bed of a "sage" who had fallen asleep over a book, and from him it imbibed a message:

> Which had kindled long ago
> Pity, eloquence, and woe. (729–730)

The reference is apparently to the death and ideas of Socrates as reported by Plato and Xenophon. The sage then repeated the message in his own works.

The fourth Spirit came from the side of a poet:

> He will watch from dawn to gloom
> The lake-reflected sun illume
> The yellow bees in the ivy-bloom,
> Nor heed nor see, what things they be;
> But from these create he can
> Forms more real than living man,
> Nurslings of immortality! (743–749)

The poet represents the imaginative, creative spirit in literature that Shelley believed heralded great social change, as had the works of Shakespeare and others in "the golden age of our literature," according to the Preface. The poet is able to project "idealisms" from the actual: "Forms more real than living man."

The fifth and sixth Spirits are clearly of particular importance because their approach is heralded in a dialogue between Ione and Panthea:

> And, hark! their sweet, sad voices! 'tis despair
> Mingled with love and then dissolved in sound. (756–757)

As the two Spirits arrive, the chorus of Spirits asks the first of them, the fifth Spirit, whether it too has "beheld the form" of the love that the first four Spirits reported. The Spirit replies that it has, but that love soon faded, to be succeeded by strife and hatred:

> And hollow Ruin yawned behind: great sages bound in madness
> And headless patriots, and pale youths who perished unupbraiding,
> Gleamed in the night. (768–770)

The Spirit then "wandered," apparently in despair, until the sad smile of Prometheus turned "the worst I saw to recollected gladness" (770–771).

The message of the fifth Spirit is clearly once more that of the Preface and of the Furies scene, for the picture that the Spirit paints is of the "terror" of the French Revolution, that terror which, Shelley believed, marked the beginning of its end and which drove the earlier English poets to despair. The revival would come with the new poetry and the new spirit embodied in Prometheus.

If the fifth Spirit is telling of the beginning of the collapse of the French Revolution, then the song of the first Spirit must, indeed, depict the rise of that revolution. The tyrants whose banners are being "torn" represent the coalition of feudal powers against the new republic, and the casting off of the "creeds outworn" refers to the attacks on the French church and the rise of the goddess of "reason." The song of the second Spirit may have specific reference to one of the naval battles of the time, of which Shelley had heard stories from his uncle Captain Pilfold, and the fraternization theme may reflect such actions as the famous Nore mutiny of 1797 led by Irish sailors, which hampered operations against the Dutch. In the "sage" of the song of the third Spirit Shelley seems to have William Godwin in mind. He saw Godwin's *Political Justice* (1793) as embodying the egalitarian and moral ideas of Socrates and Plato, as well as of the French Revolution, and for a time it had an influence, as Hazlitt testified, beyond that of any other single work:

> And the world awhile below
> Wore the shade its lustre made. (731–732)[39]

If this time sequence is correct, the reference in the song of the fourth Spirit must be to the poetry of the 1790s, that is, to the poetry of Wordsworth, Southey, and Coleridge. Some of the early works of these poets Shelley considered to be humanitarian and idealistic, both reflecting and heralding social advance, as had the writings of Milton in an earlier age. He must have considered them to be pioneers in that "peculiar style of comprehensive imagery" which, he explains in the Preface, "distinguishes the modern literature of England." If he was thinking of any particular person, as he apparently was in the "sage," it must have been Wordsworth, as indicated by the emphasis on the poet taking his inspiration from nature and the phrase "Nurslings of immortality." The songs of the third and fourth Spirits, then, seem designed to represent English intellectual life in the 1790s,—the one in thought, the other in literature.

The song of the sixth Spirit is subtle and complex:

> Ah, sister! Desolation is a delicate thing:
> It walks not on the earth, it floats not on the air,
> But treads with lulling footstep, and fans with silent wing,
> The tender hopes which in their hearts the best and gentlest bear;

Who, soothed to false repose by the fanning plumes above,
And the music-stirring motion of its soft and busy feet,
Dream visions of aërial joy, and call the monster, Love,
And wake, and find the shadow Pain, as he whom now we greet. (772–779)

The initial inspiration for the form and imagery of this lyric came from a passage in Plato's *Symposium*, which Shelley translated: "For Homer says, that the goddess Calamity is delicate, and that her feet are tender. Her feet are soft, he says, for she treads not upon the ground, but makes her path upon the heads of men. He gives as an evidence of her tenderness, that she walks not upon that which is hard, but that which is soft. The same evidence is sufficient to make manifest the tenderness of Love."[40]

In content, the lyric is clearly related to the description of the French Revolution just given by the fifth Spirit, for the sixth Spirit is answering the song of the fifth Spirit. And both lyrics are illuminated by Shelley's comments on the French Revolution in the Preface to *The Revolt of Islam*:

> The sympathies connected with that event extended to every bosom. The most generous and amiable natures were those which participated most extensively in these sympathies. But such a degree of unmingled good was expected as it was impossible to realize . . . Thus many of the most ardent and tender-hearted of the worshippers of public good have been morally ruined by what a partial glimpse of the events they deplored, appeared to show as the melancholy desolation of all their cherished hopes. Hence gloom and misanthropy have become the characteristics of the age in which we live.[41]

This passage clearly parallels the general concept of the sixth lyric, and at times the two are even close in wording. Those who had such high "hopes" of the French Revolution were mostly sensitive intellectuals—"the best and gentlest," "the most ardent and tender-hearted of the worshippers of public good"—and it was they who were most completely crushed by its failure. Their "tender hopes" for an age of humanitarian love were shattered; when they "woke," they found "the shadow pain." They were "morally ruined" by what seemed to be "the melancholy desolation of all their cherished hopes."

An earlier draft of the lyric gives further clues to its meaning. In the third line, for "treads with lulling footsteps" Shelley first wrote "seeks with unfelt footsteps." Thus, desolation was depicted as actively seeking out the "hopes" of the young idealists. In the sixth line, for "music-stirring" Shelley first wrote "dream-inspiring," and the last line originally ran: "And die like early flowers when the winds that waked them, fleet."[42] Desolation, then, like the Homeric goddess Calamity, was a force that worked on the minds of men. She maliciously sought out the hopes of the idealists, inspired them with "visions" of a future world of love, disillusioned them, and left them morally dead. The concept was that of an evil but subtle ("delicate") spirit who would ultimately produce a "desolation" of the mind—such as the fifth Spirit felt after witnessing the "terror"—deliberately leading men on in order to destroy them. Again, the initial inspiration for the lyric must have been the defection of Wordsworth and Coleridge. The poets of the past generation awoke from their dreams of a new world to find the "Pain" of disenchantment, just as Prometheus wakes each day to find (but endure) the "element" of his own pain: "pain ever, for ever" (23, 477).

Following the songs of the fifth and sixth Spirits, all the Spirits sing in chorus to Prometheus:

Tho' Ruin now Love's shadow be,
Following him destroyingly
  On Death's white and winged steed,
Which the fleetest cannot flee,
  Trampling down both flower and weed,
Man and beast, and foul and fair,
Like a tempest thro' the air;
Thou shalt quell this Horseman grim,
Woundless though in heart or limb. (780–788)

The "Ruin" of this chorus is clearly the same thing as the "Desolation" of the previous one, as the same general line of thought is continued. Shelley's meaning was more clearly indicated by his discarded last line of the previous chorus: "And die like early flowers when the winds that waked them fleet." The "tender-hearted" idealists morally died, were "morally ruined," by their own disillusionment and treachery. This, alas, is still "now" true. Such "Ruin" sows wide the seeds of hopelessness and despair, affecting the whole world with its "insidious poison." But a change is coming; Prometheus will conquer this "horseman" of moral death (a reference to *Revelations*, as in *The Masque of Anarchy*), even though it is "Woundless . . . in heart or limb," that is, it is essentially a mental or psychological force, like "Opinion," not a physical or social one.[43]

The particular weapons that would aid Prometheus in quelling the horseman of moral Ruin are indicated in the final chorus:

In the atmosphere we breathe—
As buds grow red when the snow-storms flee,
  From Spring gathering up beneath,
Whose mild winds shake the elder brake,
And the wandering herdsmen know
That the white-thorn soon will blow—
Wisdom, Justice, Love, and Peace,
When they struggle to increase,
  Are to us as soft winds be
  To shepherd boys: the prophecy
  Which begins and ends in thee. (790–800)

As the "atmosphere" which the Spirits "breathe" is that of "human thought," the concept here again is that the poets are able to sense the coming of social change—"the gigantic shadows which futurity casts upon the present."[44] As in *A Defence of Poetry* and elsewhere, the metaphor is that of the wind. Just as the herdsmen perceive in the world of nature that the "mild winds" herald the coming of spring, so too the Spirits in their mental world perceive the significance for humanity of the "mild winds" of the mind. As Shelley stated in the Preface "the cloud of mind is discharging its collected lightnings," and as in *Ode to the West Wind,* a new "spring" is coming for mankind. It is coming because "Wisdom, Justice, Love and Peace" are growing and strengthening. These are the qualities that will conquer the old order with its social and moral ruin. And they are the qualities that are embodied in the poets, in Prometheus. By means of them, Prometheus will "quell" the "Woundless" "horseman." Such is the "prophecy." With this chorus the Spirits vanish, and thirty lines later the first act closes.

The Revocation of the Curse

If the first act of *Prometheus Unbound* had been divided into scenes, there would have been three: the revocation of the curse, the attack of the Furies, and the visitation of the Spirits. The stage direction for Act I reads: "SCENE.—A Ravine of Icy Rocks in the Indian Caucasus. PROMETHEUS is discovered bound to the Precipice. PANTHEA and IONE are seated at his feet. Time, Night. During the Scene, morning slowly breaks." The "Night" and the dawn, it is now obvious, are symbolic. Night perhaps represents past society in general, but more specifically it represents the dark decades before the French Revolution. The dawn represents the coming change, suggested particularly in the final scene.

Prometheus on the precipice is depicted in accordance with the Aeschylean concept, as a heroic and suffering figure, sustained by the knowledge that the overthrow of Jupiter is inevitable. Now, added to that knowledge, comes a new wisdom. Prometheus sees "wingless, crawling hours" (48), one of which will "drag" Jupiter to:

> kiss the blood
> From these pale feet, which then might trample thee
> If they disdained not such a prostrate slave.
> Disdain! Ah no! I pity thee. (50–53)

His mood is clearly ambivalent. He takes an almost malicious joy in contemplating the coming defeat of Jupiter, yet feels that it is morally wrong to do so. Resolved to expel "hate" from his heart, he decides that he must "recall" the curse which he vented on Jupiter at the time of his binding to the precipice.[45]

In a scene somewhat reminiscent of Byron's *Manfred,* Prometheus appeals to the forms of nature by which he is surrounded—the mountains, springs, air, and whirlwinds—to repeat the curse, but they fail to do so. They state only that both nature and humanity suffered when it was uttered. This is confirmed by Earth. On the dramatic level, Earth is the Greek deity Gaia, who was both mother of the first Titans and a general symbol for earth as Mother Earth. She tells Prometheus that the forms of nature he solicited for help are afraid to utter the curse. So too is she afraid, at least to repeat it in the language of "life," for if she did, Jupiter might hear her. She then repeats the curse in a strange language, which, she tells Prometheus, is the language known only "to those who die," (151) and which Prometheus cannot understand because he is an "immortal." (150) He asks again that "mine own words" (190) be repeated. Since in classical mythology, Earth both controlled the oracular vapors and was the goddess of the dead, Prometheus' appeal to her is doubly apt. In reply to his second appeal, Earth states that there is one way whereby he may hear his words repeated:

> They shall be told. Ere Babylon was dust,
> The Magus Zoraster, my dead child,
> Met his own image walking in the garden.
> That apparition, sole of men, he saw.
> For know there are two worlds of life and death:
> One that which thou beholdest; but the other
> Is underneath the grave, where do inhabit
> The shadows of all forms that think and live
> Till death unite them and they part no more. (191–199)

In this strange underworld exist the shadowy images of Jupiter, Prometheus, and all the Titans. If Prometheus calls up one of the images, it can repeat the curse for him in the language of the immortals, which he can understand, and it need not fear the wrath of Jupiter, who cannot harm such "shades."

The exact sources for this general concept of an underworld mirroring life or for the specific one of Zoroaster meeting his own image are unknown. The general concept is ultimately Platonic or Indian, yet in the specific form given by Shelley it is neither, for Shelley's other-world is an inferior image ("shadow") of actuality, whereas in Plato or the *Upanishads* actuality is an inferior image of the One. In its shadowy grayness it is reminiscent of the Homeric underworld visited by Odysseus, but Homer did not express the metaphysical concept of the underworld reflecting life. The story that Zoroaster met his image is said to be part of Zoroastrian lore, but no one has yet cited a specific text. Perhaps it was a story that Shelley had heard from Peacock, who was interested in Zoroaster and cited a life of him in *The Philosophy of Melancholy*.[46]

Prometheus, given a large choice of shades to summon up, narrows it down to those most intimately involved, namely, Jupiter and himself, and prefers Jupiter on the grounds that he does not wish any evil to pass henceforth either from his own lips or from those of "ought ressembling me" (220), that is, his own shade. The phantasm of Jupiter then arises to repeat the curse, which Prometheus now wishes to hear again. Actually the phantasm repeats a good deal more than the curse. In fact, of the four stanzas of his speech, only one, the third, contains the curse:

> I curse thee! let a sufferer's curse
> Clasp thee, his torturer, like remorse,
> Till thine Infinity shall be
> A robe of envenomed agony;
> And thine Omnipotence a crown of pain,
> To cling like burning gold round thy dissolving brain. (286–291)

The first two stanzas voice a courageous defiance of Jupiter:

> Fiend, I defy thee! with a calm, fixed mind,
> All that thou canst inflict I bid thee do;
> Foul Tyrant both of Gods and Human-kind,
> One only being shalt thou not subdue.
>
> Ay, do thy worst. Thou art omnipotent.
> O'er all things but thyself I gave thee power,
> And my own will.

Prometheus is obviously not repudiating any of this. He remains as defiant as ever, as his later words to Mercury and the Furies show, he is prepared to undergo whatever suffering is necessary until the day of Jupiter's overthrow. What he would repudiate is the spirit of hatred and revenge, not that of firm opposition:

> It doth repent me: words are quick and vain;
> Grief for awhile is blind, and so was mine.
> I wish no living thing to suffer pain.

As soon as Earth hears these words, she cries out in horror and dismay:

> Misery, Oh misery to me,
> That Jove at length should vanquish thee. (306–307)

Earth believes, then, that Prometheus' repentance means that he has yielded to Jupiter. Ione answers that this is not so. Mercury and the Furies then appear, and the second scene begins.

Although there may not be so many problems in the revocation-of-the curse scene as in the Furies scene, there are still quite a few. What is the meaning of the revocation itself? Why cannot Prometheus understand the language of mortals? What are the two worlds? Why does Earth feel that the revocation means surrender by Prometheus? What does Earth symbolize? Why do Mercury and the Furies appear immediately after the revocation? What does Prometheus mean when he says that he gave Jupiter power over all except himself and the will of Prometheus?

The meaning of the revocation of the curse derives from Shelley's view that the French Revolution had collapsed because it became dominated by hatred and revenge:

> there was strife, deceit and fear:
> Tyrants rushed in and did divide the spoil. (663–654)

Or as he put it in *A Philosophical View of Reform*: "If there had never been war [civil as well as international], there could never have been tyranny in the world; tyrants take advantage of the mechanical organization of armies to establish and defend their encroachments. It is thus that the mighty advantages of the French Revolution have been almost completely compensated by a succession of tyrants."[47]

In essence, Shelley felt that no revolution could hold its gains and develop into a lasting egalitarian order unless people were remolded. Their self-centered urges must be turned into communal ones, their suspicions into mutual trust, their hatred into humanitarian love, their fears into hopes. The responsibility to bring about such a change lay with the leaders of the people, essentially with the intellectuals, for the intellectuals had, to a greater degree than other segments of the population, these ideals in their hearts and tried to live in accordance with them. "The change," Shelley wrote to Peacock during the period of composition of *Prometheus Unbound*, "should commence among the higher orders, or anarchy will only be the last flash before despotism.[48] By "anarchy" Shelley meant the peasant (Spencean) seizure of estates and the kind of conflicts between opposing revolutionary groups that had, he believed, prepared the way in France for militaristic dictatorship ("despotism"). By the "higher orders" he did not mean the ruling classes but the reformers, left-wing Whigs and intellectuals, from Lord Grey to Burdett, from Bentham to Byron. Of Byron, for example, he wrote in the period of composition of *Prometheus Unbound*: "He is a person of the most consummate genius, and capable, if he would direct his energies to such an end, of becoming the redeemer of his degraded country."[49] Even a comparatively small group of such men, Shelley felt, could change the psychological climate of a revolution or reform movement by "convincing" and "persuading" others, who would then persuade still others, that communal rather than selfish values must prevail.

The first step toward ensuring success must be the removal of selfishness, hatred, violence, and despair from the hearts of the leaders. They must learn, to quote the Preface to *Prometheus Unbound*, to "love, and admire, and trust, and hope, and endure"—to embody, in short, the qualities of Prometheus. And such a change was beginning: "The cloud of mind is discharging its collected lightning, and the equilibrium between institutions and opinions is now restoring, or is about to be restored." The revocation of the curse, then, reflects that "slow, gradual, silent change" toward humanitarian idealism that was taking place in the intellectual and social climate of the age.

In the revocation of the curse Shelley is not advocating individual pacifism any more than he is in *The Masque of Anarchy*. Prometheus does not "forgive" Jupiter. He says only that he no longer "hates" him and can "pity" him. He can pity Jupiter because Jupiter is himself enmeshed in evil, a victim of the social system like all "tyrants" and hence distorted psychologically and morally. For the same reason, Prometheus can refrain from hating him as an individual even though he can rejoice in his downfall and scorn both him and his emissaries. Nor does the emphasis in the final chorus on "Wisdom, Justice, Love and Peace" mean that these are the only qualities needed to overthrow Jupiter. Prometheus has not lost his former qualities of courage, hope, defiance, perseverance, and strength. All these, too, are needed. But with love added and hate expelled, they have a new significance. It is for this reason that Mercury and the Furies appear after the revocation of the curse. The ruling classes have also perceived the "discharging" of the "lightning" of the "cloud of mind" and are taking immediate measures to stop it.

The ensnarement of Jupiter in his own system and the consequent limitation of his power is reflected in the curse stanzas:

> O'er all things but thyself I gave thee power,
> And my own will. (273–274)

Prometheus, in both Aeschylus and Shelley, was the "founder" of civil society, the inventor of the sciences and arts, of speech and thought. These he turned over to Jupiter, to organize human government, and Jupiter betrayed him; the government turned despotic. The government, however, does not really have power over itself because it becomes part of a system vaster than itself, subject to the laws of necessity. Although it can conquer people by force and subdue them by deception, there is within each person a core of being that cannot be touched by external influences—the "individual" and "natural" element as opposed to the "social." In some people, the area of the "individual" circle within the mind is large. They are incorruptibly humanitarian. They cannot be broken by power, propaganda, or bribery. They keep control over their faculties and subdue the corrupting "mutiny within." Shelley is not, as is sometimes suggested, opposing necessity to free will or replacing the former by the latter.[50] When the powers of necessity begin to change society, these people, masters of their own minds and unconquered by life, will be ready to assist in making the change a humanitarian one.

Shelley's symbolic concept of Earth in the drama is illustrated in both *The Revolt of Islam* and *The Masque of Anarchy*, where Earth is depicted as an agitational, revolutionary entity. In *The Masque of Anarchy* the voice that speaks to the men of England, urging them to fight against tyranny, is introduced as follows:

As if their own indignant Earth
Which gave the sons of England birth
Had felt their blood upon her brow,
And shuddering with a mother's throe

Had turned every drop of blood
By which her face had been bedewed
To an accent unwithstood,—
As if her heart had cried aloud:

. . . . .

Rise like Lions after slumber
In unvanquishable number. (139–146, 151–152)

In *The Revolt of Islam*, following the rebellion of the sailors, the ships sail toward port to spread the revolt:

The many ships spotting the dark blue deep
With snowy sails, fled fast as ours came nigh,
In fear and wonder; and on every steep
Thousands did gaze, they heard the startling cry,
Like earth's own voice lifted unconquerably
To all her children, the unbounded mirth,
The glorious joy of thy name—Liberty!
They heard!—As o'er the mountains of the earth
From peak to peak leap on the beams of Morning's birth. (3487–3495)

In both poems, Earth urges her "children," her "sons"—humanity—to revolt. She hates the sway of tyranny over them; so, too, in *Prometheus Unbound*:

and the thin air, my breath, was stained
With the contagion of a mother's hate
Breathed on her child's destroyer; aye, I heard
Thy curse, the which, if thou rememberest not,
Yet my innumerable seas and streams,
Mountains, and caves, and winds, and yon wide air,
And the inarticulate people of the dead,
Preserve, a treasured spell. We meditate
In secret joy and hope those dreadful words
But dare not speak them. (177–186)

Earth is obviously not only the classical goddess (apparently a main character in Aeschylus' lost *Prometheus Unbound*), but also a symbol for revolt, even for vengeance, a force eager for the freedom, justice, and equality of her "children" and, hence, opposed to despotic power.[51] But she also seems to be, in part at least, a symbol for these "children" themselves, for the common people, the toilers of the earth, who in the Spencean vision (reflected in *Swellfoot the Tyrant*) would take over by direct revolutionary action, seizing the estates of the rich. Certainly Earth believes that there is no way to overthrow Jupiter except by keeping alive the hatred, born of oppression, which will one day burst out into forceful action. It is for this reason that she feels Prometheus' revocation of the curse means that he is submitting to Jupiter. She does not understand that hatred will only produce further hatred, and that love, brotherhood, and patience are also important in the struggle.

Not only in a social but in a general sense, Earth is a materialistic entity, with overtones of the Lucretian Mother Earth. When Prometheus suggests that she, too, is immortal, she answers in materialistic terms:

> I am the Earth,
> Thy mother, she within whose stony veins. . . (152–153)

Her affinity is with nature, the mountains, rivers, ocean, and air, not with spiritual or mental phenomena. She feels deeply for humanity but in a direct, primitive, "earthy" way. She knows the language of the dead, the language, that is, of mortals. Whether she also knows the language of immortals is not made clear, but the implication is that she does not. Prometheus, however, does. When Earth repeats the curse for him and he fails to hear it, she says:

> No, thou canst not hear:
> Thou art immortal, and this tongue is known
> Only to those who die. (149–151)

By the language of the immortals Shelley, to judge from *A Defence of Poetry* and other works, means the inspiration which comes to "the Poets" and is connected with the imagination and with original, creative thought. The strange shadow world of the immortals and their language seems similar to the "cave" of the "witch Poesy" in *Mont Blanc.* If so, it stands for the realm of the creative, poetic imagination.

Asia, Panthea, and Ione

Shelley first indicates his concept of Asia in the words of Prometheus to Panthea after the disappearance of the Spirits at the end of Act I:

> How fair these air-born shapes! and yet I feel
> Most vain all hope but love; and thou art far,
> Asia! who, when my being overflowed,
> Wert like a golden chalice to bright wine
> Which else had sunk into the thirsty dust. (I.807–811)

In the second act, Shelley makes the concept explicit in Panthea's description of the coming of Asia:

> The Nereids tell
> That on the day when the clear hyaline
> Was cloven at thine uprise, and thou didst stand
> Within a veinèd shell, which floated on
> Over the calm floor of the crystal sea,
> Among the Ægean isles, and by the shores
> Which bear thy name, love, like the atmosphere
> Of the sun's fire filling the living world,
> Burst from thee, and illumined earth and heaven
> And the deep ocean and the sunless caves
> And all that dwells within them; till grief cast
> Eclipse upon the soul from which it came:
> Such art thou now; nor is it I alone,
> Thy sister, thy companion, thine own chosen one,
> But the whole world which seeks thy sympathy.
> Hearest thou not sounds i' the air which speak the love
> Of all articulate beings? Feelest thou not
> The inanimate winds enamoured of thee? (II.v.20–37)

The picture of Asia arising from the sea and floating ashore on "a veined shell" clearly reflects the traditional rising of Aphrodite from the sea as depicted in Botticelli's *Birth of Venus,* which Shelley could have seen in Florence shortly before beginning *Prometheus Unbound.* He could hardly have been more explict. Asia is, if not Aphrodite herself, at least akin to her and, hence, a symbolic representation of love. Shelley must also have been aware that the Aphrodite who arose from the sea was generally considered to be Aphrodite Urania, that is, divine or spiritual love, and Botticelli's picture has been so interpreted. That Shelley is referring to the classical concept seems to be indicated also in the names of her "sister," Panthea. "Panthea," literally signifying "all the gods," must have reference to Aphrodite Pandemos, the goddess of "all the people" and the symbol of "earthly" or sexual love.[52]

However, neither here nor elsewhere in his drama does Shelley follow Greek tradition literally. Asia cannot simply be Aphrodite Urania because Shelley did not believe in the Platonic dichotomy between divine love, which was good, and sexual or earthly love, which was evil. On the contrary, he regarded sexual love as an integral part of the whole complex of love. Prometheus' almost explicitly sexual comments on his relationship with Asia are the opposite of Platonic. So, too, is Panthea's description of Asia as one who represents the love desired by "the whole world," and Asia's own comment: "Common as light is love,/And its familiar voice wearies not ever" (v.34, 40–41). Finally, when Panthea first comes to Asia, Asia addresses her as:

Beloved and most beautiful, who wearest
The shadow of that soul by which I live. (i.30–31)

Asia, in other words, is dependent on Prometheus, their relationship being in fact, one of mutual dependence. Whatever kind of love she represents, it is obviously one associated with humanity.

Yet it is also apparently a love that humanity does not at present possess but "seeks" for. Shelley's thinking on this matter is clarified in the *Essay on Christianity*:

In proportion as mankind becomes wise, yes, in exact proportion to that wisdom should be the extinction of the unequal system under which they now subsist. Government is in fact the mere badge of their depravity. They are so little aware of the inestimable benefits of mutual love as to indulge without thought and almost without motive in the worst excesses of selfishness and malice . . . The whole frame of human things is infected by the insidious poison. Hence it is that man is blind in his understanding, corrupt in his moral sense, and diseased in his physical functions. The wisest and most sublime of the ancient poets saw this truth and embodied their conception of its value in retrospect to the earliest ages of mankind. They represented equality as the reign of Saturn and taught that mankind had gradually degenerated from the virtue which enabled them to enjoy or maintain this happy state. Their doctrine was philosophically false. Later and more correct observations have instructed us that uncivilized man is the most pernicious and miserable of beings.[53]

"Mutual love," then, cannot exist in a society based on an "unequal system." Conversely, it can exist only in an egalitarian order. Shelley did not believe that there had ever been such an order. Contrary to Rousseau's doctrine, "uncivilized man" was "the most pernicious and miserable of human beings." Although the "wisest and most sublime of the ancient poets" also did not believe there had ever been a society based on equality, they perceived that love could flourish only in such a society and therefore chose to imagine it as having once existed in the past. They "represented equality as the reign of Saturn." Although this Saturnian concept was "false," it "ministered" to "thoughts of despondency and sorrow" and hence, according to Shelley's general view on such matters, was a legitimate concept to use in poetry. And this is what he does in *Prometheus Unbound*. He conceives of Asia and Prometheus as having once been together, and then separated by Jupiter: "grief cast/Eclipse upon the soul from which it came." They will come together again in a future egalitarian society. In the meantime, they have contact through Panthea.

Panthea, the "sister" of Asia, is described by Prometheus:

Sister of her whose footsteps pave the world
With loveliness—more fair than aught but her,
Whose shadow thou art—lift thine eyes on me. (i.68–70)

Shelley's concept is illustrated in *On Love*: "this is the invisible and unattainable point to which Love tends; and to attain which, it urges forth the powers of man to arrest the faintest shadow of that, without the possession of which there is no rest nor respite to the heart over which it rules."[54] In *Epipsychidion* Shelley wrote:

In many mortal forms I rashly sought
The shadow of that idol of my thought. (267–268)

If Asia is a symbol for the potential of human love that can be realized only in the future and is at present "unattainable," what is attainable is only a "shadow" of that potential. The "shadow" is love as it now exists. Such is Panthea.

Even though love is only a "shadow" of what it could be, however, it is a powerful and pervasive influence, rooted in the capacity of man to make "the pains and pleasures of his species . . . his own."[55] It can be a beautiful and inspiring force, as it is to Shelley in *Epipsychidion*, or to Laon and Cythna:

and then I felt the blood that burned
Within her frame, mingle with mine, and fall
Around my heart like fire. (2634–2636)

Similarly, the relationship of Prometheus and Panthea is strong and passionate:

I saw not, heard not, moved not, only felt
His presence flow and mingle through my blood
Till it became his life, and his grew mine,
And I was thus absorbed, until it passed,
And like the vapours when the sun sinks down,
Gathering again in drops upon the pines,
And tremulous as they, in the deep night
My being was condensed. (i.79–86)

Panthea is actually with Prometheus, whereas Asia is separated from him. Panthea thus represents the "many mortal forms" or, on the Promethean level, "all the gods" (and goddesses), in which the poets seek love. Through such a love they aspire to attain that greater love of which they feel they are capable: Panthea is the intermediary between Prometheus and Asia. But this greater love has being now only insofar as the poets can imaginatively envisage it: "the shadow of that soul by which I live."[56]

Ione is the youngest of the three sisters: "Our young Ione"(i.46). In the first act she is depicted as timid and dependent on Panthea. When the phantasm of Jupiter appears, she hides her eyes and cries out to Panthea: "He speaks! O shelter me!" (257). Again she hides her eyes when the

Furies are attacking Prometheus and is astonished that Panthea has the courage to look: "Darest thou observe how the fiends torture him?" (582). Shelley, however, gives only one direct clue to his symbolic intent. After Panthea experienced the love of Prometheus and lay in a glow of remembrance by the side of Ione—the two sisters sleep in each other's arms—Ione wakes and speaks to her:

> Canst thou divine what troubles me to-night?
> I always knew what I desired before,
> Nor ever found delight to wish in vain.
> But now I cannot tell thee what I seek;
> I know not—something sweet, since it is sweet
> Even to desire. It is thy sport, false sister!
> Thou hast discovered some enchantment old
> Whose spells have stolen my spirit as I slept
> And mingled it with thine; for when just now
> We kissed, I felt within thy parted lips
> The sweet air that sustained me, and the warmth
> Of the life-blood for loss of which I faint
> Quivered between our intertwining arms. (i.94–106)

Ione, having always known what she desired and apparently always having gotten it, is now overcome by a new, disturbing sensation. It is as though Panthea is drawing life out of her. What she feels is apparently the demands of the love of Prometheus operating through Panthea. For the first time she is having some contact with mature love. Previously love had been childlike, perhaps largely fantasizing, for otherwise she would hardly have been able to achieve all her desires. Her love life had been centered, like that of the poet in *Alastor*, on imaginary objects or the beauties of nature or art. But now she is being stirred out of herself, turning not inward to further fantasy but outward to Panthea and, through Panthea, to Prometheus, for although she is disturbed by the new sensations, she is attracted by them. "Desire" as such is "sweet"; the "life-blood" is warm. In the three sisters, then, Shelley seems to be reflecting three forms or stages of love.[57]

Demogorgon

Although Demogorgon was a creation of medieval mythologists, Shelley got some ideas for him from Aeschylus and Plato. One function of Demogorgon is to overthrow Jupiter; in Aeschylus, Prometheus stated that Jupiter would eventually be brought to reason by the power of necessity, "that which need must be." In Plato's *Timaeus* the builder of the world was the Demiurgos, who was not the force behind creation but a power that acted only on materials already present and endowed with their basic qualities.

From this concept arose the medieval legend of Demogorgon. The standard picture of him is that in the opening pages of Boccaccio's *Genealogies of the Gods*, where he was described as the first of all things, preceding all the gods, a vast, dark personification of fate and the "companion" of eternity.[58] It was mainly from Boccaccio's description that he entered literature. To Spenser he was the "Prince of darkness." To Robert Greene he was the dread, mysterious "master of the fates." He is referred to by both Marlowe and Milton.[59] Shelley's attention was doubtless turned to him by Peacock, who commented in *Rhododaphne*: " 'The dreaded name of Demogorgon' is familiar to every reader in Milton's enumeration of the Powers of Chaos . . . Natalis Comes . . . makes Pan and the three sister Fates the offspring of Demogorgon . . . He was the Genius of the Earth, and the Sovereign Power of the Terrestrial Daemons. He dwelt originally with Eternity and Chaos, till becoming weary of inaction, he organised the chaotic elements, and surrounded the earth with the heavens." Peacock and Shelley discussed *Rhododaphne* together at Marlow while it was being written, and Shelley later reviewed it.[60] That they specifically discussed Demogorgon is indicated by the fact that someone at Marlow, either a resident or visitor, was nicknamed Demogorgon.[61]

Shelley, then, when he came to write *Prometheus Unbound*, was aware of Demogorgon and the attributes of fate connected with him. He apparently assumed that his readers would remember at least the Spenser and Milton references and would know of his general nature or significance—or could find him easily enough in such works as *Bell's New Pantheon*.[62] Shelley, however, does not depict him exactly as he found him. He is no more simply the Demogorgon of Boccaccio than Prometheus is the Prometheus of Aeschylus.

Shelley's meaning in Demogorgon is indicated in several passages in the drama. For instance, he places Demogorgon's cave in "the fatal mountain," that is, the mountain of fate, thus linking him with the Renaissance "master of the fates" concept. He gives specific indications of his meaning in the semichorus of Spirits, which sings as Asia and Panthea approach the realm of Demogorgon:

There those enchanted eddies play
   Of echoes, music-tongued, which draw,
   By Demogorgon's mighty law,
   With melting rapture, or sweet awe,
All spirits on that secret way;
   As inland boats are driven to Ocean
Down streams made strong with mountain-thaw:
   And first there comes a gentle sound
   To those in talk or slumber bound,
   And wakes the destined; soft emotion

Attracts, impels them; those who saw
  Say from the breathing earth behind
  There streams a plume-uplifting wind
Which drives them on their path, while they
  Believed their own swift wings and feet
The sweet desires within obey. (ii.41–56)

"Demogorgon's mighty law" is clearly the law of necessity, which controls events and actions that individuals believe are matters of personal decision or "desires within." It is the "wind" which drives them through life, as boats are rushed seaward by the current of a river. According to *Queen Mab*, necessity "presides, apportioning with irresistable law" (VI. 162–163). When Panthea first sees Demogorgon, she describes him as "a mighty darkness/Filling the seat of power" (II.iv.2–3). Elsewhere she says of his appearance:

  A mighty Power, which is as darkness,
Is rising out of Earth, and from the sky
Is showered like night, and from within the air
Bursts, like eclipse which had been gathered up
Into the pores of sunlight. (IV.512–516)

He interpenetrates all nature—the earth, air, and heavens. As Shelley wrote in *A Refutation of Deism*, "The greatest equally with the smallest motions of the Universe are subject to the rigid necessity of inevitable laws. These laws are the unknown causes of the known effects perceivable in the Universe."[63]

Shelley perhaps thought that some readers might remember *The Daemon of the World* in the *Alastor* volume. According to the Abbé Banier, the power of "Demons" "extended over the lower World, and in particular over Man," in contrast to the power of the gods, which extended over the upper world, and the name Demogorgon means "Genius or Intelligence of the Earth."[64] Like Demogorgon, and also like necessity in *Queen Mab*, Shelley's Daemon is eternal and omnipresent. Demogorgon and the Daemon of the World, in short, are the same, and the Daemon is clearly necessity, or, what is essentially the same thing, power in its necessitarian aspect.

The power that is to bring about the new order in *Prometheus Unbound* is also the same as in Shelley's preceding major work, published in the year when *Prometheus Unbound* was begun (1818), namely, *The Revolt of Islam*:

                    One comes behind,
  Who aye the future to the past will bind—
Necessity, whose sightless strength for ever
  Evil with evil, good with good must wind
In bands of union, which no power may sever:
They must bring forth their kind, and be divided never! (IX.xxvii)

The concept of the necessitarian nature of the coming social change—"necessary because it is inevitable and must be"—also permeated *A Philosophical View of Reform*, written in the same period as *Prometheus Unbound*.[65] The revolution that Shelley sketched there as arising in Europe, Asia, and the Americas was taking place not because Shelley wished it, or because it was "just," but because the powers of historical necessity were creating it. Shelley also used the concept of necessity in *Hellas* ("The world's eyeless charioteer, Destiny"—711–712) and in *The Triumph of Life* (the charioteer of life).

Love and Necessity

Act II of *Prometheus Unbound* opens with Asia in her valley at dawn awaiting a visit by Panthea, who apparently comes regularly to convey the thoughts and feelings of Prometheus. On this occasion one would expect Panthea to tell her of the attack of the Furies and the songs of the Spirits, but instead she reports on two dreams, one concerning the transformation of Prometheus by love, the other about a strange spirit.

Shelley described his play as having "characters & mechanism of a kind yet unattempted," and Panthea's failure to report on the events of the first act shows something of what he meant.[66] The earlier action was not action in the usual sense of the word but an impressionist depiction of social and psychological change. Panthea reports on the essence of this change, as symbolized by the transformation of Prometheus, not on its details. The second act does not carry on the action of the first act but continues the atmosphere of its conclusion.

Because of the change in Prometheus, the way is opened for a change in society. Prometheus will conquer the ruin that has devastated the age. Love and wisdom are increasing; spring is "gathering up beneath." In the second act—as in the *Ode to the West Wind*, published in the *Prometheus Unbound* volume—the "spring" theme swells to symphonic proportions. Act I depicted the chaos and gloom of the period from the collapse of the French Revolution to the domination of the Quadruple Alliance—"the winter of the world," the "age of despair" of *The Revolt of Islam*—with only a final note of coming revival, of "unimagined change." Act II depicts in symbolic form the actual rise of these forces, gathering, as it were, beneath the surface of society to overthrow the old order: "But mankind appear to me to be emerging from their trance. I am aware, methinks, of a slow, gradual, silent change."[67]

The theme is struck immediately in Asia's invocation to spring:

> thou hast descended
> Cradled in tempests; thou dost wake, O Spring!
> O child of many winds! (i.5–7)

It is continued in both of Panthea's dreams. Asia, gazing into the eyes of Panthea, sees within them the transformed Prometheus of the first dream. His smile presages for her their reunion in the new world order:

> Say not those smiles that we shall meet again
> Within that bright pavilion which their beams
> Shall build o'er the waste world? (i.124–126)

The spirit of the second dream then appears:

> What shape is that between us? Its rude hair
> Roughens the wind that lifts it, its regard
> Is wild and quick, yet 'tis a thing of air
> For through its gray robe gleams the golden dew
> Whose stars the noon has quenched not. (i.127–131)

This spirit seems clearly to be a symbol of revolution: it combines roughness and impetuosity with intellectuality ("air") and hope (the "golden dew" of dawn). It bids the sisters to "Follow! Follow!"

Panthea's next speech—which in an early draft began with "I had dreams of spring"[68]—is apparently once more a symbolic representation of the rise and fall of the French Revolution:

> Methought
> As we sate here, the flower-infolding buds
> Burst on yon lightning-blasted almond-tree,
> When swift from the white Scythian wilderness
> A wind swept forth wrinkling the Earth with frost:
> I looked, and all the blossoms were blown down;
> But on each leaf was stamped, as the blue bells
> Of Hyacinth tell Apollo's written grief,
> O, FOLLOW, FOLLOW! (i.133–141)

The word "follow," as soon becomes apparent, means that the sisters are to follow mysterious voices to the cave of Demogorgon. In other words, a revolution has arisen, bright and budding in its hope, only to perish in the winds of history; but, it is implied, if the sisters will follow to the cave of necessity, they will there find new revolutionary forces astir.

"Echoes" then take up the cry of "Follow, follow" and promise the reunion of Asia and Prometheus ("Parted, to commingle now"—205).[69] They address Asia in riddling verse:

> In the world unknown
> Sleeps a voice unspoken;
> By thy step alone
> Can its rest be broken;
> Child of Ocean! (i.190–194)

The child of Ocean is clearly Asia, who, according to Hesiod, was one of the daughters of Ocean and who was associated in Shelley's mind with Love (Aphrodite) rising from the sea. The "voice unspoken" must be the voice of Demogorgon, for it is to the cave of Demogorgon that the sisters are going.

Essentially the same message is conveyed to Asia by a chorus of Spirits as she and her sister approach the cave:

> We have bound thee, we guide thee;
> Down, down!
> With the bright form beside thee;
> Resist not the weakness,
> Such strength is in meekness
> That the Eternal, the Immortal,
> Must unloose through life's portal
> The snake-like Doom coiled underneath his throne
> By that alone. (iii.90–98)

"Meekness" apparently refers to Asia, as symbol for love, one of whose characteristics is presumably "meekness." Necessity (Demogorgon), it is implied, can perform certain acts only if assisted by love. Necessity is a blind ("sightless") force, producing, with equal disinterest, good or evil. It produced the French Revolution, and then its collapse. It produced Washington, and it produced Napoleon. What Demogorgon does in *Prometheus Unbound* is to bring about a defeat of tyranny which then leads to an egalitarian world. This second step, Shelley implies, here and elsewhere, could not have come about without the assistance of Asia. Here again is the familiar idea that the French Revolution collapsed because there were not sufficient humanitarian leaders to direct it. The new revolution will succeed because there are enough such leaders—because, in short, there is enough "love" in society to prevent the murder of "kindred" by "kin" that formerly resulted in dictatorship and war. When radical intellectuals (Prometheus) renounce vengeance (in the revocation of the curse) and withstand the ideological attack of the state (the Furies), there opens the possibility of a lasting triumph over the old order. As a result, Panthea and Asia are able to begin their march to the cave of Demogorgon: love moves to join the forces of historical change. Although their trip to the cave may give the impression of timeless fantasy, Shelley must have regarded it as reflecting events beginning in his own age and continuing over the next decades.

The chorus of Spirits who speak to Asia and Panthea on their way to the cave describe the region in necessitarian terms, similar to those describing the temples of the Daemon of the World and of necessity in *Queen Mab* except that the cave of Demogorgon is situated, in accordance with Renaissance lore, "Downe in the bottome of the deepe Abysse." The injunction to Asia to go "down"—"Through the veil and the bar/Of things which seem and are"—to "Where there is one pervading, one alone" is not however simply a description of a journey under the earth but of a symbolic journey into the unknown essence that is common to all phenomena.[70] As a result of it, Prometheus "shall be loosed, and make the earth/One brotherhood" (ii.94–95).

In Scene III, as Asia and Panthea approach the cave, the revolutionary images increase. The scene opens with a speech by Panthea:

Hither the sound has borne us—to the realm
Of Demogorgon, and the mighty portal,
Like a volcano's meteor-breathing chasm,
Whence the oracular vapour is hurled up
Which lonely men drink wandering in their youth,
And call truth, virtue, love, genius, or joy;
That maddening wine of life, whose dregs they drain
To deep intoxication, and uplift,
Like Maenads who cry loud, Evoe! Evoe!
The voice which is contagion to the world. (iii.1–10)

Shelley is here using "contagion" in a revolutionary sense—the spirit of liberty seems a contagion to the rulers of the world—as in Cythna's exhortations to the revolutionary sailors in *The Revolt of Islam*:

but felt around
A wide contagion poured—they called aloud
On Liberty—that name lived on the sunny flood. (IX.iv)[71]

Shelley is recalling, as in *Hymn to Intellectual Beauty*, his excitement in his own "youth" when he first began to envisage the inevitability of revolutionary change.[72]

Just before Asia and Panthea enter the cave, an avalanche sweeps down a nearby mountain—clearly yet another revolutionary symbol:

Hark! the rushing snow!
The sun-awakened avalanche! whose mass,
Thrice sifted by the storm, had gathered there
Flake after flake, in Heaven-defying minds
As thought by thought is piled, till some great truth
Is loosened, and the nations echo round,
Shaken to their roots, as do the mountains now. (II.iii.36–42)

Similar symbols appear also in other images in the scene. The time is "dawn"; the season, spring; the "cataracts" are roaring down from "their thaw-cloven ravines"; and "the gusty sea of mist is breaking." Necessitarian images recur:

Down, down!
As the fawn draws the hound

> As the lightning the vapour,
> As a weak moth the taper;
> Death, despair; love, sorrow;
> Time both; to-day, tomorrow;
> As steel obeys the spirit of the stone,
> Down, down! (iii.64–71)

The fourth scene, the pivotal one in the act, takes place in "The Cave of Demogorgon." Asia and Panthea stand before his "seat," and Asia questions him. Shelley's flexible "machinery" for character portrayal on various levels of meaning permits him considerable range, but it is still a little startling to see Asia, who had previously seemed the embodiment of gentleness, now emerge as a vigorous-minded, Cythna-like radical. Even Demogorgon wilts before her sharp, sometimes angry probing.

Demogorgon begins arrogantly, "Ask what thou would'st know," to which Asia replies, "What canst thou tell?" (iv.7,8) That Asia's question had sarcastic intonation is indicated in Demogorgon's scornful reply: "All things thou dar'st demand." Asia questions him with a Portia-like precision: "Who made the living world?" And:

> Who made all
> That it contains? thought, passion, reason, will,
> Imagination? (iv.9–11)

Demogorgon, not seeing the trap into which he is being led, answers the first question with careless condescension, "God" (iv.9), and the second with awe: "God; Almighty God" (11). Asia's next question leads him on still further, as she asks who made the sense of love and beauty that one receives from nature or human love. The answer, "Merciful God" (18), springs the trap:

> And who made terror, madness, crime, remorse,
> Which from the links of the great chain of things,
> To every thought within the mind of man
> Sway and drag heavily, and each one reels
> Under the load towards the pit of death? (iv.19–23)

Asia is asking not merely about the origin of evil but about that "immense and uninterrupted chain of causes and effects" which acts in both "the moral and material universe."[73] Demogorgon, apparently humbled, can only reply: "He reigns" (iv.128). When Asia later returns to the point, he simply answers: "Jove is the supreme of living things" (113). By this he does not mean that Jupiter is necessarily the only source for social evil but that he is the visible manifestation of it. There may or may not be something beyond Jupiter. In effect, Demogorgon has no answer to Asia's question. He cannot answer because he is not the Creator but merely the power who administers the laws of a world that he did not make (the "master of the fates"). His cave represents not the creative source (a source about which Shelley was skeptical) but the unifying element common to life and nature, and existing not beyond them but within them. Further insight into Shelley's meaning comes from *A Refutation of Deism*:

These laws [the laws of necessity] are the unknown causes of the known effects perceivable in the Universe. Their effects are the boundaries of our knowledge, their names the expressions of our ignorance. To suppose some existence beyond or above them, is to invent a second and superfluous hypothesis for what has already been accounted for by the laws of motion and the properties of matter. I admit that the nature of these laws is incomprehensible, but the hypothesis of a Deity adds a gratuitous difficulty, which so far from alleviating those which it is adduced to explain, requires new hypotheses for the elucidation of its own inherent contradictions.

Although there may be some force beyond these "laws," at present it is unknown. Such hypotheses are outside the field of the doctrine of necessity, of Demogorgon.

Demogorgon's specific failure to answer Asia's question about the origin of evil, is illustrated in a Note to *Queen Mab*: "But the doctrine of necessity teaches us, that in no case could any event have happened otherwise than it did happen, and that, if God is the author of good, he is also the author of evil . . . we are taught, by the doctrine of Necessity, that there is neither good nor evil in the universe, otherwise than as the events to which we apply these epithets have relation to our own peculiar mode of being." In a Note to *Hellas* Shelley developed the point further:

Let it not be supposed that I mean to dogmatise upon a subject, concerning which all men are equally ignorant, or that I think the Gordian knot of the origin of evil can be disentangled by that or any similar assertions. The received hypothesis of a Being resembling men in the moral attributes of His nature, having called us out of non-existence, and after inflicting on us the misery of the commission of error, should superadd that of the punishment and the privations consequent upon it, still would remain inexplicable and incredible.[74]

It is thus apparent that no character representing necessity and its laws could answer the philosophical question about the origin of evil. His only realm is one of things as they are. Necessity in *The Revolt of Islam* (IX.xxvii) impartially winds "Evil with evil, good with good" as they appear on the surface of society. He did not create them; he simply directs them. The problem of evil, therefore, has for Demogorgon a certain irrelevance.

Asia, becoming impatient with Demogorgon's attempts to dodge the question, gives a résumé of mythology and history.[75] She begins with the reign of Saturn, which is depicted not as a golden age but as a primitive society in which people were deprived of the "birthright of their being," namely, "knowledge, power . . . thought . . . Self-empire and the majesty of love" (iv.39–42). Following this primitive state, Asia continues, there came the reign of Jupiter. Political power, as in Aeschylus, was given to Jupiter by Prometheus, with the injunction, "Let man be free" (45). Jupiter, however, established a dictatorship, and people were afflicted by famine, toil, disease, war, and psychological distortions of the human spirit: "mad disquietudes" (56). Prometheus, seeing these evils, brought hope and love to mankind, giving them fire, which enabled them to control metals, and speech, science and art, also emphasized by Aeschylus. There was peace between people: "the Celt knew the Indian." Great cities flourished. But with all these advances, man was unable to abolish inequality or religion: "the thrones of earth and heaven . . . shook, but fell not." (74–75).

Asia is saying, in effect, that evil is not inherent in mankind. What is inherent are love, thought, poetry, and science. The perversion of these elements comes from social causes. Thus, there is no need to presume any supreme power from which evil flows. "Declare/Who is his [Jupiter's] master? Is he too a slave?" (iv.108–109) That is, although Jupiter is ostensibly in charge, he is really as much a "slave" of the social system as anyone.

Asia's comments on the creation, and her résumé of history, reinforce Demogorgon's own skepticism:

If the abysm
Could vomit forth its secrets—but a voice
Is wanting, the deep truth is imageless;
For what would it avail to bid thee gaze
On the revolving world? What to bid speak
Fate, Time, Occasion, Chance, and Change? To these
All things are subject but eternal Love. (iv.114–120)

The fact that "eternal Love" is said by Shelley not to be "subject" to "Fate, Time, Occasion, Chance and Change"—that is, to the laws of necessity, to Demogorgon—has been taken by some to signify that necessity is under the control of love. But Shelley does not say this. He says only that love is not subject to these other entities, not that it controls them. That the manifestations of love in the world of nature are controlled by the laws of nature is obvious in the processes of generation, growth, and death. "There is certainly a generative power," Shelley wrote in *A Refutation of Deism*, "which is effected by particular instruments," and such "instruments" are subject to "the rigid necessity of inevitable laws."[76] Nevertheless, "eternal love" as such was neither created by necessity nor controlled by it. An individual plant or animal might be born and die in accordance with the laws of nature, but love itself, the generative force woven through the whole "web of being," would continue. Necessity might command its manifestations, but he had not created it and he could not stop it.

There is no doubt that in the references to the "voice unspoken," the "spell" being "broken," the "snake-like Doom," the opposition of "eternal love" to "Fate" and "Time," and so on, Shelley was being deliberately mystifying. He was, in effect, setting up a puzzle for his readers, but one that he felt they could solve once they grasped the meanings of Asia and Demogorgon and then related them to concepts developed fairly explicitly in Act I.

Asia asks one final question of Demogorgon:

> Prometheus shall arise
> Henceforth the sun of this rejoicing world:
> When shall the destined hour arrive? (iv.126–128)

Demogorgon answers "Behold!" and through the cave come "cars driven by rainbow-winged steeds," in each of which there stands a "wild-eyed charioteer urging their flight" (iv.130, 131). These, Demogorgon explains, are "the immortal Hours" (iv.140). One of them, he adds, "waits for thee." Asia then notices one who looks different from the others:

> A spirit with a dreadful countenance
> Checks its dark chariot by the craggy gulf.
> Unlike thy brethren, ghastly charioteer,
> What art thou? (iv.142–145)

The charioteer answers:

> I am the shadow of a destiny
> More dread than is my aspect; ere yon planet
> Has set, the Darkness which ascends with me
> Shall wrap in lasting night Heaven's kingless throne. (iv.146–149)

The "Darkness" ascending in this chariot is Demogorgon himself. As he soars upward, "blackening the night," Panthea observes another chariot drawing near:

> See, near the verge, another chariot stays;
> An ivory shell inlaid with crimson fire,
> Which comes and goes within its sculptured rim
> Of delicate strange tracery; the young spirit
> That guides it has the dove-like eyes of hope. (iv.156–160)

The chariots, as Demogorgon states, are "the immortal Hours," a concept resembling that in the *Ode to Liberty* of the "eager hours" waiting to be born in order to bring liberty to the world. The charioteer with the "dreadful countenance" who bears Demogorgon upward is the hour of the revolutionary overthrow of the old order, "the shadow of a destiny." The second chariot, meant to carry Asia and Panthea, is the hour of the beginning of the new order, its "crimson fire" perhaps symbolizing dawn, its "hope" the hope of humanity. The car of revolution goes first, bearing Demogorgon to the throne of Jupiter, whom he overthrows. The second car transports

Asia and Panthea to Prometheus, who is then "unbound." First, comes the dark hour of revolution, then the bright hour of the beginning of a new order.

The Spirit of Asia's and Panthea's chariot sings as it waits for them:

> My coursers are fed with the lightning,
> They drink of the whirlwind's stream,
> And when the red morning is bright'ning
> They bathe in the fresh sunbeam;
> They have strength for their swiftness I deem,
> Then ascend with me, daughters of Ocean. (iv.163–168)

In the next scene, as Asia and Panthea ascend with the Spirit, it sings:

> On the brink of the night and the morning
> My coursers are wont to respire;
> But the Earth has just whispered a warning
> That their flight must be swifter than fire:
> They shall drink the hot speed of desire! (v.1–5)

No two stanzas in the drama reveal so well the multiplicity of meaning in which Shelley delighted. The underlying concept of energy is both scientific and political. On the scientific meaning, King-Hele, himself a physicist, commented:

> Shelley seems to have in mind the contemporary theory which held that atmospheric electricity was drawn up from the earth by the morning sun, became quiescent at noon and returned to earth at nightfall, a theory which lent support to Adam Walker's speculation that electricity is "a child of the sun." The lines quoted may thus be paraphrased as follows. "My power unit operates by taking energy from electricity in the atmosphere. At dawn, when this elecricity is sucked out by the sun, my air intake sweeps up the ions and stores the energy. This stored energy, together with more picked up as we travel, enables us to cover hundreds of thousands of miles during the morning. But at noon we have to rest because the air is no longer active and our stored energy must not be squandered."[77]

After the Spirit has sung the second stanza, the following dialogue takes place:

> *Asia.* Thou breathest on their nostrils, but my breath
> Would give them swifter speed.
> *Spirit.* Alas! it could not. (v.6–7)

Why is there such a need for haste? And why is the power of Asia (love) unable to increase the speed of the chariot bringing the new order? The need for haste is inherent in the "warning" that the earth whispered to the Spirit, namely, the hour of revolution is at hand—the car of Demogorgon preceded Asia's—and that unless love arrives quickly, the revolution may degenerate into violence and anarchy. If love arrives close after the revolutionary hour, the new order will be born; if it does not the hour will be aborted and fade; but love can neither hasten nor retard its arrival, since this is determined by necessity alone.

Although the song embodies two kinds of meaning, social and scientific, these are clearly not on the same level. The two Oceanids, Asia and Panthea, are ascending in a chariot, whose "coursers," like those of the chariot of the Daemon of the World, represent electrical and magnetic forces, but this fact is not relevant to the action of the play. Jupiter is not being overthrown by electricity. The social meaning, implied in the importance of love being present at the birth of the new oder, is primary, the scientific is secondary.

Following the Spirit's song, the scene turns to its central theme, the transfiguration of Asia, apparently representing the new love coming to animate society as the egalitarian world order approaches. The Spirit and Panthea both perceive the change in Asia, which inspires Panthea to make the comparison with Aphrodite rising from the sea noted earlier.

Two songs follow, the first by Prometheus but sung by Panthea, the second both by Asia and sung by her. Although the two songs form a duet between lovers (part of the second song being anticipated in Shelley's "Constantia" songs to Claire Clairmont at Marlow), they reflect essentially universal and not personal love.[78] In the first song love is depicted, somewhat like the power in *Hymn to Intellectual Beauty,* as an entity that is perceived only in glimpses but which gives life its essence:

> Lamp of Earth! where'er thou movest
> Its dim shapes are clad with brightness,
> And the souls of whom thou lovest
> Walk upon the winds with lightness. (v.66–69)

Asia, inspiring love, gives love.

In the second song Asia's soul is "an enchanted boat" (v.73) guided by the spirit of Prometheus. They pass through:

> Realms where the air we breathe is love,
> Which in the winds and on the waves doth move,
> Harmonizing this earth with what we feel above. (v.95–97)

The final stanza, which follows these lines, runs:

> We have passed Age's icy caves,
> And Manhood's dark and tossing waves,
> And Youth's smooth ocean, smiling to betray:
> Beyond the glassy gulfs we flee
> Of shadow-peopled Infancy,

Through death and birth, to a diviner day;
  A paradise of vaulted bowers,
  Lit by down-gazing flowers,
  And watery paths that wind between
Wildernesses calm and green,
Peopled by shapes too bright to see,
And rest, having beheld; somewhat like thee;
Which walk upon the sea, and chant melodiously! (v.98–110)[79]

The clue to the general meaning here is contained in the final line of the preceding stanza: "Harmonizing this earth with what we feel above." The power behind nature ("above") is filled with the egalitarian essence of love, but in society as it now exists ("earth"), youth, manhood, and old age are alike filled with evil. Asia and Prometheus are, as it were, being transported by love beyond this life into the power, and as in *Hellas* and *The Triumph of Life,* the metaphor suggests transmigration. There they see the world and people as they could be. Shelley is both personifying this state and implying that in the future it will be realized—the future society will be inhabited by people of a beauty so thrilling that one cannot "rest" content after having envisaged them. This prospect, the implication runs, stimulates one to try to make the potential actual.

15

The World Transformed

Prometheus Unbound, Acts III and IV

The Fatal Child

The third act of *Prometheus Unbound* opens with the climactic scene of the overthrow of Jupiter. Seated on his throne in "Heaven," Jupiter addresses his bride, Thetis, and the other assembled deities. Speaking in hard, compact blank verse, which contrasts sharply with the preceding soaring lyrics, he complains that his ancient empire, though built on fear and superstition, has been rendered insecure, for the "soul of man" is "hurling up insurrection" (i.5, 8) against him and refuses to be subdued:

> though under my wrath's night
> It climb the crags of life, step after step,
> Which wound it, as ice wounds unsandalled feet,
> It yet remains supreme o'er misery,
> Aspiring, unrepressed. (i.13–17)

Jupiter, however, is now convinced that he is about to triumph and repress mankind completely.

Shelley indicates his basic symbolic concept of Jupiter when the Spirit of the Hour later describes the transformation of society that has taken place. It reports, "Thrones, altars, judgment-seats, and prisons" (iv164)) have been overthrown; so, too have:

> those foul shapes, abhorred by god and man,
> Which, under many a name and many a form
> Strange, savage, ghastly, dark and execrable,
> Were Jupiter, the tyrant of the world;
> And which the nations, panic-stricken, served
> With blood, and hearts broken by long hope. (iv.180–186)

Jupiter, then, is not himself only the instruments ("form") of the state, prisons, churches, armies, but the ideas ("name") that give them life and enable them to keep mankind in subjection, suffering the horrors of war and persecution—"served with blood"—and having their humanity destroyed—"hearts broken by long hope." In one aspect Jupiter is opinion, the Furies, the shadows and phantoms that emanate from the cold car of life. Basic to these are, as Jupiter declares, "eldest faith, and hell's coeval, fear" (i.10), that is, religion and superstitious fears as old as the "hell" of tyranny itself.

But Jupiter is, like Prometheus, also a character in a drama and, traditionally, "the Oppressor of mankind," as Shelley notes in the Preface. In this respect he represents the tyrants of the ages, just as Prometheus represents the rebels.

In the dethronement scene this universal tyrant aspect of Jupiter is dominant, but with special application to the tyrants of Shelley's own day. If Prometheus is a "modern Prometheus," Jupiter is a modern Jupiter. This is indicated both by his own comments and by the scene's placement in time in the drama. As the ascent of the chariot of Demogorgon was swift, with Asia having to rush to avoid falling behind, the overthrow of Jupiter must be taking place shortly after the events in Demogorgon's cave. In the opening of the dethronement scene, Jupiter is regarding the world of the early nineteenth century. The "insurrection" being mounted against him is that Shelley believed was beginning in his own day: "Well do these destroyers of mankind know their enemy, when they impute the insurrection in Greece to the same spirit before which they tremble throughout the rest of Europe, and that enemy well knows the power and the cunning of its opponents, and watches the moment of their approaching weakness and inevitable division to wrest the bloody sceptres from their grasp."[1]

The alarm of Jupiter at the "insurrection" taking place in the soul of man is similar to that of Mahmud in *Hellas* as he regards the contemporary world:

> The spirit that lifts the slave before his lord
> Stalks through the capitals of armed kings,
> And spreads his ensign in the wilderness. (351–353)

Thetis was taken by Shelley from the original Prometheus myth. She was not a character in Aeschylus' *Prometheus Bound,* and she played no major role in the traditional action of the story. She was simply the consort of Zeus who, according to the prophecy known to Prometheus, would bear a child greater than his father. When Jupiter heard of this prophecy, she was hastily wedded to Peleus. Shelley, however, makes rather ingenious use of her. The key to Thetis appears in the cryptic reference to her as the "bright image of eternity." In the *Timaeus*—the dialogue that also discusses the demiurgos—Plato refers to time as the "image of eternity."[2] Tyranny, in other words, is wedded to time. The thought is similar to that in *Sonnet: England in 1819,* where Shelley refers to the British government as "Time's worst statute unrepealed." Prometheus is linked to the eternal qualities of love and beauty, Jupiter to the passing ones of greed, hatred, and oppression.

After complaining about man's continued rebellion despite the ancient narcotics of faith and fear, Jupiter triumphantly announces that he has found a remedy:

> Even now have I begotten a strange wonder,
> That fatal child, the terror of the earth,
> Who waits but till the destined Hour arrive,
> Bearing from Demogorgon's vacant throne
> The dreadful might of ever-living limbs
> Which clothed that awful spirit unbeheld,
> To redescend, and trample out the spark. (i.18–24)

This "fatal child", a "strange wonder" and "terror of the earth," is obviously no makeshift expedient but a fundamental reactionary force that will forever "trample out the spark" of human rebellion and assume the functions of necessity (Demogorgon). The word "fatal," then, is being used for the child as it was of Demogorgon's mountain, to signify "fate,"—a child having the characteristics of fate. Jupiter also reveals that the child, the product of a mating between himself and Thetis, is a spiritual not a corporal being:

> Two mighty spirits, mingling, made a third
> Mightier than either, which, unbodied now,
> Between us floats, felt, although unbeheld,
> Waiting the incarnation, which ascends,
> (Hear ye the thunder of the fiery wheels
> Griding the winds?) from Demogorgon's throne. (i.42–48)

As C. E. Pulos argued, the "fatal child" represents the doctrines of Malthus, which were put forward in his *Essay on the Principle of Population* in 1798:

> Population, when unchecked, increases in a geometrical ration [i.e.3, 9, 27 etc]. Subsistence increases only in an arithmetical ration [i.e. 2, 4, 8 etc]. A slight acquaintance with numbers will shew the immensity of the first power in comparison of the second . . . The germs of existence contained in this spot of earth, with ample food, and ample room to expand in, would fill millions of worlds in the course of a few thousand years. Necessity, that imperious all-pervading law of nature, restrains them within the prescribed bounds. The race of plants, and the race of animals shrink under this great restrictive law. And the race of man cannot, by any efforts of reason, escape from it. Among plants and animals its effects are waste of seed, sickness, and premature death. Among mankind, misery and vice. . . I see no way by which man can escape from the weight of this law which pervades all animated nature. No fancied equality, no agrarian regulations in their utmost extent, could remove the pressure of it even for a single century. And it appears, therefore, to be decisive against the possible existence of a society, all the members of which, should live in ease, happiness, and comparative leisure; and feel no anxiety about providing the means of subsistence for themselves and families.[3]

Malthus' attack, here and throughout his essay is directed at Godwin, who had argued in *Political Justice* that the advance of the intellect was such that mankind would in time achieve an egalitarian order, in short, that man was "perfectible"—not in the sense that he would become "perfect," but that he would constantly advance toward it. In contrast, Malthus argued that whatever "necessity" was inherent in the march of the human intellect was overruled by a greater necessity: the population of the earth was increasing faster than its food supply. Hence, the population had to be kept down by starvation (poverty) and slaughter (war), and human progress was a hopeless delusion. Malthus did not mean, however, that the whole population of the earth should live in poverty. On the contrary, the status quo of a privileged few and the impoverished many would continue. "Let things be as they have ever been," as Shelley's Chorus of Malthusian Priests chanted in *Swellfoot the Tyrant* (II.ii.14). Inequality, then, was also a "necessary consequence" of the iron laws of geometric and arithmetic progression.

Malthus, therefore, was putting one law of "necessity" in place of another, and this is precisely what Jupiter proposes to do with his "fatal child." As Shelley had already hinted that Demogorgon was necessity in the Godwinian sense, presumably he thought that in view of the then current controversy over Malthus, his readers would see that the other necessity to take the place of the Godwinian necessity and repress the "soul of man" must be the Malthusian necessity. Furthermore, he apparently tucked into his description one of those esoteric references in which he delighted. Among Malthus' most bitter opponents was William Hazlitt, who charged that Malthus' name hung over the heads of the liberals "*In terrorem* like some baleful meteor," which may have been the origin for Shelley's "terror of the earth."[4]

The year after completing *Prometheus Unbound*, Shelley satirized Malthus and his followers in *Swellfoot the Tyrant*, and in *A Philosophical View of Reform* he specifically denied that Malthus' views refuted the theory of a coming egalitarian order: "The doctrine of this writer is that the principle of population, when under no dominion of moral restraint, [is] outstripping the sustenance produced by the labour of man . . . I cannot imagine how the advocates of equality would so readily have conceded that the unlimited operation of the principle of population affects the truth of these theories."[5]

Shelley was disturbed not so much by the logic of Malthus' doctrine as by its influence and practical effects. Not only had the influential theologian William Paley and the Scottish philosopher Dugald Stewart taken up the doctrine (Stewart even using it to defend child labor), but liberals and radicals such as Francis Place and Richard Carlile had been influenced by it.[6] Shelley considered the doctrines of Malthus as being particularly influential in creating that "gloom and misanthropy" which had affected the liberals of his age and were holding back social progress.

Jupiter, like Malthus, or like Satan in the Prologue to *Hellas*, is confident that the "spark" of human striving will be quenched. He therefore looks forward to the return of his "fatal child" clothed in the person of Demogorgon. But this vision of eternal human misery is not to be, for the necessity which arrives to confront Jupiter is that not of Malthus but of Godwin. The Godwinian necessity of an ascending humanity is thus the true necessity.

When Jupiter, expecting his own "child," asks Demogorgon who he is, Demogorgon answers: "I am thy child, as thou wert Saturn's child." With Paine and Godwin, Shelley believed that the conditions bred by tyranny would lead inevitably to the overthrow of the existing order: "The distribution of wealth, no less than the spirit by which it is upheld and that by which it is assailed, render the event inevitable. Call it reform or revolution, as you will, a change must take place; one of the consequences of which will be, the wresting of political power from those who are at present the depositories of it."[7] In other words, the necessity that brings about Revolution is the child of tyranny.

When Jupiter asks Demogorgon who he is, he replies cryptically: "Eternity. Demand no direr name," implying that he has a "direr name" (necessity). In both the original myth and Shelley's philosophy, necessity and eternity are linked together. According to Boccaccio, Demogorgon was "the companion of Eternity," and this concept is repeated by Peacock in his note on Demogorgon in *Rhododaphne*. In *The Daemon of the World* Shelley represented necessity as part of the eternal order of things:

> The flood of ages combating below,
> The depth of the unbounded universe
>   Above, and all around
> Necessity's unchanging harmony. (I. 288–291)

But Demogorgon's answer does not primarily signify that he is an eternal force in nature. The primary meaning is, once more, social and cultural, the "Eternity warning Time" theme, and in this instance it has direct application, for Jupiter is wedded to time (Thetis). The society that Demogorgon, with Asia's help, is to bring about is one in which the "eternal" and "natural" values of love, beauty, and wisdom shall triumph. The same general thought is expressed in *Rosalind and Helen*:

> Fear not the tyrants shall rule for ever,
> Or the priests of the bloody faith;
> They stand on the brink of that mighty river,
> Whose waves they have tainted with death:
> It is fed from the depths of a thousand dells,
> Around them it foams, and rages, and swells,
> And their swords and their sceptres I floating see,
> Like wrecks in the surge of eternity. (893–901)[8]

The charge has been made that in this scene Shelley depicts the fall of Jupiter as taking place too swiftly. But this is a scene in a symbolic drama, not a passage in a political tract. Shelley gave his views on what was actually involved in the fall of Jupiter in the Preface to *Hellas*: "Of this holy alliance all the despots of the earth are virtual members. But a new race has risen throughout Europe, nursed in the abhorrence of the opinions which are its chains, and she will continue to produce fresh generations to accomplish that destiny which tyrants foresee and dread."

In *A Philosophical View of Reform* he broadened the picture to include America and Asia: "The Great Monarchies of Asia cannot, let us confidently hope, remain unshaken by the earthquake which shatters to dust the 'mountainous strongholds' of the tyrants of the western world."[9] In this scene, even though his primary emphasis is on Europe, he no doubt has this vaster perspective also in mind. Certainly he felt that the struggle would be both long and violent, a worldwide revolutionary upheaval, which it would take several generations to accomplish. Shelley, then, was under no delusions about the scope or character of the coming conflict. In the symbolic, impressionistic context of *Prometheus Unbound,* however, he gives only one brief indication of it. Following the dethronement of Jupiter, in a dialogue between Apollo and Ocean (the god Oceanus), Apollo speaks of "the strife . . . which made dim/The Orb I rule, and shook the solid stars" (ii.2–3).

One reason that Shelley did not depict the strife in more detail may have been his view that many, perhaps most, of his readers had already been overly affected by the "gloom and misanthropy" of the age and were well aware of the immensity of the task ahead.[10] Hence, he may have wished to place the emphasis on the might of necessity, to demonstrate that once it began to exert its revolutionary power, the crash of despotism would be everywhere inevitable.

The Cave of the Mind

The first scene of Act III concerns the dethronement of Jupiter; the third scene depicts the unbinding of Prometheus. Apparently Shelley felt that it would be dramatically inappropriate to go directly from the one scene to the other, for he inserted between them the Ocean-Apollo episode. Another reason for doing so was perhaps to indicate the passage of time. Apollo suggests cryptically that a long and bitter struggle has taken place. Ocean remarks that certain positive changes will soon be evident. Naval battles (such as Trafalgar) will shortly be no more:

> Henceforth the fields of heaven-reflecting sea
> Which are my realm, will heave unstained with blood. (ii. 18–19)

The brutal despotism of the merchant marine and navy (attacked by Shelley in his early poem, *The Voyage*) will be abolished as the ships of peaceful commerce sail the seas:

> Tracking their path no more by blood and groans,
> And desolation, and the mingled voice
> Of slavery and command. (ii. 29–31)

After centuries of witnessing naval warfare and other horrors, the "unpastured sea" is "hungering for calm." Apollo, for his part, is glad that he will no longer have to observe from his sphere in the sun the general oppression and misery of man: "deeds which make/My mind obscure with sorrow" (ii. 35–36). In the new society the forces of nature and society will be in harmony.

The first car that arose from Demogorgon's cave, the dark car of the hour of Jupiter's overthrow, having accomplished its mission, in scene three the second car, the beautiful car of the hour of the beginning of the new society, arrives at Prometheus' "Ravine of Icy Rocks." This car bears, in addition to Asia and Panthea, Ione, the Earth, Hercules, and Spirits (including the "Spirit of the Earth"). In accordance with the myth, Prometheus is freed by Hercules, who symbolizes strength:

> Most glorious among Spirits, thus doth strength
> To wisdom, courage, and long-suffering love,
> And thee, who art the form they animate,
> Minister like a slave. (iii. 4.)

When Prometheus is released, he announces that he, Asia, Panthea, and Ione will retire to a cave:

> Henceforth we will not part. There is a cave,
> All overgrown with trailing odorous plants,
> Which curtain out the day with leaves and flowers,
> And paved with veinèd emerald, and a fountain,
> Leaps in the midst of an awakening sound
> . . . . .
> Where we will sit and talk of time and change,
> As the world ebbs and flows, ourselves unchanged.
> What can hide man from mutability? (iii.10–14,23–25)

In the cave they will hear "the echoes of the human world" (44) and perceive its arts:

> And lovely apparitions, dim at first,
> Then radiant, as the mind, arising bright
> From the embrace of beauty, whence the forms
> Of which these are the phantoms, cast on them
> The gathered rays which are reality,
> Shall visit us, the progeny immortal
> Of Painting, Sculpture, and rapt Poesy,
> And arts, though unimagined, yet to be. (iii.49–56)

According to a stage direction in the manuscript, Prometheus kisses the ground, whereupon Earth is rejuvenated:

> I hear, I feel;
> Thy lips are on me, and their touch runs down
> Even to the adamantine central gloom
> Along these marble nerves. (iii.84–87)[11]

Earth rejoices that man and all creatures and plants that formerly "drew disease and pain" from her "wan bosom" will now "take/And interchange sweet nutriment" (iii.94–96). Addressing Prometheus, she tells him of a cavern in which she suffered during his long martyrdom:

> There is a cavern where my spirit
> Was panted forth in anguish whilst thy pain
> Made my heart mad, and those who did inhale
> Became mad too, and built a temple there,
> And spoke, and were oracular, and lured
> The erring nations round to mutual war. (iii.124–129)

Her breath still rises from the cavern, but now it has a good effect, filling the "rocks and woods around" with a "serener light" (133) and feeding "the quick growth" (135) of the foliage. To guide Prometheus to the cavern, which she says is his, she summons a Spirit, to whom she gives explicit directions:

> guide this company beyond the peak
> Of Bacchic Nysa, Maenad-haunted mountain,
> And beyond Indus and its tribute rivers. (iii.153–155)

They will come to a temple which is reflected in a "crystalline pool" (159). Although this temple is now "deserted":

> once it bore
> Thy name, Prometheus; there the emulous youths
> Bore to thy honour through the divine gloom
> The lamp which was thine emblem. (iii.167–170)

Earth concludes: "Depart, farewell./Beside that temple is the destined cave" (iii.174–175).

In the first act Prometheus represented the qualities, intellectual and moral, of the humanitarian rebels, as well as the rebels themselves. It is this psychological or spiritual aspect of Prometheus that is primary in the episode of the cave. The "lovely apparitions" that "visit" Asia, and her sisters within the cave arise from the human mind under the influence of "beauty" and are the "progeny immortal" of poetry and the other arts. Shelley described the creative process similarly in *A Defence of Poetry:* "Poetry turns all things to loveliness; it exalts the beauty of that which is most beautiful, and it adds beauty to that which is most deformed." It comes to the mind in "evanescent visitations" of unknown origin. The cave, then, is apparently mind, and its fountain the source of artistic creation. The "progeny immortal" of the arts are the thoughts and images in the minds of "the Poets." The concept is similar to that in *Mont Blanc,* where the thoughts in the "human mind" of the poet visit "the still cave of the witch Poesy," which contains "the shadows . . . of all things that are."[12] Prometheus and

Asia, who represent intellectual creativity and love, have become part of the eternal stream of mind.

It has been argued that this scene is dramatically feeble, that from the Titan Prometheus one would expect heroic actions. Shelley, however, was not writing a regular play, with Prometheus as its "hero," but a "lyrical drama" with a new kind of "machinery." Once Prometheus is freed, there is no further part for him in the action. Since in the dramatic structure he was a Titan, an immortal, Shelley could hardly show him—as he did Laon—as going out among mankind to perform heroic, revolutionary deeds. And to have him overthrow Jupiter would have run contrary both to the classical tradition and to Shelley's concept of historical change as arising from necessity. Furthermore, Shelley was following the classical myth. There is no mention in the mythologists of Prometheus performing heroic deeds after his release. He merely returned to Mount Olympus and became a counselor and prophet for the gods. He went back, that is, to the abode of the immortals. Shelley, in having him retire to the cave, is giving his own symbolic version of this story.

Of the two temples mentioned by Earth, the first was built by men after breathing the vapor exhaled by Earth at the suffering of Prometheus and was dedicated to the oppression of mankind. The reference, as in Act I, is to the revengeful spirit of Earth (the common people, the tillers of the soil), provoked by the martyrdom of Prometheus. This vengeful spirit had the opposite effect to what Earth had anticipated, however, for it led not to the freeing but to the oppression of humanity (the anarchy-despotism cycle based on violence and hatred). The temple thus symbolizes religious oppression, religious wars, and the religious sanctioning of war. It is near the cave of Earth, in which she brooded over the persecution of Prometheus.

The second temple, which is "beside" Earth's cave, is dedicated to Prometheus. In the margin of Shelley's manuscript, opposite the passage on "emulous youths" bearing a torch to "honour" Prometheus, Shelley wrote: "The beginning of Plato's Republic." The reference is to the following passage:

> But you do not know, said Adimantus, that there is to be an illumination, in the evening, on horseback to the goddess.
>
> On horseback! said I, that is new. Are they to have torches, and give them to one another, contending together with their horses? or how do you mean?
>
> Just so, reply'd Polemarchus. And besides, they will perform a nocturnal solemnity worth seeing. For we shall rise after supper and see the nocturnal festival, and shall be there with many of the youth, and converse together.

The dialogue concerns a celebration in Athens for the fire gods, of whom Prometheus was the chief one. Shelley perhaps had in mind also the words of Pausanias: "in the Academy [of Plato] is an altar to Prometheus and from it they run to the city carrying burning torches." According to ancient scholars, there was in the academy not only an altar but a temple to Prometheus. Next to the academy stood the grove of Colonus, in which was a deep cavern thought to be an entrance to the underworld. It would seem, then, that Earth's references both to the temple of Prometheus and to the cave were specific and classical.[13] And this fits with her directions to the Spirit to lead Prometheus and the others from the Indian Caucasus through "Bacchic Nysa" (in what is now Afghanistan) and beyond the Indus, which would take them in a generally northwestern direction, that is, toward Greece.

Whether this temple of Prometheus is the same as the one that previously existed near the cave is not clear in the text, but it seems more likely that the two are separate, that the temple had been there many years before as the center of a reactionary creed, and that later a temple to Prometheus was established nearby. If the two had been the same, surely Earth would have commented on the fact that a temple once used for evil purposes was later used for the worship of Prometheus. The assumption seems to be that the first temple has vanished. The second one, dedicated to Prometheus, is "deserted" because it has not been used for over two thousand years. Are there also two caves, or is the cave Prometheus speaks of the same one he is directed to by Earth? Earth brings up the cave as though no cave has been mentioned before, but this is apparently because she has heard nothing of what Prometheus said before he kissed the ground, as indicated by her exclamation, "I hear, I feel." In the first act it was implied that Earth knew only the language of mortals, not that of the immortals. The kiss of Prometheus is what begins her transformation. The probability is, then, that the two caves are the same, that Prometheus has in mind the cave near his temple, and that Earth, not knowing he has spoken of it, begins all over again. That the caves are the same is indicated by the stage direction for Act IV: "A part of the forest near the cave of Prometheus." The "cave of Prometheus" would most naturally refer to the cave described by Prometheus as his future dwelling place. Yet the cave to which he and the others are being led at the end of Act III, Scene III, is the one described by Earth.

Before Prometheus enters the cave, he asks Ione to give to the Spirit of the hour a shell that Proteus formerly gave to Asia on her wedding day. According to classical tradition, Proteus had the gift of prophesying the future. Prometheus tells Ione that this "many-folded shell," which is presumably a large conch such as that used as a trumpet by Triton, has "breathing within it/A voice to be accomplished" (iii.66–67). The shell is apparently a symbol for the necessitarian power. Shelley had stated in the *Essay on Christianity* that a good and sincere person is ever "aware of benignant visitings from the invisible energies by which he is surrounded."[14] What Prometheus ("the Poets") is now able to do is to release these "energies" for all mankind. The shell of the prophetic Proteus becomes, in truth, the "trumpet of a prophecy."

The Awakened Earth

Scene IV opens with Panthea and Ione gazing in wonder at a new spirit that has come to seek out the cave of Prometheus, the Spirit of the Earth:

Ione. Sister, it is not earthly; how it glides
Under the leaves! how on its head there burns
A light, like a green star, whose emerald beams
Are twined with its fair hair! how, as it moves,
The splendour drops in flakes upon the grass!
Knowest thou it?
Panthea. It is the delicate spirit
That guides the earth through heaven. From afar
The populous constellations call that light
The loveliest of the planets; and sometimes
It floats along the spray of the salt sea,
Or makes its chariot of a foggy cloud,
Or walks through fields or cities while men sleep,
Or o'er the mountain tops, or down the rivers,
Or thro' the green waste wilderness, as now,
Wondering at all it sees. Before Jove reigned
It loved our sister Asia, and it came
Each leisure hour to drink the liquid light
Out of her eyes. (iv.1–18)

The Spirit runs to Asia and calls her "Mother dearest mother," although Panthea comments that "whence it sprang it knew not, nor do I" (iv.23).

As Asia is symbolic of love and as the Spirit feels a natural affinity for her, it must be connected with love. That it is, indeed, permeated with love is shown by the songs of the Earth and the Moon in Act IV, and by Demogorgon's comment on the Earth in his final speech:

Beautiful orb! gathering as thou dost roll
The love which paves thy path along the skies. (IV. iv.521–522)

The idea is a common one in English poetry, as in Spenser's *Hymne in Honour of Love;*

Ayre hated earth, and water hated fyre
Till love relented their rebellious yre. (83–84)

Shelley perhaps came across it first in his early favorite, Pope's *Essay on Man:*

Look round our World; behold the chain of Love
Combining all below and all above.
See plastic Nature working to this end,
The single atoms each to other tend,
Attract, attracted to, the next in place
Form'd and impell'd its neighbour to embrace. (iii.6–12)[15]

Shelley's concept of the Spirit of the Earth arises from his view that a generative force is inherent in universal matter, as he expressed it in *Adonais*, a "Light whose smile kindles the Universe" (478). He commonly connects light with love, as in the transfiguration of Asia, and associates magnetism with it also, as in *Epipsychidion* when speaking of the moon as Mary and the sun as Emilia, with himself as earth:

> Twin Spheres of light who rule this passive Earth,
> This world of love, this *me*; and into birth
> Awaken all its fruits and flowers, and dart
> Magnetic might into its central heart. (345-348)

The connection of electrical forces and of light with those of generation is implied in the fifth Spirit's song in Act I, when it speaks of "the form of Love" as:

> That planet-crested shape swept by on lightning-braided pinions,
> Scattering the liquid joy of life from his ambrosial tresses:
> His footsteps paved the world with light. (I.765–767)

Shelley unfortunately wrote little on his scientific views, but one passage in *A Refutation of Deism* succinctly presents his concept of matter:

> Doubtless no disposition of inert matter, or matter deprived of qualities, could ever have composed an animal, a tree, or even a stone. But matter deprived of qualities, is an abstraction, concerning which it is impossible to form an idea. Matter, such as we behold it is not inert. It is infinitely active and subtile. Light, electricity and magnetism are fluids not surpassed by thought itself in tenuity and activity; like thought they are sometimes the cause and sometimes the effect of motion; and, distinct as they are from every other class of substances, with which we are acquainted, seem to possess equal claims with thought to the unmeaning distinction of immateriality.[16]

Since in Shelley's day the distinction between organic and inorganic matter was not clear, one could conceive of electricity or magnetism as having a basic effect on biological forms ("an animal, a tree"). They produce atomic motion and are themselves affected by the motion they produce. These various views suggest that the Spirit of the Earth, who "guides the earth through heaven" (III.iv.6). is a representation of light, magnetism, electricity, and perhaps other physical forces that Shelley felt were connected with biological generation (love). These physical forces are represented in the green light on the spirit's head, which may be that color because Shelley felt that the earth, with its seas and forests, would appear green from another planet.[17] The light manifests itself as phosphorescence (in the sea spray), as swamp gases ("foggy cloud") which were believed to produce meteors (seen "o'er the mountain tops"), or as a will o' the wisp or similar phenomena (seen in fields, on rivers, and even in cities).

Shelley's concept of the Spirit thus seems to be primarily that of the forces of love or generation in nature, which are rooted in physical phenomena. Why, however, does he represent the Spirit as a child? And where had the Spirit been between its early union with Asia and their reunion as the new order of society is about to begin? Panthea's account of the early relationship between Asia and the Spirit apparently harks back to the mythic Golden Age, in which the early humanitarian spirit of mankind is imagined as being in harmony with that of the Earth. Later society, exploitive and oppressive, shut out this spirit so that it could not develop. Its place was taken by the crude, simple Mother earth. The Spirit as such was still in existence, but it had no relationship to mankind after love (Asia) was separated from its intellectual leaders (Prometheus). Once these two are brought together again, however, the Spirit returns. In the new order man will harness the forces of the earth—electric, magnetic, and so on—in order to develop their potential for serving mankind.

One of Shelley's dramatic objects in presenting the Spirit as a child was apparently to be able to show the beginning of the change in society from the point of view of a naive observer, close to the events, in contrast to the more intellectual and sweeping survey of the Spirit of the Hour. The Spirit of the Earth speaks first of the evil old society that it saw in its "walks o'er the green world" (iv.39). Some of its descriptions clearly come from Shelley's own embittering experiences with lawyers, moneylenders, bailiffs, and such:

> Hard-featured men, or with proud, angry looks,
> Or cold, staid gait, or false and hollow smiles,
> Or the dull sneer of self-loved ignorance,
> Or other such foul masks, with which ill thoughts
> Hide that fair being whom we spirits call man. (iv.41–45)

These experiences were all the more disturbing to Shelley because he saw the human potential beneath the "foul masks" of hypocrisy, pride, and arrogance.

The Spirit of the Hour's Protean shell is then sounded, rocking "the towers amid the moonlight" (iv.55), and the transformation begins. The "foul masks" float by in the air, "fading still/Into the winds that scattered them" (67–68). Even nature changes. The deadly "night-shade" has lost its poison, and snakes have become beautiful.[18]

The main description of the transformation comes from the Spirit of the Hour, who explains that in this new society man is "Sceptreless . . . Equal, unclassed, tribeless and nationless" (194–195). "Thrones, altars, judgment-seats, and prisons" (164) have all vanished, along with the writings that supported them (such as those of Paley and Malthus): "tomes/Of reasoned wrong glosed on by ignorance" (166–167).[19] The picture is similar in some respects to that of the United States in *A Philosophical View of Reform;*

"It has no king . . . It has no hereditary oligarchy . . . It has no established Church . . . It has no false representation." But Shelley also felt that the American republic was "remote . . . from the accuracy of ideal excellence," and that the founding fathers were aware of its inadequacies: "they observed the superiority of their own work to all the works which had preceded it, and they judged it probable that other political institutions would be discovered bearing the same relation to those which they had established which they bear to those which have preceded them."[20]

In *Prometheus Unbound* Shelley projects the image of this future state beyond a democratic republic. The American republic had no "established Church"; nevertheless it had a church. It had no king or hereditary aristocracy, but it was a society of economic inequality and slavery. It had prisons and a legal system, and these were used by the rich against the poor. It had no standing army; nevertheless it still had an army. Peace, security, and happiness would be possible only in a world in which not just monarchies were done away with ("Sceptreless"), but there were no longer nations ("nationless") or classes ("unclassed") and all people were equal economically and before the law.

It has been argued that Shelley's egalitarian order was anarchistic, as was Godwin's, but this is not at all clear. True, he believed that prisons and "judgment-seats" would disappear, but he did not state that governments would vanish. He was in favor of the American governmental system. However, he apparently still followed Godwin's concept of individual economic units based on equality of private property and had not adopted Robert Owen's view of a "socialized" industrial economy with balanced production and consumption, which required extensive governmental controls.

In the new society there will be basic psychological and moral changes. The new world will be inhabited by a new humanity:

> And behold! thrones were kingless, and men walked
> One with the other even as spirits do,
> None fawned, none trampled; hate, disdain, or fear,
> Self-love or self-contempt, on human brows
> No more inscribed, as o'er the gate of Hell,
> 'All hope abandon ye who enter here';
> None frowned, none trembled, none with eager fear
> Gazed on another's eye of cold command,
> Until the subject of a tyrant's will
> Became, worse fate, the abject of his own. (iii.131–140)[21]

These changes Shelley conceived of as coming about gradually and in stages, intermingled with social and political movement. Indeed, without such psychological and moral changes, mankind could not advance to the egalitarian world order. The French Revolution collapsed because social progress was not accompanied by moral progress: "The Revolution in France overthrew the hierarchy, the aristocracy, and the monarchy, and the whole of that peculiarly insolent and oppressive system on which they were based. But as it only partially extinguished those passions which are the spirit of these forms a reaction took place which has restored in a certain limited degree the old system."[22]

Just as the social changes in the new world order will be much greater than in the American republic, so too will be the psychological and moral changes. The key to the total change is equality. When no man has superior wealth or power, there will be no need for either fawning or trampling. The individual who does not have to fawn will not fall into the morass of "self-contempt," nor will the one who has no need to trample succumb to "Self-love." The "eye of cold command" will vanish because the power to command has been dissipated. The "eager fear" of sycophancy will be no more because no person will have political or economic power over another. Shelley, in essence, is depicting not a psychological miracle but a transformation resulting from social change. In this he was in accord with the most advanced social thought of his day. Ultimately the concept goes back to the contentions of Rousseau and the French encyclopedists that man is not naturally evil but good, and that social evil arises from the "institutions" of society, from which it follows that human nature is not immutable but will change if the social structure changes.

One psychological change which Shelley emphasizes is that expected to take place in women:

> And women, too, frank, beautiful, and kind
> As the free heaven which rains fresh light and dew
> On the wide earth, past; gentle radiant forms,
> From custom's evil taint exempt and pure;
> Speaking the wisdom once they could not think,
> Looking emotions once they feared to feel,
> And changed to all which once they dared not be,
> Yet being now, make earth like heaven; nor pride,
> Nor jealousy, nor envy, nor ill shame,
> The bitterest of those drops of treasured gall,
> Spoilt the sweet taste of the nepenthe, love. (iii.153–163)[23]

The potential of women in civilized society from its beginnings had, Shelley felt, been even less realized than that of men. The reason was that women were subjected to greater restrictions than were men of the same social classes. Women, like men, became what each society made them. In Periclean Athens, for instance: "The women, thus degraded, became such as it was expected they would become. They possessed, except with extraordinary exceptions, the habits and the qualities of slaves . . . They were certainly devoid of that moral and intellectual loveliness with which the acquisition of knowledge and the cultivation of sentiment animates as with another life of overpowering grace the lineaments and the gestures of every form which it inhabits."

Shelley's reason for wishing women to have "moral and intellectual loveliness" was not only that human relationships would benefit but that women could make greater cultural and social contributions to society: "and all the virtue and the wisdom of the Periclean age arose under other institutions in spite of the diminution which personal slavery and the inferiority of women, recognized by law and by opinion, must have produced in the delicacy, the strength, the comprehensiveness, and the accuracy of their conceptions in moral, political and metaphysical science and perhaps in every other art and science."[24] The character of the Periclean age, that is, would have been improved if women had been free to influence it. Women not only would have added to the existing culture in the same way as men but would have changed it, because women can add qualities that men cannot. Shelley expressed the same concept a year earlier in *The Revolt of Islam* in the character and actions of Cythna.

The repression of women, however, had made it difficult for them to develop the "wisdom" of which they were capable, presumably not only wisdom in general but also the particular kind of wisdom that they potentially possess. The same repressive forces had prevented them from fully expressing their emotions, in particular those of sexual love. The corrupting forces of society had made women, like men, proud, jealous, and envious—attitudes that they again expressed in their own special ways, particularly in the realm of relations between the sexes. Worst of all was "ill-shame," presumably the sense of shame in sexual love engendered by church doctrines and social taboos. All these factors spoilt the relations between man and woman; as a result, life was "poisoned in its wells."[25] One force that had specifically distorted and thwarted these relationships was reactionary laws:

> and love
> Dragged to his altars soiled and garlandless,
> And slain amid men's unreclaiming tears. (185–187)

The reference is apparently to executions for adultery, and there is no doubt that Shelley's new men and women in the egalitarian order would not be restrained by legal marriage ties.[26] Shelley hesitates to express this directly, because it would have brought down such denunciations on the poem as to have reduced even further the small number of "enlightened" readers anticipated.

The vision of the future ends with a passage that, before the later addition of a fourth act, was intended to conclude the drama:

> The loathesome mask has fallen, the man remains—
> Sceptreless, free, uncircumscribed, but man—
> Equal, unclassed, tribeless and nationless,
> Exempt from awe, worship, degree, the king
> Over himself just, gentle, wise—but man.

Passionless? no: yet free from guilt or pain,
Which were, for his will made, or suffered them,
Nor yet exempt, though ruling them like slaves,
From chance, and death, and mutability,
The clogs of that which else might oversoar
The loftiest star of unascended heaven,
Pinnacled dim in the intense inane. (III.iv.193–204)

The opening lines emphasize the fact that the new world order can be accomplished by "man" alone. No "God," no miracle, is required. Humanity, in the new soxiety, will still be humanity, even though transformed. In effect, Shelley is saying to his readers that they themselves can accomplish these changes; the revolution is within human power. But there is also the implication in "man" of human limitations. Accident, death, and the life cycle remain. They can be controlled by science ("ruling them like slaves"), but they cannot be eliminated. And if they exist some "grief" and "pain" will exist also. If, however, humanity could conquer "chance, and death, and mutability," those "clogs" of its spirit, it could control nature absolutely.

The Conquest of Science

Act IV of *Prometheus Unbound* is a lyrical tribute to the new society, its dominant note the conquest of the world by humanity with the aid of science. Although it is not broken into scenes it consists of three main episodes: the vision of the Hours and Spirits of the new order, the vision of the renovated Earth and Moon, and the epilogic message of Demogorgon.

The act opens with Panthea and Ione sleeping in front of the cave of Prometheus at dawn. As they wake up, they see "A Train of dark forms and Shadows" pass by, singing:

Here, oh! here:
We bear the bier
Of the Father of many a cancelled year
Spectres we
Of the dead Hours be,
We bear Time to his tomb in eternity. (10–14)

These "dark Forms and Shadows," as they state here and as Panthea tells Ione a few lines later, are the "past hours," the hours of the old order, the order of exploitation, injustice, and inequality that has existed since the beginning of civilization. On the mythological level the stanza simply signifies that Jupiter ("Father" and "Time" are in opposition) is being buried, for Jupiter was also known as the King of the Hours (Horae):

Be the faded flowers
Of Death's bare bowers
Spread on the corpse of the King of Hours! (18–20)

The Hours of the past society, then, are burying their king—Jupiter, Time—and are also symbolically burying the old order, one presided over, as Shelley saw it, by fleeting evil rather than the eternal values of love and beauty.[27]

As the past hours vanish they sing:

We melt away
Like dissolving spray
From the children of a diviner day. (24–26)

The "children" are the Hours of the new society. As the (symbolic) dawn deepens, these new Hours appear, singing in semichoruses:

Semichorus I. An hundred ages we had been kept
Cradled in visions of hate and care,
And each one who waked as his brother slept,
Found the truth—
Semichorus II. Worse than his visions were!
Semichorus I. We have heard the lute of Hope in sleep;
We have known the voice of Love in dreams;
We have felt the wand of Power, and leap—
Semichorus II. As the billows leap in the morning beams! (61–68)

Here, as in *Ode to Liberty,* Shelley imagines the Hours as awaiting their birth through the ages. Both in dreams and in fitful periods of waking they have occasionally glimpsed the "hate and care" that dominated the world under the old order of tyranny, but recently they have had premonitions of a new order of hope and love. They could not however, be born until they felt the "wand of Power" (Demogorgon, historical necessity). Now that they have, they "leap" into life.

These Hours of the new society are joined by the "Spirits of the human mind" (82), representing the psychological transformation of mankind:

We come from the mind
Of human kind,
Which was late so dusk, and obscene, and blind;
Now 'tis an ocean
Of clear emotion,
A heaven of serene and mighty motion. (93–98)

They will create a new art and a new science:

From the temples high
Of Man's ear and eye,
Roofed over Sculpture and Poesy;

From the murmurings
Of the unsealed springs
Where Science bedews her Daedal wings. (111–116)

In spite of the stylistic lightness of the verse, the emphasis is on power, the power of a freed humanity. The human mind has become one "mighty" mover, like the winds sweeping the sky or the ocean, and will soar upward on the wings of science, fulfilling the ambitions of Daedalus.

The Hours of the new society, presumably representing external social and cultural changes, and the Spirits of the mind of that society sing together in chorus of the conquests they will make together, not on earth only but in the universe:

Our spoil is won,
Our task is done,
We are free to dive, or soar, or run
Beyond and around
Or within the bound
Which clips the world with darkness round.

We'll pass the eyes
Of the starry skies
Into the hoar deep to colonize:
Death, Chaos, and Night,
From the sound of our flight,
Shall flee, like mist from a tempest's might;

And Earth, Air, and Light,
And the Spirit of Might,
Which drives round the stars in their fiery flight;
And Love, Thought, and Breath,
The powers that quell Death,
Wherever we soar shall assemble beneath.

And our singing shall build
In the void's loose field
A world for the Spirit of Wisdom to wield;
We will take our plan
From the new world of man,
And our work shall be called the Promethean. (138–158)

Shelley's interest in science did not, as is sometimes implied, cease at an early age, with Adam Walker's lectures at Eton or his reading of Erasmus Darwin. In November 1816, he and Mary were reading "Davy's 'Chemistry,'" Sir Humphry Davy's *Elements of Chemical Philosophy*, which he had ordered from Thomas Hookham in 1812. In 1820 Mary noted that she and Shelley had read "Astronomy in the Encyclopedia," probably referring to the article on astronomy in *The British Encyclopedia,* edited by William Godwin's friend William Nicholson. In February 1821 Shelley sent for the "most copious and correct history of the discoveries of Geology," adding: "If one publication does not appear to contain what I require, send me two or three." In April 1822 he sent for works by Laplace, Herschel, and Cuvier, as well as a book on geology. The astronomical scope of the above stanzas is revealed by a passage from Shelley's essay *On the Devil, and Devils:*

> The late invention and improvement in telescopes has considerably enlarged the notions of men respecting the bounds of the Universe. It is discovered that the earth is a comparatively small globe in a system consisting of a multitude of others which roll round the Sun; and there is no reason to suppose but that all these are inhabited by organized and intelligent beings. The fixed stars are supposed to be suns, each of them the center of a system like ours. Those little whitish specks of light that are seen in a clear night are discovered to consist of a prodigious multitude of suns, each probably the center of a system of planets. The system of which our earth is a planet has been discovered to belong to one of those larger systems of suns, which when seen at a distance look like a whitish speck of light; and that lustrous streak called the Milky Way is found to be one of the extremities of the immense group of suns in which our system is placed. The heaven is covered with an incalculable number of these white specks, and the better the telescopes the more are discovered and the more distinctly the confusion of white light is resolved into stars.[28]

The concepts in this passage are based, in the main, on two seminal sources, Kant and Herschel, whose ideas pervaded the science of the age. Kant was one of the first to grasp the size of the universe. Prior to his speculations, scientists, such as Galileo and Newton, had concerned themselves primarily with the solar system. The realm of the "fixed stars" was of secondary interest. Kant argued that the stars seemed to be "fixed" only because their motions were so vast that astronomers had not detected them, and in 1755 he posited a stellar space immense beyond conception.

Kant's vision was extraordinary in that it was based on the findings of the comparatively small telescopes of his day. The "improvement in Telescopes" that Shelley mentions was mostly Herschel's work, culminating in a forty-foot reflecting telescope in 1789, as a result of which Herschel was able to reveal the immensity of the universe suggested by Kant. For instance, although the distance from the earth to a star was not determined accurately until 1838, Herschel succeeded in making rough calculations, with which Shelley was acquainted.[29] It was Herschel who resolved the many nebulae —"little whitish specks of light"—into "star clusters," each consisting of suns with their planets which might be "habitable"—a theory held also by Adam Walker. And Herschel demonstrated that the Milky Way, "that shining zone," is a vast whirling wheel of which our sun is part.[30]

In addition to Shelley's picture of the immensity of the universe, the chorus of Spirits reveals two other aspects of it that are not brought out in the essay *On the Devil, and Devils,* namely, its constant motion and the nature of space beyond it. Both concepts have roots in Kant and Herschel. Kant argued that "the movement of the suns of the starry heavens goes round a common center" and that these sun systems were infinite in extent.[31] In the 1780s Herschel demonstrated that certain pairs of stars rotated around each other, that the stars of the Milky Way, including our sun, whirled in an immense orbit, and that the Milky Way as a whole was itself moving through space. It is this motion of the stars to which Shelley is referring in the third stanza. The "Spirit of Might" that drives the stars is gravitation.

As a result of his observations of nebulae, Herschel became convinced that stars were formed from them and that beyond the stars in space was "a canopy of discrete nebulous masses." Stellar space was finite, even "confined." No doubt Shelley, as Carl Grabo argued, is referring to this outer nebulous space beyond the stars in the lines:

> We'll pass the eyes
> Of the starry skies
> Into the hoar deep to colonize. (141–143)[32]

The same remote region is referred to in the phrase "the void's loose field." Grabo was also correct in contending that by "the world" in the first stanza Shelley means not the earth but the universe. That he could not here mean the earth is shown by the fact that the earth is not clipped "round" with "darkness."[33] In contrast, the stellar universe, as Herschel conceived of it, is. Shelley used "world" in this universal sense in *The Daemon of the World* (I, 225–227) and in *Ode to Liberty*: "The daedal earth,/That island in the ocean of the world" (18–19).

The Spirits of the human mind, then, are envisaged as sweeping out beyond the stellar universe to create a new "world," presumably a new planet. They will create this world through a combination of matter in its various forms ("Earth, Air, and Light"), gravitation, and human power ("Love, Thought, and Breath"). That Shelley conceives of this world as being formed from the matter of nebulae is indicated later:

> We whirl, singing loud, round the gathering sphere,
> Till the trees, and the beasts, and the clouds appear
> From its chaos made calm by love, not fear. (171–173)

The "gathering sphere" seems to describe the formation of solid matter from the stuff of nebulae, as anticipated by Kant and depicted most vividly by Shelley's early favorite, Laplace.[34] The new world will be formed by human intervention ("love"), not by the undirected, brute force of gravity, which Herschel argued was the dominant force in the formation of stars from nebulae. The essence of Shelley's concept is that humanity will in time not only run its own planet with the aid of science but will establish controls over other parts of the universe also. How he expected man actually to create a new planet beyond the known stellar universe is not clear, especially since he was aware of the extent of space involved. "Some idea may be gained of the immense distance of the fixed stars," he wrote in the Notes to *Queen Mab*, "when it is computed that many years would elapse before light could reach this earth from the nearest of them."[35]

The Earth and the Moon

Scarcely have the Spirits and the Hours left, some to conquer space, others to develop the new society on earth—"Let some depart, and some remain" (160)—than Panthea and Ione, who are still in the forest near the cave, see a new vision: a chariot and a sphere coming through "two openings in the forest" (194), out of which flow "two runnels of a rivulet" (196). The chariot, whose wheels are "solid clouds" (214), has an "orblike canopy" (210) over it, and inside sits a "winged infant" (219) of extraordinary whiteness, holding in its hand a "quivering moon-beam" "from whose point/ A guiding power directs the chariot's prow." The sphere contains ten thousand orbs, between each of which are transparent shapes. In the center of the sphere the Spirit of the Earth is laid asleep" (265). Parallelling the moonbeam in the white infant's hand is a star on the Spirit's forehead, from which whirl "vast beams" (274) that penetrate the geological layers of the earth and reveal its history: "the melancholy ruins/Of cancelled cycles" (288–289). As these descriptions and the succeeding dialogue make clear, the chariot is the moon and the sphere is the earth, the figures within them representing their "Spirits." In these descriptions Shelley obviously has scientific meanings in mind, but his colorful language makes it difficult to perceive how specific these meanings are. One example is the description of the moon's "winged infant":

> Its hair is white, the brightness of white light
> Scattered in strings; yet its two eyes are heavens
> Of liquid darkness, which the Deity
> Within seems pouring, as a storm is poured
> From jagged clouds, out of their arrowy lashes,
> Tempering the cold and radiant air around,
> With fire that is not brightness. (224–230)

This description, as Carl Grabo pointed out, is exact in terms of the scientific knowledge of Shelley's day. The hair and all other features of the infant are white because the moon has no atmosphere to act as a prism to break the light of the sun into its constituent colors.[36] The light is also "scattered in strings" because of the lack of atmosphere: if there were an atmosphere, the light would be bent, like a stick in water.[37] The eyes with their "liquid darkness" are almost certainly volcanoes. Both Kant and Herschel speculated about such volcanoes, and the subject was popularized by Erasmus Darwin.[38] The "fire that is not brightness" apparently refers to another of Herschel's discoveries, namely, that certain invisible rays beyond the red end of the spectrum (now known as the "infrared") transmit heat.[39] The "guiding power" that emanates from the moonbeams in the infant's hand is presumably, as for the earth earlier in the act, a combination of gravity, light, electricity, and magnetism.

The nature of the "sphere" of the earth, and of its whirling orbs within, presents an even more complex problem than that of the moon:

> And from the other opening in the wood
> Rushes, with loud and whirlwind harmony,
> A sphere, which is as many thousand spheres,
> Solid as crystal, yet through all its mass
> Flow, as through empty space, music and light:
> Ten thousand orbs involving and involved,
> Purple and azure, white, and green, and golden,
> Sphere within sphere; and every space between
> Peopled with unimaginable shapes,
> Such as ghosts dream dwell in the lampless deep,
> Yet each inter-transpicuous; and they whirl
> Over each other with a thousand motions,
> Upon a thousand sightless axles spinning,
> And, with the force of self-destroying swiftness,
> Intensely, slowly, solemnly roll on,
> Kindling with mingled sounds, and many tones,
> Intelligible words and music wild.
> With mighty whirl the multitudinous orb
> Grinds the bright brook into an azure mist
> Of elemental subtlety, like light;
> And the wild odour of the forest flowers,
> The music of the living grass and air,
> The emerald light of leaf-entangled beams
> Round its intense yet self-conflicting speed,
> Seem kneaded into one aereal mass
> Which drowns the sense. (238–263)

The key to this passage lies not in the astronomical but chemical investigations of the age. Chemists had begun to discover a vast number of chemical compounds and were attempting to reduce them to the "elements" of which they were formed. Lavoisier, for instance, in one of the best-known chemical textbooks of the time (1789) listed eighteen metals that became oxides by combination with the element oxygen, as well as various salts, acids, and gases that were formed by combinations of two or more elements. The first attempt in England to construct a table of atomic weights was made by John Dalton, who in 1804 listed twenty-one elements that in combination produced innumerable compounds, solid, liquid, and gaseous. All the phenomena of nature, it was becoming apparent, were manifestations of chemical compounds, which themselves were the result of combinations of elements. In a further attempt to determine what actually constituted the elements, Dalton demonstrated that they were the result of specific molecular or atomic attractions. Water, for instance, as Cavendish had shown in 1783, was a compound of two molecules of hydrogen and one of oxygen. Dalton argued that all such combinations could take place only in certain proportions. "The elements of oxygen," he wrote, "may combine with a certain proportion of nitrous gas or with twice that portion, but with no intermediate quantity."[40] Shelley probably first learned of these chemical investigations from Adam Walker, whose writings show him to have been a man of wide-ranging interests, and well aware of all major scientific discoveries and theories. Then, in Sir Humphrey Davy's *Chemical Philosophy*, he would have found passages such as the following:

> Since all matter may be made to fill a smaller volume by cooling, it is evident that the particles of matter must have space between them; and since every body can communicate the power of expansion to a body of lower temperature, that is, can give an expansive motion to its particles, it is a probable inference that its own particles are possessed of motion; but as there is no change in the position of its parts as long as its temperature is uniform, the motion if it exists, must be a vibratory or undulatory motion, or a motion of the particles round their axes, or a motion of particles round each other.[41]

This general concept of matter as essentially active is similar to ideas expressed by Shelley in *A Refutation of Deism*, except that Davy discussed such activity in terms of "particles," Shelley in terms of the "fluids," as they were then usually called, of electricity, magnetism, and light. Davy's particles" clearly referred to molecules or atoms.

These early views of matter provide the key to Shelley's description of the earth. Within the orb of the replica of the earth "ten thousand orbs" are whirling; within these whirl still smaller orbs—"Sphere within sphere"—and each of them seems to cut through the orbits of the others: "involving and involved." This picture is an impressionistic rendering of matter—gaseous, liquid, and solid—following the general lines of Davy's and Dalton's views. The larger orbs are most likely chemical compounds; the smaller ones, elements; and the still smaller ones, molecules and atoms, the difference between which was not clear at the time. The compounds are made up of elements, and the elements of molecules and atoms. Out of the total come all the phenomena of nature,—air, ocean, land, and life. By endowing his orbs with color, Shelley presumably is suggesting that all the colors of nature are inherent within them, to be brought out by light.

Between the whirling and interlocking orbs is space. In this space are "unimaginable shapes/ Such as ghosts dream dwell in the lampless deep." The "lampless deep" is apparently another reference to the cosmic space that

Herschel argued existed beyond the stellar universe. Of the shapes themselves Shelley indicates only that they are "inter-transpicuous." "Transpicuous," which literally means "to see through," is an obsolete synonym for "transparent." By "inter-transpicuous" Shelley apparently means that the shapes flow invisibly through one another. Thus, they probably represent the basic constitutients of the "fluids" of electricity, magnetism, sound, and light. This is indicated also by the earlier lines on "music and light" flowing through the apparently solid orb "as through empty space." By "music and light" Shelley must mean more than sound and light, for although both penetrate air, they do not generally penetrate solid matter. However, electricity and magnetism do.

Shelley's picture, then, is a kind of "dance of matter," with the compounds, elements, molecules, and atoms depicted as orbs whirling within orbs, the electric and other "fluids" depicted as interpenetrative shapes flowing between them. Although the image of the orbs seems to favor the particle theory of matter, this is not certain. The orbs whirling on "sightless" (invisible) axles could be regarded either as particles or as fields of force. And nowhere else does Shelley commit himself to either theory. In the Notes to *Queen Mab*, for instance, he wrote on the disputed question of the nature of light: "Light consists either of vibrations propagated through a subtle medium, or of numerous minute particles repelled in all directions from the luminous body." Apparently he held the same noncommittal attitude toward other forms and manifestations of matter, as did Sir Humphrey Davy also: "Whether matter consists of individual corpuscles, or physical points endowed with attraction and repulsion, still the same conclusions may be formed concerning the powers by which they act, and the quantities in which they combine, and the powers seem capable of being measured by their electrical relations, and the quantities on which they act of being expressed by numbers."[42] The extraordinary feature of Shelley's picture, as Desmond King-Hele, himself a physicist, pointed out, is the degree to which it anticipates modern physics, not in details but in general conception.[43] This anticipation is not simply a matter of Shelley's reflecting the experimental science of his time but of imaginatively reaching beyond it, to pick out with intelligent discrimination from a vast mass of material the essential elements.

The orbs Shelley described as whirling with "self-destroying swiftness" but as being saved from actual destruction by the brook, which they stir into "an azure mist/Of elemental subtilty, like light." This mist is apparently the "ether" that Newton had declared to be an omnipresent entity, "much subtler" than air, through which light and other waves traveled.[44] It is the same "ether" that Shelley had in mind in the "subtle medium" reference in *Queen Mab*. His general concept is that the universal energy of the earth, or the sun, or just of matter in motion would wear itself out in time if it were not somehow renewed. What renews it he does not say. The "brook" is his usual symbol for the source of life and energy, as in *The Triumph of*

Life, and here he conceives of this source as being converted into the ether by mechanical or other action, with the suggestion that the ether is the basic element of matter in all its forms.

At the end of the passage Shelley depicts the Spirit of the earth as sleeping within its orb. Panthea comments that the Spirit seems to be talking in its sleep. Ione replies: " 'Tis only mocking the orb's harmony" (269). Shelley uses "mocking" here, as in *Ozymandias,* in the old sense of "imitating." The Spirit of the earth is simply echoing or repeating words and music coming from the orb of the earth. It has no independent being and can give no answer beyond what nature and science reveal.

Shelley refers several times to the music that the Spirit echoes. Panthea and Ione hear the music before they see the orb and the chariot:

> *Panthea.* 'Tis the deep music of the rolling world
> Kindling within the strings of the waved air
> Æolian modulations.
> *Ione.* Listen, too,
> How every pause is filled with under-notes . . . (186–189)

The general reference is clearly to the "music of the spheres." Although Shelley knew that this concept as traditionally presented, had no scientific basis, he perhaps believed that there were sounds involved in planetary and atomic motion (as the "under-notes" may suggest). King Hele commented that Adam Walker in his lectures repeated Newton's argument that "the widths of spectrum occupied by each of the seven colours correspond exactly with the frequency-differences between the seven musical notes." There were also experiments in Shelley's day, published in *Nicholson's Journal,* showing that of various gases each had "its characteristic tone and quality" of sound. It seemed reasonable to deduce that motion would produce sound, and that regular motion, such as that of the planets or of whirling elements and atoms, might produce a kind of music. Shelley is also emphasizing, in the concepts of both music and color, the beauty of the various forms of chemical or physical activity that the scientists were unveiling.[45]

In Shelley's view of the earth, the star on the forehead of the Spirit of the earth shoots out rays that are able to penetrate matter. This is presumably the same star that was described on the Spirit's first appearance in Act III. In Act III, however, the beams were "emerald" and flashed out into space. Now they are "like swords of azure fire" and fill "the abyss" (the earth's center) with "sun-like lightnings," which "Pierce the dark soil" and "make bare the secrets of the earth's deep heart." Once more Shelley may be equating these beams with the "fluids" of electricity and magnetism, which penetrate matter, and he may have hoped that by their use science would be able to trace the history of the earth. As the beams flash upward—out from the interior of the earth, where the Spirit is, toward the surface—Shelley depicts their geological surroundings. The picture is divided into two parts, first "the earth's deep heart," and then the sedimentary rocks near the surface. In the light of modern knowledge, one might assume that the "deep heart" refers to the center of the earth, about three thousand miles down, but it becomes clear from the description that Shelley is using the phrase to cover everything below the surface rocks and clays. The "deep heart" contains:

Infinite mines of adamant and gold,
Valueless stones, and unimagined gems,
And caverns on crystalline columns poised
With vegetable silver overspread;
Wells of unfathomed fire, and watersprings
Whence the great sea, even as a child is fed,
Whose vapours clothe earth's monarch mountain-tops
With kingly, ermine snow. (280–287)

The concepts here stem from Leibnitz whose theories entered the popular science of Shelley's day. Leibnitz, followed by Buffon, argued that the earth had a molten core and that nearer the surface there were great caverns filled with air and water which sometimes collapsed and flooded the earth.[46] Until it was demonstrated that rainfall, past and present, would account for the seas, lakes, and rivers of the earth, the old belief in "waters under the earth" persisted, and this is what Shelley has in mind here. Although he pictures the rise of vapor from the waters of the earth's surface as turning into snow on the mountaintops, he believed with Leibnitz that the seas were fed by underground springs from deep caverns of water.

The picture of the near-surface section of the earth is a vivid if incongruous mixture of geological, archeological, and historical materials:

The beams flash on
And make appear the melancholy ruins
Of cancelled cycles—anchors, beaks of ships,
Planks turned to marble, quivers, helms, and spears,
And gorgon-headed targes, and the wheels
Of scythèd chariots, and the emblazonry
Of trophies, standards, and armorial beasts.—
Round which Death laughed, sepulchred emblems
Of dead Destruction, ruin within ruin!
The wrecks beside of many a city vast,
Whose population which the earth grew over
Was mortal, but not human; see, they lie,
Their monstrous works, and uncouth skeletons,
Their statues, homes and fanes; prodigious shapes
Huddled in gray annihilation, split,
Jammed in the hard, black deep; and over these,
The anatomies of unknown winged things,
And fishes which were isles of living scale,

And serpents, bony chains, twisted around
The iron crags, or within heaps of dust
To which the tortuous strength of their last pangs
Had crushed the iron crags; and over these
The jagged alligator, and the might
Of earth-convulsing behemoth, which once
Were monarch beasts, and on the slimy shores,
And weed-overgrown continents of earth,
Increased and multiplied like summer worms
On an abandoned corpse, till the blue globe
Wrapped deluge round it like a cloak, and they
Yelled, gasped, and were abolished; or some God
Whose throne was in a comet, passed, and cried,
"Be not!" And like my words they were no more. (287–318)

As the concluding lines reveal, the picture is based on Cuvier's famed catastrophe theory, which posited neither a divine creation nor an evolutionary progression but a series of natural creations and destructions.[47]

As the x-raylike beams on the head of the Spirit of the Earth flash upward through the strata of the rocks toward the surface of the earth, they show first the relics of past civilizations ("cancelled cycles"), including some inhabited by creatures that were "mortal but not human," which presumably derives from current speculation on the ape ancestry of man. Then come the fossils of "unknown winged things" (presumably petrodactyls), of strange fish, serpents, alligators, and mammoths.

Shelley had similarly mixed geological and historical changes in an early letter, when speaking of the English Lake District:

Imagination is resistlessly compelled to look back upon the myriad ages whose silent change placed them here, to look back when, perhaps this retirement of peace and mountain-simplicity, was the Pandemonium of druidical imposture, the scene of Roman Pollution, the resting place of the savage denizen of these solitudes with the wolf.—Still, still further! Strain thy reverted Fancy when no rocks, no lakes,—no cloud-soaring mountains were here, but a vast populous and licentious city stood in the midst of an immense plain, myriads flocked towards it; London itself scarcely exceeds it in the variety, the extensiveness of [or?] consummateness of its corruption![48]

The idea here is that the Roman civilization, combined with the society of the "Druids" or ancient Britains, whom they conquered, was preceded by a period in which there had been both a geological change, producing the mountains and lakes, and a prior civilization. Such incongruities were rationally conceivable only in terms of a series of catastrophes, in which geological and historical changes were wiped out and new cycles begun. In *Prometheus Unbound*, Shelley suggests two causes for such a catastrophe: a flood of unstated origin, but presumably coming from the caverns under the earth, or the gravitational pull of a comet passing near the earth. The second theory was approved by Sir Humphrey Davy: "We perceive the effects of this great catastrophe [the deluge], but the immediate material cause of it can never be distinctly developed. The hypothesis of Leibnitz, extended by Whiston, that it was produced by the attraction of a comet upon the waters of the ocean, is, perhaps, the most plausible that has been advanced; and when taken with limitation, the most adequate."[49]

Shelley, like Davy, presumably accepted the catastrophe theory because it made possible on the basis of unknown but not unreasonable factors what otherwise seemed impossible. Even though he accepted the theory, however, he grasped something of the essence of the evolutionary process. His picture of the "prodigious shapes Huddled in grey annihilation" and "Jammed in the hard, black deep" shows a vivid realization of the reality (revealed, for instance, in the La Brea tar pits of southern California).

In his descriptions of the earth and moon, as in his previous depiction of the universe, Shelley is not simply attempting to put science into verse but giving what he believed was a deeper picture of reality than had been available to poets of the past. The findings of Herschel, Priestley, Davy, Dalton, Cavendish, and others had, he believed, penetrated further into the forces behind the appearances of nature than had ever been done before. True, they had not revealed the full picture, but Shelley seems to have felt that certain broad truths had been established, such as that the universe was of an immensity not hitherto recognized, that matter was more space than solid and was infinitely active, and that the phenomena of the earth came not from divine creation but from vast natural processes extending over a period of "Thrice three hundred thousand years" (I. 74).

Following the description of the earth and its history come the songs of the Earth and the Moon. That the Earth is masculine and the Moon feminine and their relationship is that of lovers becomes evident in the first song of the Moon:

> Some Spirit is darted like a beam from thee,
> Which penetrates my frozen frame,
> And passes with the warmth of flame,
> With love, and odour, and deep melody
> Through me, through me! (327–331)

In view of the sexual symbolism in *Epipsychidion*, there can be no doubt that Shelley intended these lines and others to have a sexual connotation. This is indicated also in the final words of the Earth to the Moon:

> O gentle Moon, thy crystal accents pierce
> The cavern of my pride's deep universe,
> Charming the tiger joy, whose tramplings fierce
> Made wounds which need thy balm. (499–502)

These lines admit no other but a sexual meaning. The "tiger joy" connected with "pride" and "trampling" and making "wounds" must refer to sadistic excitement connected with the male sexual urge, an excitement which can be quieted only by the feminine "balm" of the Moon.

In other passages there is a combination of sexual and scientific concepts, as when the Moon sings:

I, thy crystal paramour,
Borne beside thee by a power
Like the polar Paradise,
Magnet-like, of lovers' eyes;
I, a most enamoured maiden
Whose weak brain is overladen
With the pleasure of her love,
Maniac-like around thee move
Gazing, an insatiate bride,
On thy form from every side
Like a Maenad round the cup
Which Agave lifted up
In the weird Cadmaean forest.
Brother, wheresoe'er thou soarest
I must hurry, whirl and follow
Through the heavens wide and hollow,
Sheltered by the warm embrace
Of thy soul from hungry space. (463–480)

The "polar Paradise" (363) refers to the magnetic poles of the earth and the moon, as well as to the time in which it was thought that the earth's poles would be on the same plane as the sun, so that the earth would cease to tilt and the arctic and antarctic regions would become warm.[50] It was further believed in Shelley's day that "the magnetic virtue of the earth pervades the region of the moon." "Maniac-like" refers to the eccentric movement of the moon on its axis known as "libration," caused by the dual gravitational attraction of the sun and the earth. In the final lines the "warm embrace" characterizes the power of the earth that keeps the moon from spinning off into space. This force is gravity, but Shelley may have believed that heat was also active in the process. Adam Walker had argued that the heat from the sun helped to keep the planets from breaking their orbits, and the word "warm" indicates that Shelley had a similar concept in mind here.[51]

Coupled with these scientific ideas in Shelley's mind was the picture on an altar that he had recently seen in Florence depicting the dance of the Bacchantes following the slaying of Pentheus by them and by his mother, Agave, daughter of Cadmus:

Their hair loose and floating seems caught in the tempest of their own tumultuous motion, their heads are thrown back leaning with a strange inanity upon their necks, and looking up to Heaven, while they totter and stumble even in the energy of their tempestuous dance. One—perhaps Argave with the head of Pentheus, has a human head in one hand and in the other a great knife;

another has a spear with a pine cone, which was their thyrsus; another dances with mad voluptuousness; the fourth is dancing to a kind of tambourine.[52]

This picture and his reading on the moon's librations combined in his mind with the dance of the Maenads in Euripides' *Bacchae.*

The old order—the "Sceptred Curse" (338)—gone, the Earth sings a hymn to love and humanity in the new order. Love "interpenetrates" both the earth and man, and moves from the earth to the moon. Although Shelley felt that a force resembling love might be infused in nature, he did not, of course, believe that this force would of itself remold mankind or spread from the earth to the moon as he makes clear in the final four stanzas of the Earth's song, which begin:

> Man, oh, not men! a chain of linked thought,
> Of love and might to be divided not,
> Compelling the elements with adamantine stress. (394–396)

Man, therefore, is the controlling force, not love as such—a new man in a new society. The concept of power here—implicit in the words "might" and "Compelling"—tends to be ignored because of Shelley's frequent emphasis on love and beauty. But Shelley felt that in the new order, power would be a dominant force, directed toward social, intellectual, and scientific conquest. He had admiration for and responded to the right kind and use of power, and earlier in the act he had characterized the new Spirits of the human mind" as Spirits not only of "pleasure" but of "might," and the new mind of man was envisaged as a "heaven" not only of "serene" but of "mighty motion."

The true power of Man, embodying love and beauty, could be realized only when conflict had ceased and humanity had become united:

> Man, one harmonious soul of many a soul,
> Whose nature is its own divine control. (400–401)

The vision is that of humanity, having abolished social evils and religious superstition, at last in control of its own destiny. The energies of man that in the past were dissipated in wars or social struggles are transformed into a single constructive force:

> His will, with all mean passions, bad delights,
> And selfish cares, its trembling satellites,
> A spirit ill to guide, but mighty to obey,
> Is as a tempest-winged ship, whose helm
> Love rules, through waves which dare not overwhelm,
> Forcing life's wildest shores to own its sovereign sway. (406–411)

Shelley's meaning in the third line is indicated in the fact that for "guide" he first wrote "rule."[53] When man tried by his "will" to control "the mutiny within" with its "mean passions" and other self-centered emotions, he failed; the "will," trying to force a harmony out of this psychological discord, was a poor ruler. But in the new society these destructive emotions have vanished and the will is brought under the control of the harmonious psychological unity of the new man. This is its natural function. It is a "mighty" weapon when it follows the dictates of a harmony of selfless and humanitarian motives, a harmony both beautiful and powerful ("Forcing life's wildest shores to its own sovereign sway").

The new power of man is shown in art and in science:

> All things confess his strength. Through the cold mass
> Of marble and of colour his dreams pass—
> Bright threads whence mothers weave the robes their children wear;
> Language is a perpetual Orphic song,
> Which rules with Daedal harmony a throng
> Of thoughts and forms, which else senseless and shapeless were.
>
> The lightning is his slave; heaven's utmost deep
> Gives up her stars, and like a flock of sheep
> They pass before his eye, are numbered, and roll on!
> The tempest is his steed—he strides the air;
> And the abyss shouts from her depth laid bare,
> "Heaven, hast thou secrets? Man unveils me; I have none." (412–423)

The third line (414) apparently refers to prenatal influence, as indicated by the draft, which seems to have read at one stage: "And mothers gazing weave the robes their children wear."[54] Shelley used "robes" in the sense of body and mind in *Hellas*:

> Bright or dim are they as the robes they last
> On Death's bare ribs had cast. (209–210)

His meaning in the last three lines (415–417) of this stanza is also indicated in his drafts, where he speaks of language as "a music" which "builds with mighty harmony, the throng/Of feelings and of forms which else senseless and shapeless were." In *A Defence of Poetry* he argued that in early society "language itself is poetry," and doubtless he felt that this would be so in a future society in which man was again in harmony with nature.[55] In the new society poetry would be both beautiful ("Orphic") and disciplined ("Daedal"), giving creative power to the otherwise unconnected "thoughts and forms" in the mind of the poet. In the first three lines of the stanza, then, Shelley is discussing the arts of sculpture and painting, in the second three, literature.

In the second stanza, concerning science in the new world, the references are, in order, to electricity ("lightning," with direct reference perhaps to Benjamin Franklin's famous experiment), astronomy, air travel (doubtless Shelley, like Erasmus Darwin, had heavier-than-air machines as well as balloons in mind), and geology. Desmond King-Hele commented on the stanza: "Of these four prophecies of Shelley's, three have been fulfilled, by the electric motor, by the progress of astrophysics and by the aeroplane; and the fourth has in part been fulfilled, too. For, though the secrets of the earth's interior are not yet *laid bare,* a good deal has been found out by measuring the rumbles of earthquake waves."[56] To these can now be added a fifth, for Shelley's meaning in depicting the influence of the earth on the moon is that man, having conquered earth, will next conquer the moon, as one stage of the prediction earlier in the act of the general conquest of space.

The Path to Victory

Following these songs, Panthea describes the coming of Demogorgon:

> A mighty Power, which is as darkness,
> Is rising out of Earth, and from the sky
> Is showered like night, and from within the air
> Bursts, like eclipse which had been gathered up
> Into the pores of sunlight: the bright visions,
> Wherein the singing spirits rode and shone,
> Gleam like pale meteors through a watery night. (510–516)

The necessitarian aspect of the power, that is, pervades all matter, solid and gaseous, in the earth and beyond the earth. The phrase "pores of sunlight" originally read "pores of light," which more exactly expresses Shelley's meaning, namely, that the necessitarian power resides in the elemental units of matter, which in the case of light were either particles or waves. The word "pores" perhaps originated in Newton, who spoke of the aether as being within the "pores of the earth and water."[57]

The "bright visions" subdued in the background, which suggests a stage set, are apparently those of the Earth and Moon only, not of the earlier Spirits and Hours, for the draft reads "and the bright visions/Gleam like two meteors."[58] The "Singing Spirits" are those of the Earth and the Moon.

From the dramatic point of view, Demogorgon's reappearance is a kind of epilogue, his audience being the constituent parts of the universe and man himself. First, he calls upon the Earth, the Moon, and then:

> Ye Kings of suns and stars, Daemons and Gods,
> Aetherial Dominations, who possess
> Elysian, windless, fortunate abodes
> Beyond Heaven's constellated wilderness. (529–532)

Shelley is here following the form of the Miltonic invocation to the orders of angels, but he changes it to suit contemporary scientific concepts. First come the Spirits that control the "suns and stars" (since suns are stars, perhaps "stars" refers specifically to the starlike points of light that Kant had argued were actually nebulae); and then come the Spirits that control the aether beyond the stellar universe (as envisaged by Herschel).

Next Demogorgon addresses himself to the human dead, presumably on other planets as well as the earth:

Ye happy Dead, whom beams of brightest verse
  Are clouds to hide, not colours to portray,
Whether your nature is that universe
  Which once ye saw and suffered—
A Voice from beneath. Or as they
  Whom we have left, we change and pass away. (534–539)

That by the "happy dead" here Shelley did not mean only the great creative intellects of the past, as some have contended, but all the dead is indicated by his first draft, in which the line read, "O unimagined people of the dead."[59] The draft line also explains "whom beams of brightest verse/Are clouds to hide, not colours to portray." Shelley means that one connot really imagine the state of those who have died; even the finest verse falters on the barriers of death. The dead are "happy" because death is preferable to the suffering that the mass of mankind has always indured in life. They have perhaps, like Adonais, become part of a "universe" of mind or perhaps they have simply changed into matter and vanished as living entities. As usual Shelley is non-commital on the subject of immortality.

Demogorgon next calls on the Spirits of the basic units of matter:

Ye elemental Genii, who have homes
  From man's high mind even to the central stone
Of sullen lead; from heaven's star-fretted domes
  To the dull weed some sea-worm battens on. (539–542)

The word "elemental" is clearly used in its technical sense, "of the elements," and given Shelley's scientific interests, he cannot be referring to the traditional four elements but to the new chemical elements discovered by Davy and others and listed in Lavoisier, elements that were common to all matter, solid, liquid, and gaseous, organic and inorganic, the human body and the human brain, the stars and the interior of the earth. The final reference is to the newly discovered element of iodine, which had been extracted from seaweed and was announced in England by Sir Humphry Davy.[60] The elements reply in a "Confused Voice": "We hear: thy words waken Oblivion" (543). The "Confused Voice" is intended to suggest the remoteness of the elements from the surface appearance of phenomena and their apparent mysteriousness. The reply itself indicates that chemistry is bringing light to bear on the nature of inorganic matter ("Oblivion" here meaning that which is unknown).

Demogorgon then summons what Shelley apparently intended to be the units of living matter:

Spirits, whose homes are flesh; ye beasts and birds;
  Ye worms, and fish; ye living leaves and buds;
Lightning and wind; and ye untameable herds,
  Meteors and mists, which feed air's solitudes. (544–547)

In Shelley's day little was known of the nature of living matter, for biology lagged behind chemistry and physics. The theory of the cell was not propounded until 1838, and knowledge of chromosomes, genes, and the nucleic acids lay many years in the future. There was, in fact, still considerable confusion over the biology of sexual reproduction. Shelley indicates here his belief that the same basic units are behind both biological life and such physical phenomena as wind, lightning, meteors, and mists (the last two being thought of at the time as connected). Although he was aware that the elements were also present in the various forms of matter, he apparently did not consider them as the immediately active units. His essential point is that the necessitarian laws of nature pervade matter in all its forms as well as "man's high mind."

Demogorgon finally addresses humanity:

Man, who wert once a despot and a slave;
  A dupe and a deceiver; a decay;
A traveller from the cradle to the grave
  Through the dim night of this immortal day. (549–552)

By the "night" Shelley means all societies and civilizations that have hitherto existed, for all of them have been based on inequality and injustice, distorting rather than developing the human potential. This past has been humanity's "night." In it people were either exploited ("slave") or exploiters ("despot"), the many being "duped" by the lies of the few "deceivers"—they who "hold the strings of that complicated mechanism with which the hopes and fears of men are moved like puppets."[61] The lives of all, rulers and ruled, was a journey of decay, physical and moral. The "immortal day" refers to the new society, which is "immortal" because it will last as long as mankind exists. In comparison to its vastness, the "dim" trail of the past is short and insignificant.

To the now assembled powers of the universe and society Demogorgon delivers his final message, in what is almost a separate poem with an ode-like power and sweep. The first stanza celebrates the destruction of the old order:

This is the day, which down the void abysm
At the Earth-born's spell yawns for Heaven's despotism,
  And Conquest is dragged captive through the deep;
Love, from its awful throne of patient power

In the wise heart, from the last giddy hour
Of dread endurance, from the slippery, steep,
And narrow verge of crag-like agony, springs
And folds over the world its healing wings. (554–561)

On the surface level, the "Earth-born" is Prometheus, like all the Titans a child of Earth and Heaven, but it refers primarily to the leaders of mankind who are, as it were, the essence of humanity. Shelley is emphasizing that the old order will be overthrown only by humanity's own efforts, not by supernatural intervention. "Conquest" on the literal level refers to Jupiter, but on the symbolic level it refers to all those who have conquered mankind by war or oppression. Again Shelley conveys a sense of the power required for this destruction of the old order and rejoices in it: "dragged captive through the deep." The "wise heart" is Prometheus, and hence, all those leaders of humanity who have had the courage, patience, and faith to continue the struggle to the end. The essential power that they had and which enabled them to break down the old social structure and establish the new was "Love." Taking the stanza by itself, one could interpret "Love" in a personal sense and argue that Shelley was thinking of individual moral conversion. But in context, the stanza points up the message of the drama as a whole. The first three lines summarize the overthrow of Jupiter in Act III, a long and arduous social process. The last five lines summarize the coming of the new society and the general means by which it was achieved, as depicted in the second and third acts, also a long and varied process of several stages. By "Love" Shelley means essentially the humanitarian feeling of brotherhood which, if it spread deeply and widely enough, would enable mankind not only to overthrow the old order but to consolidate the new. This love exists in its purest and strongest form in the hearts of the Promethean leaders of humanity. Even in their deepest agonies as they witnessed the oppression of mankind and watched it go down to defeat after defeat—the latest being that in France—these men and women endured and did not despair.

The new society has been achieved. The old rulers have been overthrown. But is the new order really secure forever? Cannot the old rulers, or their descendants, return to power and mankind again be conquered? Will "Conquest" ever return from the "deep"? These are the questions to which Demogorgon next addresses himself.

Gentleness, Virtue, Wisdom, and Endurance,
These are the seals of that most firm assurance
Which bars the pit over Destruction's strength;
And if, with infirm hand, Eternity,
Mother of many acts and hours, should free
The serpent that would clasp her with his length,
These are the spells by which to reassume
An empire o'er the disentangled Doom. (562–569)

For this serpent image Shelley was once more indebted, either directly or indirectly, to Boccaccio on Demogorgon and eternity in *The Genealogies of the Gods:*

Next of Eternity, whom the ancients supposed to be the companion of Demogorgon . . . What Claudius Claudianus has written concerning her in his heroic song in praise of Stilicho may be quoted: "Far off, unknown, inconceivable by our minds, hardly to be approached by the gods themselves, is a cave of immense age, the hoary mother of the years, who gives forth the periods of time and recalls them into her vast bosom. A serpent surrounds the cave, who consumes all things with quiet power; his scales perpetually grow afresh and, with his mouth turned back, he is devouring his own tail, thus in his course tracing his own beginning . . ." [The poet] speaks of her cave, that is, the unknown profundity of her bosom . . . and with back-turned mouth eating his own tail, we are to know that the cyclic lapse of time is meant.[62]

Shelley used a similar image in *The Revolt of Islam*: "as many-coloured as the snake/That girds eternity" (1445–1446). This serpent is apparently the same as the "snake-like Doom" that Demogorgon had "coiled" under his throne. And this "Doom" is not eternity but, as Boccaccio expressed it, time, the element associated with eternity. It is a time creature that necessity has coiled under his throne: he uses time and the social evils Shelley associated with it to overthrow tyranny. But he can equally well use them to overthrow a progressive, egalitarian society, to bring about a revolution, or to destroy a revolution. Presumably the doom was "disentangled" when Jupiter was overthrown. If it becomes disentangled again, it could restore the old order. The "past" might return.

Shelley felt that such a disaster could come about if mankind forgot or neglected the natural, "eternal" qualities of the human mind, such as love and courage, and reverted to qualities of time-serving selfishness. Then humanity would face a situation not of "Eternity warning Time" but "Time warning Eternity." In such a contingency the historical powers of necessity would again come into play, not as revolutionary but as counterrevolutionary action.

Although Shelley is in the stanza presumably speaking of future events, his mind is really on the present. The message of Demogorgon to the assembled powers is actually a message from Shelley to his contemporaries. He gave the essence of his thought in various passages in *A Philosophical View of Reform*, written in the same period as *Prometheus Unbound*. In one such passage his language (italicized here) is similar to that in the stanza:

A Republic, however just in its principle and glorious in its object, would through violence and sudden change which must attend it, incur a great risk of being as rapid in its decline as in its growth. It is better that they [the people] should be instructed in the whole truth; that they should see the clear grounds of their rights, the objects to which they ought to tend; and be impressed with the just persuasion that *patience and reason and endurance* [are the means of] a calm yet irresistible progress. A civil war, which might be engendered by the passions attending on this mode of reform, would confirm in the mass of the nation those military habits which have been already introduced by our tyrants, and with which liberty is incompatible.[63]

In other words, if in the future the eternal (intellectual and moral) powers of the new egalitarian society grow weak ("infirm") and release again forces (the serpent) which, getting out of control, threaten the people with "civil war" ("Destruction's strength"), matters can be again brought under control if the people fight for their rights with "patience and reason and endurance" ("Gentleness, Virtue, Wisdom, and Endurance"). The final stanza develops this thought further:

To suffer woes which Hope thinks infinite;
To forgive wrongs darker than death or night;
  To defy power, which seems omnipotent;
To love, and bear; to hope till Hope creates
From its own wreck the thing it contemplates;
  Neither to change, nor falter, nor repent;
This, like thy glory, Titan! is to be
Good, great and joyous, beautiful and free;
This is alone Life, Joy, Empire, and Victory! (570–578)

Shelley does not mean either here or in the previous stanza, that moral virtues by themselves will bring victory over reaction. He had long accepted the argument of *Political Justice* that moral virtues, if they are effectively to help humanity, must be applied politically, and he had gone beyond Godwin in substituting popular political action for individual propaganda. One must "defy Power," and defy it continuously in all its forms: "lose no opportunity of bringing public opinion and the power of the tyrants into circumstances of perpetual contest and opposition." But one must have patience also, never letting a sense of wrong push one into precipitate action. If violence is the only way out, if the tyrants leave no other path open, then one must use violence, but violence has its dangers. Although in this drama he is placing the emphasis on these dangers, it is not because he has renounced revolution ("The last resort of resistance is undoubtedly insurrection," he wrote in *A Philosophical View of Reform*), but because he felt that the reform movement was rising to a point of power where it could achieve its aims by "irresistible" peaceful pressure and might lose them if provoked into violence. He argues this position, "not because active resistance is not justifiable when all other means shall have failed, but because in this instance temperance and courage would produce greater advantages than the most decisive victory." Under some circumstances, patience ceases to be a virtue: "if they wait until those neutral politicians, a class whose opinions represent the actions of this class, are persuaded that so soon [as] effectual reform is necessary, the occasion will have passed or will never arrive, and the people will have exhausted their strength in ineffectual expectation and will have sunk into incurable supineness." For the present, the path of gradual struggle seems to be the best hope: "It is better that we gain what we demand by a process of negotiation which would occupy twenty years, than that by communicating a sudden shock to the interests of those who are the depositaries and dependents of power we should incur the calamity which their revenge might inflict upon us by giving the signal of civil war."[64]

This final speech of Shelley's drama recapitulates in verse the conclusion of the Preface. Ostensibly it spells out how one could in the future restore an egalitarian order after a hypothetical triumph of tyranny, but it is really a directive to his fellow intellectuals on the overthrow of the existing order. Until those intellectuals who are interested in "reform," which is the first step in this process, learn to have faith in the people and lead them courageously and unfalteringly—"love, and admire, and trust, and hope, and endure"—no radical movement adequate to its tasks, immediate or ultimate, can materialize.

Short Titles   Notes   Index

Short Titles

Baker	Carlos Baker. *Shelley's Major Poetry: The Fabric of a Vision.* Princeton: 1948.
Bloom	Harold Bloom. *Shelley's Mythmaking.* New Haven: 1959.
Blunden	Edmund Blunden. *Shelley: A Life Story.* New York: 1947.
Boas	Louise Schutz Boas. *Harriet Shelley: Five Long Years.* New York: 1962.
Byron	*The Works of Lord Byron: Letters and Journals,* ed. Rowland E. Prothero. 6 vols. New York: 1898–1901.
Cameron	Kenneth Neill Cameron. *The Young Shelley: Genesis of a Radical.* New York: 1950.
Clairmont	*The Journals of Claire Clairmont,* ed. Marian Kingston Stocking. Cambridge: 1968.
Correspondence	*The Shelley Correspondence in the Bodleian Library,* ed. R. H. Hill. Oxford: 1926.
de Ricci	Seymour de Ricci. *A Bibliography of Shelley's Letters.* 1927.
Dowden	Edward Dowden. *The Life of Percy Bysshe Shelley.* London: 1886.
Esdaile Notebook	Percy Bysshe Shelley. *The Esdaile Notebook: A Volume of Early Poems,* ed. Kenneth Neill Cameron: New York: 1964.
Forman	H. Buxton Forman. *The Shelley Library: An Essay in Bibliography.* London: 1886.
Fuller	Jean Overton Fuller. *Shelley: A Biography.* London: 1968.
Gisborne & Williams	*Maria Gisborne & Edward E. Williams: Shelley's Friends, Their Journals and Letters,* ed. Frederick L. Jones. Norman: 1951.
Godwin	William Godwin. *Memoirs of the Author of a Vindication of the Rights of Woman.* London: 1798.
Godwin, *Political Justice*	William Godwin. *Enquiry Concerning Political Justice and Its Influence on Morals and Happiness,* ed. F. E. L. Priestley. Toronto: 1946.
Grabo	Carl Grabo. *The Magic Plant: The Growth of Shelley's Thought.* Chapel Hill: 1935.
Grabo, *A Newton among Poets*	Carl Grabo. *A Newton among Poets: Shelley's Use of Science in Prometheus Unbound.* Chapel Hill: 1930.
Hogg	Thomas Jefferson Hogg. *The Life of Percy Bysshe Shelley.* In *The Life of Percy Bysshe Shelley,* ed. Humbert Wolfe, vols. I–II. London: 1933.
Hunt	*The Autobiography of Leigh Hunt,* ed. Roger Ingpen. London: 1903.
Hunt, *Correspondence*	*The Correspondence of Leigh Hunt,* ed. Thornton Hunt. London: 1862.
Ingpen	Roger Ingpen. *Shelley in England: New Facts and Letters from the Shelley-Whitton Papers.* London: 1917.
King-Hele	Desmond King-Hele. *Shelley: His Thought and Work.* London: 1960.
Letters	*The Letters of Percy Bysshe Shelley,* ed. Frederick L. Jones. Oxford: 1964.

Letters about Shelley	*Letters about Shelley Interchanged by Three Friends: Edward Dowden, Richard Garnett, and Wm. Michael Rossetti,* ed. R. S. Garnett. London: 1917.
McAleer	Edward C. McAleer. *The Sensitive Plant: A Life of Lady Mount Cashell.* Chapel Hill: 1958.
McNiece	Gerald McNiece. *Shelley and the Revolutionary Idea.* Cambridge: 1969.
Marchand	Leslie A. Marchand. *Byron: A Biography.* New York: 1957.
Mary Shelley, *Letters*	*The Letters of Mary W. Shelley,* ed. Frederick L. Jones. Norman: 1946.
Mary Shelley's Journal	*Mary Shelley's Journal,* ed. Frederick L. Jones. Norman: 1947.
Massingham	H. J. Massingham. *The Friend of Shelley: A Memoir of Edward John Trelawny.* London: 1930.
Medwin	Thomas Medwin. *The Life of Percy Bysshe Shelley,* ed. H. Buxton Forman. Oxford: 1913.
Medwin, *Conversations*	Thomas Medwin. *Conversations of Lord Byron: Noted During a Residence with His Lordship at Pisa in the Years 1821 and 1822.* London: 1824.
Medwin, *Shelley Papers*	Thomas Medwin. *The Shelley Papers: Memoir of Percy Bysshe Shelley.* London: 1833.
New Letters	*New Shelley Letters,* ed. W. S. Scott. New Haven: 1949.
Note Books	*Note Books of Percy Bysshe Shelley,* ed. H. Buxton Forman. St. Louis: 1911.
Notopoulos	James A. Notopoulos. *The Platonism of Shelley: A Study of Platonism and the Poetic Mind.* Durham: 1949.
Paul	C. Kegan Paul. *William Godwin: His Friends and Contemporaries.* London: 1876.
Peacock	Thomas Love Peacock. *Memoirs of Shelley.* In *The Life of Percy Bysshe Shelley,* ed. Humbert Wolfe, vol. II. London: 1933.
Peacock, *Works*	*The Works of Thomas Love Peacock,* ed. H. F. B. Brett-Smith and C. E. Jones. 10 vols. London: 1924–1934.
Peck	Walter Edwin Peck. *Shelley: His Life and Work.* Boston and New York: 1927.
PMLA	*Publications of the Modern Language Association.*
Poems	*The Poems of Percy Bysshe Shelley,* ed. C. D. Locock. London: 1911.
Poetry and Prose	Percy Bysshe Shelley. *Selected Poetry and Prose,* ed. Kenneth Neill Cameron. New York: 1967.
Prose	*Shelley's Prose, or the Trumpet of a Prophecy,* ed. David Lee Clark. Albuquerque: 1954.
Prose in the Bodleian	*Shelley's Prose in the Bodleian Manuscripts,* ed. A. H. Koszul. London: 1910.
Pulos	C. E. Pulos. *The Deep Truth: A Study of Shelley's Scepticism.* Lincoln: 1954.
Reiman	Donald H. Reiman. *Percy Bysshe Shelley.* New York: 1969.
Reiman, *Triumph*	Donald H. Reiman. *Shelley's "The Triumph of Life": A Critical Study, Based on a Text Newly Edited from the Bodleian Manuscript.* Urbana: 1965.
Reiter	Seymour Reiter. *A Study of Shelley's Poetry.* Albuquerque: 1967.
Rieger	James Rieger. *The Mutiny Within: The Heresies of Percy Bysshe Shelley.* New York: 1967.

Rogers	Neville Rogers. *Shelley at Work: A Critical Inquiry.* Oxford: 1956.
Rossetti Papers	*Rossetti Papers: 1862 to 1870, a Compilation,* ed. William Michael Rossetti. New York: 1903.
Selected Poetry	Percy Bysshe Shelley. *Selected Poetry,* ed. Neville Rogers. Boston: 1968.
Shelley and His Circle	*Shelley and His Circle, 1773–1822,* ed. Kenneth Neill Cameron, vols. I–IV. Cambridge: 1961, 1970.
Shelley and Mary	*Shelley and Mary.* London: 1882.
Smith	Robert Metcalf Smith, in collaboration with Martha Mary Schlegel, Theodore George Ehrsam, and Louis Addison Waters. *The Shelley Legend.* New York: 1945.
Trelawny	Edward John Trelawny. *The Recollections of Shelley & Byron.* In *The Life of Percy Bysshe Shelley,* ed. Humbert Wolfe, vol. II. London: 1933.
Trelawny, *Letters*	*Letters of Edward John Trelawny,* ed. H. Burton Forman. Oxford: 1910.
Trelawny, *Records*	Edward John Trelawny. *Records of Shelley, Byron, and the Author,* London: 1878.
Verse and Prose	*Verse and Prose from the Manuscripts of Percy Bysshe Shelley,* ed. Sir John C. E. Shelley-Rolls and Roger Ingpen. London: 1934
Wardle	Ralph M. Wardle. *Mary Wollstonecraft: A Critical Biography.* Lawrence: 1951.
White	Newman Ivey White. *Shelley.* New York: 1940.
White, *Unextinguished Hearth*	Newman Ivey White. *The Unextinguished Hearth: Shelley and His Contemporary Critics.* Durham: 1938.
Wilson	Milton Wilson. *Shelley's Later Poetry: A Study of His Prophetic Imagination.* New York: 1959.
Wise	Thomas James Wise. *A Shelley Library: A Catalogue of Printed Books, Manuscripts, and Autograph Letters by Percy Bysshe Shelley, Harriet Shelley, and Mary Wollstonecraft Shelley.* London: 1924.
Woodring	Carl Woodring. *Politics in English Romantic Poetry.* Cambridge: 1970.
Works	*The Complete Works of Percy Bysshe Shelley,* ed. Roger Ingpen and Walter E. Peck. 10 vols. London, New York: 1926–1930.
Zillman, *Variorum*	*Shelley's Prometheus Unbound: A Variorus Edition,* ed. Lawrence John Zillman. Seattle: 1959.

Notes

1. *The Last Years in England*

1. Lady Shelley's contention in *Shelley Memorials* (1859) that the marriage broke up by "mutual consent" was denied by T. L. Peacock in an article in *Fraser's Magazine* (1860), later published in his *Memoirs of Shelley.* Peacock was in turn attacked by Richard Garnett in his *Relics of Shelley* (1862). In 1885 John Cordy Jeaffreson wrote a two-volume diatribe on Shelley called *The Real Shelley.* In 1886 came Edward Dowden's biography. Dowden was assailed by Mark Twain in his essay "In Defence of Harriet Shelley," published in *How To Tell a Story, and Other Essays* (1897). Jeaffreson's approach was continued in *The Shelley Legend* (1945) by Robert Metcalf Smith, Theodore Ehrsam, and others. Harriet's most recent champion is Louise Schutz Boas in *Harriet Shelley: Five Long Years* (1962), perceptively reviewed by Richard Harter Fogle in *Keats-Shelley Journal,* XII (1963), 109–110. The best account, in Newman I. White's 2-volume *Shelley* (1940), suffers from a reticence on sexual and other matters and a tendency to summarize rather than to quote documents directly.

2. For the poems in these paragraphs, see *Esdaile Notebook.* pp. 82, 169. Unless otherwise indicated, Shelley's poetry is quoted from *Works.* For the Hogg-Harriet-Shelley triangle, see *Shelley and His Circle,* III, 24–34.

3. Nov. 22–23, 1813, *Shelley and His Circle,* III, 260. See also pp. 261–265.

4. To Peacock, Apr. 6, 1819, *Letters,* II, 92; Dowden, I, 380. For the Boinvilles, see Dowden, I, 378–382; for Turner, see *Shelley and His Circle,* II, 551–553; IV, 609–624, 628–629.

5. *Letters,* I, 383–384.

6. Dowden, II, 543.

7. *Shelley and His Circle,* IV, 613–616.

8. *Letters,* I, 401–402.

9. Peacock, 335.

10. To Catherine Nugent, Dec. 11, 1814, *Letters,* I, 422n.

11. Hogg, II, 145.

12. Shelley probably first met Mary two years previously when she was fourteen. She had returned from a visit in Scotland on Nov. 10, 1812; on Nov. 11, Shelley, Harriet and Eliza dined at the Godwins. Mary would normally have been present; her friend Christina Baxter, who had returned from Scotland with her, remembered meeting Shelley and Harriet, so Mary must have met them also. On June 3, 1813, Mary went back to Scotland and did not return to London until Mar. 30, 1814. (F. A. Marshall, *The Life and Letters of Mary Wollstonecraft Shelley* [London, 1889], I, 30, 31, 36, 37.)

13. *Esdaile Notebook,* pp. 165–166.

14. Peacock, 336.

15. On Claire's birth, see *Shelley and His Circle,* I, 296–297; III, 374–375.

16. *The Elopement of Shelley and Mary As Narrated by William Godwin,* ed. H. Buxton Forman (Bibliophile Society, 1911), pp. 10–13. For Mrs. Godwin's account, see Dowden, II, 542–551.

17. Mrs. Godwin to Lady Mount Cashell, Aug. 20, 1814, Dowden, II, 543; *Esdaile Notebook,* p. 295.

18. Peacock, p. 336. To this comment Shelley replied: "But you did not know how I hated her sister." *Ibid.*

19. Hogg, II, 147–148. The date, Dowden noted (I, 420n), is "fixed by Godwin's diary."

20. Dowden, I, 430.

21. *Letters,* I, 389n2. Harriet sent other letters to Hookham, which were seen by Robert Browning but subsequently disappeared. (Smith, pp. 203–207.) In one of these letters Harriet apparently stated that Shelley left her with "14 shillings altogether," but in the July 14 letter to Harriet cited earlier Shelley writes: "If you want to draw on the Bankers before I see you, Hookham will give you the checks." As Shelley deposited £1100 on July 6, there was presumably a fair amount in his account, although some of it went to Godwin. (White, I, 677–678.) Shortly thereafter Shelley apparently arranged with a lawyer to provide for a separate maintenance for Harriet. (*Letters,* I, 393.) The next year, when he started to receive a £1000 per annum allowance as a result of his

grandfather's death, he assigned £200 of it to Harriet. In his 1816 will, he left £6000 to Harriet and £5000 to each of his children by her. (*Shelley and His Circle,* IV, 702–709; Ingpen, pp. 470–471.)

22. White, I, 672.

23. Dowden, II, 88.

24. July 14?, 1814, *Letters,* I, 389–390.

25. Mrs. Godwin to Lady Mount Cashell, Aug. 20, 1814, Dowden, II, 543–544.

26. *Ibid.,* pp. 544–545.

27. Note to can. V, l. 189, *Works,* I, 141.

28. Southey to Shelley, 1820, *The Correspondence of Robert Southey with Caroline Bowles,* ed. Edward Dowden (London, 1881), p. 364: "While you were at Keswick you told your bride that you regarded marriage as a mere ceremony, and would live with her no longer than you liked her." Also in *Letters,* II, 232n.

29. Harriet Shelley to Elizabeth Hitchner, Mar. 14, 1812, *Works,* VIII, 294–295: "When I lived with my Father I was not likely to gain much knowledge, as our circle of acquaintance was very limited, he not thinking it proper that we should mix much with society. In short, we very seldom visited those places of fashionable resort and amusement which, from our age, might have been expected . . . I thought, if I married anyone, it should be a Clergyman. Strange idea this, was it not? But being brought up in the Christian religion, 'twas this first gave rise to it. You may conceive with what horror I first heard that Percy was an Atheist."

30. *Esdaile Notebook,* pp. 92–93.

31. Peacock, p. 338.

32. *Letters,* I, 259n.

33. On the title, see *Shelley and His Circle,* IV, 1048n; *Esdaile Notebook,* pp. 86, 88.

34. Cameron, p. 267.

35. Aug. 17, 1820, *Letters,* II, 231. Shelley commented further: "I regulated my domestic arrangements without deferring to the notions of the vulgar, although I might have done so quite as conveniently had I descended to their base thoughts—this you call *guilt.*" Shelley meant that he could, if he wished, have remained with Harriet and kept Mary as his mistress, to which neither Southey nor anyone else in Regency London would have objected.

36. *Shelley and His Circle,* II, 879–891.

37. Hunt, II, 32.

38. *Shelley and His Circle,* III, 443–445. Louise Schutz Boas informs me that Shelley's father also had an illegitimate child.

39. Aug. 7, 1814, *Mary Shelley's Journal,* p. 6.

40. See also Charles I. Elton, *Account of Shelley's Visits to France, Switzerland, and Savoy, 1814–16* (London, 1894); "Claire Clairmont's Journal," ed. Sir Gavin de Beer, with a map of the trip, in *Shelley and His Circle,* III, 342–375.

41. This curious piece of information was left out of their *History,* which states simply: "Finding our ass useless, we sold it." (*Works,* VI, 94.) Mary's journal for Aug. 8 reads: "We set out to Charenton in the evening carrying the ass, who was weak and unfit for labour, like The Miller and his Son." (*Mary Shelley's Journal,* p. 6.)

42. To Harriet Shelley, Aug. 13, 1814, *Letters,* I, 392.

43. *Ibid.,* pp. 391, 393.

44. Shelley wrote in Mary's journal for Feb. 22, 1815: "[Mary] is in labour, and, after a few additional pains, she is delivered of a female child; five minutes afterwards Dr. Clarke comes; all is well. Maie [Mary] perfectly well, and at ease. The child is not quite seven months; the child not expected to live." (*Mary Shelley's Journal,* pp. 38–39.) The baby died on Mar. 6. Shelley implies that the child was conceived in late July or early August, and its sickly condition suggests that it was indeed premature.

45. Dowden, I, 440.

46. July 30, 1814, *Mary Shelley's Journal,* p. 4.

47. To Catherine Nugent, Nov. 20, [1814], *Letters,* I, 421n.

48. Dowden, I, 466ff; White, I, 364, 370–371, 379, 685.

49. Oct. 25, 1814, Mary Shelley, *Letters,* I, 3. (Quoted by permission of the University of Oklahoma Press.)

50. Leslie Hotson, *Shelley's Lost Letters to Harriet* (London, 1930). Hotson (pp. 10–13) described his discovery of transcripts of these letters. In the same year (1930) Roger Ingpen published the letters from a "transcription which I made from the copies in the Public Record Office, before Dr. Hotson published his copies." (*Works,* VII, 293–307.) The originals were at one time in the hands of Shelley's sisters, Hellen and Margaret. (Boas, pp. 208, 225.)

51. Sept. 15, 1814, *Letters*, I, 395.
52. Sept. 27, 1814, *ibid.*, p. 398.
53. To Harriet Shelley, Sept. 27, 1814; Harriet Shelley to Catherine Nugent, Nov. 20, 1814, *ibid.*, pp. 398–399, 421n.
54. On Harriet's annuity, see Shelley's "Answer" in the Chancery case of Westbrook vs. Shelley, quoted in Medwin, p. 472. On the will, see *Shelley and His Circle*, IV, 605–607.
55. *Letters*, II, 454–455. See also *Shelley and His Circle*, IV, 617–624.
56. For the magazine and its editor, George Cannon, see Louise Schutz Boas, " 'Erasmus Perkins' and Shelley", *Modern Language Notes*, LXX (1955), 408–413. For the articles, see White, *Unextinguished Hearth*, pp. 45–53, 395. See also White, I, 409–411; Boas, p. 178; Jan. 29, Feb. 7, 1815, *Mary Shelley's Journal*, pp. 36, 37. Cannon ("Erasmus Perkins") also wrote a series of articles on religious persecution for *Cobbett's Political Register* in 1814 and 1815 (XXVI, 730ff, 779ff, 853ff; XXVII, 19ff, 92ff, 214ff, 250ff, 433ff). The articles were deistic rather than atheistic in tone. He praised some of Shelley's favorites: Volney's *Ruins*, Holbach's *System of Nature*, Godwin's *Political Justice*. A George Cannon, "foreign bookseller," 33 Maiden Lane, is listed in Pigot's *Metropolitan Directory*, 1828–1829.
57. *Harriet and Mary*, ed. Walter Sidney Scott (London, 1944). These letters were presented more accurately in *Shelley and his Circle*, III, 423–473, with an essay on them by Frederick L. Jones.
58. Mar. 14, 1815, *Mary Shelley's Journal*, p. 40.
59. Mary Shelley, *Letters*, I, 8. (Quoted by permission of the University of Oklahoma Press.) Shelley and Mary eloped on July 28, 1814.
60. John Harrington Smith in "Shelley and Claire Clairmont," *PMLA*, LIV (September 1939), 785–814, argued that a serious love affair between Shelley and Claire began in late April 1815. He believed that Claire played a more important role in *Julian and Maddalo* and *Epipsychidion* than had previously been thought, and that the gloom of *Alastor* reflected Shelley's mood resulting from their affair. Smith's views were assailed in White, *passim* and by F. L. Jones in "Mary Shelley and Claire Clairmont," in the *South Atlantic Quarterly* for October 1943. Smith replied in "Shelley and Claire Again," *Studies in Philology*, XLI (1944), 94–105.
61. *To Lord Byron: Feminine Profiles Based upon Unpublished Letters, 1807–1824*, ed. George Paston and Peter Quennell (London, 1939), p. 207.
62. To Mary Shelley, Aug. 7, 1821, *Letters*, II, 319.
63. To Mrs. R. B. Hoppner, Aug. 10, 1821, Mary Shelley, *Letters*, I, 148.
64. *Shelley and His Circle*, III, 438–440.
65. *Ibid.*, pp. 468–469. The letter bears a London stamp of Apr. 26, and the content indicates that it was written in the evening. This cannot have been the evening of Apr. 26 or the letter would not have caught the London mail from Salt Hill, so it must have been the evening of Apr. 25. The "Maie" and the "Pecksie" were pet names for Mary.
66. *Ibid.*, pp. 470–471. The letter bears neither address nor postmark, but the contents show that it was written just before Shelley and Mary left Salt Hill on the morning of Apr. 27. On Apr. 26 Mary wrote two letters to Hogg, one of which has an address, a postmark, and a heavy postal fee, which denotes an enclosure; Shelley's letter would have fitted inside them.
67. Smith, p. 147; Ivan Roe, *Shelley: The Last Phase* (London, 1963), pp. 141, 151–152.
68. White, I, 392, *Letters*, I, 423n (F. L. Jones). See also Mary Shelley, *Letters*, I, 7n2, White, I, 391–392, 400–401. As evidence that Mary and Hogg did not have an affair, White (p. 401) cited Shelley's remark a few months later to Polidori in Switzerland: "He married, and a friend of his, liking his wife, he tried all he could to induce her to love him in turn." But this could hardly refer to Mary because she and Shelley were not then married; it must refer to Harriet and Hogg in 1811. Shelley's letters indicate that at Keswick he tried to get Harriet to love Hogg, then safely at York.
69. Peck, I, 435–436.
70. Mary Shelley, *Letters*, I, 72.
71. Aug. 28, 1819, *ibid.*, p. 76.
72. June 8, 1819, *Letters*, II, 97.
73. *Ibid.*, p. 104n.
74. See also Shelley's 1817 poem *To William Shelley*, written when he feared that the court might deprive him of the child, as it had of his children by Harriet ("thy brother and sister dear").
75. Mary Shelley, *Letters*, I, 6, Mar. 18, 1817, *ibid.*, p. 24. (Quoted by permission of the University of Oklahoma Press.)

76. *Shelley and His Circle,* III, 435.
77. May 12, 1815, *Mary Shelley's Journal,* p. 46.
78. *Shelley and His Circle,* III, 453. Shelley feared that Mary might develop an infection because she was no longer nursing the baby.
79. *Shelley and His Circle,* II, 668–671.
80. According to some psychoanalysts, Hogg's desires and Shelley's reactions conform to a homosexual fantasy pattern in which two men have, in effect, sexual relations through a woman. Shelley and Hogg were certainly strongly attracted to each other at Oxford, but the evidence indicates nothing beyond a normal friendship. (Cameron, pp. 106–108.) This would not, of course, preclude Shelley's having fantasies—of both love and hostility—based on suppressed homosexual feelings, which to some degree dictated his behavior.
81. To Hogg, Jan. 1, 3, 1811, *Shelley and His Circle,* II, 679–687.
82. *Works,* VI, 177–178, 181–182.
83. To Hogg, Nov. 14, 1811, *Shelley and His Circle,* III, 53. See also p. 147.
84. Shelley, *Peter Bell the Third,* ll. 192–193.
85. Cornelia Newton to T. J. Hogg, Oct. 21, 1813, *Shelley and His Circle,* III, 253: "They have made an addition to their party in the person of Peacock a cold Scholar who I think has neither taste nor feeling."
86. Peacock, pp. 341–343.
87. Peacock, p. 335. In attempting to explain what he considered Peacock's bias, Shelley's son, Sir Percy Florence Shelley, claimed that Peacock and Harriet were lovers, but there is no evidence to show that they were and the indications are against it. (*Shelley and His Circle,* III, 263–265.)
88. Byron, III, 429. The letters are undated, but references in one of them (p. 427) point to at least March 1816. Claire was related by marriage to Robert George Catton Trefusis, Lord Clinton. (*Shelley and His Circle,* II, 296–297.) Her last letters to Byron, written just prior to his leaving England on Apr. 25, 1816, indicate an affair of short duration, with brief assignations.
89. R. Glynn Grylls, *Claire Clairmont: Mother of Byron's Allegra* (London, 1939), pp. 62–63. Before Claire's infatuation with Byron, Shelley had determined to leave England or at least the vicinity of London, because of "prejudice" against him for his views and actions. He also wished a respite from Godwin's pleas for money. (To Godwin, Feb. 21, May 3, 1816, *Letters,* I, 453, 471–472.) He could not leave, however, until a Chancery suit involving the estate was settled on Apr. 23. (Ingpen, p. 462.) The actual destination of Geneva was doubtless the result of Claire's pleadings. Peacock, in conformity with his picture of Shelley as a romantic eccentric, ascribed the trip to a "spirit of restlessness." (Peacock, p. 341.)
90. *The Diary of Dr. John Wm. Polidori,* ed. W. M. Rossetti (London, 1911), p. 101 (May 27, 1816). Byron and Shelley had met earlier in the day (*ibid.,* p. 99).
91. Byron accused Southey of having spread the story, but Southey denied that he had. (White, I, 716.)
92. Paston and Quennell, ed., *To Lord Byron,* pp. 211, 213. Claire was copying Byron's *The Prisoner of Chillon.*
93. Sept. 8, 1816, Byron, III, 347–348.
94. Sept. 4, 1816, Paston and Quennell, p. 215.
95. Smith, p. 234, quoted a letter from Claire to Trelawny written in 1870, revealing that Byron once voiced such suspicions to Allegra's nurse Elise. However, the letter went on: "I showed Elise's letter to Lady M[ount Cashell] and asked her advice—and she was of opinion I must go to Venice directly, withdraw Allegra from his protection and drop all intercourse with him." If there had been any foundation to the story, Claire would hardly have shown the letter to Lady Mount Cashell, who was a close friend of Shelley and Mary. In 1822 Shelley wrote to Claire: "It is of vital importance both to me and to yourself, to Allegra even, that I should put a period to my intimacy with L[ord] B[yron], and that without *éclat.* No sentiments of honour or justice restrain him (as I strongly suspect) from the basest insinuations." (*Letters,* II, 391–392.) This sounds as though Byron had been insinuating that Shelley might be Allegra's father. Nor were his suspicions unreasonable. The exact date of Claire's first meeting with Byron is unknown, but the letters apparently began in March or April, and it seems unlikely that the affair started much before the first week in April. It was probably during the first week of April that Allegra was conceived (assuming the average gestation period of 288 days). Byron perhaps suspected at the time that she was not a virgin, and his feeling that she was having an affair with Shelley was certainly in line with the lurid picture he had received from her of the Shelley circle.

96. Thomas Medwin, *The Angler in Wales* (London, 1834), II, 187.

97. Byron's note to l. 927 indicates that he wrote under the influence of Shelley's doctrine of universal love, as noted by Thomas Moore in *Life, Letters and Journals of Lord Byron* (London, 1838), p. 317, his informant probably being Mary Shelley.

98. To Peacock, July 12, 1816, *Letters*, I, 485.

99. July 24, 1816, *Mary Shelley's Journal*, p. 53.

100. Sir Gavin de Beer showed that there were at least three inscriptions: one in a book in a hut on Montenvers, seen by Southey; one at the Hôtel de Londres at Chamonix, later seen by Swinburne; and "one somewhere else, seen and erased by Byron." At the hotel at Chamonix, in answer to the question in the register, "Ou ils sont diriges," Shelley and Mary answered, "L'Enfer." (De Beer, *On Shelley* [Oxford, 1938], pp. 35–54.)

101. De Beer, *On Shelley*, pp. 38–40, 42.

102. *Journal at Geneva*, etc, *Works*, VI, 152. The passage originally was written by Shelley in Mary's Journal, Sept. 3, 1816. (*Mary Shelley's Journal*, p. 63.)

103. Paul, II, 241–242. Crabb Robinson on Aug. 30, 1819, visited Mary Hays, the feminist author: "She tells me that poor [Fanny] Imlay, who it was said died in Ireland—and about whose death I never heard anything said—in fact, died, not in Ireland, but in England, and by her own hand! She hung herself! Poor Godwin!" (Henry Crabb Robinson, *On Books and Their Writers*, ed. Edith J. Morley (London, 1938), I, 234–235.) Mary Hays was a good friend of Godwin's in the 1790s but apparently not thereafter. (Ford K. Brown, *The Life of William Godwin* [London, New York, 1926], pp. 109–111; *Shelley and His Circle*, I, 138–141, 158–161.) Where she picked up the hanging story is not known, but the Swansea newspaper account is presumably correct.

104. *Mary Shelley's Journal*, pp. 65–66. On Oct. 9 another letter came from Fanny, this one "very alarming," and Shelley set out for Bristol but could find no trace of her. On Oct. 10 he went back to Bristol and again returned to Bath. On Oct. 11 he went again to Bristol, where he found "more certain trace"—evidently information that she had left for Swansea. On Oct. 12 he went to Swansea and returned "with the worst account." He had perhaps seen the newspaper story which appeared that day. It has been argued that Fanny did stop in Bath and that she saw Shelley there. See Burton R. Pollin, "Fanny Godwin's Suicide Re-examined," *Etudes anglaise*, XVIII (1965), 258–268. But there is no evidence for such a meeting, and the indications are against it.

105. Dowden, II, 58. On Godwin's movements, see Paul, II, 243.

106. Paul, II, 242.

107. Godwin to William Baxter, May 12, 1817, White, I, 473, 720. The fact that Fanny had committed suicide nevertheless became known. Claire told Byron about it. (Clairmont, p. 74.)

108. July 9, 1820, *Gisborne & Williams*, p. 39.

109. Godwin to William Baxter, May 12, 1817, White, I, 473, 720.

110. In the spring of 1814 Mrs. Godwin feared that Fanny was becoming attracted to Shelley and sent her to stay with her aunts in Ireland. (Mrs. M. J. Godwin to Lady Mount Cashell, Aug. 20, 1814, summarized in Dowden, II, 542.) Apparently Claire Clairmont also said that Shelley was attracted to Fanny: "She expressly asserts that Shelley addressed F. before Mary and that F.——declined him." (W. M. Rossetti to Richard Garnett, Feb. 11, 1872, *Letters about Shelley*, p. 43.) Claire's journals, however, do not indicate a romantic relationship between Shelley and Fanny. (Sept. 16, Oct. 22, 24, 1814, Clairmont, pp. 43, 53, 55.) If Shelley did propose to Fanny that she run away with him, this must have been during the period of turmoil in which his marriage with Harriet was disintegrating and he was seeking rather wildly for another mate, as witness the poems to Cornelia Turner.

111. For instance, Fanny's letter to Mary on July 29, 1816 reveals a broadly inquiring mind. Her political comments show that she was both radical and practical: "At Glasgow, the state of wretchedness is worse than anywhere else. Houses that formerly employed two or three hundred men, now only employ three or four individuals. There have been riots of a very serious nature in the inland counties, arising from the same causes. This, joined to this melancholy season, has given us all very serious alarm, and helped to make me write so dismally. They talk of a change of Ministers; but this can effect no good; it is a change of the whole system of things that is wanted. Mr. [Robert] Owen, however, tells us to cheer up, for that in two years we shall feel the good effect of his plans; he is quite certain that they will succeed. I have no doubt that he will do a great deal of good; but how he can expect to make the rich give up their possessions, and live in a state of equality, is too romantic to be believed." (*Shelley and Mary*, I, 106.)

112. Shelley's fragmentary verses on Fanny's suicide have been quoted to indicate

that Shelley and Fanny were having an affair and this was what drove her to suicide. (Smith, pp. 216–219.) The draft reads:

Friend had I known thy secret grief

Her voice did quiver as we parted,
Yet knew I not that heart was broken
From which it came, and I departed
Heeding not the words then spoken.
  Misery—O Misery
This world is all too wide for thee.

Some secret woes had been mine own,
And they had taught me that the good—
The pain—
And that for whom the lone and weary
The load of life is long and dreary;
Some hopes were buried in my heart
Whose spectres haunted me with sadness.

On manuscript, these verses on Fanny appear with verses on William Shelley "in one lament. They are written together on one side of a single sheet of paper. On the reverse of the sheet Shelley has made a sketch of a grave and added the following words: 'These cannot be forgotten. It is not my fault—it is not to be alluded to.'" (*Verse and Prose*, p. 72.) Shelley's plural "these" indicates that the reference here is not to Fanny's death but either to Fanny and William or more likely to William and Clara (Shelley's daughter), for the fragment to William ends:

Thine eyes are dark, thy hands are cold
And she is dead, and thou art dead
And the

Shelley seems to be thinking of both his dead children, the thought of William leading his mind to Clara.

To build the case for an affair between Fanny and Shelley, Smith suggested that there were three assignations between them in the weeks preceding her death, on Sept. 11, 24, and 30. In a letter to Byron on Sept. 11, Shelley stated that he had seen Fanny the day before in London in connection with a loan for Godwin. On Sept. 24 Shelley again went to London to negotiate some business for Godwin and there met Fanny, apparently in a business office in Piccadilly, as Fanny informed Mary in a letter of Oct. 3. In neither of these meetings was there a hint of anything beyond business transactions. Fanny's letters, in fact, reveal a most unromantic, single-track obsession with raising money for Godwin. As for the third date, Sept. 30, on which Smith hinted that Shelley made a secret visit to Fanny in Bristol, there is no evidence that Fanny was in Bristol on that date. Her letters show her in London on Sept. 26 and Oct. 3, and the Swansea newspaper for Saturday, Oct. 12, stated that Fanny "told a fellow passenger that she came to Bath by the mail from London on Tuesday morning [i.e., Oct. 8, after traveling all night], from whence she proceeded to Bristol." The indications are that on Sept. 30 she was in London, living as usual with the Godwins from at least Sept. 23 until leaving for Bristol on Oct. 7. Why Shelley went to Bristol on Sept. 30 is not known, but as Bristol is only a few miles from Bath, the trip was probably not of great moment. Finally, since Shelley had been absent from England during May–September, a prolonged affair leading up to the suicide was impossible.

The specific meeting at which Shelley "parted" from Fanny, recorded in the poem, was doubtless that described by Fanny in the letter to Mary on Oct. 3 from London, namely, a business meeting at which Fanny was attempting to raise money for her father. Shelley apparently was evasive with her, for he knew that he could not meet Godwin's demands. As they "parted," Fanny's voice began to quiver, and he perceived that she was more upset than he had thought. Only later, however, did he realize the underlying, suicidal depth of her despair, and blamed himself for not having seen at the time that her "heart" (spirit) had been "broken" by it.

113. Dec. 17, 1816, Mary Shelley, *Letters*, I, 16.
114. Dowden, II, 50–51.
115. Oct. 3, 1816, *ibid*; p. 55.
116. *Anti-Jacobin Review*, IX (1801), 518, quoted in Wardle, p. 322.
117. Both White (I, 472) and Paul (II, 243–244) suggest that Fanny had only recently

learned of her illegitimacy. However, this is impossible, as the story of her birth and parentage was common property. She was known as Fanny Imlay, as shown in Lamb's letters and Crabb Robinson's diary, for instance, and her father himself published the story of Mary Wollstonecraft's affair with Imlay and the birth of Fanny in his edition of Mary's letters to Imlay (1798). (See Pollin, "Fanny Godwin's Suicide," p. 260.) Some of the story was also included in Godwin's memoirs of Mary Wollstonecraft (1798).

118. Oct. 20, 1814, Apr. 21, 22, 1815, *Mary Shelley's Journal*, pp. 21, 45; Medwin, p. 463; Harriet Shelley to Catherine Nugent, Jan. 24, 1815, *Letters*, I, 424n; *Esdaile Notebook*, pp. 167, 300–301. For Harriet Shelley's "last days," see also *Shelley and His Circle*, IV, 769–802; *Romantic Rebels: Essays on Shelley and His Circle*, ed. Kenneth Neill Cameron (Cambridge, Mass., 1973), pp. 228–266.

119. William Whitton wrote to Sir Timothy Shelley on Mar. 23, 1816, that Shelley was "in court" but did not mention Harriet, as he certainly would have if she had been there. (Ingpen, p. 462.) See also Shelley to Godwin, Mar. 29, 1816, *Letters*, I, 336; *Shelley and His Circle*, IV, 680–682.

120. June 5, 1816, *Letters*, I, 477n. Harriet dated the letter simply June 5; the London Postmark is June 5, 1816.

121. According to a tradition in the Boinville family, Harriet visited Mrs. Boinville at Bracknell sometime in the months before her death. (Blunden, p. 375.) As Harriet was in lodgings in London by early September and at her father's house on June 5, this visit must have been between those dates. That Harriet had been at Bracknell is confirmed in a letter from Fanny Imlay to Mary Godwin, Oct. 3, 1816, stating that Mrs. Godwin had recently been in Bracknell and happened to visit "the house where Harriet had lodged the last time she visited Bracknell." That this visit was not far in the past is shown in Fanny's remark that the lady of the house (Mrs. Boinville?) had retailed gossip about Shelley and Mary that Fanny felt had "originated with your servants and Harriet, who, I know, has been very industrious in spreading false reports against you." (Dowden, II, 54.)

122. *Shelley and His Circle*, IV, 776–777. It has been assumed that Harriet was known by the name of Smith at her lodgings. (Ingpen, p. 480.) But in saying she was "called" Harriet Smith, Hookham apparently meant only that this name was adopted for the purpose of the inquest.

123. *Shelley and His Circle*, IV, 777. The same notice appeared the next day in *The Times*. (Ingpen, p. 479.)

124. George Henry Davis, *Memorials of the Hamlet of Knightsbridge* (London, 1859), p. 112.

125. Ingpen, pp. 648–650. The fact that the inquest was held on "Harriet Smith" led Edmund Blunden to question whether "Harriet Smith" was Harriet Shelley. (Blunden, p. 160.) The evidence for this identification is decisive. Hookham's letter informed Shelley that Harriet "was called Harriet Smith," and Shelley connected her with "a groom by the name of Smith." (To Mary Shelley, Dec. 10, 1816, *Letters*, I, 521.) Davis (*Memorials*, p. 112) gave details that had not been published earlier, such as the name of the proprietor, and was obviously using local sources. The facts on Harriet Smith given at the inquest match those on Harriet Shelley. Harriet Smith was "about 21 years of age and was married about five years" but "did not live with her husband"; so, too, Harriet Shelley. Harriet Smith had taken rooms in early September; Harriet Shelley had not been living at her parents' house for some time, as noted both at the trial for the custody of the children (Medwin, p. 469) and Harriet's suicide letter and in Shelley's letter of Dec. 16, 1816. Harriet Smith left her lodgings on Nov. 9; Godwin's diary for Nov. 9 bears the notation, added later in red ink, "H. S. dies." Harriet Smith's body was found in the Serpentine on Dec. 10; so, too, was Harriet Shelley's. Finally, there can be no doubt that the *Sun* notice referred to the Harriet Smith on whom the inquest was performed, for not only do the dates and general facts coincide, but so do the addresses, even though they may not seem to at first. The inquest gave Harriet Smith's address as 7 Elizabeth Street, Hans Place; the *Sun* indicated that the body of the "respectable female" was taken to Queen's Street, Brompton. Queen's Street and Elizabeth Street were one-block streets, one running into the other just off Hans Place. (*Shelley and His Circle*, IV, 771.) The *Sun* also stated that the woman's husband was "abroad." Shelley had been in Geneva with Byron May 3–Sept. 8, and the Westbrooks may not have known of his return.

126. At the inquest Alder's occupation was given as plumber, which perhaps meant that he had a plumber's shop. Pigot's *Metropolitan Directory* for 1828–1829 lists a John Alder, proprietor of the Castle Tavern in Mark Lane. If William was related to John, this may explain how the Westbrooks came to know him. The Castle was not far from West-

brooks' the Poulterer's Arm Tavern in Cheapside. (*Shelley and His Circle*, II, 867–869.) Alder lived at the Fox and Bull, where the inquest was held, and the daughter of the proprietor there had known Harriet Shelley. (Davis, *Memorials*, p. 112.) The Fox and Bull was just across the park from Westbrook's other tavern, the Mount. Presumably it was William Alder who accompanied Harriet to her lodgings, though Mrs. Thomas said only "a Mr. Alder." William had apparently visited her at the lodgings.

127. Cyril John Polson, *The Essentials of Forensic Medicine* (Springfield, Ill., 1965), pp. 377, 400.

128. Medwin, p. 469.

129. *Shelley and His Circle*, IV, 805–806; see also pp. 806–810.

130. *Letters*, I, 520–521.

131. Thornton Hunt, "Shelley—By One Who Knew Him," in Edmund Blunden, ed., *Shelley and Keats As They Struck Their Contemporaries* (London, 1925), pp. 37–38. Thornton Hunt's article first appeared in *The Atlantic Monthly* in February 1863. Charles Armitage Brown, the friend and biographer of Keats, heard a similar story in Italy after Shelley's death "from L[eigh]. Hunt and another of Shelley's friends,—both accounts precisely alike." (Brown to Thomas Richards, Jan. 10, 1825, *The Letters of Charles Armitage Brown*, ed. Jack Stillinger [Cambridge, 1966], p. 203.) The "friend" was probably Trelawny, whom Brown met in Pisa in 1823. (*The Keats Circle*, ed. Hyder Edward Rollins [Cambridge, 1948], I, lviii.) Probably Trelawny himself had heard the story from Hunt, whom he met in Italy. The Leigh Hunt version turned up also in an account given to William Bell Scott by George Henry Lewes, who was a friend of both Thornton and Leigh Hunt. (Scott to W. M. Rossetti, Dec. 2, 1868, *Rossetti Papers*, p. 373.)

132. May 12, 1817, Smith, p. 116. Godwin habitually used one *l*, as in "Cromwel." He did not identify his unquestionable authority." Blunden (pp. 164–165) thought it was Thomas Hill, a businessman with literary interests, basing himself on the fact that two days after writing to Baxter, Godwin wrote to his wife, who was on vacation in Paris, that he had written to Shelley about "the story I had learned from Hill at the Exhibition the Monday before, which had so much disturbed me." Godwin noted that in reply, Shelley, "only said in a vague way that it was 'much exaggerated,' and that for the present explanation was superfluous." The indication is that whatever story Hill told Godwin, it had nothing to do with Harriet Shelley or her alleged infidelities. First, Godwin had already reported the infidelity story to Shelley by Jan. 11, 1817, when Shelley wrote to Mary: "I learnt just now from Godwin that he has evidence that Harriet was unfaithful to me *four months* before I left England with you." (*Letters*, I, 528.) On Dec. 15, 1816, Mrs. Godwin had told the same story to Crabb Robinson. (Robinson, *On Books*, p. 199.) Second, Godwin would not have been "disturbed" by such a story and in fact would have welcomed it—as Mrs. Godwin obviously did—as helping to justify his daughter's elopement with Shelley. Finally, Godwin would hardly have referred to Hill as an "unquestionable authority" on the affairs of Shelley and Harriet. Since stories that "disturbed" Godwin were usually connected with money matters, the probability is that Hill told him something that indicated a threat to a negotiation he had on hand with Shelley. His letters to Shelley in these weeks are mostly on his financial problems.

133. Aug. 30, 1875, *Shelley and His Circle*, IV, 788.

134. Trelawny, *Records*, II, 19–20. See also Trelawny to Claire Clairmont, July 10, 1815, Nov. 15, 1875, Trelawny, *Letters*, pp. 210–211, 251.

135. Trelawny, *Records*, II, 15.

136. *Boyle's Court Guide* was a London directory of the upper and middle classes. It included many entries for the Hans Place area.

137. Aug. 17, 1820, *Letters*, II, 231. The fact that Hunt apparently continued to repeat some version of the prostitution story does not necessarily mean that Shelley continued to believe it. The death of Harriet was so painful to him that he hardly ever spoke of her again. (Peacock, pp. 37, 347–348.) Hunt may have known nothing beyond what he learned on the first day with Shelley after the suicide.

138. Ingpen, pp. 470–472; *Shelley and His Circle*, III, 702, 709.

139. *Letters*, I, 523 (my italics).

140. Mary wrote in her journal for Dec. 6, 1814: "A letter from Hookham, to say that Harriet has been brought to bed of a son and heir [on Nov. 30]. Shelley writes a number of circular letters of this event, which ought to be ushered in with ringing of bells, &c., for it is the son of his *wife* [as Mary was not]." (*Mary Shelley's Journal*, p. 28.)

141. Dec. 11, 1814, *Letters*, I, 422.

142. *Ibid.*, p. 424n.

143. Mar. 14, 1812, *Letters*, I, 273–274n.

144. Dowden, I, 424–425.

145. White, I, 674–676.

146. White's biography came out in 1940; the Colonel Maxwell part of Godwin's letter first appeared in Smith, in 1945 (p. 116); the preceding portion was published in Dowden (I, 425) in 1886.

147. On May 21, 1813, Harriet Shelley wrote from London to Catherine Nugent in Dublin that "Mr. Ryan dines with us today," mentioning him in connection with Shelley's radical Irish friend John Lawless. On June 22 she wrote Miss Nugent, "Mr. Ryan is still in London." (*Letters*, I, 368n, 372n.) Ryan is not heard of again until Mary Shelley noted in her journal for Jan. 5, 1815, receiving a letter from "Ryan." Her entry for Jan. 3 had noted, "Creditors from Harriet." On Jan. 6: "Shelley had staid at home till 2 to see Ryan; he does not come." On Jan. 7 Ryan came. (*Mary Shelley's Journal*, pp. 34–35.) Charles Clairmont wrote to Francis Place about Harriet on Jan. 12, 1816: "She associated (I do not at all mean what the world calls criminally) with an Irish adventurer whom she commissioned to take all possible legal advantage of Shelley." (White, II, 504.) It thus appears that Ryan was the "Irish adventurer" and was connected with Harriet's "creditors."

148. *Shelley and His Circle*, IV, 790–791.

149. Ingpen, p. 481.

150. *Shelley and His Circle*, II, 871. A mews is a converted stable with a courtyard.

151. Boas (p. x) wrote: "I am grateful to the secretary of St. George's Church, Hanover Square, for her patience and help. Through her suggestion I investigated the possibility that Harriet Shelley might have been buried at the graveyard used by the church on Bayswater Road (then Uxbridge Road), where as late as 1890 there was a stone with the name Shelley among stones of the proper date; but the Chapel of Ease and many of its stones were struck by bombs and little remained; meanwhile I came to accept Roger Ingpen's discovery of the burial record of Harriet Smith at Paddington Parish Church as that of Harriet Shelley." If there was a stone bearing the comparatively rare name "Shelley" in this graveyard, it lends support to Eliza's statement, of which Boas was unaware because the manuscript was not available to her. Perhaps by special arrangement the burial was recorded in the Paddington Parish records but the actual interment took place in St. George's. Horwood's map of London (1794) shows St. George's and Paddington parishes adjoining and the line around the St. George burial ground bulging out into Paddington. (See *Shelley and His Circle*, IV, 771.) There was also a St. George's cemetery near the Westbrooks' house, but they could not have buried Harriet there if they wished to preserve secrecy. They could, however, have buried her in the other, larger cemetery of the parish on the Bayswater Road, which was some distance from their house, and thus avoided general disclosure. That matters were indeed handled with secrecy is shown by the fact that Harriet's burial place was not known to nineteenth century researchers. In fact, there is no evidence that Shelley himself knew where she was buried.

152. Peacock (p. 344) stated that Harriet's body was taken to the Westbrooks' house in Chapel Street but did not indicate where he got this information.

153. As Harriet went to the "mews" for her "accouchement," perhaps Mrs. Smith was a midwife who was willing to go along with whatever story was told.

154. Oct. 27? 1811, *Letters*, I, 162.

155. Hogg, I, 280; II, 12; see also II, 133.

156. Jan. 24, 1815, *Letters*, I, 424.

157. Blunden, p. 162.

158. Hunt, II, 33.

159. Peacock, p. 364; see also pp. 347–348.

160. *Verse and Prose*, pp. 75–77; *Shelley and His Circle*, IV, 799–801; Boas, pp. 200–201; Blunden, p. 163; Shelley, *Epipsychidion*, l. 304.

161. To T. J. Hogg, Mar. 16, 1814, *Letters*, I, 384.

162. Jan. 17, 1817, *ibid.*, pp. 529–530.

163. Cameron, pp. 102, 343–344.

164. In recent years two contentions have been made regarding the last days of Harriet Shelley: that important documentary evidence is forged (Smith, pp. 84–132), and that Shelley was the father of the child with whom Harriet was pregnant when she drowned herself (Boas, pp. 215–217). Both these theories have been shown to be groundless. On the first, see Newman I. White, Frederick L. Jones, and Kenneth N. Cameron, *An Examination of The Shelley Legend* (Philadelphia, 1951); on the second, see *Shelley and His Circle*, IV, 783n.

165. Godwin to his brother, Hull Godwin, Feb. 21, 1817, Paul, II, 246.

166. Ingpen, pp. 470–473. For the draft will, see *Shelley and His Circle*, IV, 702–709.

167. Dec. 16, 1816, *Letters*, I, 374. On P. W. Longdill, see *Shelley and His Circle*, IV, 587–589.

168. *Letters*, I, 522. Shelley wrote: "I called on you twice yesterday—I wish I had found you at home—I designed to have communicated intelligence which I am aware is painful to you, in a manner the least painful. As it is, allow me to assure you that I give no faith to any of the imputations generally cast on your conduct or that of Mr. Westbrook towards the unhappy victim. I cannot help thinking that you might have acted more judiciously but I do not doubt that you intended well." The contrast between this statement on Eliza and those in his Dec. 16 letter to Mary and his Jan. 17 letter to Byron are owing in part to the different times at which they were written. The letter to Mary was penned under the full impact of the suicide, when Shelley was prepared to believe anything, although even at this time it is doubtful that he consciously and rationally believed that Eliza had deliberately tried to "murder" Harriet. Two days later, when he wrote to Eliza, he had calmed down somewhat and doubtless could say in all conscience that he did not believe she had intended harm (although he implied, as his hostility mounted to the surface, that such was "generally" believed). His language was also no doubt moderated by the nature of his mission to Eliza. He had called at the house in order to try to secure custody of his children, and he had already received a hint, as his Dec. 16 letter indicates, that Eliza would prove baulky on the point. In any case, he was clearly prepared to be diplomatic in order to get custody of his children. Four weeks later when he wrote to Byron, Eliza had made it clear that she would not give up the children and was entering suit against him. In this situation his old venom returned in full force.

169. White, II, 509–510.

170. Jan. 17, 1817, *Letters*, I, 527.

171. Jan. 17, 1817, Ingpen, p. 492.

172. Medwin, p. 470. (pp. 463–483) includes the Chancery papers relating to the trial and the subsequent disputes on guardianship, with the exception of slightly differing versions of the children's and Eliza's complaints, which appear in White, II, 508–515.

173. Medwin, pp. 470–471.

174. Marchand, II, 577n.

175. To Mary Shelley, Jan. 11, 1817, *Letters*, I, 527.

176. Dowden, II, 84n.

177. *Ibid.*, pp. 83–84.

178. *Ibid.*, pp. 81–83. Shelley was twenty when *Queen Mab* was printed; Harriet had just turned sixteen when they eloped.

179. *Ibid.*, pp. 86–88. This declaration should be, but has not been, included among Shelley's works.

180. Medwin, p. 470.

181. Dowden, II, 90.

182. Jan. 17, 1817, *Letters*, I, 530.

183. Shelley must have been referred to Longdill by Godwin. (*Shelley and His Circle*, II, 546.)

184. Hotson, *Shelley's Lost Letters*, p. 72; cf. Medwin, p. 485.

185. To Shelley, Sept. 28, 1817, Mary Shelley, *Letters*, I, 334n; see also p. 206.

186. Note on *The Revolt of Islam*, *Works*, I, 410. Peck (I, 524) showed that Mary in her novel *The Last Man* gave an account of Shelley's charitable deeds at Marlow.

187. Hunt, II, 33.

188. Dowden, II, 121.

189. *Ibid.*, p. 122.

190. Edmund Blunden, *Leigh Hunt's "Examiner" Examined* (London, 1928), pp. 181–182.

191. *Mary Shelley's Journal*, pp. 88–91.

192. Sept. 28, 1817, Mary Shelley, *Letters*, I, 33.

193. Ingpen, pp. 524–526.

194. Blunden (p. 195) quoted an advertisement from *The Times* for Dec. 16, 1817, which indicated the size of the house: a dining room, a study, five bedrooms, two nurseries, six or seven attics, "convenient offices, good garden and pleasure-ground." On the furniture bill, see Peacock's note to Shelley's letter to him early in March 1820. (*Letters*, II, 176.) Shelley also owed money to his landlord, Madocks. (*Ibid.*, p. 177; to Peacock, Apr. 6, 1819, *ibid.*, p. 95.)

195. May 3, 1816; see also to Godwin, Mar. 6, 1816, *ibid.*, I, 472, 459.
196. *Works*, I, 198.
197. Blunden, ed., *Shelley and Keats*, p. 44. Thornton Hunt quoted *Epipsychidion*, ll. 256–266 in support of his contention.
198. Leigh Hunt, *Lord Byron and Some of His Contemporaries* (London, 1828), p. 174.
199. *Letters*, I, 572–573.
200. Medwin, p. 270. Medwin also wrote (p. 269) "He was a martyr to the most painful complaint, Nephritis, for which he had, though with no alleviation, consulted the most eminent medical men, at home and abroad, and now was trying Scott's vitriolic acid baths, much in vogue. This malady constantly menaced to end fatally. During its paroxisms he would roll on the floor in agony." See also Medwin, *Shelley Papers*, p. 64. Sophia Stacey commented in her journal in December 1819: "He was suffering much from the pain in his side . . . Mr. Shelley was talking to me when he was seized with spasms; he is in a very delicate state of health." Helen Rossetti Angeli, *Shelley and His Friends in Italy* (London, 1911), p. 101.
201. Jan. 2?, 1821, *Letters*, II, 242.
202. *Ibid.*, p. 254. Andrea Vacca Berlinghieri (1772–1826) was a well-known Italian physician residing at Pisa with whom the Shelleys became friendly. Vacca told Trelawny that "the disease Shelley suffered from was not nephretic." (*Rossetti Papers*, p. 399.) However, Mary recorded in a letter to Maria Gisborne on Dec. 13, 1820: "Vacca says that his disease is entirely nervous and nephretic." And in a previous letter (Feb. 24, 1820) to Mrs. Hunt she had written that Vacca "tells Shelley to take care of himself & strengthen himself but to take no medicine." (Mary Shelley, *Letters*, I, 120, 95.) Myopia was another of Shelley's ailments. Medwin (p. 233) reported that he was "forced to lean over his books, with his eyes almost touching them."
203. Ingpen, pp. 513–514.
204. To W. T. Baxter, Dec. 3, 1817, Mary Shelley, *Letters*, I, 46.
205. Mary Shelley stated that Elizabeth died of a "decline," which normally then meant tuberculosis. (To E. J. Trelawny, December 1831, *ibid.*, II, 51.)
206. For Thornton Hunt, see Edmund Blunden, "Leigh Hunt's Eldest Son," *Essays by Divers Hands, Transactions of the Royal Society of Literature*, XIX (London, 1942), 53–75. Thornton Hunt became a well-known Victorian journalist, favored by Gladstone and the Queen.
207. Peacock, p. 349; see also p. 350.
208. In *The British Critic*, May 1816 and *The Eclectic Review*, October 1816, both reprinted in White, *Unextinguished Hearth*, pp. 105–108.
209. See Blunden, *Leigh Hunt's "Examiner" Examined*, pp. 125–128; White, *Unextinguished Hearth*, pp. 108–109.
210. Blunden, *Leigh Hunt's "Examiner" Examined*, p. 67; White, *Unextinguished Hearth*, p. 109.
211. Blunden, *Leigh Hunt's "Examiner" Examined*, pp. 159, 170, 171; White, *Unextinguished Hearth*, pp. 117, 123, 124.
212. Kenneth Neill Cameron, "A Reference to Shelley in *The Examiner*," *Notes and Queries*, CLXXXIV (Jan. 16, 1943), 42.
213. Nov. 6, 1817, Robinson, *On Books*, I, 212.
214. Arthur H. Beaven, *James and Horace Smith* (London, 1899), p. 136.
215. William Sharp, *Life and Letters of Joseph Severn* (London, 1892), p. 116. Possibly this argument led to Shelley's *Essay on Christianity*. Severn (*ibid.*) also comments on Shelley's "fine presence . . . his tall, elegant, but slender figure: his countenance painfully intellectual . . . his restless blue eyes . . . his manner aristocratic though gentle . . . luxuriant brown hair, and a slightly ruddy complexion," adding that he "expressed himself in subdued accents." Shelley also visited Keats's printer for the 1817 *Poems*, who remembered his "peculiar starts and gestures, and his way of fixing his eyes and whole attitude." (Walter Jackson Bate, *John Keats* [Cambridge, 1963], p. 145.) Shelley was rather adept at putting on a show for printers, as Henry Slatter, his Oxford printer, noted. (Dowden, I, 92–93.)
216. *Autobiography of Benjamin Haydon*, ed. Edmund Blunden, (Oxford, 1927), p. 338. Haydon also noted that Shelley claimed Shakespeare for the freethinker's fold. See also Benjamin Robert Haydon, *Diary*, ed. Willard Bissell Pope (Cambridge, Mass. II, 1960), II, 148–166 (a diatribe on *Queen Mab*), p. 80 (his first meeting with Shelley, Jan. 29, 1817), and p. 89: "Shelley said he could not bear the inhumanity of Wordsworth in talking of the beauty of the shining trout as they lay after being caught, that he had such a horror of torturing animals it was impossible to express it." Haydon's aversion to Shelley is clear in his comments on his death (pp. 372–373) For

differences between the Autobiography and Diary accounts, see Eric George, *The Life and Death of Benjamin Robert Haydon* (Oxford, 1967), p. 321.

217. Dowden, II, 174.

218. Hunt, II, 39–41. Hunt's sketch of Shelley appeared first in his *Lord Byron and Some of His Contemporaries* in 1828.

219. Blunden, ed., *Shelley and Keats*, pp. 49–52.

220. Feb. 9, 1817, *Mary Shelley's Journal*, p. 77.

221. To William Godwin, June 3, 1812, *Letters*, I, 303.

2. *Shelley in Italy*

1. *Letters*, II, 177.

2. W. J. Stillman, *The Union of Italy, 1815–1895* (Cambridge, Eng., 1898), pp. 104–105.

3. Mar. 26, 1818, entry by Shelley, *Mary Shelley's Journal*, p. 94. Apparently Shelley eventually got his books through, because Claire noted in her journal for Apr. 8: "Chamberry Shelley is teized [teased] with his Books. He meets a Canon who helps him & who knew his father at the Duke of Norfolk's." *(Clairmont*, p. 88.)

4. Claire Clairmont to Trelawny, c. 1870, R. Glynn Grylls, *Claire Clairmont: Mother of Byron's Allegra* (London, 1939), p. 262.

5. Apr. 28, 1818, *Letters*, II, 12.

6. To T. L. Peacock, Nov. 7, 1818, *Letters*, II, 47. In previous letters to Peacock and Hogg (Apr. 20, 30, 1818, *ibid.*, pp. 8, 15) Shelley had expressed the intention of composing a drama on Tasso's life and madness. But "of this," Mary wrote, only "a slight fragment of a song to Tasso remains." (Note on *Prometheus Unbound*, *Works*, II, 268.) Perhaps it was abandoned in favor of the superior scheme of *Prometheus Unbound*. In addition to the "song of Tasso," one fragmentary scene was written, first printed in *Relics of Shelley*, ed. Richard Garnett (London, 1862), pp. 26–27). A brief sketch of the plot was found in one of Shelley's notebooks in the Bodleian. (See *Poems*, II, 502–503.) Although Shelley would doubtless have been interested in Tasso as a fellow rebel, his special interest may have resulted from conversations with Byron. Byron's *Lament of Tasso* had been published in 1817, after Byron had visited Ferrara, and he discussed Tasso's persecution also in *Childe Harold's Pilgrimage* (IV, xxxv–xxxix).

7. *Ode to the West Wind*, l. 32; see also *Ode to Naples*, l. 1.

8. *Letters*, II, 76. Mary wrote to Mrs. Hunt on Mar. 12, 1819: "He [the child William] has quite forgotten French for Elise has left us—She married a rogue of an Italian servant that we had and turned Catholic—Venice quite spoiled her and she appears in the high road to be as Italian as any of them. She has settled at Florence." In a letter to Mrs. Richard B. Hoppner on Aug. 10, 1821, Mary implied that Elise had been pregnant by Foggi and that she (Mary) had made them marry: "I would not turn the girl on the world without in some degree binding her to this man." (Mary Shelley, *Letters*, I, 64, 148.) This seems to run counter to Shelley's statement that the marriage was "very much against our advice." Perhaps Shelley was opposed to the marriage and Mary agreed with him on the principle involved but at the same time felt that the marriage was expedient and assisted in forwarding it without telling Shelley.

9. For the birth and baptismal certificates, see White, II, 546–548. On both certificates the mother is given as "Mary Godwin." (Ivan Roe, *Shelley: The Last Phase* [London, 1953], p. 169.) Shelley lived at 250 Riviera di Chiaia, one of the most fashionable streets, opposite the Royal Gardens and close to the bay, and Antonio Di Lorenzo lived at no. 223, where he perhaps had a hairdressing establishment.

10. Smith pointed out (p. 241) that if the baby was born on Dec. 27, as the birth certificate states, she would have been seventeen months and fourteen days old when she died, not fifteen months and twelve days. Fifteen months and 12 days would place the date of birth on Feb. 26, 1819. The contradiction presumably arose when the writer of the death certificate confused the date of filing the birth certificate with the date of birth.

11. *Letters*, II, 175–176, 179.

12. Mary Shelley, *Letters*, I, 108.

13. *Letters*, II, 206–207, 208, 211.

14. Byron, V, 73–74; *Lord Byron's Correspondence*, ed. John Murray (New York, 1922), II, 180–182; Byron, V, 86. By "Queen's evidence" Byron meant the lying testi-

mony given by servants and spies at the trial of Queen Caroline. Shiloh was Byron's nickname for Shelley. Byron in his works refers several times to Joanna Southcote (1750–1814), a religious fanatic who announced that she was to give birth to a new Messiah called Shiloh. In using this name for Shelley, Byron humorously implies that he could be regarded as a new Messiah preaching the gospel of a new kingdom of God upon earth. (See, e. g., Byron, III, 128–130; White, II, 306; Byron, *Don Juan*, ed. Leslie A. Marchand [Boston, 1958], pp. 2, 459.)

15. *Letters*, II, 317–320.

16. Mary Shelley, *Letters*, I, 147–149. (Quoted by permission of the University of Oklahoma Press.) Mary enclosed this letter in a letter sent to Shelley from Pisa. Shelley, at Ravenna, was to show it to Byron and forward it to the Hoppners at Venice. It was later found among Byron's papers with Shelley's seal broken, lacking a postmark, and addressed in Mary's hand, simply "A Madame, Madme Hoppner," without any street address. Shelley showed it to Byron, as Mary requested, and sealed it. Probably he then gave it to Byron to mail to the Hoppners. The indication is that Byron did not mail it, perhaps not wishing the Hoppners to know that he had let out a story they had told him in confidence. Hoppner's clerk, Richard Edgcumbe, argued that it might have been sent enclosed in an address sheet or another letter and returned in the same way to Byron, who would never have unsealed the letter because Shelley had shown him the contents before sealing it. But Byron could well have unsealed it for a second reading, after which he decided not to mail it; or it may have been unsealed by Byron's executor, John Cam Hobhouse. Certainly the weight of evidence indicates that Byron never sent the letter to the Hoppners. (*Lord Byron's Correspondence*, II, 192.)

17. Mary Shelley, *Letters*, I, 146, 147.

18. *Shelley and Mary*, II, 786–787 (in French; trans. here by Winifred M. Davis). These letters also appear in *Lord Byron's Correspondence*, II, 190–191, incorrectly transcribed. Claire met Elise on Apr. 7; on Apr. 9 she wrote asking Mary what she wished Elise to say in her repudiations; on Apr. 11 she received a letter from Mary and Shelley presumably supplying this information; and the next day Elise wrote the two letters, one to Mary, the other to Mrs. Hoppner. (White, II, 622; Clairmont, pp. 97, 274, 279, 283. The square brackets denote illegible material.

19. Medwin, p. 116; *Rossetti Papers*, p. 500; *Letters about Shelley*, p. 51.

20. Mary's journals and letters and Shelley's letters reveal that she lived a normal, not unstrenuous existence in the months and weeks preceding the birth of the child, including horseback riding in July and a climb up Mount Vesuvius on Dec. 16. Furthermore, she wrote of Clara and William as her only children in June 1819, when Elena Adelaide was still alive. (White, II, 72; to Marianne Hunt, June 29, 1819, Mary Shelley, *Letters*, I, 74.)

21. On Jan. 24, 1819, Shelley informed Peacock that Elise and Foggi had "just" married. *(Letters*, II, 76.)

22. Dowden, II, 252–253; see also *Letters about Shelley*, p 85. This story was first hinted at in 1833 by Medwin *(Shelley Papers*, p. 50). He later wrote that before Shelley left for Geneva in 1816 (Medwin wrongly wrote "1814"), Shelley was visited by "a married lady, young, handsome, and of noble connections," who told him that, attracted by his "virtues" and his "uncompromising passion for liberty", she had decided to renounce "my husband, my name, my family and friends" and "to follow you through the world." Shelley discouraged her, but she followed him to Geneva. When he returned to England, "her constancy was untiring." When he again went to the Continent in 1818, she again followed. At Naples they met, where she told him of her wanderings in his wake—of which he had been ignorant—and "at Naples—she died." (Medwin, pp. 204–207.)

23. White, I, 437, II, 71–84; Fuller, p. 233. White stated that the governmental records do not record the death of an English woman at Naples at this time; nor does *The Gentleman's Magazine*. Roe, however, stated that these records are incomplete. (Roe, *Shelley*, p. 171.)

24. Smith, p. 245–247; Roe, *Shelley*, pp. 178–179; Ursula Orange, "Elise, Nursemaid to the Shelleys," *Keats-Shelley Memorial Bulletin*, VI (1955), 24–34.

25. Marcel Kessel, "The Mark of X in Claire Clairmont's Journal," *PMLA*, LXVI (1951), 1180–1183.

26. To Peacock, July 25, Dec. 17 or 18, 1818, *Letters*, II, 25, 62.

27. Mary Berry, *Miss Berry's Journal and Correspondence* (London, 1865), II, 117; Roe, *Shelley*, p. 174.

28. Elise had been employed by the Shelleys since 1816. The first mention of Paolo Foggi is in a letter by Mary Shelley written from the baths of Lucca to Mrs. Gisborne

at Leghorn on June 15, 1818: "Signor Chiappa we found perfectly useless—he would talk of nothing but himself and recommended a person to cook our dinner for us at 3 pauls a day—So, as it is, Paolo (whom we find exceedingly useful) cooks and manages for us, and a woman comes at 1 paul a day to do the dirty work. We live very comfortably and if Paolo did not cheat us he would be a servant worth a treasure for he does every thing cleanlily & exactly without teizing us in any way." (Mary Shelley, *Letters*, I, 53.) Mary and Shelley had arrived at Leghorn on May 8 and left on June 11 for the baths of Lucca, where they apparently lived in the house of G. B. del Chiappa, who recommended Paolo. (Dowden, II, 211n.) The probability is that he was hired just after the Shelleys moved to the baths of Lucca on June 11. Elise had left the Shelley party at Milan on Apr. 28 to take Allegra to Byron at Venice. In late August she went with Shelley and Claire from Venice to Este. (Apr. 28, Aug. 29–Sept. 14, *Mary Shelley's Journal*, pp. 97, 104–105.) See also Shelley's letter to Mary at the baths of Lucca, Aug. 23, 1818 (*Letters*, II, 37): "Pray come instantly to Este, where I shall be waiting with Clare & Elise in the utmost anxiety for your arrival . . . Make Paulo take you to good Inns . . ."

29. To Mrs. R. B. Hoppner, Aug. 10, 1821, Mary Shelley, *Letters*, I, 148.

30. See also Louise Schutz Boas, "Nursemaid to the Shelleys," *Notes and Queries*, III (1956), 216–217, 309–310.

31. Medwin, pp. 204–205; see also p. 407.

32. Medwin, *Conversations*, p. 254. Byron's remark, taken in conjunction with Medwin's account, makes it almost certain that the reference is to the mysterious lady. His reference to her as "a Mrs. ——" shows that she was not a titled lady. Medwin (p. 206) gave another possible clue: "The pride of a woman—the pride of a—— might have revolted to acknowledge, much more to feel, that she loved in vain." The blank surely stands for the name of a famous family, for Medwin stated that she had "noble connections." Thus, she was apparently connected with a noble family but had married a commoner.

33. Dowden, II, 252.

34. The name of the child as well as the word "charge" may provide a clue to her identity. "Elena Adelaide" could indicate one Italian and one English parent, for Elena is the Italian form of Helen. Two possible sources for Adelaide might be noted. Amelia Adelaide of Saxe-Meiningen married the duke of Clarence in July 1818, five months before the Neapolitan child's birth; later she became Queen Adelaide. Lady Charlotte Campbell Bury was in or near Naples at this period with her daughter (apparently a child), Adelaide Constance. (Roe, *Shelley*, p. 171.) Lady Bury, knew of Shelley, having in March 1818 married the Rev. Edward John Bury, who had been at the same college at Oxford as Shelley, receiving his B.A. in 1811, the year Shelley was expelled. Lady Bury had six daughters, one named Eleanora. The eldest daughter, Eliza Cummings, born in 1797 and married in 1815, went to Naples in November 1817, followed by Eleanora in the spring. (Harriet Charlotte Beaujolois Campbell, *A Journey to Florence in 1817*, ed. Sir Gavin de Beer [London, 1951], pp. 13, 15, 126, 131, 136; Peck, I, 105–106; *Alumni Oxonienses*; for Lady Bury, see the *DNB* and the introduction to her *The Diary of a Lady-in-Waiting* [London, 1909].)

35. Dowden, II, 478–479. Shelley's letter to the Countess Guiccioli, Aug. 9?, 1821, may also have direct reference to Foggi's activities. (*Letters*, II, 325.)

36. Thornton Hunt, "Shelley, by One Who Knew Him," *Shelley and Keats As They Struck Their Contemporaries*, ed. Edmund Blunden (London, 1925), p. 48. For Clint's idealizing of material, compare his portrait of Edward Williams (*Keats-Shelley Memorial Bulletin*, IV [1952]) with Williams' self-portrait (Gisborne & Williams).

37. For Shelley's portraits, see White, II, 518–538. White used the Williams picture (now in the Morgan Library in New York) as a frontispiece (I,ii). See also *Esdaile Notebook*, frontispiece and p. 30. Other water-color miniatures by Williams appear in a notebook purchased by The Carl H. Pforzheimer Library, and their techniques and coloring are very similar to the "Shelley." A portrait supposed to be of Shelley as a boy and attributed to Hoppner appears in Walter de la Mare, *Early One Morning* (London, 1935), p. 492, and is described in Henry G. Marquand, *Illustrated Catalogue*, American Art Association (New York, 1903), no. 29. I traced this portrait through many vicissitudes to a sale at the Newhouse Galleries, New York, in the 1950's, where the trail was lost. See also Richard Garnett, "Portraits of Shelley in the National Portrait Gallery," *The Magazine of Art*, XXV (1901), 492–495; Blunden, p. 249. Shelley had a sketch made at Florence by a "Mr. Tomkins" or Tomkyns, probably Peltro William Tomkins, which is now presumed lost. (White, II, 519.)

38. *Letters*, II, 93–94. Shelley was disturbed by a similar sight in Pisa: "At other times I have seen him also very much affected by the sight of the convicts fettered two

and two who escorted by Soldiers sweep the streets—and still more so by the clank of their chains, desperate-looking criminals, hardened in, and capable of any crimes—were they, for there was not one perhaps who had not committed a murder." (Medwin, p. 268) Claire described the scene at Pisa: "The convicts, who are very numerous, work in the streets, cleaning and sweeping them; they are dressed in red; they are chained by the leg together in pairs. All the day long one hears the slow clanking of their chains and the rumbling of the cart they drag, as if they were so many beasts of burden; and if one goes to the window, one is sure to see their yellow faces and emaciated forms." (Dowden, II, 205).

39. Aug. 28, 1819, Mary Shelley, *Letters* I, 76.

40. Dowden, II, 270.

41. Aug. 24, 1819, *Letters,* II, 114. The "tower" was a "terrace roofed and glazed at the top of the house." (Dowden, II, 274.) The reference is to Peacock's novel *Nightmare Abbey,* where Scythrop, a caricature of Shelley, inhabits a tower. (To Peacock, July 6, 1819, *Letters,* II, 100.)

42. Helen Rossetti Angeli, *Shelley and His Friends in Italy* (London, 1911), pp. 96–102. The final section, beginning "Shelley was an admirable Italian scholar," is not from the journal but from a memoir written several years later. The diary has since been lost. (White, II, 586.)

43. Angeli, *Shelley,* p. 101. Mrs. Parker was a sister of Shelley's father. (Ingpen, p. 713.)

44. Mary ascribed these poems to the year 1819, stating that Shelley intended to issue a book of them. (*Works,* III, 307.) In a letter to Hunt on May 1, 1820, Shelley asked if he knew of a publisher for such a book. (*Letters,* II, 191.) The poems were probably written late in 1819, most likely about the same time as *The Mask of Anarchy,* completed late in September.

45. Paul, I, 181–182. On Lady Mount Cashell, see McAleer.

46. McAleer, p. 119; *Shelley and His Circle,* I, 49n.

47. Paul, I, 369.

48. *Advice to Young Mothers on the Physical Education of Children,* by "A Grandmother" (London, 1823); McAleer, pp. 182–184.

49. To Marianne Hunt, Feb. 24, 1820, Mary Shelley, *Letters,* I, 95.

50. To Maria Gisborne, Dec. 13, 1820, *ibid.,* p. 120.

51. Sylva Norman, *After Shelley: The Letters of Thomas Jefferson Hogg and Jane Williams* (New York, 1934), p. 46.

52. To Medwin, Apr. 16, 1820, *Letters,* II, 184. Shelley's self-confessed "extremely social disposition" was a natural outgrowth of being brought up in the social tradition of the English county families with their constant parties and entertainments. When he was in Edinburgh in 1811, he was described by Charles Kirkpatrick Sharpe as a "very gentlemanly" person wont to "dance quadrilles eternally." (*Letters from and to Charles Kirkpatrick Sharpe,* ed. Alexander Allardyce [Edinburgh and London, 1888], I, 497.)

53. May 1, 1820, *Letters,* II, 191.

54. To Marianne Hunt, Feb. 24, 1820, Mary Shelley, *Letters,* I, 96–97. "Murray my custom" is apparently a slap at Byron, who continued to publish through this conservative house, which backed the *Quarterly Review.*

55. To Leigh Hunt, Apr. 5, 1820, *Letters,* II, 180: "Much stress is laid upon a still more southern climate for my health, which has suffered dreadfully this winter, and if I could believe that Spain would be effectual, I might possibly be tempted to make a voyage thither on account of the glorious events of which it is at this moment the theatre. You know my passion for a republic, or anything which approaches it."

56. For a balanced view of Medwin, see Ernest J. Lovell, *Captain Medwin, Friend of Byron and Shelley* (Austin, Texas, 1962).

57. Medwin, pp. 233–234, 237, 250–251, 259–260, 235.

58. *Ibid.,* p. 275; to Leigh Hunt, Dec. 3, 1820, Mary Shelley, *Letters,* I, 117. Shelley had perhaps heard accounts of Coleridge's conversation from Godwin or Southey.

59. To Claire Clairmont, Feb. 18, 1821, *Letters,* II, 266–267. An examination of the ms. of this letter in the Morgan Library shows that "taught" is a preferable reading to Jones's "loyal," which makes no sense.

60. Dec. 29, 1820, Mary Shelley, *Letters,* I, 125. The reference to Burdett shows Shelley's continued admiration for his first political hero. (See Cameron, pp. 46–49 and *passim.*) "Grey Bennett" was the Hon. H. G. Bennet, parliamentary reformer. (S. Maccoby, *English Radicalism, 1786–1832* [London, 1955], p. 384.)

61. See Norman, *After Shelley,* p. xiv; Edmund Blunden, "The Family of Edward Williams," *Keats-Shelley Memorial Bulletin,* IV (1952), 50–51. Hogg wrote to Jane Wil-

liams from Naples on Dec. 6, 1825, that the Countess Guiccioli had heard "of your great secret and our great calamity." The "secret" was Jane's previous marriage and the illegality of her union with Williams; the "calamity," that her husband was still alive and hence she was unable to marry Hogg. Norman, *After Shelley*, pp. xxiii, 51–52.

62. *Byron*, V, 595–596; Jan. 13, 1821, *ibid.*, p. 173; see also Dora Neill Raymond, *The Political Career of Lord Byron* (New York, 1924), p. 142.

63. Marchand, II, 913–916; to Mary, Aug. 7, 1821, *Letters*, II, 316–317. A day or so before the Countess Guiccioli left him on Aug. 2, Byron wrote to Shelley: "If moving at present should be inconvenient to you—let me settle that—draw upon me for what you think necessary—I should do so myself on you without ceremony—if I found it expedient.—Write directly." (*Letters*. II, 314n.) Shelley's letter to Mary after his arrival at Ravenna shows that Byron also discussed his wavering plans of remaining in Italy or going to Switzerland. (Aug. 7, 1821, *ibid.*, pp. 316–317.)

64. Aug. 18, 1821, *Letters*, II, 322.

65. C. Aug. 10, 1821, *ibid.*, pp. 330–331.

66. Aug. 26, 1821, *ibid.*, p. 345, to Mary Shelley, Aug. 10, 1821, ibid., p. 324; *ibid.*, p. 323; *Sonnet to Byron* (1821); White, II, 333.

67. To T. L. Peacock, c. Aug. 10, 1821, *Letters*, II, 331; Aug. 16, 1821, *ibid.*, p. 339.

68. Feb. 25, 1819, *ibid.*, p. 81; Dec. 25, 1820, *Byron*, V, 143; Aug, 26, 1821, *Letters*, II, 344.

69. See William H. Marshall, *Byron, Shelley, Hunt and The Liberal* (Philadelphia, 1960), pp. 22–27.

70. To Moore, June 1, 1818; see *ibid.*, pp. 10–11.

71. On Taaffe see C. L. Cline, *Byron, Shelley and Their Pisan Circle* (Cambridge, 1952, 16–25, 199–202.

72. In 1878 Trelawny brought out *Records of Shelley, Byron, and the Author*, which expands on the *Recollections* (1858). See also Trelawny's letters and interviews—with Rossetti (*Rossetti Papers*, pp. 398–399, 500–502), with Richard Edgcumbe (*Temple Bar*, May 1890), and with Mathilde Blind (*Whitehall Review*, Jan. 10, 1880).

73. Gisborne & Williams, pp. 106, 111, 114–115, 116, 122, 123–124.

74. Thornton Hunt, in *Shelley and Keats*, p. 22.

75. Medwin, *Conversations*, pp. 2–4, 91–93, 290–291, 292–294.

76. May 14, 1822, *Memoirs, Journals and Correspondence of Thomas Moore*, ed. Lord John Russell (Boston, 1853), III, 352; to Leigh Hunt, Apr. 10, 1822, *Letters*, II, 405.

77. Byron, V, 496. As Byron wrote this undated letter to Moore on the back of a note by Shelley of Dec. 13 (*Letters*, II, 368–369), it must also be dated Dec. 13 or shortly after.

78. See Marchand, II, 873–874, 886, 905, 919–920.

79. Sept. 10, 1820, Byron, V, 74, 438; Trelawny, *Records*, I, 42.

80. Quoted in Byron, VI, 35; Mar. 4, 1822, *ibid.*, pp. 32–33.

81. *Ibid.*, p. 99; April 1823, *Conversations of Lord Byron with the Countess of Blessington*, 2nd ed. (London, 1850), pp. 75–76.

82. Anne Hill, "Trelawny's Background and Naval Career," *Keats-Shelley Journal*, V (Winter, 1956), 11–32.

83. Massingham, p. 14.

84. Trelawny, pp. 189–190.

85. Trelawny (p.x) recognized the similarity: "Hogg has painted him exactly as I knew him." Rossetti noted: "T[relawny] is now reading with extreme delight Hogg's Life of S[helley] (hitherto unread by him), and considers H's view of S thoroughly consistent with T's own experience." (Mar. 11, 1870, *Rossetti Papers*, p. 501.)

86. Rossetti described Shelley (from Trelawny): "His body, especially legs and thighs, was finely formed; and his powers of active exertion, as in climbing hills, distanced all the company." (Mar. 15, 1870, *Rossetti Papers*, p. 502.)

87. April 1821, Trelawny, pp. 168, 202.

88. Medwin, *Conversations*, pp. 216–218; see also Medwin, pp. 364–365. The sequel is told by Williams: "*Thursday, December* 13. Eine. Hear that the criminal is a Priest who having flown to Florence for protection was there detected, but the Grand Duke, hearing of the cruel punishment that awaited him refused to give him up. It is reported that it was actually the Queen of Lucca's intention (who is an Infanta of Spain) to burn the culprit alive, not so much for the theft of the Sacrament cup itself as for having spilt the most Holy Eucharist upon the road." (Gisborne & Williams, p. 117. See also Cline, *Byron, Shelley and Their Pisan Circle*, pp. 60–65.)

89. See Cline, pp. 91–154.

90. William's journal, Dec. 30, 1821, Gisborne & Williams, p. 121.

91. Shelley and Mary entered their house at San Terenzo on Apr. 30; the Williamses

moved in with them on May 1. (*Mary Shelley's Journal*, p. 178; Gisborne & Williams, p. 146.)

92. On June 2, 1822, Mary wrote to Mrs. Gisborne: "Trelawny chose the name of the *Don Juan*, and we acceded; but when Shelley took her entirely on himself we changed the name to the Ariel. Lord Byron chose to take fire at this, and determined that she should be called after the Poem; wrote to Roberts to have the name painted on the mainsail, and she arrived thus disfigured. For days and nights, full twenty-one, did Shelley and Edward ponder on her anabaptism, and the washing out the primeval stain. Turpentine, spirits of wine, buccata, all were tried, and it became dappled and no more. At length the piece has been taken out and reefs put, so that the sail does not look worse. I do not know what Lord Byron will say, but Lord and Poet as he is, he could not be allowed to make a coal barge of our boat." Although *Ariel* was Shelley's and Mary's choice for a name, the boat was apparently never in fact renamed. (Mary Shelley, *Letters*, I, 170n; Trelawny, *Records*, II, 4, where Mary herself refers to it as the *Don Juan*.) When Shelley saw the words *Don Juan* on the sail, he wrote to Trelawny that this was "carrying the joke rather too far . . . Does he [Byron] mean to write the Bolivar [the name of Byron's yacht] on his own mainsail?" (May 16, 1822, *Letters*, II, 422.) This indicates that Trelawny's original suggestion had some humorous connotation. Shelley perhaps intended to change the name to *Ariel*, but for the time being he apparently did not wish to cross Byron. Shelley's anger is obvious in his letter to Trelawny. Byron's action, however, may have been dictated partly by Shelley's admiration for his poem. Shelley wrote to Peacock in August 1821 about Canto V of *Don Juan*, which he had just seen, that "every word of it is pregnant with immortality"; and to Byron on Oct. 21, 1821, about the first five cantos: "Nothing has ever been written like it in English—nor if I may venture to prophesy, will there be." (*Letters*, II, 330, 357.)

93. Gisborne & Williams, pp. 146–147.

94. Shelley checked the hemorrhage by having Mary sit in ice, "so that when the physician arrived all danger was over." (To John Gisborne, June 18, 1822, *Letters*, II, 434.)

95. For the Tremadoc episode, see Cameron, pp. 205–214, which concluded that Shelley was acting out a fantasy in order to escape from an intolerable situation. (He had claimed that he was attacked by a mysterious intruder at night in a remote house near Tremadoc in Wales.) H. M. Dowling in *Notes and Queries*, July and December 1954, argued that an attack actually took place. These notes he used as the base for an article, "The Attack at Tanyrallt," *Keats-Shelley Memorial Bulletin*, XII, (1961), 28–36. Dowling (p. 34), based his theory essentially on an undated letter from Shelley's landlord, William Maddocks. Maddocks, however, told Medwin that the episode was "a delusion." (Medwin, p. 117.) And a considerable body of evidence indicates that there was no actual attack. W. H. McCulloch in "The Last Night at Tan-yr-allt," *Keats-Shelley Memorial Bulletin*, VIII (1957), 20–32, argued that Shelley was having a hallucination. But it is not psychiatrically possible for a nonpsychotic not on hallucinogenic drugs to hallucinate.

96. *Gisborne & Williams*, p. 147; to Maria Gisborne, Aug. 15, 1822, Mary Shelley, *Letters* I 180. (Quoted by permission of the University of Oklahoma Press.)

97. John William Polidori, *The Vampyre: A Tale* (London, 1819), pp. xiv–xv. Polidori recorded the episode somewhat differently in his diary for June 18, 1816: "Began my ghost-story after tea. Twelve o'clock, really began to talk ghostly. L[ord] B[yron] repeated some verses of Coleridge's *Christabel*, of the witch's breast; when silence ensued, and Shelley, suddenly shrieking and putting his hands to his head, ran out of the room with a candle. Threw water in his face, and after gave him ether. He was looking at Mrs. S[helley], and suddenly thought of a woman he had heard of who had eyes instead of nipples, which, taking hold of his mind, horrified him." (*The Diary of Dr. John William Polidori*, ed. William Michael Rosseti [London, 1911], pp. 127–128.)

98. To John Murray, May 15, 1819, Byron, IV, 297.

99. *Letters*, II, 436, 433.

100. To Maria Gisborne, Aug. 15, 1822, Mary Shelley, *Letters*, I, 180–181. (Quoted by permission of the University of Oklahoma Press.)

101. Gisborne & Williams, p. 155. Medwin (pp. 404–405) heard a similar story from Byron, which Jane Williams confirmed. Medwin's story, as Dowden pointed out (II, 516n), was a confused blending of the doppelgänger vision with the nightmare.

102. *Prometheus Unbound*, I, 191–194; see also *The Revolt of Islam*, 3982–3986; Medwin, p. 405.

103. Harriet felt that, in the Tremadoc episode, Shelley had "wanted to frighten her." See Mrs. M. J. Godwin to Lady Mount Cashell, Feb. 15, 1815, Dowden, I, 355n.

104. *Letters of Leigh Hunt*, ed. Thornton Hunt (London, 1862), I, 182. Hunt did not actually leave until a week or so later.

105. Williams' journal, July 1, 1822, Gisborne & Williams, p. 156. On Vivian, see Trelawny, p. 207. Hunt apparently arrived without funds and expected Byron and Shelley to support him and his family. (*Letters*, II, 381n.)

106. Thornton Hunt in *Shelley and Keats*, p. 22. Thornton Hunt further indicated (pp. 51–52) that the "shrill" quality of Shelley's voice was largely the result of excitement: "The weakness ascribed to Shelley's voice was equally taken from exceptional instances, and the account of it usually suggests the idea that he spoke in a falsetto which might almost be mistaken for the 'shriek' of a harsh-toned woman. Nothing could be more unlike the reality . . . When he called out in pain,—a very rare occurrence,—or sometimes in comic playfulness, you might hear the 'shrillness' of which people talk; but it was only because the organ was forced beyond the ordinary effort. His usual speech was clear, and yet with a breath in it, with an especially distinct articulation, a soft, vibrating tone, emphatic, pleasant, and persuasive." For Leigh Hunt on the reunion, see Blunden, p. 347.

107. From the June 1822 issue, quoted in Marshall, *Byron, Shelley, Hunt, and The Liberal*, pp. 47–48.

108. *Byron*, VI, 22n.

109. William Hazlitt, "On Jealousy and Spleen of Party," in Marshall, *Byron, Shelley, Hunt, and The Liberal*, pp. 41–42. Leigh Hunt's brother, John, was in prison for an attack on the House of Commons in *The Examiner*.

110. Aug. 15, 1822, Mary Shelley, *Letters*, I, 183. See also Edward Williams to Jane Williams, July 6, 1822, Gisborne & Williams, p. 162: "in fact with Lord B. it appears they cannot do anything—who actually has said as much as that he did not wish his name to be attached to the work and of course to them."

111. To Elizabeth Kent, Hunt, *Correspondence* I, 188–189.

112. *The Liberal: Verse and Prose from the South* (London, 1822), I, vi–vii (Preface).

113. *The Literary Register*, Oct. 19, 1822, in Marshall, *Byron, Shelley, Hunt, and The Liberal*, p. 100.

114. Marshall, *Byron, Shelley, Hunt, and The Liberal*, pp. 126–127, 206, 209.

115. To John Murray, Oct. 9, 1822, *ibid.*, p. 67. Byron continued: "I believe the *brothers H.* to be honest men; I am sure they are poor ones . . . The death of Shelley left them totally aground."

116. *Ibid.*, pp. 203–204.

117. The ship was found on the sea bottom somewhere between the mouth of the Serchio, 15 miles north of Leghorn, and Viareggio, about 22 miles north of Leghorn. (G. P. Frederini, governor of Viareggio, to the secretary of state of Lucca, Sept. 12, 1822, testimony of Antonio Canova, Guido Biagi, *The Last Days of Percy Bysshe Shelley* [London, 1898], pp. 81, 142–143, 163.)

118. White, II, 377; *Letters*, II, 445n; J. E. Morpurgo, *The Last Days of Shelley and Byron* (London, 1952), p. 100; Frederick L. Jones, "Trelawny and the Sinking of Shelley's Boat," *Keats-Shelley Memorial Bulletin* (Rome), XVI (1965), 42–44.

119. To Maria Gisborne, June 2, 1822, Mary Shelley, *Letters*, I, 170; Trelawny, early narrative, in Massingham, p. 163; R. Glynn Grylls, *Trelawny* (London, 1950), p. 80 (plan of boat). Trelawny in "Narrative 2," dated September 1822, gave the length as 26 feet. (Leslie Marchand, "Trelawny on the Death of Shelley," *Keats-Shelley Memorial Bulletin*, Rome, IV (1952), 1, 29.) In *Records* (I, 152) Trelawny stated that the boat was "not more than thirty feet long with a beam in proportion." Twenty-four feet seems correct, though this may not include the false bow and stern added later. James Rieger stated that among the Trelawny manuscripts acquired by the British Museum in 1964 there was a "deck plan, presumably drawn by Roberts, which shows that Shelley's yacht was not open (as is generally supposed), but fitted with a cabin enclosed to protect sofas and bookshelves." (Rieger, p. 221.) This plan must be the one described in Sotheby & Co. Catalogue, Dec. 16–17 (London, 1963), as item no. 530, "Sketch Plan and Elevation of Shelley's boat the 'Don Juan,'" as this item was purchased for the British Museum at this sale and no other plan of the boat appeared in the Catalogue. The item is noted in the Catalogue as already reproduced in Grylls, *Trelawny*, p. 80. Although this sketch depicts a small cabin, five feet long, in the stern, the 20 feet or so of the boat forward of this cabin was open; so the boat could still be swamped by waves. According to Grylls, the sketch was by Williams; but since it was with letters by Roberts, it could have been his work.

120. Trelawny, p. 207; Williams' journal, June 21–22, 1822, Gisborne & Williams, p. 155; White, II, 368.

121. Trelawny, pp. 215–216. Marchand commented in "Trelawny on the Death of Shelley," p. 13: "The dramatic dialogue with the Genoese mate is absent from both the

early manuscripts, nor is there any reference to Trelawny's sending the mate on board other vessels to make inquiries nor of his discovering oars or spars which he believed to be from Shelley's boat. Trelawny, then, may have invented this dialogue—which he was quite capable of doing—or simply left it out of his early (very short) version. The description of the vessels rushing back to port is also in the early version, and so it is probably true."

122. Mary Shelley, *Letters*, I, 183. (Quoted by permission of the University of Oklahoma Press.)

123. Gisborne to T. J. Hogg, Aug. 12, 1822, *New Letters*, p. 137. Trelawny noted at the same period that a fishing-boat captain had witnessed the sinking. (Massingham, p. 166; see also Trelawny, p. 220; Medwin, p. 398.)

124. *The Journal of Clarissa Trant*, ed. Clara Georgina Luard (London, 1925), pp. 198–199. Clarissa Trant was the daughter of Sir Nicholas Trant, an Irish soldier and diplomat. She was born in Lisbon in 1800 and traveled extensively in Europe with her father. Taaffe, also an Irishman, had been in Florence at the time of Shelley's death and heard the story on his return to Pisa, possibly from Byron or Lady Mount Cashell, both of whom he gave as sources for information on Shelley's last days.

125. Biagi, *The Last Days*, pp. 77–79, 83. Distances are calculated from a large map of the area in *A General Map of the Empire of Germany, Holland, The Netherlands, Switzerland, The Grisons, Italy, Sicily, Corsica, and Sardinia* by Captain Chauchard, etc. (London, 1800).

126. Biagi, *The Last Days*, pp. 142–144. Trelawny stated that he "engaged two large feluccas, with drags and tackling," at Leghorn to search for the *Don Juan* and that they found the ship but could not get her up. She was then, he implied, raised by Roberts. (Trelawny, pp. 220, 229.) But an early narrative indicates that they did not find the ship and that Trelawny paid them off after six days. (Massingham, p. 166.)

127. Biagi, *The Last Days*, pp. 163–164.

128. Trelawny's statements on the distance from shore at which the boat was found varied from 2 to 13 miles. (Marchand, "Trelawny on the Death of Shelley," p. 26.) But the 13 miles was in an early account written in September 1822; the 2 miles appeared fifty-one years later. Trelawny was only repeating what he had heard, for he was not present when the ship was found.

129. British Museum Ms. Ps. 5/2793, add. 52361(3). (Quoted by permission.) See also Sotheby & Co. Catalogue, Dec. 16–17, p. 122. For Trelawny's incorrect version, see Trelawny, p. 229. Trelawny gave the letter as though written to himself and dated it simply "Sept. 1822."

130. Roberts to Trelawny, Sept. 18, 1822, British Museum Ms. quoted by permission. Roberts later sailed the boat himself. (Grylls, *Trelawny*, p. 100.) In 1827 it was sold to some officers at Zante and later was wrecked. (White, II, 633.)

131. British Museum Ms. (Quoted by permission.) Trelawny (p. 229) changed the letter freely. Jones argued that the mud in the boat might have prevented Roberts from seeing the full extent of the damage. Frederick L. Jones, "Trelawny and the Sinking of Shelley's Boat," *Keats-Shelley Memorial Bulletin*, XVI (1965), 42–44. Roberts could, however, have seen all major damage by inspecting the outside.

132. Trelawny, p. 230. Jones suggested that this sentence "probably" came from "a subsequent letter" by Roberts and was tacked on to the earlier letter by Trelawny. (Jones, "Trelawny and the Sinking of Shelley's Boat," p. 43.) This is not impossible, for Roberts later argued, as indicated in Mary Shelley's letters, that the ship had been run down, and Trelawny would have had no scruples in handling letters in this loose way. However, no such letter from Roberts is known to exist, and there is no evidence that Trelawny in fact took the phrase from Roberts. The existing evidence indicates that Trelawny invented and wrote in the sentence himself. He could have justified such action to himself on the grounds of Roberts' later views.

133. Marchand, "Trelawny on the Death of Shelley," pp. 30–31. In another early narrative (*ibid.*, p. 26) Trelawny mentioned only the storm as the cause of the sinking.

134. Mary Shelley, *Letters*, I, 197; to Maria Gisborne, May 2, 1823, *ibid.*, p. 223. (Quoted by permission of the University of Oklahoma Press.)

135. Hunt, *Lord Byron and Some of His Contemporaries* (London, 1828), I, 201.

136. Hunt, *II*, 100.

137. Nov. 22, 1875, Trelawny, *Records*, I, 196, 197–199, 202–203; Grylls, *Trelawny*, p. 238.

138. Richard Garnett, "Shelley's Last Days," *The Fortnightly Review*, n.s. *CXXXVIII* (June 1, 1878), 865–866.

139. Byron, VI, 98.

140. Biagi, *The Last Days*, p. 97.

141. Medwin, pp. 392–393.

142. Massingham, p. 167. This account was written for Hunt to publish. It is undated but was clearly written after the burning of the bodies on Aug. 15–16 and before the finding of the *Don Juan* on Sept. 12. In later accounts Trelawny defended the boat and its construction; e. g. "The unfortunate Boat was afterward perchased by a naval officer and has been the whole of this boisterous winter at sea coasting Italy without accident —and it proved to be an excellent sea boat." (Marchand, "Trelawny on the Death of Shelley," p. 31.) But Medwin (p. 399) gave an opposite view: Roberts "decked her, and sailed in her, but found her unseaworthy, and . . . her shattered planks now lie rotting on the shore of one of the Ionian Islands, on which she was wrecked."

143. The hour at which the *Don Juan* left Leghorn is not clear. Trelawny named every hour from 12 noon to 2 P.M. Mary stated that they left at 1 P.M. Roberts stated that the ship was going at about seven knots and that by 3 o'clock they were 10 miles out to sea. (Dowden, II, 522n; Marchand, "Trelawny on the Death of Shelley," p. 14.) The seven knots would agree with their time on the trip from Lerici to Leghorn—about 50 miles in 7 1/2 hours. As the ship was found between 15 and 20 miles from Lerici, it would also indicate that they had been gone for at least two hours. In different accounts the hour of the wreck was given as 4 P.M. and 5 P.M. This would accord with a letter of Sept. 17, 1822, from the governor of Viareggio to the secretary of state for Lucca stating that the ship was "wrecked after a few hours' journey." (Biagi, *The Last Days*, p. 147.) Trelawny in his September 1822 narrative reported that the ship had been gone for three hours when the storm broke. (Marchand, "Trelawny on the Death of Shelley," p. 30.) Trelawny's early narratives also contained no hint of a coming storm. In one of them he mentioned a "light breeze" when the *Don Juan* left and gave the impression of good and promising weather. (Massingham, p. 167.) This was Roberts' observation also. (To Maria Gisborne, Aug. 15, 1822, Mary Shelley, *Letters*, I, 183.)

144. Trelawny implied that he saw the salvaged boat. (Marchand, "Trelawny on the Death of Shelley," p. 30.) However, he was not at Leghorn but at Rome when the boat was salvaged and auctioned. (Trelawny, p. 229.) If he saw the shell later, before Roberts had reconditioned it, he would hardly have omitted an account of it.

145. Peacock, an official of the East India Company, held the same opinion. (Peacock, pp. 358–359.)

146. Trelawny in an early narrative gave the depth as "13 fathoms"; in other accounts as 10 and 15. (Marchand, "Trelawny on the Death of Shelley," p. 26.) How the salvaging was done is not known. The fishermen simply stated that they found the ship when she was "caught in their net" and then "towed" her. This could suggest that she was towed along in the net, but obviously the narrative is contracted. The ship must somehow have been brought to the surface, presumably by block and tackle, and then a rope made fast to her for towing. After she was towed to shore, she was "beached," then pulled off the beach and towed again, this time to Leghorn.

147. Grylls, *Trelawny*, p. 238.

148. See also Trelawny (p. 220): "the captain of one of the feluccas having asserted that he was out in the fatal squall, and had seen Shelley's boat go down off Via Reggio, with all sail set."

149. Peacock, p. 358.

150. It has been suggested that two different boats were involved. (White, II, 377.) But there is no hint of this anywhere. It seems more likely that the stories—including Trelawny's (Massingham, pp. 163–165) and Medwin's (p. 398)—emanated from the same source. The divergences between them are no more than would be normal in the telling and retelling by various narrators, perhaps with elaborations by Taaffe.

151. Massingham, p. 166. Taaffe was not at Pisa or Leghorn at the time of the disaster but at Florence. He wrote to Byron asking for information. (Taaffe to Byron, July 20, 1822, Cline, *Byron, Shelley and Their Pisan Circle*, pp. 185–186.) Where he got the story that he told to Clarissa Trant is not clear. Taaffe also told Miss Trant that Shelley, while on a visit to Lady Mount Cashell the night before his departure, had "talked in such a strain of rhapsody of storms, and hurricanes, and described so minutely the sublime horrors of shipwreck that the lady did not for the whole day recover the impression, which this conversation, aided by the howling of the wind and the noise of the waves, had made upon her nerves. Her husband, who was present, said with some degree of displeasure, that he should forbid him the house if he only came to alarm Lady McCashell with his rhapsodies, adding that he would certainly lose his life in some such scene as he had been describing, if he attempted many more voyages in his little over-rigged Boat." Mary Shelley, however, told Maria Gisborne that Lady Mount

Cashell had said that on the night before Shelley left, he was "in better health and spirits than she had ever known him." (Aug. 15, 1822, Mary Shelley, *Letters,* I, 183.)

152. Trelawny, pp. 209–210.

153. Taaffe's story conforms to the picture of Shelley as a reckless romantic that he gave elsewhere, for instance in his report of a conversation with Byron: " 'The last time I ever heard poor Shelley's voice,' he said, 'was as he closed that very door. I had repeatedly urged him to defer embarking until the next day, and told him that it was madness to embark in such a gale, and in such a boat—but all my endeavours were thrown away, he had set his mind upon returning. As he was going, he turned round and said: 'Well, to satisfy you, I will not embark if the Storm increases, but I shall confess that if the Gale freshens when we are at Sea I shall not be sorry; you know how I enjoy a storm.' " (*Journal of Clarissa Trant,* p. 197.) Most, if not all, of this conversation must be sheer invention, for Byron was at Pisa, and Shelley had left Pisa for Leghorn the night before the morning of his sailing. The "gale" did not come until at least the mid-afternoon of the next day.

154. To Maria Gisborne, Aug. 15, 1822, Mary Shelley, *Letters,* I, 183 (quoting Captain Roberts.)

155. July 4, 1822, *Letters,* II, 444.

156. July 4, 1822, *ibid.,* p. 445.

157. Gisborne & Williams, p. 162.

158. Rieger, pp. 224–225.

159. Williams' journal, June, 13, 16, 1822, Gisborne & Williams, p. 154.

160. Trelawny, p. 210.

161. Aug. 15, 1822, Mary Shelley, *Letters,* I, 182. (Quoted by permission of the University of Oklahoma Press.)

162. *Ibid.,* pp. 184–185. On the internal dating, Jones noted (*ibid.*): "It is quite evident that Mary's date is one week off. The two bodies had been discovered on the sixteenth (or seventeenth) and eighteenth; Trelawny informed them of the recovery on the nineteenth; and Mary returned to Pisa on the twentieth.—See Dowden, II, 528n."

163. Trelawny to the Rev. Thomas Hall of Leghorn, Aug. 10, 1822, Leslie A. Marchand, "A Note on the Burning of Shelley's Body,"—*Keats-Shelley Memorial Bulletin,* VI (1955), 2. Trelawny confused the dates of the cremations in his various accounts. (Marchand, "Trelawny on the Death of Shelley," pp. 18–19.) On Aug. 14 Byron wrote to Trelawny that he would join him "at noon" on the next day—the day on which Williams' body was burned. (Cline, *Byron, Shelley and Their Pisan Circle,* p. 187.)

164. Trelawny to Byron, Sept. 2, 1822, Grylls, *Trelawny,* p. 95; see also to Maria Gisborne, c. Aug. 27, 1822, Mary Shelley, *Letters,* I, 187.

165. Trelawny, *Letters,* pp. 12–14. Trelawny's slip "today" may indicate that he wrote this account on the day of the cremation. Mary Shelley's letter of c. Aug. 27 shows that he had written an account by that time. (Mary Shelley, *Letters,* II, 187.) Trelawny's later claim of "snatching" the heart from the "fiery furnace" is clearly misleading. The heart was buried with Shelley's son, Sir Percy Florence Shelley. (Trelawny, p. 224.)

166. Angeli, *Shelley and His Friends in Italy,* pp. 317–319; White, II, 383, 634.

167. To Claire Clairmont, Nov. 27, 1869, Trelawny, *Letters,* p. 221.

168. Ingpen, p. 624; Grylls, *Mary Shelley,* p. 264.

3. *Political Philosophy*

1. Thomas Spence, *The Constitution of a Perfect Commonwealth* (London, 1798), p. iii. For Spence, see Olive D. Rudkin, *Thomas Spence and His Connections* (London, 1927); *The Pioneers of Land Reform,* ed. M. Beer (New York, 1920), pp. 5–16. Rudkin includes a bibliography of Spence's writings.

2. The government spy, George Edwards, put a false notice of a Cabinet dinner in the press. On Feb. 23, 1820, the night of the supposed dinner, the "conspirators" met in their headquarters in Cato Street and were raided by police officers, with a company of Coldstream Guards held in reserve. Thistlewood killed one officer and escaped but was later captured. He and his companions were executed by being hanged until they were partly unconscious and then decapitated—castration and disembowelment having been removed from the traditional "hanged, drawn, and quartered" sentence for treason in 1814. When their heads were exhibited to the crowd, a riot almost ensued.

The Whigs and reformers demanded an investigation of Edwards, fearing that his activities might lead to frame-ups against them also. As a result, Edwards was removed from the government spy roster. See *The Examiner*, Feb. 27, 1820, pp. 137, 141–143, 177–178; E. P. Thompson, *The Making of the English Working Class* (London, 1963), pp. 613–616, 700–705. The Jamaican radical was named Davidson.

3. *Works*, VII, 48. When Shelley heard of the "conspiracy" and the arrest of Thistlewood and company, his first reaction was fear that it would be used against the reform movement: "I see with deep regret in to-day's Papers," he wrote to Peacock early in March, "the attempt to assassinate the Ministry. Every thing seems to conspire against Reform." On Mar. 13 he wrote to his publisher, Charles Ollier: "I hope you are not implicated in the late plot—Not having heard from Hunt, I am afraid that he, at least, has something to do with it." That Shelley should think Hunt, a moderate reformer, and Ollier, a liberal intellectual, could be "implicated" in such a scheme indicates that the "Papers" he read in Italy made it appear that the leaders of the reform movement could be indicted. That he was both shaken by the incident yet by no means ready to condemn the Spenceans is indicated in a letter of Mar. 19 to John Gisborne: "Horrible work, this in England! Good & bad seem to have become inextricably entangled in our unhappy country." *Letters*, II, 176, 178, 179.) The "horrible work" apparently refers to the government's tactics of force and trickery.

4. *A Philosophical View of Reform, Works*, VII, 41; *Swellfoot the Tyrant*, II, ii, 42–60.

5. Robert Owen, *Report to the County of Lanark* (London, 1927), pp. 247–248. This work was first published in 1821, but some of its ideas were expressed in Owen's *New View of Society* in 1814, and others were advanced by Owen at public meetings in London in 1816 and 1817. The meeting on Aug. 4, 1817, was widely reported, creating a sensation in London political circles.

6. Fanny Godwin in two letters to Mary Shelley in 1816 discussed Godwin's friendship with Owen. (Dowden, II, 39–40, 53). Godwin's manuscript diary does not record a meeting between Shelley and Owen, but Godwin must have discussed Owen's theories with Shelley and perhaps showed him some of Owen's works.

7. To Charles Ollier, March 1817, *Letters*, I, 534.

8. To Shelley, Aug. 27, 1817, Hunt, *Correspondence*, I ,114–115; Frank Podmore, *Robert Owen: A Biography* (New York, 1907), II, 647n; see also p. 612.

9. Medwin, p. 98: "On finding that I was connected with Shelley, he made a long panegyric on him, and taking up one of the *Queen Mabs* from the table, read, premising that it was the basis of one of his chief tenets, the following passage: 'How long ought the sexual connection to last? What law ought to specify the extent of the grievance that should limit its duration? A husband and wife ought to continue so long united as they love one another. Any law that should bind them to cohabitation for one moment after the decay of their affection, would be a most intolerable tyranny, and most unworthy of toleration.' "(See Note to *Queen Mab*, V, 189, *Works*, I, 141; Medwin made some errors in transcription.) Owen printed this Note from *Queen Mab* in full in *The Marriages of the Priesthood* (1838), and the views expressed in it were taken by some of his opponents as his own. (Podmore, *Robert Owen*, II, 512–513).

10. *A Philosophical View of Reform, Works*, VII, 10.

11. Shelley commented: "One of the vaunted effects of this system is to . . . turn children into lifeless and bloodless machines at an age when otherwise they would be at play before the cottage doors of their parents." (*Ibid.*, p. 27.) For Owen's early efforts against child labor, see Podmore, *Robert Owen*, I, 187–196. William Godwin in ch. XI of his novel *Fleetwood* (1805) made a powerful indictment of child labor, with which Shelley was doubtless acquainted. (See *Shelley and His Circle*, I, 359–366.) Mary Shelley recorded reading *Fleetwood* in 1815 and 1820, and often the books on her list had previously been read by Shelley. (*Mary Shelley's Journal*, pp. 47, 134, 144.)

12. On Carlile, see G. A. Aldred, *Carlile, Agitator; His Life and Times* (Glasgow, 1941); G. D. H. Cole, *Carlile* (London, 1943).

13. *The Republican*, I (1819), ix–xvi.

14. *The Declaration of Rights* appeared anonymously in the Sept. 24, 1819, issue of *The Republican*. The Apr. 7, 1820, issue contained extracts from *Queen Mab*. An article "Remarks on the Genius and Writings of the Late Mr. Percy Bysshe Shelley" appeared in the Dec. 15, 1826, issue. See also White, II, 405–406; White, *Unextinguished Hearth* pp. 95–98, 325.

15. See *The Examiner*, May 23, 30, June 27, Oct. 17, 24, 31, Dec. 26, 1819, pp. 321, 337–338, 401–403, 657–659, 676–677, 689–691, 827. The comments in the May 23 and 30 issues may have influenced Shelley's letter. He received *The Examiner* in Italy. On Apr. 5, 1820,

Shelley rebuked Hunt for not publishing this letter: "Then on my side is the letter to Carlile, in which I must tell you I was considerably interested." (*Ibid.*, p. 181.) The letter was not printed in full until 1926. (*Correspondence*, pp. 21–30.)

16. *Letters*, II, 136–137, 143, 148.

17. E. L. Woodward, *The Age of Reform*, 1815–1870 (Oxford, 1938), p. 24; see also George Macaulay Trevelyan, *Lord Grey of the Reform Bill* (London, 1920), pp. 73–74.

18. For Place's political activities, see Graham Wallas, *The Life of Francis Place* (London, 1925), pp. 39–64, 114–156. For these journals, see Alexander Andrews, *The History of British Journalism* (London, 1859), vol. II; H. R. Fox Bourne, *English Newspapers* (London, 1887), vol. II.

19. G. D. H. Cole, *The Life of William Cobbett* (London, 1927), p. 207.

20. In his *Political Register* for Nov. 23, 1816, Cobbett announced that on the franchise issue he was deserting the moderate reformers and joining the radicals. At a reform meeting on Jan. 22, 1817, he reverted temporarily to his old position of votes on a property basis, for which he was vigorously assailed by Henry Hunt and others. (See *The Examiner*, Jan. 26, 1817, pp. 57–58; Henry Hunt, *Memoirs of Henry Hunt, Esq., written by Himself in His Majesty's Jail at Ilchester* [London, 1820], I, ix; Samuel Bamford, *Passages in the Life of a Radical* [London, 1893], II, 21.)

21. See Hunt, *Memoirs*; Robert Huish, *The History of the Private and Political Life of the Late Henry Hunt* (London, 1836). Hunt was by no means the irresponsible mob orator he is often depicted as being but a pragmatic middle-class reformer.

22. See F. D. Cartwright, *The Life and Correspondence of Major Cartwright* (London, 1826); Francis Place's review of this biography, *Westminster Review* (October 1827), pp. 253–303. Cartwright attempted to achieve parliamentary reform not by manipulations within Parliament but by building a pressure group outside Parliament, which had the dual aim of electing new members and influencing old ones. The extraordinary thing about Cartwright was his persistence. For more than 40 years as the movement grew and changed he never deviated from his position of manhood suffrage or his advocacy of the petition as the most effective weapon.

23. William H. Wickwar, *The Struggle for the Freedom of the Press, 1819–1832* (London, 1928), p. 57. Wooler was an able political journalist, whose *Black Dwarf* gave a clear view of British domestic and foreign policy from 1817 to 1824. On almost every issue Wooler showed more insight than *The Examiner*, and his style had a radical sharpness that Hunt usually lacked.

24. For Wooler's attempts to popularize Bentham's tract, see *The Works of Jeremy Bentham*, ed. John Bowring (Edinburgh, 1843), X, 490. Wooler's version lacks Bentham's individualistic, often crotchety touches but makes for more popular reading.

25. Hunt, *Memoirs*, I, vi.

26. *Political Register*, XXXI (1816), 353; see also William Cobbett, *History of the Regency and Reign of George IV* (London, 1830), par. 438.

27. The pamphlet had been written and the proofs revised by Feb. 22, as shown by Shelley's note to his publisher, Charles Ollier, on that date. (*Letters*, I, 534.) The comments in *The Examiner* occur in the Mar. 2 and 29 issues. *The Quarterly Review* attack appeared in the January issue, published in April. (Kenneth Neill Cameron, "Shelley vs. Southey: New Light on an Old Quarrel," *PMLA*, LVII [June, 1942], 489–512.) The third *Examiner* notice appeared on Sept. 19, 1819, p. 604. After referring to Shelley's pamphlet, the editors remarked that in Leeds a petition was circulated in favor of reform and was signed by "some of the most respectable inhabitants in the town . . . If these Records should, as we confidently hope they will become general, the ulterior proceeding may be a petition to Parliament, of such a nature as to become irresistible." Thus, two years later, *The Examiner* upheld the practicality of Shelley's plan. (Kenneth Neill Cameron, "A Reference to Shelley in *The Examiner*," *Notes & Queries*, CLXXXIV [1943], 42.)

28. On Shelleys' offer, *The Examiner* remarked: (Mar. 2, 1817, p. 139) "This wants no comment; or rather we ought to say, that we deny ourselves the luxury of making any, out of respect to the feelings of this noble nature, whom we have the honour and the happiness of knowing. While there are Englishmen like these, the old breed is not extinct; and when they come forth, the new cannot long remain in possession of our green and glorious country." Waithman belonged to a group of London reformers who were both active and vociferous. Kinnaird and Cochrane, friends of Byron, were associated with Burdett in his Independent Whig revolt. Ensor was an unattached radical whose ideas were close to Shelley's. (White, I, 624–626; Blunden, p. 159; see also *A Proposal for Putting Reform to the Vote*, ed. H. Buxton Forman, Shelley Society Publications [London, 1887], pp. 11–24; William H. Davenport, "Footnote for a Political Letter of Shelley," *Notes & Queries*, CLXXXVI [1939], 236–237.)

29. In April 1817, Sherwin's *Republican* was renamed the *Weekly Political Register;* it lasted until August 1817. Richard Carlile, who had become its publisher, in 1819 issued his own paper, also called *The Republican.* (Wickwar, *The Struggle for the Freedom of the Press,* pp. 69–75.) William Hone was not a leader of the reform movement but an independent radical who took up the cause of reform. In 1817 he was three times tried and acquitted on charges of seditious blasphemy. The trials, his accounts of which are masterpieces of political humor, became rallying points for liberal opinion. His *Reformist Register* ran from February to October 1817. For Hazlitt's friendship with him, see P. P. Howe, *The Life of William Hazlitt* (New York, 1922), pp. 418–419.

30. *Works,* VI, 68.

31. *The Examiner,* which represented the views of city intellectuals, feared the mass following of Cobbett, Henry Hunt, and Wooler as much as it feared the Tories. When in 1832 most intellectuals joined the Whigs against the radical reformers in blocking an extension of the franchise to the working class, the workers turned to Chartism. Chartism itself, however, had roots in Cartwright's petitions, Cobbett's mass pressure tactics, and Wooler's radical journalism.

32. Jeremy Bentham, *Plan of Parliamentary Reform, Works of Jeremy Bentham,* ed. John Bowring (Edinburgh, 1843), III, 76. Bentham was shrewd enough to perceive—as other reformers, including Shelley, did not—that the "anarchy" cry was a political red herring, pointing out that universal suffrage had not brought anarchy to the United States of America.

33. *Works,* VI, 68. Bentham, too, argued in favor of annual parliaments. (Bentham, *Plan,* p. 521.)

34. *Works,* VI, 67.

35. See *The Trials of Jeremiah Brandreth, William Turner, Isaac Ludlam, George Weightman and Others for High Treason, under a Special Commission at Derby* (London, 1817), 2 vols.; Thompson, *The Making of the English Working Class,* pp. 649–669. Thompson corrects the usual picture of the insurrectionists as simpletons by quoting (pp. 666–667) from Brandreth's last letter to his wife (printed in full in Cobbett's *Political Register,* Apr. 25, 1818), which shows him as devout and literate: "I feel no fear in passing through the shadow of death to eternal life; so I hope you will make the promise of God as I have, to your own soul, as we may meet in Heaven . . . My beloved . . . this is the account of what I send to you—one work bag, two balls of worsted and one of cotton, and a handkerchief, an old pair of stockings and a shirt, and the letter I received from my beloved sister." In *The Trials* (I, 211) Brandreth is described as a "frame-work knitter." Turner was a stonemason; Ludlam, a Methodist preacher and part owner of a stone quarry.

36. For "Oliver" and his nefarious career, see J. L. and Barbara Hammond, *The Skilled Labourer, 1760–1832* (London, 1920), pp. 341–376, Oliver was the first important labor spy.

37. *The Examiner,* Nov. 16, 1817, pp. 715, 721; *The Black Dwarf,* Nov 12, 1817, p. 687; Hunt, *Memoirs,* II, 494.

38. On Nov. 9, 1817, Shelley visited Leigh Hunt, who may then have been writing up the case for the Nov. 16 *Examiner.* On Nov. 11 Shelley had tea with Godwin and Charles Ollier, visited Hunt again in the evening, and began to write "a Pamphlet," which he finished the next day. (*Mary Shelley's Journal,* p. 86.) On Nov. 12 he wrote to Ollier: "I inclose what I have written of a pamphlet on the subject of our conversation the other evening. I wish it to be sent to press without an hours delay—I don't think the whole will make a pamp[h]let larg[er or] so large as my last, but the printer can go on with this & send me a proof & the rest of the Mss. shall be sent before evening. If you should have any objections to publish it you can state them as soon [as] the whole is printed before the title goes to press: though I don't think that you will, as the subject though treated boldly is treated delicately." (*Letters,* I, 566.) This letter shows Shelley's desire to assist the antigovernment campaign engendered by the execution while the issue was still current. The pamphlet appears to have first been published in or before 1843 (perhaps by 1830), although whether from a manuscript or an earlier edition is unknown, and no copies have survived. Dowden discovered this notation in a bookseller's catalogue listing the item as published in 1843: "The author printed only twenty copies of this Address: the present is a fac-simile reprint." (Forman, pp. 68–69.) Wise believed that this notation was false and that the 1843 publisher probably got the manuscript from a box of Shelley's manuscripts left at Marlow. (Wise, p. 46.)

39. *Childe Harold's Pilgrimage,* IV, clxvii–clxxii.

40. Shelley and Hunt may have discussed ideas for both *The Examiner* article and Shelley's pamphlet when they were together on Nov. 9 and 11.

41. *Works,* VI, 76–77; see also "On the Punishment of Death," *ibid.,* pp. 185–190.

42. *Ibid.,* p. 82. This concept may have had roots in Shelley's Whig childhood. His father's political patron, the duke of Norfolk, was punished in 1798—the year of the Irish rebellion and British terrorism in Ireland—for proposing a toast to "our Sovereign's health—the Majesty of the People." (Cameron, p. 46.)

43. July 25, 1818, *Letters,* II, 26. John Keats wrote to Tom Keats on June 25–27, 1818: "I enquired of the waiter for Wordsworth—he said he knew him, and that he had been here a few days ago, canvassing for the Lowthers. What think you of that—Wordsworth versus Brougham!! Sad—sad—sad—and yet the family has been his friend always." (*The Letters of John Keats,* ed. Hyder Edward Rollins [Cambridge, 1958], I, 299.)

44. *Letters,* II, 22.

45. To Peacock, Jan. 24, Apr. 6, 1819, *ibid.,* pp. 75, 94. For this election, see Wallas, *The Life of Francis Place,* pp. 132–139. George Lamb, the Whig candidate, was a brother-in-law of Lady Caroline Lamb. Lamb defeated Hobhouse, 4465 to 3861. Godwin, influenced by Lady Caroline, with whom he had a philosophical correspondence, supported Lamb. (Paul, II, 266.)

46. To Peacock, June 20–21?, 1819, *Letters,* II, 99. Peacock had considerable admiration for Cobbett. (Peacock, *Works,* VIII, 192–193.)

47. To Leigh Hunt, May 26, 1820, *Letters,* II, 201. Shelley apparently began the pamphlet in early November or late October 1819. On Nov. 6 he wrote to the Gisbornes: "I have deserted the odorous gardens of literature to journey across the great sandy desert of Politics." He told his publisher Ollier on Dec. 15: "I am preparing an octavo on reform—a commonplace kind of book—which, now that I see the passion of party will postpone the great stuggle till another year, I shall not trouble to finish for this season." (*Ibid.,* pp. 150, 164.) In the first chapter Shelley treats the Spanish situation as one of dictatorship and prophesies change. (*Works,* VII, 16–17; White, II, 581–582.) As revolution broke out on Jan. 1, 1820, and Shelley would certainly have received news of it by Jan. 15 at the latest, the first chapter was undoubtedly written before that date. In the third chapter he writes of the Manchester Massacre—"at Manchester on the memorable 16th of August"—in terms close to those employed in *The Mask of Anarchy* (254–372), written in September 1819. (*Works,* VII, 48–49.) In the second chapter he writes of the decrease in suffrage "in the interval between 1688 and 1819." (*Works,* VII, 23.) All this suggests that Shelley had stopped work on *A Philosophical View of Reform* by Dec. 15, 1819, and that his comment about abandoning the work to Ollier on that date held true. In May 1820, when he wrote to Hunt, his interest had revived, and he would probably have finished the work if he could have found a publisher, but there are no indications of additions to the work between December and May.

The pamphlet was not published until 100 years later. Shelley's son, who possessed the manuscript, perhaps considered its political outlook too extreme for Victorian consumption. Edward Dowden, however, was allowed to make an abstract of it, published in *The Fortnightly Review,* November 1886, and in his *Transcripts and Studies* (1888). In 1920 it was published by the Oxford University Press, edited by T. W. Rolleston, and then in *Works,* VII, 4–55. The manuscript is at present in The Carl H. Pforzheimer Library in New York.

48. To Godwin, June 3, 1812, *Letters,* I, 303.

49. *The Revolt of Islam,* l. 2212.

50. *Works,* VII, 14. Many of his views on the French Revolution were developed by Shelley at least as early as February 1812—in his Irish pamphlet *Proposals for an Association.* (*Works,* V, 263–265.)

51. Karl Marx, *A Contribution to the Critique of Political Economy* (1859), in *A Handbook of Marxism,* ed. Emile Burns (New York, 1935), p. 372.

52. William Godwin, *Political Justice,* I, 384, 450–451, II, 474–475.

53. *Ibid.,* I, 275, 289.

54. *Works,* VII, 9–10.

55. G. M. Mathews, "'Julian and Maddalo': The Draft and the Meaning," *Studia Neophilologica,* XXXV (1963), 72.

56. *Paper Against Gold,* first published in 1815, went through a number of editions; the one used here is that of 1828. The work is a series of letters, which had previously appeared in the *Political Register,* 1810–1812. Cobbett continued to write on economic subjects, and the *Registers* that Shelley received in Italy often restated the views in *Paper Against Gold.* For circulation figures, see Cobbett's Preface, p. xi. See also Kenneth Neill Cameron, "Shelley, Cobbett, and the National Debt," *Journal of English and Germanic Philology,* XLII (April 1943), 197–209.

57. Cole, *The Life of William Cobbett,* p. 86.

58. *Morning Chronicle,* Aug. 29, Sept. 20, Nov. 23, 1809. Ricardo later issued the let-

ters as a pamphlet. See also his *Proposals for an Economical and Secure Currency* (London, 1816).

59. Shelley acknowledges his debt to Cobbett in *A Philosophical View of Reform*, in remarks on the substitution of paper for gold currency: "In a treatise devoted to general considerations it would be superfluous to enter into the mode in which this has been done; those who desire to see a full elucidation of that may read Cobbett's Paper against Gold." (*Works*, VII, 338; see also William H. Davenport, "Notes on Shelley's Political Prose," *Notes & Queries*, CLXXVII [Sept. 23, 1939], 225.) Shelley's letters show a continuous interest in Cobbett from 1812 to 1820, the later letters usually showing more approval than the earlier ones. The snobbish attack on Cobbett in *Peter Bell* (ll. 152, 652n) reflects *The Examiner's* attitude, as in the issues of Sept. 28 and Oct. 8, 1817.

Claire Clairmont was also a reader of Cobbett from 1817 to 1820. (Clairmont, pp. 79, 114, 150, 151.) An anecdote on p. 80 involving Cobbett's abuse—apparently in his pre-radical days—of "Frend" refers to William Frend, the well-known radical intellectual, who introduced the young Wordsworth to William Godwin. (See Frida Knight, *University Rebel: The Life of William Frend, 1775–1841* [London, 1971].) Mary did not share Claire's interest in Cobbett, to judge from her letter to Shelley of Sept. 20, 1817, in which he is seen as a wild revolutionist. (Mary Shelley, *Letters*, I, 37.) Shelley perhaps first came across Cobbett's views on the debt and paper money between writing the *Proposal for Putting Reform to the Vote* (February 1817) and *An Address to the People on the Death of the Princess Charlotte* (November 1817), for in the first of these pamphlets, which mentions some of Cobbett's political theories, he makes no reference at all to his financial theories, whereas in the second he elaborates Cobbett's views on the historical origin and development of the national debt, its creation of a second aristocracy, and its building of an unequal tax burden. (*Works*, VI, 77–79; cf. *Paper Against Gold*, pp.7–8, 14–15, 21–22, 27–29.)

60. *Works*, VII, 34. See *Paper Against Gold*, pp. 7, 21–22.

61. Hume's essays, according to Hogg (I, 71), "were a favorite book with Shelley, and he was always ready to put forward in argument, the doctrines they uphold." From them Shelley early derived many radical ideas on social, religious, and political questions. Prominent among them were three essays on economic matters—*Of Public Credit, On Money,* and *Of the Balance of Trade*—which vigorously attacked paper money and the national debt, which even in Hume's day had assumed considerable proportions. Shelley was probably directly indebted to Hume for at least three points: the contrast between the hoarding of treasure by ancient kings and the modern expedient of devaluation of the currency; the solution to the national debt problem through the abolition of the principal; and the theory of the "second aristocracy." On the last subject the following passages typify Hume's comments:

"There are also, we may observe, in England and in all states which have both commerce and public debts, a set of men, who are half merchants, half stockholders, and may be supposed willing to trade for small profits; because commerce is not their principal or sole support, and their revenues in the fund are a sure resource for themselves and their families."

"In this unnatural state of society, the only persons who possess any revenue beyond the immediate effects of their industry, are the stockholders, who draw almost all the rent of the land and houses, besides the produce of all customs and excises. These are the men who have no connections with the state, who can enjoy their revenue in any part of the globe in which they choose to reside, who will naturally bury themselves in the capital, or in great cities, and who will sink into the lethargy of a stupid and pampered luxury, without spirit, ambition, or enjoyment. Adieu, to all ideas of nobility, gentry, and family." (Hume, *Essays Moral, Political and Literary* [Edinburgh, 1825], I, 349, 354.)

In some respects, as in the use in *A Philosophical View of Reform* of the word "set" and the concluding attack on the bourgeois stuffiness of the group, Shelley is more indebted to Hume than to Cobbett. (See also *An Address to the People on the Death of the Princess Charlotte, Works*, VI, 78–79.) In both *Paper Against Gold* and his *Political Register* Cobbett vigorously attacked the "fundholders" but nowhere developed the concept as Shelley does. Cobbett himself was influenced by Hume. (See, e.g., *Paper Against Gold*, pp. 75, 275.) Hume's theories, indeed, underwent a revival in the ranks of the reformers. For instance, a book on his theories, and reprinting his essay, appeared in London in 1817: *Insecurity of the British Funds: Essay on Public Credit by David Hume, with Observations on the Sound and Prophetic Nature of Its Principles . . . Addressed to the British People by Imlac*, London, 1817. The identity of "Imlac"—the name is from Johnson's Rasselas—is a mystery. He was a man of wide reading and possessed a trenchant pen. His attacks on Coleridge and Southey (*ibid.*, pp. 172—"I caution you against puking Poets and besotted Lay Sermons"— 261ff, 241ff.) make even

Hazlitt's diatribes seem mildly respectable. He also wrote four able articles on reform for the *Black Dwarf* in 1817 (pp. 653, 696, 746, 759). For Hume's influence on Shelley, see also *Prose*, passim; Pulos, *passim.*

62. *Works*, VII, 28–29. In *An Address to the People on the Death of the Princess Charlotte* Shelley writes on the second aristocracy: "The effect of this debt is to produce such an unequal distribution of the means of living, as saps the foundation of social union and civilized life. It creates a double aristocracy, instead of one which was sufficiently burthensome before, and gives twice as many people the liberty of living in luxury and idleness, on the produce of the industrious and the poor. And it does not give them this because they are more wise and meritorious than the rest, or because their leisure is spent in schemes of public good, or in those exercises of the intellect and the imagination, whose creations ennoble or adorn a country. They are not like the old aristocracy men of pride and honour, *sans peur et sans tache*, but petty piddling slaves who have gained a right to the title of public creditors, either by gambling in the funds, or by subserviency to government, or some other villainous trade. They are not the 'Corinthian capital of polished society,' but the petty and creeping weeds which deface the rich tracery of its sculpture." (*Ibid.*, VI, 78.)

63. *Works*, VII, 35. Cobbett argued similarly but without Shelley's emphasis on class ownership: "For, as we have seen, the Debt is nothing more than a right possessed by certain persons, called Stockholders, to draw interest from the nation; or in other words, to take annually, or quarterly, part of the taxes raised upon the people at large." (*Paper Against Gold*, pp. 76–77.)

64. *Works*, VII, 36–37. Cobbett made a similar distinction but granted a right to aristocratic privilege denied by Shelley: "It is by no means to be understood, that there should be no persons to live without what is generally called labour. Physicians, Parsons, Lawyers, and others of the higher callings in life, do, in fact, labour; and it is right that there should be persons of great estate, and without any profession at all; but then, you will find, that these persons *do not live upon the earnings of others*; they all of them give something in return for what they receive. Those of the learned profession give the *use of their talents and skills*; and the landlord gives *the use of his land or houses.*" (*Paper Against Gold*, pp. 27–28.)

65. *Works*, VII, 34–35. See also p. 30: "the lowest and the largest class, from whose labour the whole materials of life are wrought"; and *Queen Mab*, Note to V, 93, 94, *Works*, I, 139.

66. *Paper Against Gold*, pp. 76–77; *Works*, VII, 26–27; *Paper Against Gold*, pp. 5–6; *Works*, VII, 27, 30. For his theories on property and exploitation, Shelley was partly indebted to Godwin, *Political Justice*, bk. VIII, ch. 11, and Godwin, *Of Avarice and Profusion, The Enquirer* (London, 1797) p. 174. Godwin, however, was dealing not with the added burdens placed on working people by the debt and paper money but with the general evils of exploitation in a society having an unequal division of wealth. (See also *Paper Against Gold*, pp. 28–29.)

67. *Paper Against Gold*, pp. vi, 264, 324; *Works*, VII, 35. However, Shelley did not entirely reject Cobbett's suggestion for lowering the interest rate; rather, he felt it might provide a temporary alleviation of some economic evils. (To the Gisbornes, Nov. 6, 1819, to Horace Smith, June 29, 1822, *Letters*, II, 149, 442.)

68. Ricardo first suggested abolishing the debt in the House of Commons on June 19, 1819, more than a year after Shelley had left for Italy. (Hansard, *Parliamentary Debates*, XL, 1023.) *The Examiner* commented on it on Jan. 2, 1820, but Shelley had apparently finished writing *A Philosophical View of Reform* before seeing this issue. This parallel between Shelley and Ricardo was first noted in J. F. Rees, *A Short Fiscal and Financial History of England, 1815–1918* (London, 1921), pp. 44–45. Shelley, however, need not have been indebted to Ricardo, for the germ of the idea appeared in Hume's essay *Of Public Credit*, even though Hume himself disagreed with it.

69. *Works*, VII, 31. Although Shelley seemingly implies that poverty as such is the result of the national debt, he cannot mean this, for in *Queen Mab* and other works written before he seems aware of the debt and prior to the appearance of Cobbett's *Paper Against Gold* (1815) Shelley inveighed against poverty in both England and Ireland (where there was no national debt), the implication there being that poverty arises from the general inequality of the social system. Here, therefore, he must mean that the national debt caused additional burdens which increased poverty. For example, only the "peculiar" (particular or special) "misery" is caused by the debt, and it can be corrected by correcting the "defect" in the "government." Shelley certainly never believed that all social evils could be corrected by so comparatively minor an operation. Because Shelley never revised his pamphlet, some of its phrasing remains loose.

70. *Ibid*, p. 34.

71. *A Philosophical View of Reform*, ed. T. W. Rolleston (Oxford, 1920), pp. ix–x. It may have been the antimilitary agitations of Sir Francis Burdett and *The Examiner* that focused Shelley's attention on the evils of the army system. His first letter to Hunt (Mar. 2, 1811) congratulated him on his acquittal after being tried before Lord Ellenborough for an article attacking the use of flogging in the army. On May 7, 1812, he wrote to Catherine Nugent asking if she had seen Burdett's speech of May 1 in the House of Commons attacking the erection of new barracks. (*Letters*, I, 54, 297.) On Oct. 7, 1814, Shelley and Claire Clairmont talked late of "oppression and reform, of cutting squares of skin from the soldiers' backs." (Entry by Shelley, *Mary Shelley's Journal*, p. 18.) For Cobbett on the army, see *Political Register*, XXXI (1816), 46–62. Bentham bitterly attacked the standing army in his *Plan of Parliamentary Reform* but did not call for its abolition. (Bentham, *Works*, III, 442.) Godwin, too, opposed the maintenance of a large standing army. (Godwin, *Political Justice* [London 1796], II, 165.)

72. See, e.g., the list in the *Political Register*, Sept. 6, 1817, which Mary Shelley—obviously shaken—interpreted as a call for revolution. (To Shelley, Sept. 30, 1817, Mary Shelley, *Letters*, I, 37.)

73. See Lewis Melville, *The Life and Letters of William Cobbett* (London, 1913), I, 251–53; *Political Register*, XXXI (1816), 424–25.

74. The tenth duke of Norfolk, father of Shelley's would-be political patron, was himself a Catholic and in 1778 signed a petition of Catholic peers urging the king to grant Catholic emancipation. The eleventh duke converted to Protestantism in 1790 but continued to vote for Catholic emancipation in the House of Lords. (W. J. Amherst, *The History of Catholic Emancipation* [London, 1886], I, 95–97; II, 228.)

75. See W. M. Patterson, *Sir Francis Burdett and His Times* (London, 1931), II, 449–455.

76. *Works*, VII, 45–46, 47; Cobbett's *Political Register*, Oct. 19, 1816.

77. *Works*, VII, 44; Godwin, *Political Justice*, II, 312–313. Cartwright had long advocated the secret ballot and in November 1816 convinced Cobbett of its urgency. (Cartwright, *Life and Correspondence*, II, 142; *Political Register*, XXXI, 663.) Bentham's *Plan of Parliamentary Reform* advocated the secret ballot, and Burdett's reform speech of June 2, 1818, supported him. (Hansard, *Parliamentary Debates*, XXXVIII, 1148.)

78. *Works*, VII, 44; *Political Register*, XXXIV (1818), 359. Charles James Fox, leader of the more liberal Whigs, in the reform debate of 1797 cast ridicule on granting women the vote. (Hansard, *Parliamentary Debates*, XXXIII, 726–727.) Shelley, in such works as *The Revolt of Islam*, a review of Hogg's *Alexy Haimatoff*, and *Discourse on the Manners of the Antient Greeks Relative to the Subject of Love*, ardently championed the right of women to political and social equality. In spite of the fact that women's suffrage was not during the postwar years in any reform platform, there were many women in the reform movement. Women marched in all the big reform demonstrations—as at the Manchester Massacre march–and were encouraged by Cobbett and other leaders. The first Female Reform Societies were founded in 1818. When Samuel Bamford first insisted that women vote at reform meetings, it was a "new idea" and greeted with "much laughter," but it soon became established practice. (Thompson, *The Making of the English Working Class*, pp. 415–416.)

79. *Works*, VII, 47, 48, 51.

80. To Peacock, Sept. 21, 1819, *Letters*, II, 120. Shelley sent the contribution via Alderman Robert Waithman, a leading London reformer. (To Waithman, Jan. 4, 1818, *Letters*, I, 591.) Waithman was also on the list of those to whom Shelley sent a copy of his *Proposal for Putting Reform to the Vote*. Perhaps Shelley was acquainted with some of the London reformers. In hopes that Hone, a bookseller, might handle the *Proposal*, he wrote to him at the Old Bailey: "Mr. Shelley's Compts to Mr. Hone—and his Messenger will wait for an answer on the subject of the Pamphlet." (Apr.? 20, 1817, *ibid.*, p. 538.)

81. *Works*, VII, 41. Shelley probably first read of the psychology of the soldier in Godwin's *Political Justice*, II, 160–167, and his "Of Trades and Professions," *The Enquirer* (London, 1797), pp. 233–237. He quotes from the latter in *Queen Mab*, Note to IV, 178, 179, *Works*, I, 135–136. See also the commentary on "Henry and Louisa," *Esdaile Notebook*, pp. 268–269.

82. *Works*, VII, 41; cf. *The Masque of Anarchy*, 303–372. For Gandhi's interest in Shelley's pacifist views, see John Pollard Guinn, *Shelley's Political Thought* (The Hague, Paris, 1969), pp.127–128.

83. *Works*, VII, 53–54. The same general view of the French Revolution appears in the Irish pamphlets and the Preface to *The Revolt of Islam*.

84. *Works*, III, 307.

85. *A Philosophical View of Reform, Works,* VII, 51, 30.
86. To Elizabeth Hitchener, Aug. 10, 1811, *Letters,* I, 132.
87. *Swellfoot the Tyrant,* II, ii, 91; To T. L. Peacock, Aug. 24, 1819, *Letters,* II, 115.
88. *Works,* VII, 53. See also p. 45: "No friend of mankind and his country can desire that such a crisis should suddenly arrive; but still less, once having arrived, can he hesitate under what banner to array his person and his power." Shelley's general position is the same as that he presented in a letter to Elizabeth Hitchener on Jan. 7, 1812: "Popular insurrections and revolutions I look upon with discountenance; *if such things must be,* I will take the side of the People, but my reasonings shall endeavor to ward it from the hearts of the Rulers of the Earth, deeply as I detest them." (*Letters,* I, 221.)
89. *Works,* VII, 45, 41.
90. See, e.g., Bamford's account of Burdett's reception of a delegation of radical reformers and their feeling of oppression with "the dreary stateliness of this great mansion and its rich owner." (Samuel Bamford, *Passages in the Life of a Radical* [London, 1843], II, 23–24.)
91. *Works,* VII, 43, VI, 242–243.
92. May 1, 1820, *Letters,* II, 191.
93. *Ibid.,* p. 153.
94. *Queen Mab,* IX, 148.

4. *Philosophy, Religion, and Ethics*

1. The dating of some of these works has long proved troublesome. Major advances in dating Shelley's prose were made by A. H. Koszul (*Prose in the Bodleian*), James A. Notopoulos (Notopoulos, pp. 317, 320; "The Dating of Shelley's Prose," *PMLA,* LVII [June 1943], 477–498; "The Dating of Shelley's *The Moral Teachings of Jesus Christ,*" *Modern Language Review,* XXXV [1940], 215–216); Adele B. Ballman ("The Dating of Shelley's Prose Fragments—'On Life,' 'On Love,' 'On the Punishment of Death,' " ELH, *A Journal of English Literary History,* II [1935], 332–335). Koszul attempted to date *Essay on Christianity,* the *Speculations* (on morals and metaphysics), and other fragments by examining the manuscript notebooks in which they appear, which are often themselves datable. Notopoulos' main dating method was to trace parallels between the works and Shelley's readings as recorded in the journals or letters, especially his reading of the classics. David Lee Clark (*Prose*) usually dated items much earlier than Koszul or Notopoulos, but seldom gave any evidence for doing so. For instance, he dated *Essay on Christianity* 1811 or 1812 on grounds that it is "an earlier draft of the *Biblical Extracts,* which Shelley is known to have composed and sent to Hookman in 1812" (p. 196). But Koszul showed that the *Essay* appears in a notebook containing material of 1817 and 1818 (not "1814 or 1818," as Koszul stated in what may be a typographical error). (*Prose in the Bodleian,* pp. 9–11; see also Charles D. Locock, *An Examination of the Shelley Manuscripts in the Bodleian Library* [Oxford, 1903], pp. 40, 73.) The *Essay* immediately follows a comment in the notebook on Claire Clairmont's and Byron's child, Allegra, who was born on Jan. 12, 1817. The paper, manufactured by W. Turner and Son, was being used for letters by Shelley in 1817. Finally, Notopoulos showed that the works mentioned in the *Essay* were being read by Shelley in 1816 and 1817.
2. To Hogg, November 22–23, 1813, *Shelley and His Circle,* III, 260.
3. For Godwin's influence on Shelley's philosophy, see Cameron, pp. 194–195; Ross Woodman, *The Apocalyptic Vision in the Poetry of Shelley* (Toronto: University of Toronto Press, 1964), pp. 6–9. Even before their first meeting in the fall of 1812, Godwin and Shelley had a philosophical debate. In letters during the summer Godwin had argued that materialism contravened the highest principles of morality, which Shelley denied: "Altho' like you an irreconcileable enemy tô the system of self love, both from a feeling of its deformity & a conviction of its falsehood, I can by no means conceive how the loftiest disinterestedness is incompatible with the strictest materialism. In fact, the doctrine which affirms that there is no such thing as matter, & that which affirms that all is matter appear to me, perfectly indifferent in the question between benevolence and self love." (July 29, 1812, *Letters,* I, 316.) By "materialism" Shelley means the epistemoligical doctrine that "all" (including mind) is material and not spiritual. Godwin had written in 1809 that he was "more inclined to the opinion of the immaterialists than the materialists." But in either case, matter operated according to natural laws: "The belief in the reality of matter explains nothing . . . the material world goes on for ever accord-

ing to certain laws that admit of no discrimination." That he discussed these problems with his young disciple is shown in his journal notation of their early conversations: "matter and spirit, atheism." (Cameron, p. 194; Godwin, *Thoughts on Man* [London, 1831], pp. 448–449.)

Godwin argued also that "thought" is not a manifestation of matter but a special substance in its own right. He denied that there is any difference between the energy which produces physical motion, such as walking, and that which produces philosophical ideas; both are manifestations of "thought." As a result, the mind is constantly active; even in sleep it regulates the bodily processes. Finally, it is "far from certain that the phenomenon of motion can anywhere exist where there is not thought." (Godwin, *Political Justice*, I, 398–399, 414–416, 419.)

That the young Shelley differed from Godwin's idealistic approach toward mind is clear from *A Refutation of Deism*: "It is evident therefore that mind deserves to be considered as the effect, rather than as the cause of motion." In a fragment of *Speculations on Metaphysics* of 1815–1816 he writes: "It is said that mind produces motion, and it might as well have been said that motion produces mind." (*Works*, VI, 56; VII, 342.) Both passages appear to be directly aimed at Godwin's doctrine.

4. July 29, 1812, *Letters*, II, 316.

5. Preface to *Essays, Letters from Abroad, Works*, V, ix.

6. Clark argued that the *Speculations on Metaphysics* and *Speculations on Morals* were parts of one work, which he titled *A Treatise on Morals.* (*Prose*, pp. 181–182. See also Earl R. Wasserman, *The Subtler Language*, [Baltimore, 1959], p. 204.) The fragments, however, were written over a span of four years or more and were put together not by Shelley but by Mary. The content of the two sets does not suggest a unified work. Nor is there any indication of a bibliographical connection within or between the two sets. Some watermarks are English, others Italian. It is most likely that the manuscripts are just what they seem—two sets of unfinished essays on two different though related subjects, ethics and metaphysics, written at various times. (See also *Shelley and His Circle*, IV, 733–744.)

7. *Works*, VI, 48, 55, 56. In a letter to Leigh Hunt on Sept. 27, 1819 Shelley states that he first came across the phrase, "Mind cannot create, it can only perceive," as a pencil note in a copy of Berkeley owned by Southey's friend Charles Lloyd, the poet, at Keswick, where Shelley lived November 1811–February 1812. (*Letters*, II, 122–123.)

8. *Ibid.*, p. 194. *On Life* was originally in the same notebook as *A Philosophical View of Reform.* A bibliographical examination of the *On Life* manuscript, now in The Pierpont Morgan Library, shows that it was once part of the notebook, now in The Carl H. Pforzheimer Library. The manuscript of *A Philosophical View of Reform* was first described by Edward Dowden in *The Fortnightly Review* in November 1886: "The manuscript occupies upward of two hundred pages in a small vellum-bound Italian notebook. On the outer side of one of the covers is a pen-and-ink drawing by Shelley . . . At one end of the little volume is the fragment 'On Life.' " (Dowden, *Transcripts and Studies*, [London, 1896], p. 42) T. W. Rolleston later stated that the manuscript had been given to the Reverend Stopford Brooke by Lady Jane Shelley and on Brooke's death in 1916 was inherited by Brooke's daughter, the wife of Rolleston. Rolleston described the manuscript as being "contained in about 200 pages of a small vellum-covered notebook which includes also a few jottings for poems, and casual scribblings." He made no mention of *On Life.* (*A Philosophical View of Reform*, ed. T. W. Rolleston [Oxford, 1920], p. iii)

Accompanying the manuscript of *On Life* in the Morgan Library is a letter of Feb. 21, 1916, from Stopford Brooke to an unknown correspondent, stating that he had sent "to Gosse's Red Cross Sale at Christie's Shelley's MS of the Essay 'On Life,' published in Mary's Essays and letters, Vol. 1, p. 293. It is the first draft of this taken out of one of his Note Books, and given to me in 1894 by Lady Shelley." Brooke's phrasing is misleading, for what was given to him was the notebook. It must therefore have been he who cut out the pages. (Quoted by permission of the Morgan Library.)

Shelley apparently finished *A Philosophical View of Reform* by the middle of December 1819. *On Life* was probably written in 1819 or 1820.

9. *Speculations on Metaphysics, Works*, VII, 59–60. For Shelley's skepticism in these essays, see Pulos, pp. 49–53 *passim.*

10. *Works*, VII, 196.

11. *Ibid.*, p. 60.

12. *Ibid.*, VI, 195.

13. *Ibid.*, p. 196; Note to *Hellas*, ll. 197–238, *ibid.*, III, 56.

14. *Principles of Human Knowledge*, para. 7.

15. *On Life, Works,* VI, 195.

16. Shelley's interest in Drummond went through two stages. In the first, he was mainly interested in extracting anti-Christian arguments from Drummond's works. (Cameron, pp. 392–393.) In the second, he accepted some of Drummond's metaphysics. This second stage is first indicated in the Preface to *The Revolt of Islam* (1817), where after commenting, "Metaphysics, and inquiries into moral and political science, have become little else than vain attempts to revive exploded superstitions," Shelley adds: "I ought to except Sir W. Drummond's *Academical Questions;* a volume of very acute and powerful metaphysical criticism." In April 1819 Drummond visited Shelley in Rome. (Apr. 22, 1819, Clairmont, p. 108.) In a letter to Leigh Hunt of Nov. 3, 1819, when Shelley was writing *A Philosophical View of Reform,* he referred to Drummond as "the most acute metaphysical critic of the age." (*Letters,* II, 142.) In *On Life* (1819–1820) he acknowledges his debt to Drummond. (*Works,* VI, 195.) In *Peter Bell the Third* (VI, xv), also written in 1819, he refers to Drummond's knowledge of Kant, which Drummond may have displayed during their meeting. Vol. I of *Academical Questions* was published in 1805, and according to W. T. Lowndes; "A few sheets of vol. 2 were printed, but are very rarely seen." (William Thomas Lowndes, *The Bibliographer's Manual of English Literature* [London, 1834].)

17. *Works,* VI, 55.

18. Drummond was considered a Berkeleian in G. S. Brett, "Shelley's Relations to Berkeley and Drummond," *Studies in English by Members of University College, Toronto* (Toronto, 1931), pp. 170–202. But Pulos (pp. 29–37) argued convincingly that he was primarily a skeptic. See also Reiman, p. 113. On Byron and Drummond (the "professed atheist"), see Marchand, I, 195, 353.

19. William Drummond, *Academical Questions* (London, 1805), p. 244. Shelley was influenced in other ideas by Drummond. For instance, the passage quoted above giving Shelley's reasons for renouncing materialism is partly derived from Drummond. Shelley's contention that materialism seems logical at first, but that on further examination skepticism, despite its seeming absurdity, is more tenable is typical of Drummond: "Nothing, I know, appears at first view more singular or visionary, than the philosophic doctrine of ideas. The human mind does not easily abandon its early habits of association." In connecting immortality with skepticism, Shelley may also have Drummond in mind, even though Drummond went further: "Neither men, nor inferior animals, may wholly die. Their souls will awaken from the sleep of death. What they have been, they are, and will be." (Drummond, *Academical Questions,* pp. 326, 404.) Shelley may have recalled this passage in *Adonais* xxxix. Shelley is perhaps echoing Drummond in his comments on the child mind: "Let us recollect our sensations as children . . . We less habitually distinguished all we saw and felt, from ourselves." *(Works,* VI 195.) Drummond commented that if one brings a child to fire, he will perceive light and heat, "yet it cannot be supposed that he connects these with any external object." (Drummond, *Academical Questions,* p. 195.) Shelley writes (doubtless influenced by Hume and Berkeley also): "The difference is merely nominal between those two classes of thought, which are vulgarly distinguished by the names of ideas and of external objects." *(Works,* VI, 196.) Drummond wrote: "The nominal differences between physical forces, and mental faculties, concealed from the inattentive observor their common origin and their real similitude." (Drummond, *Academical Questions,* p. 176.) (See also Brett, "Shelley's Relations to Berkeley and Drummond," pp. 170–202; Pulos, pp. 24–41; Reiman, pp. 52, 113; Earl R. Wasserman, *Shelley's Prometheus Unbound: A Critical Reading* [Baltimore, 1965], pp. 4n, 25, 28, 158.)

20. *Works,* VI, 196.

21. Baron d'Holbach, *The System of Nature,* trans. H. D. Robinson (Boston, 1889), I, 11–12.

22. *On Life, Works,* VI, 196.

23. *Ibid.,* VII, 60, 61.

24. *Shelley and His Circle,* IV, 496–502, 564–565 (ll. 1064–1072). Wasserman argued that Shelley intended the passage to reflect Drummond's exposition of a Platonic concept of the "universal mind" achieving "intelligence," but this does not seem to be his object. The "main" difference between the *Queen Mab* text and *The Queen of the Universe* revisions, according to Wasserman, lies in the use of "universal mind" instead of "spirit," but the *Queen of the Universe* text shows that Shelley there first used "Spirit," then crossed it out and inserted "universal mind," so that he apparently intended both to signify the same thing. (Wasserman, *Shelley's Prometheus Unbound,* p. 25n.) Shelley appears to be arguing that the "universal mind" or "spirit" inherent in the universe achieves human significance only when human mind perceives it.

25. *Works*, VI, 186.
26. *Works*, VII, 133.
26. *Ibid.*, VII, 65, 343 ("beings" or "being"?).
27. *On Life*, *Ibid.*, VI, 195.
28. *Ibid.*, VII, 161–162. For years Shelley was considered a Platonist. (See esp. Lilian Winstanley, "Platonism in Shelley," *Essays and Studies by Members of the English Association*, IV [1913]; Grabo; Baker; Notopoulos; Rogers in *Selected Poetry*.) Others emphasized Shelley's roots in the British empiricist. (See esp. Amiyakamur Sen, *Studies in Shelley* [Calcutta, 1936]; *Prose*; Pulos.)
29. See, e.g., Alban Dewes Winspear, *The Genesis of Plato's Thought* (New York, 1940), ch. 11.
30. *Works*, VI, 235, VII, 74. Note to *Hellas*, ll. 197–238.
31. See Notopoulos, "The Dating of Shelley's Prose," p. 496.
32. To Elizabeth Hitchener, June 11, 1811, *Letters*, II, 101; *Works*, VI, 236.
33. Notopoulos, "The Dating of Shelley's Prose," p. 495; *Works*, VI, 205, 207, 208, 209.
34. June 29, 1822, *Letters*, II, 442.
35. *Works*, VI, 194.
36. *Works*, VII, 127, *ibid.*, VI, 195, 185.
37. For a different view, see Wasserman, *Shelley's Prometheus Unbound*, p. 4n; Rogers, p. 17.
38. Pulos, p. 73. Pulos (p. 88) argued that Shelley's recognition of a skeptical element in Plato made Shelley himself "a Platonist in the skeptical tradition," but the passages cited show only that there was a generally skeptical element in Shelley's poetry.
39. Shelley's Preface to Plato's *The Banquet*, Notopoulos, p. 402.
40. *Works*, VII, 114.
41. *Ibid.*, VI, 255.
42. *Prose in the Bodleian*, pp. 8–9, 14, 33, 40.
43. *Works*, VI, 227–228. In *A Philosophical View of Reform* Shelley refers to the Roman Empire as "that vast and successful scheme for the enslaving [of] the most civilized portion of mankind." *(Ibid.*, VII, 5.)
44. *Works*, VI, 231–232.
45. *A Refutation of Deism*, *ibid.*, p. 55.
46. *On a Future State*, *ibid.*, pp. 208–209.
47. *Queen Mab*, VI, 148, 197–198.
48. *Essay on Christianity*, *Works*, VI, 231, 232–233.
49. *Ibid.*, p. 235. See also p. 236.
50. *Ibid.*, VII, 59–60.
51. *Works*, VI, 242. Koszul commented that the "middle section, in which Shelley dwells on what might be called the principles of his investigation, is headed 'Introduction' and would no doubt have found a place, in a final transcript, before the chapter on 'God,' which precedes it in the MS." (*Prose in the Bodleian*, pp. 8–9.) But as Shelley himself did not rearrange the material and the Introduction does not logically lead into the "God" section, the order of the manuscript is preferable: three separate sections not yet arranged in a total pattern.
52. See to Hunt, Mar. 2, 1811, *Letters*, I, 55: "On account of the responsibility to which my residence at this University subjects me, I of course, dare not publicly to avow all that I think."
53. *Works*, VI, 244, 245, 249. According to Notopoulos (p. 330), the passage on the "genuine republic" is derived from Diogenes Laertius. (See also Rogers, p. 258.)
54. *Works*, VI, 247, 251–252.
55. *Ibid.*, VII, 147–148.
56. Trelawny, *Records*, II, 231–232; to John Taaffe, Feb. 11? 1821, *Letters*, II, 260.
57. On Hare, see G. F. McFarland, "The Early Literary Career of Julius Charles Hare," *Bulletin of the John Rylands Library*, XLVI (September 1963), 42–83. Hare's family, like Shelley's, came from Sussex. After early interests in literature and the law, Hare turned to the ministry in 1826. In 1840 he became archdeacon of Lewes in Sussex. He spent the winter of 1818–1819 in Italy and perhaps heard of Shelley there. In an article on German drama in *Ollier's Literary Miscellany* (1820) he referred to Shelley as "a great modern poet, whose genius, when he has bowed down his neck and received into himself the purifying and sanctifying of the Spirit, if such be his earthly fate, must assuredly prove a cherisher of innocent thoughts and a kindler of noble thoughts unto many." (*Works*, VII, 346.)
58. To Charles Ollier, Jan. 20, 1821, *Letters*, II, 258. Shelley continues: "I had written a Lucianic essay to prove the same thing." The only extant work of Shelley's to which

this description could apply is *On the Devil and Devils.* Yet as Roger Ingpen argued, Shelley's essay echoes Hare's article in both the quotation from Schlegel and a quotation from "Hazlitt's *Lectures.*" (*Works*, VII, 347). The reference is to *Lectures on the Dramatic Literature of the Age of Elizabeth, The Complete Works of William Hazlitt*, ed. P. P. Howe (London and Toronto, 1931), VI, 316. These lectures were delivered in November and December 1819 and published in 1820 (*ibid.*, pp. 170, 385), but there is no record that Shelley read them, and he clearly encountered the Schlegel statement for the first time in Hare's article. Whether or not Shelley had earlier written something—now unknown—on the devil and theology, he apparently did not write *On the Devil and Devils* until after reading Hare's article. His letter to Ollier implies that he had read it shortly before writing the letter, which would set a beginning date for the essay in January 1821. Furthermore, if he was inspired to write the essay by Hare's article, he probably wrote it shortly after reading the article. The probable date for the essay as a whole is thus January 1821. This general period is also indicated by the fact that the essay occurs in a notebook containing poems of 1820 and 1821. (*Works*, VII, 346.) For a parallel with *A Defence of Poetry* (1821—"The Serpent which clasps eternity") see Notopoulos, "The Dating of Shelley's Prose," p. 483; but see also *Prometheus Unbound*, IV, 565–566. (1819). For an ingenious but inconclusive argument that the essay was written in 1819, see Stuart Curran and Joseph Anthony Wittreich, Jr., "The Dating of Shelley's 'On the Devil, and Devils,' " *Keats–Shelley Journal* XXI–XXII (1972, 1973), 83–94.

59. *Works*, VII, 88–89, 90. For Paine, see Cameron, p. 278.

60. *Works*, VII, 91–92. See also Note to *Queen Mab*, VII, 135–136, *Works*, I, 153.

61. *Works*, VII, 94.

62. *Ibid.*, pp. 97, 202–203. For Paine, see *The Age of Reason*, *Works* (New York, 1925), VIII, 85: "And, on the other hand, are we to suppose that every world in the boundless creation had an Eve, an apple, a serpent and a redeemer?"

63. *Ibid.*, VI, 220; Godwin, *Political Justice*, I, 121; Note to *Queen Mab*, VI, 197, *Works*, I, 145; Godwin, *Political Justice*, I, 130. Francis Hutcheson used the phrase "the greatest happiness for the greatest numbers" in 1725. Beccaria used a phrase translated as "the greatest happiness of the greatest number" in *On Crimes and Punishment* in 1764, the exact phrase used by Bentham in 1776. (*The Cambridge History of English Literature* [Cambridge, 1932], IX, 301–302.) Shelley read Beccaria and Bentham. (*Letters* II, 469, *A Philosophical View of Reform*, *Works*, VII, 9, 44, 52.) This Beccaria, whose *On Crimes and Punishment* was read by Shelley, was Cesare, marchese de Beccaria, not to be confused with Giovanni Battista Beccaria, whose scientific ideas might also have influenced Shelley. (Grabo, *A Newton among Poets, passim*; White, II, 598.)

64. Note to *Queen Mab*, V, 177, *Works*, I, 141; *ibid.*, V, 287–288.

65. See *Shelley and His Circle*, IV, 740–744. The segments appear out of chronological sequence in *Works* (VII, 71–83) and *Prose* (pp. 183–193). The section placed first in *Works*, headed "Plan of a Treatise of Morals," and the section headed "Chapter II" comprise the later (probably 1821) material; "Chapter I" and the final section, headed simply "II," comprise the earlier (probably 1817) material. A list of writers by Shelley placed (*Works*, VII, 72) with *Speculations on Morals* is actually on the same manuscript as part of *Speculations on Metaphysics*. The list is omitted in *Prose*.

66. *Works*, VII, 72, 75–76.

67. The following passages from Adam Smith (1759) and Godwin (1793), respectively, anticipate Shelley: "As we have no immediate experience of what other men feel, we can form no idea of the manner in which they are affected, but by conceiving what we ourselves should feel in the like situation. Though our brother is upon the rack, as long as we ourselves are at our ease, our senses will never inform us of what he suffers. They never did, and never can, carry us beyond our own person, and it is by the imagination only that we can form any conception of what are his sensations." (Adam Smith, *The Theory of Moral Sentiments*, [London, 1869, p. 3.]) "To understand this let us begin with the care of an infant. Before he can feel sympathy, he must have been led by a series of observations to perceive that his nurse for example, is a being possessed of consciousness, and susceptible like himself of the impressions of pleasure and pain." (William Godwin, *Enquiry Concerning Political Justice* [London, 1793], II, 348–349.)

Shelley's views are even closer to Hazlitt's *An Essay on the Principles of Human Action* (1805): "The Imagination, by means of which alone I can anticipate future objects, or be interested in them, must carry me out of myself into the feelings of others by one and the same process by which I am thrown forward as it were into my future being, and interested in it. I could not love myself, if I were not capable of loving others. Self-love, used in this sense, is in it's fundamental principle the same with disinterested benevolence." (Herschel Baker, *William Hazlitt* [Cambridge, 1962], pp. 145–146.)

There is no record that Shelley read Hazlitt's essay, but the parallels indicate that he was acquainted with it.

68. *Speculation on Morals, Works,* VII, 77. For the manuscript and a transcription, see *Shelley and His Circle,* IV, 736, 737. Egalitarian views of a general, pre-Godwinian nature appear in Hume's *An Enquiry Concerning the Principles of Morals,* sec. III, and in Aristotle's *Ethics.* Walter Sidney Scott reproduced what he called a "Prose Fragment by Shelley," which was not, however, an original piece by Shelley but a translation by him of Aristotle, *Ethics,* IX viii. (Scott, *Shelley at Oxford* [London, 1944], pp. 48–50; *Shelley and His Circle,* II, 659–667.)

69. *Works,* VII, 79–82. The quotation is from Wordsworth's *Tintern Abbey* ("those" should read "His").

70. *Works,* VII, 81–83.

71. *Ibid.,* p. 150.

72. *Ibid.,* p. 149; Godwin, *Political Justice,* III, 219–220, 507–510; Friedrich Engels, *The Origin of the Family, Private Property and the State* (New York, 1942), pp. 54–74.

73. Notopoulos, pp. 408–410.

74. *An Essay on Friendship: A Fragment, Works,* VII, 143. Hogg (I, 30) reported that this fragment was "written not long before his [Shelley's] death," presumably on information from Mary, for he was not with Shelley in Italy (1818–1822)

75. To T. L. Peacock, Dec. 17 or 18, 1818, *Letters,* II, 58. The remark was doubtless directed at Peacock's pro-British chauvinism, but it also shows that Shelley himself was not immune from anti-Italian prejudice.

76. Notopoulos, p. 409.

77. *Works,* VI, 177–178, 182, Note to *Queen Mab,* V, 189, *Works,* I, 142. For Shelley's views on sex and love and an attack on the concept that he was an effete romantic, see Edward E. Bostetter, "Shelley and the Mutinous Flesh," *Texas Studies in Literature and Language,* I (1959), 203–213.

78. Fromm told me around 1954 that he was unaware of Shelley's prose writings on love but had long admired the humanitarianism in his poetry.

79. *Works,* VI, 201–202.

80. To Janetta Philipps, May? 1811, *Letters,* I, 89.

81. On Aug. 24, 1814, Mary recorded in her journal at Brunnen that Shelley was reading "the description of the Siege of Jerusalem in Tacitus." The next day she recorded: "We arrange our apartment and write part of Shelley's romance." The "romance," she explained in *History of a Six Weeks Tour,* was "on the subject of the Assassins," and she wrote while Shelley dictated. (*Works,* VI, 104.) As Tacitus was one of Shelley's known sources of information on the Assassins, he may have developed the idea for the book only the previous day. At any rate, the Aug. 25 entry is the first mention of it. He continued work on it for the next two days and again on Sept. 10 in Holland; then in England on Sept. 15 he read what he had written to his friend Thomas Hookham, the publisher. Apparently encouraged by Hookham's attitude, he worked on it again on Sept. 19. This is the last reference until Apr. 8, 1815, when in an entry in Mary Shelley's journal he referred to a second source of information, Gibbon: "The Assassins,' Gibbon, chap. lxiv. All that can be known of 'The Assassins' is to be found in 'Memoires of the Academy of Inscriptions,' tom. xvii, pp. 127–170." (*Mary Shelley's Journal,* p 43.) Gibbon briefly described Holagou Khan's attack on the *Assassins.*

In her Preface to *Essays, Letters from Abroad,* Mary Shelley wrote: "I do not know what story he had in view. The Assassins were known in the eleventh century as a horde of Mahometans living among the recesses of Lebanon—ruled over by the Old Man of the Mountain; under whose directions various murders were committed on the Crusaders, which cause the name of the people who perpetrated them to be adopted in all European languages, to designate the crime which gave them notoriety. Shelley's old favourite, the Wandering Jew, appears in the latter chapters, and, with his wild and fearful introduction into the domestic circle of a peaceful family of the Assassins, the fragment concludes. It was never touched afterwards." (*Works,* V, ix.) One probable source for Shelley's knowledge of the Assassins as well as for parts of his story was an anonymous French work, *Le vieux de la Montagne,* which was in Mary Shelley's reading list for 1816. (Fuller, pp. 156–161.) According to the *Encyclopedia of Religion and Ethics* (New York, 1910), II, 138–41, the Assassins attacked all religious observances, were skeptical of the existence of God, argued that mind was the original substance from which matter arose, and were persecuted for their beliefs. Shelley would clearly have been favorably disposed toward such a group.

82. *Works,* VI, 162. Newman I. White suggested that the Assassins' valley "possibly . . . owes something to the happy valley" in Johnson's *Rasselas.* (White, I, 683; see also

Cameron, "*Rasselas* and *Alastor*: A Study in Transmutation," *Studies in Philology*, XL [1943], 58–78.) Shelley was perhaps also indebted to Marco Polo: "In a beautiful valley enclosed between two lofty mountains, he [the chief of the Assassins] had formed a luxurious garden, stored with every delicious fruit and every fragrant shrub that could be procured. Palaces of various sizes and forms were erected in different parts of the grounds, ornamented with works in gold, with paintings, and with furniture of rich silks. By means of small conduits contrived in these buildings, streams of wine, milk and honey, and some of pure water, were seen to flow in every direction." (*The Travels of Marco Polo*, Everyman Library Edition [New York, 1929], pp. 74–75.) Marco Polo, however, included nothing about the philosophy of the Assassins that Shelley could have used.

Rasselas was apparently a favorite with Shelley, for in addition to *The Assassins*, he made use of it in *Alastor* (1815), the Preface to *The Revolt of Islam* (1817), and *A Defence of Poetry* (1821). For the last, see Cameron, "A New Source for *A Defence of Poetry*," *Studies in Philology*, XXXVIII (1941), 629–644. I find no record of Shelley's having read *Rasselas*, but both Claire Clairmont and Mary Shelley mention reading it. (Sept. 16, 1814, Clairmont, p. 43.) Mary, in fact, read it on Sept. 19, 1814, a day on which Shelley was writing *The Assassins*. (*Mary Shelley's Journal*, p. 16; see also p. 83.) Mary and Claire often read works that Shelley had read previously.

83. *Essay on Christianity*, *Works*, VI, 249; *The Assassins*, *ibid.*, p. 164.

84. Note on *Prometheus Unbound*, *ibid.*, II, 269.

85. *The Revolt of Islam*, 3271–3279.

86. *Works*, VI, 166.

87. Preface to *Essays, Letters from Abroad*, *ibid.*, V, ix.

88. *Mary Shelley's Journal*, p. 111.

89. Medwin, *Shelley Papers*, pp. 51–52, 127n. That Medwin was right is indicated by the description of the stranger, which suggests one of Shelley's self-portraits: "Over all was spread a timid expression of womanish tenderness and hesitation, which contrasted, yet intermingled strangely, with the abstracted and fearless character that predominated in his forms and gestures." (*Works*, VI, 299–300.)

90. *Works*, V, ix. In Plato's *Symposium*, which Shelley translated, Diotima was the teacher of Socrates. (See "Fragments connected with *Epipsychidion*," ll. 102–103, *Works*, II, 380.)

91. *Works*, VI, 279–282 (in Italian), 283–286 (in English, tran. Richard Garnett). For a collated text, see *Note Books*, III, 158–171. That *Una Favola* was written for Emilia is indicated by its proximity to poems to Emilia in one of Shelley's notebooks. (*Note Books*, I, 188–190, 204–205; Rogers, pp. 3, 241.) As Shelley did not even meet Emilia until December 1820 (White, II, 240) and their "affair" took place in 1821, the "fable" was probably written in 1821.

92. The fable also contains Petrarchean elements. (White, II, 631.)

93. King-Hele, p. 168. Grabo (p. [xiv]) and King-Hele (p. 165) quoted A. N. Whitehead: "If Shelley had been born a hundred years later, the twentieth century would have seen a Newton among chemists."

94. Trelawny, p. 199.

95. *Peter Bell the Third*, 518–532.

96. *Works*, II, 174–175.

97. *Ibid.*, I, 247.

5. *Shelley As Critic*

1. See Melvin T. Solve, *Shelley: His Theory of Poetry* (Chicago, 1927), pp. xi, 15–16.

2. Mme. de Stael, *Oeuvres Complètes* (Paris, 1820), IV. Mme. de Stael claimed (p. 17n) that she was the first to apply the concept of social "perfectibility" to literary criticism and that she was not indebted to Godwin's *Political Justice* for the idea. Her object was to study the reciprocal influences of literature and religious, moral, and legal forms (p. 25). Her book was noted by Mary Shelley on Mar. 15, 1815, as having been read by Shelley. (*Mary Shelley's Journal*, p. 40.) He may also have learned of some of her ideas from Byron, whom she knew, or from Godwin, who was an admirer of hers. (*Shelley and His Circle*, III, 339–341.)

As for August Wilhelm Schlegel's *Lectures on Dramatic Art and Criticism* (1809–1811), Mary recorded in her journal for Mar. 16, 1818: "Shelley reads Schlegel aloud to us." That the reference was to the *Lectures*, published in English in 1815, is shown by Mary's book list for 1818. (*Mary Shelley's Journal*, pp. 93, 114.) Shelley would have agreed with some of Schlegel's literary judgments, such as his attacks on Dryden, on the Restoration, and on eighteenth century drama (London, 1883, p. 477ff.), and with such general theories as the necessity for breaking away from narrow, national concepts in criticism. Schlegel's view that Christianity and chivalry together brought about "a new and purer spirit of love, an inspired homage for genuine female worth" (p. 25), may be the basis for Shelley's similar conjecture in *A Discourse on the Manners of the Antient Greeks Relative to the Subject of Love* and *A Defence of Poetry* (Notopoulos, p. 407, *Works*, VII, 127.) Schlegel's championing of the use of music and the mask in Greek drama may be the source for Shelley's similar views (*A Defence of Poetry, ibid.*, pp. 119–120).

The direct sources for *A Defence of Poetry* are Sir Philip Sidney's *Defence of Poesie* (or *Apologie for Poetrie*) and Imlac's discourse on poetry in Samuel Johnson's *Rasselas*. For Sidney, see Richard Ackermann, *Percy Bysshe Shelley: Der Mann, der Dichter, und seine Werke* (Dortmund, 1906), p. 300; Lilian Winstanley, ed., *Shelley's Defence of Poetry* (Boston, 1911), p. xvii; H. F. B. Brett-Smith, ed., *Defence of Poetry* (Oxford, 1929), xx–xxi; Lucas Verkoren, *A Study of Shelley's "Defence of Poetry"* (Amsterdam, 1937), pp 68–77. Verkoren also cited Plato and Peacock as sources.

Shelley refers to Sidney in *Adonais* (401–404) but not in his letters or prose. The editors of *Works* (VII, 372) were mistaken in identifying the "Sidney" mentioned in *A Philosophical View of Reform* as him, (*ibid.*, p. 9), for Shelley clearly means the revolutionary of 1688, Algernon Sidney, to whom he refers in a letter of Feb. 27, 1812: "My blood boils to think that Sidney's and Hampden's blood was wasted thus." (*Letters*, I, 264,)

For the influence of Johnson, see Kenneth Neill Cameron, "A New Source for Shelley's *A Defence of Poetry*," *Studies in Philology*, XXXVIII (October 1941), 629–644. The parallels with Johnson mainly involve the necessity for the poet to transcend aesthetic functions and influence his age, and to rise above the passing concepts of his age and speak in more universal terms.

Another source for *A Defence of Poetry* was Wordsworth's Preface to the *Lyrical Ballads*. (B. R. McElderry, Jr., "Common Elements in Wordsworth's 'Preface' and Shelley's 'Defence of Poetry,'" *Modern Language Quarterly*, V [1944], 175–181.) Shelley ordered the 1800 edition of *Lyrical Ballads*, which contained the Preface, from a bookdealer in 1812. (To Clio Rickman, Dec. 24, 1812, *Letters*, I, 345.) As the opening of *Alastor* shows, he was deeply influenced by *Tintern Abbey*, which was in the *Lyrical Ballads*, and his review of Godwin's *Mandeville* shows that he had read the Preface, which, he felt, established "the true principles of taste in poetry." (*Works*, VI, 220.)

Some general parallels exist between *A Defence of Poetry* and Hazlitt's lecture *On Poetry in General* (1818), such as the superiority of imagination to reason ("the flame of the passions communicated to the imagination . . . reveals to us, as with a flash of lightning, the inmost recesses of our thought"), the superiority of poetry to painting, creative, poetic tendencies exhibited by the child at play, and the interconnection between great prose and poetry. (Hazlitt, *Lectures on the English Poets*, Everyman Library Edition [New York, 1960], pp. 2, 3, 10–11, 13–14.)

3. "*The Four Ages of Poetry*, Peacock, *Works*, VIII, 6, 11, 18, 20, 21, 24.

4. Letters, II, 272–273. On Jan. 20, 1821, Shelley informed Charles and James Ollier that he had read *The Four Ages of Poetry* in their *Miscellany* and intended to write a reply. On Feb. 15 he told Peacock that he was too lazy to work on the reply, adding: "Among your anathemas of the modern attempts in poetry, do you include Keat's 'Hyperion'? I think it very fine." The implication is that Peacock had Shelley himself in mind in his "anathemas" (for *Hyperion* one might read *Prometheus Unbound*). On Feb. 22 Shelley informed Charles Ollier that he expected to finish his reply "in a very few days" but that the essay had been sent to Florence, presumably to Claire Clairmont. On Mar. 4 he wrote to the Olliers that the reply was taking longer than anticipated. (*Letters*, II, 258, 262, 268, 271.) By Mar. 12 it was finished, for Mary Shelley recorded that she began to transcribe it on that date. (*Mary Shelley's Journal*, p. 149.) On Mar. 20 it was mailed to the Olliers. (*Letters*, II, 275.)

The draft letter to the editor of the *Miscellany* must have been written between Jan. 20, when Shelley first announced his intention of replying, and Mar. 4, when he was clearly embarked on a long project. In the meantime the Olliers decided to publish no more issues of the *Miscellany*, On Jan. 26 and Mar. 7, 1822, Shelley wrote to his friend John Gisborne, then in England, suggesting that the essay be issued as a separate pamphlet. (*Letters*, II, 272–274, 387, 396). After Shelley's death, Mary proposed to John Hunt that he publish it in *The Liberal*, but for some reason it did not appear; *The Liberal* lasted for only four numbers. (William H. Marshall, *Byron, Shelley, Hunt and The Liberal* [Philadelphia, 1960], pp. 141–142.) The essay was first printed by Mary Shelley in *Essays, Letters from Abroad* in 1839 and again in 1845. (See *Works*, VII, 351.)

5. *A Defence of Poetry*, *Works*, VII, 110.

6. *Works*, VI, 250.
7. *Ibid.*, VII, 109, 107.
8. *Speculations on Morals, ibid.*, pp. 75–76.
9. *A Defence of Poetry, ibid.*, p. 111. On "taste," see John E. Jordan, ed., *A Defence of Poetry . . . The Four Ages of Poetry* (New York, 1965) p. 29n.
10. See "Common Elements in Wordsworth's Preface and Shelley's 'Defence of Poetry,'" pp. 175–181.
11. *Works*, VII, 112, 114. After Bacon, Shelley adds the note: "See the *Filum Labyrinthi* and the *Essay on Death* particularly." *The Filum Labyrinthi* (The Thread of the Labyrinth) is a philosophical fragment written in English. Shelley's annotated copy of Bacon's *Works* is in the University of Texas Library. (Peck, II, 344.)
12. Sidney contended that poets are akin to prophets and that great prose has in it the same spirit as great poetry. (Verkoren, *A Study of Shelley's "Defence of Poetry,"* pp. 71–72.) Samuel Johnson declared that a poet must write "as the interpreter of nature and the legislator of mankind," a phrase that Shelley echoed in "Poets are the unacknowledged legislators of the world." (See Cameron, "A New Source for Shelley's 'A Defence of Poetry,'" p. 635.) Hazlitt in his lecture *On Poetry in General* (p. 13) argued that some prose was "near to poetry."
13. *Hellas*, ll. 700–701.
14. *Works*, VII, 75. However, although Shelley goes beyond Wordsworth in several respects, he loses some of Wordsworth's democratic touch. Wordsworth at the time that he formulated the ideas for his Preface was an ex-revolutionary, middle-class liberal, attacking the aristocratic tradition of what he considered a false elegance in both social life and literature. His poet was a middle class democrat. Shelley was the exaristocratic revolutionary, who retained certain aristocratic concepts of which he was unaware. His poet is the radical genius, sympathetic with but not really part of the people.
15. *A Defence of Poetry, ibid.*, p. 112. For Spinoza, see the first two chapters of the *Tractatus theologico-politicus*, "Of Prophecy" and "Of Prophets." Shelley translated the *Tractatus*, and his own annotated copy is still in existence. Shelley may also have taken his theory of the superiority of imagination over reason in part from Spinoza, e.g.: "As the prophets perceived the revelations of God by the aid of the imagination, they could indisputably perceive much that is beyond the boundary of the intellect." Shelley, too, linked poets with prophets, and Spinoza's "revelations of God" means only understanding the world of nature—"Nature herself is the power of God under another name." (*Theologico-Political Treatise, The Chief Works of Benedict de Spinoza* [London, 1889], I, 25.) For the concept of the poet as prophet, Shelley was probably indebted to Sidney. (Verkoren, *A Study of Shelley's "Defence of Poetry,"* p. 71.)
16. *Works*, VII, 112, 115.
17. Verkoren, *A Study of Shelley's "Defence of Poetry,"* p. 73; Samuel Johnson, *Rasselas, Prince of Abissinia* (Troy, N. Y., n.d.), pp. 38–39.
18. *On the Revival of Literature, Works*, VI, 213.
19. Preface to *Prometheus Unbound, Works*, II, 173.
20. *A Defence of Poetry, ibid.*, VII, 116.
21. Preface to *Prometheus Unbound, ibid.*, II, 174, *A Defence of Poetry, ibid.*, VII, 117, 118.
22. *Ibid.*, pp. 20, 52. Shelley originally added Byron's name after Bentham's but later canceled it. (*Ibid.*, p. 340.)
23. To William Godwin, July 25, 1818, *Letters*, II, 22.
24. *A Defence of Poetry, Works*, VII, 116. Shelley may have been somewhat indebted to Johnson for this idea. (Cameron, "A New Source for Shelley's *A Defence of Poetry*," pp. 634–635.) But that Shelley had long had the concept of influencing future development is shown in a letter to Godwin of Mar. 18, 1812: "I will look to events in which it will be impossible that I can share, and make myself the cause of an effect which will take place ages after *I* shall have mouldered into the dust." (*Letters*, I, 277; see also *The Revolt of Islam*, 3694–3756.)
25. To Peacock, July 25, 1818, *Letters*, II, 26. Wordsworth had campaigned for an aristocratic candidate (Lord Lother) against a reform candidate (Henry Brougham) for Parliament.
26. *A Defence of Poetry, Works*, VII, 121–122.
27. Peacock, pp. 330–331. See also p. 330: "He had a prejudice against theatres which I took some pains to overcome. I induced him one evening to accompany me to a representation of the *School for Scandal*. When, after the scenes which exhibited Charles Surface in his jollity, the scene returned in the fourth act, to Joseph's library, Shelley said to me: 'I see the purpose of this comedy. It is to associate virtue with bottles and

glasses, and villany with books.'" Shelley's views on antisocial attitudes in drama were formed long before these recorded talks with Peacock, as shown by his early comment on Gay's *Beggars' Opera,* with its highwayman hero, MacHeath, who makes love to two women at once: "Can you compare Eloisa & a ruffian—Eloisa who sacrifised all *self* for another, MacHeath who sacrifised every other for himself." (To T: J. Hogg, May 9, 1811, *Letters,* I, 81.)

28. *A Defence of Poetry, Works,* VII, 123–124.

29. *Essay on Christianity, ibid.,* VI, 249.

30. *Ibid.,* VII, 125. Shelley defends Virgil's orginality in his draft Preface to *Prometheus Unbound*: "Who wd call Virgil an imitator of Homer? the conceptions had been modelled within his mind, they had been born again." (*Note Books,* I, 8.) Shelley later hints at Virgil's subservience in *A Defence of Poetry*: "Let us assume . . . that Virgil was a flatterer." (*Works,* VII, 138.)

31. *Works,* VII, 138. For Peacock on the troubadours and the age of Dante and Petrarch, see Peacock, *The Four Ages of Poetry,* Peacock, *Works,* VIII, 15.

32. *Works,* VII, 127. See also *On the Revival of Literature, Works,* VI, 213–215; *Discourse on the Manners of the Antient Greeks,* Notopoulos, p. 407. *A Philosophical View of Reform, Works,* VII, 5; cf. Mme de Stael, *De la littérature, Oeuvres Complète,* IV, 143–146, on the rebirth of literature in Italy.

33. Notopoulos, pp. 407–408; cf. Mme de Stael, pp. 135—137; *A Defence of Poetry, Works,* VII, 127–128; *A Discourse on the Manners of the Antient Greeks,* Notopoulos, p. 409; *A Defence of Poetry, Works,* VII, 128. The "other poets listed are "Ariosto, Tasso, Shakespeare, Spenser, Calderon, Rousseau, and the great writers of our own age."

34. *Ibid.,* p. 126 (see *Macbeth,* III, ii, 53), 128, 131, 130. By "modern mythology" Shelley means Christian theology. As he wrote in the Notes to *Queen Mab*: "Milton's poem alone will give permanency to the remembrance of its absurdities." (*Works,* I, 153; cf. *On the Devil and Devils, ibid.,* VII, 90–92.) Shelley wrote to Hunt, Sept. 27, 1819: "I have been lately reading this most divine writer [Boccaccio]. He is, in a high sense of the word, a poet, and his language has the rhythm and harmony of verse. I think him—not equal certainly to Dante or Petrarch—but far superior to Tasso and Ariosto, the children of a later and colder day . . . Boccaccio seems to me to have possessed a deep sense of the fair ideal of human life considered in its social relations. His more serious theories of love agree especially with mine . . . He is a moral casuist, the opposite of the Christian, Stoical, ready-made and worldly system of morals." (*Letters,* II, 122–123.)

35. *Ibid.,* p. 122; see also *A Philosophical View of Reform, Works,* VII, 5–6. Although Shelley did not consider Tasso one of the greatest poets, he admired him and thought of writing a play on his life. For his comments on Ariosto and Tasso after visiting the library at Ferrara, see his letter to Peacock, Nov. 7, 1818. (*Letters,* II, 46–47.) In a letter to Hunt in November 1819, Shelley quotes Tasso's comment on poetry, "Non c'e creatore fuorche Iddio ed il Poeta," and again in *A Defence of Poetry*: "Non merita nome de creatore, se non Iddio ed il Poeta." (*Ibid.,* p. 152; *Works,* VII, 128; Chandler B. Beall, "A Tasso Quotation in Shelley," *Modern Language Quarterly,* II (1941), 609–611.) Hogg reported that he and Shelley read *Gerusalemme liberata* in 1813–1814. (Hogg, II, 62.)

36. *A Philosophical View of Reform, Works,* VII, 6. This earlier phrasing is more explicit than *A Defence of Poetry:* "Chaucer caught the sacred inspiration, and the superstructure of English literature is based upon the materials of Italian invention." (*Ibid.,* p. 131.) Although Shelley includes Chaucer among the great English poets, he does not exhibit the same feeling for him as for Spenser, Shakespeare, or Milton. He seems to regard him as representative of the progressive spirit of the pre-Reformation, as indicated in the draft Preface to *Prometheus Unbound*: "We owe the great writers of the Elizabethan age to the fervid awakening of the public mind which shook the most oppressive form of the Christian Religion to the dust, we owe Milton to the progress & development of the same spirit. Chaucer was contemporary with Wickliff." (*Note Books,* I, 8.) Mary recorded in her journal for June 21, 1821, that Shelley read the first book of *Troilus and Criseyde* aloud, and on Dec. 10, 1821: "Shelley reads Chaucer's 'Flower and the Leaf,' and then Chaucer's 'Dream' to me." (*Mary Shelley's Journal,* p 162.) The *Flower and the Leaf,* however, was not by Chaucer; and the "Dream" may be either Chaucer's *The Book of the Duchess* or the non-Chaucerian *Isle of Ladies.* (Caroline Spurgeon, *500 Years of Chaucer Criticism and Allusion,* [Cambridge, 1923], II, 134.) Godwin's description of a poem he also called Chaucer's "Dream" fits the *Isle of Ladies,* so the probability is that this was the poem referred to by Mary. (Godwin, *Life of Geoffrey Chaucer* [London, 1803], I, 446–448.) On Dec. 20 Shelley again read Chaucer's "Dream." (Gisborne & Williams, p. 30.) For the concept of Chaucer as a reformist akin to Wycliffe and nourished by the liberal Italian poets, Shelley was probably indebted to Godwin, who treated

Chaucer as a liberal and a patriot and linked him with Wycliffe. Shelley's apparent failure to grasp the sophisticated and humanitarian irony that was the essence of Chaucer as a poet was the rule rather than the exception in the early nineteenth century.

37. *A Defence of Poetry, Works*, VII, 132, 134.

38. *Ibid.*, pp. 133, 134. Shelley seems to have felt a lack of humanitarian and imaginative scope in such thinkers as Locke, Hume, Gibbon, and Voltaire as well as in Peacock. He had made the distinction between "reasoners" and poets several years previously, as shown by his letter of July 12, 1816, to Peacock, in which he recounts that Byron, while at Lausanne (where both Gibbon and Rousseau had lived) gathered "some acacia leaves to preserve in remembrance of him [Gibbon]," but Shelley himself "refrained from doing so, fearing to outrage the greater and more sacred name of Rousseau . . . Gibbon had a cold and unimpassioned spirit." (*Letters*, I, 487–488.) The epitome of the "mere reasoner" was David Booth (lexicographer, brewer, and friend of Godwin's): "His keen and subtle mind, deficient in those elementary feelings which are the *principles* of all moral reasoning, is better fitted for the detection of error than the establishment of truth, and his pleadings, urged or withdrawn with sceptical caution and indifference, may be employed with almost equal force as an instrument of fair argument or sophistry." (To William Thomas Baxter, Dec. 30, 1817, *Ibid.*, p. 588.) Nevertheless, such "reasoners." as Hume and Gibbon were among the germinal influences on Shelley and he continued to admire them: "What! was Hume not a Deist? Has not Gibbon, without whose work no library is complete, assailed Christianity with most subtle reasoning, turned it into a bye word & a joke?" (To *The Examiner*, in defense of Richard Carlile, Nov. 3, 1819, *Letters*, II, 142; see also *A Philosophical View of Reform, Works*, VII, 8–10.)

39. Preface to *Lyrical Ballads* (1800), *Wordsworth's Literary Criticism*, ed. Nowell C. Smith (London, 1925), p. 27; *A Defence of Poetry, Works*, VII, 135.

40. *Ibid.*, p. 136.

41. The liberals and reformers of the age represented themselves as standing for the national interest. Shelley wrote in *A Philosophical View of Reform:* "The patriot will be foremost to publish the boldest truths in the most fearless manner." (*Works*, VII, 49.)

42. *A Defence of Poetry, ibid.*, pp. 135, 138.

43. *Ibid.*, p. 140; Preface to *Prometheus Unbound, ibid.*, II, 173—174. See also *A Philosophical View of Reform, ibid.*, VII, 19–20, and the early *Proposals for an Association* (1812): "But this age of ours is not stationary. Philosophers have not developed the great principles of the human mind, that conclusions from them should be unprofitable and impracticable. We are in a state of continually progressive improvement." (*Ibid.*, V, 265.)

44. Johnson, *Rasselas*, p. 39; *A Philosophical View of Reform, Works*, VII, 20; *A Defence of Poetry, ibid.*, pp. 131–133, 112.

45. *Ibid.*, VI, 220; *To Wordsworth*. Medwin (p. 251) wrote of Shelley's feeling for Wordsworth in 1821: "He was still an enthusiastic admirer of his early productions, and particularly of his inimitable lines in blank verse to his sister." The "lines" must be "Tintern Abbey," the only blank verse addressed to Dorothy by Wordsworth then published. *The Prelude* was not published until 1850.

46. *Peter Bell the Third*, ll. 378–387. See also *Letter to Maria Gisborne*, ll. 202–208 where Shelley refers to Coleridge as "a hooded eagle among blinking owls," that is a potentially superior intellect surrounded by the closed Tory minds of *The Courier* and *The Quarterly Review*.

47. To Southey, Mar. 7, 1816, *Letters*, I, 462.

48. To Mary Shelley, Aug. 7, 1821, *ibid.*, II, 323. Sell also Shelley to Byron, Oct. 21, 1821, on *Don Juan's* originality, vigor, and satirical brilliance: "Nothing has ever been written like it in English." (*Ibid.*, pp. 357–358.)

49. To Byron, Sept. 14, 1821; to John Gisborne, Jan. 26, 1822, *Letters*, II, 347, 388. Although Shelley's own sympathy for the antireligious content of *Cain* led him to exaggerate its significance, he also had a tendency to overpraise Byron in general. Shelley felt keenly his own failure in comparison to Byron's success and masochistically exaggerated both.

50. To Marianne Hunt, Oct 27, 1820, *ibid.*, p. 239 (see also Rogers, p. 257); Medwin, p. 307 (see also p. 261); Byron, IV, 491n. For *Endymion*, see Shelley's letter to Keats, July 27, 1820: "treasures poured forth with indistinct profusion." He also implies in a letter to Gifford, c. November 1820, that Keats's style was being injured by an imitation of Hunt and others: "In poetry *I* have sought to avoid system & mannerism; I wish those who excel me in genius, would pursue the same plan." (*Letters*, II, 221, 252.)

51. *A Philosophical View of Reform, Works*, VII, 52. Shelley viewed Hunt as essentially a liberal journalist, who fought regularly, fearlessly, and vigorously in *The Examiner* against all forms of social injustice. He had little regard for Hunt's poetry, however,

which he described to Trelawny as "a passionless abortion." (Peck, II, 409; see also Medwin, p. 260.) Shelley never mentions Peacock as one of the important writers of the age. Though he praises *Nightmare Abbey* in a letter to Peacock c. June 20, 1819, he could hardly have done otherwise in view of Peacock's caricature of himself in it as "Scythrop." In a letter of Nov. 8, 1820, he gives preference to *Melincourt*: "There is more of the true spirit, and an object less indefinite, than in either 'Headlong Hall,' or Scythrop." (*Letters*, II, 98, 244.) Shelley never shows the appreciation of Peacock's humor that he does of Byron's, which is aimed more widely at social and political evils.

52. To the Olliers, Oct. 15, 1819, *ibid.*, p. 127. On "imitation," see also Prefaces to *The Revolt of Islam* and *Prometheus Unbound*. (*Works*, I, 242, 244, II, 173–174.) The "piece" was the *Quarterly's* review of *The Revolt of Islam*.

53. *Works*, VI, 177, 182, 181; 273–276; see also to Hogg, Nov. 28, 1817, *Letters*, I, 426. In his review of *Rhododaphne* Shelley mostly confines himself to a descriptive account; in his letter he hints that it is largely an echo of the classics. Of Peacock's earlier long poems, he admired the necessitarian conclusion of *Palmyra* but disliked the chauvinism of *The Genius of the Thames*, which reflects Peacock's naval background: "Mr. Peacock concieves that commerce is prosperity; that the glory of the British Flag, is the happiness of the British People; that George III so far from having been a warrior & a Tyrant has been a Patriot. To me it appears otherwise." (To Thomas Hookham, Aug. 18, 1812, *ibid.*, p. 325.) Shelley frequently mixed up his "ie's" and "ei's."

54. *Works*, VI, 213–215. One other critical work should be noted, namely, an anonymous article that appeared in 1830 in *The New Monthly Magazine and Literary Journal*. (Peck, II, 421–432; Earl R. Wasserman, "Shelley's Last Poetics," *From Sensibilities to Romanticism*, ed. Frederick W. Hilles and Harold Bloom, [New York, 1965], pp. 505–508, 510–511; *Shelley's Critical Prose*, ed. Bruce R. McElderry, Jr. [Lincoln, 1967], pp. 142–157.) The article claims to record a conversation between Shelley and Byron on *Hamlet*, which includes a "kind of commentary" on the play supposedly written by Shelley and read to Byron. It is not known who wrote the article, nor is there any other record of Shelley's "commentary," yet Shelley and Byron did discuss Shakespeare, and the dialogue has parallels with Shelley's writings, as between the phrase "like a dewdrop from a lion's main is shaken to earth" and the last stanza of *The Mask of Anarchy*. (Wasserman, "Shelley's Last Poetics," p. 511; Peck, II, 429. The article, however, contains a contradiction, for in the beginning of the conversation Byron voices a criticism of Rosencrants and Guildenstern, whereas Shelley's "commentary," represented as written before the conversation, ends with an answer to Byron on this point. (*Ibid.*, pp. 421, 432.)

55. To Godwin, Jan. 16, 1812, *Letters*, I, 231; to Peacock, Jan. 23–24, 1819, *ibid.*, II, 71; Peacock, p. 421n. Peacock wrongfully referred to can. III instead of can. II in bk. V (sts. 30–54). After Artegall fails to answer the giant's communistic arguments, the giant has him thrown over a cliff.

56. Sept. 2, 1819, *Letters*, II, 96, 95n.

57. *Ibid.*, p. 331; *Works*, III, 56; Preface to *The Revolt of Islam*, *ibid.*, I, 239; Preface to *Prometheus Unbound*, *ibid.*, II, 174–175.

58. *Letters*, II, 363; June 18, 1822, *ibid.*, p. 434.

59. To Leigh Hunt, Aug. 20, 1819; see also to Peacock, Feb. 25, 1818 (for 1819), *ibid.*, pp. 112, 80–81; "A Bacchus by Michael Angelo," *Notes on Sculptures*, *Works*, VI, 329. Although in both *A Philosophical View of Reform* and *A Defence of Poetry* Shelley includes Michelangelo among the greatest artists, he preferred Raphael. (*Ibid.*, VII, 6, 133; to Hunt, Aug. 20, 1819, *Letters*, II, 112; *On the Devil and Devils*, *Works*, VII, 101.) This judgment perhaps indicates a blurring of his aesthetic faculties by his anti-Biblical feeling, for Raphael's inspiration turned more to the sentimental depiction of cherubs and Madonnas than to such Old Testament lore as the Creation, Moses, or David. *On the Medusa of Leonardo da Vinci*, a poem of 1819, contains Shelley's only reference to Leonardo. Unfortunately the painting (still in the Uffizi Gallery in Florence), although once attributed to Leonardo, is now known not to be his. See *L'opera Completa de Leonardo Pittore*, ed. Mario Pomilio (Milan, 1967), *Classici del Arte*, XII, Cat. No. 5, p. 89.

60. *Notes on Sculptures*, *ibid.*, VI, 323.

61. Medwin, pp. 243, 250; to John Gisborne after Nov. 18, 1820. *Letters*, II, 250.

62. "An illustration of this view of the subject is afforded by a circumstance in the life of Dr. Johnson,—the last man of considerable talents who shewed any serious attachment to the antient faith, and whose life and death as compared with that of his contemporary Hume, affords a just standard of the consolations of Christianity or the Infidel systems. A gentleman enquired of Johnson what he meant by *being damned*. 'Sent to Hell and punished everlastingly,' he replied. The kingdom of the faithful." (*On the Devil, and Devils*, *Works*, VII, 93.)

63. White, II, 275.

6. *New Directions*

1. Mary Shelley's Note on *Alastor.* (*Works,* I, 198.) Shelley wrote to Hogg from Bishopsgate on Aug. 26; on Sept. 10 he indicated to the bookdealers Lackington, Allen and Co. that he had just returned from the boating trip. (*Shelley and His Circle,* III, 481; *Letters,* I, 430.) In a letter to Hogg on Sept. 22, Shelley notes that he has "been engaged lately in the commencement of several literary plans." (*Letters,* I, 432.) These certainly included *Alastor,* for the *Alastor* volume was in the press by Jan 6, 1816. (To John Murray, *ibid.,* pp. 438–439.) For a bibliographical account of the volume, see *Shelley and His Circle,* IV, 496–497, 592. On Feb. 6, 1816, Shelley wrote to Messrs. Carpenter & Son, publishers, 13 Old Bond St. (neighbors of the Hookhams at no. 15): "In consequence of the advice with which you were so kind as to favor my friend Mr. *Scharper,* I have made arrangements with Messrs. Baldwin & C[o]. for the publication of the small Vol. of Poems left for your inspection a week or two ago. I expect that they will be ready for publication in the course of a few days." (*Letters,* I, 449.) A copy was in Timothy Shelley's hands at Field Place by Feb. 27. (Ingpen, p. 463.) It was reviewed in the April issue of *The Monthly Review, or Literary Journal.* (White, *Unextinguished Hearth,* p. 105.)

2. For a summary of discussion on the poem, see Bennett Weaver and Donald H. Reiman, "Shelley," *The English Romantic Poets, A Review of Research and Criticism,* ed. Frank Jordan, The Modern Language Association of America (New York, 1972) pp. 364–365.

3. *Works,* I, 173, 174; see also *An Address to the People, ibid.,* VI, 78.

4. Richard Ackermann, "Quellen, Vorbilder, Stoffe zu Shelley's poetischen Werken," *Münchener Beiträge zur romanischen und englischen Philologie* (Erlangen, 1890), pp. 1–16, showed that in *Alastor* the introductory invocation to nature contains echoes from *The Excursion* and *Tintern Abbey.* A. Beljame, in notes to his French translation of *Alastor* (Paris, 1895), indicated echoes in the poem from Wordsworth and from Volney's *Ruins.* L. H. Allen, "Plagiarism, Sources, and Influences in Shelley's 'Alastor,'" *Modern Language Review,* XVIII (1923), 133–151, contended that many of Ackermann's parallels were far-fetched. But Paul Mueschke and Earl L. Griggs, "Wordsworth As the Prototype of the Poet in Shelley's 'Alastor,'" *PMLA,* XLIX (1934), 229, noted new parallels with Wordsworth. Harold Leroy Hoffman, *An Odyssey of the Soul: Shelley's Alastor* (New York: Columbia University Press, 1933), pp. 59–125, noted parallels with *The Missionary* by Sidney Owenson and *The Life and Adventures of Peter Wilkins* by Robert Paltock. White (I, 700–701) suggested parallels with Godwin's *Fleetwood* and Wieland's *Agathon,* as well as with Shelley's letter to Elizabeth Hitchener of June 20, 1811.

In Cameron, "*Rasselas* and *Alastor:* A Study in Transmutation," *Studies in Philology,* XL (1943), 58–78, I remarked on parallels with Samuel Johnson's *Rasselas* and Coleridge's *Kubla Khan.* Although Jerome W. Archer, "*Kubla Khan: Queen Mab,*" *Studies in Philology,* XLI (1944), 576–581, pointed out that *Kubla Khan* was published later in 1816 than was *Alastor,* Shelley may have seen the poem in manuscript, for it was probably written in 1797 and was circulated and read aloud by Coleridge in the intervening years. (*Letters of Samuel Taylor Coleridge,* ed. Earl Leslie Griggs [Oxford, 1956], I, 348, 394n; IV, 639; John Livingstone Lowes, *The Road to Xanadu* [New York, 1927], pp. 353–354.) Shelley could have been shown a copy by Godwin, who was close to Coleridge for a time.

5. The general influence of Volney's *Ruins* is evident. In *Works* (I, 420) a parallel is suggested with Peacock's *Palmyra,* which Shelley first encountered in 1812. (To Hookham Aug. 18, 1812, *Letters,* I, 325.) For Shelley's early interest in the ruins of the past, see *A Retrospect of Times of Old, Esdaile Notebook,* pp. 95–97, 226–229.

6. The sexual meaning (fellatio) in *Fragment Supposed To Be an Epithalamium of Francis Ravaillac and Charlotte Corday,* ll. 82–86, is made clear in Shelley's letter to Edward Fergus Graham, Nov. 30, 1810. (*Shelley and His Circle,* II, 646–647.)

7. Shelley's father made a wry and insightful comment on receiving a copy of *Alastor:* "P.B. has published a Poem with some fragments, somewhat in his usual style, not altogether free from former sentiments, and wants to find out one person on earth the Prototype of himself." (To William Whitton, Feb. 27, 1816, Ingpen, p. 463). Sir Timothy had perhaps not read beyond the Preface.

8. *Works,* VI, 202. See also *Dark Spirit of the Desert Rude,* or *The Retrospect, Cwm Elan, 1812,* ll. 23–48, *Esdaile Notebook,* pp. 77–78, 155–156.

9. *Works,* VI, 201–202. Frederick L. Jones, "The Inconsistency of Shelley's *Alastor,*" *ELH: A Journal of English Literary History,* XIII (December 1946), 297, argued that there is a real contradiction between the Preface and the poem, not only a difference in presentation. For a convincing rebuttal, see Evan K. Gibson, "*Alastor:* A. Reinterpretation," *PMLA,* LXII (December 1947), 1022–1045.

10. Reiman (p. 38) argued that the sea is the Aral Sea, but this does not seem possible,

for the poet sees the Caucasus from it (353) and enters a cavern in a mountain in the Caucasus (377). The sea is referred to as "the lone Chorasmian shore" (272). Chormasia embraced the region between the Caspian and the Aral seas. Reiman (pp. 38, 164–165) also contended that by the Caucasus Shelley meant the Indian Caucasus, but if so, he would have specified it, as he does in *Prometheus Unbound* (stage direction to Act I). The Indian Caucasus is not visible from the Aral Sea.

11. *To Harriet*, ll. 9–10, *Esdaile Notebook*, pp. 85, 220.

12. How naturally such concepts occurred to poets of the time is indicated by Peacock's outline for his two-canto version of *Ahrimanes*, which concludes with the hero and heroine in a boat: "The boat sails securely on, though assailed by violent tempests raised by Ahrimannic spirits, imaging the course of virtue through the storm of life." (Peacock, *Works*, VII, 432.)

13. Gibson, "*Alastor: A Reinterpretation*," p. 1037. Grabo, p. 177, suggested that the boat represents the soul, but no specific details of the description fit this view, as they do the theory of the body. Perhaps Shelley's thoughts were turned to the frailty of the body of his own recent ill health. For conjectures on the symbolism in the poem in general, see Reiman, pp. 35–41.

14. *Works*, VI, 231.

15. Peacock, p. 341. Perhaps Peacock was referring to John Wilson, who in a favorable review in *Blackwood's* took "Alastor" for the name of the hero. (White, *Unextinguished Hearth*, p. 111.) White (I, 418–419) gave as the theme of the poem: "concentration upon high and lofty ideals may bring with it an avenging fury, which makes the actual world seem dark and dead to those who have pursued perfection too far." There is, however, no "avenging fury," and it is not a search for ideals that produces spiritual decay but shutting oneself off from human love. (See Dowden, I, 532.) Neville Rogers (*Selected Poetry*, p. xx) commented: "*Alastor* gives an account of the mental struggles of a poet who is pursued by good and evil daemons"—but there is nothing about "daemons," either good or bad in the poem.

16. *Dark Spirit of the Desart Rude*, *Esdaile Notebook*, p. 77; *The Retrospect*, l. 39–48, *ibid.*, p. 156; see also ll. 120–123. Ll. 120 and 121 are reversed in the *Esdaile Notebook*, though they were in the correct order on page proof. Presumably some type was dropped, and the printer reassembled it without consulting the editor. For other early treatments by Shelley of *Alastor* themes and situations, see Melvin T. Solve, *Shelley: His Theory of Poetry* (Chicago, 1927), pp. 6–7; Frederick L. Jones, "*Alastor* Foreshadowed in *St. Irvyne*," *PMLA*, XLIX (1934), 969–971. *To Harriet* ("It is not blasphemy"), II. 5–10, *Esdaile Notebook*, p. 85.

17. *Works*, I, 198.

18. See *Shelley and His Circle*, III, 481–484.

19. To Hogg, Aug. 26, 1815, *ibid.*, p. 482. For Shelleys' hinting of an unhappy situation with Harriet, see e.g., his letter to Hogg, Nov. 23, 1813. (*Letters*, I, 259–265.) The sentence following the comment on dreams and error contains a specific reference to Thomas Love Peacock, with whom Shelley was then spending much time: "One man there is, and he is a cold and calculating man, who knows better than to waste life, but who alas! cannot enjoy it." Cornelia Newton, in a letter to T. J. Hogg on Oct. 21, 1813 (Hogg, II, 115), referred to Peacock as a "cold" scholar. On Sept. 16, 1815, Charles Clairmont wrote to his sister Claire: "Peacock was here when I came; with him I was a good deal pleased from the first; I am so still, and should have been more so if Shelley had not prejudiced me." (Dowden, I, 528; see also *Shelley and His Circle*, III, 263–265.)

20. *Works*, III, 146. Mary dated the whole work "Marlow, 1817" and the longest fragment "December, 1817." (*Ibid.* p. 325.)

21. The fragments are divided here as in *Works*, III, 137–145. Shelley perhaps derived the name Athanase from Bishop Athanasius, supposed author of the Athanasian Creed, who was banished by the Arians but brought back by Julian the Apostate, who was a foe of the Christian church, and with whom Shelley apparently identifies in *Julian and Maddalo*. The classical dictionaries mention a twelfth-century Byzantine historian named Zonaras. In her Note to *The Revolt of Islam* (*Works*, I, 409), Mary Shelley stated that the hermit is a portrait of Dr. James Lind, the king's physician at Windsor, whom Shelley knew as a boy at Eton, and since in this poem Zonoras performs the same function in relation to the hero, it is likely that Shelley had Lind in mind here also.

22. Shelley intended to publish this poem with *Julian and Maddalo*, which attacks Mary for her neglect and cruelty. (To Charles Ollier, May 14, 1820, *Letters*, II, 196.)

23. According to Mary Shelley's Note on the early poems, the subject of "Oh! there are spirits in the air" was Coleridge. However, there is little doubt that it deals primarily with Shelley himself, although it may have an oblique reference to Coleridge. White (I, 329–330) noted in it specific reference to Cornelia Turner.

24. *Esdaile Notebook*, p. 79; *Works*, I, 204.

25. See *A Philosophical View of Reform* (*Works*, VII, 14) and *Lines Written on Hearing the News of the Death of Napoleon.*

26. *Ibid.* I, 174. *Queen Mab* was not "published" but was privately printed by Shelley. He had intended to publish a revised version of it under the title of *The Queen of the Universe* and had only recently changed his mind. (See *Shelley and His Circle*, IV, 487–568.)

27. Mary Shelley's Note on the poems of 1816, *Works*, III, 128. For the dates of the trip around lake Geneva with Bryon, June 22–30, see *Shelley and His Circle*, IV, 690–701. Presumably the *Hymn* was composed at the same time as or shortly after it was "conceived," for Mary placed it before *Mont Blanc* in her edition. Shelley himself put the date "July 23, 1816," at the end of *Mont Blanc*. Since Shelley first saw Mont Blanc on July 22, he presumably wrote the poem in one or two days, during which he was also engaged in sightseeing. As Shelley often composed rapidly, this timetable is not impossible, though it is also likely that he did some revising after July 23, for he had a tendency to omit revision in estimating the time of composition. As he explains in *A Defence of Poetry*, he considered revision of secondary importance; the main thing was the initial inspiration. (*Works*, VII, 135–136.)

28. White, II, 192.

29. *Works*, VII, 206, 137, 136; VI, 231; *Verse and Prose*, pp. 18, 19. The phrase "intellectual beauty" occurs in Wieland's *Agathon*, a novel read by Shelley. (White, I, 701; see also Notopoulos, pp. 196–198, 583; *Shelley and His Circle*, I, 111.) It also occurs in William Godwin's *Memoirs of Mary Wollstonecraft.* (McNiece, pp. 183, 290.) Notopoulos (p. 196) noted that the word "intellectual" is not in Plato's text.

30. The manuscript of the *Hymn* has recently been published. See Judith Chernaik, "Textual Emendations for Three Poems by Shelley," *Keats-Shelley Journal*, XIX (1970), 44–48. The poem was first published in Leigh Hunt's *The Examiner*, Jan. 19, 1817, with errors that have persisted in later texts. For instance, l. 27 reads in the standard texts, "Demon, Ghost, and Heaven." The manuscript reads "Ghosts & God & Heaven." A copy of *The Examiner* text corrected in Shelley's hand reads "God & Ghosts." No doubt "Demon" was, as Chernaik suggested, "a case of discreet censorship by Leigh Hunt." In addition, l. 51 in the manuscript reads, "I called on the false name with which our youth is fed." The "false name" is obviously "God." The standard text reads "poisonous names," which obscures the meaning but is presumably a correction by Shelley—unless he wrote in a later draft "poisonous name," which was changed to "names" by Hunt. In the manuscript, l. 21 reads "care & pain"; the standard texts, following *The Examiner*, read "fear and dream," which makes no sense. The printed texts nevertheless contain some obviously better readings. For instance, l. 2 in the manuscript reads "walks" for the usual "floats." The manuscript, though clearly not a final revision, in some respects comes closer to Shelley's meaning.

31. *Works*, VI, 231.

32. *Esdaile Notebook*, pp. 125, 250–253; *Letters*, I, 227–228; Newman I. White, *The Best of Shelley* (New York, 1932), p. 473.

33. For the source of "vale of tears" in the Bishops' Bible (1586) and other works, see *Esdaile Notebook*, p. 246n. Shelley first used the phrase in an early poem, *To the Lover of Mary, ibid.*, p. 122.

34. *Works*, VI, 198.

35. See, e.g. *Selected Poetry*, pp. 466–467; Pulos, pp. 81–83.

36. To T. L. Peacock, July 22, 1816, *Letters*, I, 496–497; *Works*, VI, 88. For analyses of the poem, see *Poems*, II, 489–491; P. H. Butter, *Shelley's Idols of the Cave* (Edinburgh, 1954), pp. 118–125; Earl R. Wasserman, *The Subtler Language* (Baltimore, 1959), 195–240; Bloom, pp. 19–35; Reiman, pp. 42–44.

37. *Works*, VI, 196.

38. *Ibid.*, p. 195.

39. *A Defence of Poetry, ibid.*, VII, 135, 137.

40. *Poems*, II, 491.

41. Godwin, *Political Justice*, I, 404, 414–416.

7. *Shelley and Mary*

1. Mary Shelley commented: "*Rosalind and Helen* was begun at Marlow, and thrown aside—till I found it; and, at my request, it was completed." Then, following a para-

graph of comment, she adds a final sentence in a separate paragraph: "*Rosalind and Helen* was finished during the summer of 1818, while we were at the Baths of Lucca." These statements have been taken to mean that Shelley began *Rosalind and Helen* at Marlow but then "threw it aside" and wrote most of it in Italy. But that Mary cannot have meant this, is apparent from Shelley's letter to Peacock from the baths of Lucca on Aug. 16, 1818: "I have finished, by taking advantage of a few days of inspiration . . . the little poem I began sending to the press in London. Ollier will send you the proofs." (*Letters*, II, 29.) And in April 1818, shortly after arriving in Italy, Shelley had written to Peacock with reference to the same work (which Ollier published in 1819): "I have ordered Ollier to send you some sheets &c. for revision." (*Letters*, II, 29, 4.) Shelley, then, had progressed on the poem at Marlow to the point of sending it to the printers. Nor could he have written most of its 1318 lines in "a few days." The indications are that it was fairly complete before he left Marlow. Perhaps Mary meant that Shelley began it at Marlow, threw it aside there, took it up again at Marlow after she had discovered it, almost completed it there, and later added to it in Italy, perhaps in proof. The first reference to the poem is in a letter from Mary to Shelley on Sept. 26, 1817, after he had been forbidden further creative work by a physician: "It is well that your poem was finished before this edict was issued against the imagination—but my pretty eclogue will suffer from it." (Mary Shelley, *Letters*, I, 31.) The "poem" refers to *The Revolt of Islam*; the "pretty eclogue" refers to *Rosalind and Helen: A Modern Eclogue*. On Feb. 18, 1818, Mary recorded: "copy Shelley's eclogue." (*Mary Shelley's Journal*, p. 92.) Apparently Shelley was about to work on *Rosalind and Helen* late in September 1817, having completed *The Revolt of Islam* on Sept. 23, had been working on it previously, and it was in shape for the press by Feb. 18, 1818. How much work he had done on it prior to Sept. 26, 1817, or just when he had done it, is not known. The Shelleys arrived at Marlow in March 1817, and Shelley apparently began *The Revolt of Islam* almost immediately. It has been conjectured that he worked on *Rosalind and Helen* in March, before beginning *The Revolt of Islam*, and dropped it as he became more interested in the longer project. (Dowden, II, 130; R. D. Havens, "Rosalind and Helen," *Journal of English and Germanic Philology*, XXX [1931], 218–219.) But it seems likely that the poem was inspired by the visit of W. M. Baxter to Marlow in September 1817.

2. In ll. 272–275 the girl is a "babe at my bosom," and the boys are standing by Rosalind's knee; in l. 406 Rosalind states that the girl was her firstborn. (*Poems*, I, 581.)

3. For Booth and the Baxters, see Dowden, II, 174–175, *Shelley and His Circle*, II, 540–544, 557–560; III, 100–105; to William Thomas Baxter, Dec. 30, 1817, *Letters*, I, 588.

4. To Shelley, Sept. 24, 1817, Mary Shelley, *Letters*, I, 30; see also Sept. 1, 4, 29, 1817, *Mary Shelley's Journal*, p. 84.

5. Dowden, II, 178. In 1823, however, when Mary returned to England, she and Isabella again became friends and remained so for the rest of their lives. Mary remembered her in her will. (To Leigh Hunt, Sept. 9, 1823, Mary Shelley, *Letters*, I, 262; Percy Florence Shelley to Mrs. Booth, February 1851, *ibid.*, II, 358.)

6. To Shelley, Sept. 26, 1817, Mary Shelley, *Letters*, I, 31.

7. Shelley wrote to Byron on Jan. 17, 1817 that in the trial for custody of his children he was being accused of being "a REVOLUTIONIST, and an *Atheist*." (*Letters*, I, 530.) Lionel was put on trial for "keen blasphemy." The link between the two trials in Shelley's mind is also indicated by the fact that the final speech of Lionel on entering prison (894–901) was repeated by Shelley in his poem on his son William in an attack on the English "tyrants" who had deprived him of his other children.

8. See also Preface to *Julian and Maddalo*: "He [Julian-Shelley] is a complete infidel, and a scoffer at all things reputed holy; and Maddalo [Byron] takes a wicked pleasure in drawing out his taunts against religion." (*Works*, III, 177.)

9. For Claire's schemes, see to Mary, Aug. 18, 20, 23, 1818, *Letters*, II, 32, 34, 36.

10. Aug. 23, 1818, *ibid.*, pp. 37. The "fourth Canto" refers to *Childe Harold's Pilgrimage*. "Foliage" was a book of poems by Leigh Hunt, which Shelley had faintly praised in a letter to Hunt on Mar. 22. (*Ibid.*, p. 2.) Byron commented to Medwin: "I shall say nothing of the critique itself on 'Foliage;' with the exception of a few sonnets, it was unworthy of Hunt." (Medwin, *Conversations*, p. 182.)

11. Aug. 23, 1818, *Letters*, II, 36, 37; Sept. 13, 1818, Mary Shelley, *Letters*, I, 58.

12. To Mary Shelley, Sept. 22, *Letters*, II, 40; to Claire Clairmont, Sept. 15, *ibid.*, pp. 40–41, to T. L. Peacock, *ibid.*, p. 42.

13. For Shelley's early reading in Gibbon, see Cameron, pp. 266, 404; *Esdaile Notebook*, pp. 309–310. Julian the Apostate was a man after Shelleys' own heart—a liberal and a republican, who wrote a book against the Christian church and defied its ministers.

John Lavelle of Monmouth College suggested to me that the name Maddalo perhaps came from Count Maddaloni, whose family was noted in J. C. L. Simondi de Sismondi, *Histoire des republics italiennes du Moyen Age* (Paris; Furne & Cem, 1840), VII, 442–443. Shelley was acquainted with Sismondi's history. Shelley also used the name Maddalo for a courtier in *Scene from Tasso* (1818).

14. Shelley told Leigh Hunt that *Julian and Maddalo* was "composed last year at Este," and Mary Shelley commented in a Note on the poems of 1818: "and here [at Este] also, he mentions in a letter, he wrote *Julian and Maddalo*." (Aug. 15, 1819, *Letters*, II, 108; *Works*, III, 219.) G. M. Matthews, however, in " 'Julian and Maddalo': The Draft and the Meaning," *Studia neophilologica*, XXXV, no. 1 (1963), 57–84, presented evidence from Shelley's notebook manuscript in the Bodleian Library to show that most of the poem was composed in or later than December 1818, and at Naples or Rome. Perhaps when Shelley told Hunt that it was "composed" at Este, he was using "composed" loosely in the sense of "conceived." But there is also an indication that part of the poem was actually written at Este, for, as Sloane Frazier indicated to me, the Bodleian manuscript of *Julian and Maddalo* does not contain ll. 287–293, 300–336, 337–383 and 408–510. As all these missing lines come from the second or "madman" section of the poem, it may be that Shelley began the poem with this section and later fitted it into the *Julian and Maddalo* framework.

15. Medwin, *Conversations*, pp. 282–283, 291; to Leigh Hunt, Aug. 26, 1821, *Letters*, II, 345. Byron's aristocratic pretensions were also noted unfavorably by the countess of Blessington at Genoa in 1823, who reported that when a playwright dedicated a play to him simply as "George Byron," he became enraged: "I was never more provoked. How stupid, how ignorant, to pass over my rank!" She also commented on the nouveau riche gaudiness of Byron's bed and carriage. (*Conversations of Lord Byron with the Countess of Blessington* [London, 1850], pp. 93, 264.)

16. Jan. 9, 13, 1821, Byron, V, 163, 173. Part of the difference between the Maddalo picture and this journal entry stems from the fact that Byron was more personally stable in 1821 than in 1818 and had entered actively into Italian politics. (To Mary Shelley, Aug. 9, 1821, *Letters*, II, 322–323.)

17. Aug. 15, Dec. 15, 1819, *Letters*, II, 108, 164.

18. See White, II, 50–54; to Charles Ollier, May 14, 1820, *Letters*, II, 196; *Prince Athanase*, ll. 121–124.

19. Mary Shelley, Note on the poems of 1818, *Works*, III, 220.

20. Two other theories have been advanced. It was argued that the woman was Harriet Shelley in H. S. Salt, "A Study of Shelley's 'Julian and Maddalo,' " *Shelley Society Papers*, ser. 1, no. 1, pt. II (1891), pp. 325–342 (on p. 328 Salt noted that Dowden wrote to him agreeing with his view); Peck, II, 104–105; Benjamin P. Kurtz, *The Pursuit of Death* (New York, 1933), pp. 145–149. The theory was first advanced in H. S. Salt, *Academy*, March 1887; Arabella Shore *The Gentleman's Magazine*, October 1887. The theory was convincingly attacked in Raymond D. Havens, "Julian and Maddalo," *Studies in Philology*, XXVII (1930), 653n; White, II, 559. Claire Clairmont was proposed in John Harrington Smith, "Shelley and Claire Clairmont," PMLA, LIV (1939), 806–810; Smith, "Shelley and Claire Again," *Studies in Philology*, XLI (1944), 94–105. But the relationship of Shelley and Claire was not that depicted for the madman and the lady and their child. Mary Shelley was proposed in Grabo, pp. 267–269; White, II, 46–56; Elizabeth Mitchie, *Mary Shelley* (New Brunswick, 1953), pp. 11–13, 211–217, and *passim*. Grabo did not reconstruct the specific biographical situation underlying the poem but assumed a general alienation resulting from Mary's failure to understand Shelley's ideas.

An influential theory on the nature of the poem was advanced by Raymond D. Havens, following a suggestion by Dowden (II, 238). Havens speculated that the madman's speech was part of Shelley's projected drama on the madness of Tasso and that, when he abandoned that project, he incorporated it into *Julian and Maddalo*. (Havens, "Julian and Maddalo," pp. 648–653; see also Baker, pp. 124–138; Matthews, "Julian and Maddalo," pp. 80–84; *Selected Poetry*, p. 424.) Matthews himself, however, noted (p. 82) that the madman is depicted as sitting near a piano, "an eighteenth-century invention," so that he could hardly be Tasso. The fact that the name Maddalo occurs also in the fragment *Scene from Tasso*, where he is a courtier who spies on Tasso and Leonora, indicates only that Shelley was attracted to the name and had abandoned the Tasso project. Furthermore, Tasso's love for Leonora does not fit the ravings of the madman in Julian and Maddalo. Leonora did not desert him or act cruelly toward him; on the contrary, she was sympathetic and lamented his imprisonment by her brother the duke.

Matthews argued further (p. 76) that Shelley would not have published *Julian and Maddalo* if it had been autobiographical because of its reflections on Mary. But reflections on Mary as "the cold, chaste moon" in *Epipsychidion* did not prevent Shelley from publishing that poem. Presumably he felt that the specific autobiographical content in either poem would not be generally understood. He published *Epipsychidion* anonymously and such was also his intention for *Julian and Maddalo.* (To Charles Ollier, May 14, 1820, *Letters,* II, 196.) He also included derogatory comments on Mary in some of his poems to Claire Clairmont and Jane Williams.

One final theory is that the "maniac" is Byron. (J. E. Saveson, "Shelley's *Julian and Maddalo,*" *Keats-Shelley Journal,* X [Winter 1961], 53–58.) But the parallels between the "maniac" and Byron do not fit the specific references and situations of the poem.

21. White, II, 47. Not only is the woman still living (*ibid.,* p. 559), but in some passages she appears to be present, and in one passage she seems to have the child with her (ll. 484–486).

22. Note on the poems of 1818, *Works,* III, 220.

23. R. Glynn Grylls, *Mary Shelley* (New York, 1938), p. 298.

24. Sept. 16, 1818, *Mary Shelley's Journal,* p. 105; to Mary, Sept. 22, 1818, *Letters,* II, 39.

25. *Rossetti Papers,* p. 500; Claire Clairmont to Fanny Godwin, May 28, 1815, Mrs. Julian Marshall, *Life and Letters of Mary Shelley* (London, 1889), I, 118, 312; Maud Rolleston, *Talks with Lady Shelley* (London, 1925), p. 41; Elizabeth Nitchie, "Mary Shelley's 'Mathilda,'" *Studies in Philology,* XL (July 1943), 456; Nitchie, *Mary Shelley,* pp. 11–13. *Mathilda* was written in 1819, perhaps only a few months after the events at Este. The hero of the novel, Lovel, is clearly a portrait of Shelley, and Mathilda is Mary.

26. Shelley wrote to Mary on Aug. 23, 1818, urging her to come "instantly" to Este but giving no reason for the request, although earlier in the letter he quoted Byron as permitting Allegra to go to Claire at Padua and then interpolated, "when he said this he supposed that you & the family were there." (*Letters,* II, 36–37.) This is not specifically advanced as a reason for haste, but Mary could have taken it as such.

27. *Ibid.,* p. 37.

28. To Peacock, Aug. 24, 1819, *ibid.,* p. 114

29. *Works,* II, 5.

30. Dedication to *The Report of Islam,* ll. 52–53. White (II, 41) argued that the skull and bones were those of Clara. It was suggested that the bones refer to Shelley's own past, which he regarded as dead, in Donald H. Reiman, "Structure, Symbol, and Theme in 'Lines Written among the Euganean Hills.'" *PMLA,* LXXVII (September 1962), 406; Reiman, p. 66. Reiman, however, saw the beach as in Great Britain and took the seven years to refer to the time between Shelley's expulsion from Oxford and his departure from England (March 1811–March 1818). For the lines from *The Choice,* see Grylls, *Mary Shelley,* p. 299.

31. White, II, 40, 558; *Letters,* II, 43. Shelley uses the word Celtic, as does Mme. de Stael, in reference to any northern, especially Germanic race. See also the "brutal Celt" of 1. 223 and the "mighty Austrian" of l. 248. In l. 223 Shelley is speaking generically, but ll. 152 and 248 may refer to Metternich.

32. For Maria Gisborne, see Paul, I, 81–83, 332–339; Dowden, II, 206–208; Gisborne & Williams, pp. 1–11. For Henry Reveley, see Dowden, II, 229n; Rogers, p. 339. John Gisborne's extensive diaries are in the possession of Lord Abinger. Henry Reveley later possessed Shelley manuscripts, some of which he reportedly destroyed. (*Rossetti Papers,* pp. 402, 432–433; *Letters about Shelley,* pp. 28–29, 88, 92.)

33. Aug. 24, 1819, *Letters,* II, 114. Slawkenbergius, in Sterne's *Tristram Shandy,* is the German author of a Latin treatise on noses.

34. To Henry Reveley, Nov. 17, 1819, *ibid.,* pp. 157–158.

35. Oct. 29, 1820, *ibid.,* p. 243; Dowden, II, 349. In later years Henry Reveley's wife is said to have declared that Shelley owed Reveley £1,000—a debt that W. M. Rossetti considered "most unlikely." (*Rossetti Papers,* p. 402; *Letters about Shelley,* p. 29.) There is no other evidence for it.

36. The Gisbornes gave this bowl to a Miss Rumble, who in turn gave it to the British Museum. (*Rossetti Papers,* 432.)

37. Mary Shelley, Note on the poems of 1820, *Works,* IV, 78.

38. The parallels between the two works are clear, no doubt intentionally so. Mercury, like the Witch, is born in a cave and is a grandchild of Atlas. (*Hymn to Mercury,* i; *Witch of Atlas,* ii, iv.) Both caves contain similar household objects. (*Hymn,* x; *Witch,* xxxv–xxxvii.) Hermes' fashioning of the tortoise into a musical instrument is similar to the Witch's fashioning of the hermaphrodite. (*Hymn,* vii–ix; *Witch,* xxxv–xxxvii.) Mercury sweeps along on magic sandals as the Witch does in her magic boat. (*Hymn,* xiii; *Witch,* xxxvii.) In general, the same puckish spirit animates both works, the one dealing

with the pranks of a god, the other with a goddess, both of them grandchildren of Atlas. Dowden (II, 334) suggested that the "playful form of speech" used in both the *Witch* and the *Hymn to Mercury* might have been influenced by Shelley's recent reading of a light-veined Italian poem, Fortiguerra's *Ricciardetto*. White (II, 220–221) pointed out that the Italian *maga* (witch) is used in Fortiguerra's poem in a good sense, the witch Stella being very beautiful, and argued that Shelley's unusual use of the word probably came from this work.

39. That the boat is love is indicated by the description of its origin (xxxi–xxxiii), which may be compared with *Fragments of an Unfinished Drama*, II, 127–150, and *The Zucca*, vi–xi. A. M. D. Hughes (Shelley's 'Witch of Atlas,'" *Modern Language Review*, VII [1912], 514) suggested that the hermaphrodite stood for imagination, "the faculty which brings the world into harmony and in which all oppositions are reconciled, fire and snow, male and female." See also Fuller, pp. 270–271, 288.

40. Baker, "Spenser and 'The Witch of Atlas,'" *PMLA*, LVI (June 1941), 477–478.

41. Dec. 29, 1820, Mary Shelley, *Letters*, II, 124; see also to Leigh Hunt, Dec. 3, 1820, *ibid.* p. 118. Emilia in her letters referred to her mother as the source of her misfortunes. (Dowden, II, 374.) Medwin's statement (p. 277) that this was her stepmother is apparently incorrect, as her mother did not die until 1826. (White, II, 604–605.) See also Emilia Viviana Della Robbia, *Vita di una donna* (Florence, 1936); White, II, 466–485 (Emilia's letters to Shelley and Mary); Fuller, pp. 260–261. Mary described Emilia in her novel *Lodore* (1835). (Dowden, II, 370–371; Frederick L. Jones, *Times Literary Supplement*, Apr. 4, 1935, p. 228.) Claire recorded in her journal for Nov. 29 that she had visited Emilia that day; Mary apparently first accompanied her on Dec. 1. (Clairmont, p. 189; *Mary Shelley's Journal*, p. 141.) Medwin (pp. 277–278) reported that, Pacchiani told him and Shelley of Emilia's plight, whereupon the three of them went to see her. But Claire's journal shows that Pacchiani first took Claire to the convent. (Clairmont, p. 189.)

42. The visit must have been before Dec. 10, because Emilia wrote Shelley a letter on that date which appears to be based on more than one visit. (Dowden, II, 373.)

43. Medwin, pp. 278–279, 283–284. Medwin also gave the Italian text of Emilia's essay (pp. 281–283).

44. *Note Books*, I, 189 (early draft).

45. Mary Shelley, *Letters*, I, 160; see also to Claire Clairmont, May 11, 1821, *ibid.*, p. 141. Emilia married Luigi Biondi on Sept. 18, 1821.

46. June 18, 1822, *Letters*, II, 434. *Epipsychidion* was written between Shelley's first visit to Emilia early in December 1820 and his sending it to Ollier on Feb. 16, 1821. (*Letters*, II, 262.) White (II, 606) argued that the period of composition must be "the first two weeks of February," because Jane and Edward Williams are addressed by "familiar nicknames" in the poem, whereas they did not arrive in Pisa until Jan. 19, and Shelley would hardly have so addressed them until he had known them at least two weeks. The "familiar nicknames" appear in the final lines (592–604), where the poem, in Chaucerian manner, is told to "haste" until it meets "Marina, Vanna, Primus and the rest." Marina is the name with which Mary signed her letters to Leigh Hunt. "Williams" also appears in the lines in one manuscript, which indicates that Vanna (Giovanna—Jane) in Jane Williams, and Primus is Edward: "imitated from the Vita Nuova, where Dante continually speaks of Guido [Cavalcanti] as his 'first friend.'" (C. D. Locock, *An Examination of Shelley Manuscripts in the Bodleian*, [Oxford, 1903], p. 11; *Poems* II, 458.) These final lines form a kind of *coda* separated by a rule from the rest of the poem; the poem proper could have been begun in December.

47. *Selected Poetry*, p. 446; Rogers, p. 245. The word "Epipsychidion" has also been interpretated as "soul out of my soul" (l. 238) or "soul within the soul" (l. 455) and "externalized little soul." (*Works*, II, 429; *Poetry and Prose*, p. 510; Reiman, p. 125.) These suggestions now appear not to be etymologically correct, although their general concepts are present in the poem. If Rogers is right and the title is built on the analogy with epithalamion, presumably the title should be pronounced—as would be natural in English—*Epi*-psychidion, and not on the Greek system, *Epip*-sychidion. Rogers places the emphasis on "soul" in a Platonic sense. When Emilia married in 1821, Shelley wrote an epithalamium for her. (White, II, 319.)

48. *On Love*, *Works*, VI, 202.

49. *Ibid.*, I, 141. Shelley probably had Mary specifically in mind in "jealous foe."

50. A draft of the poem reads "free love" for "true love." ("Passages of the Poem, or Connected Therewith," *Works*, II, 377, 1. 17.) As Fuller (p. 264) pointed out, "True Love" has reference to Emilia's essay "Il vero amore."

51. *A Discourse on the Manners of the Antient Greeks*, Notopoulos, p. 408.

52. "Shelley—By One Who Knew Him," *Shelley and Keats As They Struck Their Contemporaries*, ed. Edmund Blunden (London, 1925), pp. 30–31.

53. C. Oct. 21, 1822, Mary Shelley, *Letters*, I, 198; *Mary Shelley's Journal*, pp. 180–181. This entry perhaps marked the beginning of a biography of Shelley, later forbidden by Sir Timothy Shelley, for it appears also in the opening paragraph of her fragments of a biography. (Hogg, I, 6.)

54. See *Verse and Prose*, p. 16; Ingpen, p. 520; *Poems* II, 456. I, 522; White, II, 262.

55. In an article written before the *Esdaile Notebook* was published, with its revelation of how severe a shock Harriet Grove's rejection had been to Shelley, I argued that Harriet Shelley was the one "not true to me." But it is now clear that the "hunted deer" crisis could encompass his state at Cwm Elan in the summer of 1811 and earlier. (Cameron, "The Planet-Tempest Passage in *Epipsychidion*," PMLA [September 1948], 952n.)

56. Hunt, II, 33; Peacock, II, 347; Rossetti, *Memoir of Shelley*, p. 69.

57. *Letters*, I, 526–531; Hunt, II, 35.

58. To Byron, Jan. 17, 1817; to Mary, Dec. 16, 1816, *Letters*, I, 529–530, 521, 530.

59. Mary Shelley, *Letters*, I, 17. *Rosalind and Helen* provides a striking parallel to both the moon and the planet-tempest passages. When Lionel is introduced by Helen (Mary), the narrator, he is described as having been "stricken deep with some disease of mind" by an unfortunate love experience and nursed back to mental health by Helen (ll. 756–813). This corresponds to the breakup of Shelley's first marriage and his meeting with Mary, reflected both in the "black despair" followed by "bright Spring" of the *Dedication* to *The Revolt of Islam* and in the "hunted deer" turmoil followed by "deliverance . . . like a noonday dawn" in *Epipsychidion*. "And I hung o'er him in his sleep" (l. 836) in *Rosalind and Helen* is similar to the *Epipsychidion* "sleep" passage (ll. 293–307). Following this episode comes Lionel's "trial" for "keen blasphemy." On his release, he becomes ill, and Helen again fears for him:

> You might see his colour come and go,
> And the softest strain of music made
> Sweet smiles, yet sad, arise and fade
> Amid the dew of his tender eyes;
>
> . . . . .
>
> And then I fell on a life which was sick with fear
> Of all the woe that now I bear. (1020–23, 1047–48)

The trial corresponds to the trial for custody of Shelley's children, and the succeeding emotional-physical crisis reflects Shelley's upset state during this period. This episode thus parallels the emotional states of the poet and the moon (Mary) during the planet-tempest episode, when the moon's lips "shrank as in the sickness of eclipse."

60. As suggested by Grabo (p. 342), White (II, 266–268), and others.

61. June 19, 1822, *Letters*, II, 438. One manuscript of the poem is dated Pisa, March 1820. (*Works*, II, 423.) On the garden, see Hogg, I, 78–79; Medwin, p. 265; McAleer, pp. 148–149.)

62. *Essay on Christianity*, *Works*, VI, 231.

63. White, II, 536.

64. Gisborne & Williams, p. 142, Mary Shelley, Note on the play, *Works*, IV, 137.

65. Sylva Norman, *After Shelley: The Letters of Thomas Jefferson Hogg to Jane Williams* (New York, 1938), pp. xv-xvi.

66. *Poems*, II, 509, 472.

67. See also King-Hele, pp. 236–237; Peck, II, 169–170.

68. See Shelley, *Poetical Works*, ed. H. Buxton Forman (London, 1877), iv, 545–548; Peck, II, 206–207; White, II, 319–320; Rogers, pp. 249–250.

69. To Marianne Hunt, Aug. 28, 1819, Mary Shelley, *Letters*, I, 76.

70. Fogle, *The Imagery of Keats and Shelley: A Comparative Study* (Chapel Hill, 1941), pp. 264–266.

71. The earliest possible date of beginning composition for this poem, as for the *Letter to Maria Gisborne*, is June 15, 1820, as shown by Mary's Note that it was written at the Gisborne's house at Leghorn. (*Works*, IV, 78.) Her Note also establishes the last possible date for completion as Aug. 4, when the Shelleys left the house. But Shelley's letter to Peacock of July 12 moves the completion date back before that date: "I enclose two additional poems, to be added to those printed at the end of Prometheus: and send them to you, for fear Ollier might not know what to do in case he objected to some expressions in the fifteenth and sixteenth stanzas; and that you would do me the

favour to insert an asterisk or asterisks, with as little expense of the sense as may be." (*Letters*, II, 213–214.)

When Peacock published this letter, he added the note: "These were the fifteenth and sixteenth stanzas of the *Ode to Liberty*." Although he does not identify the second poem that Shelley enclosed, the evidence indicates that it was *To a Skylark*, which appeared in the *Prometheus Unbound* volume. The first batch of minor poems for this volume was sent out within a few days of May 14, 1820, the day on which Shelley wrote to his publisher, Ollier: "Mrs. Shelley is now transcribing for me the little poems to be printed at the end of *Prometheus*; they will be sent in a post or two." (*Ibid.*, p. 197.) Since *To a Skylark* was not written until at least June 15, it could not have been sent with this batch. There is no record of any poems being sent between June 15 and July 12, and none could have been sent later than July 12 because the volume was in the press in July and was published in August. Furthermore, Shelley's letter to Peacock of July 12 implies that the enclosed poems were a last late batch being rushed to the press, with Peacock to act as official expediter. In the *Prometheus Unbound* volume (1820) the two final poems are *To a Skylark* and *Ode to Liberty*, and a bibliographical examination of that volume by Fannie Ratchford at the University of Texas Library revealed that they are both printed in part on the same sheet. *To a Skylark* occupies pp. 201–206, sig. N5 recto–N7 verso; *Ode to Liberty*, pp. 207–222, sig. N8 recto–07 verso.

This date span can be narrowed still further, to June 15 or 16, for on June 30, Shelley wrote to the Gisbornes: "I write from Henry's study, and I send you some verses I wrote the first day I came, which will show you that I struggle with despondency." (*Ibid.*, p. 207.) Newman White took this to refer to the *Letter to Maria Gisborne* (White, "Probable Dates of Composition of Shelley's 'Letter to Maria Gisborne,' and 'To A Skylark,'" *Studies in Philology*, XXXVI (July 1939), 524–528; White, II, 594.) But this cannot be, because that poem was dated "July 1" by Shelley. The only other poem that Shelley is known to have written in this period is the *Ode to Liberty*, but a reference in it to the Neapolitan revolution (st. xiii), which did not break out until July 2, shows that it cannot be the poem referred to. This leaves only *To a Skylark*, which clearly fits the description of a "struggle with despondency."

72. King-Hele, p. 225; see also pp. 220–227; Grabo, *A Newton among Poets*, pp. 119–140, 154, White, I, 565–566. Adam Walker was a science popularizer of the time, whom Shelley encountered at both Sion House and Eton. (King-Hele, pp. 158–159, 244; Cameron pp. 8, 80, 261, 294.) Mary dated the poem "1820," but the month of composition is unknown. (*Works*, II, 425.)

73. See also to Peacock, Dec. 17 or 18, 1818, *Letters*, II, 57–64. When the poem was first published by Mary in *Posthumous Poems* (1824), it was dated "December, 1818."

74. The other poems to Claire in the series (all fragmentary) are *To Constantia*, *To One Singing*, *On Music*, and "To thirst and find no fill." These and *To Constantia, Singing* were included by Mary among the 1817 poems, but without indicating to whom they were addressed. That *To Constantia, Singing* was addressed to Claire is indicated by the fact that it was written at Marlow (March 1817–February 1818), where Shelley was enchanted by Claire's singing, with a piano he had bought for her. (Dowden, II, 111–112) If this lyric was addressed to Claire, the others must be also. Furthermore, Claire's tombstone bears the inscription "Clara Mary Constantia Jane Clairmont," her will was signed the same, and she copied part of these poems at Marlow and is reported to have discussed them in later years as being written to her. (White, I, 731–732; Clairmont, p. 13.) The text of *To Constantia, Singing* is puzzlingly corrupt. (Locock, *An Examination of Shelley Manuscripts*, pp. 60–62.) Shelley apparently took the name Constantia from Charles Brocken Brown's novel *Ormond*. (Clairmont, p. 172.)

The fact that Claire recorded in her journal for Jan. 19, 1818 that she was copying "part of verses to Constantia" (presumably *To Constantia, Singing*, as it is the only complete "Constantia" poem) perhaps means that the poems were written toward the end of the Marlow period.

Edward A. Silsbee, who talked to Claire at Florence in her old age and received the *To Constantia, Singing* manuscript from her, noted on it: "Written at Marlow 1817, wd. not let Mary see it, sent it to Oxford Gazette or some Oxford County paper without his name. Maidenhead, Bucks, Berkshire and Oxford Co. Papers." (*Works*, III, 328.) Silsbee presumably received this information from Claire. His adventures in extracting manuscripts from Claire formed the basis for Henry James's *The Aspern Papers*. (See *Shelley and His Circle*, II, 910–913.)

75. Locock, *An Examination of Shelley Manuscripts*, p. 63.

76. White (I, 732) regarded *To Constantia* as simply Shelley's "reproach at having lost a disciple," but there is no evidence that Shelley felt he had lost Claire as a disciple.

Certainly Claire's journals did not show that he had, and the language of the poems belies such an interpretation.

77. For Sophia's journal, see Helen Rossetti Angeli, *Shelley and His Friends in Italy* (London, 1911), pp. 95–99. On Nov. 17, 1819, Shelley gave Sophia *The Indian Serenade.* On Dec. 28, as she was leaving Florence, he presented her with a copy of Leigh Hunt's *Literary Pocket-Book* for 1819, in which he had written out *Good Night, Love's Philosophy,* and *Time Long Past* On another occasion, after hearing her play the harp, he gave her *To Sophia.* In a postscript to a letter from Mary to her after she had left Florence, he included *On a Faded Violet.* (Angeli, *Shelley and His Friends,* pp. 98–105.) White (II, 174) listed *"I Fear Thy Kisses, Gentle Maiden,* as also being intended for Sophia, on the basis of "obviously related fragments in Shelley's note books." Sophia later married a Mr. Catty, and her son presented Rossetti with the *Pocket-Book* containing the lyrics to her. (Nov. 12, 22, 23, 26, 1869, *Rossetti Papers,* pp. 414–416.)

78. Peck, II, 207–208; White, II, 319–323. Other poems similarly inspired include *A Lament, Remembrance, Mutability, The Fugitives,* and a *Song* ("Rarely, rarely, comest thou"), all listed among the poems of 1821.

79. *Mary Shelley's Journal,* p. 166. Edward Williams' journal for the same day reads: "Jane accompanies Mary and S[helley] to the seashore through the Cascine." (Gisborne & Williams, p. 128.)

80. White, II, 452. The guitar that Shelley gave to Jane is now in the Bodleian Library at Oxford. Another guitar, which Shelley had in England, is now in The Carl H. Pforzheimer Library in New York.

81. On dating, see G. M. Matthews, "Shelley and Jane Williams," *The Review of English Studies,* XIII (February 1961), 44–45. Matthews gave a more exact text of *Lines.*

82. One fragment of the Spinoza translation appears in *Works,* VII, 273–274. For the history of the translation, see *ibid.,* pp. 363–364; Mary Shelley, *Letters,* II, 103n; Williams' journal, Nov. 11–14, 1821, *Gisborne & Williams,* pp. 111–112. According to Williams, who assisted Shelley with part of the translation, Byron was to write the Preface.

83. Dowden, II, 474; see also Theodor Vetter, "Shelley als übersetzer des homerischen Hymnes," in *Festgabe Hugo Blummer* (Zurich, 1914), pp. 523–539. Vetter emphasized Shelley's capacity for capturing the humor of the original.

84. Salvador de Madariaga, *Shelley and Calderon and Other Essays* (London, 1920), pp. 46–47; see also Rogers, pp. 319–323; James Fitzmaurice-Kelley, *Chapters on Spanish Literature* (London, 1908), p. 198.

85. Goethe, *Faust,* trans. Bayard Taylor (New York, 1870), p. 306; see also *Works,* VII, 277–278; Rogers, pp. 77–79; Philo M. Buck, "Goethe and Shelley," *The Goethe Centenary at the University of Wisconsin* (Madison, 1932); C. D. Vail, "Shelley's Translations from Goethe's *Faust,*" *Symposium* (November 1949), pp. 187–226.

86. F. Seymour Smith, *The Classics in Translation,* New York, 1930, p. 159. For the text of the first canzone of Dante's *Convivio* (earlier called *Convito*), as taken from the Bodleian manuscript, see Jean de Palacio, "Shelley and Dante," *Revue de litterature comparée* XXXV (January–March 1961), pp. 105–112. For Shelley's marginal notes on *Convivio* II and III, see Rogers, pp. 340–341. On Shelley and Dante, see Corrado Zacchetti, *Shelley e Dante* (Milan, 1922). On the *Marseillaise,* see *Esdaile Notebook,* pp. 144–146, 270–273.

87. Notopoulos, p. 396. For the Greek prose translations, see *ibid.,* pp. 375–603; Benjamin Farrington, "The Text of Shelley's Translation of the Symposium of Plato," *Modern Language Review,* XIV (1919), 325–326.

88. To Mary Godwin, Oct. 24–Nov. 8, 1814, *Letters,* I, 408–421; see also to Hogg, Oct. 4, 1814, *ibid.,* p. 403; to Mary Godwin, Dec. 16, 1816, *ibid.,* p. 521. "Extensively beneficial" was no doubt inspired by *Frankenstein,* on which she was then working. (Mary Shelley to Shelley, Dec. 5, 1816, Mary Shelley, *Letters,* I, 14.) Victor Frankenstein seems intentionally like Shelley: Shelley used Victor as a pseudonym in *Original Poetry;* both had sisters called Elizabeth; both read Albertus Magnus and Paraselsus in their "votary of romance" periods then turned to science, especially electricity; Frankenstein's science teachers resemble Shelley's (Lind and Walker); Frankenstein too lamented the loss of early enthusiasms. Mary's ambivalence toward Frankenstein, whose Shelleyan desire to change the world ended in failure and hurt others, may reflect her ambivalence toward Shelley.

89. Aug. 10, 1821, Mary Shelley, *Letters,* I, 149.

90. To John Gisborne, *Letters,* II, 435; E. E. Williams to Jane Williams, July 6, 1822, Gisborne & Williams, p. 162; Jane Williams to Leigh Hunt, Apr. 28, 1824, Mary Shelley, *Letters,* I, 209n.

91. *Letters,* II, 445; Gisborne & Williams, p. 161. "Buona notte" may refer to Shelley's

1820 poem *Buona Notte,* which opens; "'Buona notte, buona notte!'—Come mai/La notte sara buona senza te?" The Italian is more direct than the English: "Good-night ah! no; the hour is ill/Which severs those it should unite."

92. To Claire Clairmont, Apr. 3, 1870, Trelawny, *Letters,* p. 229. By suggesting that Mary had tried to make Shelley like Tom Moore, Trelawny meant that she wished him to be a successful society poet. In a letter to Claire of Apr. 7, 1829, Trelawny called Moore and Medwin "mercenary literary vagabonds." (*Ibid.,* p. 129.)

93. To Claire Clairmont, Nov. 9, 1872, *ibid.,* p. 239. The word "tease" in the early nineteenth century had a much stronger meaning than today, signifying to harass or seriously irritate. The intensity of emotion intended by Keats in the "tease us out of thought" in *Ode on a Grecian Urn* is usually lost on the modern reader.

94. June 28, 1869, Mar. 11, 1870, *Rossetti Papers,* pp. 398, 500; to W. M. Rossetti, May 6, 1878, Trelawny, *Letters,* p. 259; see also Trelawny, *Recollections,* p. 186; which noted the "utter loneliness in which he was condemned to pass the largest portion of his life."

95. Mary Shelley, *Letters,* I, 209n.

96. Aug. 17, 1823, in, Donald H. Reiman, "Shelley's 'The Triumph of Life': The Bibliographical Problem," *PMLA,* LXXVIII (December 1963), 543.

97. *Shelley and Keats As They Struck Their Contemporaries,* pp. 56–57.

98. As Hogg was not with the Shelleys in Italy, Jane must have been his main source of information on the last few months of Shelley's life. Jane was opposed to Mary's returning to England. (To Leigh and Marianne Hunt, Aug. 13, 1823, Mary Shelley, *Letters,* I, 249.)

99. Grylls, *Mary Shelley* p. 298.

100. See also Mary's letters to Claire Clairmont of Aug. 16, 1842, where she called her temper "quick and brooding," and of Aug. 12, 1845: "I have been pursued all my life by lowness of spirits which superinduces a certain irritability which often spoils me as a companion—I lament it & feel it & know It—but that does not suffice." (Mary Shelley, *Letters,* II, 161, 250.)

101. "A cold heart! Have I a cold heart? God knows! But none need envy the icy region this heart encircles; and at least the tears are hot which the emotions of this cold heart forces me to shed." (Nov. 10, 1822, *Mary Shelley's Journal,* p. 185.)

102. Oct. 1822, *ibid.,* p. 182; see also to Byron, Oct. 21?, 1822, Mary Shelley, *Letters,* I, 198: "now I am truly *cold moonshine.*" Mary had apparently discussed the *Epipsychidion* references to her with Byron.

103. Hogg, I, 270.

104. See, e.g., *Dark Spirit of the Desart Rude, Death-Spurning Rocks,* and *The Retrospect, Esdaile Notebook,* pp. 77–78, 81–82, 155–160.

8. *The International Scene*

1. Dec. 11, 1817, *Letters,* I, 577. Brian Wilke, *Romantic Poets and Epic Tradition* (Madison, 1965) specified (pp. 123–128) ten "epic" characteristics of *The Revolt of Islam.* Not all of these, however, are associated only with the epic; some are used in narrative poetry in general. Wilkie gave examples of influence on the poem from Milton and Southey (pp. 126, 141). For the influence of Southey's *Thalaba,* see also Benjamin Woodward Griffith, Jr., "The Writing of *The Revolt of Islam,*" Ph.D. diss., Northwestern University, 1952.

2. Mary first noted that Shelley was working on the poem on May 13. (*Mary Shelley's Journal,* pp. 79, 84.) But as Shelley indicates in his Preface that the poem occupied him for a "little more than six months," he must have begun it in April. (*Works,* I, 246.)

3. Dec. 3, 1817, *Letters,* I, 571. The publishing firm that turned the poem down was probably Longman & Co. (*Ibid.,* p. 563.) "M'Millan" was Buchanan McMillan, who ran a large, established printing business at 6 Bow St., Covent Gardens. (Pigot's *Metropolitan Directory,* 1828–1829.) As he had printed William Godwin's *Essay on Sepulchres* and was favorably disposed toward Godwin, he presumably had liberal leanings. (William Godwin, Jr. to Mary Shelley, June 24, 1822, *Letters,* II, 425n.)

4. Forman, pp. 76–80; Peacock, p. 345; *Letters,* I, 579–580.

5. To Ollier, Dec. 13, *ibid.,* pp. 581–582. The sequence of events shows that Peacock was exaggerating, no doubt partly for comic effect, when he wrote that as "Shelley was for some time inflexible" and "for a long time refused to alter a line . . . the whole of the alterations were actually made in successive sittings of what I may call a literary committee." (Peacock, pp. 365, 345; see Frederick L. Jones, "The Revision of Laon and Cythna," *Journal of English and Germanic Philology,* XXXIII (1933), 366–372; Marcel

Kessel, *Times Literary Supplement*, Sept. 7, Nov. 9, 1933, pp. 592, 774.) Peacock's memory may have failed him on the time element. (H. F. B. Brett-Smith, *Times Literary Supplement*, Sept. 21, 1933, p. 131.) Exaggerating in the other direction, Shelley told Tom Moore on Dec 16 that he "hastened" to make the changes "as soon as" their effects were pointed out to him. (*Letters*, I, 582.) For a comprehensive study of the texts of the poem and their relation to the manuscript, see Donald J. Ryan, "Percy Bysshe Shelley's *Laon and Cythna*: A Critical Edition of the Manuscripts in the Bodleian Library," Ph.D. diss., New York University, 1972.

6. *Letters*, I, 582. Why Shelley first made the lovers brother and sister is indicated in the Preface: "In the personal conduct of my Hero and Heroine, there is one circumstance which was intended to startle the reader from the trance of ordinary life. It was my object to break through the crust of those outworn opinions on which established institutions depend." He adds, "The sentiments connected with and characteristic of this circumstance, have no personal reference to the Writer." (*Works*, I, 247.) Incest, Shelley implies, is not morally wrong if it is a legitimate expression of love. It is only wrong according to the distorted values and laws of society. But as a result of the general slanders circulating about his own life, especially the story about a "league-of-incest" at Geneva, he assures his readers that he himself has not practiced incest. I have been told by Willard Bissell Pope that Benjamin Robert Haydon, who was hostile to Shelley, asserted that Shelley had an incestuous relationship with one of his sisters, an assertion for which there is no evidence. However, Shelley was perhaps aware of such rumors. Certainly he was aware that such rumors were being spread about Byron (to Byron, Sept. 29, 1816, *Letters*, I, 506), and this doubtless added to his sensitivity on the matter. Yet the Laon and Cythna theme (repeated in *Rosalind and Helen*) must have had psychological roots.

In the restricted circle of Field Place, the young Shelley may well have turned to his sisters, especially Elizabeth, for love, but was restrained by the moral code from its sexual expression, which he felt would in an ideal society have been a natural aspect of it. He perhaps expressed such feelings unconsciously in his wavering attempts to encourage a romance between Elizabeth and Hogg.

For the changes in the poem, see *Works*, I, 422–424. I follow the *Laon and Cythna* text but retain the changed title—which Shelley agreed to—as better expressing the social essence of the work. *Laon and Cythna* suggests a personal narrative. It is unfortunate, though, that Shelley dropped his original subtitle, "A Vision of the Nineteenth Century," which indicated his perspective and purpose. Perhaps the Olliers feared its revolutionary implications.

7. *Works*, I, 240.

8. *A Philosophical View of Reform*, *ibid.*, VII, 53–54, 14.

9. *Letters*, I, 563–564.

10. Preface to *The Revolt of Islam*, *Works*, I, 240–242. Byron expressed a similar view in *Childe Harold's Pilgrimage*, III (31–33), which Shelley had taken in manuscript to England from Geneva a few months before beginning *The Revolt of Islam*, but Shelley had expressed the concept in his Irish pamphlets and other early works.

11. George McLean Harper, *William Wordsworth* (London, 1929), p. 300.

12. *A New Translation of Volney's Ruins; or Meditations on the Revolution of Empires, Made under the Inspection of the Author* (Dublin, 1811), p. 92; see also Kenneth Neill Cameron, "A Major Source of *The Revolt of Islam*," *PMLA*, LVI (March 1941), 175–206; L. Kellner, "Shelley's *Queen Mab* and Volney's *Les Ruines*," *Englische Studien*, XXII (1896), 9–40. Medwin (p. 92) listed Volney's *Ruins* among the books Shelley read shortly after leaving Oxford. Hogg (I, 373; II, 3) reported that it was a favorite of Harriet Shelley's, from which she used to read aloud. In *Frankenstein*, completed in May 1817, Mary Shelley wrote: "The book from which Felix instructed Safie was Volney's Ruins of Empire . . . He had chosen this work, he said, because the declamatory style was framed in imitation of the eastern authors. Through this work I [the monster] obtained a cursory knowledge of history, and a view of the several empires at present existing in the world; it gave me an insight into the manners, governments, and religions of the different nations of the earth." (Mary Shelley, *Frankenstein, or, The Modern Prometheus*, ed. M. K. Joseph [New York, 1969], p. 119.)

13. Volney, *Ruins*, p. 106. Two other works that must have influenced both the subject and content of the poem are indicated in Mary Shelley's Journal. On Aug. 28, 1816, she noted that Shelley had read " 'Histoire de la Revolution, par Rabaut' "; on Sept. 29 she wrote that he had finished "Lacretelle's 'History of the French Revolution.' " During the period from the spring to the fall of 1817, when Shelley was writing the poem, she noted on Apr. 17, 22, 23, and May 3, 14, 15, and 19 that he was reading "History of the Cythna," *Journal of English and Germanic Philology*, XXXIII (1933), 366–372; Marcel

ley's Journal, pp. 61, 65, 78, 79, 81.) These works were correctly identified by Frederick L. Jones as Jean Paul Rabaut Saint-Etienne, *Précis d'histoire de la Révolution française*, and Jean Charles D. de Lacretelle Jeune, *Histoire de la Révolution française*. (*Letters*, II, 483, 477–478.) Jones, however, is mistaken in asserting that Rabaut's work is a continuation of Lacretelle's. Rabaut wrote his history in 1792 covering the early events of the Revolution from May 1789 to September 1791 in one volume. Lacretelle's history, in five volumes, was published from 1801 to 1805 and covered the later events of the Revolution. The two men and their histories were very different. Rabaut was a moderate revolutionary who was executed by the Jacobins. Lacretelle was a royalist who was asked by Rabaut's publishers to continue the work. Shelley's attitudes toward the Revolution were similar to Rabaut's. A sampling of Rabaut, however, does not disclose more than a possible general influence on Shelley. See also McNiece, pp. 30–31, 119. For some of these facts I am indebted to Lily Feiler, who wrote a term paper on Rabaut and Lacretelle for my Shelley seminar at New York University in 1967.

14. *Letters*, I, 563. For *Henry and Louisa*, see *Esdaile Notebook*, pp. 131–143, 260–270. Woodring (pp. 238–239, 349–350) argued correctly that the campaign described in the poem was not against the Turks in 1807 but against the French in 1801. The "impious" enemies that Henry is to fight (ll. 72–78) are the anticlerical French rather than the infidel Turks. Shelley is attacking British political and religious conservatism. Henry's "Tyrant of the World" (l. 72) is Napoleon. Although it might seem strange that Shelley should in 1809 write about the 1801 campaign rather than the 1807 campaign, the earlier campaign was historically more important. Woodring (p. 350) also argued correctly that Louisa, unlike Henry, was lacking in "chauvinistic" sentiments. Louisa's comments on patriotism (I, viii) should not be taken literally, as they are clearly sarcastic. Louise Lafferty, librarian at The Fleming School, New York, pointed out to me that the "flower" which is "sacrificed" (ll. 135–142, *Esdaile Notebook*, p. 263) is not an actual flower but an oblique reference to Henry.

15. See Kenneth Neill Cameron, "Shelley and *Ahrimanes*," *Modern Language Quarterly* III (June 1942), 287–295. For text of *Ahrimanes*, see Peacock, *Works*, VII, 265–282; *Shelley and His Circle*, III, 318–326. *Ahrimanes* was probably completed by late 1815, for one manuscript contains part of a draft of *Headlong Hall*, which was published in December 1815, and was certainly completed by the summer of 1816, for in a letter to Peacock on July 23, 1816, Shelley seems to echo the poem and writes: "Do you who assert the supremacy of Ahriman [as Shelley did not] imagine him throned among these desolating snows." (Peacock, *Works*, VII, 514; *Letters*, I, 499.) Shelley's letter was written in Switzerland during his stay there near Byron. In Byron's *Manfred* (1816), some passages on "Ahriman" seem to reflect the influence of Peacock's poem. Perhaps Shelley had a copy of the poem with him at Geneva. (See *Shelley and His Circle*, III, 226–244.)

16. Both the prose outline and the verse fragments exist in two versions, one designed for a 12-canto work, the other for a 2-canto work. The outline in the text is from the 2-canto version, which is much closer to *The Revolt of Islam* than is the 12-canto version. (Peacock, *Works*, VII, 283–286, 428–432.) On the complex problem of sequencing and dating these versions, see *Shelley and His Circle*, III, 226–244.

17. *Shelley and His Circle*, III, 235–236.

18. On the strange language, see *Prometheus Unbound*, I, 137–139.

19. See *The Masque of Anarchy*, ll. 114–117.

20. See also the conclusion of ch. I of *A Philosophical View of Reform*, where Shelley envisages a new revolutionary upsurge. Shelley, however, was indebted to *Ahrimanes* for some of his lines. (Cameron, "Shelley and *Ahrimanes*," p. 252.) Shelley and Peacock may both have been somewhat indebted to their mutual friend, John Frank Newton, who contributed four letters on his astrological and vegetarian theories to *The Monthly Magazine* or *British Register*, XXXIII (1812), 18–22, 107–109, 318–321, 408–409. Although he mentioned the Zoroastrian system only briefly at the end of the second letter, he was much obsessed by Zoroaster. Peacock (pp. 324–325) later mocked his views, but earlier he had taken them more seriously, as *Ahrimanes* shows.

21. Volney, *Ruins*, p. 250n. For the Gnostic influence, see Grabo, pp. 135–136; Rieger p. 162. Rieger's speculations, however, went well beyond the evidence. Grabo noted that Shelley also refers to the Gnostics in *The Assassins*, but his sources of information on the sect are not known. Shelley's failure to discuss Gnosticism in either his prose works or letters and the lack of specific references to it in his poetry indicate that it was a peripheral influence. These concepts from the Gnostics and Volney, however, were likely blended in Shelley's imagination with the symbolic uses to which the snake was put during the American Revolutionary War. The most famous was the insignia used by the Culpepper Minutemen, depicting a coiled snake with the words "Don't tread on me"

emblazoned below it—an emblem to which Shelley may refer in *The Mask of Anarchy* (ll. 226–229) and *Hellas*, (ll. 425–426.)

22. Volney, *Ruins, pp. 332–223. See On the Devil, and Devils:* "Among the Greeks the Serpent was considered as an auspicious and favorable being . . . In Egypt the Serpent was an hieroglyphic of eternity." (*Works*, VII, 103.) The general concept of the "serpent in a circle to denote eternity" could have been found by Shelley in Lord Monboddo's *Of the Origin and Progress of Language* and elsewhere. (Notopoulos, pp. 186–187.) But the colorful serpent seems to come from Volney.

23. *Works*, VII, 52. Shelley had classical models for a battle between an eagle and a serpent: *Iliad*, XII, 200–207; *Aeneid*, XI, 751–756; *Metamorphoses*, IV, 714–717; as well as *The Faerie Queen*, I, v, 8. (Baker, p. 73n.) He was also doubtless acquainted with the description of a serpent in Ovid's *Metamorphoses*, III, 31–34.

24. From l. 666 on, the man tells the story in the first person as Laon; the woman could hardly be any other than Cythna.

25. Mary Shelley, Note on *The Revolt of Islam*, *Works*, I, 409.

26. See Peacock, *Ahrimanes*, II, 3; Volney, *Ruins*, p. 71.

27. To Peacock, c. Aug. 24, 1819, *Letters*, II, 115; *Works*, V, 265.

28. *A Philosophical View of Reform*, *Works*, VII, 13; *Hellas*, ll. 729–730: "Revenge and Wrong bring forth their kind,/The foul cubs like their parents are." On Hogg and Harriet, see *Shelley and His Circle*, III, 24–60, 67–71.

29. Volney, *Ruins*, p. 105. For further parallels, see Kenneth Neill Cameron, "A Major Source of *The Revolt of Islam*," *PMLA*, LVI (March 1941), 178–182. On revolutionary fetes, see McNiece, pp. 116–126. The three words were *equality*, *liberty*, and *justice*.

30. Volney, *Ruins*, pp. 103, 104n. The Declaration, in fact, upheld the rights of property.

31. *A Discourse on the Manners of the Antient Greeks Relative to the Subject of Love*, Notopoulos, p. 408.

32. The scene is indebted to Volney's *Ruins* (pp. 70–71), and to Sir James Lawrence's free-love romance *The Empire of the Nairs.* (See Walter Graham, "Shelley and 'The Empire of the Nairs.'" *PMLA*, XL, [1925] 881–891.)

33. Mary Godwin to T. J. Hogg, Mar. 6, 1815, *Shelley and His Circle*, III, 453.

34. Arthur H. Beavan, *James and Horace Smith* (London, 1899), p. 173. Either Smith was oversimplifying or Shelley was discussing matters in a more limited context than Smith indicated, for Shelley did not attribute all social evils to false religious views, as *A Philosophical View of Reform* shows.

35. *The Rights of Man*, in Cameron, p. 59.

36. Preface to *The Revolt of Islam*, *Works*, I, 243.

37. W. P. Cresson, *The Holy Alliance* (New York, 1922), p. 31.

38. Frederick B. Artz, *Reaction and Revolution, 1814–1832* (New York, 1934), p. 117.

39. *Works*, VII, 32; Preface to *Hellas*, *ibid.*, III, 9.

40. Shelley wrote Byron that at the trial for custody of his children he was arraigned as "an atheist & republican." (Jan. 11, 1817, *Letters*, I, 527.)

41. White, *Unextinguished Hearth*, pp. 140, 132.

42. *Ibid.*, pp. 117, 124.

9. *Political Poems*

1. May 1, 1820, *Letters*, II, 191; *Works*, III, 307.

2. Medwin, *Shelley's Papers*, p. 68; see also p. 344. When Shelley first published the poem in the *Prometheus Unbound* volume of 1820, he entitled it "An Ode, written in October, 1819, before the Spaniards had recovered their liberty," presumably in order to get it published, for in 1820 the situation in England was still highly inflammable, and although a poet could get by with an ode anticipating a Spanish revolution, he could hardly get by with one virtually calling for an English revolution. Shelley doubtless hoped, however, that the implications of his ode would be clear to his radical readers. When Mary reprinted the poem in 1839, she entitled it "An Ode, to the Assertors of Liberty," which was probably Shelley's original title.

3. *Works*, V, 261.

4. To Peacock, Sept. 9, 1819, *Letters*, II, 119. On Sept. 6 Shelley wrote to the Olliers: "The same day that your letter came, came the news of the Manchester work, & the torrent of my indignation has not yet done boiling in my veins. I wait anxiously [to] hear how the Country will express its sense of this bloody, murderous oppression of its de-

stroyers. 'Something must be done. What, yet I know not.'" (*Ibid.*, p. 117.) As Shelley stated earlier in this letter that he had received the Olliers' letter "yesterday," he must have first received news of the massacre, presumably from Peacock, on Sept. 5. On Sept. 23 Mary Shelley recorded in her journal: "Shelley's Poem goes to Hunt." (*Mary Shelley's Journal*, p. 124.) On the next day she wrote to Hunt: "Shelley has for these last days been so occupied with our friends here from various causes—that with that, and his poem which you will have received . . . his time has been fully taken up." In a postscript she added: "As you talked of moving at Michaelmas I direct this letter to the Examiner office—a letter was sent yesterday with a poem in it directed to York Buildings." That this poem was *The Masque of Anarchy* is indicated by Mary's letter to Mrs. Hunt on Nov. 24: "A few days before we left Leghorn which is now 2 months ago Shelley sent a poem called the mask of anarchy Hunt does not mention the reception of it—it was directed to York buildings—and he is anxious to know whether it has been received." (Mary Shelley, *Letters*, I, 80, 81, 84.) On Sept. 27, Shelley wrote to Hunt and then canceled the passage: "I omitted in the transcription of my poem which you will have received, the following verse, which comes after the line." Shelley does not quote or designate the line, but the intended verse clearly belongs to *The Masque of Anarchy.* (*Letters*, II, 123.)

These excerpts establish that *The Masque of Anarchy* was written between Sept. 5, when Shelley first heard of the massacre, and Sept. 23, when the poem was sent to Hunt; and Mary's comment on Sept. 24 that Shelley had been "so occupied" with the poem "for these last days" probably means that it was written mainly in the latter part of the period. That Shelley's indignation was high in these days is shown by a letter to Peacock of Sept. 21: "I have received all the papers you sent me, & the Examiners regularly, perfumed with muriatic acid. What an infernal business this of Manchester! What is to be done? Something assuredly. H. Hunt has behaved I think with great spirit & coolness in the whole affair." (*Ibid.*, p. 120.) Mary commented in a Note to the poem that Shelley was "writing 'The Cenci' when the news of the Manchester Massacre reached us," but *The Cenci* was finished by the middle of August and was printed in Italy by Sept. 9. (*Works*, III, 307; to Hunt, Aug. 15, 1819; to Peacock, Sept. 9, *Letters*, II, 108, 118.) Perhaps Shelley was correcting proofs for *The Cenci* on Sept. 5.

Hunt did not publish *The Masque of Anarchy* in *The Examiner*, for which he gave his reasons in 1832 in a Preface to the first edition of the poem: "This Poem was written by Mr. Shelley on occasion of the bloodshed at Manchester, in the year 1819. I was editor of the Examiner at that time, and it was sent to me to be inserted or not in that journal as I though fit. I did not insert it, because I thought that the public at large had not become sufficiently discerning to do justice to the sincerity and kindheartedness of the spirit that walked in this flaming robe of verse. His charity was avowedly more than proportionate to his indignation; yet I thought that even the suffering part of the people, judging, not unnaturally, from their own feelings, and from the exasperation which suffering produces before it produces knowledge, would believe a hundred-fold in his anger, to what they would in his good intention; and this made me fear that the common enemy would take advantage of this mistake to do them both a disservice. Mr. Shelley's writings have since aided the general progress of knowledge in bringing about a wiser period; and an effusion, which would have got him cruelly misrepresented a few years back, will now do unequivocal honour to his memory, and shew everybody what a most considerate and kind, as well as fervent heart, the cause of the world has lost." (*Works*, III, 225.) That Hunt really feared the inflammatory properties of the poem is dubious, for previous issues of *The Examiner* had contained much incendiary material. It is more likely that by early October, when the poem arrived from Italy, he had been intimidated by the reprisals of the government, especially the indictment of Sir Francis Burdett, whose "seditious" letter Hunt had printed, and he hesitated to risk prosecution. In a letter to Shelley on Dec. 2, 1819, he side-stepped the issue, simply thanking Shelley for his "kind letters" and "other enclosures." At the same time he seems to have been considering a separate volume, which would presumably have included *The Masque of Anarchy*: "I will write more speedily, and tell you about your political songs and pamphlets, which we must publish." (Hunt, *Correspondence*, I, 152–153.)

5. *The Examiner*, Sept. 19, 1819 (with reference to Shelley's advocacy of petitions). See Kenneth N. Cameron, *Notes and Queries*, CLXXXIV (Jan. 16, 1943), 42.

6. Samuel Bamford, *Passages in the Life of a Radical*, ed. Henry Dunckley (London, 1893), II, 150, 151–152, 155–157.

7. *The Examiner*, Aug. 22, 1819, The "pathetic court poet" was Wordsworth, whose chauvinistic *Ode, 1815*, published in 1816, contained the oft-attacked phrase, "Carnage is thy [God's] daughter." Wordsworth's previously printed sonnets on Waterloo had

been attacked in *The Examiner* in February 1816. (Edmund Blunden, *Leigh Hunt's "Examiner" Examined* (London, 1928), p. 57.)

8. Shelley's poem was most influenced by an open letter from Burdett in the Aug. 29, 1819, issue of *The Examiner* (p. 551). Both Shelley and Burdett begin with the receipt of the news, Shelley's "voice from over the Sea" (2) being apparently a direct reference to *The Examiner.* They then describe the tyrannical governmental forces trampling down the people of England. Burdett urges the "gentlemen of England" to express their indignation "loudly"; Shelley urges the "Men of England" to do the same (147). Burdett urges the English not to stand idly by while tyrants "rip open their mother's womb" (England) but to "join the general voice" of protest; Shelley urges the English, whose "own indignant Earth" gave birth to them in a "mother's throe," to protest (139–140). Burdett urges them to call a series of meetings, emphasizing one in particular; Shelley urges them to call a "vast assembly" (299). Burdett cries dramatically, "Is this . . . freedom?" Shelley asks, "What is freedom?" (156). Burdett states that a man should be willing to die in order to vindicate "the laws" of England; Shelley urges the English to die bravely before the bayonets of their opponents and to hold to "the old laws of England" (335). For one aspect of Shelley's poem, however, there is no parallel either in Burdett's letter or in any other item on the massacre in *The Examiner,* namely, his emphasis on the sufferings of the working class. Burdett, as a member of the radical aristocracy, had no deep interest in this class and addressed his appeal to the "gentlemen." Shelley's disagreement with the narrower outlook of Burdett is perhaps indicated in his substitution of the more general "Men of England" for Burdett's "gentlemen."

On the page facing Burdett's letter is an excerpt from a pamphlet by the well-known radical William Hone. Hone depicts the miseries of the workers and their families, in vivid contrast to the conditions of the aristocracy, and stresses that the "rights of man" are connected with economic rather than with political welfare. This concept apparently inspired Shelley, who develops the economic theme in his stanzas on freedom. Hone's comments on freedom also apparently influenced Shelley: "Their [the laboring classes'] habits render them averse from the examination of abstract rights and political theories . . . Have they been harangued into the belief that they and their families are starving? The wretches hunger; their wives and children waste with disease and penury . . . [in] foul cellars or miserable garrets."

Finally, Shelley was indebted to *The Examiner* for a letter from Henry Hunt, the popular hero of "Peterloo," who commented (p. 558): "I fear that it [the massacre] will never be forgiven, and that there will be but too strong disposition to demand 'blood for blood.' Our enemies will not now, I hope, say anything about assassination; they have taught the people how to assassinate by wholesale." Apparently this threat of bloody revenge was what caused Shelley to urge the people to abandon such a policy and adopt passive resistance (195–196).

One important section of *The Masque of Anarchy,* the pageant or procession with which it opens, may have been derived, at least in concept, from a report in the Aug. 22 issue of *The Examiner* (p. 535) on a welcoming procession for the representatives of Bavaria by their constituents—a report that immediately precedes comments on the Manchester Massacre. The representatives are greeted with enthusiastic acclaim by "multitudes of all ranks," who lead them to a city where they entertain them with a fete. Although the throngs are not led to the Parliament, as in Shelley's poem, that word is introduced almost immediately in the comment on the Manchester Massacre. Perhaps the ironic contrast between this procession in honor of governmental representatives and the actions of such representatives in Shelley's own country gave him the initial idea for his pageant.

To read these issues of *The Examiner* with *The Masque of Anarchy* provides a fascinating insight into the creative process, for Shelley evidently read them in the first heat of indignation mentioned in Mary's Note. The poem was also influenced by Byron's *Ode from the French* (*Shelley and His Circle,* IV, 640–641).

9. Note on the poems of 1819, *Works,* III, 307.

10. When Shelley sent the poem to Hunt in September 1819, he apparently spelled the word "Mask." (*The Mask of Anarchy,* ed. H. B. Forman, Shelley Society, [London, 1887], p. 16.) Mary Shelley also used "Mask" in her letter to Mrs. Hunt on Nov. 24, 1819, and in a second copy of the manuscript. (Mary Shelley, *Letters,* I, 84; *Works,* III, 342.) Shelley, however, spelled the word "Masque" in a letter to Hunt of Nov. 14-18, 1819. (*Letters,* II, 152). Hunt spelled it "Masque" when he published the poem in 1832, as did Mary in her 1839 edition of the poem.

11. Shelley, *Selected Poems and Prose,* ed. Geoffrey M. Matthews (New York, 1964), p. 197. Although the British slave trade was abolished in 1807, slavery continued in the

British Empire until 1834, and the slave trade continued elsewhere. In 1814 there was great but unsuccessful agitation in Britain for the abolition of this trade by other countries, and it was not abolished at the Congress of Vienna nor at that of Aix-la-Chapelle in September 1818, the year before *The Masque of Anarchy,* though it was again discussed. Shelley supported the West Indies revolutions against "the degradation of slavery" in *A Philosophical View of Reform. (Works,* VII, 19.) In his early *Henry and Louisa* poem (1809), Shelley wrote of "slavery's everlasting moan." *(Esdaile Notebook,* p. 138.)

12. For "white horse," see *Rev.* 6, 8: "And I looked, and behold a *pale horse: and his name that sat on him was Death,* and Hell followed with him. And power was given unto them the four horsemen over the fourth part of the earth, to kill with sword, and with hunger, and with death, and with the beasts of the earth." Apparently Shelley also had in mind Rev. 19, depicting another figure on a white horse followed by a great multitude: "And I saw heaven opened, and behold a white horse; and he that sat upon him was called Faithful and True, and in righteousness he doth judge and make war. His eyes were as a flame of fire, and on his head were many crowns; and he had a name written, that no man knew, but he himself. And he was clothed with a vesture dipped in blood; and his name is called The Word of God. And the armies which were in heaven followed him upon white horses, clothed in fine linen, white and clean. And out of his mouth goeth a sharp sword that with it he should smite the nations: and he shall rule them with a rod of iron: and he treadeth the wine-press of the fierceness and wrath of Almighty God. And he hath on his vesture and on his thigh a name written, KING OF KINGS AND LORD OF LORDS."

13. Sympathy for the poor is expressed in Shelley's early poetry, for instance—in rather Wordsworthian form—in *A Tale of Society As It Is,* enclosed in a letter to Elizabeth Hitchener in January 1811. (*Esdaile Notebook,* pp. 62–66, 198–199.) In *Queen Mab* this sympathy animates several passages and embraces city as well as country poor; but again the emphasis is on the poor as such rather than on the industrial working class. It is possible that Shelley later (as in his reform pamphlets) became more conscious of the working class by reading the works of his "new counsellor," Robert Owen. (To Shelley, Aug. 27, 1817, Hunt, *Correspondence,* I, 114–115; see also Dowden, II, 39, 53.)

14. *Works,* VII, 49; see also *Ode to Naples,* ll. 77–80.

15. J. P. Guinn, *Shelley's Political Thought* (The Hague, 1969), pp. 127–131.

16. Mary Wollstonecraft wrote in her *Historical and Moral View of the Origin and Progress of the French Revolution* (London, 1794), p. 213: [It was] "the dawn of a new day, when the Bastille was destroyed; and freedom like a lion roused from his liar, rose with dignity, and calmly shook himself." This picture perhaps blended in Shelley's mind with a comment in the leading article in *The Examiner* for Aug. 22. "They [the people] would have risen in the irresistible might of their numbers." Mary Shelley noted in her journal for Dec. 23, 1814 that Shelley read to her from Mary Wollstonecraft's *View.* (*Mary Shelley's Journal,* p. 31.)

17. *The Letters of John Keats,* ed. Hyder Edward Rollins (Cambridge, 1958), II, 83–84; see also A. E. H. Swaen, "Peter Bell," *Anglia,* XLVII (1923), 139–140; Mary Moorman, *William Wordsworth; A Biography, The Later Years, 1803–1850* (Oxford University Press, 1965), pp. 364–372; Reiman, pp. 104–110; Woodring, p. 268.

18. Swaen, "Peter Bell," pp. 141–142. Wordsworth's *Peter Bell,* though not published until the spring of 1819, had been written in 1798. Reynolds' poem is not a parody of Wordsworth's *Peter Bell* but a take-off on Wordsworth's narrative style in his shorter poems, such as *Simon Lee.*

19. For Keats's review, see *Letters of Keats,* II, 93–94; Keats, *Poetry and Prose,* ed. H. Buxton Forman (London, 1890), pp. 49–52, 145–150. For Hunt's review, see Swaen, "Peter Bell," pp. 159–162. In the May 9 issue of *The Examiner* Hunt contrasted Wordsworth and Shelley, to the advantage of Shelley. (Baker, pp. 165–166.)

20. Mary Shelley, Note on the poems of 1819, *Works,* III, 307. *The Examiner* usually came by sea. Only when there was a special event, such as the Manchester Massacre, was it sent overland by letter post. The sea route took about two months, the land route about two weeks. That the magazine was arriving by sea at this time is shown by a letter from Mary Shelley to Mrs. Hunt, Aug. 28, 1819: "We see the examiners regularly now four together just two months after the publication of the last." (Mary Shelley, *Letters,* I, 76.)

21. That Shelley read Wordsworth's *Peter Bell* before writing *The Witch of Atlas* (August 1820) is indicated by the influence on it of the first section of Wordsworth's poem. Shelley also refers to Wordsworth's poem in the Dedication. That Shelley had read Wordsworth's *Peter Bell* before writing his own is shown by his quoting in his Dedica-

tion a phrase from Wordsworth's Dedication, which did not appear in the reviews (King-Hele, p. 152; Reiter, p. 214) and by references in the poem itself directly to Wordsworth's text (*Works*, III, 347). The time of composition is also suggestive. *The Examiner*'s reviews of Reynold's and Wordsworth's poems appeared respectively in the Apr. 25 and May 2 issues, which Shelley would normally have received in Italy by at least July 2. But there is no indication in either Mary's journal or Shelley's letters of any work on *Peter Bell the Third* in June or July. The first references in Mary Shelley's journal occur in October. She noted on Oct. 24: "Shelley finishes 3rd volume of Clarendon aloud, and reads 'Peter Bell' "; on Oct. 25–28: "copy 'Peter Bell' "; on Oct. 30: "Shelley reads Clarendon aloud. Writes 'Peter Bell' "; and Nov. 2: "Finish copying 'Peter Bell,' which is sent." (*Mary Shelley's Journal*, pp. 125–126.) The first reference is most likely to Wordsworth's *Peter Bell*, for Mary seems to be recording Shelley's reading of the works of others. If it had been Reynold's *Peter Bell*, she would have noted it as such. Moreover, Leigh Hunt had sent a copy of Wordsworth's poem to Shelley. (Moorman, *Wordsworth: The Later Years*, pp. 370–371.) The entry of Oct. 25–28 probably means that within a day or so of reading Wordsworth's *Peter Bell*, Shelley had written enough of his own work for Mary to begin copying it. Shelley states in the Dedication that he wrote the poem in "six or seven days," which is borne out by Mary's journal, and he sent it to Hunt on Nov. 2 to pass on to Ollier for publication. The probability is that Shelley wrote it between Oct. 25 and Nov. 1. As he continued to compose while Mary copied, he evidently wanted to send the poem to England for publication as soon as possible. He told Hunt on Nov. 2 that he wished "that it should go to press and be printed very quickly." Although the poem was finished and mailed on Nov. 2, the Dedication is dated Dec. 1. As Frederick L. Jones suggested, Shelley was doubtless anticipating the approximate date of publication. He perhaps also wished the poem to bear a later date so as to prevent any suspicion that either he or Byron was the author; too early a date might suggest that it was written by a poet residing abroad. He asked Hunt in his Nov. 2 letter to "tell Ollier that the author is to be kept a secret." In the final paragraph of the Dedication he implies that the author is living in London. (*Works*, III, 256; *Letters*, II, 134–136.)

22. Keats, *Poetry and Prose*, pp. 50–51. On Reynolds' poem see George L. Marsh, "The *Peter Bell* Parodies of 1819," *Modern Philology*, XL (1943), 267n.

23. *Works*, III, 346. Hunt's review of Wordsworth's *Peter Bell* noted with disapproval the "P.L." dedication to Southey. (Swaen, "Peter Bell," p. 162.)

24. *Works*, III, 307–308. Shelley also emphasized this view in his sonnet *To Wordsworth*, published in the *Alastor* volume (1816):

> In honoured poverty thy voice did weave
> Songs consecrate to truth and liberty,—
> Deserting these, thou leavest me to grieve,
> Thus having been, that thou shouldst cease to be.

25. To Hunt, Nov. 2, 1819, *Letters*, II, 135.

26. *Works*, III, 255. "Ultra legitimate" refers to monarchical legitimacy, the supporters of which, such as the French "ultras," were notoriously reactionary.

27. The reference is to the "butt of sack" traditionally given to the laureate.

28. Shelley's Note to Pt. Three, l. 40. See Note to Queen Mab, V, 189: "Prostitution is the legitimate offspring of marriage and its accompanying errors." At the conclusion of Shelley's review of Hogg's novel *Alexy Haimatoff*, Shelley observes that a true theory of "sexual relations" can be developed only by a "mind pure from the fashionable superstitions of gallantry." (*Works*, I, 142, VI, 182.)

29. See, e.g., Shelley's letter to Hunt of Nov. 2, 1819: "I have only expended a few days on this party squib & of course taken little pains." (*Letters*, II, 135.) But he was anxious to have the poem printed, and perhaps even hoped that Hunt would print some of it in *The Examiner*. On Nov. 24 Mary Shelley wrote to Mrs. Hunt inquiring about the receipt of the poem. (Mary Shelley, *Letters*, I, 86.) In the middle of December, Shelley wrote to Ollier: "Pray, what have you done with *Peter Bell?* Ask Mr. Hunt for it and for some other poems of a similar character I sent him to give you to publish. I think *Peter* not bad in his way; but perhaps no one will believe in anything in the shape of a joke from me." On Apr. 30, 1820, he expressed pleasure at hearing from Hunt that Ollier would publish the poem. (*Letters*, II, 164, 189.) The poem, however, was not published until 1839, in the second edition of Shelley's poems, edited by Mary Shelley.

30. William Cobbett, *History of the Regency and Reign of King George the Fourth* (London, 1830), para. 33. (The book is numbered by paragraphs instead of pages. The

title page gives the date as 1830, but some sections were written as late as 1834; see para. 403, 465.) William Dodgson Bowman, *The Divorce Case of Queen Caroline* (New York, 1930), pp. 13–25; Sir Edward Parry, *Queen Caroline* (London, 1930), pp. 60–72, 245.

31. George Macaulay Trevelyan, *History of England* (New York, 1929), p. 623; cf. Cobbett, *History of the Regency*, para. 425. *The Examiner*, June 11, 1820, pp. 372–373.

32. *The Examiner*, June 11, 1820, pp. 378, 370; June 25, 1820, pp. 406–407. For similar comments in the House of Lords by Lord Holland, see McNiece, p. 68n.

33. See Newman I. White, "Shelley's *Swellfoot the Tyrant* in Relation to Contemporary Political Satire," *PMLA*, XXXVI (1921), 332–346. White argued that Shelley saw two cartoons on the green bag theme. They could either have been sent to him, perhaps by Peacock, or been shown to him by his English friends in Italy.

34. See *The Poetical Works and Other Writings of John Keats*, ed. H. Buxton Forman, (London, 1883), II, 488, 494n; *The Poems of John Keats*, ed. E. de Selincourt (London, 1912), pp. 560–561. Keats wrote all he did of the poem before the queen arrived in England, which shows the great interest the case had aroused even before the proceedings began. Claude Lee Finney, *The Evolution of Keats' Poetry*, [Cambridge, 1936], II, 732, 736–737.)

35. Peck, II, 394. Daniel Isaac Eaton's *Politics for the People or a Salmagundy for Swine* had popularized the "swine" concept in reform literature. Shelley appears to use *The Examiner's* comments on the feeding of swine in Purganax's speech at the opening of Act II.

36. To Amelia Curran, Sept. 17, 1820, *Letters*, II, 235. In a letter to Byron on the same day Shelley wrote: "Do you take no part in the important nothings which the most powerful assembly in the world is now engaged in weighing with such ridiculous deliberation? At least, if Ministers fail in their object, shall you or not return as a candidate for any part of the power they will lose? Their successors, I hope, & you, if you will be one of them, will exert that power to other purposes than their's." He had written to Medwin on July 20, 1820: "I wonder what in the world the Queen has done. I should not wonder, after the whispers I have heard, to find that the Green Bag contained evidence that she had imitated Pasiphae, and that the Committee should recommend to Parliament a bill to exclude all Minotaurs from the succession. What silly stuff is this to employ a great nation about. I wish the King and the Queen, like Punch and his wife, would fight out their disputes in person." (*Ibid.*, pp. 236, 220; see also Mary Shelley to Maria Gisborne, July 19, 1820, *ibid.*, p. 216; *Swellfoot*, II, i, 156; ii, 103.)

37. The date when Shelley began the play is given in Mary's journal as Aug. 24 or 25, 1820. (*Mary Shelley's Journal*, p. 137.) When it was completed is not known, but it was published by at least Dec. 16, 1820. (Forman, *Shelley Library*, p. 98.) The writing, therefore, cannot have taken long, for the work had to be sent to England and then printed. Mary Shelley described the inception of the play in her Note: "We were then at the Baths of San Giuliano. A friend came to visit us on the day when a fair was held in the square, beneath our windows: Shelley read to us his *Ode to Liberty*; and was riotously accompanied by the grunting of a quantity of pigs brought for sale to the fair. He compared it to the 'chorus of frogs' in the satiric drama of Aristophanes; and, it being an hour of merriment, and one ludicrous association suggesting another, he imagined a political-satirical drama on the circumstances of the day, to which the pigs would serve as chorus—and Swellfoot was begun." (*Works*, II, 350.) But he had conceived of the Minotaur theme by July 20. See n.36.

38. Arthur H. Bevan, *James and Horace Smith* (London, 1899), p. 176. See also the annotation by an unknown "M.G." in a copy of the play, stating that the alderman was named Rothwell. "M.G." also noted that the case did not come before a jury because the publisher gave up the whole impression "except 7 what he said was the whole number sold." He confirmed Horace Smith's statement that Smith had refused to reveal the name of the author, but hinted that it might be either Shelley or Byron. (Forman, *Shelley Library*, p. 98.) Medwin (p. 254) indicated that Shelley told him that "on the first day of its being exposed for sale in the City, the then Lord Mayor of London, who was a friend of the gentleman who corrected the proof sheets, advised him [the gentleman] to withdraw it."

The Royal Kalendar: and Court and City Register for 1820 reveals that Richard Rothwell, Esq., King St., was alderman for the ward of Cheap as well as one of the two city sheriffs, and that Georges Bridges was the lord mayor. It was doubtless in his capacity as sheriff that Rothwell acted as agent for the Society for the Suppression of Vice. Pigot's *Metropolitan Directory* for 1828–29 lists a Samuel Rothwell, printer, of 26 Little Eastcheap. Although the printer of the play is given as C. F. Seyfang, 57 Fleet Market, it could be that Samuel Rothwell corrected the proofs. The publisher was J. Johnson, 98 Cheapside.

The Society for the Suppression of Vice, established by Bishop Wilberforce, suppressed works that the members considered obscene or blasphemous. They must have found Shelley's scene of the priests worshiping the Goddess of famine blasphemous, and some details on the life of the "swine" obscene, but were probably most alarmed by the general agitational aspect of the work. The following year the society suppressed Shelley's *Queen Mab* when it was brought out by Richard Carlile's former employee, William Clark. (White, II, 304–305.)

39. Medwin (p. 254), to whom Shelley gave a copy of the play and with whom Shelley discussed it, identified Purganax as Castlereagh, Laoctonos as Wellington, and Dakry as Eldon. Todhunter suggested that Solomon represented "finance, in the person of Rothschild"; Moses, "some politician of Malthusian proclivities." (Todhunter, *A Study of Shelley* [London, 1880], pp. 207–208.) Baker (p. 179) pointed out that Purganax "is a Greek transliteration of Castle-reagh (*Purg* meaning tower or castle and *Anax*, king)," that Dakry comes from "Greek *Dakru*: a tear," and that Laoktonos "appears to be derived from Greek *Laos*, or people, and *Ktonos*, or slayer." White demonstrated that Liverpool is Mammon and that the Leech, the Rat, and the Gadfly are the members of the Milan Commission (respectively, Leach, Browne, and Cooke) on the basis of parallels in contemporary political burlesques. He further noted that as Solomon, Zephaniah, and Moses "have no discoverable parallels in the other satires of the day," it is doubtful whether they represented real persons. (White, "Shelley's *Swellfoot the Tyrant*, pp. 341–346.) Milton Millhauser suggested that Moses was Ricardo on grounds that his *Principles of Political Economy and Taxation* gave support to Malthus. (*Notes and Queries*, CLXXVI [Jan. 14, 1939], 25–26.)

"Moses, the Sow-gelder," however, is more likely Malthus himself, for Shelley shows little interest in Ricardo, but a great deal in Malthus. As early as 1812 in *Proposals for an Association* he commented: "Many well-meaning persons may think that the attainment of the good, which I propose, as the ultimatum of Philanthropic exertion is visionary and inconsistent with human nature: they would tell me not to make people happy, for fear of overstocking the world, and to permit those who found dishes placed before them on the table of partial nature, to enjoy their superfluities in quietness, though millions of wretches crowded around but to pick a morsel, which morsel was still refused to the prayers of agonizing famine." Following the word "morsel," Shelley inserted the note, "See Malthus on *Population*." In the Preface to *The Revolt of Islam* (1817) he refers to "sophisms like those of Mr. Malthus, calculated to lull the oppressors of mankind into a security of everlasting triumph," adding: "It is remarkable, as a symptom of the revival of public hope, that Mr. Malthus has assigned, in the later editions of his work, an indefinite dominion to moral restraint over the principle of population. This concession answers all the inferences from his doctrine unfavourable to human improvement, and reduces the 'Essay on Population' to a commentary illustrative of the unanswerableness of 'POLITICAL JUSTICE.'" (*Works*, V, 265–266; I, 242.) On Dec. 7, 1817, he wrote to Godwin, who was then working on his "answer" to Malthus: "What you say of Malthus fills me, as far as my intellect is concerned, with life & strength." On Oct. 8, 1818, he informed Peacock that he had read "Malthus in a french translation," and considered him "a very clever man." In June 1819 he commented to Peacock: "Ah, but that ever-present Malthus Necessity has convinced Desire—that even though it generated capacity its offspring must starve." (*Letters*, I, 573; II, 43, 98.) In the Preface to *Prometheus Unbound* (1819) he remarked that he would "rather be damned with Plato and Lord Bacon, than go to Heaven with Paley and Malthus"—a comment that Claire noted in her journal for Nov. 8, 1820, as being typical of Shelley. (*Works*, II, 174; White, II, 602.) In *A Philosophical View of Reform* he excoriated Malthus and his doctrines in similar terms to those implied in *Swellfoot*, e.g.: "A writer of the present day (a priest of course, for his doctrines are those of a eunuch and of a tyrant) has stated that the evils of the poor arise from an excess of population, and that after they have been stripped naked by the tax-gatherer and reduced to bread and tea and fourteen hours of hard labour by their masters . . . [they] are required to abstain from marrying under penalty of starvation." (*Works*, VII, 32.)

40. Woodring, p. 270.

41. Cobbett, *History of the Regency*, para. 438.

42. *Works*, VII, 41.

43. Samuel Taylor Coleridge, *Conciones ad populum: Essays on His Own times*, ed. Sara Coleridge (London, 1850), p. 5; see also Kenneth Neill Cameron, "Shelley and the *Conciones ad populum*," *Modern Language Notes*, LVII (December 1942), 673–674. The *Conciones* was published in 1795. Shelley was probably indebted to it for other suggestions. Two stage directions read: "A magnificent Temple, built of thigh-bones and death's-heads, and tiled with scalps," and "The interior of the Temple of Famine. The

statue of the Goddess, a skeleton clothed in parti-coloured rags, seated upon a heap of skulls and loaves intermingled." They seem to have been suggested by Coleridge's "temple of despotism," which, "like that of Tescalipoca, the Mexican deity, is built of human skulls, and cemented with human blood." Some characteristics of Famine—"Goddess of fasts and feasts, starving and cramming"—may derive from the *Conciones*: "they [the ruling class] deprecate the anger of Heaven by a FAST! . . . and after these, a turbot feast for the rich, and their usual scanty morsel to the poor."

This parallel raises the further possibility that Coleridge in his early, radical period, exerted a political influence on Shelley. The political outlook of the two works is similar, especially on a subject that formed a central part of Shelley's social philosophy: the lessons of the French Revolution for England. Coleridge argued (pp. 14, 16–17, 21, 27) that though the revolution had produced some admirable leaders, they were unable to restrain the masses from violence; therefore, before any major change could take place in England, the overriding problem was to eradicate "retribution" from the hearts of the people and to transform them with "benevolent affections," which could best be done by "a small but glorious band" of educated reformers who envisaged "a glorious period when justice will have established the universal fraternity of love." Although Shelley scorned the "small band" concept and Coleridge's underlying Old Testament prophet approach, a similar concept is expressed in such diverse works as *An Address to the Irish People*, *The Revolt of Islam*, *The Masque of Anarchy*, *Prometheus Unbound*, and *Hellas*, in addition to *Swellfoot the Tyrant*. It doubtless formed part of the message of the early lost novel *Hubert Cauvin*, which included an "inquiry into the causes of the failure of the French Revolution to benefit mankind," and which Shelley informed Godwin on Jan. 10, 1812, that he was engaged on. (*Letters*, I, 229; to Elizabeth Hitchener, Jan. 2, 1812, *ibid.*, p. 218.)

10. *The Lightning of the Nations*

1. "Methinks, those who live now have survived an age of despair." Preface, *The Revolt of Islam*, *Works*, I, 241.

2. *A Philosophical View of Reform*, *Works*, VIII, 16–17. The "tyrant" who was "not a hypocrite" was Napoleon. See also Shelley's early poem *To the Emperors of Russia and Austria* (*Esdaile Notebook*, pp. 48–49). The change in *Paradise Lost*, I, 597–598, from "perplexes" to "perplexing," may, according to the editors of *Works*, echo an editorial in *The Examiner*, Aug. 21, 1814, where Hunt made a similar change when discussing the revival of priestcraft in Spain.

3. *The Examiner*, Mar. 26, 1820, pp. 193, 195. *The Examiner* first reported the Spanish revolution on Jan. 30 (p. 73), noting that "the Creature" Ferdinand was prepared to assent to a constitution. Further reports came on Feb. 6, 13, 20, and 27; and on Mar. 5 two documents of the insurgents were reprinted. On Mar. 12 came the triumphant announcement: "The noble cause of Spanish freedom holds up its head in every part of Spain." It was reported on Apr. 2 that the constitution had been proclaimed, and on July 23 that it had passed through the Cortes with Ferdinand swearing allegiance to it.

4. To Leigh Hunt, Apr. 9, 1820, *Letters*, II, 180. Shelley's feelings were shared by Mary, who on Mar. 26 exulted in a letter to Mrs. Gisborne: "What does the Spanish Consul say to the distress of his Monarch?" On Mar. 31 she wrote to the same correspondent: "I suppose however that you have heard the news—that the Beloved Ferdinand has proclaimed the Constitution of 1812 & called the Cortes—the Inquisition is abolished—The dungeons opened & the Patriots pouring out—This is good. I sh[ou]ld like to be in Madrid now." (Mary Shelley, *Letters*, I, 103, 104.)

5. Stanza 13 indicates that Shelley was working on the poem later than July 3, 1820, and probably later than July 7. In it he exhorts England to join the movement for liberty that had begun in Spain and was continuing in Italy:

England yet sleeps: was she not called of old?
  Spain calls her now, as with its thrilling thunder
Vesuvius wakens Aetna, and the cold
  Snow-crags by its reply are cloven in sunder:
O'er the lit waves every Aeolian isle
   From Pithecusa to Pelorus
   Howls and leaps, and glares in chorus:
They cry, Be dim, ye lamps of heaven suspended o'er us.

This refers to the Neapolitan revolution, on which Shelley later wrote his *Ode to Na-*

ples. The Aeolian isles extend between Sicily and the Italian mainland (then the kingdom of Naples); Pithecusa is an island in the Bay of Naples; Pelorus, a cape in Sicily; and the two volcanoes are respectively at Naples and Sicily. On July 2, revolution broke out in the kingdom of Naples, which included all southern Italy and the island of Sicily; on July 7 the monarchy was compelled to proclaim a constitution. The news did not reach Sicily until July 14, but there was a high hope on the mainland that Sicily would join in the revolution. Moreover, a letter from Shelley to Peacock on July 12 shows that he was anxious to have the ode published immediately, which suggests that he had just finished it. (*Letters,* II, 213–214.) Even at Shelley's rapid rate of composition, he would have taken several days to write it. It seems most likely, then, that the ode was written between July 3 and 12 (at Leghorn).

6. Shelley liked this image so much that he used it again the following month in *The Witch of Atlas,* ll. 513–516 and the next year in the small poem *Evening: Ponte Al Mare, Pisa.* See *Prometheus Unbound,* III, iii, 159–162, from which perhaps developed the "crystalline sea" image (also on Greece) in *Hellas,* ll. 696–699. Its origin is doubtless Wordsworth's *Peele Castle,* st. 2.

7. *A Philosophical View of Reform, Works,* VII, 5. In st. 7 Shelley praises the heroes of the Roman republic, Regulus (Atilius) and Camillus, which is strange as both were militarists and, even though living in the republic, imperialists. He seems to have in mind their firm moral character, enshrined in legend, perhaps in implied contrast to contemporary British leaders. The *Ode* is paralleled in its depiction of history by the first chapter of *A Philosophical View of Reform.*

8. *A Philosophical View of Reform, Works,* VII, 6; Preface to *Prometheus Unbound, ibid.,* II, 173; *A Defence of Poetry, ibid.,* VII, 130–131.

9. Shelley, *Lines Written on Hearing the News of the Death of Napoleon.*

10. Leigh Hunt's review of *Prometheus Unbound* in *The Examiner,* June 16, 1822, in R. Brimley Johnson, *Shelley-Leigh Hunt* (London, 1928), pp. 65–66; White, *Unextinguished Hearth,* pp. 248–249, 311–319.

11. *The Examiner,* July 23, 1820, pp. 473, 475; July 30, p. 481; Mar. 4, 1821, p. 137; Mar. 18, 1821, p. 161.

12. Medwin, p. 253; see also Mary Shelley, Note on *Hellas, Works,* III, 63–64; to Mary Shelley, July 30, 1820, *Letters,* II, 223. The first reference among the Shelley circle to the Neapolitan revolution is a diary entry by Claire Clairmont, which shows the enthusiasm in the household at the news: "Report of the Revolution at Naples; the King ordered his troops to fire upon them and disperse the crowd; they refused, and he has now promised a Constitution . . . This is glorious, and is produced by the Revolution in Spain." (July 16, Clairmont, p. 156.)

13. To Mary Shelley, Sept. 1, 1820, *Letters,* II, 234. The preceding sentence reads: "At Naples the constitutional party have declared to the Austrian minister that if the Emperor should make war upon them, their first action would be to put to death *all* the members of the royal family. A necessary & most just measure when the forces of the combatants as well as the merits of their respective causes are so unequal!" Shelley, like the young Wordsworth but unlike most English radicals of the time, supported executions that seemed necessary for the survival of a revolutionary state.

14. To Peacock, Feb. 15, 1821; see also to Charles Ollier, Feb. 16, 1821, *ibid.,* pp. 261-263. The attiude of *The Examiner,* Mar. 18, 1821, pp. 161–162, was similar: fearing the defeat of the Neapolitans, but still hoping that their "freeman" courage and uprisings elsewhere in Italy might turn the tide. On Mar. 23, the editors in a lead article bitterly denounced the British government for its nonintervention policy toward the Neapolitan revolution.

15. Mary Shelley recorded in her journal for Aug. 24–25, 1820: "On 24th . . . Shelley writes an Ode to Naples." (*Mary Shelley's Journal,* p. 137.) Claire Clairmont quoted two lines from it (87–88) on Sept. 3. (Clairmont, p. 173.) As the poem was not sent to the publishers until Feb. 16, 1821, however, there is the possibility of revision until that date. (To Charles Ollier, Feb. 16, 1821, *Letters,* II, 262.) Indeed, such revision is likely, for ll. 137–148 refer directly to the Austrian invasion of Italy, which began on Feb. 5. Shelley could, it is true, have been anticipating that invasion. *The Examiner* reported as early as Aug. 30, 1820 (pp. 538f), that the Austrians had 45,000 men ready to invade Italy; and in a letter to Hunt on Dec. 3, 1820, Mary Shelley spoke of "the war threatening Naples." (Mary Shelley, *Letters,* I, 118.) But Shelley's language—the army crossing the Alps, the destruction of cities, and the final "They come!" (l. 147)—suggests an invasion already underway. Moreover, it is similar in tone to his comments on the invasion to Peacock on Feb. 15. (*Letters,* II, 261–262.) Perhaps this passage was added, revised, or substituted for a previous one between Feb. 5 and 16.

The poem was first published in a paper called *The Military Register and Weekly*

Gazette, Oct. 1 and 8. (White, *Unextinguished Hearth*, p. 389.) White argued that Shelley himself could not have sent it to this publication because he later (Feb. 22, 1822) offered it to Ollier for his *Literary Miscellany*. However, Shelley may have thought that a poem published in a journal aimed specifically at a military audience could bear republication in a literary periodical. To send the poem or agree to have it sent to a military journal was in keeping with Shelley's hope that it might help the opponents of Castlereagh's foreign policy. The military could both put pressure on the government and give individual aid. Shelley (or Ollier) may have conceived the idea of sending it to such a periodical from reading the *The Examiner's* accounts of a British general, Sir Robert Wilson, who had offered to go to the assistance of the Neapolitans. That Wilson's position was recognized by the government as dangerous to its interests is shown by the fact that he was later dismissed from the army, whereupon *The Examiner* started a subscription fund for him.

16. Mary Shelley, Note on *Hellas*, *Works* III, 63.

17. To Peacock, Feb. 15, 1821, *Letters*, II, 262. See also the "Sonnet to Italy" in the Apr. 8, 1821 issue of *The Examiner* (p. 219) by "Arthur Brooke," who was actually John Chalk Claris, the author also of a sonnet to Shelley in the Nov. 5, 1820, *Examiner*. (See White, *Unextinguished Hearth*, p. 343.)

18. Jan. 9, 1821, *Byron*, V, 163.

19. To Claire Clairmont, Feb. 18, 1821, *Letters*, II, 267.

20. W. Alison Phillips, *The War of Greek Independence, 1821 to 1835* (London, 1897), pp. 47–48; *The Cambridge Modern History*, X, 169–204.

21. For the philhellenic movement, see Artz, *Reaction and Revolution*, pp. 207–208.

22. *The Examiner*, Apr. 15, 1821, p. 231; Nov. 4, 1821, pp. 689–690.

23 George Finlay, *A History of Greece from Its Conquest by the Romans to the Present Time* (Oxford, 1877), VI, 132. Shelley, who was receiving *The Examiner* regularly in Italy, also got information from the Italian press and from his Greek and other friends in Pisa. On Ali Pasha, see *Childe Harold's Pilgrimage*, II, 415–423; *Byron*, I, 246–252 and *passim*.

24. Phillips, *The War of Greek Independence*, p. 48; *The Examiner*, July 29, p. 468. For the naval expeditions, see Phillips, *The War of Greek Independence*, pp. 65–71; Finlay, *History of Greece*, pp. 172–182.

25. *The Cambridge Modern History*, X, 179; see also C.W. Crawley, *The Question of Greek Independence* (Cambridge, Eng., 1930), pp. 17–29.

26. Finlay, *History of Greece*, p. 237; Phillips, *The War of Greek Independence*, pp. 84–87.

27. *Mary Shelley's Journal*, pp. 149, 151. On Mar. 14 Mavrocordato had called on the Shelleys, and Mary enjoyed "an interesting conversation with him concerning Greece." In view of Mary's comment in her Note to *Hellas* that Mavrocordato had "often intimated the possibility of an insurrection in Greece," this conversation probably dealt with the coming revolution, of which he may have had hints from his cousin Ypsilanti and others. (*Works*, III, 63.) As early as Dec. 29, 1820, Mary had recorded a conversation with Mavrocordato in which he attacked British foreign policy toward Greece. (To Leigh Hunt, Mary Shelley, *Letters*, I, 125.) *The Examiner*, Apr. 15, 1821, pp. 231–232, reprints the proclamation, datelined "Jassy, Feb, 23 (March 7), 1821."

28. To Maria Gisborne, Apr. 5, 1821, Mary Shelley, *Letters*, I, 137. Mavrocordato was Mary's Greek tutor, hence, "My Master." See also to Claire Clairmont, Apr. 2, 1821, *ibid.*, p. 136. On Apr. 7, 18, and 24 Mavrocordato called with further news, announcing on the 24th that the Morea had been freed. (*Mary Shelley's Journal*, pp. 151–153.) During this period Mavrocordato seems to have been with the Shelley's almost every day.

29. Mary Shelley, Note on *Hellas*, *Works*, III, 63; to Byron, Apr. 16, May 4, July 16, 1821, *Letters*, II, 283–284, 289–291, 308–310. The Neapolitan revolution is referred to on pp. 290–291. No other letters of the period up to Aug. 9 mention the Greek war.

30. To Mary Shelley, Aug. 10, 1821, *ibid.*, pp. 324, 350. In this second letter, in his Dedication to *Hellas*, and in a letter to Claire Clairmont on Dec. 11, 1821, Shelley praises Mavrocordato: "The news of the Greeks continues to be more & more glorious—It may be said that the Peloponnesus is entirely free, & Mavrocordato has been acting a distinguished part, & will probably fill a high rank in the magistracy of the infant republic." (*Ibid.*, p. 368.) Medwin also noted that Shelley "entertained a sincere regard" for the prince, who "had very enlarged and enlightened views of the state of Europe." (Medwin, p. 264.) However, Shelley earlier commented to Claire, "The Greek Prince comes sometimes, & I reproach to my own savage disposition that so agreable accomplished and aimiable [a] person is not more agreable to me"; and again, "A vessel has arrived to take the Greek Prince & his suite to join the army in the Morea. He is a great loss to

Mary, and *therefore* to me—but not otherwise." (May 14, June 8, 1821, *ibid.*, pp. 292, 296–299.) Shelley's aversion was probably a jealous reaction to Mary's exuberant enthusiasm: "Do you not envy my luck, that, having begun Greek, an amiable, young, agreeable, and learned Greek Prince comes every morning to give me a lesson of an hour and a-half?" (To Maria Gisborne, c. Feb. 12, 1821, Mary Shelley, *Letters*, I, 134.) On balance, however, Shelley's rather petty reservations concerned Mavrocordato only as a person and were voiced in private letters to a correspondent with whom he was on intimate terms. Shelley clearly admired and respected him as a political leader, especially as he saw the role he was playing in the unfolding revolution.

31. Gisborne & Williams, pp. 103–104; see also to Byron, Oct. 21, 1821, *Letters*, II, 357–359; Ernest J. Lovell, Jr., ed., *His Very Self and Voice* (New York, 1954), pp. 321, 447.

32. *Letters*, II, 363–364. On Oct. 26 Williams recorded in his journal: "He [Shelley] asked me yesterday what name he should give to the drama he is now engaged with. I proposed 'Hellas' which he will adopt." (Gisborne & Williams, p. 106.) Williams' suggestion was made on Oct. 25, but by Oct. 22, as Shelley's letter to Gisborne shows, he had already named his play *Hellas*. Moreover, the postmarks show that Shelley's letter was received in England on Nov. 8, so Shelley's date of Oct. 22 is almost certainly correct. Williams' journal entry is perhaps incorrectly dated. Like other diarists, he may have made entries together in a group and mixed up his days. Possibly, however, Shelley gave Williams some leads on a name he had already considered and then let him have the satisfaction of believing that he had really named the play.

33. *Letters*, II, 365. For the date of completing *Hellas*, see also Williams' journal: "Tuesday, November 6th . . . Commence writing out for S[helley] a fair copy of his Hellas"; "Wednesday, November 8th . . . Continue writing in the evening": "Friday, November 9th . . . Continue writing and finish"; "Saturday, November 10th . . . Finish the notes and preface to 'Hellas.' " The manuscript that Shelley mailed on Nov. 11 to Ollier for publication was Williams' transcript. (Bennett Weaver, "The Williams Transcription of 'Hellas,' " *Essays and Studies in English and Comparative Literature*, University of Michigan Publications, Language and Literature, VIII [Ann Arbor, Michigan, 1932], pp. 152–153.) Weaver showed (pp. 153–168) that this MS was revised by Shelley, but as the revisions were minor, Shelley must have finished the work in all essentials by Nov. 6. Weaver also noted changes and omissions by Ollier, who left out the paragraph in the Preface beginning "Should the English" as being too revolutionary, and some passages in the Notes as being anticlerical. Williams' transcript is in the Henry E. Huntington Library, San Marino, California.

When the drama was begun is not known. Mary commented in her Note on *Hellas* that it was "written in a moment of enthusiasm," and Shelley wrote to Gisborne on Apr. 10, 1822: "It was written without much care, in one of those few moments of enthusiasm which now seldom visit me." (*Works*, III, 64; *Letters*, II, 406). As there is no mention of the composition of the poem in Mary's journal, it is likely that Shelley did not consult her while writing it, and that her comment simply re-echoes his remark to Gisborne, for the letter to Gisborne subsequently came into her possession and was reprinted in her *Essays and Letters from Abroad* (London, 1840), II, 336. That *Hellas*, however, was written neither "carelessly" nor "in a moment" is clear, for Shelley expended on it some of his hardest work and later took the trouble to send a list of errata to his publishers. (To Ollier and Co., Apr. 11, 1822, *Letters*, II, 410–411; Weaver "The Williams Transcription," p. 154n.) If the drama was planned and written as a whole, the earliest possible time for beginning composition would be early August 1821, because ll. 528–529 refer to the Russian ambassador's withdrawal from Constantinople, which took place on July 31, and it would have required several days for the news to reach Italy. Shelley also describes the burning of the Turkish battleship (ll. 509–514), which took place on June 19. From about Apr. 19 to June 22, moreover, he was occupied with writing *Adonais* and seeing it through the press. His letters of July still show him centering his attention on *Adonais*. There is no hint that he was working on anything else, and it seems unlikely that he would begin another major work immediately after completing *Adonais*. From Aug. 6 to about Aug. 22 he stayed with Byron at Ravenna, where his schedule seems too full to allow for literary work. But he and Byron discussed the Greek war, and indications are that these talks greatly increased Shelley's interest. The probability is, therefore, that Shelley did not begin *Hellas* until he arrived back in Pisa on Aug. 22, but in view of the length and intricacy of the drama, it was probably not long after that date.

34. To Charles Ollier, *Letters*, II, 365, 372. Gisborne replied to Shelley on Feb. 19, 1822: "The 'Hellas,' they tell me, will be out in a few days." Shelley received a copy on Apr. 10. (Gisborne & Williams, pp. 81, 142.)

35. *Works*, III, 8; see also Gisborne & Williams, pp. 103–104; to Byron, Oct. 21, 1821, *Letters*, II, 357–358. See also Shelley's Notes on *Hellas*: "A Greek who had been Lord Byron's servant commands the insurgents in Attica. This Greek, Lord Byron informs me, though a poet and an enthusiastic patriot, gave him rather the idea of a timid and unenterprising person. It appears that circumstances make men what they are, and that we all contain the germ of a degree of degradation or greatness, whose connexion with our character is determined by events." (*Works*, III, 56–57.)

36. See *The Examiner*, Oct. 7, 1821, p. 625: "The Monarchs . . . long to appropriate Greece . . . but . . . they fear their own people." There are other parallels between Shelley's Preface and this article. For instance, *The Examiner* reads: "But the Greeks! the Greeks! what do we not owe to them? . . . We are Greeks when we speak of nautical matters with the sailor, of arithmetic with the merchant, of stratagems with the soldier, of theatres and dramas with the playgoer, of poetry and philosophy with the man of letters, of theology with the churchman . . . we cannot paint, sculpture, write poetry or music . . . without having a debt of gratitude to the Greeks." Shelley's Preface reads: "We are all Greeks. Our laws, our literature, our religion, our arts, have their root in Greece." *The Examiner* went on to assert that present-day Greeks retained some qualities of the ancient Greeks: "The Greeks are Greeks to this day." Shelley writes: "The modern Greek is the descendent of those glorious beings." This resemblence may be simply the result of like minds thinking alike, but Shelley could have read the *Examiner* article before writing his Preface. If it had been sent by land post, as was sometimes the case, he could have received it by Oct. 25; the Preface was dated Nov. 1 and could have been added to until Nov. 10. This issue was, in fact, probably sent by land post because of the reference in another article to "Alexander Mavrocordato, nephew of Prince Caraya, [of whom] we heard a short time since in Italy, where he was reading Greek with some friends of ours," namely, Shelley and Mary, followed by a quotation from *The Revolt of Islam*, V, xi.

37. *Works*, III, 9–10. That liberals were generally convinced of growing revolution in Germany is shown by *The Examiner*, Mar. 12, 1820, p. 174: "The discontent in the Rhenish Provinces is greater than ever, and the least disturbance in France will rouse them . . . The spirit of freedom becomes all powerful in Germany, and neither the Prussian stays nor the Austrian corporal's cane will be able to arrest its programs."

38. Richard Garnett, *Relics of Shelley* (London, 1862), pp. 4–11. Garnett found the MS of the Prologue in "the same book as the original MS. of 'Hellas.' "

39. Shelley told Gisborne that *Hellas* was "a sort of imitation of the Persae of Aeschylus." (Oct. 22, 1821, *Letters*, II, 364.)

40. June 20, 1811, *Letters*, I, 110; see also King-Hele, p. 327; Shelley, *Selected Poems, Essays and Letters*, ed. Ellsworth Barnard (New York, 1944), p. 434n.

41. *Works*, III, 56.

42. *Ibid.*

43. Shelley had heard of the battle of Dragashan at first hand from Greeks who had been with Ypsilanti's army. (Oct. 21, 1821, Gisborne & Williams, pp. 103–104; to Byron, Oct. 21, 1821, *Letters*, II, 357–358.) Nevertheless, it is unlikely that the account in the poem was based on these stories. Shelley must have seen these Greek soldiers in Pisa only a day or so prior to Oct. 21, for in his letter to Byron he said they had been in Pisa "the other day," and he told Williams that they "are now passing through Pisa." His comment to Gisborne on Oct. 22 that he was "just finishing" the play shows that by Oct. 21 he must have been well past the half-way point, where the battle is described. Although he could have later added to this speech, the verse gives no evidence of this. As all accounts of the battle emphasized the same things, the speech was probably based on a report he had earlier heard or read.

44. See *The Examiner*, July 1, 20, Oct. 7, 1821, pp. 402, 468, 631.

45. See Finlay, *History of Greece*, p. 194. The ambassador left Constantinople on July 31. (Crawley, *Question of Greek Independence*, p. 18n.)

46. *The Examiner*, July 22, Oct. 7, 21, Dec. 9, 1821, pp. 456, 631, 660, 777.

47. See Cameron, *The Young Shelley*, pp. 34–35, 306–313; *Shelley and His Circle*, II, 649–659.

48. *Works*, VI, 195, 194.

49. Shelley refers in a Note to Gibbon on the siege of Constantinople. (See Gibbon, *Decline and Fall* [New York, 1880], VI, 519–527.) He also makes use of Gibbon in ll. 814–841, where Mahomet's vision presages a new siege by the Greeks.

50. *The Examiner*, Aug. 12, Nov. 4, 1821, pp. 505, 689.

51. Grabo, *A Newton among Poets*, pp. xiv, 167–168.

52. Locock pointed out that the "evening land" (land of the west) refers to the United

States. (*Poems*, II, 471; see also Raymond D. Havens, "*Hellas* and *Charles the First*," *Studies in Philology*, XLIII [July 1946], 545–550; *The Revolt of Islam*, ll. 4414–4440.)

53. *Works*, III, 57; *Essay on Christianity*, *Works*, VI, 250. See also *Works*, III, 57: "Saturn and Love were among the dieties of a real or imaginary state of innocence and happiness."

11. *Shelley As Dramatist*

1. St. John Ervine, "Shelley As a Dramatist," *Essays by Divers Hands, Transactions of the Royal Society of Literature of the United Kingdom* n.s., XV, 90 (London, 1936); Ervine's review of *The Cenci* in *The Observer* (London), Nov. 19, 1922.

2. *Works*, IV, 129–136.

3. For the purposed structure of *Tasso*, See Shelley's notebook outline of scenes, *Poems*, II, 502–503. For the social message of the poet's struggle against tyranny, which the drama would probably have conveyed, see Shelley's letter to Peacock, Nov. 6–7, 1818: "There is something irresistibly pathetic to me in the sight of Tasso's own hand writing moulding expressions of adulation & entreaty to a deaf & stupid tyrant in an age when the most heroic virtue would have exposed its possessor to hopeless persecution, and—such is the alliance between virtue & genius—which unoffending genius could not escape." Shelley also told Peacock on Apr. 20, 1818, that he intended to devote a year to the play. (*Letters*, II, 47, 8.) Apparently, however, it was either crowded out when the concept of *Prometheus Unbound* took hold of his imagination, or it was dropped because of the appearance of Byron's *Lament of Tasso*. (Mary Shelley, Note to *Prometheus Unbound*, *Works*, II, 268; Richard Garnett, *Relics of Shelley* [London, 1862], p. 26.) There is no evidence that Shelley had read Goethe's *Tasso*.

Shelley's interest in Tasso is first revealed in T. J. Hogg's account of their joint reading of *Jerusalem Delivered* in the fall and winter of 1813–1814. (Hogg, II, 62.) The journals and reading lists indicate Shelley's continued interest in the poet. (*Mary Shelley's Journal*, p. 226.) This interest later declined somewhat, as indicated in a letter to Leigh Hunt on Sept. 27, 1819, a conversation with Thomas Medwin probably in the fall of 1820, and *A Defence of Poetry* in 1821. (*Letters*, II, 122; Medwin, p. 262; *Works*, VII, 118, 128.) Mary in a Note on *Prometheus Unbound* stated that *Tasso* was to have been a "lyrical drama." (*Works*, II, 268.) But the fragment and the notebook outline suggest a play along the lines of *The Cenci*.

4. For *Job*, see *Works*, II, 268. For *Timon*, see Williams' journal entry of Dec. 30, 1821: "S[helley] who is thinking of a tragedy to be founded on the story of Timon of Athens, but adapted to modern times." (*Gisborne & Williams*, p. 121.) See also Trelawny (p. 199): "He thought a play founded on Shakespeare's *Timon* would be an excellent mode of discussing our present social and political evils dramatically, and of descanting on them." For *Troilus and Cressida*, see to Charles Ollier, Oct. 11, 1821, *Letters*, II, 357. As boys, Shelley and a friend, while in the lower forms at Eton, used to write and act plays, as reported by the friend, Andrew Amos. (White, II, 494.) Shelley's sister Hellen remembered that he and their sister Elizabeth once wrote a play together and sent it off to a theater manager, who turned it down. (Hellen Shelley to Lady Jane Shelley, c. 1856, in Hogg, I, 26.) It may be, however, that Hellen's memory was not exact, for in a letter to Graham in August (?) 1810, Shelley speaks of a tragedy that apparently he had written alone, and a "farce which my friend [probably Elizabeth] is composing." Both were to be sent to Covent Garden and the Lyceum. (*Letters*, I, 14.)

5. Trelawny, p. 198.

6. Medwin, p. 39; Hogg, I, 138; Peacock, p. 330; Mary Shelley, Note on *The Cenci*, *Works*, II, 157. For Dora Jordan, see William Charles Macready, *Reminiscences*, ed. Charles Frederick Pollock (New York, 1875), pp. 48–49. *The Country Girl* was played at Covent Garden on Nov. 23, 1805, and on June 11, 1811. (Henry Saxe Wyndham, *The Annals of Covent Garden Theatre* [London, 1906], I, 312, 353; see also Malcolm Elwin, *The Playgoer's Handbook to Restoration Drama* [London, 1928], p. 77.) The provincial performance that Shelley and Medwin saw was perhaps related to the 1805 London production. Apparently Shelley accompanied Harriet Grove to the theater on Apr. 26 and 27, 1810. (*The Diary of Harriet Grove*, *Shelley and His Circle*, II, 577.) It was perhaps this occasion that set Shelley to writing his tragedy and sending it to Covent Garden and the Lyceum.

7. *Mary Shelley's Journal*, p. 20. William Whitton wrote to Timothy Shelley on Nov. 30, 1815, that Shelley had acted on the Windsor stage. (Ingpen, p. 458.) W. G. Bebbington

argued that this was unlikely. (Bebbington, "Shelley and the Windsor Stage," *Notes and Queries*, n.s., II [May 1956], 215–216.) But Whitton, a careful man, must have had some basis for his report. Perhaps Shelley intended to act at Windsor, rehearsed there, or acted in some other town.

8. *Mary Shelley's Journal*, pp. 76, 77, 92; Clairmont, p. 84; Leigh and Marianne Hunt to Shelley and Mary, Nov. 16, 1821, Hunt, *Correspondence*, I, 174. Peacock, p. 330. On Jan. 29, 1817, Shelley also saw a melodrama called *The Ravens; or the Force of Conscience* by Isaac Pocock. (Stuart Curran, *Shelley's Cenci: Scorpions Ringed with Fire* [Princeton, 1970], p. 158.)

9. Peacock, p. 330. Shelley's attendance at the *School for Scandal* is not recorded in the journals of Mary Shelley or Claire Clairmont, but presumably it was sometime in 1817–1818. Genest recorded performances at Drury Lane, Sept. 6–9, 1817, and Covent Garden, Dec. 12, 1817. (John Genest, *Some Account of the English Stage from the Restoration in 1660 to 1830* [Bath,1832], VIII, 633.) Since Shelley was at Marlow on Dec. 12, according to Mary, and could have been in London between Sept. 6 and 9, the September period is more likely. (*Mary Shelley's Journal*, pp. 84, 87.)

10. Dowden, II, 184. Genest cryptically noted that *The Castle of Glyndower* was "acted but once." (Genest, *Some Account of the English Stage*, VIII, 642–643.) "In point of sheer stupidity," wrote *The Courier* critic, "it leaves all other plays at an immeasurable distance." (*Dowden*, II, 184.) *Clairmont*, pp. 82, 83, 85, 86; *Mary Shelley's Journal*, p. 92; Peacock, p. 349; Mar. 23, 1818, *Mary Shelley's Journal*, p. 94, app. IV.

11. "When in Rome, in 1819, a friend put into our hands the old manuscript account of the story of the Cenci," Mary Shelley wrote in her Note on *The Cenci*. (*Works*, II, 156.) But in her journal entry for May 18–29, 1818, she noted: "Finish copying the Cenci MS. on Monday, 25th." (*Mary Shelley's Journal*, p. 98.) From May 9 to June 11, 1818, the Shelleys lived in Leghorn, where they first met the Gisbornes. It seems likely that Mrs. Gisborne was "the friend" who showed them the Cenci manuscript and that when Mary wrote her note twenty years later, she made a mistake on place and time. This is natural enough, for it was not until they visited Rome the following year that Shelley became really interested in the subject, when he "found that the story of the Cenci was a subject not to be mentioned in Italian society without awakening a deep, and breathless interest." (Preface to *The Cenci*, *Works*, II, 70.) On Apr. 22, 1819, Mary recorded: "Visit the Palazzo Corunna and see the picture of Beatrice Cenci," which was supposed to be by Guido Reni, but which is neither Beatrice nor by Guido. (*Mary Shelley's Journal*, p. 120; F. Marion Crawford, "Beatrice Cenci, the True Story of a Misunderstood Tragedy," *The Century Magazine*, LXXV [1908], 460–461.) On May 11, Shelley and Mary visited the old Cenci mansion in Rome. By May 14 Shelley had begun work on his play, and Mary recorded him as working on it on Aug. 4, 7, and 11. (*Mary Shelley's Journal*, pp. 121, 122–123.) There seems to be no evidence to place the starting date of composition as early as Mar. 4, 1819, as in *Works*, II, 416. On about July 20 Shelley wrote to Peacock intimating that he would send him the play within a month and asking that he attempt to get it produced at Covent Garden. (*Letters*, II, 102–103.) On Aug. 8, Mary recorded that it was "finished." (*Mary Shelley's Journal*, p. 123.) But on Aug. 15 Shelley informed Hunt that he was "on the eve of completing" it, and on about Aug. 20 he told him that he had finished it and intended to dedicate it to him. On Sept. 2 he wrote the dedication, and on Sept. 6 he informed Ollier that it was being printed in Italy. On Sept. 9 he mailed a copy to Peacock; the bulk of the 250 printed copies were sent to England in December by ship. (*Letters*, II, 108, 112, 95n, 116–119, 126.) The manuscript of *The Cenci* is lost, but there was a forged manuscript of part of the play in circulation in the early 1950s.

12. C. July 20, 1819, *ibid.*, pp. 102–103.

13. Hazlitt to *The Examiner*, Nov. 19, 1815, *The Complete Works of William Hazlitt*, ed. P. P. Howe (London, 1934), V, 256–258; see also Macready, *Reminiscences*, *passim*. See also *DNB* (under Eliza Becher), and Wyndham, *Annals*, *passim*.

14. Peacock, p. 330. Mary Shelley wrote on *The Cenci*: "While preparing for our departure for England, however, he saw Miss O'Neill several times; she was then in the zenith of her glory, and Shelley was deeply moved by her impersonation of several parts." (*Works*, II, 157.) Shelley perhaps also saw her in *The School for Scandal*. (Curran. *Shelley's Cenci*, p. 158.) She was under contract at Convent Garden. On Oct. 13, 1814, Shelley apparently tried to get Peacock to see Kean in *Hamlet* at Drury Lane but Peacock went to Covent Garden instead, where O'Neill was playing Belvidera in *Venice Preserved*. (Clairmont, p. 50; Genest, *Some Account of the English Stage*, VIII, 446, 474.) Ervine, "Shelley As a Dramatist," p. 87.

15. Peacock, p. 352. On Mar. 13, 1820, Shelley wrote to Charles Ollier that *The Cenci*

"was refused at Drury Lane." On Apr. 5 he wrote to Hunt: "The very Theatre rejected it with expressions of the greatest insolence." As "very" makes no sense, it is presumably a misreading for Drury. (*Letters*, II, 178, 181.) Peacock wrote that at Covent Garden "great admiration was expressed of the author's powers, and great hopes of his success with a less repulsive subject." (Peacock, p. 352.) Mary Shelley stated in her Note that Henry Harris at Covent Garden "pronounced the subject to be so objectionable, that he could not even submit the part to Miss O'Neill for perusal." (*Works*, II, 158.) Hassis cannot have received the play from Peacock until late September, as Shelley did not mail it to Peacock from Italy until Sept. 9, and O'Neill gave her last performance on July 13, 1819. (*Letters*, II, 118.) Since in December she married an Irish member of Parliament and retired, she could not have performed the part even had the play been accepted. (Wyndham, *Annals*, I, 382; Macready, *Reminiscences*, pp. 136, 155.)

16. White, *Unextinguished Hearth*, p. 168. Curran, *Shelley's Cenci*, p. 10.

17. For the stage history, see Kenneth Neill Cameron and Horst Frenz, "The Stage History of Shelley's *The Cenci*," *PMLA*, LX (December 1945), 1080–1105; Arthur C. Hicks and R. Milton Clarke, *A Stage Version of Shelley's Cenci* (Caldwell, Idaho, 1945), pp. 11–29; William White, "An American Production of Shelley's *The Cenci*," *Modern Language Notes*, LXIV (1949), 178–179; Bert O. States, Jr., "Stage History of *The Cenci*," *PMLA*, LXXII (1957), 633–644; Marcel Kessel and Bert O. States, Jr., "*The Cenci* As a Stage Play," *PMLA*, LXXV (1960), 147–148; King-Hele, p. 135; Curran, *Shelley's Cenci*, pp. 183–257.

18. On Oct. 7, 1814, Shelley asked Claire Clairmont if she had read Joanna Baillie's play. Maturin's *Bertram* and Milman's *Fazio* were listed as having been read by Shelley in 1816. (*Mary Shelley's Journal*, pp. 18, 223.) That Shelley had little regard for Milman is clear from his letter to Byron on May 4, 1821 and the Preface to *Adonais*. (*Letters*, II, 290; *Works*, II, 388.) He wrote to Peacock on Apr. 20, 1818, that his projected play on Tasso "shall [have] better morality than Fazio, & better poetry than Bertram, at least." He referred to *Remorse* in another letter to Peacock in July 1819. (*Letters*, II, 8, 102.) Of foreign dramas, Peacock wrote that Schiller's *The Robbers* "took the deepest root in his mind, and he had the strongest influence in the formation of his character." (Peacock, p. 328.) In the Preface to *Adonais*, Shelley mentions John Howard Payne, but apparently only in reference to the *Quarterly Review*'s remarks on his play *Brutus* in the April 1820 issue, and there is no evidence that he read any of Payne's plays. (*Adonais*, ed. William Michael Rossetti [Oxford, 1891], p. 98.) In a letter of May 4, 1821, to Byron, Shelley refers to Barry Cornwall (Bryan Waller Proctor) as a playwright, but his letter of Sept. 25, 1821, to Ollier shows that he had not then read Proctor's only acted play, *Mirandola* (performed at Covent Garden in January 1821), even though Shelley's letter of Aug. 22, 1821, to Medwin passes unfavorable judgment on it. (*Letters*, II, 290, 354, 342.) Presumably he had read a review of it or spoken to someone familiar with it. In addition to the four currently acted plays, Shelley had also read several of Byron's that were later produced, such as *Marino Faliero, Manfred, Cain, Sardanapalus*, and *Werner* (the only one that achieved sustained success). (*Works*, X, 255, 306, 354; Williams's Journal, Jan. 8, 1822, Gisborne & Williams, p. 123; Medwin, p. 340; *Letters*, II, 470–471.) Shelley apparently also read Godwin's ill-fated *Antonio*, which ran for one night in 1800. (Peck, II, 364; *Shelley and His Circle*, I, 238–245, 364.)

19. Charles Maturin, *Bertram*, in *The British Drama*, ed. John Dicks (London, 1870), III, 685.

20. That Shelley himself was aware of the shoddiness of contemporary theater is clear from his comment to Byron on May 4, 1821: "We look to you for substituting something worthy of the English stage, for the miserable trash which, from Milman to Barry Cornwall, has been intruded on it since the demand for tragical representation." (*Letters*, II, 290.) *The Cenci* echoes Shakespeare, especially in the parallel of IV, iii with *Macbeth*, and also echoes other Elizabethan or seventeenth-century plays, such as Massinger's *The Unnatural Combat*, Webster's *Duchess of Malfi* (with its atmosphere of tragic pathos developed around a beautiful, persecuted woman), Ford's *'Tis Pity She's a Whore* (with its incest theme), and Shirley's *The Cardinal* (in which the unscrupulous, scheming cardinal plans to rape the young heroine). (See Bates, *A Study of Shelley's Drama*, pp. 48–57; David Lee Clark, "Shelley and Shakespeare," *PMLA*, LIV [1939], 277–286; Sara Ruth Watson, "Shelley and Shakespeare: An Addendum. A Comparison of *Othello* and *The Cenci*," *PMLA*, LV [1940], 611–614; Beach Langston, "Shelley's Use of Shakespeare," *Huntington Library Quarterly*, XII [1949], 163–190; E. M. M. Taylor, "Shelley and Shakespeare," *Essays in Criticism*, III [1953], 367–368; King-Hele, pp. 137–138; Curran, *Shelley's Cenci*, pp. 35–41. Curran argues cogently that the Shakespearean influence has been exaggerated.)

21. May 18–25, 1818, *Mary Shelley's Journal*, p. 98; *Works*, II, 156–166.

22. A. Bertolotti, *Francesco Cenci e la sua famiglia* [Florence, 1877]. For Bertolotti, see Bates, *A Study of Shelley's Drama*, pp. 31–34; Clarence Stratton, "The Cenci Story in Literature and Fact," *Studies in English Drama, Publications of the University of Pennsylvania*, XIV (Philadelphia, 1917), pp. 143–160; Crawford, "Beatrice Cenci," pp. 449–466.

23. Stratton, "The Cenci Story," pp. 153–154, 130–132; Henry Peyre, *Shelley et la France* (Cairo, Egypt, 1935), p. 215; Cameron and Frenz, "The Stage History," p. 1097n; Newman I. White, "An Italian 'Imitation' of Shelley's *The Cenci*," *PMLA*, XXXVIII (1922), 683–690; Bates, *A Study of Shelley's Drama*, p. 31n; Crawford, "Beatrice Cenci," pp. 461–464; Ricci, *Beatrice Cenci*, II, 287–317; Curran, *Shelley's Cenci*, p. 42n.

24. *Works*, II, 159, 161, 162, 164.

25. *Ibid.*, p. 67. On the date of this Dedication, see *Letters*, II, 95n. Shelley had written similarly to Godwin on July 25, 1818: "I wish that I had health or spirits that would enable me to enter into public affairs, or that I could find words to express all that I feel & know." (*Ibid.*, p. 22.)

26. *Works*, II, 72, 73. For Shelley's identification with Beatrice, see Melvin R. Watson, "Shelley and Tragedy: The Case of Beatrice Cenci," *Keats-Shelley Journal*, VII (1958), 13–21.

27. Arthur C. Hicks, "An American Performance of *The Cenci*," *Stanford Studies in Language and Literature* (Stanford, 1941).

28. Shelley left out the statement that Cenci forced his wife to witness his debaucheries, and he changed the charge of sodomy to that of murder. (Bates, *A Study of Shelley's Drama*, p. 49.)

29. Hicks, "An American Performance," p. 293.

30. *Works*, II, 160.

31. White, II, 139; Curran, *Shelley's Cenci*, pp. 85, 91, 92n.

32. On the self-contempt theme, see *Prometheus Unbound*, I, 510; II, iv, 24–25; *The Revolt of Islam*, VIII, xxi, 3; *Adonais*, XXXVII, 7; *Rosalind and Helen*, 1, 479; see also Wilson, p. 91. The theme is a surprisingly obsessive one with Shelley, in view of his basically confident self-image. Even though he may have felt that he did not always live up to his highest ideals, he always attempted to do so. But there were doubtless times in his life when he felt revolted by his own actions. Perhaps one was his experience with the prostitute at Oxford. (See Cameron, pp. 125–126.)

33. *Works*, II, 161–162.

34. Hicks, "An American Performance," p. 307.

35. *Works*, II, 163.

36. *The Graphic*, CVI (Nov. 25, 1922), 724; Cameron and Frenz, "The Stage History," p. 1087.

37. To Charles Ollier, Sept. 6, 1819, Mar. 6, 1820, *Letters*, II, 116–117, 174. The first edition was sold out and a second edition published in 1821. By 1827 the work was popular enough to warrant the publication of a pirated edition by William Benbow. (Forman, pp. 92–93.)

38. William Godwin to Shelley, June 8, 1818, *Shelley and Mary*, I, 281–283. The book was to be called "The Lives of the Commonwealth men." Godwin later wrote a four-volume *History of the Commonwealth of England*, published 1824–1828. Shelley commented to Mary on Sept. 22, 1818: "remember Charles the Ist & Myrrha—I have been already imagining how you will conduct some scenes." (*Letters*, II, 40.) *Myrrha* is a play with an incest theme by the radical Italian nationalist Vittorio Alfieri, which Mary was to translate. In her Notes to the poems of 1822 Mary stated that Shelley had "encouraged me to attempt a play" on Charles I. (*Works*, IV, 210.) In 1817, Mary wrote two short plays. (Mary Shelley, *Prosperine and Midas*, ed. A. H. Koszul [London, 1922], pp. xi–xiii.)

39. July 20, 1820, *Letters*, II, 220.

40. Shelley started to write the play in early January 1822. In the spring of 1821 Godwin had sent Mary a box, which for a time was thought to be lost but was located by June 8. (Mary Shelley to Maria Gisborne, Mar. 21, Apr. 5, May 28, June 8, 1821, Mary Shelley, *Letters*, I, 136, 138, 143, 145.) On about June 5, 1821, Shelley wrote to the Gisbornes: "My unfortunate Box! it contained a chaos of the elements of Charles the first. If the idea of the *Creator* had been packed up with them, it would have shared the same fate: & that, I am afraid, has undergone another sort of shipwreck." (*Letters*, II, 294.) By a "chaos of the elements" Shelley does not mean a rough draft of the play but the reference books out of which he was to make it. In Plato's concept, which Shelley here burlesques, the world was formed by the Idea working on the raw materials of uncoordinated matter;

hence, the implication is that Shelley's own work exists only in idea and that the box contained the raw materials from which to form the actual work. Godwin had apparently been asked to follow up his suggestions of June 8, 1818 for a work on the Commonwealth leaders and had shipped some books to Shelley. Shelley implies that even his concept for the work—"the idea of the Creator" (i.e. Shelley himself)—will not crystallize (has "undergone another form of shipwreck"). Hence, this letter shows that nothing of *Charles the First* had been written by June 5, 1821. (For Dowden's mistaken notion that "the Creator" was a work by Shelley, see Elizabeth Nitchie, *Times Literary Supplement*, Apr. 30, 1938, p. 296; White, II, 609.) Nor had any of this play been written by Sept. 25, when Shelley wrote to Charles Ollier: "*Charles the First* is conceived but not born. Unless I am sure of making something good, the play will not be written." On Oct. 21 he told Ollier to "expect Charles the Ist or Troilus & Cressida in the spring." (*Letters*, II, 354, 357.) Since by Oct. 21 he had not decided which play to write, the probability is that he had written nothing of either.

The first evidence of beginning composition is an entry in Williams' journal for Jan. 8, 1822: "As to S[helley]'s 'Charles the First'—on which he sat down about 5 days since, if he continues it in the spirit [of] some of the lines which he read to me last night, it will doubtless take a place before any other that has appear[ed] since Shakspeare, and will be found a valuable addition to the Historical Pla[y]." (Gisborne & Williams, p. 123.) This indicates a beginning date of about Jan. 3, 1822, which is supported by Shelley's letters. On Jan. 11 he told the Olliers that the play "promises to be good" and "is not coloured by the party spirit of the author." On about the same date he wrote to Peacock: "I have long been idle,—& as far as writing goes, despondent—but I am now engaged in Charles the *Ist* & a devil of a nut it is to crack." On Jan. 12 he asked Gisborne to see whether Ollier would "buy the copyright." On Jan. 25 he told Hunt: "I am at present writing the drama of Charles the *Ist*, a play which if completed according to my present idea will hold a higher rank than the Cenci as a work of art—" (*Letters*, II, 372–373, 375, 380.) The definiteness of Shelley's language in January 1822, in contrast to his vagueness the preceding year, suggests a difference between merely planning a work and actually writing it. Although Medwin stated (p. 340) that Shelley worked on the play "at the end of" 1819, this comment, unlike Williams', cannot be based on observation, for Medwin did not arrive in Pisa until the fall of 1820, and it is contradicted by Shelley's letter to Medwin himself on July 20, 1820. (*Letters*, II, 219–220.)

41. To the Olliers, Jan. 11, 1822,*ibid.*, p. 372.

42. To Gisborne, Jan. 26, 1822, *ibid.*, p. 388. This letter, in conjunction with one to Hunt on Mar. 2, 1822, makes it almost certain that Shelley did not work on the play beyond January. On Mar. 2 he wrote: "So you think I can make nothing of Charles the Ist—Tanto peggio. Indeed I have written nothing for this last two months; a slight circumstance gave a new train to my ideas & shattered the fragile edifice when half built." (*Ibid.*, p. 394.) This statement, together with Mary's comment that "he proceeded slowly [with *Charles the First*], and threw it aside for one of the most mystical of his poems, the *Triumph of Life*, on which he was employed at the last," show that the "new train of ideas" must have been for *The Triumph of Life*. (Works, IV, 210.) Another reason for his not later resuming composition was perhaps a letter of Feb. 19, 1822, from John Gisborne in London, informing him that his publishers, the Olliers, "decline paying any price whatever for 'Charles Ist.' " (Gisborne & Williams, p. 80.)

43. Medwin, p. 341. Whitelocke's book was first published in 1682. The edition used here is in four vols., issued at Oxford in 1853. Whitelocke was recommended by Godwin in his letter of June 8, 1818, proposing that Mary write a book on the Commonwealth men. (Kenneth Neill Cameron, "Shelley's Use of Source Material in *Charles I*," *Modern Language Quarterly*, VI [1945], 197–210.) In a notebook containing notes for the play, Shelley wrote "W" in the margin after passages derived from Whitelocke. (R. B. Woodings, "Shelley's Sources for *Charles the First*," *Modern Language Review*, LXIV [1969], 269.) Hume's essays had been favorites of Shelley's since his Oxford days and had influenced his thinking in philosophy, political science, and economics. As early as Dec. 17, 1812, he ordered a copy of "Hume's History of England (Cheapest poss. Edit.)" from his bookseller, Thomas Hookham. (*Letters*, I, 342.) In July and August 1818 Mary recorded his reading it. (*Mary Shelley's Journal*, pp. 101–102, 104.) For his use of the book in preparing *Charles the First*, see Medwin, pp. 341–342; Rogers, pp. 274–275; Woodings, "Shelley's Sources," p. 268. For parallels with Hume, see Walter Francis Wright, "Shelley's Failure in *Charles I*," *ELH: A Journal of English Literary History*, VIII (March 1941), 41–46.

Mary recorded reading Macaulay's 8-volume history (London, 1763–1783) on July 18 and Aug. 25, 1820, and on Sept. 4 she recorded "Shelley finishes Mrs. Macaulay," which shows that Shelley had been reading it also. (*Mary Shelley's Journal*, pp. 136, 137.) Although the Bodleian notebook does not show him as reading the history at the time he was making notes on it for the play, Shelley nevertheless reflects influence from Macaulay, whose concept of the historical significance of the period is closer to his than is Hume's, so that even though Shelley may not have made specific notes from her work, he must have remembered many scenes and comments. On Macaulay, see Mary Wollstonecraft, *Vindication of the Rights of Women* (London, 1792), p. 235. Boswell noted that Samuel Johnson regarded Macaulay as a dangerous radical and "leveller." (Boswell, *Life of Johnson* [New York, 1933], I, 299.) Mary Shelley recorded that Shelley read Clarendon in October and November 1819). (*Mary Shelley's Journal*, p. 220.) Even if he did not reread it later, he doubtless had memories of its vivid pages.

44. *Works*, VII, 7, 22; see also pp. 14–15, 51. Medwin (pp. 342–343) misinterpreted Shelley's views on Charles and the Puritans. Although he was doubtless correct in stating that Shelley "abhominated" Cromwell's Irish massacres and disliked the general intolerance of Puritan fanaticism, Shelley considered such matters to be secondary to the great political advance of the Commonwealth.

45. To the Olliers, Jan. 11, 1822, *Letters*, II, 372. It may be that by Jan. 11 Shelley had not written enough to know how far his own views were dominating the play's tone; and he would in any case have wished to underplay this aspect of the work to publishers already wary of his radical philosophy. The January 1821 issue of the *London Magazine* commented on the projected play: "A friend of ours writes us from Italy, that Mr. Shelley, the author of that powerful drama, 'The Cenci' is employed upon an English Historical Tragedy. The title, we believe, is to be Charles the First; at any rate, that monarch is the hero or principal person of the story. We hear that Mr. Shelley has expressed his determination to paint a true portrait of the unfortunate English King (it may be made a very captivating one) and to exclude from his work all prejudice, political as well as moral." (White, *Unextinguished Hearth*, p. 272.) This again sounds like Medwin and was doubtless the result of conversations in which Shelley expressed his intention of presenting a "true portrait" of the king, but he did not intend Charles to be the "hero" in any conventional sense. Medwin himself (pp. 342–343) was partial toward Charles and thus would tend to exaggerate some of Shelley's comments and to play down others. Woodings also argued that Shelley intended to present a "sympathetic" picture of the king, supporting his view by marginal markings of passages in what is said to have been Shelley's copy of *Reliquiae sacrae*, which contains letters and documents by Charles, and the forged *Eikon basilike* that provoked Milton's antiroyalist tract *Eikonoklastes*. (Woodings, "Shelley's Sources," p. 272; Peck, II, 363–364.) These markings, however, show only that Shelley was interested in ascertaining the king's point of view for his play. The book contains only one marginal comment, "a lie," written opposite Charles's declaration, "God knowes I did not then think of a Warre."

46. Prynne spoke of "woman actors" as "notorious whores." Laud showed this remark to the queen after she had acted in a pastoral and suggested that Prynne had intended it for her. (Whitelocke, *Memorials*, I, 52.)

47. *Ibid.*, pp. 52, 56–60. Neither Clarendon nor Hume mentioned the masque, and Macaulay devoted only one paragraph to it. (Macaulay, *History*, II, 161–162.)

48. For some of his antiroyalist comments Shelley seems indebted to Macaulay and, to a lesser extent, Hume. (Macaulay, *History*, II, 32–53, 100–102, 155–156; David Hume, *The History of England* [Boston, 1850], V, 74, 76.) Only Macaulay noted that Leighton had been branded. (Macaulay, *History*, II, 96–100.)

49. The four gentlemen, Whitelocke reported, were sent "to attend the king and queen in the name of the four inns of court, to return their humble thanks for their majesties' gracious acceptance of the tender of their service in the late mask." The thanks were given by Finch, and the king answered "with great affability and pleasingness." (Whitelocke, *Memorials*, I, 61–62.) Shelley had perhaps read Clarendon's comment on St. John as a "man reserved, of a dark and clouded countenance, very proud," for that is his character in the play. (Edward Hyde, earl of Clarendon, *The History of the Rebellion and Civil Wars in England* [Oxford, 1849], I, 261; see also p. 198.)

50. There is no hint of this lecture or reply in Whitelocke, who noted simply that after the four gentlemen saw the king, they were taken before the queen, who apparently acted with similar graciousness, saying that she "never saw any mask more noble or better performed." (Whitelocke, *Memorials*, I, 62.)

51. Macaulay, *History*, II, 455–456.

52. This episode could have been based either on Hume or Macaulay. Hume wrote: "Archy, the king's fool, who by his office had the privilege of jesting on his master and

the whole court, happened unluckily to try his wit upon Laud, who was too sacred a person to be played with. News having arrived from Scotland of the first commotions excited by the liturgy, Archy, seeing the primate pass by, called to him, 'Who's fool now, my lord?' For this offence Archy was ordered, by sentence of the council, to have his coat pulled over his head and to be dismissed the king's service." (Hume, *History of England,* V, 88; cf. Macaulay, *History,* II, 251.) The development of Archy's role during the latter part of this scene and in Scene V is indebted to *Lear* and possibly to Calderon's *Cisma de l'Inglaterra.* (Medwin, pp. 243–244.) On Macaulay and Hume, see Woodings, "Shelley's Sources," pp. 270–271.

53. Macaulay, *History,* II, 133; see also pp. 16–17, 56, 57, 88, 106, 129–130.

54. Hume, *History of England,* V, 66, 379; Clarendon, *History of the Rebellion,* IV, 539.

55. Suggestions perhaps came from Macaulay's statements that Laud "railed with the utmost gall and bitterness against the unhappy prisoners whilst he magnified his own religious patience in bearing injuries" and that "Laud whilst he was sitting in the Star Chamber, being told of Prynne's harangue, moved that he might be gagged," a suggestion that the court waived. (Macaulay, *History,* II, 246, 248n.)

56. *Ibid.,* pp. 253–254. Hume developed the concept of a new freedom in America more than Macaulay, from which may have come the suggestion for Hampden's speech: "The Puritans, restrained in England, shipped themselves off for America, and laid there the foundations of a government which possessed all the liberty, both civil and religious, of which they found themselves bereaved in their native country." (Hume, *History of England,* V, 84.)

57. Cf. the eulogies of America in *A Philosophical View of Reform, The Revolt of Islam,* XI, xxii–xxiv, *Ode to Liberty,* 159–165, and *Hellas,* 66–71, 1027–1030.

58. A song by Archy, which was thought to be a fifth scene, has been shown to be a separate lyric probably inspired by Jane Williams. (R. B. Woodings, "Shelley's Widow Bird, *The Review of English Studies,* XIX [1968], 411–414.)

59. *Note Books,* III, 104–105, see also pp. 19–20.

60. Whitelocke, *Memorials,* I, 85.

61. To John Gisborne, Jan. 26, 1822, *Letters,* II, 388.

12. *The Poet and the Critic*

1. Aug. 22, 1821, *Letters,* II, 341.

2. *The Examiner,* Dec. 1, 1816, in Edmund Blunden, *Leigh Hunt's "Examiner" Examined* (London, 1928), pp. 125–128. On *The Champion* and *The Examiner,* see *The Letters of John Keats,* ed. Hyder Edward Rollins (Cambridge, 1958), I, 191, 195–196, 199, 201; II, 93–94. On Southey and Hazlitt, see to Leigh Hunt, May 10, to Haydon, May 10–11, 1817, *ibid.,* I, 137–138, 144.

3. To George and Tom Keats, Dec. 21, 27? 1817, *ibid.,* p. 191: "Hone the publisher's trial, you must find very amusing; & as Englishmen very encouraging;—his *Not Guilty* is a thing, which not to have been, would have dulled still more Liberty's Emblazoning—Lord Ellenborough has been paid in his own coin—Wooler & Hone have done us an essential service." When subscription lists for Hone were published (including "Percy B. Shelley, Marlow, £5.5.0.,"), Keats wrote to his brothers: "There are fine Subscriptions going on for Hone." (Jan. 5, 1818, *ibid.,* p. 199; *Letters,* I, 591.)

4. Keats early broke away from orthodox Christianity and attacked its church and believers. To Hunt, May 10, 1817, to George and Georgiana Keats, Feb. 14–May 3, 1819; to Fanny Brawne, July 5 (?), 1820. (Keats, *Letters,* I, 137, II, 62–63, 304.) Although he wished to believe in immortality, he did not. (To Fanny Brawne, June (?) 1820, *ibid.,* p. 293; Amy Lowell, *John Keats* [Boston, 1929], II, 444, 516, 520.) Severn believed that Shelley was "one of those friends who had most helped to take away the means of hope from Keats." (William Sharp, *The Life and Letters of Joseph Severn* [London, 1892], p. 117.) As Shelley and Hunt were the two outstanding freethinkers among Keats's friends, and the orthodox Haydon was alarmed at their influence over Keats as early as March 1817, Severn may be right, but Keats had earlier held antireligious views. (Walter Jackson Bate, *John Keats* [New York, 1966], pp. 134–136; Eileen Ward, *John Keats; The Making of a Poet* [New York, 1963], p. 82.)

5. To George and Georgiana Keats, Oct. 14–31, 1818, Keats, *Letters,* I, 396–397: "Notwithstand[ing] the part which the Liberals take in the Cause of Napoleon I can not but think he has done more harm to the life of Liberty than any one else could have

done: not that the divine right Gentlemen have done or intend to do any good—no they have taken a Lesson of him and will do all the further harm he would have done without any of the good—The worst thing he has done is, that he has taught them how to organize their monstrous armies." To Reynolds, Apr. 9, 1818, *ibid.*, 267.

6. To George and Georgiana Keats, Oct. 14–31, 1818, *ibid.*, p. 396.

7. Medwin, pp. 178–179; Hunt, II, 41–42; to Benjamin Bailey, Oct. 8, 1817; to George and Tom Keats, Jan. 23, 24, 1818; to George and Tom Keats, Dec. 21, 27 (?), 1817; Keats, *Letters*, I, 170, 214, 194.

8. To Shelley, Aug. 16, 1820, *ibid.*, II, 323.

9. To Shelley, Aug. 16, 1820, *ibid.*, p. 322; to John Keats, July 27, 1820; to Marianne Hunt, Oct. 29, 1820; *Letters*, II, 221, 239, 240; Medwin, pp. 260–261.

10. *Selected Poetry and Prose of the Romantic Period*, ed. George R. Creeger and Joseph W. Reed (New York, 1964), pp. 249–250; see also William Michael Rossetti, *Life of John Keats* (London, 1887), pp. 84–85; Bate, *John Keats*, pp. 368–370.

11. *Letters*, II, 252. The previous fall Shelley had begun a similar letter to the *Quarterly* for its "slanderous" attacks on him in the "Sept. No." The excerpt he gives from the review, however, shows that he was referring to the April number. (*Ibid.*, p. 130; White, *Unextinguished Hearth*, p. 142.) The *Quarterly* was frequently two months late in appearing, and Shelley, in Italy, apparently did not see this number until early October. (To the Olliers, Oct. 15, 1819, *Letters*, II, p. 126; Medwin, pp. 225–226, 501.)

12. Sir William Hale White, *Keats As Doctor and Patient* (Oxford, 1938), pp 31–35.

13. Mar. 26, 1821, *The Keats Circle*, ed. Hyder Edward Rollins (Cambridge, 1965), I. 232. John Hamilton Reynolds was one of Keats's closest friends. (Robert Gittings, *John Keats* [Boston, 1968], p. 406.)

14. Edmund Blunden, *Leigh Hunt's "Examiner" Examined*, p. 153.

15. Maria Gisborne's journal for June 23, 1820, recorded a meeting with Keats: "he had lately been ill also, and spoke but little"; and on July 12: "I was much pained by the sight of poor Keats, under sentence of death from Dr. Lamb. He never spoke and looks emaciated." (Gisborne & Williams, pp., 36, 40.) "Dr. Lamb" was Dr. William Lambe, known also to Shelley and Harriet Shelley, a vegetarian and specialist on tuberculosis. (*Letters*, II, 15n; *Shelley and His Circle*, III, 259, IV, 681.) Shelley wrote to Keats on July 27 that he had heard from John Gisborne that "you continue to wear a consumptive appearance." (*Letters*, II, 220.) The letter from Gisborne is apparently lost.

16. On May 4, 1821, Shelley wrote to Byron: "The account of Keats is, I fear, too true. Hunt tells me that in the first paroxysms of his disappointment he burst a blood-vessel; and thus laid the foundation of a rapid consumption." (*Letters*, II, 289; see also to Byron, Apr. 16, 1821, *ibid.*, p. 284.) This is clearly the same story that underlay the November 1820 letter to Gifford: "The agony of his sufferings at length produced the rupture of a blood vessel in the lungs, & the usual process of consumption appears to have begun.' '(*Ibid.*, p. 252.) It is also the same story as in the Preface to *Adonais*: "The savage criticism on his Endymion, which appeared in the Quarterly Review, produced the most violent effect on his susceptible mind; the agitation thus originated ended in the rupture of a blood-vessel in the lungs; a rapid consumption ensued." (*Works*, II, 387.) Shelley, therefore, received the story from Hunt prior to the November 1820 letter to Gifford. He perhaps heard it also from the Gisbornes after their return to Italy in October 1820, for if Hunt passed the story on to Shelley, he may also have told it to the Gisbornes. (Gittings, *Keats*, p. 400.) All this conjecture, of course, was in the days before the bacterial basis for tuberculosis was known.

17. *Don Juan*, XI, 60. Byron's short but savage "Who Killed John Keats?" was not published until 1830; the *Don Juan* canto was published in August 1823. (Byron, *Poetical Works*, ed. Ernest Hartley Coleridge [London, 1903,] VI, 76, xvi.) On Aug. 6, 1821, Shelley visited Byron at Ravenna, where they talked until five in the morning. On Aug. 7 Byron, who had previously been skeptical on the point, wrote to Murray of "poor Keats now slain by the *Quarterly Review*." (*Byron*, V, 338.) Shelley had earlier, attempted to convince Byron in a letter of Apr. 16, but apparently without success. On Aug. 22, 1821, Shelley wrote to Medwin: "I am just retu[rned] from a visit to Lord Byron at Ravenna, whom I have succeeded in rousing to attack the Quarterly." (*Letters*, II, 342.)

18. To Charles Ollier, c. Aug. 20, 1819, *Letters*, II, 111; see also to Charles and James Ollier, Sept. 6, 1819; to Marianne Hunt, Oct. 29, 1820; to Peacock, Nov. 8, 1820; to John Gisborne, June 18, 1822, *ibid.*, pp. 117–118, 239, 244, 434. It is curious that in none of these letters does Shelley mention the "great odes" nor *The Eve of St. Agnes*, which also appeared in the *Lamia* volume. Presumably it was the humanitarian theme in *Hy-*

perion that particularly aroused him. So, too, with Byron: "His fragment of *Hyperion* seems actually inspired by the Titans, and is as sublime as Aeschylus." Ms. note, Nov. 12, 1821, *Byron*, IV, 491.

19. To Claire Clairmont, *Letters*, II, 268, 284. On Mar. 28 Horace Smith wrote to Shelley: "You never said anything of Keats, who, I see died at Rome under lamentable circumstances." (*Shelley and Mary*, II, 600, where the letter was wrongly dated Apr. 3. The Ms. in the Abinger collection shows the correct date to be Mar. 28.) This letter bears a Pisa receipt postmark of Apr. 11. Mary Shelley noted the arrival of a letter on Apr. 11 "that overturns us." (*Mary Shelley's Journal*, p. 152.) This was Horace Smith's letter, as shown not only by the postmark but also by the fact that it contained news of the (temporary, as it turned out) cutting off of Shelley's allowance. It was this news that did the overturning rather than Keats's death. Keats's death was noted in *The Examiner* of Mar. 25. If this issue or a clipping from it had been sent to Shelley by overland mail, he could have learned of Keats's death by Apr. 8. He had certainly not received news of it by Apr. 5, for on that day Mary Shelley wrote to Maria Gisborne: "Keats, they say, is dying at Rome." (Mary Shelley, *Letters*, I, 138.) This appears to echo a letter from Leigh Hunt of Mar. 1: 'Poor Keats! have you heard of him? They send word from Rome that he is dying." (*Shelley and Mary*, p. 592.) That Apr. 11 was almost certainly the day on which Shelley received news of the death is, curiously enough, indicated by the fact that it is not recorded in Mary's journal. If it had been received on any other day, it would surely have been recorded; but on Apr. 11 she could have omitted it in the flurry caused by the shattering news of the loss of income.

20. Shelley made somewhat contradictory statements on the time of beginning *Adonais*. On July 16, 1821, he wrote to Byron, enclosing a copy of the poem: "I send you—as Diomed gave Glaucus his brazen arms for those of gold—some verses I wrote on the death of Keats—written, indeed, immediately after the arrival of the news." On June 5 he wrote to the Gisbornes: "I have been engaged these last days in composing a poem on the death of Keats, which will shortly be finished." He wrote to Claire Clairmont on June 8: "I have lately been composing a poem on Keats." On the same day he informed Charles Ollier: "My poem is finished and consists of about forty Spenser stanzas." (*Letters*, II, 308, 293-294, 296, 297.) He thus implies to Byron that he wrote the poem in a few days in mid-April, and to Gisborne that he wrote it in a few days in early June. Both statements are apparently the result of Shelley's penchant for implying more rapid composition than was the case, and both are slightly ambiguous. Shelley does not state to Byron that he actually finished the poem in the days following the news of Keats's death. "Written" could imply that he simply began it then and continued to work on it later. Nor does he state to Gisborne that he actually began the poem these "last days," only that he was working on it then. His "lately" to Claire is even more vague.

In the notebook manuscript of *Adonais*, which is obviously an early draft, the last stanza is st. 43. (Ingpen, pp. 671–687.) Apparently the poem originally contained only forth-three stanzas, and it was this version that Shelley was writing about to Gisborne, Claire Clairmont, and Ollier. But when he wrote to Byron on July 16, the poem was published and he was referring to its final length of fifty-five stanzas. Despite Shelley's skill and speed in composition, it would have been impossible for him to compose either forty-three or fifty-five Spenserian stanzas of *Adonais* in a few days in either April or June. The notebook manuscript also shows that he had difficulties in composition and did much revising. The probability is that he began *Adonais* in April and had completed forty-three stanzas by June 8. However, the word "immediately" in the letter to Byron should not be taken literally, for it is unlikely that Shelley began an elegy on Keats "immediately" after hearing of his death, because he was too greatly upset by news of the stoppage of his income; but on Apr. 13 a second letter from Horace Smith made him believe that the threat to his income was a "false alarm." (To Claire Clairmont, Apr. 13, 1821, *Letters*, II, 281.) On Apr. 16 he wrote to Byron: "Young Keats, whose 'Hyperion' showed so great a promise, died late in Rome." (*Ibid.*, p. 284.) And on Apr. 17 Mary wrote to Leigh Hunt: "We have been much shocked by Keats' death—and sorry it was in no way permitted us to be of any use to him since his arrival in Italy." (Mary Shelley, *Letters*, I, 139.) In view of this interest in Keats on Apr. 16 and 17 and Shelley's recovery from the shock of Smith's first letter by Apr. 13, Shelley's July 16 statement to Byron indicates a date of Apr. 15–20 for the beginning of *Adonais*. That Shelley was at work on the poem in early May is perhaps indicated by a letter to Byron on May 4, containing parallels in theme and language with *Adonais*: the reviewers as the cause of Keats' death; the delicate nature of Keats, making him especially susceptible to such attacks; Shelley's own "indifference" to such attacks; the contrast of Keats's response with Byron's counterattack in *English Bards and Scotch Reviewers.* (*Letters,* II, 289.)

As for the date of finishing composition, on June 8 Shelley wrote to Charles Ollier: "My poem is finished, and consists of about forty Spenser stanzas." On June 16 he informed Gisborne: "this day I sent it to the press"; and on the same day he wrote to Claire Clairmont: "My elegy on him is finished . . . I send it to the press here [at Pisa], & you will soon have a copy." On July 4 he wrote to his Irish friend, John Taaffe, at Florence: "I do not await the slow progress of Rosini [the printer of *Adonais*] before I thank you for your kind letter . . . Accept also my thanks for your strictures on *Adonais.* The first I have adopted, by cancelling in the preface the whole passage relating to my private wrongs." He refused a second suggestion by Taaffe, to eliminate in st. 34 the "introduction of the name of *Christ* as an antithesis to *Cain.*" (*Ibid.,* pp. 297, 300, 302, 306.) Thus, Shelley was still making changes in the Preface and considering changes in the poem itself as late as July 3. Taaffe was also seeing his own translation of Dante through the printer at Pisa that was handling *Adonais,* and Shelley was helping him with the proofs. (Ibid., p. 293; Richard Harter Fogle, "Dante and Shelley's *Adonais,*" *Bucknell Review,* XV [December 1967], 11–21.) Apparently, as a return courtesy, Shelley allowed Taaffe to see proofs of *Adonais.* The first copy of the volume was ready by July 12, when Mary recorded for the first time: "Read Shelley's 'Adonais' "; and on July 13 Shelley wrote to the Gisbornes: "I send you the only copy of Adonais the printer has yet delivered." (*Mary Shelley's Journal,* p. 158; *Letters,* II, 307.) Thus, the poem was sent to press about the middle of June or shortly thereafter but was not printed until or shortly before July 12. As Forman (p. 103) remarked, this is "a long time for the printing of a thin pamphlet [25 pages in quarto], and seems to indicate some trouble given to the printer in the shape of corrections while at press." No doubt Shelley thought the poem was finished on June 8 in about forty, probably in forty-three, stanzas, then revised it until June 16, when he sent it to the printer, probably still in about forty stanzas. Between sending it off and its final printing he composed another twelve stanzas or so and revised the proofs. Mary noted in her journal that Shelley went to Pisa on several days during the period in which the poem was in the press: on June 16 (when, he informed Gisborne, he sent it to the press), 18, 20, 22 (with Mary), 27, and July 7. (*Mary Shelley's Journal,* pp. 156–157.) If Shelley took the manuscript and proofs to the printer himself, as Mary's journal indicates, his last journey to Pisa on July 7 was probably the last date on which new or corrected material was given to the printer. Thus the composition of *Adonais* probably spanned about April 15 to July 7. Mary's journal and letters make no mention of *Adonais* during this period, which must mean that Shelley did not show the poem to her until it was finished. The Preface shows that Shelley also intended to publish a separate "London edition" of *Adonais,* but no such edition appeared. (*Works,* II, 387.) The poem first appeared in England in *The Literary Chronicle,* Dec. 1, 1821. (Forman, p. 104; White, *Unextinguished Hearth,* pp. 285–286.)

21. *Works,* II, 387.

22. *Ibid.,* p. 406; *Letters,* II, 251; *Works,* II, 408. The fact that these remarks were at first retained on proof shows how strongly Shelley felt about then.

23. See Kenneth Neill Cameron, "Shelley vs. Southey: New Light on an Old Quarrel," PMLA, LVII (June 1942), 489–512. The January issue of the *Quarterly* did not appear until April, and Mary recorded reading it on May 29 and 30, 1817, while she and Shelley were on a visit in London from Marlow. Southey's authorship of his *Quarterly* articles was well known in literary circles.

24. For parallels between the *Quarterly* article and Southey's letters on Shelley, see Cameron, "Shelley vs. Southey," pp. 494–505; *New Letters of Robert Southey,* ed. Kenneth Curry (New York: Columbia University Press, 1965), II, 20, 156, 240, 249. The pseudonym "The Hermit of Marlow," under which Shelley wrote the pamphlet, would not have been difficult for Southey to penetrate, for Shelley was the only inhabitant of the little village of Marlow capable of producing such a work, and he had not attempted to keep his identity a secret. He sent the pamphlet to almost every prominent liberal in London and informed Hogg, the Olliers, J. J. Stockdale, William Hone, Leigh and John Hunt, Thomas Hookham, Peacock, and Godwin of his authorship. Southey's antagonism toward Shelley in this period is shown by a letter he wrote to Wordsworth, May 5 and 8, 1817: "Hunt with all his family is on a visit to—Shelley [at Marlow], and in a fair way of becoming as infamous in his domestic conduct." (*Ibid.,* II, 249.)

25. *Quarterly Review,* XVI (January 1817), 538–539, 540–541.

26. *Crabb Robinson on Books and Their Writers*, ed. Edith J. Morley (London, 1938), I, 212; *Quarterly Review*, XVIII (January 1818), 328–329; to Leigh Hunt, Dec. 20, 1818, *Letters*, II, 65–66; see also White, *Unextinguished Hearth*, pp. 124–125. The review of *Foliage* was probably written by either John Wilson Croker or Sir John Taylor Coleridge.

27. Robert Southey to the Editor of *The Courier*, Dec. 8, 1824, in *Byron*, VI, 396; Leigh Hunt to Mary Shelley, Mar. 9, 1819, *Shelley and Mary*, II, 368.

28. White, *Unextinguished Hearth*, pp. 133–142. In 1876 Archibald Milman, son of Henry Hart Milman, wrote to Lady Shelley that this review was not by his father (as Shelley later suspected) but Sir John Taylor Coleridge. Its general approach toward Shelley and its specific charges, however, are remarkably parallel to Southey's 1817 *Quarterly* attack on the "Hermit of Marlow." It pictures an arrogant, impulsive young man of low moral character who embraces radicalism without adequate thought, e.g.: "These are indeed bold convictions for a young and inexperienced man, imperfectly educated, irregular in his application, and shamefully dissolute in his conduct." The review also hints at the "desertion" and suicide of Harriet: "if we might withdraw the veil of private life, and tell what we *now* know about him, it would be indeed a disgusting picture that we should exhibit." (White, *Unextinguished Hearth*, pp. 137, 142.) The similarities between these two articles explain Shelley's conclusion that Southey wrote the second one also; indeed, it seems likely that Southey had talked over these matters with Sir John Taylor Coleridge.

29. To Leigh Hunt, Nov. 2, 1819; to *The Quarterly*, October ? 1819; to Southey, June 26, 1820, *Letters*, II, 134, 130, 204.

30. *The Correspondence of Robert Southey with Caroline Bowles*, ed. Edward Dowden (London, 1881), pp. 359–360; *Letters*, II, 205n, 230–231.

31. *Correspondence of Robert Southey*, pp. 364–365; *Letters*, II, 232–233n. Following Shelley's death, Southey wrote to Joseph Cottle on June 25, 1823: "Probably you are not acquainted with half his [Shelley's] execrable history. I know the whole, and as he gave me a fitting opportunity, read him such a lecture on it as he deserved." (Southey, *New Letters*, II, 249.)

32. *Works*, IV, 65–66; see also Rogers, p. 217.

33. *Works*, II, 407; see also to Hunt, Dec. 22, 1818, *Letters*, II, 66: "I am almost certain that Southey, not Gifford, wrote that criticism on your poems. I never saw Gifford in my life, & it is impossible that he should have taken a personal hatred to me."

34. *Works*, II, 387–388; *Letters*, II, 230.

35. To the Editor of *The Courier*, Dec. 8, 1824, *Byron* VI, 397n.

36. The edition of Bion and Moscus I have used is that in the Loeb Classical Library: *The Greek Bucolic Poets*, trans. J. M. Edmonds (New York, 1912).

37. For a mythological and metaphysical interpretation, see Earl R. Wasserman, *The Subtler Language* (Baltimore, 1959), pp. 311–318, e.g. p. 313: "Consequently, here *Adonais* is not only Keats, but also the tragic Lord of a religion of materialistic monism, and the death of the divinity therefore appears to contain in itself the death of Nature." Nothing in the poem indicates that Shelley had such concepts in mind.

38. See Milton, *Paradise Lost*, ed. A. W. Verity (Cambridge, 1929), II, 686–688; Baker, pp. 241–242. Shelley was certainly aware of the invocations to Urania by Dante (*Purgatorio*, XXIX, 40–42) and Milton (*Paradise Lost*, VII, 1–12.)

39. Feb. 15, 1821, *Letters*, II, 261. Baker (pp. 246–247) argued that Urania is the Platonic One: "When Adonais enters the realm of the immortals, he is permanently reunited with Urania who, in the meantime, has been dissolved in light and transformed from an incarnated goddess into the mystical 'One,' or the World-Soul." (See also Wasserman, *The Subtler Language*, pp. 350–355.) There is no evidence, however, to associate Urania with the Platonic One, and if Shelley had intended Adonais to be reunited with her after death, presumably he would have said so.

40. July 16, 1821, *Letters*, II, 308–309. The same fear that he would be considered to be exaggerating Keats's claims as a poet motivated Shelley's announcment in the Preface that he would "subjoin to the London edition of this poem, a criticism upon the claims of its lamented object to be classed among the writers of the highest genius who have adorned our age." (*Works*, II, 387.) He informed Ollier on Sept. 25, 1821, that he had not written the criticism because he had mislaid the *Lamia* volume (*Lamia, Isabella, The Eve of St. Agnes and Other Poems*, 1820), which contained *Hyperion*. (Letters, II, 355.) The volume found after his death had been lent to him by Leigh Hunt. In writing to Byron, however, Shelley softened his own view of Keats, knowing of Byron's skepticism on the subject. A letter to John Gisborne on June 18, 1822, comes closer to Shelley's real feelings: "The 'Adonais' I wished to have had a fair chance,

both because it is a favourite with me and on account of the memory of Keats, who was a poet of great genius, let the classic party say what it will." (*Letters*, II, 434.) Byron's admiration of Dryden and Pope, allied him to the "classic party," and he had been attacked by Keats along with that "party" in *Sleep and Poetry* (ll. 181–247), which Byron resented. (Marchand, II, 846, 873–874.)

41. Shelley uses a similar metaphor in *A Defence of Poetry*: "Poetry is a sword of lightning, ever unsheathed, which consumes the scabbard which would contain it." (*Works*, VII, 122.) The source of this strange metaphor of a sword or scabbard being consumed by lightning, especially of the sword being consumed before the sheath, was found by John Lavelle of Monmouth College, New Jersey, in Sir Charles Morell's *Tales of the Genii* (London, 1808), a book from which Shelley had derived an early poem, *Sadak the Wanderer*. (Cameron, *The Young Shelley*, p. 384.) In the story called "The Talisman of Oromanes; or, the Adventures of Merchant Abudab," Abudab, seeking for the talisman, comes in contact with a school of astrologers and "alchemysts," one of whom tells him (p. 60) that the "secret which I am now preparing, is what gave the great Demogorgon power to dissolve all nature." This mixture, however, fails to work, so they try again(p. 63): "'I have a cold fusion,' answered Abraharad, 'though a hot one is denied me; for I will send the lightning, which melts the sword, and leaves the scabbard unhurt, through that stubborn piece of mechanism [the crucible].'" Shelley most probably read this passage in his early youth, and it emerged from his memory ten or more years later in *Adonais* and, in a modified from, in *A Defence of Poetry*. Possibly the image blended in his mind with some lines from the third canto of Byron's *Childe Harold's Pilgrimage* (st. 97):

All that I would have sought, and all I seek,
Bear, know, feel—and yet breathe—*one* word,
And that one word were Lightning, I would speak;
But as it is, I live and die unheard,
With a most voiceless thought, sheathing it as a sword.

Possibly he was also echoing st. 6 of the same canto. It was this third canto that Shelley took to England for Byron in the fall of 1816 to give to the publisher, John Murray. He must have read it often because many passages from it have penetrated his poetry.

42. Keats wrote to Shelley on Aug. 16, 1820: "I remember you advising me not to publish my first-blights [*Poems*], on Hampstead heath." (Keats, *Letters*, II, 323.) Shelley also hints in a letter to Keats of July 27, 1820, that Keats should not have published *Endymion*, at least not without further revision. (*Letters*, II, 221.) Shelley implies in the second part of st. 17 that if Keats had waited until he had completed the *Lamia* volume before publishing, he would have been acclaimed by the critics.

43. *Verse and Prose*, pp. 39, 36. One fragment has been assumed to be a reference to Scott. (*Ibid.*, p. 36.) But its parallel to Shelley's *Peter Bell the Third*, IV, ix–xiv, and V, xii, shows that it refers to Wordsworth. Shelley was always ambivalent about Wordsworth, admiring the early humanitarian poetry but despising the later Tory sentiments. He apparently once thought that Wordsworth the poet could justifiably be placed among the mourners but later perhaps feared that his inclusion might be misunderstood and perhaps disclaimed by Wordsworth. The Fragment reads:

Next came a spirit beautiful and strong,
Wrapt in the guise of an uncomely form,
Who sometimes like a pedlar limped along
With packs upon his back, and did deform
. . . . .
Clothed in the skirts of a Scotch Puritan
With wilful . . .

44. Dec. 8, 1821, in White, *Unextinguished Hearth*, p. 287.

45. *Works*, II, 408.

46. The "unknown land" refers to the true realm of poetry. Shelley also represents himself as carrying "a light spear topped with a cypress cone" (291). He wrote in *Notes on Sculptures*: "another [maenad] has a spear with a pine cone, which was their thyrsus." (*Works*, VI, 323.) Shelley propably had in mind not so much the "divine madness" of the poet as his own maenadlike rage at human persecution and injustice. The pounding of his heart shakes the spear in his hand (294–295).

47. Either Shelley's rage made him forget that Adonais had previously been killed by

"the shaft which flies in darkness" (11–12), or he was not interested in a literal consistency.

48. Medwin, *Conversations*, pp. 182–183. Byron, in view of his own hatred of Southey—see the Dedication to *Don Juan* and *The Vision of Judgment*—doubtless rejoiced in Shelley's attack. On Aug. 30, 1821, Horace Smith acknowledged receipt of *Adonais* with high praise: "It reminded me of 'Lycidas,' more from the similarity of the subject than anything in the mode of treatment. You must expect a finish stab from Southey whenever he has an opportunity." (*Shelley and Mary*, III, 690.) As Smith received his copy of *Adonais* personally from the Gisbornes, who were then passing through Paris, he may have heard from them about the attack on Southey in the poem.

49. *Works*, III, 56.

50. *Isabella* is referred to in st. 6, and *Ode to a Nightingale* also in st. 17. (See Reiman, p. 136.) The picture of the dead Adonais and the visit of Urania to his bier generally parallels the picture of the dead Adonis and the visit of Venus to his bier in the second book of *Endymion*.

51. The phrase "the one Spirit's plastic stress" (l. 381) apparently echoes Coleridge's "Plastic and vast, one intellectual breeze" in *The Eolian Harp*, l. 47, and perhaps *Religious Musings*, l. 405, and *Sonnet to W. L. Bowles*. (See Notopoulos, p. 160.) A source for both Coleridge and Shelley could be Pope's *Essay on Man*, III, 6–12. (See to T. J. Hogg, Jan. 3, 1811, *Letters*, I, 35.)

52. Rogers, p. 263.

53. To Shelley, July 1820, *Correspondence of Robert Southey*, p. 360; *Letters*, II, 205n.

54. Aug. 17, 1820, *Letters*, II, 232; *Correspondence of Robert Southey*, p. 363.

55. Shelley may have been indebted for the dome image to Dante and to Southey's *Thalaba*—"many-coloured domes." (Notopoulos, p. 299; see also *Childe Harold's Pilgrimage*, III, xxxiii; Wasserman, *The Subtler Language*, pp. 336–339.)

56. Shelley was indebted in this stanza to the concluding speech of Act III of George Chapman's *The Conspiracy of Charles, Duke of Byron:*

> Give me a spirit that on this life's rough sea
> Loves t'have his sails fill'd with a lusty wind,
> Even till his sail-yards tremble, his masts crack
> And his rapt ship run on her side so low
> That she drinks water, and her keel plows air.
> There is no danger to a man, that knows
> What life is; there's not any law
> Exceeds his knowledge; neither is it lawful
> That he should stoop to any other law.
> He goes before them, and commands them all,
> That to himself is a law rational.

Shelley quoted this speech in part as the motto for *The Revolt of Islam*. (*Works*, I, 249.)

13. *Masks and Shadows*

1. Mary Shelley and Medwin placed the beginning date as February–March 1822. "Shelley had at this time," wrote Medwin, "also begun *The Triumph of Life*, of which we have a fragment. It advanced very slowly." (Medwin, p. 352.) "At this time" refers to the final period of Medwin's 1821–1822 visit to Pisa, which terminated on Mar. 8. If by Mar. 8, Shelley had progressed so far that Medwin could comment on his rate of composition, it is probable that the work had been underway for some weeks at least. This evidence fits Mary Shelley's statement that Shelley "threw it [*Charles the first*] aside" to begin *The Triumph of Life*, for indications are that Shelley had finished all major composition on *Charles I* by the end of January. (Note on the poems of 1822, *Works*, IV, 210.) Shelley wrote to Leigh Hunt on Mar. 2, 1822: "So you think I can make nothing of Charles the 1st. Tanto peggio. Indeed, I have written nothing for this last two months: a slight circumstance gave a new train to my ideas, and shattered the fragile edifice when half built. What motives have I to write? I *had* motives, and I thank the God of my own heart that they were totally different from those of the other asses of humanity who make mouths in the glass of time." (*Letters*, II, 394.) The "new train" of ideas, as shown by Mary's comment, must mean *The Triumph of Life*. "Written nothing" should not be taken literally, for Shelley is expressing a mood, although it prob-

ably indicates slow composition. For a similar glass image, see *The Triumph of Life,* ll. 245–251. The nature of the "slight circumstance" is not known. Perhaps it had to do with Shelley's interest in Jane Williams, which was developing about this time.

Donald H. Reiman argued that composition was probably not begun until the end of May or middle of June, but Shelley could hardly have written the poem's 548 terza rima lines between the middle of June and July 1, when he left Lerici for Leghorn and almost certainly left his manuscript behind, and it is most unlikely that he could have done so between the end of May and July 1. The state of the manuscript, with numerous cancellations and revisions, does not suggest rapid composition. In particular, Shelley seems to have had difficulty with the opening pasage of thirty-eight lines, which was rewritten three times. Reiman also argued that the state of the manuscript indicates that Shelley had all of it with him as he composed, moving back and forth to make changes, and that this "would seem almost to preclude his having written the bulk of 'The Triumph' while sailing as Mary ('Notes on poems of 1822') and Lady Jane Shelley *(Shelley Memorials)* suggested." (Reiman, *Triumph,* pp. 250, 234–238, 248.) Mary Shelley, however, did not say "the bulk of" but "much of." (Note on Poems of 1822, *Works,* IV, 211.) And the nature of Shelley's boat, with its book shelves and writing table, shows that he could have had his whole manuscript with him in it.

2. Note on the Poems of 1822, *Works,* IV, 210–211; Preface to the Posthumous Poems, *ibid.* I, xvi. Mary's statement on the final period of composition is borne out by the manuscript. Leaf 46, verso, consists of a "letter cover" postmarked May 15 at Pisa and addressed to Shelley at Lerici. It contains ll. 438–450 of *The Triumph of Life.* The date of the letter must be May 15, 1822, for only in 1822 was Shelley at Lerici. Leaf 48, verso, contains the beginning of a draft letter by Shelley to Captain Daniel Roberts, written between June 19 and 24. Leaf 49, recto, contains ll. 479–488 of *The Triumph of Life.* (Reiman, *Triumphs,* pp. 231, 249; *Letters,* II, 440.) Other leaves contain poems written to Jane Williams at Lerici—*Lines Written in the Bay of Lerici* and *To Jane:* "The keen stars were twinkling."

3. See especially Reiman, *Triumph,* and G. M. Matthews, "'The Triumph of Life': A New Text," *Studia Neophilologica,* XXXII, no. 2 (1960), 271–309. See also: F. Melian Stawell, "Shelley's *Triumph of Life,*" *Essays and Studies by Members of the English Association,* [Oxford, 1914], V, 104–131; A. C. Bradley, "Notes on Shelley's 'Triumph of Life,'" *Modern Language Review,* IX (October 1914), 441–456. In 1960 Reiman completed as a dissertation at the University of Illinois a variorum edition of the poem, which contains a valuable compilation of critical opinions omitted from his published edition. The text quoted from here is in Reiman, *Triumph,* pp. 136–211, with occasional readings from Matthews, "'The Triumph of Life.'" Both editions are based on Shelley's manuscript, which was deposited in the Bodleian Library in 1946.

4. Reiman, *Triumph,* p. 147.

5. On May 8, 1811, Shelley wrote to T. J. Hogg, of "the tremendous Gregory: the opinion of the world," apparently referring to the dictatorial policies of Gregory I. *(Shelley and His Circle,* I, 777, 779.) The best known of the "Johns" was John XXII, whom Shelley would have particularly detested for his brutal use of the Inquisition against his enemies, a number of whom he had burned at the stake, a form of punishment in which Shelley took a special interest, as shown by the conclusion of *The Revolt of Islam.*

6. See Baker, pp. 265–266. Reiman *(Triumph,* p. 60) suggested that by "cavern" Shelley meant "canyon," but that the cavern has a roof is indicated in ll. 360–361.

7. A suggestion of femaleness about the figure is especially strong in the discarded line, "And over it like a widow's veil of crepe." Life is later referred to twice as feminine (ll. 240 and 438).

8. June 29, 1822, *Letters,* II, 442.

9. To Hunt, May 1, 1820, *Letters,* II, 191; *Essay on Christianity, Works,* VI, 249.

10. See also *Queen Mab,* I, 59–60, 212–217.

11. Notes on *Queen Mab,* VI, 198, *Works,* I, 144; *A Refutation of Deism, ibid.,* VI, 49. The meaning is even clearer in a partly crossed-out first reading: "banded eyes could scan the sphere/Of the to come, the present & the past." Shelley perhaps rejected the second line because it echoed *Hellas,* l. 148.

12. Reiman, p. 27.

13. *Works,* I, 174.

14. *A Discourse on the Manners of the Antient Greeks Relative to the Subject of Love,* Notopoulos, p. 408.

15. Notes to IX, 189, *Works,* I, 142.

16. Preface to *Alastor, Works,* I, 174.

17. Reiman (*Triumph*, p. 36) suggested Milton, Dante, and Petrarch.

18. "Mutiny" provides an excellent example of the necessity of establishing a text before speculating on meaning. Until Matthews' " 'The Triumph of Life' " (1960), the word had been read as "mystery," and interpretations were offered on this basis. That Matthews' reading is correct is shown by the canceled words "rebels in their hearts" above the line. (Reiman, *Triumph*, p. 165.)

19. Reiman (*Triumph*, pp. 43–44) first suggested this sonnet as a parallel. When Mary Shelley first published it in the *Posthumous Poems of* 1824, it was titled *Political Greatness*, but in the Harvard Notebook it is titled *Sonnet to the Republic of Benevento* in Shelley's hand. (*Works*, IV, 410.) The reference is presumably to the small state of Benevento, northeast of Naples, which in 1815 was returned to the papal states.

20. Shelley also uses "will" in a pejorative sense when voicing thoughts aroused by the downfall of Napoleon: "And much I grieved to think how power and will/In opposition rule our mortal day" (228–229). See also *Prometheus Unbound* I, 354 (on Jupiter's "will"), and I, 273–274 (on Prometheus' "will"). A conflict of wills produces nonprogressive violence; hence, "will," even in Prometheus, is evil. For "will" one must substitute "Gentleness, Virtue, Wisdom and Endurance" (*Prometheus Unbound*, IV, 562–578), at least until society is changed (*ibid.*, ll. 406–411).

21. *Works*, VI, 244. The spaces indicate blanks left in the manuscript by Shelley.

22. The epigram appears also (in Plato's Greek) on the title page of *Adonais*.

23. Rousseau, *The Reveries of a Solitary* (London, 1927), pp. 37, 46, 120. Shelley read the *Reveries* in 1815; Mary Shelley, in 1816. (*Mary Shelley's Journal*, pp. 49, 55–56.)

24. To T. J. Hogg, May 14, 1811, *Shelley and His Circle*, II, 785. See also *Works*, V, 265.

25. L. 249. Shelley uses "wilderness" in the same symbolic sense in *Triumph of Life*, l. 426, and *Epipsychidion*, l. 189.

26. *Queen Mab*, VIII, 6; *Daemon of the World*, ll. 321.

27. It was also Rousseau's aim in *Reveries of a Solitary*, see e.g. his "Seventh Promenade."

28. See Bloom, pp. 265–272; Bice Chiappelli, *Il pensiero religioso di Shelley* (Rome, 1956), pp. 105, 108; Rieger, pp. 211–213; *Selected Poetry*, p. 461; Reiman, p. 157.

29. "On Love," *Works*, VI, 201.

30. Baker (pp. 267–269) and King-Hele (p. 267) argued that the phrase "touched with faint lips" means that Rousseau did not drink the nepenthe. But Bloom (p. 269) commented aptly: "If Shelley meant to indicate that Rousseau did not drink, he would surely have made so important a point a bit clearer. As it is, he employs an idiom, to touch a cup with one's lips, which means that one drinks."

31. *A Defence of Poetry*, *Works*, VII, 128; see also p. 133 and *A Philosophical View of Reform*, pp. 9, 13. Shelley's early condemnation of Rousseau in *Proposals for an Association* (1812) is not representative, for he had probably read little of Rousseau at the time. (*Works*, V, 265.)

32. To T. L. Peacock, July 12, 1816, to T. J. Hogg, July 18, 1816, *Letters*, I, 485, 487–488, 494; *Works*, VI, 124, 247–248.

33. Voltaire, however, who was usually considered as important a precurser of the French Revolution as Rousseau, is shown as chained (l. 235). The explanation must lie in Shelley's different attitude toward the two. While he considered Rousseau a "poet," a positive, creative thinker who felt for mankind as a whole, he put Voltaire among the lesser "reasoners and mechanists." (*A Defence of Poetry*, *Works*, VII, 133, 131.) Nevertheless, Shelley admired Voltaire and linked him with Rousseau in *An Address to the People on the Death of the Princess Charlotte*. (*Ibid.*, VI, 74.)

34. *Works*, VI, 164.

35. The indications from Shelley's letters are uncertain. On Oct. 22, 1821, in writing of current misinterpretations of *Epipsychidion*, he commented to Gisborne: "I intend to write a Symposium of my own to set all this right." Eight months earlier, on Feb. 16, 1821, when dispatching *Epipsychidion* to Ollier, he had written: "I am employed in high and new designs in verse; but they are the labours of years, perhaps." Again he wrote to Ollier on Feb. 22, 1821, in discussing his plans for *Charles the First*: "My thoughts aspire to a production of a far higher character; but the execution of it will require some years." If all these references are to the poem of which *The Triumph of Life* is the only extant part, then the whole work would have been of great length and would have centered around the theme of love (a modern "Symposium"). However, Shelley stated to Leigh Hunt on Mar. 2, 1822, in regard to *Charles the First*: "a slight circumstance gave a new train to my ideas and shattered the fragile edifice when half built"—the "new train of ideas" being *The Triumph of Life*. (*Letters*, II, 363, 263, 269,

394.) As Shelley ended his work on *Charles the First* in January 1822, the new ideas must have come to him at that time. Moreover, chariots are described in the opening scene of *Charles the First,* the basis for which Shelley found in Bulstrode Whitelocke. It can hardly be a coincidence that chariots are featured in both the play and the poem. Perhaps the chariots in Whitelocke reminded Shelley of Petrarch's *Triumphs* and influenced him to reread it. At any rate, the indication is that the specific idea for *The Triumph of Life* did not come to Shelley until at least January, 1822. This does not, of course, mean that the chariot and other specific concepts could not have been enveloped in a larger work on the subject of love for which Shelley only had a general concept earlier, but the "Symposium" and other references cannot be a plan for the existing fragment of *The Triumph of Life.* (See William Cherubini, "Shelley's 'Own Symposium,' *The Triumph of Life, Studies in Philology,* XXXIX [July, 1942], 559–560.)

36. Bradley, "Notes on Shelley's 'Triumph of Life,'" pp. 441–442; see also Dowden, II, 506; Stawell, "Shelley's *Triumph of Life,*" pp. 110, 114, 122–123, 130–131; White, II, 372–373, 630–631.

37. Reiman, *Triumph,* pp. 82–83. Before Matthews' edition, "fold" was misread "gold."

38. *Works,* II, 175.

14. *The Contemporary World and Its Promise*

1. For Shelley's later views on *Queen Mab,* see Cameron, pp. 405–407. On *The Revolt of Islam,* see to Charles Ollier, Feb. 16, 1821: "Is there any expectation of a second edition of the 'Revolt of Islam'? I have many corrections to make in it, and one part will be wholly remodelled." See also to Charles Ollier, Sept. 25, 1821. (*Letters,* II, 263, 354.)

2. Shelley considered three subjects for his projected work: "the story of Tasso," "the book of Job," and "Prometheus Unbound." (Mary Shelley, Note on *Prometheus Unbound, Works,* II, 268.) With his classical schooling Shelley no doubt had long been acquainted with the Prometheus legend. He referred to it in 1813 in *A Vindication of Natural Diet* and in the Notes to *Queen Mab.* (*Works,* VI, 6; I, 158.) There is no evidence however, that he was seriously interested in the legend until the appearance of Mary Shelley's *Frankenstein* in 1818, subtitled *The Modern Prometheus.* As *Frankenstein* was conceived and partly written at Geneva in the summer of 1816, when Byron was writing his own *Prometheus,* perhaps Byron impressed Shelley with the legend's possibilities for symbolic humanitarian representation. It seems likely that Byron showed Shelley his own poem at Geneva. Certainly Shelley must have read it in *The Prisoner of Chilon* volume later in 1816, for its concept of Prometheus is similar to his own, and it is verbally echoed in Shelley's play. (Compare, e.g., the last two lines of Byron's *Prometheus* with *Prometheus Unbound,* I, 700–701.) But Shelley apparently got the actual idea for the play when he and Mary were crossing the Alps on their way to Italy in 1818. On Mar. 26, 1818, Mary Shelley recorded of Les Echelles: "The scene is like that described in the 'Prometheus' of Aeschylus; vast rifts and caverns in granite precipices," (*Mary Shelley's Journal,* pp. 94–95.) Five years later on her solitary journey back to England, she passed the same mountain and wrote to Leigh Hunt that its "dark high precipieces [sic] towering above, gave S the idea of his Prometheus." (Aug. 1, 1823, Mary Shelley, *Letters,* I, 239–240.)

Mary's Note on *Prometheus Unbound* reveals that Shelley "meditated the subject of his drama" during the succeeding months at Milan, Pisa, Leghorn, and the baths of Lucca. (*Works,* II, 268–269.) As for the date of beginning composition, Mary's journal reads: "*Monday* Sept. 2–14. In four days, Saturday 5th, arrive at Este. Poor Clara is dangerously ill. Shelley is very unwell, from taking poison in Italian cakes. He writes his Drama of 'Prometheus.'" (*Mary Shelley's Journal,* p. 105.) In her Note on the poems of 1818 she indicated that *Prometheus Unbound* was begun at Este, and as Shelley arrived at Este on or about Aug. 25, the earliest possible time of beginning composition would be late August. Although the journal entry is not specific, it suggests that when Mary arrived at Este on Sept. 5, Shelley was already at work on the drama for she recorded not that he "begins" but that he "writes" it.

Shelley continued writing until Sept. 21, for Mary recorded in a collective entry on Sept. 22 that "Shelley writes." Apparently he wrote at a good rate of speed, for on Sept. 22 he asked Mary to bring his manuscript to him at Venice, which he told her consisted of twenty-six sheets. On Sept. 22 Shelley went to Venice, where the ensuing days were taken up with the tragedy of little Clara's death. On Oct. 8 he wrote to Peacock that he had "just finished the first act." On Nov. 5 the Shelley ménage left on the long journey to Naples, where they remained Dec. 1–Feb. 28, 1819. On Jan. 24, 1819, Shelley wrote to Peacock: "At present I write little else but poetry, and little of that. My 1st Act of Prometheus is complete." (*Letters*, II, 39–40, 43, 70–71.) This comment may indicate further work on Act I up to that date, but if so, it was slight. The probability is that Act I was begun in late August and completed by Oct. 8, 1818.

On Mar. 5, 1819, the Shelleys arrived at Rome, where they remained until June 10. "At last, when at Rome," wrote Mary in her Note on *Prometheus Unbound*, "during a bright and beautiful spring, he gave up his whole time to the composition." The drama, Shelley states in the Preface, "was chiefly written upon the mountainous ruins of the Baths of Caracalla." In her Preface to the *Posthumous Poems*, Mary stated that it "was written among the flower-grown ruins at Rome." (*Works*, II, 269, 172; I, xvi.) On Mar. 13 Mary recorded a visit to the baths of Caracalla. (*Mary Shelley's Journal*, p. 117.) On Mar. 23 Shelley praised them to Peacock. On Apr. 6 he informed Peacock that "My Prometheus Unbound is just finished & in a month or two I shall send it." (*Letters*, II, 84–85, 94.) On Apr. 25 Mary recorded: "Read Shelley's drama." (*Mary Shelley's Journal*, p. 120.) This entry suggests that the first three acts were completed by Apr. 25. But there is the possibility of revision until Sept. 6, when the poem was being transcribed for shipment to the publisher. (To the Olliers, *Letters*, II, 116; Sept. 10–12, *Mary Shelley's Journal*, p. 124.)

On Oct. 2 the Shelleys moved to Florence. "At first," wrote Mary in her Note on *Prometheus Unbound*, "he completed the drama in three acts. It was not till several months after, when at Florence, that he conceived that a fourth act . . . ought to be added." (*Works*, II, 269.) On Dec. 23 Shelley wrote from Florence to the Gisbornes at Leghorn: "I have just finished an additional act to Prometheus which Mary is now transcribing." (*Letters*, II, 165; see also to Charles Ollier, c. Dec. 25—given in *Letters*, II, 162 as Dec. 15, but shown to be later by the letter to the Gisbornes on Dec. 23). Act IV, therefore, was written sometime between Oct. 2 and Dec. 23, 1819. As Shelley was engaged during late October and early November on *Peter Bell* and the letter in defense of Richard Carlile, and as Mary gave birth to their son, Percy Florence, on Nov. 12, it is probable that the act was mainly composed between the middle of November and Dec. 23. Shelley thus worked on *Prometheus Unbound* over a period of about fifteen months, during which he also wrote *The Cenci, The Mask of Anarchy, A Philosophical View of Reform, Julian and Maddalo, Peter Bell* and the open letter on Richard Carlile.

There has been some uncertainty over the shipping of the manuscript to England. On Sept. 21, 1819, Shelley informed Peacock that he was sending *Prometheus Unbound* (the first three acts) to John Gisborne, who had left Italy for England on Sept. 12, to deliver to Peacock. Peacock was to pass it on to the publishers (Olliers) when so directed. But on Oct. 13–14 Shelley told Maria Gisborne, who was still in Italy, to send a copy of the poem by ship to the publisher along with printed volumes of *The Cenci*, and the ship for some reason did not actually sail until mid-December. On Dec. 23, 1819, Shelley informed the Gisbornes, then both in Leghorn, that he was sending them the manuscript of Act IV for their inspection. (*Ibid.*, II, 120, 126, 165.) This final act the Gisbornes were to send to the Olliers in London, and in a letter of Dec. 28 to them Mary assumed that they were doing so. (Mary Shelley, *Letters*, I, 92.) On Mar. 6, 1820, Shelley informed the Olliers that they should soon receive the package shipped by sea in December, which included both printed books of *The Cenci* and the manuscript of *Prometheus Unbound*, Acts I-III. Both in his Letter of c. Dec. 25 to the Olliers, Shelley noted that Act IV would be received "in a few days" (i.e., about Jan. 15) and that "Prometheus" should be "printed without delay," which indicates that Act IV was sent by land mail and not, as were Act I-III, shipped by sea. (*Letters*, II, 174, 164.) Shelley's sending of Acts I-III by sea and Act IV by land—so that the two packages would hopefully arrive in London at about the same time—suggests that he had formed the intention of writing Act IV before he shipped off Acts I-III in mid-October 1819.

The first edition (1820) of *Prometheus Unbound* contains many printer's errors. Fortunately there is a manuscript in Shelley's hand in the Bodleian Library, as well as several early drafts of parts of the drama. (See Zillman, *Variorum*, Appendix A.) Zillman's *Shelley's Prometheus Unbound, The Text and the Drafts* (New Haven, 1968) presents an eclectic text. The manuscript text was printed in *The Reader's Shelley*, ed. Carl H. Grabo and Martin J. Freeman (New York, 1942), pp. 111–195, and is the edition basically used here.

3. *Letters*, II, 127, 174. See also to Peacock, Apr. 6, 1819: "I think the execution is better than any of my former attempts"; and to Charles Ollier, c. Dec. 25, 1819: "My *Prometheus* is the best thing I ever wrote." His remark of May 4, 1821, to Byron that

the "'*Prometheus*' is also a very imperfect poem" should not be taken literally, for his comments on his own works to Byron were often derogatory. Nor should his remark to Charles Ollier of Sept. 25, 1821, that *Adonais* "is the least imperfect of my compositions" be misread. He states not that *Adonais* is his most significant poem but only the "least imperfect." (*Ibid.*, pp. 94, 162, 290, 355.)

4. To Hunt, May 26, 1820: "Have you read my Prometheus yet? but that will not sell—it is written only for the elect. I confess I am vain enough to like it." (*Letters*, II, 200.) Again Shelley's statement should not be interpreted literally, for his failures had led him into a self-deprecatory pose. Certainly Shelley hoped that his poem would reach the best minds in the liberal intellectual reading public and would have a wide audience in future generations.

5. See James George Frazer, *The Myths of the Origin of Fire* (London, 1930), pp. 193–200; Zillman, *Variorum*, pp. 723–724.

6. Hesiod appears in *A Vindication of Natural Diet* (1813) and in Shelley's reading list for 1815. (*Works*, I, 6; White, II, 541.)

7. Hesiod, *Theogony*, *Works* trans. Hugh J. Evelyn White, Loeb Classical Library (Cambridge, 1914), pp. 87–90.

8. Hesiod, *Works and Days*, *Works*, p. 11; see also *Prometheus Unbound*, II, iv. 86.

9. *Theogony*, *Works*, pp. 105, 117. The two imprisonments are not in Hesiod but, as they are in Aeschylus, must have been an early tradition. For a brief account of the myth as it was known in Shelley's time, see Lemprière's *Classical Dictionary*, under Prometheus.

10. See *Hygini Fabulae*, ed. H. J. Rose (London, 1933), p. 45. Hyginus, though living in Roman times, made use of early Greek sources that are now lost.

11. For a reconstruction of Aeschylus' *Prometheus Unbound* from the extant fragments, see Aeschylus, *The Prometheus Bound*, ed. George Thomson (Cambridge, 1932), pp. 18–32.

12. Aeschylus, *Prometheus Bound*, ed. and trans. Gilbert Murray (London, 1959), pp. 20, 25, 29, 43, 44, 63, 68.

13. Zillman, *Variorum*, pp. 727–728.

14. In announcing to Peacock on Oct. 8, 1818, that he has just completed Act I of *Prometheus Unbound*, Shelley asks: "Will you tell me what there is in Cicero about a drama supposed to have been written by Aeschylus under this title?" (*Letters*, II, 43.) The apparent parallels between the Cicero fragment and Shelley's opening scene, however, suggest that he had either previously read it or read about it.

15. *Poems*, I, 597; see also *Prométhée Délivré, ed.* and trans. Louis Cazamian (Paris, 1942), pp. 13–14. For the transference of the locale of Prometheus' suffering from the Caucasus to the Hindu Kush Mountains, see Strabo, *Geography*, Loeb Classical Library edition, trans. Horace Leonard Jones (New York, 1917), I, 12–15. The Hindu Kush Mountains are west of the Himalayas. Shelley, however, may have thought of both as one chain because there was considerable confusion in his day over the term Indian Caucasus. Curtius, e.g., referred to the whole "central chain from E. to W." as the Caucasus. (William Smith, *Dictionary of Greek and Roman Geography* [London, 1854], II, 552; see also Joseph Raben, "Shelley's *Prometheus Unbound*: Why the Indian Caucasus?" *Keats-Shelley Journal*, XII [Winter 1963], 95–106.)

16. See Raben, "Shelley's *Prometheus Unbound*," p. 102. Shelley had read of the Vale of Cashmere in Lady Morgan's novel *The Missionary* in 1811. He used it also in *Zeinab and Kathema* and *Alastor*. (*Esdaile Notebook*, pp. 275–277.) In the map of Hindustan in Abraham Rees's *Cyclopedia*, a work Shelley consulted, the valley of Cashmere is shown between the Himalayas and the Hindu Kush ranges. In an early draft manuscript Shelley referred to the Indus and to Lahore with its cave temples. (Zillman, *Variorum*, pp. 644, 645, 646; *Works*, I, 159; Cameron, p. 390; see also *Prometheus Unbound*, III, iii, 155.)

17. See Zillman, *Variorum*, pp. 313–316.

18. *Works*, II, 171–172.

19. See Aeschylus, *The Prometheus Bound*, ed. Thomson, p. 6. The main political thrust of Aeschylus' play was to condemn despotic rule. Various phrases, however, left open the possibility for a compromise between Jupiter and Prometheus.

20. *Works*, II, 174–175. "A Passion for Reforming the World" was the title of ch. XVI of Robert Forsyth, *The Principles of Moral Science* (Edinburgh 1805). (Zillman, *Variorum*, p. 307.)

21. To Leigh Hunt, May 1, 1820, *Letters*, II, 191.

22. Zillman, *Variorum*, p. 641; *Works*, II, 173.

23. The interpretations of the poem may be followed most succinctly in Zillman,

Variorum, pp. 27–112, 302–630. Since Zillman wrote, the only full-scale interpretation is that in Earl R. Wasserman, *Shelley's Prometheus Unbound: A Critical Reading* (Baltimore, 1965).

24. *Works*, VII, 53–54.

25. Shelley is perhaps echoing and compressing passages on the French Revolution from his old favorite, Volney's *Ruins*, which he had previously used in *The Revolt of Islam*. (See Kenneth Neill Cameron, "A Major Source of the 'Revolt of Islam,'" PMLA, LVI [March 1941], 178–183.)

26. To Elizabeth Hitchener, Jan. 2, 7, 1812, *Letters*, I, 218, 223.

27. *Works*, I, 240–242; see also *Proposals for an Association*, *Works*, V, 264–266; *A Philosophical View of Reform*, *ibid.*, VII, 13–15; Byron, *Childe Harold's Pilgrimage*, III, 765–796, and IV, 856–882.

28. *Works*, VII, 19–20, 51–52.

29. Zillman, *Variorum*, p. 727.

30. London (1740), III, 78, 81. For Banier's influence, see Edward B. Hungerford, *Shores of Darkness* (New York, 1941), pp. 177–178, 183.

31. *Queen Mab*, IV, 33–70; see also Cameron, p. 251.

32. Shelley had a particular interest in religious mania. See *Queen Mab*, V, 111–112: "or religion/Drives his wife raving mad," to which Shelley adds the note: "I am acquainted with a lady of considerable accomplishments, and the mother of a numerous family whom the Christian Religion has goaded to incurable insanity. A parallel case is, I believe, within the experience of every physician." (*Works*, I, 140.)

33. Burnings of religious rebels are also depicted in the execution of Laon and Cythna in *The Revolt of Islam*.

34. Zillman, *Variorum*, p. 163.

35. *Queen Mab*, VII, 219–224, as noted in Rieger, p. 69.

36. The character of Shelley's Mercury was not suggested by Aeschylus' Mercury, who is bullying and arrogant, but was perhaps derived in part from his Hephaestus.

37. *A Philosophical View of Reform*, *Works*, VII, 7, 20; *Works*, II, 173; *A Defence of Poetry*, *Works*, VII, 140.

38. *Ibid.*, pp. 140, 112.

39. Hazlitt wrote in his essay on Godwin in *The Spirit of the Age*: "No work in our time gave such a blow to the philosophic mind of the country as the celebrated enquiry concerning *Political Justice*. Tom Paine was considered for the time a Tom Fool to him; Edmund Burke a flashy sophist." (Everyman Edition [New York, 1960], p. 183.)

40. *Works*, VII, 189.

41. *Works*, I, 241–242.

42. Zillman, *Variorum*, p. 643.

43. *The Masque of Anarchy*, st. 4; see Ch. 9 above, n. 12.

44. *A Defence of Poetry*, *Works*, VII, 140.

45. For the controversy over whether "recall" means remember or revoke, see Zillman, *Variorum*, p. 350n. That it here means remember is indicated a few lines later: "What was that curse?" See also l. 137.

46. *Ibid.*, pp. 361–363; *Shelley and His Circle*, III, 234.

47. *Works*, VII, 53.

48. Aug. 24, 1819, *Letters*, II, 113.

49. Preface to *Julian and Maddalo*, *Works*, III, 177.

17. See Zillman, *Variorum*, pp. 313–316.

51. *The Prometheus Bound*, ed. George Thomson, pp. 20–21.

52. Zillman, *Variorum*, pp. 486–487; H. W. Janson, *History of Art* (New York, 1965), pp. 344–345 and Plate 36; Zillman, *Variorum*, p. 331.

53. *Works*, VI, 249.

54. *Ibid.*, p. 202.

55. *A Defence of Poetry*, *Works*, VII, 118.

56. *Ibid.*, pp. 136–137.

57. First suggested by A. H. Koszul in 1925. (Zillman, *Variorum*, pp. 333–334, 756.) I was incorrect in earlier identifications of Panthea and Ione in my "The Political Symbolism of Prometheus Unbound," *PMLA*, LVIII (September 1943), 738–741.

58. Boccaccio apparently derived his knowledge of Demogorgon from Theodontius and Lactantius Placidius. (Charles G. Osgood, *Boccaccio on Poetry* [Princeton, 1930], pp. xxv; xliv.)

59. Zillman, *Variorum*, pp. 313–316.

60. Peacock, *Works*, VI, 94. To T. J. Hogg, Nov. 28, 1817, *Letters*, I, 569. In November 1817 Shelley was living near Peacock in Marlow and writing *The Revolt of Islam*, which

echoes Peacock's *Ahrimanes.* The two writers were in close personal and literary association at this time. (See *Shelley and His Circle,* III, 235–244.) For Shelley's review, see *Works,* VI, 273–276. Mary recorded copying it on Feb. 20, 1818, at Marlow. *(Mary Shelley's Journal,* p. 92.)

61. Hogg to Peacock, Sept. 8, 1817; Peacock to Hogg, Sept. 26, 1817; in W. S. Scott, ed., *New Shelley Letters* (New Haven, 1949), pp. 98, 101.

62. Woodring, p. 290. *Bell's New Pantheon* was a standard reference work of the time.

63. *A Refutation of Deism, Works,* VI. 48.

64. Abbé Banier, *Mythology and Fables of the Ancients Explained from History* (London, 1740), I, 467; II, 549n.

65. *Works,* VII, 4.

66. To T. L. Peacock, Apr. 6, 1819, *Letters,* II, 94.

67. The *Prometheus Unbound* volume also contained *Ode to Liberty* and *Ode to the Assertors of Liberty* (on Peterloo). *Revolt of Islam,* l. 3685; Preface to *The Revolt of Islam, Works,* I, 242.

68. Zillman, *Variorum,* p. 643.

69. Mary Shelley, the year after Shelley's death, found in these "follow, follow" songs a new and sadder meaning. (To Maria Gisborne, May 2, 1823, Mary Shelley, *Letters,* I, 223–224.)

70. Zillman, *Variorum,* p. 315 *(Faerie Queene,* IV, ii, 47). Boccaccio had suggested Mount Aetna or Taenarus as possible entrances to Demogorgon's realm. (Edward B. Hungerford, *Shores of Darkness* [New York, 1941], pp. 183–184.)

71. See also *Ode to Liberty,* ll. 1–4.

72. As expressed in *I Will Kneel at Thine Altar* (1809), *Esdaile Notebook,* p. 126.

73. Shelley, Notes to *Queen Mab, Works,* I, 144.

74. *Works,* VI, 48–49; I, 145; III, 56.

75. Shelley is partly indebted to Hesiod's description of the golden age of Saturn in *Works and Days;* to Aeschylus' *Prometheus Bound,* II, 436ff, Loeb Classical Library, pp. 255–259, on the contributions of Prometheus to mankind; and to Plato's *Statesman.* (Lillian Winstanley, "Platonism in Shelley," *Essays and Studies by Members of the English Association,* IV [1913], 98–99.) Shelley is also indebted to Lucretius and to Rousseau's *Essay on Inequality among Mankind.*

76. *Works,* VI, 48.

77. King-Hele, p. 181. Shelley gave his view that sunlight is a form of energy in the Notes to *Queen Mab:* "Light consists either of vibrations propagated through a subtle medium, or of numerous minute particles repelled in all directions from the luminous body." (*Works* I, 135.) This solar energy created the coursers and will sustain them after their task of drawing the car of the hour is done. They will then seek (III, iv, 108–110):

> their birth-place in the sun,
> Where they henceforth will live exempt from toil
> Pasturing flowers of vegetable fire.

The "coursers" normally "rest from long labours at Noon." Later, the Spirit of the earth asks Asia (III, iv, 28–29):

> May I play beside thee the long noons,
> When work is none in the bright silent air?

Both references are to the current theory that the sun drew up electricity in the morning but by noon, once the atmosphere was saturated, the process ended.

78. Zillman, *Variorum,* p. 496.

79. *Ibid.,* pp. 498–500.

15. *The World Transformed*

1. *Works,* III, 10.

2. *Timaeus,* 37d. Shelley perhaps also had in mind *Childe Harold's Pilgrimage,* IV, clxxxiii (on the sea):

> Dark-heaving—boundless, endless, and sublime,
> The image of eternity, the throne
> Of the Invisible.

Thetis was a sea goddess and, hence, part of this mirror of the sky (eternity). See also *Hellas*, l. 926.

3. T. R. Malthus, *An Essay on the Principle of Population As It Affects the Future Improvement of Society* (London, 1798), pp. 13–17; see also C. E. Pulos "Shelley and Malthus," *PMLA*, LXVII (1952), 113–124; Zillman, *Variorum*, pp. 507–508.

4. Zillman, *Variorum*, p. 507, quoting Pulos.

5. *Works*, VII, 33. See also Ch. 9 above, n. 39, on Shelley and Maltus.

6. Pulos, pp. 56–57.

7. "Fragments on Reform," *Works*, VI, 295.

8. Shelley repeats these lines in *To William Shelley*.

9. *Works*, III, 9, VII, 17.

10. Preface to *The Revolt of Islam*, *Works*, I, 242.

11. Zillman, *Variorum*, p. 240.

12. *Works*, VII, 136, 137; *Mont Blanc*, ll. 37, 44, 45–46.

13. Zillman, *Variorum*, p. 245; *The Republic of Plato*, trans. D. Spens, Everyman Library (New York, 1927), p. 2; Pausanius, *Description of Greece*, xxx. Pausanius' comment was general knowledge; see, e.g., "Prometheus" in *Rees' Encyclopedia*. On these and related matters see also Edward B. Hungerford, *Shores of Darkness* (New York, 1941), pp. 196–199. For the academy and its environs, see William Smith, *Dictionary of Greek and Roman Geography*, I, 303. Pausanius indicates only that there was an altar to Prometheus, but some scholars, following a scholium on l. 56 of *Oedipus at Colonus*, have contended that there was a temple and not merely an altar. (J. G. Frazer, *Description of Greece* [London, 1898], p. 391.)

14. *Works*, VI, 231.

15. Shelley wrote to Hogg on Jan. 3, 1811: "I confess that I think Pope's 'all are but parts of one tremendous whole' something more than Poetry, it has ever been my favourite theory." (*Letters*, I, 35.) Pope's text reads "stupendous whole." (*Essay on Man*, I, 267.)

16. *Works*, VI, 50.

17. See *Prometheus Unbound*, IV, 461: "Green and azure sphere." Grabo (*A Newton among Poets*, ch. VIII) argued that the Spirit of the Earth is simply electricity, but it is more likely that Shelley had a combination of forces in mind. His science teacher, Adam Walker, had argued that "fire, light, heat, caloric, phlogiston, and electricity" are "but modifications of the same principle." (Peter Butter, *Shelley's Idols of the Cave* [Edinburgh, 1954], p. 143; see also pp. 151–153.) Grabo (*A Newton among Poets*, p. 126) argued that "green" refers to the green light given off in a Leyden jar with copper terminals.

18. In *Queen Mab*, VIII, 129–130, as part of the rejuvenation of society:

> Like passion's fruit, the nightshade's tempting bane
> Poisons no more the pleasure it bestows.

Shelley's interest was probably the result of encounters with poisonous berries or laurel when at Keswick in 1811. (See *Esdaile Notebook*, pp. 180–181.)

19. See Woodring, p. 302.

20. *Works*, VII, 10–11, 12.

21. The manuscript has "frowned" in l. 133 and "fawned" in l. 138. (Zillman, *Variorum*, p. 254.) I follow the first edition text.

22. *A Philosophical View of Reform*, *Works*, VII, 14.

23. This passage was attacked in a review in *The Londsdale Magazine or Provincial Repository*, November 1820: "But this is not all, the very decencies of our nature are to vanish beneath the magic wand of this licentious REFORMER. Every modest feeling, which now constitutes the sweetest charm of society is to be annihilated—and women are to be—*what God and nature never designed them.* But his own description alone can paint the lasciviousness of his own heart." (Zillman, *Variorum*, p. 703.)

24. Shelley, *A Discourse on the Manners of the Antient Greeks Relative to the Subject of Love*, Notopoulos, pp. 407–408.

25. *The Revolt of Islam*, l. 3315.

26. Zillman, *Variorum*, p. 563, quoting A. M. D. Hughes.

27. See *The Assassins:* "Time was measured and created by the vices and miseries of men, between whom and the happy nation of the Assassins, there was no analogy nor comparison. Already had their eternal peace commenced." (*Works*, VI, 162.)

28. *Mary Shelley's Journal*, pp. 67, 143, 218; to Thomas Hookham, July 29, 1812; to Charles Ollier, Feb. 22, 1821; A. & W. Galignani to Shelley, Apr. 25, 1822, *Letters*, I, 319;

II, 270 458–459 (the geology book ordered was *Traité de geognosie* by J. F. Daubuisson de Voisins); *Works*, VII, 96–97.

29. In a Note to *Queen Mab* (*Works*, I, 135), Shelley gives the distance to the star Sirius as 54,224 billion miles, citing the article on light in *Nicholson's Encyclopedia*, but this figure does not appear there. (Cameron, p. 400.) The figure is remarkably close, however, the distance to Sirius being 51,000 billion miles. (King-Hele, p. 39—using "billion" in the British sense.) The calculation is in line with those made at the time by Herschel. Possibly Shelley heard it from Adam Walker. Herschel lived at Salt Hill, now Slough, where Shelley and Mary vacationed in 1815.

30. Grabo, *A Newton among Poets*, p. 84; Cameron, pp. 8, 294; William Herschel, *On the Construction of the Heavens* (1785), in Milton K. Munitz, *Theories of the Universe* (Glencoe, 1957), p. 264.

31. Munitz, *Theories of the Universe*, pp. 235, 240.

32. *Encyclopedia Britannica*, 11th ed. (New York, 1910), XIII, 393; Munitz, *Theories of the Universe*, pp. 267–268; Grabo, *A Newton among Poets*, p. 166. Butter (*Shelley's Idols of the Cave*, p. 160) disputed this point, but Grabo was clearly right.

33. Grabo, *A Newton among Poets*, p. 166; Butter, *Shelley's Idols of the Cave*, p. 160.

34. Shelley, Notes to *Queen Mab*, *Works*, I, 143n.

35. Grabo, *A Newton among Poets*, p. 82; *Works*, I, 135. When Herschel first began to examine the stellar universe, he believed that it was finite. In June 1818, however, three months after Shelley left for Italy, Herschel wrote an important paper withdrawing this view and arguing that the universe was "fathomless." As Grabo noted, in *Prometheus Unbound* Shelley is clearly presenting Herschel's earlier view in his notion of a bounded universe of stars with nebulous ("hoar") space beyond. (Grabo, *A Newton among Poets*, pp. 85–86.) Shelley expresses the concept also in Demogorgon's final speech to the "Aetherial Dominations," who are said to exist "Beyond Heaven's constellated universe" (530–532), that is, beyond the constellations of stars. In those regions of space there is still "aether," that entity more subtle than light which Newton and others had posited, and which was apparently the raw stuff of the nebulae. But even though Shelley does not follow Herschel's latest theory in *Prometheus Unbound*, perhaps he heard of it by 1820–21 when he wrote *On the Devil, and Devils*, for there he does not mention the finiteness of the universe. On the contrary, he speaks of the "incalculable number" of nebulae. Moreover, it had been argued that these nebulae were flattened suns. Kant, however, disagreed: "It is far more natural and conceivable to regard them as being not such enormous single stars but systems of many stars, whose distance presents them in such a narrow space that the light which is individually imperceptible from each of them, reaches us, on account of their immense multitude, in a uniform pale glimmer." (Munitz, *Theories of the Universe*, p. 236.) Shelley seems to have been influenced by this view of Kant's. (*Works*, VII, 97.)

36. Grabo, *A Newton among Poets*, p. 152.

37. *Ibid.*, pp. 153–154. Butter (*Shelley's Idols of the Cave*, p. 154n) again dissented. King-Hele (p. 189) assumed that the white light "scattered in strings" is that emitted only from the volcanoes on the moon, but Shelley means the moon's reflected light in general.

38. Grabo, *A Newton among Poets*, pp. 88, 45–46. Kant wrote a treatise *On the Volcanoes in the Moon* in 1785.

39. *Ibid.*, p. 88–89; see also King-Hele, p. 189.

40. *Encyclopedia Britannica*, 11th ed., VII, 778. This edition is extremely useful for surveys of early science, both by subject and scientist. Much valuable information has been omitted from later editions.

41. Grabo, *A Newton among Poets*, p. 142.

42. *Works*, I, 135; Davy, *Elements of Chemical Philosophy*, in Grabo, *A Newton among Poets*, p. 142.

43. King-Hele, p. 190–191. In interpretating the passage in "the modern idiom," however, King-Hele inadvertently gave the impression that Shelley's interpretation of matter is closer to the modern than it actually is.

44. Grabo, *A Newton among Poets*, p. 92.

45. King-Hele, p. 191; Grabo, *A Newton among Poets*, p. 143.

46. On July 24, 1816, Shelley in a letter to T. L. Peacock from Switzerland referred to concepts in Buffon's *La theorie de la terre* (1749). (*Letters*, I, 499.) He may have read the book, or he may have known Buffon's theories from encyclopedias and other general works. He was doubtless also acquainted with Leibintz' geological theories, as they were general knowledge at the time.

47. At the same time as geological theories—catastrophic or gradualistic (James Hut-

ton)—were being presented, similarly advanced theories on related biological matters were being formed, for instance, those of Lamarck and Erasmus Darwin, who was early read by Shelley. (Cameron, p. 392.) Darwin's anticipation of his illustrious grandson are indeed extraordinary. He argued that "all warm-blooded animals have arisen from one living filament" (the biological cell then being unknown). From this elementary filament came all the forms of life, first the simpler, then the more complex:

Organic Life beneath the shoreless waves
Was born and nurs'd in Ocean's pearly caves;
First forms minute, unseen by spheric glass,
Move on the mud, or pierce the watery mass;
These, as successive generations bloom
New powers acquire, and larger limbs assume.

(Grabo, *A Newton among Poets*, pp. 63, 67.) Darwin was also intrigued by the theory, which he attributed to Helvetius and Buffon, "that mankind arose from one family of monkeys on the banks of the Mediterranean" who somehow developed the opposable thumb, which enables the hand to grasp. (*Ibid.*, p. 65) Lord Monboddo, also read by Shelley, had previously suggested that the orangutan was an earlier form of man. (Cameron, p. 394.) Darwin looked also to future evolution: "Perhaps the productions of nature are in their progress to greater perfection!" (Grabo, *A Newton among Poets*, p. 65.)

Shelley's interest, however, is not primarily with these evolutionary views but with the catastrophe theory, as put forward, for instance, in James Parkinson's *Organic Remains of a Former World*, published in 1811. According to Parkinson, in the floods of the past the world had been "desolated and rendered one vast mass of seeming ruin . . . torn up and carried away by the force of the tremendous torrent, the trees of the mountains . . . laid on those of the valleys, and . . . together buried by the subsequent subversion of the mountains themselves." (Cameron, p. 248.) In such catastrophes various strange animals of the past were "entombed": "Thus you will behold the bones of an animal, of which the magnitude is so great as to warrant the conviction, that the bulk of this dreadful, unknown animal, exceeded three times that of the lion; and to authorize the belief, that animals have existed, which have possessed, with all the dreadful propensities of that animal, its power of destroying, in a threefold degree. You will also view the remains of a being of the magnitude, at least, of the elephant; which was armed with tusks, equally dreadful, as a weapon, with those borne by that animal; possessing, in addition to these, enormously huge grinders, supposed to bear the distinctive marks of those creatures, which gain their food, by preying on those of inferior powers and size. The jaws of an animal bearing a near resemblance to those of a crocodile, you will perceive to be armed with teeth, not widely different from those of the shark. In a word, you will be repeatedly astonished by the discovery of the remains of animals, of which no living prototype is to be found." (Grabo, *A Newton among Poets*, p. 179, quoting Parkinson.) Despite the incorrectness of the catastrophe theory, leading proponents of it such as Cuvier uncovered many fossils and grasped something of their essence—as Shelley does in the above passage. Shelley was also indebted to Keats' *Endymion* (III, 119–136) in the passage. (Zillman, *Variorum*, p. 595.)

48. To Elizabeth Hitchener, Nov. 23, 1811, *Letters*, I, 189. Shelley's source here is not Parkinson, for he told Elizabeth Hitchener on Dec. 26, 1811, that he had never heard of Parkinson but would send for his work. (*Ibid.*, p. 214.)

49. John Davy, *Memoirs of the Life of Sir Humphry Davy*, in Grabo, *A Newton among Poets*, p. 176.

50. Zillman, *Variorum*, p 672; Grabo, *A Newton among Poets*, pp. 163–164. Shelley doubtless was influenced by Adam Walker, who argued in *A System of Familiar Philosophy in Twelve Lectures* (London, 1802), I, 15–16, that "the solar impulse" will in time straighten the earth up. In Plate III, fig. 12, he illustrates this happening.

51. William Gilbert, in Grabo, *A Newton among Poets*, p. 94; King-Hele, p. 194; Butter, *Shelley's Idols of the Cave*, p. 152.

52. *Notes on Sculptures in Rome and Florence*, *Works*, VI, 323. Shelley visited the art galleries in Florence in October 1819. (*Ibid.*, p. 375.)

53. Zillman, *Variorum*, p. 669.

54. Grabo, *A Newton among Poets*, p. 194; Zillman, *Variorum*, p. 669.

55. Zillman, *Variorum*, pp. 669–670, 610.

56. Erasmus Darwin, *The Botanic Garden*, I, 289–296, in Grabo, *A Newton among Poets*, p. 36; King-Hele, p. 192.

57. Zillman, *Variorum*, p. 674; Grabo, *A Newton among Poets*, p. 97.

58. Zillman, *Variorum*, p. 674.
59. *Ibid.*, pp. 297, 676, 617–619.
60. Grabo, *A Newton among Poets*, p. 162. Butter (*Shelley's Idols of the Cave*, p. 156) expressed doubts.
61. *A Philosophical View of Reform*, *Works*, VII, 47.
62. Henry G. Lotspeich, "Shelley's Eternity and Demogorgon," *Philological Quarterly*, XIII (1934), 310.
63. *Works*, VII, 41.
64. *Ibid.*, pp. 48–49, 50, 52, 53. Shelley continues (p. 53) "The right of insurrection is derived from the employment of armed force to counteract the will of the nation."

Index